HOME
HANDYMAN

HOME
HANDYMAN

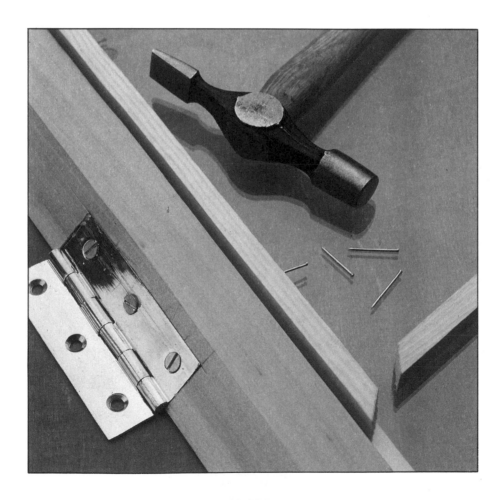

Colour Library Books

CONTENTS

CLB 1950
This edition published 1988 by Colour Library Books Ltd,
Godalming Business Centre, Catteshall Lane,
Godalming, Surrey GU7 1XW.
Original material © 1985 – 6 Marshall Cavendish Ltd
This arrangement © 1987 Marshall Cavendish Ltd
Prepared by Marshall Cavendish Books Ltd
58 Old Compton St, London W1V 5PA
Printed in Italy
ISBN 0 86283 553 4

INTRODUCTION

HOME HANDYMAN is the complete manual of do-it-yourself skills and projects—an essential guide for every home improver that can help you get professional and economic results, fast. Whether you're installing double glazing, fitting a new sink or fixing a faulty fuse, you'll find the information here that can help you get the job done quickly and efficiently.

Divided into six sections for easy reference, *HOME HANDYMAN* covers virtually every task that the home improver could want to tackle. Each job contains all the background information you need to understand the subject— even if you are starting a job for the first time. Clear, detailed colour drawings and step-by-step photographs help you follow the job through from stage to stage. They help you understand what is going on before you start, and make sure you know what you're after when you need to buy parts and materials. *WATCHPOINT* panels spread throughout the book give you vital 'inside information' on tricky points that are bound to crop up in any job.

An indispensable guide for the expert and beginner alike, *HOME HANDYMAN* gives you all the know-how you need to make your house and garden look good and wear well.

While every care has been taken to ensure that the information in *HOME HANDYMAN* is accurate, individual circumstances may vary greatly. So proceed with caution, especially where electrical, plumbing or structural work is involved.

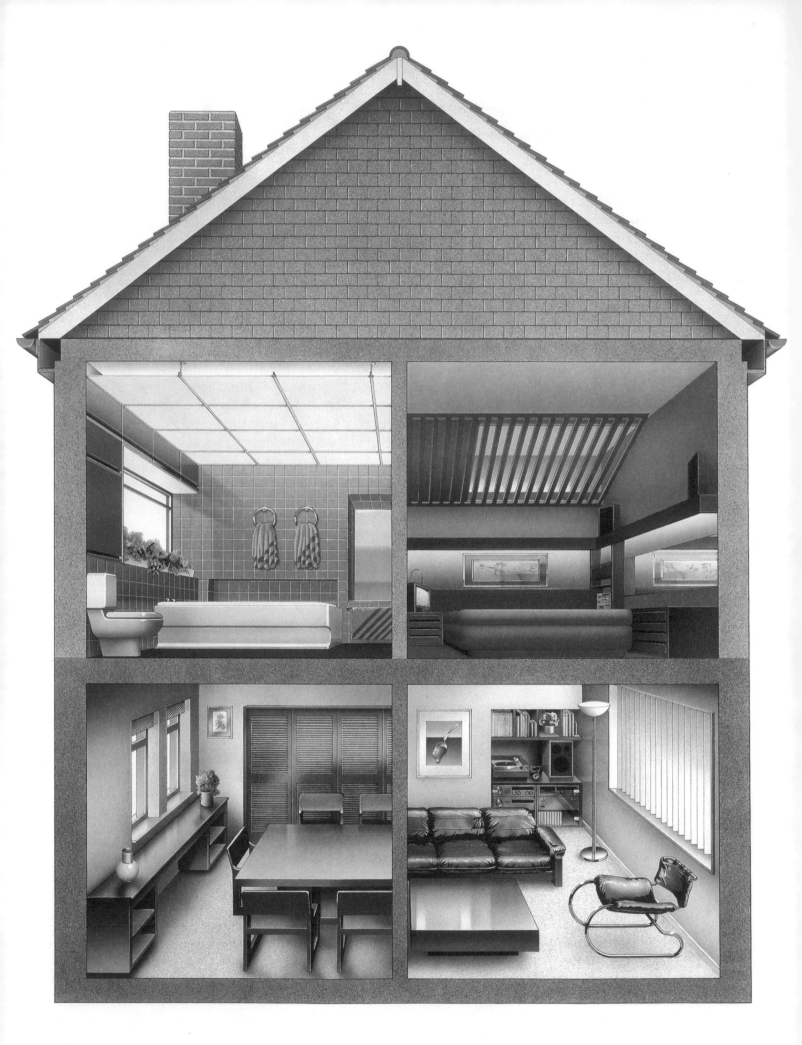

CHAPTER 1

HOME BUILDER

Basic skills and repairs like painting, tiling and plastering, combined with money-saving projects like DIY double glazing, draughtproofing and opening up a fireplace

DEFENCES AGAINST DAMP

Brick is a porous material and moisture can penetrate it. If the brick walls of a house are properly built, then damp should not be able to get through to the inside surfaces. But if the walls are defective, then damp can strike.

The tell-tale signs are damp, discoloured patches frequently accompanied by a white salty deposit called efflorescence and perhaps a fungal growth. However, condensation has much the same symptoms—so you should check first that this is not the cause.

Unfortunately, when penetrating damp becomes visible it is already too late to prevent some damage to the plaster and wallcoverings. But prompt action will keep this to a minimum.

Tracing the source

Damp can penetrate the exterior fabric of a house in all kinds of places. If you discover that a DPC is at fault or that a roof covering is leaking badly, wholesale replacement of the defective material may be the only answer. But most penetrating damp problems are due to smaller defects and can be cured a great deal more easily.

External cures

These vary, according to the nature and location of the damage.

Around chimney stacks: Older types of chimney stacks, particularly those which are exposed to the elements, provide a common place for damp to enter and work its way down the internal walls. Flue gases condensing inside the stack cause the mortar joints to expand, and this, combined

Below: *Damp patches should be left to dry out and then sealed before redecorating*

with wind and rain, results in rapid deterioration of the brickwork. Damp can also penetrate the flashings around the roof if these have been neglected or badly installed.

If, after investigation, you discover that the mortar joints are at fault, it is worth repointing the entire stack using a 1:3 mortar mix with waterproofing agent added.

If the flashings are suspect, cut them out and replace them completely. Apply waterproof mastic at all the joints.

Parapet walls: Very badly pointed or damaged parapet walls give rise to similar damp problems. They should be carefully checked and thoroughly cleaned before broken bricks are made good. Repoint using the 1:3 mix with waterproofer added.

In some older houses, the parapets were not fitted with a DPC. In this case, you may have no choice but to remove the copings and first few courses, then insert your own

1 *A transparent silicone-based water-proofer can be applied to outside walls to prevent damp seeping through bricks and mortar*

2 *Flaking plaster and fungal growth on walls should be thoroughly cleared by the vigorous use of a wire brush all over the area*

3 *Mark around the outside of the affected area so that all of the unsound plaster can be chopped out with a hammer and wide bolster*

4 *Cut out all the affected plaster until the brickwork underneath is exposed. This can be cleaned down and left to dry out*

5 *Before and during the period of drying out—which may take a few weeks—a fungicide should be applied to the whole area*

6 *Once all signs of damp have disappeared, coat the brickwork with bitumastic paint before filling the gap with sound plaster*

DPC of bituminous felt.

Another common fault is that rainwater runs off the top of the copings, down underneath them, and so on into the brickwork below. To stop this, you must cut a 'drip' groove along the underside of the coping stones on the side which faces the roof, 25mm from the edge. Do this either with an electric angle grinder or with a small bolster and club hammer. Be sure to wear safety goggles to protect your eyes from flying masonry.

Sometimes, cutting an accurate groove in this way is impossible. In this case a less satisfactory solution is to secure a 15mm square batten to the underside of the stones. Make sure that the wood is well soaked in preservative, then secure it with an epoxy resin adhesive. Do not use screws or

★ WATCH POINT ★

When you are searching outside, do not assume that the entry point of the damp is directly adjacent to the damp patches on the internal walls. Damp can often enter well away from the point where it eventually manifests itself, so a thorough inspection of the external walls and their junction with the roof is essential.

masonry pins as these will split the wood and allow damp to penetrate it. Remember, though, that this is only a short-lived cure and shouldn't be treated as a lasting repair.

Gutters and downpipes: If you find after periods of heavy rain that damp patches appear adjacent to a gutter or downpipe, start by making a thorough check of your rainwater system and remove blockages.

Ogee-section guttering—which is screwed directly to the fascia boards—often splits along the back vertical face and is a particularly common source of damp. So, too, are old cast-iron and galvanized steel downpipes: these may look to be sound but a closer inspection often reveals that the backs have rotted away. Long, rust-stained water marks down the brickwork are often the most obvious signs of rot in the guttering.

The only satisfactory solution to these problems is to renew the offending section.

Rendering: If your house is rendered, damp may still have penetrated even though the surface appears to be sound. Constant expansion and contraction due to weathering can cause the render to detach itself from the brickwork and craze.

Check whether this is the case by tapping the rendering in several places with a hammer handle—a hollow sound will reveal where it is loose. When the render is 'blown' in this way, you must cut it back to sound edges and fill the hole with new render.

Bridged DPC: A very common cause of penetrating damp, especially around floor level, is that the DPC has been covered or bridged outside the house. Soil or debris may be piled high above DPC level if you have been gardening or building near outside walls, so allowing damp to find its way into the brickwork. Timber and other objects stacked against the outside walls are another possible source of dampness: they too should be removed.

Remove any such material immediately and make sure that a gap of at least 150mm is left between the DPC and ground level.

Dirty wall ties: Random patches of damp which appear after heavy rain may be an indication that debris such as brick-laying mortar has collected on the metal ties between the inner and outer leaf of a cavity wall, causing damp to penetrate along them. This is typically the result of careless building or repair work carried out on the walls.

The only remedy is to cut away the brickwork around each patch, identify the offending tie, clean it and make good. This can be a laborious process: you may be able to save time by cutting only the bricks around a central patch, then poking a stick along the cavity to clean the other ties.

7 *The small gaps around doors and window frames which allow damp to enter must be stopped by forcing mastic between the joints*

8 *Once the mastic has been applied, the surface can be smoothed down with a small piece of rounded stick periodically doused in water*

12 *Seal the wall with a primer and then cut the laminate to length, allowing extra at the top and bottom for trimming*

13 *Brush water evenly and liberally on to the back of the laminate so that it becomes thoroughly saturated and tacky to the touch*

Repairing brickwork

One of the most common causes of penetrating damp is brickwork which has been allowed to deteriorate. In this case the damp can appear suddenly and cause damage over a wide area.

In less serious cases, the pointing breaks down and falls out and the bricks become badly pitted due to weathering. In the worst cases, in very cold conditions, the bricks become *spalled*—water enters the cracks, freezes, then forces the faces off.

If bad pointing is the problem, repoint the wall and cut out and replace any bricks which are badly damaged. Powdery mortar and brickwork should be sealed with PVA bonding solution after you have raked out the joints.

★ WATCH POINT ★

If you want to keep the existing brick finish, an alternative to the conventional exterior paints is transparent, silicone-based waterproofer. This protects the brickwork but does nothing to detract from its appearance. And though it prevents damp entering the wall, it allows the moisture already there to escape freely.

When using this type of waterproofer, take extra care with your initial surface preparation as it is this which affects the quality of the final finish.

Where the state of the brickwork is generally poor but still intact, consider applying a cement- or stone-based paint. This can often improve the appearance of the house and, providing it is regularly maintained, is effective at keeping out damp.

Before you apply the paint you must thoroughly prepare the surface, first by running over it with a wire brush to remove loose debris, then by painting on a fungicide to kill any mould growth which still remains. Repoint any areas of loose mortar and apply bonding solution to suspect areas.

Doors and windows

Another site of penetrating damp is around door and window frames, where gaps have

9 *Use a hammer and bolster to cut a drip groove along the underside of a masonry window sill so that it runs in a line 25mm from the edge*

10 *As an alternative, a 15mm square batten of wood soaked in preservative can be secured under the sill with an epoxy resin adhesive*

11 *Before applying a damp barrier, rub down all damp patches to remove flaking paint and allow the wall to dry out thoroughly*

14 *Fold the laminate over on itself towards the middle with the wet side inwards and leave it in this state for one hour*

15 *Once primer has dried, paint the adhesive evenly and thinly on to the wall, covering an area wide enough for one length of laminate*

16 *Apply the wet side of the laminate to the wall, brushing it into place and starting from the top. Subsequent rolls should overlap by 12mm*

appeared due to shrinkage or weathering. Putting mastic in the gaps can cure this.

Start from the top of the frame, working the point of the applicator right into the gaps and making sure that they are well filled (fig. 7). Then use a small piece of dowel, which has been wetted, to force the mastic deep into any smaller cracks and wipe away the excess (fig. 8).

A less obvious cause of damp around windows is that the drip groove beneath the sill is blocked or damaged, causing water to run along the underside of the sill and into the brickwork. Make sure that it is cleared, cut a new one with hammer and chisel, or, for a temporary cure only, fit a 15mm square wood batten under the sill, about 25mm from the edge. The batten must first be coated with preservative, then secured with an epoxy adhesive (figs 9 and 10).

★ WATCH POINT ★

Remember that drying out walls will take some time—often a number of weeks—so do not get impatient or try to speed the process by using heating in the room; this is likely to give a false impression of how successful you have been with your external cures.

Internal cures

It is wrong to believe that you can cure penetrating damp internally: you must first stop it at source by working on the external walls as has already been described. Though temporary repairs are sometimes possible, any work you do on the inside should be regarded as an addition to the work you have done outside, rather than as a final cure.

Always avoid the temptation to cover up areas of dampness which appear internally with paint or wallcoverings—the damp will only reappear later.

The general practice is to carry out remedial work outside the house and then allow the inside to dry out thoroughly. Give this as much encouragement as possible by opening windows and doors; if you have carried out the work properly, you should see the patches of damp recede.

Once you are convinced that the wall has dried out, you must remove all the wallcoverings and cut away any patches of damp or blown plaster with a hammer and bolster. If only sections of the wall are affected, the bare brickwork should be cleaned and painted with bitumastic paint, then covered with sound plaster. But if the damage is more extensive, it is best to dry line the whole wall or alternatively cover the affected area with a protective damp-proof barrier.

Applying a damp barrier: If areas of damp persist on internal walls, you can apply a damp barrier. This comes in kit form and consists of a waterproof laminate which is stuck directly to the affected wall, once the surface has been prepared with a special primer. Though not as complete a treatment as dry lining, it has the added advantage that you do not have to go to the trouble of removing all the old plaster before you install it.

First prepare the walls by removing old existing wallpaper, making good any blown or damp plaster and smoothing down high spots with glasspaper (fig. 11). You should also remove the skirting board since the damp barrier must be carried down behind it.

After sealing the wall with primer, the laminate can be hung in strips much as you would with wallpaper (see figs 11 to 16).

Dry lining the wall: This involves covering the bare brickwork with a pitch-impregnated fibre sheet to shut out the last traces of damp and protect new decoration. The sheet, which is corrugated, comes in rolls 1m wide by 5m long (fig. A).

Having stripped off all the affected plaster, fix the sheets to the bare brickwork with galvanized clout or masonry nails. Firmly drive the nails through the corrugated valleys at spaced intervals of about 300mm.

Where the sheets join, line the wall behind them with 100mm wide pieces of bituminized felt laid vertically to stop the damp getting through, then overlap the sheets by one corrugation. Where the lining material is cut to fit around pipes or other wall fixtures, fill the gaps with a waterproof mastic.

When you are lining only one wall, stop the damp getting round the edges of the sheets by continuing the lining some way around the corners of the adjacent walls. For the same reason, you should try also to carry the lining 150mm below floorboard level. At the junction with the ceiling, leave about a 150mm gap to allow air to freely circulate—this can be easily covered later with coving.

Once the lining is in position, you can either replaster the wall or else fit sheets of foil-backed plasterboard.

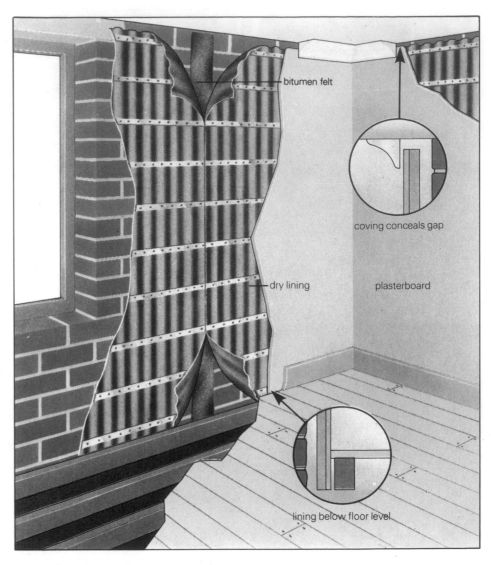

Labels: bitumen felt · coving conceals gap · dry lining · plasterboard · lining below floor level

A. *To dryline a wall, you will need to cut away all the damp plaster and cover the exposed brickwork with pitch-impregnated sheeting*

Basement walls often suffer from damp. The cure may be a simple matter of patching up with waterproofing compound, repairing pipes, clearing out drains, or taking steps to cure condensation. If the basement has been damp for a long time and the damp is quite extensive but cannot be traced to a single source or location, then you have a reasonably major job on your hands.

In the long term, in many cases, the only way to cure severe dampness in a basement is to 'tank' it. This involves waterproofing the entire basement—walls and floor—with a continuous membrane. You treat the basement literally as a tank—except it keeps water out rather than in.

The waterproof membrane can be several layers of a bituminous coating, with extra coats of bituminous paint, or rolls of bitumen impregnated felt fixed with a hot bitumen adhesive. In both cases particular attention has to be paid to joints and corners, and you'll have to take great care not to puncture the covering when attaching fixtures afterwards.

An alternative is to use a proprietary waterproofer. However, it is essential to plaster the walls and lay a floor screed afterwards.

Another approach is to fix pitch impregnated fibre material to the walls.

Before installing this, the floor slab has to have a waterproof membrane which is run up the wall for 100mm or so.

In very serious cases, the pressure of ground water may be enough to force off any waterproofing. If this happens, you will have to build a second wall in brick or concrete—what is in effect a box—within the basement with the water barrier actually sandwiched in between the two main walls.

REPAIRING GUTTERS

Gutters and downpipes play a vital role in protecting your house from the effects of rain, but if they are to work properly they must be regularly checked for blockages, cracks and leaks. Even if they show no obvious signs of damage, you should still make a point of inspecting your gutters and downpipes once, or preferably twice, each year.

You will find that leaves and debris accumulate in the gutters, particularly during the autumn months, and if you don't clear this out, you could end up with a blocked downpipe. If left, blockages allow water to flow over the edge of the gutter and down into the wall of a house to cause penetrating damp.

Basic maintenance

Clear out the rubbish with a hand brush and trowel or, in the case of plastic guttering, with a piece of hardboard shaped to fit the curve of the guttering and attached to a piece of wood. Try to keep the debris well away from the downpipe outlet.

If you have cast-iron guttering, check carefully for signs of rust. Use a wire brush to remove loose flakes of paint and rust and treat the surface with a proprietary rust-inhibiting chemical. Ideally, you should follow up with one or two coats of bituminous paint to form a strong, protective surface.

Ogee-section guttering is often attached directly to the fascia, rather than held in brackets. Here, rust is most likely to be

Above: *Debris soon accumulates in gutters if they are often left unattended. Cleaning them out is an easy and worthwhile task*

found around the fixing screws. The affected section must be removed and refixed with galvanized screws.

Leaking joints

Next check the joints for leaks: cast-iron gutters are particularly prone to this. A quick and easy remedy is to apply mastic to the defective joint. This is only a temporary repair, however, and the joint should be undone and resealed as soon as possible.

Resealing metal joints

Sections of cast-iron guttering are held together by a nut and a bolt with a wide, slotted head. A proprietary sealing compound (often a mixture of putty and red

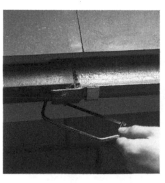

1 *If the bolt has completely rusted up, you'll have to cut it off with the help of a hacksaw*

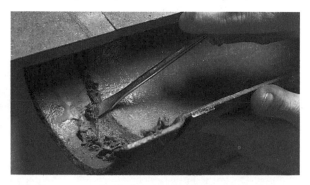

2 *Try to get off all the old pieces of sealant that still remain on the gutter section before you actually start to reassemble the joint again*

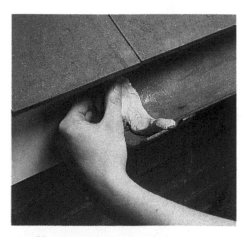

3 *You can use mastic or putty to seal the joint—don't skimp with how much you use; you can always clear off any excess*

4 *Use a spanner to hold the nut firmly in place as you screw the new, replacement bolt right through the piece of guttering*

5 *As you tighten the bolt, putty will start to ooze out—you can scrape off the excess with the aid of a putty knife*

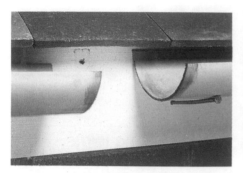

6 *Support the guttering while the bracket is removed—nails will easily take all the weight*

7 *Clean off the ends of both sections of guttering—petrol is very useful to remove particles of rubber*

8 *Reassemble the joint and then snap the bracket back into position around the guttering*

lead, or a mastic sealer) is sandwiched between the ends of adjoining sections to make the joint watertight. If a joint starts to leak, one of the sections will have to be removed, and the ends of both parts cleaned thoroughly and resealed. If the section you need to remove comes in the middle of a run, you'll have to undo and reseal the joints at both ends of it.

Start by removing the bolt which holds the joint together. If this has rusted and seized, try applying some penetrating oil. If this fails, saw through the bolt with a junior hacksaw (fig. 1), then lift out the loosened section and take it to ground level.

Chip away all traces of old sealing compound from the ends of both sections of guttering and scour them thoroughly with a wire brush. Apply fresh sealing compound to the socket section of the joint, spreading it in an even layer about 6mm thick and re-assemble the joint. Fit a new bolt through the hole from above and screw on the securing nut. Tighten up with a screwdriver and spanner until the joint closes completely and the sealing compound begins to squeeze out.

Scrape away the excess sealing compound from both the face and underside of the gutter (fig. 5).

Resealing plastic joints

Nearly all new houses are fitted with lightweight plastic guttering which will not rust and is much cheaper and easier to replace if you do have problems.

Sections of plastic guttering are connected by union clips lined with replaceable rubber seals. In some cases, the seal is positioned in the end of one section of gutter with a separate clip used to secure the joint. When the clip is sprung home, the gutter ends compress the seal to form a watertight joint. However, if silt finds its way in the seal may leak and have to be cleaned out or a new seal fitted.

To do this, release the clip by pulling the lip at the back over the gutter edge and squeezing the front edge. Peel off the old seal. If particles of perished rubber stick to the clip, you can remove this with petrol. Remember, too, to clean the face and underside of the two end sections of gutter. After cleaning, fit the new seal, then squeeze the ends of the gutter slightly and snap on the union clip back over each edge.

Some systems use a combined union and bracket, with these a silt bridge is fitted into the union to ensure that grit and dirt cannot

get between the union and the gutter. Leaks in this type of joint are usually caused by cracks either in the bridge or the union bracket and can be remedied by replacing the defective part.

Start by removing and examining the silt bridge. If this is free of cracks, you need to unscrew the union bracket—but make sure the gutter is supported by nails driven into the fascia before you do so. Ease the ends of both sections of gutter out of the union bracket, clean both the surface and underside of the ends of each section.

Secure the new bracket to the fascia—use longer screws if the holes have become enlarged—and refit the silt bridge by hooking one end under the front of the bracket, then snapping the other end under the lip at the back of the gutter.

Clearing a downpipe

Before you attempt to clear a blocked downpipe, first put a plastic bowl under the base of the pipe at the discharge into the drain to prevent any debris being pushed further into the drainage system.

If the downpipe is fitted with a hopper head, carefully clear by hand any debris

9 *Start by clearing the loose debris out of the hopper head—try not to push it down*

10 *Tackle the blockage with a suitable implement to try to clear it*

11 *Finally flush the pipe with water—a garden hose is ideal if it will reach*

12 *An offcut of wood will make it easier to lever away fixings*

which has collected. Try not to push any waste down or it could cause a more serious blockage (fig. 9).

With plastic hopper heads, wipe the inside with a cloth and soapy water once the rubbish has been cleared. And when clearing a cast-iron hopper head wear rubber gloves to protect your hands from any rough edges.

If you are dealing with a straight downpipe, try poking it clear with a piece of wire.

A. *A swan neck makes it slightly more difficult to clear a blockage—try using stiff wire*

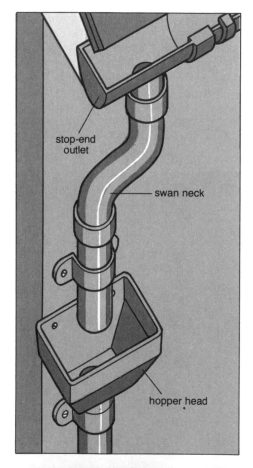

stop-end outlet

swan neck

hopper head

If this doesn't work, try washing it out with a garden hose. For a really stubborn blockage, you can use a flexible wire drain rod, which can be fed up or down and rotated to shift the debris. In the absence of one of these, tie a rag firmly to one end of a long pole and poke it down the pipe (fig. 10). Once the blockage has been dislodged, flush the pipe thoroughly with water (fig. 11).

With some systems, the guttering is positioned some way out from the wall and water is directed into the downpipe through an angled section known as a *swan neck* (fig. A). To clear a blockage here, use a length of fairly stiff wire.

If you are dealing with a downpipe on a two- or three-storey house and the blockage is situated close to the bottom of the pipe, you may not be able to clear it using a long pole. In this case, you will have to start removing the bottom sections of downpipe until you trace where the blockage lies. To do this, follow the same procedure used when dealing with a loose downpipe bracket.

Once you've cleared the debris and reassembled the pipe, make sure you fit a grille over the downpipe outlet and regularly clear out hopper heads and gutters to prevent the same thing from happening in the future.

Securing a loose downpipe

Downpipes are secured to the wall by brackets which are held in place by pipe nails—long round-headed nails driven into metal, lead or wooden plugs bedded into the brickwork. If the pipe is inadequately secured it is under stress and there is a risk of it breaking—particularly if it is made of cast-iron.

To refit the loose bracket, you will need to remove any brackets which are fitted

underneath it, starting with the one nearest the ground, and also remove the section of pipe.

Place an offcut of timber against the wall to give you enough leverage to remove the nails holding the bracket in place, then remove the section of downpipe and lay it aside. Repeat the procedure until you reach the defective bracket.

Once you have removed the loose bracket, dig out the old plugs from the masonry and make up replacements which are slightly larger than the existing holes. Cut these from a piece of 12mm dowel, then extend the holes using a 12mm

masonry drill bit. Drive in the replacement plugs until they are flush with the wall, replace the last section of downpipe removed, and refit the bracket. Repeat this procedure moving downwards, replacing any plugs which have become loose. Before you start replacing the sections, check each one thoroughly for rust and renew them if necessary.

Plastic downpipes are much lighter and the securing brackets are less likely to become loose. If they do, however, follow the same procedure—working from the base of the pipe upwards—to reach the defective bracket. Sections of plastic downpipe are joined by a socket and spigot type of connector and there is no need to seal the joints.

13 *If the pipe won't separate, heat the joint to melt the old sealant*

14 *Take care when removing the section of downpipe—it is heavy*

15 *Hammer the new plug into the masonry—use the old plugs if they feel secure*

16 *When the joint is re-assembled, scrape off any excess sealant*

PAINTING THE OUTSIDE

The skill and experience you require to make a good job of painting the outside of your house are fairly minimal. However, what you do need in good measure are patience, tenacity and, unless you live in a bungalow, a head for heights.

Outdoor maintenance is a time consuming and, at times, messy job. Painting (or repainting) is only half the story; much of the time and effort is spent on preparation. Do this properly and the job may not need doing again for five years; skimp on the preparation and you will be back up the ladder in eighteen months time.

It's because the time element is such a big factor compared to the cost of materials that you can save so much money by doing the job yourself. The main disadvantage is that it will eat into your leisure time—to do a three-bedroom house properly from top to toe will take at least four weekends.

For a house that is in poor condition

you've no alternative but to tackle the whole job at once to get the paintwork back in order. But once you've got a reasonable finish, or if the house is not too bad to start with, it makes sense to split the house into areas and to deal with these by rotation each year—start at one end and work your way round. This approach makes the chore an annual one, but it keeps the task more manageable. Tackling the job in this way also ensures that no part deteriorates too badly before it gets attention.

It is the combined effect of moisture and sunshine that causes paint failures so, before you start, have a good look around the outside of your house to check its condition. Pay particular attention to those sides

Below: Repainting the outside of your home will really brighten it up and, more importantly, really protect it against all the adverse weather conditions

which bear the brunt of the elements.

Weighing up the job

Divide the job into woodwork and masonry.
Woodwork: Start by carefully inspecting the lower corner joints of window and door frames. This is where paint usually deteriorates first and where wood starts to rot. Test for rot with an old knife: if the wood is soft and wet you'll have to sort it out before starting to repaint (see Preparation). While looking at your windows, check the condition of the putty holding the glass in the frames. If it is cracked or missing, replace it first

The only satisfactory way of closely inspecting woodwork at roof height—the bargeboards, soffits and fascias—is on a ladder. If you don't own a ladder yourself, borrow one from a friend—it's not worth

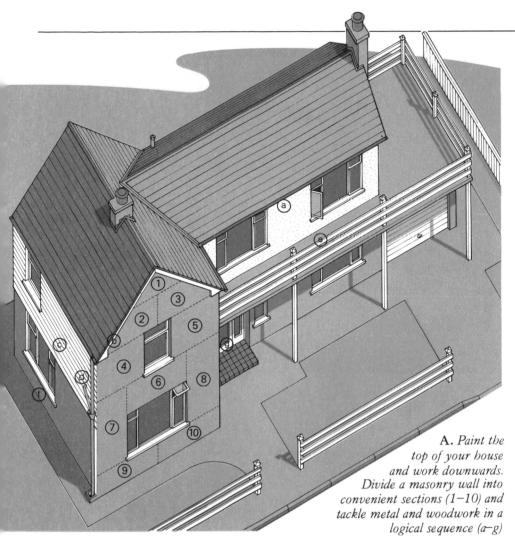

applied over a darker one.

You can also buy water-based gloss topcoat finish paints, which last at least as well as the best alkyd-resin based paints. The manufacturers claim that these paints allow the wood to breathe slightly by letting moisture through the paint film. Water-based topcoats tend not to be as glossy as alkyd-resin topcoats but they are well worth considering. Always buy primer and topcoat paint from the same manufacturer. Apart from giving better results, it may affect any guarantee.

On *masonry* the best choice is masonry paint, which contains crushed rock or synthetic fibre to reinforce the paint film and fill any small cracks. Another option is to use cement paint, which is sold as a powder for home mixing; however, it tends to be expensive and can't be used on a surface which has already been painted.

A. *Paint the top of your house and work downwards. Divide a masonry wall into convenient sections (1–10) and tackle metal and woodwork in a logical sequence (a–g)*

hiring one at this stage as, if you're lucky, the woodwork may not need repainting. As a last resort, you could try using binoculars to get a better view from ground level.
Metalwork: Rust is the main cause of peeling paint, so check downpipes and guttering (on a ladder) for blisters and cracks.
Masonry: A possible reason for badly flaking paint is damp. Don't attempt to cover such flaking, call in professional help to find the root cause. Mildly peeling paint can be scraped off and the masonry sealed with a stabilizing solution.

Types of paint

For *wood* and *metalwork* always examine the surface to see if it needs priming. Generally speaking, you will get the best performance by using separate special purpose primers for woodwork and for metal but if you use a universal primer you can do both wood and metal surfaces from one tin. A third choice are the quick-drying acrylic primers. These water-based paints cope with all surfaces and most can be

★ WATCH POINT ★

While examining your gutters, clear out any debris that may have collected in them over the years —blocked gutters are a main reason for damp walls.

overpainted in just three hours.

Gloss paint is traditionally used for the topcoats. There are two types of gloss paint —non-drip and liquid. Non-drip paints are applied in two coats over a primer; liquid glosses are conventionally applied as one coat on top of an undercoat applied over a primer. However, there is a school of thought which believes that undercoats are not only unnecessary but actually cause the paint to fail more rapidly because they are not flexible enough to take up movement by the wood and tend to crack. For this reason some professionals use two topcoats over primer for most exterior wood and introduce an undercoat only when the paintwork will be under particularly close scrutiny or if a light-coloured paint is being

Tools and other materials

● You'll need access equipment for high-level work. An extension ladder—about 7m long for a two-storey house—will do, but you need a good head for heights to work at the top of a ladder. An access tower is safer and more comfortable if you have room to use one—you need a flat area next to the house at least 0.6m wide. Access towers are so much safer than ladders that it is worth making space where possible. You can hire access towers in easily assembled kit form.

When working aloft have an eye for safety—for the people below as well as yourself. Make sure that nothing can fall off the ladder or access tower. Never deliberately drop things to the ground. If necessary, cordon off the whole area.

● To prepare wood and metal surfaces, a stripping knife, hot air stripper (or blowtorch), wet and dry abrasive paper and filler are essential. You may also want to use a paint stripping chemical for fiddly areas around windows, such as the glazing bars, putty, sugar soap and possibly something to treat rot with—proprietary kits are sold for the purpose.

● To prepare masonry surfaces for

★ WATCH POINT ★

A butcher's hook enables you to hang your paint pot from a convenient rung of the ladder instead of holding it. They're available from DIY and decorating shops.

painting, all you need is a stiff brush and maybe stabilizing and fungicidal solutions to treat dusty, powdery surfaces and eradicate mould spores respectively.

● What you use to apply the paint with is largely a matter of personal preference. If you prefer to use a brush for trim surfaces, a 50mm brush is the largest you will need although for narrow surfaces a 38mm or 25mm brush would be better. For edges you can use a cutting-in brush (sometimes called a sash brush), which has the bristles cut at an angle.

Paint pads are the other main option for painting woodwork and metalwork. Their chief advantage is that they don't splash. Their major disadvantage—that they give a disappointing finish with gloss—is often not important out of doors. Paint pads often come with a tray for loading, but if you use a brush you will need a paint kettle or some other wide-mouthed, shallow, easy-to-carry container to decant the paint into.

● For masonry paint, a paint roller or spraying equipment (fitted with a special nozzle) is faster than a brush but a brush is better for covering uneven surfaces. There are special brushes for masonry paint but the crushed stone in the paint will ruin good tools so use cheaper ones you don't care about or are prepared to throw out.

● Protective clothing is a must. You need gloves to protect your hands when using chemicals such as strippers or sugar soap and goggles when using chemicals or abrasives in a power tool of any sort.

Planning the job

The best way to work is from the top down (fig. A)—that way debris and splashes won't fall on parts you have freshly painted. It also gets the worst over and done with first—and if you're going to hire a ladder or access tower, it means you can take back the equipment as soon as possible to cut down on hire costs.

Aim to paint when it has been dry for a few days and looks set to stay fair for a few more. Paint can be damaged by frost and by blistering sun so avoid days when either of these is forecast. On sunny days try to work in the shade. Above all, avoid windy days as the wind will pick up debris and deposit it on wet paint. If dirt particles do settle on the surface, you will have to let the paint dry before sanding them off and repainting.

If you are painting the walls as well as the trim—the woodwork and metalwork—think about a logical order which will suit you. Painting the walls is probably more

1 *When the paint starts to blister, you will need to scrape it off, doing one layer at a time*

2 *Brush a wood hardener over any rotten or decaying areas of woodwork before you apply the filler*

4 *The quickest and easiest way to remove any flaking rust is with a disc sander*

5 *For downpipes, wrap wet and dry paper around a sponge—it will accommodate the curve*

★ WATCH POINT ★

Old bedspreads make ideal dust-sheets. Jumble sales are a good source. Plastic sheeting is an alternative but needs to be firmly weighted down.

---

splashy so do them first and then the trim. Whatever the order, work carefully to avoid splashes and cover vulnerable areas with large dustsheets. Paving and flowerbeds in reach of splashing also need covering.

Preparation

Although it is tedious, thorough preparation is the key to successful results: before you start painting, carry out the necessary surface repairs.

Woodwork: Deal with peeling areas first by taking off all the loose and flaking paint.

The best way to do this is with an electric hot air stripper (fig. 1) or to burn it off with a blowtorch. Provided you have a long enough extension lead, the electric tool has several advantages; it can be used closer to glass, can cope with mouldings and won't scorch the wood. It is also safer than a naked flame.

Play the hot air or flame over the paint and, once it has melted, scrape it from the surface. If you do use a blowtorch, keep a plastic bottle of water handy in case of fire and take particular care at the eaves of the house where birds' nests may be hidden—they ignite in a flash and can set the whole roof alight. Around the glass of window frames you will have to resort to paint stripper, use abrasive paper wrapped around a block or use a dry-stripping tool.

If you discover any rotten wood, don't despair. The traditional way of dealing with rotten wood is to cut out the bad and replace it with a new section of preservative-treated wood. As most bits of wood are shaped mouldings, this usually means chiselling or

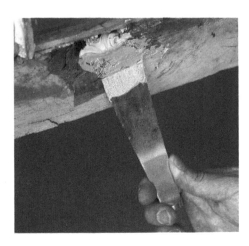

3 *Patch the damaged area with the repairing filler as smoothly as possible, then treat with preservative rods*

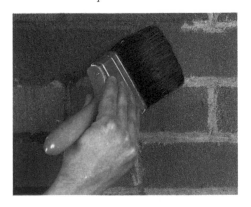

6 *Brush down masonry and, if it's still flaky and dusty, prime it with a stabilizing solution*

routing it to match the existing frame. However, for do-it-yourselfers who aren't skilled in carpentry, there are now two easier methods: one is to squirt a resin into the damaged wood and to let it harden, thus restoring strength to the wood; and the other is to use a rot treatment system: these typically include a hardener, a filler and preservative rods. To use a kit, first cut away the rotten wood before painting the hardener on to the surface (fig. 2) and filling the hollow (fig. 3). The preservative rods are inserted into the wood in drilled holes around the repair to protect it from further damage.

Fill any cracks or holes in sound wood with an exterior-grade wood filler. Where a good finish is important—such as on a ground-floor window sill—use the filler to raise the level (where the paint has been removed) back to the level of the sound paint. The difference is only a fraction, but if you are too hasty, it will always look patchy. If the joints of a frame or door have moved apart, force a flexible mastic-type filler into

the gaps. The resilience of this type of filler will allow it to take up any further movement in the wood.

If you come across cracked or damaged putty, don't be tempted to paint over it; it's much better to scrape it away and reputty (see Renewing putty).

Rub down the stripped wood and filled patches with a fine grade—120g—glass-paper. Wood that has been exposed for even a short while will have developed a weathered surface which must be sanded off.

Before painting over sound paintwork use an old paintbrush and a weak solution of sugar soap to clean off dirt. Other washing solutions such as detergent, soap powder or washing soda can be used, but sugar soap is easiest to rinse off completely—this is important because any residue will slow down or even prevent the paint from drying. Remember to clean (and later on, paint) the inside edges of opening windows. Rinse and then use wet and dry abrasive paper and water to rub down the surface. Rinse again to remove the grey flecks of abrasive and let the surface dry.

Metal frames: If paint is flaking off metal-work, the surface below will probably be rusty. This spells trouble and means a lot of work getting it back to a clean surface. There are special treatments for painting over rust which are claimed to inhibit its spread, but there is really no substitute for sanding it off.

For quick results use a silicon carbide disc fitted to a sanding attachment on a power drill. Where the disc will not reach or fit, try a small wire brush in a power drill and as a last resort for really fiddly or intricate areas use coarse wire wool by hand. Wash off all the debris and let the surface dry before priming with zinc phosphate primer.

Sound paintwork over metal can be cleaned with a sugar soap solution, as for woodwork, and repainted.

Apart from rust problems, there will be no need to remove paint from metalwork unless a build up of coats is causing an opening window to stick. If this is the case find out whether the window is plain steel or galvanized—if you've no problems with rust on any other metalwork (or when in doubt) assume that it is galvanized. It is best to leave galvanized steel alone as any stripping could damage the galvanizing coat and cause rust later on. For plain steel use a chemical paintstripper: wear gloves and goggles and stipple the stripper on to the paint with an old brush. Leave the stripper for the specified time—usually ten minutes —and then scrape it off carefully.

As with wood windows, look out for crumbly, loose putty on metal frames, too. Replace with new putty before repainting the frame (see Renewing putty).

Metal guttering and downpipes: If any metal guttering is in bad condition, consider replacing it with plastic, which never needs to be painted—it will be worthwhile in the long run. Otherwise treat rust as described above, by removing flaking areas with an abrasive disc attachment to an electric drill (fig. 4). For downpipes, wrap wet and dry abrasive paper round a sponge—it accommodates the curve (fig. 5).

Wash down sound paint with sugar soap solution. Check whether black paint is bituminous or not. If it is, and it's in good condition, leave it alone: bituminous paint forms a valuable protective layer. If you want to paint over bituminous paint, you must seal it first with aluminium primer or the original surface may bleed through your new finish.

Masonry: Use a stiff fibre or plastic brush (not a wire brush) to clean down the masonry and remove any loose bits. If the brush pulls a lot of material off, it shows that the surface is friable (decaying to powder) and will need priming with a stabilizing solution (fig. 6). Algae on masonry will stop the paint from adhering and will need to be washed with a fungicidal solution or diluted bleach.

If the wall is rendered or pebble-dashed make good any damage before proceeding. With brickwork check the pointing.

Renewing putty

Make sure that you buy the right putty for your window—they're not all the same. Metal frames require a different kind to the usual linseed oil-based wood putty, called metal casement putty.

Glaziers use a special hacking knife for removing defective putty but if you haven't got one, use an old chisel to prise off loose or cracked material (fig. 7). Remove only as much as you need and then clean out the rebate with a brush. Paint the inside of the rebate with primer and leave it to dry out thoroughly.

If you have a wooden window, take the opportunity while the putty is removed to have a good look at the sprigs—the small metal nails which hold the glass in place. If any are loose or rusty, knock in replace-ments with a pin hammer. Be very careful, as it's all too easy to smash the pane.

A professional glazier will roll a small handful of putty into a ball and, holding it in

7 *Remove cracked putty by levering it off with an old chisel or screwdriver*

8 *The easiest way to apply putty is to roll sausages and use them to line the rebate*

9 *Bevel the putty to form a seal against the glass. Let putty dry out before painting*

10 *Apply shellac knotting to seal 'live' knots which have never been painted*

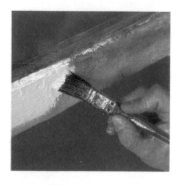

11 *Prime bare wood and if you are renewing putty, paint the rebate*

12 *Sand down lightly after each coat with wet and dry paper on a block*

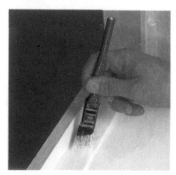

13 *Brush on the topcoat with even strokes to get a really smooth finish*

14 *Use a brush for painting uneven masonry. If necessary, apply two coats*

the palm of his hand, feed the putty through finger and thumb into the rebate. This is more difficult than it sounds and if you can't handle it try rolling out a sausage of putty first and use that to line the rebate (fig. 8).

Fresh putty is often wet with oil and tends to stick to your fingers instead of becoming pliable. Work in any oil which is noticeable on the top of a new tin and if it is still sticky, roll it out on a clean stone to remove any excess oil.

Level off the putty to form a bevel against the glass. A putty knife is normally used for this (fig. 9) but almost any flexible knife will do. Putty dries by contact with the air so don't paint over it for two weeks or so. When you do overpaint, carry the paint right over the edge of the putty by about 3mm to form a compact seal against the pane of glass.

Starting to paint

Before you start repainting, lay down your protective dustsheets on the ground below—they will save you a lot of time and bother clearing up any unwanted splashes of paint afterwards.

Wood: Apply shellac knotting to any knots which have never been painted (fig. 10) and then prime all bare wood (fig. 11). When you paint around glass hold a piece of card or a proprietary plastic or metal paint shield along the edge.

Most outdoor wooden surfaces are narrow so they are not too difficult to paint. For the best results spread the paint fairly thickly, taking particular care to cover the edges. Load the brush by dipping one-third of the bristle length into the paint and remove the excess by pressing both sides of the brush against the side of the container. Starting with the primer, put dabs of paint on the surface at 50mm to 60mm spaces. Then join the dabs together with several firm brush strokes, followed by light strokes parallel to the length of the frame. These last strokes should then just pull the top

surface right into line.

When the primer is dry—about 24 hours with an alkyd—use a fine-grade abrasive to rub down. Don't apply a lot of pressure and take care not to rub the paint thin (fig. 12). Follow the primer with the undercoat or first topcoat (fig. 13). Allow each coat to dry before rubbing it down lightly with a fine abrasive. Take most care with the application of the topcoat as it will be the layer on show, but remember not to skimp on the earlier stages.

Metalwork: Pipes and gutters are painted in much the same way as wood if you are using gloss paint. Bituminous paint goes on in two or three fairly thick coats with a large brush—it will ruin a new brush so use an old one.

Masonry: Brush, roll or spray on the paint, working on an area about two square metres at a time (fig. 14). One coat may be enough cover for some walls but it is often advisable to do two for a better, more professional finish.

For the bottom 300mm or so of the walls, you can use a bituminous paint to give a black plinth. Not only does this look effective but it also hides splashes which would otherwise disfigure a light coloured masonry paint.

REPOINTING BRICKWORK

The mortar joints in brickwork protect a wall from the damaging effects of rainwater. So if the mortar shows signs of decay, replace it with fresh mortar to make a new seal.

So long as brickwork is correctly designed and well built, it does not require much in the way of maintenance or repair work. But, as a building ages, the mortar joints between the bricks may begin to decay and crumble. Flaking joints in brickwork allow water to penetrate the wall and should never be neglected. The remedy for crumbling joints is repointing—clearing out the old mortar a short way and replacing it with fresh mortar to make a new waterproof seal.

Types of joint

The mortar between bricks can be finished in one of several ways; wherever possible, you should try to match new joints to the existing ones. However, if the old mortar is particularly badly decayed, you may not be able to see what type of joint has been used.
Weather-struck joint (A): The horizontal joints of this type have sloped surfaces which are slightly recessed below the upper brick and slightly overhanging the lower one. This slope allows water to run off quickly and prevents it from lodging on the lower edge of the joints, thus giving the wall further protection from rain and moisture. The vertical joints slope from one side to the other and match the angle of the horizontals above and below. Other types of joint commonly used in brickwork include:
Flush joint (B): When the mortar has almost dried, it is rubbed over with a piece of wood or old sacking to produce a surface flush with the surrounding brickwork. This type of pointing looks particularly effective when used in conjunction with smooth-surfaced bricks.
Keyed or rounded joint (C): This is produced by running along the surface of the mortar with a semi-circular piece of metal to form a shallow, curved depression.
Recessed joint (D): This is formed by scraping out the freshly laid mortar to a depth of about 6mm below the brick surface, then smoothing the surface of the

Right: This mortar is in bad need of repair—if left for very much longer rainwater will seep through and damp problems will occur

remaining mortar with a piece of wood the width of the joint. Recessed joints look best on rough-textured bricks but should be used only where they match the existing pointing. If used on external walls in cold climates, the bricks must be hard and durable, otherwise water may collect and freeze on the ledges causing pieces of brick to flake off.

Equipment

For repointing brickwork, even if you are working over quite a small area of wall, you need a spot board on which to mix the

mortar and a hawk for carrying the mortar to the work area. For applying the mortar to the joints, you need a pointing trowel, which resembles a small bricklayer's trowel and for clearing out the old mortar, use an old shavehook with its pointed end cut off square or a special plugging chisel, made for the purpose.

If you are applying weather-struck joints, you also need a tool called a *frenchman* for trimming away the excess mortar at the bottom of the horizontal joints.

To guide the frenchman neatly along the joints when trimming, you need a straight-edged piece of timber which is held immediately below the top edge of the lower brick. Attach two pieces of hardboard to each end of the piece of wood so that when it is held against the wall, there is a slight gap allowing the trimmed mortar to fall through (fig. E).

Wherever possible, the mortar for repointing should be mixed to match the composition of the existing mortar. If you do not know the mixing proportions of the original mortar, use a 1:1:6 (cement:lime:sand) mix or 1 part of masonry cement to 3 parts of sand. An

A. *The slope of weather-struck joints allows water to run off quickly, protecting the wall from rain*

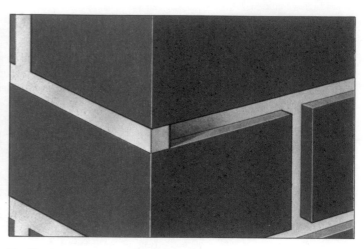

B. *Flush joints are produced by rubbing the mortar with a piece of wood to form a smooth surface*

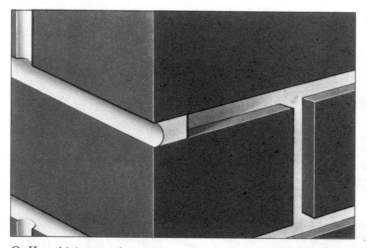

C. *Keyed joints are formed by smoothing the surface of the mortar with a rounded piece of metal*

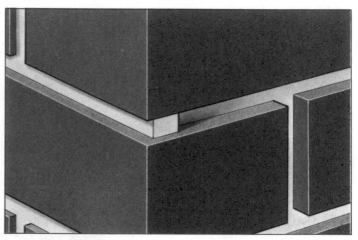

D. *The mortar in recessed joints is scraped out to a depth of about 6mm below the brick surface*

exception to the rule is the softer type of facing brick, where you should use a weaker 1:2:9 mix.

Use as fine a grade of sand as possible. If the only sand available is coarse, work it through a fine-meshed sieve to remove any pebbles.

Working considerations

Repointing is generally best undertaken during warm weather, as newly laid mortar is easily damaged by frost, particularly if you are using a weak mortar mix.

If the area to be pointed is large, tackle the work in stages, finishing off the joints over an area of about 2m² before moving on to the next. Start work at the top left hand corner of the wall and move across and downwards.

Mortar for pointing should be mixed in small batches and then used immediately. If you do mix too much, and some begins to

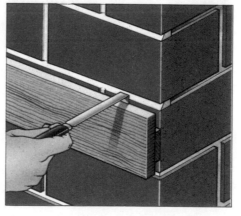

E. *To trim the excess mortar from the bottom of the weather-struck joints, use a frenchman and draw it along the top edge of a straight length of timber held just below the top edge of the lower brick. Attach a thin block of wood to each end of the timber to let the trimmed mortar fall through the gap. Make a frenchman from an old kitchen knife*

dry out and harden before you come to use it, discard it and mix a fresh batch. Do not try to reconstitute hardening mortar by adding more water to it.

Preparing the surface

If there is paving below the wall to be repointed, lay down a large sheet of polythene before you start work to protect the concrete path from mortar droppings.

With the protective sheeting in place, gently scrape any lichen and moss from the surface of the brickwork, taking care not to damage the faces of any bricks.

When the brickwork is clean, start raking the joints, using the cut-back shavehook or a plugging chisel, to a depth of between 12mm and 20mm—if you clear out the mortar further than this, you may damage the wall. Rake out the vertical joints—called *perpends*—first and then the horizontal, or *bed*, joints again taking care as you work not to damage the bricks.

Make sure that the recess formed in the joints is absolutely square and that no traces of old mortar remain on the edges of the bricks (fig. 1). If you fail to remove all the old mortar, the fresh mortar will not adhere properly and will soon flake and crumble.

When all the joints in the area to be repointed have been raked out, brush them thoroughly with a stiff hand brush to remove any remaining particles and dust (fig. 2).

In order to prevent too much moisture being absorbed by the surrounding brickwork from the fresh mortar, dampen the wall by flicking thoroughly clean water over the surface with a distemper brush (fig. 3). However, take care not to use too much water or you will soak the brickwork and the fresh mortar will not adhere properly.

Handling the trowel

Opinions vary on the best way of using a pointing trowel, so it is best to experiment until you find a style that suits you before you start.

You may find that the easiest method is to roll the mortar down the hawk and divide it into 'strands' as long as the trowel and about 12mm thick (fig. 5). Pick up each strand on the back of the trowel, along one edge, and flick it firmly into the waiting joint (fig. 6).

Weather-struck joints

Although slightly more difficult to construct than other types of brick joint, weather-struck joints are well worth the extra trouble as they give the wall added protection against water penetration.

To fashion weather-struck joints, start by transferring a manageable amount of mortar from the spot board to the hawk and carry it to the work area. Using the pointing trowel, force some mortar well into the first few perpends. Use the trowel to form a sloping angle by drawing it down the edge of the brick on the right-hand side of the joint, then cut off the excess mortar neatly with the edge of the trowel (fig. 7).

Move on to the bed joints above and below the filled perpends. Holding the trowel point upwards, press in more mortar, so that it is recessed to a depth of about 3mm at the top of the gap and slightly overhangs the edge of the brick at the bottom (fig. 8).

When you have used up the first batch

1 *To prepare the surface of brickwork for repointing, rake out some of the old mortar from the joints with an old shavehook*

3 *Dampen the surface of the brickwork with a distemper brush and clean water to make sure that the new mortar will bond*

of mortar, make the rough slope already formed in the perpends neater by trimming off any remaining excess with the pointing trowel so the mortar is recessed 3mm on the right-hand side.

Next, take the frenchman and straightedge to the wall. Holding the straightedge immediately below the lower edge of the bed joints, run the frenchman along the wall, with its tip pointing downwards, to cut off the excess mortar (fig. 9).

When the mortar has begun to harden, rub the joints with a dusting brush to remove any remaining waste then move on to the next section.

Flush and keyed joints

Pointing brickwork with flush joints pro-

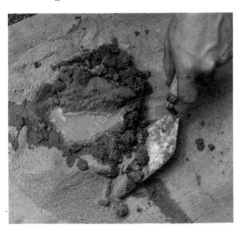

2 *Make sure that no traces of old mortar are left at the edges and brush down the joints to remove any remaining dust*

4 *Mix up your first batch of mortar taking care not to prepare too much. Try to match the composition of the mix with that of the old mortar*

vides a neat finish and can be particularly useful on old brickwork, where the outer corners of the bricks have crumbled and the wall surface is to be redecorated.

Start as for weather-struck joints by filling perpends then bed joints. Press the mortar firmly into place with the pointing trowel, until it protrudes slightly out from the surface of the brickwork.

When the mortar starts to harden, rub along the joints with a piece of wood or old sacking working in the same direction, until the mortar is flush with the surrounding brickwork. When completely dry, scrape over the mortar with a stiff piece of plastic to remove any excess particles of mortar dust.

To form a keyed joint, press the mortar well into the joints with the trowel, then smooth it to shape with a piece of metal rod, wooden dowelling or a piece of unridged

5 *Transfer a manageable amount of mortar to the hawk and divide it into strands as long as the trowel and about 12mm thick*

6 *Carry the hawk to the work area and pick up strands of mortar with the back of the pointing trowel. Force the mortar into the joints*

7 *If you are making weather-struck joints, form the sloping angle in the perpends by drawing the trowel down the edge of the brick*

8 *Tuck the mortar into the beds of weather-struck joints so that it is recessed under the top brick and slightly overhangs the lower one*

9 *Trim off the excess mortar at the bottom of the weather-struck joints with a frenchman, then brush the joints to remove waste*

10 *If you are making recessed joints use a shavehook, with its point cut off, to scrape out the freshly laid mortar*

garden hose. After rubbing the joints, trim the surplus mortar with the trowel.

Cleaning the brickwork

Although all the joints should be cleaned off as thoroughly as possible during the pointing process, it is difficult to achieve a completely clean finish by this means alone and some mortar will probably be left adhering to the edges of the bricks.

If marks still remain on the brickwork because the mortar has penetrated the surface, they can be removed with a very dilute solution of hydrochloric acid—1:10 by volume for clay bricks and 1:2 by volume for calcium silicate bricks. Saturate the brickwork with clean water, then apply the solution sparingly with an old paintbrush, taking great care not to get any on

★ WATCH POINT ★

Never try to remove mortar which has been spattered on bricks while it is still wet, or attempt to wash it off with water. Instead, leave the excess mortar to dry out completely then use a stiff scrubbing brush to brush the soiled bricks. Remove large lumps of mortar on clay bricks by scraping with the side of a trowel. With calcium silicate bricks, lightly abrade the surface with a brick of the same colour to remove large pieces.

your skin or in your eyes. When the area has been thoroughly treated, hose down the brickwork to remove every trace. The surface of some types of brick can be affected

by acid so, if in doubt, seek expert advice.

Colouring joints

To produce a matching or decorative effect in finished brickwork, proprietary colourants and special coloured cements are all available from builders' merchants and can be added to the mortar mix if desired. But because the colour will be altered by the texture of ordinary sand, you should use white sand in the mix, if possible. Remember also that cement with colour additives requires less water.

If you are repointing part of a wall and want the colour of the fresh mortar to match that in the existing joints, rub the joints around the area with candlewax to prevent them from absorbing the colouring in the new mortar mixture.

OPENING UP A FIREPLACE

Fires have always been a centre of attraction but, as central heating became more popular, many people blocked off their fireplaces and disposed of the decorative surrounds and mantelpieces. In doing so, they often lost a distinctive visual feature which radiators, efficient though they may be, cannot replace.

Nowadays, real fires are finding favour once more and there are also authentic looking solid fuel-effect gas fires, which offer a 'cleaner' form of direct heating, and which you can install yourself.

If you feel you've been rash in banishing the fireplace from your home's decorative scheme—or you've moved into a house which has suffered this fate—don't despair; reinstating a disused flue and installing a new decorative surround is quite straightforward.

Choosing a fireplace

Whether you search for a discarded original in junk shops, on demolition sites and at house clearances, or buy a brand new or reproduction model from a specialist supplier, you're sure to find a fireplace to suit your style of decor and—equally important—the proportions of your room.

The most basic type consists of a tiled concrete slab, often with a stepped profile, fixed against the wall, complete with a matching hearth. The fireback is usually made out of fireclay and the grate is a separate metal fitting.

Other more decorative fireplaces consist of a timber, marble or metal surround and mantel. These generally have an ornate cast-iron insert incorporating the grate and fireback.

If you opt for the home-made touch, kits are available containing special bricks, blocks or stones, which you can use to construct your own fire surround.

Types of finish vary considerably. Tiled surrounds may be plain or decoratively patterned, timber ones painted or varnished (to enhance the wood grain); metal surrounds are also commonly painted, but may be blacked and burnished.

Cast iron metal inserts were traditionally painted matt black—fireback, grate and all. This type looks particularly elegant when fitted with a surround and mantel featuring mouldings or carvings. You can usually mix and match tiles from the side channels,

and some antique dealers specialize in exchanging (and selling) original fireplace tiles—many of which are quite valuable.

If you want an original cast-iron fireplace and surround, be prepared to have it renovated—it's likely to be fairly rusty after being stored outside in all weathers. Examine it before purchase for missing or badly corroded parts that might affect its looks or performance, and which you might not be able to replace.

Not all fireplaces are the same size: they can measure anything from 300mm across to about 1200mm or more. So it's important that you choose one which will fit in your fireplace recess, and which is not so

large that it would completely dominate the room in which it will go.

Measure the overall width of the chimney breast so you can look for a mantel and surround that's not too large or too small. Also, accurately note the height, width and front-to-back dimensions of the recess.

Fireplace formats

Before you start to open up a blocked off fireplace, it's useful to understand how each part fits into place.

Most fireplaces consist of a constructional hearth (**A** in the diagram, overleaf)

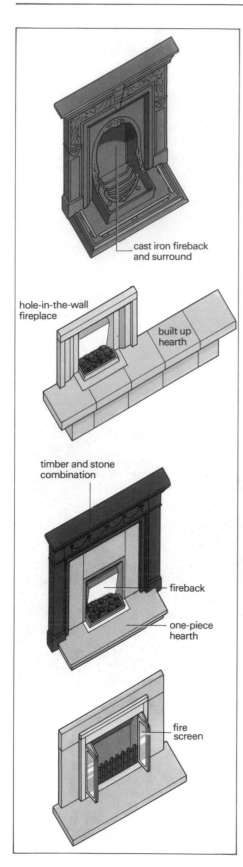

Fireplaces can be bought in all sorts of shapes and sizes and a variety of materials. Apart from looks, the ways in which they are assembled differ too

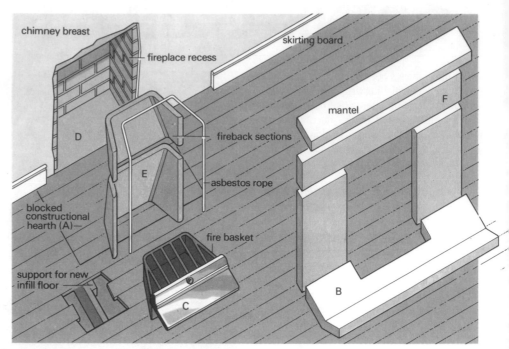

built to a standard size directly on the over-site concrete to prevent the spread of fire. The decorative (or superimposed) hearth (**B**) is set on top of the hearth.

The fire itself—contained in a grate or basket (**C**)—usually sits on a back hearth (**D**) within the recess. An angled fireback (**E**) channels smoke and fumes up the chimney while protecting the masonry of the flue from the heat of the fire. Ventilation needs serious thought—some fires draw air from the room while others are fed from vents built into the fire itself. You may need to reinstate the original ventilation.

The fire surround (**F**) is the decorative part of the fireplace, and usually includes a mantel; the surround may be made of tiled concrete, timber, cast-iron or marble (or an imitation product). It's usually fixed to the chimney breast around the recess with metal lugs and screws, or retained by metal ties; timber types are screwed to a batten framework fixed to the wall.

Some older types of surround include a cast iron insert, which combines grate, fireback and flue throat in one unit.

First steps

To find out how your fireplace was blocked off, tap the wall around the ventilation grille with your knuckles.

Roll back the floorcovering: on a timber floor, the hearth may have been broken up and new floorboards laid to continue the existing run, or the hearth may have been screeded level with the boards. With luck,

Common fireplace formats include integral front hearths—you may have to rebuild the constructional hearth as well as the fireback

the original hearth may be intact. On a solid floor, screed cement may have been used to level off the hearth with the surroundings.

The rest of the structure is more difficult to analyse from the outside. You may be able to remove the vent and peer inside the recess using a torch and mirror but most likely you'll have to break through the infill (see Opening up the recess).

Remove a small portion of the infill at the top of the blocked off opening to check on the condition of the lintel supporting the span: you may find a concrete beam, a metal bar or even a timber lintel has been used, and in some cases the opening will be supported by a brick soldier arch.

Remember, the full weight of the chimney breast for all the floors above will bear down on this point if it's left unsupported. Seek expert advice if you're not sure what to do.

The requirements for recommissioning a fireplace are simply that the flue and chimney breast are in serviceable condition (see Checking the flue) and that adequate ventilation is reinstated for the flue to 'draw'.

In addition to the fireplace, surround and fireback or firebricks you'll need fire cement and asbestos rope (for sealing gaps or bedding down firebricks or backs), gypsum plaster (for making good) and plenty of tough polythene sacks for disposing of the inevitable debris.

Opening up the recess

Start to open up the fireplace recess at a top corner, so you can examine the condition of the lintel or arch supporting the masonry above, plus its side bearers. First of all you have to locate the perimeter of the opening.

Roll back any carpeting from around the chimney breast and spread polythene dust sheets over the floor. Strip off any wall-covering from the area of the fireplace opening and look for a telltale ridge or variation in plaster colour. If you can't readily spot the perimeter, tapping with your knuckles may enlighten you. Score through the wall-paper around the perimeter to avoid tearing it back further than necessary.

Chop into the plaster at one of the top corners, using a club hammer and cold chisel until you reach the brick, block or plasterboard infill. Chop away more plaster to expose about a 600mm section of lintel, then chop down about 300mm to reveal the condition of the lintel bearers.

You should then be able to see how the infill is attached to the sides of the opening. If bricks have been used, and they're toothed into the side walls, seek professional advice before continuing.

So long as the lintel or arch bears down on at least a half brick at each side, you can go ahead and remove the infill. Hack off the rest of the plaster within the perimeter using a bolster chisel and club hammer, then start to chop out the individual bricks or blocks.

1 Drive a cold chisel into the corner of the new plaster to reveal the type of blocking and the lintel over the opening

2 Fully remove the blocking to reveal the exact size of the fireplace recess. Roll back carpets to expose the hearth

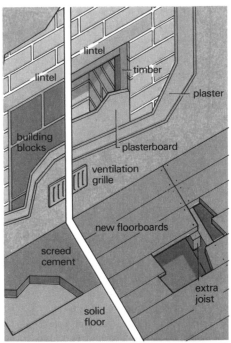

The recess blocking may have been made with plasterboard or with bricks or blocks. Floorboards or screed may cover the hearth

structure of the chimney for ventilation these must be replaced with solid bricks.

Now go outside and look up at the chimney stack. Check that the masonry is in good repair, that it isn't leaning and that the pot is undamaged.

The pot may have been fitted with a metal or ceramic cap, which is intended to

---

★ WATCH POINT ★

If you're certain the structure of the fireplace is sound, you'll find it far easier to chop out the bricks or blocks from the ventilation grill, working outwards.

Where plasterboard has been used, the job's much simpler—just expose the edges of the panel and lever it from its timber frame (set within the opening) using a crow-bar. Prise away the timber frame from within the opening, after first checking that it isn't helping to support the bricks and masonry above.

Bag up the debris straight away—but save whole bricks for re-use elsewhere—and dispose of it. Clear any debris from the recess and if the fireback is still in place, examine it for damage. If it's badly deteriorated, or your replacement fireplace has its

own (sizes do vary), hack it out and lever it away with a crowbar. Clean up the recess.

Examine the flue for suitability (see Checking the flue), then measure up the opening for the new fireplace. The vital statistics you'll need to take include the height of the opening, its width and the front-to-back depth. Also note the overall width of the chimney breast so you can obtain a suitable mantel and matching decorative surround.

Checking the flue

If you intend to install an open fire (or a gas solid fuel-effect type) you must ensure that both the fireplace and flue are sound.

Examine the brickwork around the open-ing, then peer up the chimney to look for blockages or faults in the masonry. Check the flue lining at the same time—it will probably be a layer of fire cement.

If any airbricks have been let into the

★ WATCH POINT ★

Simply looking up the chimney (armed with a torch) is the best way to examine the structure, but if the flue is too small, use a mirror to reflect the inside of the chimney.

---

seal off the flue from rain yet keep it venti-lated. You'll have to remove this before you can re-use the fire.

In some cases, the pot may have been re-moved and the stack sealed with a concrete slab, with airbricks fitted around the sides for airflow; the stack may even have been cut down in size to a mere stub when the fireplace was blocked off.

Reinstating the chimney in this case will mean substantial rebuilding of the stack and the fitting of a new pot—not a job to be undertaken lightly or without adequate access to the roof.

Remaking the hearth

How you fit your new decorative hearth depends on the way the original one was removed. It may simply be a matter of cutting back the surface and bedding tiles in mortar—or you may have to rebuild the constructional slab and back hearth.

If the original fireplace had a decorative hearth of tiles set flush with the floorboards, and these are still fixed and in good order, you may be able to retain them.

Sometimes, however, they're set at an angle at the back to fit along the line of the original surround. Your new surround will probably not match this profile exactly, so you may prefer to replace them with new ceramic or quarry tiles.

Break up the tiles and remove them using a bolster chisel and club hammer.

Fireplace tiles commonly measure about 110mm × 52mm, although versions about

3 *Most hearths need rebuilding to provide a fireback at the new hearth level. Remove boards and erect formwork*

4 *Rebuild the old constructional hearth to the level you need to match the fireback and the new hearth—use a stiff concrete mix*

50mm square are also available, so you shouldn't have any trouble refitting new ones on the hearth.

Remove all traces of old mortar (or tiling adhesive if this has been used) and clean up the base of the hearth.

Brush out any dust and debris, then wet the concrete surface to improve the adhesion of the mortar and prevent it from drying out too rapidly. Mix up a bucketful of fairly dry ready-mixed bricklaying mortar and spread this on the hearth to a depth of approximately 6mm.

Bed each tile in place, starting at the outer corners and working inwards to fill the hearth. Laying hearth tiles is exactly like laying quarry tiles.

If the original hearth has been cut back so that floorboards could be continued up to the chimney breast, prise these up with a club hammer and bolster chisel and remove the extra joists that will have been fitted to support them.

Clean up the hacked-back surface of the constructional hearth, removing loose debris and dust. You'll need to rig up a timber formwork box to mould and retain a new concrete mix while it sets. Measure the dimensions of the hearth—average size hearths are about 980mm × 360mm—and cut out panels of thin plywood or hardboard.

Wedge the panels between what's left of the slab and the walls surrounding it—nailing them to the timber plate on top if possible. Pin together the corners or fix them with battens so the concrete can't seep out.

Prepare a concrete mix of 1 part cement, 2 parts sharp sand, and 3 parts aggregate so it's stiff but workable. Wet the top of the original slab, then tip in the wet concrete.

Level off the concrete about 50mm below

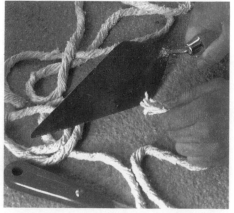

5 *Continue the concrete into the base of the recess. Place asbestos rope between the hearth and the fireback concrete*

the finished surface of the hearth to allow for a mortar screed plus tiling. Use a straight-edged length of timber cut to fit between the formwork to compact the mix using a chopping action. Draw the timber across the concrete to smooth it, and check that it's level. Leave the concrete for about 48 hours to set before adding a screed.

Add a mortar mix of 1 part cement to 4 parts sand, and smooth it off level with the floor surface if you're fitting a raised hearth, or bed tiles in the top for a recessed hearth. Take the screed into the fireplace recess itself, if the back hearth is damaged.

If your fireplace includes an integral hearth, like the one shown, there's no need to rebuild the constructional hearth as long as the back hearth is rebuilt to the new height and the gap between the two is sealed with asbestos rope and fire cement.

Rebuilding the fireback

The fireback protects the masonry of the chimney from the intense heat of the fire, channels smoke and fumes up the flue via its angled throat, and throws heat out into the room. Firebacks are either a single unit or separate bricks, which you cement into place. The type you'll need depends on the fire you've chosen.

If you're fitting a tiled slab fire surround, or the type without an integral flue and fireback, you'll probably have to install a completely new fireback. The type you'll need is probably the single unit.

Firebacks are sold in standard widths—commonly 406mm and 457mm, although larger sizes are available. If the original one is still there, measure the inside front open-

6 *With many firebacks, you need to cut the unit into two pieces along a pre-formed line. Use a bolster and hammer to do so*

7 *Use fire cement and asbestos rope to site and level the fireback. Place corrugated card behind—it chars away later and forms a gap*

8 *Trowel a layer of fire cement on to the top of the lower section. Make sure you cover the asbestos rope at the sides with fire cement, too*

9 *Bed the top section on the lower one and continue the rope and fire cement around the joint between the wall and fireback*

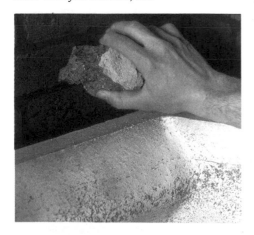

10 *Fill the gap behind with hardcore and weak mortar. Build up flaunching at the top to match the shape of the fireback throat*

ing to give you the size for the replacement. Otherwise, measure the width of the recess and order the size that corresponds.

Some one-piece firebacks must be split in two along a pre-formed weakness line, then cemented back together again when fitted; this joint allows for expansion to prevent cracking. Make sure you know which sort you're buying. To split the fireback, tap along the break line very gently (it will take quite some time) using a club hammer and bolster chisel, until it splits in two. You'll then have two parts: a bottom section and a top section.

Mix up a little mortar and trowel a 19mm thick screed along the bottom of the recess on which to bed the lower section of the fireback. The top and sides of the opening—between the walls and the fire-

back—must be sealed with asbestos rope to provide a non-combustible buffer to prevent cracking due to expansion. You may need to test fit the fireback and build out the sides of the recess for a tight fit. Cut the rope to length and tack it in place with masonry nails at the top.

Lift the lower fireback section into place and tap it down evenly on the mortar, using the handle of your club hammer. Check with a spirit level that it's horizontal at the top and vertical within the opening. Pull it forward against the asbestos rope, so it compresses it slightly against the top and sides.

The space behind the fireback—back and sides—must be filled with a weak mortar mix of one part cement to nine parts sand.

Tip in the mix and add some rubble to bulk it out—old bricks or pieces of the damaged original fireback will do. Compact the mix lightly behind the fireback—make

---

★ WATCH POINT ★

Before you add the mortar, tuck one or two sheets of corrugated cardboard behind the fireback. This chars away later and provides an expansion gap.

---

sure you don't dislodge the lower section and that it remains flush at the front.

Trowel a 19mm thick layer of fire cement—it's available in tins from builders' merchants—along the top of the lower fireback section, and lift the top section into place, pressed against the asbestos rope attached at the sides and top.

Point in the sides over the rope with fire cement then run a wet paintbrush over it to leave a smooth finish.

Tip more weak mortar mix and rubble into the gap behind the fireback, then build up mortar flaunching over it at the back so that its slope matches that of the fireback's angled throat. Smooth the mortar flaunching with a damp trowel.

Cast-iron fireplaces with integral flue throats usually have firebricks cemented in at the base, around the grate, where the fire sits. Often these bricks—flat or U-shaped—are intact on old fires, but new ones are readily available from builders' merchants and hardware stores. Simply measure the size you need across the front opening, then check it for fit against the fire, before you fit the metal insert in the opening.

Clean up the rim of the opening where the brick fits and trowel new fire cement onto the brick. Press it against the metal rim. Point in the front joint for neatness.

Fitting the surround and mantel

Whether you're installing a tiled slab surround, a brick or stone frontage, or a cast-iron insert with separate side pillars and mantel, the procedure is virtually the same: the components must be held against the wall with integral lugs. Timber and marble surrounds are the exception. The former are sometimes fixed with screws to battens; the latter need special metal ties to hold them in place.

To fix a tiled slab surround, measure the height and width, transfer these dimensions to the wall and cut back the plaster with a 25mm margin all round, using a club hammer and bolster chisel.

Lift the surround into place and rest it against the wall. Check that it's central on the chimney breast, then drill holes through the integral lugs (usually about 75mm from the top; sometimes at the bottom) to take the fixing screws. Secure the surround to the wall in the appropriate manner.

Set the tiled hearth slab on the constructional slab using a bed of 3:1 sand/cement mortar, about 20mm thick.

Cast-iron surrounds with separate pillars and mantel are more complicated. Sometimes the metal inserts have to be bolted to the wall, and details depend on the exact type. More usually, the unit simply rests against the wall without the need to attach it.

When you're measuring up for the metal insert, the vital statistics are the height and width of the projecting fireback/flue throat section: this must fit within the recess easily so that the insert's flat front panel rests against the front of the chimney breast. Check the dimensions before you buy. The unit usually incorporates a throat closure plate: make sure there's room to open this.

11 *Level or attach the hearth with fire cement before adding the side pillars (these are fixed in a number of ways, shown below)*

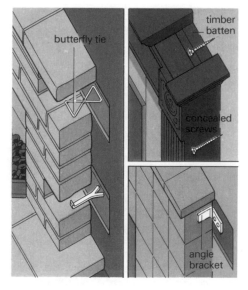

Fixing methods for pillars may be any of those shown—make sure the pillars are vertical and the correct distance apart

Prepare the fireplace opening for the insert by hacking back the plaster all round, then lift it into position.

Types of surround to fit round metal inserts vary considerably: they may be a

single unit or separate components such as side pillars, mantel and front cross panel (which fits under the mantel).

If your surround has integral lugs, simply offer it up to the wall and mark how much plaster you'll have to remove around the perimeter. Chop away the plaster, then screw the surround to the wall.

Marble surrounds (or those made from simulated materials) probably won't have any lugs so you'll have to attach the components with metal ties. You can use wire butterfly ties, as used in cavity wall construction, or right-angled strips of galvanized metal with screw holes on the upstanding part of the fixing.

Side pillars usually incorporate a recess at the top, into which you can mortar the tie.

Prop the pillars upright with long timber battens, then check them for level and make sure they are plumb. Adjust the props to set the pillars vertically.

To use butterfly ties, chop out the mortar joint between two bricks, level with the pillar recesses. Slot one wing of the tie into the joint and rest the other in the pillar recess. Mix up some mortar and trowel it into the recess, covering the tie. Fill in the mortar joint.

Galvanized strips are fixed similarly. They're screwed to the wall, saving you from having to rake out the mortar joints.

Fit the cross panel when the mortar holding the pillars has set. The panel rests on a ledge formed in the side pillars, usually on small corbels. You don't need to stick these in place, although you can bed them in a little fire cement.

Centre the mantel within the width of the chimney breast and mark the wall to indicate how much plaster you'll have to cut back so it can fit flush against the masonry. Remove the mantel, chop out the plaster, then trowel some fire cement around the top rim of each pillar. Return the mantel to the pillars and tap it down gently but firmly. Scoop off any excess cement that's squeezed out, then check the shelf for level—across its width and from front to back. Adjust the thickness of the cement bed if necessary.

To complete the fireplace—whichever type of surround you've fitted—make good the channel around the perimeter with a one-coat plaster application.

Timber surrounds often require slightly different treatment: they may be screwed directly to the wall, the screw heads concealed by mouldings or wood pellets, or they may include fixing lugs. Alternatively, you might have to nail timber battening to the wall first, then screw the surround to this length of battening.

REMOVING A FIREPLACE

A disused or unsightly fireplace can be an annoying waste of space and spoil the general scheme of your decor by serving as an obsolete centre of attention. Removing the fireplace itself—but leaving the chimney breast intact—leads to a better use of space and also helps to prevent expensive heat loss at the same time.

The job itself isn't difficult but it is messy, disruptive and can involve some heavy lifting. It's best to work with an assistant to remove the bulk of the debris.

The necessary sequence of steps will largely depend on the construction of your fireplace—the materials used, method of fixing, type of fireback, and how the surround is attached to the hearth at the base.

After the job's done, it's a matter of repairing the damage to walls and floors caused by the removal, redecorating and arranging for the chimney pot to be capped.

Planning considerations

Before you begin any detailed planning, examine the fireplace—get the chimney swept first and you'll minimize any mess.

Try to familiarize yourself with how the fireplace is constructed and how it's likely to be fixed to the chimney breast or wall (see diagram on page 35).

Consider what to use for blocking the opening. Lightweight concrete building blocks and mortar are best because they provide comparable stability but if your fireplace is made of brick you can save money by using those you take out (as long as you clean them before re-using them). On the other hand, using plasterboard nailed to a timber framework would allow you to decorate more quickly—although you still need to 'skim' the surface with plaster to disguise the false front.

The removal itself will be messy, so protect furnishings or furniture and remove curtains. Make sure you have dust sheets, plastic sheets or something similar to cover those items you can't take out of the room.

You'll also need a large plastic sheet (heavy duty) to cover the carpet from the point where you fold it back round the hearth area.

Debris: Getting rid of the debris is worth some advance thought. Some of the concrete can be taken out in one piece but much will have to be broken up, so make

sure that you have a supply of heavy duty plastic bags at hand—they're available from builder's merchants. A wheelbarrow is useful for carrying out the bags and smaller debris. Clear a path to the nearest outside door and protect the carpet.

Materials and tools

You only need a few tools; long cold chisel, crowbar or nailbar, club hammer, bolster, screwdriver, hacksaw, plane or planer file, drill and assortment of bits, bricklayer's trowel, plasterer's trowel and spirit level.

Materials will depend on the method you use. For blocking with building blocks or bricks, you need to re-use the old bricks from the fireback or surround or buy new lightweight building blocks. Various sizes of aerated blocks are available but the one most commonly available measures 440mm × 215mm × 100mm. Measure the area to be filled and work out how many you need—you may not be able to do so ac-

curately until you've removed the fire surround. You also need a three-brick high airbrick, a medium size bag of ready mixed bricklaying mortar (about 2kg should be sufficient), browning and finishing plaster (a 50kg bag of each is more than enough though you could use modern one-coat plaster too), steel mesh plastering strips to cover the join between the old and the new, 19mm flat topped galvanized nails and an adjustable ventilator cover to fit on the room side of the fireplace.

For panelling you'll have to measure up and see what size of plasterboard is required. You'll also need 50mm × 25mm battens for a framework, 50mm countersunk screws, wall-plugs, scrim mesh to cover the joins between panel and fireplace, galvanized nails to secure the plasterboard to the frame and finishing plaster only.

Whichever method you use to block the opening, order extra matching skirting board to fill the gap created by the removal of the fireplace—it's easiest to remove the boards from either side and install a completely new run of skirting rather than patching in.

If the floor is solid you'll need extra sand and cement to fill the holes left by the hearth. If it's made of timber, you'll need extra floorboards.

Removing the fireplace

Protect your eyes against flying fragments—wear goggles, gloves and protective clothing. First clear a space and protect furnishings against dust and damage. Provide a clear route to the outside. Work in the order surround, fireback, hearth.

Begin by removing any skirting boards on either side of the fireplace—gently lever

off with a bolster or claw hammer to avoid damage to the surrounding plasterwork. How you remove the rest of the surround depends upon how it's constructed and fixed to the wall (see diagrams opposite).

Tiles on a concrete slab: Metal lugs with securing screws are usually located about 75mm from the top of the surround on either side of the fireplace. To release the fixings some damage to the surrounding plaster is inevitable. Minimize it by cutting into the plaster with a bolster and hammer all the way round appoximately 25mm from the edge of the surround. Chunks of plaster will then be less likely to fall off later or as you prise away the surround—this can happen if you remove plaster from around the fixings only.

Different fixing methods

When you have exposed the fixings, remove the screws. If they are tight—and penetrating oil doesn't do the trick—try inserting the blade of an old screwdriver into the screw slot and tap firmly—the vibration may dislodge the screw's hold. If not, drill out the screw head with a high speed steel (HSS) drill bit of the appropriate size.

If you find nails securing the fixings instead of screws, prise them out. The end of a crowbar may come in useful here—a sharp blow with a bolster and hammer will probably be needed to start the nail off.

With the screws or nails removed, the surround will be ready to come out. In general, surrounds come out in one piece so get an assistant to take the weight.

What you find when the surround comes away depends on the age and quality of the original installation. You may be deluged by dust and rubble from the bricks that supported the fireback or you may find this brickwork intact—the latter is more convenient but have sacks handy anyway.

Place a crowbar between the surround and the wall and lever gently. Prise at a number of points to loosen the whole surround at once—it should release itself fairly easily. Make sure you have an assistant to take the weight as it moves away from the wall. Then lower the surround gently to the ground until you are ready to dispose of it.

If the surround won't come away in one piece, break it up with a cold chisel and club hammer. Cut through any reinforcing bars with a hacksaw and put the debris into bags or straight into your wheelbarrow.

Cast iron fireplaces: Fixings for these types are likely to be lugs and screws buried behind the plaster at the edges—perhaps four instead of two. If there is a separate section of cast iron framing the opening, you'll have to loosen the nuts and bolts securing it or cut through them with a hacksaw. Move the surround in one piece if you can. Remember that attractive fire surrounds may well have considerable second-hand value. Check locally to see if there is an architectural salvage merchant in your area—they might be interested in your surround.

Timber surround fireplaces: Any separate mantle section must be loosened with a club hammer and lifted out first—it may be plastered into the wall or just fixed to the top of the surround. The main surround will be screwed to battens—the screws may be countersunk and filled or plugged with wood. Tap the surface until

1 Prise away the skirting board carefully from both sides. You'll fit a new section later

2 Chip off plaster to expose lugs. Unscrew these or drill out the screws if rusted in

3 Prise away the surround—take care as it is heavy and may move surprisingly easily

4 Remove the fireback. One-piece backs may need breaking up to get them out. Built-up backs come apart easily

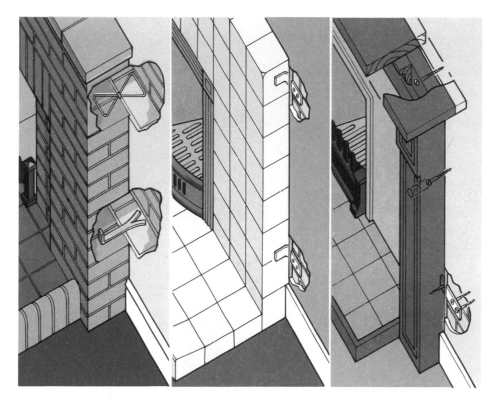

chimney breast. If one won't move try another—they may be interdependent. If they still won't move, search around for fixings and remove them before continuing —use one of the variety of methods suggested earlier.

Back boilers

A living room or kitchen fireplace may have a back boiler built into it (see diagram).

If you block up the fireplace, the boiler must be removed otherwise there's a risk of water in it freezing in cold weather and causing bursts and leaks that will be almost impossible to repair.

Don't be tempted to leave the feed pipes connected to the hot water cylinder by cutting them at the boiler end and blanking them off—you must disconnect them at the cylinder end to prevent all possibility of potential leaks and bursts.

Boiler removal: The boiler is linked to the hot water cylinder by two pipes—the flow and return pipes. You must drain the

Built-up surrounds have lugs mortared into the wall. Dismantle bit-by-bit.
Tiled or iron surrounds have lugs at the side buried in plaster and fixed with screws.
Timber surrounds may be screwed directly to the wall or fixed with side lugs

you hear a change of sound, scrape off the filler and undo the screws. Lift the surround away from the wall.

If you can't find the screws it may be that the surround is fixed to side lugs similar to those already described, so remove them in the same way. But if neither of these fixings seem obvious, use a crowbar to level the surround away. You may need to chip off any tiled inner sections to reveal any concealed fixings on the inside.

Brick or stone fireplaces: Dismantle this type bit by bit and clean the bricks if you intend to re-use them. Start by forcing the bolster into the top course of mortar. Tap free each brick in turn and take it out. Continue working downwards. If you come across metal ties between brick and wall, release them by knocking out the mortar and working the ties loose by pushing them backwards and forwards until they pull free.

Just above the fire opening, you may find a steel plate acting as a lintel for the material of the surround itself (don't confuse it with the lintel for the chimney breast which you **must** leave in place). Take out the surround's lintel, then continue work.

Removing the fireback

The fireback is the portion of the fireplace behind the opening—it contains fire-resistant material to support the fuel and reflect heat. It's wise to remove the fireback so that you can provide the necessary space for blocking the opening.

There are different types of fireback (depending on the age of the fireplace and the builder) so the dismantling process will vary slightly from one case to another.

Fireproof clay shell: This is in one piece and you will have to chip away at the mortar holding it to pull it away from the chimney breast. It may not pull out easily so your only alternative is to break it into sections and remove it in pieces.

Once it's out there will be rubble, infill and soot, so carefully clean this out.

Firebrick backs: Some fireplaces—even fairly modern ones—have a construction of individual firebricks rather than a one piece shell. Start chipping away from a cold chisel and club hammer or a small crowbar until you get all the bricks out. Once you manage to break up the first two bricks you should be able to lever away the others without too much difficulty. Clear away the rubble in the same way.

Solid steel castings: These are to be found in older fireplaces (especially cast iron ones) and are in three pieces—back wall, sides and surround. Prise each part away from the

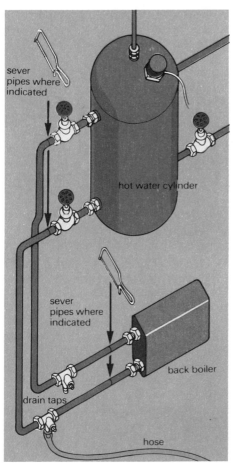

If there's a back boiler, turn off the supply and drain the pipes. Then cut the pipes at boiler and cylinder and cap off

system to remove the water then cut the pipes at the cylinder end and blank them off.

First empty the hot water system—turn off the mains water stop tap and open all the basin and bath taps to drain the water and allow air in. The boiler drain taps are generally in the wall next to the fire surround—attach hoses to these, run them outside and then open the taps.

When the system is empty, disconnect the feed pipes from cylinder to boiler at the point where they leave the cylinder. Joints may be compression joints or capillary joints. In either case, use a hacksaw to cut through the pipes about 50mm from the joint. Blank off the pipe ends from the cylinder with compression-type pipe blank caps of a matching size—use PTFE tape for a fully watertight fit. Refill the hot water system by turning on the mains stop tap and adjusting the basin and bath taps to give only a steady trickle. When the trickle is fluent and has stopped spluttering, turn the taps on and allow the system to fill up. Check the pipe blanking caps for leaks.

Remove any firebricks around the boiler and lift out. You don't need to remove the feed pipes from the wall—as long as they are empty. Remove any boiler accessories—like the flue—at the same time.

5 *Lever up the hearth. On wooden floors there's a concrete or brick shelf beneath the mortar bedding of the hearth itself*

leave the base alone. Fill any holes or cracks in the mortar with a 3:1 mix of sand and cement to the level of the surrounding floor. Add a little waterproofing agent to the screed to prevent damp penetration from below. Finish off with a steel float.

Blocking the opening

You can close the opening left by the removal of the fireplace with building blocks or with plasterboard—but before you do so you must arrange for enough ventilation inside the chimney.

Adequate ventilation is important if you are to avoid condensation and stale air—both of which can cause external staining and expensive rot.

There is a further consideration, too. At some stage—preferably when you're working on the roof—you should either remove the redundant chimney pot and block off the stack so that water won't seep downwards, or simply cap the pot. In neither case should you seal the chimney breast totally—some air must be allowed to circulate freely.

With or without this measure, the free flow of air may cause an uncomfortable draught and a corresponding heat loss. You must decide at this stage—before you block the chimney—whether you can make a compromise between the vital ventilation and the possible discomfort of the heat loss. The ideal situation is to install an adjustable ventilator grille at the fireplace and to allow controllable ventilation inside the chimney. Block the opening with your ventilator

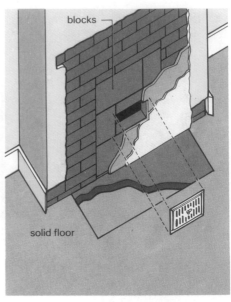

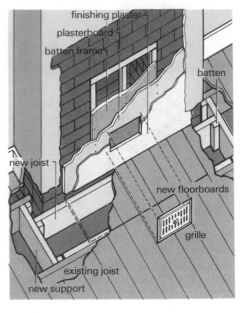

Fill solid floors with concrete. Fill the opening with lightweight blocks or panel in with plasterboard—always include a vent. Fill a wood floor with extra boards

grille in mind—place an airbrick in the blockwork as you proceed.

Aerated blocks: Measure the opening to find how many blocks you need to use—you'll probably need to cut at least one. Spread a 10mm layer of ready mixed bricklaying mortar across the opening. Insert a layer of heavy duty polythene as a damp proof course, then spread a further layer of mortar on top. Start building up your blockwork, remembering that approximately 100mm from the bottom you must install an airbrick—later to be covered with the ventilator grille.

★ WATCH POINT ★

It's easiest to tackle the job of lifting the hearth from two sides at once—lever one side up, push a piece of wood under it to keep it off the floor, then do the same to the other side.

Levelling the hearth

On a solid floor, the hearth itself is bedded with a thin layer of mortar—you need to remove it to make the floor level with the rest of the room. On timber floors there may be something different—the hearth may sit on a 'shelf' of concrete projecting from the chimney breast or on a brickwork projection.

You should be able to lift out the concrete bedding in one piece. Drive a cold chisel under the hearth and break the bond. When a good size gap has opened, push in your crowbar and lever the whole thing away from the floor. You'll need help to lift the hearth out.

If the hearth is recessed and has a layer of tiles flush with the floor, all you need do is take them off with a hammer and chisel and

Mark and cut a block at the appropriate place to accept the larger sort of airbrick (three bricks in height). Use a bolster and hammer or a masonry saw to cut the block.

As you add subsequent courses, check that blocks or bricks are aligned by holding a straightedge or a spirit level against the face of the blockwork.

When the work is complete, make a final check with your straightedge or spirit level that the blocks are flush and then leave the mortar to dry.

Plasterboard and framework: Measure the perimeter of the opening and cut 50mm × 25mm battens to make a simple frame. Fix in the battens, recessing them to take account of the thickness of the board —the frame must be set back from the face of the wall so that the plasterboard finishes flush. Use 50mm No. 8 screws and wallplugs. Cut the plasterboard to fit the opening then cut a hole 100mm from the bottom of the board to accept the ventilator grille—use the grille itself to mark the size of cut. Drill holes at the corners of your marked area and insert a padsaw to join them and remove the waste. Screw or nail the board to the frame.

simpler to use but it is more expensive.

In the case of block or brickwork, you can plaster 12 hours after the mortar is dry. First clean up the brickwork around the opening. Before you begin plastering, spray some water over the surface with a plant spray container or brush on some water.

Traditional plaster: Rake out the mortar between the new brick or blockwork to a depth of about 10mm to ensure a good key. Apply a first coat of plaster (browning) with a plastering trowel—don't cover the ventilation area. Next apply a skim of finishing plaster, making quite sure the new plaster is flush with the existing wall.

When the plaster is thoroughly dry, fit a ventilation grille over the airbrick.

For plasterboard, either use jointing tape and compound or 'skim' the surface with a thin layer of finishing plaster.

DIY one coat plaster: For a small job like this, you can use a ready mixed plaster such as Polyplasta, in place of both kinds of traditional plaster and for laying the blocks. It takes four hours to set, so there is plenty of time to get a really smooth finish for decorating right away. If in any doubt about the finish, try bringing the first coat of plaster

Use a ready-mix bag of fine mortar, or make your own with one part of cement to three parts of sharp concreting sand.

Trowel the mix onto the base and work it roughly into position. Use the surround to give you the level by working a straightedge across from side to side with a sawing action. After establishing a level, finish off with a wood or metal float.

The important thing to avoid is over-trowelling. This brings the cement to the surface which will tend to be dusty and crumbly as a result. After a few hours, the water will have risen to the surface by itself. This is the moment for a few finishing strokes with the float. If the weather is hot or the house is well heated, cover the screed with polythene or wet sacking for twenty-four hours to cure properly. A final coat of dilute PVA will reduce the tendency to dust even further.

After about 24 hours (less for ready-mixed plaster) you should be able to replace skirting boards and other fixed woodwork but a fully plastered wall will take a considerable time to dry out enough to decorate. In the meantime, apply a coat of emulsion paint.

6 *Arrange a layer of polythene over the first course to act as a DPC*

7 *Position the airbrick flush with the surrounding plaster—not the blockwork*

8 *To improve the adhesion of the plaster, rake out the mortar joints*

9 *Bring the browning coat of plaster close up to the final level. Skim when hard*

Cover the join of the frame and existing wall with fibre scrim if you intend to finish with a thin skim of finishing plaster. If you don't want to finish in this way, screw a timber moulding through the board and into the frame battens behind. Tidy up by restoring the surrounding plaster.

Finishing off

When finishing off, you have a choice of plasters. You can either mix your own or buy a DIY one coat type—available ready-mixed in various sizes of tub. The latter is

up almost to level, and then putting on either a final coat of ready-mixed skimming plaster, or a thin coat of the general purpose variety that you can work until you have a smooth finish.

Screeding a hearth: The final work is screeding over the hearth to bring it up to level, if you are not going to sand the floor.

Clean off all dust and rubble from the surface of the concrete underfloor and remove all loose material. Damp down with plenty of water and prime the surface with some PVA adhesive.

In either case, add some more PVA to the mix that you prepare for the screeding.

Timber floors: If your floor is stripped and sanded you'll want to match the exposed hearth area to the surrounding floor. Break up the concrete base, take it up and remove any rubble and infill underneath. Fix a new joist close to the wall between the joists on either side; this will enable you to nail a batten to the existing joists and nail the new joist to the battens.

Cut back the existing floorboards to the nearest joists and nail a 100mm × 50mm timber to the existing joists to support the ends of the new floorboards. Trim them to size and fit. Treat the new timbers with preservative.

WHY INSULATE?

If your house is cold in winter, or you find your fuel bills are too high, then thermal insulation may be the answer. However, it's a fairly complex subject, and before you start worrying over much about *how* you do it, it's important to know a little about *why* and *where* you should insulate.

So long as the temperature outside your house is lower than that inside, your house will be losing heat—precious heat that you have paid for. You can't stop this heat loss entirely, but you can slow it down by lining your house—or parts of it—with insulation materials. The slower the heat is lost from your house, the lower your fuel bills will be.

stout board laid across two or three joists—not on the joists themselves, and certainly not on the ceiling of the room below as this will not bear your weight.

Heat lost through walls

You lose a great deal of heat through walls —perhaps as much as through a totally uninsulated roof. The problem is that insulating walls can be a very expensive job, so it is not nearly as worthwhile in terms of saving money as insulating the roof.

For houses with brick or blockwork

external cavity walls, the simplest method is to fill the cavity with an insulation material. This is a job best left to the professionals.

An alternative method, which can be used with almost any house construction, is to line either the inside or the outside surface of the exterior walls with insulation. You can line walls internally with panels of polystyrene bonded to plasterboard—for example, gyproc thermal board. This can be fixed either with adhesive or by nailing. Or you can use the interlocking Epsicon polystyrene panel system—see page 41. Another method is to nail battens to the wall, fill the space between with rolls of

Insulating the roof space

If you have no insulation at all in your loft or roof space, then you should certainly put some in—a lot of heat is lost through the roof, yet it's one of the easiest areas to insulate. In the UK, you can get Government grants covering some of the cost of roof insulation, if there is none to start with.

For most people the best choice of material to use is glass fibre, or mineral fibre blanket, which is laid between the joists forming the ceiling of the room below the loft space. The material comes in rolls of a width that suits the normal joist spacing, and it is a relatively simple matter to unroll them directly into place in the loft. For safety, fix up a light in the loft and stand on a

Shown (right) are the main trouble spots where you will lose heat from your home. Up to 20 per cent of home heating can be lost through the roof space (1)—insulation can save as much as 16 per cent. There are a variety of methods you can use. The most popular is to lay insulation material—glass or mineral fibre—in between the joists over the top ceiling. Don't insulate directly under the storage cistern (2) as the heat that rises through the ceiling helps to prevent the water from freezing. Outside walls (3) are responsible for 25 per cent heat loss. Insulating foam can be pumped through holes drilled into the mortar joints of cavity walls. If you have solid walls these can be insulated with panels of suitable materials fixed to the inside face. Hot water cylinders (4) should be lagged—quilted jackets are sold for this purpose. Windows (5) and doors (6) account for another 20 per cent heat loss. Windows can be double glazed; doors and letterboxes (7) can be draughtproofed. Floors (8) don't lose heat all that fast but can be insulated

The most common way of insulating a roof space is to lay rolls of glass fibre. The material comes in widths which will fit in between the joist spacing

glass or mineral fibre loft insulation material, then nail plasterboard over the lot.

External insulation is very expensive, mainly because the materials have to be weatherproof. It is usually done by professionals, and is really not worth considering unless the house needs major repairs to the external walls anyway.

Windows and doors

Windows and doors are poor insulators, and lose heat rapidly—mainly because they are so thin. However, external doors do not form a large part of the house, so there's no need to worry too much about insulating either your front or back door.

Windows, on the other hand, can be responsible for up to 20 per cent of the heat loss from a house. The usual method of insulating these is with double glazing, and there are many systems available for either do it yourself or professional installation (see pages 48 to 50)—many of them, however, are expensive. A cheaper, and perhaps more attractive solution, is to hang heavy lined curtains at the windows. Provided you are conscientious about drawing these every night they are almost as effective as double glazing.

Shutters are another effective solution to insulating windows, but can be very expensive—and, like curtains again, you have to remember to close them.

Insulating floors

Uninsulated ground floors do not lose heat very fast but they can still be insulated and, because of the large area they cover, this can save significant amounts of heat.

Suspended floors are the easiest to insulate if you can get at the undersides. Simply tack glass or mineral fibre blanket to the joists, using garden netting to hold the insulation material in place.

Solid floors are more difficult. The usual answer is to lay slabs of polystyrene over the existing floor, and then cover the lot with sheets of flooring grade chipboard (you can get Epsicon flooring panels with the chipboard already bonded to the polystyrene).

Other means of heat escape

As well as losing heat by conduction through the fabric of the house (walls, roof and so on) you lose it also by ventilation—the warm air in a house is continually being

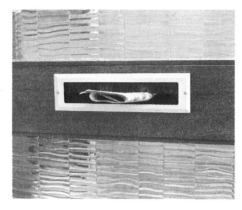

A seal comprising a casing and two nylon brushes prevents letter box draughts

replaced with cold air from outside, which then has to be heated. To reduce this heat loss, you have to slow down the rate at which warm air escapes from the house, by blocking off gaps—a process called draughtproofing or weather-stripping. Check all the house for gaps. As well as the obvious gaps between the opening parts of windows and doors and their frames, you will probably also find gaps between window and door frames and walls; around loft hatches and where pipes and cables run into the loft; in ground floor floorboards, and round the skirting board. Letter boxes are also likely to be draughty, and so are open fireplaces.

There are many types of draughtproofing equipment. For gaps between opening parts of windows and doors, use some form of flexible strip; for many other gaps, a proprietary filler or mastic is best.

Cylinder insulation

If your hot water is heated in a hot water storage cylinder, then you must make sure this is properly insulated. If the cylinder is bare, then insulate immediately; if you already have some insulation, but less than about 75mm, it's a good idea to top it up.

The usual insulation for the traditional British hot water cylinder is a special **lagging jacket**. Alternatively, you can build a box around the cylinder with plywood or something similar, and fill the space between this and the cylinder with some form of loose-fill insulation—but this is a more expensive method.

Cold water pipes that pass through insulated lofts, or under insulated ground floors must be insulated—otherwise they may freeze and burst in cold weather. It is probably also worth insulating hot water pipes that run through these areas, to save on heat loss. On the other hand, it is rarely

Gaps around windows and door frames should be sealed with a flexible filler

worth insulating pipes that run through the house itself, though.

You can insulate pipes either with pipe wrap (long strips of glass fibre insulation that you spiral round the pipe) or foam plastic tube with a split along one side that you simply slip over the pipe. Pipe wrap is cheaper, but probably more fiddly to fit.

Water cisterns in the loft must also be insulated to prevent their contents freezing—cover the sides and top with blanket insulation. But don't insulate underneath—this is difficult anyway and the heat rising from below is useful because it stops the water getting too cold.

The important areas to insulate

The purpose of insulating is to save fuel and reduce your heating bills—or make you

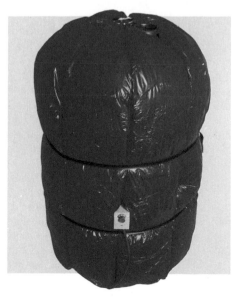

A hot water cylinder should be lagged with a purpose made insulating jacket

warmer without spending any more money on heating bills. So there is rarely any point in insulating unless the savings you make on your bills quickly repay the cost of the insulation materials.

Unfortunately, it is not too easy to predict how much you will save by any particular piece of insulation; it depends on your house construction, the amount you heat, and what fuels you use. In general, though, the priority for people living in the UK should be as follows:
•lag your hot water cylinder, or increase the insulation on it,
•draughtproof thoroughly,
•put in some loft insulation if you have none already—you should be able to get a Government grant to cover most of the cost, and
•consider cavity wall insulation if you can use a cheap form of material.

The following things will be much less worth while doing in financial terms, unless, perhaps, you heat the whole of your house to a very high temperature all day, and use one of the more expensive fuels:
•increasing the amount of loft insulation, if you have some already,
•installing floor insulation,
•installing interior wall insulation,
•fitting double glazing, unless it is of the cheapest kind—using, for instance, plastic film rather than glass.

Insulation problems

Unfortunately, insulating your house can give rise to many problems. Perhaps the most common is **condensation**. Particularly if you draughtproof too well, there may not be enough ventilation to get rid of steam and moisture from cooking, bathing, heating appliances, and just living and breathing. The answer in most cases is to fit a powerful extractor fan in the kitchen and bathroom, and not to use mobile gas heaters and paraffin stoves that do not have a flue. Another safety point you should remember is not to use an extractor fan if there is a conventional-flued boiler in the room.

Heating appliances (except electric ones, and balanced-flue heaters) need a flow of air to burn properly. If you over-do draughtproofing, they may not get enough air—the result may be a build-up of toxic or explosive gases that could kill you.

After insulating the loft, there is a greater chance of condensation forming on the roof timbers, which could give rise to rot. To prevent this, you should ensure the loft is well ventilated. Drill plenty of holes along

External cavity walls can be filled with foam or other insulation material

the length of the soffit, and on the sides of the roof. When laying the insulation, don't tuck it under the eaves, but make sure there's a gap between the roof and the insulation material.

If you insulate walls by fixing timber battens to them, make sure that these are pressure-impregnated with preservative.

Cavity wall insulation can give rise to damp on the inside of walls if the material has been installed incorrectly. In the UK, you should have no problems if you use a firm that has an **Agrément certificate**, or which holds **BSI registration**.

The cheapest and most widely used cavity wall insulant is **UF foam**. This gives off a gas for a week or so after filling, which some people may find irritating to breathe. But so long as UF foam is used only in traditional UK-type brick or block cavity walls, then there should be no long-term problem presented by the foam.

The problems of solid wall or block insulation are mainly ones of installation. The material can thicken walls and floors by up to 100mm or more—so doors and architraves will have to be moved and shortened, and skirting boards and possibly electric sockets repositioned. This can naturally involve a lot of work—so give the matter a great deal of thought before you start work.

Insulation in new houses

The most recent new houses are very much better insulated than those built only a few years ago. In many cases, there will be very little extra that is worth doing. But it's a good idea to check that the draughtproofing is well done—check especially areas like the loft hatch cover, cracks in upstairs ceilings, letter boxes and so on.

Don't worry if your cavity walls are not filled—the builder might have used highly-insulated blockwork to give an effect which will be nearly as good.

If you are in the process of having a house built, then it would be worth checking what levels of insulation are to be adopted, and to see whether it would be worth increasing them—it is easy, for example, to incorporate insulation in the floor during the building process.

If you are living in an older house, there are no regulations which compel you to add any insulation to what (if anything) is already there. Newly-built houses have to comply with the current building regulations, which lay down insulation levels for lofts and walls and so on. These are minimum levels and as such are uprated from time to time.

CURING A COLD HOUSE

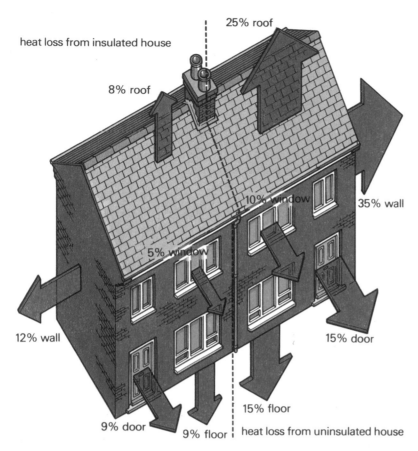

heat loss from insulated house

25% roof

8% roof

10% window

35% wall

5% window

12% wall

15% door

9% door

9% floor

15% floor

heat loss from uninsulated house

The benefits of insulation

Heat escapes from nearly every part of a house—roof, walls, windows, doors, even the floor—adding substantial amounts to your fuel costs. Insulating the major problem areas can make a great deal of difference to your comfort and your costs.

Draughtproofing openings like windows and doors is simple, cheap and effective. This is covered on pages 45 to 47. But walls, roofs and floors can account for greater losses of heat because of their large area.

The diagram on the left illustrates the difference that good insulation can make.

Roofs are always a major culprit but they're areas where you can dramatically reduce the loss without spending a great deal of money or causing an unnecessary upheaval.

Walls—especially older solid external walls—lose even more heat and can frequently cause condensation inside the house, too.

Together these two areas lose more heat than all the others combined, so it makes sense to insulate them first

Insulating floors

Surprisingly enough, the heat loss from a floor area can be quite considerable—cutting it down is a worthwhile job.

Floorboards: With a wooden floor, check for gaps between the boards. Small ones can be filled with the appropriate mastic. For larger gaps, cut tapered wooden 'wedges' to fit, coating both sides with PVA adhesive

before placing each wedge between the boards and tapping gently to get a snug fit. Any projecting edges should be planed off flush with the other boards.

Holes in floorboards where old pipes or wire came in can be patched with pieces of wood, but larger ones are best dealt with by removing the relevant section of board and replacing it with a new piece cut to fit.

Skirtings: If the floor and the skirting don't quite meet, fill in with a wooden

moulding pinned and glued into position. Pin to the floor, not the skirting.

Concrete floors: Insulation has been made simple with new systems such as that made by Epsicon, which have been introduced to the DIY market for use over solid floors, walls, and ceilings. The Epsicon system consists of 1200mm × 450mm interlocking panels of polystyrene available separately or bonded to a finishing material—the panels being laid loose and neatly connected

1 *Make a wedge from a thin piece of wood, apply adhesive to both sides and tap into the gap*

2 *Allow the adhesive to dry, then plane the excess flat. Level the edges of raised boards, too*

3 *Pin small mouldings to the gap between skirting boards and floorboards—nail to the floor*

4 *Remove skirtings to insulate solid floors. Epsicon polystyrene panels save time and effort*

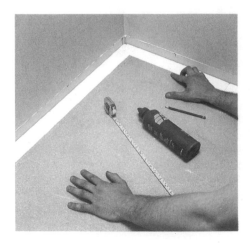

5 *If you use unbonded panels, add a 'floating' layer of flooring grade chipboard*

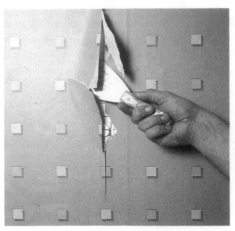

6 *Remove wallpaper and scrape off loose paint. You can either remove skirtings or panel over them*

7 *To cover old skirtings, first remove the polystyrene backing from the base of the board*

or 'clicked' together by plastic inserts. For floors buy the chipboard finish or cover the panels with a separate 'floating' layer of flooring grade chipboard.

To lay Epsicon board, first check if the floor is damp and if it is coated with a waterproof agent, otherwise you will have to check for damp and possibly install a new damp-proof course before starting work.

Level out any uneven patches with a self-levelling screed. Remove any doors in the room. Later you will cut them to match the higher floor level. Prise off existing skirting boards and replace them later.

Lay the boards straight onto the concrete, working from one corner of the room. Begin alternate rows with panels cut in half to get a 'brickwork' effect for extra strength. Before butting the panels together with the interlocking inserts, coat the edges with PVA adhesive to give extra bonding and rigidity.

Cover unbonded panels with a continuous layer of flooring grade chipboard. Refix doors and skirtings at their new height.

Where changes in floor levels occur, cut a strip of board to form the rise and fit together to ensure continuous insulation.

Dealing with solid walls

Cavity wall insulation is a job for the professional. But when it comes to solid external walls through which heat escapes, DIY insulation is a practical proposition.

Lining the wall with polystyrene in 5mm roll form is cheap and simple, but although it reduces condensation, it won't cut the heat loss dramatically. But other similar methods can do so very effectively.

Dry lining: Modern technology has

brought this well within the scope of the home do-it-yourself enthusiast by introducing simpler methods and materials to the DIY market. Boards and battens have largely been superseded by various thermal boards which fix directly to the wall:

Gyproc thermal board, for example, is attached to the wall with 863 Gyproc adhesive and comes in standard 1200mm widths, three lengths and several thicknesses of insulation.

To use Gyproc thermal board, first remove wallpaper or sand down paintwork with a coarse grade paper then brush off any dust. Remove any skirtings and anything else attached to the wall surface.

Alternatively, fix the boards directly above existing skirtings by removing a section of polystyrene backing. Apply in the following way before attaching new skirting boards to the wall lining.

Light and plug sockets will have to be relocated to accommodate the new lining and wooden window sills should be extended to accommodate the thickness of the wall board. If the existing sill has a curved edge, plane it square and glue and pin a new piece of wood to the edge.

Next draw out the board sections on the wall. Start from a door or window and remember to allow for the thickness of the board which will line the window or door recess. Add 2mm to the overlap to allow for the thickness of the adhesive.

Cut the boards to size with the wallboard suface uppermost. Use a fine tooth saw and cut at a shallow angle.

Mark the first board at the nine points shown in the diagram on the right for the secondary fittings. Lay the board on the floor and place a spare piece of wood under the board to prevent damage to the floor

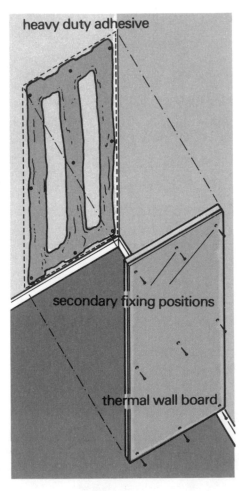

Fixing procedure for each board is a combination of heavy duty adhesive available from the board manufacturer and screws or special 'plugged' nails driven through the board.

Drill nine holes at the points shown for the secondary fixings. Adhesive should then be applied to the wall in bands 200mm wide

surface from the drill bit, before drilling for screws or nailable plugs. Use either method to fix boards to the old wall surface.

Put the board against the wall and get someone to hold it in position while you mark the fixing points on the wall through the drill holes. Take the board away and drill the holes in the wall using a masonry bit if you intend to use screws. Now cut sections out of the board for switches or electrical sockets.

Apply adhesive to the wall—in bands 200mm wide as shown on the diagram—with a trowel. Spread with an applicator.

Place the board in its position against the marked wall, making sure the vertical edge is plumb and tamp it firmly into place. Put in the secondary fixings—nailable plugs or screws—as illustrated in the diagram.

The sides of the window and door recesses should also be lined with the board. If the exposed framework of the window or door is not wide enough to accommodate the thickness of the board, the existing plaster should be removed from the recess and the background thoroughly cleaned.

It will be necessary to remove the polystyrene from the wall panel where it overlaps the recess in order to allow the plaster edges to meet. Fix the lining with adhesive and provide support for the top piece for 24 hours to allow it to dry.

When all the boards are in position, fill in between the joints with a joint filler—fill the screw heads too. The method is the same as that used for jointing ordinary taper edged plasterboard.

Use jointing tape to cover the filled joints. This comes in 150m rolls, 53mm wide.

About an hour after applying the filler and tape, apply Gyproc joint finish—stir 5kg into two litres of cold water or amounts in the same proportions, spread in a broad 200mm wide band down the joint, feathering out the edges slightly with a damp sponge or cloth.

To finish the job apply a coat of dry wall topcoat over the boards and refix the skirting board to the wall.

Insulating the loft

The job of laying loft insulation is not a difficult one and it provides very worthwhile savings in fuel costs.

Preparation: Apart from clearing the loft of anything you have stored there, little preparation work is necessary. However, this is the time to tackle repairs you've been putting off—closing any roof tile gaps, for example, which could later expand, let in water and cause a build up of damp in the insulation. Seal any holes where birds or vermin can enter, especially at eaves and gutters. But DO NOT cut off all ventilation because this can encourage dry rot.

Inspecting timbers for woodworm is also worthwhile at this stage. Access to joists will be difficult after the insulation is laid, and, if there is any woodworm present, any

---

★ WATCH POINT ★

Cover ventilation gaps with a fine wire mesh to keep birds out.

---

insulation must be removed to treat it.

For ease and safety, make a platform to work from by laying a number of boards across three or four ceiling joists, moving them along as you work.

Insulation materials

There is a variety of loft insulation products. Prices vary so check to see which is the best buy locally.

Blanket: Made either of glass fibre or mineral wool, this comes in rolls wide enough to fit into the 350mm to 400mm spacing between joists.

Various thicknesses are available: the thicker the material, the better the heat retaining properties. Regard 75mm as the absolute minimum although some firms are now making material 150mm thick.

To lay blanket insulation, you just place the roll between the joists and unroll it. Wear gloves, goggles and a dust mask to prevent irritation. Be careful not to compress the material as you work. Cut at the end of one run and start again. Lay under pipes and wire for easy access to them later should you ever require it. When you get to the eaves or awkward areas, a long handled brush may help push the material in. Don't insulate beneath your cold water tank.

Quilt: This is wider than the rolls and in the same materials. It's intended to be draped over joists and because it traps a layer of air between itself and the ceiling below, it has better heat retaining qualities.

The disadvantage of quilt insulation is that it can cause access problems later and you will also need to make 'walkways' of

8 *Cut the thermal board from the face side— use a fine tooth panel saw to cut both layers*

9 *Cut holes for light switches and power sockets—drill holes and join them with a padsaw*

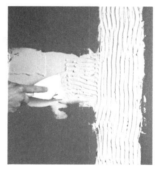

10 *Spread the adhesive on to the wall in 200mm bands—use a notched spreader*

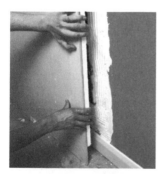

11 *Drill secondary fixing holes and offer up the panel to the wall. Adjust as necessary*

12 *Nailable plugs are useful secondary fixings—drive them through the holes*

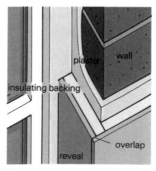

Reveals need special attention. Remove the thermal backing so that you can overlap the boards

13 *Blanket insulation can be unrolled between the joists—wear protective clothing*

14 *Don't forget the trap door through which heat can escape. Cover the blanket with polythene sheet*

15 *Loose fill insulation is even easier —pour it between the joists in the attic and level off*

boards screwed to joists above the quilt.

Foil: Foil with a reflective face comes in quilt form for laying over joists, but used on its own it is not as effective as the other materials mentioned.

Loose fill: Some people find this the easiest insulating material of all to work with. You buy loose pellets or pieces—vermiculite or mineral fibre—by the bag and simply tip them into the spaces between the joists.

Aim for a depth of 100mm and, to get it level, make up a spreader from a piece of board. Incidentally, if your joists are more widely spaced than normal you can use a combination of blanket and loose fill—use the loose material to fill the gap.

When working, some of the materials can cause irritation to skin, nose and eyes. So, to be safe while you work, wear a mask, gloves and safety goggles.

Insulating the tank

Make sure the pipe joints of the cold water tank are in good order. If the ball valve needs changing (or its washer), now's the time to do it. Check that the overflow works as it should. If your tank doesn't already have a cover, make one from chipboard cut to size.

Take some blanket insulation and lay pieces over the top of the tank so that they overhang the sides. Then wrap more pieces right round all four sides of the tank, enclosing the top overhangs and overlapping at the join. Secure with string. The 'cover' should go to the floor, but not underneath the tank.

Alternatively, using block polystyrene of the correct size, build a container closely round the cistern. Hold the corner joints with plastic adhesive tape.

16 *Pipe wrap is the cheapest method but you may need to release pipes to attach it*

17 *Flexible foam plastic tube is easier and quicker when insulating pipes —it just slips over the pipe*

Three methods for insulating cold water cisterns in the attic. Don't insulate beneath the tank

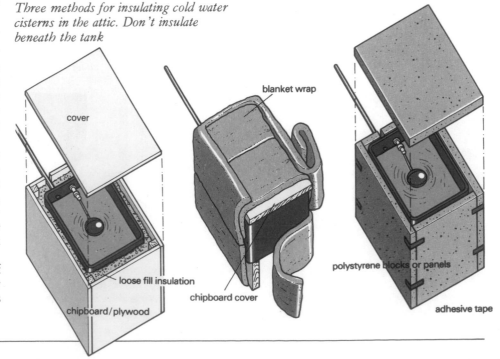

cover

loose fill insulation

chipboard/plywood

blanket wrap

chipboard cover

polystyrene blocks or panels

adhesive tape

DEALING WITH DRAUGHTS

Good ventilation is essential in any home—to prevent stuffiness or a build-up of condensation. But proper ventilation generally allows a degree of control over the passage of cold air from outside or hot air from within. Draughts, on the other hand, apart from being irritating and often uncomfortable, are uneconomic and wasteful. It's been estimated that up to 15 per cent of all household heat losses can be blamed on wasteful draughts.

In centrally heated homes, draughts are often unnoticed, but in homes where rooms are heated from a single source, such as a coal, gas or electric fire, they are much more noticeable and annoying.

There are numerous causes of draughts in any home, and your first job is to find them. First look for the obvious ones—a badly fitted outside door, missing mortar around door or window frames, a weakly sprung letter box. All these can allow unwanted currents of cold air into the house.

If you suspect gaps or cracks around a door or window frame, you can often feel the draught of incoming cold air simply by running your hand up and down the length of the door frame.

For draughts that are more difficult to locate use a lighted candle or smoking taper to detect the slightest breath.

If you use a taper, simply light it and, once alight, blow it out. Move it gently over the area where you suspect there's a draught and watch closely for any obvious change in direction of the smoke.

If you do the same with a lighted candle, the flame will flicker when cold air hits it—but take care not to touch curtains or any other inflammable material.

Once you've located the draught, mark the spot with a pencil or crayon. Curing it depends on where the cold air is getting in. If it's just a small crack around a frame, for example, you can probably effect an immediate cure by filling it with a wood filler, mastic or a flexible sealant as appropriate. Otherwise you may need to fit one of a variety of special draught excluders.

Check each room in turn, but make sure you close all doors and windows, and cover over any ventilators as you do so.

Warning: Don't be over enthusiastic in your efforts to keep out cold air. Never seal opening windows or ventilators. It's important that a room has adequate ventilation—particularly if you use a fuel burning appliance such as an open fire or gas heater. Without ventilation, the flame will rapidly use up all the oxygen in the air, possibly with harmful effects in the room.

Sealing windows

Draughtproofing strips will solve most draught problems with opening casement windows and often with doors, too (sash windows need slightly more treatment—see below). But how long your draughtproofing will last depends on the quality of the materials you use. At the cheapest end of the scale are proprietary draught proofing strips of self adhesive foam plastic. Don't be too cost conscious when buying this, the cheaper foam tends to rot quite quickly, and it's best to buy one with a liner or coating which prevents it stretching. These foam strips can be fitted at the contact points of a window so that when the window is closed,

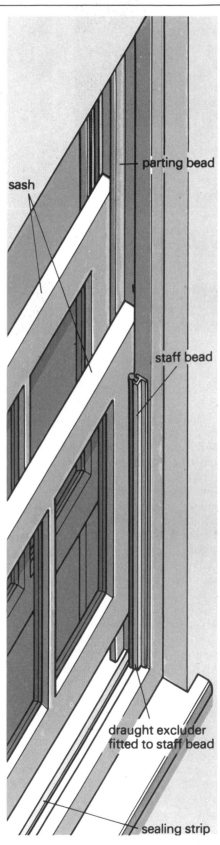

parting bead

sash

staff bead

draught excluder fitted to staff bead

sealing strip

Sash windows need several types of draughtstripping

1 *You can detect draughts along window and door frames*

2 *A smoking taper or joss-stick also reveals draughts*

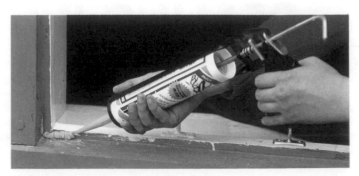

3 *Apply foam strip to the frame*

4 *Press the foam in with your finger*

5 *Seal frames by applying a flexible silicone sealant*

6 *Remove the staff beading and sash before fitting sprung strips*

7 *Offer up the strip to check its position on the pulley stile*

8 *Nail it in place, with the sprung edge facing outwards*

9 *Nail a strip to the upper sash, sprung edge facing down*

the foam is compressed to form a draught-excluding seal.

Make sure that the area the foam is being attached to is thoroughly clean—if it's not, the foam won't stick properly.

Cut a length of strip to the exact length required, and offer it up to the window to check it's been correctly cut.

Peel back about 50mm of the back tape and push the sticky side of the strip into place. Work down—or across—the window frame securing the strip and pulling off the backing tape as you go.

Use your thumb to compress the foam down its length to ensure that the strip hasn't lifted anywhere, then pull off the liner.

Even the best foam hasn't got an extensive life, and another alternative which is probably better suited to warped timber or rusted steel frames is one of the silicone sealants often sold for sealing baths.

Open the windows and apply a thin bead of sealant from the applicator nozzle on the tube, all along the contact points on the frame. This will take up any irregularities between the window and frame and can, if needed, be easily removed. The material takes up to 24 hours to dry fully, but in most cases windows can be closed after an hour or so.

For a longer term solution to window

draughts, you can use rigid weatherstripping made of polypropylene, vinyl, phosphorbronze or aluminium. These strips have a slight in-built springiness which forces them outwards against the frame.

★ WATCH POINT ★

Always apply strip or silicone sealants on a warm, dry day. This reduces the risk of trapping moisture and causing rot or rust as a result.

Cut the strip to length and offer it up to the frame to check it is a snug fit top and bottom or widthways.

Tack the strip to the frame using either galvanized pins or tacks. There are usually holes pre-punched at regular intervals. Always tack from the bottom and at regular intervals. Excessive space between tacks might cause the strip to ripple and reduce the draught proofing effect.

Although it's fairly easy to draught proof the top and bottom of a sash window—you can use foam strip for this—dealing with the sides and middle can be a problem. The sliding action of the window tends to rub against most types of excluders.

The one type of excluder which works

well, particularly at the sides of the window, is a sprung metal or plastic weatherstripping. To fit it, you need to remove the staff beading and parting beading which hold the sashes in place from the inside of the frame.

To do this, ease a screwdriver tip under the staff beading and gently knock it with a hammer. This will loosen the nails holding the beading in place and you should be able to prise it off. The parting beading is usually fitted into a slot in the frame but can be removed in the same way. If the beading is damaged, you can take this opportunity to replace it with new beading which can usually be bought from most timber yards or DIY stores.

Once the beading has been removed, fit the strip inside on the pulley stiles.

In the middle, nail the strip inside the gap to the rail of one of the sashes. Make sure you fit it the right way up so it doesn't get caught up when you slide the sashes.

If only the gap in the middle is causing problems, you can fill this with self-adhesive nylon pipe which should be fitted to the rail of either sash. This is a lot easier to apply, as you don't have to dismantle the window.

Another simple way to seal sash windows is to fix flexible strips to beads around the frame, both inside and out. This is simple and cheap and doesn't require you to remove and replace the staff beading.

Sealing doors

For the tops and sides of doors, follow the same procedures as for windows. Again, the better the quality of the sealant strip, the longer lasting and neater in appearance it will be. But with doors, the biggest draught problem is usually created by a gap at the bottom. A speedy, but only temporary, solution to this problem is to tack a strip of rubber along the bottom of the door above the floor.

Cut a strip of rubber or vinyl from a sheet to the width of the door and about 30mm deep all the way along.

Offer up the strip so that it just touches the floor and mark where the top of the strip falls on each side of the door.

Hold the strip in place and secure it at the centre with a tack. Adjust the strip so that it is parallel to the door and secure it with tacks at 30mm intervals.

There is a great variety of proprietary versions of strips to seal doors. Some have brushes instead of a continuous strip, and others have a mechanism to lift the strip as the door opens. These are much neater, though not necessarily more effective, than a home-made strip.

These generally come in standard sizes, and for internal doors the best arrangement is to use the brushpile type of strip. Here, the suspended bristles compress against the floor to form an effective seal and are ideal with exposed plank, parquet or tiled floors and can be used if the floor is uneven.

The strip is fixed with pins or screws, but first you must adjust it for height.

Offer up the excluder so that when the door is closed, the fibres are slightly bent. This will give enough 'play' in the bristles to maintain a seal as the door is opened and closed. Any strip of this type depends on contact for its efficiency—so there is bound to be some wear.

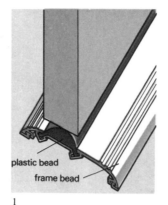
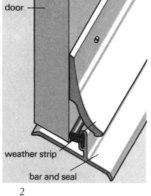
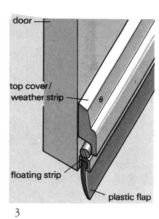

1
2
3

1 Bottom-sealing replacement sills are a worthwhile investment
2 Two-part face-sealing excluders are good for outside doors
3 Automatic lifting excluders seal well but can be troublesome to fit
4 Combination excluders come in two parts, but offer a good seal
5 Bottom-sealing excluders fill the gap and are very simply fitted
6 Brush-type excluders are cheap, simple and effective for all doors

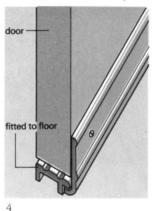
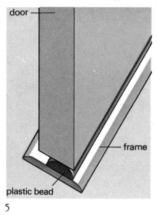
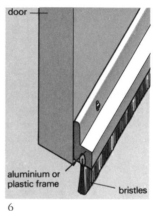

4
5
6

Strips such as these can wear quite quickly and, for a long term solution, it may be better to tackle the sill and fit a ready-made metal or plastic door sill which is fixed to the outside of the door. There are various types of these. Some are in one part which fixes to the sill with a springy seal that presses against the door. Other versions are in two parts, fitted to both door and sill so that they interlock.

The sprung weatherstrip used for sash windows can be used on doors. Offer up lengths of the strip to the door frame, the sprung edge facing in the direction the door opens, and mark the positions of the door hinges onto the strips.

If the strip lies over the hinges, cut that small portion of it away, then tack the strip into place following the instructions of the manufacturers.

10 *The strip should seal without fouling*

11 *Screw the strip to the door, keeping it parallel to the floor*

12 *Fit sprung strip around door frames*

CHOOSING DOUBLE GLAZING

Most people install double glazing in the hope that it will dramatically reduce their fuel bills. While it may not be the magic answer that some manufacturers claim, there's no doubt that it will provide effective insulation for your home—both thermal and acoustic—provided you choose the right double glazing system.

There are a number of systems loosely known as double glazing from sheets of polyethylene or PVC taped to your window frame to a professionally installed replacement window. There is a wide price range —you can pay a relatively small sum for a home made system or you can outlay vast amounts of money for the sort of good looking systems that are backed by extensive advertising.

Different types of double glazing

There are two main types of double glazing: **sealed units** or **secondary glazing**.

Sealed units consist of two panes separated all round by a spacer. They are held rigidly together and sealed all round. The space—or air gap—between the panes is normally filled with a dry inert gas to prevent condensation. Apart from the seal around the outside—hidden once the glass is framed—a sealed unit looks much like a single piece of glass.

Sealed units commonly appear in two different applications. Replacement windows of the type heavily publicized by the major double glazing companies use sealed units for the actual glazing. But you can also buy the units separately made-to-measure for reglazing existing frames. Doing this has some of the advantages of installing complete replacement windows —however, it's unlikely that the frames themselves will have the same standards of insulation or draughtproofing.

The thickness of the air gap between the panes of a sealed unit is usually from 6mm to 12mm and the thickness of the glass can vary between 4mm and 10mm. Once you have measured your window frame, the manufacturer or your stockist should be able to advise you which thickness to use. The air gap will be determined by the size of your window reveal. The units can be supplied with patterned or safety glass—even solar control glass—as well as conventional float glass. As these units

Replacement windows come in many styles and sizes with factory made sealed units fitted into a frame—made from wood, aluminium or PVC. Metal or plastic windows are generally installed inside a hardwood sub frame. You can fit them yourself but patio doors and larger windows are probably best installed professionally

replace existing panes they are suitable for nearly all types of window.

Sealed units are available in a wide range of standard sizes as well so you should be able to find a model which fits your window exactly. It must be a tight fit to the existing frame otherwise draughts will completely undermine the efficiency of the system.

Most sealed units consist of two panes of glass of the same size. But because the complete panel is quite thick, you may have problems reglazing a window with narrow rebates in the frame. For this, you can get what is called a stepped unit where the inner pane is smaller than the outer one and so fits into the rebate.

With **secondary double glazing**, an inner pane of glass is added to the existing window—in its simplest form, you can stick plastic film on the inside of the window.

Sealed units are available with conventional, patterned and even leaded-glass

This method is cheap, surprisingly efficient at eliminating condensation and it is also very simple to remove.

A more permanent form of secondary double glazing consists of a second pane of glass in its own frame—metal, wood or plastic (UPVC)—secured to the existing window frame or to the inner or, in very rare cases, the outer sill.

DIY enthusiasts can fit their own secon-

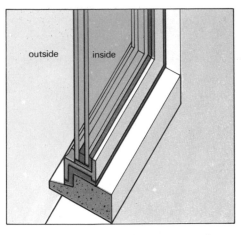

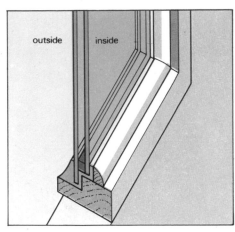

Unstepped sealed units have inner and outer panes of glass of the same size

Stepped sealed units with one smaller pane are used for windows with narrow reveals

dary double glazing using plastic channelling. The second pane is fixed to the window frame by U-shaped channelling and held in place by clips. If you are fitting to sash windows, you can fix the plastic channel to the inside of one pane and the outside of the other so that the sashes still work. It will be much more effective if you draughtproof the gap between the panes of glass—to do this, use sprung metal strip.

If you want sliding secondary glazing you can fit a track with two channels all the way round the reveal. These can either have two or more pieces of smooth edged glass sliding in the track or they can be purchased as panel systems where the glass is mounted in rigid frames—this type tends to be more expensive.

The other main type of secondary glazing also has the glass mounted in a rigid frame —generally aluminium—with a seal which is fitted to the main frame of the window. This supplementary frame may have separate sliding sashes or be hinged so you can open it for ventilation. Alternatively, it can be mounted on clips allowing it to be removed completely. Panels of all these types can also be mounted separately on a sub-frame away from the existing window.

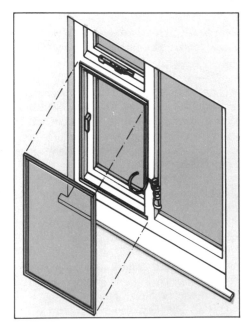

Another system uses self adhesive steel on the frame and magnetic strip on the glazing
1 Use vertical double glazing on sliding sash windows
2 Some systems are designed to slide horizontally
3 Hinged systems are attached to the existing frame

The best system

There's no easy choice, because so much depends on price and your own individual requirements. In general, sealed units—especially if you install complete replacement windows—are the most expensive option and the hardest to fit. However, they are generally far neater than secondary glazing.

Other factors you might consider are:
• With replacement windows you get a new frame. If your windows are in bad shape,

you may have to replace them soon anyway.
• If you want to cut down noise, choose secondary double glazing with a substantial air gap and a good seal.
• If you're aiming to cure a condensation problem, choose sealed unit glazing, since its heat insulating properties are better.

If you're considering replacement windows, it is of course possible to buy these and install them yourself. However, the work involved and the tools you'll need to hire means that it is often worth leaving the job to manufacturers.

Buying double glazing

You can buy from a specialist company or purchase a double glazing kit and do the job yourself. The best way to begin is to visit some of your local firms—there should be no shortage of these—and get them to show you what's on offer. Selling double glazing is a very competitive business—many firms will make up frames and systems to suit your needs exactly—but it is still a good idea to shop around. A visit to your local glass merchant may also prove fruitful—but do beware of exaggerated claims.

In any event it is well worth getting a few free estimates and then making up your own mind which system of double glazing you want and can afford.

DIY double glazing kits

Most kits vary in detail but work on the same principle—you fit an additional frame to the wall or the existing window frame. The material you choose for the frame depends more on how you want your windows to look rather than one material having inherent advantages over another. What is more important is the way you assemble the system you choose. For example fitting to wooden frames is relatively straightforward while metal frames are more of a problem in that you can't use conventional screws.

1   2   3

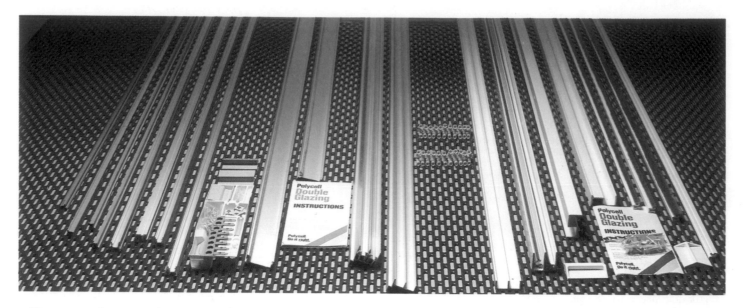

You can, of course, fit a secondary wooden frame around the window and fix the glazing to this, but this does require careful measuring and even more careful carpentry on your part as everything must be squared exactly.

Joining the corners of the frame can cause problems depending on which kit you choose. Some come with L-shaped corners which you simply slot into position, others require you to make 45° cuts before you join everything up, and some frames have to be square cut so that they can interlock automatically into corners.

If you've got metal framed windows they will almost certainly have a very narrow rebate. In this case it's probably best to fit a sub frame to the reveal—a sealed unit is unlikely to fit; alternatively you can use one of the self adhesive systems.

Dealing with condensation

Install double glazing on a dry day—this prevents condensation forming—important if you are fixing a secondary system. Double glazing is not normally cost effective unless you install one of the cheaper systems yourself. In any event it will take a considerable length of time to get your money back if you are merely looking to reduce your fuel bills. Certainly other methods of insulation—draughtproofing in particular—are more effective and are more easy to justify in terms of expense.

However, this is not the only way to look at double glazing. In terms of reduced draughts, noise reduction, increased warmth and perhaps in the increased value it can put on your house when you come to sell it you should find that double glazing is

A typical DIY kit includes height and width tracks. You buy the glass separately

worth the trouble as well as the expense.

With single glazed windows condensation is always a problem. Over a period of time it can damage your furnishings and can even cause the wooden framework of your windows to rot.

With double glazing, the inner pane is insulated from the outer pane so that the inner surface, warmed by the air in the room, is virtually at room temperature and condensation is less likely to occur.

So although double glazing does not always eliminate condensation, provided it is fitted properly it goes a long way towards solving the problem. However, if it still continues after installation you can place a moisture absorber (silica gel) in the air gap. Sealed units normally have a filling of inert gas between the panes so condensation should never appear there. If it does, it means that there is a fault in the seal itself.

Noise reduction

This depends on the width of the air gap between the two panes of glass. To be really effective at reducing noise you'll need a gap of at least 100mm—preferably 150mm—with 4mm glass. However, this sort of gap is not possible on most domestic windows—there just isn't the room—and anyway a very wide gap reduces the amount of thermal insulation that your system will give. When you remember that most sealed units have a gap of around 12mm you'll understand why they are not particularly effective at reducing noise.

A cheaper kit uses plastic film and sticky tape. The hair drier removes wrinkles

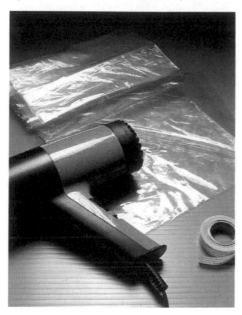

Ultimately you are going to have to compromise between thermal and acoustic insulation but it's worth remembering that if you install secondary glazing yourself you control the size of the air gap and therefore the quality of noise reduction you can expect.

Double glazing safety

Any system (whether you fit it yourself or have it professionally installed) which does not allow for an escape route in the event of a fire is a hazard. So make sure that your double glazed windows can be opened or, if fixed, that the inner pane can be quickly removed.

DIY DOUBLE GLAZING

Properly installed double glazing is a sure way to cut down heat loss and eliminate draughts through your windows. In certain cases, it can also help soundproof your home against exterior noise.

The chief advantage of DIY double glazing systems, however, is cost—at least half that of professionally installed units. But you also have flexibility—you can double glaze your windows as and when you feel like it. Naturally, as 'bolt-on' accessories rather than custom-made windows, DIY systems don't give you quite such a high standard of finish. But that's not to say that with a little care and patience you can't create perfectly respectable double glazed windows that may well add to the value of your home.

What's available

The most substantial DIY double glazing kits fall into two groups—sealed unit panes and secondary glazing systems. The first consists of two sheets of glass (normally 3mm) sandwiched together with a sealed air gap of 5mm−6mm in between. Providing your window casement has rebates wide enough to accommodate the overall 11mm−12mm thickness of this replacement 'pane', fitting should not present any problems.

Secondary glazing simply means fitting a second window inside the original, but within its own sub-frame. Fixed, sliding (horizontally or vertically) and hinged versions are available, to suit various different types of windows.

Sealed unit panes have the best insulating properties, so they're the ones to go for if you have a large area of heat-conducting glass within an otherwise reasonably draughtproof frame. They are also the most efficient at cutting down condensation. On the other hand, secondary glazing comes into its own if your window has many small panes or if the frame itself is ill-fitting and admits a lot of draughts. The larger air gap which normally results from using this method means slightly reduced insulating efficiency (20mm is a practical maximum gap), but better sound-proofing. In fact, with an air gap of 150mm, you should notice a significant reduction in the level of noise outside your house.

With secondary glazing kits, the important considerations are safety, convenience

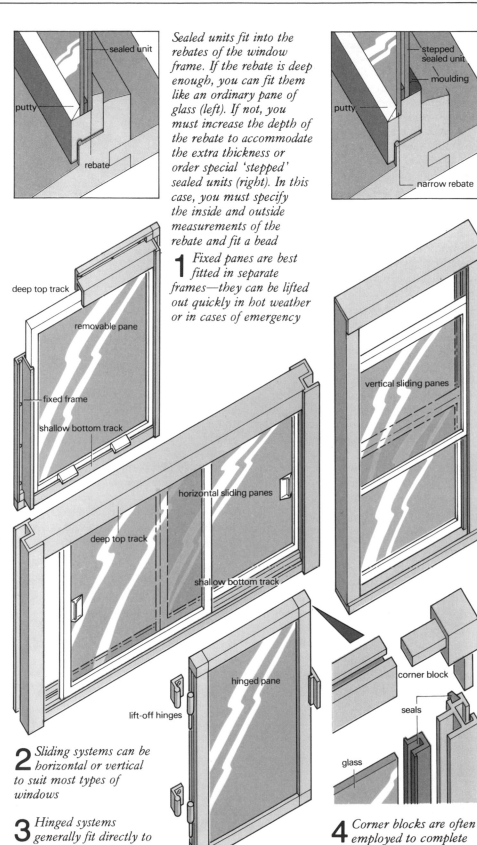

Sealed units fit into the rebates of the window frame. If the rebate is deep enough, you can fit them like an ordinary pane of glass (left). If not, you must increase the depth of the rebate to accommodate the extra thickness or order special 'stepped' sealed units (right). In this case, you must specify the inside and outside measurements of the rebate and fit a bead

1 *Fixed panes are best fitted in separate frames—they can be lifted out quickly in hot weather or in cases of emergency*

2 *Sliding systems can be horizontal or vertical to suit most types of windows*

3 *Hinged systems generally fit directly to the existing window frame via lift-off hinges*

4 *Corner blocks are often employed to complete the glass edging frame*

and the sub-frame material (which contributes to the look of the finished job). As regards safety, **there is one point that cannot be overstressed**. You must make sure that the system of your choice can be removed easily and quickly—or at least opened sufficiently wide—to provide an escape route in the event of a fire. Carefully examine the range available until you're satisfied that there's one to safely suit your original window.

When it comes to convenience, you will naturally want to ensure that you can still open the window as and when you want to. The cheaper and simpler kits have fixed panes, so if you take the easy way out you may well find yourself with a poorly ventilated—and possibly unsafe—home.

The most common sub-frame materials are white plastic (uPVC), and aluminium (in plain or brushed form). The aluminium types are more durable and tend to look better, but of course they are more expensive. The uPVC type can be painted, to blend unobtrusively with the surrounding window frame.

Most secondary systems are sold in the form of individual 'packs' corresponding to different heights and widths of windows, and there are also extension packs for splitting larger panes into more manageable sections. In each pack you can expect to get the appropriate sub-frame sections, plus the corresponding slide sections. Fixings, handles, hinges and other accessories may also be included, though in some kits they come as another separate pack.

Glazing options

What you don't get is the glass: this must be ordered separately. With some fixed and all sliding kits, you measure up for and order the glass once you've installed the sub-frame; with other fixed kits and all hinged systems, calculate the glass area at the time you measure up the existing window opening, after making the allowances specified in the kit instructions.

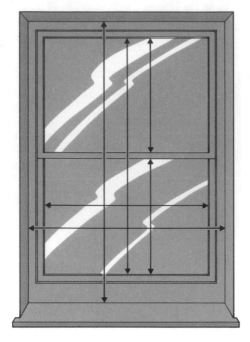

Measure your panes as well as the reveal so that you can choose a suitable system

Surveying your windows: The first thing to ask yourself before double glazing a window is whether it's worthwhile. If the frame itself is badly warped or rotten, then it should be replaced entirely, in which case you have the option of fitting a complete, double glazed replacement window.

Next, decide whether your priorities are better insulation against heat loss and condensation, or improved draughtproofing and soundproofing; this could determine whether you choose sealed units or secondary glazing, though the size and type of window in question also has to be taken into consideration.

Sealed units: If you go for these, check that the rebate in the window casement is deep enough (at least 11mm) to take what is

For large windows panes must be measured to coincide with window members, while frames and seals must be fixed the right way round

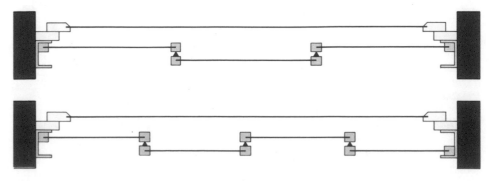

effectively a thicker pane of glass. If the existing pane is glazed with putty, the rebate width should be immediately apparent, but you may not be able to calculate the depth until you've removed the glass. You may need to increase the depth with a chisel and plane.

Measure up the pane from the outside edges of the rebates. Start with the diagonals; if these are equal you know the window is truly square. Then measure the height and width at three points across the pane and deduct 3mm from each figure to allow for expansion and contraction of the window frame.

When you come to order, it is customary to give the height before the width. If you need a special type of glass—safety, or one with a pattern, for instance—ask your supplier if these options are available.

Apart from the new pane, you'll need a supply of glazing putty and sprigs (wooden frames) or steel clips (steel frames). For the job itself make sure you have some stout working gloves, a putty knife, pin hammer and an old wood chisel for gouging out the existing putty.

Secondary systems: First of all decide whether you want fixed, hinged, or sliding double glazing, then choose a kit system and obtain an instruction leaflet telling you from which points to measure the window. (Even though most sub-frames are fixed either to the window frame surround or to the reveal and sill, kits do vary in details.) At the same time it's worth measuring the diagonals of your window to check whether it is out of square. If it is, and your sub-frame fits inside the reveal, you'll need to pack the frame sections to bring it back to shape. Start by adding small packing pieces to bring the frame level and plumb, then fill in with other pieces to support the frame along its length.

On the other hand, if the kit of your choice is attached to the surround, you should have enough room for manoeuvre to be able to square it up as you fit it.

Having measured the window, these are the points to consider:

• Number of frames—most manufacturers recommend that no single frame should cover more than 1.85 sq m (20 sq ft), that the width of the frame should be no more than three times the height, and that no frame should be more than 1.5m high. The diagram (left) shows some examples of how larger windows can be divided.

• Fitting room—depending on the kit make and type, a minimum width of window surround or reveal will be needed on which to fit the sub-frame. This should be given in the manufacturer's leaflet, so make sure you check it at this stage.

If you can't meet the width requirement, you can either choose a different type of kit or system, or modify the surround/reveal with extra woodwork. Unless you are a proficient carpenter, the latter option could look messy and is probably more trouble than it's worth.

• Existing window stays and handles— depending on how the kit of your choice fits and the resulting air gap, these may protrude too far inwards. Either replace them with smaller fittings or attach packing battens to the surround to enlarge the gap between the old and new glazing.

• Air gap—where thermal insulation or condensation are the overriding factors, the air gap should be as small as is practical unless specifically stated otherwise in the instructions. For soundproofing purposes the ideal air gap is 150mm. To achieve this you will probably have to fit packing battens to the window surround or reveal (depending on the kit). In this case mitre the ends for a neat finish and make sure that all the wood is thoroughly primed and painted before you fit it—the packing will be highly susceptible to rot, particularly if condensation is present.

• Selecting height and width packs—both types come in a range of sizes to suit standard window measurements; select the nearest sizes above the dimensions of your window. The same applies to extension packs, should you need them.

• Tools and materials—most kits supply all the materials and hardware you need in one or more packs, with the possible exception of plastic wallplugs for fixing into masonry.

As regards tools, you will almost certainly need a junior hacksaw, electric drill, screwdrivers, steel rule, metal file, hammer and wood block (or mallet), spirit level, try square, and masonry and twist drill bits.

Installing a sealed unit

Providing the rebates in your window casements are wide enough, this job is perfectly straightforward—the same, in fact, as re-glazing a broken window.

If the casement is hinged, unscrew the hinges at the frame and remove it. Lay it on a thick blanket of soft material.

On all windows, carefully gouge out the old facing putty around the pane using an old wood chisel. Then, if you've removed the casement, wrap the blanket over the pane and smash the glass with a hammer.

From now on, wear a pair of stout work-

1 *Gouge out the old putty with a chisel*

2 *Tape over the entire pane to smash the glass—wear tough gloves*

3 *Thumb fresh putty into the cleaned out rebate*

4 *Press the unit into the bedding putty. Tap in sprigs to secure it in place*

5 *Trim off the facing putty and the putty on the inside*

6 *Saw the sections to length to fit the window reveal*

ing gloves—to protect your hands from barely visible splinters of glass.

Pull the broken glass out of the frame with great care and dispose of it immediately in a safe place. Follow by brushing away the splinters, then take your old chisel and trim away the old bedding putty from the rebate.

When the rebate is completely clean, thumb a layer of fresh bedding putty into the corner on all four sides; aim for a thickness of about 3mm. Then offer up or lay the new sealed unit on top of the putty and press it firmly home, ensuring that it is the same distance inside the rebate all round.

On a wooden window, tap glazing sprigs into the rebate at 300mm intervals to hold the glass in position. Hold the flat-sided sprigs against the glass as you tap them home—slide the hammer across the glass to avoid cracking and to keep the sprig parallel.

On a steel window, steel clips hold the glass. You'll find pre-drilled holes in the frame for them to clip into—space them at 600mm intervals.

You can now thumb the fresh facing putty right around the rebate to cover the sprigs/clips and seal the pane. When you've got more or less an even thickness all round, wet the blade of your putty knife and strike off any surplus so that the surface is flat and angled away from the pane. Follow by trimming off any excess bedding putty.

Allow two to four weeks for the putty to harden (it does so faster in warm, dry weather) before you paint it. When you do, overlap the paint about 2mm onto the glass to provide a fully weatherproof seal.

Installing a secondary sub-frame

Many fixed pane secondary systems, and all sliding systems, employ a sub-frame into which the framed glass is fitted. You install the sub-frame before you measure up and order the glass itself.

Start by laying out the sub-frame sections on the floor, in front of the window, exactly as they will be fitted. Then measure up the

★ WATCH POINT ★

If the pane is fixed, you can prepare the glass for breaking by applying lengths of masking tape criss-cross fashion over the whole of one side. An even quicker alternative is to tape pieces of thick blanket securely to both sides. This done, break the glass with one or two firm, but controlled, blows with a heavy object.

7 *Screw the side sections firmly to the inside of the frame*

8 *On many kits, you cut the cross pieces to interlock*

window surround or recess exactly as specified in the manufacturer's instructions. Measure the diagonals too, to see if the window is square.

Before you mark the sections for cutting, be sure to deduct the specified amount for clearance; then mark each section individually using a try square and felt tip pen. Both uPVC and aluminium frames are cut using a junior hacksaw. However the sections join together—they may butt, interlock or use corner pieces—it is essential that they are cut square. You can ensure this by laying each one on a firm, flat surface (or against a bench hook) and then wrapping a piece of stiff cardboard around it to act as a guide for your saw.

When you've cut each section, take a metal file and remove the burrs around the cut to leave a smooth, clean edge.

At this stage make sure you know what preparatory work must be done on the sections before you screw them into place.

Aluminium sections usually require screw fixing holes to be drilled not less than 50mm from the end and then at 125mm–150mm intervals; with some double glazing kits you have to insert the fibre slide seals and then trim them to length.

On kits where the sections butt or interlock, you generally fit the side sections first, then saw small cut-outs in the ends of the top sections before you fit these. Exact guidance will be given on this point in the instructions.

On kits employing corner pieces, you assemble the sub-frame on the floor and then fix it as one complete unit.

In either case, if you are fixing to masonry, be sure to hold a spirit level against the section/frame as you mark the fixing holes.

After marking the wall, drill holes with a No. 8 masonry drill bit to take standard plastic wallplugs.

If you are fixing to wood, simply locate the section/frame, check for level/plumb with your spirit level, then make pilot holes through the fixing holes in the frame sections.

Screw the sections/frame in place in the order given in the kit instructions and then check yet again that it is square. Minor discrepancies can be dealt with by packing behind the sections. Note that on horizontal

sliding systems it is most important that the top and bottom sections are parallel along their entire length. On vertical systems the same applies to the side tracks.

Preparing the glass

Depending on the kit, you either measure up for the glass against the sub-frame or directly against the window surround. Be sure to do it strictly according to the manufacturer's instructions.

Having noted the dimensions, order the glass and ask your glass merchant to remove the sharp edges. When you take delivery, make sure that this has been done and check that the pane has been cut to within 1.5mm of the correct size.

On all kits the glass is framed with uPVC or aluminium sections, these being cut and assembled in much the same way as sub-frames. Measure and mark them for cutting strictly according to the kit instructions, then saw them to length with a junior hacksaw using a piece of stiff card wrapped around the cutting line to guide you. Remove all burrs with a file.

uPVC fixed pane with sub-frame: Stand the glass upright on edge and rest it on an old blanket (to act as a cushion). Take the top frame section, clip one end over the edge

9 *Saw edging strips to length and cut any gasket or brush strips*

10 *Rest the glass on a blanket to tap edging strips into place*

11 *Corner blocks are normally plastic mouldings*

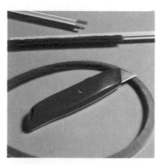

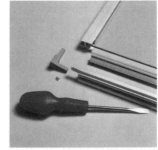

12 *Lift sliding panes up into the top track*

13 *Fit stays, catches or handles as indicated in the maker's instructions*

14 *For hinged panes, you need to align the hinges and stays*

of the glass, centre it, then take a hammer and wood block and tap it gently home over the glass, working from one end of the frame to the other.

Now take the bottom frame section, make sure its seal faces the same way as that of the top, and tap it home as described above. The two side sections may have to be notched before fitting to clear the top and bottom sections. Do this with a junior hacksaw, remove the burrs, then fit them as before—making sure their seals are facing in the right direction.

uPVC sliding pane: In this case the glass is framed in the same way as a fixed pane kit, but take particular care to ensure that the seals face the right way round. On horizontal sliding systems you need to distinguish between front and back panes; on vertical systems it's between upper and lower panes.

Self-adhesive handles are usually provided for fitting to horizontal sliding panes; with vertical systems, don't forget to clip the ratchet catches—which engage in the side tracks of the sub-frame—into the frame sections.

Aluminium sliding systems (and fixed pane systems with sub-frame): Most kits of this type have individual frame sections which you cut to length according to the kit instructions and then assemble around the frame with screw-on corner pieces. The sections are tapped onto the edge of the glass using a hammer and wood block, as with uPVC systems, but in this case they go over a PVC glazing gasket.

Make sure you cut the sections squarely and deburr them afterwards. Fit the sections in the order given, with the glass resting on edge on a blanket. Lay the PVC glazing gasket in place, then lay the section on top and gently tap it home.

Some kits have slide rollers which slip in to a channel in the bottom section and are held by setscrews. On others, the handles must be added before you fit the relevant frame section to the glass.

The corner pieces are normally loose-fitted as you go; then, once the frame is complete, you tighten the securing screws of the corner pieces.

As with uPVC sliding systems, make sure that the seals on each section face the same way and that you have distinguished between front and back panes.

Hinged systems: these are always aluminium, and there is no sub-frame—the frame around the glass holds the hinge posts and the seals locate against the window surround.

Assembly of the frame is the same as for other aluminium types. When complete, the hinge posts can be slid into channels in the side sections and secured with setscrews. Some aluminium fixed pane kits also do without a subframe. In this case locking catches simply replace the hinge posts.

Installing the panes

This is usually the simplest part of the operation, but before you go ahead check that all the sub-frame and frame parts are correctly butted and that, where fitted, the seals between panes have been positioned the right way round.

Sliding systems: If the system is uPVC, simply lift the back pane into the sub-frame and up into the top track; then lower into the bottom track. Check that it slides freely, then repeat for the front pane.

Use the same procedure on aluminium systems, but check first that all the correct seals are in position—with some kits you fit them separately to the completed pane. Also, if your system employs PTFE runners rather than rollers, fit these to the corner pieces on the bottom frame section at this stage.

On vertical sliding systems, start by fitting lengths of ratchet sash guide into the right hand track. They are a simple press fit, but you may need to cut the final length to size. Follow by fitting just one length of sash guide into the left hand tracks.

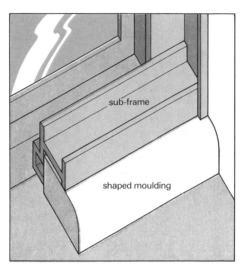

To finish off the frame neatly where a subframe is fitted, you can pin and glue a wooden moulding along the edge

Now insert the window side pane into its tracks with the left hand ratchet catch above the guide; operating both catches, gently lower it to engage in the guides on both sides. Repeat this procedure for the room side pane, then fit the remaining lengths of ratchet guide on the left hand tracks. Finally, measure and cut the top track insert to fit and press it in position on the inside of the top track.

Hinged and fixed systems: With hinged systems there is no sub-frame—installation is simply a matter of hanging the hinges, then fitting stays and catches.

Separate the hinges and screw the posts/sockets to the window surround. Hang the frame, then fit stays/catches where indicated in the instructions.

On fixed pane systems employing a subframe, you fit the pane inside as for a sliding system. If the system doesn't have a subframe, fit the locking turncatches as for a hinged pane.

Finishing off

On some systems, the look of the sub-frame can be improved by pinning and gluing lengths of wooden moulding against the surround in front of it (see diagram).

Check carefully that the completed installation contains no air gaps between parts—particularly if the room is subject to heavy condensation. Such gaps can be filled by piping in a thin bead of silicone sealant.

If the sub-frame is uPVC and you want to paint it, rub over the surface first with fine abrasive paper to provide a good key.

SKIRTING TROUBLE

Skirting boards can be fixed to a wall in several ways. In timber-frame construction, they are simply nailed through the plasterboard and into the studs, or vertical timbers, behind.

In masonry walls, nails can be hammered at an angle through the board and its backing of plaster into the brickwork (fig. 22). Alternatively, strips of wood called grounds can be used. These are firmly attached to the wall and act as a fixing base for skirting boards placed over them. A continuous strip is supported at intervals by small upright pieces called soldiers (fig. B).

With either system, some plaster damage must be expected as the old skirtings are removed, and usually needs to be made good with plaster or filler before new boards are fixed.

In rare instances, the skirting is fixed to wedge-shaped uprights bedded into cavities in the brickwork (fig. C). Installed at the time the wall was made, these are held in place by a mortar filling which often decays over a period of time. Excessive force on the skirting—such as that required to remove it—is often sufficient to dislodge these uprights. If this happens, mortar them back in. A new upright can be made by tapering a suitable length of batten.

The golden rule to bear in mind when dealing with skirting board is to be careful; the bedding plaster is easily chipped by a casual knock.

Replacing boards

To remove a length of skirting, start at one of the corners and place a bolster on the top edge where the skirting meets the wall. Using a claw hammer, hammer the bolster gently down. This will prise the skirting away from the wall at that point. Continue this action along the length of skirting to be removed. Where greater resistance is met, the skirting is nailed to the wall.

With the top edge prised away from the wall you can start to remove the skirting completely. For this you need a claw hammer and a small, thin piece of plywood or hardboard to protect the wall finish. Place the claw of the hammer down behind the

Right: *Damaged skirting boards can be easily replaced with new boards. Several different methods can be used to fix the boards to the wall*

top edge of the board and slip the timber between the claw and the wall. Lever gently upwards on the handle, pressing the hammer head against the timber. This forces the board further away from the wall and draws out the nails at the same time.

Always use timber or a piece of hardboard to protect the wall or the hammer may leave an indent. Do not use a crowbar as this can damage the wall plaster.

Once the skirting is removed the nails should be pulled out. Use a pair of pincers to draw out the nails from the back of the

---

★ WATCH POINT ★

With the top edge of the board free, insert a timber wedge between the board and the wall at the place where the first cut is to be made. The wedge should have one sloping face and be thick enough to push the board out by about 40mm. Position the wedge with the flat face to the wall so that as you hammer it down, the sloping face pushes the skirting away from the wall.

---

board. This keeps the paint surface intact, as the face of the board often splinters if the nails are hammered through and drawn out from the front.

Partial removal of skirting

When the area of damaged or decayed skirting is relatively small, partial replacement is more economical. Measure the length of board to be replaced and buy or make a new piece to match. First, prise the damaged part of the board away from the wall with a bolster (fig. 1).

To cut out the damaged length of board, make a mitred cut at each end using a mitre block or box. There are no set rules for positioning the direction of the mitres: they can be parallel or they can face in opposite directions, and lean either inwards or outwards.

Position the mitre block with its back against the face of the skirting and the top level with, or above, the top of the skirting. If necessary, put some suitable packing material under the block to raise it to this level. Make the first cut at the end of the

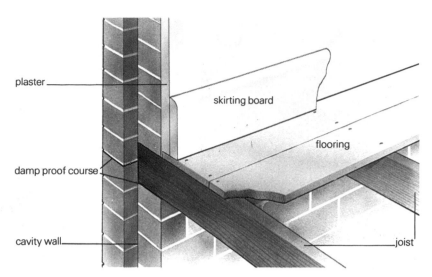

A. *Skirting fixed directly to a wall. On a plastered brick wall, plaster damage usually accompanies the skirting board's removal, especially if the nails securing the board have rusted*

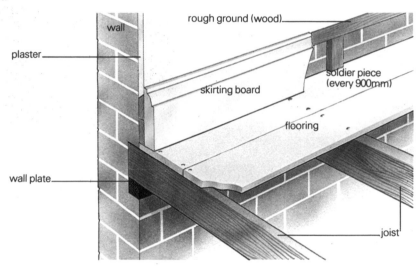

B. *Skirting fixed to a rough ground supported clear of the floor. Board removal may cause partial collapse of the ground and plaster base it supports*

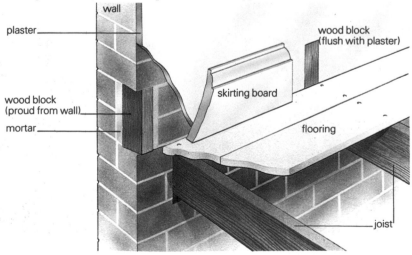

C. *Skirting fixed to wood blocks set in the wall at the time of building. Retaining mortar may have decayed, and both this and damp soldiers have to be made good before replacing skirting*

damaged area using a panel saw in short rapid strokes (fig. 6). Only the first few teeth of the saw are used so these teeth must be extremely sharp or they will just damage the wood.

Continue the rapid strokes until the teeth of the saw reach the base of the block. Remove the block in order to complete the cutting down to the floor, taking great care to maintain the straight line of the cut. Pull out the wedge and reposition it where the second cut is to be made at the other end of the damaged piece of skirting. The second cut is made in exactly the same way. Once free, lift out the damaged piece of board from the skirting.

Fitting the new board

Using the mitre block, cut a mitre at one end of the new board. Make sure that the direction of the cut is the same as that of the first cut, made when removing the damaged piece. After cutting the mitre, measure the inside edge of the area to be fitted with new skirting and transfer the measurement to the replacement board. Use the mitre block again to cut the second mitre. Check that the direction of the cut matches that in the skirting. Fit the replacement piece in the gap to check its compatibility. If adjustment is necessary, use a plane with the blade set finely and remove a few shavings from the end grain.

★ WATCH POINT ★

You can use masonry nails to fix the skirting into the brickwork behind. In this case, a piece of timber the same thickness as the plaster should be placed behind to overlap the old and new pieces of skirting at each end. This ensures that the skirting will not be pushed out of its vertical position should it be knocked at all from the bottom.

Fixing the new board

An easy method of fixing the new length of board is to use 38mm oval pins and skew nail them through the mitre joints. This way, you will nail through both thicknesses of skirting. Punch the nail heads below the surface, so that you will end up with a better finish, and then make good the indentations with a little woodworking filler.

1 *Place a bolster behind the top edge of the skirting board. Hammer the bolster down gently. Repeat along the length of skirting*

2 *Place the claw of the hammer behind the skirting and slip the protective board between it and the wall. Lever the board away*

3 *If a board proves particularly stubborn, hammer a row of wedges down behind it. This reduces the risk of splitting the board*

7 *You may have to match new board to old skirting. For a 'pencil round' mark a line 6mm from the front top edge and plane it round*

8 *For splayed skirting, mark the desired thickness on the top of the board and the end of the incline on the face. Then plane down*

9 *For splayed and rounded skirting, mark off the top of the board as for a pencil round and plane and sand the edge*

13 *Next, mark a mitre across the top of the board, joining this mark to the one on the back. Make sure the mitre slopes the right way*

14 *Cut through the board to form the mitre—either 'free-hand', as here, or using a mitre box or mitre block. A true cut is essential*

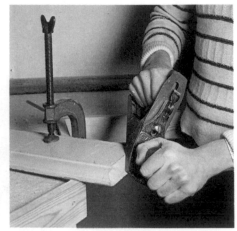

15 *Position the board to check for fit, remembering to remove bits of plaster or other obstructions. If necessary, trim it with the plane*

4 *When the whole length of skirting has been levered from the wall, draw out the nails from the board using a pair of pincers*

5 *If a damaged length is to be removed, first drive in a wedge, then place a mitre block against the skirting while you start your cut*

6 *Now continue the cut to the bottom of the board, having first ruled a vertical pencil line to help keep the cut straight*

10 *For an angled board, mark the correct thickness on the top of the board and the angle required on both the end grains. Plane down*

11 *A variety of skirting styles can be manufactured from ordinary board or from a combination of board and moulding*

12 *To join a new section part-way along a wall, first measure the length you need and mark it on the back of the replacement board*

16 *Another technique of fitting boards is to drill a well for the nail head and then fill this with filler after the nail has been hammered in*

17 *Nail the board into place once a fitting check has been made. Use suitable filler to conceal the nailwells you have drilled*

18 *The completed section should join inconspicuously with existing skirting if the job of matching and fitting has been properly done*

Matching new skirting to old

New houses usually have one of the following types of skirting: pencil round, splayed, splayed-and-rounded, or chamfered. These are easier to obtain than the elaborate older boards but fill-in pieces can be made from a square-edged board.

For pencil round skirting, for example, mark a line along the face of a square-edge board, about 6mm down from what will in effect be the top leading edge. Carefully round this edge as you plane down to the 6mm mark. It helps to start with the plane level, at the top, curving round the edge as you plane down the edge along its length.

Splayed skirting—where the face of the board is sloped slightly upwards—is almost as straightforward. Mark the desired thickness at the top, and where you want

the face to end. Then plane down between these two lines.

Skirting a room

Skirting a whole room is in many ways much easier than repairing existing skirtings. You do not have the problem of matching new skirting to old and, as skirting can be purchased in full lengths to suit room walls, you will have no joints to make in the length of the boards.

The one rule when skirting a room is that external corners have a mitred joint and internal corners have a scribed one. Apart from that, it is sensible to work round the room in rotation. Doing this gives you a scribed cut at one end of a board. The other end will be either square cut (for another scribed joint) or mitred, depending on whether the board meets another internal or external corner.

When using masonry nails always wear plastic goggles as the nails are brittle and are inclined to break off if they meet resistance in the brickwork.

External corners

Mitred joints pose no problem if made carefully with a cutting guide such as a mitre block. However, once placed against the wall, the inevitable irregularities in the plaster may cause a few small gaps to develop. Fill these with filler paste: when they are dry and have been decorated they will not show.

If you can, make these mitred cuts with a mitre box and panel saw. If not, use a jig saw with an adjustable sole plate. First, mark a piece of board to length and cut it 50mm oversize. Hold it in place against the wall

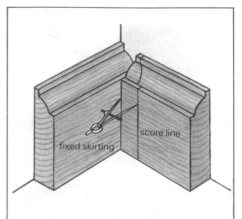

D. *Dividers can be very useful to scribe complex shapes of moulding to a new board*

19 *For an external corner, hold the board against the wall and mark in pencil the end of the wall with a straightedge*

20 *Add to this the thickness of the board. Draw a line across the face. Set the jig saw blade to the width of the sole plate*

23 *Cut a mitre on a second length of board. Measure off and cut to length, leaving a square end to go into the inside corner*

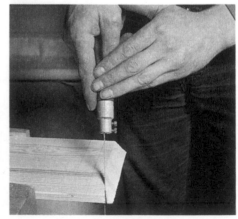

24 *Using a keyhole saw, cut along the outline on the face of the board which has been displayed by cutting the mitre first*

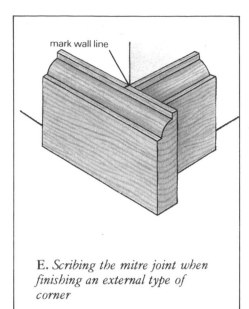

E. *Scribing the mitre joint when finishing an external type of corner*

and carefully mark the inner measurement of the mitre joint. To do this, hold a straightedge or try square at right-angles to the board and close against the other wall. Add the width of the board to this measurement and mark off in pencil, continuing the line all the way down the face of the board.

Set the sole plate on the jig saw to an angle of 45 degrees (instructions for this accompany the different makes of saw). Cramp the board firmly—face upwards—and set the jig saw blade against the pencil line. Mark on the board the right-hand edge of the jig saw sole plate and extend this line across the board. Measure the gap between the lines at both ends to check that the line is straight.

Take a small timber offcut and cramp it firmly in place against the line. This provides a straight and secure edge against which to press the sole plate. Saw across the board keeping the plate pressed closely against the offcut and the result will be a perfectly cut mitre.

Cut a second mitre on the adjoining length of board, using the jig saw in exactly the same way.

Now position the first length of board against the wall and measure right from the tip of the mitre to the wall to determine the exact length you will need. Transfer this measurement to the board and then cut a square edge for the butt joint with a panel saw.

Before nailing the skirting to the wall, a replacement ground must be fitted if the old one is no longer intact or has rotted. Use masonry nails to fix the grounds into the brickwork, below the plaster (see fig. B). Mark the position of the soldiers on the floorboard below, so that you know where to nail when the skirting board has covered them. Use nails to fix the skirting to the ground support and punch the heads below the surface so that they can be concealed with filler.

Internal corners

A scribed joint is used on internal angles. You cut one board to length with a square end, then cut the second to a shape that fits against the curved or moulded end of the first board. This joint is used because, unlike a mitre, it cannot open up—leaving a gap between the boards—as you nail the skirtings to the walls.

There are two ways of obtaining the scribed shape on the second board. One is to use a pair of dividers to trace the profile of one board onto the other. Then cut out this profile with a coping saw, keyhole saw or jig saw.

A better way is to start by fixing the first board (the square-ended one) in place. Then, on the second board, cut a mitre. This leaves a profiled outline on the surface of the board. So cramp the board firmly and cut around this outline—at right-angles to the board's surface—with your coping saw, keyhole saw or jig saw.

However you fix the skirting to the wall or ground, make sure the board is firmly in place—particularly where knocks are common, such as near doorways, sockets and external corners that are always in an exposed position. A firm fixing can prevent considerable additional damage to plaster and grounds that ought really to have been replaced a long time before they even worked loose.

21 *Cramp an offcut to this mark and set the saw blade to 45°. Saw along the pencil line, pressing the sole plate firmly against the offcut*

22 *Fix this board to the wall with masonry nails. Take care when hammering to avoid brickwork or plaster damage beneath*

25 *Join the two boards with two or three nails, nailing through one mitred edge into the other. Punch the nail heads down*

26 *Measure and cut the board to length to fit over the square end of the previous length of board. To get a perfect fit, tap it down*

PLASTERING THE DIY WAY

Alternatives to plastering

Faced with the need to replaster, you have two choices of how to go about the job: conventional plastering or drylining. Drylining consists of covering the wall with sheets of plasterboard—usually fixed to a framework of battens. This guarantees you a smooth surface, but it will only be level over the whole wall if the framework is level—and achieving this is no easy task.

Drylining becomes progressively more difficult the more corners, recesses and door and window frames you have to deal with. But there are also times when it is the only choice, for example if you want to plaster a painted brick cellar wall (plaster does not adhere readily to paint). Usually, the decision boils down to whether you feel happier working with wood and boards or a trowel and hawk.

Removing the old plaster

DIY plastering is a major undertaking, so divide it into two stages: removing the old plaster and replastering. It does mean that you'll have to live temporarily with a lot of mess, but this is infinitely preferable to a job that turns into a disaster because it's been completed in haste.

Start by removing as much furniture and as many fittings from the room as possible. Cover what you can't take out with dust sheets, and spread more dust sheets along the route to the nearest exit—either at the front or back of the house.

Next work out where to dump the debris. The plaster rubble from an average size wall

Plastering or replastering an entire wall is not something to approach lightly. First you must be sure that it really is necessary. And then you should check that there isn't an easier alternative—drylining for instance.

Why replaster?

Patching a plastered wall is a great deal easier than replastering it from scratch. But if the patches are large or extensive it simply is not worth doing—you will never get a surface good enough for an acceptable finish—either paint or wallpaper.

Large-scale DIY jobs present the same problem: if you have hacked the plaster off half a wall it will probably be better to replaster the whole of it rather than simply making good the damaged area.

Walls which are intact but have a poor surface because of previous patching could be another candidate. But in this case you need to assess whether it's worth the trouble. Remember too that ready mixed skimming plaster is available for resurfacing sound but uneven plaster. This has good adhesive qualities, so you can apply it to painted plaster—something you can't easily do with ordinary finish plaster.

One of the most common reasons for replastering is damp. Plaster which has been badly soaked either disintegrates or 'blows' (comes away from the wall). You can check this by tapping the plaster with a piece of wood; a hollow sound indicates damage.

There are several cures for damp walls, depending on what the cause is. While most of them call for plastering skills, it cannot be stressed too highly that there is no point in replastering until you are certain that the damp has been eliminated and the wall given at least several weeks to dry out.

The other all too common reason for replastering is that the existing plaster has failed—a problem that can manifest itself in several ways. Cracking is found in all plaster—especially new plaster—because the material has only limited elasticity. But if the cracks become really severe and the plaster blows in some places, it has been incorrectly applied and should be renewed.

Plaster can also fail if it is the wrong type for the wall. It may simply blow, or it could suck all the moisture out of the wall and produce efflorescence—white salty deposits —on the surface. As replastering is the only solution when faced with this problem make sure, therefore, that the plaster you apply is the correct type for the job in hand.

1 *Cut a V-shaped groove in the middle of the wall, then work gradually outwards*

takes up plenty of space: if you haven't got the use of a skip or dump, get some strong plastic bags—such as fertilizer or ballast bags—in which to store the rubble until it can be collected.

The wall itself must be as clear of fixtures and fittings as possible. Have radiators unhooked and folded down (or better, capped and removed) by a plumber. Where possible the same should be done for any other pipework likely to obstruct you later.

To deal with power points and sockets, first turn off the electricity at the fuse board or consumer unit main switch. Then remove the faceplates to reveal the backing boxes. These can be left where they are, to be plastered around later. If you suspect that cables are buried in the plaster, make a note of their approximate locations at this stage and remember to go carefully when you start clearing the wall.

Finally, remove all skirtings, picture rails and coving or cornice moulding by prising them away from the wall with a claw hammer or crowbar held against a block of wood. Don't worry about damaging the wall plaster—you're about to strip it.

2 *Try to push the bolster behind the plaster so you can ease it off the wall in large sheets*

To remove the old plaster, you need a club hammer and a sharp bolster; if the plaster turns out to be a cement-based render, you'll also need a drill and masonry bit to help loosen it. The ideal dress is a pair of overalls—plaster dust gets everywhere. To protect your hands wear heavy work gloves and make sure you wear a pair of plastic safety goggles to protect your eyes from dust and flying chips.

Start your demolition in the middle of the wall by cutting a V-shaped channel in the plaster until you reach solid masonry. (If

there are any obvious weak points in the plaster you can start there instead.)

★ WATCH POINT ★

If cutting the channel proves really hard work, the wall is probably rendered. In this case drill a series of closely spaces holes in it to give yourself a start.

The purpose of cutting a channel is to give you enough room to angle your bolster in behind the plaster coats and prise them away from the wall. Do this, working outwards in all directions, by tapping the bolster gently—there's no need to use great force, even with tough render.

Using this method causes most of the plaster to fall away in large sheets. Continue along and across the wall, packing the rubble as you go, until most of the surface is clear. Then hack off the stubborn patches that are bound to remain in cracks and crevices in the masonry.

If you come across any cables or electrical fittings make sure that they are firmly attached to the wall before continuing.

Preparing the wall: Although the fresh plaster will take up most of the unevenness in your brickwork or blockwork, it's no good for filling large holes. Unsound mortar joints could cause the plaster to fail later, so initial preparation of the wall is important.

Rake out any crumbling mortar joints to a depth of 25mm with your bolster then brush away debris. Dampen them with a little clean water and repoint flush with the surrounding masonry using a mortar mix of one part cement to three of soft sand.

Large holes can be patched with pieces of brick. Brush out and dampen them with water before setting the bricks in place with a 1:3 mortar mix.

Preparing for plastering

Professional plasterers have four important advantages over amateurs: they know what plasters to use on any given wall; they have help—in the form of a plasterer's mate; they instinctively know when the plaster is mixed to the right consistency; and their experience teaches them how to use a trowel—something which can be taught, but perfected only after a lot of practice.

Against this, the do-it-yourselfer has time on his side. If he takes it and uses it well, it is possible to produce an acceptable finish. But

if he rushes or tries to imitate the professionals, the result is likely to be a disaster. The preparations described below may seem laborious, but they are necessary all the same if you want perfect results.

Choosing and buying plaster

Selecting the right plaster for the job is part of the plasterer's art: it can make all the difference between a good and bad finish.

Repair plaster of the type sold in small bags at hardware and DIY stores is no good for this job: you need to go to a builder's merchant where you can be sure of getting the right materials—in bulk at a competitive price.

Plasters vary in type, but also from region to region—like sand. To add to the confusion, the terminology is different too. So although the terms below are in general use, always state exactly what you want the plaster for to avoid misunderstandings.

Plaster is nearly always applied in two coats. The undercoat—or *floating coat* as it

Plastering tools: the only tool you really need to buy is a plasterer's laying on trowel—and it's well worth buying a good quality model while you are at it. You may also need one or more angle trowels (see above) to finish off any internal or external corners neatly. All the rest of the tools—the scaffold square, scratcher and hawk—can be home-made using a few odd offcuts of timber

is generally called—makes up the bulk of the job; the usual thickness is about 12mm. On top of this goes the *finishing coat*, with a thickness of around 2mm. Hence the following classifications.

Browning: This is the standard floating coat plaster for semi-porous surfaces such as brick and light aggregate block. It has a good filling capacity and does not suck too much moisture out of the wall.

Bonding: The floating coat plaster to use on less porous surfaces such as concrete and dense concrete block. It has good adhesive qualities, which makes it easier to apply than browning. But if you use it on brickwork which is any way damp—and most external walls are—it will suck the moisture straight out to ruin the surface finish.

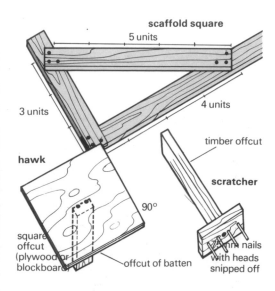

Use the materials and dimensions above as a guide when making your own plastering tools

Finish plaster: Used for the finish coat, it is very fine and hence has good smoothing qualities. But use it to any great thickness and you'll be in trouble. Finish varies in colour from brand to brand and area to area.

Quantities: All plaster comes in bags of varying size, but it's the overall quantities that should concern you. The material is cheap, so always overestimate. As a rough guide, for every 600mm square of wall, allow 3kg of floating coat plaster and 1.3kg of finish.

Cement render: Don't let this confuse you. Render is a mixture of cement and sharp sand, not a type of plaster. Its main use is on external walls, but it is sometimes applied in place of floating coat plaster—usually with waterproofer added—to protect from damp.

Tools and other materials

First and foremost you need a plasterer's *laying on trowel*. Most professionals have at least two: one for the floating coat and one for the finish. Assuming that you won't be doing a lot of plastering you can get by with one, but make sure it is the best quality you can afford—the cheap types found in hardware stores simply aren't any good for proper plastering. Internal and external *corner trowels* are also a good investment: you may be able to scrape by without them, but the extra trouble this causes isn't really worth the saving.

The rest of the equipment should cause no problems. You need a *spotboard* to put the mixed plaster on—a piece of chipboard, plywood or blockboard about a metre square and laid on bricks will do. Make up your own *hawk* for holding the plaster from two offcuts of timber, as shown below.

For scoring the floating coat plaster prior to finishing you need a *scratcher*: knock about six oval nails through the end of an offcut of timber and then snip or saw the heads off.

You need two standard size plastic buckets—one for mixing the plaster and one for carrying water. And a spirit level is a vital piece of equipment—for aligning the setting out battens.

Other materials: Requirements here will vary according to the nature and scope of the job. For the setting out battens, buy lengths of 12mm square sawn softwood to match the height of your wall. You need enough to divide the wall into bays of approximately 1.3m width. To go with the battens, get a 1.5m length of timber to act as a straightedge—a length of planed 75mm × 25mm is suitable. Sight along the piece you choose to make sure that it *is* straight. And if you decide to plaster an external corner the traditional way, you will need a 100mm × 25mm board.

The modern solution is to use galvanized steel corner strips which you pin in place and then plaster around.

If there are window reveals or recesses in the wall, a scaffold square will be needed. You can make your own, as shown left.

Finally, buy masonry nails for securing the setting out guides, boards and strips.

Setting out the wall

If you haven't already done so, prepare the room as you did when stripping the old plaster. Set up your spotboard reasonably

near the site so that you don't have to travel too far with the hawk.

Start with the setting out battens. Take the first one and nail it to the top of the wall. Then lay your spirit level against the side, adjust it until it is plumb, and nail it at the foot of the wall.

3 *Begin by fixing each of the vertical battens into mortar joints using masonry nails*

4 *Check that each batten is plumb. Pack out low spots with card and scraps of ply*

5 *Then check that the front face of each batten is level using the timber straightedge*

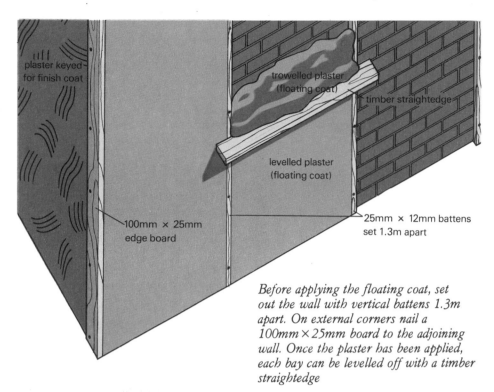

plaster keyed for finish coat

trowelled plaster (floating coat)

timber straightedge

levelled plaster (floating coat)

100mm × 25mm edge board

25mm × 12mm battens set 1.3m apart

Before applying the floating coat, set out the wall with vertical battens 1.3m apart. On external corners nail a 100mm × 25mm board to the adjoining wall. Once the plaster has been applied, each bay can be levelled off with a timber straightedge

6 *On external corners nail a board to the adjoining wall. Level it off with the battens*

7 *Before you start, dampen the brickwork using water mixed with PVA adhesive*

Now lay your level against the face of the batten and check that it is plumb in this plane; if it isn't, ease it from the wall slightly and pack out the low spots with scraps of card or wood. Refix the batten and recheck that it is plumb along both the side and the face with the level.

Repeat this procedure for all the setting out battens, spacing them at rough 1.3m intervals. When they are all up, take the longest straight edged board you can find and lay it across the battens at the top, the middle and the bottom. If any are conspicuously proud or recessed, pack them as described above and recheck with the board. When all the battens are level, you know you've got a perfectly true framework against which to apply the floating coat.

The next step is to fix any other guide boards or strips. Cut corner strips to size with a hacksaw and nail them in place where needed, checking that they are plumb with your level as you go. If you use an external corner board, nail it to the ad-

> ### ★ WATCH POINT ★
>
> Immediately prior to plastering, mix up half a small tin of PVA bonding adhesive in a bucketful of water and use this to dampen—NOT soak—the entire wall. This prevents over-rapid drying of the floating coat and aids adhesion.

joining wall so that it is plumb, with exactly 12mm protruding on the side you are intending to plaster.

Mixing plaster

If you can, get a helper to do the mixing: it's hard work and if you have to do it yourself you're likely to get hot and bothered—which is not conducive to good plastering.

Floating coat and finish plaster are both mixed in the same way—in a bucket—in batches of a third of a bucketful at a time.

Put the water in the bucket first, filling it about a third full. (Do it the other way round and the plaster will clog and go lumpy.) Then add the plaster, a little at a time, stirring quite vigorously as you go.

Continue stirring and adding plaster until the mixture in the bucket reaches the consistency of thick cream—really thick and 'porridge-like' in the case of floating coat plaster; a bit thinner for the finish coat.

When the batch is the right consistency, empty it out onto the spotboard, clean the mixing bucket thoroughly, and start mixing the next. Be warned however: you won't know how much to mix until you know how much you can handle, so start with small amounts only—the most important thing is to avoid the plaster drying before you get a chance to use it. Always reject a batch which looks as if it is 'going off'.

Applying the floating coat

When you are absolutely ready to start, mix up the floating coat plaster and transfer it onto the spotboard. Then scrape a manageable amount off the spotboard onto your hawk with the laying on trowel.

Carry the hawk to the first bay—aim to start in the middle and work outwards. Adopt the following procedure each time you apply plaster to the wall:
- Tilt the hawk slightly towards you.
- Cut into the load on the hawk with the trowel blade, separating an amount which is roughly the size of the trowel.
- Slide this up the hawk with the trowel blade, so that it rolls onto the trowel blade in the process.
- Press the plaster hard against the wall and sweep the trowel upwards in a curving movement. Keep your arm fairly rigid so that you work from the shoulder rather than the wrist. Hold the trowel blade almost parallel to the wall, but with the upper edge slightly tilted towards you so that more plaster is fed onto the wall as you move it.

You will find that the finish plaster spreads and smoothes more easily than the floating coat. Take extra care not to let the edges of the trowel blade dig in and you should get a reasonably flat finish.

Inevitably, though, there will be trowel marks all across the surface. Leave these for the moment, until you have covered the entire section to the correct thickness.

You remove the marks and do the final smoothing with a combination of your trowel and a paintbrush dampened with clean water. The exact method is a matter of personal preference: some people wet the trowel blade then smooth the plaster; others wet the plaster before applying a dry blade.

There are two golden rules about smoothing—or 'polishing' as it's often called. The first is that your trowel must be perfectly clean and flat; the second is that

8 *Work on one bay at a time. Apply plaster and then level off with the straightedge. Start at the bottom and move the straightedge up*

9 *Leave the plaster to dry for one hour, then roughen up the surface with the scratcher. Follow by removing the battens and filling the gaps (inset). Level off neatly*

★ WATCH POINT ★

As you flatten the plaster, it will smooth out. But if you keep pressing and spreading, cracks will appear. At this point stop: it is time to reload the trowel.

Continue in this way until the bay is filled just proud of the battens. You now have to level it using your timber straightedge.

Hold the timber hard against the battens, at the foot of the wall. Run it up the wall, shifting the straightedge from side to side in a scissoring motion, so that the high points on the floating coat are cut off.

Once you have levelled the bay, fill any obvious low points with more plaster, clean the trowel, and smooth off any places where the plaster has 'caught'. If necessary, re-check that the bay is level.

Repeat the entire plastering and levelling procedure on each subsequent bay. At internal corners, use the full length of the trowel blade—or your cornering trowel, if

★ WATCH POINT ★

Always work upwards to cut off any excess; if you work downwards the plaster is certain to pull and could possibly drop off the wall.

you have one—to cut the new plaster neatly. On external corners scrape the plaster against the corner strip or edging board so that you leave a depression about 2mm deep—to allow for the finish coat.

After about one hour, by which time the plaster should be semi-dry, take up your scratcher and swirl it across the entire surface to leave score marks similar to those in step 9. Take care not to apply too much pressure on the scratcher—start gently and increase it gradually.

When the scratching is completed, dig out the setting out battens by prising them away against the floor and the ceiling. Fill the trenches that are left with fresh floating coat plaster and smooth this off level with the surrounding surface. Take care not to disturb the surrounding floating coat plaster more than is necessary.

Leave the floating coat to dry for at least another four hours before attempting to apply the finish plaster.

Applying the finish plaster

This is applied in the same way—and using the same technique—as the floating coat. But the job is much more difficult, because you don't have any battens to work against.

Aim to make the finish coat about 2mm thick. If you are plastering a large wall, do it in two or more complete sections—you can sand where they join later—rather than risk the plaster drying before smoothing it.

10 *Give the wall a final polish, wetting the surface first*

you must dampen the plaster only enough to remove the ridges and marks—any more, and you will stop it from hardening

You have quite a long time to work on the wall—about half an hour—but don't push your luck. If there are some spots that you just can't get flat, leave them for sanding later rather than risk ruining the newly-plastered surface.

Finishing awkward corners

Window reveals, alcoves and recesses can be plastered in the normal way, but it's very hard to get them level. The answer is to separate them from the main job so that you have an edge to work to. Then, when you apply the floating coat, use a scaffold square to check that the plaster is at right angles to the other surfaces; skim off the excess and smooth corners with a corner trowel.

TILING A WALL

Imaginative tiling in anything from cool ceramic to imitation brick can make all the difference to a wall. And it's certainly not just a job for the experts. Providing you follow a few simple rules, there's no reason why you shouldn't be able to achieve a fully professional finish.

Tiles look good in practically any situation in the home, partly because you can get them in such a variety of materials and textures and partly because you have a wide variety of laying patterns open to you now that tiles are produced in such a mix of shapes. From providing easy-to-clean surfaces in kitchens and bathrooms to ultra-smart finishes in living rooms and hallways, tiles provide a decorative feature that you should exploit at every opportunity. One of the great advantages of tiles is that should any get spoiled or damaged they can be replaced individually; you don't have the whole surface to do.

Surfaces to tile

Most surfaces are suitable for tiling as long as they are flat and sound. Plain plaster and plasterboard walls are suitable, old ceramic tiled walls are too. And you can tile over blockboard, plywood, chipboard and laminated surfaces. You'll have to strip walls which have been papered or painted with emulsion, and gloss paint will need to be checked to make sure that the surface is sound. It's not a good idea to tile a hardboard panelled wall with heavy ceramic or mirror tiles—it almost certainly won't be strong enough to stop buckling—but cork and some imitation brick tiles should be suitable.

Choosing tiles

Visit plenty of suppliers when choosing tiles. Some tiles are mass produced while others are only made to order. There is a variety of different types of tile, depending on how they are made.

Ceramic: The most up-to-date universal tiles have chamfered edges of which at least two are glazed. The chamfer produces the grouting line when they are laid butted up against each other and the glazed edges do away with the necessity of having to buy some extra round-edged tiles for finishing off external corners.

Above: *Tiling need not be complicated. By following a few basic guidelines a professional finish can be achieved*

Some traditional tiles have built-in spacer lugs but with most you have to insert spacer slips to provide a grouting gap. You will also need matching round-edged tiles for corners.

You don't, of course, have to stick to ceramic or wall tiles. **Quarry tiles** are thicker and much denser and really made for heavy-duty flooring and industrial use. But they can look very good on walls. Sizes vary from 100mm square to 250mm × 125mm.

Mosaic tiles come on sheets of stiff reinforced paper with the faces of the tiles stuck to the paper ready spaced. You glue the sheet of tiles to the wall and when the adhesive is set peel off the paper before grouting. There's also a type which has a backing of rough hessian. With these, you just stick the backing to the wall. The size of

mosaic tiles varies from less than 25mm square right up to conventional 108mm square size. They can be practically any material from ceramic to steel to mirror. The only disadvantage with mosaic tiles is that they tend to be very expensive.

Cork, vinyl and carpet tiles can be used on walls to great effect. You can buy ordinary floor tiles—or in the case of cork, slightly thinner versions of the flooring grade. Sizes range either side of 300mm square.

Mirror tiles are now readily available and in a range of sizes from 108mm square up to three and four times that size. They are normally stuck to the wall with self-adhesive pads.

Metallic tiles are available in the same range of sizes as ceramic tiles. They are essentially thin pieces of stainless steel or aluminium or other metals with a self-adhesive backing. They can normally be bent around corners although they look better if they are cut conventionally.

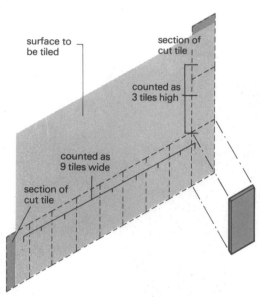

A. *To calculate quantities, divide the height and width of an area by the height and width of a tile. Multiply the figures together. This area needs 27 whole tiles*

Brick and stone tiles can either be thin pieces of real brick and stone, or may be based on concrete or even polystyrene, coloured to look like the real thing. They are most widely used for fireplaces but there is no reason why you should not face an entire wall with them—they particularly complement stripped pine furniture.

Adhesives

There is, unfortunately, no universal adhesive for the whole range of tiles. Some tiles are self-adhesive, some require special adhesives which come with the tile packs and some use widely available adhesives. To find out which adhesive to use, read carefully what the manufacturer recommends and follow the advice given.

Additional materials

When budgeting to tile a wall, don't forget the extras you will need. The notes given here apply to conventional ceramic tiling. If you are using another type of tile, check the manufacturer's recommendations carefully before you proceed.

Adhesive: Use special ceramic tile adhesive which you should be able to get at the same time as the tiles and grout. Allow roughly one litre of the ready-mixed kind for one to one and a half square metres of tiles.

If you are tiling an area which gets wet—and remember that in Europe tiled walls tend to get wet from condensation even when there isn't water about—make sure that you buy *waterproof* adhesive (and grout) not water resistant. There's not much difference in price but it could make a big difference to the state of your tiling in a few years.

Grout: Get it at the same time as the adhesive and follow the same rule about using a waterproof type. You may care to use coloured grout to match another colour in the room and you can buy powder colourings or in some cases ready-mixed coloured grout in tubs. If you are tiling in a kitchen buy a grout with an added fungicide for hygiene's sake.

Spacers: Use small squares of stiff card or matchsticks unless you have bought universal tiles or tiles with spacer lugs. You can often buy packets of spacer slips or cards ready cut. They are worth buying because they are of a standard thickness.

You may need to buy some special quadrant tiles which you use to make a neat finish to edges in exactly the same way as quadrant moulding in carpentry. Try to avoid them as they look old fashioned but they can be useful for sealing around baths.

Estimating for tiles

Don't just take a rough guess. Many tiles are costly so you could soon end up out of pocket. It's better to estimate accurately how many tiles you need.

Measure the area to be tiled and divide by the area of one tile. Allow for any cut tiles, counting each cut tile as a full one. Add at least five per cent to the results to allow for breakages—more if this is your first attempt.

A more accurate method, however, is to divide the height and the length of the wall to be tiled separately by the length and width of one tile, then round up to the next whole number. Multiply these numbers together and, once more, add five per cent to account for breakages.

Preparing walls for tiling

The important thing about walls is that they should be true and flat and that their surface should be good enough for tiles to stick permanently. That means that you will have to strip off any wallpaper, fill any depressions or holes with general purpose interior filler and remove flaking paint.

If you are tiling over an old tiled wall make sure that you check that the old tiles

1 *During the course of your preparations fill any holes or dents in the wall—an uneven surface will only lead to unstable tiles and a bad finish*

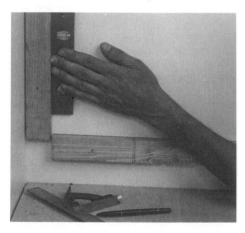

4 *Next, fit the vertical batten in the corner to mark the position of the last row of full tiles. Double check with a spirit level that it is vertical*

★ WATCH POINT ★

Test a painted wall by sticking long lengths of sticky tape to four or five sections. Rub them down then pull them off quickly. If any paint comes off with the tape you will need to remove all the paint.

are firmly fixed. If you find any loose ones remove them carefully, clean off their backs and refix them with new adhesive. Use a tile cutter to score the surface of the old tiles to give a key for the adhesive. It's a good idea with painted or stripped or plaster surfaces to give them a coat of stabilizing solution after sanding them down with coarse abrasive paper.

If the wall is in terrible condition when

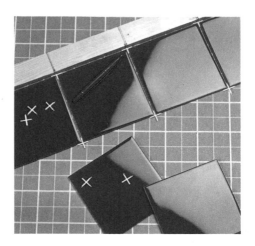

2 *Lay your measuring rod on the floor against a row of tiles—and spacers if you are using them—and then mark across onto the batten*

3 *Mark the position of the bottom of the last row of complete tiles and nail a horizontal batten to the wall to act as a support and guide*

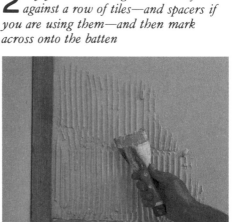

5 *Use a serrated spreader to get the necessary even coverage of adhesive on the wall. Do not use too much as it will just be wasted*

6 *Start laying the tiles in the corner of the wall against the two temporary support battens, so that you start to build up straight lines*

height of a wall and discover that the ceiling is uneven or slopes at a slight angle, you may have to cut an additional row of tiles to fit. Whatever the case, always draw a level line at the top and measure down from it.

Mark the position of the bottom of the last row of full tiles using another line on the wall. Check that it is level and straight. Nail a batten the same length as the wall along this. This is the support for the first row.

Normally you will find the width of the wall doesn't coincide with the module of the tiles either and you will have to run cut tiles up the sides as well. If you have internal angles at each end it looks best if you run a row of cut tiles up each side. Try to make them even on either side. If you have an external angle you should use full tiles at the corner and use cut tiles at the other end.

When you have decided about the

★ WATCH POINT ★

To mark the measuring rod accurately, lay a row of tiles on the floor, inserting spacer cards if they have no lugs or are not universal tiles. Mark off the rod directly from the tiles.

---

positioning of cut tiles, mark off the fixed batten into tile wide divisions. Draw a line up the wall marking the last row of full tiles and fix another batten to the wall aligned on this vertical mark. Check that it is vertical with a spirit level and make sure that it is at right-angles to the bottom horizontal batten. Once you have marked up and fixed the battens you are ready to start tiling.

Fixing the tiles

If you've prepared the walls properly, fixing the tiles is a straightforward job but take your time to achieve a good finish.

Start by spreading adhesive over an area of about one square metre in the corner where the two battens join. Use a notched spreader to get the adhesive reasonably even. Start laying the tiles from the corner working out in a triangular pattern and butting up the edge rows hard against the battens (fig. 6).

Depending on the type of tiles you have chosen butt the lugs of the tiles to adjacent tiles or slip spacers between them as you lay. When you have laid all the full tiles, clean off any excess adhesive and wait for a day.

When the adhesive has set, remove the

you have got back to a sound surface, you have the option of replastering or lining the wall with new plasterboard—or one of the man-made boards such as chipboard or blockboard or ply. If you are using a timber board don't use a thickness of less than 12mm for ceramic tiles—anything thinner will eventually sag and loosen the tiles.

In wet areas, such as shower compartments, the best backing is waterproof ply or exterior grade ply. Don't use chipboard or blockboard—they will swell if they get wet. Remember in wet situations that you must use *waterproof* adhesive and grout—*not* water resistant.

Setting out for tiling

With the surface of the wall prepared, plan the pattern of the tiles. Start by making a

measuring rod from a long batten. Mark it off in divisions of one tile, not forgetting to allow for the thickness of the grouting gap between each tile (fig. 2).

The most common—and glaring—mistake some people make when they tile a wall is to start from the bottom against a skirting or edge of a bath. The chances are that neither is truly horizontal with the result that the subsequent rows of tiles lean off at an angle. The only way to guarantee a perfect arrangement of tiles is to start against a level batten.

Draw a line on the wall marking the top of the area you want to tile—this may be at the ceiling. Use the rod to measure down to the bottom—the floor or skirting board or the edge of a bath. The chances are that this will show you that you will have to use cut tiles in one row. This row should be at the bottom, but if you are tiling the complete

battens and start on the more time consuming part—measuring and cutting tiles to fit the borders.

Walls are rarely absolutely even or vertical so you need to mark and cut each tile individually and fix it in place before moving on to the next. An alternative is to mark and cut a group of tiles and number them and their positions on the wall. Then fix the tiles in batches of half a dozen. Always mark cut tiles individually.

Start measuring and cutting along the bottom row and work up the sides afterwards. Make sure that the grout lines line up with the main tiling. This is the time to fix any special fittings, such as soap or toilet roll holders, as well.

Leave the adhesive to set for a day and get ready for grouting. You'll need two sponges and a thin dowel with a rounded end. You'll also need to remove any spacer cards before you start. Wipe the grout over the face of the tiling, rubbing it well into the joints with a slightly damp sponge. Wipe off excess grout with a dry sponge as you go. After 20 minutes run along each joint with the rounded dowel, pressing the grout in firmly and leaving a neat finish (fig. 9). Don't be tempted to use your fingers to round off the joints as the grit in the grout will more than likely wear extremely painful holes in your skin and may even lead to dermatitis. If you suspect that you have sensitive skin, it's always a good idea to wear protective rubber gloves.

After a couple of hours wipe off the dried remaining grout which will look like the 'bloom' on fruit skins.

If you use coloured grout make sure that the floor or bath at the bottom is protected—grout's quite difficult to get off and it is better to prevent against it in the first place.

Dealing with problem areas

Make an assessment of any problem areas before you start work—it will speed the tiling process later.

Problem areas can arise in any room. You may want to put things like soap holders and towel rails in a bathroom or tile around a power socket in a kitchen (fig. 10).

Special fittings

In bathrooms you will probably want to incorporate such things as soap holders into your tiling. Most manufacturers now make them in the same sizes as a tile or a pair of

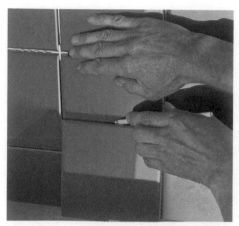

7 *When the adhesive has firmly set for the first few rows of tiles, remove the battens and mark and cut the bottom row of tiles*

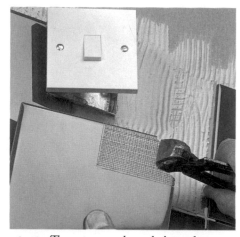

10 *To cut an awkward shape from a tile, score the area in a criss-cross fashion and then nibble away at the section with a pair of pliers*

tiles. Fix these at the same time as the cut tiles around the edges.

When you are laying the full tiles decide where the fitting is to go. Lay an ordinary tile at that position and continue tiling—but go back before the adhesive has completely set and carefully remove it. You need it there to get the joints even and straight for the rest of the tiles in the row and above. Hold heavy fittings in place with masking tape until the adhesive has set.

Light fittings

Make sure you turn off the electricity at the mains before you tile around light fittings or switches. With flush-mounted fittings unscrew the face plate of the fitting and cut tiles to the edge of the metal box fixed to the wall. Your cutting doesn't have to be perfect but make sure that there is plenty of

8 *Liberally wipe the grout over the face of the tiles forcing it into all the gaps as you go along. A sponge is the best applicator to use*

11 *Cut tiles are best left to internal corners where they will blend in and be less obtrusive. If possible, turn the corner with the tile offcuts*

room for the face plate and its attached wires to go back freely. Don't skimp on grouting the joints behind the face plate before you screw it back in place. When you have cleaned off the grout turn the mains on again.

Internal and external angles

The basic rule is that you should use full tiles at external angles and corners, cut tiles in internal angles. The rule applies to window and door reveals as well.

At external angles it is a good idea to nail a batten on the return wall leaving a little overlap to provide an edge to butt the last row of square-edged tiles against. When they are in position remove the batten and lay round-edged tiles—or universal tiles—on the return wall to overlap the edges which are exposed.

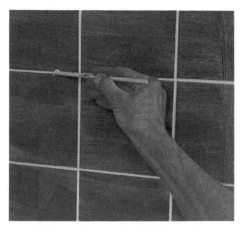

9 *Tidy up the grouted joints with a length of dowel and then thoroughly polish the tiles with a clean cloth to get rid of any excess grout*

12 *At external corners, lay one row of tiles flush with the edge of the wall and overlap their sides with the adjacent row for a neat finish*

If a corner is likely to get rough treatment you should consider fixing a timber batten or L-shaped moulding permanently to the corner of the wall and tiling up to it on both sides. The timber will tolerate much more bumping and scuffing than the relatively fragile tiles.

Changes in thickness

If you are tiling over an old area of tiling which goes only half way up the wall, you will have the problem of a step. There is a variety of ways of dealing with this. One is to stop your own tiling at round about the same level filling in behind any overlap with plaster and finishing off with either a ceramic quadrant tile or a hardwood strip. If you use a wooden strip in a bathroom, play safe and seal it with varnish before you fit it.

If you want your tiles to continue right up

to the ceiling or to a higher point, you will either have to accept the visual break—and make a design feature of it in the form of a small shelf or a band of tiles in another colour—or line the upper part of the wall to the same thickness of the old tiling and continue up on the new base. Hardboard stuck with contact adhesive to a sound wall will provide an adequate lining material (use tempered or waterproofed hardboard in a bathroom or kitchen) and should approximate the thickness of the original tiles.

Measure and cut the sheet or sheets to fit the area of wall and start fixing the pieces one section at a time.

Take the shine off the polished side of the hardboard with coarse sandpaper and, paying particular attention to get even coverage along the edges and corners, add the adhesive with a serrated spreader.

While the adhesive is still wet on the board, smooth the sheet in position on the wall to get a transfer of glue—this will indicate the exact area on the wall that needs to be coated with adhesive. Spread the adhesive on the wall and when both surfaces are touch dry firm the hardboard permanently in place. Once the hardboard is fixed, you are in a position to start laying the tiles.

Fixing non-ceramic tiles

Non-ceramic tiles won't need the same kind of physical support which the battens provide. But it is still a good idea to use them for all the other kinds of tiles, simply because it is easier to align against an edge than to a pencil mark.

Below: *The gap between mosaic panels must be the same as between the tiles themselves (left). Cut the backing off mosaic tiles for awkward shapes (right). Use dowelling to 'point' brick tiles (inset)*

Although some non-ceramic tiles such as cork, vinyl and carpet will be much bigger than their ceramic counterparts, use the same setting-out procedure—marking the top and measuring down in increments of one tile height.

Cork is laid using cork flooring adhesive and **vinyl** and **carpet** may be too—unless they have a self-adhesive backing.

Mirror tiles are fixed with self-adhesive pads. They are not always exactly the same size so it is a good idea to lay them out on the floor first. Mirror tiles call for flat and true walls but remember that you can often move the pads around on the back of the mirror tile. Position the pads, therefore, so that they lie in the flattest position.

Metallic tiles don't reflect very much although their surface is shiny. They can be laid on walls which are not flat without it showing too much. They have either a self-adhesive backing or self-adhesive pads.

Mosaics have the advantage that the tiles are automatically spaced and are laid in quite large areas in one go. But you have to be careful in lining up the joints of adjacent panels of mosaic. Tear off a narrow strip of the backing around the four sides so that you can see the joints for lining up. A strip only a few millimetres wide is enough. You must also make sure that the distance between sheets is the same as the spacing between tiles on the sheet.

Brick and **stone** tiles are laid in the same way as ceramic tiles except that the courses will not be in a grid but in a conventional masonry bond. You'll have to work this out on paper first as if you were building a real brick or stone wall. As with ceramic tiles you fix this kind of tile to the wall and when the adhesive has set fill in the joints with grout—or mortar. Filling the joints between brick or stone tiles is more like pointing than grouting—take care not to get the surface of the tiles contaminated.

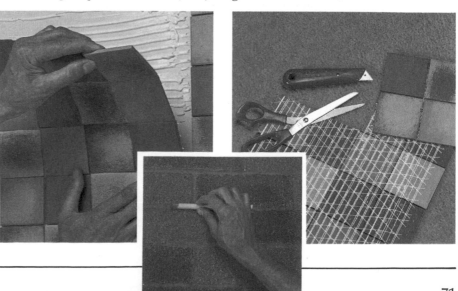

WORKING WITH WALLBOARD

Panelling walls has recently become a popular alternative to wallpapering and painting. Apart from the decorative aspect, you can use wallboards to create a brand new surface—even if the existing walls appear to be in bad condition.

Wallboards (such as Laconite) are purpose made sheets of hardboard or sometimes plywood. One side is coated with a polyester finish which is coloured or moulded to create different effects: tiles, timber planks, hessian and a whole range of plain and textured patterns—there is a design for every sort of room. They are practical too; you can clean them with a damp cloth and they are resistant to most household stains and knocks, including

★ WATCH POINT ★

A good way to insulate a wall for either heat or sound is to fit battening and then sandwich insulating material—either polystyrene sheeting or glass fibre quilting—in the gap between the wallboard and the wall.

splashes of boiling water and spills from pots and pans.

If your walls are in good condition, you can simply stick them on with adhesive or, if you want to straighten up an old wall, fit them over a battening framework. However, if your walls are damp for any reason, don't be tempted to use wallboards to cover it up. The problem is certain to recur unless given specialist treatment.

Choosing wallboards

Decorative wallboards come in a variety of patterns and finishes; Laconite, for example, is made in a range of textured or plain woodgrain, tiles and decorative prints. Good DIY stores have sample swatches to help you make your choice. Tiles are always a good bet for bathrooms and kitchens, whereas simulated wood or hessian are ideal for living rooms or bedrooms.

When you buy your wallboards, check that all the panels are colour matched and, if they are patterned, that the patterns all line up when the boards are placed side by side. Checking the panels before purchase will help to ensure a satisfactory finish.

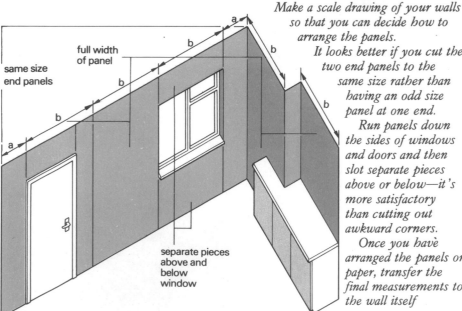

Make a scale drawing of your walls so that you can decide how to arrange the panels.

It looks better if you cut the two end panels to the same size rather than having an odd size panel at one end.

Run panels down the sides of windows and doors and then slot separate pieces above or below—it's more satisfactory than cutting out awkward corners.

Once you have arranged the panels on paper, transfer the final measurements to the wall itself

Planning

Have a good look at your walls and decide which method of fixing you are going to use. If your walls are flat and sound, you can stick the wallboards on with neoprene contact adhesive or flexible mastic based adhesive; if they are lumpy or out of plumb, you must use the battening method—basically you build a lightweight frame onto the wall and then fit the wallboard on top.

You can use either adhesive or panel pins to secure the boards to the battening. Pinning is cheaper and less messy but is only really successful on tiled or planked wallboards where the pins can be hidden in the grooves between the panels.

If you choose to batten your walls, check whether your walls are masonry or stud and plasterboard—it will make a difference to how you go about the job.

Wallboards normally come in 2240mm × 1220mm sheets so measure the height of your ceiling—the walls may be more than 2240mm high; if they are, don't worry as you will be able to make up small differences between the height of the panels and the ceiling with a skirting at the bottom or a cornice at the top.

Laconite also make boards in smaller sizes —1830mm × 610mm and 1220mm × 610mm which are useful for panelling above a worktop or around a bath.

> ### ★ WATCH POINT ★
>
> Don't be tempted to add bits on the end of a panel to make up the height of the wall—it's unlikely that you will be able to conceal the join. If you have a very high ceiling, panel up to a picture rail.

Wallboards are always put on vertically and, unless you are very lucky, you will have to cut panels to fit your walls. Decide how you want to arrange them by first drawing up a plan of your walls on paper.

> ### ★ WATCH POINT ★
>
> You can always use the architects' 'flashgap' technique: leave a space of 4–6mm between the edges of the board and paint the exposed backing wall or battening in a contrasting or matching colour.

Materials

Joints: Dealing with the joints in a planked or tiled board is easy—just fill them with a matching grout. To cover joints in plain boards, you can buy wooden strips or plastic extrusions—these are particularly useful for external corners (see page 75).
Adhesives: Unless you choose to nail on your wallboards, you will need an adhesive.

Manufacturers normally recommend a special adhesive—either mastic or contact —to be used with their brand of wallboard.
Battening: If you decide to use battening, buy planed all round (PAR) 50mm × 25mm softwood. While sawn timber is cheaper to buy, it is not so easy to line up accurately.

To fix the battening, use either 38mm masonry nails or 38mm No. 8 screws and the appropriate wallplugs—you won't need plugs for a stud wall as you can screw into the timber. The advantage with screws is that they can be loosened to get the battening plumb, but they are more expensive and fiddly to fit than nails.

Additional materials you may need

After planning how your wallboards are going to fit along the walls, decide how to treat skirtings, cornices and picture rails.
Skirtings: Providing they are in good condition, re-use your original skirtings. If needs be, you can always buy lengths of skirting from your local timber yard.
Cornices: You can get strips of coving (for cornices) from your DIY shop. Fix to the wall with adhesive or plasterboard nails.
Picture rails: Picture rail moulding is sold by the metre priced according to the design. You need panel pins to fix the rails; their length depends on the wood's thickness.

Estimating

Calculate the number of wallboards you need with a length of batten cut to the width of a sheet. Go around the walls counting off the number. If you are using battens, to calculate the length you need for a masonry wall, multiply the number of wallboards by three and add one for each corner, door and window. Multiply this number by the height of the room. Add to this the distance round the room multiplied by three.

For a stud wall divide 400mm into the height of the room multiplied by its length. Note that you need one screw or nail per 400mm length of battening.

One cartridge of mastic adhesive will fix two 2240mm × 1220mm panels; a litre can of contact adhesive, one panel. Always play safe by buying a little more adhesive than you calculate.

It is impossible to give a precise estimate for the number of 15mm panel pins needed to fix one sheet of wallboard—it will be something between 30–40 on average.

Coving strips, skirting, and picture rail moulding is sold by length, so buy them according to the size of your walls. Fix them in place with either plasterboard nails or panel pins spaced 1m apart.

Tools for the job

To cut the wallboard use a fine toothed panel saw; for fixing, a spirit level, plumbline, square, tape measure and hammer. Other useful things to have around will be a nail punch, plane or rasp, sandpaper, hard roller, a straightedge, stepladder or hop-up, drill and bits, and a padsaw. You may also want to use a mastic gun, an adhesive spreader, a stripping knife and a filling knife.

Preparing the walls and boards

Two days before you intend to start hanging the wallboards, stack them loosely in the room so they get conditioned to the temperature in which they will be hanging.

How you go about the next stage of preparation depends on whether you are fixing the boards with adhesive or on battens.
Preparing for fixing with adhesive: The surface of the walls must be sound, so strip off wallpaper and old paint and fill any hollows. Then sand down the walls.

Mark off the spacings of the boards across the walls. The first board to be fixed will be the one in the middle—use a chalked plumbline to mark its position. You won't have much leeway to reposition the panels once they are glued, so have accurate and clear guidelines from the start.
Preparing for fixing on battens: first, remove architraves and skirtings—you will be able to re-use them later on.

The sort of framework you fix up will depend on the nature of the wall: on masonry walls the battens run vertically; on stud walls they are horizontal (see page 74).

For a masonry wall, start by cutting lengths of batten to the height of the ceiling or picture rail—one for each corner and one for the sides of each door and window. Fix them with either masonry nails or 38mm screws and wallplugs every 600mm. If you use screws, drill clearance holes and mark through them the positions of the wallplugs. Check with a spirit level that the battens are vertical—if not insert packing pieces. Next cut and fit the top and bottom battens.

1 *Fill any holes and then smooth down*

2 *Mark the position of the first board with chalk*

3 *Lever skirtings off carefully to avoid damage*

4 *Screw the end battens to the wall first*

5 *Insert packing pieces to get the battens vertical*

6 *Next, secure the top and bottom battens in place*

7 *Fix intermediate battens about 400mm apart*

8 *Use a cartridge gun to apply mastic adhesive*

The rest of the vertical battens are spaced so that each sheet is supported along its edges with two intermediate battens in between—every third batten must be positioned to straddle the joints; the intermediate battens are added at roughly 400mm intervals. Cut these battens so that they fit tightly between the ceiling and floor battens and screw or nail them into place. Stretch a piece of string between the two outside battens to make sure that the frame is in line. For extra support, skew nail horizontal battens halfway up the vertical ones, using 38mm oval nails.

If you have a stud wall, all the battens are horizontal and spaced at 400mm intervals up the wall (see illustration). Make sure that you fix them into the studs and not into the plasterboard which will not be strong enough to take the weight of the boards.

On stud walls, run the battens horizontally (left); on masonry walls set them vertically (below right)

Hanging the wallboards

Start fixing panels in the middle of a wall and work outwards to each side, cutting the end panels and any tricky bits last.

How you treat joints in the panels will vary according to the finish: wood effect panels can simply butt together while tiled boards can be caulked later. Plain boards will need cover strips which are either pinned or glued into position.

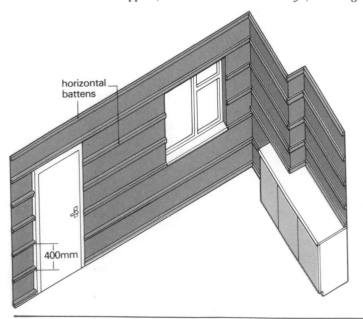

horizontal battens

400mm

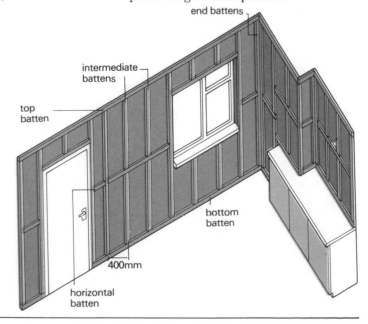

end battens

intermediate battens

top batten

bottom batten

400mm

horizontal batten

If you decide not to use cover strips at internal corners, arrange the junction of the boards so that the open joint is least obvious from the most used part of the room.

External corners need corner mouldings; it is difficult to mitre the boards accurately and corners need protection from knocks.

Adhesive fixing: Apply *mastic adhesive* from a cartridge gun; form a continuous strip or 'worm' right around the perimeter of a board, followed by a series of blobs—the size of a marble in parallel lines 400mm apart.

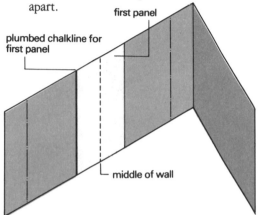

Fix your first panel starting in the middle of the wall

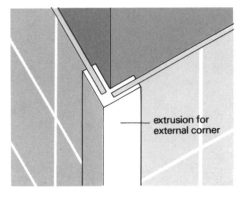

External corners are dealt with by fitting special mouldings made for the job

this is not easy to do in practice.

Fixing to battens: If you are using mastic adhesive to fix panels to battens, apply a strip from the cartridge gun to the battens and then offer the panel up.

If you have decided on contact adhesive, an easy way to work out where the battens line up on a panel is to coat the battens first and to hold the wallboard up against them to get a transfer of glue. After removing the panel, apply contact adhesive to the back following the pattern of the battens.

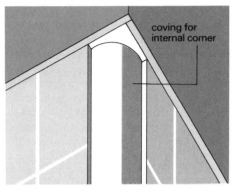

Internal corners can be finished off with a coving strip to cover the joints

If you want to nail on your panels, start by holding one in position against the battens—a wooden wedge placed on the floor will help you balance the sheet. Using 15mm panel pins, nail the middle of one edge to the batten behind. Then working fanwise, nail the rest of the panel to the battens—pins should be spaced about 150mm apart on the edge and 300mm apart on the intermediate battens. Always pin through the grooves of timber planking or tiling-style board.

9 *When gluing follow the lay of the battens*

10 *Pin the panels in place through the grooves*

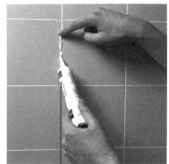

11 *Use a grout or sealer to fill tiled boards*

12 *Pin on scrap pieces before the skirting*

Press the panel up to its mark with the top edge tight against the ceiling. Smooth it over and then immediately take it off; half the adhesive will be stuck to the wall in the same pattern. Leave the adhesive to dry for about 20 minutes and then replace the panel to its mark and smooth it over with a hard roller. The adhesive works immediately so make sure you get the positioning right first time.

Spread *contact adhesive* over the whole of the back of the wallboard, and the wall, and then leave it to dry for 15–20 minutes. When the adhesive is touch dry, position the panel against its mark and firmly roll over it. Some contact adhesives allow you to make small adjustments but with big panels

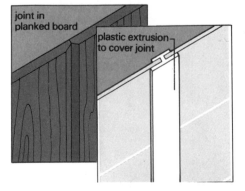

Wood effect boards are simply butted together (left)
Flush joints can be bridged very effectively with plastic strips (right)

Finish off by punching the pin heads home and filling in the holes—use a waterproof filler in a bathroom or kitchen.

Skirtings, architraves and trouble spots

At some stage you will encounter problem areas like light switches and, when you have finished, refitting the skirting.

The most complicated situation is where you have to cut a hole in the centre of a panel—as when fitting over electrical outlets and switches. In other cases you can generally refix fittings over the top of the panelling.

Switches and sockets: If you are sticking your wallboard directly onto the wall, you won't have much trouble; you simply cut out a rectangle that fits over the switch. To mark up where to cut the rectangle, align the panel to be cut next to the switch. Against a straightedge, draw two parallel lines across from the top and bottom of the switch plate. Then measure the distance from the preceding panel to the sides of the switch plate and mark off the two measurements on your parallel lines. Join up the points where the lines cross and cut out the rectangle. For the neatest result, cut the hole fractionally undersize. Switch off the mains and remove the faceplate before boarding the wall. Then refix the plate over the board.

With a battened wall, the problem is more elaborate. The best way to solve it is to bring the switch forward so that it is flush with the surface of the wallboard.

Turn off the electricity at the mains and remove the switch plate. Then unscrew the mounting box and pull it out. Construct a simple frame of battening around the opening and secure the switch box to a batten offcut. Measure up and cut out a rectangle from the panel and then fit it over the switch box before replacing the plate.

Radiators: The only satisfactory way of dealing with radiators is to remove them before hanging the panels and then to refit them when you have finished. If you are using the battening method, provide extra battens to support the radiator brackets; wallboard is not a structural material.

Windows and doors: Run full length panels down the sides of windows and doors and fill in with cut panels below and above, giving them adequate support if you are using battens.

Skirtings: When you come to refix these, nail or glue scrap pieces of wallboard across the wall or the battens below the bottom of the panels. Make chalk marks on the floor in front of the battens if you have used them, and then nail on the skirting.

Architraves: Like skirtings, architraves are simply nailed on. If you have used battening, sandwich a piece of packing—the thickness of the batten plus the thickness of the wallboard—between the architrave moulding and the door frame (see above). You can use hardboard as a packing material—simply pin or glue it in place and then paint over it in a matching colour.

Re-fix the mounting box to an offcut of batten set back into the recess. Construct a simple frame to secure the box in place before fitting on the panel

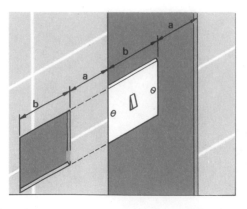
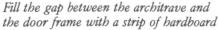

Mark off the measurements (a) and (b) and cut out a hole for the switch plate

Fill the gap between the architrave and the door frame with a strip of hardboard

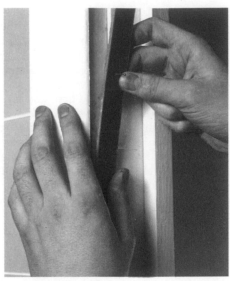

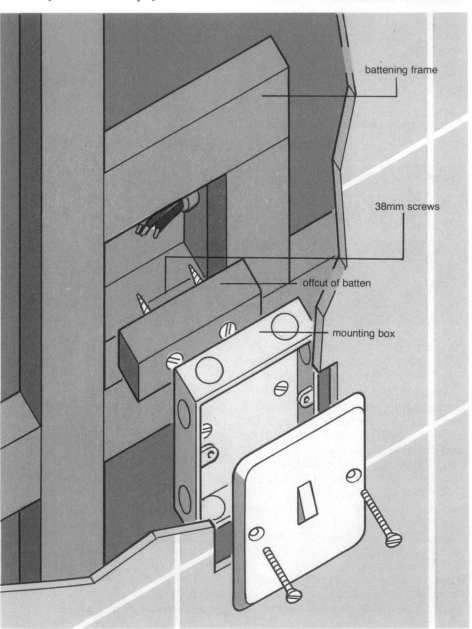

battening frame

38mm screws

offcut of batten

mounting box

CHAPTER 2

HOME PLUMBER

Basic plumbing skills using copper and plastic pipes
and fittings with projects such as installing a
bathroom suite, fitting an outside tap and plumbing-in a shower

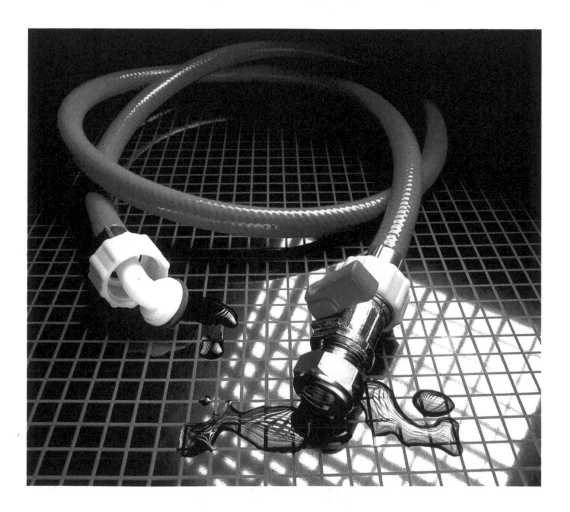

LEAKS AND DRIPS

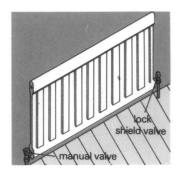
The radiator can be isolated for repair or replacement by turning off both valves

1 Tightening the nut under the manual (or wheel head) valve may be enough

2 If you don't have a lockshield key, use a spanner with care

3 Finally, turn off the manual valve at the other end by hand

Curing a leaking radiator

A leaking radiator should be looked at without delay—to avoid damage to carpets and floorboards. If it is leaking at the coupling to the pipe there's little cause to worry. Tightening the nut may be enough to stop the leak. If not, you need to undo the cap nut, take off the fitting, then replace the olive.

You'll have to drain the radiator before you can tackle this job. And if you need to carry out repairs to the valve, you'll have to drain at least part, if not all, of the system.

If the leak is caused by corrosion, the only cure is to fit a new radiator. You can make a temporary repair, however, using a plastic resin filler.

To work on the radiator you will need to isolate it, by turning off the valves at each end. To turn off the lockshield (see diagram), remove the cap which holds it in its set position then fit a key onto the top.

Next turn off the manual valve at the other end. You can then take the radiator out to replace it or carry out a temporary repair more easily.

If you install a new radiator, you can avoid further corrosion problems by adding a rust inhibitor to the water after flushing out the system with clean water.

Replacing a WC connection

A leaking joint between a lavatory pan and its soil pipe should be attended to immediately—even if you can only carry out a temporary repair.

As an emergency measure, clean and dry the area thoroughly and wrap it tightly with heavy duty sealing bandage such as Sylglas. This is a temporary solution, so remake the joint as soon as possible.

The soil pipe will be connected to the pan in one of three different ways.

The oldest method used for earthenware and iron soil pipes was to caulk the joint with tarred hemp and then fill it with cement and sand mix.

In later years these joints were often packed with putty; most recently plastic connectors have been used to join the pan and soil pipe.

To reseal a sand and cement joint can pose some severe problems. It entails chopping out the cement, which is very difficult to do without breaking either the pan outlet or the collar of the soil pipe.

If the joint is packed with putty this will have set hard but it is not too difficult to scrape out using an old screwdriver.

The easiest way to remake the joint is to fit a plastic Multikwik soil pipe connector. To do this, you'll need to take the lavatory pan right out.

Unless you are dealing with a close-coupled lavatory pan start by disconnecting the flush pipe at the back of the pan. This is usually held by a plastic sleeve which you

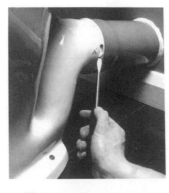
1 If putty seals the waste joint, scrape it off with a screwdriver

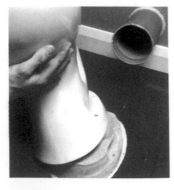
2 The pan may wriggle off the mortar base, or it may be screwed

3 Fit the Multikwik connector into the end of the soil pipe, then to the WC

4 Use the grease—it will make the job easier and help get a better join

simply roll back.

Remove the screws holding the base of the pan to the floor and lift the pan out of the way—be careful, though, it's heavy. If the lavatory has a solid floor, the pan will probably be bedded into a mound of mortar to keep it level. The only thing you can do in this case is to try to wriggle the pan free—prising it from underneath could break it.

Clean the outlet of the pan, and the collar of the soil pipe before fitting a flexible plastic connector such as a Multikwik. One end of this fits into the soil pipe socket. The other end fits over the pan waste outlet.

You can then replace the lavatory pan and screw back to the floor. The plastic connector has enough flexibility to allow for any slight discrepancies in the alignment of the pan outlet and the soil pipe.

Resealing leaking pipe joints

The weakest points in any pipe-work are the joints. If copper pipe is involved, resealing a leaking joint is either a simple matter of tightening a nut, or soldering a joint. Joints in lead pipe are not really a DIY job.

Copper pipework is often connected by compression joints. With these a slight turn of the nut will generally compress the olive inside sufficiently to cure the leak.

Soldered joints are more of a problem as they cannot be resealed without first emptying the pipe and this means draining at least a part, if not all, of the water system. If you are dealing with a hot water pipe (other than central heating), tie up the ball valve in the cold supply tank so that the water can be drained off at the taps. For central heating turn off the boiler and open the drain cock. A cold water pipe only needs the water turned off at the main stop tap. But even with the system drained, there may still be some water in the pipe.

There's no point in simply trying to re-solder the joint—the pipe will be dirty inside the fitting, and you need a clean and shiny pipe if the solder is to grip. You also need a new capillary joint that does the same job as the old. But you may not need an identical fitting: if the original was the type that uses a separate solder supply, buy the pre-soldered kind instead as they are very much easier to use.

The best method of taking the joint apart is to make a cut right through the centre of the fitting with a hacksaw and let any water out. Then heat the pipe fitting with a blow-torch to melt the solder; this will allow you to pull out the ends of both sections of pipe. You may have to loosen some pipe clips in order to spring the pipe enough to allow you to free it.

When using the blowtorch, you must take great care not to damage the wall behind the pipes. The best way to do this is to tape a piece of asbestos to the wall. The type of asbestos mat used by plumbers is expensive, and an excellent substitute is an asbestos simmering pad found in most good kitchenware shops.

Clean the pipe thoroughly with wire wool or abrasive paper making sure that all the old solder is removed. Smooth the cut ends with a file.

Coat the pipe with flux to keep it clean. Clean the new fitting before sliding it over the ends of the section of pipe.

When it is in place heat it with a blow-torch until the solder appears around the

1 *Start by cutting straight through the centre of the joint at right angles*

2 *The old joint will come away once the solder is melted with a blowlamp*

3 *Clean the pipe thoroughly with wire wool or glass paper to remove grease*

4 *Then coat both ends of the pipe with flux. Apply flux with a matchstick*

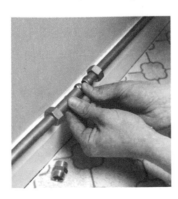

5 *Protect the wall behind when using a blowtorch with a special mat*

6 *First push the nut, then the olive, onto the pipe. Apply jointing compound*

7 *Next fit both ends of the pipe into the fitting. Push them hard into the ends*

8 *Finally, tighten up by hand then use an adjustable spanner*

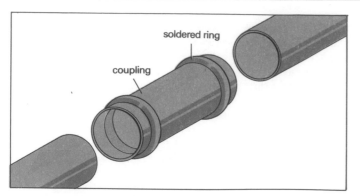

Presoldered joints are easy to fit, but must be heated

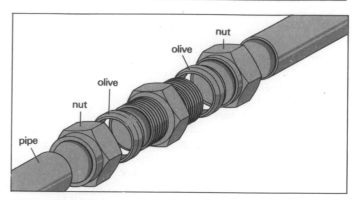

Compression joints can be undone with spanners

end of the fitting, indicating a fully soldered joint. Remove the heat as soon as you see the solder appear. Never continue to heat the pipe after this point.

An easier solution may be to replace the existing solder joint with a compression fitting which needs no heat.

The compression fitting has a nut at each end with a ring, or olive, inside. First push the nut and then the olive onto the end of the pipe which must be clean and smooth.

Push the pipe into the fitting as far as the moulded stop, then push the olive into the end of the fitting.

As you screw the nut up, the olive is forced into the fitting and compressed onto the pipe, forming a water tight joint. Tighten the nut as far as you can go by hand—then give it a further 1½ turns with an adjustable spanner.

Lead pipe is more difficult to repair. You must scrape the pipe clean and cover the bright area with tallow flux. You then melt a plumber's solder onto the pipe and wipe it in to the traditional shape using a coarse cloth coated with tallow.

Don't tackle this job unless you feel confident you can handle it—use an epoxy filler to make a temporary repair, then call in an experienced plumber.

Dealing with a leaking overflow

Although you only fill a sink up to the overflow infrequently, it's important that overflow connections are well sealed. A leaking connection will cause a great deal of mess but it's often difficult to determine whether it's the overflow connection or the sink waste that's leaking. So before you do anything, fill the sink up to the overflow outlet and check underneath to see just where the water is coming from.

Most modern kitchens and inset sinks have a flexible pipe leading from the overflow outlet to the waste pipe, just above the trap connection to the sink. If the leak is at the connection to the outlet in the side of the sink, take off the pipe by unscrewing the little grid inside the sink.

On some of the more recently produced kitchen sinks, the grid is incorporated in the sink itself and to undo the overflow pipe to reseal the connection, all you need to do is to unscrew the nut which the plug chain is attached to. And a few sinks don't even have an overflow outlet.

Clean the outlet and the end of the pipe then screw the grid back in position, making sure it's as tight as possible. If the leak is around the grid, seal it with a little silicone sealant before screwing it back.

When you cut the nozzle of the sealant tube, make sure the opening is not too wide. For once you apply the sealant and tighten up the grid, if you have applied too much, it will ooze out of the side of the grid and may look unsightly.

The other point where a leak can occur is at the connection to the sink waste. This connection may push on or take the form of a collar which fits around the metal outlet from the sink. To undo the connecting nuts, you will need a large adjustable spanner or wrench.

Undo the connection and clean the joint thoroughly. Check the order in which any washers are fitted as you remove them and also check and replace any damaged ones. You can then reconnect the waste and overflow and test the connection with a sink full of water.

These joints are not under any pressure, so they should be water-tight without excessive tightening of the nuts. If the connections still leak once the joints have been cleaned and re-tightened, undo the defective joints and apply a thin squeeze of sealant before reassembling the connections.

1 *On some sinks, there's only a screw holding the overflow. Undo it with pliers*

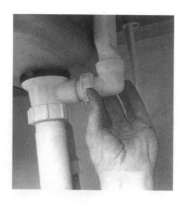

2 *Loosen the waste fittings with an adjustable spanner, then free by hand*

3 *Don't cut the nozzle too large to avoid too much sealant*

On modern sinks you buy the whole overflow fitting as one unit

WC AND BATHROOM REPAIRS

Clearing a blocked trap

When a bath or basin becomes blocked it is usually the trap underneath that is at fault. Loose hairs are the most common cause of trap blockages and, if conventional plunging fails to shift them, you have no choice but to remove the offending material by hand. How you do this depends on the type of trap installed. If you are dealing with a bath, you will have to unscrew and remove the panelling to gain access to the trap.

Old-style U trap: These are generally of brass or lead, and must be handled with care to avoid damage.

Start by placing a bowl underneath the trap and a piece of wood in the U part. Holding the wood in one hand, to counteract the turning force, use a wrench to unscrew the clearing eye which you will find at the base of the trap.

Hook out any debris remaining in the trap with stiff wire. Then clean the thread of the clearing eye and wrap a few turns of PTFE joint tape around it. Replace the eye, turning it a fraction over hand tight.

Plastic U trap: In this case you must dismantle the entire trap.

Unscrew the locknuts either side of the trap by hand, wrapped around a cloth. If they won't budge, boiling water should shift them.

When you reassemble the trap, a few turns of PTFE tape around the locknut threads will prevent leaks.

Bottle traps: These are the simplest of all to clear.

Hold the waste pipe in one hand and unscrew the cover with the other, wrapped in a piece of cloth.

Having allowed the debris to fall out into your waiting bowl, poke some stiff wire into the waste pipe to clear any residue then refit the cover. Again, a little PTFE tape wrapped around the cover thread will prevent leaks and save you having to tighten the cover too hard. Run the taps to check the repair. Also check that the waste is tightly connected and does not leak.

Changing a tap washer

When a tap starts to drip from the spout, it's usually the washer that's at fault. Replacement washers are available cheaply from hardware stores but, like the taps they fit, most are still in Imperial sizes—½in for basins, ¾in for baths. Only imported Continental models and the more unusual modern designs are Metric, the equivalent sizes being 15mm for basins and 22mm for baths and sinks.

Tap washers seldom fail when the shops are open so it pays to dismantle one of each of your tap types while they are still in good order and take the washers to your local stockist so that spares can be matched up.

Start the job by isolating the water supply to the tap concerned. Look for a stop valve on the pipe supplying the tap and turn this clockwise to cut off the water. If there are no such valves, what you do to drain the system then depends on whether the tap is for the hot or cold water supply.

Cold taps: If your plumbing system includes a cold storage cistern, look for a stop valve on the supply pipe running from the base. Otherwise tie up the ball valve to stop water entering the cistern, then open all your cold taps to drain it. (Note: this

applies to bathroom cold taps; kitchen cold taps are plumbed direct to the rising main, in which case turn off the main stop valve to isolate them.) If you have a direct system with no cistern, simply shut off the main stop valve and open all the cold taps. With this type of system you will only wait a few seconds for the pipes to drain.

Hot taps: Look for a stop valve on the cold supply entering the base of your hot water cylinder or water heater. You may be surprised to find that this stops any hot water leaving the cylinder: simply open the tap being repaired, to drain any water still left in the supply pipe.

To get at the washer, start by removing the tap handle. Old-style crutch-type handles are held on by a small screw—either under the colour button, or underneath the handle where it joins the tap stem. Follow by unscrewing the shroud below the handle with a pair of self-grip pliers—put some cloth in the jaws of the pliers to protect the tap chrome.

1. New-style plastic handles either simply pull off or are held on by a screw fitted under the colour button.

2. The next step is to unscrew the entire stem assembly from the tap body. Get a spanner, self-grip pliers or a plumber's wrench around the large nut where the two meet and apply force. As you do so, take care not to move the tap body itself or you

1 *Remove handle*

2 *Unscrew stem assembly*

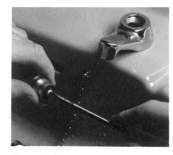

3 *Release the old washer*

4 *Fit new washer in its place*

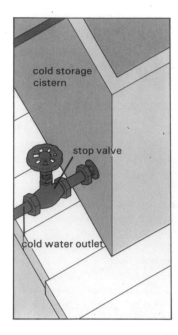

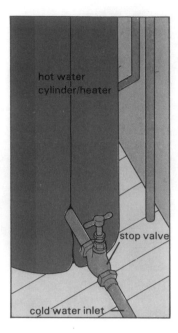

Stop valves: cold water cistern (left) and hot water cylinder

1 *Remove pin to release arm*

2 *Unscrew piston cover*

3 *Juggle out and remove piston* 4 *Dig washer out of piston*

may disturb the pipe joint below. If the nut is tight, wedge the body with a length of wood against something solid so that you counteract the turning force.

3, 4. You will find the offending washer on the end of the stem unit. The older rubber sort are held in a mounting plate by a small nut or screw. Undo this and dig out the washer, then slot in the new one, replace the nut and tighten.

Newer nylon washers simply snap into place on the end of the stem or onto a mounting plate—prise the old one off with the end of a screwdriver.

In both cases, reassembly is an exact reversal of the dismantling procedure. Turn on the water and test.

Toilet cistern overflow

Overflows here are caused by a failure of the ball valve washer controlling the water flow.

Most probably your problem valve is an old one. In this case the replacement washer will be rubber, in an Imperial size—almost certainly ½in (to match the supply pipe).

Start the repair by shutting off the water supply to the ball valve.
1. Now disconnect the ball arm from the valve by removing the split pin and then juggling the end free of the washer piston.
2. With the arm removed, unscrew the piston cover.
3. Stick a nail in the slot where the ball arm entered the valve and flick the washer piston out through the end of the valve.
4. On the other end of the piston is the washer. Dig it out of its seat and fit a new washer.

Fitting a new toilet seat

You can rarely repair a damaged toilet seat satisfactorily—it is usually easier to replace

1 *Slide end block onto bolt and tighten from below*

2 *Fit pivot rod into block and fit on other block*

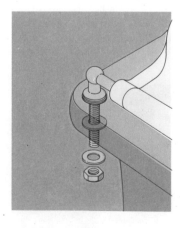

Ball-headed bolts are generally found on older fittings

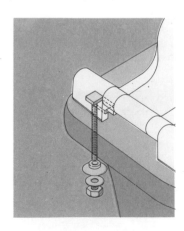

Modern fittings are usually the sliding end block type

it. Seats and lids are normally sold as a set, though some manufacturers will supply them separately. Remember that some lids are only designed as covers and are easily damaged if any weight is put on them—others are sturdier, and will withstand the weight of the average man.

1. To fit a new seat, you need to bolt it through the existing holes in the back of the pan rim (see diagram). Check the diameter of the bolts and the distance between them (if this is not adjustable) to make sure the new seat will fit your pan.

2. If the damaged seat is bolted into place with metal bolts which are rusted over, you will need to soak them in penetrating oil before trying to remove them. Modern units are fitted with plastic bolts which will not rust and should always be tightened only finger tight.

A common problem in many lavatories is that the seat fails to stay up as the cistern sticks out too far. If you have this problem, ask whether you can get a cranked fixing bolt for the new seat. This allows the seat to be moved forwards by up to 50mm, while using the existing holes in the pan rim to bolt the fittings securely in position. Fitting is simple and quick.

Unblocking a WC

The correct tool for dealing with this is a cooper's plunger—a plain rubber disc on the end of a T bar—NOT a plunger with metal disc, which would damage the pan.

· You can get by using a conventional sink plunger, though this will not be the right shape to create full pressure—it can only force short, sharp surges of water through the trap to clear the blockage.

To this end, insert the plunger in the trap and move it up and down vigorously in 30

household mop is a good substitute. Or you could try wrapping a toilet brush in rags and then enclosing it in a plastic bag tied with string. Use both as you would a plunger and see if this frees the blockage. If not disconnect the trap and clear the U bend by hand.

Flush pipe repairs

The flush pipe that connects a WC cistern to the pan is liable to leak from either of its connections at some time.

At the cistern end the water will seep through the nut and run down the pipe. Often the first sign of a leak is a wet patch behind the WC pan which may be mistaken for a leaking soil connection.

If you're not sure where the water is coming from, wrap a piece of toilet tissue around the flush pipe at the top end and then flush the cistern. If the tissue is wet you may safely assume the source of the leak is above it.

There is no absolute need to empty the cistern to carry out repairs to the flush pipe and, therefore, no need to turn the water supply off or tie up the ball valve provided you do not disturb the backnut on the cistern siphon.

Gently try to undo the lower nut securing the flush pipe on the threaded section protruding through the bottom of the cistern. If it's an old nut that has been painted, this may be difficult. Rather than exert undue force, apply paint stripper around the nut and leave it for a few minutes. In most cases, the nut will then undo easily.

Once you have slipped the nut down the flush pipe you can examine the seal. Old cisterns may have hemp wrapped around a swivel joint which looks like a large tap connector.

(available from plumbers' merchants) several times around the connection. It's a good idea to knot it in position. Smear some plumber's putty around the hemp and retighten the nut.

On some copper and plastic pipes, you'll find a rubber O-ring instead of a hemp joint. Between the rubber and the backnut is a ring of plastic or metal which prevents the rubber from being distorted when the nut is tightened.

If the rubber seal is perished or damaged,

★ WATCH POINT ★

If the flush pipe is lead, tie it at the top end with a piece of string wrapped around the cistern bracket—this will stop it falling down and bending out of shape.

replace it with a new one. Before tightening the backnut, smear a little silicone grease or washing-up liquid around the assembly. Plastic nuts can usually be sealed by hand—a piece of rag wrapped around the nut will help you gain a good grip.

If you have to use a wrench on a plastic fitting, do so with care as you may easily distort the nut. There is no pressure in a flush pipe, so the seal doesn't have to be too tight. If the leak is occurring at the lower end of the flush pipe, you'll probably find that a rubber joint called a flush cone has perished. To remove the flush cone you will have to gain some free movement on the flush pipe by undoing the top connection.

Once the flush pipe is loose, gently work it out from the back of the pan and remove the perished rubber cone.

Universal rubber cones are available from plumbers' merchants. If the one you buy

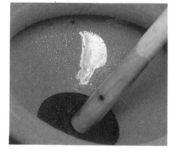

Using a plunger to siphon the WC trap

1 *The seal round the flush nut may need replacing*

2 *Use a knife to remove a perished flush cone*

3 *A new cone can be made to fit by inverting it*

second bursts. When the blockage clears, flush the cistern to refill the trap.

If you haven't got a plunger, an ordinary

Carefully cut away all the old jointing material and leave the mating surfaces clean. Then wrap a new length of hemp

doesn't fit your pan, simply turn it inside out to give you another size. Slip the flush cone onto the lower end of the pipe first and insert the pipe into the pan. You can then pull the cone forward, easing it onto the chinaware as you go. A lubricant such as washing-up liquid will help to make this procedure a good deal easier if the cone is a fairly tight fit.

Some old installations with lead flush pipes have a putty and bandage connection at the pan end. Often the china socket is not evenly formed and a new rubber cone fails to make a good watertight seal.

In this case, cut away all the old putty, being careful not to damage the pipe. Repack the joint with linseed oil putty and wrap a new gauze bandage around the joint in a similar fashion to the old one. Truss the joint with string to hold it in place while it dries. After a week, apply an oil-based paint around the whole joint to make a final seal that is also easy to wipe clean.

If you find the old flush pipe is faulty you can replace it with a new plastic assembly which will need no further maintenance once installed.

High level flush pipes come in two patterns to suit rear-mounted or side-hung cisterns—the pieces slot inside each other and need no sealing compound. You may have to shorten the spigot ends of the pipe to suit your installation. This is easily done by cutting with a fine-toothed saw.

Renewing a cistern

If your cistern is cracked or rusted through it will have to be replaced.

To make the job easier try to select one that matches the dimensions of the old one. The important measurement is that

between the overflow pipe and the top of the flush pipe, since it will save you having to make alterations to the plumbing.

Turn off the water supply and drain the old cistern.

Disconnect the cold supply and oveflow pipe and undo the flush pipe connection.

Cast iron high-level cisterns are quite heavy. To avoid accidents, hand the cistern down to an assistant on the floor.

New cisterns come with their workings packed inside, so before connecting to the plumbing the cistern must be made up. This entails fitting the siphon and flush handle assembly. To determine whether this goes on the left or right you will need to fit the ball valve to match your existing supply. The ball valve and overflow connector are interchangeable in their respective holes. Once these are in position, it will become clear which way the siphon fits.

On most new cisterns a dual flushing option is available to comply with local water regulations. This allows only half the water content of the cistern to be discharged by releasing the handle immediately after flushing. To obtain a full flush the handle must be held down until flushing ceases. If you do not require a dual flush facility a small plug must be fitted in the top of the siphon.

When the cistern is fully assembled, offer it up to the pipework and mark the position of the brackets and fixing holes in the back.

Drill and plug the holes, making sure they are level. The cistern can then be hung in position on the wall.

Screws inside the cistern must be rustproof—either electroplated or brass.

When you are satisfied that the cistern is

secure connect the supply to the ball valve and the overflow connector.

On plastic ball valves, wrap a few turns of PTFE tape around the end of the threads as well as fitting the fibre washer.

Connect the flush pipe, taking care not to twist the siphon out of line with the flush lever. Finally, turn on the supply and adjust the water level to coincide with the mark in the cistern.

★ WATCH POINT ★

On china cisterns use a couple of tap washers to protect the cistern from being damaged by screw heads.

Improving flushing

Poor or unreliable flushing can be attributed to a number of different things.

First make sure the water level comes up to the line indicated on the inside of the cistern. If it is too low, it can be raised by adjusting the ball valve.

Adjustment on brass valves can be achieved by bending the arm upwards. Hold the arm near the valve body with one hand and bend up gently with the other.

The flushing mechanism is fairly simple. When the handle is pulled down, the plunger pushes water through the siphon and into the flush pipe. As the float drops with the water level, the ball valve opens and draws in water from the supply pipe

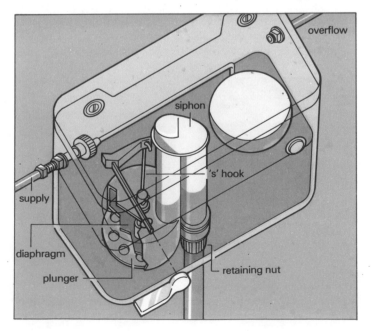

1 Fit a plastic plug over the siphon to prevent dual flushing

2 Support a low level cistern on your lap while offering it up

3 Wrap some PTFE tape round plastic ballvalve shanks

Plastic ball valves have an adjustment screw either at the float end or near the valve body.

Once you're satisfied the water level is correct, try the cistern again. If it still doesn't flush satisfactorily, the fault is probably with the diaphragm inside the siphon mechanism.

To change this you will have to empty the cistern. Turn off the supply to the ball valve and remove the water from the cistern. If you cannot flush it, you may be able to siphon it with a short hose pipe which you can discharge into the WC pan. Alternatively, bale out the cistern with a small pan and mop out any remaining water with a sponge.

Once the cistern is completely empty, undo both nuts underneath—this should leave the siphon mechanism free to pull up and out. You will also need to detach the siphon mechanism from the lever mechanism. Usually, it is possible to manoeuvre the brass 'S' hook out of the centre spindle—the siphon should then be easily removable.

Examine the siphon for cracks or holes. If it appears faulty, take it to a plumber's merchant and purchase a replacement of the same size.

If the siphon is sound, the likelihood is that the rubber or polyethylene diaphragm is torn or perished.

This is removed by sliding the plunger backplate and spindle out of the housing.

If the diaphragm is in any way misshapen or torn, you'll need to replace it. A new diaphragm can be purchased from a plumber's merchant, but should you have any difficulty obtaining the correct size and shape you may find it easier to make one.

A heavy gauge piece of polyethylene from something like a fertilizer sack will make a perfect diaphragm. Simply cut out a new one with some scissors using the old one as a template.

When re-assembling the diaphragm, remember to replace the small rubber washer that holds it down on the spindle. Check the seal on the underside of the siphon. If it's perished, it's well worth replacing while you have the cistern apart—ensure that no dirt is trapped under the seal as it might cause a leak.

On porcelain cisterns, a protective washer must be fitted between a metal back nut and the cistern to prevent cracking.

Close-coupled WC cisterns sit directly on the pan without the need for a flush pipe.

Occasionally, a leak may occur where the cistern meets the pan. First check that the two wing nuts underneath the pan are secure. If the leak persists, you will need to replace the rubber seal.

Shut off the water and drain the cistern. Disconnect the overflow pipe and remove the screws holding the cistern on the wall. Next undo the wing nuts and lift the cistern off the pan.

After purchasing the correct replacement, fit the new washer around the back nut so the threaded section of the siphon is poking through.

Ball valve troubles

On modern WC cisterns, the margin between a correct water level for satisfactory operation and a leaking overflow is very little. It is therefore necessary to maintain the ball valve in perfect working order.

If your cistern is overflowing, turn off the water supply and remove the ball valve assembly—but first check the float itself has no water in it.

Older style ball valves made of brass may have hard water scale deposits stopping their smooth operation. Dismantle the ball valve by removing the split pin and sliding out the piston. Gently remove all traces of debris from the moving parts of the ball valve. You can do this with fine emery paper or a proprietary scale remover such as the type used on kettles.

Check the rubber washer in the piston—if it is even slightly perished, replace it with a new one. The piston unscrews into two parts, enabling the washer to be removed, but these may be somewhat corroded. A good pair of adjustable grips will help you do this, but take care not to squeeze the piston out of shape.

Next check the seating onto which the washer closes. If this is pitted or worn, even a new washer will not seal it. Often the water will have worn minute grooves into its edges. In most cases the seating is replaceable with a new hard plastic insert.

New inserts come in three sizes. The smallest hole is for high-pressure cisterns fed directly from the mains, a middle-sized hole is for low-pressure cisterns fed from the cold water tank in the roof space, and the largest hole is for 'fullway' ball valves installed in flats where the cold water storage tank is only a couple of feet above the WC cistern.

If you use the wrong size orifice, you may experience problems with the cistern filling too slowly—which is annoying—or too quickly, which can result in a perpetual flushing of the pan. This happens when the cistern is filling so fast that the siphon never

has a chance to draw air because the water level is always too high.

Newer style plastic ball valves are now common on many WCs. Some designs have proved unreliable and have since been discontinued. An indication of this is the difficulty experienced when obtaining a replacement washer. Most WC manufacturers now fit plastic valves of a good design. A small screw is located at the end of the float arm to give precise adjustment of the water level in the cistern.

Plastic ball valves generally have the advantage of being quieter than the older style brass variety. This has obvious advantages for WCs.

If you wish to replace a brass valve with a plastic valve there are a few details which you should consider.

The new ball valve arm must go around the siphon—plastic arms are rigid so they cannot be bent to achieve this. A Torbeck valve has a very short arm only 50mm or so long—this is often a way of overcoming the space difficulty.

The threaded section of the ball valve known as the tail comes in 38mm and 50mm lengths; the longer tails are necessary on china cisterns, which have

---

★ WATCH POINT ★

When fitting a new ball valve, incorporate a small Ballofix-type stop-valve into the supply pipe. This will give you a means of isolating the ball valve during future maintenance.

---

particularly thick walls.

Ball valves are either bottom or side entry. Bottom entry valves are attached to a stand-pipe. The cistern will have to be drained to change this. Often you will find the new valve doesn't reach the existing pipe-work, but a 12mm tap extender may overcome this problem.

Oil-based sealing compounds should not be used on fittings with plastic threads.

It's a simple matter to fit one of these valves into an existing pipe run. Measure the depth of the shoulders within the fitting, subtract them from its length, cut out this much from the pipe and insert the valve. Tighten the couplings.

Dirt in the ball valve: small pieces of rust and scale tend to collect in ball valves, causing slow filling and damage to the washer. A small filter may be fitted in the pipework to collect the debris without interrupting the supply.

HOT WATER PROBLEMS

Inspecting your system

Hot water cylinders or tanks are invariably fed from a cold water storage cistern in the loft. In flats, some hot water cylinders are fed from an all-in-one cold water cistern that sits directly on top of the hot water cylinder.

The water can be heated in one of three ways: by a direct system; by an indirect system or by an immersion heater. Before replacing your tank, you must know which system is in use in your house, so go into the loft and make an inspection.

In a **direct** system, the domestic hot water is heated by a boiler, back-boiler or gas circulator. Water flows from the cold water cistern in the loft to the base of the hot water cylinder. From there it passes to the boiler, is heated and rises back to the top of the cylinder. Heavier, colder water from the base then flows from the hot water tank to the boiler and the process repeats itself in a continuous loop.

In an **indirect** system, the water in the hot water cylinder is not heated directly by the boiler: there are two separate circuits. The boiler is connected to the 'primary' circuit; the water in this circuit passes through a coil of pipe inside the hot water cylinder (known as the 'calorifier') after being heated by the boiler. This coil passes heat to the domestic hot water which forms the 'secondary' circuit: the two do not mix.

An **immersion heater** can be added to these systems or fitted on its own to a hot water cylinder. It is simply an electric heater, thermostatically controlled, which is immersed in the water inside the cylinder to heat it.

Replacing an immersion heater

The majority of hot water cylinders have a screwed hole, known as a *boss*, to take an immersion heater. There are two main types of heater: **vertical**, which fit into the top of the cylinder and **horizontal**, which fit into the side.

Single and dual element vertical heaters are available. The dual element type has elements of unequal length. This allows you to select, by means of a changeover switch, whether to heat the water in the whole tank or just that at the top (for the occasions

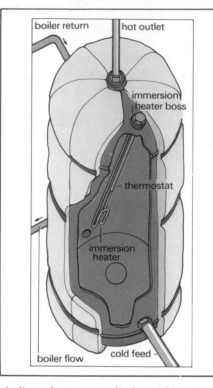

A direct hot water cylinder with an immersion heater

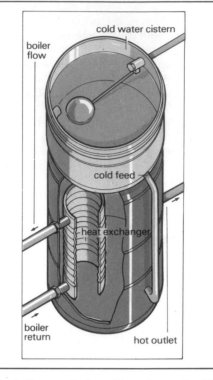

An indirect cylinder with an integral cold water tank

when you only need a small amount of hot water for washing or bathing).

Dual element horizontal heaters do not exist. Instead, you fit two heaters, one to the top and one to the bottom of the tank. If one only is to be fitted, position it at the bottom.

Immersion heaters are generally rated at 3kW and wired on their own circuit, which is protected by a 15 amp or 20 amp fuse. All are fitted with a thermostat which turns the electricity supply to the heater on or off depending on the temperature of the water. Thermostats are often supplied, separately, so make sure you've got one and that it is the right length to fit inside your own particular immersion heater.

Apart from the appropriate immersion heater (and thermostat, if necessary), you'll need some plumber's putty or PTFE tape for sealing the threads of the heater, an immersion heater spanner (these can be hired, but are fairly cheap to buy), a small or adjustable spanner for unscrewing the drain cock and electrical tools (screwdrivers, wire strippers, pliers) for connecting the flex to the heater.

The first steps are to turn off the electrical supply to the heater (switch off the electricity *and* remove the fuse if it's on its

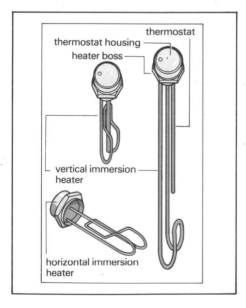

Vertical or horizontal heaters can be fitted to the cylinder

own circuit) and turn off any additional heating supplying the hot water cylinder, such as a boiler or gas circulator.

The gate valve on the supply from the cold water cistern should be closed next—this is likely to be near the hot water cylinder rather than near the other gate valves in the loft.

If there isn't a gate valve, you'll have to drain the cold water cistern after the water has been turned off or the ballvalve tied up to a piece of wood across the cylinder. Fit a gate valve before refilling the system.

Once the gate valve has been closed (or the cold water cylinder drained), connect a piece of hose to the drain plug (positioned next to the cylinder or by the boiler if you have a direct hot water cylinder) with the other end run to an external gully, and open the plug gently with a spanner—don't use pliers which will chew up the plug.

You don't need to drain all the water out of the cylinder—only enough so that water won't come out when you remove the immersion heater. The actual amount will depend on whether your immersion heater is fitted at the top or bottom of the cylinder. It will not be necessary to open the hot taps to drain the system, but it might help to get rid of water in the vent pipe.

The existing heater can now be disconnected from its electrical flex and unscrewed carefully from its boss with an immersion heater spanner.

Once the heater is screwed firmly in place, it can be wired up using three-core heat-resisting flex. The thermostat needs to be positioned carefully inside the heater (after removing the cover) and set to the right temperature before the cover is replaced.

Before refilling the cylinder, all drain taps must be closed and the upstairs hot taps opened to avoid any air locks.

Open the gate valve on the cold supply and watch the immersion heater boss as the cylinder is filling: if there's a leak, tighten the heater until it stops or, if this doesn't work, turn off the valve, drain the cylinder and refit the heater.

If there are no leaks, keep filling until water is running happily out of the hot water taps and then turn these off.

If all is well, the immersion heat can now be turned on. The neon light on the fused flex outlet will tell you that the electricity is connected to the heater—within a short time you should be able to feel the cylinder warming up. Relight the boiler.

Wiring an immersion heater

An immersion heater should have its own circuit from the consumer unit wired in $2.5mm^2$ two-core and earth cable and protected by a 15A or 20A fuse. The cable is run to a double-pole switch from where a length of two-core and earth heat-resistant 13A or 15A ($1.25mm^2$ or $1.5mm^2$) flex connects it to the heater.

A convenient type of double-pole switch would be a switched fused connection unit with a neon indicator, though there are special 20A double-pole switches (with a neon indicator) marked 'water heater'.

If you have a dual element or two separate elements you will need a special changeover switch (often marked 'bath/sink') and two lengths of flex will need to be run to the heater. Inside this type of switch, you will need an extra piece of insulated single conductor cable (take a bit from spare $2.5mm^2$ two-core and earth cable) to connect the two parts of the switch together.

You may want to have a time-switch connected to the immersion heater so that it comes on before you get up in the morning and perhaps before you come home from work in the evening. There are special time-switches for this, wired in as shown below. Don't use a plug-in timer to control an immersion heater—it simply is not robust enough to handle the job.

Fitting the new heater

Before fitting the new immersion heater, smear plumber's putty on the threads (or wrap PTFE tape around them) so that the joint won't leak afterwards.

When wiring the double-pole switch, the cable from the consumer unit is connected to the terminals marked 'SUPPLY' or 'MAINS' and the flex to the heater to the terminals marked 'LOAD'. At the heater end, there are terminals helpfully marked L and N for the brown (live) and blue (neutral) wires and E for the earth wire.

Renewing a hot water cylinder

Houses built before about 1939 may still have an old-fashioned rectangular galvanized steel hot water tank, together with its associated lead plumbing. This type of tank has a circular inspection hand-hole on the front and is not fitted with a boss for an immersion heater.

Most hot water cylinders these days are copper, either uninsulated (though you should fit your own insulating jacket) or pre-insulated with a thick layer of polyurethane foam. The pre-insulated kind is much better at keeping the water hot and only costs a little more.

The standard size of copper hot water cylinder is 458mm in diameter and either 915mm or 1066mm high, holding around 140 litres. Other diameters include 300mm, 406mm and 508mm; other heights include 1220mm, 1525mm and 1828mm. The 1525mm × 300mm size is particularly useful for replacing a rectangular tank, since a standard-size won't fit if the tank is in a cupboard. It is generally the tallest made in a pre-insulated version.

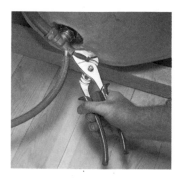

1 *Using an adjustable spanner, drain down the cylinder through a length of hosepipe*

2 *Switch off at the mains before disconnecting the heater flex from the thermostat*

3 *Apply PTFE tape or plumbers' putty to seal the new immersion heater threads*

4 *Screw the new immersion heater to the tank boss tightly using an immersion heater spanner*

As well as choosing the size and type, you will also have to choose between a direct and an indirect cylinder, depending on what hot water system you have or want to have installed.

In addition, you will have a choice of where the bosses are for fitting immersion heaters—most cylinders on display in shops have a top fitting designed to take a vertical immersion heater.

Kits are available for converting direct cylinders to indirect ones and for fitting immersion heater bosses if your cylinder doesn't have one.

plus a drain cock at the cylinder, and that this pipe should feed *only* the hot water cylinder. You will need the appropriate number of 22mm elbows and 'T' fittings plus pipe clips to support the pipe, and expanded foam lagging to protect any cold water pipes in the loft.

Typical layouts are shown in the drawing above left. All hot water pipes must be taken off the vent pipe *above* the level of the cylinder and the pipes must fall slightly away from the vent pipe to avoid air locks.

The tools you need will be the same as for installing an immersion heater, plus a large

Spread some old sheets on the floor to catch any spills of dirty water. Old tanks can be very heavy—particularly the rectangular galvanized kind—so get help to carry them downstairs.

Fitting the new tank

Once the old tank has been removed, run any new pipes that are necessary for the cylinder. If you're running a new cold water feed, the cold water cistern must be drained so that the pipe can be connected into it.

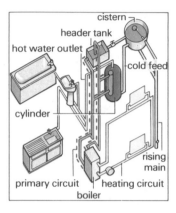

A separate electrical circuit should be run from the consumer unit to power the immersion heater

1 If the drain cock is damaged or rusted solid, siphon out the water with a hose

2 After laying down drip sheets around the tank, disconnect all the pipes using a Stilson wrench

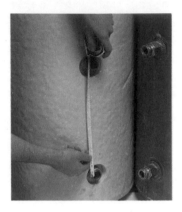

3 Compare the position of the pipe connections on the old cylinder with the new ones

What you'll need

The different types of hot water cylinder are described on page 87. If you're going for a replacement, it would be worth trying to find a cylinder that has its pipe connectors in the same place to avoid having to alter any of the existing pipework.

If you're putting in an indirect cylinder to replace a direct one, make sure that the connections will be accessible when the cylinder is in place.

If the cylinder is heated only by an immersion heater, it would still be worth fitting an indirect cylinder so that a central heating boiler connection can be made in the future. Make sure that the new cylinder will fit in the place taken up by the old one (allowing for insulating jacket or pre-insulation) and that there is adequate support.

If you need to run any pipework for either the hot water supply from the cylinder or the cold water supply to it, stick to 22mm tube—it will give much better flow rates than 15mm and will help to avoid air locks.

Remember that there should be a gate valve on the cold supply from the cistern

plumber's wrench if you're removing an old rectangular tank or any direct cylinder, since the joints will be very stiff to undo (hire a wrench if you haven't got one – 900mm isn't too big for this job). You'll also need the normal plumbing tools if there's any pipework to renew—pipe cutters, spanners, a blowlamp (if you're using capillary fittings), a bending spring (or, for 22mm pipe, a hired pipe bending machine) plus a tape measure.

Removing the old tank

For this job, the entire cylinder will have to be drained down and, if necessary, the pipes back to the boiler (for a direct system). Take the hosepipe from the drain tap outside if possible and proceed as for replacing an immersion heater.

Removing an old tank can be strenuous work and you may have to take measures such as sawing through pipes with a hacksaw if you can't get the old, corroded nuts undone: if you weren't planning to change the pipes this will, of course, mean that you now have to.

After you have taken the old cylinder out, and before you have installed the new cylinder, stand the cylinders against each other and measure—from the centre of the holes—the distance between the primary circuit flow and return.

When you install the new cylinder, offer it up first and arrange it so that drain cocks, immersion heater bosses, gate valves, and all the other things to which you may need access are easy to get at. The old pipework needn't necessarily be moved to suit the new cylinder: simply use flexible copper pipe to join the pipework and cylinder. Be careful to keep bends in the tubes gradual, to prevent air locks.

If putting in an immersion heater for the

★ WATCH POINT ★

You'll need to do a couple of dummy runs first to ensure that the pipework goes together properly, before installing the cylinder for real. As you fit each pipe, label it clearly for identification later.

first time, run the electric wiring at this stage. If you're not having one, check that the blanking plate is screwed tightly home—some plumber's putty or PTFE tape will stop it leaking.

Put the new cylinder in position on its platform and connect the pipes—again using plumber's putty or PTFE tape on the indirect screwed connections to and from the boiler if they're being used. The cylinder can now be filled and the immersion heater connected to its switch, following the procedure described in Replacing an immersion heater (page 86), and the

boiler. A horizontal heater can be positioned below these, a vertical one at the top and as near the centre as possible so that it points down the middle.

If the cylinder has foam insulation, cut this away with a handyman's knife first.

The hole you need is fairly large and can be cut in one of two ways—either using a hole saw or tank cutter fitted to an electric drill, or by making a series of small holes in a circle and then removing the waste and filing the large hole to shape. If you're adopting this method, it might be better to remove the cylinder completely to avoid

fitting the heater and, if necessary, replacing the cylinder.

Insulation and scaling

Whatever method you use to heat your hot water, there's little point in allowing it to cool down before you can use it. An insulating jacket should be fitted to all plain copper cylinders, and it won't hurt to lag hot pipes within the airing cupboard as well, using slip-on lengths of foam pipe insulation tied or taped securely at bends to keep it in place.

4 *When fitting flexible copper pipe bend the pipe gently, a little at a time, to avoid fractures*

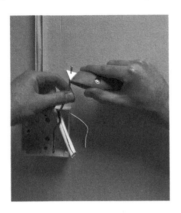

5 *Fix the switch to control the immersion heater in a place where you can turn it on and off easily*

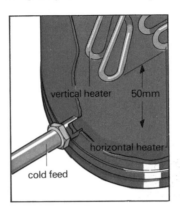

Ensure the immersion heater is at least 50mm above the base of the clinder to guarantee safe operation

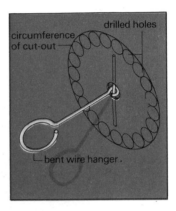

A clean hole can be cut in a cylinder using an ordinary drill but it is laborious work. It is easier to use a hole saw

system inspected for leaks before turning on the electricity or lighting the boiler.

Don't forget to fill the primary circuit if you have an indirect boiler, which may mean bleeding the radiators if it is connected to the central heating system—see page 178 for details.

Cylinder conversion

If you want to put an immersion heater in a tank that hasn't got a hole, or you want to put a new one in a different position in the tank, you'll have to make a new hole for it (there's a standard size for this in the UK— 2¼in. BSP). After the cylinder has been drained, the job consists of two parts: making the hole and fitting the boss.

Making the hole

If you have an indirect cylinder, you will have to be careful about where you position the hole for an immersion heater. Do not drill it in the space between the two tappings for the primary flow and return from the

getting a lot of copper filings inside it.

With the drill-and-file method, you'll have to drill a small hole in the centre of the cut-out and secure it with a piece of bent stiff wire to stop the 'waste disc' falling inside the cylinder. If you're using a hole saw, stop cutting when you're almost through the cylinder wall and prise out the disc as if you were opening a tin, bending it to break the remaining metal. Remove all the waste and clean around the outside of the hole.

Fitting the boss

The boss with all its necessary washers (and a template for making the hole) comes in a complete kit with full fitting instructions. There are different versions, depending on whether the boss is to be fitted on the side of the cylinder or on the top domed section—make sure you get the right one.

When fitting the boss, hold it securely with a length of wire to prevent it falling inside the cylinder as you tighten the whole assembly up.

When you've fitted the boss successfully, follow the procedure already described for

Hard water problems

If you live in a hard water area, two problems will arise to reduce the efficiency of your immersion heater and ultimately to shorten its life. Scale will build up comparatively quickly inside the cylinder and on the immersion heater itself, and if this build-up becomes too thick the heater will need to be on for longer and longer periods. You can reduce the incidence of scale by setting the heater thermostat to no more than 60°C.

Hard water can also corrode the heater element's cover, leading to early failure. If this is a problem in your area, fit a special corrosion-resistant type of heater which will have a far longer life. As a long-term aim, you could consider fitting a water softener.

Other alternatives for dealing with hard water include a **chemical scale inhibitor** (a bag of chemicals suspended in the water tank) which will stabilize the water, and a **magnetic conditioner** which generates a strong magnetic field and so counteracts the effect of impurities in the water. A **water filter** eliminates many of the problems associated with hard water.

MODERN STYLE TAPS

Many old taps have seen better days, and if they are in kitchens or bathrooms which have been upgraded, they may well now look old fashioned and out of place. Yet the business of replacing them with completely new taps can be daunting simply because it may involve quite complicated plumbing in a confined space.

Tap conversion kits eliminate the plumbing problems. You simply unscrew the head of your old tap and replace its handle and working parts with new ones. It's a simple job which can transform your kitchen sink, hand basin or bath. In the bathroom it means you can co-ordinate the style of all your taps. And because a new mechanical action—the gland—is included with most kits, you will have effectively renewed the life of your tap. The only tool you should need is a spanner.

Practical considerations

You will find that most old taps can be converted—although not all: kit manufacturers only make provision for the most common types. Obviously, the screw threads of the converter and sizes of the parts must be compatible, and it is not immediately obvious how this can be checked. In the UK, manufacturers sometimes specify the

British Standards Institute code number (normally BS 1010) of taps for which their kits are suitable. The difficulty is finding the BS code number on your tap. It is usually not visible—although a 'Made in Britain' stamp or British Standards Institute kitemark can usually be found in some unobtrusive position.

The rule of thumb is that if your tap is British made and the kit you are using is British too, then it will almost certainly fit. If you are at all uncertain, write a note to the manufacturers of the kit describing your tap and any marks on it including brand names—they should be able to advise you.

If your taps are suitable, the other main thing to look out for is their size—whether they are bath or basin taps—and make sure your kit matches. Normally bath taps are ¾in while kitchen, laundry and hand basin taps are ½in. In Britain new taps are still mostly reckoned in Imperial sizes and an old tap certainly will be. The new size refers to the diameter of the supply pipe and its connector to the bottom of the tap. So to make certain look under the back of the structure.

Fitting the new gland and head

The first thing to do is to turn off the supply of water to the tap. This may simply involve turning off a stop valve somewhere in the pipe leading to the tap—or it may be easier to turn off the whole system at the mains. But most household plumbing systems are more complicated than that and you will probably have to do some investigation—usually under the sink—with a torch.

If you are converting a hot water tap look for a stop valve between your tap and the hot water cylinder. A cold water tap should have a stop valve somewhere between it and the storage tank in the roof. If you can't find any stop valves you will have to turn off at the mains and drain the tank or cylinder supplying the tap. If you are draining a cylinder remember to turn off any heating element—boiler or immersion heater—for the duration of the job. When you are satisfied that no more water can come from the open tap, give it an extra twist anticlockwise to make sure it is fully open.

If you are very unlucky it may be that there is no stop valve at all inside the house. In this case the supply can be turned off at

the water authority stop valve which is usually situated under a metal cover flap somewhere between the house and the road and operated with a key. You may have to ask the authority to do this for you; in some areas you can do it yourself with a piece of wood cut to a V-shaped notch at one end.

With the water turned off, unscrew the bell shaped outer casing of the tap body using an adjustable spanner. The cover should have a thin octagonal or hexagonal rim at its bottom for this purpose. This may need considerable effort to shift if it has corroded in place over the years (see When it won't budge).

Slide the freed casing up the spindle of the handle to expose the hexagonal nut around the base of the spindle. You shouldn't need to remove the handle to do this. Adjust the spanner to fit the nut and unscrew it to remove the mechanical part (the gland body) from the tap. Once again, this may not be easy to do. Pull the spindle to lift away the loosened gland body.

Take this opportunity to clean the base and spout of the tap thoroughly. On chromium plate use a proper chrome cleaner and a gentle action.

Screw in the replacement gland until it is firm, making sure you include any seals or washers. Follow the maker's instructions about final tightness. If the body is plastic—as many are—be careful not to deform it with the spanner.

The new head may be a press fit on the gland body or it may be held with a screw concealed under a pressfit cover. Rotate it until the internal splines on the head line up with the grooves in the top of the spindle. Check that any symbols on the head are the right way round when the tap is closed and —elementary but easy to forget—that the Hot and Cold heads are on the appropriate sides of the tap.

Turn the water on again and check that the taps work properly. Leave them to run for a while to allow any air bubbles to work their way out of the pipes.

When it won't budge

Dirt, corrosion and scale can all make it hard to undo plumbing threads such as those on a tap's outer shroud or gland body.

Before you start to apply any force, take care to prevent the tap from turning. If it is

1 *When turning off water, look for a stop valve—usually under the sink*

2 *You may need to remove the handle and shroud to get a spanner in*

3 *With the shroud off, unscrew the gland unit. Do not use excessive force*

4 *Remove the gland, leaving just a bare casing. Clean the base thoroughly*

5 *Fit the modern style nylon gland in its place. Screw tight with a spanner*

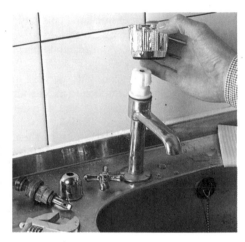

6 *Press on the head making sure that the splines line up with the spindle*

at all loose and turns in its socket, there is a strong risk of damaging the bath or basin. Stop it turning by locking a piece of sturdy batten across the spout.

Use a spanner which fits the nut properly, or a well fitting adjustable one. If it is too short to apply enough force you can extend it by locking another spanner or wrench onto the end.

If a steady pressure doesn't release the nut easily, don't immediately apply more force. There are several things you can try to release the threads first.

Start by trying to *tighten* the nut slightly. This often breaks the grip of the threads so that you can then unscrew them in the conventional way.

If this fails, you can try heat, which will expand the parts slightly. Wrap them tightly in cloth and pour boiling water carefully over the cloth. Try the nut both while it is hot and when cold again.

Penetrating oil is well worth trying, but

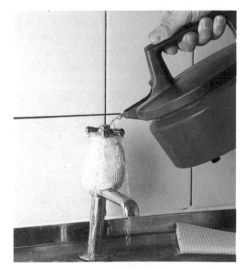

Hot water is a great tap loosener

do allow *plenty* of time for it to soak in.

If all these methods fail you can try jarring the end of the spanner to shock the

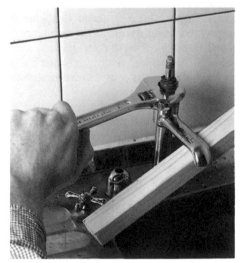

Use wooden props to stop a tap moving

nut free, but take extreme care on ceramic basins where there is a definite risk of cracking if you use excessive force.

FITTING AN INSET SINK

Old style kitchen sinks, bracketed to the wall or set on top of their own special units, are items that traditionally you don't move. In a small kitchen that has been progressively modernized this often means the positions of the surrounding appliances and units are a poor compromise between the desire for space and the need for efficiency.

The way to solve the problem is by taking advantage of the latest trend in sinks—recessed units that you set into an existing or custom-made worktop.

Inset sinks have one major advantage—flexibility. You don't need a special unit, so you can do away with the existing one and install a straight run of worktop. This could go over extra units to match those you've already got, giving you the added bonus of increased storage space.

Alternatively, you might decide to change the position of the sink to make your kitchen more convenient. And if your worktops are the usual laminated sort, fitting one or more inset sinks in them generally calls for no more than jig-sawing a hole and a few minor alterations to the base unit and waste system below.

Choosing a sink

Most inset sinks are designed to be accommodated within the standard worktop depth of 600mm–610mm. Sink depths generally range from 170mm–200mm. But when it comes to form and accessories, the choice is vast. The most popular combinations are:

•**Single sink**—impractical unless space is tight and you can hang a draining rack above the sink.

•**Double sink**—a better bet, particularly as some models incorporate lift-off bowl covers doubling as chopping boards or drainers. Choose a two-hole mixer tap which you can site centrally between the two bowls.

•**Sink and drainer**—choose a double sink and drainer if you've got the space.

•**Sink and waste disposer**—the waste disposer bowl can be teamed with a single or double sink, but you should allow for the extra depth taken up by the disposer unit itself (this will be sold separately).

•**Sink materials:** The traditional sink materials are stainless steel, vitreous enamel (over cast iron or pressed steel), and ceramic (usually vitrified clay). The last two have been improved enormously in recent years

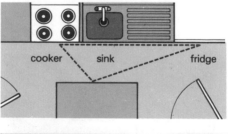

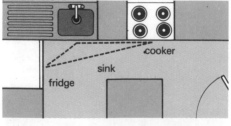

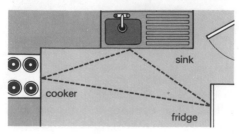

and now come in a wide range of colours and styles to suit most kitchens.

The newcomers are reinforced plastic (ICI's Sylac, Resan) and cast synthetic stone (Du Pont's Corian). These are well worth considering if you want an up-to-the-minute look, although Resan is not 100 per cent heat resistant and Corian, though tough, is a very expensive choice.

Making a choice: This is largely a matter of balancing personal taste, washing up habits and the space you have available against what you can afford. But bear in mind that very shallow sinks are alright for rinsing—not for washing; and that round and oval bowls swap capacity for stylish looks.

Choosing taps: Some inset sinks come with taps (or at least tap fittings); on others it is left to you to fit your own taps direct to the worktop. If you opt for a mixer tap, make sure that the model you choose has water authority approval. Water by-laws usually stipulate that there must be no

Position your sink wisely—it is an integral part of your kitchen 'work triangle'

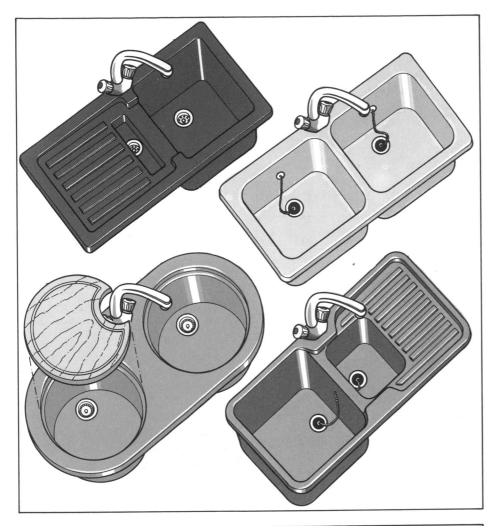

Sinks come in all shapes, sizes and colours. Some have detachable chopping boards, convenient if you have a waste disposer

waste disposer you might have to sacrifice a shelf as well.

New laminated post-formed worktops are normally 600mm wide and are sold by the metre, though some dealers will supply them cut to size. The worktop can be teamed with ready made non-drawer base units, or units to match those already installed in the kitchen.

If you plan to tile the worktop, do this after you have cut the recess and tap holes but before you fit the sink.

Plumbing and drainage

Once you have decided on the ideal location for the new sink, work out how to get the existing plumbing to the site with as few modifications as possible.

Drainage fittings: What you need here depends on your new sink and on whether or not you're moving it. If you take the latter option your aim must be to stick as close to the original waste pipe run as possible, with no bends. Some local authorities do permit bends in waste pipes providing a clearing eye is fitted on the crown in case of blockages (see diagram). But others don't, and you should avoid them if you can.

If the existing waste pipework is in copper or lead, you may as well replace it completely right back to the stack or gully. The same may apply if your pipes are plastic and you can't match the brand or they are of an odd size—it's not worth risking leaking joints for the sake of buying a few feet of plastic waste pipe.

It's worth getting a waste system manufacturer's catalogue and then sketching out what new parts you need. You may have the choice of push-fit, solvent welded and screw coupled joints, but only the connection at the trap need be semi-permanent. Standard pipe sizes for sink wastes are 38mm and 43mm. Don't forget to bear the following points in mind:

- If you're connecting to an older, open gully with new pipe, buy a plastic grid and carry the pipe outlet below it. If the gully's the modern back inlet sort, you can sever and connect it to the existing pipe above ground level.
- Use the manufacturer's recommended adhesive and cleaner for making solvent welded joints in the pipe run.

Your supplier should be able to help you

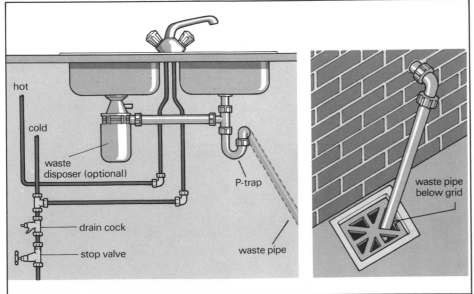

danger of stored hot water mixing with the mains cold water inside the tap—possibly contaminating the supply.

Worktops and base units: If you're fitting the sink into an existing wooden or laminated worktop over drawered base

A typical plumbing layout with the waste run directly to a convenient gully

units, you can discard the drawers, saw off the fronts, and screw or glue and pin these back on from behind. Only in the case of a

with traps and sink fittings—many sinks are sold with their own 'plumbing kit' which includes everything you need in this area. Double sinks normally connect to a single double-sink trap and onto a single waste pipe. Otherwise you have the choice of P or S traps, both of which can be swivelled round to adjust the direction of the pipe run. Avoid bottle traps: although easy to clear, they are also easy to block—especially when used in the kitchen.

Waste outlets are nearly always available from your supplier, although you may have to buy them separately. Most now incorporate a built-in overflow; separate overflows, if you need one, connect between the waste outlet and trap.

Water pipework: If you sever the existing supply pipes near to the old sink and you're not changing its position, it should take no more than a single bendable connector on each pipe to link up to the new taps. Buy connectors with a capillary or compression joint at one end (see below) and a screw tap connection at the other, to match the taps. Remember that British taps still take an Imperial (½in.) fitting, while imported European ones are usually the 15mm size. One hole mixers have two 10mm tails which need adaptors (usually supplied with the taps) to take them up to 15mm.

Even if you are moving the sink, the flexibility offered by bendable connectors—which are 540mm long but can be cut to suit at 180mm intervals—means that you shouldn't need more than one extension length per pipe. Make this up with 15mm pipe and compression or capillary fittings.

WARNING: The cold supply to your sink will come direct from the rising main, and in the UK some authorities insist that all such pipes are joined with soldered capillary fittings—so before you buy the materials check with your local building control office if you are in any doubt.

Tools and other materials

There are no special requirements here, other than a good supply of plumber's putty, PTFE tape and silicone sealant. Make sure that you have a pair of wrenches, grips or adjustable spanners for pipe jointing —or a blowlamp, if you're making capillary rather than compression joints.

If you don't have a jig saw for cutting the sink recess, it's worth hiring one—the alternative is to use a padsaw, which is very hard work and likely to be much less neat.

Removing the old sink is the easy part of the job, but it still needs to be done with care

if you are to avoid problems later.

Start with the waste pipe as this will give you more room to work underneath the sink. If the trap is plastic, place a bowl underneath to catch the water and then simply unscrew each joint to dismantle the run. If the trap and pipe are metal, cut through the pipe at a convenient place— you'll be replacing them anyway—and dismantle the rest of the run when the sink is out of the way.

> ### ★ WATCH POINT ★
>
> To ensure a square cut, make a mark on the pipe and wrap some thin card around the pipe at this point. Align the edges of the card, then use it as a cutting guide.

Removing an old sink

Now work out where best to sever the supply pipes, bearing in mind that you need enough access to work with a junior hacksaw. If the new sink is going in more or less the same position, cut as near to the old taps as possible; if you are extending the pipes to a new location, cut them at a place where a join will be easy, well clear of the sink and/or sink unit.

Note that if your main stop valve is under the sink, as many are, you must cut **on the tap side** or you'll flood your kitchen.

Shut off the water supply to the pipes next. The cold supply is isolated by closing the main stop valve; the hot by closing the valve on the cold feed pipe at the base of your hot water cylinder or water heater. Empty the hot water pipes by turning on all

the hot taps in the house. Work from the top downwards to avoid airlocks. Make sure that any heating apparatus is switched off. When you cut the supply pipes, make sure you cut them square.

If your old sink is the heavy earthenware sort, support it on bricks before unscrewing or sawing through the brackets holding it to the wall. Get several helpers to assist with removal—old sinks are very heavy.

Newer stainless steel sinks are held to their base units by brackets so you should have no difficulty unscrewing these.

Before lifting the sink away, break any seal along the back with an old screwdriver. If you have a tiled splashback, pull the sink out and up towards you to avoid cracking the tiles.

Installing the new sink

Whether you're modifying an existing worktop, or adapting a new post-formed one, it must be cut to accept the new sink and drilled for separate tap holes.

2 *Use a piece of tape or card wrapped around the pipes as a cutting guide*

1 *Place a bowl under the trap—to catch any drips—before you unscrew the waste connection*

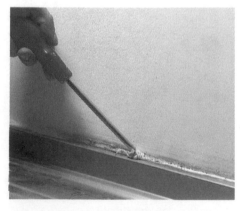

3 *Remove the seal around the old sink by using an old screwdriver or an old knife*

4 *If no template is supplied, mark the position of the sink on the worktop*

5 *Lay the seal against your mark and draw a cutting line on the inside*

With the hole completed, try the sink for fit and make any minor adjustments with a rasp or planer file.

Cutting the tap holes

Position the tap hole or holes parallel with the back of the sink recess. If you're fitting a single mixer, you should locate it centrally behind a single bowl or midway between a double sink.

6 *Use a flat bit to drill a hole—large enough for a jig saw blade—on the inside of your cutting line*

7 *Score the cutting line and insert the jig saw blade carefully into the hole. Cut around the marked line*

Arranging the plumbing

Do as much of the plumbing work—including equipping the new sink with its fittings—before you install the sink and refit the worktop. Once they're in position, you won't have much room in which to work.

If you're installing new units, start by setting them in place so that you can mark off where the pipe runs must be led through them. Then drill or notch the backs as appropriate.

Preparing the sink: Unless plastic or rubber washers are provided for the purpose, you bed the waste and overflow outlets on plumber's putty and then screw them in place by tightening the backnuts from behind. Continue tightening until the putty squeezes out around the rims, then wipe or scrape away the excess.

If the overflow is a separate unit, connect it to the waste outlet at this stage, making sure that you get any washers or seals that come with it in the right order (see diagram). Follow by wrapping one or two

If the sink is to go into an existing worktop, remove the worktop at this stage by unscrewing the brackets holding it to its base units and removing the screws securing it to adjoining runs.

If the worktop is new, cut and prepare it for installation before embarking on any of the sink modifications.

Manufacturers often provide a template for cutting the sink recess. Use this to mark cutting lines on the worktop, which should be firmly supported on trestles or stools. If no template is provided, mark out the surface carefully with the dimensions given in the instructions. Alternatively, you can mark out the exact position by using the sink itself as a template as shown in steps 4 and 5. Use a try square to ensure that your marking out is at all times square with the worktop edge.

The basic cutting technique for thick laminated worktops is to drill holes within the perimeter of the marked out recess large enough to insert a power jig saw blade. You then saw along lines drawn between each of the holes in turn and finish off any corners with a rasp.

Drilling holes in laminate isn't easy. Either drill pilot holes with a twist drill and then enlarge them with a flat bit, or else drill a series of small holes and join them up. In either case, use a piece of masking tape over the hole marks to stop the drill slipping. And take great care that your holes don't extend outside the marked line.

Before using the jig saw, score along the cutting lines with a laminate cutter.

As you saw, keep the sole plate hard against the cutting guide and let the blade find its own way through the wood—don't be tempted to force it. If it overheats, stop sawing and let it cool down. After you have completed the first line, remove the guide and set it up for the next one—and so on.

8 *Assemble the waste system in a dry run and measure before cutting*

9 *File off burrs at the end of cut pipes before connecting them up*

10 *Push-fit joints are the simplest way of connecting the supply pipes*

11 *Washing up liquid acts as a good lubricant on push-fit waste pipes*

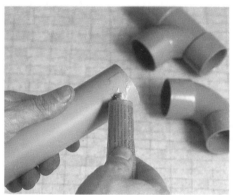

12 *On solvent weld pipes, spread the adhesive and join quickly*

turns of PTFE tape around the waste outlet thread, then screw on the plastic trap—there's no need to tighten it for the moment.

Fitting the taps: If these are separate, they can be fixed to the prepared worktop. Like the sink fittings, they may well be provided with sealing washers; if not, bed them on a generous layer of mastic and trim away the excess when you've tightened up the backnuts. You'll find it easier to use a box spanner or basin spanner for this.

The next stage is to locate the worktop and sink temporarily in position so that you can measure up underneath for the waste and supply pipes. Where the latter are concerned, accuracy isn't essential—you simply make sure that you bring the bendable connectors you'll be fitting to the pipe ends 'within range' of the tap shanks.

It is important, however, to get the waste pipe lined up perfectly with the trap on the sink. If you are replacing the entire run, you'll have some room for manoeuvre; otherwise you need to direct-measure the first length against the trap at this stage.

Remove the sink and worktop. Tackle the supply pipes first. If you need to extend the runs, measure up two extension pieces in 15mm copper pipe, not forgetting to allow for the amount that gets 'lost' inside the joint fitting. Cut the pipes with a junior hacksaw, taking care to get the ends square, then file off any burrs inside and out.

If you're using compression joints, fit them to the severed supply pipes first. Tighten one and a half turns above hand tight and then repeat the procedure on the extension pieces. Finish off by compression-jointing on the bendable tap connectors in the same way.

If you're making soldered capillary joints, see page 97.

Now deal with the waste pipe. If you're joining straight to the existing pipe, measure up and cut a length to run to the new trap. If you're solvent welding the

General arrangement for push-fit supply and waste connection. You may need a straight connection capillary joint to connect the rising main (inset)

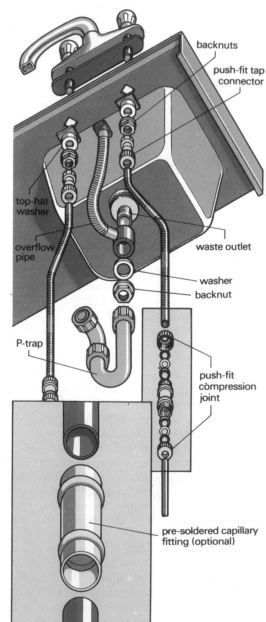

backnuts

push-fit tap connector

top-hat washer

overflow pipe

waste outlet

washer

backnut

P-trap

push-fit compression joint

pre-soldered capillary fitting (optional)

joint, try the pipe for fit in a dry run first. Trim as necessary, then file off the burrs, clean the pipe ends, apply the solvent cement and join. On a push fit joint, apply lubricant to the pipe ends.

If you're replacing an entire run, use solvent weld joints. Dry-assemble the run and check the fall—not more than 1 in 48, not less than 1 in 24. When all is well, cement the joints and fill the gap in the wall with non-setting mastic. Complete the run outside to below the level of the gully grid or join it up to a waste stack.

Finally, secure your pipe runs to the walls with brackets—every 500mm for copper, every 900mm for plastic.

Capillary joints

Some authorities insist that you use capillary joints on plumbing jobs involving the rising main. In this case, opt for pre-soldered (Yorkshire) fittings which don't require extra solder.

To make the joints, you'll need a blowlamp, flux, wire wool and a heat-proof board or large tile with which to protect surrounding fixtures and fittings.

As with compression joints, it's vital that the pipe ends being joined are cut square and burr-free. Inspect the fitting beforehand to check that the solder rings inside are continuous—reject it if they're not.

When you are ready, follow the procedure below exactly.
•Clean the pipe end and the inside of the fitting with wire wool until the copper shines. Remove dust.
•Coat the pipe end and the inside of the fitting with a thin but even layer of flux, applied with an old toothbrush.
•Bring pipe and fitting together.
•Adjust your blowlamp flame until the centre is clear blue. Play it gently over the fitting and the pipe end, moving it all the time, until the flux starts to bubble and spit.
•At this point, ease off slightly but keep the flame to the joint; after a few seconds you should see the solder that was inside the fitting appear around the pipe end. When the ring is complete remove the flame and then allow it to cool.

Preparing the worktop

Fit the worktop first, screwing into adjoining surfaces and securing the brackets to the base units as necessary. Follow by laying the rubber seal supplied with the sink in position; in some cases this must be laid on a

Clean the ends of the pipes with wire wool

bed of silicone sealant to prevent drips.

Fit the sink strictly in accordance with the instructions, tightening the clips or brackets that secure it to the worktop.

Working from underneath, connect the bendable connectors to the tap shanks and

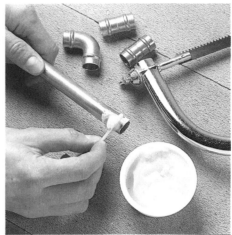

Use a matchstick to spread the flux

tighten with a wrench or adjustable spanner. Finish by push-fitting or screwing on the waste pipe to the new trap and hand-tightening the joints on the trap itself. Reinstate the water supply and test all joints for watertightness before making good.

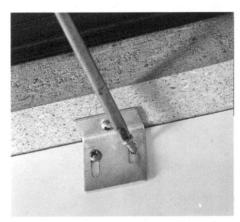

13 *Secure the worktop to the units with the slotted angle brackets*

14 *Push the seal firmly in place on the underside of the sink*

15 *Tighten the brackets so they grip the under side of the worktop*

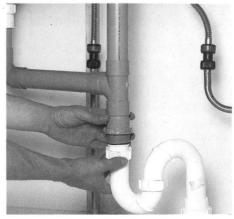

16 *Finally, connect up the waste pipes before turning on the water*

INSTALLING A WASTE DISPOSER

Waste disposal units are the modern answer to smelly rubbish bins; they keep your cooking—and your kitchen—clean and pleasant. Initially they had a poor reputation for reliability but waste disposers have come a long way since then, and today's machines can be relied upon to give many years of safe, trouble-free service—providing, of course, that they're used properly and serviced regularly.

All waste disposers work on more or less the same principle: the waste is flushed through the sink drain hole into a grinding compartment where blades driven by a powerful electric motor convert it into semi-fluid effluent to be carried away along the waste pipes into the main drain. On most units the grinder is activated by a switch fitted near the sink; on a few more sophisticated models, it comes into operation automatically when the grinding compartment receives a full load and water.

Modern disposers will cope with most kinds of organic waste—fish bones and skin, vegetable peelings and such like—which are unpleasant to dispose of by conventional means. About the only things they can't handle are large bones, tough fibrous stringy items and large amounts of fat, but these are easily thrown away.

The chief enemies of the waste disposer are things made from plastic, metal or ceramic. Nowadays, however, there are plenty of drainage stoppers and rubber trap accessories to prevent items such as cutlery and small bowls from falling into the machine and damaging the blades.

The system

The typical modern waste disposer is fitted under the kitchen sink, suspended from the drain outlet bush by a series of clamps and plates. The machine itself is in two parts: the upper half is the grinding compartment and has a standard 38mm outlet pipe in the side; the lower half houses the blades and motor and has a flex to connect it to the power source. The halves are normally held together by adjustable spring clips or screw bolts, enabling the lower half to be removed easily for clearing or servicing. A blanking plate can be fitted to the top half under such conditions, so that you can still use the sink in the conventional way.

The power can be taken from a conventional 13 amp plug and socket fitted at least 1.5m from the sink, but this is not advisable since it tempts you to operate or even unplug the unit with wet hands. It's far better to install an independent switch fused connection unit as a spur from another socket in the kitchen.

Drainage arrangements are made by connecting a standard U-trap to the unit's outlet pipe, followed by a run of ordinary 38mm piping as far as the stack or gully to which the existing sink connects. If your sink is currently fitted with a bottle trap you need to replace it with a U-trap since it might restrict the flow of what will be slightly denser waste matter. Likewise, if your existing drain run has an old metal trap and lead or iron pipe, this is a good time to replace it with the more modern PVC waste fittings.

Usually the only problems related to drainage occur because the unit's outlet is lower than that of the original sink trap—which in turn affects the fall of the waste pipe. The ideal fall for a waste disposer waste pipe is 1:12 and it may be that you can't meet with this requirement unless

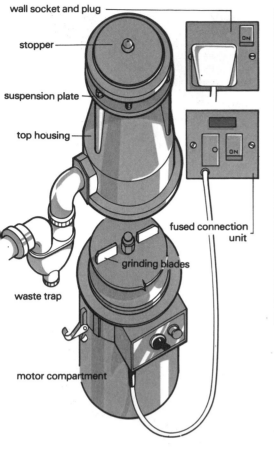

wall socket and plug

stopper

suspension plate

top housing

fused connection unit

grinding blades

waste trap

motor compartment

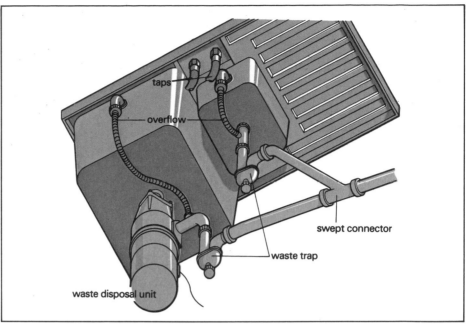

taps

overflow

swept connector

waste trap

waste disposal unit

The vital connections: a waste disposer has two halves—the top half is bolted to the sink outlet hole via a series of plates and seals and connected to the waste trap and pipes. The lower motor compartment—complete with grinding blades—is secured to the top with adjustable clips and is connected to the power supply by a flex. The best source of power is via a fused connection unit taken as a spur from the nearest power socket

you lower the entire pipe run by dismantling it and drilling a new hole in the wall. This doesn't normally involve changes to where the waste pipe discharges. But if the outlet is over an open gully, you would be well advised to fit an extension to the pipe and carry it below the level of the grating—if your existing grating is iron, simply buy a new one in plastic and cut a hole in it to allow the waste pipe to discharge safely into the gully.

Sinks and sink outlets

Waste disposal units can be fitted to most sinks—but you should think carefully before making a final decision.

Waste disposers are most useful if they

have their own separate sink bowl or, failing that, if they are fitted to one half of a double sink. This gives you a disposal facility while you are actually doing the washing-up.

The standard inlet size for a waste disposer is 90mm, as opposed to a conventional sink outlet's 38mm; the larger size doesn't affect the disposer's efficiency, but it does make it easier to get waste into it, particularly if you're dealing with large amounts at a time.

Most modern kitchen sinks can be ordered with a 90mm outlet in one of the bowls, and many have the format of two large bowls plus a separate small disposer bowl (with a large outlet) to one side (often covered when not in use by a chopping board). Such arrangements are easily plumbed in to a single drain waste pipe using double traps. So all in all, if you're thinking of replacing your kitchen sink it's a good job to do in tandem with fitting a waste disposer.

If you want to fit a waste disposer to an existing sink with a 38mm outlet, you have two alternatives. The first is to take advantage of the fact that most machines are available with special small-outlet adaptors that are no more difficult to fit than the usual 90mm sort. The second is to enlarge your sink outlet to 90mm. This job involves removing the existing bush and buying a new one, then cutting a hole for it using a large hole saw. You also need to hire a special recessing tool to make a recess so that the new bush sits flush with the sink's surface to prevent leaks.

In view of what's involved in relation to what you gain in convenience, there really

Drainage arrangements for a double sink must be planned in advance—you'll need a wider range of waste fittings.

It's best to incorporate separate traps for each basin (right) though you could use the same trap for both outlets.

Waste pipes from the disposer unit must be provided with a fall of at least 1:12 and any changes of direction must be gentle to avoid blockages—swept bends and connectors should be used in preference to right angled elbows.

Keep the arrangement simple to aid servicing and avoid blockages

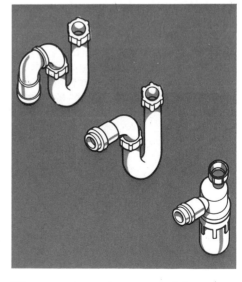

Waste traps come in a range of shapes. Bottle traps (bottom right) must be replaced with S-traps (top) or P-traps (centre) otherwise the denser effluent may cause blockages

is little point in taking the second option—it's far better to fit a new sink with a disposer compartment or at least with a 90mm outlet.

Nearly all types of sink are strong enough to take a waste disposer and to absorb the slight vibrations made by the unit when it's operating. The only exceptions are some thin plastic and aluminium sinks or old ceramic sinks—consult the sink manufacturers if you are in any doubt—and it is possible to add an extra support made from offcuts of board.

Planning ahead

This is one job where it pays to buy the actual unit some time before you plan to install it. Doing so gives you the chance to check what modifications, if any, must be made to the existing drainage layout and you can also take advantage of any specific recommendations which are made by the manufacturer of the unit.

With waste disposers, you get what you pay for. Most models now feature rubber jaws on the inlet boss to guard against accidental entry of unwanted objects, plus some sort of stopper should you want to use the sink in the normal way. The better units on the market have an automatic overload cut-out to stop the motor overheating and a reverse-run facility for clearing minor blockages. You will, of course, pay more for automatic operation.

When you buy a waste disposer it should come complete with outlet pipe, flex and its own special sink boss. But before you part with any money, make sure that you are also given the correct fitting for your sink.
Electrics: For this part of the job you'll need a surface-mounted switched fuse connection unit with indicator light, enough 2.5mm sq twin and earth PVC sheathed cable to connect it to a nearby ring or radial socket (see The power supply, page 102), and a supply of plastic conduit (mini-trunking) to carry both the cable and the flex from the unit. Surface mounting is generally much easier to arrange in a kitchen (where there may be a tiled splashback). You may need a flex connector and extra cable to extend

the length of the flex—bear in mind that the colour code is different for cable than for flex.
Drainage: Start your assessment of requirements here by inspecting the existing layout. Metal pipework and bottle traps must be replaced with a U-trap as a matter of course. If you already have a plastic U-trap, place a bowl underneath, unscrew it from the sink and waste pipe, then test-fit it on the disposer outlet pipe: if it is a non-standard size, it too must be replaced, together with the pipe run.

The next thing to check is the fall of the waste pipe. Offer up the complete disposer unit into position and check how much lower the outlet is than the existing waste pipe. You should be able to tell by eye if the pipe needs lowering. In this case, if the joints are solvent welded, you'll need to sever the pipe and buy new sections to deal with the pipe where you make a new hole in the wall; if the pipe joints are push-fit, re-use the old rather than buying new ones.

After your inspection, make a sketch of the proposed new pipe run and note down the extra parts you need. If you're buying a new trap, make sure it has the same fittings —overflow connection, washing machine inlet, and so on—as your existing trap. If you're connecting the disposer into part of a new double sink arrangement, you'll need parts to make up a trap layout like the one shown in the diagram on page 99.

Apart from the electrical and drainage materials, you need a supply of non-toxic plumber's putty to fit the new sink boss. Installing the disposer itself should call for no more than a wrench and a screwdriver. You will, of course, need more tools—drill, masonry bit, mains tester screwdriver, hacksaw, wire strippers—for the wiring.

Preparing the sink

This part of the job is straightforward enough—it's mainly a matter of removing existing fittings—but if you're going to re-use the existing waste pipe and trap, do not disturb them more than necessary.

Start by placing a basin under the existing trap. If it's a bottle or U-trap, you can simply unscrew it by hand; metal traps must be severed on the waste pipe side with a hacksaw and then disconnected from the sink boss by unscrewing the retaining nut with a large wrench. Replace metal pipework with new PVC pipe and fittings.

Now turn your attention to the sink boss itself. Some are loosened by unscrewing the retaining nut from below, using a wrench,

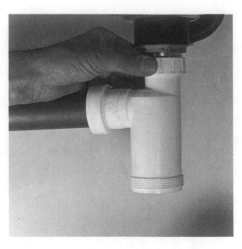

1 *Remove the existing waste trap. Drain first to avoid a mess. Bottle traps must be replaced with more efficient S, P or U-traps*

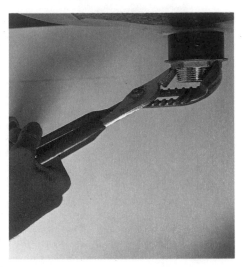

2 *Release the sink boss retaining nut using a large wrench. Considering the options, now is a good time to change your sink for the type with a wider 90mm outlet hole.*

then prising or gently tapping upwards to break the putty seal. Others are in two halves, which you separate by unscrewing the screw in the centre of the outlet from above—again prise or tap to break the seal. With the boss removed, scrape or scour away all traces of old putty from around the recess and from below the sink.

If you need to lower the waste pipe this is a good opportunity to make a new hole in the side of your sink base unit. The easiest way of doing this is with a hole saw, set to about 40mm. Alternatively, mark the hole using a spare piece of waste pipe as a template, drill a series of holes around the circle, then join them with a padsaw.

Installing the unit

Though nearly all waste disposers are connected to the sink in a similar way, the actual connection method on your unit may vary slightly in detail from those given below—always consult the manufacturer's instructions for your particular model.

Start by separating the two halves of the unit. Take the upper part, note carefully how the various plates, clamps and seals are arranged, then dismantle them.

Prepare the sink outlet by laying a generous layer of non-toxic putty around the boss recess, then slip the new boss into the correct position.

Most 90mm connections follow the sequence shown in the diagram opposite.

3 *Before you attach the new sink boss, spread a layer of non-toxic plumber's putty around the boss recess*

Using standard 38mm outlets (right) means fitting an adaptor plate to the sink bush. The adaptor plate is held in position by extra sink bush retaining nuts. Apart from the inconvenience of the narrower outlet, the waste disposal unit is just as efficient in use

Wider sink outlets—90mm—are specially designed for waste disposers (below). The unit attaches to the bush by way of a series of plates and seals—the top is bolted to a suspension plate. Grub screws force the clamp plate against the seal

Working from underneath the sink, slip the sealing gasket over the boss, followed by the clamping plate. Next, offer up the suspension plate, locate the grub screws on it with the corresponding holes in the clamp plate, then hold it in position by snapping the steel circlip supplied onto the boss thread (on some models there is a screw-on retaining nut instead of a circlip).

The next stage is to tighten the grub screws on the suspension plate so that the clamp plate and the gasket above it are forced hard against the underside of the sink to create a watertight seal. This done, offer up the top half of the unit (check that its seal is in position around the lug on the inlet), locate the lug in the boss and the retaining bolts in their holes in the suspension plate, and slip on the nuts and washers provided.

Hand tighten the nuts, then swivel the unit until the outlet pipe points in the desired direction. When you're satisfied with the arrangement, tighten the bolts fully to pull the unit hard against its seal.

If you are using a 38mm outlet, the procedure is slightly different. First of all, secure the sink bush by slipping on its seal

and then tightening the retaining nut from below. Follow by screwing on the suspension plate upper retaining nut — about two

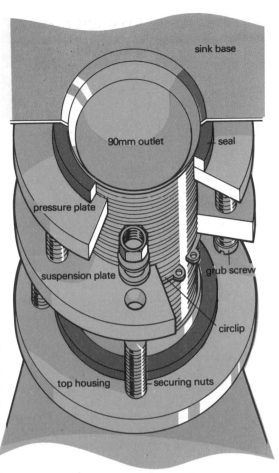

sink base

90mm outlet

seal

pressure plate

suspension plate

grub screw

circlip

top housing

securing nuts

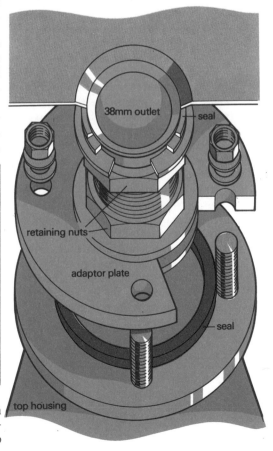

38mm outlet

seal

retaining nuts

adaptor plate

seal

top housing

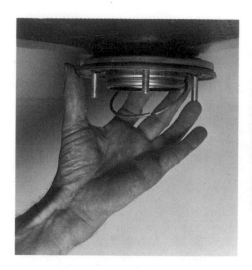

plastic grid and cut it to accommodate the pipe. If all is well make any permanent joints that are necessary by pulling the joints apart, deburring and degreasing the pipe ends; then apply solvent cement and reconnect.

If you haven't had to alter the pipe run, simply mark off against the trap how much pipe has to be removed, trim it with a hacksaw, then juggle it into the trap joint to make the appropriate connection.

In all cases, resecure the pipe run to the wall with clip brackets every half metre. Seal around any new holes with mastic, inside and out. Double check that all the joints are secure, especially those either side of the trap and on the unit itself.

4 *Fit the sink bush and slip the seal, clamp plate and suspension plate into place. A steel circlip completes the arrangement of this particular design. Tighten the grub screws substantially in order to form a tight seal*

5 *Fit the waste outlet pipe to the top half of the unit, then slip the bolts of the housing into the holes of the suspension plate. Adjust the position of the waste disposal unit so that it suits your drainage layout*

The power supply

These instructions are for installing a fused connection unit—by far the safest way of getting power to your new waste disposer.

thirds of the way up the remaining thread on the bush.

Now slip on another seal, the suspension plate itself, a further seal, and finally the lower retaining nut. Tighten this nut with a wrench to hold the plate firmly. Then simply bolt the upper half of the unit to the plate to complete the job.

Arranging the drainage

What's involved here depends very much on the location. The critical part of the job is ensuring that the waste pipe ends up with the recommended 1:12 fall.

If you think you can use the existing pipe as it stands, start by loosening all the wall brackets holding it in place.

Screw or push-fit the U-trap to the disposer outlet pipe, then hold the waste pipe against the trap and check the fall. If it is out by any appreciable degree, you'll have to lower the entire run of the waste pipe.

In this case, dismantle the existing pipework as far as the drainage outlet. If the pipe joints were glued, cut through them squarely using a hacksaw and a piece of card as a template. Now make up a new set of pipework in a dry run to extend from the trap as far as the wall and adjust the fall using the method described above. When it is correct, mark where the pipe must pass through the kitchen unit or the outside wall (or both).

Make the hole in the wall by working from both sides in turn and using the old

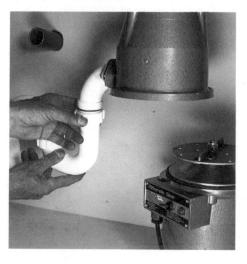

6 *Fit the new trap to the outlet pipe from the waste disposer. Use PVC fittings and run the pipework to join up to the existing waste fittings—in most instances, the new pipes will be much lower than the old*

hole as a reference point. It is good practice to use a piece of larger-diameter pipe as a channel for the new pipe: cut it to the thickness of the wall and set it in the hole with exterior filler. Block up the old hole at the same time using repair mortar or filler.

Now reassemble the entire pipe run in another dry run, cutting and joining it where necessary. Lead it through the wall and join it to the trap at the sink, then re-check the fall. If you don't already have the facility, arrange for the waste pipe to discharge into the gully *below* the grid—buy a

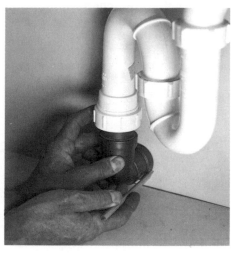

7 *Attach new pipe sections—with bends or sweeps—to the waste trap. Try to lead the pipes as near as possible to the old waste fitting—mark the base units so that you can cut a new exit hole*

Fused connection units are almost like extra sockets—and they're installed in the same way, by taking power from another socket. If you have not already done so, select a site for the unit: it can go above or below the sink, but if you put it above, it should be out of arm's reach of anyone standing directly at the sink, and at least 150mm above the height of the kitchen worktop surface.

Make a start by unscrewing the body of the unit and offer up the backing plate to the wall—check that there's enough flex from the disposer itself. Mark the screw posto it without first seeking the advice of a qualified electrician.

If you have a radial system an inspection of the socket will reveal one or two sets of wires. If there is only one, you should be able to connect to it providing there aren't too many sockets further down the circuit —but consult an electrician if in doubt. If there are two sets, it is not advisable to connect to the socket.

Connecting the unit: Once you have found a suitable socket, arrange a run of plastic conduit between here and the new connection unit. Fix the backing with screws and plugs, masonry pins or impact adhesive (whichever is most convenient) and use angle pieces where changes in direction are required. Afterwards prise the existing socket's backing box away from the wall, knock out a new cable entry hole and —unless it's surface-mounted—fit a rubber grommet to protect the cable.

Prepare the ends of your 2.5mm sq cable, lay it in the plastic conduit and snap on the conduit cover pieces. Sheath the bare earth wires with green and yellow sleeving and connect the cable to the appropriate terminals on both the socket and the connection unit faceplate (often labelled MAINS)—red to live (L), black to neutral (N) and bare wire to earth (E)—as shown in the diagram on page 104.

Having arranged an exit point for the cable into the conduit, replace the socket faceplate.

Connecting the waste disposer: Fit the lower half of the unit to the upper half following the manufacturer's instructions. Now feed the flex up to the connection unit.

Loosely pass the flex to the fused connection unit by the most convenient route— along the base units of the kitchen and up through the worktop is generally best. Avoid stretching the flex. If it is long

8 *Drill a series of holes around the marked exit route for your waste pipe. Cut out the waste with a padsaw or trimming knife and saw blade*

9 *Measure the distance from the old exit hole to the new. Use this dimension to cut a hole through the wall for the waste pipe. Use a drill and masonry bit or a cold chisel*

itions, then fix it in place. If the flex is too short, fit a flex outlet plate.

Now turn off the electricity at the mains switch on the consumer unit or fuseboard.

Unscrew the faceplate of the socket you propose to take the power from. If you have a ring main system, the back of the socket reveals two sets of wires (red, black, and green and yellow PVC sheathed) and you can safely take power from it. But if you find three sets of wires, the socket already has a spur drawn off it and you can't connect into it. If the socket has only one set, it is itself a spur. In this case it's inadvisable to connect

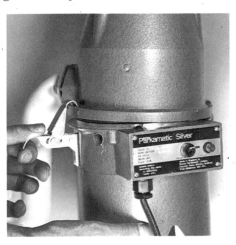

10 *Fit the motor compartment to the top housing of the unit. Ensure that the seal is in place, then adjust the clips to form a tight seal*

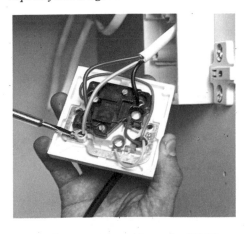

12 *Connect new cable to the FEED side terminals, noting that the terminals are different for cable and flex*

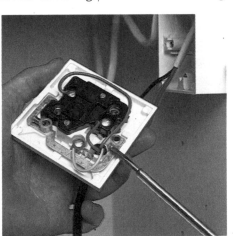

11 *If the flex is too short to reach the fused connection unit, fit a flex outlet plate underneath the sink. Connect the flex to the LOAD—tighten the cord*

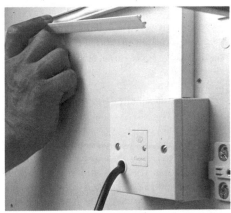

13 *Protect the cable inside surface-mounted plastic conduit—nail, screw or glue the conduit to the walls*

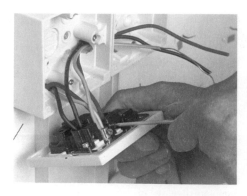

14 *Switch off at the mains. Connect new cable from the flex outlet to the LOAD side of the fused connection unit*

15 *Make a spur connection between the fused connection unit and the nearest suitable power socket (see diagram)*

enough to reach the connection unit, connect it in the manner shown below. Knock out an entry blank in the backing plate and connect to the terminals marked 'LOAD' as follows: brown to live (L), blue to neutral (N) and green/yellow to earth (E). Make sure the flex is held in the flex grip, then secure it with cable clips.

If the flex is not long enough to reach the connection unit you must join the flex to some new 2.55m sq twin and earth cable to extend its length. You need a flex outlet plate for a safe, reliable join between the flex and the cable.

Use an unswitched flex outlet plate with a surface-mounting box and fit it out of the way underneath the sink somewhere—as far from the water supply as length allows. Connect the flex to the 'LOAD' side and the new cable to the 'FEED' side in the manner described for fitting direct to a fused connection unit. You must then join this new cable to the fused connection unit in the manner shown in the diagram below. Cable colour codes are as follows: black for neutral (N), red for live (L), unsheathed copper for earth (E). Sheath the earth with green/yellow PVC sheathing.

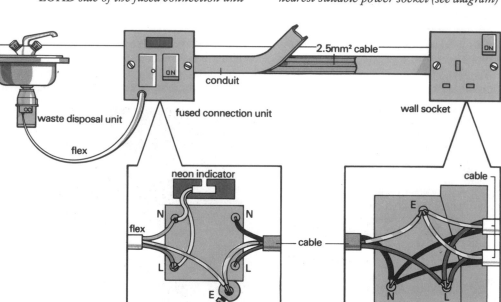

Ideal connection to the power supply: the flex from the unit connects to a fused connection unit at least 1.5m from the

sink. Power comes from the nearest socket—make a spur extension and protect the new cable inside conduit

Using a waste disposer

Waste disposers need to be treated with respect if they are to work properly so follow the guidelines below to make sure that you get trouble-free service from your unit.

• Always operate the disposer with a strong flow of COLD water. Never use hot water: it can melt fats in the waste, which then solidify and block the drain pipe.

• Never force waste into the disposer with your fingers or any other object—use a jet of water instead.

• Keep the stopper on when the machine is not in use, to reduce the risk of objects accidentally falling in.

• Always turn off the power supply to the machine before dismantling it or attempting to unblock it by any other means than reverse winding.

• If the cut-out operates, be sure to investigate the cause of the trouble and leave the machine for a while before pressing the reset button.

• When grinding, keep the machine running and the water flowing until you hear only the sound of the motor and swirling water.

• On no account feed the disposer with inorganic materials, large bones, scallop shells or large quantities of fat—these will only damage or block the machine.

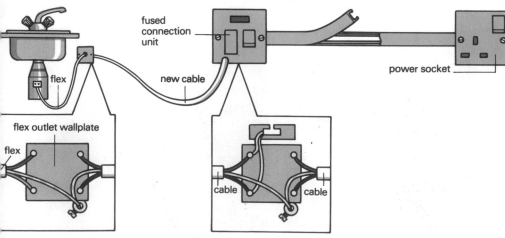

Where the flex will not reach comfortably to the fused connection unit, extend the flex via a flex outlet plate under the sink.

Electrical connections are similar to page 103 except at the fused connection unit—cable joins to cable here

HOW TO CLEAR BLOCKED DRAINS

How drainage systems work

Before you attempt to unblock main drains, make absolutely certain what system you have and get to know how it works.

Two pipe systems are still very common on houses built before the Second World War. There are two separate waste stacks running down the outside of the house—one for waste water and one for soil (waste from the WC). The waste pipes from your plumbing fittings run into the waste stack either directly or via a hopper head

Below: typical single stack system with an extra soil pipe (plus rodding eye) joining the main flow at a manhole

Right: older two pipe system with hopper on the waste stack. The combined flow is joined by a gully at the interceptor

(now obsolete, but still very common). Pipes from ground floor fittings often connect to the stack underground. But if they are far away from the stack they run instead to a separate gully—a kind of underground U trap. This joins the underground pipe from the waste stack at an inspection chamber, covered by a manhole.

Soil from the WC always runs to the soil stack direct. The underground pipe from the stack joins the waste water pipe at the inspection chamber.

Rainwater may be collected at a gully to join the waste water system. It may run from the gully to the inspection chamber via a separate pipe. It may be dispatched to a separate gravel-filled pit or soakaway. Or, in areas where water is in short supply, it may run to a separate stormwater drain.

From the inspection chamber, the combined waste and soil water flows toward the main drain, normally in the road. Before it gets there it may well pass through another

chamber—the interceptor—containing a large U trap.

Interceptors were once used to cut houses off from the main drains; this is no longer done, so they are no longer fitted. But you may find that you share an interceptor with one or more neighbouring properties Interceptors are easily distinguished from ordinary inspection chambers by an air inlet terminal nearby.

The single stack system is the one now in common use. As its name implies, waste water and soil pipes all connect to the same stack. Until recently the stack had to be inside the house, but the rules have since been relaxed to allow outside stacks. Ground floor appliances too far away from the stack to connect to it have their own sub stack or run to a closed (back inlet) gully. All underground pipes run in a straight line to meet at an inspection chamber.

Variations: There are as many of these in drainage as there are in plumbing. Houses

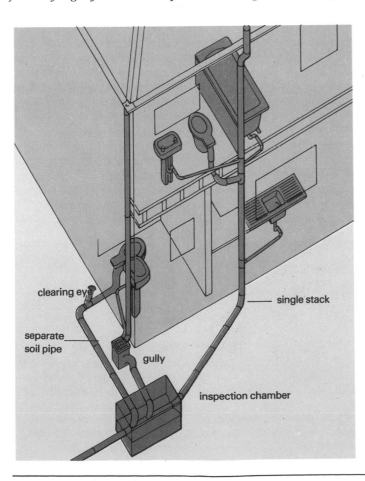

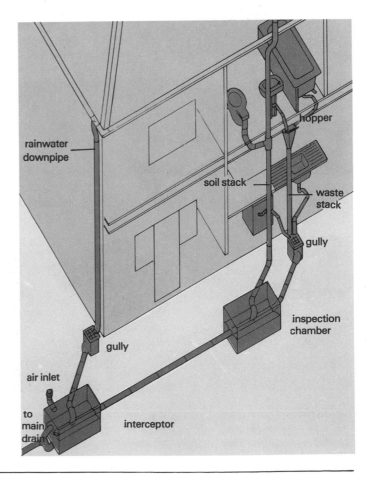

105

with the two pipe system which have been modernized may also have an internal single stack or sub stack.

Some larger houses have the **one pipe system**, in which a single stack runs on the outside of the building.

Some early single stack systems have additional old-style gullies.

And you may find you have more than one inspection chamber: they must be installed wherever pipes join and where the gradient or direction of the drain changes.

The only way to be really sure how your drains are laid out is to piece them together on a sketch plan, using the information above as a guide.

Locating blockages

Your first check is always to see if the trap on the fitting itself is blocked. If you are sure the blockage is in the drains, adopt the following procedure.

Open the manhole nearest the house. If this is empty the fault is in the fitting waste pipe, the stack or the gully trap (in the case of a backed-up gully).

If only one fitting on a stack gives trouble, the fault is in its own waste pipe. If several

If the handles are intact, use timber and rope to lift cover

do, the blockage is in the stack—probably low-down, towards the chamber.

If the manhole is full of effluent, don't immediately assume that this is where the blockage is. Try if possible to lift all other manholes between there and the main drain in the road—particularly if the drain includes an interceptor, which give more trouble than ordinary inspection chambers. It may be that the last one in the line has blocked, causing effluent to back up as far as the first.

> ## ★ WATCH POINT ★
>
> Remember that drains nearly always run in straight lines between fittings, stacks, gullies and inspection chambers. Fill these in first on your plan, join them, and it's a good bet that this is where the pipes run.

Lifting a manhole cover

You have to lift the manhole cover to check the drains, so this is always the first job. It's not easy: cast iron manhole covers are heavy, so get some help.

Frequently the cover is rusted in its frame. Scrape around the join with a screwdriver then tap the cover gently with some wood—the vibration should be enough to release it from its seating.

Special keys are available for lifting covers but if you don't have one a strong hook or a piece of steel bent in a vice will do the job just as well.

Some covers have handles consisting of small bars across indents. In this case loop several turns of string or wire through the bars and around stout pieces of timber. With someone on either side of the cover and using the timber as handles, lift the

cover and swing it free. If necessary, as a last resort, use a garden spade to lever up the cover over a fulcrum made from wood or bricks. The easiest way is to lift one end first and support it across the opening on a broom handle or similar. You can then lift the other end onto another support and use them both as rollers to push it clear of the opening.

Some covers are secured by screw bolts, in which case soak them in penetrating oil before attempting to undo them. Remove the bolts with a spanner or wrench.

On all manhole covers a little grease smeared around the frame before replacement will stop future rusting.

Blocked inspection chambers

The only really effective tools for this job are a set of rods. You could try plunging with a mop or poking with a bamboo stick, but because the outlets and inlets will be hidden by effluent, you really need something more flexible.

Drain rods can, of course, be hired, but this is inconvenient. If your drains block regularly or you are worried that they could, it really is worth buying a set of 'unbreakable' polypropylene rods and attachments—they are now very cheap. Among the attachments you can get are a plunger (for gullies), a worm screw (for retrieving debris), a scraper (this unfolds when you withdraw the rods), a flexible wire leader (for acute bends) and a small wheel (this screws onto the front rod to stop it catching on joints).

Screw two rods together and lower them into the chamber. Keeping the diagram in this panel in your mind's eye, feel for the inlet or outlet where you think the blockage is, and try to slide the rods into it.

When you feel them go in, screw on

1 *Lay out your rod attachments before assembling the first rods*

2 *Try the plunger head first, working it vigorously*

3 *After the blockage has cleared hose the chamber thoroughly*

4 *Chambers vary in size, but all demand the same procedure*

another rod and keep pushing. Continue in this way until you feel an obstruction.

Now turn the rods clockwise and at the same time keep manoeuvring them back and forth until you feel the blockage 'give'. You may have to do this for several minutes—and quite vigorously—before it has any effect.

After you have cleared the blockage, always flush the chamber thoroughly with water to remove the last traces of debris.

Interceptor problems

Interceptor blockages are nearly always in the trap. Above this is another pipe—the clearing eye—which should be closed by a clay stopper on a chain.

When confronted with an interceptor full of effluent, the first thing to try is removing the stopper. You won't be able to see

stopper chain breaks and the stopper falls into the trap where it acts like a butterfly valve and causes periodic blockages. If you think this has happened, call in professional help. If the stopper is simply missing from your interceptor, you can buy a new rubber one from a plumber's merchant.

Clearing gullies

Gullies, particularly the old open sort, are very common sources of blockages. If the blockage is in the trap, you can usually clear it from the gully itself. But if all else fails, rod in a plunging motion up the inlet in the inspection chamber that leads to the gully.

Small gullies can be baled out by hand. Lift the grid, then, wearing rubber gloves, scoop out the debris into a bucket. Check that the outlet is clear with your finger: if it isn't try poking some coathanger wire up it.

Gullies receiving sink waste get clogged with grease. This can usually be shifted with boiling water or scraped out by hand.

If this doesn't work try pouring down a solution of caustic soda. But take care and follow the instructions to the letter—caustic soda is dangerous.

Deep gullies and blockages on the other

gully itself with polyethylene bags rammed tightly in place—the extra pressure this creates will help the water do its work.

Blockages in stacks

These are rare in single stack systems and simple two pipe arrangements, but common in older, complicated drainage layouts. Fortunately there are often clearing eyes at junctions and direction changes.

The procedure is to soak eye covers (or their bolts) in penetrating oil before attempting to remove them.

You can then either insert a rod with a head to match the stack diameter, or else feed in a screw clearing wire. Use the same procedure as for an inspection chamber.

Hopper stacks can be cleared from above with a worm screw rod.

Tree roots

These can work their way through a joint in a drain pipe, in which case no amount of plunging will shift them. You may be able to clear them partially with a powered screw augur similar to the type used by pro-

Some gully pipes have rodding eyes at changes of direction. Unscrew the cover for access

Some waste pipe clearing eyes are unscrewed with a wrench. Soak in penetrating oil if stiff

Feed in a screw clearing wire to unblock the waste pipe. Use the same procedure as for an inspection chamber

Hopper stacks which are blocked up can usually be cleared by hand or with a worm screw rod

it—you must feel for the handle with a piece of wood and try hooking it out of its socket.

If you succeed and the blockage is in the trap, the chamber will clear and you can set about clearing the trap itself. Plunge it vigorously with your rods—preferably using a plunging head—until the debris shifts.

If removing the stopper has no effect, the blockage is further down the drain; in this case rod through the clearing eye.

An all too common problem is that the

side of the trap can be shifted by plunging—you can get an attachment like a sink plunger that screws onto the end of an ordinary drain rod. A household mop makes an effective standby, as do old rags wrapped in a plastic bag and tied to a broom handle, but only if there is enough bulk to fill the gully neck completely.

You could try threading a garden hose around the bed in the gully trap to flush the blockage with water. In this case stop up the

fessional drain clearers—they are available at some hire stores. But a more satisfactory solution is to excavate the drain.

Find out where this is by making a note of how many rods it takes to reach the obstruction. Then lay the same rods out at ground level and see where they end.

Dig down to the pipe, hack away and pull out the offending roots, then make good the damage to the joint with a strong mix of one part cement and two of sharp sand.

INSTALLING A NEW SUITE

Bathroom fittings have improved enormously in the last decade, with more styles, colours and choice of fixtures available than ever before. Your existing bath, basin and WC may function perfectly adequately, but swopping them for a new set could give your bathroom that special individual touch it probably lacks. And more importantly, an up-to-the-minute bathroom adds significantly to the value of your home.

If you're far from convinced about your ability to tackle the job yourself, take heart: there's no denying that it's a major undertaking, but thanks to the range of plumbing fittings and attachments now made specially for the do-it-yourselfer it's not half as difficult as it sounds. Such fittings add a little to the cost, but the saving in effort is worth it in the long run.

Planning your approach

Removing the old bathroom equipment may seem the easy part of the job—it is—but before you rush in and start pulling out the fittings, avoid potential headaches by planning your approach.

Firstly, lay aside ample time to complete the job and, if need be, get a friend to help you out: an extra pair of hands can save a lot of time removing the bath and disposing of the rubbish. A day to remove the old suite and two days to install the new one should give you some leeway, and allow for inevitable stoppages which are bound to occur.

Secondly, assess your bathroom with a view to how the new suite, when you buy it, is going to fit in. By siting the new bathroom equipment exactly where the old used to be, there should be no need for extensive modifications of the existing plumbing. Inevitably, you will have to reposition the pipework slightly, as the new suite will not match the old. But modern accessories—flexible copper pipe for tap connections and adapters for waste outlets—make this task simple by comparison with running new drain and supply pipes.

If you have a high wall-mounted WC cistern which is fed from above by a pipe that comes through the ceiling, you will have to remove the pipe and install a new feed. But this too is relatively simple and is covered in detail on page 114.

If you discover that your existing plumbing is made of or includes lead, now is the time to replace it with modern materials—a job best left to a professional. It is not a good idea to join lead pipe to copper because the water flowing through will encourage electrolytic action—like a car battery—and cause one or the other to decay rapidly.

Before you buy your new suite, make a sketch plan of the existing fixtures and a floor plan (on graph paper) of the room as it stands. As well as the overall dimensions, measure the height, length and depth of the bath, basin and WC, and mark them on the drawings. Then consider if you want the new equipment to be larger or smaller, bearing in mind that space is often at a premium in bathrooms.

It is also helpful to make a sketch of how the WC is connected to the soil outlet (see the diagram below) so that you can ensure you get a similar fitting on the new unit. Slight variations in the angle and dimensions of the WC outlet can be overcome by fitting an adapter, but try to get the new WC trap as close as possible to the existing outlet for ease of connection.

Your old WC pan will have one of the outlets illustrated above. Whichever type it has, you should be able to buy plastic adapters to connect your new WC pan to the old soil pipe. Make a sketch and take measurements of your particular outlet.

Most modern WC pans have horizontal outlets (top) which are connected to the soil pipe with adapters. Some old styles have S-trap outlets which go vertically through the floor (centre). There is a third type, P-traps (bottom), which go out through the wall to be discharged into a soil stack on the outside of the house

Choosing a new suite

Bathroom equipment is continually being updated and re-styled, but assuming that you know what you want there are still practical considerations to be borne in mind.

Baths are normally made and sold in one of three materials: acrylic, pressed steel and cast iron.

Before—an efficient but rather dingy bathroom. The high wall-mounted WC and old-fashioned suite give the room a 'dated' atmosphere

After—simply replacing the suite and redecorating gives the bathroom a new lease of life and makes plumbing connections easy

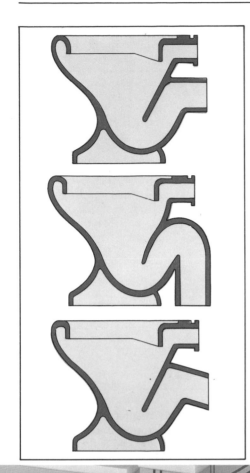

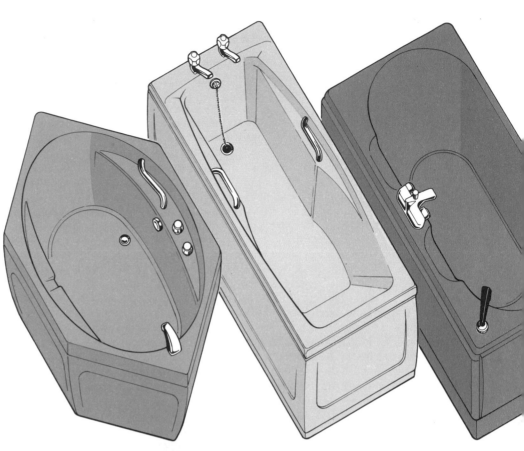

There are plenty of modern bath designs worthy of consideration before you make your final choice.

Corner baths (left) add elegance to a bathroom as well as being more economical on space than the traditional rectangular bath (centre). But, don't forget that rectangular baths can vary both in length and width, and some have sloping backs for greater comfort.

The position of the taps on the bath is also worth thinking about—taps on the side of a bath are more accessible (right) than the conventionally placed ones.

The choice in bathroom suites is very large and so you should take a good look around before making a final decision.

Acrylic baths are supported in a cradle which is assembled around the bath before installation. They are light, easy to fit and are comparatively cheap to buy. Panels are normally included in the kit, although they may be offered only as an optional extra.

The problems once associated with acrylic—creaking and poor heat retention—have now virtually been eliminated; in fact, modern acrylic retains heat better than most other materials. Their chief drawbacks are that they are easily scratched—particularly during installation—and are vulnerable to high temperatures, so take care if you are using a blowlamp near one.

Acrylic baths are available in a variety of shapes—round, square, rectangular and corner-shaped. But a word of warning: before buying a shaped bath, consider the plumbing side of the job first and check that the tap and drain connection points are easily adapted to match your existing pipework and wastes.

Pressed steel baths are also light and easy to install but they are not available in such a range of shapes. The other snag with pressed steel baths is that they are easily chipped and damaged if knocked accidentally with something hard.

Cast iron baths are very heavy and are extremely cumbersome to install, though they do have a feeling of superior quality. These baths stand on adjustable legs and it is important to spread the weight of the bath by placing wooden battens under the feet (it is a good idea to do this on all baths, but essential with cast iron). The disadvantages of cast iron baths are that they conduct heat away from hot water more quickly than others, and they are expensive.

Basins are almost always made from glazed china, which makes them vulnerable during installation. Most modern basins stand on a *pedestal* which takes the weight while the basin itself is held in position against the wall by either brackets or screws. The pedestal also serves to hide the feed and drain pipes.

Wall fitted basins release the floor space

below but they must have a strong wall to support them. On a frame wall, this means removing a section of wall boarding and adding a timber noggin—say 150mm × 50mm—where the fixing will go.

Vanity basins are incorporated into a framework which is boxed in to provide storage space below and room for sundries on either side. Some basins come complete with units, others have compatible units available as optional extras. If you don't like what's available, bear in mind that making your own will take up extra time.

Basins, like baths, are available in a range of styles and shapes but again beware: although some styles look very attractive,

Choose your basin from the wide selection available. The standard pedestal basin (below left) is very stable when in position and is a safe bet. Square and oval basins (below) make a striking alternative to the normal shape but make sure that they are practical to wash in as well as good looking. Basins are usually made from vitreous china so take extra care during installation.

Close coupled WCs (near right) may be relatively more expensive than the traditional low level WC (centre right) but they are quieter and look neater. WC pans can be shaped (far right) for a more streamlined effect.

Although you can get plastic cisterns, most, like the pans, are made from vitreous china—so take care

they are not always practical to wash in.

While considering the bath and basin, think about the taps and outlets that are to go with them. These may have to be bought separately, though you should be able to purchase them at the same time. Mixer taps are an obvious option but they cannot always be plumbed into a cold water supply coming directly off the rising main. If you are in any doubt about whether or not you can fix mixer taps, consult your local water authority.

Pop-up waste attachments make the old fashioned plug-and-chain obsolete. There are no problems involved in fitting pop-up wastes—so long as your basin is designed to take them—and full instructions are given when you buy them.

WCs are made up of two parts; the pan and the cistern. Both are usually made from vitreous china although you can now get lightweight plastic cisterns.

With WCs, you get what you pay for. The most basic type has a *low level* cistern which is connected to the pan via a *flush pipe*. Although this does its job perfectly well, a more attractive—and expensive—alternative is the *close coupled* type which is bolted onto the pan. The most quiet, efficient and expensive type of WC employs what is called a *siphonic flush system*.

The water supply to the new WC cistern can be fed from underneath or from either side—a point worth thinking about when you make your choice, remembering that your existing plumbing has to be connected

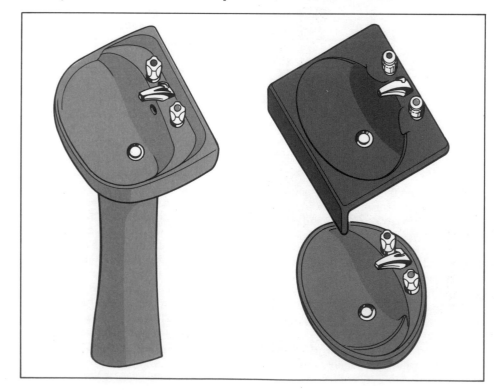

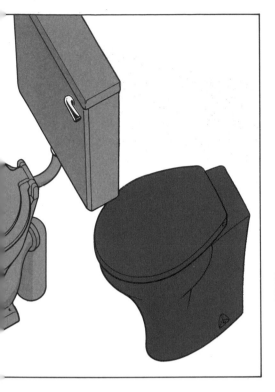

To help remove the taps and other fittings, you must have a supply of penetrating oil; the type which comes in aerosol tins is easier to apply in awkward corners.

If you are unable to complete removal and installation on consecutive days, or if you want to use your water supply elsewhere in the house at the halfway stage, you can temporarily cap the severed supply pipes with a soldered or compression cap. By doing this you can be sure that the rest of your water system will be perfectly safe.

You will certainly have a lot of debris and rubbish to dispose of once you have removed all the old fixtures—so get a supply of plastic rubbish bags and arrange to take the old suite to a local rubbish tip.

★ WATCH POINT ★

Use a basin spanner to unscrew the tap fixings. You can get better leverage by gripping the bottom with an adjustable spanner.

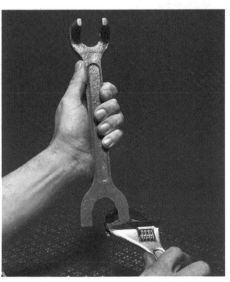

Preparing the bathroom

Even if you intend to keep the bathroom decor as it is, temporarily remove as many wall fittings—mirrors, cabinets and so on—as possible before the upheaval begins.

Which fixture you remove first largely depends on how your bathroom is arranged: you may, for example, have to remove the basin in order to get at the WC. However, once the bath is removed there will be a lot more space so all things being equal this is probably the place to start.

Before you tackle any pipework, turn off the hot and cold water supplies and switch off any water heating apparatus. The supply

pipes may well contain stop valves to isolate them locally but these are not always completely reliable: it is usually quicker and easier in the long run to shut off the supply at the cold water storage cistern (if you have one) or to close the main stop valve and open up all your taps for a few minutes to drain everything down.

The first thing to do is remove the bath panel. This may be made from any number of materials—from hardboard to marble.

Panels are usually secured underneath the lip of the bath at the top and screwed to battening at the bottom. To get at the screws you may have to pull away skirting: this is easily done with a crowbar or claw hammer, levered against a block of wood. If you don't intend to salvage the panelling, breaking it up on the spot will make it a lot easier to carry away. If pipes pass through the panelling, take care not to wrench them out of position as this could dislocate the joints. Where necessary, provide extra clearance by cutting away part of the panel with a padsaw.

Once the panelling has been removed, you have access to the feed and waste pipes. Rather than unscrewing the taps at this stage, it is easier to cut through the feed pipes—a maximum of 300mm from the taps—with a hacksaw: the gap between the sawn off pipe and the new tap connections can be bridged later with copper bendable connectors. If you decide to keep the existing taps, they can be removed more easily with a basin spanner once you have lifted the bath out.

If the waste is connected to a lead pipe, your best bet is to cut through it and renew the piping all the way to the waste stack or gully: lead has a limited life span and it will have to be renewed sooner or later. Plastic waste pipes and traps are easily unscrewed and may be worth keeping to fit to the new bath if they are in good condition.

If the waste pipe is made from iron or copper, and providing it is 38mm in diameter, you can buy a plastic connecting unit which allows new plastic pipe to be jointed onto it.

Remove the waste overflow at the bath or at the trap—whichever is the most convenient to get at.

Some baths are anchored to the wall with brackets and screws, so check this possibility and if necessary remove them before attempting to move the bath itself. If you want to keep any tiling around the bath, unscrew the legs and lower the bath onto some baulks of timber so that it is free of the sealant or grout around the edges. If the tiles are not important, lever them off with an

to it in the most convenient way. If your old cistern was fed from above and you intend to install a new feed, it is obviously neater to have a cistern that is fed from below. The overflow and inlet connection points on either side of new cisterns are interchangeable, so you won't have to re-route your plumbing from one side to the other.

Tools and materials

It's impossible to give a comprehensive tool list for a job like this: so much varies according to circumstances and the chances are you'll end up using every tool you've got. However, make sure that you have a hacksaw to cut through pipes, an adjustable spanner for compression joints, a basin spanner to remove taps (see diagram right), a long screwdriver for taking out the securing screws on the WC pan and a tape measure to measure up the old and new equipment and pipes.

You may also find it useful to have the following: a crowbar to lever the old WC pan if it proves obstinate; an old wood chisel to remove any tiles or sealant that secure the bath to the wall; a pipe wrench to unscrew ancient waste outlets and steady pipes; a club hammer and cold chisel to chip away at the WC soil pipe seal; a stepladder or hop-up to reach a high mounted cistern, if you have one; goggles and gloves if you have to break up a cast iron bath; and a sponge to mop up water in the WC cistern.

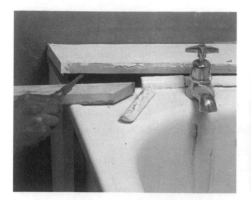

1 *Remove panels with an old screwdriver levered on a block of wood*

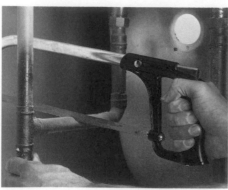

2 *Cut squarely through the tap supply pipes with a hacksaw*

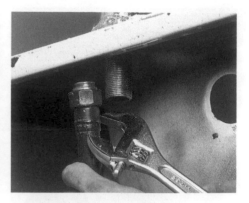

3 *Alternatively, unscrew connections with a spanner or basin spanner*

4 *Disconnect the overflow from the bath by unscrewing the locking nut*

5 *The locking nut on the waste pipe will probably be inaccesible so cut through it with a hacksaw*

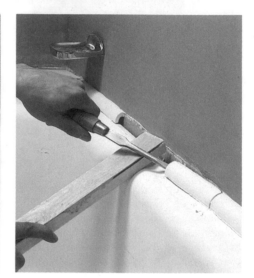

6 *Lift off any quadrant tiles or sealant around the bath with an old screwdriver levered on scrap wood*

7 *Acrylic or pressed steel baths are quite light but are awkward to handle —so get a friend to help you do the removals. Cast iron baths are very heavy and must be broken up on the spot. But take necessary precautions first: protect your eyes with goggles and lay an old blanket over the bath to contain splinters of enamel*

old wood chisel and then chip away the sealant. If there are quadrant tiles around the bath, they will have to go.

Cast iron baths are best broken up on the spot as they are so awkward and heavy to move. Cover the entire bath with an old blanket to contain splinters, protect your eyes with goggles, and start breaking off small pieces with a sledge hammer, beginning at the edge and working inwards.

Both acrylic and pressed steel baths are light and can easily be carried away by two people—they are awkward to manoeuvre though, so pad the corners with rags.

★ WATCH POINT ★

When you sever the supply pipes, make sure that you cut them squarely to save jointing problems later.

Removing the basin and WC

The procedure for removing a basin is similar to that for a bath. Again, it is much easier to sever the supply and waste pipes near the fixture and then strip it of its fittings (if you need them) on the ground.

If the basin is wall mounted, chip away any sealant around the edges and then locate the fixings, or bracket fixings, on the wall. Undoing them is likely to prove difficult, even if you can get sufficient purchase on the screw heads. You may need to loosen them by driving in a screwdriver or old wood chisel between the basin/brackets and the wall itself. This may well cause the wallplugs to pull out, so make sure the basin is supported from underneath at this stage. Having removed all the fixings, lift the basin clear.

Deal with the fixing on the basin part of a pedestal basin the same way, then chip away any cement around the joint between the two parts. Having lifted the basin clear, you should have more than enough room to tackle any screws holding the pedestal to the floor—you will need a large screwdriver to shift these. Finally, remove the pedestal which can then be disposed of.

Taking out a WC sounds like a really unpleasant task. In fact it isn't that bad, but plumbers will nevertheless charge a fortune to do it for you.

Start by flushing the cistern to empty it, then mop up any water left inside with a sponge. Disconnect the supply pipe at the the aid of your assistant before removing the brackets themselves from the wall.

Lastly, pull whatever remains of the old flush pipe out of the pan.

Removing the pan: If the pan itself is joined to the soil pipe via a polypropylene sleeve, or the pan trap is held in the soil outlet collar by mastic/putty, you are lucky: having removed the pan fixings you simply pull it away.

However, it is more than likely that the trap is cemented into the outlet collar, in which case you have to smash the trap—NOT the outlet socket—with a hammer and cold chisel. Wear protective goggles when you do this.

Afterwards, stuff a large piece of rag down the open soil outlet to stop debris falling down and smells rising up; make absolutely certain that there is no chance of the rag itself getting lost down the pipe. Don't bother to chip away the rest of the pan trap debris and seal from the outlet collar at this stage: the job is best left until later, when you know how the new WC pan is going to join it.

With the old fixtures removed and disposed of, you quite literally have to pick up the pieces. Now is the time to make good any defects revealed by their removal.

Holes in plasterwork will be obvious, but you may have more problems with a

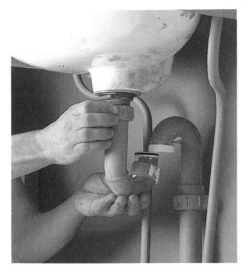

8 *Unscrew the basin trap and waste pipe. Watch out for spillages*

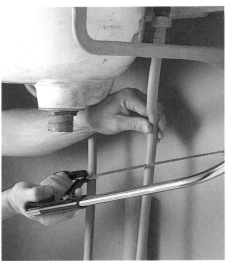

9 *Cut through the supply pipes at right angles with a hacksaw*

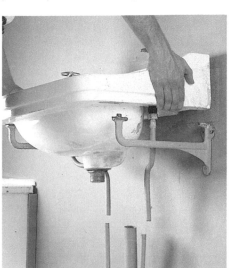

10 *You can then lift the basin free from its brackets or fixings*

ball valve by undoing the connector nut with an adjustable spanner, then do likewise for the overflow pipe.

You disconnect the flush pipe where it joins the siphon unit at the base of the cistern. There should be a large nut holding the pipe to the siphon outlet, and you can undo this with a wrench. But if the flush pipe is an old lead or iron one, you can simply saw through it.

Before starting to remove the cistern, support its weight as best you can. Low level ones should present no problems, but for a high level one you may need steps and a helper standing by to be sure of avoiding any accidents.

Search right around the cistern until you have located all its fixing screws. If it is screwed directly to the wall, remove the screws using the largest screwdriver you've got, then lift it up and away from the site.

If the cistern is on brackets, disconnect them and lower the cistern to the floor with

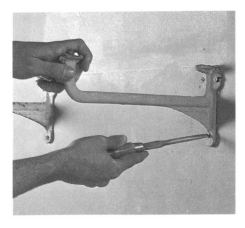

11 *Unscrew the basin supports from the wall taking care not to pull out any plugs or damage the wall*

Now undo the fixing screws holding the pan to the floor. If they prove reluctant— or if the joint has been sealed—use a crowbar to lever the pan free. Finally, remove it from the site with the aid of your helper.

12 *Spray penetrating oil (such as WD40) on the tap fixings and then unscrew them with a basin spanner*

wooden floor. Check all the boards—but especially those where the bath was—for defects and rot. If you suspect dry rot, call in a specialist immediately and be prepared to have to halt proceedings.

Removing the WC

1 *Use an adjustable spanner to unscrew the cistern inlet. A high level wall-mounted cistern is shown here*

2 *Disconnect the flush pipe from underneath the cistern. An adjustable wrench should free it*

3 *Pull the flush pipe away from the WC pan. In most cases this will be a rubber connector*

4 *Use a long screwdriver to remove the securing screws. There will be one screw on each side of the base*

5 *Break the pan trap with a sharp hammer blow if it cannot easily be removed in one piece*

6 *Chip out any residual debris from the soil pipe. Stuff a rag down the open soil outlet*

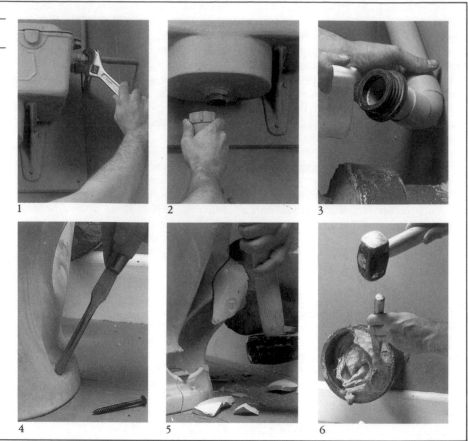

Capping a pipe

Capping severed copper supply pipes is a useful way of making the rest of your water system serviceable in the interim or permanently sealing a pipe you may have had to cut in the roof space. Apart from compression caps themselves—½in. or 15mm for basins and WC supplies, ¾in. or 22mm for baths—all you need are spanners, flat and round files, and some jointing compound or PTFE tape.

After cutting the pipe, file off the burrs, inside and out, and slightly chamfer the outside edge. Push the securing nut over the end of the pipe followed by the olive—the brass ring—and smear some jointing compound over the end of the pipe. Push the cap on as far as it will go and screw the nut hand-tight. Give the nut an extra one and a half turns with an adjustable spanner to seal the joint completely.

Installing the new fittings

Careful planning is the essence of a job like this: once you start, you don't want to have to stop to make a dash for the plumber's merchant because something doesn't quite line up. Nor do you want the family's washing and toilet facilities out of action for any longer than you can possibly help.

New suite: As soon as this is delivered, check that the fittings which go with it are all there.

• The WC should have a lid—although you may have to buy this separately—and fixings. Inside the cistern in a bag you should find the handle, ball valve assembly, siphon unit, overflow outlet and various nuts and washers. There should also be an instruction leaflet telling you precisely what goes where.

• Acrylic baths are generally supplied with a frame (which you assemble yourself), wooden carcase (to which you attach the panel) and a moulded side panel. Fittings are separate, but you should have ordered them at the same time. Remember that you need an overflow, drain outlet and taps.

• With a basin, again check that you've got the taps, drain outlet and overflow. If your taps incorporate a pop-up waste, check that the fitting instructions are there.

If possible, put the new suite in a room near the bathroom and assemble the fittings in there—it avoids confusion.

New plumbing: This is the most difficult part of the job, so it pays to take as much time over it as you can afford—installation is easy if you are using the right parts.

Although it's laborious, the safest way is to locate each part of the new suite in turn in its proposed position. You can then take accurate measurements or draw sketch plans of how to bridge the gap between new fittings and old pipework.

• With the WC, your main problem is getting the new pan trap to line up with the old soil outlet. The connection will be made using one of the patent sleeve connectors now available for this purpose ('Multikwik' is the best known brand), and these can take up slight variations. Offset connectors will cope with slight differences from side to side. And the 90° type easily convert a modern horizonal outlet into the older P type outlet.

However, if the new pan is too low, you must build it up to the level of the soil outlet with a platform of plywood, blockboard or chipboard. Stand the pan on your chosen material, draw around it, then cut the board to shape and finish the edges with a planer file or sandpaper.

If you have a problem with the WC connectors it always pays to take a sketch plan with you as well as accurate measurements: plumber's merchants usually have a fitting to cope with most common difficulties.

• With the bath and basin, drainage traps

are the main consideration; it's worth replacing your existing ones if they are metal (vital if the new bath is acrylic) and it generally makes the job simple anyway because you can 'tailor' the new trap to match your exact requirements.

You have a choice between conventional U and P traps and bottle traps—the latter are easier to unblock but discharge water more slowly. Often it comes down to what fits best. U and P traps have interchangeable halves, providing for numerous variations.

Traps are available to match all sizes of outlet pipe (note this down before you buy) and come with a screw connector to the waste fitting on one end and a compression or push fitting to the waste pipe on the other. There is normally no restriction on depth, except that in the UK a trap connecting to a combined soil/waste stack must be the 75mm (deep seal) type in case of any back-siphonage.

Any remaining gap can be bridged with a length of compatible plastic waste pipe, compression-jointed into the existing pipe. If you have an old waste system in metal pipe, see Joining to old pipework.

•Before measuring up for the supply pipes, decide what plumbing system to use. Copper is still the most widely available. And if you use flexible tap connectors on all the connections, this could well be all the fittings you need.

However, you may find it pays to cut back the existing supplies and run new ones by a slightly different route. Again you could use copper—with push-fit or compression joints and fittings. Or you may prefer plastic: some systems are flexible, enabling you to clear obstructions easily; others rely on fittings for changes in direction. You have the choice of push-fit or compression joints both of which have their pros and cons.

One thing is certain. If you plan the route carefully enough and take accurate measurements, you should be able to rule out the need for traditional plumbing—blowlamps, pipe bending and so on—altogether.

Bear in mind that baths (unless fed directly from the mains) take 22mm pipe; basins and the WC take 15mm pipe. One hole basin mixer taps have 10mm flexible connectors which can be joined to the supply pipes by means of compression jointed adapters.

Before you order the supply pipes, consider the material you are connecting to—usually either copper or lead pipework. If the existing pipes are Imperial copper, a 15mm compression fitting can go straight

on to ½in. pipe but a 22mm fitting needs a special olive to connect a ¾in. pipe. If your existing pipes are galvanized iron you cannot join copper to them—use plastic instead, with the relevant adapters. If your supply pipes are lead, it's probably worth replacing the entire run—at least to the main feed from the cold storage tank.

Coping with disruption: If you only have one WC, consider hiring a chemical one so that you aren't rushed into completing. These are available at hire stores and sometimes from your local authority health department. You may also be able to avoid disruption by capping off pipes temporarily (see page opposite) or by planning to install the WC first, straight after the bath.

If you need to do the installation work in stages, start with the bath: this is bulkier than the other fittings, so putting it in first lessens the chances of damaging it and gets one large component out of the way.

Specialized equipment

Your requirements here are certain to vary according to circumstances. You will of course need a supply of wrenches and adjustable spanners for the fittings and supply pipes, but you may also need to hire one or two specialized items.

If your existing WC soil outlet is vitrified clay or cast iron you will probably have to cut it to fit. This is best done with an angle grinder or cutting wheel attachment for your power drill. And if you need to make a new hole in the wall for the WC overflow, hire a heavy duty masonry bit—and possibly an industrial drill—at the same time.

Make sure that you have supplies of both PTFE tape and plumber's putty (such as Plumbers Mait)—they are used practically everywhere.

Check too that you have enough fixing

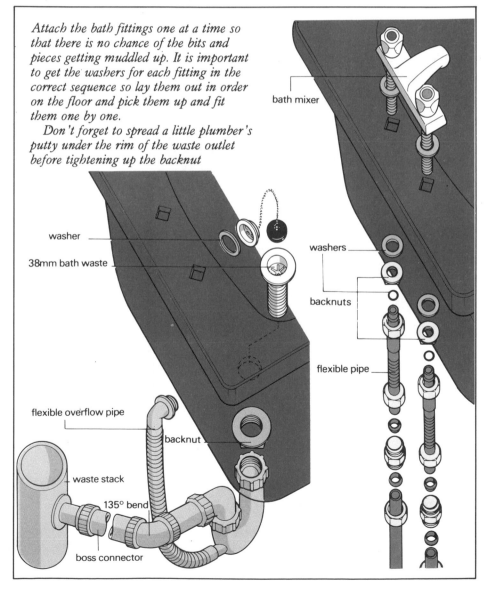

Attach the bath fittings one at a time so that there is no chance of the bits and pieces getting muddled up. It is important to get the washers for each fitting in the correct sequence so lay them out in order on the floor and pick them up and fit them one by one.

Don't forget to spread a little plumber's putty under the rim of the waste outlet before tightening up the backnut

bath mixer

washer

38mm bath waste

washers

backnuts

flexible pipe

flexible overflow pipe

backnut

waste stack

135° bend

boss connector

screws and wallplugs to fit the new suite. Recommended sizes should be given in the manufacturer's instruction leaflets.

Preparing the suite

Equipping the bath, basin and WC with their relevant fittings is best done before installation. And if you add the tap connectors as well, you may be able to cut down on a lot of fiddly plumbing later.

Start with the bath taps. Whether single or mixer, the fitting procedure is much the same. Bed the taps or tap unit on the rubber seals provided—if none are, lay a bed of plumber's putty—insert the tails through the holes in the bath, and slip on the sealing washers from underneath. Follow with the backnuts, which you can tighten with a basin spanner or box spanner.

Now screw a 22mm bendable connector to each tap tail and tighten with a wrench. Leave the connectors hanging straight down.

The overflow will probably connect to the waste outlet via a flexible plastic pipe. Spread a little plumber's putty around the underneath of the waste outlet rim and insert it in the bath. From underneath the bath, slide on the overflow pipe collar (making sure it aligns with the hole in the outlet), then the O ring seal, and then the plastic locknut that secures the fitting. Tighten gently with a wrench.

Spread more putty around the overflow plate, insert it in its hole, and screw on the free end of the overflow pipe. To tighten the plate, you can hold it with two screwdrivers arranged in a 'crossed swords' pattern.

Pop-up wastes: The fitting procedure here will vary slightly from the one above, but full instructions are always given. Make sure that everything is properly bedded.

Installing the bath and basin

If your new bath is acrylic or pressed steel, assemble the frame around it according to

1 *Use a basin spanner to tighten the bath tap backnuts*

2 *Bed the overflow washer in putty before tightening up*

the manufacturer's instructions. Lift the whole assembly on-site with the aid of an assistant if possible.

The bath will have an in-built fall, so the sides must be level. Check this with a spirit level along both the length and the width and adjust the frame feet acordingly. Then crawl underneath and mark the wall bracket fixing points on the wall. Remove the bath, drill and plug the holes, then replace the bath and secure the fixings.

Basin fittings are secured in much the same way as those for a bath. Bottle traps take up less room than the conventional type and are ideal for basins.

The sequence of washers is important, so make sure they're in the right order. Screw up the backnuts hand tight and then give them another 1½ turns with a spanner—don't be tempted to overtighten them as they could well damage or crack the basin

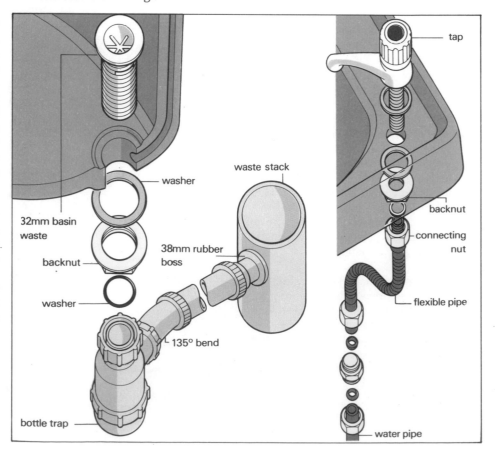

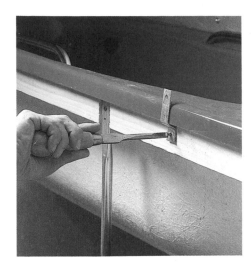

3 *Attach the wall brackets securely to the frame battens*

4 *It's as well to fit flexible connectors to the bath and basin taps at this stage*

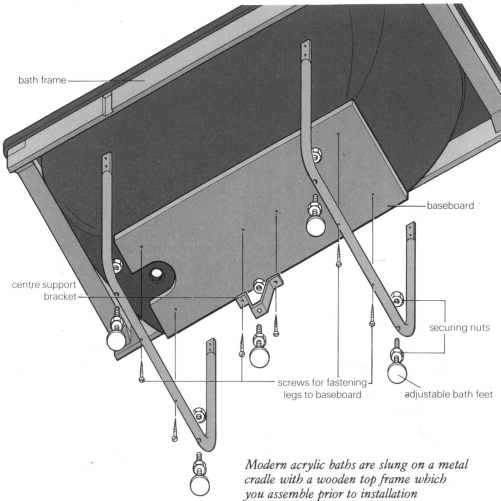

bath frame

baseboard

centre support bracket

securing nuts

screws for fastening legs to baseboard

adjustable bath feet

Modern acrylic baths are slung on a metal cradle with a wooden top frame which you assemble prior to installation

If your bath is cast iron, prepare four offcuts of board to place under the feet. Locate these on-site, then get one or more assistants to help lift the bath into position. Cast iron baths are very heavy, so you're certain to need help. Level up as above.

Fit the trap next, wrapping PTFE tape around the waste outlet thread before screwing on the connector. You should now be able to assess what needs to be done to bridge the gap to the existing supply and waste pipes.

Unless it's going to obstruct you unduly, you should install the basin next, then deal with all the supply pipes at once.

On a pedestal basin, start by positioning the pedestal and mark its fixing positions on the floor. Drill pilot holes, then screw it securely in place.

Locate the basin on top of the pedestal and mark the wall, then refit the basin and secure (not forgetting the putty in the socket trick—see Watch Point).

For a wall mounted basin, mark the bracket positions on the wall at the desired

height—get an assistant to help you, so that you can check that they are level and plumb with a spirit level. Drill and plug the wall and secure the brackets. Then place the basin on top and secure it.

Supply pipes: If you are lucky, the bendable connectors you have fitted will reach the severed pipe ends; if not, you must add straight sections of pipe joined with push-fit or compression fittings to bridge the gap.

With copper pipe:
• When measuring up for a new section don't forget to allow for the length of the fittings—not forgetting the 20mm of the pipe that gets 'lost' in the joint fitting.
• All pipe ends being joined must be cut absolutely square; if you find one that isn't, recut it rather than risk leaks later.
• Deburr cut pipe ends thoroughly—use a round file on the inside, a flat file on the outside. For a compression joint, chamfer the outer edge of the pipe end slightly.
• Smear jointing compound or wrap PTFE tape around compression joint threads before assembly, to guard against leaks and protect against overtightening.
• Assemble compression joints hand-tight

and then tighten one and a half turns further with your wrenches.
• Try not to bend a bendable connector more than once in the same place—it'll split. Avoid tortuous bends, too, especially in two places as connectors are easy to snap.

For plastic pipes:
• Always cut square and deburr.
• Whether you use compression or push-fit connectors, you need to strengthen the end of the plastic supply pipe with a metal insert.
• Smear silicone lubricant or washing up liquid on the pipe end before making a push-fit joint, otherwise the fitting may be damaged.

All pipe runs should be as unobtrusive as you can get them. On a pedestal basin, bend the connectors back towards the front of the basin and run the supply pipes to meet them, up the inside of the pedestal itself.

Drainage: Make up any gap between the new trap and the waste outlet with a new section of pipe. Use compression joints, rather than welded, as these will take up the slight variations in pipe size that occur between brands. Make sure the pipe ends are cut square and deburred; lubricate with

5 *Level the bath by adjusting the feet*

6 *Secure the bath to the wall by its frame brackets*

7 *Use a level to position the battens on the floor*

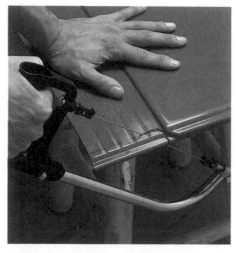

8 *Shape the bath panel, if necessary, using a saw*

9 *Secure the panel under the lip of the bath*

10 *Screw the basin or its brackets firmly to the wall*

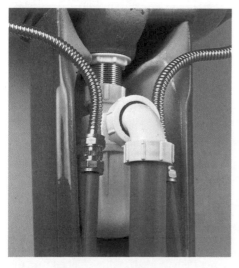

11 *On a pedestal basin, you can run the supply and drainage pipework unobtrusively behind the pedestal*

12 *When sealing around fittings, push the sealant ahead of you, gently squeezing as you go*

washing up liquid before fitting.

It is quite conceivable that the old and new pipes are at different heights. On a bath, you ought to be able to get them level by readjusting the bath feet or even packing under the feet with scraps of plywood. Where a basin outlet passing through a wall is concerned, you can get various sizes of P traps, one half of which can be trimmed down to fit. Although you may have to cut back the existing waste pipes in order to

★ WATCH POINT ★

Fill the screw sockets with plumber's putty before tightening, then stop screwing in when the putty is almost all squeezed out—it stops the china cracking accidentally.

insert new sections, there should be no need to (and you mustn't) alter the fall to the stack or gully to any appreciable degree.

Installing the WC

With the pan temporarily in position, your first job is to measure and mark off what needs to be done to the existing soil outlet pipe. If it is too near or too far from the pan spigot, it must be cut to size.

Before you commit yourself, however, double check the relation of the pan as it stands to the cistern and the wall. On a close coupled suite in particular, there must be enough room to fit the cistern between the pan and wall, but not so much as to leave an unsightly gap behind the cistern once it is in its final position.

If you can re-use the soil pipe socket, chip out what remains of the old pan spigot and joint very carefully with hammer and cold chisel; keep going until it is completely clear of debris.

If the pipe is too short or too long, it must be cut using an angle grinder or cutting wheel attachment. Wear goggles to do this.

Angle grinders are dangerous tools: make sure that you grip the tool firmly and

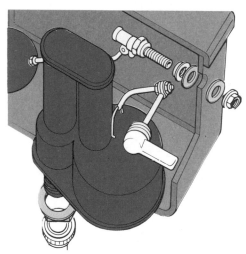

Assemble the inside of the cistern, watching out for the washers.

★ WATCH POINT ★

If the pipe is vitrified clay, wrap a piece of thick cardboard around the cutting line you have made and score against it, right around the pipe, using a tile cutter. The score will ensure a clean cut.

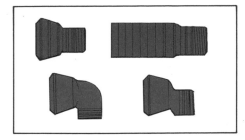

Above: you can connect the WC outlet to the soil pipe using a range of different adapters

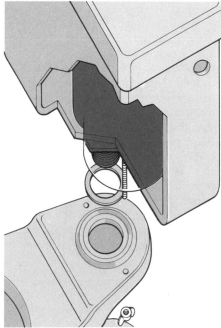

Bolt the cistern of a close coupled WC to the pan with wingnuts. Don't forget the washer

don't let it run away from you.

Once you have cut the pipe, slip the patent connector onto the end of the pan spigot and offer up the pan. (Do the same if you are reusing the socket.) Slip the other end of the connector onto (or into) the soil pipe and juggle the position of the pan until you get a perfect fit. Now mark the positions of the pan fixing holes.

Remove the pan to drill the holes (and plug them, if the floor is solid). Then replace the pan and connector, adjust as necessary, and screw the pan in place. Don't forget to fill the screw sockets with putty prior to tightening or the china may be cracked.

Now you can fit the cistern. On a close coupled suite, centre it on the pan, mark the wall fixing holes and remove. For a low level cistern, offer it up to the wall and get an assistant to help you centre it while you mark the fixing holes. Screw the cistern to

13 *Use an adapter to fit your new WC pan to the soil pipe*

14 *Secure the pan to the floor with brass or plated screws*

15 *Level the cistern and mark screw holes through it on the wall behind. Drill and fix*

16 *Use an adjustable spanner to tighten up the compression joint that connects the water supply to the WC cistern. Check for leaks*

17 *Follow the manufacturer's instructions when you assemble and fit the cistern, paying particular attention to the washer sequence*

the wall. Then, where necessary, screw the flush pipe to the siphon outlet, slip the other end into the pan, and fit the plastic sleeve that seals it.

All that remains is to connect the supply and run out an overflow. The connection for the water supply at the ball valve may be a compression joint or, more likely, a screw joint like the taps. The overflow should be 22mm copper or plastic. Drill the hole through the wall before assembling the run; seal it afterwards by forcing in some non-setting mastic from a gun and patch the hole on the outside wall with exterior filler.

Adapters for both feed and waste pipes will enable you to join modern Metric pipes to old Imperial ones

Connecting to old pipework

This is often the greatest plumbing problem in an old bathroom. On a job of this size it is usually easier to replace an old run in its entirety, rather than trying to extend it.

Supply pipes: If your supply pipes are exclusively lead, scrap them completely and replumb new runs in copper or plastic back as far as the cold storage tank. If they are only partially lead, they will have copper stubs wipe-jointed onto them—in which case connect to these in the normal way. Making your own wiped joints between copper and lead is difficult, and is best left to a professional. In any case, the lead pipes will have only a limited life.

If the supply pipes are galvanized iron, you should be able to buy adapters enabling you to tee-joint new runs in plastic pipe. But don't join iron to copper: the electrolytic action which this sets up will cause the pipes to decay prematurely.

It is quite likely that any existing copper supply pipes are Imperial rather than Metric. You can check—½in. and ¾in. Imperial pipe is measured across the internal diameter, Metric 15mm and 22mm across the external diameter—but in practice it can be quite tricky to be sure of the difference.

If you use a compression joint, you can join 15mm pipe to ½in. pipe without difficulty. To join 22mm to ¾in. requires a special olive. All capillary fittings require special Imperial-Metric adapters.

Drainage: If your waste pipes are lead, your house almost certainly has a two pipe drainage system. In this case, it should be fairly simple to fit a complete new waste pipe in plastic to a hopper head or gully.

If you are connecting into plastic pipes, take a sample with you to the plumber's merchant and get the brand matched—each brand has very slight size variations.

Adapters are available to connect modern 32mm and 38mm pipe to Imperial 1½in. and 1¾in. pipe and also to deal with other, more obscure, Metric sizes, such as 40mm.

If you are not sure of the brand but know the diameter and can match it, use compression fittings with a flexible rubber seal inside (rather than solvent welded joints) to take up any minor variations.

Finishing off

Once you have reinstated the water supply and checked for leaks, the new suite is ready for use. But you should make sealing around the bath and basin a top priority to protect the wall and floor behind.

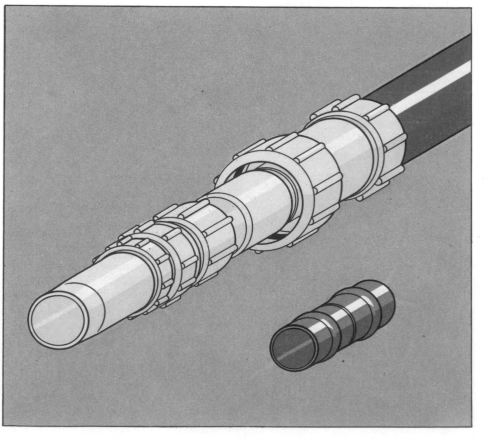

PLUMBED-IN SHOWER

Not only does a permanently plumbed in shower add significantly to the value of your home, but a shower is a hygienic and refreshing way to wash. Another convincing reason for having a shower is that they are economical to use—a five minute shower uses only a quarter of the water needed for the average bath.

Choosing a shower

The simplest type of shower is undoubtedly a rubber push-on hose which is little more than a glorified handspray. This type requires no plumbing but is clumsy to use.

A much better option is a **bath/shower mixer**. This replaces the existing bath taps and has two outlets for the water—one downwards through a single spout into the bath and one upwards to the shower. Changing from one to the other is simply a matter of moving a lever. Bath/shower mixers are sometimes sold complete with a wall bracket or rail for mounting above the bath. These allow the height of the shower to be varied to suit individuals.

Before buying a bath/shower mixer, make sure that it will fit—or can be adapted to fit—the tap holes in your bath.

A third alternative is a **shower-only mixer** which has its own independent hot and cold water supplies. This type gives a

 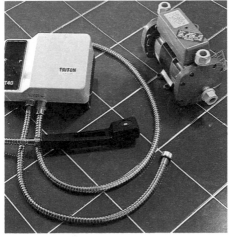

better flow rate than a bath/shower mixer and can be mounted over a bath or in a separate shower cubicle. However, the snag is that, depending on where you put it, there may be a lot of extra plumbing to do.

Shower-only mixers can have one of

You can provide a good shower by fitting a shower-only valve (with blue rose) or a bath/shower mixer unit. Poor water pressure can be improved by fitting a spray booster (above left) or a booster pump (above right)

three types of control: either two knobs with one to regulate the temperature and one to regulate the flow; or hot and cold taps; or a single control to regulate temperature only.

You can get two designs of shower-only mixers—exposed and concealed. With an exposed design, the valve is surface mounted, together with some or all of the connecting pipework; with a concealed design, the pipework and valve are hidden.

Shower mixers have either a rigid or flexible hose which is mounted on the wall to either a bracket or rail.

The last option is an electric shower, which is easy to fit and connect but does not usually give the same flow that a fully plumbed in shower will guarantee.

Siting the shower

You have a choice of putting your new shower over the existing bath, or in a separate cubicle with its own shower tray.

The main advantage of installing a shower over a bath is that the plumbing will be simpler—you won't have to put in a separate waste pipe. On the other hand, if you're prepared to put in the extra pipe-work, there are several benefits to a separate shower cubicle—chiefly that you can put one almost anywhere in a bathroom or small cloakroom, for example.

Plumbing considerations

For bath/shower mixers and separate shower mixers, there are several requirements which will affect whether you can install them and, if you can, the amount of plumbing that you will have to do.

• The hot and cold supplies to the shower must be at the same pressure. With the majority of houses this won't be a problem since they have a cold water cistern which supplies both the cold taps—apart from the kitchen tap—and the hot water cylinder.

However, you may have a system where the hot water cylinder is supplied from a cistern, but all the cold taps are supplied from the rising main. With this type of plumbing, there's a good case for installing an instantaneous electric shower directly to the rising main.

The other type of plumbing system you may have is where all the fittings are connected to the rising main, the hot water being supplied by means of a multipoint gas heater. Again this may mean using an electric shower.

• The second requirement is that the pressure of water for non-electric showers must be sufficient to give a decent flow of water—5 litres per minute. The pressure is measured by the 'head' of water which is taken as the vertical distance between the shower rose and the bottom of the cold water cistern. The minimum head you need is 1m. If you have an insufficient head, it's best to install a shower pump which will boost the flow.

• The third consideration when fitting a shower is safety. If the cold supply to the shower is on the same pipe run as other fittings, the cold supply will be affected when the other fittings are used. This can mean the person using the shower could get scalded when the WC is flushed. The two ways of avoiding this are to provide a new and separate supply pipe for the shower from the cold water cistern; the other is to buy a thermostatically controlled shower mixer valve. With this type of mixer the outlet temperature is controlled so that if

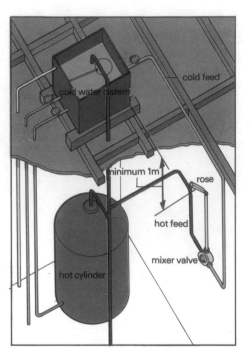

Water supplies can be taken from the cold cistern and the hot cylinder. You need at least 1m of 'head' above the rose for a good shower

the pressure on the cold side drops, the hot flow is reduced accordingly.

The reverse situation can occur with the hot supply—resulting in the shower running cold when a hot tap is turned on somewhere else in the house. This is annoying rather than dangerous, but can be avoided by making sure that the hot connection to the shower is the first from the pipe leading out of the top of the hot water cylinder, before the take-off to any hot taps.

Additional materials and tools

Apart from the shower fitting itself, which should come complete with instructions and all the nuts and washers you need to install it, you may need certain extra materials and fittings.

For a bath/shower mixer, you will certainly want PTFE tape and possibly flexible push-fit tap connectors. For a shower-only mixer, you will want lengths of 15mm flexible piping plus sufficient elbows and T-connectors to complete the supply runs. You may also use wall plugs, pipe clips and either plaster or filler to make good the installation.

If you decide to incorporate a booster pump into the pipework, you have a choice of fitting two types. One goes between the

mixer and the shower spray, while the other is fitted before the mixer to both the hot and cold supply pipes.

To save yourself a lot of extra wiring, it's best to buy a pump which switches on automatically when the shower is used—otherwise you will have to install a ceiling mounted pull-cord switch. It is possible to buy some pumps which have a built-in transformer and operate off low voltages—either 12V or 24V. With these, switches can be wall-mounted and within reach of the shower.

For a bath/shower mixer, the one essential tool is a bath/basin spanner, and you will probably need an adjustable spanner as well, to tighten up the tap connectors. You'll need several tools for a shower-only mixer including a drill and bits, saws and screwdriver.

★ **WATCH POINT** ★

If neither of the supply pipes has a gate valve, drain the cold water system by tying up the ballcock in the cold water cistern and opening both bath taps. Don't turn off the main stopcock or your kitchen tap will be without water.

Fitting a bath/shower mixer

Installing a bath/shower mixer is a straightforward job, as there is no extra plumbing to do. Fitting the mixer is very much like installing any other sort of tap. Before removing the old taps, close the gatevalve on the cold water feed from the cistern and drain down the small amount left in the pipe by opening the cold bath tap. Similarly, turn off the water heating and close the valve supplying the hot water cylinder.

Getting at the bath taps can be awkward—there's not much space at the end of a bath and you'll have to remove the bath side panel to give yourself access.

Disconnect the tap connectors with an adjustable spanner and then use a bath/basin spanner to undo the backnuts holding the taps in place. Be careful not to damage the bath and, if necessary, get someone to hold the taps so that they don't swivel around as you loosen the nuts.

When you've got the old taps off, clean any dirt or old compound from around the holes and polish the ends of the supply pipes with wire wool.

Before attaching the new fitting to the

bath, push on the gasket which goes between the bath and the mixer.

If you need to move the positions of the tap connectors because the shanks on the mixer are either too long or too short, cut back the supply pipes and fit lengths of flexible copper pipe which have tap connectors at one end.

The mixer is fixed to the bath by two large backnuts—these usually need plastic washers and sometimes metal ones, too, between them and the bath. Put the plastic washers on first, followed by the metal washer and then the nut. Tighten up the nuts with a basin spanner.

Before screwing on the tap connectors, wrap a strip of PTFE tape three times around the threads on the shanks of the mixer to seal the joint.

Fix the hose by simply screwing it to the top of the mixer valve—again using PTFE tape to get a watertight join.

If you have one, fit the wall bracket or sliding rail next. Measure the optimum height for the rail—or bracket—and mark its position on the wall. Check that the rail is vertical with a spirit level. Drill clearance holes for suitable wallplugs and fix the fitting in place with chromium plated screws to avoid rusting.

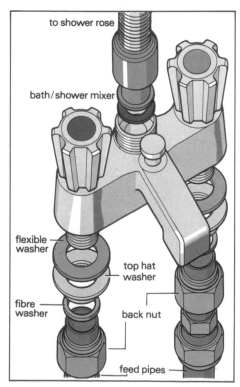

A bath/shower mixer (right) can replace existing taps if the hole separation is suitable. The feed pipes are connected in the same way with a back nut tightened onto the tap tails

After fixing a shower over a bath, you'll need some kind of shower curtain or screen to protect the surrounding idea.

1 *The first step in replacing pillar taps with a bath/shower mixer is to loosen the tap connectors*

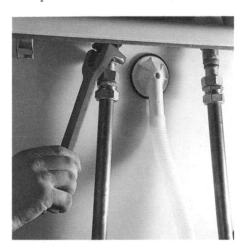

2 *With the tap connectors disconnected, use a bath spanner (crowsfoot) to undo the backnuts holding the taps*

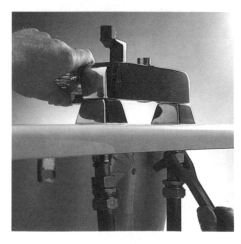

3 *Position the mixer unit, and tighten the back nuts and tap connectors*

4 *Screw the shower rose support bracket to the wall, slip on the chromed shroud and press the rose into place*

Connecting to the supply

New cold water supply: First turn off the water supply to the cistern or, alternatively, tie up the ballcock. Drain the whole system by turning on the bathroom cold taps.

Near the base of the tank, mark the position of the new hole. If you haven't got a tank cutter or hole saw, drill a series of small holes inside a 22mm circle and file the edges clean.

The new pipe is connected to the cistern with a 22mm tank connector. Make sure that you put a nylon washer on either side of the cistern before tightening up the flanged nut on the outside.

Cut, and then fit, a 150mm length of 15mm pipe to the compression end of the connector.

To the other end of the short pipe, fit an isolating wheel valve—again a compression fitting—and from this run 15mm piping to the cold inlet of the mixer.

Tee-ing into an existing pipe: After draining down the system, mark on the pipe where you want to put the fitting—remember that this should be closer to the hot cylinder or cold cistern than any other of the branches.

The gap you need to cut in the pipe to take a tee fitting is somewhat less than the length of the tee—to allow for the length of the pipe that slots inside.

Mark the gap on the pipe with a pencil and cut at right angles.

Insert the 22mm × 22mm × 15mm reducing tee into the gap and tighten up the securing nuts on each end of the tee.

Connect the 15mm pipe to the reducing tee and run this to the appropriate inlet on the mixer valve.

INSTALLING A SHOWER TRAY

A shower is economical and quick to use, more convenient—and less wasteful of water—than taking a bath; it also occupies very little space. If you want the shower to be a completely independent fitting, you must install some type of shower tray, an enclosure or splashback, and a new waste drainage system.

Providing you've got the space you can still install your self-contained shower unit in the bathroom. But if you can arrange the drainage there's no reason why you can't fit it elsewhere—in the bedroom, inside a fitted cupboard, or even in a room of its own—and add considerably to the value and luxury of your home in the process.

Planning considerations

Where you position your shower depends largely on how you're going to dispose of the waste water. Most modern waste systems have the 'single stack' arrangement: all soil and waste pipes discharge directly into a large pipe connected to the drain. But in many older houses the soil waste is dealt with by a separate pipe. The baths and basins upstairs discharge into an open hopper head at the top of another pipe, or downstairs into a gully. Both of these lead in turn to the same drain. In fact, whether you have a one or a two-pipe system, it's usual for sinks and basins on the ground floor to discharge into a convenient gully.

If your shower is to be on the ground floor it's simplest to dispose of the waste water direct into a gully; if it's on an upstairs floor you can either take the new waste pipe to an existing hopper or connect it into the combined waste/soil stack.

Depending on the age of your house, the stack may be made of cast iron or PVC. Leading a waste pipe into a PVC stack is straightforward, although you must identify the make and buy compatible connection fittings—systems aren't usually interchangeable. Cast iron stacks cause more problems: you'll need special connection fittings for these.

Check with your local authority on the recommended pipe fittings—they may specify certain types. Some authorities don't accept push-fit connections and may demand that the first 2m of soil pipe is cast iron.

Once you've worked out how you're going to deal with the waste you can plan your pipe run. This shouldn't exceed a length of three metres for efficient drainage and it should have a slope downwards of between 1° and 5°—equivalent to a drop of between 18mm and 90mm per metre length. Avoid too steep a slope; this can siphon water from the waste trap under the shower tray and such a seal is necessary to prevent smells from entering the house.

A shower tray and surround can be fitted almost anywhere. If you want to build your own plinth, see page 127

Choosing and siting a tray

Shower trays are commonly made in acrylic plastic or glazed ceramics, although you can also buy pressed steel or cast iron types. Acrylic trays are light in weight and come in a variety of colours to match standard ranges of sanitary ware. There's a range of shapes and sizes—triangular, quadrant and square are typical—to suit most locations.

Most types are set on legs and have detachable side panels, giving space underneath for the outlet connections, and some have a raised flange on two sides for fixing the tray direct to the masonry before you start tiling over.

Ceramic trays are also made in various designs and colours, although they don't usually incorporate space underneath to accommodate the trap. Also, they're very heavy and you'll need help to fit one.

The waste outlet—like an ordinary plug-hole but without the plug—may be in the centre of the tray, at one side, or in one corner, so you can position the tray exactly where you want.

The trap should be the shallow 38mm diameter shower/bath type, with a 70mm seal for single stack drainage or a 50mm seal for two-pipe drainage. Use a P-trap where the waste pipe exits direct to the outside, or an S-trap where the pipe must include an internal drop. If your chosen tray doesn't include space underneath for the trap you'll have to cut a hole in the floor—if it's a timber one—and run the trap and waste pipe in the space below. Alternatively

you can mount the tray on a plinth (see Constructing the plinth) to accommodate the trap and pipe. Include an inspection panel for access.

Don't lead the pipe across the joists: you'd have to cut a notch about 40mm deep in the timber, and this would seriously weaken it.

Don't forget to allow sufficient space outside the shower for drying off: you'll probably need about 700mm on the opening side of the tray.

The best place for your shower tray is in a corner—the walls can form part of the enclosure, as long as they're properly water-proofed. For this you can either tile the

surface or fix sheet plastic, glass, or water-proof decorative wallboard.

Ready-made enclosures are available in kit form. They usually consist of an aluminium framework with plastic or glass panels, which you attach to the wall on top of the tray. Most types are adjustable to fit various tray sizes, and some incorporate a system to align the enclosures on out-of-true walls. They generally have sliding or concertina-type doors, which you can also buy separately for fitting to a home-made surround. Various designs of enclosure are made for the different types: freestanding, corner or built-in showers.

It's important to make sure that the

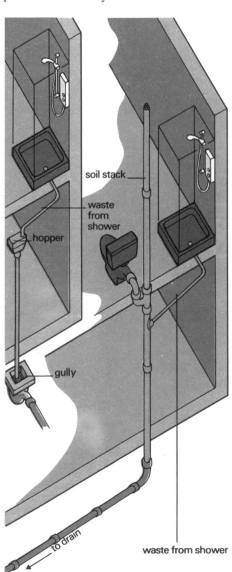

Plan your shower tray's waste disposal. In most modern houses, all soil and waste pipes discharge into one soil stack; in older houses, the shower will need to be fixed up so that it discharges into a gully via an open hopper head

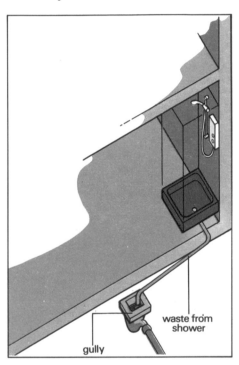

Regardless of the age of the house, it is usual for sinks, basins and showers on the ground floor to discharge directly into a gully. This is usually for simplicity's sake —connecting into a soil stack can be tricky unless there is a convenient hopper head to use

joints between the wall and tray and the surround and tray are sealed against water seepage, using quadrant tiles or a flexible non-setting mastic to fill the gap, followed by an acrylic or silicone sealant. If you fit a shower surround, this too must be sealed so that water cannot get in (see page 132).

Fitting the shower tray

Once you've planned the route of your shower waste pipe you can install the tray in

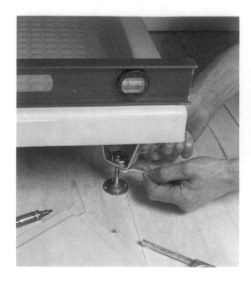

1 *Put the tray in position and adjust the legs until it sits level*

2 *If your tray is fitted with wall brackets, mark their position*

3 *With the tray's position finalized, mark around the feet with a pen*

4 *Remove the feet from the tray and secure them to the floor*

5 *Relocate the tray on its feet, add the securing screws and check for level*

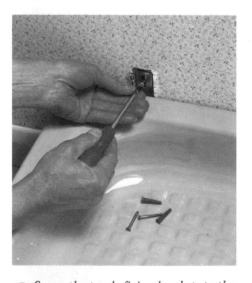

6 *Screw the tray's fixing brackets to the wall. You can make good later*

7 *When you have made the waste connections, fit the side panels*

its final position and attach the trap.

If you're installing an acrylic shower tray with its own plinth all you have to do is fit the waste outlet and trap, attach its short legs and set it on the floor in the position which you require.

The type of supporting leg varies from make to make but they usually consist of angled metal brackets which screw or clip onto the underside of the tray, with threaded feet that can be adjusted for level. Attach the legs first.

Place the tray against the wall. Mark the area of skirting board that needs to be removed so that the tray can be placed flush with the wall. Remove the tray then mark the skirting for cutting. Prise away the skirting board with a claw hammer or bolster chisel to give yourself room to cut

down the lines with a small saw. Protect the wall by levering against a scrap of wood.

Reposition the tray against the wall and adjust the nuts on its feet so that it sits level on the floor; check with a spirit level. If your tray includes a wall bracket, mark its position on the plaster. Hack off a band of plaster so that the tray can be fixed to the

★ **WATCH POINT** ★

It's a good idea at this stage to temporarily assemble the waste connections to your stack or gully, and make any adjustments that may be necessary to avoid straining the pipes or connections.

masonry and the bracket plastered over. Mark around the position of the feet on the floor with a pen.

Turn the tray upside down and remove the feet. Place them over your marks and fix them to the floor with screws (and plugs on a solid floor). Drill and plug the wall to take the wall brackets. Carefully locate the tray on its feet and add the securing nuts. Screw the brackets to the wall.

Reconnect the waste fittings and pour some water into the tray to check for leaks. Separate side panels usually clip onto the tray and locate on the floor battens. Fix these when you've finished making all the waste connections.

Ceramic shower trays sometimes have separate outlet inserts. To fit one of these, press a sausage of plumber's putty around the underside of the fitting then insert the outlet into the hole in the tray and fit its metal washer. Wind PTFE sealing tape around its thread. Screw on the retaining backnut and tighten with an adjustable wrench. This will squeeze putty from the perimeter of the outlet, which you should remove immediately for a neat finish.

Making a water-tight seal around the outlet is one area where many DIY enthusiasts come to grief—but there is no reason why they should. Apply plenty of plumber's putty to the fitting and ensure that it is evenly distributed. Be thorough in your use of the PTFE tape too and then, when you tighten the backnut, you should have a good seal.

On trays that have no built-in plinth you'll have to construct your own (see Constructing a plinth). This is not difficult but you must give careful thought to the position of the waste outlet and any other features peculiar to your room alone.

Cutting a hole for a pipe

When cutting a hole for a waste pipe, you cannot afford to adopt a hit or miss attitude—so draw up a plan.

Basically, you need to construct a square on the interior wall using a reference point common to both sides of the wall—a window for example—and then, using the measurements of the square, draw an identical square on the exterior. Then knock the hole through from both sides, so that you create a neat opening in the middle of the wall.

To cut a hole in your wall to take the waste pipe, first mark its position. Do this by temporarily attaching a short length of pipe to the waste trap so that it touches the

Using a 15mm masonry bit, drill a series of holes around the waste pipe guidelines

Knock through the wall with a club hammer and chisel. Work from both sides

Test fit the waste pipe in the hole— remove it when you're satisfied

wall. Mark the wall neatly around the pipe.

On a thick cavity or 225mm wall it's best to mark the position of the hole inside and out, and then tackle the cutting from both sides. To do this you'll need a common reference point on both sides of the wall, such as a window or another pipe passing through nearby. Measure the height of the reference point from inside floor level and transfer this measurement to the outside. You now have the floor level marked on the outside wall.

Using a spirit level draw a vertical line from the floor level inside to your reference point. You can then transfer this line to the outside wall.

Draw a second vertical line from the inside floor level to pass through your pipe exit point. Measure the distance between the two vertical lines and transfer this line to the outside wall. Inside, measure from floor level to the centre of the waste pipe exit point and transfer this measurement to the outside wall. This gives you a reference for marking the pipe exit point on the outside of the wall.

To cut the hole, starting at one side of the exit point use a 15mm masonry drill to make a series of holes around the perimeter of the guideline. Hack off the plaster from within the guidelines using a slim cold chisel and club hammer. Start to cut out the masonry from the hole, then move to the other side of the wall and repeat the procedure until you break through. Try to keep the sides of the hole as square as possible.

If you're working up a ladder when knocking through from the outside, keep a lookout for people passing below you or cordon off the area.

Constructing the shower plinth

If your shower tray has no integral base with room to take the waste trap, you can make a timber plinth and tile it to match the shower surround or splashback. In this way the plinth is completely integrated.

The plinth is made from four pieces of 150mm × 50mm PAR softwood and one piece of 100mm × 50mm softwood held together with proprietary joint blocks or battens that you can make yourself.

Its overall height—150mm—leaves ample room for the shallow waste trap and there's a gap in the frame to provide access in case of blockages or leaks; you can fit a trap door or leave the access point open.

First take the measurements of the base

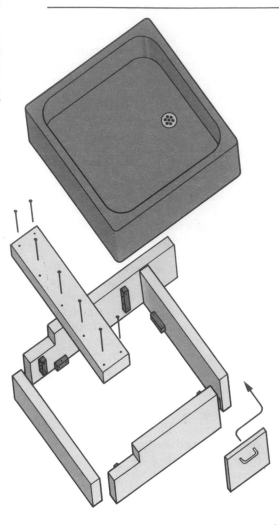

A basic plinth design. Note the access panel and the side panels which are notched for the step

of your shower tray. Turn the tray upside down and measure the distance from the edge of the tray to the inside edge of the outlet. Add on about 50mm for clearance. From this point measure to the front of the tray. Add on 150mm for the step.

Mark out and saw two pieces of timber to this length to form the sides of the plinth. Use a try square when doing this.

Measure the width of the shower tray and subtract 100mm—twice the timber thickness. Cut one piece of 150mm × 50mm and the piece of 100mm × 50mm to this length, to form the front and back of the plinth.

So that the step can be set flush with the top of the plinth, cut a notch in the front edge of both side pieces 150mm wide by 50mm deep.

Assemble the frame with two joint blocks per corner to form a square, with the two notches at the top front edge. As the plinth is to be a permanent fixture you should use the one-piece joint blocks instead of the two-part knock-down type.

1 *Fit a separate outlet insert with plumber's putty*

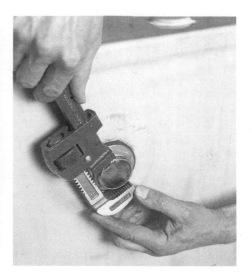

2 *Screw on the retaining back nut and tighten it with an adjustable wrench*

3 *Use the tray as a guide to mark the sides of the plinth for cutting.*

4 *Lay the sides in position and use them to mark the front and back for cutting*

5 *Cut a notch in the top front edge of each side piece ready for the tread*

6 *Use joint blocks or battens to assemble the plinth framework*

7 *Lay the trap on top of the plinth. Adjust until the two are aligned as accurately as possible*

8 *Secure the plinth framework to the floor with joint blocks or battens*

9 *Cut and fit the tread and riser for the plinth step. Hammer all nails home fully for a secure fixing*

★ WATCH POINT ★

Mark out and cut the notches in the two side panels together, by clamping the pieces to a flat surface such as a table top or bench. This not only saves time but also ensures that both notches are identical.

Lay the assembled frame on the floor and place the shower tray on top. Mark the position of the plinth and then remove the tray. Place joint blocks inside the plinth and screw them to the floor and frame.

Return the tray to the plinth and make the waste connections so they are tight and free from any possible obstruction.

Cut a piece of 150mm × 50mm timber to fit across the plinth and attach it to the notched section with waterproof adhesive and 75mm long nails to form the step.

Finish off the plinth with paint or by cladding it with ceramic tiles to match the walls or splashback. If you tile it's best to recess the plinth by the tile thickness so they're exactly flush with the sides of the shower tray.

★ WATCH POINT ★

To fix the joint blocks accurately, lay one of the side frames on the floor with one end butting up to a wall, door or cupboard. Rest one of the shorter lengths on top of the side frame, end on and resting against the upright surface. Place the joint blocks in the angle and mark through their screw holes with a bradawl. Insert the screws. Repeat the procedure for each of the other corners.

Arranging drainage

There are various drainage arrangements you can have for your new shower, depending on its location (see diagram right). If the shower is on the ground floor, simply lead the pipe from the waste trap through the outside wall into an existing gully; if the shower is upstairs you can lead the waste pipe into a hopper head or make a separate connection into the soil stack. Each of these leads in turn to the same drain. If you use plastic solvent-weld or push-fit plumbing connections, the job is very straightforward and requires no special tools or equipment.

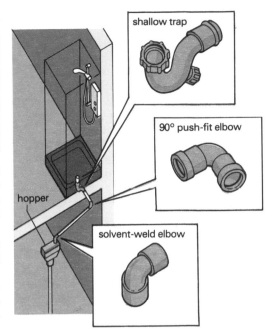

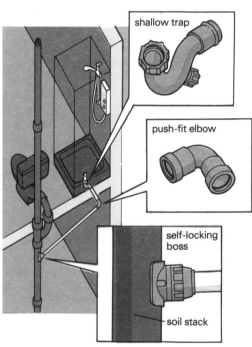

The waste connections for an independent shower are easy to make if you use plastic push-fit and solvent-weld fittings. You need few components to lead the waste to a hopper or gully (above left); even the soil stack connection needs only one extra component. The pipework is all made in 38mm plastic—so be sure to buy fittings compatible with pipes this size

There are, however, some special requirements to bear in mind when you're planning your waste run from the shower:
• for efficient drainage, the waste pipe shouldn't exceed a length of three metres;
• the pipe should slope downwards between

1° and 5° (a drop of between 18mm and 90mm per metre length);
• the waste trap should be the 75mm shallow type made especially for showers and baths;
• the waste pipe must not enter the soil stack within 200mm of a soil branch pipe connecting to the WC (unless you fit a specially designed deflector);
• don't take pipe runs across joists—the size of notch you would have to cut would cause a serious weakness in the timber.

Fitting a shower enclosure

There are many types of shower enclosure you can fit. They're available in kit form and fitted with patterned glass or acrylic panels in various colours.

You can buy various designs of shower surround depending on the location of your shower. These are commonly the corner surround, which consists of two panels (the walls act as the other sides); the built-in type (only one panel fits over a fitted unit) and the freestanding surround, which consists of three panels (the wall makes the fourth side). Some special panels include niches—often on both sides of the panel—to hold soap, towels, cosmetics and other bathing accessories but these tend to be expensive. You can usually fit the door in whichever panel you want for convenience, or even in two sides if there's sufficient room outside for drying off. Doors can be operated in a variety of combinations, usually concertina and sliding.

Before deciding on any particular type of surround, pay a visit to one of the large bathroom or DIY retailers to see what there is on offer. Many of the surrounds will actually be on full display in the store.

Once you've fitted the tray you can make up the waste pipe connections and erect the surround to complete the job.

Making the waste connections

When you've secured the shower tray to the floor, you can make the waste pipe connections into the soil stack, gully or hopper according to your domestic arrangements.

Once you've positioned the tray, cut an exit hole in the wall to take the pipe (see Cutting a hole for a pipe, page 127). To connect the tray to the trap, pass a length of 38mm plastic pipe through the hole from

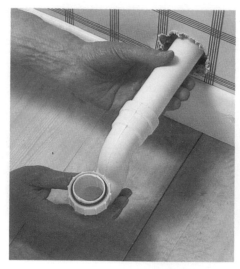

1 *Once you've cut a hole through the outside wall to take the waste pipe, fit the trap to the pipe and test the fit against the tray*

2 *Outside, if you're on the first floor, cut the waste pipe to allow for a 90° elbow to be fitted to divert the waste to a convenient hopper*

3 *Attach a 90° elbow (here, a push-fit) to the protruding pipe then fit a short length of pipe to lead towards the hopper*

4 *Fit a 45° elbow on the end of the pipe to discharge into the hopper. Ensure that the pipe doesn't slope too steeply*

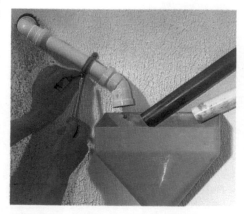

5 *Secure the pipe run at intervals with special plastic brackets which simply clip over the pipe and fix to the wall*

6 *To connect into a plastic soil stack, cut a hole in the stack, and stick in the entry piece of a self-locking boss*

7 *Attach the screw-on section of the boss, the collar, the rubber grommet and the push-fit connection*

8 *Cut a length of waste pipe to lead from the boss connection to the waste outlet, allowing for a 90° elbow conection*

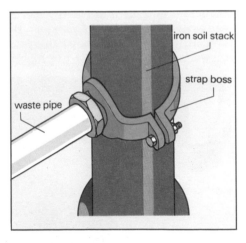

iron soil stack

strap boss

waste pipe

Connecting a waste pipe into a cast-iron soil stack is fairly straightforward, but you'll need a special strap boss connection

the outside. Connect it to the trap, making sure it's fully seated. Mark the pipe on the outside of the wall. You will need to cut it at this point so that you can fit a 90° elbow fitting on its end. This will divert

the pipe so that it runs to the drainage point.

Cut the pipe and attach the elbow using solvent-weld connections, or push-fit sockets. If you use a solvent weld fitting make sure it includes an access plug in case of any blockages.

Connecting to a hopper or gully: Measure how much pipe you'll need to join up the elbow to the hopper or gully, and cut a length to fit. If the pipe is leading to a grating over the gully you'll probably also need to fit a 135° elbow above the grating so that you can attach a pipe from this to below grating level. Make sure that the pipe through the grating stops short of the water level in the gully. You'll probably need to buy a new plastic grating and cut it to take the extra pipe.

If the pipe is going to a hopper, fit a 45° elbow where it discharges into the hopper head itself.

Clip the pipes in place with proprietary brackets at the required points—roughly 500mm intervals is ideal—and ensure that the pipes are aligned without any strain being exerted to hold them.

Connecting to a plastic soil stack: There are basically two methods of connecting your waste pipe into a plastic soil stack. You can lead the pipe to a convenient 'boss branch', a section of the stack which includes a spare entry point, or you can fit a special self-locking boss connection.

To break into a boss branch you have to cut out the circle of plastic within the entry point and fit a special socket adaptor. The procedure may vary slightly according to the make of pipe but usually consists of solvent-weld fittings.

Cut the hole in the pipe using a special 38mm diameter hole cutter attachment to an electric drill. If you haven't one of these you can drill a row of holes at the perimeter of the entry point in the boss and insert a padsaw blade to cut out the section. Be sure that the circle of plastic doesn't accidentally fall into the soil stack.

To fit a self-locking boss, cut a hole to take the entry piece and attach the collar piece and pipe entry section. Fittings vary from make to make but usually consist of solvent-weld connections and adapters.

Connecting to a cast iron soil stack:

There are similar fittings for connecting up a plastic waste system to a cast iron stack. But most involve either cutting a hole in the stack to take the pipe and adapter, or the fitting of a special conversion socket or 'strap boss', which is clamped around the cast iron stack.

Cast iron isn't easy to cut without special tools so the easiest solution to the problem is to remove an entire section of the stack between the two joints and replace it with a plastic section. For this you'll have to fit an adapter at both ends of the run to take the new pipe. You can then fit a new boss branch in the run and connect your shower waste to it, as previously described.

Erecting the shower surround

Proprietary shower surround kits are available to suit most types of tray. The type you choose depends on whether you want a completely freestanding cubicle or just a corner arrangement.

There are many designs of shower enclosure but your choice will be governed, to some extent, by the position of your tray —in a corner arrangement, freestanding, or built-in. The basic corner arrangement consists of two panels—one or both including doors—which are each fixed to a wall. The walls make up the other two sides of the enclosure and then the shower head can be fitted on to whichever wall suits you better.

Freestanding surrounds consist of three panels (with various door arrangements) fixed against a single wall.

The third basic arrangement is used where the shower is fitted into an existing cupboard or alcove and is simply a single panel with door which completes an enclosure already three parts constructed.

When buying an enclosure, bear in mind that the panels containing the doors (sliding or folding) should be fitted in the best position for you simply to step outside where you can dry off.

Methods of assembling kit surrounds vary considerably from make to make but most consist of an aluminium frame with glass or plastic panels. Many include a feature that enables the frame pieces to be adjusted to suit different sizes of tray, and have easily assembled slot-in corner brackets—often made of plastic.

Fitting a surround usually involves the following procedure. Mark the position of the wall uprights on the wall using a spirit level to ensure they're truly vertical.

1 *Complete your shower tray plinth, once you've made the waste connections, with a tiled panel providing access to the trap*

2 *To erect the surround, place the first upright against the wall, check its level with a spirit level and mark the fixing positions*

Attach the uprights with screws—usually provided in the kits—driven into wallplugs.

If you're fixing the surround to a tiled wall, stick a piece of masking tape to the tiles below the fixing hole positions. This enables you to mark the surface more easily and will prevent the drill bit from sliding on the glazed finish.

Attach the first side panel—which might contain the door—to the upright and adjust the length, if necessary, to fit the tray. Add the second panel and adjust its size. Locate the top and bottom runners in the corner brackets and again check that the frame is perfectly square. If the tiles haven't been fixed truly vertically you should adjust the level of the surround uprights to follow the line of the grouting. Otherwise the surround will appear crooked—even if it's not.

If you're making a corner cubicle you can then locate the door on its runners and check that it opens smoothly. If you're making a completely freestanding cubicle you'll have to add the front panel. Again check the operation of the door.

Should the door not slide smoothly you can lubricate the runners with a little vaseline although you should also check that there isn't any distortion of the frame.

Rubber seals in the frame may require lubricating with silicone lubricant—although you can use washing-up liquid—before you insert their panels.

To complete the cubicle you'll have to seal the joins between frame and wall, and frame and tray, with a proprietary sealant. Use a flexible waterproof sealant for this, taking care to apply it in one continuous bead along the full length of each join. Be particularly careful around the plinth area as that will be the most likely source of trouble.

3 *Drill and plug the wall in the marked fixing positions, return the upright to the wall and screw it in place. Take care not to damage wall tiles*

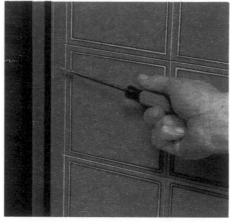

4 *On a flat surface, first assemble the top and bottom frames with the plastic corner brackets and then attach the glazed panels*

5 *Lift up the frame and panel assembly onto the tray making sure it's perfectly square and level. Adjust the screws to alter the level*

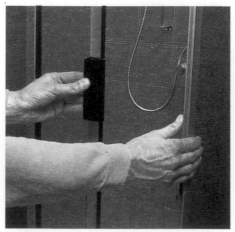

6 *Install the door panels in their tracks, fit the screw-on handle and test the operation of the door. Make any adjustments which are necessary*

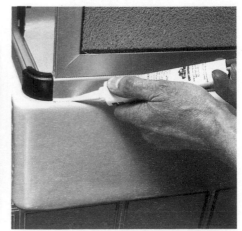

7 *Carefully seal the join between the shower surround and the tray, and the surround and wall, using a flexible mastic sealer*

TOWEL RAIL

A heater not only gives a special touch of comfort to a bathroom—ensuring warm, dry towels—but also helps prevent condensation. Many different types of bathroom heater are on the market, so you should be able to find one to suit your home.

Types available

Which type of bathroom heater you should choose depends a lot on your current heating arrangements and on the size of your family, so consider the various options before you start work. Listed below are the most common heating systems.

• **Wet central heating:** If you have a 'wet central heating system'—one with radiators—then arranging a bathroom towel heater is usually quite simple. You may already have a radiator in the bathroom—in which case all you need to keep towels warm and dry is a clip-on towel rail. These are relatively cheap, come in different styles and

sizes to fit almost any make and size of central heating radiator, and are very easy to fit: they just clip round the radiator without the need for any extra plumbing.

If you have no heater in the bathroom, you might like to add one. This is usually a relatively simple plumbing job consisting of connecting a couple of branches of new pipework to nearby central heating pipe runs. In this case, there are three types of heater you could install. The first is an **ordinary radiator**, probably with a clip-on towel rail. This is often the most sensible solution—radiators are relatively cheap, and because they come in a wide range of sizes you can be sure of getting one large enough to heat the bathroom thoroughly. The second type is a simple **heated towel rail**. This is basically a number of chrome-plated pipes joined together to form a towel rail. They give lots of space to hang towels on, but generally give off little heat; they can also be expensive. A **radiator/rail** is a combination of the two other types—a towel rail mounted on (or alongside) an ordinary radiator.

Whether you have a radiator in the bathroom or not, you might prefer to connect a heater into the hot water circuit—there are several definite advantages for this method depending on your plumbing system.

• **No central heating or hot water boiler:** Some houses, especially in countries other than the UK, do not have water boilers—heating may be provided by warm air units or electric storage heaters; hot water by immersion heaters or instantaneous boilers. Here, the usual answer to keeping towels in the bathroom warm is to install an electrically-operated oil-filled towel rail—see page 135. These are easy to install, but in most countries, electricity is an expensive form of heating.

• **Hot water boiler:** Some houses without a central heating system heat the hot water with a boiler of some sort which feeds a hot water cylinder. You should tap into the pipes connecting the boiler and cylinder and run a heated towel rail from this.

Even if you have central heating, this method has several sound advantages over plumbing in a radiator in the normal way. The rail stays hot even when the heating is switched off in the summer. And in most houses, the pipes between the boiler and the hot water cylinder pass close to the bathroom, so installation is easy and relatively inexpensive to carry out.

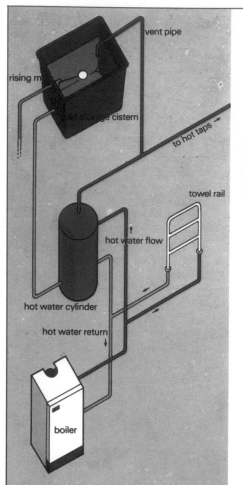

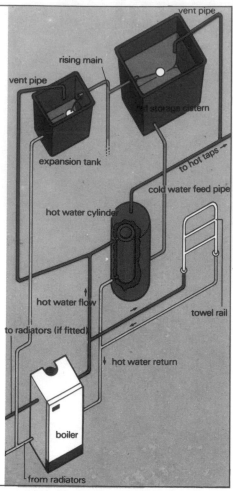

A normal hot water heating system consists of a boiler on the ground floor connected by flow and return pipes to the hot water cylinder on the floor above. The water in the cylinder constantly circulates through the boiler, being heated as it passes through—this is known as gravity flow and is entirely automatic (left).

If a radiator is connected across the flow and return pipes, then the water will circulate through this, too—warming the radiator and so the bathroom.

The system show (left) is the direct heating type—the water that circulates through the boiler is the same as that which comes out of the hot taps. You cannot use normal steel panel radiators with this sytem: they would quickly corrode. You can use only heated towel rails which are designed for connection to a direct system—these are made of copper and therefore you will find that corrosion isn't a problem.

The system shown (right) is the indirect heating type—the boiler water circulates through a coil in the cylinder, heating the water that comes out of the taps indirectly —wet central heating systems use this

arrangement, but you may also find it on a hot water only system.

Once filled, the boiler water is more or less unchanging, so corrosion isn't a problem. You can use any form of radiator, radiator/rail or heated towel rail, connecting it across the flow and return pipes as shown.

You may have a fully pumped indirect system—there is a pump on the flow or return pipes. You must fit the towel rail connections before the pump in either case—on the boiler side of the flow pipe, on the cylinder side of the return pipe.

Planning ahead

Your first job is to find out what plumbing system you have, so you can decide which types of bathroom heater you can install. The connections at the water cylinder won't help you much—they look the same for direct and indirect systems. You must look elsewhere for other clues and signs.

If you have wet central heating you can assume you have an indirect system, unless the heating system is very old. You can also

assume the system is indirect if it has an **expansion tank**—a small cistern (in addition to the cold water cistern) usually in the loft, connected to the hot water flow and return pipes as shown above.

This leaves systems without central heating or an expansion tank. These will usually be direct, but could use a form of indirect cylinder called a **single feed**, of which the Primatic is the best-known brand in the UK. If it isn't labelled as such, the only way you can be sure is to unscrew the immersion heater after draining down the system (see Draining down, page 138) and peer inside with a torch—any sign of tanks or pipes within the cylinder means it's the indirect type.

Now trace the thick flow and return pipes between the boiler and hot water cylinder. Note the points where you could easily cut into them to form branches: somewhere accessible, and preferably just below the level of your proposed heater. The easiest place is likely to be near the hot water cylinder where the thick flow and return pipes enter and exit from the cylinder (see left). These will generally be in the airing cupboard next to the bathroom itself.

Aim to put the towel rail (or radiator) close to the point you intend to have the branch connections—at the least, ensure the run has as few bends, twists and horizontal sections in it as possible.

Some 'fully pumped' systems have a pump on the flow or the return pipes of the boiler to help the circulation of hot water around the entire system. It's wise to connect the pipes **before** the pump—on the boiler side of the flow pipe, on the cylinder side of the return.

There may also be a fixture called a 'diverter valve' that decides whether to send the hot water to the radiators or to the hot water cylinder. It's important to connect the towel rail pipework **before** the diverter so that it receives hot water whenever the boiler is working. If you're in any doubt, always seek professional advice.

Check the size of the boiler pipes. They are likely to be at least 28mm diameter and could be 35mm; modern, fully-pumped central heating systems may use 22mm (it's easiest to measure the circumference: 28mm pipe is 89mm in circumference; 35mm is 110mm; 22mm is 70mm).

What you need

Apart from the towel rail, the major item you need is piping. The usual choice for this is 15mm pipe, but if you use a radiator

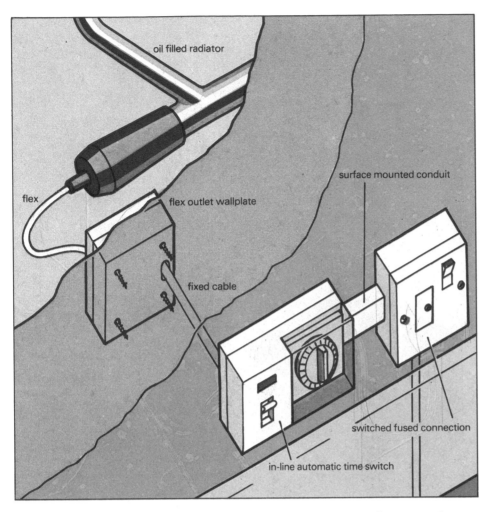

oil filled radiator

flex

flex outlet wallplate

fixed cable

surface mounted conduit

switched fused connection

in-line automatic time switch

it joins directly to the towel rail or runs along skirtings. But if you don't use it, you could paint the copper pipe to match the colour of your skirting boards instead.

★ WATCH POINT ★

Check the towel rail in the position you want it before screwing it home. Make sure there are no obstructions, such as joists, which might make fitting the pipework more difficult than it need be. Nails will indicate the position of the joints below.

Fitting the heater

It's easiest to start at the end, by first fixing the towel rail firmly into place.

On a timber-framed wall, make sure any wall mounting points will be into studs, not hollow cavities.

Towel rails are mounted in various ways, though it's usually fairly straightforward. Some are screwed to the wall and floor using mounting plates. Others are mounted like ordinary radiators—you fix brackets to the wall, then hook the fitting itself over these. Measure off both the brackets and the hooks on the towel rail carefully, so you can work out exactly where to fit the brackets: there is only a little room for error here.

On timber-framed walls, you should try to screw into the studs, because towel rails are heavy fixtures. But with ones that sit on the floor you can use cavity wall fittings.

Electric oil-filled radiators are connected directly to the main supply. In the UK, you must wire the radiator to a proper fused connection unit. The unit can be connected into the power circuit in the same way, and following the same rules, as for an ordinary power outlet.

You can't have a switch inside the bathroom where it could be reached by anybody in the bath, so it's best to switch from the outside. Fit the switched connection unit outside and a flex outlet wallplate inside. An in-line automatic time-switch provides automatic control.

Alternatively, use an unswitched unit and a pull-cord switch

rather than a towel rail, and if it is a long way from the boiler pipework (more than three metres, say) a better choice is 22mm pipe. To take advantage of this, you would need a radiator with larger than normal connections: ask your supplier for guidance on this. Copper pipe is the most widely used, but in the UK plastic pipe can sometimes be used as well.

You will need tee connectors to form the branch with the boiler pipes. You cannot

use the easy-fix types of connector because they are unlikely to be available in large enough sizes to allow the circulation water to flow freely enough under gravity. Again, because boiler pipes are so big, you probably will not be able to use the modern plastic and push-fit types of connector. In most cases, ordinary **compression tees** are what you will need—with 28mm ends (or whatever your boiler pipes are) and 15mm in the branch. If you have, and can use, a blow lamp you could use soldered **capillary tees** instead. After this connection, you can change to plastic pipe and fittings if you find them more convenient.

At the towel rail end, use radiator valves: make sure these suit the connections on the rail and will mate with 15mm pipe. The easiest type to fit can be screwed into the radiator using an ordinary spanner; other types need a large Allen key for this job.

In between, you should need hardly any fittings—you will have to decide where, and which ones, for yourself. Pipes that run along walls or parallel to joists will need supporting frequently with clips.

Stainless steel 15mm pipe might look neater at the towel rail end—at least where

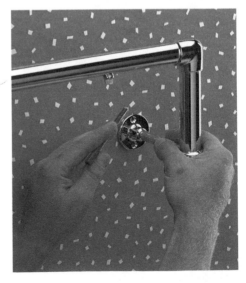

1 *Fit the wall brackets to the towel rail then mark fixing holes at wall or floor level for screws and wallplugs*

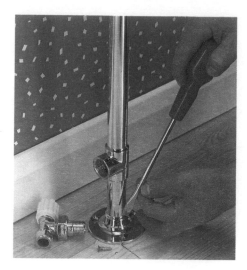

2 *Adjust the position to avoid floor joists, then drill, plug and fix at floor and wall. Use a spirit level to make sure the towel rail is upright*

Routeing the pipework

Careful routeing of the pipework between the boiler pipes and the radiator is vital if you want the job to look good, and the rail to work satisfactorily.

The basic aim you should follow in running the pipe is to ensure that it rises gradually, but consistently, from its connections with the boiler pipes to its connections at the towel rail. Any dips in this circuit could stop the gravity flow circulation of the heating water round this circuit, and could also cause airlocks at the top of the rail.

If the only place you can make the boiler pipe connections is **above** the level of the towel rail, you could still have a satisfactory system—but it would be sensible for you to

3 *Underfloor routeing is best—try to run the pipes parallel to the joists. Use pipe clips to secure the pipes along their length, preferably at 450mm intervals*

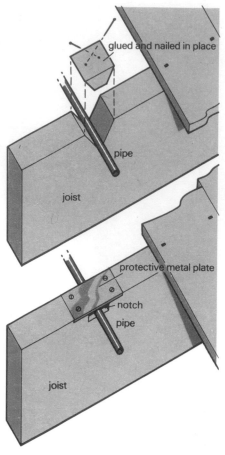

Crossing joists means cutting notches— you may not have room to drill holes

get professional advice first.

The easiest arrangement is to run the pipework along the wall at skirting board level. The amount of rise you need is not very great: a few millimetres per metre run is usually sufficient—so the pipe runs, even though exposed, will still look fairly neat. It is best at this stage not to fix the sections of

4 *If it's inconvenient to clip the pipes to the sides of the joists, use battens as shown to support the pipes between them. Allow a small gap for expansion*

pipe permanently together—fit only the main lengths of pipe, clipping them to the wall with plastic pipe clips. Leave yourself plenty of leeway to work round the boiler pipe and rail connections. If you have to run the pipes under a suspended floor, then you should still be able to arrange for a rise so long as they run parallel to the joists. Again, clip the main lengths of pipe to the sides of the joists—or at least support them underneath with carefully driven nails.

Running pipes **across** the joists is a little more tricky. You must make notches in the tops of the joists to take the pipes, and it is often difficult to make these so that the pipe lies snugly with the correct rise in it. One answer is to cut the notches a fraction deeper than needed, and pack out to the correct depth with pieces of felt or old carpet. Packing round the pipes like this is a good idea in any case—it helps reduce the creaking noises when the pipes heat up or cool down. However, take great care not to cut the notches deeper than absolutely necessary, for it weakens the joists.

★ WATCH POINT ★

Making the preliminary connections to the towel rail—called **dressing**—is often easier if you do it before fitting the rail in place. It also makes it easier to see exactly where the pipes will run before you cut the floor.

Making connections

The bulk of the work of installing a towel rail is in making the connections at either end of the pipe run.

Make the connections at the towel rail end first—then you will only need to interrupt the existing plumbing for a short time.

Radiator valves usually come in two parts. One part is a straight connector which screws into the towel rail or radiator bottom connections. Wrap a good measure of PTFE tape round the screw thread, and then screw tightly home. At the top of an ordinary radiator, there are other connections to be made up. One is a blanking plug, simply to fill in an unwanted hole; the other is an air vent plug which has a bleed nipple in it which you can open to allow trapped air to escape. These are similarly screwed in place after wrapping PTFE tape round the thread. You will almost certainly need a large Allen key for these.

In some cases, you will be supplied with

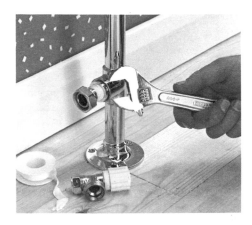

5 Fit the valves to the inlet and outlet holes of the towel rail—use PTFE tape on the connector only so that you can adjust the position of the valve to meet the pipework

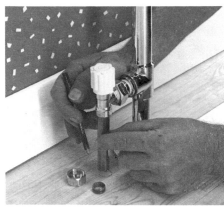

6 Mark the floor where you need to drill holes for the pipes—use an offcut of pipe to mark the hole position and make sure that it is immediately below the valve opening

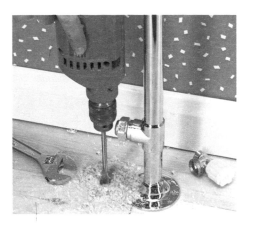

7 Remove the valve itself to drill the hole. Use a 16mm flat bit and power drill. Hold it upright to avoid damaging the valve connector when the drill breaks through the surface

8 Start the connections at the towel rail end. Assemble the first elbow joint and slide the pipes into place. Connect one end to the valve and support the pipes with clips

9 Connect the other end of the towel rail in the same way—direct the pipework along the same route as the first. You'll need to cross a joist to do so (see Routeing pipes on page opposite)

10 At the cylinder end, drain the pipes and mark them for the connectors on the flow and return pipes. You may need to use special 'crossovers' to avoid obstructing pipes

11 Cut through the pipes with a hacksaw and deburr the ends, inside and out. Fit the connectors—you may need to loosen the pipes in order to slide them into place

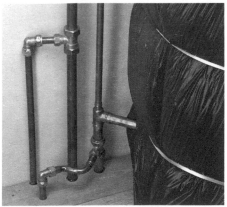

12 Connections at the boiler/cylinder circuit should look like this—the flow pipe connection should be higher than the return pipe connection to aid the circulation

two valves—one control valve for the flow into the towel rail and one for the return out of the towel rail. Make sure you fit them the right way round—if necessary, label the valves and pipework to avoid confusion.

The radiator valves themselves fit on the end of the straight fitting—the connection here, which is part of the fitting, is a type of compression joint: you can do it up loosely and still move the valve around to line it up with the pipework. When making the joint, smear the metal mating surfaces with a coat of jointing compound or PTFE tape. The other end of the valve has a normal compression joint to connect it to the pipe. Connect this one loosely by tightening by hand—without jointing tape or compound —until you're absolutely ready to make the rest of the connections to the flow and return pipes on the radiator.

At this stage, you should be ready to connect the whole new system to your boiler pipes. It's also worthwhile running through the job to anticipate problem areas such as changes in direction and boiler pipe connections.

First, drain down the relevant part of the system (see this page). Then begin connecting the pipes between the towel rail and the boiler pipes (see page 136). Work from the towel rail back towards the boiler/cylinder circuit, using any type of joint you prefer—there's really not much difference between them on a job like this. Compression joints are generally the easiest to make—especially for underfloor routeing where there's the risk of starting a fire.

With your tee-fitting in hand, measure the amount that you will have to cut out of the boiler pipework—this is the length of the body of the fitting less twice the amount that the pipe will disappear into the connector when it is inserted.

Mark this distance on the boiler pipes at the exact point that you want the towel rail pipes to branch from, and cut out the section of pipe carefully with a hacksaw.

Your next problem is going to be inserting the long body of the fitting into the short gap you have cut out. There may be some 'slack' already in the pipes, or you may have to remove some pipe clips to give you a bit of leeway. In extreme cases, you will need to dismantle a whole section of pipe by unscrewing at the nearby compression joint.

Before tightening your new tee, connect the branch run to it, and make sure all the pipework aligns neatly and without strain. If the pipes don't lie easily and loosely in the fitting, the chances are that the joint will not be watertight. Faults like this are easier to remedy now than at a later stage, even if it means you have to remake a whole section of pipework.

Double-check your joints; refill the system; and test with cold water before relighting the boiler. Then heat the water, and check again—keep your eye on the joints for a couple of days after installation: leaks may take a little time to show up.

★ WATCH POINT ★

Before starting work on the existing system, double-check that the rest of your installation is finished and sound. Then check that you have all the tools and materials that you might want for the next stage.

Draining down

The procedure for draining the boiler pipes varies a little depending on whether you have a fully indirect system or not.

With a fully indirect system you should first switch off the boiler and let it go cold.

Cut off the water to the expansion tank by closing the valve, or tie up the ball valve using a stick and a piece of string.

Locate a drain tap on the lower boiler pipe, usually close to the boiler. Attach a hose to the drain tap and lead it outside. Open the tap and let the system drain for a few minutes.

The hot water cylinder will remain full, and if you have an immersion heater you can still use it to provide hot water for baths or for washing up.

With any other sort of system you follow the same procedure, except that you cut off the water by closing a valve on the pipe between the cold water storage cistern and the hot water cylinder. If you haven't got a valve on this pipe, you must cut off the flow into the storage cistern, or tie up its ball valve. You will be emptying the hot water cylinder, so you will have no hot water until you refill. And, if you have to cut off the flow to the storage cistern, you will have no cold water (except in the kitchen).

13 *Tie up the ball valve at the expansion tank (or the cold water tank in a direct system). This will prevent the tank from refilling when drained*

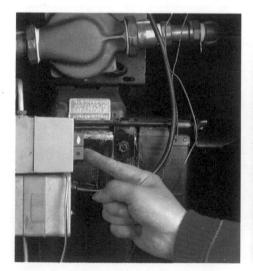

14 *Switch off the boiler and allow it to cool. With an indirect system, you can still use the hot water but with a direct system you should also switch off immersion heaters*

15 *Drain the boiler. Attach a hose to the lower drain plug and unscrew the plug. Allow the system to drain down—it may take some time to clear all the pipes, so be patient*

INSTALLING AN EXTRA WC

An extra WC can be a real asset in a home if, for example, you have an elderly or disabled person living with you. But it isn't always easy to install a new WC exactly where you want it because of the need to accommodate a bulky 100mm diameter waste pipe, which links the pan with the soil stack, and so the drain. In addition conventional waste discharge from a WC works on a gravity principle, which limits the length of the waste pipe (6m maximum) and requires a positive 'fall' to ensure that the waste drains away efficiently.

It is now possible to buy a device that eliminates the need for a large-diameter waste pipe with its limited length and steep 'fall'. Basically, it's a compact pump and shredder unit, which connects directly to the back of the WC pan and liquidizes solid waste before discharging it through small bore copper or solvent-weld PVC pipe to the soil stack. The pumped discharge allows a much longer pipe run between the amount of fall needed. However, the unit is only

meant for those locations where conventional drainage is impossible. Because of the special nature of the system you must have planning approval from your local authority before you begin the installation.

Operation of the device is automatic following the flushing of the WC. As the waste flows into the unit, it triggers a pressure switch, which operates an electric motor to drive the stainless steel shredder blades and pump. A fine mesh filter limits particle size before the slurry is pumped away through the outlet.

The discharge pipework needs a minimum bore of 18mm, which equates with the kind of pipework used in central heating systems. This makes it suitable for running floor/ceiling voids, hollow partition walls or along skirtings.

The system offers considerable flexibility in siting of the WC, making it ideal for garage or loft conversions, extensions and so on. It is advisable to site your new WC as close to the existing soil stack as possible to

minimize the amount of disruption to your home during the installation.

Planning considerations

The most important point to remember is that the installation of a new WC, or any plumbing work that involves modifying or adding to the building's existing waste system, must have the approval of your local building inspector. So, consult him with your plans before you begin work; he will probably want to inspect the finished installation.

You must have access to a suitable electrical circuit to provide power for the unit and a suitable cold water supply to feed the WC cistern.

The unit can be positioned up to 30m from the soil stack, but ideally it should be near an outside wall, through which the cistern's overflow pipe and the unit's vent pipe can be passed if that is acceptable to your local authority. Plan the pipe run carefully, keeping it as straight as possible and bearing in mind the need for a slight fall of 5mm in every metre.

The unit will pump the waste vertically, if required, but the maximum distance is limited to 2m—an important consideration if you're installing it in a basement.

Ample ventilation is essential, and if there is no openable window nearby, you'll have to fit an extractor fan. Also, remember that a room containing a WC must not open directly on to a living room or a kitchen; there must be a ventilated lobby in between.

Tools and materials

The exact tools you require will vary from one installation to another and with the pipe materials chosen. However, the following are essential: spirit level, steel measuring tape, pencil, electric drill, masonry and wood bits, bradawl, screwdriver, junior hacksaw, flat and half-round files, wire wool, two adjustable wrenches, long cold chisel, club hammer, wire strippers or a sharp knife. A small electrical screwdriver is also necessary.

If you plan to use copper pipe with capil-

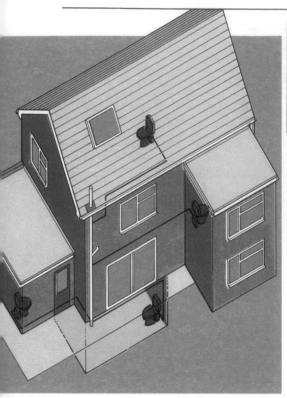

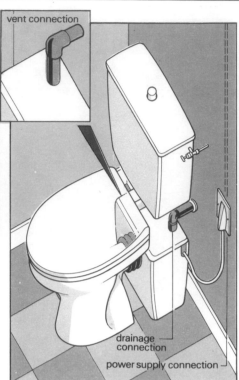

vent connection

drainage
connection

power supply connection

An extra WC can be installed in several locations around the house. If you have an elderly or disabled person living with you an added WC in a 'granny' flat is a great help. If you are planning a loft or basement conversion, an extra WC is well worth considering. The pump in the unit enables you to locate a WC below your existing drainage run provided that the distance is less than 2m. Locate the new WC with care to allow for as little structural change as possible

lary fittings, you'll also need a blow torch, flux, solder (if you're using end-feed fittings), protective gloves and a flame proof mat (to protect skirtings). If you're using plastic solvent-weld pipe and fittings, you'll need a tin of cleaning fluid and a tin of solvent cement.

For the actual plumbing, you'll need sufficient lengths of copper or PVC pipe and the appropriate fittings to make the vent and waste runs from the unit, the feed pipe to the cistern and to take the overflow pipe from the cistern.

Jubilee clips are needed to connect the vent and waste outlets of the unit to the appropriate pipe runs and to secure the flexible coupler to the pan outlet. If there is no convenient boss branch on the soil stack to connect into, you'll want a suitable strap or saddle boss to make the connection.

The unit needs a 3 amp fused connection unit with front flex outlet suitable for use in bathrooms and this, in turn, can be fed from

In most situations local authorities insist that the unit be vented to an external wall or into the existing soil stack. In some cases it is possible to vent the unit internally but the air inlet cowl must be above the height of the WC pan

a lighting circuit (with 1.5mm² cable) or a ring main (with a 2.5mm² cable). If you're not taking the power directly from the back of a socket or loop-in ceiling rose, you'll also need a three-terminal junction box of the appropriate rating.

Other items you may need are: a length of conduit, cable clips, wall plugs, a small bag of ready-mixed mortar and some all-purpose filler for making good.

Installing the unit

The shredder unit is freestanding, so there's no need to make any mounting holes; simply position it where you want the WC and connect up the outlet pipes.

Stand the shredder unit in the appropriate position close to the wall, allowing enough clearance so that it won't be wedged in place by the pan when that is installed.

Connect the vent pipe first; exactly what you do here depends on the requirements of your local authority. Generally, it should be taken through an outside wall or connected to the soil stack so that it can be safely vented to the atmosphere.

You can use either copper or solvent-

weld PVC pipe for the vent. Cut a short length and push this into the moulded vent outlet on the top of the unit, securing it with a jubilee clip. If the unit is against an outside wall and you are not required to connect the vent to the soil stack, you can simply take the pipe back through that wall: cut a suitable hole with a cold chisel and club hammer, keeping it as small as possible to reduce the amount of making good needed later. Run a length of pipe through the hole and connect it to the short length already attached to the vent outlet with an elbow fitting. On the other side of the wall you may be required to run the pipe to above eaves level, so fit another elbow and run the pipe vertically upwards. Clip it at 1.2m intervals and fit the cowl supplied with the unit to the top.

If there's no outside wall nearby, or if your local authority requires you to connect the vent pipe to the soil stack, run the vent pipe alongside the waste pipe.

The unit's waste outlet is an elbow fitting on the top, which may be turned as necessary to face the direction of the waste pipe run. Adjust its position and then take the flexible pipe supplied and push one end over the elbow's spigot, securing it with a jubilee clip. The other end of this pipe should be taken to the rigid waste pipe run, making sure that any bend in it has as large a radius as possible to prevent it becoming kinked and causing a blockage. Push the end of the flexible pipe over the end of the waste pipe and secure it with a jubilee clip.

Make the pipe run to the soil stack, keeping it as straight as possible, with any bend being of large radius. Keep the number of fittings to the minimum and clip the pipe to the wall at 1.5m intervals so that it's supported adequately.

When running pipes beneath the floor,

★ WATCH POINT ★

Lubricating the lip of the coupler will help in fitting it to the pan outlet. Use petroleum jelly or a little washing up liquid to make the job easier.

clip them to the sides of the joists or to battens fitted between the joists. If they need to cross the joists, this should be done at right angles to the joist run. Cut notches for the pipes in the tops of the joists so that they're positioned beneath the centres of the floorboards above; this will reduce the likelihood of them being accidentally pierced by a nail when the boards are

★ WATCH POINT ★

Draw a pencil line on the floor round the base of the pan to mark its exact position. You will then be able to align it more accurately after the holes have been drilled.

replaced. Don't cut the notches any larger than they need be, otherwise you run the risk of weakening the joists.

Allow a fall on the pipe of 5mm in every metre, and after about 13.5m you'd be wise to connect into pipework of larger bore (about 40mm is adequate), which will reduce the load on the pump. If you have laid out the pipe run so that the unit pumps vertically upwards at first, the discharge pipe should be connected to a pipe with a minimum bore of 30mm and a positive fall immediately after the vertical run. This will ensure that the waste flows away freely and that there's no possibility of backflow or back siphonage.

Run the waste pipe as close as possible to the soil stack before breaking through the outside wall (assuming, of course, that the stack is not run in a duct inside the house). Cut a short length of pipe to run through the wall and connect it to the pipe from the unit with an elbow fitting. Add another elbow and straight length of pipe to link to the soil stack itself. Run the PVC vent pipe to an external wall or the soil stack using the same method as you have for the waste pipe.

When all the pipework has been completed, the pan and cistern can be installed.

You may be faced with connecting into either a plastic or cast-iron soil stack, and the former is much easier than the latter due to the 'workability' of the material.

If you are lucky, there may be a convenient boss branch with a spare entry point on a plastic stack, but even if there isn't, connection is still straightforward with a self-locking boss connection.

If there is a spare entry, simply open it up with a hole saw—or drill a series of holes round the edge and cut out the blanking piece with a padsaw—and fit a special connector. The waste branch must be solvent-welded to the connector.

A self-locking boss is fitted by cutting a hole in the side of the stack, inserting one half of the boss and screwing the outer half to it. The waste branch is fitted as before.

The methods of breaking into a cast iron stack are similar to those used with plastic stacks. However, since the material is more difficult to cut, it may be easier to remove a

1 *Position the shredder unit. Attach the internal vent or mark the external vent position; clip into place*

2 *Attach the flexible pipe to the waste outlet fitting of the shredder unit. Secure it with a jubilee clip*

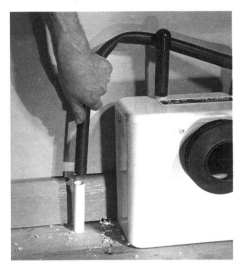

3 *Fix the other end of the flexible pipe to the end of the rigid waste pipe run. Keep curves to a minimum*

4 *Run the rigid waste pipe under the floor boards to the soil stack, clipping the pipe to the joists where necessary*

★ WATCH POINT ★

Although not essential, it is a good idea to fit a stopcock to the inlet pipe just before it reaches the cistern, simplifying any future maintenance by eliminating the need to drain the entire cold water system to be able to work on the WC cistern. Fit a short length of pipe to the ballvalve inlet connector and then install the stopcock at a suitable point.

★ WATCH POINT ★

In some instances, you may find it easier to cut the pipe with a flexible Abrafile rather than a conventional hacksaw. This can be passed round the pipe and used to cut it without fear of damaging either the wall surface or skirting.

complete section and replace it with a length of plastic pipe. It is probably better to replace the entire top section of the stack as

you will have only one connection to make. Remove a convenient section and use it to mark the length of the new plastic pipe, remembering to subtract the length of any new connectors. Use a special fitting, of which there are many types, to connect the

Join the plastic waste pipe into the stack by taking out a spare entry blank on a boss branch. Solvent weld the pipe

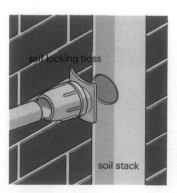

Use a self-locking boss if you don't have a convenient boss branch on the stack, or if all the entry holes are in use.

5 *Connect the flexible coupler to the WC pan and partly tighten the jubilee clip holding it in place*

6 *Check the pan for level using a spirit level. Secure it tightly to the floor using brass screws*

★ WATCH POINT ★

If you are using a drill and padsaw to remove a disc of material from the stack, drill a hole in the centre of the disc first. Bend a piece of stiff wire so that one end is hooked and the other is formed into a hand loop. Insert the hook end through the hole with the hook uppermost and hold the loop while you cut between the drill holes. This will prevent the disc falling into the stack, where it could possibly cause a blockage.

old and new stacks. Break the plastic waste pipe into the stack in the same way as described before.

Installing the WC pan and cistern

Once you've installed the shredder unit, you can position the WC pan and cistern and make the plumbing connections.

Set the pan in front of the shredder unit and slide it back so that you can pull the unit's flexible coupler over the pan outlet. Make sure that it isn't distorted or under any strain—positioning the pan square on to the unit will help here.

When the pan is sited properly, mark the positions of the mounting screw pilot holes on the floor by pushing a bradawl through the screw holes in the base of the pan. If you haven't a bradawl, or if the blade isn't long enough, you can use a long nail or even a skewer to mark the position.

Remove the pan temporarily and drill the pilot holes; if the floor is solid concrete, drill

the holes with a masonry bit and fit plastic wall plugs.

Replace the pan and draw on the shredder unit's flexible coupler. Screw the pan to the floor, using brass screws with lead washers beneath their heads—these will prevent you overtightening the screws and cracking the pan. Before you fully tighten the screws, lay a spirit level across the top of the bowl—from side to side and from back to front—to check that it's sitting perfectly level. If it isn't, insert some slivers of wood below the base of the pan to level it. Fully tighten the screws then clip the flexible coupler to the pan outlet.

Next, offer up the cistern to the wall, following the manufacturer's advice on its height above the pan. If none is given, fit the cistern at about waist height so that the flush handle will come comfortably to hand. Mark the position of the cistern on the wall, using a spirit level for accuracy.

Remove the cistern and position its supporting brackets so that they coincide with the marks you've just made. Mark the screw holes then drill and plug them; screw the brackets to the wall. Place the cistern on its brackets—checking once more that it's level—and mark the positions of the upper screw holes; drill and plug these before screwing the cistern to the wall.

Fit the fall pipe between the cistern and the pan, checking that the rubber seals are properly located; you may have to trim one or both ends of the pipe for it to fit, so offer it up first just in case.

Assemble the internal flushing mechanism, according to the manufacturer's instructions, then attach the float arm assembly. Complete the installation by fitting the flush handle and linkage.

You are now ready to connect the cistern to the water supply, and you can make the pipe run in 15mm copper or plastic pipe.

Continue running the pipe back to the point where you intend breaking into the existing cold water supply, clipping at 1.2m intervals and using as few bends and fittings as possible.

When you reach the point where you intend to break into the supply, cut the last piece of pipe so that it's a little too long. Turn off the main stopcock or tie up the cold water storage cistern float arm and drain down the system by opening all the cold taps (except the one over the kitchen sink, which is connected directly to the mains supply).

When the system has been drained, offer up a tee fitting to the supply pipe and mark the latter for cutting, using the depth stop mark on the body of the fitting as a guide.

With the supply pipe cut, spring the tee fitting into place and then mark the new pipe to length to fit neatly in the branch of the tee. Before restoring the water supply, connect the plastic overflow pipe to the cistern and run it to an outside wall.

Allow the system to fill and check for leaks at all the pipe joints.

Powering the unit

To complete the shredder unit installation, you need to connect the unit itself to the power supply. You can take power either from a nearby lighting circuit or from the ring main in the house.

Whichever method of powering the shredder unit you choose, you **must** remove the fuse controlling that circuit from the main consumer unit before you start work.

First mark the position of the connector unit's box on the wall and cut a recess for the box with a bolster chisel. Screw the box to its recess, having removed the

7 *Fit the cistern making sure that the fall pipe and rubber seals are properly located and do not leak*

8 *Assemble the internal flushing mechanism. Attach the float arm and fit handle. Adjust the arm*

9 *Connect the water supply pipe to the cistern; carry it to the existing water supply. Connect up the overflow*

10 *With the water turned off, mark, and then cut, the pipe you'll tee into. Try to exit at right angles*

appropriate knockout in its side to allow cable entry. Then, chop out a cable chase from that knockout to either the ceiling or the floor, depending on where the cable is to run from. Although you can clip the cable into the chase, it's safer to run it in a length of conduit. Make a hole through the ceiling or floor as necessary.

Having identified the appropriate circuit cable, cut it and insert a three-terminal junction box. Add the branch cable, connecting like core to like core. Alternatively, you can connect directly into the back of a power socket or to a loop-in ceiling rose.

Run the cable to the connector unit, connecting the cores to the appropriate terminals. Don't forget to run an earth core from the terminal of the mounting box to the earth terminal of the faceplate. You can make good the wall before connecting the flex from the shredder unit to the faceplate. Check that the correct size fuse is fitted, fit the faceplate and restore the power.

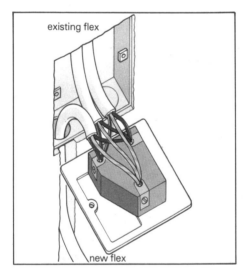

To wire into a ring circuit remove the face of a convenient socket. Check to see that there are two sets of three core cable and connect the matching colours together

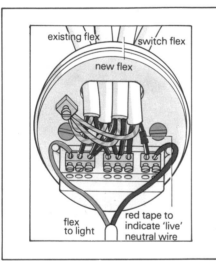

It is possible to wire into a loop-in ceiling rose by doubling up like cores in the supply terminals. However, it is easiest to wire into the last rose on a line and use its entry set of terminals

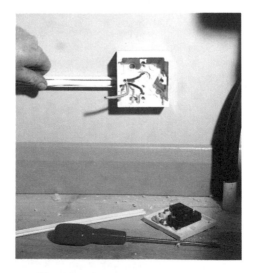

1 *Fix a fused connection unit to the wall and run cable to it*

2 *Tap into the power supply at a joint box, socket or rose*

3 *Connect the flex to the supply at the connection unit*

FITTING AN OUTSIDE TAP

Having an outdoor tap puts an end to traipsing through the house every time you want to fill a bucket or attach a hose. And as well as being an invaluable gardening aid, it's a boon if you're doing regular building work or regular cleaning, like washing a car. If you invest in an automatic hose reel as well, you can fit this next to the tap, ready-connected, for greater convenience.

As plumbing jobs go, installing an outdoor tap is about as simple as it could be: you've only got one supply pipe to worry about, plus the fairly easily solved problem of piercing a hole in an outside wall. Using conventional plumbing materials and techniques the job's straightforward enough. But there are complete kits on the market, similar to those for plumbing to a washing machine, which are designed specifically with the do-it-yourself enthusiast in mind.

At their simplest, such kits consist of the tap, wall fitting, stop valve and supply connector. But the latest include almost everything that you're likely to need, including easily workable plastic supply pipe, push-fit connectors for jointing, and an automatic supply connector for breaking into an existing pipe without having to turn off the water.

Planning and preparation

When choosing a site for an outdoor tap, bear in mind the following points:
• The tap should be sited where it's going to be of most use. For example, if you need to use a hose front and back, don't position the tap so far round one side of the house that it's impossible to get the hose to the other.
• Try to site the tap over a gully, pathway or at the very least hard ground: there's bound to be some spillage and grass or soil could quickly turn into a mud patch.
• For maximum water pressure, the tap should be connected to the rising main. This means finding out where the main runs, and then reconciling the most convenient connection point with the ideal site for the tap to give you the shortest possible pipe run.

The rising main is usually easy to find because a branch from it will run directly to the kitchen cold tap—this rule applies irrespective of whether your plumbing is direct (when all fixtures are fed direct from the main) or indirect (in which case you'll have a cold storage tank).

Starting under the sink, trace the route of the rising main and make a note of possible connection points along the way. When you find what looks like the best spot, check that from there to where you will break through the wall gives you enough room to fit an unobstructed pipe run with stop valve and sufficient space to drill through the wall itself. This isn't as obvious as it sounds: there's nothing more frustrating than starting the job only to find that you can't complete it without tearing out half your kitchen fixtures.

When you've settled on a location for the tap and chosen a suitable connection point on the rising main, you're almost ready to start. But before you buy any materials, get in touch with your local building control office or water authority. In some areas, work on the rising main must be left to an authorized plumber; in others, there may be bylaws specifying what materials you can use—for example, some authorities still insist that you use metal pipe and soldered joints. You'll almost certainly have to pay an extra charge on your water rates for the extra tap.

Tools and materials

If you buy a kit you get all you need except the extension pipe (see opposite). If you decide to opt for individual components rather than a kit, purpose-made garden taps are available from builder's merchants and garden centres. They're normally made of brass for maximum weather resistance, have crutch-type handles for ease of operation, and should come complete with wall brackets and fixing screws.

As well as the tap itself, you must fit a stop valve on the supply pipe inside the house so that the tap can be isolated and drained in the event of a frost. Traditional stop valves are all brass with compression or capillary connections at each side. Plastic pipe manufacturers include push-fit jointed valves in their ranges.

Subject to local water authority restric-

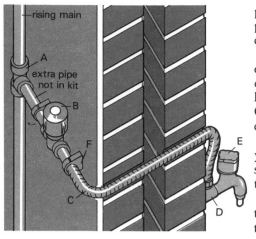

An outside tap kit contains: push-fit tee (A); stop valve (B); pliable copper pipe (C); wall elbow (D); tap (E); pipe clips (F)

tions, the connection at the rising main can be made with a capillary, compression or plastic tee fitting, or with an automatic connector; of the latter, choose the water authority approved type, in which the hole is cut by a small firing pin that traps the resultant metal swarf (which can cause damage) permanently in the fitting.

Note that if you connect to an old type rising main, you'll need a 22mm tee reducing to 15mm for the new branch; if you connect to the kitchen cold tap branch, buy a standard 15mm tee.

You need enough 15mm pipe to make the connection, plus elbow and slow bend fittings and copper bendable connectors in your chosen jointing system to take care of bends. You also need a wallplate elbow tap connector to connect the new tap to the wall and to its supply.

Pliable copper pipe can be run directly through a 15mm hole in the wall—seal around it with mastic. Alternatively, you can arrange a protective conduit through the wall: 22mm plastic pipe is best for this —buy about 300mm, plus non-setting mastic and repair mortar or exterior grade filler to make good the hole.

Tools for the plumbing work are straightforward: a hacksaw and tape measure for plastic pipe, plus a pair of wrenches, grips or adjustable spanners if you're making compression joints. For capillary joints you'll need a blowlamp, resin-cored solder, flux, wire wool and a heat-proof tile.

Running pipe through the wall

Cutting a hole in the wall to take the supply branch pipe is the first, and most daunting,

part of the job. But if you measure up properly you can tackle any sort of wall with confidence.

You can cut the hole for the pipe using an electric hammer drill fitted with a heavy duty masonry bit and extension (the bit will have to be 15mm or 22mm in diameter). Or you can hack through the wall with a club hammer and long cold chisel.

Unless you're using a very long drill, you'll most likely have to work from both sides of the wall. It's therefore important that the holes are aligned exactly.

Start by marking on the outside where the tap is to go, then select a reference point that will be visible from the inside as well—a

window or door are the most obvious.

Measure from the reference point to the tap location in straight horizontal and vertical lines, using a try square or spirit level to guide you. As you go, make a note of the measurements. Then move back inside the house and repeat the measuring procedure exactly, working from the same reference point. Where you end up marks the point at which you drill or cut through the wall.

If you are using a drill, set it on the lowest speed setting and start drilling from the inside to keep damage to the plaster to a minimum. Make sure you drill at right angles to the wall.

1 *Drill a hole through the exterior wall to take the pipe using a hammer drill with a large diameter masonry bit. A number of holes may be needed*

2 *Widen the mouth of the hole so that you can bend the pliable copper pipe to meet the water supply without too sharp an angle*

3 *Insert the pliable copper pipe through the hole in the wall. Go outside and work out how much you need*

4 *Hand-bend the pliable copper pipe in the direction of the rising main, being careful not to form too tight an angle*

On a cavity wall, you'll feel the drill
suddenly free itself as you break through the
inner leaf. If you haven't a long extension
piece for the drill, stop at this point and drill
through from outside. On a solid wall,
stop when you've drilled to a depth of
approximately 110mm.

Using a hammer and cold chisel, your
priorities are to keep the hole straight and as
near 22mm as you can. As when drilling,
start with a hammer and chisel from the
inside. You'll cut down damage to the
plaster if you start off by drilling a series of
holes through it using an ordinary masonry
bit. As you get into the wall proper, stop
every so often and clear out the debris with a
piece of wire.

However you break through the wall,
don't forget to wear goggles so that you are
protected against flying chips of masonry.

When the hole is finished, take your piece
of pipe (or conduit) and try it for fit. Drill or
chisel out more masonry where needed.
With conduit, re-insert the pipe in the hole
and cut it with a hacksaw to the exact
thickness of the wall plus plaster.

Finally, make good any damage around
the hole inside and out with repair mortar
or filler. This should leave you with a neat
hole or conduit through which to run the
new supply pipe to the outside tap.

Connecting to the rising main

There are four ways of doing this job—with
a soldered or compression tee, with a push-
fit tee, or with an automatic connector.

Before you do anything else, double
check that you've got the right pipe and
mark on the connection point in felt-tip pen
so that you don't get confused later.

Conventional tee branch

Drain down the rising main by turning off
the main stop valve and opening the kitchen
cold tap. Place a bowl under the connection
point and then cut through the pipe using a
junior hacksaw. Take care that you keep the
cut absolutely square.

Measure and mark along from the cut the

width of the fitting; don't forget to allow for
the amount that will slot inside it at both
ends. At this point, make a second square
cut through the pipe. Afterwards, file off the
burrs on the cut pipe ends—inside and out
—and in the case of a compression tee shape
the edges to a slight bevel.

5 *Hold the push-fit tee against the
rising main and mark off on the pipe
how much you'll need to remove; this is
denoted by ridges on the tee*

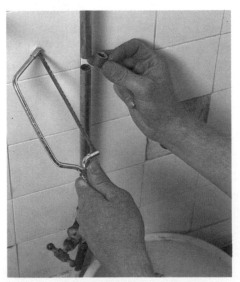

7 *Make the second cut through the
rising main and remove the offcut.
Prepare the cut pipe ends for fitting into
the tee*

Before you fit the tee, you may need to
remove one or more pipe brackets so that
you can ease it into the gap.

Compression tee: Slip the capnuts onto
the pipe ends, followed by the olives, which
should go about 12mm down the pipe.

Insert the pipe ends into the fitting, screw
on the capnuts and tighten about one and a
half turns above hand-tight using a pair of
adjustable spanners or wrenches.

Soldered tee: Clean the pipe ends with
wire wool until they're shiny, then smear
them with flux. Slip the pipe ends into the

6 *Drain down the rising main by
closing its stop valve and opening
cold taps; cut through the pipe using a
junior hacksaw*

8 *Loosen the pipe clips retaining the
rising main and slot on one side of the
push-fit tee. Ease the other cut pipe end
into the socket*

tee. Place a tile or heat-proof board behind
the pipe run to protect the surrounding area
from the blowlamp flame.

Run a blowlamp over the first joint until
the flux starts to bubble, then ease off
slightly. When a small ring of solder appears

right around the edge of the fitting, cut the flame and leave the joint to cool.

Plastic push-fit tee: Lubricate the pipe ends and the inside of the tee, then slot it on the pipe run.

Automatic connector

This method is simplicity itself—you don't even have to turn off the water.

Clamp the connector over the pipe at the connection point and tighten the four clamp screws using the Allen key provided. Check that the outlet hole is pointing in the direction of the run.

This is literally all you do at this stage. The charge which cuts through the main is activated when you've assembled the run.

Installing the pipe run and tap

This final stage of the job is perfectly straightforward, providing you take care to make each joint properly—in this way you will avoid leaks.

When installing the pipe run and tap, take your time. Professional plumbers may work quickly but they generally have years of experience behind them.

Conventional copper plumbing: Measure, mark and cut sections of pipe to allow for the inclusion of a stop valve at a convenient point. If you need to start with a bendable connector at the tee, fit this and bend it to shape, then measure on from here as far as the stop valve. Before you assemble the run, pin pipe brackets to the wall at least every 1m, plus one each side of the valve itself. Then make compression or pre-soldered joints, according to preference.

9 *Push the stop valve on to the prepared end of the pliable copper pipe. Mark the wall to take a plastic pipe retaining clip*

11 *Measure the distance between the stop valve and tee fitting, allowing for the small amount to be inserted into each of the fittings*

From the stop valve, measure and cut enough pipe to take you to the elbow that turns the run through the hole in the wall. Then, before you fit the elbow, cut another length of pipe to run through the wall so that it protrudes about 25mm on the outside. Fit this to the elbow before fitting the elbow to the rest of the run. Check that the pipe run is held rigidly in its brackets and that all the joints are properly made, then move outside.

Solder or compression-joint a tap connector to the bare pipe end, then check the tap fitting instructions. If the tap has a bracket, mark the fixing holes, then drill and plug

10 *Swing the pliable pipe and stop valve out of the way and screw a plastic pipe clip to the wall. Clip the pipe in place*

12 *Cut a length of flexible plastic pipe to size and push a special metal insert into each end. Insert the pipe tightly between the fittings*

the wall. Fit the tap to its connector simply by tightening the capnut with an adjustable wrench or spanner. Where necessary, secure the tap bracket to the wall with the screws provided.

Plastic plumbing (push-fit joints): Start off the run by fitting a straight tap connector or bendable tap connector to the automatic connector outlet or tee on the rising main.

From here you simply assemble a run of push-fit-jointed plastic pipe including a stop valve and a 90° elbow fitting to take it through the wall. Cut the sections of pipe running through the wall to protrude 25mm on the outside and fit it to the elbow

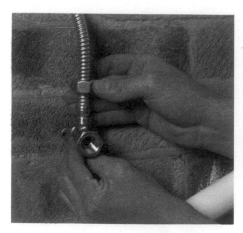

13 *Outside, slot the compression wall elbow onto the copper pipe. Fit capnut, olive then elbow body and then tighten the capnut*

14 *Mark, drill and plug the wall for the elbow fixing screws then fasten it to the wall using the screws which are provided in the kit*

15 *Finally, screw on the bib tap to the end of the wall elbow. You may need to wind on PTFE tape so the tap will be vertical*

before joining the elbow to the rest of the run. Secure the pipe run with clips every 1m, plus two each side of the stop valve (see Plastic pipe and push-fit joints). Some kits include pliable copper pipe instead of plastic.

Now move outside and fit a push-fit straight tap connector to the free end of the pipe. Drill bracket holes for the tap itself (if needed) then screw the tap to the connector.

The final job with plastic pipe is to activate the automatic connector on the rising main. Check that the new tap is turned off, then remove the plastic firing pin cap on the fitting and strike the firing pin sharply with a hammer: you'll hear a loud crack when the charge goes off to pierce through the pipe.

Check carefully for leaks around the automatic connection. Retighten the nuts around the connector if necessary. Also check the tightness of the other connections.

Plastic pipe and push-fit joints

Assembling a run of plastic pipe with push-fit joints is very easy if you follow a few simple rules:
• Cut the pipe squarely using a hacksaw and a piece of card as a template. Afterwards, remember to smooth off any burrs on the cut edges using the emery cloth provided with the pipe or by using the de-burring tool fitted to the end of a pipe cutter.
• Smear the cut end to be joined with silicone lubricant (also provided) before pushing it home into the joint with a slight twisting motion. Make sure the pipe goes right into its seating.
• If space is too limited to push the pipe home, unscrew the joint fitting. Slip the cap over the pipe end, followed by the grab ring and O-ring seal. Then screw the cap down tightly to the other half of the fitting.
• Don't disturb the joint once you've made it. If you do have to take it apart, unscrew the fitting and fit a new grab ring and seal prior to reassembly.
• When using copper bendable connectors, avoid bending them more than once and keep the bend to as large a radius as possible. If you have to cut the connector, do so on a plain section only and leave 25mm for connection to the next push-fit joint along the run.

Final moves

On a conventional installation, start by re-instating the water supply. Then, in all cases, operate the new tap and check the entire run for leaks. Test the stop valve, too, which you should close if a frost is expected.

Finish off by filling the small gap between the new supply pipe and its plastic conduit —inside and out—with non-setting mastic.

Push-fit joints can be used with either plastic or copper supply pipes

Deburr the ends of copper pipe with emery cloth or wire wool

Lubricate the pipe end with a little silicone lubricant to help insertion

Lubricate the inside of the fitting and insert the pipe firmly

Flexible plastic pipe needs a metal supporting insert for fixing

PLUMBING TOOLS

Having the right tool for a plumbing job not only makes things easier, it also reduces the possibility of things going wrong. For example, it's all too easy to damage a nut with the wrong spanner, making it impossible to remove. Other jobs, like installing an immersion heater, just cannot be done if you don't have the proper tool. So knowing what's available and what you need for a particular job will really pay dividends.

Tools for jointing copper pipes

For compression fittings spanners are necessary; for capillary ones a blowlamp is needed. Compression fittings are easier to use and can be easily undone and reused if mistakes are made. However, capillary fittings are neater and the job of melting the solder to make the joint isn't difficult once you've mastered the technique.

For one or two joints only, a blowlamp with an integral gas cylinder can be used, but if you're making a large number of

joints—as when installing central heating, perhaps—a **blowtorch** connected by a flexible hose to a large refillable gas cylinder will be much more economical. A flame-guard accessory for the burner is useful as it concentrates the flame around the joint and away from the surface behind. A glass fibre mat is a useful alternative for the job of protecting the surrounding surfaces.

To tighten the nuts on a compression fitting, two spanners are necessary—one to hold the fitting and the other to turn the nut. You're most likely to be making joints in 15mm and 22mm pipe, so it's best to have spanners in these two sizes. Add a couple of **adjustable spanners** to cope with any odd-sized fittings.

Adjustable pipe wrenches can be invaluable. It's worth owning a small pair; larger ones are expensive, and can be hired whenever you really need them. The ser-

Cut metal pipes with a saw or, more neatly, with a pipe cutter (centre). Bending pipes is easy with a pipe bender or a bending spring

rated jaws give a powerful grip, but may damage fittings if a lot of force is used.

Tools for cutting and bending pipes

For cutting pipes, both copper and plastic, you will need a **hacksaw**; a junior one will cope well unless you have a lot of cutting to do. Fit a fine-toothed blade. If you don't fancy hacking your way through a lot of pipe, buy a **pipe cutter**. This tool clamps the pipe between fixed jaws and a cutting wheel that trims the pipe neatly as the tool is rotated around it, leaves no swarf (rough metal) and can cope with all common pipe sizes—15mm, 22mm and 28mm.

If you're using a hacksaw, you'll need a fine **file** to remove the swarf and burr left after making the cut plus some steel wool to clean up the pipe ends before filling.

There are two tools for bending copper pipe. The first is a **bending spring**; this is a coiled steel 'snake' which slips inside the pipe to support its walls and prevent kinking while you bend it, and is then pulled out once the bend has been made. The springs come in different sizes to suit the commonest pipe diameters, up to a maximum of 22mm—pipes larger than this cannot be bent by hand.

For larger projects (and larger pipes) you need a **pipe-bending machine**, which you can easily hire. With this, the pipe is placed across the bottom plate of a former and is bent by the top plate as it is pulled down into position by a lever.

Using **unkinkable copper pipe** avoids the need for bending tools. This is pipe with straight ends for making connections, but with the centre portion made flexible by corrugations in the pipe wall. It can be bent without a spring or former and is useful for making tap connections where you want to bend the pipes in awkward situations— behind a basin pedestal, for instance. However, it is more expensive than buying ordinary pipe.

Tools for baths and basins

Taps are often tucked tight against a wall, making it impossible to use a spanner in the usual way. In these cases you will need a special **basin spanner**, sometimes called a **crowsfoot spanner**; it can be used hori-

Fit taps to baths and basins with a basin spanner (top), and immersion heaters with an immersion heater spanner (bottom)

zontally where space permits, but will also turn nuts when held vertically. There's a larger version called a **bath wrench** for bath waste back nuts, and a double-ended version that will cope with both sizes.

Another tool that can be used vertically is the plumber's **adjustable wrench** (not to be confused with a pipe wrench). This tool is far less common than the crowsfoot spanner and also more expensive, but it is very useful in certain situations. It is supplied with two or three universal heads (small—for 15mm nuts; medium—for 22mm nuts; and large—for 35mm and 42mm nuts) which can be used at more or less any angle to the shaft. It's a self-tightening tool which takes a stronger grip the more it is turned and will sometimes shift nuts that other spanners won't budge. As with other expensive tools, it's probably best to hire one when you need it rather than to buy it for your tool kit.

Tools for installing a WC and immersion heater

The tools you need for installing the bowl of the WC depend on where it will be sited and the material of the soil pipe to which the bowl will be connected. The WC-to-soil pipe connection is usually made with a flexible plastic connector which simply pushes on to the pipes and requires no special tools. The connection between the bowl and the cistern is usually a push-fit assembly too. You will need screws and a screwdriver for securing the bowl to the floor and fixing the cistern to the wall. You may need a **bolster chisel** and **club hammer** if you are removing an old WC which was mortared to the soil pipe.

To install an immersion heater you need all the usual tools plus a special large spanner to screw the immersion heater into the boss which is normally provided on the dome of a hot water cylinder. This spanner is 2¼in wide and may be open-ended or ring pattern. Builders' merchants usually sell them, or you can hire one from a local hire shop if you prefer.

General-purpose tools—including a power drill, screwdrivers, a file for smoothing off pipe edges and a handyman's knife—will be needed for most plumbing jobs

Tools for plastic pipework

Like copper, plastic is easily cut with a fine-toothed saw, but you're likely to be cutting much larger diameter pipes for soil and waste runs and it will be important to get the cut exactly square. A set square is useful for this, but you can get a very good line by wrapping a sheet of paper round the pipe and using its aligned edge to cut the pipe at right angles.

You'll need a handyman's knife to trim large pieces of swarf from the cut and a file to rub off the burrs. You may also need a small brush for applying the solvent-weld cement which glues the joint; however, many cements come with an applicator attached to the lid of the container.

You can also cut rigid cPVC (chlorinated polyvinyl cloride) pipe (used for water supply and central heating runs on some very modern installations) with an ordinary pipe cutter; for polyethylene and poly-butylene pipe, special shears are ideal but a hacksaw will do the job quite adequately.

To hire or buy?

If a tool is fairly cheap then it's usually worth buying rather than hiring. Although this adds a little to the cost of the job, you have the tool for future use and you can do the current job in your own time without worrying about hire charges clocking up.

Larger, more expensive tools are another story. It usually won't be worth buying a pipe bender, for instance, but might well be worth hiring one for a day or so if you've got a lot of work to do.

It is also well worth hiring the more specialised tools, like immersion heater spanners, which you're fairly certain you won't use more than once in a long while.

General-purpose tools and materials

Many of the tools in your toolbox will be useful for plumbing. You'll probably have a hacksaw suitable for cutting copper or plastic pipe (invest in a new blade if you've been using the saw for other jobs). A file is a must for smoothing pipe ends. For fitting pipe clips securely and accurately you'll also need a drill and screwdriver.

Plumbing can involve lifting floorboards to run pipes below the floor, so a saw will be useful and also a bolster chisel for levering

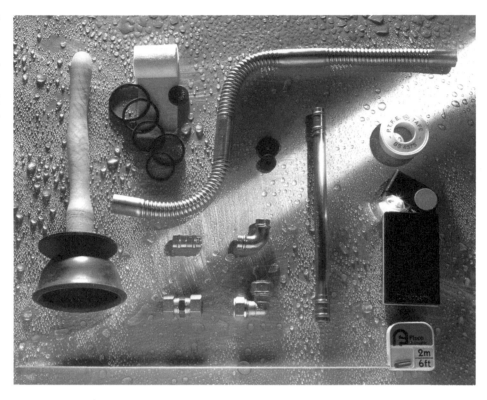

up the boards. A bolster chisel and club hammer will be useful if you have to chase walls, and if you're taking pipes through a wall you'll need a large masonry drill bit.

There are also plenty of sundries you will need. These are cheap to buy, so it is worth investing in supplies of the following:
• A roll of **PTFE tape**—a turn or two of this low-friction plastic tape will also help to give a good seal at joints.
• **Jointing compound**—a smear on the meeting faces of a fitting prevents leaks.

If you're using capillary fittings you will need **flux paste** and for plastic solvent-weld joints, you will need the special **solvent-weld cement**. **Hemp** is the only other specialist jointing material you are likely to need and then only for large joints and those near central heating boilers.

Pipe clips are essential with long runs of pipes; some come complete with screws or masonry pins. **Pipe lagging** in foam or glass fibre is useful for all hot water supply pipes and for cold pipes that rub through unheated areas—as well as insulating the pipe it stops condensation forming on cold pipe walls.

Plumbing emergencies

Burst pipes are the most common plumbing emergency and as they can cause a lot of damage, it makes sense to be prepared, by keeping an emergency repair kit.

A small emergency kit containing a sink plunger, some spare joints, tap washers and 'O' rings will prove invaluable

The first thing to do is to limit the amount of water that can flood out. Stop water coming into the house by turning off the main stopcock and drain the cold water cistern and pipes before tracing the burst.

Copper pipes often fail at joints and, if you're competent at joint making, your repair kit should include spare joints to fit in place of a damaged one. To remake a leaking compression joint you'll need some new olives in 15mm and 22mm sizes—the old one will be crushed, and will have to be cut off with a hacksaw. For a quicker but less permanent repair, which doesn't need tools, you can use a leak-sealing paste to patch up a joint. Most of these are two-part products—you mix together resin and hardener to get a working paste which will rapidly set to seal the burst. You usually use them in conjunction with some sort of re-inforcing tape.

You can make a more permanent repair with a burst pipe coupling—a length of pipe with a joint at either end—which you fit in place of the split length.

A plunger is a useful gadget to have in the house—use it for clearing blocked sinks and waste pipes. Lastly, keep a few washers to stop dripping taps, plus 'O' rings for mixer taps and solid washers for the ballvalve of the WC cistern.

SILENCING NOISY PLUMBING

Air in pipes

Vented systems such as central heating and the hot water supply can suffer from air problems if they are not well designed. If your system suffers from this, the symptoms will be all too apparent.

In hot water services you may notice spluttering taps especially when running large quantities quickly. Usually, this is due to air being drawn down the vent pipe. This happens when cold water from the tank is not flowing fast enough into the bottom of the hot water cylinder.

Check first that the valve controlling this supply is a gate valve, and not a stopcock, which makes it unsuitable for low pressure systems. If you have the right type of valve, ensure it is fully open. Too many bends in the pipe run will also result in a poor flow.

A quick test to check whether air is being drawn down the vent pipe is to run the hot bath tap and at the same time gently place the palm of your hand over the open end of the vent pipe in the loft. If you detect any sucking this is conclusive proof; take your hand away immediately before any damage occurs to the plumbing system.

Cylinders are designed to take a 28mm cold-feed pipe. If yours is smaller, this may be the problem, and you may need to increase the flow by replacing the pipe with a larger one.

A build up of scale in the cylinder may also contribute to a poor supply. There are no easy answers to this problem. The entire system will need to be drained and the cylinder disconnected. It can then be flushed through with a hose pipe.

Air in central heating systems

Air in central heating systems is a major problem. It causes banging noises, howling or even whistling in cast iron boilers, and also increased corrosion of the boiler and radiators. If you find yourself having to bleed air from radiators at frequent intervals it is an indication that something is wrong with the system.

The best way to overcome this problem is to fit a de-areator to the vent pipe. If you do not wish to use soldered capillary joints choose a de-aerator which is suitable for connection to compression fittings. The unit itself is made of copper and is shaped rather like a bottle.

It works by causing turbulence which 'beats' out the air in the water. It is fully automatic in operation and requires no maintenance. The additive should be mixed according to the maker's instructions and added to the expansion (header) tank for the central heating.

Anti-corrosion additives for central heating systems will help to quieten down boiler noises caused by air on rough castings. They will also preserve steel-panelled radiators.

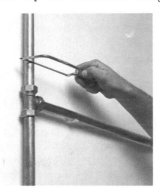

1 *Drain the system before you cut into the vent pipe. Allow plenty of room*

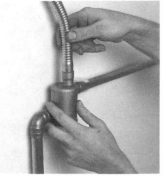

2 *Fit the de-aerator according to the maker's instructions. Make the joints strong*

3 *Bleed air from pumps on a horizontal pipe run by turning the bleed screw half a turn*

A typical central heating system showing the general layout, pipe sizes and the direction of flow of the water in the pipes. The boiler warms the cylinder, too

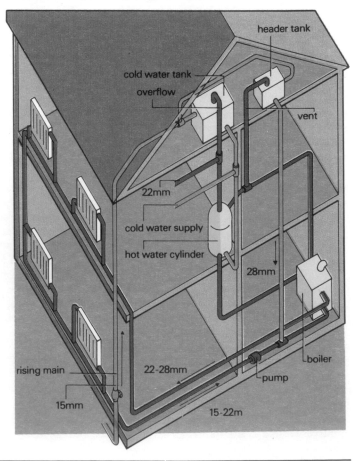

header tank
cold water tank
overflow
vent
22mm
cold water supply
hot water cylinder
28mm
rising main
15mm
22-28mm
pump
boiler
15-22m

Eliminating water hammer

When a fast flow of water through a pipe is halted abruptly (by turning a tap from full on to full off quickly, for example), shock waves are set up which carry back along the pipe and sometimes result in an audible banging. This *water hammer*, as it's known, often becomes progressively louder as the shock waves bounce back and forth and only quietens down very slowly.

Common causes of water hammer are faulty taps or stop-cocks, too fast a flow of water, and a faulty ball valve in the cold water storage tank. The problem can be aggravated by loose pipe securing clips or pipes which are not secured at regular enough intervals.

Curing water hammer is not always drawn into a string, around the spindle pushing it down in to the body of the tap. Then screw down the gland nut, tightening until the spindle is firm. The idea of this is to stop the spindle turning too quickly causing the flow to stop suddenly.

The jumper is the brass or plastic plate holding the washer in place. Take the tap apart as if you were changing a washer and remove the jumper. It should slide in and out of the spindle but have no appreçiable sideways movement. Replacement tap jumpers are available from plumbers' merchants. Alternatively, you could fit a new tap and body.

Stopcocks suffer from the same problems as taps. The packing becomes loose and jumpers wear out.

Servicing a stopcock is no more difficult than a tap but you will have to shut off the but the pipes will be weakened.

Manufacturers overcome this by fitting flow restrictors inside the connecting pipes. The installation instructions supplied with the machine will indicate their whereabouts and may also tell you how long the machine should take to fill. Reduce the flow at the valve where the flexible hose joins the main plumbing if the machine is filling too fast.

Similarly, electric showers should have some restriction upon the input. Many manufacturers recommend the fitting of a valve which does not have a jumper. The Ballofix valve is one of these, and may be fitted at a convenient point in the supply. If the pipework is surface-run chrome-plated or stainless steel tube you can buy a chrome-plated version of the Ballofix.

Faulty ballvalves: Where water hammer only occurs when a ballvalve is operating,

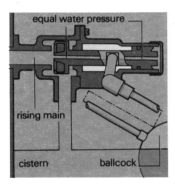

The equilibrium ballvalve uses water pressure in the valve body to eliminate the shock waves

1 Tighten loose spindles on taps and stopcocks by tightening the gland nut with a spanner

2 If the jumper looks to be badly worn, replace it and the washer with new ones

3 Ballofix valves are very easy to fit, maintenance free, and easily adjustable by screwdriver

straightforward, so you must be prepared for a little trial and error.

First, turn the stopcock down to reduce the flow. If this solves the problem and still leaves you with enough water at the taps, you need do no more.

More persistent water hammer will need further investigation. Start by fixing any loose pipes securely with clips.

Where pipes pass under wood floors, notches or holes are usually made in the joists to take the pipes. Use soft packing material—rubber, carpet pieces, rag, felt—to pad the pipes and help stop any vibration.

Taps and stopcocks: Noises heard when taps are running can be attributed to one of two things: loose spindles and worn jumpers. Before starting work turn off the supply to the tap concerned.

Tighten a loose spindle by turning the gland nut. If the spindle is still loose, undo the gland nut and slide it up the spindle. Wind a few turns of wool, or PFTE tape supply from outside the house. This is usually done at the Water Authority's stopcock just inside your boundary. Strictly, you should ask their permission to use it, but it is highly unlikely that they would object to you using it in an emergency.

If any one tap seems to be responsible for water hammer but there is no convenient way of restricting the flow to it, fit an additional stopcock.

If the supply pipe is on the surface of a wall, you can fit a special Ballofix valve rather than the more conventional stopcock. Ballofix valves are much neater in appearance and require no maintenance.

Solenoid valves such as those used inside automatic washing machines and instantaneous electric showers are designed to shut off in a fraction of a second. On mains supplies they can produce extremely violent water hammer.

With washing machines, the flexible hoses take most of the impact and you may not know that the hammer is taking place, the cause will probably be the ballvalve itself.

If a ball bounces up and down on the water's surface it will open and close the valve rapidly causing even more waves and more bounce. The result may well be extremely violent banging in the pipes.

Fit a damper to the ball to eliminate the bounce. Dampers are available from some plumber's merchants but you can make your own.

Wrap a stiff wire around the arm of the ballvalve just next to the ball. From this suspend a plastic disc or empty plastic yoghurt carton open end up. This will form a damper under the surface of the water and smooth its operation.

An equilibrium ballvalve, which is designed to operate under varying pressures, will also eliminate bounce without the need for a damper. These valves operate in the same way as a lock gate. By equalising the water pressure on both sides the valve will open and close with maximum smoothness.

A new version of this equilibrium valve is the 'Torbeck' valve which is silent in operation. It is therefore ideal for fitting to noisy-filling WC cisterns.

Modern PVC cold water tanks are less rigid than their steel counterparts. For this reason an alloy or galvanized steel plate is supplied to clamp the ballvalve to the tank. This provides increased rigidity around the mounting, so the ballvalve will be braced as it shuts off. The supply pipe to the valve must be clipped securely to a joist to eliminate any movement.

Similarly, many PVC tanks have substantial stiffening ribs on the bottom which prevent the water 'swilling about', and thus prevent ballvalve problems.

Severe water hammer

Severe cases of water hammer that resist cure by more simple measures can be dealt with by installing a form of shock absorber in the mains system. The ideal position for this is at the top of the rising main.

your kitchen tap and then refilling.

Similar commercial units are called Hydropneumatic accumulators. Unlike the home-made air chamber they contain sealed vessels of helium.

Blowing out airlocks

On indirect systems—that is those fed from a cold water storage cistern—occasional air-locks can be blown out by connecting a hose pipe between the affected supply and the cold water tap in the kitchen.

Turn on the air locked supply first, then the mains tap. It may take several minutes to blow out the air during which time a lot of 'gurgling' noises may be audible.

Air will collect at any high point in pipe runs. You must therefore make the pipes rise progressively to an open end. This means in effect that pipes should fall away from the cold water tank, taps, ballvalves and vent pipes. In some cases this is impossible to arrange so an air vent may be the best answer. By careful positioning on the

cold water storage tank. The vent tube need only be 15mm bore.

If you want to use this system on pumped central heating circuits you should seek professional advice on the positioning of the tube since it may produce an adverse affect.

Central heating pumps: If you hear a lot of noise coming from your central heating pump it may be air that is causing it. This only occurs on pumps mounted on horizontal pipe runs.

Turn the system off and look for a bleed screw on the uppermost part of the pump. Undo the screw by about half a turn until water seeps out then tighten it before turning the systems on again.

If the problem is pump vibration try fitting pipe brackets either side of the pump. On variable speed pumps you may stop the noise by turning the speed down. You must turn off the system before doing this.

Pipe sizes: The accurate sizing of pipes is crucial in achieving silent plumbing. Full calculations are complex, especially in heating systems, but a rule of thumb guide—set out below—may help.

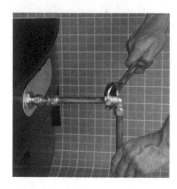

1 *Disconnect the elbow joint next to the cold water cistern*

2 *Replace the elbow with a tee joint, one half of the 'T' pointing upwards*

3 *This air chamber is simply made from 28mm tube and a blanking cap*

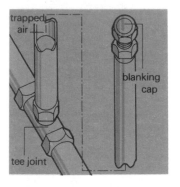

The principle—and the practice—of an air chamber is very simple

By continuing the pipe run above the tank you can produce an air chamber to cushion the shock waves of hammering. Make the piece of pipe as long and large as you can sensibly manage, the only restriction being that it must remain vertical. As an example, 600mm of 22mm copper tube would be the sort of requirement for an air chamber. Cap the top with a blanking-off fitting; tighten it properly and seal it with jointing compound. When you fill the system air will naturally collect and become trapped in the vertical pipe. This air will absorb the shock waves.

After a while the air may become displaced by the pressure of the water. You can recharge the chamber by turning off the main stopcock, draining the pipe through

pipe air will rise towards the valve and be omitted through the top.

If you choose the manual type of air cock operated by a radiator bleed key be sure to run a foot or two of pipe vertically up before fitting the cock.

This will act as an air bottle to collect the air in greater volumes before its release is necessary.

If you would rather fit an automatic version there are several makes on the market. They are designed to go on emitting air indefinitely. Their use is restricted to removing air from pipe runs and they are no substitute for a boiler or cylinder vent.

A third way of removing air from pipe runs is to provide additional vent pipes at high spots. This is done by fitting a tee to the pipe and running a vent tube up to the

Gravity flow and return pipes to and from the boiler should be a minimum of 28mm in diameter. Any less will give rise to a noise resembling a boiling kettle.

Pumped circuits should be a minimum of 22mm in diameter when serving more than three radiators, after which they may be reduced to 15mm on short runs. Bore sizes of less than 15mm must only serve individual radiators.

The cold feed to the cylinder should ideally be 28mm, and definitely not less than 22mm in diameter, especially where the base of the cold water supply is less than one metre above the top of the cylinder.

The hot supply should be 22mm in diameter reducing to 15mm to serve a sink or basin. Indirect cold water supplies must be 22mm.

CHAPTER 3

HOME HEATING

Precise and detailed information on all types of central heating plus how to install your own system and fit a wide selection of heaters and stoves

HOW CENTRAL HEATING WORKS

There are various ways to heat an entire house, from storage heaters to warm air ducting. But in the UK, most systems are of the 'wet' central heating type.

Wet central heating

The essence of a wet central heating system is simply that water is the medium which is used to pass heat from the boiler to the rooms of the house. The water is pumped electrically around the house giving off its heat via a network of radiators. As the water in the system cools, it returns to the boiler where the cycle begins again.

Types of boiler

Central heating boilers can be run off gas, oil, solid fuel (this is generally coal) or even off-peak electricity.

In the UK, gas is a good choice of fuel—it is relatively inexpensive and the boilers can be quite small and neat. As well as this, there's no storage problem with the fuel. If you cannot use gas, oil is more expensive, but convenient; coal is quite cheap, but needs frequent attention.

Gas and oil boilers are available with a **balanced flue**. The boilers don't need a chimney, and can be mounted on most outside walls. **Conventional flue** models are a little cheaper; the waste either runs up the chimney or through an external wall.

System organisation

There are many ways in which the radiators can be connected to the boiler, but the most common on modern domestic systems is the **two-pipe pumped** system. Here, each radiator is connected to the boiler by a **flow** pipe, which brings water to the radiator, and a **return** pipe, which takes it back to the boiler—these pipes sometimes have branch pipes to other radiators. Water is forced around the circuits by means of an electrically driven pump, placed either in the flow or return pipe close to, or in, the boiler.

Even without the use of a pump, water can flow round the circuit by natural circulation—this method of gravity flow is widely used for heating domestic hot water. It is rarely used for radiator circuits because it requires large-diameter pipes with

relatively short and simple pipe runs and preferably no horizontal sections. Even so, most radiator circuits, especially those upstairs, will circulate by gravity to some extent when the pump is switched off, unless a control valve is fitted into the pipework.

Hot water circuits need not be on gravity flow, and pumping can be useful: you can have smaller pipes in this circuit, water-heating time is greatly reduced and the cylinder need not be sited near the boiler (but with a solid fuel boiler, either the hot water cylinder or some large radiator must

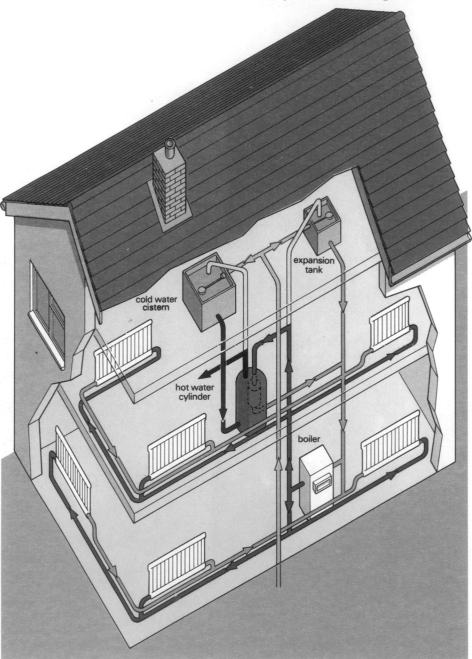

This is a typical two pipe 'wet' system. Cold water enters the house via the rising main and passes via the expansion tank to the boiler, or direct to the hot water cylinder. Hot water then goes to the radiators and the hot water taps. As it cools it returns to the boiler via the cold water return pipe. Vent pipes allow for expansion into the cold water cistern or expansion tank

be on gravity flow. This is because this type of boiler always produces some heat which must not be allowed to build up. The only way round this restriction is to provide a fairly complicated control system).

Types of radiator

Most modern radiators are made of two sheets of corrugated steel joined face to face,

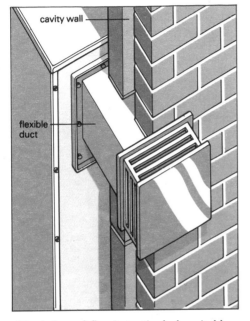

The balanced flue is particularly suitable for use with wall mounted boilers. The unit draws in fresh air and expels flue gases

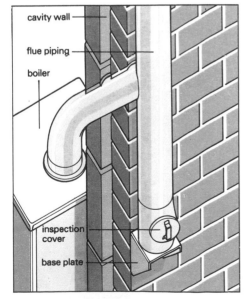

With conventional flues waste gases either run up prefabricated piping mounted on an outside wall (as shown) or up the chimney

with the corrugations forming the water channels. This forms the basic single panel radiator—two of these placed back to back, form a double panel radiator. Some single and double panel radiators have extra metal fins welded to the back surface; these are often called convector, or **high-output radiators**. These variations produce more heat for a given frontal area than a single panel does, so they are particularly useful if you have a restricted wall space. For example, a single panel radiator about 600mm high and producing 1500 Watts would be about 1.9m long; a single panel convector radiator of the same height and output would be only 1.5m long; a double panel radiator about 1.2m; and a double panel convector radiator about 0.8m.

Not all panel radiators have a corrugated front: some special types are smooth in appearance. You can also still buy the old fashioned column radiator, and various types of modern-looking radiators.

Other heaters

Convector heaters (these are different from convector panel radiators) take up much less space than panel radiators. Here, the heating element is enclosed in a box—convection currents carry cool air in through a grille at the bottom, and warmed air flows out at the top. Many convector heaters have a fan which boosts the heat output—but these can be very noisy when they are on their maximum setting.

One particular form of convector heating is skirting heating. This gives a good heat distribution, but heat output is low, so long lengths are needed.

Pipework

Nearly all central heating systems use copper piping. When this is in short supply, stainless steel is sometimes used instead, but this is more difficult to work with.

Fittings for copper pipe can be either compression joints or some form of soldered joint. If you are installing your own central heating it makes sense to use soldered joints: a large number is needed and they are much cheaper than compression joints. Plastic pipe approved for central heating systems is available in the UK. It is easier to cut than copper and it has the added advantage that it can often be routed around curves without having to make a joint.

The **size** of pipe used depends largely on the design of the system and the amount of heat demanded by the radiators that each pipe feeds. Usually, radiators are fed from 15mm pipe (often called **smallbore**) although near the boiler, where all the branches join up, 22mm or even 28mm pipe is needed. A gravity flow hot water circuit will need at least 28mm pipe. With

From left to right are five different radiators: a skirting heater; two single panel; one double panel and a convector radiator

modern pumps, even 15mm pipe is often larger than necessary, so you can use smaller sizes—10mm, 8mm and even 6mm diameter. These **microbore** or **minibore** pipes have the added advantage that they are a little easier to install and are less obtrusive than smallbore pipes. Microbore piping is often used in a design where separate pairs of pipes radiate from a central point out to each radiator; at the central point, the pipes are connected together in one special plumbing fitting called a **manifold**. But microbore pipes can also be used in a conventional branch-type design.

Designing a system

For best results, a central heating system has to be properly designed. This involves working out how much heat each room needs to keep it at the required temperature, and therefore how big a radiator you'll need; what size diameter pipes are needed for each branch of the pipe run; and how large (in terms of heat output) the boiler has to be. The calculations are not too difficult, and there are books available to help you. Alternatively, some central heating equipment suppliers are willing to carry out the calculation for you.

Getting the sums right is important—if you install undersize radiators, pipes or boiler, then you will not be warm enough in cold weather and if you size them too large, your system will cost more to buy and it will be expensive to run.

Radiator valves

It is useful to be able to control the flow of water through a radiator (or convector) for a number of reasons, and each radiator should be fitted with two valves. One valve (called a **wheel head** or **hand wheel valve**) should have a control knob on it—you can use this either to shut down the radiator completely, or to reduce its temperature by restricting the flow of water into it. The other valve (called a **lockshield**) should not be easily adjustable. This is set up after installation during **balancing** to make sure each radiator has the correct amount of water flowing through it to heat each room properly. If you do need to adjust it you'll have to unscrew the cover and turn the valve with a spanner wrench.

You can turn off both valves to isolate the radiator—for example, if you want to remove it for decoration. If you do this, count the number of turns needed to close

Copper pipe for central heating comes in several sizes. Also shown are a manifold and three types of radiator valve

From left to right: room thermostat, programmer, hot water cylinder thermostat, motorized valve and a time controller

the lockshield valve, so that you know how much to re-open it again later.

Heating controls

Good controls are important if you want to keep your fuel bills down. The basic control is a **boiler thermostat** though the main purpose of this is to prevent the boiler from overheating, rather than for economy. Nevertheless, you can use it to turn the boiler down or (except with solid fuel) off when the house becomes too warm, or when you are out. If you have **radiator valves**, you can use these to turn off the heat room by room.

These manual controls are cheap, but most people like some automatic controls—these are convenient and, especially if you are a forgetful type of person, can save you more money. The basic automatic temperature control is a **room thermostat**. This turns off the heating in the whole house when one room (usually the lounge or hall)

has reached the temperature you set on the thermostat. To control individual groups of rooms (upstairs separately from downstairs, say) you have to connect room thermostats to electrically operated **motorized valves** placed in the piping runs. If you want to control temperatures in each room individually, you can fit **thermostatic radiator valves (TRVs)** in place of the hand wheel valves on radiators. You'll find that TRVs are particularly useful in rooms that are also heated from other sources—a lounge with an open fire, or a kitchen with a cooker for example.

To control the times at which the heating is on or off, you need a programmer. Most allow you two on and two off periods every 24 hours—some are even more flexible.

Great sophistication in controls is usually a waste of money—a reasonable system would consist of a simple programmer, a room thermostat perhaps with one or two rooms separately controlled with TRVs, and some control for domestic hot water temperature.

Domestic hot water

Almost all wet central heating systems also heat the **domestic hot water**. The principle that is used is much the same as for heating rooms—but instead of a radiator, the hot water cylinder contains a coil of pipe or something similar (often called a **heat exchanger**) that gives off its heat to the domestic hot water in the cylinder.

It may seem simpler to have the domestic hot water heated directly by the boiler. But this would mean that every time you drew off water at the hot taps it would have to be replaced in the heating system by fresh water from the mains which would cause rapid corrosion, particularly of the radiators. Indirect hot water heating systems avoid this.

It is important to control domestic hot water temperatures—water that's too hot can scald. Also, in hard water areas, it gives rise to scale. A simple non-electric valve can be fitted in gravity-flow circuits; or a cylinder thermostat can be wired to a motorized valve: this can be used on pumped circuits, too. With a motorized valve, you can also have control of the time during which hot water is heated (though if you want to do this totally independently of the heating circuit, you will probably need another programmer). It is not usually possible to fit hot water controls in situations where the boiler runs off solid fuel, however.

DESIGNING YOUR SYSTEM

Installing your own central heating is not a job to be undertaken lightly. It creates a lot of upheaval throughout the whole house, and it takes quite a lot of time (best spent in large lumps, rather than spread over weekends and the odd evening). But it is not all that difficult—if you have some plumbing experience—provided you plan the work properly in advance.

The first thing to do is to get a broad idea of how a central heating system operates, and some of the terminology used. At the same time, you need to know what are the main options open to you, and their pros and cons. This is dealt with under the heading, Understanding central heating.

Next, you must find out about the actual hardware involved—the brands, prices, availability and so on. There are so many bits and pieces involved that you need to browse through the possibilities for some time—so the best plan is to start by looking through catalogues, rather than trying to see all the components in a shop or builders' merchants. There are a few firms that operate a mail-order supply of central heating components, and some of these produce thick, fully-illustrated catalogues of components, often including very useful descriptions of what each one does and its advantages and disadvantages over other choices. These catalogues are well worth sending for.

The final pre-installation stage is to plan and design the system. Design is not all that difficult, but many people feel that it is better to hand this part of the job over to an expert—they feel in this way they can be confident that the finished job will actually work and keep them warm. There are two main ways in which you can get your heating system designed for you. Firstly, there are professional design consultants who specifically deal in domestic central heating. They will visit your home, measure it, and prepare detailed plans and specifications, based on everything they can find out about you, your house and your lifestyle. Such consultants can be expensive. Alternatively, you can use the services of the mail-order firms, some of whom offer a design service for a relatively small fee (often refundable if you then buy your components from them). If you take up this service, you will have to draw plans of your house, and be responsible for telling the firm about the system you want; they are unlikely to visit you. To do this part of the job successfully, you need to know a little bit about why a design is important, and what is involved in creating one—see What's involved in design (pages 161–2).

Understanding central heating

In the UK, the most usual form of central heating to install, particularly in a house that's already built, is wet central heating.

Here, there is a central boiler where water is heated; this hot water passes through pipes to radiators in each room. The radiators give off the heat from the water to warm the room and the cooler water then passes back to the boiler for re-heating. This sort of central heating system is described in detail on pages 156 to 158. The most usual form is the *two-pipe* system shown on this page.

Boiler: Can be gas, oil, or solid fuel. May

A typical two-pipe central heating system includes a pump and motorized valve to push hot water around both the circuits—the radiators and the domestic hot water circuit. Other systems can be designed to suit your plumbing

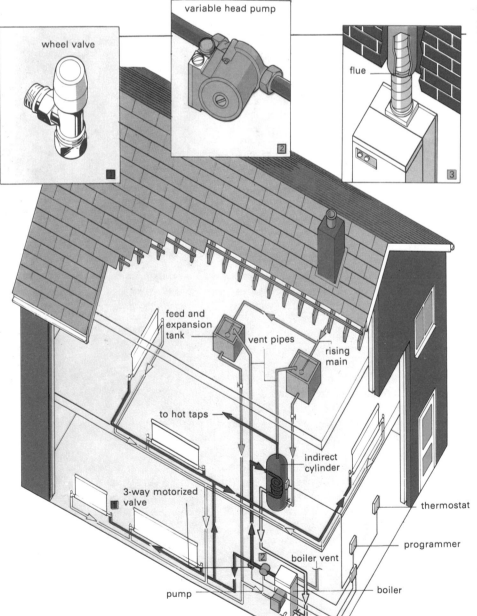

wheel valve

variable head pump

flue

feed and expansion tank

vent pipes

rising main

to hot taps

indirect cylinder

3-way motorized valve

thermostat

programmer

boiler vent

pump

boiler

be free-standing or fitted into a fireplace as part of a room heater.

Flue: The easiest solution to the problem of flues is to fit a *balanced flue* boiler. This is a cheap method of getting a flue and is easy to install. You must be able to mount the boiler on a suitable outside wall—see the drawing on page 167. You cannot get balanced flue solid fuel boilers. The alternative is to use a *conventional flue* boiler, which needs a proper chimney. An existing chimney can be used, but unless this was built after about 1965, it will almost certainly need *lining*. Lining is easy for a gas boiler—a lightweight flexible stainless steel liner can be used. More complicated linings are needed for other boilers.

Pump: Forces water around the system, and means that you can use small-diameter pipes. Get one with *valve* fittings on either end, not plain unions: it makes it easier to remove the pump for repair or replacement.

Flow pipe: Takes the water from the boiler to the radiators. In most systems, each radiator is connected individually to the end of a 'branch run' of flow pipe bringing water from the boiler.

Return pipe: This takes the water back to the boiler, and is connected in branch runs identical to the flow pipes.

Radiator: The usual form of radiator in the UK is the *panel radiator*: a large panel of steel with channels in it through which the water flows. The basic version is the *single panel*; other types are the *single panel convector* or *high-output* radiator, which has extra fins welded on to it; the *double panel* radiator; and the *double panel convector* radiator. These variations give increasingly more heat output for a given surface area—or to put it another way, occupy less wall space for a given heat output.

Convector: An alternative to a radiator. The heating element is enclosed in a box and heating is purely by convection. These are very compact. Most have an electric fan to increase the output—but these fans can be noisy.

Skirting heating: A type of convector heater, which gives a very good heat distribution, but long lengths are needed.

Valves: for turning radiators on and off, and for balancing the flow of water to each heater so that it will heat the room correctly.

Feed and expansion cistern: UK systems are normally *open* to the atmosphere; if there is a fault and the water boils then it can easily expand or boil away without causing an explosion. The feed and expansion cistern (often called an f&e tank) is mounted as high as possible above the rest

of the system, and is linked to the boiler through the *feed pipe*—there must be no valves fitted anywhere between the cistern outlet and the connection with the boiler. The cistern receives its water from a *ball valve* connected to the rising main.

The f&e tank has several functions: it ensures the system is open to the air and not sealed; it provides a small pressure head to ensure the radiators remain full of water; it provides a source of water to the boiler (to prevent explosions) if there should be a leak; and it provides somewhere for the water to expand into when it is heated. In normal circumstances, fresh water does *not* flow into the system—it's important to ensure that this does not happen to avoid corrosion.

To provide an easy passage for any steam to escape, the system also has a *vent pipe* connected to the boiler. The free end of this rises above the f&e tank so the tank would catch any escaping water.

Domestic hot water (dhw): The boiler usually also heats the hot water using an *indirect* copper hot water cylinder. This works in much the same way as a radiator—inside the cylinder is a coil of pipe, connected to the boiler by feed and return pipes (called *primary pipes*). The hot water from the boiler flows through the coil, heating the water in the cylinder; this is drawn off at the top through *secondary* pipes to the hot taps. The cylinder is refilled through a *feed* or *make-up* pipe from the *cold water cistern*, and as with the boiler, there is a *vent pipe* for safety.

Usually, the dhw primary circuit is operated by natural *gravity flow*—the water circulates without the need for a pump. This is simple, but requires large-diameter pipes and a careful layout—with the cylinder more or less directly above the boiler.

Alternatively, the dhw circuit can be pumped using the same pump as in the radiator circuit. It is neater, and means you will be able to re-heat the water quickly.

Microbore: Most systems use *smallbore* tubing—rigid pipes down to 15mm diameter. For some of the piping to the radiators, you could use instead *microbore* tubing. This is smaller in diameter (10mm, 8mm and 6mm) so looks less obtrusive if you fix it to wall surfaces; it uses clips like those for electric cables, too, which are simpler to fit than normal pipe clips. It is also flexible to some extent, so you may find it easier to thread under floorboards and through walls.

You can use it for the final branch run to each radiator (unless the radiator is very large) in much the same layout as an ordinary system, but main runs will still

Panel radiators (above) need valves and drain taps—radiator foil improves efficiency. Convector radiators need special attention

Wall-mounted balanced flue gas boilers are available in a range of sizes and capacities to power the facilities of your system

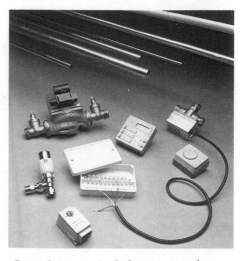

Control systems include pumps and thermostats as well as electrical fittings for the programmer—pipe sizes are important

need to be the larger smallbore pipes. Alternatively, you can use a different sort of layout, in which radiator branch pipes all run to a single central point, rather than joining up along the way. At this point, the microbore pipes all join up in a single fitting called a *manifold* which is connected to the central heating boiler.

Control system: All boilers have a boiler thermostat to prevent overheating. But you need other controls if you want to keep fuel bills as low as possible. Control systems to provide economical running can become very complex—and the danger might be that you spend much more on the controls than you would save in lower fuel bills. Most people, however, would appreciate a *timer*—sometimes called a *programmer*—which will switch on the boiler or the pump (depending on the design) only when you want heating.

Besides controlling time, you also need some way of controlling temperatures. The usual way is by a central *room thermostat*—this is sited usually either in the hall or living room and can be pre-set to a particular temperature; when the room reaches this temperature, the heating in the whole of the house goes off. Much more flexible, but more costly, is to fit each radiator with a *thermostatic radiator valve* which enables you to control the temperature in each room individually.

Hot water needs controlling for safety reasons—if it is too hot, it may scald (especially when it's going to be used by old people and children). The simplest control for hot water is a thermostatic valve that fits in the primary pipe work and cuts off the flow (whether pumped or gravity) whenever the temperature of the water in the cylinder rises above a pre-set limit. With gravity flow systems, this is the only control usually fitted—water is otherwise heated whenever the boiler is not switched off.

If you want independent control of the hot water timing, you will have to fit *motorized valves* in the primary pipework, and check that the timer you use is capable of controlling all the components in the hot water supply independently.

You cannot normally fit hot water controls of any type to a solid-fuel fired system. If you do want to do this, you will need to fit a special, and rather complicated set of controls.

Fuel supply: A gas boiler is connected to the mains gas supply—a job best left to a qualified gas engineer after you've put in the rest of the system. If you use a design-and-supply firm, they may be able to arrange for the work to be done. An oil boiler needs a large oil tank and fuel delivery line. Ask your local authority about the regulations governing the position of an oil tank and the fire safety regulations involved. For a solid fuel boiler, you will have to provide a bunker.

What's involved in design

Whether you plan to hand over the design work to a mail-order firm, or hire a domestic heating consultant, it's sensible to have some idea of what goes into central heating design—so that you can brief your designer with your requirements.

Proper design is not a haphazard process but involves careful and systematic calculation taking account both of your needs and the limitations of any system. This is normally divided into four stages.

Stage 1: Calculate the heat loss from each room of the house in turn.

As long as the outside of a house (or even an adjacent room) is colder than the room you are considering, then heat will flow out of it—and to stop the room growing cold you have to supply heat to it at the same rate. The rate of heat loss varies, partly depending on how cold it is outside, and how warm you want it to be inside. So the first step in the heat loss calculation is to decide inside and outside *design temperatures*.

If you want a cost-effective heating system, it is important to pick both temperatures carefully. If you choose too high an outside temperature, then your heating system will not be able to warm rooms properly in the coldest weather, and you will have to top up with some other, perhaps more expensive, form of heating. If you choose too low a temperature then the system will be bigger than it needs to be, with excess heating capacity for most of the year and it will be more expensive to run. In the UK, a good compromise outside design temperature is −1°C: a system designed for this will cope with most normal winter conditions, and only rarely will you need to top up with other heating. In parts of Scotland, a design temperature of −2°C is more sensible; and in the West Country, 0°C may be sufficient.

Many of the same considerations apply to inside temperatures—if they are too low, you will feel cold; if they are too high then your system is bigger than it needs to be. Inside design temperatures are largely a matter of personal preference. Many designers use these temperatures:

Living rooms, etc: 21°C.
Bedrooms: 18°C.

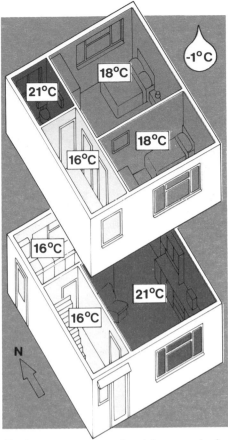

Design temperatures depend on nominal outside temperature together with your preference for inside temperatures in each room

Halls and passages: 16°C.
Bathroom: 21°C.

Other designers prefer to use 21°C throughout, on the grounds that, particularly in modern houses, almost all rooms may be used as living rooms at some time or another.

The calculations will also take into account the materials from which the house is built—some are better at retaining heat than others. Insulation will affect this, too.

Stage 2: Decide on the positioning of the radiators.

As a general rule, the best positions for radiators is on external walls, preferably underneath windows—this gives the best heat distribution in the room, especially around the window area.

However, there may not be enough room under the window for a normal radiator of sufficient heat output. In this case, the designer will normally opt for one of the higher output types. Where there definitely is not space under the window for any type of radiator, another position on an outside wall can be tried—perhaps alongside the window; or the radiator could be split into two, one half on each side of the window.

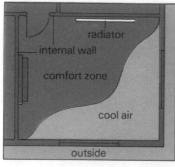
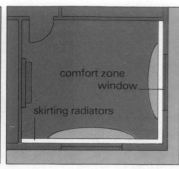
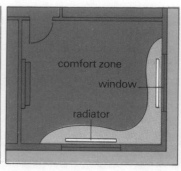
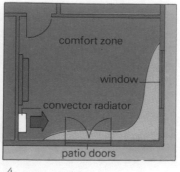

1

Radiator siting and choice is important for efficient operation and control of room temperatures. You must site them to ensure the maximum circulation of warm air as well as to offset any areas of heat loss

Panel radiators mounted on internal walls (1) are less efficient—warm air can't offset heat loss.

Panel radiators are most efficient on external walls, especially under windows (2)

Skirting radiators (3) give good overall room temperatures but, like convector types (4), are more difficult to install. Both offset the heat lost to the outside and aid the circulation of warm air round the room

Only if all these approaches fail should radiators be placed on inside walls.

In a large room, or a long one such as a through lounge, you should use two or more radiators to give a good heat distribution.

Stage 3: Decide on a sensible pipe run and then calculate pipe sizes.

The best pipe runs are as short as possible—taking into account the construction of the house. Where possible, pipes underneath floors should run along the joists rather than across them. Doors, and to a lesser extent, walls and fitted furniture may mean the pipes have to make detours, and branch runs may have to be connected rather differently from the layout that appears to make most sense.

Having sorted out what appears to be a sound and realistic pipe layout, it is then necessary to calculate the sizes of pipes needed. Choose too small a pipe, and it will not be able to carry enough heat to the radiators to provide the required design heating load—no matter how carefully the radiators are sized, the room could be too cold. Too large a pipe would be wasteful of materials, and is more difficult to install.

In most cases, sizing small bore piping is not too difficult: 15mm pipe is usually big enough for all but the largest main runs nearest the boiler. For these runs, and for pipes leading to the hot water cylinder, 22mm or 28mm pipe is used.

Sizing a microbore layout can be more difficult, partly because there are more main pipe sizes to choose from.

Stage 4: Decide on pump sizing.

The pump has to be capable of pushing water quickly enough round the circuit to supply the heat required, and powerful enough to overcome the resistance of the pipes themselves. Pumps are usually

variable head: they can be set to provide a number of different flow rates. So this part of the design is not usually critical—a 'normal' pump will do for most smallbore circuits in ordinary houses; a *high-head* pump will probably be needed for any circuit with microbore piping in it.

You need to draw up a plan of the various floors in your house, together with details of its construction, level of insulation and so on, decide what sort of a system you want, and tell the firm of any particular requirements you have.

• Mark in, on your plan, the position of all

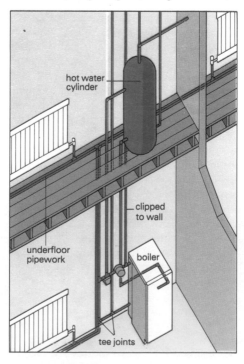

Sensible pipe runs are short and straight with the pipes concealed, or at least running along the same route so you can box them in

doors and windows, built-in cupboards, fixed equipment such as baths and washing machines, and any other obstructions that might hinder radiator or pipe positioning. Mark the direction of joist runs (almost always at right angles to floorboards). State if the ground floor is solid or hollow. Mark in window sizes and window sill heights. Note all room heights.

• Give the construction of all external walls —whether they are solid or cavity masonry (and if so, whether the cavity is filled with any insulating material) or timber framed. If the wall is cavity masonry, tell them if the inner leaf is brick or lightweight block.

• Tell them whether any windows are double glazed, and how much insulation there is in the loft. Adding insulation *before* installing central heating is worthwhile.

• Decide on the temperature you want in each of the rooms.

• Decide whether you want a conventional or a balanced flue boiler. If you intend to use an existing chimney tell the firm about it: when it was built; whether it is lined (if you can tell); how tall it is and if there are any other walls or trees within a couple of metres radius. Ask them for their recommendations. If you need an entirely new chimney, explain where it will have to go and again give details of any likely obstructions. If you want a balanced flue boiler, you can check yourself whether there are any problems in positioning it.

• Decide on whether you want the hot water circuit pumped or on gravity flow. This may be a matter of personal preference, or may be dictated by your plumbing.

• Decide on your control system. Unless you are confident you know a lot about controls, it is best to go for a package system that will come with all the instructions for wiring up and labelled junction boxes.

RADIATORS AND FLUES

Use your design plans and specifications to order all the components you need. Some of the firms which undertake design also supply all the hardware, but it may be worthwhile to shop around for comparable items at local heating supply shops or from mail order firms.

Make sure that you specify the exact items you need in all cases—if you're in any doubt, take your plans along with you and ask for advice in the shops.

There's a wide range of items and fittings you need to make a comprehensive check-list of the numbers of each item, the sizes

Assemble the fittings for each radiator and lay them alongside each one. Check that you've got everything you need

and any other special considerations (some design firms supply such a checklist). Whatever the exact nature of the component, divide the list into identifiable related areas and check off the items within each of the following areas:
• A boiler and flue (possibly with a pump) and a three-way motorized valve to divert heated water from the domestic hot water circuit to the radiator circuit;
• A number of radiators in different sizes and types with valves, lockshields, vent plugs, fixing brackets and, if you prefer, drain taps that you can attach to one of the valves on each of the radiators;
• Feed and expansion tank;
• Supply and connection pipes and cables;
• A control system of thermostats, programmers and valves.

You need a number of accessories for installing the radiators and boiler: an assortment of screws and wallplugs for fixing; valves, taps and vent plugs for each radiator; radiator foil to minimize heat loss through walls and contact adhesive or double-sided tape to secure it; PTFE tape and jointing compound and hemp; boiler flue accessories (see under heading, Installing boiler and flue); fire cement and material for making good and post-installation decoration.

When all the materials are delivered, check them off against your list and stack them as neatly as possible in a place where they won't impede your work. Stack them together in their five main groups as specified above.

When you're satisfied that all the components you ordered have arrived, check

your design plans yet again, then carry the radiators to their intended positions. Prop the radiators in position and lay the fittings for each one alongside so that you can check that they're all ready for the installation. Make sure that you've got fixing screws and brackets, valves, vent plugs and blanking plugs for each one.

As you lay out the components, take the opportunity to estimate any difficulties that may face you—for example, check again the direction of the joists and the nature of the wall (stud partition or solid masonry). Don't forget to check that you've ordered the right size of radiator to fit the space available and to give the correct heat output.

The boiler itself may need to be assembled on site—follow the manufacturer's instructions for doing so and complete the assembly before you attempt to install the boiler. If it's a wall mounted type, bear in mind that you may need help to lift it into place, and that arranging the flue outlet can be quite a difficult and messy job.

Hanging radiators

The first job of installation is to hang the radiators, mainly because it gets them out of the way quickly—but partly because it gives you a boost that the job is well under way.

Radiators usually clip onto metal brackets that you screw to the wall. Working out the height at which to fit these brackets is crucial—if the radiator is too high, it may foul on window sills and so on; if it is too

1 *Measure from the bottom of the radiator to the bottom of the fixing bracket, then measure the distance between brackets*

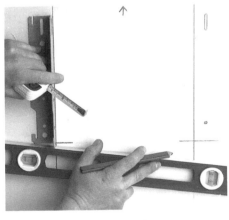

2 *Find the centre beneath the windows, and transfer your measurements on to the wall. Use a spirit level to mark fixing positions*

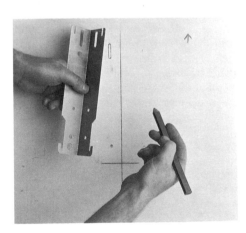

3 *Align the brackets with your marks. Draw on top of the fixing holes—there's normally a slotted hole and a screw hole*

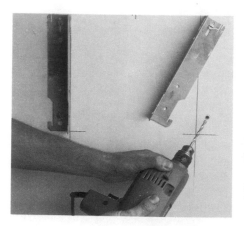

4 *Drill holes and attach the brackets with wallplugs and screws—fit the slotted end first so that you can adjust as necessary*

5 *It's easiest to remove the brackets, fit radiator foil (see opposite), then refit the brackets to the original fixing holes*

6 *Lift the radiator on to the brackets and check that it won't foul. A drain tap may help to avoid fouling against a joist*

★ WATCH POINT ★

Before you hang the radiators, think about painting or papering behind them—the job will be much easier now than when you have finished the installation. Paint the back of the radiators, too.

low, there will not be room to fix the radiator valves and pipework, and the brackets may foul on the skirting boards.

You need a minimum height from floor level to the bottom of the radiator of about 100mm—about 175mm if you are running the pipes along a skirting board rather than under the floor. A minimum 50mm clearance below the window sill is needed, too.

Lay the radiator face down on the floor and clip one of the brackets into place. Measure down from the bottom of the radiator, and add on whatever height you want the radiator to be above the floor. Do the same from the top of the bracket, and finally from the top of the radiator.

Check all these measurements against the wall, and make sure that both the radiator and bracket will sit in place happily. If not, alter the height of the radiator, and try again. When you are satisfied with the position, work out the height above floor level that one of the screw holes on the radiator bracket will come—use the centre of the elongated hole if the bracket has one.

Having worked out the vertical positioning of the radiator, the next job is to work out the horizontal positioning. In most cases, you will want the radiator to sit centrally under a window. But there are two things to check out before you commit

yourself to the position. One is that the pipework from the radiators may foul on the joists—if you can, shift the radiator slightly sideways to avoid this.

Secondly, on timber-framed walls you should try, if at all possible, to mount the brackets on studs. If you can't, it's better to screw stout wooden battens horizontally across the studs and fix the brackets onto these, rather than rely on cavity wall fixings.

Screw one bracket into place, using a No. 10 screw at least 50mm long. Use

★ WATCH POINT ★

Some people find it easier to dress radiators before they are hung on the wall. It also makes it easier to see exactly where the pipes will run.

sturdy wall plugs on a masonry wall. Fit the other bracket similarly. Check with a spirit level on a batten that the clipping points on both brackets are level. Some people like to ensure that there is a **slight** rise towards the end of the radiator that the vent plug is fitted to.

Make sure the brackets are hanging truly vertically, then fix them firmly in place through their bottom screw holes. You can now clip the radiator over the brackets.

The next stage is to **dress** the radiator—that is, you must add any valves, taps or fittings that are necessary. Standard radiators have four screw-threaded holes, or **tappings**, one at each corner. These are used for connecting valves and so on—you have to do this yourself because the radiator manufacturer does not know exactly what

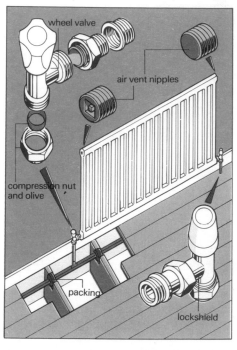

Radiator dressing involves fitting valves and air vents before connecting up. Wheel valves and locksbields can be fitted on either side, flow or return. Fit air vents to both top corners, or just one with a blank plug on the other

★ WATCH POINT ★

If you have a number of radiators of the same size to fit, make a note of the height of the first screw hole in the bracket, so that you don't have to re-measure every radiator. Do the same for the horizontal spacings between the two brackets on each radiator of the same size.

If you can't align the radiator without fouling against a joist, consider whether you can add a drain tap to either of the valves—that way you won't have to make an unsightly bend in the pipe. The drain tap might be enough to move the valve and its pipe to one side of the obstruction. Fit it between the valve and the radiator. You can then remove a radiator for decoration.

component you want in which corner.

Your design will show you what goes where, but the pattern is usually as follows:
• The bottom two tappings are fitted with valves that connect the radiator to the pipework. One valve is normally called a **wheel-head** or **hand-wheel** valve—it has a handle on the top so that you can easily turn the radiator on and off.

The other valve—the **lockshield**—is usually identical, but has a cover over the top so that the valve setting cannot be altered easily. The setting is fixed during commissioning of the system, and is altered only if you want to isolate the radiator completely so that you can remove it, say for repair or so that you can redecorate the wall behind it. Normally, the hand-wheel valve is fitted to the flow tapping, and the lockshield to the return tapping (see page 164), but this isn't essential, and in any case, if you are using matched valves they are usually interchangeable. So it doesn't

Remove the brackets to fit the foil behind the radiators. Tap pins into the holes to mark their positions

normally matter to which of the bottom tappings you fit these valves. If you are using thermostatic radiator valves, fit them in place of the hand-wheel valve.
• One of the top tappings is fitted with a **vent plug**, from which you can easily bleed air that will be trapped in the radiator during filling, and that may build up from time to time when the system is in operation. Again, it does not matter which tapping the vent plug is fitted to—use the one that will be easiest to get at.
• The remaining tapping is not used, and is fitted with a **blanking plug**.

All these are **screwed** fittings, and are made watertight by wrapping PTFE tape round the thread before screwing them into place.

Useful tools

You will need a variety of tools to dress the radiators. Vent and blanking plugs are usually screwed up using a large square-headed Allen-type key. Radiator valves come in two parts: the union to the radiator is fitted either with a spanner or a large hexagonal key, depending on brand; the valve part, which is fitted later, is usually a compression-type fitting.

But as a final check, mount the radiators on the wall loosely. Fit the valves by hand without using PTFE tape to check whether you're satisfied. When you are sure of the final position, dress each radiator properly using PTFE tape and the necessary tools.

Radiators that are fitted on external walls

Cut the foil to size by laying it on top of the radiator—leave a margin around all four edges

can lose quite a lot of heat to the outside through the wall. You can trap much of this heat loss, and reflect the heat back into the room, by fitting radiator foil to the walls before you hang the radiators. The job is quick and easy.

You will get the most benefit where the walls are solid brick and you are using single panel radiators; if the walls are well insulated, and you use double panel radiators, much less heat is lost so the benefit of radiator foil is much smaller, and the task may not be cost effective.

Special radiator foils are sold, but ordinary aluminium cooking foil is almost as good and much cheaper. Fix either, using double sided adhesive tape (or a contact adhesive or sticky foam pads), over the whole area of the wall that will be covered by the radiator.

Installing the boiler and flue

Installing the boiler itself is usually a matter of following manufacturer's instructions. The same goes for flues, too. But an idea of what's involved will help you decide whether you feel up to tackling this job.

The firm who carried out your design work should have already taken into account the requirements of the various regulations covering boiler installation, but if you are in any doubt, you should check that your installation will comply with all the regulations.

Use double-sided tape or sticky pads to attach the foil to the wall—make sure the pins are visible

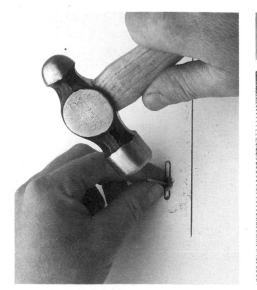

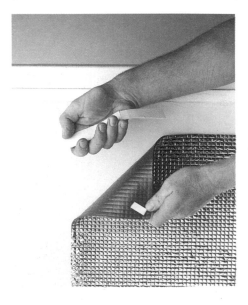

There are two main points. First, walls and floors close to the boiler should be non-combustible—for example, a solid floor with quarry tile covering and a thick masonry wall. The regulations on fire protection are a lot more strict for solid fuel boilers than for gas or oil ones.

Second, all boilers with conventional flues need adequate ventilation in the room they are sited in—starving a boiler of air could kill people. Openable doors and windows are not enough—there must be some permanent ventilation opening in the room. Your design firm should tell you exactly how much you need, and how to provide it: usually by fitting airbricks at both low and high level close to the boiler.

Besides these points, make sure you position the boiler where you can easily get to all the connection points, door hatches and so on, and where the pipework running to and from it will be easy to install.

You could connect a gas boiler to the gas supply yourself, but it is better to hand the work over to a qualified gas engineer—if only for the peace of mind this will bring. Have this done last, just before commissioning and testing the system.

Flue installation depends on the type:

Balanced flue: This is mainly a matter of chopping a horizontal hole in the wall through which the flue will poke. If the wall is a cavity one, make sure that debris doesn't fall down the cavity. Slide the flue

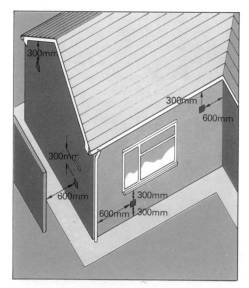

Balanced flue terminal positions (above) are more flexible than for open-flue systems but it's still important to allow a free flow of air at all times. If the terminal depends upon a natural draught it's likely to be affected by the proximity to eaves, gutters, corners and nearby walls. Distances indicated are the minimum

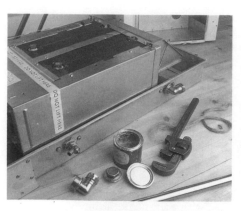

7 Assemble the boiler according to the manufacturer's instructions. Attach the fittings with compound and hemp

into place and seal the hole according to the manufacturer's instructions.

Existing lined chimney: Assuming the boiler is not being placed in an existing recess, you must cut into the chimney some height above the top of the boiler so that you can fit a piece of vitreous enamel flue pipe into the chimney at an angle of 45° to take the flue pipe sections from the boiler—your firm should have supplied you with drawings showing what components to use. Make a bed of asbestos rope and fire cement at the bottom of the opening you have cut and bed the flue pipe on this. Continue the asbestos rope round the top and sides of the pipe. This will ensure that the joint between the flue and the brickwork is flexible, to allow for expansion. Then pack any large holes with a 1:3 mortar mix and allow the mortar to dry.

If you want to mount a free-standing boiler in an existing recess, you will have to have a **register plate** made up—a metal plate that is fitted horizontally into the flue above the level of the recess. The boiler flue pipe pokes vertically into a hole cut in the plate. You also need to have an inspection hatch cut into the plate to allow for chimney sweeping—make this as large as possible. Seal all joints between the plate, inspection hatch, flue, and chimney with fire cement.

• **Unlined chimney:** For a gas boiler, this can be lined with a flexible stainless steel liner. To install this, you need to climb on the roof and work on the chimney: get someone to do this if you are not confident of your abilities. You will probably need a **condensate drain** at the bottom end of the liner—best done by fixing a Tee-piece to the liner, with the bottom connection to the drain, and the side connection to the boiler flue pipe. If you can, fit the Tee-piece in the chimney itself, for neatness; you'll also need to cut a hole in the chimney breast.

8 Attach the flue duct to the inside wall with stout screws—wall-mounted boilers hang from the wallplate of the duct

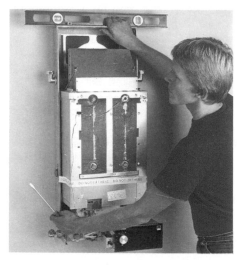

9 Lift a wall-mounted (or manoeuvre a floor-mounted) boiler into place. For balanced flue installations, this means attaching it to the flue duct. Check that the boiler is steady and level—you may need to attach it through fixing holes at the bottom too

Now go on the roof and remove the existing chimney pot and the mortar it is bedded in (called **flaunching**). The pot will be very heavy, and must be lowered carefully to the ground. Take the liner onto the roof, fitted with its 'nose cone'—a conical block in the lower end which makes it easy to thread the liner through the chimney. Drop a weighted rope down the chimney to an assistant and tie your end to the nose cone. Have your assistant carefully pull the liner down the chimney as you feed it in.

The top of the liner is held with a fixing plate that you mortar into place on top of the chimney stack. You then slide a terminal into place. Make sure the seal between the chimney and the liner is absolutely gas tight.

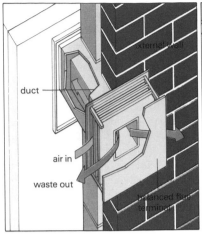

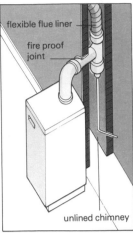

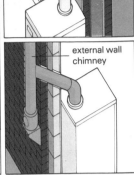

Flue arrangements will vary from one installation to another. Balanced flues (left) are the most convenient and adaptable because there's no need for a chimney. Conventional types need a flue liner fitted inside a chimney. If the chimney is

unlined (centre), use a flexible flue, fed from top to bottom. Lined chimneys (top right) need no flue liner, just a joint between boiler and chimney. If there's no chimney, a pre-fabricated flue can be attached to an external wall (bottom right)

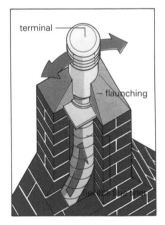

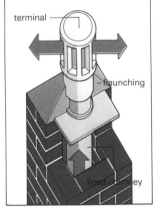

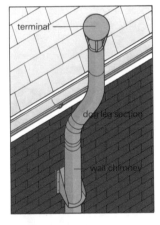

Flexible flue liners run from the boiler to the top of the chimney stack where the terminal is sited

Lined chimneys only require a top plate and the installation of an approved type of terminal

If there's no chimney, or it's in the wrong place for your boiler, fit a prefabricated chimney

Use PTFE tape for small threads and fittings—wrap at least three layers clockwise

Larger fittings require compound and hemp—apply acidic types with a spatula

Wrap a layer of hemp round the threads and compound, then apply another coat of compound

At the boiler end, seal the Tee-piece to the liner and the boiler flue pipe with fire cement, plus asbestos rope if the gap is very large. Lead the condensate drain through the wall and out of the house.

Lining a chimney for types of boiler other than gas is really a job for professionals.

• **Prefabricated flue:** The installation of these differs enormously, depending on where you intend to install it and on the type and brand you use. You should get full manufacturer's instructions when you buy —in fact, it would be a good idea to ask for these before you decide which type to install. Bear in mind that they're not very attractive and that they'll need to be routed up an external wall.

All-in-all, balanced flues are the best choice. They involve less installation work, yet provide greater flexibility for boiler positioning—they're certainly best for wall-mounted boilers. As long as you carefully choose a position that provides ventilation and safety (see illustration), the only work involved is that of cutting an access hole through the wall—there's no need to erect scaffolding because you don't need to get on to the roof, and there's no need for a lining or any ugly pipes. If you are not able to fix your boiler directly to an outside wall, you may be able to fit a fan-assisted flue with a moveable duct to take advantage of a balanced flue.

Screwed joints

Screwed plumbing joints are made simply by screwing the two components together, like a nut and bolt, until they are tight. But this won't make them **watertight**, so first a wrapping of PTFE tape is applied to the thread of the 'bolt' component. Make sure you wind this in such a direction that it doesn't become undone as you screw it home—clockwise as you look at the end of the 'bolt'. You need three or four layers.

PTFE tape is easy to use and works well on small threads. But on the larger threads —such as on an immersion heater—and on boiler tappings, you must use jointing paste and **hemp**. Coat the thread of the fitting with the jointing paste (use a spatula, not your fingers if the paste is the acidic type) then wrap several fine strands of hemp into the threads in the same direction as for PTFE tape. Work some more paste on top of the hemp, then screw the fitting home.

Screwed joints are still referred to in imperial BSP (British Standard Pipe) sizes. A ½in BSP is equivalent to 15mm pipe size; ¾in to 22mm; and 1in to 28mm.

CYLINDER, PIPEWORK AND CONTROLS

As long as you have some experience of plumbing, you should not find fitting pipework difficult, though it's almost certainly the largest and most time-consuming plumbing job you'll ever do. It's also a job that occupies every room in the house, so if you can, work full-time on this stage of the installation, rather than only at weekends or in the evenings.

There are two main parts to the pipework: the connections between the boiler, the new expansion tank and the hot water cylinder; and those between the radiators and the boiler cylinder circuit.

All the connections are quite complicated, so study your design plans and the illustrations on the following pages until you're confident that you know exactly which component is connected to which. Only when you're fully satisfied should you begin this stage of the plumbing and pipework installation.

The next stage is to install your control system and the wiring that supplies the power—a job made much easier by modern 'packaged' systems. Finally, you can fill the system, then hire a qualified engineer to fire the boiler and check all your work.

Boiler and hot water cylinder pipework

The most complicated section of pipe work is that around the boiler. Here, you have the large pipes from which branches run to the radiators, the hot water primary circuit

Boiler/cylinder connections —also called the primary circuit—will vary according to the shape of your house and the system that has been designed for you.

The circuit must be vented properly, both from the boiler and from the domestic hot water cylinder.

The pump/motorized valve arrangement must be sited in the most convenient position on the circuit—it's often easiest at the boiler end but could equally well be placed alongside the cylinder

to the cylinder, and the feed and expansion pipes to and from the new cistern.

Your designer will have offered you one of a variety of layouts, depending on your house and the type of system you are installing, and the plans should show in detail the layout of the pipework in this area. But you can't rely on this to be perfectly accurate and you may have to make minor modifications as you go along. This will probably involve buying odds and ends of fittings—best done locally.

Start by installing the feed and expansion cistern in the roof space. This cistern should be placed as high as possible—at least 1m above the top of the highest radiator, or the hot water cylinder if this is higher.

Run the feed pipe down to the point where it will connect with a return pipe to the boiler (or right to the boiler itself if this has a separate feed pipe connection). The vent pipe should be crooked over the top of the cistern, and taken up as high above the

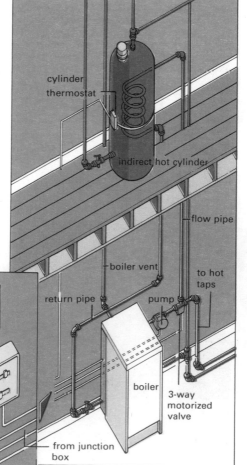

tank as there is room for. Again, run this pipe down to the connection with the piping round the boiler (it may be connected in a number of places, depending on your design or space).

You might want to take this opportunity to install a new cold water cistern as well—the procedure is much the same as for a feed and expansion tank, except it's larger.

Now you can install the new hot water cylinder. Run the flow and return pipes from it to the boiler connections. Commonly, the boiler has separate tappings for the hot water cylinder circuit, so you can connect the pipes directly into it. With a fully pumped system, you effectively treat the hot water cylinder as another radiator—regard the flow and return pipes as branch pipes off the main radiator run and blank off any unused tappings. In these pipe runs there are likely to be a number of control valves and perhaps an air-vent—your design will show you where these go and explain how to install them.

With a gravity flow primary circuit, make sure the pipes have a continuous rise from the boiler to the cylinder—there should be no horizontal or downward-sloping sections of pipe.

You can now make all the connections at the boiler, which include the first section of radiator feed and return pipes; again, your design will show you what goes where. The boiler will have large-diameter screwed tappings. Use bushes to reduce these to the size of the pipes entering the boiler. Screw into these either straight or elbow fittings that are screwed on one end, and have compression joints on the other—known as **male iron to compression**, or **MI× comp**. All the screwed fittings should be made with hemp and jointing paste.

Installing cisterns

Most modern cisterns are made of plastic and must be supported on a sturdy, continuous surface, such as chipboard or floorboards laid close together. If you want to raise the height of a cistern, make sure that the platform you build is also sturdy, especially for a cold water cistern which is large and very heavy when it is full of water.

Holes must be cut in the cistern for the various pipes which have to be fitted—these

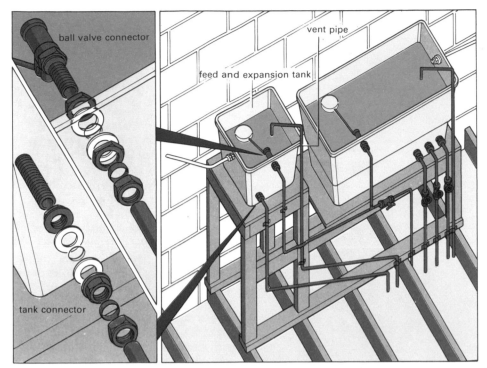

ball valve connector

vent pipe

feed and expansion tank

tank connector

1 *Make connections to the tappings of the boiler—the flow and return pipes from the cylinder, and the cold feed from the expansion tank, often connect to it. Having made the first run, install a new hot water cylinder*

2 *You may need special reducing fittings where the larger pipes of the primary circuit meet with smaller pipes— they're generally shown on your plans though you may have to make slight alterations to get them to fit*

are the same for either the feed and expansion cistern, or a cold water cistern. By far the easiest way of cutting the holes is with a **hole saw** fitted to an electric drill. Other methods are very time-consuming and, if they involve cutting at the sides of the hole with a knife, can weaken a plastic cistern. Do all your hole cutting at ground level, rather than up in the roof. But try out the cistern in the loft first, so that you can check that you will be making the holes in sensible places and not, for example, where the pipes coming out of them would foul on rafters or beams, or where the connections to the cistern would be hard to get at.

The holes that are needed should be made in the following places:
• About 75mm from the top, to take the ball valve.
• Slightly below the level of the first hole, for the overflow pipe.
• 50mm up from the base, for the outlet.

The ball-valve hole, and the hole for the outlet from a feed and expansion tank, should be the old Imperial ½in diameter; other holes should be ¾in diameter—but check these measurements in case the fittings on your cistern are metric or different from the usual ones.

Fit the outlet hole and the overflow hole with **tank connectors**, the threaded end pointing out of the cistern. Seal the joint between the cistern and the connector with plastic washers: on a plastic cistern you must **not** use any form of jointing paste or compound.

Fit the ball-valve in place, too. This

usually comes with its own version of a tank connector already fitted. Put a plastic washer on the inside wall of the cistern; push the tank connector end of the ball-valve through the hole; fit a large metal plate over the connector (this piece should come with the cistern, and is used to strengthen the cistern walls); then another plastic washer; and finally the securing nut. The pipe generally joins the fitting via a compression fitting.

Take the cistern into the loft, and place it in position on its support. Then connect the various pipes up to it. These must be well supported—clipped to the roof timbers or the cistern's platform. There must be no strain on any of the connections to the cistern—pipes must be of just the right length and at just the correct angle—otherwise the cistern might leak.

Fitting the pump

Either your first or second section of radiator pipework—the pipes that run from the boiler to the radiators—will take you up to the position of the pump specified on your plans. Fitting this requires some care.

Pumps come with two fittings, one for each end. These are different from those used in other parts of a plumbing system— one end has a standard compression joint, for connecting to the pipework, but the other has a flat flange which makes it easy to slide the pump out when it needs repairing or replacing. You cannot use jointing com-

pounds to make a watertight joint between the flange on the fitting and that on the pump—you have to rely on a thin sealing washer—so it's vital that the pump, and the pipework on either side of it, are accurately in line.

Follow the instructions provided with the pump carefully—some have to be fitted in particular orientations. Clip the pipework just either side of the fitting so that the pump is supported properly. Compression-joint the fittings to the pipes, but only hand-tighten the cap nuts, and do not apply any jointing compound. Then slide the pump between the flanges, with the sealing

3 *Connect the flow and return pipes— you may have to bend them. Fit the valve to the flow in order to connect radiator pipework*

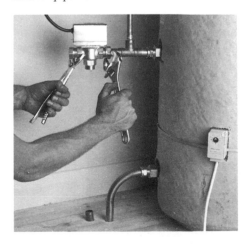

washers in place. Loosely screw up the flange nuts and check that all the pipework is not only of the correct length but is also accurately aligned.

For the time being, remove the pump and its unions and replace it with a short piece of pipe held in place with normal straight compression couplings. This ensures that no debris gets into the pump when you flush the system later.

Installing a cylinder

You will almost certainly want to install a new hot water cylinder along with your central heating system. For one thing, you will need one with an indirect heating element in it, and if you don't have central heating at present, your current cylinder is likely to be of the direct type. Although you can convert these, fitting a brand-new indirect cylinder is likely to be easier and more efficient.

It's important to plan the change-over of cylinders carefully, so that you are not left without hot water for long periods. The night before, switch off any hot water heater —a solid fuel boiler should be raked out. There should be a draincock at the point where it enters the cylinder; if you already have a boiler of some sort, the drain cock may be at the lowest point of the boiler return pipe. You can drain the cylinder from either of these points. If there is a valve at the outlet of the cistern on the feed pipe, turn this off to stop the cylinder refilling; if there is no valve here you will have to turn off the supply to the cistern, either at the main stop-valve on the rising main or by tying up the ball-valve; you will also have to drain the cistern as well.

After draining, undo all the fittings connecting the pipes to the cylinder (or cut the pipe if you have to). Disconnect any immersion heater at the nearest junction box— **not** at the heater itself—and be sure to **switch off** at the mains first.

Undo the immersion heater—you will need a special large spanner for this, or a

4 *Fit the pump at the point specified on your plans—generally on the flow pipe before the three-way motorized valve*

pair of slip-joint pliers, which you can hire. If the heater is in good condition you can re-use it in the new cylinder—you may still want the ability to heat water separately with an immersion heater even if you fit central heating.

Try to do all this work early in the day, so that you can then put the new cylinder in

place and decide what fittings you will need to connect it up—unless you are very lucky, you will have to move, shorten, or extend at least some of the pipes and it's unlikely that you will be able to plan this in advance.

At this stage, you need to connect up only the domestic water side of things—the inlet from the cold water cistern and the outlet to the hot taps.

As yet there is no need to connect up the central heating flow and return tappings: because these lead to an enclosed coil inside the cylinder, there is no possibility of the cylinder leaking when you fill it.

The inlet pipe should have a drain tap fitted to it, and according to how your pipes are placed and the amount of space you have, this may have one screwed end, for screwing directly into the cylinder, or two compression ends, for fitting a little way away from it. In either case, the drain tap may be a straight or elbow type of fitting. Make up the screwed ends of all fittings with hemp and paste. With the cylinder connected, test this part of the circuit before you continue.

Connecting up radiators

Though technically one of the easier jobs of installation—if you have done any plumbing previously—connecting the radiators to the boiler involves a great amount of upheaval in every room in the house.

Plan the order in which you fix the pipework to the radiators so that you disturb each room for as short a time as possible: it's probably best to do the most far-flung branches first, then work your way back to the boiler.

Start at the radiator end. If the pipes are to run underneath floorboards, lift these first so that you can check on the position of the joists. Don't try to lift the board closest to the wall the radiator is on (if the boards run parallel to the radiator) as it is easier to lift the next one.

Screw the radiator valves hand-tight onto the unions you fitted to the radiator earlier

1 Turn off the supply to the old cistern— you may need to tie up the ball valve in order to drain it down

2 Disconnect the fittings and remove the immersion heater—you may find you need to hire a large spanner

3 Fit the new cylinder in the same way, but remember to include tappings for the flow and return pipes

1

2

3

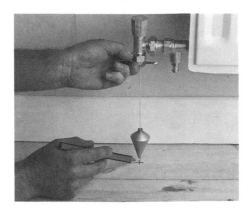

5 *Use a plumbline or spirit level to mark the floorboards so that you can connect the radiator to the pipework*

6 *Remove the radiator from the wall brackets to drill the hole—use an 18mm bit if you're using 15mm pipe*

7 *Lift the floorboard adjacent to the one you have drilled—use a lever to prise up from one end to the other*

8 *Loose lay the pipework to mark the floor joists—notch them before you make the final connections to the radiator*

9 *Use a compression fitting underneath the floorboard. It's easiest to fit this joint before you connect to the radiator*

10 *You may need to bend pipes or use special fittings to connect to the appropriate pipe*

and mark the floorboard directly underneath the other end of the valve. Remove the valves to prevent them from being damaged, and drill holes about 18mm diameter through the floorboards (assuming you are connecting to the radiator with 15mm pipe). Drill smaller holes if you're using one of the small-bore types (see Working with micro-bore).

Replace the valves, this time smearing a little paste on the metal mating surfaces. Then slip a length of pipe through the hole in the floorboard and into the valve to check that all is well and that there is no strain on the valve or the pipework.

You will almost certainly have to change the direction of the pipework under the floorboards from vertical to horizontal at this point. Don't try to bend the pipe—there isn't usually enough room under the floorboards for this. Instead, use an elbow fitting. Both compression and capillary fittings are difficult to use in this position unless you assemble them first then wiggle them into position—you may find a push-fit connector is well worth while here.

Again, be prepared to make modifications to the design—especially in the exact pipe runs and the fittings used. Ensure that pipes do not have dips or peaks in their length—these could trap air. All pipes run from boilers to radiators should have a slight constant rise or fall along their length.

Pipes under floorboards

There are various ways you can saw through floorboards to lift them. But whatever you use, take great care: there may be electric cables just beneath the surface.

•**Circular saw:** Adjust this to just cut through the thickness of the board—experiment in a concealed corner. Set the saw

---

★ WATCH POINT ★

Replace the floorboards, but don't fix them down. You'll need to lift them later to check there aren't any leaks.

---

going before lowering into the board, and stop when you reach adjacent boards. You can cut either to one side of a joist or on top of a joist—on top would be better because it makes it easier to fit above the old joist. Finish off the cut at each side either with a hand saw or (if you have cut over a joist) with a narrow chisel.

•**Jig saw:** You can't cut over a joist with this, but only to one side, and you have to take even greater care that there are no cables or pipes beneath. Drill a hole for the blade on one side and set the saw going before you lower it into the wood. You can cut neatly right up to the adjacent boards.

•**Flooring saw:** This is a hand saw specially shaped so that you can make cuts in a laid floorboard. If you can hire one, it could be a useful tool.

After cutting the end, lift the board by carefully levering under the side with a wide bolster chisel. If the boards are tongued and grooved, you will first have to saw or chisel through the tongue along one side of the full length—avoiding intervening joists—before you can lever the board free.

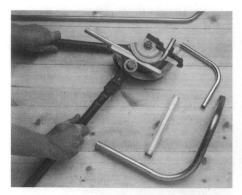

11 *Hire a pipe bender. You may need to bend pipes to avoid other pipes or to skirt round obstructions*

12 *Fit the room thermostat at the most convenient position—follow the manufacturer's instructions*

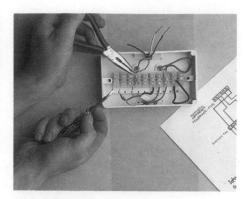

13 *All the wires meet at the junction box—follow the wiring diagram and the colour codes*

You will have to cut notches in joists if you want to lay pipes across them. This is easily done by sawing down both sides of the notch, then chiselling out the wood. Take care not to go too deep—say 5mm more than the diameter of the pipe—and make sure the pipe will run along the centre of a floorboard, not close to one edge where you might accidentally nail into it as you refit the board. If possible, have separate notches for each pipe—a single wide notch may weaken the joist.

Lay the pipe in the notch, making sure it is not binding against the sides. Help prevent creaks and noises by packing the notch all round with pieces of insulation material.

Control system and wiring

Control systems can get complicated—the easiest way to deal with them is to buy a packaged system, and follow the manufacturer's instructions.

Even the simple system of programmer and room thermostat described here can involve fairly complicated wiring runs, with many joints. The packaged systems usually come with a central junction box—you simply run the cables from all the components to this and then make the connections on a longer terminal strip, following the manufacturer's instructions.

First, decide on positions for the components. A programmer is usually mounted in the kitchen near the boiler—but it can go wherever in the house would be most convenient for you to set it—by the front door, so you can check its settings before you go out for the day; or even by your bed if you like, so you can adjust the controls at the same time as you set your alarm clock.

There is no really good place for a room thermostat—but the best compromise is

★ WATCH POINT ★

Protect the pipe by screwing a metal plate across the notch—chisel a rebate to make the top surface flush.

probably the living room. Place it about 1.5m high, away from heat sources, draughts and so on, but in an open position where it can best sense the temperature of the room.

To keep the wiring runs short, place the junction box as close as possible to the programmer, thermostat, boiler and pump—but more importantly, install it where it will be easy to work on, and where the resulting mass of wires won't look too obtrusive.

Connect the programmer and thermostat to the junction box using 1.0mm² cable—the same as is used for lighting circuits. The final section of wiring to the boiler, pump and any motorized valves should be in heat-resistant flex; run these flexes clear of the heat then, via a proper joint box, continue the run to the junction box in 1.0mm² cable. Note that many of the components need more than two conductors—motorized valves can use up to six wires—so you will probably have to use three-core and earth cable, or even two or more cables to each component (in which case label each carefully so you know which conductor of each goes to which terminal). Almost certainly, all components will need to be properly earthed. If you're not sure of the procedure, leave this part of the job to an electrician or heating engineer.

The junction box is the only component which is connected directly to the mains. It's best to connect this to the power supply from a fused spur connection unit.

The hot water circuit should be control-

led at the very least by a mechanical valve fitted in the primary pipework—though this will give no control over the timing of the hot water supply, it will at least ensure that the hot water never gets dangerously hot. Such a valve will have been fitted when plumbing in the hot water cylinder.

Working with microbore pipe

Flexible microbore pipe can be easier to work with than conventional rigid copper tube, but only if you know how to handle it.

To cut it, use a junior hacksaw. Ream out the inside carefully—you cannot afford to

Wiring diagrams are simpler than they seem—the wires are colour coded and the terminals in each component are numbered

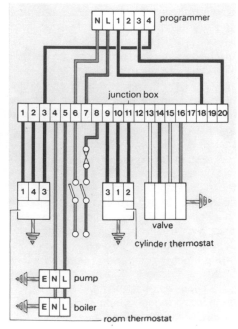

make the diameter any smaller than it already is. It is better to use solder fittings if you can get them—compression fittings are a little fiddly and delicate at this small size. Before making a joint, use a **re-rounding tool** to make sure the tube end is properly circular—it is very easy to squash it slightly as you cut it. The tube can be bent easily by hand, but for the tightest, neatest bends you should use a **bending spring**. Once the tube has been bent, it tends to harden up and it is more difficult to bend again.

It is quite easy to pull the tube through holes drilled in floorboards—something that is very difficult to do with conventional tube—but only if you have an assistant to help wind the tube off the roll as you do so. Never try pushing the tube—you'll only kink it. A kinked piece of tube is useless.

Commissioning the system

Commissioning simply means getting the system working for the first time, and naturally you'll be keen to feel your heating working. But don't let impatience prevent you from taking care at this stage.

The first step in commissioning is to fill the system so that you can check for leaks and flush out debris. Start by attaching hosepipes to all the drain cocks (on the heating side—there's no need to touch the hot water side) and open the cocks.

Open the tap to the feed and expansion tank (or release the ball-valve if this is tied up) and let this start filling. Once the water reaches the outlet pipe, part of the heating system will start to fill—how much depends on the position of the drain cocks. If all is well, close off the drain cocks and let the system fill completely. Check continuously for leaks at all the joints; small leaks in compression or push-fit joints can usually be cured by **carefully** tightening up the fitting a little; soldered joints will have to be re-made after the pipe has drained and dried, so try to bear with any such leaks until such time as the whole system has been filled and emptied.

Check also that the ball-valve in the feed and expansion tank is working properly: it's likely that the tank will fill, and the ball-valve shut off, several times during the filling session. When the ball valve does shut off, check the level of the water in the tank: it should be no more than 100mm, to allow for the expansion in volume when the water in the system heats up. As the system fills, air will become trapped in the branch pipe runs, preventing the system from filling further. Bleed off this air by opening the

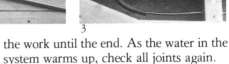

1

2

3

1 Microbore pipe can be cut with a hacksaw. You will find connections at the valve are often more complicated

2 Some valves are connected to both the flow and return pipes—a length fits into the radiator very neatly

3 Thread the pipe through drilled holes— use a bending spring to prevent kinking the bore—kinked tube must be replaced

vent nipples on the radiators one by one, starting at the lowest. Hold a rag under the nipple and be ready to shut it as soon as you see water dribbling out.

Open the drain cocks and drain the system. Mend any leaks, then refill and empty again to flush the pipework thoroughly.

Next fit the pump in place. Making sure everything around you is dry, connect up the pump to the control system wiring. Fill the system yet again, and set the pump running for a few minutes. Drain and refill; you should now be ready to warm up the whole system.

You should call in a qualified engineer to light the boiler for the first time. The engineer will be able to test and alter the flue draught, and check that combustion is safe. With a gas boiler, you could get all this work done at the same time as the gas supply is connected if you leave this part of

14 *Drain the system from its lowest point—often at the boiler. Attach a hose to the drain cock and lead it outside*

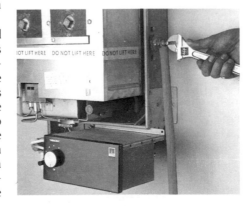

the work until the end. As the water in the system warms up, check all joints again.

The final job is to **balance** the radiators — alter the flow of water through them so that the correct temperatures are achieved in each room. To do this properly, you need two clip-on thermometers (which you may be able to hire from your stockist). Check that the pump is operating on its designed setting, and that the boiler is at full operating temperature—usually 80°C. Starting with the radiator furthest from the boiler, open both the lockshield and handwheel valves and clip on the thermometers, one on each end of the radiator just above the pipework. Then close down the lockshield valve until the outlet thermometer reads 10°C less than the inlet one (if you can't achieve something close to this, come back to the radiator when you have balanced the others). Do this on each radiator, then check them all.

During the first few weeks of operation, you may need to bleed one or two of the radiators a few more times, but if you have to continue doing this, it suggests a fault— perhaps a leaky joint that is sucking air in, or a more serious design fault. Once you are sure the system is working properly, you should add some corrosion inhibitor to the water. This is usually introduced into the feed and expansion tank, and means draining off some water. See instructions.

15 *As the system fills, bleed the trapped air from the radiators. Special keys are provided for the nipples*

CENTRAL HEATING PROBLEMS

When a central heating system ceases to function properly, it becomes an expensive liability. But it does not always take an expert to repair it. Many common faults can be cured just as easily by the householder.

The most complicated part of the average domestic central heating system is the boiler. This may require specialist knowledge and tools to put it right should it fail—but failures in boilers which are regularly serviced are rare. More prone to trouble are circulation pumps, thermostats and radiators.

Faults here are usually easy to identify and even if a specialist has to be called in, being able to pinpoint a problem will help keep repair bills to a minimum.

Wet central heating systems

In order to identify a particular fault in a central heating system, it is worth having some idea of how the system works.

In most modern systems, hot water flows from the boiler to the radiators and hot water cylinder, releases its heat and returns to be reheated. The flow is created artificially by an electric circulation pump which is normally mounted adjacent to the boiler. The pump is controlled by a time clock and, in most cases, by a room thermostat as well.

At pre-selected times, the mechanism in the clock switches on the pump. The pump then sends hot water to the radiators, heating the house.

Maintenance of the system

Although all central heating systems should be serviced at least once a year by qualified engineers, you can keep the system running reliably by correct use and regular maintenance.

It is not advisable to switch off heating at night during cold weather. A small amount of heat—to ensure that the temperature throughout the house never falls below 10°C (50°F)—cuts the time needed to reach full operating temperature and may, in the long run, save fuel. It will also help to reduce condensation and prevent frost damage to the system.

The boiler should never be run at too low a thermostat setting. There is no economic advantage to be gained and it can shorten

Above: *A central heating system is a great asset to a home, but it needs to be regularly serviced and maintained*

the life of the boiler. The boiler thermostat in a conventional small bore system should be set at up to 82°C (180°F) in winter. In summer, when the system is required for hot water only, it should be kept at not less than 54°C (130°F).

If the system is oil-fired, the oil tank should be examined annually. Any external rust should be removed with a wire brush and glasspaper and then painted over with black bitumen paint. Keep the vent pipe on top of the tank clear, removing any obstruction with a stiff piece of wire. A piece of fine wire mesh can be fitted over the end of the vent pipe to ensure that leaves do not enter the tank and restrict the flow of fuel to the boiler.

To clean the oil filter on an oil tank, turn off the stop cock and remove the filter bowl. Clean the element with paraffin, dry it and refit. At the same time check the oil line

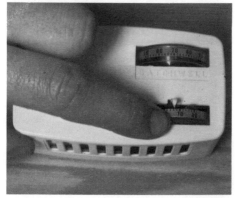

1 *To check a room thermostat, turn it to its lowest setting. Turn it back up again, listening for a click as the pump is switched on*

5 *To free an air lock in the pump, unscrew the vent valve located at the top. When water begins to trickle out, close the valve*

from the tank to the boiler for leaks, tightening joints where necessary.

When a solid fuel boiler is not in use it should be left clean. Remove sooty deposits from the combustion chamber and flue and leave the damper and boiler doors open to allow a current of air to pass through. Have the flue cleaned at least once a year.

If a central heating system has to be left drained for any length of time and stop valves are fitted on either side of the circulation pump, you can close the valves, remove the pump and dry it thoroughly to prevent rusting.

Overheating

Overheating is one of the most common faults found in wet central heating systems. In all cases of overheating, if the fault cannot be rectified at once, the supply of gas or oil to the boiler should be cut off as a precaution. If you can run the circulation pump with the boiler off, keep it circulating water so that the heat is dissipated through the radiators. With a solid fuel boiler, rake the fire into the ashpan and remove it.

If the house feels abnormally hot, check the time clock and, if there is one, the room thermostat. These may be failing to turn the pump off when they should or have had their settings accidentally advanced. Start by turning the time clock down to the present setting. If the radiators do not cool

★ WATCH POINT ★

To find out whether the pump is working, hold one end of a screwdriver against the casing with the other end to your ear and listen for the hum of the rotor inside (fig. 2): if there is no noise, this is probably stuck.

down at the time they are supposed to, the mechanism of the clock has probably jammed and will have to be replaced with a new one.

To check a room thermostat, turn it down to its lowest setting and then back up again. A click should be heard as the switch inside turns the pump on. If there is no click, the unit will have to be replaced.

If the whole system is overheating seriously, the radiator pipes may make prolonged knocking or hissing noises and there will be excessive temperature in the boiler delivery pipe. One possible reason for this is failure of the circulation pump.

On pumps with a screw-on glass inspection cover, the rotor can be freed quite easily. Turn the pump off, unscrew the cover and insert a screwdriver into one of the slots in the rotor. If the rotor does not spin freely, it should be possible to free it by levering gently with the screwdriver (fig. 4).

On pumps which have all metal casings, the water supply must be cut off before

2 *To find out whether a circulation pump is working, hold one end of a screwdriver against the casing with the handle to your ear*

3 *On pumps with all-metal casings, you may have to drain the system and remove the unit before you can unscrew the casing*

4 *If the rotor has seized, you may be able to free it by inserting a screwdriver into one of the slots and levering gently*

6 *To check the boiler thermostat, turn the dial down and then back to its maximum setting. If there is no click, the thermostat is jammed*

7 *If the sender bulb on the end of the copper capillary has come out of place, reposition it and replace its securing clip*

8 *Make sure that the level of water in the expansion tank is not more than 150mm from the valve outlet. If it is, add more water*

opening the cover. In most cases, there are stop valves on each side for this purpose but where no such valves are fitted, the system will have to be drained before carrying out any work on the pump.

If the pump is heard to be working but water is evidently not circulating, there is probably an air lock. At the top of the pump you will find a vent valve—operated either by a key or a screwdriver—from which the pump can be bled (fig. 5).

To do this, turn the pump off and leave it for a few hours to allow the water in the system to settle. Then open the valve to bleed off the air. A hiss of air will be followed by a trickle of water: when the trickle becomes constant, you can close off the valve.

If the fault is not in the pump, the boiler thermostat may have failed. The thermostat, a small box with a dial on the top, is located behind the boiler casing. Remove the casing and check that the electrical connections on the thermostat are sound. Check also that the sender bulb on the end of the copper capillary from the thermostat to the boiler has not fallen out of its socket (fig. 7). If so, reposition it and replace the securing clip.

Note the setting on the boiler thermostat dial and turn it down low. After a few minutes turn it back towards its maximum setting and listen for a click. If there is no click, it may mean that the thermostat has become jammed and you should call in a qualified engineer to give it a thorough maintenance check.

If the boiler thermostat appears to be working, check to see whether the boiler flue outlet outside has become blocked in some way. Depending on the nature of the blockage, expert help may be needed in order to clear it.

If the flue is free of any obstruction, the next thing to check is the expansion tank. The ball valve supplying it may have become jammed or seized, in which case there may not be enough water in the system to absorb the heating action of the boiler. If the level in the tank is more than 150mm from the valve outlet, free the valve and introduce more water into the system. Where the valve is completely seized, replace it with a new ballcock, arm and piston unit.

Central heating too cool

If all the radiators are cool and the boiler is working correctly, the fault probably lies with one of the thermostats, the time clock or the circulation pump. Carry out checks outlined above under 'Overheating', paying special attention to the position of a room thermostat if fitted. This reacts to the temperature around it, and a nearby heat source can cause it to give a false reading even though the mechanism may be perfectly sound.

To work efficiently, the thermostat should be mounted on an internal wall at least 1.5m above the floor and away from draughts, radiators and direct sunlight. It should not be placed in rooms which are in constant use—such as lounges—because people generate extra heat, nor in kitchens, because of the heat from cooking and appliances. However, it should be accessible so that changes in setting can be made conveniently.

Draining the system

Before doing any major repairs or modifications to your central heating, you will have to drain, or partially drain, the system. Start by turning the boiler off and leaving the system for a few hours to cool down. Turn off the electricity supply to the time clock and the immersion heater—if the system includes one (fig. 9).

Shut off the water supply to the boiler by closing the stop valve on the pipe into the expansion tank (fig. 10). If no stop valve is fitted to the system, lash the ball valve in the expansion tank to a piece of wood laid across the tank.

When the system has cooled, return to the boiler and identify the main drain cock. This is usually at the front end of the boiler near the pump where it is always built into the lowest pipe. Alternatively, it may be found on a ground-floor radiator. Attach one end of a garden hose to the nozzle and run the other to an outside drain. Open the drain cock by turning the nut beneath with a spanner or adjustable wrench and allow as much water as you require to drain away (fig. 12).

Refilling the system

Before refilling, close the main drain cock securely. Open the valve on the pipe leading to the expansion tank, or untie the ball valve, to admit fresh water into the system. Regulate the position of the valve so that the tank fills slowly—keeping the risk of air locks to a minimum. Also check the drain cock for leaks.

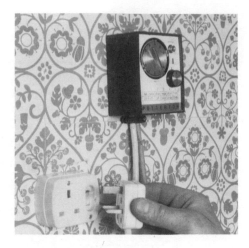

9 *Before draining a central heating system, turn off the electricity supply to the time clock and also to the immersion heater, if fitted*

12 *Run the other end of the hose to an outside drain, then open the drain cock by turning the nut beneath with an adjustable wrench*

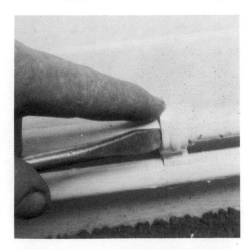

15 *Metal pipe brackets are another common source of noise. Bend them back slightly and stuff pieces of felt into the gaps*

Noise

Noise is another common problem with wet central heating systems. Creaking under the floorboards and around radiators is caused by pipes—which expand and contract according to the temperature of the water—rubbing against the floor joists on which they rest. Creaking can also occur where a pipe rises through the floorboards to feed a radiator.

If the noise persists, take up the floorboards around the suspect area. Eventually you will find a point where one or two pipes cross a joist and are notched into the woodwork. If the notch is so small that it causes the pipes to rub against each other, enlarge it to give a better clearance. Make sure, though, that the notch does not exceed one sixth of the depth of the joist or it will seriously weaken the timber. Use a piece of rubber pipe lagging, felt or carpet, trimmed to the approximate size of the notch, to cushion the pipes (fig. 13).

Where a pipe rises through a gap in a floorboard, either enlarge the gap by filing it away or pack the space around the pipe with padding (fig. 14). Metal pipe brackets—another common source of noise—can be bent back slightly, and stuffed with felt to prevent them making direct contact with the pipes (fig. 15).

Creaking behind radiators is usually caused by the hooks on the back of the panels rubbing against their corresponding wall brackets. For serious cases, on smaller radiators, special nylon brackets can be fitted in place of the normal pressed steel type. A simpler solution is to place pieces of felt or butyl rubber between each hook and bracket. This can be done, with the help of an assistant, by gently lifting the radiator away from its brackets, slipping the pieces of felt into the hooks and then replacing it.

Immersion heaters

In many systems, hot water for sinks and baths is heated by a thermostatically controlled immersion heater in addition to the boiler-fed heat exchanger. The thermostat is pre-set to turn the heating element off when the water reaches the selected temperature. If the water is unbearably hot, the thermostat may simply need adjusting.

The thermostat control is found at the top or on the side of the hot water cylinder (fig. 16). To adjust it, turn off the electricity supply to the heater then unscrew the element cover where you will find a small

10 To shut off the water supply to the boiler, close the stop valve tap on the pipe which leads into the expansion tank

11 When the system has cooled down, attach one end of a garden hose to the nozzle of the main drain cock on the boiler

13 Pipes often creak where they run through a notch in a floor joist. Cushion the pipes with felt or carpet to stop the noise

14 A pipe may rub against wood where it rises through the floor. Pack the gap round the pipe with pieces of suitable padding

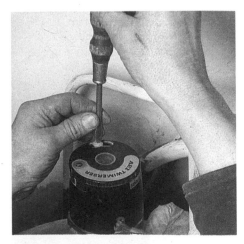
16 To adjust the thermostat control of an immersion heater, unscrew the element cover on the top or side of the cylinder

17 Remove the cover to locate the temperature dial. Turn the dial by hand or with a screwdriver to the desired temperature mark

dial marked centigrade, fahrenheit, or both. By hand, or with a screwdriver, turn the regulator screw to the desired temperature—normally 60°C (140°F) in hard water areas or 80°C (180°F) in those with especially soft water.

If the water heats up slowly, or the hot tap cools too quickly, check that the cylinder is sufficiently lagged and that the lagging is in good condition. If it is, try adjusting the thermostat. When water fails to heat up at all, either the thermostat control or the heating element is defective and will have to be replaced.

Radiator controls

Most radiators are fitted with two valves—a *handwheel* and a *lockshield* valve. The handwheel allows radiators to be shut down individually or the temperature of a radiator to be reduced by restricting the flow of water. The lockshield valve is set when the system is installed, to give a balanced flow of water through the radiator.

★ WATCH POINT ★

Creaking from the radiators can often be reduced by turning the boiler thermostat down so that the radiators remain switched on for longer periods instead of constantly heating up and cooling down.

Above: *Most radiators are fitted with two valves, called a handwheel and a lockshield valve, which control the flow of water*

There is no basic difference between the two valves except that the lockshield valve is locked into position to prevent casual adjustment. A lockshield valve should normally need adjusting only when a radiator has to be removed for decoration or repair. When this is necessary, both the lockshield valve and the handwheel should be closed. To close a lockshield valve, unscrew the cover and turn the valve with a spanner or a wrench.

In some cases, thermostatic radiator valves are fitted in place of handwheels. A radiator thermostat can be pre-set to maintain any desired temperature and is controlled by temperature-sensitive bellows. As the water temperature falls, the bellows contract to allow more hot water into the radiator. Radiator thermostats are usually only suitable for use in a two-pipe type of system.

Bleeding a radiator

When air accidentally enters a wet central heating system, it can find its way to a radiator and prevent this from functioning

Right: *To bleed a radiator, undo the valve screw and release the trapped air until water spurts out*

efficiently. All radiators should be bled of air once or twice a year to clear the small amounts that inevitably get into the system. But if a radiator becomes cold while others are functioning normally, the cause is probably a substantial air lock and the radiator should be bled immediately. The top of a radiator remaining cold while the bottom is scalding also suggests an air lock.

On most radiators a square-ended hollow key—obtainable from ironmongers—is needed to open the air vent valve at the top. To prevent air being sucked into the system, turn down the room thermostat and switch off the time clock so that the pump stops working.

Place a towel underneath the radiator to catch any drips, then open the valve by turning the key anticlockwise until a hiss of escaping air is heard. As soon as water begins to flow, re-tighten the valve.

If air locks occur frequently in a certain radiator, you can fit a screw bleed valve or an automatic air eliminator. These save you the nuisance of constantly having to bleed it by hand.

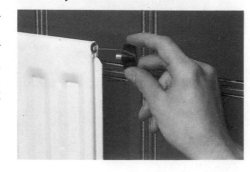

CENTRAL HEATING REPAIRS

Dealing with cold radiators

If one or more radiators are cold, or significantly cooler than the rest, an airlock caused by air getting into the system or the presence of gas due to a chemical reaction between air, water and metal may be responsible.

Simple airlocks can be removed by bleeding using a special key to open the bleed valve on the top of the radiator.

Before you start, turn the system off and give the air a chance to settle. Hold a container under the valve to catch any drips and then open it very slightly with the key. If there is an airlock, you should hear a hiss of escaping air which will be followed by a dribble of water which gradually becomes a steady flow. When this happens, close the valve immediately.

Occasionally, because of leaks, lack of water in the system, or a design defect in the pipework, the airlock may be more serious. In this case bleeding the radiators could have no effect.

Open the bleed valve on the affected radiator and get one or more assistants to stand by with containers to catch the drips.

Find the pump (normally near the boiler) and locate the flow regulator. Note what setting it's on and then, using a screwdriver, turn it full on and then off in 15 second bursts.

If you still have no success, the only other thing to try is bleeding the pump itself.

You should find the bleed valve on top of the pump casing: open and close it again very briefly using a screwdriver—a hiss of air betrays the fault.

If the radiator valve itself has seized up, drain the system and dismantle the valve. Clean the jumper gently with wire wool and reassemble it; if you can't get a replacement rubber O-ring use PTFE tape instead.

Note that you'll almost certainly get airlocks if you've had to drain and refill the system. But you can minimize them by adopting the correct procedure.

However, if you are constantly plagued by airlocks or you have to bleed a radiator every week, suspect another fault. Check that the expansion tank is at the right level: if dry, the ball valve has probably jammed.

Balancing: Sometimes, what seems like an airlock in a radiator is in fact caused by an incorrectly set lockshield valve. These balance the flow between one radiator and another and are preset during installation. But if the radiator has been removed for any reason, the setting could have been disturbed.

If you suspect that this might be the case, remove the cover and with an adjustable spanner open or close it a few turns to admit hot water to the radiator.

Most central heating systems will look like this. Pipework problems are less common than pump and radiator faults, though old age and hard water take their toll of pipes, radiators, valves and boilers. While the majority of problems are minor ones and easily dealt with, prevention is always better than cure

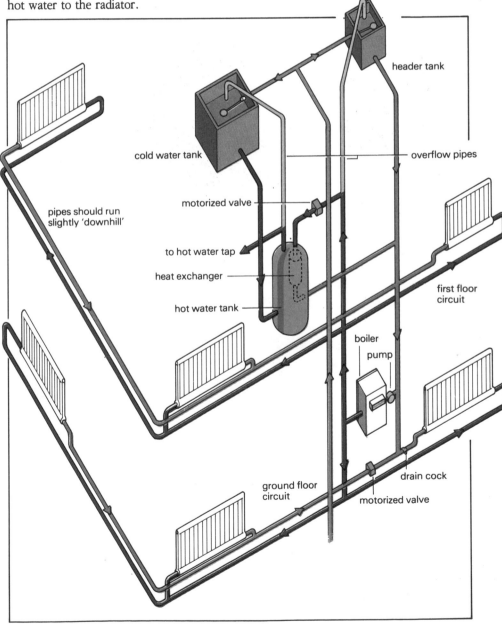

header tank

cold water tank

overflow pipes

pipes should run slightly 'downhill'

motorized valve

to hot water tap

heat exchanger

hot water tank

first floor circuit

boiler

pump

ground floor circuit

drain cock

motorized valve

Faulty thermostats and time-switches

When all your radiators go cold—or get hot when you don't want them to—the first thing to check is your room thermostat.

Make sure it is on the right setting—15°C in a hallway, 21°C in a living room. If you turn the dial back and forth, you should hear a click as the thermostat operates: no click means that it is faulty and should be checked or replaced.

Check, too, that the thermostat isn't giving a faulty reading because of some outside source: a strong draught, a fire nearby or sunlight can all affect it.

If all is well, move to the programmer/ timeswitch. Start by checking that it shows the correct time: a momentary power cut could have zeroed it while you were out.

Next make sure that the programme settings are correct—they're easy to get wrong or knock out of adjustment.

If the programmer seems 'dead', turn off the power supply and unscrew it from its backing box. Check that the power 'in' connections are sound and that plug-in connections between the unit and backing box haven't become dirty or loose.

If turning the programmer to 'constant' has no effect on the boiler or pump, check the connections to these two components— again making sure the power is switched 'off'. Loose terminals or frayed flexes should be easy to spot: if necessary, replace the defective wires using heat-proof flex.

If your system includes thermostatic control valves on the hot water primary circuit supplying the cylinder, or motorized valves to distribute boiler-heated water

may be able to dismantle it and free the temperature-sensing bellows controlling the flow, but drain the system before doing so.

It may be stating the obvious, but check the boiler thermostat as well. Instructions on the boiler unit will tell you the correct setting, while you can check it's working by turning the dial and listening for a click. Check the sender capillary between the thermostat and heat exchanger—it mustn't be kinked or dislodged. Replace or renew it and test the system.

Boiler and pump faults

A faulty circulation pump may result in cold radiators, over-heating or an excessively noisy system.

You can tell if a pump is running by switching the programmer to 'constant'

1 *Check all wiring and settings, especially in central heating programmers*

2 *The connections in motorized valves can vibrate and so loosen*

3 *Don't forget to check thermostatic radiator valves too*

4 *Check the sender capillary is located correctly and not kinked*

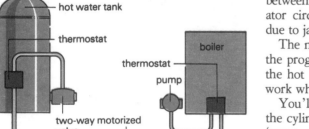

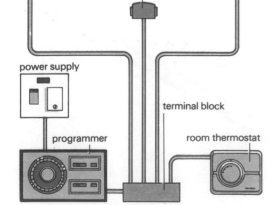

between the hot water circuit and the radiator circuit, you may experience trouble due to jamming or failure of the motors.

The most common symptom, assuming the programmer is working, is that either the hot water or the heating valves don't work when they should.

You'll find such valves near the boiler of the cylinder. With the system switched to 'constant', feel by hand that hot water is being distributed through them.

On a motorized valve, check that the electrical connections to the motor haven't become loose.

On some systems, thermostatic valves are fitted to individual radiators to give localized heating control. These are mechanical in operation, and sometimes they may jam.

Depending on the make of valve, you

Electrical connections and cable runs are basically simple; keep wiring diagrams and maker's instructions handy to deal with problems quickly

and holding a screwdriver to it, like a stethoscope: if you hear a noise, suspect some other fault—like an airlock; if there is nothing, either electricity isn't reaching the pump, the motor's burnt out, or the pump rotor is jammed.

Assuming that you've checked the power supply and programmer, the fault lies with the pump.

On some pumps, such as the common *Commodore*, it's possible to check the rotor without removing the unit, providing stop valves are fitted either side.

Shut off the power supply and close the stop valves on either side of the pump by turning them clockwise. Loosen the screws securing the casing and remove.

The rotor underneath should spin freely: if it doesn't, you may be able to free it by *gentle* levering with your screwdriver.

In all other cases the pump must be removed and taken to a heating suppliers to be checked.

If there are no stop valves, the system must be drained completely before removal.

Diagram labels: hot water tank, thermostat, boiler, thermostat, pump, two-way motorized valve, power supply, terminal block, programmer, room thermostat

1 *Listen for the sound of the pump motor turning by touching the blade of a screwdriver to the body*

2 *Use the valves on either side to isolate the pump from the water supply before removal*

3 *Check the connections inside the pump itself. Some of them may well have shaken loose*

4 *When you re-fit the pump, replace the O-ring or hemp seals on the coupling joints*

The pump will probably be connected to the pipework by threaded screw couplings: loosen these with a pair of plumber's wrenches or adjustable spanners and it should come straight out.

Before removing the pump completely, you must sever the electrical connection to the programmer. On some pumps you can get to the terminals easily having first removed a small cover on the motor casing.

With other types the motor is sealed, so disconnection must take place at the programmer end.

Fitting a new pump is a straightforward reversal of the removal procedure. But be sure to seal any screw coupling joints with hemp and jointing paste before you finally tighten them up.

Certain types of connector (especially those which incorporate a shut-off valve) may not require hemp; instead, replace the rubber O-ring seals.

★ WATCH POINT ★

Before you disconnect the wires make a note of which goes where and label them for reference.

Corrosion

Modern central heating systems in which the radiator and hot water cylinder primary circuit water is constantly recirculated should not suffer from scaling.

In areas with exceptionally hard water it is possible that the secondary hot water circuit could be affected.

Some corrosion in a system is perfectly normal—it's what turns the water black. Most systems have a proprietary corrosion inhibitor added to the primary circuit water via the expansion tank: replace it when you

Faultfinder chart

If your central heating goes wrong, consult this chart first—it should help you get straight to the root of the trouble

One radiator cold:
Check valves
Bleed radiator
Check for air locks
(see Dealing with Cold Radiators).
Check radiator thermostat
(see Faulty Thermostats and Time-switches).

Overheating:
Check boiler thermostat
(see Faulty Thermostats and Time-switches).
Check pump (see Boiler and Pump Faults).
Check water supply (see Dealing with Cold Radiators).

All radiators cold:
Check room thermostat and time-switch/programmer
(see Faulty Thermostats and Time-switches).
Check boiler (see Boiler and Pump Faults).
Check pump operation (see Boiler and Pump Faults).
Check water supply (see Dealing with Cold Radiators).

Excessive noise:
Check pipe/radiator brackets and notching in joists/floor.
Check pump (see Boiler and Pump Faults).
Check for scale and corrosion (see Corrosion).

Fumes in house:
Check boiler (see Boiler and Pump Faults) and ensure flue is not blocked.

drain the central heating system.

Excessive corrosion will only occur if large amounts of air are present in the system or the primary circuit water is too

cool. So deal with leaks and airlocks immediately, and set the boiler thermostat above 60°C. This should help to eliminate corrosion in a relatively short time.

REPAIRING FAULTY BOILERS

Troubles with pilot lights

The pilot light on a gas boiler is intended to light the main burner when gas is released through the main automatic valve.

So that no gas is released through the burners when the pilot is out, a fail safe device—the thermocouple—is incorporated into the valve. This prevents the boiler literally blowing up.

The pilot flame is intended to heat up the tip of the thermocouple sufficiently to produce a tiny electrical current which opens the pilot's magnetic gas valve.

If the pilot flame on your boiler is too small to heat the thermocouple it will keep going out. Adjustments can be made by turning a small screw on the gas valve. The screw is usually situated adjacent to the pilot gas supply line. In cases where turning the screw doesn't make the pilot flame large enough, it will be necessary to examine the pilot burner.

To do this you may have to remove the main burner assembly before you can dismantle the pilot burner and injector. Often the problem will be a simple blockage which can be removed easily with a fine wire pricker. The hole is purposely very small and should not be enlarged.

If the burner itself shows signs of wear it can be replaced relatively cheaply.

Examine the deflector shield which directs the pilot flame on the thermocouple. Replace this if it is damaged or badly misshapen through heat.

When replacing or refitting pilot parts *sealant must not be used* since there is a risk of it blocking the small hole and necessitating replacement again.

1 *Adjust the pilot jet on the gas valve using a screwdriver*

2 *Clean the pilot nozzle using the appropriate wire pricker*

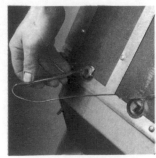

3 *If the jet is blocked it may need to be replaced with a new one*

it, first make sure that the electricity supply to the boiler is off. It's usually taken from a switched fused connection unit nearby.

Look for some small screws holding the thermostat onto the control panel. These are often located behind the thermostat knob and when they have been removed it should be possible to take the switch away from the casing. Make a note of the wiring arrangement before you disconnect the wires running into the switch.

A replacement thermostat should be readily available from spares stockists. Always quote your boiler make and model number when buying so you are sure of getting the right thermostat.

When fitting the new thermostat make sure the copper capillary tube is not kinked or damaged. Always test the operation of a thermostat throughout its range before leaving the boiler to run unattended.

On some older boilers non-electrical thermostats are used. In these a small amount of gas is drawn off the main supply through an electrically operated valve and this opens the main gas valve when the room thermo-

stat is calling for heat. Renewal of these units is no more complicated.

First, turn off the gas to the boiler and undo the nuts that connect the gas supply. Withdraw the sensor rod from the boiler water jacket and replace it with a new unit—make sure that the open ended gas tube discharges over the top of the burners. Finally, tighten the nuts and test the unit.

The type of gas valve used in these boilers differs significantly from those used in boilers with electrical thermostats. In either case you shouldn't try to cure problems in the gas valve by yourself—they are intricate and expensive items and best left to experts.

Fitting a thermocouple

If, when lighting a gas boiler, the pilot light will not remain alight after the manual reset button is released it may be that the thermocouple is at fault.

Before you try fitting a new one make certain that the pilot flame is correctly adjusted—its flame must envelop the tip of

Renewing a faulty boiler thermostat

Thermostats have no serviceable parts; the only way of remedying a fault is to replace the whole thermostat unit.

On electric thermostats a small phial is housed in a dry pocket of the boiler's main water jacket. Its removal is a simple matter of undoing the retaining screw or split pin and sliding the narrow copper phial out by pulling the copper capillary tube which is attached to the phial.

At the other end of the tube is the thermostatic switch itself. Before removing

The thermostat capillary runs from the water jacket to the thermostat control knob

The non-electrical thermostat's two capillaries run from the water jacket to the gas valve

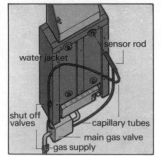

4 *The thermostat phial slips easily out of its housing in the boiler water jacket*

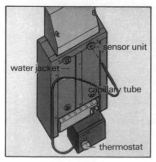

the thermocouple. At the point where the thermocouple enters the gas valve make sure the small nut holding it in place is tightened properly.

Most central heating merchants stock universal thermocouples for use with practically all boilers. But—just to make sure—take a note of the make and model number of your boiler.

If your boiler is one with a conventional flue you may be able to reach the pilot light without removing the burners. Balanced flue boilers are completely sealed so you will have to withdraw the burner and pilot assembly in one piece.

The tip of the thermocouple is held in place by a small split gland nut or circlip. At the other end—where it enters the gas valve—another split gland nut holds it in place. Once these nuts are undone the thermocouple will be easy to pull out.

Placing the old thermocouple to one side choose two split nuts from the new one's packet. Gently uncoil the new thermocouple and look along the length of copper for a flattened section. Slip the open end of each nut over the flat part and slide them along to their respective ends.

The new thermocouple should now resemble the old one. Any excess length can be coiled up again before fitting. Avoid making any sharp bends or kinks in the wire. Insert the tip into the pilot flame area first and then connect the other end to the boiler's gas valve.

Cleaning the flue and heat exchanger

An annual cleaning of the boiler is essential to maintain safe and efficient operation. All that is needed is a purpose-made flue brush and a vacuum cleaner.

Before starting work switch off the gas and electricity supplies to the boiler and, if the boiler was in use at the time, give the water jackets and heat exchanger a chance to cool down.

At the top of the boiler is a cover plate. In most cases it is held by a couple of wing nuts. Remove the nuts and lift the plate, complete with the gasket, away from the boiler. With the bottom cover plate and burners removed you should have a clear view through the main body of the boiler. This is the heat exchanger where the heat from the burnt gas warms the water. When this is clean the maximum efficiency is derived from the burnt gases and the combustion products will pass safely into the boiler's flue.

5 *Unscrew the control unit's face plate to gain access to the capillary tube*

6 *Before disconnecting any wires make a note of how they are linked to the control unit*

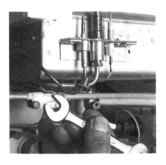

7 *Disconnect the thermocouple at the pilot end using a spanner of the appropriate size*

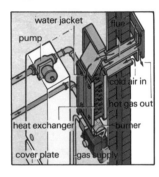

Don't be intimidated by your boiler—its construction is very simple. So is cleaning it

8 *Fit the split nuts to the new thermocouple, taking care not to kink the capillary*

9 *Don't over-tighten the nut which holds the thermocouple in place at the gas valve end*

10 *Clean the heat exchanger with a stiff-bristled brush, working from below*

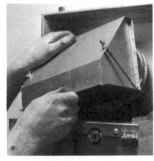

11 *The flue cover is easily removed for routine cleaning with a proper flue brush*

12 *Use a vacuum cleaner to remove all the dirt you have dislodged from the boiler*

If your boiler has the gas valve and thermostat at the bottom, below the heat exchanger, cover them with a cloth to prevent dirt affecting them.

At the top of the boiler, the flue will be protected by a cover plate of some kind—either a wedge shape or a curved bend which forms part of the flue itself. These should be easy to remove; most are held in place only with a couple of butterfly nuts.

With the cover plate removed check the gasket between flue and boiler. If this is defective, exhaust gases may leak into the boiler room.

Start by brushing inside the flue with a non-metallic bristled flue brush to remove any sooty deposits. Then brush down through the heat exchanger letting all the dirt fall into the bottom of the boiler.

Using your vacuum cleaner nozzle remove all traces of dirt and dust from the entire boiler area including the area inside the casing.

Examine the seal around the flue pipe—if it is cracked or defective a repair can be made using fire cement, which is obtainable in small tins. There is no need to let the fire cement dry before relighting the boiler.

Check the flue where it passes through the outside wall as well. Clear any dirt and leaves clogging up its protective grille and check the pointing around the flue aperture.

Safety valves

Safety valves on central heating systems are incorporated to relieve excessive pressure within the boiler or the primary circuit. Normally, pressure is released through the vent pipe at the top of the system and the safety valve is installed as a back up in case the vent is blocked by ice or other objects.

Unfortunately, many safety valves are not of very good quality and leaks occur around their seating—a small drip should not be ignored as it could result one day in a major leak. The best course of action is to renew the safety valve. To do this you must first drain the system.

Draining the system: This is done by tying up the ball valve on the feed and expansion tank. Attach a hose pipe to the lowest drain cock and run the hose out of the building to discharge at a level lower than the boiler. Open the cock fully.

When the system is empty unscrew the valve body with an adjustable spanner or wrench. The valve may be fitted to a spare housing in the boiler itself, or on the primary circuit close to the boiler. The male thread is usually ½in or ¾in BSP (a traditional British screw size). Wrap the thread with PTFE tape before screwing it home. If it is being fitted to a brass tee hold the tee with a wrench to prevent any distortion of the pipework.

When you refill the system, check for leaks. If a drip occurs on the valve turn the cap nut on the valve until it stops. Tightening the nut too much will prevent it working properly.

If your safety valve blows—letting out steam—turn the boiler off immediately and examine the system. In cold weather check that the vent pipe and the feed pipe from the expansion tank haven't frozen.

If they have, first try to warm up the loft temporarily with a small portable heater while you thaw out the pipes. When they are clear refit the safety valve and then lag the pipes and expansion tank.

If the cause of the blow-out is less obvious, call an engineer.

Removing the burner

In order to carry out proper servicing and cleaning of your gas boiler it is necessary to remove the main burner from beneath the heat exchanger. This is not difficult as burners are designed for easy removal.

Turn off the gas supply at the main cock before the boiler gas valve. Undo the union nut on the main gas supply line—this lies between the cock and valve. Remove the nuts or screws (there are usually four) from the cover plate at the bottom of the boiler.

Carefully withdraw the cover plate and then simply slide out the burners and gas valve. Often the plate and burners are fixed together—it is not necessary to separate them. In most cases there will be enough spare electrical cable to remove the burner without disconnecting the electricity supply to the gas valve.

If there isn't turn off the electricity at the mains before undoing the cover plate on top of the valve. With the burner removed you can carry out work on the pilot burner or thermocouple as well as checking the ignition device.

Use a vacuum cleaner attachment to remove dust from the gauze filter around the gas injector nozzle. This is vital to maintain the correct gas and air mixture entering the burner. Reverse the dismantling sequence to replace the burners.

Ignition devices

Spark generator—piezo: On boilers with permanent pilot lights a piezo-electric spark ignition system is often used.

When a fault occurs it will be in either the unit's high tension lead or its generator. Check the electrode is firmly positioned next to the pilot flame—examine the lead for damage which may cause shorting.

The piezo generator unit may be tested by unplugging the lead and holding an earthed screwdriver so that it is very nearly touching the piezo terminal. Fire the unit and look for a spark. If none occurs remove the piezo spark unit by undoing the screws that secure it to the bracket.

If the spark generator is proved to be working, replace the electrode complete with high tension lead. On some boilers this may entail removing the burners.

Ensure the high tension lead is kept below the level of the burners to prevent charring of the insulation on the cable.

Spark generator—mains electric: On some boilers the spark is produced by sending an ordinary current down the wire to the electrode. This may be used to ignite the pilot whenever the boiler is fired, thus avoiding the need for a permanent pilot. the generator may be tested by running a well-insulated cable from the electrode and shorting it against the earthed boiler casing.

13 *When fitting a new safety valve wrap PTFE tape round threads*

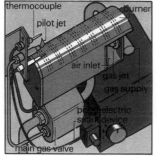

14 *The typical burner and pilot layout is simple and logical*

15 *Remove the retaining screws to slide the burner out*

16 *Remove the gauze filter and clean it with a vacuum cleaner*

17 *To check the lead disconnect it and try to get a spark*

18 *If there's no spark, disconnect it and test the piezo device*

MOVING A RADIATOR

There are many good reasons for repositioning a radiator. It may be, for example, that you intend to improve your home by knocking two rooms into one or by replacing a window with sliding patio doors. If this is the case, you may not have any option but to re-organize your central heating layout.

In many houses, radiators were originally positioned to suit the convenience of the installer rather than to suit the occupier. This can mean that a radiator lies along a wall exactly where you want to put a sofa. Or you may just want to exchange an old radiator for a more streamlined or efficient model. Whatever your particular reasons are for moving a radiator, plan your approach to the job with care so that you can avoid potentially messy disasters. Make sure you have plenty of dust sheets to hand.

Planning considerations

The two most important points to consider are the type of system you have and where you intend to put the radiator in relation to the existing layout.

The system: The pipework which connects the radiators to the boiler will be **smallbore** (15mm or 22mm in diameter) or **microbore** (6mm, 8mm or 10mm).

Smallbore pipework will follow one of two different types of layout. In a one-pipe layout, a single 22mm pipe runs around the house to and from the boiler and each radiator is joined to it via two connections. However, the majority of houses have a two-pipe layout where there are separate pipes for flow and return with the radiators connected to bridge across them (see diagram on this page). In a two-pipe layout, more than one radiator can be connected to the bridging branch.

With a two-pipe smallbore system, the size of pipe decreases as it gets further away from the boiler—it starts off with 22mm and reduces to 15mm, whereas in a microbore set up, the pipes connect the individual radiator to a centrally placed manifold.

In order to identify exactly which system you have, you will inevitably have to lift a few floorboards so that you can trace the flow and return pipes back to their source.

Choosing the new position: Unless you have double glazing—or plan to install it—it's best to put the radiator directly underneath a window. This is so that the heat from the radiator can counteract the cool downdraught from the window.

If you have double glazing, put the radiator where it is most convenient or where you will have to use the least amount of extra piping.

With smallbore systems, you may be able to use the existing branches if the new site is near to the original one—it's simply a matter of extending the pipes with the aid of elbows or straight connectors.

If the new site is some way from the old one, you'll have to break into the main flow and return pipes (two-pipe layout) by installing tee fittings and connecting new branch pipes. The old pipes can be blanked off either at the old radiator position or where you tee off (you can re-use the old pipes if they are in good condition).

Once you have decided where to put the radiator and where to break into the circuit, work out what you need to buy in terms of tees, elbows and new piping. To help in your calculations, it's a good idea to make a scale drawing of your room. If you are connecting metric sized pipe to imperial, 15mm compression fittings will fit both pipe types but 22mm won't, so in this case you'll have to use a special capillary adaptor to make the join.

With a microbore system, you have the additional choice of re-routing the pipes

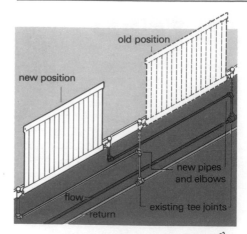

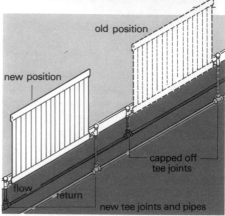

With smallbore systems, use whichever of the methods shown above is most convenient to run the pipework to the resited radiator

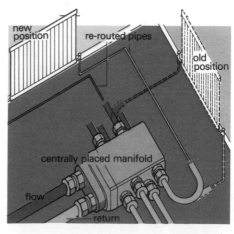

With microbore systems, each radiator is connected to a centrally placed manifold so run your new pipework back to that

from the manifold. This may be easier than trying to connect to the existing pipes. Microbore is notoriously thin and fragile and unless you are used to handling it, you will be better off buying a new coil of pipe which will be much easier to work with than the old piping.

If your microbore supply pipes are to be clipped to the wall or skirting (as opposed to running underneath the floor), a good way of protecting them is to encase them in plastic conduit. Cable conduit is adequate but check that it can take the diameter of the pipe.

Tools and equipment: For removing and fixing the radiator, you will need little more than a screwdriver, an adjustable spanner, some jointing compound and some PTFE tape. However you will also want tools for cutting and jointing pipe, lifting floorboards and drilling holes through joists. A garden hose will prove invaluable when it comes to draining down the system you can carry waste water from the house without spillage.

Removing the radiator

Before you start disconnecting the radiator, turn off the boiler and let the water cool down. Then drain the system.

To drain the system, turn off the valve in the supply pipe to the feed-and-expansion cistern in the loft—this is smaller than the main cold water tank. If there isn't a valve, tie up the ballcock.

Next, find the draincock which will be located at the lowest point in the system, probably next to the boiler. Push one end of a garden hose over the nozzle on the draincock and lead the free end to a gully or drain outside the house. The level of the drain must be below that of the draincock.

Turn off all the radiators before opening

the draincock and letting the water flow out.

When the pipes are empty, make sure that the handwheel valve on the radiator you want to move is tightly shut and close down the lockshield valve with an adjustable spanner. As you twist the lockshield nut, count the number of turns necessary to close the valve as you'll need to open it by this number of turns later.

The next step is to undo the two compression nuts which connect the supply pipes to the valves. Residue water will probably come out of these as you loosen them, so pull any carpet away from under-

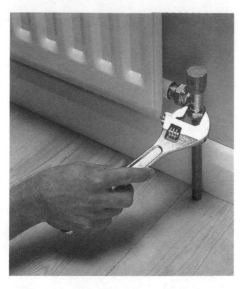

2 *Undo the compression nuts which secure the supply pipes to the handwheel and lockshield valves. Be prepared for leaks*

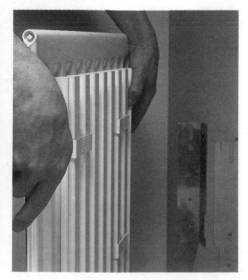

1 *To drain the system, find the draincock, push a garden hose onto its outlet and then open it with an adjustable spanner*

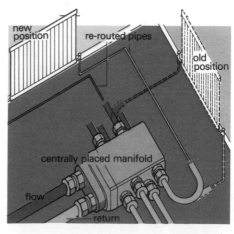

3 *Free the radiator from the pipes and lift it clear of its mounting brackets. Remove the brackets and make good their fixing holes*

4 *If you're going to re-use the radiator, take the opportunity to flush it through with a strong burst of water from your hose*

5 *Cut back the supply pipes to the radiator in its old position so that you're ready to run the new piping in later*

neath the radiator and put a bowl below the nut. Free the radiator from the pipes and lift it clear of the brackets.

If you are fitting a new radiator and want to salvage the old lockshield and wheel-valves, now is the time to remove them. However, some old radiator valves are not compatible with their new counterparts, so check before you start setting to with a spanner. If the nuts prove very obstinate—which is likely to be the case if the radiator has not been handled for a long time—try heating the joint with a blowtorch. So as not to damage the valves them-

selves, play a gentle flame onto the radiator side of the joint for a few seconds.

Hanging the radiator

Hang the radiator in its new position before you lay down the connecting pipework—that way you will know exactly where to lead the pipes.

A new panel radiator has four screwed tappings—one at each corner. Only three of these are used—the remaining one is blanked off. Normally, the flow and return pipes are connected to the bottom two tappings and an air bleed valve screwed to one of the top tappings.

6 *If you're upgrading as well as resiting a radiator, measure up for the fixing brackets and transfer your measurements to the wall*

8 *Fit the brackets. Now is also the time to fit heat reflecting foil especially if you're installing the radiator on an outside wall*

You need to fit the brackets to the wall so that the bottom of the radiator is just above the skirting board. If you are siting the radiator underneath a window, you also need to leave a 50mm clearance below the sill. To site the radiator properly, lay it on the floor and clip on the brackets. Measure and make a note of the exact distances of the brackets from the bottom and sides of the radiator. Transfer these measurements to the wall and mark where to drill fixing holes.

Before you screw the brackets to the wall, check beneath the floorboards for joists. If necessary, shift the radiator to one side so that the joists won't obstruct the connecting pipes. A second consideration—if you are fixing to a timber framed wall—is the position of the studs. If you can't screw

7 *With the radiator fitted to the wall and the valves fitted to the radiator, mark on the floor the entry points for the pipework*

9 *If you've invested in a new radiator, it's worth fitting a thermostatic valve as it will give you greater temperature control*

directly into wood, mount a horizontal batten between studs and secure the brackets firmly to this. Large radiators may require three brackets.

Once you are satisfied, drill holes in the wall, insert appropriate wallplugs and screw the brackets home using a quantity of 50mm No. 10 screws.

Hang the radiator on the brackets and, if

★ WATCH POINT ★

If they are in good condition, there's no reason why you can't re-use all the original fittings, but this is a good opportunity to fit a thermostatic wheel valve.

you have a wooden floor, use an offcut of pipe as a guide to mark holes directly underneath the two valves. Drill clearance holes through the floorboards for the pipes.

Running the pipes

The amount of work you will have to do will depend on how far you are moving the radiator. It's a good idea to lay all the pipes and fittings out in a dry run—from the connection points to the radiators—before you start connecting up. Remember to run pipes parallel with, or at right angles to, the joists.

Cut the pipes to length and when you are happy with the layout, start joining them together—see Handling copper pipe. Leave the final connection to the radiator until last—the flow pipe should lead to the hand-wheel valve.

On a solid floor, chase the pipes into the wall above the skirting. Running pipes underneath a suspended wooden floor is not so easy and you will have to lift floorboards to gain access. Downstairs, all the pipes can be run below the level of the joists; upstairs you'll have to cut some slots in the joists to take pipes running at right angles to them.

Microbore pipe can be pushed through 10mm holes drilled through joists in much the same way as electric cable but, with smallbore, you'll have to cut a slot to take the pipe. To protect pipes that run through joists from floorboard nails, either screw metal plates along the top of the joists or fill each slot with a vee-section cut-out.

Secure the pipes with plastic clips screwed to the sides of the joists (or to the wall if there's a solid floor) at 1m intervals.

Make the connections to the radiator by leading the pipes through the holes in the floorboards and up to the valves. Be sure to apply jointing compound to the end of the

pipe before tightening up the compression nuts. Don't be tempted to over-tighten the nuts as this will crush the pipes and weaken the joint, and may cause leaks. If joints don't work it is best to separate and re-make them.

Re-filling the system: Close down the draincock and double check that you have capped off any severed pipes. Open up the wheel valve on the radiator and twist open the lockshield valve the same number of turns that were needed to close it down when you started the job.

Open up the supply valve to the feed-and-expansion cistern (or untie the ballcock). As the water starts to flow through the system, go round the house bleeding all the radiators to get rid of any air. If you turned off all

the other radiators when you drained the system, they should still be full of water but it's best to make a thorough check and to bleed them as well.

Bleeding is usually done by turning the bleed screw with a special key and letting the air out—as soon as water spurts out of the hole, you know that the radiator is full. Some modern radiators have specially designed air vents which are opened and closed by hand—thus making the use of a key obsolete.

As the system is filling, check carefully for leaks and tighten any suspect connections. It helps to have someone in the loft who can turn off the water quickly if you discover a major leak.

When the radiator and system are full, switch on the boiler and nail all the floorboards back into place.

Should the re-filled system start vibrating (known as 'knocking') when you turn on the heating, don't despair as the chances are that an air lock will be the cause. The

simple cure for knocking is to bleed all the radiators once again; if necessary, bleed the valve on the electric pump too.

Handling copper pipe

It's easiest to cut copper pipe with a special pipe-cutting tool. This has a hardened steel wheel which scores a line around the pipe as you rotate the tool. The score gradually gets deeper and eventually slices through the copper. Use the pointed bit on the end of the tool to remove any burr you've made.

When cutting into a length of existing pipe to make a tee-joint, remember that the section you cut out is less than the overall length of the tee—the shoulders on com-

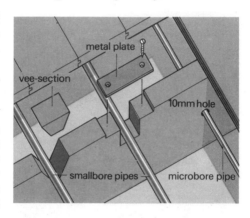

Always protect pipe when running it at right angles to joists. Microbore can be run through joists, smallbore must be notched into them

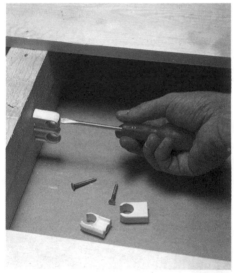

10 *When you know where you want to run the new pipework, screw pipe clips to the joists at 1m intervals*

11 *Run new piping to the point where you cut back the old, adjust its length and then make the connections*

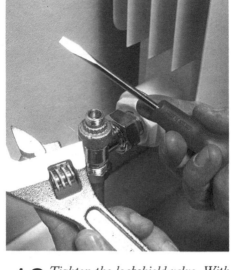

12 *Bring your pipework up through the floor and make the connections to the radiator valves—be sure to use jointing compound*

13 *Tighten the lockshield valve. With older radiators you'll need an adjustable spanner, but newer types may need a screwdriver*

14 *The final stage of the job is to bleed the radiators. When water spurts from the bleed valve, turn the key or replace the nipple*

pression tee fittings show you where the pipes should end. You will have to flex the supply pipes apart so you can slip the fitting into place.

When it comes to joining pipes together or capping off severed ends, compression fittings are the easiest type to use—especially in confined spaces.

To make a compression joint, first slip the capnut and olive over the end of the pipe and then wipe on some jointing compound. Push the pipe into the fitting until it butts up against the end of the recess. Twist on the capnut until it is hand tight and then give it a final half turn with a spanner—it's important not to overtighten the nut.

Scrape away any burr on the inside of the pipe using the point on the pipe-cutter

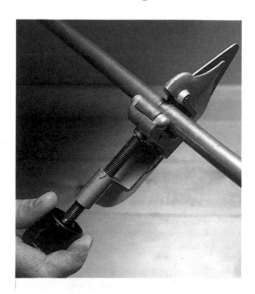

A pipe cutting tool is well worth hiring if you've got a lot of joints to make

Compression fittings are the easiest to use. Smear plumber's putty on the pipe end first

CHOOSING A HEATING SYSTEM

Most people, when they think of home heating, think in terms of a central heating system. But it is not the only choice, and some other type of heating system may be a better bet for you in certain circumstances.

The first consideration is whether to go for some form of central heating system (sometimes called whole-house heating) or to rely solely on individual heaters in each room.

Adding a **central heating system** to your house makes sense:
• If you own your own house—while central heating costs a lot of money to install this cost is usually recouped if you sell the house.
• If your house or flat is of a reasonable size—in very small homes central heating is not usually necessary.

If you decide on a central heating system, you may still want a few individual heaters as well—for when you are in a room only a short time and turning on the central heating isn't worth while; for 'topping up' central heating during very cold weather; or to provide a focal point in a room, which is something that central heating does not really provide.

Individual room heaters make sense:
• If you live in rented accommodation—most types can be taken with you when you move; fixed heaters are relatively inexpensive, so you don't lose much if you have to leave them behind.
• If you live in a very small flat or house, the capital costs of installing a full central heating system are not usually justified. Individual heaters will be able to warm the whole place adequately, and will cost much less to buy and install.

Whatever sort of heating you decide on, good insulation and draughtproofing are essential. It's best to install this *before* installing the heating—you'll then need a smaller system with perhaps no radiators or heaters at all in some rooms. The savings you make in this way will help to offset the cost of the insulation materials.

Choosing the best fuel

The decision over fuel is largely one of balancing convenience, availability, and cost. The relative costs of different fuels vary—from time to time and from area to area. Use the details below only as a guide, and check up on your local prices.

Gas-fuelled or electric 'coal effect' fires look attractive and give instant heat

• **Gas** is usually one of the less expensive fuels to use and if you have a supply readily available, it is also very convenient.
• **Electricity** is very convenient, and almost certainly easily available. It is usually very expensive, but you may find special tariffs which greatly reduce the cost. In the UK, for example, there is an 'off-peak' tariff —used in conjunction with storage heaters (see opposite) this can provide central heating with the same sort of running costs as gas or solid fuel. Electric heaters need no flue or ventilation, which all other types do. This is a major advantage as flues are expensive to construct from scratch.
• **Oil** is usually quite expensive, and storage space is needed. Heating oil, except in its paraffin (kerosene) form, is generally used in central heating boilers.
• **Solid fuel** appliances are less convenient than other types—they need regular stoking and cleaning and storage space is needed for the coal. Open fires are very inefficient, and consequently relatively expensive to run, but they are nice to sit by. Closed room heaters are efficient and can be as cheap to run as gas heaters. Wood is usually cheaper than other solid fuels, but needs more attention and greater storage space. If you live in a smokeless zone, you

may not be allowed to burn wood anyway.
• **Bottled gas and paraffin (kerosene)** are quite expensive fuels, used in portable heaters. Bottled gas can also be used in fixed heaters as a substitute for piped gas, but it is usually very much more expensive.
• **Solar heat** from the sun is not entirely free—it costs a lot to collect it—but it can be a useful way of heating water even in the UK. It is still too expensive to be used for space heating.

Types of central heating

There are two common forms of central heating. In a **wet** system, a central boiler heats water which is then passed through pipes to radiators in each room. This system is described in detail on pages 4 to 6. It is widely used in homes in the UK, and can be fitted into existing homes reasonably easily. Most fuels can be used in a wet system— even electricity, though this requires storing water in very large hot water tanks, and heating it overnight on the special off-peak tariff.

In a **warm air** system, a central 'furnace'—gas, oil, or electric—and fan unit blow warmed air through ducts connected to each room of the house. This system is widely used in North America. It's best suited to timber-framed houses, or those with lots of insulation on the *inside* of masonry walls. It is very clean, because the air that circulates in the rooms is constantly being filtered. However, the system uses large air ducts and it is usually impracticable to install these in an existing house.

Though **electric storage heaters** are generally classed as 'central heating', they can be taken with you when you move; they are relatively cheap; and you can buy just one or two units, so they can be treated as individual room heaters as well. The heaters contain a number of solid brick-like pieces (this makes them rather bulky) with an electric heating element running through. The element is switched on at night, 'charging' the bricks with heat which is then given off slowly to heat the room. If the heater size is chosen carefully, and the element switched on for sufficient time, the room will be warm all day—although the highest temperatures will be reached in the morning, and by later evening the room may feel a little chilly. Some models incorporate booster fans to enable the heat output to be varied and controlled.

The reason for the popularity of storage heaters is that, in the UK, overnight electricity can cost very much less than on the daytime rate, and it is only this which makes electric storage heating worth con-

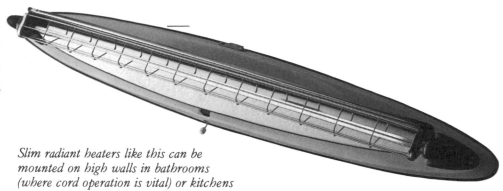

Slim radiant heaters like this can be mounted on high walls in bathrooms (where cord operation is vital) or kitchens

sidering from the cost point of view.

Storage heaters are extremely simple to install. No flues or piping are needed—just a simple wiring job. So the cost of having a system installed for you is rather less than with a wet system. In most cases, a whole-house system consists of storage heaters in some rooms, with panel heaters or infra-red heaters in the other rooms. These operate on full-price electricity, and so you should try to use them as sparingly as possible. Because these are individual heaters, they have no central control, so if you want them switched on and off in unison, you will have to install some additional time clocks and perhaps more wiring as well.

There are two other forms of heating which are usually thought of as whole-house systems, but which can be installed in individual rooms. **Ceiling heating** uses an electric element mounted in special ceiling panels. This system works on full-price electricity, can be very expensive to run, and it is rarely installed.

Underfloor heating is also rarely installed. However, there are various possibilities, including simply running pipes connected to a wet central heating system within the floor. Many systems use electric heating cables. These are laid on top of an insulated concrete floor, and covered with a concrete screed. The whole floor acts as a storage heater, so this system can run off cheap electricity. But it isn't as effective as a proper storage heater, so an afternoon boost is usually required to keep temperatures up.

Choosing individual room heaters

You should first decide whether the heaters are to provide the main heat in your house, or just quick extra heat on odd occasions. If they are to provide the main heat, then you should look for something that is reasonably cheap to run and, particularly if you rent your home, that can be easily taken with

you if you move.

With heaters for additional heat, portability is probably more important than running cost, and, for something that has to provide heat quickly, look for a **radiant** or **fan** heater rather than a **convector** type. It's also useful to have something that uses a different fuel from your main heating system, so you have a back-up in case of power cuts (remember that almost all central heating systems, whatever fuel they burn, use electricity to run the pump or air fan and time clock).

Electric room heaters

Many electric fires are light and portable, so they are a useful way of providing back-up heat in almost any room of the house. Fixed heaters, mounted on the wall or ceiling, are generally easier to install than heaters running off other fuels.

There are several types of electric heater:
• **Electric fires.** Most electric fires are of the **radiant** type: these heat objects in direct view of the heater but do not heat the air. So provided you can sit directly in front of the heater you feel the heat very quickly. Simple radiant fires are very cheap, but you can get quite elaborate ones for mounting in a fireplace opening that are more expensive (though these won't warm you any better, or be less expensive to run).
• **Convector heaters** warm the air in the room first, so it's some time before you feel the benefit—but the whole room is eventually evenly warmed.
• **Fan heaters**, like convector heaters, heat the air. But they have a built-in electric fan which pushes the warmed air around the room, helping to heat the room more quickly. In summer, the fan can be used without the heater elements to help cool a warm room.
• **Oil-filled radiators** work by convection —despite their name—in the same manner as central heating radiators. They take some

Small wall-mounted convector heaters are excellent for back-up or emergencies

time to warm up and cool down, so they are not the best choice if you want to heat a room intermittently.

•**Infra-red heaters** are radiant heaters but with a different type of element that can cope with being splashed by water. They can be used, fixed to the wall or ceiling, in a bathroom or kitchen.

All these fires are 100 per cent efficient, so they all cost the same to run for a given heat output. The heat output is quoted in kilowatts—it's usually 1, 2 or 3kW. Although you need a 3kW fire in only a very large room, it's often a good idea to buy one this large so that you can warm a room very quickly—a larger fire usually has more than one heat setting so you can turn it down if you want to. Even better are fires with thermostatic controls.

Gas heaters

Individual gas fires can be a very good buy; one of the most popular is the **convector** type, which does not have a visible flame and so is a good choice for halls and dining rooms. These heaters can be linked together to a central clock to give some of the controllability of a central heating system.

The main alternative type of gas fire is the **radiant/convector**, with a visible glowing element which might appear more comforting in, say, a living room (they are often installed in a hearth). As their name suggests, these provide some of their heat by radiation, and some by convection. They are not quite as efficient as convector-only heaters, so cost a little more to run for a given heat output.

Some gas radiant/convector fires have the gas flame playing over imitation coals or logs, which can look quite effective. However, some types are extremely inefficient and are excessively costly to run: check carefully before buying.

All gas heaters need proper flues. A **conventional flue** is some form of masonry or prefabricated chimney. Unless this has been built recently, it will need lining with a flexible stainless steel liner—not a particularly difficult job. If you have no chimney, providing one for a conventionally-flued gas heater would be very expensive. A **balanced flue** is a short horizontal duct mounted on the back of the heater and which protrudes through an external wall of the house. This restricts positioning in one sense—the heater must be on an outside wall and not all outside walls are suitable—but a balanced flue is much cheaper to install than building a

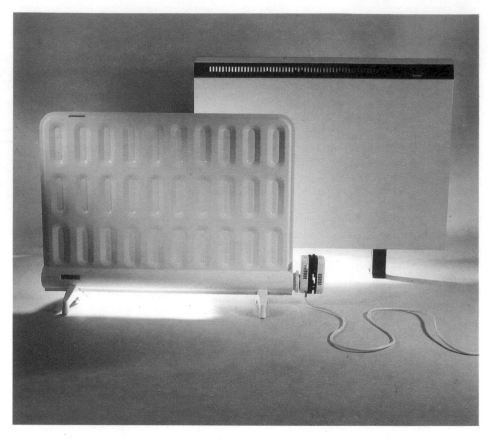

Storage heaters (back) work on cheap rate electricity—oil-filled radiators do not

chimney from scratch. A radiant/convector heater can be fitted with either a balanced flue or a conventional chimney of some sort, but convector-only heaters are available only with balanced flues.

Blocking off open fires

If you have open coal fires, it's a good idea to retain them—they are useful in power cuts and many people find them very attractive to sit by. Fit a **closable throat restrictor** in the flue so that you can close off the chimney and prevent draughts within the room and dust coming down the chimney when you are not using the fire.

Open coal fires are not very efficient, and they are rarely the best choice for your main heating source. However, a modern grate, which has better control over the air supply to the fuel, is more efficient than older types, and is well worth fitting. These come in different sizes to match the fire opening size and are usually easy to drop into position within the existing fireplace.

To reduce draughts in the room when you are using a coal fire, an under floor air supply is a good idea. This is easy to arrange if the floor is suspended timber, but would

involve a lot of upheaval with a solid floor.

If you intend to use a coal fire regularly it is sensible to install a **closed room heater** —these cost much less to run. They can be fitted into an existing fireplace opening, and usually have a back boiler to provide hot water and perhaps central heating.

Other types of room heater

Bottled gas and paraffin heaters are useful in power cuts and, because they don't need flues, they are as portable as electric heaters. But they must be provided with good ventilation, and they do cause condensation.

Paraffin heaters are usually of the convector-only type. One point to bear in mind is that they are relatively light in weight and can be easily knocked over. All modern heaters have a cut-out device which smothers the flame and reduces the risk of fire if the heater is accidentally knocked over or even just tipped.

Bottled gas heaters are now very common. There are many types: radiant-convector, convector-only, radiant-only, and **catalytic** heaters which have no flame. All of them have a large cylinder of LPG (liquid petroleum gas) or propane gas within the casing, which makes the heater quite bulky. The cylinders have to be changed regularly and they are fairly heavy to lift.

FIT A GAS WALL HEATER

The reputation of gas heaters has suffered in the past as a result of the greater flexibility and control offered by central heating systems. But modern thermostatically-regulated gas wall heaters offer the choice of manual or fully automatic controls (the latter with built-in programmer) and so are now sophisticated enough, and versatile enough, to take up the challenge.

A gas wall heater—known technically as a balanced flue convector heater—can be fitted to any suitable *external* wall, whether it's on the ground floor or several storeys high. There's no need for a chimney because the balanced flue (see pages 165–167) deals with the air intake *and* the burnt gases.

You can use the heaters on an economic low setting to take off the chill in a hallway or set them in advance to warm a whole room to a comfortable level. You can even install several together or over a period of time so that you can programme them to heat the whole house to pre-determined temperature levels.

The installation procedure is relatively straightforward—it's largely a question of mounting the unit and connecting a fuel supply. In the case of the automatic models, you'll also need an electrical connection. However, there are limits to which jobs you can tackle by yourself.

In the UK, the regulations governing the installation of gas appliances demand that they're fitted by competent technicians. However, there's no reason why you can't install the unit, then connect back the pipework and wiring *before* calling in a qualified technician to commission and test your end of the installation. Let the technician make the final connections to the mains.

What's available

Most large stockists of heating equipment carry a range of gas wall heaters. All are fitted with balanced flues which need to be mounted on an external wall.

Simple manual models need no electrical supply—a piezo spark generator like those fitted to ordinary gas fires governs the ignition. The controls consist of simple on/off switches with a manual setting, or there may be one knob for ignition and another for temperature control. The controls may be concealed inside the case of the unit or on the top or sides. Manual models are simpler to install than their automatic counterparts.

Automatic models offer greater flexibility and temperature control. Some are only available with a built-in timer so that you can programme the heater to come on and go off when necessary. With these models, you determine the heat manually.

Top of the range are automatic heaters that contain a thermostatic control as well as a timer—these are fully automatic, coming on and off when you require them to and also adjusting their output to suit the room temperature.

Though most heaters operate on a convection process, some models are fan-assisted. They're advantageous if you need to warm a room rapidly, but they may have the drawback of being noisy.

The choice is so great that you may end up choosing the one that looks best. A closer look may reveal some important differences. The position of the outlet grille varies. Top grilles are likely to mark wallpaper with black heat stains, but they may be preferable if there is a chance of something being placed in front. The shape of the grilles themselves may also be important. To most young children, louvred grilles resemble letterboxes—scorching paper may be the first signs of their correspondence.

Planning considerations

The chief restriction on fitting a gas wall heater is likely to be on the wall itself—it must be an outside wall to enable the balanced flue to discharge the combustion products and draw in air for the burners.

Walls made of combustible material, including brick walls that have cavity insulation, must be fitted with an additional liner to protect them from heat.

If your wall is on a boundary with a neighbour you will have to obtain their permission before carrying out the installation.

If it is within reach of children, protect the flue terminal with a proprietary mesh guard. Some thought may need to be given to protecting it from accidental damage by cars and so on it if projects into a driveway.

Some models have flues which can be fitted from the inside only, without the need for outside access—particularly useful when fitting heaters in upper storeys. Because the outside diameter of the flue is only about 125mm it is unlikely to be an eyesore, and even smaller flues are available.

Sufficient clearance for ventilation must be allowed around the flue terminal on the outside of the house. Minimum recommended distances for natural draught balanced flues are shown in the diagram (right).

Planning your heat requirements. Heaters come in a couple of different capacities around two and three kilowatts (2–3kW) and are adjustable within that range. Large lounges with three outside walls may need two heaters unless they are well insulated.

A big advantage of gas wall heaters is that you can add to the system at any time in the future if your heat requirements increase later. However, bear the following in mind.
• Insulation and draught proofing will dramatically reduce your heating requirements and, of course, your gas bills.
• Because of the heat generated by a cooker, kitchens will need less heat.
• In rooms only used occasionally, you will need to choose a more powerful model or a fan assisted heater, to warm the room more rapidly. In hallways you may wish only to keep the chill off over long periods, so a small heater can be left on a low setting.

If you are planning to wire more than one heater to a central time switch, you must choose models with mains electric ignition (see page 193 for details). In this case, you will also need a simple central heating timeswitch and a wall mounted room thermostat.

In all cases, you will need enough 15mm copper pipe to run a supply from the main gas pipework to the heater. You will also need fittings for the pipes, including a gas cock and a reducer from 15mm to ¼ inch BSP internal.

You may prefer to run the final lengths of pipework in chrome plated fire tube. Apart from its more attractive appearance, it is made from soft copper which is easier to bend neatly than ordinary copper tube. Don't forget to include pipe clips on your list of what is needed for the job.

To simplify the job of cutting the flue hole through the external wall, hire a heavy duty power drill and core cutter from your local tool hire shop.

Planning pipe runs. The main requirement is **safety** and, for this reason, copper pipe must not be run through notched joists where it may be damaged by floorboard nails or carpet tacks—instead run through or along joists.

Surface-run copper pipe along walls or skirtings is safer since it can be seen, so it is

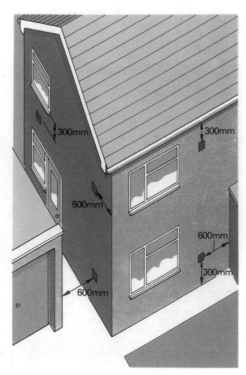

Flue terminal positions are important for venting the heater. Dimensions above are generally acceptable, but check instructions carefully

less likely to be damaged and, if it is, the leak is more readily detectable.

You may also consider the option of threading 15mm soft copper tube through holes drilled in the joists. The tube is easily bent and fewer joints will be necessary.

Installing the heater

It's important that the heater is mounted in the correct place and that it's securely fixed to the walls. Most models are supplied with a template to mark fixing and flue holes.

Bearing in mind the planning considerations for positioning the heater, tape the maker's fixing template to the wall. Make sure the screw holes are level. This will give you the positions for drilling the screw holes and the flue hole. Once the positions are marked on the wall, remove the template. Remember that the dimensions for the heater positioning are essential to its efficient operation—take care to follow them exactly.

After marking the relative position of your flue hole to the heater mounting holes, drill and plug the wall ready to receive the screws for the heater.

To cut the hole for the flue, you have a choice between using a core drill or a hammer and cold chisel. If you are drilling

the flue hole, start by making a pilot hole. This will provide a useful guide for the core cutter as well as easing the load on the drill. Make sure that the drill goes through at right angles to the wall.

When you are satisfied the hole is in the right position, follow through with the core cutter fitted to a pneumatic drill—hire both from a tool hire shop.

Select a low speed on the drill and take your time—bricks vary greatly so be prepared for the job to take a little longer if the going is tough.

On cavity walls you may be unlucky and hit a metal wall tie in which case you have no choice but to cut it out with a hammer and chisel. After removing the tie you can resume with the core cutter until you are finally through both leaves of the wall.

If you decide to use a hammer and cold chisel, drill a pilot hole and cut through from both sides using as small a chisel as possible. Remember, the neater the hole the less making good you will have to do.

Balanced flues are designed to fit a variety of wall thicknesses. Provided your wall is within the tolerances specified by the manufacturers, you will find it easy to adjust the flue so that it fits the exact thickness of your wall—a sleeve duct slides apart or together like a concertina.

Measure the overall wall thickness and, taking care to follow individual instructions supplied with the heater, adjust the flue length. Bear in mind that the flue terminal itself must project forward of the outside wall surface; the duct must be adjusted to fit the thickness of the wall.

This is normally a simple matter of sliding the telescopic section of the flue until you reach the desired length. In most cases, a small self-tapping screw must be inserted into the flue wall and secured to maintain the correct length when fixing. A length of heat resistant tape is supplied which must be wrapped around the joint to form a seal— the duct must be relatively airtight so that the waste gases and the air necessary for combustion will flow properly.

When the flue is correctly adjusted— check it through the wall—it may then be attached to the heat exchanger connection on the back of the fire.

If the controls are front mounted, lay a couple of timber battens on the floor to prevent them being damaged. There should be some form of gasket between the flue and the heat exchanger. Position it between the flanges before screwing or bolting the flue on.

When the unit is assembled it must be hung on the wall. Prepare the site first so you can pick the heater straight up and insert the flue through the wall without damaging the unit—you may well require the help of an assistant at this point.

You must have some means of propping up the heat exchanger while you are screwing it to the wall. Simply letting it hang on the flue may damage the seals.

If the flue incorporates an external rubber seal there will be no making good to do on the outside wall provided the hole has not been cut too large. If it has, fill the gap later with a damp mixture of sand and cement in the proportions of 3:1.

Some models require the gap around the flue to be made good with sand and cement. In doing this you must be careful not to let the sand and cement clog the air intake. The air intake should not be recessed in the wall so an allowance should be made for render when you adjust and secure the flue.

★ WATCH POINT ★

If your gas supply is coming up through the floor, drill the hole before proceeding to fit the heater.

Before filling the gap around the flue, wrap masking tape around the mesh to prevent clogging—be sure to remove the tape before turning on the heater.

Adjust the position until you can secure the unit to all the fixing holes you have made. Make a final check for level.

Making gas pipe joints

There are three types of joint used to connect gas pipes—capillary, compression and threaded. Which you use depends on personal preference and ease of access.

Capillary: Cut the ends of the pipe square and remove all burrs. Clean the pipe and fittings with steel wool. Smear the ends of the pipe with flux and insert the pipe into the fittings. Heat the fittings gently with a blowlamp until a ring of solder appears around the mouth of each side of the joint.

Compression: Cut the ends of the pipe square and remove all burrs. Slide the nut and olive onto each pipe and smear the mouth of the fitting with a small amount of jointing compound. Tighten the nuts gently with a spanner—take care not to over-tighten nuts, especially on soft copper pipe.

Threaded fittings: Wrap PTFE tape around the thread and tighten the fitting with a wrench or pair of grips. Never use hemp on gas fittings as it will develop leaks.

1 *Most manufacturers supply a fixing template with the unit. Use it to mark the flue hole and fixing hole positions on to the wall*

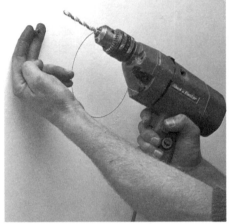

2 *Drill and plug the fixing holes first. Make sure that the drill does not wander; check the hole positions when you finish*

3 *Use a core cutter fitted to a pneumatic drill to cut the flue hole—drill a small central hole first. Otherwise, cut the hole by hand with a cold chisel and hammer*

4 *If running underfloor pipes, drill an access hole now—before you fit the heater on to the wall*

5 *Measure the wall thickness, then adjust the telescopic duct length to suit. Seal the joint with the tape provided*

6 *Assemble the unit according to the instructions provided. Take particular care when attaching the seals*

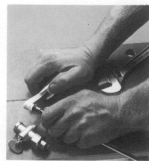

Pre-soldered capillary joints are generally best for gas pipes and fittings

Compression joints may be easier but don't overtighten nuts

Threaded joints must be sealed with winds of PTFE tape

Running the pipes

Providing you are competent at installing water supply pipes, you will find no difficulty in running pipes to convey gas.

Capillary fittings are favoured by the gas authorities because they form a positive seal which cannot be loosened.

You will find pre-soldered joints (Yorkshire fittings) ideal for the job. Select slow bends, rather than sharp elbows, for changes in direction. If possible hire a pipe bender to reduce the number of joints you will need—the fewer joints, the less likelihood of a leak.

Starting at the fire, attach a union to the ¼ in BSP fitting, shown in the instructions as the inlet connection. A smear of jointing compound on the union faces will help form a good joint.

Next, you should install a small gas cock which will isolate the heater for the purposes of maintenance. It is not necessary for this cock to be readily accessible and, from the point of view of neatness, it is best sited inside the casing.

If you prefer, you can make the first connections with chrome plated fire tube—the type used on ordinary gas fires—before enlarging the pipe size to 15mm copper pipe for the main installation pipework.

Chrome plated fire tube can be bent into large radius curves by hand, but, particularly for tight bends, an internal bending spring will reduce the risk of kinking and help you to make neater bends.

Continue running the pipework back to the meter or branch of the existing gas installation—secure the pipe with clips at 500mm intervals. If you need to cross over joists, notch the top of the joists and protect the new pipe by one of two methods. Either screw a metal plate over the top of the notch, or sleeve the pipe with a larger diameter iron pipe at the appropriate places.

If you have to pass the pipe through a wall, the hole should first be sleeved and the ends sealed around the gas pipe with mastic. This will prevent leakage into the cavity and help protect the pipe from damage.

Don't make the final connection to the mains supply—leave this part of the job to a

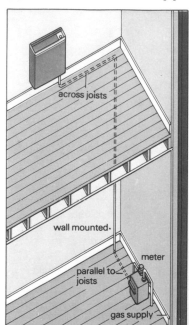

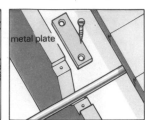

A metal plate will protect the pipe from damage

Unprotected pipe in a notch may be punctured by nails

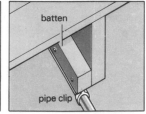

Better still, drill a hole for the pipe and sleeve it with larger iron pipe

Attach underfloor pipes to battens then nail to the joists

7 *Attach the assembled unit to the fixing holes at all the relevant points. When complete, check for level*

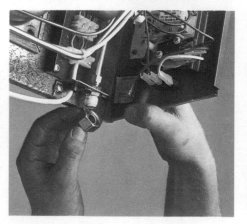

8 *Attach a male to female union to the gas inlet pipe at the base of the water heater*

9 *A stoptap followed by a flexible fire tube begins the pipe run back to the gas supply*

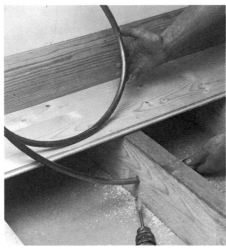

10 *If you're lucky, you can run pipework in line with the joists— use pipe clips to attach the pipes to the sides of the joists*

11 *Soft copper tube can be threaded through holes drilled in the joists —make sure it's below the level of any flooring nails*

12 *Run the pipe back to the meter— or suitable connection point—and leave final connection and testing to a technician*

technician. Run the pipework from the heater to a point as near as possible to an appropriate connection or to the meter.

To avoid taking gas from the individual supply pipes to other appliances, the connection for the wall heater should be made as close as possible to the meter and, preferably, into the meter itself.

The mains connection must be carried out by a qualified technician. Before any of the new pipework is joined to the main supply, the existing system should be tested for leaks and pressure using a U-gauge. The usual place for connecting a U-gauge is on the test nipple after the meter. If the existing system is proved to be sound, the new work can be connected. Where the existing pipework is in iron, you can substitute a short length of pipe with copper to enable a standard copper tee to be incorporated from which the new work may be run.

When the work is complete, the whole system must be checked by connecting up the U-gauge again and testing for leaks.

Test suspect joints with a solution of soapy water applied around the joint with a brush. If the joint is leaking the solution will change into quite noticeable bubbles.

When the installation is proved sound, turn the heater on, let the air escape from the pipe and then light the gas. On long runs of pipe, it may take several minutes before a flame can be established and the heater tested for operation and control.

The best method for running the electrical supply is to take a spur from the back of an existing socket to a new socket or a new fused connection unit to which you connect the heater. Even though the heater's elec-

tricity consumption is only about 50 watts, the power supply should be run in 2.5mm² cable (thinner cable of a lower current rating will not be protected sufficiently by the circuit fuse in the main consumer unit).

Switch off the power supply at the consumer unit, unscrew the face plate of the existing socket and thread your new cable through. If you plan to run your new cable on the surface and your existing socket is flush mounted you will have to chase out a channel from the wall.

Take off about 75mm of the outer cable casing and expose the three wires. Sheath the bare wire with green/yellow earth wire insulation up to about 20mm from the end. Bare the live and neutral wires to match. Double the copper ends over individually before inserting each one in its correct terminal. Secure with the screws and give the wires a *gentle* tug to ensure they are caught firmly. The new cable can be run along the top of the skirting to connect with a new socket and box adjacent to the fire.

1

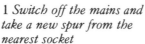
2

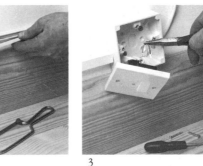
3

1 *Switch off the mains and take a new spur from the nearest socket*

2 *Run the new cable along the wall in surface mounted conduit*

3 *Connect the flex from the heater to the cable via a fused connection unit*

4 *An existing wall socket supplies power to a new connection unit*

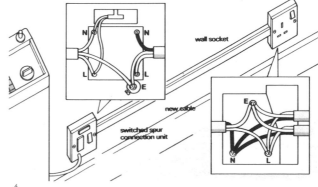
4

ELECTRIC WALL HEATER

Wall heaters are the ideal solution for rooms which are used intermittently—such as bathrooms. You turn the heater on only for as long as you need it and, because the heater is radiant, it warms you rather than everything else in the room.

Fitting a wall heater is easy but, because you can't have an electrical socket in the bathroom, you can't just plug one in. Don't worry, all you have to do for a safe connection is take off a spur from your power circuit and wire the heater into that via a fused connection unit.

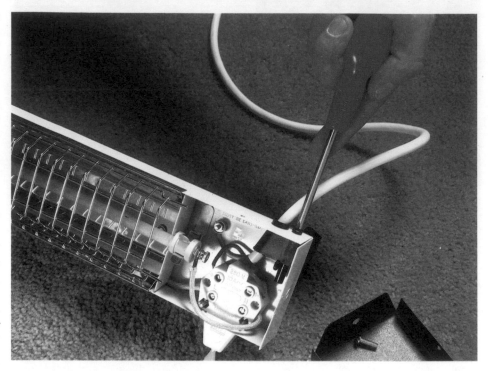

Choosing a wall heater

Wall heaters are readily available and inexpensive so it's worth going for a neat design which will blend with your bathroom decor.

If you are installing a wall heater in a bathroom it must be unswitched or have an integral cord operated switch—it's unsafe to have ordinary switches in a moist atmosphere and this is prohibited by wiring regulations. Some heaters have their pull switch in the middle, others at the side. If you use an unswitched model, it must be controlled by a switch fitted outside the bathroom—a very inconvenient option—or by a separate pullcord operated switch introduced into the circuit. In either case, you are likely to have much more cable routing to do—so choose a switched heater if at all possible.

Sizes for the most powerful types of wall heater are around 700mm to 800mm long with a depth of up to 200mm. You can buy them with ratings of between 750 watts and 1kW for single element models—double that for double element heaters. The size generally increases with the power rating.

Which kind you choose will depend on your preferences about appearance—and on how warm you want to be—but a 1kW heater is sufficient to warm up the average small bathroom.

As always when installing any electrical equipment—especially in a bathroom—safety should be your prime consideration. Check the following points before you start:
• **Siting the heater:** The important thing to remember about positioning a wall heater in a bathroom is that it must be impossible to touch while you are using any of the taps or when you are having a bath or shower. High up on the wall opposite the bath is the best position. Of course, it shouldn't be so high that you can't reach the cord.
• **Wiring:** The heater should be wired up

with 0.75mm² three-core sheathed flex to an adjacent fused connector unit which is then connected with 2.5mm² twin-and-earth electric cable to the back of a nearby socket. The only complicated part is deciding on the route of the cable and which socket to use. You have the choice of running the cable in the wall or of using surface mounted mini-trunking. However, the first thing to do is to find out which socket you can wire up to.

So that there is no danger of you overloading your circuit, start by working out if it's a ring or radial type; it may affect whether or not you can install a heater. If you don't already know, investigate by examining a number of your sockets in the following way. Turn off the electricity at the mains. Unscrew three or four socket outlets from their mounting boxes and look at the wiring: a ring main socket will have two sets of cable attached to it, a radial circuit will have only one. However, some radial cir-

cuits have several sockets strung together so you may find two cables attached to any one socket. Similarly, some ring circuits have spurs extending from them. If you open up one of these, you will see only one cable. The answer is to look at three or four sockets to establish a general pattern.

Once you have established which type of circuit you have, the rule is that on a radial, use a socket which has only one cable leading to it, and on a ring, use a socket which has two cables leading to it.

Ideally, borrow power from a socket in the room above. Don't put the heater above the bath or too near the ceiling

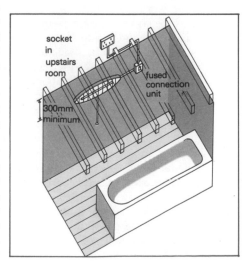

socket in upstairs room

fused connection unit

300mm minimum

•**Locating the best socket:** The socket you select should be chosen not only for its electrical suitability but also for convenience in terms of routing the cable. The shorter the distance, the less work you will have to do.

The ideal is a two gang socket in a room directly above the bathroom, because you can then run the cable straight downwards for a short distance—a relatively simple job. However, the chances are that your bathroom is on the top floor. If so, pick a socket in the room next door. Whatever your choice, you will have to make a hole for the cable, either through the wall or through the ceiling.

•**Routing the cable:** There is one golden rule to follow: the runs must be vertical and horizontal—never diagonal. You have a choice of two methods of routing the cable so that it is protected—either in a surface mounted conduit or concealed in a channel in the wall.

•**Surface mounted conduit:** Can be used on any type of wall—it is the easiest method of running cable. You can make it less obtrusive by careful routing and by painting it to match the walls or skirting.

•**Concealed routing:** Is neater and gives you two options depending on your wall construction. You can tell the type of wall by tapping it with the handle of a screwdriver: a solid and fairly flat thump indicates a plastered masonry wall, a hollow sound means a timber frame wall. On a masonry wall, you can channel out a groove which can be filled and redecorated; on a stud wall, you can drop the cable behind the plasterboard and thread it out through holes at the connection points.

•**Additional materials:** You will certainly

It's likely that you'll have to wire up the fused connection unit to a socket next door which means a longer cable run

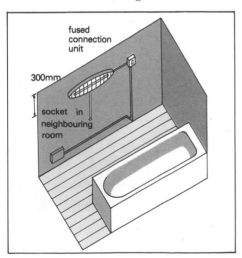

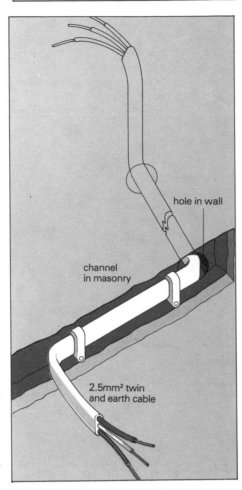

need to have a fused connection unit—choose an unswitched type fitted with a 13A fuse—a surface mounting box to fit it, a sufficient length of 2.5mm^2 twin-and-earth cable and 0.75mm^2 three core sheathed flex. You will also need cable clips, rubber grommets—which protect the cable in the mounting boxes—and yellow/green earth sleeving.

And, depending on how you decide to fix the cable, you may need plastic conduit, 25mm No. 8 wood screws, plus wallplugs and cellulose filler.

•**Tools for the job:** The only essential tools are an electrician's screwdriver, spirit level, drill and bits and a trimming knife. For cutting conduit, a hacksaw is useful and, if you are channelling out a groove in a masonry wall, a bolster and club hammer will be handy. You need decorating equipment to

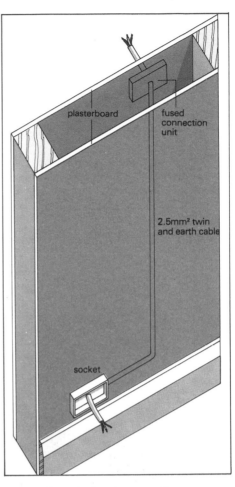

Above: In a timber frame wall you can run the cable through the cavity although you may have to pass it through some timbers
Left: in a masonry wall you can conceal the cable in a channel. Secure it with cable clips and plaster over later. Drill a hole straight through the wall at a convenient point

make good any channels when the job is done and the heater is in place.

Routing the cable

Once you have decided on the cable route, mark it onto the wall together with the position of the heater and its new fused connection unit.

Make a final check to see that both the heater and unit can be securely fastened to the wall and that the marks are level. You don't need to channel in the flex from the heater to the unit, but mount them close together to keep the flex short.

Fix the surface mounting box for the connection unit to the wall using impact adhesive (if the wall surface is sufficiently sound) or wall fastenings and screws.

Measure and cut the channelling for the mini-trunking and fix it to the wall.

At your chosen break-through point, use a 10mm masonry bit to make a neat hole for the cable to go through the wall. Prepare the cable route to the socket by cutting a channel to the socket and entering its box from the side or by threading the cable through from behind and up the plasterboard, or by using conduit.

Push the cable through the hole in the wall and take it to the socket. Then feed the cable into the channelling securing it with clips every 100mm or so and through to the back of the connection unit mounting box. Make sure that there is enough cable at both ends to allow for the odd mistake in cutting or wire stripping—and for working on the ends of the wires.

It's convenient at this stage to connect the end of the cable to the fused connection unit. It isn't necessary to turn off the power while you do this—you won't be connecting to any live wires until everything else is wired up. But don't under any circumstances try to connect the cable to the socket that you are drawing power from at this stage—you **must** turn off the power before doing so.

Connecting to the fused connection unit: Thread the end of the cable through the most conveniently positioned knockout panel in the connection unit mounting box and fit a grommet. Cut the cable to a convenient length and strip back the outer sheathing by about 75mm. Remove about 10mm of insulation from the wires and slip a yellow/green sleeve over this length of the exposed earth wire.

Insert the wires into their terminals in

the connection unit. The unit will have separate live and neutral terminals for the mains cable (labelled feed) and for the flex leading to the heater (labelled load). The earth terminal is common to both (see right). Connect the red wire to the live (L) terminal on the feed side and the black wire to the neutral (N) terminal. When you've done this, connect the sleeved earth wire to the earth terminal.

Fixing the heater

With the fused connection unit wired up you can now fix the heater to the wall. Working overhead is awkward so get someone to help.

Mark the position of the fixing holes with a pencil and drill the wall for the fixings. Use the same type of plugs as you used for the connection unit box.

Cut the heater flex to length allowing some extra for connection, strip back about 75mm of the outer sheath and 20mm of the insulation from the three wires and connect them up to the terminals in the heater. The brown wire goes to the live (L) terminal, the blue to the neutral (N) and the green/yellow to the earth terminal. You may also need to fit the element to its screw terminals.

With the heater on its marks, screw

3 *Drill through the wall at a convenient point for connecting in to the socket. If you are drilling close to the socket be very careful not to drill into a live wire. If you don't know where the wires go, switch off and make a hole by hand with a cold chisel*

1 *Decide the position of the heater—not over the bath and more than 300mm from the ceiling—and mark onto the wall*

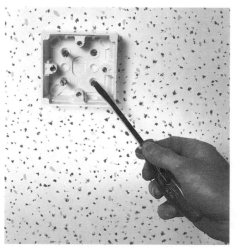

2 *Fix the connection unit mounting box to the wall close to the position of the heater so the connecting flex will be short*

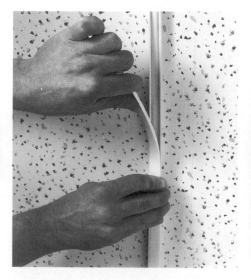

4 *Surface mounted conduit avoids the need for any further holes in the wall*

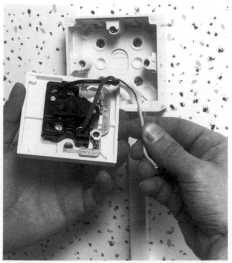

5 *Connect the supply cable to the correct terminals on the feed side*

6 *Wire up the heater flex to the correct terminals and refit the cover*

7 *Screw the heater brackets to the wall and adjust the angle to suit the room*

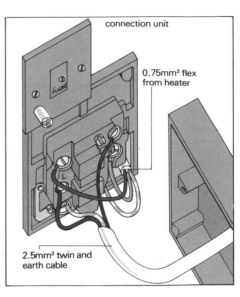

The connection unit has two sets of terminals for the supply cable (feed) and heater flex (load). The flex outlet has a flex clamp to prevent straining the lead to the heater. Fit a 13A fuse

Below: the supply cable can be connected to the same terminals as the existing wiring. Make sure you connect it the right way round

8 *Lead the flex into the front of the unit and connect to the terminals on the load side*

9 *Switch off the mains, then connect the supply cable to the back of the chosen socket*

through the fixing brackets into the wall fixings. Adjust the angle of the heater so that it will radiate diagonally down into the room. You might have to adjust this later.

With the fused connection unit face plate unscrewed from the mounting box, loosen the flex clamp, slip the flex through it, strip the end and fix the wires into their terminals. The brown heater flex wire goes into the live (L) load terminal corresponding with the red spur cable in the live feed terminal, the blue heater wire into the neutral (N) load terminal corresponding with the black spur wire in the neutral feed terminal and the yellow/green earth wire with the yellow/green sleeved earth wire of the spur cable to the earthing screw. Tighten up the flex clamp making sure that it grips the outer sheath of the heater flex. Fit a 13 amp fuse and screw the plate back on to the mounting box.

★ WATCH POINT ★

To double check that the mains supply is off, plug a table lamp into the socket and attempt to switch it on.

Connecting the power

With the heater fixed up and all the wiring connections made inside the bathroom you can make the final connection to the power supply in the house.

Before you attempt to do this **you must ensure that the electricity is switched off at the mains.** As an extra precaution, remove the relevant fuse. With this done you can unscrew the faceplate of the socket and pull it forward out of the way.

Feed the end of the cable through an appropriate knock out panel in the box and fit a protective grommet.

Cut the cable to the same length as the existing wiring and strip back about 75mm of the outer sheathing and about 10mm of insulation from the red and black wires. Don't forget to slip a length of yellow/green sleeving on the bare earth wire which you have just exposed.

Unscrew the terminals at the back of the face plate and insert the new wires. Connect the red wire into the live (L) terminal and the black into the neutral (N) terminal. Connect up the earth wire to the earth plate at the side. Replace the faceplate and any

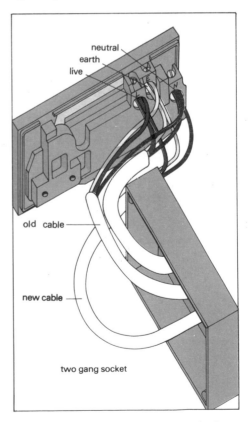

conduit cover strips, turn the power back on then test the heater. If it does not operate properly, switch off at the mains and recheck all your connections.

MULTIPOINT WATER HEATER

Gas powered multipoints have come a long way since the single spout geysers that perched above the bath or kitchen sink—they're now simple to operate, fully controllable, powerful, quiet and efficient. They'll provide instant hot water for the entire house—as much as you like for as long as you like, at temperatures you regulate by the turn of a knob. Yet the instant you turn the taps off, the water stops heating. There's no need to wait for the water to get hot, and there's no need to pay for water you don't use. In fact, multipoints are remarkable for what you don't use and what you won't need.

You won't need a hot water cylinder because you won't need to store hot water —cold water becomes hot water as it flows through the heater en route to the taps. So not only do you save money, but also space.

Because you don't need a hot water cylinder, you won't need the pipes that supply it—the multipoint is best fed direct from the high pressure rising main pipe. In some cases, you may even be able to dispense with the cold water storage cistern in the attic altogether—some local authorities permit all the cold water appliances to be fed direct from the mains.

There is no need for timing devices, thermostats or pumps; the casing of the heater conceals everything it needs to do its job—it doesn't even need an electricity supply.

These features make a new installation less expensive and far easier than a conventional system. But it's not much more difficult to instal one instead of, or alongside, your existing hot water system.

The only feature modern multipoints do need is a flue. However, this is only of minor significance as these units use a balanced flue to draw in air and to exhaust waste gases. The flue passes through the wall behind the multipoint.

Even if you have a central heating system, a multipoint may still be a money-saving proposition. By transferring your hot water load on to a separate unit, you can gain extra capacity for your heating from the existing boiler. This is a boon if you're planning a home extension—at least you won't need to upgrade the size of the boiler and the system.

Alternatively, if you install a multipoint in combination with your central heating system, you can use the multipoint during the summer months when the heating's not working, but use conventional stored hot

Fit isolating valves to the inlet and outlet pipes—use gate or Ballofix valves. Fitting the flue is probably the most difficult job

A typical installation: cold water comes from the rising main feeding the sink; the new hot outlet joins the existing hot pipework

water when the heating's in use during the winter. This is particularly advantageous when the system is powered by a very large or solid fuel boiler which runs inefficiently when heating domestic hot water only.

The different models

A number of well known companies manufacture multipoint instantaneous water heaters. Their sales literature gives a good idea of the capabilities of the various models. A wise choice may be made by comparing flow rates (how much hot water over a given period of time), temperature range and minimum head (for indirect feed from a cold water storage cistern).

As a guide, an average adult bath will require something like 115 litres of hot water, at a temperature of about 43°C. Flow rates on certain models may be as low as 3.2 or as high as 12 litres per minute. Operating temperatures are always given as a range—anywhere from 30°C to 57°C. And because winter water is colder than summer water, some models include a compensator.

The main concern is not how much water you require, but how quickly and to how many different taps at the same time—compare model specifications and relate them to your own needs.

A number of further refinements are available, including thermostatic temperature controls, automatic temperature stabilization—particularly good for showers—and water pressure stabilizers. Check with your local water authority to see if there are any special byelaws relating to the installation of showers or washing machines, because these may apply to multipoints too.

The most common—and convenient—flue arrangement is a balanced flue (see above). Balanced flues are adjustable over their length, making them suitable for installation into walls between 100mm and 600mm thick—the telescopic duct can be adjusted to fit. Manufacturers also supply liners to protect combustible walls, and terminal guards for low level installations.

An important aspect of multipoint installation is water pressure regulation—it must remain virtually constant, especially if you intend to supply a shower or automatic washing machine. Some models include a pressure stabilizer in their design, but others may require a governor to be fitted independently in order to even out pressure fluctuations. Governors are expensive items, so if you want a shower or washing machine connection, or if you share a cold water supply with other dwellings, check that the model includes a pressure stabilizer.

Dimensions vary considerably and this may influence your choice. If you intend to install one in a confined space, check the method of access for maintenance purposes. Most require the removal of the front casing, so allow enough room for clearance.

1 *Trace pipe routes throughout the house until you're entirely familiar with the layout. Check and note every tee and stoptap*

2 *Mark the hole for the flue duct. Adjust the position to match mortar courses in order to make the job of hole cutting easier*

3 *Adjust the flue duct to fit the thickness of the wall. Attach seals and any fixings, then secure the duct firmly in place*

Apart from the planning, the most difficult part of the job will probably be cutting the hole through the wall to insert the flue duct. Once that's complete, and the heater unit is mounted, you just need basic plumbing skills using copper pipes and standard compression or capillary fittings to connect the multipoint.

Routing and connecting gas and water supply pipes is the same in either case—run the pipes back from the heater to suitable connection points with the mains. Connecting the pipes to the taps (or other fittings) is exactly the same in this case as in any other, except that most of the pipework will already be installed.

The only part of the job you won't be able to complete is the final connection to the mains gas supply. You must leave this to a qualified plumber or gas board technician who can also test and commission your part of the installation. Never attempt to do this part of the job yourself.

Vital first steps

You may be able to install a multipoint without changing all the existing pipework in the house, but you won't know what's involved until you undertake some routine investigation.

Begin by looking at a site for the heater, connection points for the gas and water supply, connections to appliances and ways to speed up your work. Trace the existing pipe routes throughout your house until you're entirely familiar with which pipes supply which appliances.

Don't skimp on your checks—lift floorboards and remove panelling to find where one pipe joins another. Note the positions of stoptaps and gate valves.

★ WATCH POINT ★

Don't assume that concealed pipes supply only one appliance—they often supply more. If you're unsure, trace back to the nearest stoptap, turn it off and open the taps on each appliance in turn.

Where you place the heater is determined primarily by the flue—you must choose an outside wall for balanced flue models. Make sure the passage of air across the flue terminal will be unrestricted.

A vitally important factor in your choice of site—and one which will affect how much work you need to do—must be whether to take a **direct** cold water feed from the rising main or an **indirect** cold water feed from the storage tank in the attic. If it's at all possible (and allowed by your local water authority), it's generally far easier and less restrictive to take the water supply from the rising main pipe. This always feeds the cold tap on the kitchen sink and the storage tank in the attic anyway, but may also feed other appliances. If you take a supply from this pipe, there'll be no problem about feeding all the taps.

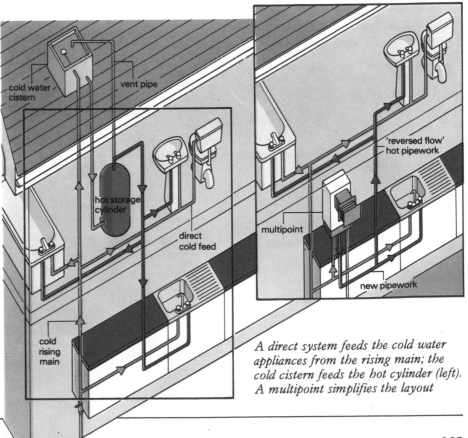

A direct system feeds the cold water appliances from the rising main; the cold cistern feeds the hot cylinder (left). A multipoint simplifies the layout

4 *The multipoint generally attaches to both the wall and the internal flanges of the duct—attach it at each fixing point*

5 *Make good the hole on the outside as well; use a 3:1 mortar mix. Mask the grill with paper and tape to prevent any blockages from dust or dirt*

If you can't connect the heater to the rising main, make sure that you check the minimum head of water required. Bear in mind that the head is measured from the bottom of the storage tank to the highest draw-off point.

Direct feed

Another factor is how much of the existing hot water pipework you will be able to use. This will depend entirely on the route and arrangement of the existing hot water pipes —make sure you know where everything goes and the sequence of the connecting pipework. Draw a rough circuit diagram.

The sink is the most frequently used appliance and is fed by the rising main's

cold water pipe, so it makes sense to mount the multipoint as near to it as possible in order to avoid long 'dead legs' of hot water going to waste.

If you want to mount the multipoint above the kitchen worktops, the two inlet pipes (gas and water) and the outlet pipe (hot water supply) can be taken through neat holes drilled in the worktop—leave the connections to the mains, and the connection to the existing hot water pipe, until later.

In this case, you should be able to join the outlet pipe from the multipoint to the existing hot supply to the sink. And as the sink's hot pipe is already connected—in one way or another—to all the other hot taps, the pressure of the rising main water will simply 'reverse the flow' in order to provide hot water to all the other hot taps.

If the existing hot supply is from a storage cylinder and immersion heater, the cylinder can be disconnected and removed and the pipework cut and capped.

But if you want to keep the existing hot water facilities—particularly if it's part of a central heating system—there's no reason why you can't leave the cylinder in place. But you must ensure a means of turning off the water supply from the hot cylinder—do this by inserting an isolating valve on the cylinder outlet pipe as near to the hot tap supplies as possible.

Using a direct feed from the pressurized mains in this way will override changes in pipe sizes and means that even the highest tap can be supplied with hot water.

Indirect feed

If you choose a cold supply from a storage tank, make sure that you can obtain the minimum operating head of water needed to open the gas valve in the heater as the water flows through it. This can be as much as 11 metres. Bear in mind that the head is

measured from the base of the cistern to the highest hot tap, not to the heater itself. In most houses, this requirement will make it impossible to use an indirect feed.

If it is possible to use the existing cold feed to the cylinder as a cold feed for the multipoint, the heater can be mounted and its supply pipe can be run back to meet the pipe that feeds the cylinder.

However, there are additional problems that need careful consideration. On indirect systems such as this, the pipe sizes do matter. The diameter of the supply pipe to the heater must be 22mm to minimize pressure losses, but the diameters of the supply pipes to the taps must also be carefully examined.

If the multipoint is serving more than one tap, the hot water pipe must be run in 22mm diameter copper pipe. When it branches off to connect to individual basin or sink taps, it should be reduced to 15mm pipe. But if it's serving a bath tap, the pipe must be 22mm from the heater all the way to the bath.

Hence, because of the extra work involved and the considerable restrictions, it is far better to opt for a feed from the rising main.

Whichever feed you choose, the gas

In this system, the cold cistern feeds everything but the sink. If you supply a multipoint from the cistern too, a sufficient 'head' between cistern and taps is vital

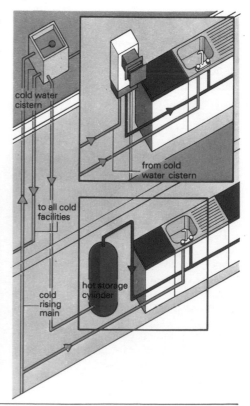

cold water cistern

from cold water cistern

to all cold facilities

cold rising main

hot storage cylinder

★ WATCH POINT ★

First mark the flue hole and remove the template. Use a bolster and hammer to remove a small amount of plaster until you can see the mortar courses between bricks. Replace the template and align it with the mortar courses, then make a new mark that will be easier to follow. Remove the template and drill out the mortar with a large masonry bit and electric drill.

6 *Drop a plumbline from the inlet/outlet unions so that you can mark and drill holes for the first sections of pipework*

7 *It's always better to bend pipes rather than use elbow joints. Use a pipe offcut to mark right angled bends accurately*

8 *Hired pipe bending machines help to control the radius and position of bends—useful when routing through floorboards*

supply is the same—15mm copper pipe is run back from the heater to a suitable connection point with an existing gas supply pipe. **Don't** attempt this part of the job—leave it to a plumber or gas board official, who will be able to test the installation too.

Attaching the heater

Use your drawings and measurements to calculate the best method for making the supply connections and to work out what materials you need. Bear in mind that pipes can be mounted on wall surfaces, buried in

the plaster or routed underneath floors or through cavity walls.

Mounting the heater on an outside wall should be the first part of the job of attaching the heater—a template is generally supplied as a guide for the flue hole and fixing hole positions.

Use a spirit level to position and level the template on the wall. Temporarily attach it with adhesive tape to prevent any movement. If no template is provided, use the dimensions specified in the instructions and mark out the flue hole.

When the hole is complete, re-check the position of your marks by replacing the template. Drill and plug the fixing holes so that

the flue assembly can be fitted.

Measure the wall thickness, including any cement render or plaster. Telescopic flues can then be adjusted to match the wall thickness precisely.

Some models have a self tapping screw to fix the flue at the correct length; others rely upon a heat resistant tape to hold the flue steady and at the right length.

Insert the flue through the hole in the wall and check it sits squarely in position. Attach it in place with two of the appropriate screws, then examine the flue from outside the building. Look from all angles to see if it is square in the hole—now is the last chance to make any adjustments. When you're satisfied, fix all the screws that hold the flue plate.

If the flue has external fixing screws, these may also be secured and any gaps around the duct made good with a 3:1 mix of sand and cement—keep mortar out of the flue terminal. Use masking tape and sheets of newspaper to prevent the mesh guard from becoming clogged.

Carefully remove the casing from the heater making sure you don't damage any seals in the process. Set the casing aside where it cannot be knocked or scratched.

Most heater units hang on the internal flue terminal by means of bolts and are light enough to be fitted by one person, but it is a good idea to have a helper standing by if only to hand you the nuts and washers.

The flue terminal seal fits either to the terminal or a recess in the back of the heater. Most are self adhesive strips which fit in much the same way as draught excluder—peel off the backing and press the strips home.

Once the flue terminal seal is in place, the multipoint heater unit can finally be bolted to the locating points.

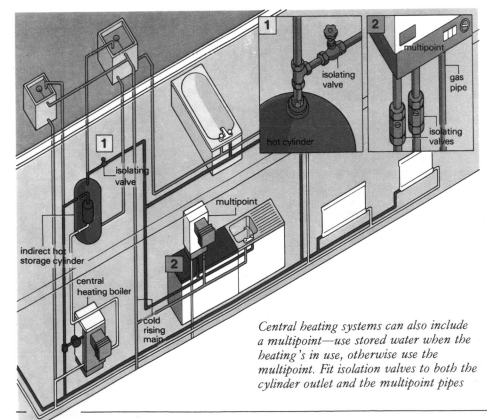

Central heating systems can also include a multipoint—use stored water when the heating's in use, otherwise use the multipoint. Fit isolation valves to both the cylinder outlet and the multipoint pipes

Making the connections

Once you've calculated the best places to make the connections for the gas and water supply, and the changes you need to make to the feed pipes to the taps, the connections are just like any other plumbing job.

There are three connections to be made: the incoming cold water supply, the gas supply and the outgoing hot water supply to the taps. Work backwards from the heater in all three cases. You can use capillary or compression fittings and joints for all three pipes. And the pipes can be surface mounted, concealed or buried in channels cut into the plaster of the wall surfaces.

Try to avoid burying joints in plaster chases where leaks may be difficult to locate or remedy. If you do so, make joints in the normal way, but don't make good until the installation has been tested.

Changes in direction can be made using a bending spring or bending machine. Alternatively, you can use plastic pipe for pipes carrying water, but not for gas.

Concealed pipework should be run horizontally or vertically—never diagonally.

You must fit an isolating valve to the incoming water supply near to the heater. If one is not supplied with the unit, use a 'Ballofix' valve, which needs no maintenance, rather than an ordinary stopcock.

The correct connection points inside the heater should be shown in the manufacturer's literature and will probably be marked inside the unit itself. Angle unions should be supplied with the heater to enable the first connections to be made. Don't fit the fibre washer or 'O' ring until you've completed the pipework and are ready to make the final connections. Tape them to the body of the heater until you've flushed the pipework.

Run the cold water supply back to the rising main pipe or other supply pipe, but leave the connection at this point until you're ready to test the water side of the installation. Connect the entire water side and as much of the gas pipework as you can before calling in a plumber to connect the gas supply and test the installation for you.
Hot water cylinders: What you do with the existing hot water cylinder depends upon whether you want to keep the cylinder as part of a combined system or remove it entirely from the house.

If you intend to leave the cylinder in place, you still need to install a stopcock on its feed side so that you can choose whether to use its stored water or water from the multipoint. In this case, you turn off the isolating valve on the multipoint and open the valve on the cylinder feed to the taps in order to use the water in the cylinder. If not, open the isolating valve on the multipoint and close the valve on the cylinder to use water from the multipoint. You'll need to drain the cylinder to fit this valve.

To drain and remove the cylinder entirely, empty the water through the drain cock at the bottom of the cold feed—turn off the supply pipe from the cistern or tie up the ball valve to prevent it refilling. Don't forget to remove the immersion heater.

Cut the cold feed pipe short and cap it as near to the cold water cistern as possible. Use a blanking off compression fitting or a gate valve for this purpose. If a gate valve is already fitted here, simply turn it off and disconnect the pipe to the cylinder.

Undo the vent pipe connection and cap off the old hot supply at the appropriate place—before it begins to feed the individual taps and appliances. The vent pipe and the cylinder can then be removed entirely. Remember to connect any earth bonding tags to the new hot supply. If you're using plastic pipe, get an electrician to alter the bonding arrangements.

When you've made the necessary arrangements at the cylinder end, return to the cold supply pipe to make the final connection to the feed. Turn off at the main stopcock (for indirect feeds, at the storage tank) to make the joint between the feed and the supply.

Disconnect the new pipework at the heater end and flush the pipework through to remove bits of solder or jointing compound—you may need assistance here. Refit the union with the seal or 'O' ring provided then run the new gas pipe back to the meter or existing gas supply ready for final connection by a qualified plumber or gas board technician.

9 *Run the inlet pipe back to the rising main (or indirect cistern supply), the outlet pipe to the existing hot water pipe*

10 *When fitting a multipoint to central heating, fit an isolating valve to the cylinder outlet*

11 *Flush the new pipes before finally fitting the seal at the inlet union—get an assistant to turn on the supply*

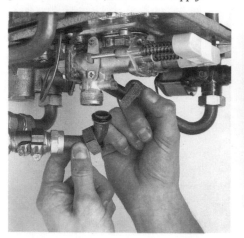

12 *Adjust the flow if necessary. Leave all the other adjustments and the gas connection to a qualified technician*

FITTING A FAN CONVECTOR

Apart from being far smaller than a radiator of the same output, a fan convector heater —fitted into your existing central heating system—offers a number of special advantages. One of the most obvious is that there's no limit on where you can put them; they'll fit above or alongside doors or windows, they'll fit on the walls in all the normal places and there's even a type that fits into the kick space below kitchen work units. There are high level and low level types, horizontal and vertical types and a range of miniature models. But such adaptability and versatility is only half the story.

Areas of the house that are difficult to heat by natural convection from an ordinary radiator can be warmed up rapidly by forced convection. Fan convectors literally force warm air to circulate, thus offsetting more of the heat loss from doors or windows.

Ordinary radiators are also often ill suited to kitchens. Modern fitted kitchen units rarely allow enough wall space for a radiator. Even if they do, the heat generated from cooking appliances may result in uncomfortably high temperatures. The rapid response of the thermostatically controlled fan and good siting will solve both problems.

Rooms which need heating quickly for short periods are also better served by fan convectors—warm-up periods are dramatically reduced by the vigorous air circulation.

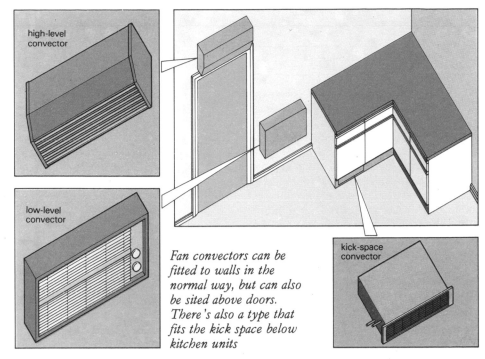

Fan convectors can be fitted to walls in the normal way, but can also be sited above doors. There's also a type that fits the kick space below kitchen units

How they work

Fan convectors can only be fitted to closed circulation two-pipe pump-assisted central heating systems. They take their heat from the central heating boiler in the same way as ordinary radiators—hot water is pumped in through the flow pipe and back out to the boiler by the return pipe. What makes them different is a heat exchanger and the principle of forcing air across the hot 'radiator'.

The principle is identical to that of a car heater—an electric fan blows air through a finned copper radiator where it becomes very hot indeed. The hot air is then blown across the room to produce a rapid change in temperature. When the room reaches the pre-set temperature you have chosen, the fan cuts out. But when the temperature drops below it, the fan automatically restarts.

Apart from the electricity consumed by the fan—which is no more than you need to power a small light bulb—the running costs are the same as those for a radiator of the same heat output.

Sophisticated controls—such as a multispeed fan and a thermostat sensitive to the room temperature—ensure that the unit can match your heat requirements, reducing problems of overheating and long warm-up periods.

A clever device called a low limit thermostat also senses the incoming temperature of the water from the boiler. If the water temperature is too low, the fan will not operate and as a result will not blast cold air into the room. Controlled by the low limit thermostat, the fan waits until the water is hot enough to provide comfortable heat. This also prevents the fan heater operating when the boiler is switched off, so the boiler controls still govern the fan operation.

On some models, an over-ride switch will allow the fan heater to be used in the summer to cool the air. In this respect, fan convectors can also be used as 'air conditioning' units.

What's available

There are basically three types of fan convector—the categories are based on their mounting positions. Within each category, there is a range of heat outputs which ensure that you'll be able to select one to match your needs. Heat output is based on the size of the unit, the three fan speeds— boost, medium and low—and the difference between the temperature of the radiator water and the air in the room. Select a model capable of heating the room on a low fan speed—the higher speeds and temperature difference (that controls the heat exchange) can be used for rapid heating or in excessive conditions. Take the room measurements to your dealer.

Low level wall mounted heaters: These units are positioned in the same places as ordinary radiators and are ideal for hallways, lounges and kitchens (where space permits). They come in a variety of dimensions.

High level wall mounted heaters: The best position for a high level convector is above a door, partly because it counteracts draughts and partly because it is a space rarely required for anything else.

Kick space heaters: To overcome the space problem in kitchens, a special heater is available to fit inside the plinth of a fitted kitchen base unit. The unit directs heat across the floor of the work area and forces upward air circulation. The fan speed control knob is designed to be fitted in a remote position, such as on a nearby wall. Consequently, there are no controls on the face of the heater that could be damaged.

Because of the problems associated with electricity in a damp atmosphere, none of the heaters are suitable for a bathroom.

An important feature of all fan convector heaters is a washable filter. Grease and general dust will inevitably collect around the air intake. Occasional cleaning of the filter will help its operation.

What's involved

When you've made a provisional choice of location for the heater, take a closer look at the fitting requirements and iron out any snags before you begin the work. Aim to fit the heater first, then the pipework.

The proximity of an existing central heating pipe run may influence your choice of position—but don't sacrifice future comfort for a few metres of copper tube. Install the heater where the prospect of air circulation is greatest and where heat loss from draughts is most noticeable. The unit itself is not difficult to install and you may be able to use flexible tube for connections that require awkward bends—otherwise hire a pipe bending machine from a hire shop or use a bending spring.

General considerations applying to central heating pipework are equally relevant in supplying a fan convector. Avoid high points in the pipework which may trap air. If you can't avoid them, fit small air vents at the highest points to bleed the system.

Fan convectors offer high resistance to the hot water flow, so additional resistance in the pipework may overload the pump. Try to make as few bends as possible, and consider running some of the longer lengths in 22mm pipework to reduce the strain on the pump. You can do so by taking connections from a 22mm section of the flow and return pipes from the boiler and running the new pipes as near as possible to the heater before reducing down to the more standard

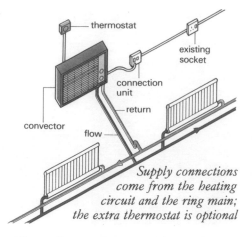

Supply connections come from the heating circuit and the ring main; the extra thermostat is optional

15mm diameter—you can buy compression or capillary fittings to reduce from 22mm to 15mm.

On some of the larger models, 22mm pipework is required anyway—this may mean going further back towards the boiler to find a 22mm run or substituting an existing section of 15mm pipe with the larger size. The important thing to bear in mind is that water will take the easiest route possible. Consequently, if the new pipe run is long and winding there will be a natural tendency for the water to go to the other radiators in the house.

Kick space heaters require pipes to be run under or through the kitchen units, which may be difficult if the units are not standard.

★ WATCH POINT ★

Check the bottom edge of the template is parallel to the skirting. If there is a discrepancy, it will probably be better to align the heater with the skirting for the sake of appearances.

Choosing the correct capacity: The size of your room, together with the quality of insulation in the house, will determine the correct capacity of your heater—your own experience is probably a good guide. Kilowatt ratings on these heaters compare directly with other heaters, such as electric fires—3kW is usually enough for larger rooms. The thermostatic control prevents waste of heat.

Electrical connections: A basic electrical connection via a fused connection unit or a plug and socket (with a 2 amp fuse) is a simple job and quite adequate to operate the unit. However, there are some modifications that can be made to the existing central heating wiring that will give you greater control.

In cases where the pump is controlled by a single wall thermostat in another room, a situation may occur where the fan heater is calling for heat when the wall thermostat is satisfied. This can be overcome by wiring a second thermostat in parallel to the existing one and placing it nearby.

Checking boiler capacity: Always check that the boiler is large enough to cope with the extra demand from any fan convector which you fit.

Modern boilers are adjustable within a range of outputs, so there may be no difficulty in increasing it to supply the fan heater. If your boiler thermostat periodically shuts the boiler off even though it is operating below the highest temperature setting, it is likely you have some spare capacity in the system.

In cases where the boiler is already working to its limit—where the boiler is firing continually on its higher settings—you must seek an alternative. You could turn off the radiators in the bedrooms.

In any event, the boiler should be

1 *Use the template or the instructions to mark fixing holes on to the wall—make absolutely sure that your lines are level*

2 *Mount the heater on 65mm No. 8 screws but don't tighten them yet. For stud walls, screw into the studs or onto a surface batten*

3 *Attach the valves and the first sections of pipework. Don't complete the joints until you've run the pipes through floors or walls*

struggling only during very cold weather or when the domestic hot water cylinder is refilling with water.

If you have any serious doubts, it is best to consult a heating engineer or the boiler manufacturers. They will probably want to know the volume of each room in the house and the total area of your radiator surfaces to make an accurate calculation.

Fitting a wall mounted heater

Mounting the heater is the first part of the job—it's largely a question of levelling the unit and attaching it to the wall with screws and wall plugs. Make sure there are no obstructions in front of the grille position.

Use the template supplied with the heater to mark the fixing holes on the wall. A spirit level and tape measure will ensure the correct position of the template. If there's no template, make your own by measuring fixing hole positions on the back plate.

Low level heaters are generally easier to install—there's no need for ladders or such like and it should be a job which one person can easily tackle.

Mark and drill the holes to take 65mm No. 8 screws and the correct size plastic wallplugs. If you're fitting it to a stud partition wall, make sure you can screw into the studs themselves. If you can't, screw sturdy battens to the studs and attach the heater to them.

Remove the template and insert the screws—leave approximately 9mm protruding from each screw on which to hang the heater chassis.

Following the manufacturer's instruction, take off the casing and hang the heater chassis on the screws. Don't tighten them fully until you've made arrangements for the first sections of pipework.

Most heaters are supplied with a pair of valves to isolate them from the pipework. Fit the valves, using jointing compound and the compression nuts provided, to the copper tails of the heat exchanger.

Connect copper pipe of the recommended

4 *Kick space heaters attach to the floor—you may need to pack beneath to centre the front grill. Cut the grill hole from the kick board with a jig saw*

size to the other end of the valves and run the pipework away from the heater.

There is usually the option of either going straight down through the floorboards or out through the back of the heater and the wall.

Whichever method you use will require the drilling of two holes—one for the flow pipe and one for the return. Once you have marked the holes clearly, slip the heater off the mounting screws to allow easier access for the drill.

High level heaters: The procedure for fixing the heater to the wall is similar to the low level wall mounted unit. Make sure you observe the minimum clearances specified in the instructions.

The pipes enter and leave the heater through the top of the heat exchanger. For neatness they should pass directly through the ceiling above. However, as this is sometimes inconvenient, they can be run on the surface along the wall. It is important to avoid dropping them to a lower level along their route as this will result in air being trapped in the high spots. If you can't avoid doing so, fit two small air vents at the highest point—make certain they are accessible because even after initial bleeding some air is bound to collect there.

Fitting a kick space heater

The first thing to do is prepare the cupboard to give yourself ample room for working—remove the drawers and shelves. At the same time, remove the adjacent kick boards in the direction of the pipe run.

Depending on the type of unit, the base can be removed in one of two ways—either by unscrewing the fixings or by cutting a large removable trap door in the bottom of the unit. You will have to decide which is

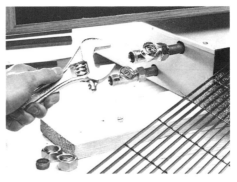

5 *Re-fit the top plate and attach the valves to the inlet and outlet pipes, preferably pointing forward. It's easiest if you screw the packing itself to the floor*

most practicable after careful examination of the unit. If in doubt consult the manufacturers.

When you have removed the base, cut an aperture in the kickboard to receive the heater grille. Mark the area carefully, leaving enough room at either side of the unit to make the plumbing and electrical connections—make sure you use exact dimensions.

Drill four holes at the corners of your marked area and join the holes with a padsaw or power jigsaw. Remove the cover plate from the top of the unit and position the heater in the hole in the kickboard. To prevent vibration and noise during operation, screw the heater to the floor. Place the kickboard and heater together on the floor and mark through the position of the heater's fixing holes or lugs.

Ensure the heater is high enough from the floor to provide a small, level clearance below the grille—small packing pieces of plywood may help achieve the ideal height. Connect the pipework to the heater using the isolation valves provided.

For difficult pipe runs through units, it may be easier to use flexible polybutylene pipe suitable for high temperature use.

After the electrical connections have been completed, the cover plate can be refixed. Test the heater thoroughly before refitting the unit base.

★ WATCH POINT ★

When fixing the heater above a door, either open the door fully or make sure that it is locked so that there is no chance of being knocked off your stepladder by somebody walking in while you're working.

★ WATCH POINT ★

To reduce the frequency with which you need to bleed the pipes, small upstands can be extended from the high points to act as air chambers. Fit the air cocks in the top of the upstands.

6 *Fit a drain cock to the lowest section of pipework so that you can empty the pipes either for repair or for maintenance purposes*

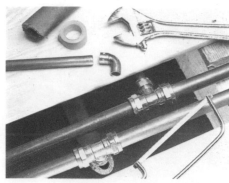

7 *To connect to the flow and return pipes, fit a compression tee to each—you'll need to use ones that reduce from 22mm to 15mm*

into a gully or drain. When you're satisfied the pipes are empty, mark and cut the flow and return pipes to receive the new compression tees—it's difficult to drain central heating systems completely, so place a rag or small dish under the pipes you intend to cut to catch any drips.

Capillary joints should not be used on these two connections since the slightest trace of water in the pipes will prevent the solder running evenly around the joints.

Once you have made the connections, close the isolation valves on the heater and undo the connections at the heater side.

Fill the system by turning off the drain cock and releasing the header tank ballvalve. When the water stops running in, place a bucket under the valves near the heater and open each one cautiously. By running a small quantity of water through the pipework you will flush out any solder or jointing compound that may block the heat exchanger.

When the pipes are clear, these con-

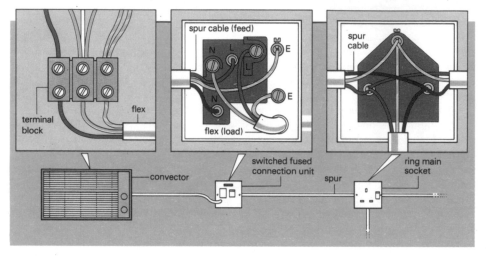

terminal block

flex

spur cable (feed)

N L
L
E

N
E

flex (load)

spur cable

convector

switched fused connection unit

spur

ring main socket

Electrical connections via a spur; the flex generally attaches to a simple terminal block

Running the pipes

Pipe runs should be supported every 900mm by clips to prevent movement. If the new pipes are lower than the existing circuit, incorporate a drain cock at the lowest point on the new pipework.

Continue the pipe run along the neatest and most convenient route—notching through joints where necessary—until you reach a connection point.

Joints on copper pipe can be made with compression or capillary fittings—try to use long radius bends rather than elbows.

All pipework running under floors or through other unheated areas must be insulated with foam tubes or lagging tape to prevent heat loss or pipe bursts.

Connecting to the system: When you are ready to connect into the main pipe run (with a compression tee joint), fully drain the heating system by tying up the ballvalve on the small header tank at the top of the house. Attach a hose pipe to the drain cock at the lowest point of the system. This may be on a pipe run or on the boiler itself. Run the hose pipe out of the house to discharge

nections can be re-made (with jointing compound) and the isolation valves opened fully. Check the pipe runs for signs of leaks and bleed the air from the heat exchanger by opening the small air vent at the top. When water appears, close the air cock.

Electrical connections: The power supply for all heaters must incorporate a fuse of the correct rating—usually two amps. Connection may be made via an ordinary plug and socket or through a fused spur connection unit.

The electrical connections are the same in this case as for any other fixed electrical appliance; you may add another outlet or extend an existing one.

1 *Increase the flow on the radiator circuit to cope with the extra load—you may be able to adjust the pump speed*

2 *Shut down all the other radiators then open them in turn to balance the system. If in doubt, employ a heating engineer*

1

2

ELECTRIC WATER HEATER

Point of use electric water heaters are designed to provide small amounts of hot water at the place it's needed, whenever it's needed. They can be used either as an independent means of heating water or as a supplement to a larger system (a conventional hot water cylinder with immersion heater or central heating system, for example) which is only operated for the limited periods when the whole family needs hot water.

Rapid recovery times and good insulation ensure economy and convenience in use, and because they are situated so close to the sink or basin, long hot water pipe runs are avoided. This offers great savings in installation costs and eliminates the waste which occurs when hot water is left to go cold in the pipework.

A built-in thermostat keeps the water at an even temperature allowing the heater to be left switched on for long periods without wasting electricity. By incorporating a time-switch into the electricity supply even greater economy can be achieved.

The heater may be plumbed directly into the rising main or connected to a tank-fed supply. Each manufacturer's literature specifies the minimum static head required for tank-fed heaters—this is generally about one metre from the base of the tank to the base of the heater but you'll need to check before buying as models vary.

A great advantage of using electric point of use heaters is the versatility of plumbing installation. By plumbing them into the mains, hot water can be supplied to rooms at a higher level than the cold water storage tank. This is especially useful for attic rooms and loft conversions where washing facilities would not be possible using a conventional hot water system. Such heaters also enable the quick and easy installation of hot water in garages and outhouses used as utility rooms.

What's available

A range of sizes to suit both sink and basin applications is available in a variety of shapes. Over-sink heaters can be square or cylindrical with a swivel spout and come in 1kW and 3kW versions. Both heat the water to a good temperature but the lower-powered model takes longer. A 3kW model heats at about the same rate as a modern electric kettle.

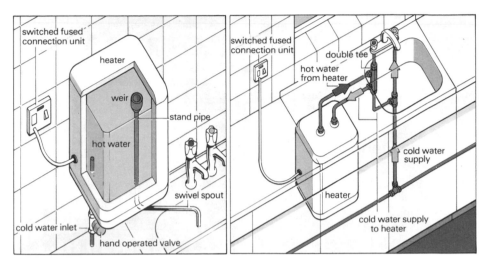

The smallest size is approximately 7 litres—a convenient size for most domestic kitchens. If your requirements are above average, sizes up to 15 litres are available from some manufacturers.

If the heater is mounted centrally, swivel spout models can be used to supply two adjacent sinks. Varying lengths of spout can be ordered to cope with different locations where the heater may have to be mounted away from the sink or basin—some makes offer a telescopic spout.

For neatness and convenience of operation, a range of heaters can be mounted inside a sink base or basin vanity unit. These models must be used with special taps supplied by the manufacturer.

The heating elements are guaranteed for anything up to five years and a thermal cut-out device may be incorporated in the circuit to protect the element should the heater be accidentally drained whilst the power is on. If the element does burn out, changing it is an easy matter of unscrewing a few bolts and withdrawing the whole electrical assembly.

For handwashing only, instantaneous sprays are available for mounting above the basin. These heaters are very economical because they heat water only when it is needed. Some models have a sophisticated proximity switch that turns them on and off when hands are placed beneath the spray.

Other electronic models use a touch switch. Both these systems are well suited to the garage or workshop where you may wish to avoid turning knobs by hand.

Although these heaters are termed 'instantaneous', a few seconds delay will be experienced before delivery of the hot water to allow warming up.

The basic difference between over-sink and under-sink heaters is that in the latter special taps and valves must be used

How they work

When you turn on the tap of an over-sink heater, cold water enters at its base and displaces the hot water inside. The hot water then spills over a weir inside the top of the heater and discharges through a swivel spout above the sink or basin. The flow is regulated by a hand operated valve on the cold supply leaving the spout completely unrestricted to allow expansion and venting of the hot water. A characteristic of this type of heater is the tendency for a drip to appear at the spout during the heating up period caused by the expansion of the water. This will cease when the water reaches its pre-set temperature.

Under-sink water heaters operate in a similar way to the over-sink type, but the swivel spout and control valve are incorporated in a special tap system located on the sink or basin in the conventional manner. The cold supply is fed into the bottom of the hot tap and is redirected into the under-sink heater via a short pipe. The cold water forces hot water out through another pipe that runs from the top of the heater back to a third connection on the tap—the water is discharged through the spout of the tap into the sink or basin. A matching cold water tap is supplied to be connected directly to the cold supply in the usual way.

Instantaneous hand spray heaters work like electric showers, heating up cold water as it passes through the unit. This is achieved by a powerful element and a thermostatic restriction on the flow of water making sure the water is delivered at an even temperature.

Generally, instantaneous water heaters are only suitable for connection to mains pressure, because the minimum static operating head is approximately 11m.

Power for all models can be taken from an existing switched socket or, and better, a switched fused connection unit.

Planning

Finding a suitable position for mounting the heater is the first consideration. If there is a window immediately above the sink, the heater will have to be mounted to one side. A better option is to choose an undersink model and buy the special taps.

If the heater is to be installed in a garage or outhouse, select a model with frost protection and protect all pipework.

Electrical connections can be made through a surface mounted spur outlet or in a flush mounted box with concealed wiring.

Avoid making joints in buried pipework and protect the copper from the corrosive elements in cement. This can be done by applying oil based or bituminous paint or by wrapping the pipe with tape. Always run concealed pipework and cables horizontally or vertically across the wall.

Fitting an over-sink heater

Mounting the heater couldn't be simpler—it's the plumbing and electrical work that demands more effort.

Once you have determined the heater's position, mark out the fixing points on the wall. Measure the centres to coincide with the holes in the heater and check they are level before you start drilling.

Plug the holes and fix the screws for the top two holes. Hang the heater in place and mark the third retaining screw position at the bottom of the heater. Remove the heater and drill and plug this hole. The heater may then be fixed in place.

Connecting the pipework: Attach the swivel spout temporarily to make sure the new pipework will not foul its operation. In most cases the connection is behind the swivel spout and the pipework runs down the wall and through the worktop.

★ WATCH POINT ★

If you have a spare hole in the sink top where the hot tap would normally go, it can be used for running the cold feed through—a large rubber grommet will seal the hole and make a neater job.

If the sink meets the wall, you will have to find a way of getting the pipework through the sink top unobtrusively.

Alternatively, you can chase out the brickwork using a club hammer and cold chisel and bend the pipework behind the back of the sink. If this is difficult the pipework can be run horizontally along the wall to enter the base unit at the side. In some cases, you may be able to connect up to the cold supply outside the base unit.

★ WATCH POINT ★

It may be possible to avoid cutting the pipework by replacing an existing compression elbow or straight connector with a new tee.

The pipe must be connected to the control tap on the heater inlet with the tap head facing outwards. Where this necessitates a tight bend, a male to female capillary elbow will make it easier. The pipework should be supported by brackets to prevent any vibration, especially on a mains supply.

When you have run the pipework to a position out of view, connect a 15mm stopcock before carrying on to the main pipe run. Select a point to break into the main pipe run that offers you good working access—this may not always be the nearest position. Mark where to cut the main pipework by offering up a compression tee.

Turn off the water and catch any residue from the pipe when you've cut it in a small bowl. Connect the compression tee in position and tighten all the nuts. If it is difficult to insert the tee into the fixed pipework you may have to undo a joint further up the line to give some lateral movement. You may be able to loosen some pipe brackets to allow the pipe to be temporarily pulled out of line.

Before turning the water back on, make sure the fibre washer 'O' ring is fitted to the tap on the heater. Open all taps fully and flush out the pipework before making this final connection. A momentary delay will be experienced before any water appears.

1 *Check that there are no electricity, gas or water services buried in the wall before fitting the bracket and hanging the heater*

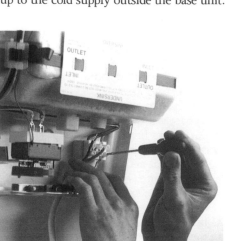

2 *After clamping the outer sheathing of the flex in the cable grip, make the correct connections to the clearly marked terminals*

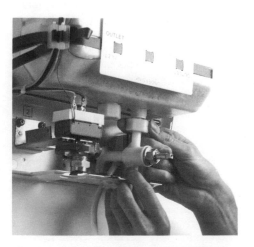

3 *Assemble the inlet control valve and its associated fittings and connect it up to the plastic inlet boss. Check that all the fittings are tight before you continue*

4 *Run the supply pipework back to the rising main and connect it via a tee. Add a stopcock so you can isolate the water heater*

5 *Assemble the spout fittings and slide on the grommet before attaching the swivel spout assembly to the outlet boss. Check that the spout moves freely*

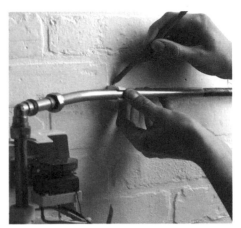

6 *Before connecting the cold water feed to the heater, offer up the pipework to mark the position of its supporting brackets on the wall*

7 *When connecting the pipe from the hot tap to the heater, be very careful not to overtighten and damage the plastic nut*

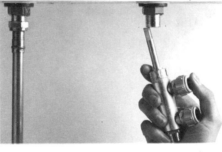

8 *The connector fitted below the hot tap has an upper connection for hot water from the heater and a lower one for the cold feed*

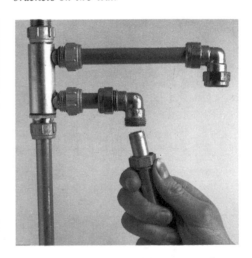

9 *After linking the cold water supply to the connector, make up the pipe runs to and from the heater. You can use either compression or soldered joints*

Plumbing in under-sink heaters

If you want to fit an under-sink heater you'll need to buy the special taps too. The added expense will be more than justified, however, by the neater look of the finished job.

Under-sink heaters must never be connected to any taps other than those supplied by the manufacturers. The taps may be single pillar taps or of the mixer variety.

Connect the new taps to the sink or basin in the normal way. The cold tap can be connected to the mains supply using the standard plumbing techniques.

The hot tap must also be connected to the cold water supply at the inlet designated 'cold water in'. Models vary in the arrangement of pipes but in all cases you should find the connections clearly labelled.

The second connection on the hot tap is from the tap to the heater. This is controlled by the tap washer.

Connect a length of 15mm pipe between the compression fittings making sure you select the cold feed into the heater itself.

The final connection is from the heater outlet back to the hot water tap. This should be marked—'hot water in'. This connection has a clear way through to the spout of the tap to provide a vent for the heater.

Some taps have soft copper tails for connection to compression reducers—take care not to overtighten the nuts on these.

Test the plumbing before making any power connections—see Connecting the power (right) for details.

Some undersink heaters are in fact dual-purpose models which can be installed the other way up as well to function as an over-sink unit. Such heaters usually have fitting instructions for each mode securely taped to the unit when you unpack the heater; make sure that you're following the correct set for your installation.

Connecting the power

Connections between the heater and the fused spur outlet must be made in heat-resistant flex. This can have butyl rubber or special PVC sheathing.

Remove the cover plate from the heater to expose the wiring terminals. A small wire link from the thermostat to the live terminal should be connected. In some cases a thermal cut-out is incorporated into the live supply—this protects the element if the heater is accidentally drained whilst still being switched on. Consult the manufacturer's instructions regarding the thermal cut-out and other features including a low limit frost thermostat.

Connect the flex to the appropriate terminals which are clearly marked Earth, Live and Neutral, and tighten the screws.

Run the flex through the cable clamp and tighten down until secure. Arrange the flex neatly so it doesn't foul the swivel arm (if fitted) and run it back to the spur point.

The flex should be clamped inside the spur housing and the wires bared to provide just enough to make good contact inside the terminals. Attach the socket box to the wall with at least two screws.

Run the 2.5mm cable inside conduit or mini-trunking along the wall.

If the cable is to be run beneath floorboards drill the joists rather than using notches. To be doubly safe write 'cable under' with a felt tip pen on the top of the boards as you replace them, and screw them down rather than nailing them so they can be raised easily if necessary for future repairs or maintenance.

Low powered heaters of under 3kW can be connected directly to an existing ring main via a socket outlet.

Turn off the electricity at the mains and remove the appropriate circuit fuse.

Undo the faceplate and poke the new cable into the back or side of the box. Con-

10 *Position the hand spray heaters so that the spout is at a convenient height above the sink. Use a spirit level to check its alignment*

nect the cable to the terminals, remembering to sheath the bare earth wire with green/yellow PVC sleeving first.

Replace the socket faceplate and circuit fuse, and test that everything works.

If a spare fuseway is available, simply run the new circuit cable from it to a double-pole isolating switch (rated at 20 amps). Further cable links the switch to the water heater

11 *Use copper or stainless steel tubing to connect the heater directly to the rising main. Then wire up the electrics*

Fitting a hand spray heater

Instantaneous hand sprays are fitted in the same way as over-sink heaters, but they require a much greater water pressure and for this reason they must be connected to the cold rising main.

The control valve for the water is powered by electricity and is sealed inside the case, so the water supply can be connected directly to the heater without worrying about taps.

It is, however, recommended that some form of isolation valve be fitted in a convenient position for servicing, but this will not need to be accessible by the user.

The electrical connection should be made through a permanently connected double-pole switch. As most of these heaters are rated at 3kW, probably the most convenient way of doing this is to use a switched fused connection unit fitted with a 13 amp fuse. You can then isolate the heater from the mains for repairs. Connect the heater with a 2.5mm² three-core flex, and link the unit to a nearby ring main socket with a spur of 2.5mm² two-core and earth cable.

Installation in outbuildings: It can be extremely useful to have hand-washing facilities in a garage or outbuilding, and hand spray heater units are ideally suited to this purpose. However, make sure you choose a model with frost protection and take steps to protect and insulate all the pipework which is located outside the house. A drain cock at the lowest point of the run will allow the pipe to be emptied during particularly severe weather.

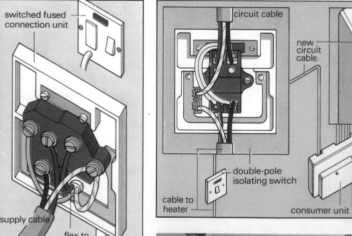

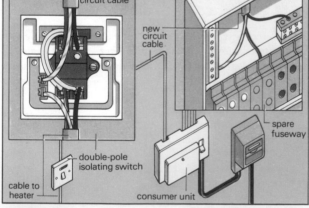

1

1 *A switched fused connection unit can be used on heaters rated at less than 3kW. Fit a 13 amp fuse in the fuseholder*

2 *For complete safety, cross-bond the new pipework to the old with 6mm² single-core earth cable*

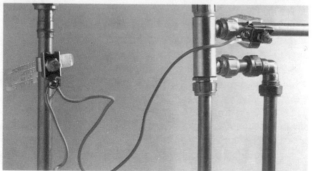

2

CHOOSING A SOLID FUEL STOVE

There are two kinds of modern solid fuel 'super stove'—those used for heating and cooking in the kitchen, and those used as room heaters elsewhere. Either type is capable of providing hot water to your taps, and many can also serve as a boiler for a central heating system.

Both solid fuel stoves and heaters combine the advantages of a traditional fire on the one hand with efficient modern technology on the other. The result is an economical heater that can be regulated to give precise heat levels—a quality not normally associated with solid fuel burners—and many models are so efficient that clearing the ash is only necessary every few days.

Most solid fuel stoves can be fitted to a fireplace in a single day with no messy or expensive structural alterations. And, if that's not possible, prefabricated flues ensure they can be fitted into houses without chimneys.

Solid fuel cookers offer an unrivalled performance in the kitchen. The cast iron construction of the ovens ensures an even temperature for baking and roasting—an asset which has made them a highly prized piece of very durable kitchen equipment.

The two-oven system of the more sophisticated models allows you to stew, braise, roast and bake different dishes at the same time; one oven operates at a different temperature to the other. In the warming oven, a meal may be left all day without drying out and slow cooking casseroles can simmer from morning till night. The hot oven is ideal for baking cakes and bread as well as roasting meat.

The two plates set into the hob likewise operate at two different temperatures to allow boiling and simmering; special insulated covers close down the cooking surface to retain the heat when not in use. The large top surface is especially useful for cooking more lavish meals—they're generally capable of heating six pans at once.

Some new designs offer a griddle for cooking so you can enjoy the charcoal flavour of a barbecue all the year round. A few Scandinavian models even boast a smoke chamber for curing fish and meats. Features like these will certainly increase the scope and range of your cooking.

The ovens and hotplates also help to keep themselves clean—the surfaces remain hot so that spills simply burn to a dust which you can remove with a stiff brush.

Old style stoves

You can buy authentic black cast iron stoves that are faithful reproductions of the traditional top plate cooker and heater. UK, continental and American manufacturers produce a range of the early designs using castings of higher quality than the originals and with more efficient internal workings. The price, however, is high. Always be suspicious of cheaper versions of a similar appearance—the quality of the casting is probably inferior.

It's quite common to find local stove centres stocking a range of solid fuel stoves. They can also provide information and advice. Make sure that you compare several brochures if you can't inspect the models themselves. Whatever you do, don't order one on the basis of the information in the brochure alone.

Solid fuel and wood-burning cookers come in a wide range of designs; most are capable of providing hot water and central heating. With fine control of temperatures and ample top plates and oven facilities, they're a useful alternative to conventional stoves (some people think they cook better, too)

A more modern but 'traditional' design in the UK is the legendary cooker made by Aga-Rayburn and Esse. They're sold in several rich enamelled colours as well as the original cream or black, they also run on fuels other than coal or wood—gas, liquid petroleum gas (LPG) and oil.

Second-hand models of many of these cookers can be sought at reclamation centres, house clearance sales or auctions. It's wise to contact a reputable dealer beforehand for advice about what to look for. Many dealers are willing to move one of their stoves from one house to another too—a valuable service if you intend to move home.

Drawbacks of solid fuel cooking

The drawbacks of solid fuel cooking are easy to see. The need to refuel, or even to stock fuel, may be inconvenient in a busy kitchen and some forward planning is necessary to ensure the cooker has warmed up to the required cooking temperature prior to use. Allowing a solid fuel cooker to go out is a culinary disaster since it can take several hours for the cooker to heat up again to the required temperature. Hopper-fed cookers, which take in fuel as and when the fire needs it, reduces the risk of this.

In the summer the kitchen is likely to get uncomfortably hot; while this is very pleasant in the colder months, it can be a nuisance during warm weather.

In most cases, you'll also need some back-up facilities to provide grills and spits, though the solid fuel cooker is ideal for roasting, baking and casseroling. Unlike gas or electric cookers, even models with automatic control and fan assistance take time to adjust to changes in temperature.

Choosing a stove

There is a surprisingly varied range of solid fuel and woodburning stoves available. Apart from the cookers, there are also stoves that are primarily room heaters but which contain a limited facility for simple cooking—hotplates and accessories for toasters, for example.

Stoves specifically designed as room heaters are available in an extraordinary selection of styles and appearances. Some look like the old kitchen ranges or pot-bellied stoves, others look like modern gas fires, yet others have a design entirely of their own—exciting geometric shapes (cylindrical, spherical, triangular or square) with bright enamelled surfaces or stainless steel finishes.

Direct comparisons between various models are difficult to make because the operating conditions of solid fuel appliances are bound to differ, not only in the types of fuel used but also in the characteristics of the chimney. Most manufacturers admit that outputs are approximate and allowances must be made.

Features such as top or front loading may have a bearing upon your final decision—top loaders require space above them but may also have a reasonably large top surface for limited cooking: front loaders may have solid or glass doors.

Some stoves operate as either open or closed fires. If you wish to see the fire but gain the optimum efficiency, choose a model with a glass front. Opening solid doors to enjoy the fire will mean uncontrolled greater heat loss.

How heaters work

The stoves achieve their high efficiency by carefully controlling the air flow to the fire. Few moving parts, high-quality insulation and efficient door seals maintain this efficient control.

On models designed to burn wood only, the air enters the burning chamber level with the fire. The logs burn on a bed of ash that is left to provide a reservoir of heat—the danger of the fire going out is reduced because the bed of ash stays red hot for a long time.

Some Scandinavian companies produce a stove that burns logs from end to end rather like a glowing cigar. They burn for up to twelve hours on a single filling.

Modern solid fuel room heaters are available in traditional stove black or exciting enamel finishes—shapes and designs vary. Many include limited cooking facilities (left)

Multi-fuel stoves that burn coal operate on the old fashioned principle of an under-draught rising up through the fire. This means the grate must be cleared of ash to allow the draught through. Many models incorporate rotating riddles (sieves) that sift the burnt fuel into an ash pan. Apart from having to turn the handle and empty the pan, they are no more trouble to use than other woodburning stoves.

Features which improve the operation of the stove include items such as secondary combustion chambers to burn flue gases, tar filters to help keep the chimney clean, twin draught ports to control the burning rate and updraught, and thermostatic controls to automatically adjust the heat output. Some models include a hopper fuel feed which takes one large load then gradually feeds it into the fire. Others may include fan assistance to reduce 'warm-up' time and aid combustion and heat output.

Special chimney regulations

The flue pipe for your solid fuel stove should be purchased at the same time as the stove to make sure that you obtain the right size and adaptor. If you plan to run the flue into an existing chimney, you should ensure the chimney has been swept and make sure that it is in good working order prior to installing any kind of solid fuel heater.

If it is old, you may find it needs lining. Flexible liners such as the kind used for gas boilers are *not* suitable for solid fuel. However, many special liners are available from stove merchants. Follow the advice of the merchant in selecting the correct flue.

For wood burning stoves, a liner is essential. Tar deposits from wood smoke will rapidly eat their way through the mortar between the bricks and produce dark stains on the chimney breast. If this is allowed to go unchecked, the structural stability of the chimney will be impaired. Ask the dealer about special grades of liner for wood burning.

If you have no chimney or fireplace, stoves may be operated as free-standing appliances by using a special prefabricated chimney system. There are many types available which can be erected quickly and easily inside or outside the building. Some are specially designed to be exposed on the inside—they're finished to match the stove.

Adding a cowl to the top will help keep the chimney dry and prevent draughts which sometimes blow smoke back into the room in which the stove is located.

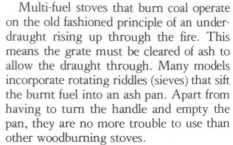

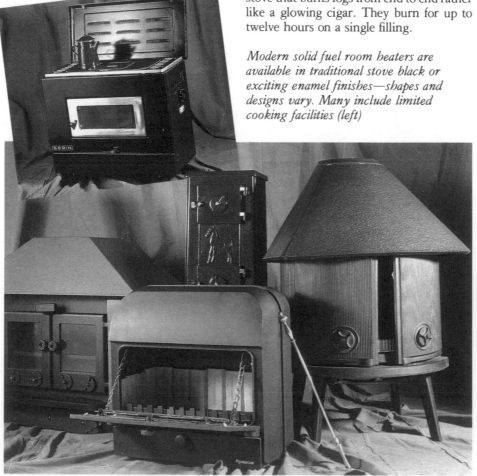

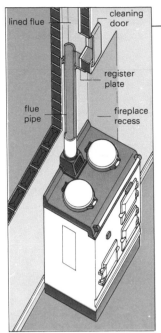

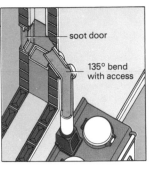

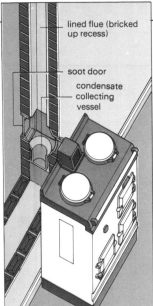

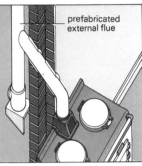

Central heating from a stove

There are a great many stoves that are specifically designed to run central heating systems. These are available in three types: purpose-built boilers, combination cooker/boilers and heaters with back boilers.

Free-standing boilers do nothing but run central heating and provide hot water. Some are available with enamelled casings for standing in a kitchen, but most look functional rather than decorative. The casings are often insulated to reduce heat loss to the room, so they can be located in an outhouse or cellar without a lot of heat going to waste.

Combination boilers and cookers are purpose made for the kitchen and are only marginally more bulky than their cooker/heater counterpart. The enamelled casings are available in a number of bright colours as well as the traditional cream and brown finishes. These models can be left free-standing between units or in an inglenook fireplace.

Room heaters are decorative living room appliances built to replace the open fire. The fires themselves may be stove-blackened, bright enamel or stainless steel with solid or glass doors. These may be purchased with or without high output back boilers.

The efficiency of all these types of boilers depends upon the fuel. Wood gives approximately half the calorific value of coal, so you must be prepared to burn twice the weight to gain the same heat. Since wood is also more bulky, finding the storage space needed to keep it dry is a major problem—

Flue arrangements are very important and depend on the house structure and where you want to install the stove. Your supplier should give you the necessary help and advice

you may need to build a large shed just to house your log supply. For most people it is impractical to run central heating boilers on wood alone.

Solid fuel central heating systems differ in a number of ways from more modern systems (see pages 156–158). Some alteration in controls and pipe sizes will probably be necessary if you wish to adapt an existing system. A solid fuel boiler should never be used on a fully-pumped system because pump failure would result in the boiler overheating. If you intend using a direct system either for central heating or domestic

Fireplace-fitting room heaters may include back boilers capable of running a full central heating system and hot water

hot water, make sure the boiler is rustproof; the best types are coated internally with enamel.

Options other than full central heating are available. It is possible to combine an automatic modern central heating control system with a solid fuel boiler but a fairly sophisticated control system will be necessary—you will need to call in an expert to design the layout.

Choosing a site

Most houses have sites which are suitable for the installation of a solid fuel stove, whether an existing chimney is used or a factory-made flue is erected so that the stove can be free-standing.

The fundamental requirement is a fireproof hearth or floor. The building regulations require minimum dimensions for this and carpets and rugs must be kept outside this area. Wood floors can be covered with a sand and cement screed laid on expanded metal mesh. Since stoves tend to be rather heavy, check that the floor is strong enough.

The stove can be positioned within an inglenook fireplace or immediately in front of the chimney breast. By choosing the right size of model you can avoid costly alterations later.

Equally important is a flue outlet to take waste gases to the outside. Some models offer a choice of flue positions to make installation easier. The top outlet is best for an inglenook, whilst the rear outlet suits a stove mounted in front of a fireplace. If there's no fireplace at all, you'll need to erect a prefabricated chimney inside or on an outside wall. In the first case, you'll need to run it through the ceiling and roof: in the second, the flue must run to eaves level.

If you intend to heat your water with a stove, consideration will have to be given to the relative position of the water cylinder—it must be immediately above the stove.

Installation

Many room heaters can be installed in a single day with the help of comprehensive instructions usually supplied by the maker (see pages 218–222). If the appliance is to be used with a conventional brick-built chimney, you will need a register plate to cover the opening and an access door.

Most room heaters are delivered ready assembled. If they include firebricks, these come in a separate pack and are simply placed in position around the interior.

INSTALLING A SOLID FUEL STOVE

Although usually installed by the supplier, there are now solid fuel stoves that are specifically designed for the DIY market. These types are quite straightforward to fit, so long as you're meticulous in your preparatory work. You'll also need to be competent at basic plumbing if you want to utilize the cooker's hot water or central heating facility.

How they work

A solid fuel cooker works on the principle of heat storage: the cast-iron ovens are indirectly heated by the burning fuel—typically coal, smokeless fuel, wood or peat.

The appliance is kept burning continuously, efficiently and economically (thermostatically controlled to use the minimum of fuel) so heat is always instantly available for whatever cooking you want to do.

The hotplate or plates—some cookers have a single large one, others two smaller ones—are graded according to the heat they emit. The plate (or section) that's located directly over the heat source is fiercely hot for grilling, toasting or rapid boiling whereas its neighbour is intended for simmering and low heat. The plates are covered, when not in use, by insulated lids, which conserve the heat.

Oven temperature and fuel-burning rates can be adjusted by a damper control for the most efficient use of the appliance, and there's a door permitting access to the firebox for re-fuelling during use.

The cooker has a flue connected to the house chimney, which removes combustion gases from the chamber and unwanted cooking smells from the room. You may have to insert a liner to protect against staining. If there's no convenient chimney, you'll need to erect a prefabricated flue on an outside wall.

Some solid fuel cookers incorporate a built-in boiler behind the firebox, which can provide full central heating for up to twelve radiators—ample for the average household —plus all the hot water you'll need for washing-up and baths for the whole family. Other types require a separate, matching, boiler, which sits alongside the cooker.

Choosing a cooker: Don't assume that a single appliance offering so much will be an ugly, bulky and purely functional unit: a typical solid fuel cooker measures only about 900mm wide, 850mm tall by 600mm deep.

Colour choice is more adventurous than most conventional cookers, offering the classic cream, or bold red, blue, green, brown, black or white (two-tone types are also made). The finish is a durable glossy enamel which, with chrome trims, assures a style to suit your taste.

Efficiency and economy are important considerations when you're thinking of buying a solid fuel cooker. Per 24 hours, you can expect a cooker/boiler to consume about 22kg of coal (60kg of wood) during winter and 12kg of coal (39kg of wood) during summer, producing the equivalent of 35,000Btu/h and 10,500Btu/h maximum respectively (20,000 and 9,000 for wood). Over 24 hours your cooker/boiler will produce about 450 litres of hot water.

Planning considerations

Take time to examine what's available—different models offer labour and fuel saving devices like hopper feeds, fan assistance and draught controls.

Installation of a solid fuel cooker demands

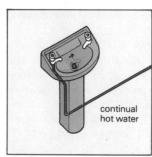

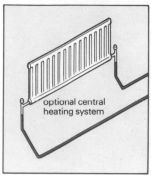

Modern solid fuel cookers are capable of supplying all your hot water requirements and some can also fire full central heating systems. Primary circuits must be the unpumped 'gravity flow' type

optional central heating system

that you comply with the building regulations, which ensure that the appliance is properly fitted and will be safe to use.

The cooker must be set on a solid, level concrete constructional hearth, which is intended to separate the appliance from the combustible parts of the room, such as a suspended timber floor. A hearth must conform to certain size requirements (see Assessing the site). In a house with a concrete floor, no hearth is required.

If the existing hearth isn't big enough you'll have to extend it, or lay a new one. This can be quite a complicated job, as it requires you to cut back the existing timber floor and joists beneath to accommodate the new hearth.

Siting the cooker

In a typical room with one chimney breast there are three possible positions (see diagram on page 60).
• In an existing fireplace recess (space permitting—see below).
• Against a bricked-up chimney breast.

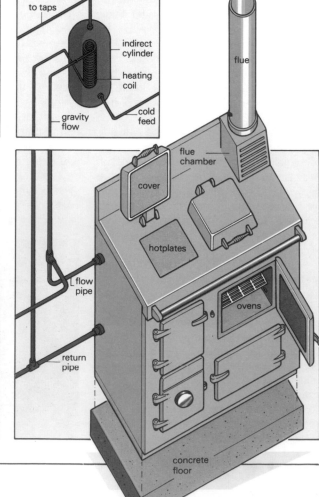

• In an alcove at one side of the chimney.

The flue from the cooker can enter the main chimney in one of three ways.

• Rising vertically if the cooker is in a recess.

• Running directly back through the bricked-up chimney breast.

• Entering through the side or front of the chimney breast via bends in the fluepipe.

If there's no chimney in the room, you may be able to install a new insulated chimney or an external prefabricated chimney. Consult your dealer or the local Building Control Office for details of suitable types of prefabricated chimney.

In all types of chimneys the minimum height for the correct operation of the cooker is 5.5m. The stack should terminate above the roof in accordance with regional statutory requirements, which in effect means a suitable cooler or pot must be fitted at the top. Choice depends to some extent on local conditions, and advice should be taken from the supplier of the cooker.

If you're planning to install your cooker in an existing fireplace recess you must take stock of the dimensions of the opening (see Assessing the site). Your main consideration is the structure of the flue which must be adequately lined to cope with efficient disposal of fumes. Suitable linings consist of terracotta or cement, usually standard in homes built after about 1965. Aluminium flexible liners are not suitable for this type of installation. If your flue does need lining, it's best to leave this to a specialist whom you should call in to help.

Assessing the site

The cooker must be set on a non-combustible, solid and level concrete hearth, which must conform to specified dimensions. Care must also be taken to position the appliance a recommended distance away from any combustible materials. Your first job is to assess these various details.

If you're setting the cooker on an existing hearth, first measure it to check that it's large enough. Regulations state that a hearth must be at least 125mm thick, must project beyond the chimney breast by at least 500mm and must extend past the builder's recess by at least 150mm on each side (note that these are minimum dimensions).

A hearth not built in conjunction with a chimney breast must be 840mm square. But in a house with a concrete floor, no special or additional hearth is required.

Now consult the manufacturer's specifications for your model of cooker to make sure there will be sufficient clearance for the

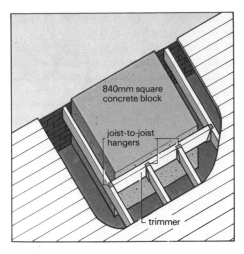

Timber floors must be strengthened below the cooker by replacing joists with a concrete block of the correct size. Use trimmers and joist hangers to rebuild the floor

appliance on the hearth. If there's not enough room, you'll have to extend the concrete slab or break up the old one and lay a new, larger one. This, however, requires considerable rearrangement of the components in the floor structure (see diagram above for details).

The fireplace recess must also be big enough to take the cooker. Important dimensions are the height, width and depth (front to back) of the opening; minimum sizes should be 1680mm, 1080mm and 343mm respectively. These dimensions permit access to the boiler flow and return connections (see Running central heating) and for rear boiler flueway cleaning.

When the cooker is installed in a recess it must be totally freestanding. Any combustible material, such as kitchen furniture and units, must be a minimum of 150mm away from the appliance on each side and 225mm from the front.

If the rear and oven-side walls of the recess are 200mm thick or more (and non-combustible) you can position the cooker in the angle without having to leave a space. For thinner walls you should aim to allow a 100mm gap (150mm for combustible walls, such as any internal hollow stud partitions).

Once you've decided on a suitable location for the cooker, you can work out its flue layout. In a top flue outlet you have to make the connection from the cooker's flue chamber using a length of 150mm diameter vitreous enamel or cast-iron fluepipe. Measure up the wall from the flue chamber position, as given in the manufacturer's details, and work out the length and pos-

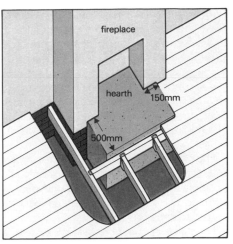

ition of the pipe—it's generally necessary to allow the fluepipe to project at least 150mm beyond the opening into the existing flue.

Square bends mustn't be used: only 135° bends are permissible. The flue must be sealed where the fluepipe enters with a metal register plate, which you'll have to make up yourself.

With a flue outlet you must make provision for a 'condensate collecting vessel' under the flue outlet, within the chimney. This constitutes a small pipe discharging into a receptacle to collect moisture formed during the combustion process when the fuel is burning.

To enable you to clean a conventional lined flue periodically, it's also necessary to include a 'soot door' in the chimney breast —this can be a hole about 225mm × 225mm (about one brick wide by three deep) cut in the face of the bricked-up recess or in the back wall with access from outside on an external wall. The hole should be lined with a frame and fitted with a proprietary, close-fitting door—it's generally best to include the soot door below the end of the fluepipe and above the register plate.

Running central heating

Some solid fuel boilers incorporate a boiler for use in heating domestic water and powering radiators. Some models can run up to twelve radiators.

Most cooker/boilers can be used to replace an existing central heating boiler and to run your existing radiators. However, you cannot use a solid fuel boiler for fully pumped central heating systems—the domestic hot water circuit must be a natural gravity feed between boiler and cylinder. You may need to alter the pipe layout to use larger diameter pipes on this circuit and you may need to alter the position of the pumps and zone controls. If you're not familiar with central heating systems, it's wise to leave this to a qualified heating engineer.

The central heating system should comprise the following.

• 28mm diameter primary flow and return pipes connected to the cooker/boiler tapings. The flow pipe should have an open vent at a feed and expansion tank and should rise continuously from the cooker/boiler to a hot water cylinder.

• The cylinder should be a 190 litre capacity indirect double-feed type. It should be positioned above and as near as possible to the cooker. The cylinder should be well lagged to conserve heat.

• The radiators should be fed by a system of 22mm diameter copper heating flow and return pipes.

• The heating return pipe must be connected to the primary return with an injector tee or a non-return valve.

• There must be a drain cock at the lowest point in the system.

• A reverse acting thermostat fitted to the cylinder or primary flow pipe and electrically connected to the pump will help to prevent boiling and overheating.

Summer/winter settings

Solid fuel cookers with water heating and radiator facilities are usually adjustable for summer and winter economy use. This is typically accomplished by repositioning the fire bricks inside the firebox but will vary from one make or model design to another.

The oven-side firebricks are permanently fixed with fire cement but the two boiler face side bricks are removable.

For winter use—where central heating, hot water and cooking are required—lift out the boiler back brick and store it until summer. Lift out the two boiler face side bricks and relocate them on or over the ovenside firebricks. This arrangement allows heat to be distributed throughout the cooker and boiler set-up and up to the maximum capacity possible.

For summer use—where only cooking and hot water are needed—replace the boiler back brick in its locating channel and replace the side firebricks on the boiler side of the firebox: these bricks are rebated to interlock, one on top of the other. This arrangement in effect restricts the passage of heat to the boiler, so cutting down on the amount of heat generated.

Firebricks are expendable and can be easily replaced with new ones if damaged.

Positioning the cooker

Positioning the solid fuel cooker on its prepared base is quite straightforward

Radiator circuits can be pumped but hot water must be unpumped gravity flow. Sizes and components are important

Flue arrangements will vary with your choice of position and the existing structure. If the chimney's suitable, run the flue into it; if not, build a prefabricated flue to the roof

(although you'll need some help to man-handle it). Before you connect it, check that all of its various components are fitted correctly.

Haul the cooker into place, then lift out the hotplate or plates. Run your fingers around the joints between the underside of the hob and the top of the cooker to check that the joints are intact. If any joints have opened up, run a bead of fire cement along them. It's probably best to use your fingers to insert the fire cement, so as to ensure a good, smooth seal.

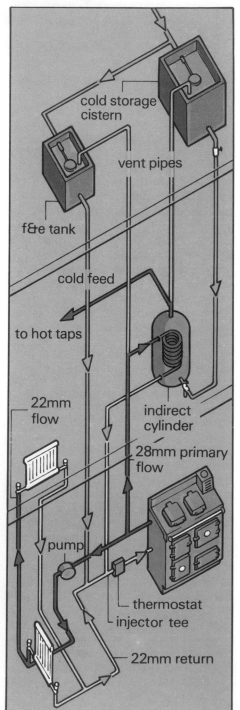

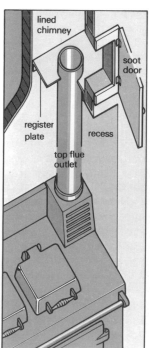

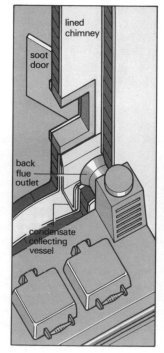

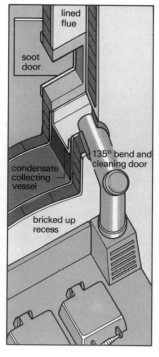

Check that the boiler/cooker flueway dampers are working properly, following the sequence of operations in the manufacturer's instructions precisely.

Replace the hotplate in the recess in the top of the hob and make sure it is resting evenly on the asbestos rope seal. The plate should protrude from the top of the enamelled top by about 1.5mm and be positioned centrally in the recess.

If you're using the cooker for hot water and central heating you must connect the pipework at this stage (see Running central heating). The BSP (British Standard Pipe) connections take 28mm diameter copper flow and return pipes.

The flue chamber, which fits on top of the cooker, and into which the fluepipe is inserted, can be fixed in place at this stage.

Smear 1mm of fire cement on to the underside of the unit—some types can be positioned to exhaust vertically or horizontally—then position it over the outlet. Insert the screws provided and fasten the chamber to the cooker top.

Finally, open the firebox and ashpit doors and operate the riddling lever on the front of the appliance. This shuffles the bottom grate bars, which sieve the spent ash from the grate into the ashpan for removal. Adjust the grates if necessary to ensure efficient working. Check that all the doors close tight.

Fitting the flue

Connecting the cooker's flue outlet to the main chimney flue depends on the position of the appliance. Basically installation involves running a length of fluepipe between the two.

Mark out the length of fluepipe required and cut it to size using a hacksaw. Offer it up to the cooker's chamber. If the fluepipe is to rise vertically into the chimney there must be 150mm clearance between its open end and any overhanging brickwork, for free passage of waste gases.

Measure up for the sheet metal register plate that's used to seal the chimney flue. Note the dimension of the opening and add 25mm to each to allow for a fixing flap all round (see diagram, overleaf).

Sheet metal is difficult to cut (suppliers use powerful guillotines) so you'd be wise to order the correct size, and have the flaps bent too at the same time.

Hold the plate in position just inside the flue to check its fit, then mark out the fluepipe exit hole, using the pipe itself or an offcut as a template.

1 *Check that all the components fit properly. Hotplates and doors generally lift off to reveal the oven's inner chambers*

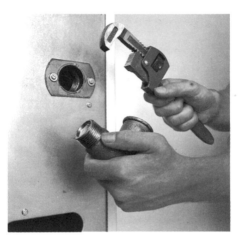

3 *Screw the elbows or connectors into the tappings for the flow and return pipes. Use hemp and compound*

Drill a hole through the sheet at the perimeter of the exit hole so that you can then insert a hacksaw blade or saw file to cut out the waste metal.

Drill 4.5 mm diameter holes at 150mm intervals along the flaps and screw the plate

2 *Check the joints between the hobs and the cooker body. If necessary, remake them with asbestos rope and a bead of fire cement*

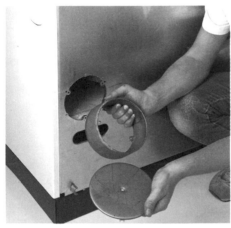

4 *There's more than one choice for a flue outlet—remove the blanking plate to fit the pipe spigot*

to the masonry, located in wallplugs. Seal the gap between the two with fire cement.

Insert the fluepipe into the plate's hole and slip on a proprietary sealing clamp or seal the join with asbestos rope and fire cement. Feed a length of asbestos rope bedded in fire cement around the flue chamber socket then slot in the lower end of the pipe. Make good the seal with a further bead of cement and polish the surface.

If the fluepipe is to enter the chimney breast at the front or side via a 135° bend, insert the pre-cut length loosely in the cooker's flue chamber, then mark the wall where the exit point will be.

Tidy up the perimeter of the hole and check that the fluepipe fits. Smear the end of the pipe generously with fire cement, then bind it with asbestos tape.

Slot the top end of the pipe into the hole and the lower end into the cooker's flue chamber (which you've lined with fire cement and asbestos rope). Make good the seal with more fire cement.

Cut the hole for a soot door, line the perimeter and fit a close-fitting door.

Commissioning the cooker

Here is a guide to a typical operation procedure for a cooker firing central heating. But bear in mind that one solid fuel stove may vary greatly from another, so follow manufacturer's instructions with care.

Turn the boiler thermostat knob, which may be located at the back left hand corner of the top plate, from low (No. 1) to high (No. 8)—remember, the higher the number, the hotter the water produced.

Check that the system is full of water and free from air locks. Double-check that draincocks fitted into the pipework are closed and stoptaps fully open.

To light the cooker pull the flue chamber damper open to maximum. Place paper and kindling onto the bottom grate, with a little fuel, through the fuelling aperture. Close the firebox door.

There's normally a slight adjustment necessary concerning the choice of flue outlet you've made. You must open or close a 'gate'—normally by turning a specified screw—to direct the waste gases from one flue outlet towards the one in operation. Make sure you check which position feeds which outlet, then adjust the screw.

Open the ashpit door below and apply a lighted match or taper to the fuel. When the fuel is well alight, close the ashpit door and check that the boiler thermostat knob or the spinwheel control on the ashpit door is at the required setting: you should allow the cooker to heat up as gradually as is possible for the initial lighting.

Make up a metal register plate to fill chimney openings

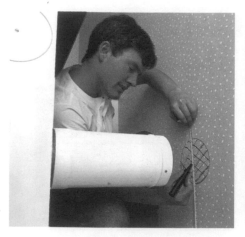

5 *Mark the wall or chimney for the flue hole. Its position will vary from one installation to the other (see diagram on page 60)*

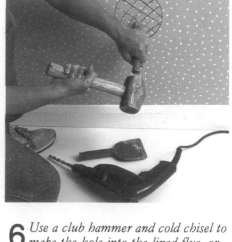

6 *Use a club hammer and cold chisel to make the hole into the lined flue, or hire a core cutter if you are using an electric drill*

7 *Seal the gap between the fluepipe and the wall with asbestos rope and fire cement to make it heat resistant. Smooth it flush*

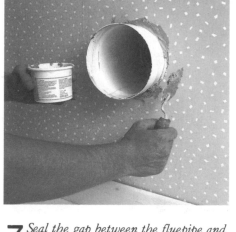

8 *Prepare the joint between the flue-pipe and spigot before you finally manoeuvre the cooker into place, then fill gaps with cement*

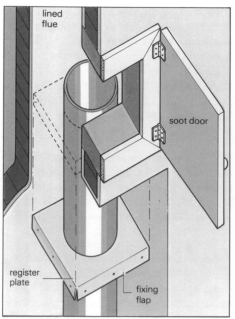

lined flue

soot door

register plate

fixing flap

9 *Light the fuel in the firebox to test the operation of the thermostats and the draught. Adjust the flue outlet gate accordingly*

MAINTAINING GAS APPLIANCES

Working with gas

Working with gas requires care as there is no room for error without prejudicing your safety. Always plan ahead and never start work if you are not fully confident of your ability to complete the job safely.

In the interest of safety, the authorities in the UK require that the connection of any gas appliance to the gas supply is left to a fully trained and approved technician.

As a general rule, however, you can buy and position gas appliances in your home and run any pipework to the supply, provided that you leave the final connection to an engineer. In this way, the gas fitter can inspect and adjust your work before finally connecting the appliance to the gas authority's supply.

Safety aspects

If you work carefully, you should experience few, if any problems, but it's worthwhile knowing what to do in the event of a gas leak; even if you only suspect a gas leak, take all of the following precautions.

• Extinguish naked flames, including cigarettes.
• Turn off the main stopcock at the gas meter.
• Open all windows and doors to provide good ventilation.
• Do not use electrical equipment or light switches.
• Try to keep all the occupants of the house away from the suspected leak.

In the event of serious leaks, carry out as much of the above as is possible, then evacuate the house and call the authority.

Cooker maintenance

Cleaning the cooker is a familiar, if unwelcome, chore but day-to-day cleaning often fails to remove the grease and debris that can gradually reduce a cooker's efficiency. Stripping down the burners and pilots on an occasional basis, however, will help restore and maintain your cooker's performance.

Turn off the gas supply and any electricity to your cooker.

Remove the pan supports from over the burners next. They may simply lift off although some are secured by clips.

Check to see if there are any fixing screws

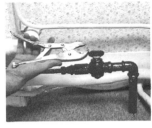

2 *You may need a wrench to shut stopcocks to appliances*

3 *Remove the pan supports, burner rings and flash tubes*

1 *Make sure you know where the main gas stopcock is located. Keep the key—or a spanner—nearby to turn it off. Remember that you should never, at any time, attempt to remove or tamper with your gas meter. This should be left to a fully-trained and qualified gas fitter*

4 *Undo screws or release clips to remove the top tray*

5 *Clean the burners with a degreasing agent and brush*

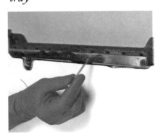

6 *Clear burner holes with a pin or nail of suitable diameter*

7 *Unscrew the pilot nozzle in an anticlockwise direction*

that you need to undo and then lift off the top tray so that you can see the internal workings of the burners.

You should be able to lift the burner rings away from the supply pipes although some are actually built into the pipes, in which case the whole section will lift away—you may need to undo locating screws.

With all the burners out, clean all the dismantled parts with a nail brush and degreasing agent, such as soda or detergent.

Prick out the holes or channels on the burner rings to remove carbon deposits—use a thin wire or pin of suitable size.

Once everything is clean and dry, the burners and pilots may be re-assembled, provided you are satisfied that the pilot or spark ignition is functioning correctly.

Overhead grills are less likely to require

this sort of attention, but oven burners may well do. You can treat these in exactly the same way—lift out the burner column to clean it and the tray into which it fits.

Clearing cooker pilot lights

There are various arrangements of cooker pilot light. On hobs, some are centrally mounted with flash tubes to the burners while on ovens and grills they are usually arranged as individual pilot flames adjacent to the burner ring or tube.

The pilot jets normally get their gas supply from a manifold mounted under the cooker top cover and some adjustment mechanism—a tap or screw—may be incorporated in this manifold. This adjustment can only be used to change the size of all the pilot flames together if they all need adjustment.

If one pilot is troublesome when others are working well, turn off the gas at the meter (you could disconnect the supply hose if it's the bayonet type, see: Fitting a new cooker hose) and dismantle the components until you can see the pilot assembly.

Remove the malfunctioning pilot jet—the nozzle from which the flame appears—by unscrewing it anti-clockwise with a small adjustable spanner.

Clear the jet with a very thin piece of wire or a blow lamp nozzle pricker. Blow through the jet to remove the debris. If the jet still fails, buy a new one from your gas appliance supplier or order one from the maker of the cooker. Replace the pilot jet by screwing it back into place.

When re-assembling cookers with centrally mounted flash tubes, make certain that the tube is correctly aligned. Poor alignment hinders the flow of unburnt gas along the tube to the pilot light and ignited gas back to the burner. There are often locating points on the burners to help you to re-position the tubes.

If ignition depends upon an electrically produced spark, it may be that the spark generator, rather than the pilot, is at fault. In this case see the information entitled Replacing a spark generator (right).

Fitting a new cooker hose

If the flexible supply hose at the back of your cooker is worn or damaged, replace it immediately before a serious leak occurs. Fitting a new one is a quick and easy job.

There are two types of flexible hose available. The older style has a screwed union at each end which must be undone with spanners. The second, more modern kind, has a bayonet plug and socket arrangement which can be connected and disconnected from the supply pipe by hand in a similar way to putting in a light bulb. Bayonet-fitting hoses are self sealing when disconnected, so when doing this repair there is no need to turn off the gas.

For older style hoses, turn off the gas at the main cock near the meter, unless an intermediate shut-off cock is incorporated in the pipework.

Ignite one of the burners to use up the remaining gas—don't forget to turn it off—then pull the cooker away from the wall just enough to reach the union.

Using two spanners, hold the pipe section firm with one and turn the large nut on the

8 *Clean the jet with a nozzle pricker or needle threader*

Individual pilot lights ignite each of the burners on older cookers and oven grills

Flash tubes may be set into the top tray, running from the centre pilot light to each of the burners. Others may run between each pair of burners. All must be correctly aligned with the pilot

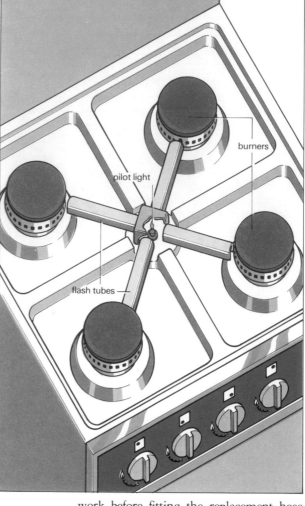

union anticlockwise with the other.

Once any additional fixings have been disconnected—there's often a wire that protects the hose from being stretched—the cooker can be slid further out from the wall.

The other end of the hose is screwed into a female elbow connector on the back of the cooker. Hold the elbow firm and undo the hose with a wrench or adjustable spanner.

If the unions on the new hose are not identical to the old ones you will need to remove the remaining halves from the pipe

work before fitting the replacement hose and matching unions. Simply unscrew them from the pipework—you may need to use a self-locking wrench.

When fitting the new hose to the cooker end, wind a few turns of PTFE tape around the threads before you screw them in. Do not use jointing compound and hemp on natural gas installations as the gas tends to dry out the hemp and cause leaks.

The union faces at the supply pipe end of older hoses are machined to provide a seal and at the very most may require a smear of jointing compound (Boss White) before

9 *Unscrew the hose with a wrench or adjustable spanner*

10 *Dispose of damaged hose—even small holes are dangerous*

11 *Wind PTFE tape anti-clockwise round each male joint*

joining. There is no need for fibre washers or anything similar.

If a steel hose protection wire is supplied, it should be fitted in such a way that it prevents the hose from being strained when pulling the cooker away from the wall. Loop the ends over the pipe fittings prior to fixing, or attach a chain as shown.

The ideal arrangement for the hose, when the cooker is pushed back against the wall, is for it to hang down in a loop from both the cooker and the supply pipe. The bottom of the loop should be far enough from the floor to prevent it touching when the cooker is in position.

Modern bayonet unions only need be pressed home and carefully turned to the 'lock' position.

On ovens with drop-front doors, an anti-tilt bracket should be fixed to the wall in such a way that the cooker locates upon it when in position. Most cookers have a hole in the back to receive this bracket. A small L-shaped shelf bracket will do the same job.

Look for a suitable hole in the cooker

12 *Fit an anti-stretch wire—or make one from a chain*

13 *Bayonet fittings are 'push and turn' connections*

14 *Brush on a soapy mixture—bubbles indicate a leak*

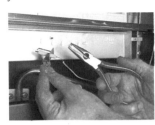

15 *Release the sparking end of the electrode from the casing*

16 *Test the action of the electrode against the metal casing*

17 *If faulty, remove the other end and replace with a new one*

back and fix the bracket onto the wall so it slides into the cooker when pushed back.

Checking for leaks: When the hose is connected, a simple test for gas leaks can be carried out before positioning the cooker prior to use.

Mix up a strong solution of washing-up liquid and water in a small jar.

Turn the gas supply back on at the mains and paint the bubble mixture around the newly made joints. Any leak will cause the bubbles to balloon.

If tightening does not stop the leak, remake the joint.

Replacing a spark generator

If the spark ignition on your boiler, gas fire or cooker will not light, check the electrode is sparking correctly across the pilot light —the spark should jump across the pilot jet nozzle.

Similar battery powered generators are fitted to some ovens and fires. If the problem is merely worn out batteries you will find

them easy to replace. On fires they are located inside the casing at the bottom of the appliance. On ovens they are usually inside the bottom plinth or oven drawer.

If it is not the power supply that's at fault, then you may need a new electrode—the component from which the ignition spark 'jumps' to light the gas.

The sparking end of an electrode is held in place by a bracket and screw. If you remove this screw and draw the tip out of the pilot area you will be able to test its function against the main body of the gas fire as long as it's made of metal.

Hold the bracket on the metal casing and with the tip of the electrode a few milli-metres from the casing, fire the spark igniter button in the usual way.

If no spark is produced, remove the push-fit terminal from the igniter and substitute a small length of thin insulated wire for the electrode.

Hold the bared end of the wire near the body and fire the igniter again. This should produce a spark which will prove the elec-trode is at fault. If no spark is produced, the igniter or generator itself may well be the faulty component.

The generator may be a mains supplied unit or, more commonly, a 'piezo' crystal spark unit. Whichever it is, a whole replace-ment unit is available.

Most igniters are simply held in place by a couple of screws. Take the complete unit to a gas stockist who may test it for you before supplying the new part required. Fit the new component by simply reversing the dismantling procedure above.

Boiler and fire flue problems

If you see black stains on the wall around your gas fire or sooty deposits around your boiler, it probably means the flue is not working properly.

Any major problem must be referred to an authorized service engineer, but a pre-liminary check will help determine whether the air flow has been blocked or if there is a more substantial failure.

Two types of flue arrangement are avail-able for gas boilers and fires. The **conven-tional flue** rises from the back or top of the boiler or fire to discharge the combustion products above the roof of the building. An unfortunate feature of conventional flue boilers is their tendency to draw dust in around the burners. If allowed to build up, the dust itself may become a fire hazard.

Regular removal of this dust is best carried out with a vacuum cleaner. First make sure the boiler and pilot are off.

Clean the nozzle around the burners using a small flue brush to reach the more inaccessible parts behind the radiants.

An increasingly common flue arrange-ment is the **balanced flue**. The appliance is sealed from the room and air is drawn in from outside the building. The products of combustion are discharged through a separate channel in the same flue.

It is essential for efficient and safe operation to avoid obstructing the flue terminal on the outside of the building. Any leaves or foliage that are restricting the flue terminal must be removed.

INDEPENDENT HEATER FAULTS

Cleaning a convector heater

An electric convector heater has a large, heavy-duty spiral-type element in its base, which you can't replace yourself. If the element fails, or is damaged, take the heater to a dealer for replacement.

You can clean the element periodically (every two or three months will do) to get rid of dust and fluff; this may cause the element to spark when it heats up and give off an unpleasant singeing smell as the debris burns. It can also be dangerous.

Unplug the heater, invert it and release the cross-head screw fastening the base grid to the body of the unit. Lift out the grid and clean it thoroughly with a vacuum cleaner nozzle attachment. Wipe over the surface with a damp cloth.

Dust the inside of the heater lightly, taking great care not to dislodge the spiral element inside.

★ WATCH POINT ★

Pressurized containers of air, used by photographers for cleaning their cameras, are ideal to use in cleaning dust and fluff from the delicate element of a fire without risk of damage. Buy a canister from a photographic supplier and use it sparingly. Do take care with it as the propellant is inflammable.

Before you refit the heater's grid, it's worthwhile dismantling the body of the unit and giving it a thorough wipe down with a damp cloth. Allow all parts to dry completely before reassembling and using the convector heater again.

Maintaining a paraffin heater

Paraffin convector heaters are commonly used as an economical way to heat bathrooms, hallways and even the greenhouse. Positioned where it's not likely to be knocked over, a paraffin heater is safe in use. It does, however, need regular attention to keep it clean and efficient.

The heater is basically a fuel tank with a burner attached, and a chimney mounted on the top, through which the heat is

1 *Disconnect the heater from the mains and remove back panel*

2 *Use a vacuum cleaner fitted with a nozzle to suck out accumulated fluff*

3 *Wipe the inside of the body with a damp cloth and allow to dry*

channelled out via the top vent.

To strip down the heater for cleaning, remove the front and lift out the fuel tank. Dismantle the components starting with the chimney and gallery below it. Brush out dust and carbon deposits from inside the gallery then wash with warm water and mild detergent. Dry thoroughly.

Examine the flame spreader and wick tube for fluff. Pull it off and wipe away any carbon. The wick will need to be trimmed occasionally, using the special trimming device supplied. Place the trimmer over the wick, on top of the burner. Wind up the wick by turning the side wheel until it is visible in the trimmer's aperture. Revolve the trimmer clockwise to clean off carbon and trim the wick evenly.

A wick that's badly carbonated will burn sluggishly and you should replace it. Before you do, however, empty the fuel from the tank and store it in a closed container.

There are two types of wick—one for Aladdin and the other for Valor heaters. To fit an Aladdin wick, lift off the burner, flame spreader and outer wick tube (disengage the

latter with a quarter-turn anticlockwise). Wind up the wick until it disengages from the cogs, remove the carrier rack and dispose of the old wick.

Feed the new wick between the winder cogs and the centre tube by pulling the winder wheel outwards slightly. Refit the carrier rack in its slots and realign it with the winder cogs.

To renew a Valor heater wick, remove the chimney, flame spreader and gallery—plus any sealing washer there may be. Wind up the wick using the side wheel and release the attached ratchet from the cog wheel.

Valmin wicks, a variation of the Valor type, have a plastic wick applicator, which must slot into the top of the centre tube. Position the replacement wick on the tube and align the ratchet with the adjusting cog wheel. Wind the wick down to expose the plastic applicator, remove it and refit the flame spreader, gallery and chimney.

The heater's chimney is fairly flimsy and can easily be bent out of shape by the heat of the burner. You should be able to hand-bend it back into shape.

1 *Wash away the carbon deposits in the gallery, then allow it to dry*

2 *Use the special device provided with the heater to trim and clean*

3 *Fit a new wick. The rack engages with the cog on the winder*

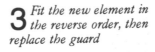

1 *Release the element rod by sliding the sleeves off the terminals*

2 *Unscrew the tiny milled nut then lift the rod out*

3 *Fit the new element in the reverse order, then replace the guard*

If the mica window at the front of the chimney is cracked or discoloured so that you can't see the burner clearly when adjusting the flame, replace it.

Release the metal frame from over the mica by loosening its screws, slip out the old mica and slot in the new one. Screw the frame back carefully to retain the heater's new window.

To light a paraffin heater, the wick must be set at the correct height in its carrier. Wind the wick out about 12mm and apply a lighted match all around it.

Let the flame burn until it's established, then slowly wind down the wick until all you can see is a rim of blue flame around the wick carrier.

When you are storing a paraffin heater, drain off the fuel tank first and burn the wick outdoors (in a sheltered position) to use up all the fuel.

Replacing an enclosed-rod element

Electric element fires either have an exposed element or elements enclosed in a silica-glass tube, which makes them suitable for use in a bathroom where the element would otherwise be exposed to a damp, steamy environment. You can replace the element easily.

Disconnect the fire from the mains and

remove the metal mesh guard from the front of the fire by squeezing the bars gently, or release the retaining screws.

The element rod will be fixed to terminals at each end and these will be protected by sleeves. Simply applying finger pressure should release the sleeves, which can then be removed by sliding them along the element rod.

Release the tiny milled nut holding the enclosed rod element in the terminal, lift out the rod and take it to a local electrical supplier to obtain a matching replacement. Fit the new element-rod in the terminals, refit the nuts and sleeves, then refix the wire guard. Restore the power and test the operation of the fire.

If the fire hasn't been used for a long time, take this opportunity to clean the reflector before switching the fire on.

Flame-effect fires

Flame-effect fires use low-wattage bulbs beneath the coal- or log-effect display, with a mirror or 'windmill' of polished metal, which spins in the heat of the bulb to create mock flames.

New bulbs specially made for the purpose are available from electrical shops, and can be fitted like an ordinary bulb. Turn off the power to the fire at the mains and replace the dead bulb or bulbs.

1 *Replace a burnt-out bulb in exactly the same way as a normal light bulb*

2 *Polish the light dappler with a soft, fluff-free cloth and re-assemble the heater*

Finally, check that the windmill spins freely on its pivot, and is not bent out of shape. If it is, try to correct the shape by carefully bending the windmill back into the right position.

Using a bottled gas radiant fire

Portable radiant gas fires fuelled by bottled butane gas are popular space heaters that provide back-up heating where you don't want to put on the central heating, or for other areas such as bathrooms, playrooms, halls or garages.

They are perfectly safe to use, so long as you exercise some caution, particularly when changing the gas canisters and in siting the heater sensibly.

Most three- or four-radiant appliances take a 15kg canister; other smaller heaters are also available.

Exact methods of connecting up the cylinder vary in detail between makes of fire, although the basic procedure applies for all. One popular model is connected in the following way.

To connect the regulator/adapter onto the top of the gas cylinder, first haul the cylinder into the back of the fire body—be careful: it's very heavy when full and you may need help to lift it into position.

Rotate the plastic cap on the cylinder valve so that the arrow on the top points through the gap in the valve shroud. To release the cap, pull the attached lanyard out and upwards to release the wire clip. Lift the cap off the valve and leave the cap dangling.

Check that the regulator switch is pointing in the correct direction—in this case, downwards. Press the regulator down onto the cylinder valve. Turn the switch on the regulator to lock it to the cylinder valve (here, you turn the switch clockwise, so that the switch points to the left; this is the 'off' position). You will know when the lock has been made when you hear a 'click'.

To turn on the gas, swivel the switch clockwise (to point upwards). The cylinder valve is now open. Some models with a screwed cylinder connection require you to turn the cylinder valve to switch on the gas.

To light the fire, lightly depress the control knob at the top of the fire and rotate it fully clockwise to the first burner position. Now push down fully and turn the knob to the ignition symbol.

The pilot light and centre burners should ignite. If they don't, repeat the procedure until they do. Hold the knob down for about

If there's air in the gas supply line after you have fitted a new cylinder, depress the control knob for about another ten seconds, then repeatedly operate the spark igniter until the radiant lights.

1 *Press the regulator/ adapter on to the top of the cylinder until you hear a 'click'*

2 *Turn the cylinder valve clockwise to switch on the gas flow to the fire*

3 *Having disconnected the old gas cylinder, replace the protective valve cap*

ten seconds for the flame safety device to heat up, then release it.

Control the heat output by slightly depressing and turning the knob to the second or third burner positions, which will ignite them automatically.

To switch off the heater, either turn the cylinder valve clockwise (where a screwed connection is used) or turn the regulator switch anti-clockwise so it points horizontally. You shouldn't attempt to re-light the fire for five minutes.

When you want to disconnect the empty cylinder and fit a new one, you depress a central button in the regulator switch (you mustn't depress this when the burner is alight) and, with this still pressed, turn the switch anti-clockwise to the downwards-pointing position. Lift the regulator valve off and fit the new cylinder.

Replace the plastic cap on the cylinder valve to protect the threads during transit.

Safety with bottled gas

Although bottled gas heaters are quite safe, butane is dangerous if misused, so be very cautious when using it.

Never smoke or work near naked lights when you are changing the cylinder—an explosion could seriously injure you.

Never drape clothes over the heater or rest anything on top—not only would this hinder the efficient operation of the heater but also it could start a fire.

Never attempt to move the heater from room to room when it's alight.

Do not position the appliance alongside curtains or in a corner, or too close to furniture.

The room in which you use the heater must be well-ventilated to remove the combustion by-products and allow fresh air to enter. This also discourages condensation.

Escaping butane gas is quite insidious, making you become slowly drowsy. So if you find yourself affected by increasing lethargy you should turn off the heater immediately and check it thoroughly for leaks. If you fail to find anything untoward, have

the heater checked by an approved dealer or service engineer.

Whenever you fit a replacement cylinder, check that the rubber hoses and clips feeding the heater are soundly fixed; avoid excessive bends in the main gas line and keep a look out for perishing rubber. Replace any suspect pipes.

If you suspect a leak from your bottled gas heater, turn the gas off at the cylinder. Extinguish all naked lights. Examine the connections and brush them with soapy water or liquid detergent: turn on the gas slowly and look for bubbles, which indicate a leak. If you find a leak, inform your gas supplier immediately.

Lubricating a fan heater

Electric fan heaters consist of spiral elements positioned behind the front grilles: air is drawn by fan blades through side vents, passed over the heating elements and

blown out of the front of the appliance. Some types have a single fan, others have two. Alternatively, there may be a two-speed motor.

Most fan heaters incorporate a cut-out facility in case the air vents are obstructed so it's not possible to turn on the heating element without the fan's blowing. But if, when the fan is running, you notice the elements glowing red, it could be that the motor bearings need lubricating to increase the fan speed. By dismantling the appliance you can combine internal cleaning with lubrication. Unplug the fan heater and dismantle its casing to reveal the motor. You might have to release the screws holding a fan cover, or else disconnect the flex connections.

Use a soft, medium-sized paint brush (or an air canister: see Cleaning a convector heater) to dust off the motor and the interior of the fan. It's usual to find a mass of fluff that's been sucked inside through the vents at the side of the heater.

Lubricate the motor bearings with a few drops of light machine oil, then re-assemble the heater and test its operation. If the glowing element persists you should take the heater to a reputable dealer and have it checked.

1 *Unplug the heater and dismantle its casing to reveal the motor, fan and elements*

2 *Use a soft paintbrush to clean dust and fluff from the interior of the heater*

3 *Lubricate the motor bearings with a few drops of light all-purpose oil*

BOTTLED GAS APPLIANCES

Bottled gas fuel presents no special problems except perhaps one of carrying heavy equipment tanks about. Installing and using such equipment correctly and safely requires some know-how and care but the connecting and operating principles of many bottled gas fuelled appliances are very similar. Because it can be stored as a liquid it's main advantage over natural gas is that it takes up less storage space. In some instances, such as when camping, bottled gas is the only safe way of heating and lighting and in other cases, as with a blowtorch, it is the most convenient fuel to use. It also has the advantage of being a clean as well as odourless fuel.

Gas types

There are two types, propane and butane, both of which are usually made during the refining of crude oil to produce petrol. Propane tends to be used in large domestic appliances; butane in small cylinders for blowtorches, camping equipment, and the like. In many respects, these are effectively the same—both are stored in metal bottles under pressure, which turns the gas into a liquid. Because it's stored in bottles, it is often called 'bottled gas', but the more correct name is *liquified petroleum gas* or LPG for short.

There are some important differences, however. Propane turns from a liquid to a gas at a lower temperature, so it is under greater pressure in the cylinder than butane. Almost all appliances can use either propane or butane as long as they are fitted with the appropriate **regulator**, or **adaptor**.

For easy identification, propane is stored in red cylinders, and butane is stored in blue or green ones.

Using bottled gas

Bottled gas performs in just the same way as mains gas but costs more. If you have a mains gas supply, therefore, it's much more economical to use it.

If you live in a remote area where mains gas is not available, bottled gas could be an alternative fuel for cooking. It may work out cheaper than electricity and in any case you may prefer gas.

Central heating with LPG is very little

different in any respect from using oil: it costs about the same, and it is delivered to your fuel tank in much the same way. But both solid fuel and electric storage heaters would be cheaper alternative fuels to bottled gas in the UK.

If you want a portable room heater, LPG would work out slightly less expensive than full-price electricity (but the heaters are bulkier and require a lot of ventilation).

Using LPG

Almost any domestic appliance that runs off mains gas can be run off LPG—althought you must, of course, buy appliances which are especially adapted by manufacturers for the job. There is a whole range of cookers —including split-level hobs and oven units —that look and perform identically to mains-gas types. Similarly, there are fixed room-heaters, both conventional-flue types (that must be installed under a working chimney) and flueless models which can be fixed to any wall. There are gas fridges and fridge/freezers, and water heaters—both the single-outlet type and the 'multipoint', which can feed continuous hot water to a number of different places. Finally, there are central heating boilers with a range of heat outputs to suit anything from a small flat to a large country house: some have conventional flues, while others operate with balanced flues. All these appliances are supplied with LPG from a bottle or tank mounted outside the house.

There are also portable room heaters. These carry their gas with them, in a large cylinder kept in the back of the heater cabinet. There are different types—convector heaters which warm air passing through them; radiant heaters which provide direct heat; radiant-convectors and catalytic heaters in which the heat is generated by chemical reaction between the gas and a platinum mat resulting in no flame. Portable heaters are flueless.

LPG and mains appliances

The only difference is in combustion level— so only the burner jets and pipework are different. This means that it is often possible to convert a mains gas-cooker to LPG if, for instance, you move from an area with mains gas to one without and don't wish to buy a

LPG containers range in size from large, red, outside propane cylinders to small disposable butane cartridges. Propane gas can also be stored in large outside refillable tanks

completely new cooker; similarly, you can convert from LPG to mains. But there is quite a wide variety of LPG appliances available, so there is no need to do this if you are buying a new appliance.

Storing gas

Portable heaters carry their own supply of gas in a 15kg cylinder, which is usually delivered to you in exchange for the empty cylinder. The weight refers to the net weight; the total weight of a cylinder filled with gas is about 30kg. These are quite heavy but the heater itself will be on wheels so it is not difficult to move around—never move a heater once it is alight. Smaller cylinders are available, but you will probably find that the gas works out to be more expensive.

If you have just one or two fixed heaters, cooker, or fridge, then these will usually be run from cylinders placed outside the house and connected to the appliances by flexible hoses. These cylinders will invariably be propane, and they are available in various sizes from 3kg to 47kg. You choose a size which relates to your consumption of gas but the bigger cylinders work out cheaper. Whatever size you pick, however, it is a good idea to use two cylinders in tandem, linked by a **changeover valve**. This allows gas to flow out of one cylinder, and automatically changes over to the other when the first is empty. You can then have the empty cylinder changed at leisure by your supplier, and you are never without a supply of gas.

With a central-heating system you may still have your gas supplied from a set of cylinders, in which case you will need four of the largest type, linked as two pairs. But more likely the gas will be supplied from a larger tank. Your gas supplier will know from records of your consumption when this is running low, and will come and fill it without your having to tell him—much

along the same lines as with an oil-fired installation. The tank and equipment linking it to your central heating boiler almost always remain the property of the gas supplier, who will install and maintain it in return for an annual rental charge.

How long a bottle or tank lasts depends on individual circumstances but, very roughly, a tank feeding the central heating system for a three-bedroomed house might need filling about four times a year. If you use only a portable bottled gas heater to heat a single room, you might get through 20 bottles in a year.

If I have to change bottles myself, what is the procedure?

For safety reasons it's important that you connect and disconnect cylinders correctly. Start by turning the control on the cylinder off—there is usually either a handwheel which you screw down, or a 'switch-on valve' that you move to the off position. Except for twin-cylinder installations with

an automatic changeover valve, you must now wait until the burner or pilot light has gone out—this is your safeguard that the cylinder control is working properly. If the control isn't working correctly, and the appliance still continues to burn, then you should contact your supplier and not attempt to remove the cylinder. With twin-cylinder installations, the fact that the changeover valve has operated should mean that the cylinder you are to replace is empty and can be disconnected safely.

You can now disconnect the cylinder from the pressure regulator or hose connecting it to your appliance. With handwheel valves, this connection is made with a nut that you undo with a spanner—the nut has a left-hand thread so be ready for this. With switch-on valves, you turn the valve to the disconnect position and simply lift off the connector. Finally, replace the safety cap or plug over the cylinder outlet.

Fitting the new cylinder is the same operation in reverse. But always check that there is a sealing washer at the connecting point, and that this seal is not damaged: if in doubt, replace it.

Portable and fixed room heaters, cookers and water heaters, some with a shower attachment, will all run off LPG. This makes them particularly versatile

The attachments for LPG blowlamps include (from front to back): a precision burner, a soldering bit, a torch kit attached to its propane cylinder,

a cyclone burner for plumbing work, a fan-tail paint stripping burner, a disposable cartridge-powered blowlamp and a cyclone burner

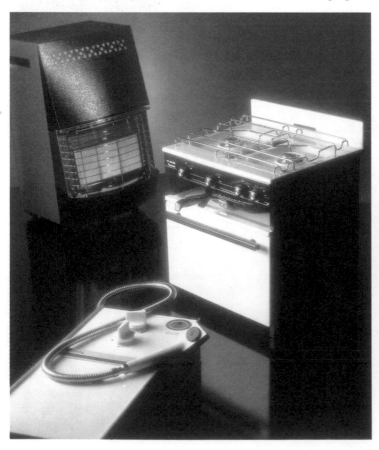

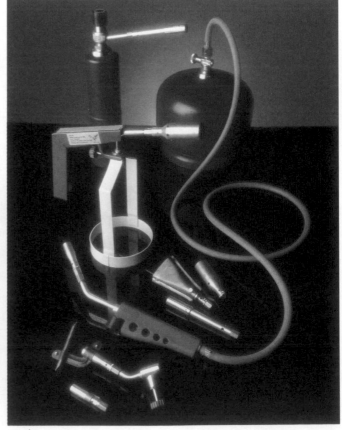

LPG and safety

LPG is perfectly safe if used properly. But there are safety precautions that should be followed. The main risk from LPG is that it is highly inflammable and, as it is stored under pressure, any small leakage from the system can allow large amounts of gas to escape. So keep in mind the following.
•Don't store or carry cylinders upside down—you may damage the valve.
•Don't store cylinders below ground level: LPG is heavier than air, so if a leak should occur, the gas would be trapped.
•Make sure outside storage tanks and pipework cannot be damaged—by a car, or garden tools, for example. Domestic-sized tanks must be kept at least 3m away from any buildings or boundaries.
•Make sure you have a means of lighting an appliance *before* you turn it on, so that gas isn't escaping while you are looking for matches.
•All flexible hoses must be of the correct type and approved for use with LPG (which attacks, for example, natural rubber). They should be checked frequently for damage.
•Never look for leaks with a naked light. If you suspect a leak—LPG has a 'smell' added that can be detected only when there is a leak—switch off the gas, open windows and make sure there are no naked lights around. Check hoses and connections and, if you can't find the trouble, contact an authorised service engineer.

If an LPG cylinder is heated, the pressure of the contents will increase and even though safety devices are fitted to release excess pressure, there is a risk of explosion. It is essential, therefore, to take the following precautions:
•Never subject a cylinder to heat.
•Never store or use propane indoors, because propane is stored under higher pressure than butane.
•Do not use cylinders in high-rise flats where a piped gas supply is not allowed.
•Never tamper with any pressure regulators fitted to your system.
•Do not surround an external storage tank with inflammable material—keep the area within 3m of the tank clear of fences or sheds. As long as there is plenty of ventilation around the tank, it is safe to have a slatted screen or flowers and shrubs within this safety distance.

The third possible risk is the same as that with any fuel-burning appliance, including mains gas, solid fuel and paraffin (kerosene). The gases produced by burning LPG are normally harmless, but if the appliance is not burning correctly, or if the ventilation to the room is restricted, then dangerous fumes can be produced.

The ventilation requirements you must provide in each room where there are appliances are quite strict—details of the regulations are as follows.

Conventional-flue appliances must have free ventilation at least equal to the area of the appliance flue outlet, with a minimum of $0.75m^2$.

Flueless appliances must have a free ventilation of at least $200mm^2$ for each kilowatt rating of the appliance (half of it at a low level, and half at a high level) with a minimum of $1m^2$.

Modern flueless heaters are fitted with **atmosphere sensing** and **flame failure** devices. These switch off the gas supply automatically if the flame goes out or if the ventilation is insufficient for proper combustion. If you have an older heater it is a good idea for safety's sake to install a compatible sensing device.

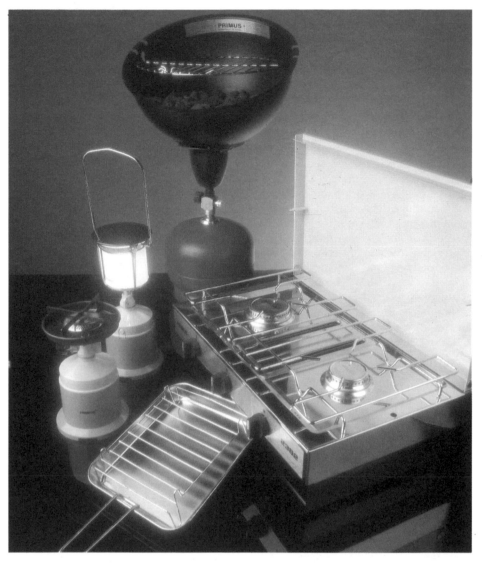

Camping equipment (clockwise): gas ring and lantern, a gas grill and a stove

Gas-fired tools

The most obvious is a **blowtorch**. There are two main types. One uses disposable butane-filled cartridges fitted with a self-sealing safety valve to which you attach a burner with its own on/off valve. Several patterns of burner head are available—a standard one for general work, such as soldering plumbing fittings; a paint removal burner which gives a broad flame for paint stripping and fine flame burners for hobby and delicate work. The second type of blowtorch consists of a hand-held burner attached to a length of flexible hose; the other end of the hose is attached to an LPG cylinder.

Industrial-type space heaters and LPG powered **site lights** are both useful for working in places with no electricity.

REPAIRS TO OPEN FIREPLACES

Dealing with throat restrictors

Otherwise known as dampers or registers, a throat restrictor is basically a hinged metal flap which can be set in various positions across the throat of the flue to regulate the flow of air up the chimney.

Because open fires draw in air from the room in which they are situated, they have a reputation for creating draughts. So by 'restricting' the amount of hot air passing immediately up the flue the fire doesn't draw in as much air from the room, hence draughts are reduced. And the overall effect is that more heat is thrown into the room for the amount of fuel being burnt.

To set the position of the flap, keep closing it down until smoke just starts to enter the room rather than go up the chimney, then open it slightly so that smoke is drawn smoothly upwards into the flue and out of the chimney.

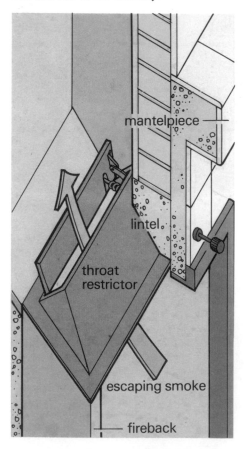

Throat restrictors cut down draughts from open fireplaces by regulating the amount of air drawn in from the room

Throat restrictors come in a wide range of designs, but they usually consist of a metal frame from which a flap pivots upwards into the flue. There are a number of different handle mechanisms to hold the throat restrictor in the required position.

If possible remove the restrictor to clean it. This may mean having to take off the handle first. A quick investigation should reveal how this can be done. Sometimes it's a matter of tapping out a small fixing pin.

With the handle out of the way the flap may simply lift out. However, some pins protuding from the bottom edge may still be located in holes in the side frames. There should be enough tolerance to slide the restrictor from side to side to work it clear. Once free, give it a good clean on both sides with a stiff wire brush. If you can't remove it, you'll have to work on it while it's in place. Also check that the framework of the restrictor is firmly mortared in position to the top of the fireback.

Not all fireplaces are fitted with restrictors, yet it is possible to fit them even if you aren't intending to replace the fireback. Channel a groove in the base of the flaunching, manoeuvre the frame into position (a slightly awkward job) and then mortar it securely in place.

It is possible that the throat restrictor will impede access to the top of the fireback when you need to replace it. In this case you must remove the restrictor, if possible, and either look up the chimney or feel with your hand to find out whether the two are in contact. It is unlikely that the throat restrictor will make that much difference, but if you are in any doubt, get the advice of an expert before you start.

When fitting a throat restrictor, whether you've fitted a new fireback or not, ensure that no infill blocks the flap or prevents the restrictor's adjustment mechanism from working properly.

Sweeping a chimney

Many of the problems associated with open fires often come down to the fact that the chimney has not been cleaned regularly. Once a year is the usual advice, but ideally it should be swept twice. This becomes essential if you burn a lot of wood, because this can give rise to the formation of a build-up of creosote in the flue.

Soot, tar and creosote are all highly in-

flammable so the risk of a chimney fire increases considerably. Tar deposits can even penetrate the brickwork of chimney breasts and stain walls, which must then be treated with a sticky-backed foil or foil-backed plasterboard and redecorated to conceal the staining.

There is much to be said for getting hold of a professional chimney sweep to clean the flue for you. He will have all the necessary equipment—a powerful vacuum cleaner besides the traditional brushes—and it will only take him about 20–25 minutes to do the job. Furthermore, it's surprisingly inexpensive (although it pays to shop around for quotations).

However, if you decide you would like to have a go yourself the brushes can be hired, although you may have a problem finding the vacuuming equipment. But you can get by without this if you work carefully.

If you intend to do the cleaning yourself on a regular basis, it will be more cost effective to buy a brush head and rod sections. It's not a bad investment as you can also fit other heads to use the rods for unblocking drains. The main thing to check is that the brush has polypropylene or natural bristles. Stiff wire can scratch flue liners (increasing the risk of corrosion) and it can also dislodge mortar in a brick-built chimney, which could lead to smoke seepages.

To give you some idea of when the chimney needs cleaning, watch the speed at which smoke rises up into the flue. If it moves slowly, even when the throat restrictor is fully open, it suggests that the chimney is becoming clogged with soot and the like or that there is some obstruction—a bird's nest, for example—obstructing the smooth upward passage of air. Also inspect the base of the flue with a torch to get an idea of the thickness of the build-up.

Wherever possible work from the fireplace to clean the chimney. It's far easier—and safer—than having to clamber onto the roof to work downwards.

Close the doors and windows in the room with the aim of creating an updraught of air in the flue. You may have to reopen a window slightly to get the necessary flow.

As a precaution, cover the surrounding furniture and flooring with plastic sheets so that no spilt soot can penetrate through. Be careful, though, as they tend to be a bit slippery to walk on.

Mask off the fire surround with newspaper and masking tape, particularly if the

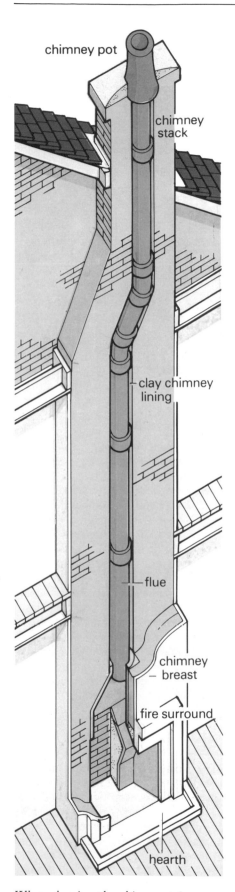

chimney pot

chimney stack

clay chimney lining

flue

chimney breast

fire surround

hearth

When cleaning the chimney take care not to damage either the flue lining or the chimney pot

surround is ornamental, as this will prevent extra cleaning.

Remove the grate and fireback, if it's the metal moveable kind, and detach or open the flap of the throat-restrictor (see diagram, page 232). Push the first section of rod through a large square of polyethylene and screw on the brush head.

Next push the brush through the restrictor. Then stick the polyethylene to the surround and weight it down at the bottom so that no soot can cascade into the room. Work the brush head up and down a few times and then add the next section of handle. Continue doing this until you come to the top of the stack.

Where the brush has to travel round a bend in the flue you may have to use extra pressure. But don't be too enthusiastic with the up-and-down action as you could push a cowl from the chimney pot. A sudden decrease in pressure on the rods as a rule heralds the arrival of the brush head at the top of the flue.

As you work the brush, it's worth rotating the rods clockwise so there is no danger of an individual section unscrewing and becoming trapped in an inaccessible position in the flue. The other thing to remember is not to rush. By working the brush up and down too quickly you could cause a downdraft which may lead to unnecessary mess.

Once you've brought the brush down the chimney you can shovel the soot and debris into buckets, cover it over with damp cloths and carry it outside for eventual disposal.

If there is no flaunching from the top of the fireback to the flue there will be what's known as a smoke shelf. A lot of dust and muck will collect on this and you will have to reach up by hand and sweep it clear with a banister brush.

If the chimney is on an outside wall, there may be an access plate at the bottom through which it can be cleaned, but the fireplace and internal flue will still have to be brushed from inside.

To make sweeping easier you could try using chemical cleaning agents. These come either as a liquid or powder which you may have to sprinkle onto the lighted fire. The resulting gas rises up the chimney and combines with the soot to form a flaky scale which breaks away from the sides of the flue. Whichever method you use, chimney-cleaning is a very dirty job. Wear old clothes, keep children and pets out of the way and have a vacuum cleaner handy to deal with the inevitable mess.

Repairing and replacing firebacks

Continual expansion and contraction over long periods, coupled with accidental knocks from pokers prodding the fire, often cause cracks to develop in the fireback. These should be dealt with as soon as they are noticed.

If the fireback is made up of individual firebricks, you may be able to rake out the crack with the edge of a trowel and pack the crack with fire cement, which is available in small tins.

The procedure is the same for a one-piece fireback. The important point to remember is that you must brush the crack and the surrounding area liberally with water before applying the cement so that it sets fairly slowly, forming a stronger bond.

For a more permanent repair you may decide to replace the cracked brick or bricks. First drill along the mortar lines to loosen the brick as best you can and then chop out with a bolster and club hammer. The less hammering you have to do the better, as vibrations could loosen other sound bricks.

Depending on the size and the tightness with which the bricks fit together you may be able to use fire cement buttered round the opening and round the new brick to secure it in place when it is pushed home. Smooth the pointing so that it is flush with

1 *Tape down newspaper to protect the fire surround*

2 *Fix the brush to the rod and push it through clear sheeting*

3 *Gradually work up the chimney by adding sections of rod*

233

4 *Break the new fireback in two along the grooved line*

5 *Use the correct mortar mix to fill behind the fireback*

6 *Fix the top section on a bed of cement above the bottom half*

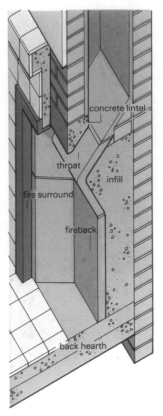

7 *Carefully brush on a weak solution of hydrochloric acid for cleaning*

8 *Apply heat-resistant adhesive to the bed and tile-back when replacing ceramic tiles*

9 *Clean marble fireplaces with a proprietary paste which lifts dirt as it is wiped off*

Modern firebacks are usually made of fire-resistant clay

the rest of the fireback.

To replace a one-piece fireback, lift out the grate or unscrew it from its fixing to the back hearth. Then use a club hammer and chisel to break up the back. If it's badly cracked this won't be too difficult.

Clear the opening of all rubble backfill, but don't remove the bead of asbestos rope that runs up the side and across the top at the mouth of the recess. Often it is fixed to the back of the surround itself. The new fireback will butt against this, allowing an expansion gap to be created.

The new fireback should be exactly the same size as the old, as measured across the inside front edges. You may be able to manoeuvre it into place in one piece, but if not break it into two by tapping along the grooved break line which is cast across the middle of the fireback.

Position the bottom section in the opening on a mortar bed, making sure it rests against the asbestos rope. Then slot a sheet of corrugated cardboard down the back of the fireback to form an expansion gap between the back and the infill (the card usually disintegrates in the heat).

Ideally the infill should consist of a fairly dry mix of 1 part lime to 4 parts vermiculite, but often an ordinary fairly dry 1:7 mortar mix can be used with some old back-

fill rubble mixed in.

Next run a fillet of fire cement round the rim of the bottom section and set the top section in place. You can then gradually replace the backfill.

Now is also an excellent opportunity to fit a throat restrictor to the chimney, the frame of which usually has to be mortared onto the top of the fireback itself. Consequently you can incorporate this into the flaunching when you lay it. Note that the angle of the flaunching as it slopes upwards from the fireback to the back of the chimney flue must be parallel to the slope of the throat-forming lintel.

To finish off the opening you may want to fit a metal fire frame—in effect an 'L' sectioned metal beading. These are available in copper, brass and stainless steel and are made to fit all standard openings. They are simply mortared into place.

When all the repair work has been completed, leave the fireplace for a day or so to dry out and settle. Even then, only start a moderate fire. After about a week, you should be able to have a blazing fire in the grate once again.

If any cracks appear between the top and bottom pieces of the fireback, fill them with more fire cement.

Metal firebacks: these are often heavy cast

iron affairs which usually just stand in place against the sides and back of the opening to protect it from intense heat and, at the same time, to throw more heat forward into the room. Some of them are also quite decorative, but this feature is often hidden behind soot, tar and the like. Lift them out of the opening (you may have to remove the grate first) and give them a good brushing down with a wire brush. Then give the fireplace a good rub down with wire wool. Again you may need some methylated spirits to get rid of any tar deposits. A wash with a bucket of soapy water is then all that's needed to remove the rest of the dirt and grime.

Surround and hearth care

Fire surrounds and hearths are made or faced with a wide range of materials. These usually provide a hardwearing finish that is virtually maintenance-free apart from the small running repairs that are necessary from time to time.

To avoid damage, don't stand on the hearth or rest scuttles or pokers on it. And resist the temptation to rest cups or glasses here—at best they leave 'rings', at worst spillages can cause ugly stains. The same applies to the mantelpiece.

CLAD A CHIMNEY BREAST

Every room needs a focal point to catch the eye and draw together the various decorative elements within it; in many homes it is the fireplace which provides this natural centre of attraction.

Even if the fire's been blocked off in favour of central heating, the chimney breast itself is likely to remain the most pro-minent structural feature in the room and the most obvious point around which to base a co-ordinated decorative scheme.

You could decorate the chimney breast with paint or a wallcovering to emphasize it as a focal point, but there's a range of tex-tured brick or stone cladding that can help you to create a really spectacular effect which will enhance even the plainest room.

Fixing the cladding is straightforward; you just stick the individual brick or stone tiles onto the chimney breast to imitate a natural finish—it's certainly much easier than exposing the real thing and it will do just as much to enhance your fire surround. With the added benefit of a wide choice of textures, colours and shapes—and your own choice of a pattern to use—there's bound to be something for every room and every taste.

Although you can achieve a similar effect by hacking off all the plaster from the wall, it is a messy and time-consuming job, and there's really no guarantee that the masonry beneath will be worth displaying. Doing the job this way guarantees good looks and solves any problems that might occur at the points where the mantel and surround meets the wall—brick and tile cladding can be fixed directly on top of the plaster surface.

Planning considerations

The only requirement for fixing masonry cladding is a fairly smooth, dry and sound wall, although most types will accommo-date slight irregularities.

Strip off any wallcovering and remove the skirting board, picture rail and coving; you may choose to refix these later.

Examine the plasterwork for soundness. Tap the surface with your knuckles and listen for a hollow sound, which could indi-cate that the plaster has 'blown'—lost its grip with the masonry. In this case, you'd be wise to hack off the loose material back to sound edges, undercut the perimeter of the hole and refill with new plaster—you can buy this in small bags ideal for making minor repairs.

Electrical socket outlets are sometimes fixed on the return wall of a chimney breast, within the alcove; if these are surface-mounted you can easily cut the tiles to fit around them, but if they're flush-mounted you'll have to bring the outlets forward to the finished level of the cladding (see Deal-ing with socket outlets).

The fire surround shouldn't present too much of a problem, whatever it's made from. As the tiles are only about 15mm thick, they won't encroach on the mantel-shelf unduly, or protrude beyond the sides or side pillars.

When you're planning the bonding arrangement for the tiles (see below) make sure that a row of whole tiles will coincide with the top of the mantelshelf: don't try to cut them lengthways to run along the top. If there's likely to be a gap at top or bottom that's smaller than a whole tile, conceal the discrepancy with skirting board or coving.

If the fire surround is a rectangular or stepped design, simply cut out the tiles to fit around it. But if it incorporates curves, you'll have to make a template and carefully nibble the tiles to shape using a pair of pincers for the job.

Types of cladding

• **Brick tiles** not only look authentic but also feel real. This is because they're actually genuine brick slips—thin slivers sliced from kiln-produced bricks.

Tiles come in a diverse selection of colours to imitate popular brick types—commonly rich red-browns, pinks, buff and sandy tones, whites, greys and burnt mottled finishes. Textures range from fairly smooth to cracked or heavily ridged faces to mimic bricks both old and new. Some types also have irregular chipped edges like old bricks to add an extra touch of realism.

The tiles are aproximately brick-sized—215mm × 65mm—but are only about 15mm thick. They're sold in boxes typically containing about 30 tiles—enough to cover an area of about 1m × 500mm.

In addition to flat tiles you can also buy angled external corner tiles, which incorporate a stretcher (long) and a header (short) face. For the same reason, some tiles can even be bent to cope with corners: you just heat the tile with a hair dryer or hot air paint stripper—or dip it in hot water— and then bend it to shape. Check which method is recommended for the tiles you choose.

• **Stone tiles** are reconstructed from moulds to resemble natural stone blocks and they're actually made from reconstituted stone. They're either irregularly-shaped for a random effect, or rectangular for a more formal, coursed finish. Various sizes of both types are made, from about 100mm across to about 300mm across. Colour choice is intended to imitate local stone types—with varying degrees of success—and is typically white, buff or grey, although weathered versions of these are also available.

Bonding patterns

Brick tiles can be laid in a host of different bonding arrangements to give the effect you want. You're not limited by any structural requirements, so you can create a flamboyant, dramatic effect that would be impossible to build from real bricks—perhaps fixing the courses vertically, diagonally or in a parquet design—or just opt for a more conventional bond. Remember, complex patterns may look striking but they demand a lot of cutting of tiles—which can be wasteful as well as time-consuming, and can create problems at corners. The more dramatic they are, the less realistic they'll look.

Random stone tiles are easier to arrange on the wall: just position them where you want to achieve a pleasing pattern. Aim for a blend of different sizes and shapes for the most realistic-looking effect.

Coursed stone tiles are more suited to a formal, geometric arrangement, but again a good mix of small and large, square and rectangular faces gives a more true-to-life finished effect.

It's a good idea to experiment beforehand by laying tiles out on a flat area approximately equivalent to the area of the chimney breast. Rearrange the tiles until you're satisfied, taking corners and obstacles into account, then number the tiles in the order you wish to lay them.

Tools and materials

Fixing brick or stone tiles can be carried out with few tools. You'll need a claw hammer for attaching (and removing) temporary framing battens plus some 25mm masonry nails. Cutting some tiles will be necessary to maintain the bonding pattern at the edges, and this can be done using a club hammer and bolster chisel, or a tile cutter—although some tiles can be cut with a sharp pair of scissors or simply snapped. If you plan to

Bonding arrangements need not be hampered by structural considerations —you can copy common brick bonds or devise your own. With tiles, almost any pattern is possible, though corners need careful planning

Natural weathered brick or stone tiles are available in a range of colours, sizes and textures. The wide choice guarantees endless possibilities for decorating with all the warmth and charm of local materials

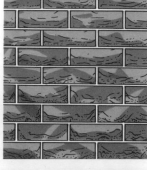

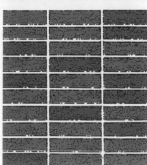
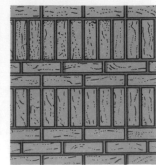

finish off the mortar joints with a decorative profile you'll also need a pointing trowel and some ready-mixed pointing mortar.

In addition to the tiles you'll need to buy sufficient adhesive for fixing them to the wall. This usually comes in 2.5 litre tubs with a notched applicator, although some makers recommend any reputable tiling adhesive for attaching their tiles. You'll need a wide-bladed filling knife for applying adhesive for stone tiles.

Wall preparation may require a number of tools, from stripping knives and chisels to plastering trowels.

Preparing the walls

Imitation brick and stone tiles must be stuck to a clean, sound and dry bare wall. If you're hanging brick faces or coursed stones you'll need to attach temporary battens to the wall as a positioning guide for the cladding, and as a support to help keep it in position while the adhesive sets.

Strip off any wallpaper as far back as the edges of the area you wish to tile. Score through the paper along this border using a trimming knife—strip off to the scored line. You may need to hire a steam stripper if sponging the wallpaper doesn't soften it sufficiently for you to strip it.

You can generally clad on top of painted surfaces as long as the paint is sound. Scrape off the loose parts and lightly abrade the surface as a 'key' for the adhesive.

Wash down the wall with warm water and a little detergent to remove dust and grease, and allow it to dry. Meanwhile, cut lengths of 19mm × 12mm softwood to fit around the chimney breast as a baseline support for the courses of tiles.

Before you fix the battens, measure the wall from the ceiling down to check that a number of whole tiles plus 10mm mortar joints will fit; measure from the top of the mantelshelf to the floor to ensure that a course of whole tiles will run along the top. Position the support battens accordingly.

Drive masonry nails into the battens at

300mm intervals so that they just break through on the other side, then hold each batten in place—with a spirit level on top to ensure it's horizontal. Tap the nails all the way in to secure the battens to the wall.

If the old skirting board is narrow enough, it's easiest to use it as the support batten, then to fix a wider skirting on top.

Irregular-shaped stone faces don't require any support or course battens, but it's important that brick tiles (and stone rectangles) are laid perfectly level to avoid a lopsided effect, so you should mark the course positions on the wall in pencil. Alternatively, set up stringlines tied to nails on vertical battens fixed where the chimney breast meets the wall, and held away by blocks at its external corners. Check that the strings are horizontal with a spirit level. To save having to set up strings for each

1 *Strip off wallpaper back to the bare plaster. Wash the surface to remove dust and grease and allow to dry*

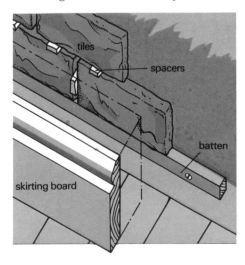

tiles

spacers

skirting board

batten

Calculate how many courses you need—remove skirtings to avoid undue cutting and so that you can refix them on top of the tiles later

course, simply move the same string and corner blocks higher after you complete each course.

Stringlines and battens can get in the way when you're cladding a chimney breast with these tiles, so cut a single batten to reach from floor to ceiling and mark it off in increments of brick courses plus mortar joints. Hold it against the rows as you fix them, as a levelling guide.

It's also important to work out where the vertical joints fall—bear in mind that the external corners of the breast must be clad with special corner tiles (or bent tiles) so that any cutting can be done on the less obvious internal corners. Use the tiles—in the pattern of your choice—to mark the positions of the joints of the first few rows. Subsequent rows of tiles will take these as their guide.

Once you've prepared the chimney breast for hanging the tiles, roll back the floorcovering or, if this isn't possible, lay down dust sheets to catch any adhesive or mortar droppings.

Dealing with socket outlets

Surface-mounted sockets can simply be tiled around without you having to reposition them or you can remove them (switch off at the mains first), tile the wall behind, then refix them to the new surface. Flush-mounted types will have to be removed and refixed at the new level.

Turn off the power at the mains—or remove the relevant circuit fuse—then unscrew the socket faceplate and draw it forward. Disconnect the cable cores and set the faceplate aside. Unscrew the mounting box and remove it from the wall.

Cut a piece of 15mm thick chipboard to fit snugly within the recess and drill a hole through which to feed the cable (if necessary). Screw the chipboard into wallplugs set into the masonry.

Cut tiles to fit around the recess, then refix the mounting box within the recess, screwing it to the chipboard fillet. This will set the faceplate forward by the required amount. Feed the cable through the mounting box, making sure it passes through a rubber grommet to prevent chafing, then reconnect the cable cores to the terminal on the back of the faceplate.

Screw the faceplate back on to the box, then restore the power and test the socket.

Attaching brick tiles

Brick tiles are easy to stick to the wall using a thick, mortar-coloured adhesive, which you apply with a notched spreader. First of all you have to prepare and measure the wall, then decide on a bonding pattern.

Unpack the boxes of tiles and lay them near the chimney breast. Clear a space and dry-lay several rows of tiles to experiment with patterns. Mix tiles from different boxes for a more even distribution of colours, as

batch tones can vary slightly.

The 'joint' spaces between the tiles are set by small 25mm × 20mm pieces of expanded polystyrene, which you cut to size with a trimming knife from a sheet of packing material provided with the tiles. Insert these between the tiles at each corner and vertical joint for a regular spacing.

Starting on one of the chimney breast side walls, spread on adhesive using the notched plastic applicator provided with the adhesive. Cover an easily manageable area of about 1 square metre. Press the first tile onto the adhesive, resting it on the batten. Use a slight wiggling motion to bed the tile into place—make sure it aligns with the vertical joint marks you have made. You may have to cut a tile—using a bolster and hammer—to fit up to the return wall.

Place a polystyrene spacer against the outer edge of the tile, then position the next tile on the batten. Continue in this way to the external corner.

At the corner you can either use a pre-formed angled corner tile, which you stick on as previously described, or bend a tile to turn the corner.

To bend a tile, first mark on its rear face where you want to bend it, then place it on a

2 *Attach a support batten at the lowest level possible. Apply adhesive to the wall with the notched spreader provided*

3 *Press the tiles into the adhesive and place spacers between each. Check the coursing as you go, especially at corners*

4 *At corners, alternate the long and short faces of the special corner tiles to match the bonding of real brickwork*

5 *Fit the spacers between the brick tiles throughout to ensure regular vertical and horizontal joint thicknesses*

heat-proof surface (a concrete step, for example). Play the jet of a hot-air paint stripper (or the flame of a blowtorch) over the surface for a few minutes.

Put on some thick gloves, or wrap the tile in thick cloths, then bend it gently into a right angle at your mark. You'll find it easier to bend it around a corner of the wall.

Continue to work up the chimney breast, sticking on tiles with spacers between. Whatever the bond, you'll certainly have to cut some tiles to fit internal corners. Do this using a club hammer and bolster chisel.

First mark the tile by laying it on top of the last whole tile. Place a second dry tile on top, butting up against the wall. Mark the middle tile where the top tile overlaps it. Scribe both faces of the tile using your chisel, then place the tile on a thin bed of sand. Tap the chisel gently on both sides of the tile until it eventually snaps.

You can also use a conventional tile cutter to cut brick tiles, or a hired tile cutter for thicker ones, though some can be cut with a sharp pair of scissors.

Trimming the tiles to fit round the fire surround can be awkward, especially if the surround is embellished with decorative mouldings, or has complex curves.

Use a profile gauge to judge the shape or make a template from thin paper, by pushing it into the profile of the surround, then cut out the shape. Transfer it to the tile. Score the cutting line with a tile cutter, then nibble away the waste using a pair of pincers. Be careful not to try to break off too large a portion of the tile, or it may snap unevenly and you will not be able to use it.

If the surround is just too fiddly to cut tiles to fit around, fill in the gaps with car body filler. While it's still soft, flick on some dust from ground tiles for an invisible patch.

ERECT A FUEL STORE

The need for outside fuel stores and sheds diminished when oil and gas central heating systems became ever more popular and 'off peak' electricity storage heaters were heavily promoted. Now, solid fuels are making a comeback and, with efficient central heating boilers, the return to the pleasures of an open fire and growing enthusiasm for both coal and wood-burning stoves.

This means that fuel—wood, coal or anthracite—must be stored in large quantities, and that signals the need for a bunker or fuel store of some kind.

Various models of bunkers are available including pre-constructed galvanized steel bunkers and pre-formed concrete types. You could even build your own from bricks or timber, but the work involved and the cost of materials hardly warrants the effort compared to what's available in self-assembly kits.

You can choose from a number of finishes for most bunkers—typically a pebbledash front panel with terracotta or stone grey sides. Some bunkers even come with polished metal or wooden lids.

Most bunkers are suitable for storing timber for a wood stove as well as coal. What you must make sure of is that the bunker is sited in such a way that ground water can't enter and you must choose a type which has an adequately weatherproofed access lid. Put it in a handy place for unloading, too.

Some bunkers come with non-spill hopper doors, which prevent coal dust or small particles of coal spreading around the mouth of the bunker. These are well worthwhile as they cut down the risk of picking up coal dust on your shoes and walking it into the house. These features can only be used where the bunker comes with a precast base. An interior baffle plate is also provided, which prevents the hopper overspilling when coal is unloaded.

Despite the weight and size of the panels supplied for kit bunkers, assembling them is not a particularly daunting task. More important is the care and attention you give to siting them, choosing the right size for your needs, the fuel the bunker will house, and preparing the site.

Siting the bunker

Even the most aesthetically designed bunker looks like a bunker, so for many

Single coal bunkers are available in pre-fabricated kit form for easy assembly. The panels are simply bolted together and a fixed lid section just sits on top of the basic box. The fuel is loaded via a hinged lid section, which may be of wood or metal, and the coal is taken out from a sliding door. Depending on the model, the bunker may come with its own precast concrete base

Twin fuel stores are similar in construction to single bunkers, although they incorporate a central panel to separate the loads of fuel—ideal if you plan to use wood and coal for your heating needs. You can also fit a non-spill hopper to the conventional opening to prevent the coal spilling out

people the need to position it out of sight is paramount. But often this means tucking the bunker around the side of the house or positioning it in an obscure part of the garden. While this might be more visually pleasing than having the bunker outside a back door, remember that trudging any great distance when snow is lying thick or rain is pouring down, means that collecting fuel will be a misery.

Ideally the bunker should be located as near to your back or side entrance as possible. It must also be sited in such a place that fuel deliveries aren't hindered. Your coalman will not thank you if he has to undertake an obstacle course with a heavy

sack over his shoulder. Access considerations apart, don't position the bunker so that it comes into contact with the house walls: you could introduce damp problems by bridging the damp-proof course. So if the bunker is located near the house, make sure that it stands at least 50mm from the wall.

A favourite location is to position the bunker behind a garage wall. Here, more often than not, access for deliveries is satisfactory, you'll not have too far to go to collect fuel, and it leaves the rear of your house without any unsightly obtrusions. The only disadvantage is that you'll probably not have a concrete apron already laid on which to stand the bunker. But, so long as you have the space for the bunker, casting a concrete slab on which to sit it is not difficult (see Casting a concrete slab).

Choosing the size

In the UK, volumes of coal are still measured in imperial units, whereas bunkers are sold in metric capacities. Conversions to metric for standard bunker capacities are easy to work out, however. Simply start from the basis that 1cwt roughly equals 50kg and work from there. If you regularly store 6cwt of coal, you will need a bunker of 300kg capacity.

If you are using solid fuel to supplement an existing heating system such as gas central heating, perhaps with just one open fire used on special occasions or particularly cold days, you'll only need minimal bunker capacity. In most cases a 300kg capacity bunker is ideal. At the other end of the scale, where solid fuel is to provide all your heating, then a twin bunker of up to 1220kg (24cwt) capacity is best. With twin bunkers you can run down one half of the unit, ordering a fresh supply of fuel when it becomes empty; the capacity in the remaining bunker will ensure a continuing supply of fuel to allow for delivery times and to spread the financial load more evenly.

In cases where you have a mixed fuel system, such as wood and coal or anthracite, then a twin bunker provides compact storage while allowing for the mixed fuels.

Before you order a new bunker, it's a good idea to have your first load of coal or anthracite delivered loose. Keep the volume as small as possible and carefully monitor the amount of fuel you use each day. Now relate this to the frequency of fuel deliveries and you'll soon see what is the minimum practical capacity of fuel you'll need to store. It's always a good idea to add on 50 per cent volume to cope with unforeseen cold spells or problems over fuel deliveries.

Preparing the base: If you intend to locate the bunker on an existing concrete apron outside your house, much of your preparation work will have been done for you. Some bunkers come with a pre-cast concrete base, but this should still be set on firm, level ground. This will raise the bunker and keep ground water out of the fuel store.

The best type of support for the bunker is a concrete slab, although well-compacted hardcore will do if you're using a pre-cast base section; alternatively, use a paved area.

Assembling the bunker

Once you've prepared the base you can start to erect the bunker. Most prefabricated types consist of bolt-together sections, which you can assemble with only a few tools. Assembly of coal bunkers varies from make to make, although the basic construction details are generally similar.

If you're using a precast base, you should lay this first. Position the base of the bunker

---

★ WATCH POINT ★

Any movement in the precast base can be taken up by laying a layer of sand over the sub-base and by partially rotating the precast base. You can then work the sand around so that it fills any small voids underneath.

---

onto the main sub-base, smooth side uppermost. Try to rock the panel, to ensure that it is bedded evenly on the slab. If there's any unevenness, the weight of the coal will cause cracks to appear.

Offer up the first, back panel of the bunker to the base. Be very careful—this is not a lightweight component—and you may need assistance to lift it (and the other panels) into place. Remember the golden rule when lifting heavy objects: always bend your knees, using your leg muscles, *not* your back muscles, and keep your back as straight as possible.

Hold the panel in place, either with someone's help or by means of timber struts. Offer up the left-hand panel and secure it in place with the bolts, nuts and washers provided in the kit.

Next, offer up the front panel and bolt it into place. Don't over-tighten any of these fixings at this stage: some slackness will allow you to make slight adjustments until

---

★ WATCH POINT ★

Grease the bolts liberally or spray with a releasing agent first. Should you ever wish to demount the bunker it will make dismantling much easier.

---

all the panels are squarely in place. Never force the bolts through the fixing holes if they don't properly align—you could easily crack one of the panels by overstraining them. Instead, use small wooden wedges hammered underneath the panels to align the bolt holes.

Secure the right-hand panel in the same way then fit the access door. This is usually held in place by two brackets, one on each

1 Once you've laid a suitable flat, level base for the bunker you can start to assemble the panels

2 To assemble the kit, slot a bolt through the connecting holes and fit two washers and a nut

3 Tighten the bolt and nut using two spanners. Don't overtighten the bolt or it will crack

4 *Fit the front textured panel, which contains the hopper doorway, followed by the final side panel, bolting them together loosely*

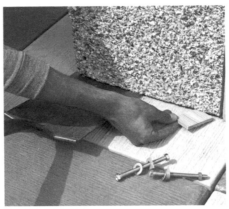

5 *If the base is slightly uneven you'll have trouble aligning the connecting holes; wedge up the panels with a spade and wood offcuts*

6 *An interior metal baffle plate can be fitted inside the bunker around the top edge of the hopper to stop overspilling of the fuel*

side of the access hole into which the door slides. The brackets are again usually secured using nuts and bolts. Before fitting, grease the inside of the track.

Attach the brackets and slide the door into place, making sure that it does not bind or jam. If this happens, slacken the nuts on the brackets and adjust them so that the door opens properly. If, after this, the door still jams, remove it and run a file down each side edge (or use an angle grinder) until you've removed enough metal to provide a smooth-running fit. It's unlikely, though, that this problem will occur with most kits.

Finally, place the top of the unit into position then bolt on the lid. Lightly oil the hinges and make sure that the lid opens and closes freely without snagging against any of the side panels.

For twin bunkers the construction is much the same except for a probable increase in weight for the panels and the addition of the centre dividing partition.

There's very little you need to do to keep your bunker in good order. Keep the hinges and sliding tracks well oiled. Periodically check the panels to make sure that no cracks have appeared due to the assembly being sited on an uneven base. Once a year, when the bunker has been run down, hose it out to clear away deposits of coal dust.

Casting a concrete slab

Mark out the site for the concrete slab by driving timber pegs into the ground at about 600mm intervals. Make this area at least 150mm larger than the precast base on all sides to allow room to work and the setting up of formwork to mould and retain the wet concrete while it sets. You can remove the formwork later and fill the gap left.

Dig out the area to a depth of over 150mm and infill to a depth of about 80mm with hardcore. Compact the hardcore using

a sledge hammer, stout timber post or garden roller, then use a long length of timber with a spirit level on top to check the fall or rise of the site. Use wedges of wood to raise the straight edge on its lowest side until the length of timber is level.

Drive a peg into the excavation so that its top is level with the required top of the slab. Repeat this procedure over the area of the excavation at 500mm intervals.

Fix lengths of 75mm × 25mm timber to pegs around the perimeter of the excavation as formwork then check the level across the top—there's no need to incorporate a drainage fall for a slab of this size—most of it will be covered by the bunker.

If there are any voids in the hardcore layer, you'd be wise to spread a 'blinding' layer of sharp sand over the surface to fill the larger gaps, or you'll waste a lot of concrete.

Fill the excavation with a concrete mix of one part Portland cement to five parts all-in-ballast. Tamp down the wet concrete to just

7 *Bolt on the non-spill hopper onto the front panel and fit the metal door in its recess*

8 *An ordinary hopper door simply slots into two metal brackets bolted to either side of the doorway*

9 *Next, fit the concrete top panel and then firmly screw on the galvanized steel access lid*

above the level of the formwork using a stout plank edge-on, then draw the plank back across the slab with a sawing motion to dispel air bubbles and compact the mix level with the top of the formwork.

Cover the slab with a polythene sheet (to stop it drying out too quickly) and leave it to set for about two days before removing the

★ WATCH POINT ★

If the slab is much larger than the base area of the bunker use a thin strip of timber or dowel to groove small gullies. Make these deeper towards the outside edge, to allow surface rainwater to drain away quickly.

formwork and pegs. Leave for a further two days before erecting the bunker on the slab, but be careful at the edges—they'll be crumbly. If there's a risk of frost, you must protect the slab from freezing; the best method is to sprinkle soil onto the polythene sheet covering the newly-laid slab.

To cast a concrete slab dig out the soil to about 15mm and level it using datum pegs. Set framework around the perimeter to mould and retain the wet mix. Add a layer of hardcore, top with sand then shovel in the concrete and compact

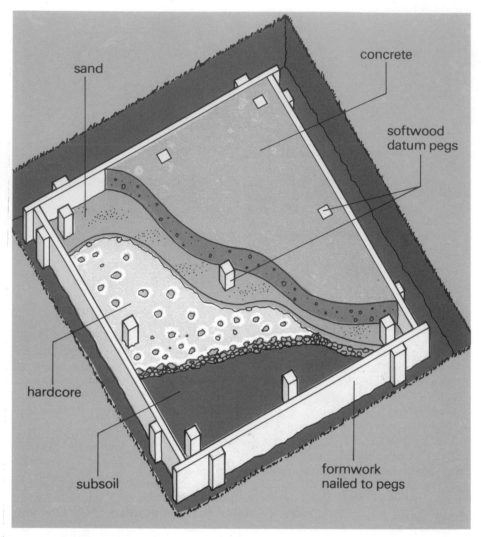

sand

concrete

softwood datum pegs

hardcore

subsoil

formwork nailed to pegs

CHAPTER 4
HOME ELECTRICS

All the information you need from how to wire a plug to installing a new electrical system. Plus details of all types of lights, switches and electric fittings

ALL ABOUT HOME ELECTRICS

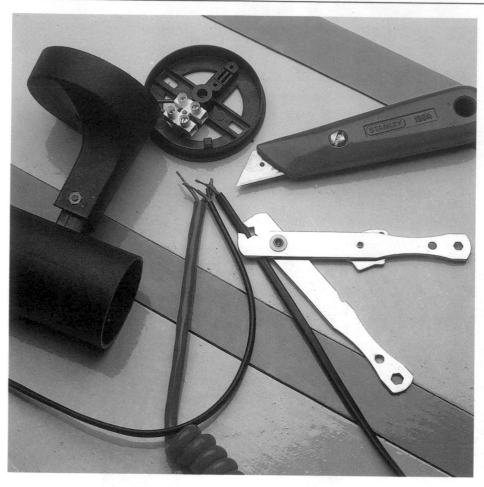

The two most important things to understand about home electrics are the technical terminology used to describe the electricity itself, and the nature of the system which is actually installed in your home.

Volts, amps and watts

Try to think of electricity in a wire as water in a pipe. The water must be under pressure or it will not flow. In electrical terms this pressure is known as the **voltage** and is measured in **volts**. The higher the pressure —or voltage—the harder the electricity is 'pushed' along the wire. In the UK, domestic electrical systems operate at 240 volts. This gives enough 'push' to get the electricity right around the house and through to any of your appliances.

Going back to the water pipe, it would be possible to measure how much water is flowing through it. In the same way you can measure how much electricity is flowing along a wire. This measurement is called the current and is measured in **amperes**, or **amps** for short. How big the current is depends on two factors. In a water system these would be the pressure and the size of the pipe. In the same way the size of an electric current depends on the voltage and what it is flowing through. This is why

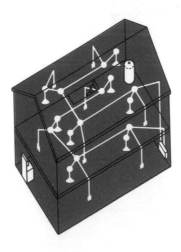

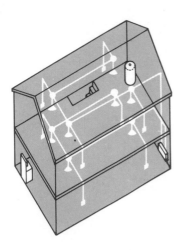

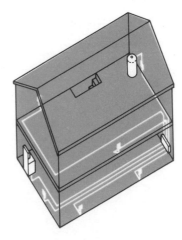

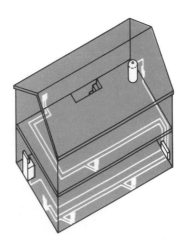

In older junction box lighting circuits the cable runs from the fuse board to junction boxes above the ceiling. Separate cables run to the ceiling roses and switches.

In a modern loop-in system the wiring is continuous, running from the fuse board to each ceiling rose in turn. The switches are wired directly to the roses, which act as junction boxes.

In older UK houses, a radial system runs separately from the main switch to each wall socket. There may be three or four fuse boxes connected to the meter with more than one main switch.

UK houses wired since 1947 use a ring main system with the power running from the consumer unit to each wall socket and back again. There is usually only one fuse board and one main switch

wires and appliances have a current rating —to tell you how much electricity can safely flow through them.

It is the size of the current that can make electricity dangerous, which is why you can still get a nasty shock from a car battery rated at only 12 volts. For a given voltage, it is also the current capacity which determines how much work an appliance can do —a kettle with a bigger element will boil the water faster. This capacity for work is measured in **watts** and takes into account both voltage and current by multiplying them together. So a 240 volt, 5 amp appliance consumes 240×5, or 1,200 watts. Working backwards, you can also find out that a 240 volt, 720 watt appliance will have a current rating of 3 amps. (1,000 watts is 1 kilowatt, 1 kW for short.)

Domestic electrical systems

Before the Second World War, British houses were wired on the radial system. Houses wired since 1947 employ a ring main. In the radial system all outlets—lights and sockets—are wired separately on circuits of various current ratings. Normally the wiring goes direct to a central point—the fuse board—but often one outlet is wired off another one for convenience. If the system has been abused, long spidery chains of outlets will have built up, each demanding more current than the wiring connecting them can safely handle.

In the ring system, the sockets on each floor of the house are connected by a separate 'ring' of wiring with a single current rating—normally 13 amps. The 'ring' starts at the consumer unit—the modern version of the fuse board—and then passes through each socket in turn before returning to the unit again. The lights in the house have their own separate radial circuit, and appliances demanding large amounts of current—cookers, showers, water heaters—are each wired direct to the consumer unit. This is also the case on radial-type circuits.

Wiring

The wiring is done with **cable**. Cable consists of a red insulated live wire, a black insulated neutral wire and a bare earth wire —all encased in a thick outer sheathing. Until the immediate post-war years this sheathing was rubber which has a safe life of only 25 years, after which time it starts to

perish. If this happens the current-carrying wires may touch and there is a serious risk of fire. So if you find any such cable in your system today, it must be replaced immediately.

The tough PVC sheathing that has replaced rubber lasts much longer—round about 70 years—but not indefinitely. Most authorities recommend that modern cable installations should be tested for deterioration every five to ten years and that most houses need to be completely rewired every 30 to 40 years.

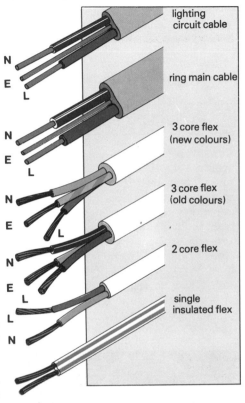

Cable is semi-rigid and carries electrical current in circuits. Flex (short for flexible conductor) carries the current from a socket via a plug to an appliance.

Finding out which system you have

The difference between radial and ring circuits may not be immediately obvious. The sockets originally installed with radial circuits were those of the round pinned types and had different current ratings— normally 10 amp, 5 amp and 2 amp. But in many cases these will have been replaced with the square pin type, found on all ring circuits, in the course of partially updating the system. So the place to start your investigation will be at the fuse board.

Ring circuit consumer units have the

fuses neatly in a row, each one guarding a separate circuit. In a typical two storey house there will be two socket ring circuits, for upstairs and downstairs, a lighting circuit, one to two spurs for larger appliances and one or two spare 'fuseways'. These are gaps to allow for the addition of new circuits.

Radial circuit fuse boards (which may be boxed) are by contrast confusing. It is very likely that there will be more than one board and they may all look very different. However, the number of cables running from them should give the game away.

The only way to be certain which system you have is to examine the socket wiring. Start by turning off the electricity at the main switch. Then unscrew the faceplates of at least three sockets around the house and examine the wires running into them.

Sockets wired on a ring main will have two sets of three wires. Each set will have a red live, a black neutral and an earth. The earth wire, which runs bare in the cable supplying the socket, should be insulated locally at the socket with a length of green and yellow PVC sheathing.

Sockets wired radially **should** have only one set of wires, however, you may be unlucky enough to choose a socket which is an extra socket itself or a power source for somewhere else. So you should continue opening up sockets until you have established a definite pattern and are certain which system you have.

Safety

Electricity, if not controlled, can pose a real danger and many household fires are a direct result of faulty installations. To cut down the worst risks, two safety measures are incorporated into the wiring—fuses and an earth.

A fuse is a deliberate weak link introduced into the live wire of an electrical circuit. Older-type fuses are simply lengths of thin wire fitted on to a porcelain body. Modern fuses enclose the wire inside a sealed cartridge to make replacement easier. If, for any reason, too much current flows through the fused circuit, the thin wire will melt, or 'blow', and shut off the current. Without a fuse the current would continue to flow until the circuit overheated and burnt out.

The house wiring system actually has a number of fuses to protect individual circuits. The whole house is protected by a **service fuse** fitted in a sealed box close to the meter. This is the responsibility of the Electricity board and cannot be repaired or replaced by the householder. However, it is only in exceptional circumstances that the service fuse will blow since each circuit has its own individual fuse which will almost certainly blow first if a fault develops.

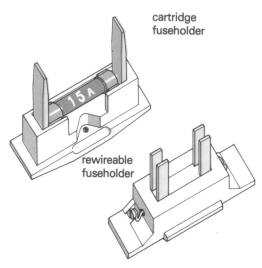

cartridge
fuseholder

rewireable
fuseholder

Fuse wire may be encased in a replaceable cartridge or run through a tube in the holder

Recognizing the individual fuses

Fuses are fitted in the consumer unit (or fuse board in older installations). Each circuit has its own fuse which is matched to the current rating of the circuit it is fitted in. Modern fuses and fuse carriers are colour coded: 5 amp is white (for lighting); 15 amp is blue (for immersion heaters and other 3 kW circuits); 20 amp is yellow (for some types of shower heater); 30 amp is red (power ring circuit) and 45 amp is green (for cookers). Old-style porcelain carriers have the current rating written on them and must be rewired with a correctly rated wire.

Alternatives to the conventional fuse

Some of the newer electrical installations have miniature circuit breakers (MCBs). These look like ordinary switches or push buttons but instead of blowing in the event of a fault, MCBs 'trip' and switch off the supply. Once the fault has been repaired, the circuit can be brought back into use simply by pressing the switch or button to reset it, thus eliminating the need to replace the fuse. Like fuses, MCB's are current rated for different circuits.

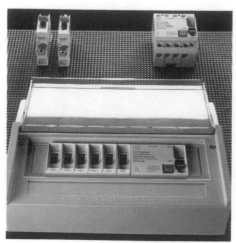

A modern consumer unit uses miniature circuit breakers instead of fuses

Protecting appliances

In modern installations the flexes to each appliance are also protected by their own fuses. These are fitted inside the plug, or spur connector for fixed appliances. They are always cartridge fuses and are current rated at either 3 amp (coloured red) or 13 amp (coloured brown). You may also find older 1 amp and 5 amp fuses. It is these fuses which will blow if anything goes wrong with an appliance or its flex—the most frequent cause of trouble. Older round-pin plugs do not have them, which in itself is a major reason for replacing them.

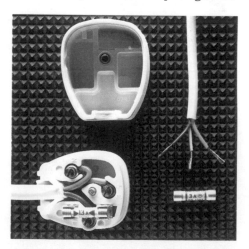

Earth wires

The purpose of an earth wire is to provide an escape path for the electricity—which quite literally runs back down this wire into the earth in the event of a fault. Though fuses protect the wiring from burning out, the earth wire directly protects **you**.

Some types of electrical faults on an appliance can make touchable parts live—for instance if an uninsulated wire is dropped onto a metal case. The earth wire is connected to the casing, so that if this were to happen, the electricity would instantly flow away down it. The large 'fault' current that this creates will blow the fuse, shutting off the supply and telling you that there is a fault. Earth terminals in an appliance are identified by the letter E, or sometimes by the symbol.

If you have old equipment with no earth wire it may be potentially dangerous. If you are at all uncertain you should have the appliance checked. But some modern equipment is designed not to need an earth. Its safety comes instead from **double insulation**, which means there is no possible way for a fault to put you in contact with live parts. Such equipment will be clearly marked DOUBLE INSULATED, or will carry the symbol ⊔ on the rating plate.

Electric shocks

If all your appliances and circuits are **properly** earthed or double-insulated, you should not get a shock even in the event of a fault. But if the earth is poor—perhaps because a contact is not secure—it is still possible that a lethal current could flow to earth through you. And there are some circumstances—for instance, if you drill through a buried cable and touch the chuck —where even a sound earth may not protect you.

Such possibilities are rare, but you can be protected against them if earth leakage circuit breakers (ELCBs, or sometimes called RCDs) are fitted to the circuit. These react very quickly to the leakage of any current to earth—quicker than the current can harm you—and shut off the supply. They are also very sensitive, and will trip if even a tiny current is detected. A fuse or MCB needs a fairly substantial current to cause it to trip, and this might well be enough to cause a fatal shock.

An ELCB can be wired to protect the whole installation—either fitted between the meter and the main switch, or used to replace the main switch entirely when it doubles as the main isolating switch. Individual ELCBs can also be installed to protect a single circuit or appliance. You can get sockets which incorporate them, and also portable, plug-in versions.

However, an ELCB should be regarded as a back-up device and is no substitute for ensuring that your installation or appliances are properly earthed in the first place.

CABLE AND FLEX

Electricity flows easily through certain materials—these are called conductors. Other substances—insulators—will block its progress. These two simple facts can be harnessed to control the flow of electricity around your home and direct it so that it goes where it is wanted.

Domestic wiring consists of a good conductor—usually copper—which carries the electricity around, surrounded by an insulator to contain it. Pages 244–6 give details of the wiring system in general. But all household wiring is not the same. Different types of wiring are suitable for different types of circuit. One major division is between flex and cable, but within each category are many types.

The difference between flex and cable

Flex and cable are terms which are often confused and yet there is a very precise difference. Both consist of a number of insulated conductors colour coded for classification—and both carry electricity from A to B. But flex, as its name suggests, is a flexible cord. Cable on the other hand is semi-rigid; although it can easily be bent by hand, it will take up a set unless bent again.

Broadly speaking, cable is used for the permanent, fixed wiring which carries the electricity around the house to sockets, ceiling roses and fixed appliances like wall heaters. Flex is used for the final connection between a piece of electrical equipment and its plug, or a light fitting and its rose.

Colour codes for flex and cable

Since 1969 flex has had brown insulation for its live conductor, blue for the neutral and green and yellow for the earth if there is one. Cable is different: red insulation covers the live conductor and black covers the neutral (the only exception is three core and earth cable or strapping wire which is used for two way switching—for a light on the stairs for example. The conductors are insulated in red, blue and yellow, but only for purposes of identification). The earth is bare inside the sheath, but should be covered with a sleeve of green and yellow insulation wherever the sheath is stripped

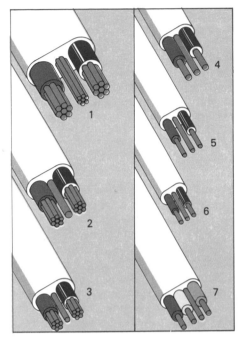

Types of cable: (1) 10mm². (2) 6mm². (3) 4mm². (4) 2.5mm². (5) 1.5mm². (6) 1mm². (7) 1mm² three core and earth cable

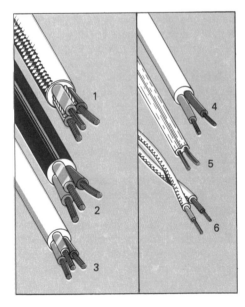

Types of flex: (1) Unkinkable. (2) Rubber sheathed. (3) 1.5mm² PVC sheathed three core. (4) 0.75mm² PVC sheathed two core. (5) Parallel twin flex. (6) Twisted flex

back to make a connection—inside a socket or ceiling rose for example. The earth is a safety device. It carries current only when a

fault develops in the circuit. If this happens the fuse protecting the circuit blows and for the short time that current flows along the earth conductor, the outer sheathing of the cable is sufficient protection.

Cable for lighting circuits and sockets

The cable commonly used for all modern house circuits is called **twin and earth**. This is PVC-sheathed cable containing two PVC insulated cores with a bare earth. Twin and earth cable has a flat rather than round cross section—a feature of electric cable which is unique to the UK but does have the advantage of being neater for surface wiring. You'll find that the only difference between the cable used for a lighting circuit and the cable used for a circuit supplying electricity to your sockets is in the actual size.

The size of a cable is measured by the thickness of its cores and is given as the cross-sectional area of a core in square millimetres—for example, 1.00m² cable is commonly used for lighting circuits. The size of cable—and flex—is important because it determines the amount of electric current that can be carried. If a cable is too small for the current it has to carry, it will overheat, melt the insulation and expose the metal core. This can result in fire—around 3,000 fires a year in the UK (6 per cent of all domestic fires) are caused by faults in the permanent wiring.

The power sockets in a house are usually connected to a cable which runs from a fuse in the fuse-box around the sockets and back to the fuse again. This is a ring-circuit. The circuit is normally run in 2.5mm² cable and is protected by a 30 amp fuse. In every house there are also special circuits which draw a lot of current. These are best wired with their own cable from a separate fuse. The size of cable depends on the equipment.

Choosing flex

As flex is used for connecting electrical equipment you'll generally have a particular appliance in mind when you come to buy it. The most important thing you need to know is whether the equipment needs to be connected to earth. Appliances like irons and electric heaters and such things as metal light fittings always do, but nowadays a lot of equipment has a double protection of insulation and does not need an earth connection. You'll find that such appliances—hair driers, lawnmowers and electric drills for example—will be clearly marked or will carry the double insulation symbol ⊞ .

You will also need to know how much current the equipment will draw as this determines the size of the flex. And it is worth considering whether there are any special conditions which might point towards a special type of flex.

Different types of flex

There are two core and three core flexes: the first for double insulated equipment, the second for appliances that require an earth. Two core flex is usually round sheathed with colour coded connectors, but there are also thinner twin flexes which are sometimes used for light fittings. There is a parallel and a twist type—neither has colour coding so care is needed to identify the conductors.

Three-core flex is always round sheathed with colour coded conductors. As well as the ordinary PVC types there are three main other types—heat resistant for storage heaters and immersion heaters, unkinkable for irons, and tough-rubber-sheathed (TRS) for lawnmowers and other equipment whose flex may be subject to rough treatment. This type of flex is often sheathed orange but you should not assume that this is always so.

It is vital to choose flex with the right number of cores. Always use three core if there is an earth and note that extension leads should always be made from three-core flex. This is because you cannot guarantee that an extension lead will never be used with a piece of equipment which needs to be earthed.

Other types of wire

Coaxial cable is a strange type of wire—not strictly a cable since it is flexible—used only for connecting television aerials or, in the thinner gauges, for hi-fi systems. It has a central copper core surrounded by sheathing designed to cut out interference with the television or audio signal. Another type is bell wire—more properly called extra low voltage wire. This is used to connect things like door bells which run on a very low voltage supplied either from a battery or

from the mains via a transformer which reduces your voltage supply from 240V to around 12 volts or even less.

There is one other cable you may come across—called mineral insulated copper sheathed (MICS). This is used for outside circuits and very occasionally indoors. Using MICS is something you should not attempt until you have considerable experience with wiring, and even then you may think twice. The mineral insulation surrounding the copper cores absorbs water so the ends of the cable must be sealed.

Getting the right size

In most parts of the UK the voltage is 240V so you can reckon that for every 1,000W a piece of equipment will draw you are going to need a flex current capacity of 4 amps.

Remember the larger the size of cable or flex that you buy, the greater its current carrying capacity and the higher its cost. But don't skimp as your safety is at risk.

The current carrying capacities of the most common sizes of flex and cable are:

mm^2	0.5	0.75	1.0	1.25	1.5	2.5	4
Amps	3	6	10	13	15	20	25

Always buy the next size up to the one you actually need.

Note that with pendant flexes for ceiling lights you also need to think about the weight the flex will have to carry—a 3 amp flex can support 2kg, a 10 amp flex can support 3kg and larger flexes 5kg.

When choosing cable you will find that most of the circuits in a house are run in one or two sizes—1.0mm^2 for lighting and 2.5mm^2 for ring circuits. It is only for fixed appliances that you'll need thicker cable.

Apart from choosing the right size and type, you should make sure that all the connections are well made with only as much insulation and sheathing stripped off as is necessary. You should also avoid tight bends when installing cable and you should unravel flex before you use it. Make sure that the flex is properly anchored at both ends—in the plug and to the piece of equipment it supplies.

Tools for handling flex and cable

A minimum of tools are necessary—just a trimming knife for stripping the sheath and insulation and a screwdriver for making the connections. However, there are two other tools which are handy and will help you to

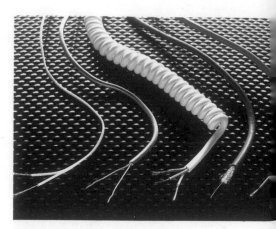

Other types of wire (from left to right) include bell wire, MICS, coiled flex, coaxial and orange tough rubber sheathed

do a more professional job—a pair of strippers and a pair of long nosed pliers.

The wire strippers strip both cable and flex much more quickly than a knife and can be set so that the copper cores are not damaged in the process. The long nosed pliers help to bend the cores at the end when making the connections—this is most useful with larger cables whose large cores can be well-nigh impossible to bend with your bare fingers.

Cable or flex exposed on the surface of a wall can be held to the surface with wrap-around clips called buckle clips—these have the advantage that they can easily be undone—or with the better looking plastic hoop and pin type of clip. They should be spaced every 300mm or so. Surface cables can also be run in plastic channelling which protects the cable as well as securing it.

Stripping cable

To strip cable slit the outer sheath lengthways with a sharp penknife or trimming knife. Don't cut back too much—about 75mm should be adequate. Peel back the sheathing like the skin of a banana and cut off the waste.

The best way to strip the live and neutral wires is with a wire stripper—a cheap, easy-to-use tool you can buy from any DIY store. At a pinch, you could cut around the insulation with a knife; but take extra care not to nick the wires. Don't use pliers—they are too difficult to control accurately.

Adjust the wire stripper until the blade just begins to cut through the insulation; then pull gently towards the wire ending so that the insulation is removed and a length of the inner core exposed. Trim back about 20mm on both the live and neutral wires.

FIXING FUSES

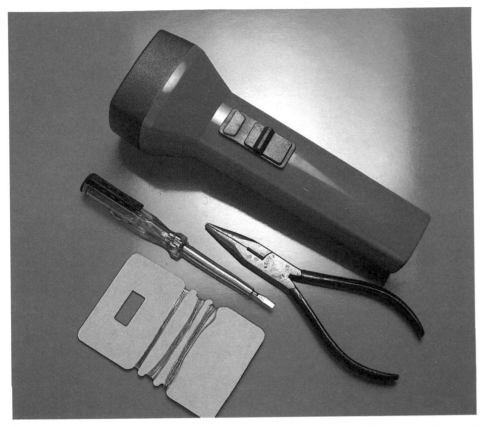

Domestic electrical fuses are deliberate weak links in the system, designed to break when a fault occurs. Electrical faults take many different forms and can occur almost anywhere in the wiring, but most have one thing in common: they cause an abnormally large amount of current to flow in the adjacent flex or cable.

Simple fuses are wires combining high resistance—which means they heat up fast —with a low melting point. So when an abnormal current flows through a high-resistance fuse, the fuse melts and breaks the circuit. Current is measured in amps, which is also what fuses are rated in. Consequently a 5 amp fuse would melt if a current of 13 amps were passed through it; a 13 amp fuse would not.

In Britain, household fuse systems are designed to provide several lines of defence which protect both you and the electrical hardware. The two main weapons in this system are the fuses themselves, which halt a dangerous build-up of current—and the earthing system which disposes of it safely.

Although some appliances have their own built-in fuse, the first line of defence is generally the cartridge fuse that is found in the plug.

Plug fuses are rated at 3 amps for small appliances consuming under 750 watts— toasters, hi-fi and lamps for example—and 13 amps for over-750 watt appliances, like fires, kettles, televisions and videos. Confusingly, other ratings of fuse are available (such as 5 amp), but they are not required for home use.

Most people happily operate small appliances on a 13 amp plug fuse—happily, that is, until the appliance fails. Although it's not really dangerous to do so, it does make sense to give your equipment as much protection as possible—especially when it comes so cheaply in the form of a fuse.

As well as being fitted in plugs, plug fuses are also found in fused connection units— the fixed sockets used to supply kitchen appliances, wall heaters and the like.

After that comes the circuit fuse — they're the ones you'll find in a row in your fuse box or consumer unit. Each lighting and socket circuit in the house has a circuit fuse and there are additional ones for the individual circuits supplying high power equipment such as the cooker and immersion heater.

Circuit fuses are rated according to the current flowing in the electrical circuit which they are protecting:
- Lighting circuits are 5 amps.
- Socket (power) circuits are 15 amps.
- Small cooker, shower and immersion heater circuits are 20 amps.
- Large cooker, shower and immersion heater circuits are 30 or 45 amps.

Conventional fuses can be of two types. Older, rewireable fuses consist of a thin strand of fuse wire running between the terminals of the fuse holder. The wire is current-rated according to the list above.

Newer fuses have a cartridge similar to a plug fuse, only larger—easier to replace than rewireable fuses, but you can't quickly tell if they've blown.

Both these types have their fuse holders colour coded:
- White—5 amp.
- Blue—15 amp.
- Yellow—20 amp.
- Red—30 amp.
- Green—45 amp.

In more sophisticated modern consumer units miniature circuit breakers (MCBs) are fitted instead of fuses.

What causes fuses to blow

It's essential to know what can cause the current build-up that eventually melts a fuse before you set about faultfinding.

Short circuit: This is the classic electrical fault. It means, quite simply, that the outgoing live current is allowed to run straight into the returning neutral current, bypassing the appliance in the process. This allows a massive flow of current.

Short circuits are usually caused by faulty connections or by deterioration in the wiring, though outside factors such as dampness or a stray drill bit can have the same effect.

Insulation failure: Though poor insulation can create a short circuit, an insulation failure within an appliance may result in part or all of it becoming live. This causes a current build-up which the fuse should halt, before you get a shock.

Poor connections: When a connection becomes weak or loose, it may cause the current to surge across it; fuses respond to this and blow accordingly.

Appliance failure: If the electrical circuitry in an appliance breaks down—say, when the element of an electric kettle fails—the impedance of that appliance falls to a low level. The result is very similar to a short circuit: a current build-up, then a blown fuse.

Over-extensions: Electric cable and flex sizes are carefully determined not only by the amount of electrical current they can handle but also by how far they can carry it. Consequently, overlong flexes and extension leads, or circuits which extend further than the guidelines laid down by the IEE can result in current surges which blow fuses—sometimes after many years of trouble-free service.

Overloading: This is perhaps the most common cause of blown fuses. When an electrical wire is asked to carry more current than it can handle it heats up. Hopefully, as they are designed this way, the wire that heats up fastest is the fuse.

It is a common fallacy to suppose that just because a 15 amp power circuit can supply several sockets, so a single socket should, via an adaptor, be able to supply two or even three appliances. Often, the socket connections, adaptor and plugs simply cannot handle all that is asked of them. They heat up, the insulation begins to break down and the circuit fuse blows.

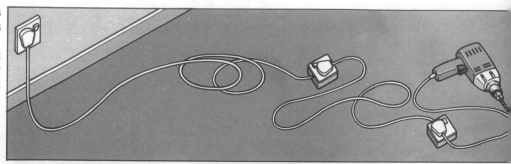

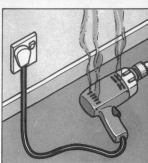

Blown plug fuses are caused by a variety of reasons: among them are using too many extension leads (top); overloading a single wall socket by abusing a multi-adaptor (left), accidentally knocking fluid over an electrical appliance (centre) or by plugging a faulty appliance into the circuit and then switching on

Before a fuse blows

You can save yourself a lot of trouble later by taking two simple measures as soon as you move into a property.

First turn off the main switch at the consumer unit and remove all the fuse holders but one (on MCBs press the small 'off' button below the reset button).

Turn on the electricity and note what lights, sockets or appliances are served by the fuse that you've left. Note the information down and stick it to the fuseholder. Then check that the fuse's colour coding is correct.

Repeat this procedure for each fuse in turn, always remembering to shut off the main switch between times. Once you have circuit information on all the fuse holders you won't be in the dark if a fuse blows.

Secondly, make sure that you have fuse wire or cartridges (as applicable), a screwdriver, pliers and torch in a handy place near the consumer unit. Rummaging around in the dark can be dangerous.

Faultfinding—plug fuse

If an appliance goes dead but none of the others fed from sockets on the same circuit are affected, suspect a blown plug fuse.

1. If you have not already done so switch off before opening up the plug. The fuse may look charred, or it may not—but in any case you must check the appliance, the flex and the plug for faults before fitting a new one.

First of all check the rating of the fuse—and then the wattage of the appliance. If the former is only 3 amps and the latter is over 750 watts, you've found the fault.

2. Follow on by looking at the plug connections: they should all be tight and there should be no stray strands that could short from one to another.

Check the plug in the socket. If it is a loose fit, one or the other may be badly worn and in need of replacement.

Move on to the flex. It should be tightly held in the plug's cord grip. Along its length there should be no evidence of fraying, splitting, kinking or twisting—any of which may cause a blown fuse.

3. Finally, check the appliance. Start with where the flex enters it—the rubber grommet should be intact and there should be no appreciable movement when you pull it. If there is, this indicates loose terminals or cord grips inside.

Often, misuse or maltreatment of an appliance can blow a fuse. For example, an excessive buildup of dust or dirt can cause overheating, and the same problem results from restricting the airflow around it—particularly on hi-fis and videos. Foreign objects, too, cause problems and bear in mind that something may have fallen in accidentally.

Charring indicates a blown fuse—first check the rating. Too much bare wire plus stray strands may cause shorting.

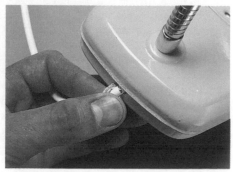

Worn grommets often lead to damaged flex insulation. You need to replace both the flex and the grommet.

1 *Too many spurs from one socket will overload the circuit*

2 *Cracks in sockets are a tell-tale sign of trouble within*

3 *Make sure that the fuse wire is of the correct rating*

4 *Check pendant light fittings for loose wires and reconnect*

Faultfinding—circuit fuses

With a bit of luck, your observations at the time the fuse blows should give you more than an inkling as to where the trouble lies—more often than not it happens when you switch something on.

For this reason, and hopefully to save you having to conduct a systematic survey of your house's electrical system, the checks below are grouped according to the most common individual trouble spots.

Overloading: If a socket is overloaded, you'll almost certainly recognise the fault as soon as it happens. Three-way adaptors (which do have their own plug-type fuse) are a particularly common source of trouble and their use should be avoided.

If you must have a three-way adaptor, make sure you never run high-power appliances—such as a kettle—from it.

Circuit overloading is harder to recognise, but it can easily happen if you have all your high-power appliances—washing machine, spin drier, TV, fan heater, kettle—running at the same time. If the problem recurs frequently, have the circuit checked by a qualified electrician.

Appliance failure: Serious faults within an appliance can cause a circuit fuse to blow as well as the plug or connection unit fuse.

Light switches: In the case of a suspect switch, turn off the mains electricity.

Remove the switch faceplate and inspect the connections behind. The red and black wires should be held tight in their terminals—with no stray strands to cause short circuits—and the insulation should be complete, without nicks.

Now look at the earth wire. This should be attached to a terminal on the switch box and covered with a length of green and yellow plastic sheathing. A loose earth terminal means the switch may not be properly earthed: a bare earth wire can cause a short circuit.

Sockets: These suffer from more or less the same problems as light switches—loose connections or shorting via an uninsulated earth wire (in this case live, neutral and earth wires are held in terminals in the back of the socket faceplate).

Having made sure the electricity is turned off, unscrew the faceplate and make a thorough inspection.

Incorrect fuse rating: This may seem obvious, but it's a common fault. Even if the colour code on the fuse holder is correct, you should also check the cartridge. And if the fuses are rewireable don't assume that the blown wire was of the correct rating. Check the figure stamped on the fuse with the ratings on the fuse wire packet to make sure you use the right one.

Among the other faults to look out for are: cracking or worn terminals, in which case the socket must be replaced; kinking of the cable where it enters the backing box, in which case the cable must be pulled through and trimmed.

Light fittings: Turn off the electricity and remove the rose or the body of the fitting. Be on the lookout for loose wires, stray strands and perished or broken insulation.

Mending a fuse

Plug fuse: Simply open up the plug, flick out the old fuse with a screwdriver and slot the new one in. In the case of fused connection units, the fuseholder either unscrews or is prised out with a screwdriver. Slot in the new fuse and replace.

Circuit fuse (cartridge): Remove the fuseholder of the circuit that has failed. Dig out the old fuse and slot in its replacement.

Circuit fuse (rewireable): These may be one of several patterns, notably open or enclosed, but the principles are the same.

Remove the relevant fuseholder and loosen the screw terminals at either end to release any burnt wire.

Cut off sufficient new wire of the correct rating to stretch the length of the holder and wrap around the terminals.

Wrap one end clockwise round one of the terminals and tighten. Feed the wire across or through the holder as necessary.

Wrap the other end round the other terminal—again in a clockwise direction—and tighten. Replace the fuseholder.

MCBs and ELCBs: Simply press the reset button once the fault has been put right.

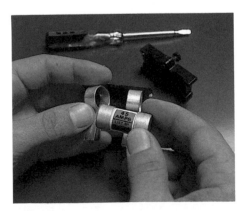

5 *Make sure you use the correct rating of cartridge fuse*

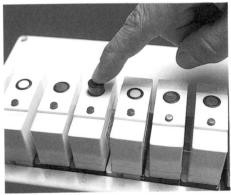

6 *Only reset a circuit breaker after correcting the fault*

ADD AN EXTRA SOCKET

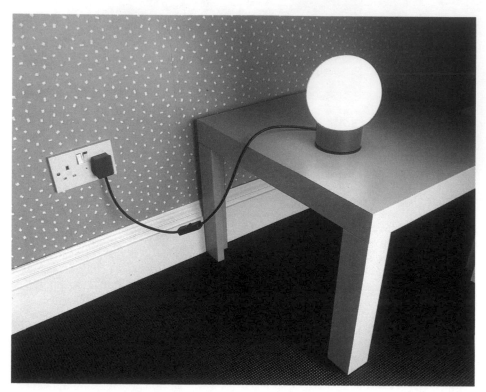

Where the power comes from

If you want to add a new socket outlet, the power does not have to come all the way from the consumer unit or fuse board—it can be drawn from any suitable existing outlet as long as you do not overload the circuit.

Start by determining whether you have a ring or a radial circuit. If you do not know already, switch off at the mains. Unscrew the faceplates of three sockets around the house. Pull each faceplate away from the wall and examine the wires carefully. Sockets wired on a ring main have two sets of cable, each consisting of a red live wire, a black neutral wire and a green/yellow earth. Those on a radial main have just one set of wires. You may be unlucky enough to choose a socket which is an 'extra socket' itself or is the power source for somewhere else. So continue opening up sockets until you have established a definite pattern.

Before you add an extra socket, make sure that you do not overload the circuit.

On a ring circuit you can safely add a socket provided that the existing circuit you intend to 'tap' does not exceed a floor area of 100 sq m—and that you do not go outside this area when you fit the new socket outlet.

On a radial circuit the floor area served

There are a number of different types of socket outlet so make sure that you choose the right one before you start. Flush-mounted outlets are the most common and obviously the neatest. They consist of a steel backing box recessed and fixed into the wall and a faceplate which screws on to the front.

Surface-mounted outlets are installed where it is difficult or impractical to cut a hole in an existing wall. They have a square backing box which is fixed directly to the wall and a faceplate—identical to the flush mounted plate—which is screwed on to the front. Most surface-mounted sockets are made of white plastic but you can also buy strong, impact-resistant metal boxes and faceplates for a garage or workshop.

Even if you fit a surface-mounted outlet you still have to hide the cable. The obvious way is to cut a channel for it through the wall. But you can avoid the bother that this entails by using *plastic conduit* or *mini-trunking*. Here the cable is led through a neat surface-mounted plastic channel which runs along the top of the skirting board or up the side of an architrave. Many conduit systems come complete with their own surface-mounted socket outlets as well as angled adapters which allow you to turn corners and right angles. Note, though, that

Trailing wires are messy and dangerous. Tidy them up by installing new sockets

existing flush outlets have to be converted to the surface mounted type if power is taken from them (see page 254).

Whatever type of socket you decide to fit remember that it is always possible to install a double rather than a single outlet—although you will need to cut out a larger recess to fit a flush-mounted socket.

Fused connection units

If you want to install an extra outlet in a bathroom—for a wall heater or towel rail, for instance—it would be dangerous (and in Britain against the electrical regulations) to use a plug and socket. Instead you must install a *fused connection unit*—a fitting which links the appliance directly and permanently to the power supply.

The unit is fitted and wired in a similar way to a socket outlet and can be either flush or surface mounted. A number of different faceplates are available—so examine the range carefully before you buy. For instance, some are switched and some have a pilot light which tells you when the unit is on or off.

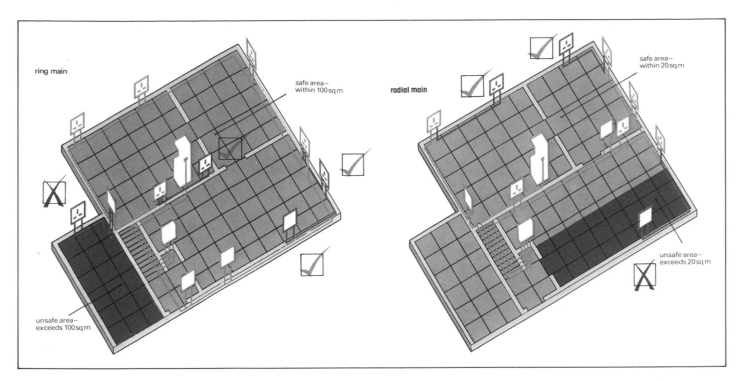

ring main

safe area—
within 100 sq m

radial main

safe area—
within 20 sq m

unsafe area—
exceeds 20 sq m

unsafe area—
exceeds 100 sq m

by the existing circuit must not exceed 20 sq m. Any new socket must be fitted inside this area.

Never draw power from a fused connection unit or from an appliance which has its own individual supply.

Once you have found out whether you have a radial or ring circuit refer to the diagram, then wire up according to the following rules:
• On a radial circuit system draw power only from a socket with one set of wires (that is, the last socket in that circuit).
• On a ring circuit system draw power only from a socket with two sets of wires (that is, a socket not previously added to).

Siting the new socket

The next step is to decide exactly where you want to put your new socket. As a general rule, try to position it at a minimum of 150mm above the level of the floor or worktop and well out of reach of anyone working at a sink.

For flush-mounted sockets and installations where the cable is to be hidden in the wall, you must take into account the type of wall construction. On a solid masonry wall you can fit the socket almost anywhere; but on a timber framed (stud) wall a new crossmember or trimmer needs to be added between two studs to take the backing box. The cable is then fed behind the skirting to the socket.

If you are not certain what type of wall

you are working on, test it by tapping the surface with the handle of a screwdriver—a hollow sound will indicate that it is a stud or timber frame construction, a dull thud that it is solid (probably plaster on brick or building block).

If you discover that you are dealing with a frame wall, 'sound out' the whole area you want to work on. By trial and error you should be able to work out roughly where the timber uprights (studs) and crossbearers are sited (bearing in mind that they are probably at rough 400mm or 450mm centres) and mark their positions in chalk across the face of the wall. Once you have a good idea of where you want to install your new outlet, plan the best route to take the cable from there to the socket that is your power source. Run the cable along the top of the skirting board as far as you can. If one of the sockets is higher than the other, avoid the temptation to plan the run so that the cable runs diagonally across the wall—if you do, it is much more likely that someone may accidentally puncture the wires at a later date. Mark out the route, including the new socket position, using a piece of chalk and a wooden straightedge. Measure and note the distance between the outlets.

What you need for the job

As well as the new socket and fixings you will need a length of cable to take power from an existing supply. Ask for 2.5mm² 'twin and earth' and always get a few

Deciding whether it is safe to add an extra socket will depend on whether you have a ring main (above left) or a radial main (above). On a ring main it is safe to add extra sockets providing the circuit does not exceed 100 sq m. On a radial main the circuit must not exceed 20 sq m. Take care not to exceed these limits

metres more than you actually need. You will also need to buy some PVC earth sleeving. This is green/yellow in colour and is used to cover the earth wire and prevent it accidently touching one of the other wires or the backing box. Buy a box of cable clips to hold the cable in place, and a rubber grommet to protect it where it enters the new socket.

Any damaged areas must be made good afterwards with plaster. Use either ready-mixed plaster which you can buy in large tubs from most DIY stores or purchase a small bag of finishing plaster to mix up your own. If you are installing a flush socket in a stud or timber frame wall you will also need a small piece of plasterboard and some clout nails to patch up the damaged wall before you finish it by plastering the cracks.

Starting work

Before you start work, cut the power at the mains consumer unit. Remove the relevant fuse and keep it with you just in case someone switches on the power accidentally while you are working. Just to make sure that you really have cut off the supply, test the existing socket with a mains tester screwdriver or plug in an appliance such as an electric lamp.

Using plastic conduit

Start by fitting the backing box in place using impact adhesive or plugs and screws. Then measure and cut the backing pieces to length—use a junior hacksaw—and fix them in position as you did the box.

Feed the cable into place making sure

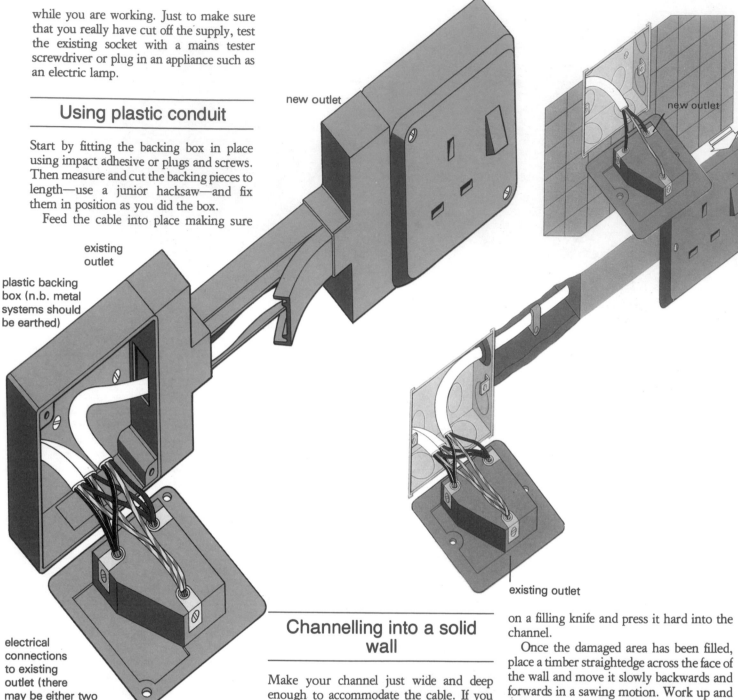

new outlet

new outlet

existing outlet

plastic backing box (n.b. metal systems should be earthed)

electrical connections to existing outlet (there may be either two or three sets of cables)

existing outlet

there are no twists or kinks (some manufacturers supply small clips which are spaced along the top of the conduit to hold the cable tightly). Lead the cable into both backing boxes, strip the ends and make the electrical connections to each socket (see Wiring the sockets).

Trim the conduit covers to length and snap them into place on top of the backing pieces (fit angled adapters as well, if these are supplied). Screw both faceplates into position, then turn the power back on at the mains.

Channelling into a solid wall

Make your channel just wide and deep enough to accommodate the cable. If you are fitting a flush-mounted socket, cut out a recess about 7–8mm deeper than the backing box. Fix the box in place using screws and wallplugs.

Thread a length of cable into the channel and secure it every 300mm with cable clips. Knock out one of the cable entry blanks, add a grommet, and feed the cable into the backing box of each outlet. Strip the cable, bare the wires and attach them to the terminals on both sockets (see Wiring the sockets).

To repair damaged areas, load your plaster onto a small board and stand near the wall. Pick up a small amount of plaster

on a filling knife and press it hard into the channel.

Once the damaged area has been filled, place a timber straightedge across the face of the wall and move it slowly backwards and forwards in a sawing motion. Work up and down the wall so that the plaster is smoothed off neatly. Sand any ridges when it is dry.

Frame wall insulation

On a frame wall, start by cutting away a section of wall boarding around the proposed outlet with a sharp knife and straightedge. The hole should be about 300mm high and just wide enough to half overlap the uprights on either side. Skew nail a trimmer between the uprights to accommodate the backing box then cut a

1 *Cut the chase, angling the chisel in the direction you want to go*

2 *An easy way to cut a recess for the backing box is to loosen the brickwork first by drilling a number of closely spaced holes 7–8mm deeper than the box*

3 *Level the plaster with a straightedge. Draw it back and forth in a sawing motion*

4 *On a frame wall make sure the trimmer is correctly aligned then skew nail it firmly on both sides. Cut a recess for the backing box and screw it to the trimmer. Make sure that the leading edge of the box is level with or just below the original wallcovering*

5 *If you cannot reach the cable when you drop it down the cavity, retrieve it with a piece of coathanger wire*

recess for the box itself with a mallet and wood chisel.

If the existing socket is directly below the new outlet, making the correct electrical connection is relatively easy. Simply drop a length of cable down the cavity. Then remove the existing socket faceplate and backing box and pull the end of the cable through the gap in the wall.

In most cases, however, you will want to lead the cable to an existing socket some distance away. The easiest and quickest way to do this is to drop the cable down the cavity and then lead it behind the skirting board.

Push a bolster or large-bladed

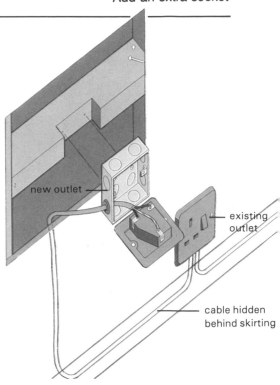

A trimmer is a length of 100mm × 50mm sawn timber nailed between the studs

screwdriver down behind the skirting board and lever it gently away from the wall. Drop the cable down from above and retrieve the end. On most walls there will be a small gap between the wall boarding and the floors—if not, cut away a section with a trimming knife large enough to reach the cable. Then lead the cable along the wall. Secure it with cable clips as close to floor level as possible. This will avoid nailing through the cable when the skirting board is replaced. Make the electrical connections to each outlet (see Wiring the sockets).

Patch up the damaged area around the socket with a small piece of plasterboard. Cut out a small square hole in the middle of the board to accommodate the backing box and nail it to the uprights and to the new trimmer with clout nails. Then make good the area around the socket with filler.

Wiring the sockets

Connect the wires to the back of the faceplate as shown above. Cut off a 55mm length of sleeving and slip it over the end of the bare earth wire. When wiring the new socket (or fused connector) double over the end of each wire so that it is gripped more tightly (and safely) in the terminal.

On the existing socket, twist each pair of wires together with pliers before making the electrical connections to the relevant terminals.

FITTING WALL LIGHTS

Lighting is just as much a part of interior decoration as wallpaper, wall colours, furnishings and furniture. Ordinary ceiling mounted lights are a convenient way of illuminating rooms but there's usually less scope for creating interesting light effects. Also, it isn't so easy to tailor the lighting to your individual requirements—for example to provide extra lighting for a dark corner.

The creative use of lighting effects has never been easier to achieve than now, with a myriad of lamps, spotlights and designs on the market. Whilst table lamps and standard lamps are easy to fit, they all have disadvantages: table lamps are often positioned at unsatisfactory eye levels as well as occupying useful table surfaces; standard lamps are awkward and take up valuable floor space. And both types need connection to power sockets which means flex trailing dangerously across the floor.

Wall mounted lights are a much better choice—they're permanent and can be positioned at ideal heights and in places where light is most needed, for instance, to illuminate a picture.

Planning for wall lights

You should always try to avoid any lighting arrangement which causes glare. This is the biggest problem with ceiling mounted lights which need high wattage bulbs to illuminate a room of any size. It's far better to have a number of lower wattage sources providing the same overall level of illumination but without being over-bright at source. Here wall lights ideally fit the bill. For best effect, choose wall lights with their own integral switching so that you can switch in or out any combination of lights. In a room measuring 5m × 4m two wall lights rated at 60 watts will provide adequate light for most purposes.

Where should they go? As a rule of thumb the ideal location is about two-thirds of the way up a wall. In a conventional oblong room, it makes sense to mount two lights on each of the longest walls—about a quarter of the way in from each end. However, not all rooms are symmetrical and if you have any alcoves, beams, nooks and crannies, try highlighting them for interesting effects.

There are various ways of wiring up wall lights. How complicated you make it depends on the degree of flexibility you want in controlling them. From an operational point of view, the simplest arrangement is to wire the lights so that when you turn on the main light switch the wall lights come on too. And by choosing fittings that have integral switches you'll be able to control the lights individually as well. However, with this simple system you can't have the wall lights on and the main light off. To do this you'll have to install another master switch for the wall lights alone. Although this may sound a more involved job ironically it could make the overall wiring job that much simpler (see page 260). When you come to position this new switch make sure you set it by the entrance door to the room to avoid the dangers of feeling your way across a dark room after the lights have been turned out.

In some situations, and particularly those where you can't get access to the lighting circuits in the ceiling void, it may be easier to take the power for the wall lights from the power circuit via a fused connection unit (see page 260).

Fitting wall lights will mean chasing cables into a wall and pulling up floorboards to pick up the power source. For these reasons it's not a good idea to introduce wall lights soon after new wallpaper has gone up or major painting has been completed. So plan well in advance and remember that in both practical and decorative terms, wall lights are an integral part of interior design.

Bear in mind that the type of wall in the room—timber frame or solid masonry—will affect how the lights will be fitted and the ease with which cables are channelled in. But these will not affect your choice of wall light fitting, the cable you use or the location for the new lights.

What you need for the job

Apart from the light fittings themselves, fortunately you won't need much in the way of materials. Use 1.0mm² PVC sheathed twin core and earth cable for the wiring. How much you need will depend on how you decide to connect the lights, but measure the runs fairly accurately and add

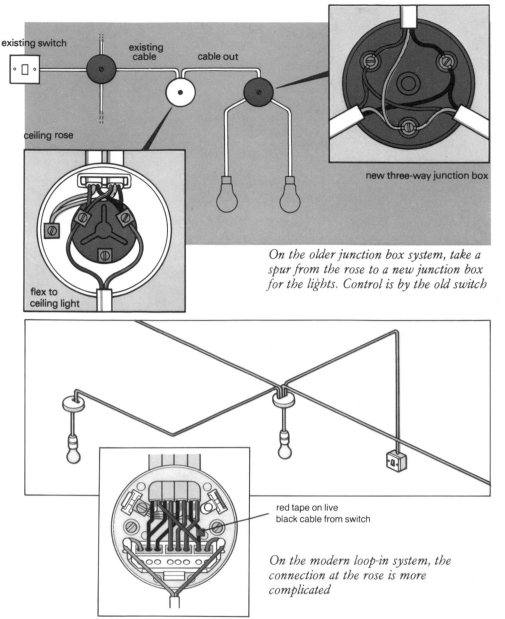

On the older junction box system, take a spur from the rose to a new junction box for the lights. Control is by the old switch

new three-way junction box

red tape on live
black cable from switch

On the modern loop-in system, the connection at the rose is more complicated

The cable runs below ceiling level are the simplest of all—the cable should run vertically up the wall from the light and then into the ceiling void. This will ensure that anyone drilling into the wall at a later date will have a good idea of where there is likely to be concealed wiring and so avoid it.

Before channelling the wall use a bradawl to make a small hole at the ceiling/wall junction directly above the light fitting. After breaking through the plaster it should go in easily. If you hit a joist then you can move the run slightly to one side to miss it.

Once you have established the best route, chalk it off on the floor. You have to lift enough floorboards to feed the cable along or through the joists beneath. For the best way to do this see Lifting floorboards. Where cable runs along the joist, it can be fixed to the side of them with cable clips. Where it crosses them, they must be drilled to pass the cable through. Use a 10mm or larger wood bit. Because the joists are close to one another, you won't be able to get the drill in between them. Either drill through at an angle or cut the drill bit off short to fit between the joists. Alternatively, you may be able to get hold of a right angle drilling attachment for an electric drill.

★ WATCH POINT ★

When you drill the holes in the joists, be sure that they are at least 25mm below the top—that way there is no danger of the cables being punctured by nails.

Lifting floorboards

It's easy to make a mess of lifting floorboards unless you know what you're doing. Stick to these rules and you won't have any trouble.

•First remove the skirting boards with a crowbar or stout screwdriver levered on a block of wood.

•If you have a fitted carpet, don't try to pull it up—it will tear or snag on the grippers. The only safe way of releasing the carpet is to force it away from the teeth of the grippers with a bolster or screwdriver underneath.

•Have a look at the boards you want to lift and see if they are complete lengths or if they run underneath a partition wall. In both cases you will have no option but to saw through the floorboards before you can lift them out.

on 10%. You may also need an oval conduit as well as light switches, and three- and four-terminal junction boxes. And don't forget the little things like green/yellow earth sleeving and red insulating tape to mark any switch drops.

It is extremely difficult to channel cable into reinforced concrete or stone walls. If your walls are like this, the best option is to go for surface mounted plastic conduit.

For cable channelling in masonry walls, you need cellulose filler or plaster to patch up the grooves. In plasterboard walls you may additionally need plasterboard for patching.

Depending on the nature of the walls, you will use either masonry plugs, cavity wall fixings and woodscrews to screw the lights to the walls. The size of the screws

will vary according to the type of wall lights you are installing and are often supplied.

A good general tool kit should safely see you through the job—the only addition you may have to get are a cold chisel and club hammer if you are channelling into a masonry wall.

Routing the cable

Weigh up the wiring options before deciding which one to go for and always keep the cable runs as simple as possible. Plan carefully how you expect to run the cables from the lights to the power supply—and switch if you choose to have one. Try and anticipate the snags you might come across.

1 *Mark the light position and extend a vertical line*

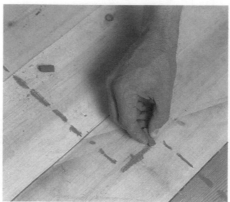

2 *Chalk out the cable run on the floor above*

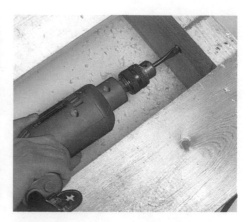

3 *Lift floorboards along line of cable. Drill through joists*

4 *To cut a board drill holes so you can insert the blade of a padsaw*

5 *Lever up with a bolster or crowbar against a block*

6 *Screw support battens to the sides of the joists*

● If you have to cut the boards, the golden rule is to saw across them near a joist—preferably one near a wall rather than in the middle of the room.

● Locate the joists by sliding a narrow blade between the floorboards. Mark a cutting line across the boards in line with the side of the joist and parallel to the wall.

● If you haven't got a special floorboard saw, drill out a series of 5mm holes along the line so that you can insert a padsaw to cut the boards.

● To free the boards, lever them up on both sides with a bolster. If there are any signs of the boards cracking, ease off—you may be forcing the nails at too tight an angle. Try again on the other side of the offending nails.

● With the boards free from the joists, pull out all the nails with a clawhammer; they can be dangerous—and painful—if trodden on.

● Before replacing the boards, screw 50mm × 25mm support battens to the

joists directly underneath the saw cuts.

● Nail the boards back with flooring brads—they are less likely to split the wood—and then refit the skirting and carpet.

Fixing the cable

Use clips spaced every meter to secure the cable along the joists. Leave plenty of slack where you run it across the joists. Then start channelling the cable where you have marked the position of the wall lights.

There are three options for concealing the cable. Choose whichever is most suitable.

Channelling into a solid wall: Use a cold chisel and club hammer to cut grooves into the wall from the ceiling to where you have marked the position of the wall lights. Cut the channel just deep and wide enough to accept the cable. Take extra care when you cut the channel at the point where the

ceiling joins the wall. Use a small chisel to work from both above and below the ceiling and continue the channel to about 15mm above ceiling level. This will avoid an unsightly bulge in the ceiling where the cable bends into the wall channel. Pull a length of cable down from above and tack it in place in the channel with clips—or better still run it through oval conduit. Plaster over the cable and finish it flush with a straight edge drawn over the wet filler.

Frame wall installation: At the points where you want to fit the lights, drill holes big enough to accept the cables. You may be able to drop the cable through a hole drilled in the top plate into the cavity and pull it out through the holes by hooking it with a piece of still wire. If you encounter an obstruction, it's probably a noggin—a horizontal frame member between the studs. Mark it, then cut out a small section of plasterboard over this point. Cut a notch in the noggin to pass the cable, nail back the plasterboard and patch with filler.

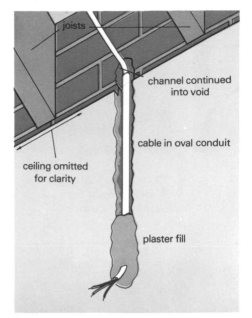

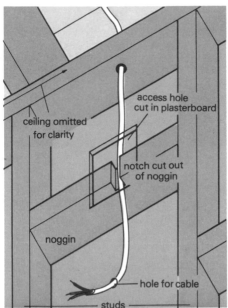

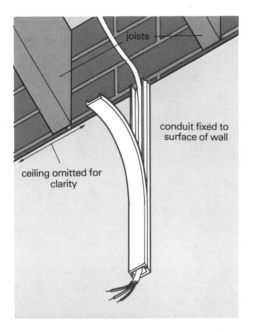

7 *On a masonry wall, channel cable into the plaster. Continue the run above the ceiling*

8 *In a frame wall, pass through the cavity. Cut out to clear any frame cross members*

9 *Alternatively, on any wall, use surface mounted plastic conduit—not so neat, but very easy to fit*

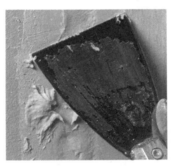

10 *First run the cable above the ceiling. Fix it every metre and leave slack between joists*

11 *Then on a masonry wall, chisel a channel down to the light. Carry it right up into the ceiling void*

12 *Feed the cable into the channel and secure it with clips. Leave plenty spare for connection to the light*

13 *Fill or plaster over the cable and finish off flush with the surrounding wall surface*

Using conduit: Above the light positions drill holes in the ceiling for the cable and screw or glue the backing part of lengths of conduit to the wall—the bottom of the conduit should be just above the place where you want to fit the lights. Feed the cable into the conduit and snap on the cover strips.

★ WATCH POINT ★

It is a good idea to mount the new lights onto wooden backing blocks the same thickness as the conduit. Holes drilled at right angles to each other in the backing blocks will enable the cables to pass straight from the conduit into the wall light.

Wiring up the lights

It makes sense to start off by connecting and fixing the cables to the lights. Only then should you wire up the other ends of the cables into the supply via the junction box. In this way you don't need to turn off the supply until you make the final connections.

Offer the lights up to their marks and use a spirit level to ensure that they are plumb. When you are absolutely sure of their positions, pencil in and then drill the screw holes—it's easier to do this now before the wires are connected.

Cut the cables protruding from the wall back to length which will allow the light fitting to sit snugly against the wall.

Strip back the outer sheathing of the cables by about 50mm and trim off 10mm of insulation from the wires. Slip lengths of green/yellow sleeving over the earth wires and connect up to the appropriate points in the terminal box in the light units—red to L, black to N and green/yellow to E.

With the lights wired up, fix them to the wall using screws and either wallplugs or stud wall fixings.

Before you start connecting to the supply, turn off the electricity at the mains.

If you're installing two wall lights, link their cables together at a three-terminal junction box to simplify the wiring. Set the junction box at a convenient point in the ceiling void or loft space. Connect the red cores of the cables to one terminal block, the black cores to another and the earth cores to a third. From here you can take one cable to connect into the existing lighting circuit.

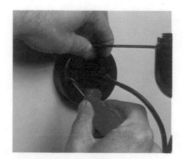

14 *Mark the positions of the fixing holes with the light held in position over the channel*

15 *Strip the cable and screw to the terminals in the light fitting. Remember to sheath the earth wire*

16 *Screw the light into drilled and plugged holes in the wall and check it is secure*

17 *Switch off, then you can connect the new cables into the existing power supply*

Wiring to the existing switch: If you want to use the room's main switch, then you'll have to link the cable from the junction box to the ceiling rose. It doesn't matter if the rose is on a loop-in or junction box system. For ease of working unscrew the rose from the ceiling but keep the cores in their terminals. Feed the new cable through the access hole, taking care not to damage the sheathing.

On a junction box rose take the red core to the live terminal, the black to the neutral and the earth (sleeved in green/yellow PVC) to the earth terminal.

On a loop-in rose first check that there are only one or two power cables going into it together with a switch cable. If there is also a branch supply looped into it then you shouldn't overburden the rose by adding yet another cable. If a connection is feasible then take the red core to the switch terminal and the black to the neutral block. The earth goes to the earth terminal.

Wiring to an independent switch: The best way of wiring is to install a four-terminal junction box at a convenient point on the main feed cable of the lighting circuit. You can then link the wall light cable to this as well as a new cable to a new switch which will give you control of the wall lights independent of the main light (see diagram).

Wiring to a ring circuit: Finally, if you can't take the power from a lighting circuit you can wire the wall lights to a ring circuit. First install a fused connection unit fitted with a 5 amp fuse. Then run 2.5mm² cable to a three-terminal junction box set under the floor. Then take 1.00mm² cable to the wall light.

Before making good the ceiling, walls and floorboards, try the new lights—if they don't work, recheck the wiring.

Finally patch up any holes or damage using plaster or cellulose filler and redecorate around fittings and switches.

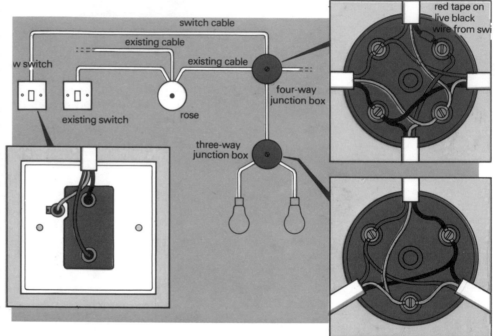

To fit a new switch that controls the wall lights independently of the original switch, cut the existing cable and insert a four-way junction. Connect both the switch cable and the supply for the lights to this. A second junction box divides the supply between the individual wall lights

To power lights from a ring main, break in and insert a junction box. Lead a spur cable up from the junction via a fused spur connector fitted with a 5 amp fuse

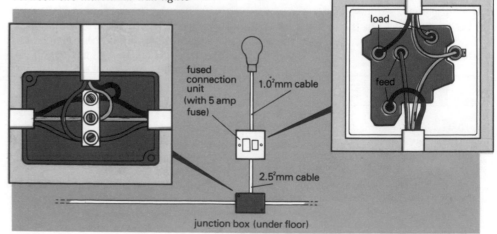

REPAIRING LIGHT FITTINGS

A fluorescent light should operate without trouble for thousands of hours. And after it's been working normally, it's very unlikely that it will suddenly fail completely to come on. If a fault does occur, look at the tube, because the way this reacts will point you to where the problem lies. Remember, it doesn't have to be with the tube, it's often with the starter. The starter is a small drum-shaped device which is usually fitted to the side of the tube.

Recognising starter failure: First make the basic check of inspecting the fitting to confirm that it is a switch starter type and not a quick start tube which doesn't need a starter—a typical starter model is shown in the illustration. Then turn on the light and watch the ends of the tube. If both elements glow white but the tube doesn't light you've got a faulty starter which will need to be replaced. But don't confuse this with only one element glowing, as this indicates a fault with the respective lampholder. Similarly, if the tube flickers, or if it comes on and then goes off every few seconds, the problem is likely the starter. But a very old

tube can sometimes show these symptoms.

If you think you've identified a fault with the starter, it'll need to be replaced, as it can't be repaired. The starter socket is often located inconspicuously on the side of the casing towards one end. This enables you to remove it without having to take out the diffuser or the tube. On some small types of fluorescents, though, you may find that you have to remove these in order to gain access to the starter.

Push the starter in slightly and then rotate it anticlockwise so that it is free to be lifted out. Replace it with one of exactly the same type. The commonest kind is a two-pin 'glow' starter. Insert the new unit, push it fully home and then rotate it clockwise to lock it in position.

Replacing an old flex

The procedures for replacing the flex on a standard lamp, table or desk light are virtually the same. They may have to be modified slightly depending on the design of the light.

Usually the flex is concealed within the fitting and has an outlet point on the side near the bottom so that base of the light can stand flat on the table or floor. Sometimes a standard lamp has feet so the flex can be taken under the base and then up the central column to the lampholder at the top. With a desk lamp, the lampholder and switch mechanism are fixed to a bracket which in turn is fixed to the metal cone

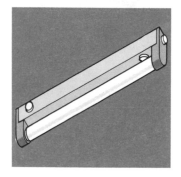

1 *Starters may be located at various points on the light fitting*

2 *To remove the starter push it in slightly and rotate it*

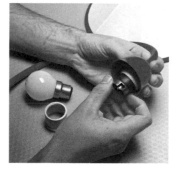

3 *Take out the bulb and then gently ease down the lampholder*

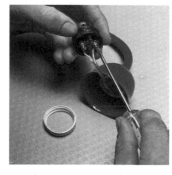

4 *With a screwdriver unscrew the terminals to release the flex cores*

5 *Tie a string to the old flex before you draw it out, as shown here*

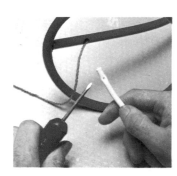

6 *Pierce a small hole in the end of the new flex and thread the string through it*

7 *Draw the new flex up through the fitting, then cut off the damaged end*

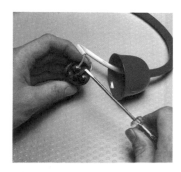

8 *Secure the new cores to the lampholder and reassemble the lamp*

shade with self-tapping screws.

To remove the old flex, take out the bulb and take off the lampshade or cover. On table and standard lamps this is held in place by a screw-down ring or the skirt of the lampholder. On desk lamps unscrew the bracket from the cone and then ease down the lampholder so the flex connections are exposed. Unscrew the terminals to free the cores from the lampholder.

With standard and table lamps you need to unscrew the top half of the lampholder to get to the terminals. Do this by holding the

---

★ WATCH POINT ★

Use a bradawl to pierce a small hole through the flex very near to one end. Thread the draw wire or string through the hole and tie it back on itself. This makes a more secure fixing than if you just tied the wire or string round the top. It also means that the flex is less likely to catch as it is drawn round any bends which occur along its path.

---

flex you should upgrade this anyway. As a general rule, if the lamp has any exposed metal parts then it should be earthed.

Draw the new flex up through the light fitting using a draw wire.

On some lamps a draw wire may not be necessary and the 'stiffness' in the flex may be sufficient for it to be pushed through the base unit. And on some china lamp bases you may be able to remove the felt pad from the bottom so you can get your hand inside to feed up the flex to the lampholder.

5. Once the flex has been drawn through, cut off the end beyond the hole to release the draw wire. The insulation on the flex cores in all probability will have been damaged by the bradawl so this section must be discarded.

6. Next, prepare the ends using the old flex as a guide for the amount of insulation and sheathing to remove. Then secure the cores, including the earth, to the terminals. However, before doing this it's worth checking to see if the cores need heat-resisting sleeving.

Now screw the terminal housing and cover back together. With table and standard lamps, you may once again find it

---

push the cap of the bulb against the spring pins in the lampholder, rotate it to clear the fixing cups and then pull it free.

First, turn off the light switch and the power to the circuit. If there is sufficient glass left you may still be able to take out the bulb as you would do normally. But wear a thick gardening glove, and grip the bulb as near to the base as possible.

Unscrew the skirt from round the socket to expose enough of the metal cap of the bulb for you to grip in a gloved hand. If this proves awkward, push pliers into the end of the cap to depress and rotate it. Open the jaws a little as you do this so the outside edges of the pliers make contact with the inside of the cap.

★ WATCH POINT ★

Alternatively, cover the broken bulb with a **thick** polythene bag and tap away the remaining glass, including the centre spindle carrying the filaments. The bag will stop splinters flying into the air.

9 *If you can get a grip, use a glove to protect your hand*

10 *Use pliers to grip the base of the broken bulb*

11 *Hold the fuse against the casing and the battery*

12 *Hold the bowl with one hand and undo the screws*

---

top half and rotating the bottom section attached to the base unit. You may find it easier doing it this way round because the flex won't twist and kink as much as you are working.

Once the flex is free, you should be able to draw it back through the unit. But before you do this, tie some string or thin wire to the end of one of the flex cores so that it can be pulled through the lamp as the old flex is removed and then used to draw the new flex into the lamp.

Measure out the length of new flex you need. This may be two- or three-core depending on whether the lamp needs to be earthed. If the light has the original flex then use this as a guide—although with very old lights that have obsolete types of

easier to rotate the base rather than the socket to prevent kinking the flex. Then fit the shade and the skirt that prevents you from touching metal parts of the socket while you're changing a bulb. On desk lamps you may have to fit the skirt before attaching the headgear to a bracket which in turn is screwed inside the metal shade.

At the other end of the flex fit a three-pin plug with a **3 amp** fuse (colour-coded red).

Removing a broken bulb

How you go about this job depends on how much of the bulb is broken and the type of socket it is fitted to. So be prepared to improvize. Basically, what you have to do is

Testing a plug fuse

If you are unsure whether a fuse in a plug has blown or the appliance it serves is at fault, you can check the fuse using a metal-cased torch.

First switch on to check that the torch is working. Then hold the torch upside down and unscrew the bottom cap to expose the base of the batteries. Put the torch in the on position and hold the fuse so that one end touches the battery and the other the metal casing. If the torch lights (i.e., the fuse completes the circuit), you'll know that the fuse is in working order. You will then need to look elsewhere for the fault: first recheck the flex and bulb as shown above.

Bowl light fittings

There are various types of bowl light fittings which fully, or partially, encompass the light bulb.

Many modern decorative bowl fittings are suspended from a single chain. To release the bowl look for the screws on the side of the metal cup into which the rim is inserted. When done up, these screws locate under the lip of the rim. Undoing them will allow the bowl to drop down. The procedure is trickier than it sounds because you need one hand to support the bowl and the other to turn the screws. So there's no free hand to steady yourself, say, if you're working over a stairwell. Therefore, slacken all the screws first with a screwdriver, so you can undo them fully later with your fingers.

Another type of fitting also encloses the bulb, but can be close mounted either to a wall or, more usually, on a ceiling.

There are some elaborate fixings which invisibly hold the bowl in place. One type, for example, has a metal backplate which acts as a base for the lampholder. The bowl

Fitting a torpedo switch

Most table, desk and standard lamps incorporate a switch in the lampholder. But access to the switch could be awkward. The neat answer to the problem is to fit a slimline torpedo switch.

With the plug removed and by your side, unscrew the cover and hold the torpedo switch against the flex in the exact place you want to fit it. Mark the position of the cord clamps on the flex with insulation tape and cut a 'window' in the flex as shown. Take extra care that you don't cut through the core insulation.

Using the switch as a guide, cut the live (brown) core and possibly the blue (neutral) core—this depends on the design of the switch—so they will fit into their respective terminals.

Note that the switch is wired into the live core, so connect the brown cores to the two terminals on the switch housing. The blue cores go to the terminals to one side of this. Usually, torpedo switches don't need to be earthed, so any earth core can run through unbroken. You can also leave the neutral

take off the diffuser, if one is fitted. Support the tube with one hand while easing back the spring-loaded end plate and socket with the other. This will free the tube from the socket. Lower it slightly to pull it from the other end. Fitting a new tube follows the reverse order.

Bayonet-type tubes: If you're replacing a tube which has a bayonet end fitting similar to an ordinary light bulb first pull back or remove the protective cover to reveal the sockets. Then push the tube into the spring-loaded holder at one end and rotate to free it. Do likewise at the other end. Push the new tube into the sockets first and then turn to secure. Finally fit the diffuser back in place.

Renewing a pull-switch cord

The easiest way of replacing a dirty or frayed cord is to cut it off near the switch and then use a plastic cord connector to join on a new length. Slip the cup of the connector over the stub of old cord and tie a knot so that it can't drop off. Similarly, slip the other section of the connector over the

13 *Cut a window in the flex at the point you have marked*

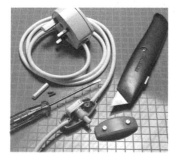

14 *Wire up the live core to the terminals and fit the cover*

15 *First remove the diffuser in order to gain access to the tube*

16 *Release the tube from the socket at one end and lift it down*

fits over the plate and then a lever is activated to move catches under the rim to keep it in place.

To remove the bowl, at ceiling level you should be able to see the slightly bent end of the recessed lever. Pull this out towards you. Push the bowl upwards to clear the catches then push the lever round to retract the catches leaving you free to lower the bowl to expose the bulb.

★ WATCH POINT ★

If there's any risk of the bowl slipping free without warning, tape it securely to the fitting to stop it dropping.

uncut if you prefer and if there is room.

Screw on the cord clamps and the cover before testing.

Replacing a fluorescent tube

Before touching the tube make sure that the light has been turned off.

Bi-pin tube: This is now the most common type of tube. At each end there are two small pins which project from insulated caps. These pins locate in the sockets on the casing. As these are also well insulated it's virtually impossible to come into contact with a live connection.

To remove an old tube of this kind first

end of the new cord and again tie a knot. Then screw the two sections together to hold the cord in place.

If you wish to replace the cord entirely, then you'll have to dismantle the switch. First, turn off the light and the power to the circuit. Undo the faceplate and disconnect the circuit cable. This will free the switch.

Carefully undo the screws holding the switch mechanism to the back of the faceplate. You'll find that the cord is threaded up through two concentric springs, a metal contact plate and plastic cover. It is prevented from being pulled out by a knot which rests inside a plastic bush. Before dismantling this section make a sketch of it so you know the exact order in which to reassemble the bits and pieces.

FITTING DIMMER SWITCHES

The surprising thing about dimmer switches is not that they are now so popular but that they have taken so long to become readily available to the householder.

Different activities in the home call for different levels of light: low, reassuring levels in the nursery, soft light for watching TV, mood lighting for supper parties, and background light for specific tasks such as writing or sewing where you need a concentrated source.

The expensive solution is to have numerous lights, each one tailored to your needs. The low-cost answer is to fit dimmer switches and get more mileage from your pendant lights. And where your room has more than one light you can create an even level of light rather than having to make do with bright and dark patches in a room.

Because fitting dimmers creates lower levels of light using less electricity, it means that you can afford to leave hall and stairway lights on—an important safety feature—and time-delay dimmers make it possible to leave security lights on when you go out for the evening without burning a hole in your household budget.

Dimmer switches are easy to install. You simply turn off at the mains, take out your old switch, connect the dimmer to the existing wires and switch on. All you need is a screwdriver and perhaps a pair of pliers. It shouldn't take you much more than half an hour.

Buying a dimmer switch

The difficult part of installing a dimmer switch is deciding which one you want from the variety that are available. Almost all are designed as straight replacements for ordinary light switches. The most common type (featured here) has a square plastic cover plate with a rotary knob mounted in the middle; the on-off switch may be built into the control knob or separate.

But there are many variations. They come with decorative faceplates in different materials, and with pairs of knobs or sometimes none at all.

Some dimmers incorporate a separate on-off switch which allows you to set the level of lighting the day before; others have auto-matic on-off operation when the room starts to get dark. The control knob may be very large, or it may be set at 90° to act as an edge wheel control. Some switch plates glow in the dark. The more sophisticted dimmer switches consist simply of a plain or decorative plate which changes the level of light according to how long you touch it. Others of this type turn on and off when you tap the plate with a finger and yet others can be controlled remotely—from your armchair for example. Many dimmers have a facility for two-way wiring—such as on a landing light.

Fitting restrictions

There are a few restrictions to bear in mind when you go window shopping or look through the manufacturers' brochures. For example, if you have fluorescent lights you need to get a special fluorescent dimmer. Depending on the model you buy you may also have to make modifications to the lights themselves. These usually involve fitting a new ballast and an extra resistor to the switch circuit; unless you know about fluorescent lights it's probably easier to buy new lights, ready adapted.

If the switches you want to replace are the two-way type make sure that you specify that the dimmers are suitable for this application and can take the extra wire (the cable between two-way switches is three core and earth instead of the standard twin core and earth—see page 266).

If your switch plate has several switches in it there shouldn't be any problem. You can normally control several lights from one dimmer providing you do not exceed the dimmer's total wattage rating and can fit the wires safely in the terminals at the back.

On the other hand you may prefer to control each light separately. You can buy two-gang dimmers which have two control knobs on a standard square plate, and bigger switch plates with more control knobs are also available. But remember that unless you are prepared to cut a hole for a larger metal switch box in the wall you should buy a dimmer whose plate is the same size as your present conventional light switch.

It's important to check the depth of your present switch box. Some dimmers won't fit in shallow plaster-depth boxes, others are slimline fittings. Switch off the mains at the

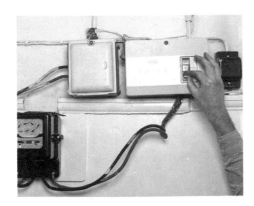

1 *Make absolutely sure that you shut off the main switch before opening the existing switch*

2 *Double check by testing the light before you unscrew the faceplate of the switch*

3 *With the switch opened, use a mains tester screwdriver to check again for live wires*

4 *If the earth wire is bare, disconnect it and slip on a length of green and yellow sheathing*

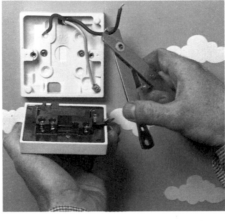

5 *Test fit the wires against the dimmer switch then trim them back and strip them as necessary*

6 *Connect the mains feed and switch line wires to the terminals specified by the makers*

7 *On this example, you switch on and then vary the brightness via a separate rotary control*

your dimmer, make sure its thickness (excluding the faceplate) doesn't exceed this depth.

Fitting a one-way dimmer

First of all switch off the house power supply at the main fuse board or consumer unit. The whole job shouldn't take you more than half an hour, so there's no danger of the fridge or freezer defrosting seriously. Electricity is dangerous so follow a strict safety procedure before you disconnect the existing light switch. Make sure that the switch you are about to replace really is disconnected by trying it. Then, with the switch safely isolated from the mains, unscrew the two screws on either side of the faceplate and gently pull it away from its mounting box. From now onwards check all the bare wires you come across with a mains tester screwdriver. You hold the bare blade of the insulated screwdriver against the bare wire and touch the plate built into the end. If the small neon in the handle lights up you have a live wire. Don't touch it until you've made sure that the main switch on the fuseboard really has been turned off.

Using a small screwdriver, unscrew the terminals to free the attached red and black wires from the back of the switch plate. It is likely that the copper earth wire is screwed to the metal box. There's no need to disconnect this unless it has been left bare. If it has, it's a good idea to sleeve the earth before you refit the switch (it cuts down the risk of short circuits in a crowded switch box). To this end, unscrew the terminal and remove the wire. Cut a length of green and yellow striped PVC sleeving to slip over the wire—leaving enough bare at the end to connect to the box terminal screw.

fuse board or consumer unit and then unscrew the switch faceplate. Pull the switch out far enough to insert a ruler and gauge the depth of the box. When you buy

Now check that the new dimmer switch fits comfortably in the backing box. If all is well, loosen the screws on the back of the switch and test-fit the wires. If the new terminals are less deep than those of the old switch, trim the wires so that the insulation butts up hard against the outside of the terminals with no bare wire visible.

When the wires have been trimmed correctly connect them to the switch. Always follow the maker's instructions about which terminals to use. In a one-way switch both the red and black cable covers are 'live' because the switch is simply a break in the live part of the lighting circuit. For the purposes of following the manufacturer's instructions treat the red wire as the 'feed' from the mains and the black wire (the switch line) as its extension to the light. As a reminder, put a short piece of red tape around the black wire to indicate that this too is live when the switch is on. Finally, screw the PVC sheathed earth wire to the backing box.

If you have bought a metal faced dimmer switch there will be an earth terminal on the back. Make sure that this is connected to the earth terminal on the metal box using an offcut of cable core. Like the cable earth wire, it's best to sheath it in green and yellow PVC sleeving.

Screw on the dimmer switch. The manufacturers will supply the screws and these should fit into the threaded adjustable lugs on the sides of the metal box without difficulty.

When the screws are almost home, adjust the switch plate so that it is square then tighten them up hard.

Faultfinding: Turn the switch off, rotating the knob anticlockwise until it clicks. Now turn on again at the mains and check that your new dimmer operates correctly. If it doesn't, go through this checklist below until you manage to track down the fault.
• Are your other lighting and power circuits working?
• Have you more than one main switch and have you switched them all on?
• If you have fuses has one of them blown?
• If you have miniature circuit breakers, has one of them been tripped off?

If the problem is clearly only with the circuit you have been working on, switch off at the mains again, following the same procedure as before, and unscrew the dimmer switch.

Check that the wires are tightly fixed in their correct terminals, that there are no loose wires in the box and that no bare wires can touch each other or (the earth wire excepted) the metal box.

Check that the back of the dimmer is not fouling a wire or that a screw or a sharp edge has not accidentally cut the insulation to wires. Replace, switch on at the mains and retest the switch.

Two-way and multi-gang dimmers

Two-way and multi-gang dimmers are fitted in exactly the same way as a simple one-way

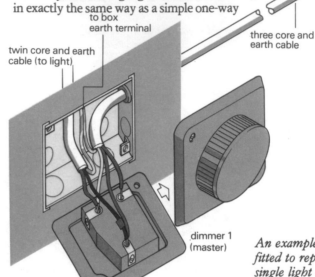

one, but the extra wires involved can cause confusion.

Two-way switch systems are commonly used for lighting the stairs—they're controlled from either the hall or landing. When you dismantle either switch in a two-way system you'll find three core and earth cable instead of the usual two core type. Three core has a red wire, which you can regard as live 'feed' from the mains, and yellow and blue wires which distribute the 'feed' to the light itself between the switch that you are working on and the other two-way switch.

The maker's instructions should be quite specific about which wire goes to which terminal on the new dimmers, so fitting them should present no problems. There is nothing to stop you fitting a dimmer in place of one switch in a two-way system and retaining the existing conventional switch on the other part of the circuit.

If the dimmer is replacing a switch controlling two or more lights on the same circuit, the only restriction is that the dimmer's wattage rating isn't exceeded. Similarly, you can replace a double switch with a single dimmer, although you will of

An example of how two dimmers can be fitted to replace two switches controlling a single light source such as a landing light. It is vital that the red, blue and yellow cores on the three core cable go to the same terminals in both switches—the maker's instructions will specify which they are. The mains feed (red) and switch line (black) cores of the two core light cable connect to the master only. The earths run to the box terminal.

Bear in mind that dimmer switches can be fitted to all types of ordinary lights, but should not be fitted to fluorescent lights. Read the manufacturer's instructions carefully to ensure that the switch you buy matches the output of the light.

course sacrifice individual control: simply make sure that the same wires from each cable are connected to the terminals specified in the instructions.

Problems arise if you try to fit more than two sets of wires to a single dimmer—the terminals simply aren't large enough—and in this case you'd be better to opt for a multigang dimmer retaining individual control. As with all multi-gang switches, the red ('mains live feed') wires from each cable are connected to a common terminal (usually marked C) on the switch backing box. The black switch lines should be connected to separate terminals, one for each control knob.

NEW CEILING LIGHT

The lighting arrangements in many houses amount to just one ceiling rose in the centre of each room with a single pendant lampholder hanging from it by a length of flex. But if you want something better looking or more efficient, you need to know both what's available and just what's involved in making the wiring connections.

Depending on where you go to buy your lighting, you may find a small confusion over the terms used: what you probably know as light bulbs are more correctly called **lamps**; the bits they fit (or screw) into are known as **lampholders** and the whole fitting (excluding the lamp) is known as a **luminaire**. For a normal pendant light the bit hanging on the bottom of the flex is both a lampholder and a luminaire.

Whatever you call them, there's an incredible range of light fittings. A visit to a specialist light shop (or the lighting department of a large department store) or looking through some of the larger lighting catalogues will leave you reeling with the choice. The light fittings that you choose are mainly a matter of taste and design, but the fittings available do divide into a number of types, each of which has its merits and each of which has its own requirements for fitting and wiring up.

Pendant lights: The normal type of pendant light consists of a plastic heat-resisting lampholder suspended from the ceiling rose by a length of two-core flex. (Metal lampholders are not common, but if you have one, bear in mind that any exposed metal parts must be earthed. Alternatively, replace with a plastic type). There's not much you can do with these to make them more interesting apart from choosing interesting lampshades.

Decorative pendant lights: These include lanterns, harp-lamps (styled like old-fashioned oil lamps) and chandeliers. The majority of these will be too heavy to suspend from the flex attached to the ceiling rose and will need some kind of additional or alternative support. With many decorative pendants, the supporting chain and associated hook will be an integral part of the fitting's design. Rise and fall lights should be treated in the same way and fixed to a BESA box mounted in the ceiling.

Spotlights: Spotlights for mounting on ceilings can be single spots or two or three spots mounted on a baseplate or a stalk. Spotlights can produce interesting effects

because the light can be directed. The effect created will depend on the type of lamp (bulb) fitted—an ordinary light bulb (GLS or General Lighting Service lamp), a wide-beam Internally-silvered (IS) lamp or a narrow-beam Crown-silvered (CS) lamp. Spotlights generally have an open baseplate which will mean a special fitting must be used at the ceiling to replace the existing ceiling rose.

Track lights: This system, which is popular in shops, enables a number of spotlights or other lights to be used. The tracks, which are attached to the ceiling, have continuous conductors inside them and the lights are mounted on adaptors which 'plug' in to the track using special clips.

You can position the lights anywhere you like on the track which only needs to be connected to the electricity supply at one end. There are two types of track: single-circuit where all the lights go on and off together, and multi-circuit where you can switch them on and off in two or three groups. Both types come in a variety of lengths and are available in kits.

If you're replacing a single pendant light with track lighting, be careful not to overload the circuit—lighting circuits are generally designed to cope with up to 12 lamps, assuming that each one is 100W. If the number of lamps you intend using is going to overload the existing circuits, you'll have to run a new circuit from a spare fuseway in the consumer unit. If there is no spare, fit an additional consumer unit.

Track lighting can be fed with flex from

★ WATCH POINT ★

If you want to use track lighting in conjunction with your existing rose, why not pick a colourful curly flex? You can buy curly flex from specialist dealers.

the existing ceiling rose. But if you want to conceal the connections you'll have to remove the existing ceiling rose and, if you've got loop-in wiring, replace it with a junction box.

Fluorescent lights: In terms of light output per unit of electricity, fluorescent lights are by far the most efficient type of light—most other lamps generate more heat than they do light. Fluorescent lights are particularly suitable for kitchens as they throw light over a large area, but the tubes tend to be rather 'cold' in appearance for other rooms.

It's essential that fluorescent lights are **earthed**, which may mean running an earth wire from the consumer unit or electricity board earth—*not* from water or gas pipes—if your lighting circuit doesn't have an earth conductor. Otherwise, the wiring restriction is similar to track lighting (above) except that ordinary dimmer switches can't be used with fluorescent lighting and will have to be replaced by ordinary switches.

Enclosed lights: This type of light is a must in bathrooms, where special safety provisions apply. Most bathroom lights are fairly ordinary globe lights, but there is a range of opal and crystal enclosed lights suitable for living rooms. These will all require the ceiling rose to be removed.

Downlighters: This type of light, which gives a narrow downward beam is mostly used in kitchens, particularly over work surfaces. The downlighter itself is usually in the form of a cylindrical tube which is fully or partially recessed into the ceiling. This means that you cannot use an existing ceiling rose and that you will have to engage in more complicated wiring arrangements as well as cutting holes in the ceiling.

What you need

Apart from normal electrical tools—wire cutter and strippers, pliers, cutting knife and a selection of screwdrivers—you'll need some woodworking tools for cutting and drilling holes in wood and either plasterboard or lath-and-plaster ceilings, depending on what you've got. A stepladder will be handy for obvious reasons.

The electrical accessories you'll need apart from the new light fitting itself will depend on the type of light you are installing. Check through Installing the light, to find out what you need. You'll almost certainly want some plaster or cellulose filler for making good the ceiling if you remove a ceiling rose.

Regulations

In the UK all wiring in houses should be carried out in accordance with the IEE Wiring Regulations. One regulation that is particularly important for replacing ceiling lights is the requirement that the wires and connections to them must be made inside an incombustible enclosure. A ceiling rose meets the requirement, but you're not allowed to have wires waving around in the space above the ceiling since this constitutes a possible fire risk.

Understanding your wiring

Modern lighting circuits are radial—that is the wiring starts at the fuse box (or, more commonly, consumer unit) where it is protected by a 5 amp fuse or circuit breaker and goes from one lighting point to the next until it comes to the last one where it terminates. Normally there will be two lighting circuits in a house—one for the upstairs lights (run in the loft space) and one for the downstairs lights (run between the downstairs ceiling and the upstairs floorboards).

The systems used for the wiring are—**junction box** (also called joint box) and **loop-in**.

In the junction box system, the 'circuit' consists of a cable going from the consumer unit to each box in turn. If this system is fitted, you should be able to spot the boxes.

Each junction box has a supply cable IN and a supply cable OUT—except the last one on the circuit which has only one supply cable going in. There are two other cables connected in to each junction box: one to the light switch and one to the ceiling rose which supplies the light fitting. As

two-core and earth cable is used, the black return wire from the switch is usually sleeved with red PVC insulating tape inside the junction box to show that it is live.

The terminals in the **junction box** are wired as follows:
1. Live supply IN (red).
   Live supply OUT (red).
   Live supply to switch (red).
2. Neutral IN (black).
   Neutral OUT (black).
   Neutral to ceiling rose (black).
3. Live return from switch
   (black & red sleeve).
   Live supply to rose (red).
4. All earth wires (bare & green/yellow sleeve).

The ceiling rose for junction box wiring uses just three terminals—one each for live, neutral and earth. The flex for the light is connected to the appropriate terminals: brown to live, blue to neutral and green/yellow to earth.

In the loop-in system of wiring lights, the ceiling rose also acts as the junction box and all the connections are made there. So there should be three cables in the ceiling rose: one IN, one OUT (except on the last rose in the circuit) and one to the switch. The connections are exactly the same as for the junction box given above except the light flex replaces the cable to the rose.

You can easily tell which system you've got by **turning off the supply** at the mains (it is not enough to turn off the light switch) and then looking inside a ceiling rose and counting the cables coming into it. If there's only one, you've got junction box wiring; if there are three, you've got loop-in wiring. If there are two, it is either the last

The wiring in a junction box rose (below left) is straightforward; a loop-in rose (below) acts as a junction box

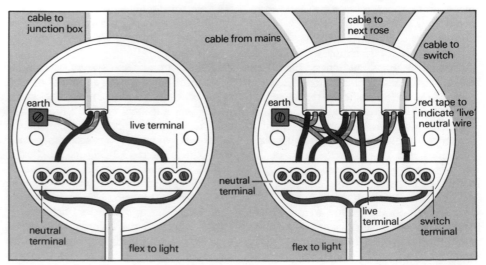

rose on a loop-in system or is a junction box system with an extra light run off the same switch. If it's not obvious, check another rose.

Removing a ceiling rose

You probably won't be able to connect the new light directly to the existing ceiling rose and so you'll have to remove it.

Removing a ceiling rose wired with the **junction box** system is straightforward, since there is only one cable to worry about. Once you've turned off the electricity at the mains and disconnected the existing pendant, the main problem is likely to be in unscrewing the cap of the ceiling rose which may be gummed up with paint. Since you're removing the rose, it won't matter too much if you damage it. Now is the time to check that your wiring is sound. If the cable insulation has started to perish or go brittle, don't go any further but consider having your house rewired—electrical faults are a fire hazard.

If you're using the length of cable that's left poking out of the ceiling—for a fluorescent light or track lighting—there's nothing more to do. But if you're shortening or lengthening the cable to reposition the light fitting, you'll have to continue the work from upstairs—or in the loft, which is much easier.

Shortening isn't much of a problem; lengthening either means putting in an extra junction box (see Fitting a junction box) above the old ceiling rose or running a new length of cable from the junction box for that light.

After you've pulled the cable through the ceiling and done one of these things, make good the hole in the ceiling with plaster or cellulose filler.

★ WATCH POINT ★

If the hole is very large, push in some screwed-up paper or wire mesh for the plaster to hang on to.

Removing a **loop-in** ceiling rose is a different story: there'll probably be three cables to cope with. To avoid getting them confused when you unscrew the terminals, it's best to twist them together if they come out of the same terminal block. As an extra precaution, work out which cable is which and label them before pulling them up above the ceiling and re-connecting them to a junction box—see Fitting a junction box.

Installing the light

How you fix the light to the ceiling and wire it up will depend on the design. Most lights come complete with a ceiling plate but this may or may not include terminals for the supply connection which must be made in an incombustible enclosure.

A consideration worth bearing in mind before you fix the light is its weight: the maximum weight you can suspend on a 3 amp flex from a standard ceiling rose is 2 kg—anything greater than 2 kg and you must install a special support. But whatever the weight, play safe and attach the fitting to the underside of a joist.

Close-mounted fittings: These are the easiest type to wire up if you have junction box wiring. First screw the support bracket to the joist and then wire up the cable direct to the terminals in the back of the baseplate.

However, if you have loop-in wiring there will be no facility to connect up all the cables and you must fit a junction box to the side of the joist above and lead off a separate cable to the light.

Track lighting: Both track and fluorescent lights must be adequately supported. This inevitably means finding where the joists are.

★ WATCH POINT ★

The simplest way of locating the joists is by tapping the ceiling with the handle of a screwdriver—a hollow note indicates a void, a solid noise a joist.

You can run the fitting either along or across the joists. If you choose to run it along a joist, you can screw the frame directly into the timber—but make sure that there's enough space to get the cable down through the ceiling.

If you decide to run the fitting across the joists, you will probably find that the screw holes don't coincide with the joists. Get over this problem by screwing an appropriate length of 50mm × 25mm batten to the joists. You can then fix the fitting to the batten.

Track lighting fittings have no facility for wiring loop-in cables so you will have to fit a four-way junction box to an adjacent joist and wire up accordingly—see Fitting a junction box.

Light fittings without terminal blocks: If there are no terminal blocks at the back of the fitting—whichever type you have

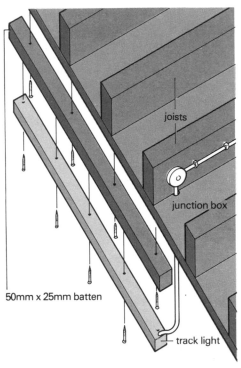

If you decide to run a track system across the joists (above), screw a batten to the underside of the joists first and then fix the track to this

got—you must make the necessary connections to the supply in an 'incombustible enclosure'. The best type is a BESA box (pronounced 'beeza'). This is a plastic terminal conduit box which can be recessed into the ceiling. Choose a BESA box which best suits your location—some have cable outlets in the side, others through the top.

It's best to mount the BESA box to a batten which is fixed between two joists.

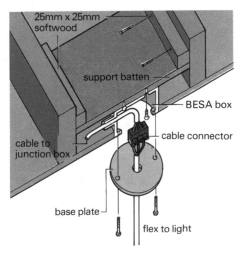

The best way of fixing a recessed BESA box between two joists is to screw it to a support board which bridges the gap. Use two offcuts to join the board to the joists

First locate the joists and then mark the outline of the box on the ceiling between them. Use a padsaw for cutting.

Screw the BESA box to the batten before fixing it in place between the joists. You will need someone else in the room below to make sure that the box is flush with the ceiling.

The electrical connections in the BESA box are made using a 'chocolate bar' cable connector. In theory, both loop-in and junction box connections can be made in the box. However, although you won't have any problem if you have a junction box system, you will probably find that there isn't enough room in the box to make all the connections for a loop-in system. If this is the case, install a junction box nearby and then lead a cable from this to the BESA box where you can connect the cable to the light flex.

Rise and fall lights: More often than not, rise and fall lights are designed to be fitted directly to a BESA box.

Once the BESA box is in place, all you have to do is screw on the bracket, hook on the fitting and wire up the connections.

Chandeliers and heavy pendant lights: These are sometimes sold complete with a hook and bracket but no terminal block. If this is the case, it's best to fit a BESA box for the connections and then fit the bracket and hook to an adjacent joist.

However, there is a device called the Ceiling Master Unit specifically designed to support light fittings (if you have loop-in wiring, you must install a junction box as well).

The Ceiling Master comes in two parts: one incorporates a terminal block for the cable and is screwed to the ceiling; the other slots into it and has a hook for the light fitting together with a second terminal block for the flex. When the two parts are slotted together, electrical contact is made by three spring loaded pins onto three contacts. The Ceiling Master comes in several different finishes.

Fitting a junction box

Junction boxes allow you to tap the power supply from either a loop-in or junction box circuit—safely and securely.

Fitting one is more awkward than difficult and, if there is a room above where you want to install the new light, you will inevitably have to lift floorboards.

Before you start on the job, double check that you have turned off the electricity supply at the mains.

You can fit the junction box directly to a joist—which is more convenient—or to a 75mm × 25mm batten which straddles the void.

How you connect up the cables will depend on the type of lighting circuit you have—junction box or loop-in. The wiring methods are illustrated in the diagrams below. If you want a longer cable in a junction box system, either lead a new cable from the old box or add an extension to the existing cable—making the connections in a three-way junction box.

Points to watch out for are that you use 1mm two core and earth cable; that the bare earth wires are sleeved with yellow/green insulation; and that the neutral return wire from the switch is taped red to show that it is live.

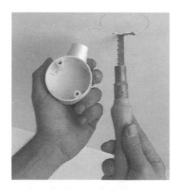

1 *Pencil the outline of the box on the ceiling and cut the shape with a padsaw*

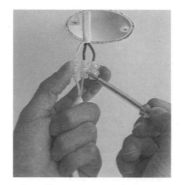

2 *After mounting the BESA box, use a connector strip to join the flex to the cable*

3 *In a Ceiling Master, wire up terminal blocks before slotting the sections together*

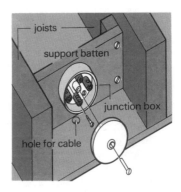

4 *If the hole for the ceiling rose lies between two joists, fit a support board*

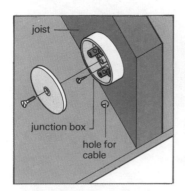

5 *Whenever possible, you will find it best to fix the box to the side of a joist*

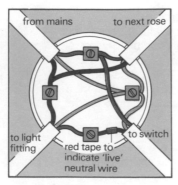

6 *In a loop-in system, install a four-way junction box to replace the old rose*

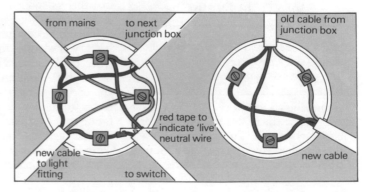

7 *There are two options in a junction box circuit; either run a new cable from the existing junction box (left) or connect an extension to the old cable in a three-way box (right)*

ILLUMINATED CEILING

All too often, ceilings are simply ignored when it comes to planning decor—a great pity, since most of them are a lot less than perfect. Perhaps the ceiling is too high—a common fault in smaller rooms or bathrooms—or is cracked and marked, or maybe it has a rather old fashioned or unsightly heavy cornice.

One of the obvious advantages of an illuminated ceiling is that it enables you to install more diffused, or exciting, lighting—downlighting spotlights, fluorescent tubes (plain or with coloured sleeves) or swivel eye ball lights can all be incorporated. But with different panels and lighting effects to choose from you can, in effect, design your own quite individual ceiling.

If your ceiling is wider than the largest size in the kit range of your choice—it's worth checking because they do vary—you can usually order additional sections of frame to fill out the extra space. In wider rooms, it may also be necessary to give additional support to the structure. The manufacturer's instructions will give guidance as to the spacing of any such supports and indicate the method used. Special brackets normally strengthen extra joins while suspension wires support the span at other points, these being attached to the original ceiling.

Safety is an important consideration, so always choose a kit with panels which have passed the British Standard fire tests (in the UK)—especially if you are putting a ceiling in the kitchen.

Apart from the kit, you need accessories for special lighting effects; most importantly, fluorescent fittings to provide diffused illumination across the entire ceiling. Both these, and direct-light swivel spots which can be recessed into the acoustic type of panel, must be ordered separately. A number of smaller components you'll need for the ceiling assembly must also be specially ordered once you've planned the spaces involved—items like wallplugs, joining brackets, support wires and clips to hold the panels securely in position. You may also need a fine toothed hacksaw to cut the metal supports, plus an electric drill.

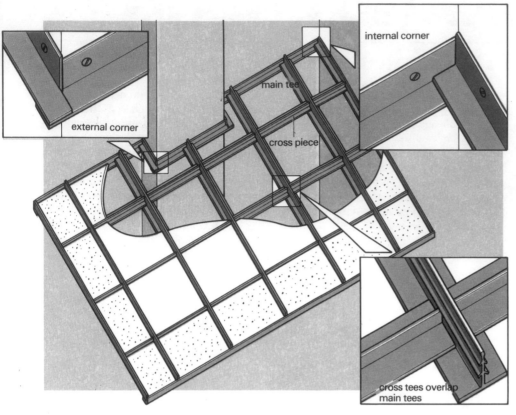

external corner

internal corner

main tee

cross piece

cross tees overlap
main tees

Illuminated ceiling kits consist of a series of translucent or insulating panels laid on an aluminium framework. The main tees are supported by a side framework screwed to the walls; the cross pieces rest on the main tees. There is normally no need to secure the panels—they simply rest in place on top of the aluminium framework. To avoid high spots of light, the fluorescent tubes should be positioned so they run directly above the main tees

Planning considerations

The first thing to consider is the height of your new ceiling. Building regulations in the UK require a minimum of 2.3m from the floor over at least half the area in a habitable room. Because of the fixing and lighting requirements, the illuminated ceiling must be at least 100mm below the level of the existing one (50mm will suffice if you use the acoustic panels without lighting).

Bear in mind that the height of the top of the existing window recesses may affect your intended ceiling height—you must install the ceiling *above* window recesses to avoid unnecessary work, or blocking the light and even creating changes in level.

Measure the ceiling, make an accurate scale plan, then divide it into squares to represent the panels. Some firms supply a ready-squared diagram as part of their order form so that you can transfer your ceiling measurements on to it. Always check your measurements twice.

If your ceiling will not take an exact number of whole panels—and the chances are that it won't—calculating the number of panels you need is slightly more tricky. You don't want to have part panels at one side of your ceiling only—they should be evenly spaced at both borders for a balanced look. So find the centre of the room by measuring across between walls. Take recesses into account—the centre of the new ceiling should be centred on the widest part of the room.

You don't normally need to provide details about the framework when you order. Give the firm the ceiling size and they will send you appropriate framework.

Next decide on the colour, pattern and texture of panels you want. Here, bear in mind the existing decor and colours in your room and the finish of the framework you've chosen. You don't have to use the same type of panel across the entire grid. The whole ceiling can be covered with translucents, you can have a patchwork effect by mixing them with acoustics, or you might want illumination in the central portion and opaques round the borders. And you can mix and match any number of different colours, too.

Supports: How many and what type you'll need depends on the kind of kit you have opted for—so check the manufacturer's brochure for distances between supports (it could be anything from 1,220mm to 3m).

If a system of brackets is used at joins in the main framework, calculate how many you'll need by looking at your measurements and the maximum length in which the components are supplied. Wire supports are available in packets of ten, each one 1m long. Here again, work out how many you need by taking the length of your main runners and checking how many supports are recommended for that length. Then you must multiply by the number of main tees you have in your framework.

Screw eyes to secure the suspension wires to the ceiling must also be ordered—sufficient to cope with the wires and perhaps a couple of extra ones.

Lighting: Allow about 1.5 watts per square foot of ceiling when working out how many lights you'll need.

Decide now whether you want to have all fluorescents or a mixture of these and downlights round the edges, for example. If you pick fluorescents make sure you get the correct type of fitting for your ceiling level—batten units with a full-length bracket-type fixing are best for a drop of 150mm or more, compact units which have the tubes fixed directly to the ceiling with clips are useful for lesser drops.

Ventilation: To avoid condensation problems later insert a plastic ventilation grille into a panel at either end of the ceiling.

Preparing the ceiling

Before you begin to prepare the existing ceiling, clear the room as much as you can. Take out any furniture which can be moved, cover the rest and either take up floorcoverings or cover them with a large sheet of polythene or a dust sheet.

First, find the joists and mark them so that if you want these for fixing support wires or lights later, you won't have to waste time trying to locate them. Take a screwdriver and tap the ceiling with the handle. When you hear a dull thud instead of a hollow sound, you know you've hit the joist. Mark it in pencil and then proceed to locate the others. You'll find in most cases that joists are 400mm to 450mm apart.

Next, check on the condition of your ceiling and decide whether some renovation work is required at this point. Fill any cracks with fine surface interior filler and

sand smooth. If the paint or whitewash
appears to be flaking off in parts, rub it down
and give the whole area a coat of stabilising
solution.

When this had dried—or if your ceiling
hasn't required an application of stabilising
solution—give it a coat of brilliant white
emulsion paint (two coats are even better).
The white paint helps to reflect a maximum
amount of light through the panels of the
new false ceiling.

The next marking up job is for the side
framework to be fixed round the walls. You
should have already decided at what height
to install your illuminated ceiling. Don't
consider changing the level at this point
because you will already have ordered the
appropriate light fittings for the level you
originally chose.

Mark where the line is to go, after
measuring carefully. Continue the line right
round all four walls of the room. It's
extremely important to get it absolutely
horizontal, so don't rush this marking
job—use a spirit level as you go along and
use a straight edge (like a timber batten) to
rule the line. Use as long a spirit level as you
can. If you haven't got a builder's level, or
cannot hire one, simply tie a long batten to a
small level and use that. Using a small level
on its own invites awkward discrepancies.

Light fixings

Before you start putting up the ceiling
framework, the lights must be positioned
and then wired up. Mark the positions
where these are to go. If they are not near

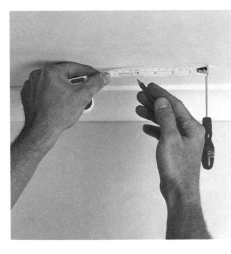

*1 Locate the first joist, mark its
position with a bradawl and measure
to next joist*

*2 Establish the lowest point of the
ceiling then mark round the walls for
the side frame*

*3 Snap chalk lines to show where the
tees fit. Light fittings should always
align with them*

joists, drill the ceiling plaster carefully
where you have marked it, insert a toggle
type cavity plug and screw the fittings into
the ceiling. The clips which hold the
compact type units will require similar
plugs so that you can screw their clips in
place.

If the gap between the old ceiling and the
new is less than 100mm, position the lights
where the struts of the frame will go to
avoid any risk of overheating and damage to
panels. You can check the relevant strut
positions by referring back to your original
scale plan of the ceiling.

The next step is the wiring and since the
light units are all pre-wired this should be
fairly straightforward. First switch off the
electricity at the mains. Some pre-planning
is useful here so that the supply is disconnected for the minimum length of time.

Undo the cover of the ceiling rose and
take a look at what sort it is. If it is an old-
fashioned two terminal rose, remove it and
replace it with a three terminal junction
box. You simply undo the wood screws
which hold the rose to the ceiling and take
out the mains wires from the terminals.
Take care that you don't push the cable out
of reach into the ceiling cavity. There will
be some slack in the mains cable so ease it
out of the ceiling cavity.

Secure a three terminal junction box
where the rose was located, fastening the
mains wires, one to each of the terminal
blocks (if there is no earthing wire, you
must run one from the main consumer unit
to the junction boxes).

Modern type rose: If you have a modern
loop-in kind of ceiling rose (this will have a
terminal block with three separate sections
set into it and an earth connector), you can
leave it in place. Replace the pendant flex
with a length of new 1mm^2 twin and earth
cable and run this to a new junction box as
before. Make sure that the new box is firmly
secured to the ceiling.

In the case of either kind of rose, the new
cables run to the ballast starter units for
each fluorescent—fly leads connect the
starter ballasts to the individual tubes.
Secure the new cable to the ceiling with
cable clips at 300mm intervals.

Using this method the lights will be
controlled from the existing switching
arrangement.

Though the wires of the switch are
colour-coded (red for live, black for neutral)
they are both effectively 'live'. For future
reference and safety, stick red tape round
the ends of the black wire to indicate that it
is a 'switched live' wire.

Independent control of the lighting

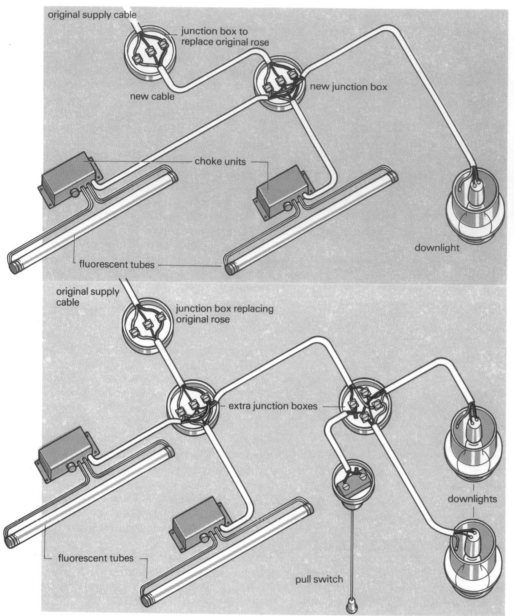

original supply cable

junction box to replace original rose

new cable

new junction box

choke units

fluorescent tubes

downlight

original supply cable

junction box replacing original rose

extra junction boxes

fluorescent tubes

downlights

pull switch

4 *Switch off the electricity, unscrew the rose cover and remove the pendant flex*

5 *Secure the heavy ballast units to a joist or a batten run between two joists*

Top: The simplest wiring arrangement. Take a feed for each light from a new junction box. The lights are then controlled by the original switch

Above: To give independent control of downlights, you can incorporate a pull switch in our wiring arrangement. You will need to buy an additional junction box for this, however

circuits can be achieved by duplicating and extending the above wiring circuit with additional four-terminal junction boxes. A cable is taken from the three-terminal junction box to each of any number of four terminal junction boxes (see diagram above). A pull-cord switch is wired into each four-terminal box in the manner

described above. Finally the units to be controlled by each pull switch are wired into the junction box.

Wiring for the downlighters should be done at the same as that for fluorescents although the lights will not be connected until the ceiling panels are added.

Installing the framework

Start with the right angled edge trim round the walls. Measure the distance along the line you have already marked out, from corner to corner on the first wall—measure twice to be sure you get it right.

Having established the length of metal angle you'll need, cut it with a hacksaw, filing off any rough edges. Sections which

6 *Run the cable from the ballast unit to a new junction box and make the connections*

7 *Go round the wall marking the fixing positions for the side framework. Make sure they are absolutely level*

8 *Position the main tees. For accuracy use the cross tees or panels as a spacing guide*

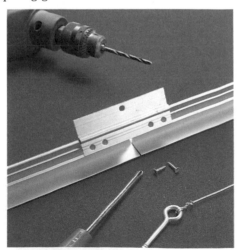

9 *You may need to extend the main tees. If so, use the brackets supplied by the manufacturer*

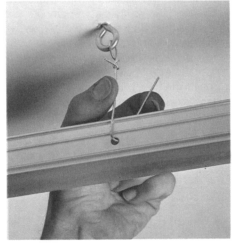

10 *Add suspension wire supports as required. Fix the screw eye into the nearest joist*

butt together should be cut straight using a try square as a guide.

When you have cut the first piece, drill holes in it at 550mm intervals, file off any burrs then place the section against the wall along the line. Mark the hole positions, remove the frame and drill for fixing with suitable wallplugs. For solid walls any kind of plastic or wallplug will do; for stud partition walls get the cavity fixing with a butterfly flange. As you put up each section, do a quick check with a spirit level to make sure the alignment is correct.

Main tees: With the edge support installed, add the main tees. To avoid joins, place these across the shortest span of the room.

Start by marking their positions on the edge framing. Unless the ceiling is a regular shape that matches a whole number of 600mm square panels then you will have to cut panels at the borders, so you must take account of this in marking for the tees.

Measure between opposite walls, find the centre point and work from that. Use either a cross tee or a panel to check the spacings between components as you go.

When the points are marked, measure between corresponding marks on opposite walls so that you can cut and install the first tee. Before you do any cutting, check the manufacturer's instructions to make sure that there are no special indents or slotting-in points in the main tees to accept the shorter cross tees.

If the manufacturer recommends suspension wire supports over specific distances (this varies according to the type of framework), add these as you go along. Drill a hole in the tee at the recommended distance, loop the wire through and attach it to a screw eye fixed into a ceiling joist at the nearest appropriate point.

Joining framework

Joins on the main tees must be supported by brackets. These will not be so obvious when the ceiling is completed, but joins on the edge trim—either in a straight run or at corners—will be visible from below, so it's worth taking the time and trouble to achieve a really neat join. There are different ways of cutting for different joins.
For a straight length: To join two straight lengths you need a butt joint. Make sure that the angle on both pieces is 90°. Use a square as a guide and mark your cutting line, preferably with a metal scribe or with a very sharp pencil.

Support the section to be cut on a stable surface. It's best if you can sit it firmly against a wooden stop or bench hook to prevent the angle moving.

Cut along the line with a fine toothed hacksaw—through both faces at once. Then take a fine flat file and remove rough edges and burrs.
At a corner: You have a choice of two cutting and joining methods here. Use an overlap join for an internal corner—it's made in the same way as a butt joint, except that you measure up to remove extra material to make the overlap.

Adding the panels

Once the main tees are in position, the cross tees and panels can be slotted into place.

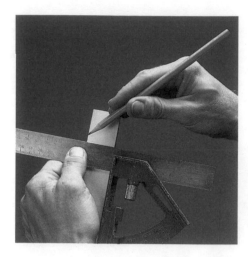

To get a true 90° cut for a butt joint use a square and with a metal scribe mark your cutting line

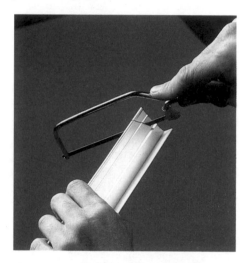

Cut across with a fine toothed hacksaw. Then cut the rib back slightly so it fits easily

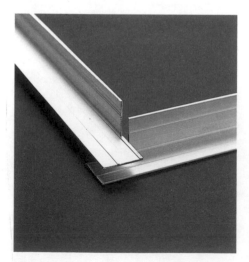

External joints should overlap. They require careful marking and cutting for neat results

Remember that you will, no doubt, have part panels at the border so start with the cross tees and panels at the centre of the room and work outward. First find the centre point.

Mark the position of your cross tees from the centre point and then slot in a cross tee and its panel—the panel generally sits on top of the tees. Check instructions on the exact way to fit the cross tees—some slot into the main tees, others just sit neatly on top of them.

You can, of course, fit all the cross tees first and then slot in the panels, but since you will almost certainly have to move the tee to position the panel it's usually easier to put in one cross tee, one panel, slide the next cross tee into place, put in another panel and so on.

Although not essential, panel clips will hold the panels securely in place, so if you've ordered them with your kit, use them as you proceed from panel to panel.

Border panels: Cut these to size after the central section is complete. Measure the gap between the centre of the last tee and the edge trim on the wall.

Don't, whatever you do, cut them too small or they may simply fall through the framework. Transfer these measurements onto the panels using a felt-tipped pen. Measure twice, cut once. Don't assume every panel to be the same measurement; do each one individually.

Ventilation: It's worth providing ventilation with two plastic grilles. Install them in complete tiles once the panels are in place and you're sure that they all fit.

Downlights: To fit these in acoustic panels, take out the appropriate panels and cut a hole in the centre of each fractionally smaller than the light's external diameter.

Cut the hole with a padsaw, smooth the edges and then put it back in position on the ceiling grid. Cut two wooden battens to fit across the top of the main runner on each side of the hole, then gently push the lamp through the hole you've cut and adjust its fixing prong so that they sit securely on the battens. Assemble the rest of the light and it can then be wired to the connections which you have already prepared.

★ WATCH POINT ★

Try to keep the panels clean—PVC ones in particular mark easily. Wear a pair of cotton gloves or use pads of cloth to hold the edges as you slot in the panels.

11 *Lay the panels in position adjusting the cross tees for each one as you work if necessary*

12 *Use a padsaw to cut acoustic panels ready for downlights or ventilation grilles*

13 *If you need to cut translucent panels, cut oversize and fold up edge as a supporting rib*

INSTALL A SHAVER UNIT

For those who use an electric razor, it's unfortunate that it isn't just a simple matter of plugging the device into the most convenient three-pin socket outlet. Instead, it has to be operated from a special point which will accept the continental-style two-pin plug that is invariably moulded onto the end of its flex.

Rather than installing a proper outlet unit, you may be tempted to buy a three-pin socket converter. But at best this can only be a temporary measure. You still won't be able to use the razor in the bathroom—you aren't allowed any sockets there—and in other rooms most sockets will be at floor level, which means that if you use the razor standing up in front of a mirror, then the flex could well be over-strained. Sooner or later you'll find it makes sense to install a proper shaver outlet unit, or units, which are permanently connected to the fixed wiring of the house.

Types of shaver outlet

Outlet units come in several forms and the terminology used to describe them sometimes varies among the manufacturers. What you must be aware of, though, is that there's one type that can be used in any room, including bathrooms and cloakrooms, and another, which must not be used in a bathroom. So when you go to buy a shaver socket, make doubly sure you get the right one.

The reason for having two types has to do with the UK IEE wiring regulations regarding the use of appliances in bathrooms (and in cloakrooms with showers); the regulations are geared to making it impossible for you to touch anything electric since there's always a chance that you'll have wet hands.

This is where the shaver outlet unit approved for bathroom use comes into its own: it contains a double-pole isolating transformer and the outlet supply is taken from the secondary winding, which is effectively separated from the earthed mains supply. This safety feature eliminates the risk of getting a shock in a 'wet environment' and also prevents anything but a razor from being powered by the outlet.

Shaver outlet units without a transformer are naturally cheaper, but they're definitely

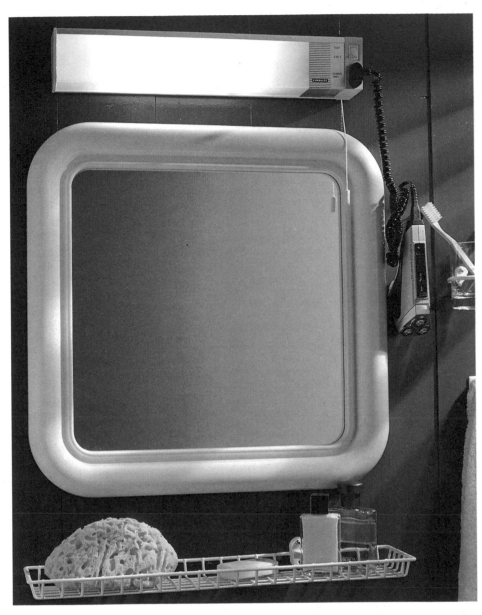

not safe if there's any chance of them being touched by wet hands.

Fitting a shaver socket and light

If you plan to install a shaver outlet in a bathroom, then it's well worth considering using one that also includes a light in a neat casing. From a practical point of view, bathroom lighting is often far from satisfactory —a central, close-mounted and encased fitting being the norm, with many fittings taking nothing more than a 60W bulb. For most of the time you're in the bathroom

you tend to stand with your back to this light, so washing, shaving or applying make-up are done in your own shadow. With a shaver socket/light unit fitted over a mirror you'll be able to get round this problem by providing excellent, close-quarters illumination.

Outwardly, all these units look similar, consisting of a tubular lamp and a socket—either at one end or underneath—for the razor. The light works independently of the socket and is operated by a short pull-cord switch. Some units use a small fluorescent tube with a 15W, 20W or 30W rating, while others use a 60W tungsten filament striplight. These lamps are nearly always

Four types of shaver socket. Only the two largest, each fitted with an isolating transformer, are suitable for use in bathrooms

covered by a diffuser, which spreads the light evenly and stops discomforting glare from the mirror.

Safety is the keynote with these units and nothing is left to chance. For example, even without a diffuser, special shields prevent you from touching the live parts of the lampholders when changing the fluorescent tube or striplight. In fact, as an added precaution the power to the light is often automatically cut off as the diffuser is lifted out or you start to turn the fluorescent tube to remove it.

Another point to look at on these units is the socket outlet itself. Some units have what's known as a dual-voltage facility, which means they can accommodate razors that run off 115 volts as well as those running on the standard European 230–250 volts. The socket on this type of unit has three holes arranged in a line, the centre hole being common to both voltages. Note that the safety shutters on the holes operate the on/off mechanism; when the razor plug is inserted, the power automatically comes on—there's no separate switch as there is on other units.

Standard shaver outlet units

If you're happy with your lighting, or if the mirror you shave at extends well above head height, you might as well install a straight-forward shaver supply unit. These, too, are available with dual voltage facilities, the required voltage being determined by the

flick of a switch rather than the selection of the appropriate holes on the socket panel. (In fact, these are the only rocker switches that are allowed in a bathroom.) There's also a separate on/off switch.

The best place to site such a unit is probably at chest height and to one side of your shaving mirror.

All the units mentioned so far contain transformers and are therefore intended primarily for bathroom or cloakroom use—although this doesn't exclude them from being used elsewhere in the home. However, the fact that the units without transformers are cheaper makes them attractive alternatives for bedroom use. They also tend to be smaller, with less obtrusive faceplates, so they aren't such a conspicuous feature next to, say, a dressing table or dress mirror. Such outlets are protected by a 1 amp or 2 amp fuse and they, too, contain a thermal overload device to restrict their use to shavers.

Power supply

Finding a power source for a shaver socket is not difficult. For the types incorporating an isolating transformer and thermal overload device, you can take the power from the lighting circuit, the power circuit or a junction box linked to the power circuit.

If you are installing the shaver socket in your bathroom, it's probably easiest to take the power from that room's lighting circuit as the nearest power socket will certainly be outside the room. All you need to do is fit a three-way junction box close to a lighting cable (the 1.00mm² size), switch the power off and make the connections.

When taking the power from a power circuit, you can either take it direct from a socket or fit a junction box into the nearest power cable. Once again, however, always check that the power is off.

In all cases, double check your wiring before turning the power on again.

Shaver sockets not incorporating an isolating transformer must be wired via a fused connection unit and must never be installed in a bathroom.

If you're taking the power direct from a power socket, this calls for some care in organising your wiring. From the power socket to the fused connection unit, run 2.5mm² cable, but from the connection unit to the shaver socket, you must use the lower rating 1.00mm² cable.

To ensure that this has proper fuse protection, you need to fit the fused connection unit with a 3 amp fuse.

Tools and materials

In all cases, screwdrivers, wire strippers, a trimming knife and an electric drill with bits are essential items (note that for drilling through ceramic tiles you'll need a spear point bit). You're also certain to need a supply of wall fixings and screws.

For flush installations, have a club hammer, sharp bolster and cold chisel to hand, plus a bag of plaster for making good.

If you decide on surface mounting, you'll need plastic conduit (mini trunking) together with a means of fixing it—screws, masonry pins or impact adhesive.

Electrical connections to the shaver unit are made using 1.00mm² PVC sheathed two core and earth lighting cable. If you're wiring into the lighting circuit, you will also need a three way junction box and cable clips.

If your shaver unit has a transformer and you're wiring it on a direct spur from the main power circuit, buy 2.5mm² cable. Non-transformer units must be wired in 1.00mm² cable as far as a 3 amp fused connection unit and then on to the power circuits in 2.55m².

Fitting the unit

First decide exactly where the unit is to go and mark its position on the wall. From here onwards the procedure may vary depending on whether the cable and unit are flush or surface mounted.

If you're wiring into the lighting circuit, mark out the cable drop from the ceiling, using a plumbline to get a true vertical. Then push a bradawl into the junction of the ceiling and the wall on the proposed route to check that it isn't obstructed by a joist. Now bore a hole in the ceiling at your chosen point.

If the cable is to be surface mounted, cut a run of plastic conduit to stretch from the unit to the point where the cable enters the room and fix the back section to the wall.

For flush mounting, mark out the edges of a cable channel 18mm–25mm wide and also the recess for the unit's backing box with a sharp bolster chisel. Cut out the channel and recess, using both the bolster and a cold chisel to a depth of at least 38mm, then square off the sides.

Feed the cable through its entry point into the room. At the unit, allow about 150mm extra for connections at this end. Place the cable in its conduit and clip on the cover or lay it in the channel and replaster.

On a conventional shaver unit, lay the backing box against the wall and mark the fixing holes. Drill these to take plugs or cavity fixings as necessary.

On a combined light/socket unit, remove the diffuser and take out the lamp. Underneath there will either be fixing holes, or screws holding the body of the unit to its mounting bracket. Having gained access to the holes, place a spirit level on the unit to check that it is horizonal then mark their positions on the wall. Drill and plug the holes to take the appropriate fixings.

On a conventional unit, fit a rubber grommet to the cable entry hole, feed in the cable and screw the unit to the wall. On a light unit, check that the cable feeds in neatly through the entry point on the backing plate as you screw it home.

Connecting the power

If you're breaking into the lighting circuit in the roof space, finding an appropriate cable should be easy. At first floor level, you may have to raise a few floorboards before you track one down.

Lighting cables are going to be the only cables running in your roof space, so all you need do is select the one passing closest to the bathroom. Depending on how the wiring is arranged, you may need to lift some insulation to follow its route, so a pair of gloves will come in handy especially if your skin is sensitive to glass fibre.

If you have any doubts about a particular cable being part of the lighting circuit, simply trace its path. The cable should lead you to a ceiling rose. If you don't come to a ceiling rose quickly, find the nearest rose you can and then determine whether any of its cables will be suitable for your purposes.

If you are breaking into the lighting circuit running between the ground floor ceiling and the first floor, don't simply lift floorboards at random. The chances are that this will be awkward anyway—the degree of difficulty depending on the type of floor covering you have. Before you lift any boards, make sure you know where the nearest ceiling rose is.

Start wiring up at the unit end. Strip back the sheathing of the cable and then strip about 6mm of insulation from the live and neutral cores. The exposed earth core should be sheathed in green/yellow PVC tube. Connect the three cores to their appropriate terminals, following the maker's instructions. On some units you may find a two-part terminal block, to make the wiring easier.

1 *Begin wiring up by stripping back the cable's outer sheathing and about 6mm of insulation from the live and neutral cores*

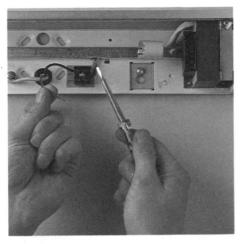

2 *Connect the wires to their appropriate terminals. Do not forget to sheath the exposed earth core in green/yellow plastic tubing*

3 *Keep the wiring neat when connecting to a flush unit. Slack wiring may get nipped by the backing box*

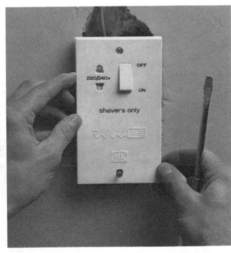

4 *With the connections completed, screw on the faceplate, check that it is level and then make good the chase*

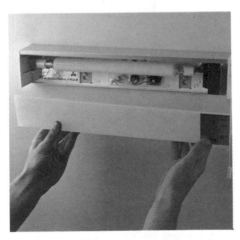

5 *If the fitting includes a strip light, complete the wiring, fit the bulb in place and then position the diffuser*

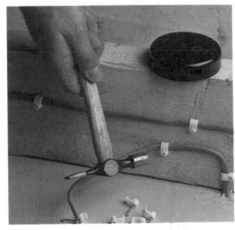

6 *Run the supply cable for the shaver socket to the lighting cable. Secure the new cable with clips at regular intervals*

7 *Fit a three way junction box to the joist in the most suitable position for your connections; then check that the power is off*

On a conventional unit, complete this end of the job by screwing on the faceplate and checking that it is switched off.

8 *Cut the lighting cable and connect it to the junction box terminals. You then simply connect the shaver socket supply cable*

On a combined light unit, refit the body or cover, followed by the lamp and then the diffuser.

At this stage turn off the electricity supply at the main switch and remove the fuse from the circuit on which you'll be working. Remember that you'll need a torch if you're making the connections in the dark recesses of a roof space.

Note that the instructions given here are for breaking into a lighting circuit; taking a spur from a ring or radial power circuit is covered in detail on pages 252–255. For a shaver unit, you have three basic choices when connecting into a power circuit. For units fitted with an isolating transformer, you can take the power directly from the mains circuit using 2.5mm² cable. To do this, you can either run cable to the back of an existing socket and connect in (see the diagram below left), or you can fit a junction box into an existing power cable and take the power from there. For units without an isolating transformer, you'll need to run 1.0mm² cable to a fused connection unit and then 2.5mm² cable onto the power circuit.

Clip the cable neatly to the joists as far as the break-in point on the existing power supply cable. When you reach it, screw a three way junction box to the nearest adjacent joist, then strip and prepare the cable as you did at the unit end.

Plan your location for the junction box carefully. Strictly speaking, it's not advisable to bury cables and junction boxes beneath insulation, as the materials may allow excess heat to build up. If you've fitted the minimum recommended depth of insulation, then screwing a junction box to the side of a joist may not be possible without partially covering it. The answer is to fit the junction box between joists using a batten.

To accommodate a junction box comfortably, you'll need at least a 75mm × 25mm batten and two 25mm × 25mm offcuts to use as joint blocks at either end. Screw the offcuts to the joists, and then screw the batten to the offcuts. Fit the junction box to the batten and then carry on with your wiring. The main point to note with this method is that you may need to reroute some of the existing cable slightly. If the existing cable is held in place with clips, remove some and check to see if there is enough slack or flexibility in the route to allow you to pass the existing cable close to the new junction box.

Connect all three sets of wires to their appropriate terminals in the junction box, exactly as shown in the diagram left. Check that the terminals are right and refit the junction box cover. You are now ready to reinstate the supply and test the unit.

Finding a power source for a shaver socket is not difficult. For the types incorporating an isolating transformer and thermal overload device, you can take the power from the lighting circuit, the power circuit or a junction box linked to the power circuit

junction box connected to lighting circuit

isolating transformer

shaver socket with isolating transformer

existing socket

junction box

AUTOMATIC CUPBOARD LIGHT

A small striplight in a display cabinet instantly enhances ornaments and glass-ware and similar lights in deep, dark kitchen cabinets are an invaluable practical aid.

In many instances it's sufficient just to be able to turn on the light when it's required, but there are situations where it is extremely useful to have a light that comes on automatically, for example, when a cupboard door is opened. The facility has been standard on refrigerators for a good number of years and is now a common feature on drinks cabinets.

Automatic lighting is made possible by a device known as a push-to-break switch. This consists of a spring-loaded plunger which is held depressed by a cupboard door when closed. In this position it 'breaks' the circuit to the light which therefore goes off. But when the door is opened, the plunger springs out and the circuit is connected.

Automatic lights have a number of applications. Kitchen units, for example, are an obvious choice—particularly the floor cupboards where you have to bend right down to see into the back of them. But understairs cupboards, bathroom cabinets, walk in wardrobes and writing bureaux can all benefit too.

Choosing a light fixture

Automatic switches can be used to control most types of light fitting, but for many of the locations where you'll be fitting cupboard lights, small striplights or fluorescent tubes are the obvious choice.

Striplights tend to be more popular, but this is probably due to the fact that they are much cheaper to buy than a fluorescent unit. However, there are a number of advantages in using a fluorescent tube, once the initial cost has been absorbed. For example, you only need a tube rated at a quarter of the wattage of a striplight to give out roughly the same amount of light, and the tube will last up to five times longer, so they are more economical to run. Unlike a striplight a fluorescent tube doesn't heat up which is a point well worth bearing in mind if you're not too sure about the quality of the veneer or melamine finish of the cupboard you're fitting the light to. The heat

from striplights can lift veneers and discolour melamine.

Fluorescent tubes are also sometimes fitted with diffusers to help give an even spread of light, and added protection against the effects of steam.

When you buy the fitting, check the maximum size of the lamp it will take. Remember, you are lighting a confined space, so in most cases you're only going to need low wattage lights. Small cupboards may only need a 15W striplight, with larger ones needing 25W or 30W lamps. Sometimes in very large cabinets you may even need to wire two 30W fittings together to give a good spread of light. What you must never do, however tempting, is to exceed the maximum wattage of the fitting when you want to produce more light.

The simplest way of providing an

automatic light, both from the installation and wiring point of view, is to use a fitting which combines the lamp and switch in one unit. Naturally, these units are more bulky, and therefore slightly more conspicuous than a separate switch and light, but this is a minor disadvantage. The units incorporate a heat deflector and a reflector under the bulb so that the maximum amount of light is thrown into the cupboard, and there is no damage from heat to the cupboard's surface.

If you are mounting a light in the larder or understairs cupboard, you need something more than a small striplight or fluorescent tube to illuminate it. In this instance, there's nothing to stop you connecting an automatic switch to an ordinary battenholder to which you can fit a 100W light bulb. The battenholder could

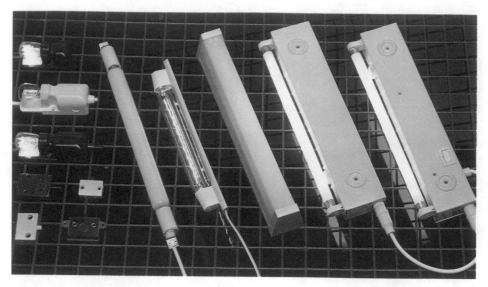

A variety of fittings can be used for cupboard lighting. 'Pigmy' lights (on the left) may be fitted with their own switch. Otherwise you need a separate switch (bottom left). These will also control strip and fluorescent lights (centre and right)

be set on the ceiling, although there is a type with an angled socket which enables you to mount the light on the wall. Try to pick a spot in the cupboard that will minimize the amount of shadow cast by any shelves. Again, the wider spread of light from a fluorescent light fitted with a diffuser will help alleviate this problem.

If required, you can operate more than one light from the same automatic switch. So if you have a cupboard with three solid shelves and you want to illuminate each one, you can loop together three 15W or 30W fittings and then connect these to the switch. The actual wiring involved will depend on the method you use to obtain the electricity supply. However, if you want to connect fluorescent lights, it's not just a simple matter of looping together the terminals in each fitting. By far the easiest method is to buy fittings that can be joined using special connectors.

The main factor governing the number of lights that can be controlled from one switch is the amp rating of the switch itself. Usually this is 1 amp. Because domestic electricity in the UK is supplied at around 240 volts this means that such a switch can control up to 240W of light or eight 30W striplights, for example. But the situations where you'll need this capacity are extremely rare.

However, there is one other thing to remember if you are taking the power from a lighting circuit. A modern domestic lighting circuit has the capacity to supply power to light fittings which in total don't exceed 1200W (light bulbs under 100W counting as 100W). So calculate the wattage of the lights on the circuit you intend adding to just to make sure you're not going over the limit. But unless you've already made considerable additions to the circuit it's doubtful that you'll exceed the maximum load.

Tools and materials

Aside from the light fixture and switch there is very little else that you will need for this job. If you are going to take your power from an existing socket you will need a 3 amp plug and a length of flex. When calculating the amount of flex that you will require, measure fairly accurately and add a 10 per cent allowance to arrive at the total amount of flex to buy. If you want to change the colour of the flex at some point along the run, you will also need a flex connector to join one length to another.

If you are going to break into a circuit to obtain your power supply, then you will need a four terminal junction box. In a bathroom you will need to use an unswitched fused connection unit to take a spur from a nearby outlet.

In the way of tools, you'll need a cold chisel and club hammer to cut a channel in a masonry wall as well as conduit and cable clips. The screws you require will most likely be included with the fixture and switch. Don't forget a bit of red PVC tape to mark a live neutral returning to a junction box from a switch, and a little filler to make good any channels you have cut. Also have to hand a small screwdriver, drill, wire cutters, a sharp knife, and a filling knife to finish off.

Installing the switch and fixture

Usually there is little more to mounting a switch and light fixture than screwing them into place through the insulated screw holes moulded into the casing. But for them to work effectively, it's the positioning that's all important.

It's usually not critical how you site the switch and light in relation to one another —although the closer they are, the neater you can make the wiring runs. And if you can take the wiring in a corner or under a shelf, so much the better. See Wiring up the circuit, for what's involved.

Fitting the switch

Site the switch on the cabinet or door frame so that the top leading edge of the door or flap closes against the plunger. This means the light will come on almost immediately and turn off later than if the switch was mounted on the hinge side of the cupboard.

In the case of a door frame, you'll probably have to cut a notch in the door stop to conceal and protect the switch as much as possible. Hiding switches in cabinets is a little more difficult, but if you use one with a white casing on white or light-coloured furniture and one with a brown casing on a natural wood finish, they shouldn't be too conspicuous once they are installed.

Depending on the design of the cabinet, however, you may be able to mortise the switch into the frame, concealing the mechanism almost entirely. The plunger may protrude through a metal plate (which should be earthed) which holds the switch in place. If you are building your own cabinet you may also be able to incorporate the switch into the design, so that a baffle at the front concealing the light fitting can also house the switch.

Fitting the light

If you are making or assembling a cabinet, it's relatively easy to incorporate the light into the design. One favourite place is a cutaway at the back of a shelf so that light can be thrown up and down the back panel. It's an economical arrangement as well because one fitting can effectively light two bays of the cabinet.

But if you're fitting lights into a cabinet

1 *Position the switch where it will be operated by the door's outer edge, and mark around the case*

2 *You may need to saw or chisel out a housing to allow the switch to fit neatly and to protect it from knocks*

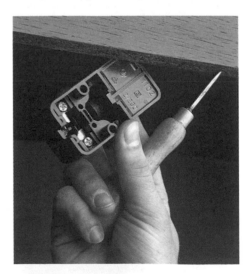

3 *Position the light in a convenient spot and mark fixing holes through the case using a bradawl*

that initially wasn't designed for them, siting the lights here isn't really a practical option unless you are prepared to alter the structure. Instead you'll have to look for an alternative location. Remember, it's the effect of the lights you'll want to see and not necessarily the fittings themselves. Wherever possible try to hide the lights unless you are using a light which is attractive to look at. You can, for example, buy a striplight with an opal tube that obscures the tungsten element and in so doing gives a less glaring light. This is particularly valuable where you only want illumination for aesthetic purposes.

The easiest method of concealment is to fit a baffle under the top front edge of the cabinet and screw the fitting to this. If you can match the finish of the baffle to the rest of the cupboard it will look as though it's part of the original design. The baffle will also help direct light into the cupboard. And for greater effect in a drinks cabinet cover the base with a mirror so that light is also reflected back under the glasses. Baffles are particularly important in kitchen units because they protect the light from being knocked accidentally as you put away cans and saucepans and other awkward objects.

Making a baffle

If the cabinet you want to light has adjustable shelves then it is quite simple to create an arrangement where you can light two bays with one light fitting. You can cut the baffle from one of the shelves. Remove the upper shelf to the two bays you want to light and mark a line along the length approximately 65mm from the back edge. Carefully cut along this line using a panel saw. Use this offcut as the baffle. You will have to finish the rough edge of the baffle to match the rest of the surrounding surface. The easiest method is to use iron-on tape.

Mark the baffle so that it is centred along the edge of the shelf and so it projects the same distance above and below the shelf. Drill countersink holes at approximately 200mm centres along the length of the baffle. Drill pilot holes and screw the baffle to the shelf. You may find that the shelf no longer fits on its supports properly therefore you may also have to readjust the position of the shelf supports. Once you have the shelf-baffle combination completed, you're ready to wire up the light fitting and switch in the ordinary way. However, you will find it easier to fix the light fitting to the baffle if you remove the shelf/baffle from the cabinet. Also if you have to drill through

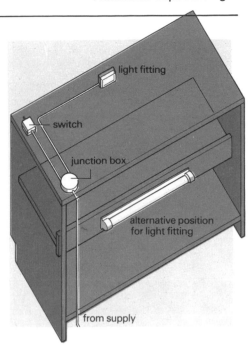

There are several alternative positions for the light and switch. Decide the best and then work out neat routes for the wiring using a junction box as necessary.

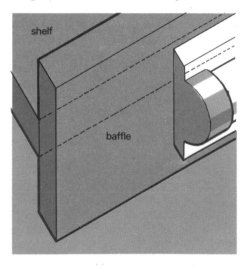

You can fit a striplight to the back of a shelf if you cut away a section and then add a baffle to protect the fitting

the back wall of the cabinet for the flex entry, you should drill the hole opposite the baffle so that it is hidden.

Wiring up the circuit

Once the switch and light fitting are positioned, you've got the task of connecting them to a suitable power source.

Basically, you've got three options on how you provide a supply of electricity.
Plugging into a socket outlet: By far the easiest and simplest method of providing

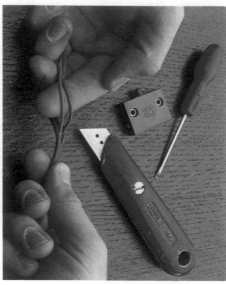

4 *Drill a hole in a concealed corner at the back of the cabinet in order to admit the flex which connects to the power supply*

5 *Strip away the sheathing from the flex to form a 'window' for the switch. Take great care not to cut the inner insulation*

power is to plug into a three-pin 13 amp socket outlet. It's a means most commonly used for wall units, cupboards, cabinets and wardrobes in the living room, dining room or bedroom.

Usually there's a free socket near floor-level which is close enough to provide a supply. And because the plug can be easily pulled out you've got no problems of disconnection should you want to change the units around. You simply find another convenient socket to plug in to.

The three-pin plug must be fitted with a 3 amp fuse and wired with 0.5mm² flex. Whether you use two-core or three-core flex depends on the type of switch and fitting being installed. If they are double insulated, they don't need to be earthed, so two-core

flex can be used. But if the light fitting, for example, has an exposed metal base, and the switch is held into a mortise with a metal plate, these will need to be earthed so use three-core flex. This is not very common on most new light fittings and switches because they are held in place with plastic casings which eliminates the problem.

From the plug, run white-sheathed flex clipped along the top of the skirting to the back of the unit or cabinet. Here you may want to fit a flex connector so you can change the colour of the sheathing. A brown-sheathed flex, for instance, will look less conspicuous against a natural wood surface than white flex, which is better used on white melamine.

Run a flex up the back of the unit and drill

a small hole through the back panel where the side and top panels meet. Thread the flex through the hole and neatly run it along this join until you reach the switch position. Here you have to make what's known as a 'window' in the flex. This entails removing a section of sheathing very carefully without damaging the insulation on the cores underneath.

To make the window, use a sharp cutting knife to slice down the length of the flex and then to circle round it at each end. How much sheathing you have to remove depends on the size of the switch. Don't overcut, as you can always remove a little more sheathing as required—you can't add it. Next, test that you haven't nicked the insulation on the cores by doubling the flex over to see if there are any splits revealing bare metal.

Now you can make the connection to the switch itself. Cut the 'live' (brown) core and strip back about 6mm of insulation from the ends. Secure these ends in the terminals either side of the plunger/switch mechanism. The neutral (blue) core doesn't have to be cut, it is just looped round (see diagram below).

Draw the sections of flex each side of the 'window' together and set them under the cord clamp so that the flex can't be pulled from the body of the switch. Run the flex

---

★ WATCH POINT ★

You will be dealing with small terminals and pieces of equipment set in awkward corners so you may find it easier to remove the switch and light temporarily while you make the wiring connections.

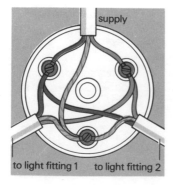

Use a three terminal junction box to wire up more than one light fitting controlled from the same switch. Connect all the like cores

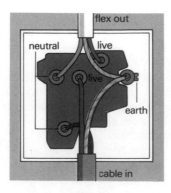

To take your power supply from a fused connection unit connect the supply cable to the feed side, and the flex to the load side

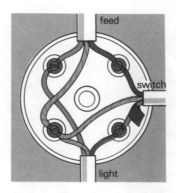

Use a four terminal junction box if you are running a separate flex to the switch and light fitting. Flag live/neutral with red PVC tape

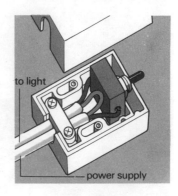

Most new switches do not need earthing as they have plastic casings. Cut a window in the flex and connect split live cores to the switch

onto the light fitting, strip back the sheathing and insulation from the cores and connect them to the relevant terminals.

If earthing is required either at the switch or light, run the circuit in three-core flex. At the switch you may have to improvise a little if there is no earthing terminal to connect the mortise fixing plate to the earth continuity. You could wrap the earth core round one of the fixing screws but make sure you don't break the continuity to the light. If this needs to be earthed, there's usually a terminal for it near the live and neutral terminals.

Only after all the wiring is complete and all the protective covers set in place should you plug in to test the light.

Connecting to a lighting circuit: This is an ideal method of providing power if you are installing an automatic light in kitchen wall units, a bathroom cabinet or an under-stairs cupboard. In a kitchen, for example, you'll probably want every socket outlet there is for running electrical appliances, so taking one over permanently for automatic cupboard lights isn't satisfactory. If you've got a spare socket at floor level, you've still got the problem of concealing the flex as it runs up into the cupboards, whereas by taking the power from the lighting circuit above, the cable can drop down neatly into the top of the units unseen.

For ease of wiring, use the junction box system. Decide on where to site the switch and light, then run 1.0mm² two-core and earth cable back from these to a four-terminal junction box fixed in the top corner in the picture. Ignore the earth core if it isn't needed and cut or tape it back; if it is make sure it is sheathed in green/yellow sleeving. And remember that both the cores in the cable leading to the switch are 'live' so the black core should be flagged in red PVC insulating tape to indicate this. Connect one core to the terminal on one side of the plunger and the other to the terminal opposite.

From the four-terminal junction box run a 1.0mm² cable back to the lighting circuit and connect it into the main supply with a three-terminal junction box. Make sure that power to the circuit has been turned off before you do this.

If you're installing the light in a larder, however, you may find it easier to insert a four-terminal junction box directly into the main lighting circuit and then run a cable to the light and another to the switch.

In a small bathroom cabinet you may be able to get away with a third variation in this system of wiring. In fact it's virtually the same as the wiring from a socket outlet.

6 *Cut the brown 'live' core and strip the ends so you can connect them into the two terminals of the switch*

7 *Strip the ends of the flex back so that you can connect them into the terminals in the light fitting*

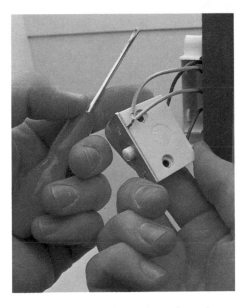

8 *On metal-cased switches where there is no earth terminal, connect an earth wire to one of the case fixing screws*

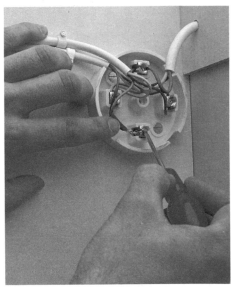

9 *If you fit two lights, use a junction box to split the supply to each of the fittings and the light switch*

You have to cut a 'window' in the 1.0mm² cable to fit the switch and then the cable is taken on to connect to the light. The cable should then be joined to the lighting circuit in a three-terminal junction box.

Power via a fused connection unit: You may be faced with the situation where there are no convenient socket outlets (as in the case of a bathroom) and where access to the lighting in the ceiling void is not very easy. If you're installing the automatic light in, say, the living room then the obvious thing to do is to fit a new double socket at the end of a spur from the ring circuit. But you

can't do this in the bathroom. Here the answer is to fit an unswitched fused connection unit at the end of a spur from the ring circuit and then to run a 0.5mm² flex from the load side of the unit to the push-to-break switch and then onto the light as if you were wiring the system from a socket outlet. The connection unit should be fitted with a 3 amp fuse. Ideally it should be sited as near to the cabinet as possible which, unfortunately, may mean cutting a long chase for the spur cable if you are flush mounting the wiring. Any surface wiring should be run in wall-mounted, plastic trunking.

CENTRAL HEATING CONTROLS

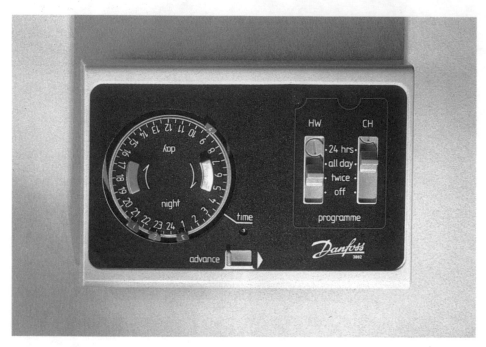

Central heating systems, even new ones, tend to be fitted with the bare minimum of controls. This means that they are often running inefficiently, either by giving out heat where it isn't needed, or by not heating rooms adequately. By adding supplementary controls to the system, it is possible to obtain a more balanced performance and make substantial savings in running costs into the bargain.

How this is achieved depends upon the individual design of the system and the type of controls already in use. To see where your system is lacking, compare it with the schematic diagram of an ideal fully automated system opposite.

None of the schemes mentioned below, however, is suitable for solid fuel boilers. Also, low water content gas boilers with copper heat exchangers may require a bypass valve to prevent a build-up of heat when the controls are off. Any boiler manufacturer's recommendations on how you adapt your system must take precedence over the advice given here.

Areas to consider

Work your way through your existing system, looking at its functions and making a note of any obvious deficiencies.

The boiler: Both gas and oil boilers are now controlled by an integral electrical thermostat. This keeps the water inside the heat exchanger at a constant temperature—igniting the burners as the temperature falls and extinguishing the flame as the temperature is restored.

Domestic hot water: On conventional systems, the domestic hot water is stored in a cylinder. The control of the water temperature is primarily through the boiler thermostat. On the crudest gravity systems, this is the sole means of controlling the water temperature at the taps. This has two major disadvantages.

When the central heating is turned on, the water in the cylinder is automatically heated to the same temperature as the water in the radiators. There are many occasions when you need a different temperature in each individual circuit.

When the heating is turned off, the boiler will remain hot all the time the domestic hot water circuit is switched on. This means that although the cylinder may be full of hot water the boiler will be switching on and off under the instruction of its own thermostat merely to keep the water in the boiler hot. Because the boiler is not insulated this cycling effect will continue every few

minutes as heat is lost through the flue and through the casing.

What is needed is a means of telling the boiler that the cylinder is hot enough. An electrical cylinder thermostat is designed to do this by sensing the temperature of the water in the cylinder and sending a signal to shut off the boiler.

This is a perfectly adequate arrangement as long as the hot water only is required. But as soon as the radiator circuits are brought into use the water temperature in the cylinder is once again governed by the boiler thermostat. To overcome this a valve (mechanical or electro-mechanical) is needed to shut off the water returning from the cylinder circuit, thus giving independent temperatures in the radiators and at the taps.

The programmer: Central heating programmers are designed to control all the different components of a central heating system, giving an automatic switching operation through the timeclock.

The radiators: The majority of radiator circuits are assisted by an electrical pump which greatly accelerates the speed of water passing through the system. Switching the pump on and off is the simplest method of controlling the room temperatures. Usually, a room thermostat mounted on the wall is used to control the pump. But inevitably this leads to a compromise.

The answer lies in local control. Depending on the layout of the pipework one of two methods may be adopted.

The most effective is to fit individual *thermostatic radiator valves* which control the temperature of each radiator.

The other method is control by *zone valves*. A fundamental requirement of this is that pipework must be easily divided into separate runs. A careful examinination of the system will determine the feasibility of this scheme.

Where the pipework branches to supply the upstairs and ground floor on two separate circuits, zone valves may be effectively employed to operate each circuit independently.

In some cases this cannot be done. Many systems installed in houses with solid ground floors drop individual radiator circuits from the first floor. Individual thermostatic radiator valves are the best bet if you have this type of system.

If it's decided that a zone valve is feasible, a means of switching it on and off will be required. A simple room thermostat located within the zone is probably the best method; alternatively a time clock may be used so the upstairs circuits are automatically switched off when the bedrooms are not in use.

Any plumbing work will entail draining the system—but don't do this before you have established which pipes are which. Often, this can only be done by feeling which pipes become hot and in what order. Electrical work is best tackled separately.

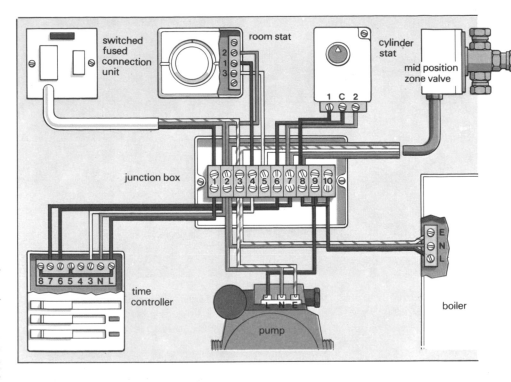

Tools for the job

Most systems can be worked on with relatively few tools. For plumbing work you will need a junior hacksaw, an adjustable spanner, a radiator valve key and something to raise floorboards—a brick bolster or crowbar, for example.

Electrical work requires a small screwdriver and a pair of pliers. You may need to use a battery and bell continuity tester to trace the more complicated circuits.

Fitting thermostatic radiator valves

When fitting thermostatic radiator valves to an existing system, it is essential to maintain an open circuit for the pump. This can be done by leaving one radiator with a manual valve always open or by fitting a bypass pipe between the flow and return on the heating side. The result of this is to stabilize the load on the pump, and it also helps to overcome noise problems.

Thermostatic radiator valves will only work if they are connected to the flow —you'll need to find the flow pipe on each radiator before you drain the system.

To find out which is the flow, turn the system off and allow it to cool, then turn it

The wiring circuit has heat-resistant PVC or butyl rubber cable within the boiler casing and standard 1.5mm^2 cable to link all the components to the junction box

back and feel both the pipes on each radiator. The flow pipe is the one which gets hot first—label it.

The system can now be drained by tying up the ball valve and opening the drain cock at the lowest point. Also open the air cocks on the radiators to allow water to drain down more easily.

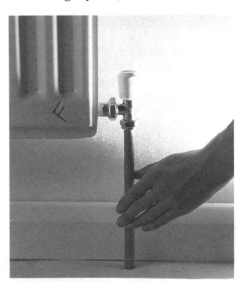

1 *Determine which pipe is the feed by turning the system off, letting it cool then turning it on and feeling which pipe heats up first*

2 *Remove the standard valve and copper pipe if it's too short; then wrap PTFE tape around the threads of the new valve body*

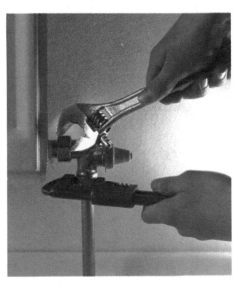

3 *Tighten the threaded connections, avoiding distortion to the pipework by holding the valve body firmly with a spanner*

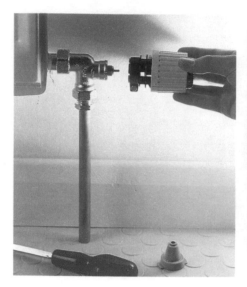

4 *Attach the actuator to the valve body, screwing the knurled nut finger-tight; then fill the system and check for leaks*

When the system is empty, hold the valve steady and undo the nuts on the pipework and radiator. You should then be able to slip off the old valve and place it on one side. Remove the threaded shank from the radiator using a radiator valve key.

The nut and olive on the pipe can be removed either by tapping the nut gently upwards until the olive is forced off or by carefully cutting through the olive with a junior hacksaw—be sure not to cut the pipe.

Offer up the new valve to the radiator and check that the copper pipe is long enough to locate correctly inside the valve body. If you find the pipe is too short there may be enough free play to draw it up a little. If not, the pipe will have to be cut further down and a new section joined in. The neatest way of doing this is to solder a new capillary connector on to the existing pipework.

The next step is to fix the new shank into the radiator. Wrap some PTFE tape around the threaded section and screw it into the radiator with a hexagonal radiator spanner. Fit the valves as shown, then fill the system once more and check for leaks.

Fitting an electrical cylinder thermostat

A cylinder thermostat does not require any plumbing work. The thermostat is held against the outside of the cylinder by means of a metal strap or curtain wire.

The position of the thermostat on the cylinder will determine the volume of water heated before the sensor operates. The usual position is somewhere around the

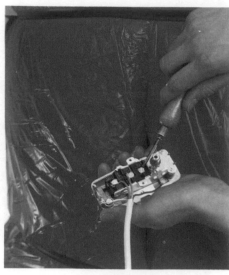

5 *Switch off the electricity and connect a three-core cable from the cylinder thermostat to the controller*

6 *Secure the thermostat to the hot water cylinder with the metal strap provided or a length of curtain wire*

middle of the lower half.

If the cylinder is factory-lagged with urethane foam, a cutout must be made with a sharp knife to expose a small section of the copper surface. Use the body of the thermostat as a template.

Run a three-core cable from the cylinder thermostat to the programmer and connect them up. Before removing the cover on the programmer, however, make sure that you switch off the electricity.

You will now have to find which wire goes from the programmer to the boiler. Many programmers have a small diagram to help identify the terminals. The terminal will be named 'hot water on'. Disconnect the live wire from this terminal and connect

the new wire from the cylinder thermostat terminal marked 'make on fall in temperature' or 'demand'.

Join the 'common' terminal on the cylinder thermostat to the live supply for the boiler.

The remaining terminal on the cylinder thermostat marked 'make on rise' must be connected to the central heating terminal that supplies power to the pump. It may be joined on the room thermostat terminal or anywhere between the room thermostat and the pump.

This will supply an alternative route to power the boiler when the cylinder thermostat is off and the heating is on.

Fitting a thermostatic cylinder valve

The ideal position for a cylinder valve is on the return pipe from the cylinder to the boiler. Often lack of space makes this impractical and another position must be sought. It is essential that the valve does not restrict the open vent or cold feed from the header tank. Note also that this valve is only for use on indirect systems.

You may need to reposition the cold feed to join the return pipe after the valve. You can do this fairly easily using compression fittings but you'll need to blank off the original cold feed pipe with a compression stop end.

The remote sensor must be placed against the copper of the cylinder and held firmly in position by the tape provided. The temperature adjustment is made by revolving the head of the valve, so this must be accessible.

Turn off the boiler and drain the system completely before commencing the installation. Offer up the valve and clearly mark two cutting lines on the pipe. Using a junior hacksaw, cut out the section between the lines and clean up the cut with a file.

Provided there is some free play in the pipework you should be able to slip in the valve and the compression joints.

If you find this impossible, disconnect the pipe at the cylinder union and reconnect

---

★ WATCH POINT ★

Incorporate an air cock into the blanking-off fitting so you will be able to bleed the system easily when you are refilling it.

7 *Gently uncoil the connecting pipe, place the remote capillary sensor against the cylinder and secure it with the tape provided*

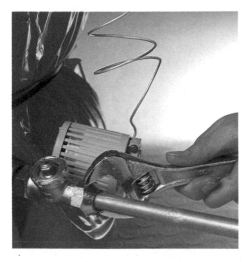

8 *Having drained the system, cut a section from the cold feed and insert the valve, tightening the fittings on either side*

when the valve is in place. Tighten the compression fitting on each side of the valve and fill the system with the valve fully open. Check the operation of the valve.

Fitting a wall-mounted thermostat

A wall-mounted thermostat can be used to control a pump, a diverter valve or a zone valve. The basic wiring principle is the same for all three in that the thermostat interrupts the electricity in exactly the same way as an ordinary light switch.

Because the switching action is activated by air temperature, the positioning of the thermostat is critical in obtaining an accurate sensing of the room temperature as a whole.

The most common position is either in the hall or the lounge. A case can be argued for either of these areas being better than the other, but really it is a matter of personal preference, since neither is perfect. In the end your decision may be influenced by which place offers the easiest route for running the cable, especially if you want to conceal it.

However, there are a number of positions that are *not* suitable. The unit must be kept clear of any heat source such as a radiator, a table or wall lamp, a television set or the direct rays of the sun. It must also be mounted away from draughts. The recommended height from the floor is 1500mm so when you have taken all these things into consideration your choice may be limited.

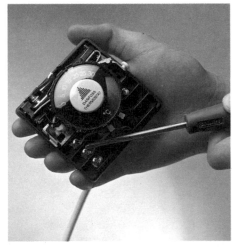

9 *Run a cable from the thermostat to the junction box and mount the unit in a hall or lounge away from any heat source*

With the mains power off, connect the 'heating on' terminal at the programmer to the room thermostat 'common' terminal. The wire leaving the thermostat must be connected to the 'demand' or 'calling for heat' terminal. This will pass a live current to power the component.

Modern room thermostats incorporate a tiny heating element in the unit to improve the response of the heat sensor. The element requires a neutral connection, which can be taken from the programmer junction box.

Frost thermostat: A variation of a room thermostat is made to provide frost protection during very cold weather. If your boiler is located in an outhouse or you are likely to leave home for more than a few days during the winter, a frost thermostat can be fitted to fire the boiler when temperatures fall to 5°C.

All that is required is a live supply run through the frost thermostat to the boiler and pump (see page 287).

Fitting a zone valve

Fitting a zone valve involves the same plumbing work as fitting a cylinder valve.

After draining the system, cut through the pipe with a junior hacksaw and secure the valve by means of the compression fittings. The system can be filled and tested

10 *Having drained the system, cut through the supply pipe at the appropriate point, insert the valve and tighten the fittings*

11 *Run a cable from the valve plug to the junction box; then simply connect the plug, fill the system and check for any leaks*

before commencing the electrical work.

If you're fitting a 22mm valve to old imperial ¾in. copper, change the olives in the fittings for ¾in. olives which are still available from good plumbers' merchants. You can fit a 22mm valve to 15mm pipe by inserting reducing sets into the ends of the fittings and tightening just like an ordinary joint.

Zone valves are available in two different types: spring return valves which require power only to open, and fully motorized valves requiring power to switch on and off.

Whether you intend to switch the valve by means of a thermostat, an ordinary light switch or directly from the programmer, the wiring is the same; all motorized valves require a neutral connection and an earth.

Some valves have an auxiliary wire to supply current to another component when the valve is fully open. This is useful in ensuring that the pump is open. It may also be used to power an indicator light.

Fitting a new programmer

Modern programmers are made in two parts —the backplate, which screws on the wall and takes the wiring, and the control box which all the timing circuitry and clips on when the wiring is complete.

Cables can enter the box either through the back or the sides, giving you a choice of surface-run or concealed wiring.

The power supply for the programmer should be from a 3 amp fused connection unit or a plug and socket. Some programmers have a built-in junction box; others have a separate one.

All the neutrals and earths can be run directly from the junction box to the components. Switching is carried out on the live pole only (see page 287).

The terminals in the programmer are designated for switching power to the heating and hot water circuits. Where thermostats are fitted, the terminals will be connected to the thermostats first, and then on to any motorized valves and finally to the pump and central heating boiler.

When switching on for the first time, many solid state programmers have to charge their batteries before normal operation is achieved—so an initial lack of activity is not always an indication that you have put a wire in the wrong place.

Types of programmer. There are essentially two types of programmer: the analogue and the digital time switch.

The analogue type can be used to programme the on and off times of the central

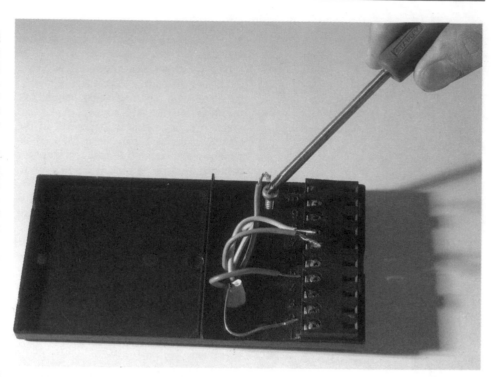

12 *Feed all the necessary wires through the backplate of the programmer and mount it on the wall in the most convenient position*

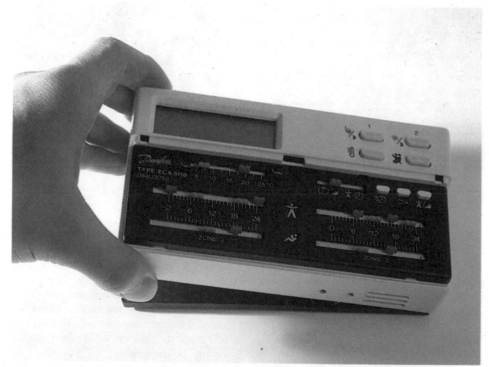

13 *Connect the wires to the appropriate terminals, then fit the control box to the backplate and then reconnect the power supply*

heating and domestic hot water systems independently. In addition, remote timer/night thermostats are available which can be used to maintain a temperature at night.

The more sophisticated digital types can display the temperatures both inside and outside the house and in different zones, and feature an override button for parties and late-night gatherings plus zone change-over buttons to swap the operation of the zone regulators.

FIT A DOOR BELL

As you may know to your cost, the sound produced by a door knocker does not always carry well inside, particularly if the internal doors are closed and the TV is on: what you need is a far more versatile announcing system—an electric door bell.

The great advantage of an electric bell is that you can site it where it can be most easily heard. You can fit an extension bell to make the system more audible, and have bell pushes for both front and back doors.

Types of bells: Electric bells operate off very low voltages and the simplest types are battery powered (see Battery-powered bells). They're available individually or in kits, complete with a length of special thin two-core (twin) bell wire to connect to the power source, a bell push and all the fixings. You should be able to install a simple battery-powered bell system in about half an hour.

Door bells can also be powered from the mains, but you must fit a suitable transformer to reduce the mains voltage. If you decide on this system, you'll find there's a wider range of bells to choose from, but the initial costs are inevitably higher: a bell transformer can cost more than the bell kit itself. Installation will also take longer, because you have to make a connection into the mains supply.

Both battery and mains-powered electric bells are cheap to run. Batteries last about two years while a mains-powered bell will have little effect on your electricity bill.

Buying a bell

When you go to buy a bell, visit a store with several different types on 'live' display so that you can try them out and buy the one that suits you best. Bells, buzzers and chimes are all available while the more complex types can play a short peal and some models containing a cassette or programmed microprocessor can play a short tune.

If you want to fit two bell pushes, it's worth considering a unit which gives one signal for the front door and a slightly different one for the back.

A simple chime unit consists of an electromagnet wound round a sliding bar; at each end there's a striking plate or tube—these often hang down below the housing. When the bell push is depressed,

the bar is drawn through the electromagnet coil to strike one of the tubes. It's held in this position until the bell push is released when a spring throws the bar back through the coil to hit the chime tube on the other side—hence the familiar 'ding-dong'. Some models also incorporate a 'repeater' mechanism for keeping this action going as long as the bell push is depressed.

Probably the most familiar of door bells is the 'trembler' bell, so called because the sound it makes is created by a hammer vibrating furiously against a metal gong. The bell will continue to ring as long as the bell push is kept down.

With trembler bells, an electromagnet is again used to activate the striking arm, but as the arm moves 'make-and-break' contacts are opened, so closing the circuit. The arm returns to its starting position once it has struck the gong. Because the make-and-break contacts are now closed, the circuit is remade so the process repeats itself—at many times a second—until the circuit is finally broken when the bell push is released; the volume of the bell can be adjusted via a screw on the make-and-break contacts.

Trembler bells can operate off the direct current (DC) of batteries or the alternating current (AC) of the mains via a transformer. But you can also buy mains-operated trembler bells, which harness the alternating nature of the current to cause

the hammer to vibrate against the gong. These bells don't require make-and-break contacts so they're much easier to maintain.

If you aren't keen on a piercing ringing bell, then you can opt for a buzzer instead. This works in a similar way to the trembler bell, but the sound is made by a metal bar striking the electromagnet itself, rather than a gong. Again, battery and mains types are made.

Bell pushes

To operate any door bell you need a basic switching mechanism and this, simply, is what a bell push is. When you push the button you complete the circuit made with the bell wire; when you remove your finger a spring pushes the contacts apart.

The most basic types consist of a plastic base plate on which the switch mechanism is mounted; this is protected by a push-on cover, which also conceals the fixing screws. You can also buy brass and other ornate bell pushes to match your door furniture: they work in exactly the same way as the basic type. Some of the more elaborate pushes include a light, which illuminates the button or a name tag; useful features on a poorly lit doorstep. Because the light will stay on continuously illuminated pushes should only be used when the bell is run off the mains; a battery would run flat within two or three days. The miniature bulb inside may require occasional replacement.

Choosing a transformer

It's safest and easiest to buy a purpose-made transformer for your bell. These units normally contain a 1 amp fuse. The instructions with the bell will tell you what voltage it should be run on—commonly 3, 5 or 8 volts—and you'll find that most bell transformers have output (Secondary) terminals to match. Chimes usually have to be connected to the 8 volts terminals; bells and buzzers to the 5 or 3 volt terminals. You can also get transformers which supply higher voltages—commonly 4, 8 and 12 volts.

Siting the housing

Obviously, the bell push will have to be sited right by the door. The best place to site the bell housing is often in the hall where it can probably be heard throughout the house. An extension bell can be installed in a garage or shed, and if someone is hard of hearing then it's also worth putting another bell in the living-room, kitchen or other room that's used frequently.

Mount the bell high up on the wall so that it's inconspicuous and can't be knocked accidentally. This is particularly important for chimes with striking tubes that protrude down from the housing. Once you've determined the site, you can work out how you're going to run the bell wire to the bell push, and to the transformer. Fortunately, because bell wire is very thin its easy to conceal behind picture rails, skirting boards and architraves.

Obtaining power

There are basically four ways to connect your transformer. The simplest is to plug it into a three-pin socket outlet, replacing the plug's 13 amp fuse with a 3 amp one instead. But to avoid an unsightly run of flex, the transformer should be fitted next to the socket and this leaves it vulnerable to knocks. In addition, hallways, where bells are usually installed, tend to be short of sockets and you may have to unplug the transformer each time you want to operate your vacuum cleaner for example. To get around this, you could install a switched

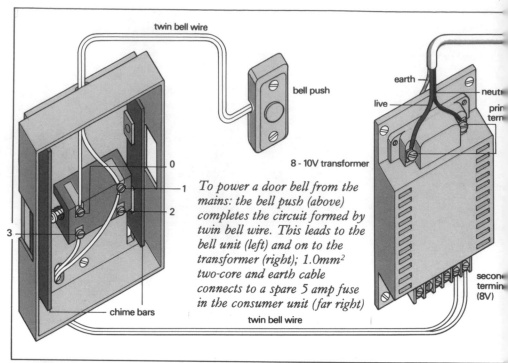

twin bell wire

bell push

earth

live

neut

prim tern

8 - 10V transformer

0

1

2

3

chime bars

secon termin (8V)

twin bell wire

To power a door bell from the mains: the bell push (above) completes the circuit formed by twin bell wire. This leads to the bell unit (left) and on to the transformer (right); 1.0mm² two-core and earth cable connects to a spare 5 amp fuse in the consumer unit (far right)

fused connection unit, fitted with a 3 amp fuse, specifically for the transformer. This unit should be connected to a spur run in 2.5m² two-core and earth cable from the main power circuit; then 1.00mm² two-core and earth cable should be run to the primary terminals of the transformer itself. For full details on how to install a fused connection unit, see Add an extra socket, pages 252–255.

Similarly, you could break into the lighting circuit either by linking into a loop-in ceiling rose or by running a branch from a new three-terminal joint box installed on the supply cable. Unfortunately, to carry out the wiring you'll have to raise a few floorboards.

However, this does allow you to mount the transformer neatly by the side of the bell housing, especially if it's set high up on the wall. But as you're likely to be installing the bell close to the consumer unit—usually in the hallway—it makes sense to make your mains connection here.

If your consumer unit has a spare fuseway or spare miniature circuit breaker (MCB) the best way to obtain power for the transformer is to connect it to its own circuit protected by a 5 amp fuse or MCB.

Safety first

Electricity is potentially lethal if you don't treat it properly. So long as you make sure that the current is switched off before you touch any electrical fitting you cannot

possibly get a shock. But, although turning off the main switch will render the live parts dead, in some consumer units the mains terminals to which the meter leads connect aren't recessed, and there's still a risk of you receiving a shock. To be safe, it's wise to ask the electricity board to cut off the mains supply before you carry out any work on the consumer unit. When they restore the power they can also test your new circuit.

Installing a bell push and housing

When it comes to fitting a mains-powered door bell, all the work entails is installing a simple electric circuit. This consists of the bell push to activate the circuit, the wire to carry the current to the bell itself—and a transformer to provide the correct voltage.

Start by fitting the bell push. This is normally sited on the door frame at about chest height. It should be conspicuous, yet protected from the weather.

Hold the backplate of the unit to the frame and mark the position of the fixing holes and the bell wire entry using a

---

★ WATCH POINT ★

Bed the bell push on non-setting mastic if there's a danger that it might be exposed to rain.

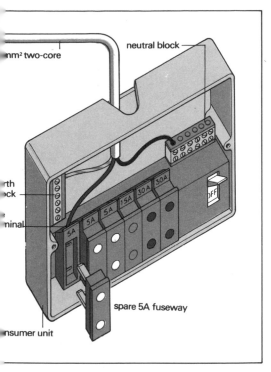

the bell wire is kinked, running it quickly through your hands a few times will warm and smooth it.

Keep the wire in place at 600mm intervals either with bell wire tacks, which you tap between the insulated cores, or with small cable clips that lap over both cores. You can also buy bell wire with a sticky strip on one side that you just press down to hold in place.

Remove the decorative cover from the bell housing and hold the backplate, which contains the bell mechanism, against the wall. Mark the fixing holes using a bradawl then drill and plug them. Run the bell wire from the push to the housing. Separate and strip back the insulation of the cores then connect them to the relevant terminals.

Fix the backplate, and connect to the transformer, then replace the cover.

Installing a bell transformer

The transformer reduces the mains voltage to the low level required for a doorbell. There are various ways to connect it—from simply plugging it into the mains at a three-pin socket to providing its own circuit from the consumer unit.

A bell transformer has two sets of terminals. At the top of the box the 'primary' terminals take the cable linking into the 240V mains supply; at the bottom the 'secondary' terminals take the twin bell wire from the bell housing. Make the connections by attaching the exposed bell wire cores to the correctly-rated screw-down terminals.

To connect into a spare fuseway in the consumer unit, first turn off the main switch (or have the mains supply cut off temporarily); remove the consumer unit cover and check that there's a spare (unconnected) fuseway the correct rating

for the transformer: 5 amp.

Once you have the correctly-rated fuseway installed, mount the transformer next to the consumer unit.

Attach a length of twin bell wire to the secondary terminals of the transformer and run it to the bell housing. Make the connections and attach the decorative cover.

★ WATCH POINT ★

If there's not a spare fuseway, you'll have to unscrew the live busbar and slide the existing fuseways along the busbar to make room for a new one. The fuseways must be arranged in the correct current rating sequence: highest (45 amp) next to the main switch; the lowest (5 amp) at the opposite end.

Strip and connect the live (red) and the neutral (black) cores of a length of 1.0mm² two-core and earth cable to the primary terminals of the transformer. If the transformer doesn't need to be earthed, then ignore the earth core and tape it back out of the way.

Run the cable to the entry point of the consumer unit, fastening it down with cable clips. Remove enough of the cable's outer

★ WATCH POINT ★

It's best to make all the connections—from the push to the bell housing and on to the transformer—before you make the mains connections. This lessens the time you'll have to have the power switched off.

bradawl. Then drill a 6mm diameter hole through the frame so the bell wire can be fed into the back of the push. Screw the backplate in place using woodscrews—they're usually provided—and thread the bell wire through the hole in the door frame.

Separate the two insulated wire cores enough to allow them to reach the terminals on the backplate. Strip about 6mm of insulation from each of the cores and connect them to the terminals (it doesn't matter which way round they go), using a small electrician's screwdriver. Now draw any extra bell wire back through the hole—avoid straining the connections—and then clip on the bell push cover.

Next run the bell wire back to the site of the bell housing choosing the most inconspicuous route, usually along skirting and picture rails and around door frames. If

1 *To fit the push, drill through the door frame from both sides using tape guide*

2 *Feed a length of twin bell wire through the door frame and connect up the bell push*

3 *Slot the bell wire into the housing, screw the unit to wall and connect the terminals*

4 *Run in more bell wire from the housing to transformer and make the connections*

sleeve so there's about 25mm remaining inside the box. Strip off about 10mm of insulation from each core. Connect the live core to the terminal at the top of the spare fuseway and take the neutral core to the neutral block. Link the earth core (which must be sleeved in green/yellow PVC) to the earth terminal.

Have the supply restored and turn on the main switch. Test the bell to ensure that everything works properly.

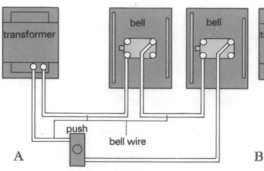

Wire an extension bell: in series (A)—both bells in the same circuit so one won't rob the other of power; or in parallel (B)—if one should fail the other will still function

Alternative ideas

You might not be able to hear the front doorbell from certain parts of the house—especially if the internal doors are shut, or you're in the garden. The answer here is to fit an extension bell.

You can either wire the two bells in 'series' or in 'parallel' (see diagrams). The advantage of the first method is that the two bells are connected in the same circuit, so one bell won't rob the other of power. You'll need to reconnect the bell wire in the transformer to higher voltage terminals.

To wire two bells in series:
- connect the push to the transformer with a single core of bell wire
- connect the push to one bell with a single core of bell wire
- join the two bells with another single core
- run a single core from the second bell to the transformer.

The advantages of bells wired in parallel is that if one breaks down the other will still work. Both bells must be of the same type and while strictly you don't have to double the operating voltage, it is advisable to do so.

To wire two bells in parallel:
- connect twin bell wire to the transformer
- split one core and connect up the push
- run the twin bell wire on to the first bell

- run a further length of twin bell wire on to the second bell and make the connections.

Battery-powered bells

If you don't want to go to the trouble and expense of fitting a transformer, a battery-operated door bell is the answer. With most chimes and some bells, the batteries fit inside the unit.

Rather than using one large battery, usually two or four 1½V 'baby' or 'mono' batteries are used instead. These are arranged in series to give the required voltage. They're slotted into place against spring terminals, and the direction in which they should be set is clearly marked with arrows and positive and negative symbols. The doorbell won't function unless the batteries are the right way round.

Many bells and most buzzers don't make provision for the batteries to be housed internally. Instead they run off a larger battery (usually 4½V) which have to be mounted nearby.

To wire up a bell to a battery, connect a

length of twin bell wire to the terminals inside the bell or buzzer unit. Run one core to the bell push and then link a separate single core from the push to the negative (−) terminal of the battery. The two cores of the bell wire are easy to separate simply by pulling them apart. Next run a single core of bell wire from the positive (+) terminal of the battery to connect up the free end of the bell wire from the bell housing.

You can't connect two trembler bells together if the circuit is run off batteries: the first bell would prevent the second one from operating properly. To get round this problem either fit an AC powered bell or join the make-and-break contacts of the second bell with a core of bell wire.

You'll need twice the voltage to power an extension bell. Either fit a more powerful battery or connect two 4½V batteries in series (negative to positive) with bell wire.

★ WATCH POINT ★

High power (HP) batteries last longer than ordinary ones: make sure you use the sealed type. When the batteries run down, change them immediately—don't leave them in the unit, where they may corrode.

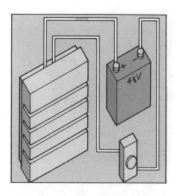

A battery circuit consists of battery, push and bell connected with twin bell wire

To power an extension bell you'll need two 4½V batteries wired in series

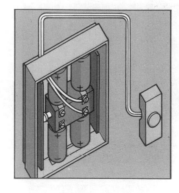

Four 1½V batteries will power a single bell, and can be fitted inside the unit

Bell wire cores are easy to separate: nick the sheathing then pull apart the cores

DOOR ANSWERING SYSTEM

Door answering systems are generally found in blocks of flats, where the occupants can identify and admit callers without having to descend several flights of stairs to the door. But such a system can also be equally suited to any home: it's an excellent complement to a burglar alarm, stout door and window locks and any other home security devices.

A typical system

A door answering system is a simple intercom facility. It basically comprises a telephone-style handset, which is mounted in the house where it can most conveniently be answered—the kitchen, for instance, or hallway, study or living room.

Multi-core flex runs from the handset to a push-button external unit, which you fix onto the wall outside by the front door (or with some units, actually set within the door). The external unit contains a microphone, a receiving amplifier and a speaker (which may have volume control).

When a caller presses a button on the external unit, a buzzer sounds on the handset. By lifting the telephone receiver, the occupant opens a channel to the speaker and receiver. The occupant can then enquire who is there and also hear the caller's reply.

The system operates on low voltage, provided via a transformer, which you must mount out of harm's way (next to the consumer unit is both safe and convenient). The transformer can be connected to the mains by wiring it into a spare 5 amp fuseway although it is possible to run it off a spur fused connection unit, wire it into the lighting circuit or simply plug it into an ordinary socket outlet.

Siting the system

Exactly where you site the system depends on the layout of your house. Aim to site the handset where it can most conveniently be reached.

The external unit can be positioned directly outside your front door or, if you live in a house with a long driveway

surrounded by a wall or fence, the unit can be fitted on the gate or doorway at the boundary.

The flex connecting the unit and handset can be run inconspicuously along the inside walls in plastic conduit, or with more trouble be neatly located in channels cut in the wall.

If the cable is to run to a gate outside, bury it in a trench dug in the ground for neatness. This also prevents accidental damage from garden tools, although as the answering system runs on low voltage, there's no danger of receiving a dangerous electric shock.

Tools and materials

To install a door answering system the only

materials you need, apart from the kit, are: a quantity of multi-core telephone cable to reach from the outside panel to the handset and transformer; a length of 1.0mm^2 two-core and earth PVC-sheathed cable if you plan to connect to the mains; and if necessary, a fused connection unit to tee into the ring main.

You'll need few tools to install the unit: a tape measure, marking knife, chisel, mallet, screwdriver, and an electric drill with wood and masonry bits (bit size depends on the kit so consult the manufacturer's instructions) is ample for fixing the panels to the wall and drilling the cable holes in the front door frames, if necessary.

Secure the multi-core cable runs in place or you may find yourself tripping over them. Ordinary telephone cable securing clips will do.

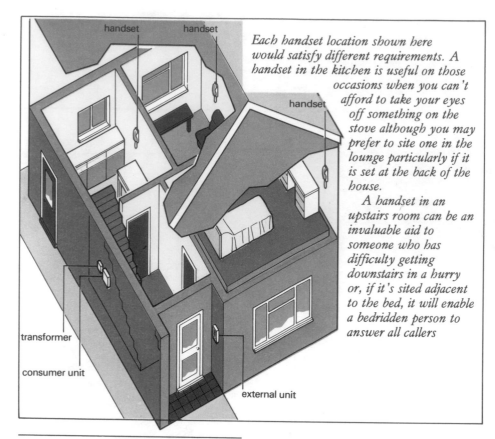

Each handset location shown here would satisfy different requirements. A handset in the kitchen is useful on those occasions when you can't afford to take your eyes off something on the stove although you may prefer to site one in the lounge particularly if it is set at the back of the house.

A handset in an upstairs room can be an invaluable aid to someone who has difficulty getting downstairs in a hurry or, if it's sited adjacent to the bed, it will enable a bedridden person to answer all callers

If you're surface-mounting the external unit on the wall by your front door, you can simply screw it into pre-drilled and plugged holes. Remove the cover from the unit and hold the base box against the wall in the required position.

Mark through the fixing holes with a pencil (or bradawl if the holes are too small). Remove the box and drill holes at the marked positions. Insert wall plugs then return the box to the wall and screw it into place.

★ WATCH POINT ★

Surface-mounted panels usually have plastic cases that are water resistant, but you should, where possible, site the unit where it won't be exposed to driving rain. You may think it worthwhile constructing a wooden box around the panel as extra protection.

Answering systems intended for flush-mounting have metal—not plastic—base boxes like those used for conventional mains electrical appliances, incorporating knock-outs for cable entry and fitted with lugs for fixing to the wall. The knock-outs may be situated all round the base box to give you plenty of choice when running the cable. Only punch one out when you've decided.

To fit a flush-mount box, hold the box, faceplate removed, against the wall and draw round it in chalk. Try to position the

Fitting the door panel and handset

The first job is to position the external unit and the handset. There are basically two ways you can fit the external unit: by surface-mounting it, or recessing it in the wall for neatness. The handset is simply surface-mounted inside the house.

For comfortable use, the external unit should be positioned about 1.4m above the ground, so that callers will be able to introduce themselves and receive your reply without having to stoop unduly. If you can, position the unit in a sheltered location so that visitors receive some protection from the rain during wet weather.

1 *Position the external unit about 1.4m above the ground. Mark the wall, through the fixing holes, with a bradawl making sure the unit is straight*

2 *At each mark, drill out a hole using a masonry bit. Plug the holes and then secure the external unit with the screws provided*

3 *Screw the handset's backplate to a wall at a chosen location inside the house. Prepare the wires ready for connection*

unit so that you will not have to cut too many bricks; position it between horizontal courses, too, for this reason.

Chop out a hole in the wall using a club hammer and bolster chisel. Keep the sides of the hole as smooth as possible to save unnecessary making good later. Don't cut too deeply, either: you need only go as deep as the box itself, and this is likely to be approximately 75mm.

Clean up the inside of the hole and try the base box for fit: if it fits well, simply mark the wall through the screw holes, drill and insert wallplugs, and then screw the box to the masonry.

Don't forget to knock out the blank circle in the metal box to accommodate the cable at the point of entry. At this stage you can leave the unit without mortaring it in place, in case any adjustments need to be made at a later stage.

The next job is to fit the handset to the wall inside the house. Aim to fix it about 1.5m above the floor for convenient use. Remove the cover then hold the backplate against the wall. Mark the fixing holes, drill and insert wallplugs, then screw the unit to the wall.

Now position the transformer between handset and the external unit. The two units are now ready for connecting up. However, if your set includes an automatic door latch this must be fitted first. Remove the old latch before you start.

Fitting a remote control door latch

You can fit an automatic door latch, which can be operated by depressing a button on the system's handset. Latches can be either set on the architrave or recessed into the door frame, depending on the type of lock in use—check when you buy.

Basically, most door answering systems are designed to work with rim locks. There are mortise lock versions but they are rarely used in ordinary domestic installations. With both types, when the button on the handset is depressed, the latch is electrically activated and the door can then be pushed open by the caller in order to enter.

Whichever type you're fitting, first hold it in position against the door frame and draw around it in pencil, to indicate where you'll have to cut the frame.

For a rim latch type, use a bevel-edged chisel to chop a recess for the device; for a mortise latch type (should you happen to have obtained one of these) you'll have to drill a series of holes within the marked out

4 *If you're fitting an automatic door latch, your first job must be to remove the old latch from the door frame*

mortise, then use a chisel to remove the waste, forming a square-sided slot. Fix the device in its recess with the screws provided.

The cable to the mortise type of automatic latch enters the device from the rear, so you'll have to drill a small hole through the door frame to slot it in. Feed the end of a length of multi-core cable into the hole and connect two of the cores to the terminals on the latch. Slide the latch into position and make sure you secure it firmly.

With the mechanism fixed to the frame, close the door and mark the position of the keep plate or the bolt box. Screw the keep plate inside the face of the door or cut a recess for the bolt box on the more rarely used mortise type latch.

Manually test the operation of the latch to make sure the action is smooth and make any necessary adjustments.

Making the electrical connections

You can power your door answering system by simply plugging the transformer into a spare 13 amp socket outlet. Alternatively, run a spur from the lighting circuit or a branch from the ring main. By far the best arrangement however, is to site the transformer next to the consumer unit and simply run a length of 1.0mm² two-core and earth cable from it to a spare 5 amp (lighting) fuse. With a double insulated transformer, you won't need to use the earth core so just cut it right back out of the way.

If you just want to run the door

5 *Hold the new latch over the old recess and mark it with a pencil. Enlarge the rebate with a bevel-edged chisel*

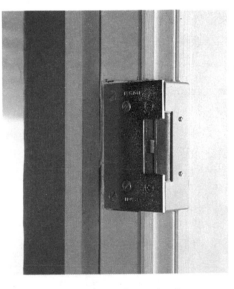

6 *Check that the lock on the door engages cleanly with the latch before tightening up the securing screws*

answering system transformer from an existing socket outlet, connect the live (brown) and neutral (blue) cores of a length of 1.0mm² two-core flex to the relevant terminals of the transformer—following the manufacturer's instructions fully—and wire up the other end to a three-pin plug, then make the connections from transformer to door answering system as described later on.

To run a branch from the ring circuit, first switch off at the mains, or remove the relevant fuse. You'll need to fit a fused connection unit between the mains supply and the transformer (see page 280). Break into the ring circuit at the nearest available power socket. Most transformers don't

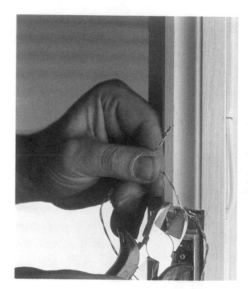

7 *Connect the wires from the unit and telephone to the remotely-controlled latch. Strip back the wires and connect according to instructions*

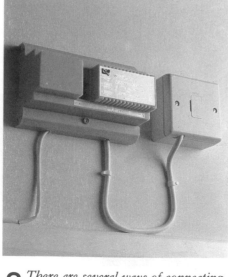
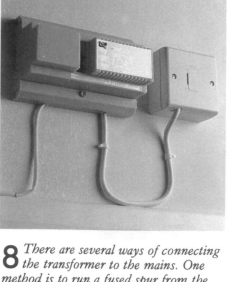

8 *There are several ways of connecting the transformer to the mains. One method is to run a fused spur from the ring main*

relevant terminals in the handset. Run the cable to the external unit and connect the cores to the terminals there. Run another length of flex from the handset to the transformer, this time connecting only the blue core and taping back the others.

Connect the blue, green and pink cores of another length of cable between the transformer and external unit. Finally, run another length of cable between transformer and external unit, connecting only the blue core to the terminals indicated in the kit instructions.

Although this method involves quite a few separate runs of cable, it's preferable to the alternative's splitting the individual cores with additional lengths of bell wire.

When you're satisfied that the connections are good, replace the terminal cover on the transformer, then secure the runs of cable between units using small cable clips or, for neatness, insert them in plastic conduit. If you've chased out the wall, fit in

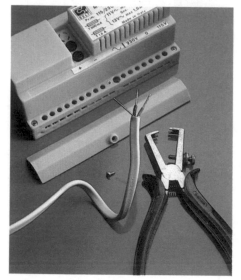

9 *Use 1.0mm² twin core and earth cable to connect the transformer to the mains*

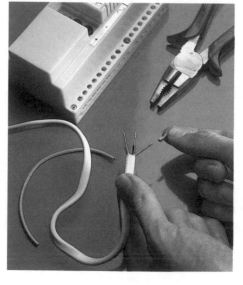

10 *If you need to use the earth core, sheath the exposed core with green and yellow sleeving*

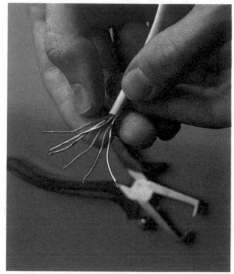

11 *The wires in telephone cable are not very robust so take care when you prepare the cores*

need to be earthed, so you can just ignore the earth core.

Alternatively, you can connect the cable into an existing loop-in ceiling rose and run it to the transformer.

For more details on identifying ring main circuits, loop-in ceiling roses and installing junction boxes, see pages 277–280 and 267–270.

The connections to the door answering system's handset and the external unit are made with multi-core telephone cable. This typically has blue, red, orange, yellow, green, pink, black and white cores but as the core colours vary so much it's difficult to

give categoric guidance. The best thing to do is study the diagram opposite, note which wires lead where and then run your own wires to match those routes exchanging the colours used in the diagram for the core colours in the cable you are using.

First run a cable between the automatic door latch and the transformer: only two cores are necessary here, so cut back the others. Insert the cores in the terminals.

Now connect the red, orange and yellow cores (or whatever colours you've chosen from those on your cable to fulfil this purpose) of another length of cable to the

the cable and make good the channels with plaster.

Switch on the power at the mains (or replace the circuit fuse) then test the system.

Reinforcing the door

Although an automatic door latch offers a degree of security, it means you won't be able to fit other locks, except for night-latches. In this case it's worth reinforcing the door frame.

At its simplest, reinforcement can mean

fitting good quality hinge bolts, which won't strengthen the opening side of the door but will ward against forced entry from the hinge side.

To fit the bolts, first mark the position of the bolt on the hinge edge of the door and drill a hole—likely to be about 10mm diameter and 38mm deep—to take the ribbed part of the bolt.

Hammer in the ribbed end of the bolt then partially close the door so the bolt will mark the jamb. At this point drill a 12mm diameter hole for the depth of the bolt, mark up for the mating metal plate, then chisel a recess in the jamb for it.

Screw the plate into position then test the operation of the door to make sure it doesn't bind.

There are various proprietary devices available for strengthening the door without hindering its action: anti-jemmy plates are small metal strips which you can hammer

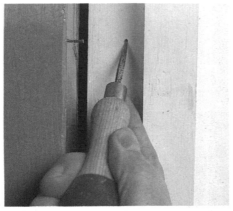

Tap a nail into the door's edge—it will leave a mark opposite on the frame

Drill out a hole in the door and hammer in the ribbed end of the bolt

Chisel a recess in the frame to take the plate and drill another hole for the bolt

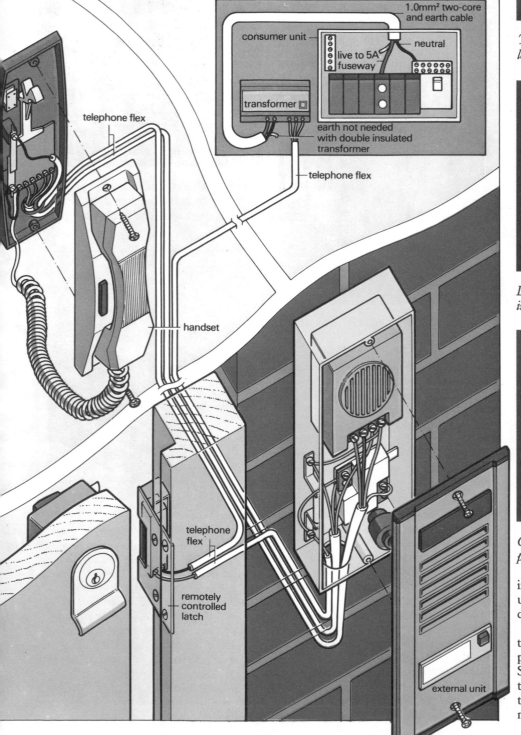

1.0mm² two-core and earth cable

consumer unit

live to 5A fuseway

neutral

transformer

earth not needed with double insulated transformer

telephone flex

telephone flex

handset

telephone flex

remotely controlled latch

external unit

into the door jamb to deter thieves from using a jemmy or crowbar to force open the door.

Reinforcing strips, which you fit around the door frame, are also a good method of protecting the door frame from forcing. Simply measure around the frame, order the relevant amount of strip and screw it to the timber, as described in the manufacturer's instructions.

FIT A NEW CONSUMER UNIT

An old electrical installation is typically a jumble of switches and fuse units, with old, decaying cables and inadequate capacity

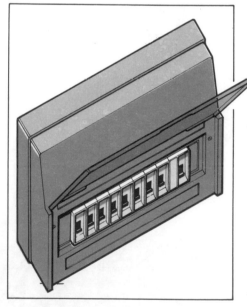

A modern consumer unit consists of a neat plastic or metal box containing all the terminals. All that's visible from the front is a row of MCBs and the main isolating switch; there's a plastic cover over these

From cookers to videos, the list of electrical equipment used in the home seems almost endless and it's placing an increasing burden on the domestic electrical system. If the wiring of your house is more than about 25 years old, the chances are that it needs replacing anyway—so you can increase the capacity of the system then. But if your home's wiring is satisfactory, you can increase its capacity simply by installing a new, larger consumer unit.

The job's not especially complicated—more a matter of being careful and methodical about making the connections. And since the final connection to the mains has to be done by the electricity board, you never have to deal with any live parts.

Types of distribution point

In older installations, the house circuits will probably originate from separate switch and fuse units, which allow individual circuits to be isolated from the mains supply. Alternatively, you may have a fuseboard which is controlled by a separate main switch and fuse or individual fuseboards which deal separately with the lighting and power circuits.

But by far the best way of distributing electricity to where it's needed in the house is to use a modern consumer unit containing a number of fuseways and a double pole isolating switch. Both from a safety and practical point of view, modern consumer units have a number of advantages. And if you've got an old distribution system, it's worth bringing it into line with current wiring practice.

On the safety front, old switch and fuse units and fuseboards themselves often have double pole fusing, which means that the live (phase) and neutral of each circuit have separate fuses. It's possible for a situation to arise in which a fault on the circuit causes the neutral fuse to blow but leaves the one on the live side intact: the result is an ineffective safety device, as part of the circuit could still be live. So if you've got double pole fusing it's important for reasons of safety that you replace it.

Consumer units have single pole fusing, which means that the fuse is connected to the live side of the circuit only. When this blows as a result of a fault or an overload all

power to the circuit is cut off; no part remains live.

But don't imagine that simply fitting a new consumer unit will by itself renew the safety standards of an old wiring system. If the wiring is old, it's potentially lethal. If you intend to upgrade your installation by installing a new consumer unit, then it's **vital** that you inspect the existing wiring very carefully (see Checking the wiring). Unless it's run in PVC sheathed and insulated cable you shouldn't attempt the conversion. Old wiring **must** be replaced in its entirety—for your safety and the fulfilment of legal requirements—and you can then install the consumer unit as part of an overall rewiring job.

Checking the wiring

Before you carry out any electrical work, it's absolutely essential you get to know your wiring system. And top of the list should be a check on the state of the cables themselves. Don't be misled by modern light switches and fittings, square pin sockets and a modern consumer unit. It's not unknown for these parts of a system to be renewed leaving the old cables in place.

If you've got lead or rubber-sheathed cable this will virtually be at the end of its life and will almost certainly need replacing in its entirety. The insulation will have deteriorated almost to dust, which, when disturbed, will leave the cores of the cable exposed and extremely dangerous. A rewire is essential and you can then install a new, larger capacity consumer unit as part of the job.

If you've got grey or white (or possibly the older black) PVC-sheathed-and-insulated two-core and earth cable, then you should be able to upgrade your installation by installing a consumer unit in place of switch fuse units, for example. If you're in any doubt get the wiring checked by the electricity board or a qualified electrician.

Also check for sockets and light fittings with poorly fitting cables and insecure terminal fittings. And make sure that any flexes aren't frayed: if exposed cores should come into contact this could lead to short circuits—and possibly even fires. Attention to detail may prevent accidents later on.

Choosing a consumer unit

It's worth spending a little time and seeking professional advice when deciding what consumer. unit is best for your house; individual requirements can vary quite considerably.

From a practical point of view, installing a consumer unit with more fuseways than you require at present will make extending

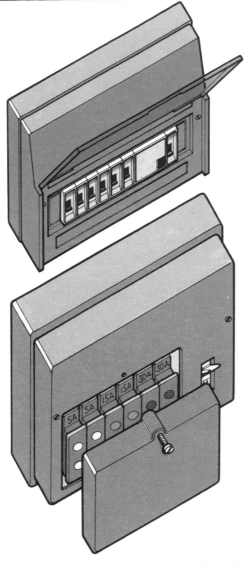

A modern consumer unit with MCBs and ELCBs (above), can detect most faults and shut down the system in milliseconds; a consumer unit with fuses (right) is cheaper but not as efficient

the system in the future that much easier. For example, you may at some time want to run a new circuit to a loft conversion, a back extension or a garage. You could install a modern switch-fuse unit (in effect a mini consumer unit), but the cost, time and extra wiring it entails makes the relatively simple connection to a spare fuseway in a consumer unit a far more attractive proposition. It also contains the connections in one unit— a far more convenient arrangement.

If you've got a fairly new installation, or the house has been rewired recently there'll probably be a consumer unit fitted already. But it's still worth considering whether it's likely to meet your future needs. If not, it'll need to be upgraded.

A standard six-way unit will deal with six circuits. Yet, while it will cope with a basic

installation of two lighting circuits. two power circuits, a cooker and an immersion heater, it's obvious that it's lacking in capacity as far as modern day needs are concerned. However, there are units with far more capacity—some have as many as twelve ways, but eight to ten ways are normally sufficient. If there are fuseways you're not going to use for the time being then fit them with empty fuse carriers, miniature circuit breakers (MCBs)—see Using MCBs and ELCBs—or you can use special blank fuses.

Fuses and circuit breakers

The other important point to consider is whether you want the unit fitted with rewireable fuses, cartridge fuses or with MCBs. The most common types are still the ones fitted with rewireable or cartridge fuses. They give serviceable performance protecting the circuit against faults, overloads and fire risks, as well as giving some protection against electrical shocks.

MCBs are a more expensive alternative but they're a more efficient safety device than fuses, since they respond more quickly to faults.

For example, a fuse rated at 5 amps needs a current of more than 10 amps passing through it (a 100 per cent overload) before it will blow. A cartridge fuse rated at 5 amps will take a current of 7.5 amps (a 50 per cent overload). But best of all is a comparable MCB, which will 'trip' at just over 6 amps (a 25 per cent overload) when there's a fault or an overload on the circuit.

Some consumer units are made specially

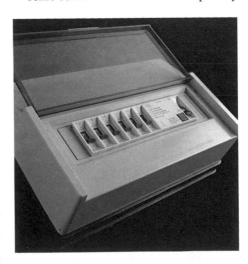

A modern consumer unit containing MCBs with toggle switches and an ELCB for efficient, safe electrification of your home

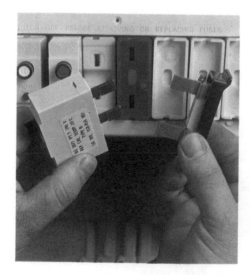

In many consumer units you can replace the rewireable fuses with MCBs, although you'll also have to fit special holders to take the MCBs

to take the traditional type of fuse, and likewise there are units that will take only MCBs. If you already have a consumer unit with fuses you may be able to replace the fuse carriers with MCBs that plug into the fuseways.

The best (but most expensive) consumer units, apart from using MCBs, also incorporate an ELCB (earth leakage circuit breaker—see Using MCBs and ELCBs). This is a sophisticated device, which besides acting as a double pole on/off switch to isolate your supply from the mains, also gives greater protection against the risk of electric shocks and electrical fires than is given by an existing solid earthing system. They're also available as separate units and have to be installed if the electricity board's main earthing arrangements are altered. If you want to fit a consumer unit with an ELCB then it's vital you contact the authorities, who will advise you on the type to use.

Using MCBs and ELCBs

Basically, an MCB is an automatic single pole switch, and the most up-to-date have what's known as a 'high speed current limiting action'.

Inside an MCB there are two mechanisms for cutting off the current. The first is a bimetallic strip. When the circuit is moderately overloaded this heats up, bends and touches a trip bar, which then sets off the trip mechanism, and so renders the circuit dead.

But if there happens to be a short circuit

and a sudden surge of current which exceeds the MCB's rating, then a solenoid activates a plunger, which in turn releases the trip mechanism. Because it operates so quickly (3–5 milliseconds) it shuts down the supply before the fault current has time to damage the installation, hence the description 'current limiting action'.

Once a fuse has been installed in its fuseway, the circuit becomes operational, but this isn't the case with an MCB. This has to be set either by depressing a button or by pushing a toggle switch to the up position. Consequently, you can use an MCB to turn off a circuit without disturbing the other MCBs connected to the consumer unit. You can then work on that circuit safely.

★ WATCH POINT ★

MCBs and ELCBs incorporate a test button, which you should operate from time to time to make sure they're working. Sometimes the contacts in MCBs and ELCBs can stick if they haven't been 'exercised' regularly.

With MCBs, the circuit that's at fault is instantly recognized because either the toggle switch will have dropped to the off position or the setting button will have been pushed out. And if you try to reset the switch without first correcting the fault the MCB will not function.

Earth leakage circuit breakers (ELCBs) are ingenious devices, which can detect a potentially dangerous earth fault current and turn off the main supply before it has a chance to do any harm. They're used where there's poor mains earthing for an installation. And they also provide greater protection against shocks and fires.

Many electric shocks occur when someone touches a live wire or a faulty appliance resulting in a current passing through the body to earth. But the most sensitive ELCB will trip the shutdown mechanism in less than 30 milliseconds if it detects a current leaking to earth of over 30 milliamps. This is well below the power and duration needed to give you an electric shock.

Similarly, it only takes a small current leaking to earth, even less than 1 amp, to start an electrical fire. But the ELCB will detect this and turn off the supply before the fire can start.

However, ELCBs will not detect live/neutral short circuits or overloads, so they're not a substitute for fuses or MCBs.

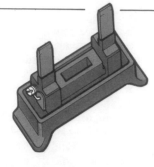

A push-button MCB (above); a replaceable cartridge fuse (right)

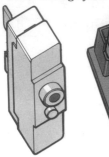

An old rewireable fuse has the fuse wire stretched across

An ELCB will detect even the slightest earth fault

ELCBs come as separate units or they can be incorporated in a consumer unit. There are two types: a voltage-operated model and a residual current version, which is also known as a current-operated ELCB. Which type you use depends on local earthing facilities.

The ELCBs incorporated in consumer units are mostly the residual current type. They contain a transformer and a detector winding, which can sense if there's an imbalance in the current between the live (phase) and neutral conductors.

In contrast, the voltage-operated ELCB detects earth fault currents in the earthing circuit itself and will then shut down the installation. But this relies on the earthing system working efficiently, and if the current finds another way to earth, say via metal pipework, then it may go undetected.

Installing a consumer unit

Installing a consumer unit isn't a time-consuming job, nor is it difficult. The only practical skill you need is the ability to strip cable and to anchor the cores properly in their terminals.

What's most important when you're installing a consumer unit is that you work carefully and methodically, running all the cables and their cores to the right place. If you have the slightest doubt about what you're doing, seek professional advice.

For complete safety, get the electricity board to disconnect your supply before you start to carry out any work. You'll need to give them at least two days notice for this, and at that time arrange for the reconnection and a test to be made on the installation. This is a vital check that you've carried out the work properly. Pay particular attention to the earthing of the installation (see diagram opposite). On some units there's still a potential shock risk even with the double pole switch turned off, particularly if the faceplate is removed and you're changing the cable to the new consumer unit. So safety, as always, is the key word.

Replacing fuse boxes: If your circuit wiring is in PVC sheathed and insulated cable and you've got a number of switch-fuse units you want to do away with, then first check what each unit controls and label the cables. Remove the fuses and faceplates from the units in turn to give you access to the terminals securing the live, neutral and earth cores of the cables. On older installations you may find that the lighting circuits don't have an earth core. The wiring regulations now insist that they do, so this is a good opportunity to run single core 1.5mm² green/yellow cable to all the mounting boxes and fittings on the circuit; with all the cables disconnected you can unscrew the units from the back board. Also remove the main switch and fuse unit and any distribution board.

At this stage you'll probably be faced with a confusing array of wires, but if they're all labelled carefully you shouldn't lose track of what you're doing. Because of the positioning of the fuse boxes or fuseboard, some of the cables may not reach to the site of the new consumer unit so you'll have to install junction boxes and

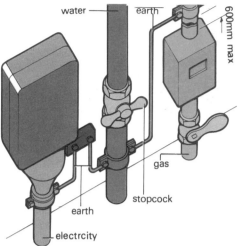

Bond any metal—pipes and radiators, for instance—that could come into contact with electricity to the earth terminal. 'Crossbond' gas and water pipes to earth

extend them. But it's best not to do it yet.

Position the new consumer unit as near to the electricity board's sealed fuse as possible. But if this is in, say, a cellar and you want the unit in a more convenient place you'll have to install a main switch-fuse unit rated at 80 or 100 amps and then run 16mm² two-core and earth cable to the new consumer unit.

When it comes to mounting the unit the best fixing is a fire-proof back board. A piece of 12mm thick fire-resistant chipboard is the best material to use.

Once the unit is firmly in position you can start making the connections. The circuits must be arranged in sequence with the highest circuit ratings nearest the main switch and the lowest furthest away. A common sequence, for example, is to have a 45 amp cooker circuit nearest the switch, followed by 30 amp radial or ring circuits, 20 amp radial circuits (to an immersion heater, for instance) and then the 5 amp lighting circuits.

If you're installing a unit specially designed for MCBs you may have to lift the mounting plate up and out and then take out the busbar so the MCBs can be simply slid along the rail to get the correct order. You don't have to do this with MCBs and fuses that just plug into the unit.

Now you can start to connect up the cables to the terminals in the unit. Work logically beginning with the cooker circuit (if you have one). If the cable won't reach then you'll have to install a junction box and run a cable of the same size to the unit. In this case it could be 4mm², 6mm² or 10mm² two-core and earth cable, depending on your type of cooker.

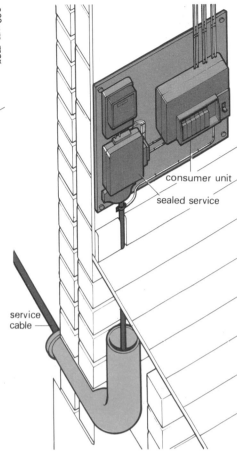

Everything up to and including the meter is the responsibility of the electricity board (top); arrange fuses or MCBs in order with highest loadings next to main switch (above)

At the unit you may have to tap out a knock-out to admit the cable. Modern consumer units are designed with a reasonable amount of space for the wiring up, so don't cut the cores too tightly and avoid making sharp bends in them, which may weaken the insulation and the conductor.

Next strip about 6mm of insulation from the ends of the live and neutral cores and slip a length of green/yellow PVC sleeving over the earth core. Connect this core first to its terminal, then take the black neutral core to the neutral block and the red live core to the top of the fuseway.

When connecting to the terminals, make sure that no bare metal of the conductor is left exposed and it's not good practice to fold over the end of the conductor in a mis-

1 *Label and disconnect the circuit cables, remove the old consumer unit and offer up the new consumer unit*

2 *Arrange the cables near their terminals. Try to keep all the wiring as neat as possible*

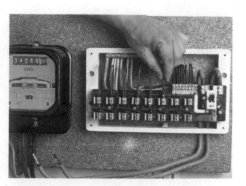

3 *Connect the circuit cores to their terminals in a methodical order working from one side to the other*

4 *Make sure the sleeving is held close to the terminal. Bare wires should not be visible working from one side to the other*

5 *If you're running in a new circuit, feed in the cable and then strip off the insulation*

6 *Arrange the MCB holders in their correct positions and screw the terminals down securely*

7 *Push in the MCBs, replace the unit cover then get the authority to make a test*

guided attempt to get a better fixing.

Repeat this operation for the other circuits, and remember that for ring circuits there'll be two red cores going to the same fuseway terminal.

When all the circuits are in place clip the cables neatly in position and check to see that the sheathing of each cable passes a little way into the consumer unit.

If there isn't going to be an intermediate main switch and fuse, and the consumer unit is right by the meter, then you can connect up the meter tails to the unit and attach the earth core from the electricity board's earthing point. However, if the tails can't be reused because they're not long enough, you'll have to fit red and black 16mm² single core insulated cable to the relevant mains terminals in the unit and leave the other ends free for connection to the meter by the electricity board; they can do this when they come to reconnect the supply.

Follow the same procedure if you install a main switch and fuse, but you will be able to link it to the consumer unit using 16mm² two-core and earth cable.

If you're just replacing an existing consumer unit with a more modern version, then the wiring is even simpler. Once the electricity board have disconnected the supply, you can disconnect the cables methodically, labelling them as you go. Check that they're in the right order and don't need to be rearranged. Disconnect the power and earth cables from the unit and then fit the new consumer unit in position and replace the wires as before.

There's also another situation where you

may have to install a consumer unit, and that's if you intend to run night storage heaters on an off-peak supply. While you can fit the unit and wire up the radial circuits to the separate heaters, you'll also need a time clock and a special meter, which the electricity board will have to install and connect up.

When the electricity board come to reconnect the supply they may wish to check the earthing of the installation. See page 87 for details of earthing the system.

See page 87 for details of earthing the system.

★ WATCH POINT ★

Allow enough length so that the sheathing can be stripped back about 300mm. Then make a trial run to the relevant terminals and cut the cores to the correct length. You should leave at least 25mm of core on the end of each wire so that it can be gripped tightly and screwed down. Once you have checked the length of the earth cable make sure it is correctly sheathed before fitting.

NEW POWER CIRCUIT

Some people try to get round a shortage of sockets by using multi-way socket adaptors, or worse still by wiring two pieces of equipment to one plug, but these practices are dangerous and can result in electrical fires. If you face this problem, the only safe solution is to extend your existing fixed wiring system.

How you upgrade the circuitry depends on a number of factors. First you must investigate the present wiring. If it's old (run in lead or rubber sheathed cable with sockets that take unfused round pin plugs) don't tamper with it. There's a good chance that the insulation will crumble, leaving exposed live conductors. In this instance a complete rewiring job is necessary, and you will be able to specify as many power points and light fittings as you want. Rewiring a house in full is covered in detail later.

However, homes with wiring less than 30 years old will probably have modern ring circuits, with separate rings for each floor of the house (see All about home electrics, pages 4–6). The usual way of adding extra sockets here is to break into the ring (see Add an extra socket, pages 74–77) but you're restricted with this method as to the number of sockets you can add. If you want to install several sockets, your best option is to supplement the existing circuitry by installing a separate modern *radial* circuit. There's nothing to stop you putting in another *ring* circuit, but this will involve you in extra work and the use of more cable than might be necessary. A 20 amp radial circuit will serve all the socket outlets you need providing they are contained in a floor area of not more than 20 square metres. And using a 30 amp radial circuit can serve a floor area up to 50 square metres. Apart from supplying power to socket outlets, radial circuits can also be used to serve individual high capacity fixed electrical appliances such as cookers and instantaneous showers. Note that the cable size needed depends on the current rating of the circuit and the type of fuse used.

Power for the circuit

Whether you're adding extra sockets or providing power for a fixed appliance via a radial circuit, you must consider how to supply the new circuit with power. If there's a spare fuseway in the consumer unit, you can link the appropriate size cable to this and fit a fuse or MCB of the correct rating.

If your consumer unit has no spare capacity for another circuit, you can always replace it with one that has more fuseways (see: Fit a new consumer unit, pages 84–88). But it may be easier to fit a switch-fuse unit or extra consumer unit alongside the present one. If you intend to add more circuits in the future, a small consumer unit is your best option and you'll have to choose this if you are installing night storage heaters.

Planning the new circuit

If you're installing a radial circuit to provide more socket outlets, you'll be taking a cable from the consumer unit and running it to the first socket, looping from here to the next point and so on until you reach the last one.

First decide where you want the sockets and mark them lightly, in case you have to move them later.

Traditionally, sockets have been set above the skirting about 150mm from the floor, although on very deep skirtings special fittings are sometimes set into them. But there is nothing to stop you siting them higher up the wall.

In kitchens, always keep sockets over 150mm above the work surfaces so they are unlikely to be affected by spills. Never site them over cooker hobs and keep them more than arm's length from sinks.

If you're going to the trouble of installing a new outlet point, it's far more sensible to fit a double socket than a single (unless you're installing a fused connection unit). Switched sockets are useful as you don't have to withdraw the plug to isolate an appliance from the mains.

As with all electrical fittings, buy the best you can. One important point to look for is on the back of the faceplate. Check if there's a metal strap that links the screw holes to the earth point. Its presence means that the screws and the metal mounting box are automatically earthed when the faceplate is fixed on. Cheaper sockets don't incorporate this so you have to earth the mounting boxes separately.

How many sockets you need depends on

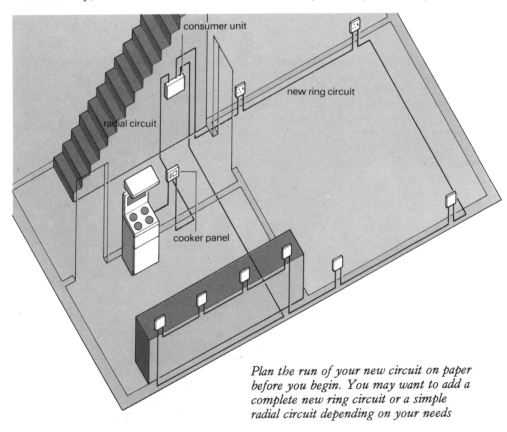

Plan the run of your new circuit on paper before you begin. You may want to add a complete new ring circuit or a simple radial circuit depending on your needs

your existing installation and the electrical equipment you want to use. In kitchens it's often better to install fused connection units to serve some appliances. An *unswitched* fused connection unit is ideal for a freezer as there is no risk of being accidentally turned off except by the freezer's own switch. Fixed appliances like washing machines, dishwashers and waste disposers are best run from their own *switched* fused connection units. The double-pole switch means that they can be isolated from the mains for servicing without having to be disconnected.

Once you've placed the outlet points, work out how to run the cable back from the last point via all the others in turn to the consumer unit or switchfuse unit. It's slightly easier if the circuit serves just one major appliance like a cooker or electric shower. Commonsense, expediency and a willingness to compromise are what's needed. Plan to avoid as many problems as you can foresee, even if it makes the run slightly longer.

The first decision is whether you run the cables on the surface or conceal them wherever possible. Concealing cable runs means cutting some horizontal and vertical chases in the wall—which means a fair amount of making good and redecoration. But you can compromise by surface mounting the run for part of its route before taking it under the floor in some convenient place, inside a cupboard perhaps, and back to the consumer unit.

In a room with a solid floor you may have no choice other than to surface mount most of the run. But in kitchens you should be able to conceal a lot of it behind fitted units and use mini-trunking to disguise the rest.

The alternative with a solid floor is to run the circuit above the ceiling void, then bring the cable down to the socket positions. Again you can use wall cupboards to conceal most of the drops.

Tools and materials

Listing the electrical fittings required is quite straightforward. But make yourself a checklist to ensure you don't forget anything. The biggest problem you're likely to have is in working out how much cable to buy. Measure the proposed run, being generous rather than skimping, and then add a 10 per cent 'detour' allowance. It may also be worth getting a spare junction box just in case you are forced to join two lengths of cable, although you should always try to avoid doing this. Buy plenty of

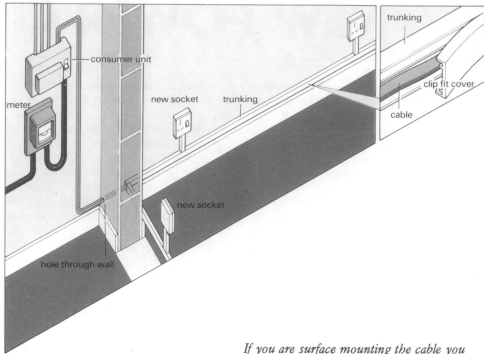

If you are surface mounting the cable you can simplify matters by drilling through a wall to continue the run on the other side. The trunking system consists of a channel and snap-on cover

cable clips for securing the full length of the run.

Simple tools including a screwdriver, wire cutters, a sharp knife, a drill and bits, will see you through most of the work. If you want to cut chases you will also need a cold chisel and club hammer.

Concealing cable runs

Aim for a professional finish when running the cables. It's the only way to blend the additional wiring in with the existing system.

Mark the position of the sockets exactly (use the mounting boxes to draw an outline on the wall), then mark out the proposed route for the cable. Check that horizontal runs don't cross any cables, water or gas pipes already set below the surface. If you can't avoid them you'll have to take extreme care when working near them and you might prefer to consider surface mounting.

Where a cable has to travel some distance up the wall, plumb a line from the socket to the floor. At this point lift back any carpets and raise part of a floorboard to see that there is no obstruction in the subfloor cavity.

Where the cable run has to cross the joists, you'll need to raise a longer length of

floorboard so you can drill a series of holes 50mm below the top of the joists and in the centre of the floorboard run so that the cable is well clear of the fixing nails. A 15mm diameter hole should be sufficient for most cable sizes. However, don't cut the holes at this stage in case you have to change the route later.

With suspended timber ground floors, the gap underneath will enable you to clip the cable to the underside of the joists. There may even be sufficient space for you to crawl underneath which will make the job easier.

Where the cable has runs parallel to the joists, it should be clipped neatly to their sides. Initially, just raise a section of floorboard at each end of this part of the cable run and then check with a mirror and a torch that there is no obstruction to the route from debris left when the house was

★ WATCH POINT ★

For ease of working, and to cause the minimum disruption possible, especially to fitted carpets, plan the run so that it travels round the perimeter of the room even though it may not be the most direct route back to the consumer unit.

built or from water or gas pipes.

When you come to laying the cable here you can either pull it under the floorboards using stiff wire, or you can raise some intermediate boards and stretch an arm under the floor to draw the cable along.

Once you've checked the cable run, you can drill the necessary holes through the joists and chop out the chases for the runs down the walls using a bolster chisel and club hammer. Angle the chisel inwards slightly towards the groove you're cutting. By doing this you'll get a much neater edge, particularly if you are working on soft plaster.

If you're flush mounting the fittings, now is the time to chop the recesses and don't forget to channel down behind the skirtings to take the cable below floor level.

After the route has been prepared, you can start to lay the cable. For added protection where the cable is set in the wall, run it in oval PVC conduit, otherwise fix the cable in place with cable clips positioned every 150mm–225mm.

Now work the cable under the floorboards in sections if the run is parallel to the joists and clip it to the sides. You may have to feed it through the predrilled holes or clip it to the underside of the joists.

Surface mounting the cable

Work out and check the route for the cable. It may be possible to drill through the walls to pick up the run in another room, thus keeping the overall route as short and as practical as you possibly can.

Next measure and cut the various sections of trunking you'll need to conceal the wiring. Corners should be mitred, although you can use special internal and external fittings. Drill and plug the fixing holes and then screw the channel section onto the wall, along the top of the skirting and round door and window frames as dictated by the route.

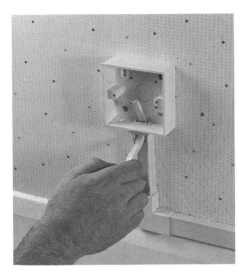

1 *Fix surface mounted boxes carefully, then feed the cable and clip on the trunking cover*

3 *Drill holes along the marks to the depth of the box. Chisel out the rest of the waste*

Now set the cable in the channel and clip on the cover. Remember to leave sufficient cable at the starting point for making the necessary connections.

If you surface mount cable you'll almost certainly be surface mounting the sockets or switch panels, and you can use special adaptors to make a neat join between them.

Fitting the new outlets

How you fit the new outlets depends on the type you are using, but always double check that you are satisfied with their position before starting work.

When you are marking the fixing holes for surface mounted sockets, it's essential

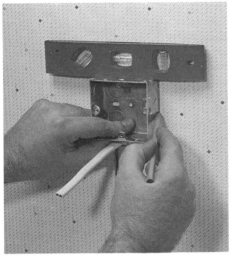

2 *Mark the position of flush mounted boxes using a spirit level to check that they are straight*

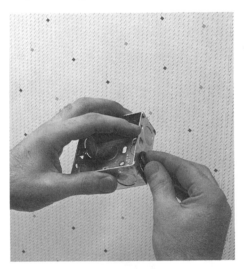

4 *Knock out the cable entry from the box and fit a protective rubber grommet*

that you get the box absolutely level as there is no fine adjustment for getting the faceplate square after the box has been set in place. Next, drill and plug the fixing holes. On a stud wall, if you can't screw into a stud, use cavity wall fixings to hold the box. Before fixing, snap out the cable entry using a small pair of pliers.

Flush mounting sockets

For flush mounted sockets, first check that the wall is suitable. Ideally the wall should be constructed of brick or blocks, though you can recess sockets into a stud frame partition wall. Rest a spirit level on top of the mounting box as you pencil its position on the wall. Next, hold a drill bit against the side of the mounting box and tape the depth of the box on it. Then drill to this depth just inside the four corners of the mounting box's site, and at 2mm intervals along the inside of the guidelines. This will help you chop the recess to the correct depth using a bolster chisel and club hammer. Test with the mounting box at intervals to avoid over-cutting.

★ WATCH POINT ★

If you do over-cut, either pack out the back of the hole with mortar or set the box in place and use extra long screws to reach the fixing holes on the box.

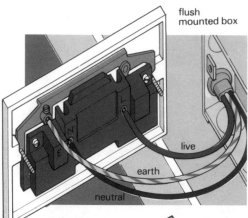

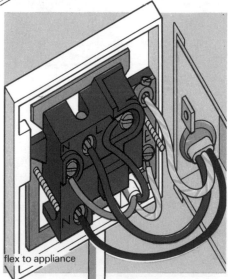

Fix the cores of the cable to the appropriate terminals on the socket faceplate (top). For a fused connection unit (above) or cooker panel (right), connect the cores of the supply cable to the feed side of the box, and connect the appliance flex or cooker cable on to the load side of the box

Mark, drill and plug the fixing holes, tap out the knockout for the cable entry, fit a rubber grommet and then screw the box in place. Don't worry if the box is slightly askew because the adjustable fixing lug allows the faceplate to be straightened.

Feed the 2.5mm² cable (or cables, if the circuit is being continued to another socket) and then strip back about 150mm of sheathing. Sleeve the earth in green/yellow PVC and take off about 6mm of insulation from the ends of the live and neutral cores. Fix these to their respective terminals on the back of the faceplate, and check that you don't have to make a separate earth connection to the metal box. Arrange the cores neatly in the box so they will avoid the fixing screws. Push the faceplate back so that it is flush with the wall and secure.

Fitting a fused connection unit

Fused connection units are fitted in exactly the same way as a socket—they fit onto a single socket mounting box. However, there are special boxes which allow you to fix a fused connection unit directly by the side of a single socket. But you have to run the power supply through one to the other. connections to the appliance go to the 'load'

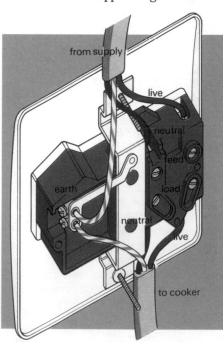

The main thing to remember about wiring any fused connection units is that the circuit cables go to the 'feed' terminals. These are usually the socket type where you just push the exposed cores in and a screw clamps them secure from the side. The flex

terminals. In contrast, these are usually screw down terminals. Wind the flex cores anti-clockwise round the shaft so they are drawn tightly when the screw is tightened.

Mounting a cooker panel

A cooker should be supplied by its own radial circuit run in 6mm² or 10mm² PVC sheathed and insulated two-core and earth cable and protected by a 30 or 45 amp fuse or MCB respectively. Which size of circuit you install depends on the rating of the cooker, anything above 11kW needs the larger circuit.

There are two main types of control panel for a cooker. There is the *cooker panel* which contains a 45 amp double-pole switch for isolating the cooker from the mains and a 13 amp switched three-pin socket. The alternative is the *cooker switch* which just contains a 45 amp double-pole switch. Both are connected in exactly the same way and can either be flush or surface mounted. But for flush mounting remember that the control needs a deeper recess than the ordinary 13 amp socket.

Installation is very similar to fitting a fused connection unit, except that this time you use the same size cable to feed the cooker as you do to supply the control. The supply to the cooker can either be chased into the wall and then fed through an outlet plate below worktop height and connected to the cooker, or it can be run via a connection block if you find it easier to run the cable in two sections. In any event, the cooker panel or switch shouldn't be more than 2 metres away from the cooker.

Set the mounting box in the wall, with grommets protecting the cable entry points. Make sure the box is set square as there are no adjusting lugs. Feed the circuit cable and cable to the cooker into the mounting box and prepare their ends. Remove the faceplate from the panel and then connect the circuit cable to the mains side of the unit. Next connect the cooker cable to its terminals and then run an earth core from the terminals on the mounting box to the earth terminal on the switch. Finally fit the mounting box and faceplate.

The connections at the cooker end are equally straightforward. If you run one length of cable to the cooker, all you have to do is remove the back panel from the cooker to give access to the terminals, then prepare the cable ends and connect them to those terminals. If you install an intermediate connection unit all you have to do is link the cores to the appropriate terminals.

Powering the circuit

Power for the new circuit can be taken from the existing consumer unit or a new unit. Which you use depends on your circumstances, but in all cases turn the power off before connecting into the existing system.

The rating of the fuse or MCB that you have to fit to protect the new circuit will govern where the fuseway should be positioned in relation to other fuseways. The larger the rating, the nearer to the double pole main switch it should go. A common arrangement is a 45 amp cooker circuit, two 30 amp ring circuits, a 30 amp circuit for an instantaneous water heater, a 15 amp circuit for an immersion heater (when the heater is rated at 3kW or higher) and two 5 amp lighting circuits.

In order to make space for the new fuseways, you may have to rearrange the existing MCBs or fuseways. Depending on the type of consumer unit you've got, you may either have to remove the busbar and slide the fuseways along the mounting bar to provide a slot, or, if the fuseways aren't manoeuvrable, you'll have to reorder the live cores going into them and then change the position of the fuse-carriers accordingly.

Feed the cable into the unit and cut it back until you have 200mm spare to work with. Strip the sheathing right back to free the cores and then sleeve the earth core in green/yellow PVC. Then connect the earth to the earth block. Strip off 6mm of insulation from the ends of the other cores and take the black core to the neutral block and the red to the live terminal at the top of the spare fuseway or fitted MCB. Make sure no bare metal of the core is left exposed. Next fit the cover back onto the consumer unit and press in the fuse-carrier or MCBs.

Fitting a switchfuse unit

A switchfuse unit is just a very small consumer unit containing one, or perhaps two, fuseways. Fitting one is a two stage operation—first you have to wire in the new circuit and then the unit has to be connected to the mains supply.

Remove the faceplate from the unit to reveal the fixing holes and screw the unit to a fire-resistant backboard.

The new circuit connections are identical to those for a consumer unit with the cable being fed through a knockout in the top of the unit protected by a rubber grommet. The red core goes to the live, the black to the neutral block and the earth core goes

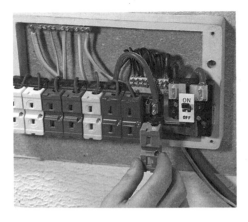

5 *You may have to rearrange your consumer unit to accommodate the new circuit*

7 *Position the distribution board between the consumer unit and the new switchfuse unit*

★ WATCH POINT ★

Ideally, mount the board on blocks. This will keep it away from the wall and reduce the dangers of damp.

to the earth terminal.

The second operation is to get power to the switchfuse unit. Because this entails working on the supply side of the installation it means that you can only do part of the work yourself. The electricity authority **must** make the final connections.

Essentially, what happens is that the power supply is divided into two after it leaves the meter with a feed going to the consumer unit and another to the switchfuse unit.

What you can do is fix the distribution board next to the switchfuse and then link this to the terminals of the unit using red, black and green/yellow 6mm² single core cable. The authority must make the final

6 *Fix the new switch fuse unit to a fire resistant board and wire the circuit into it*

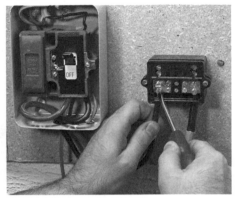

8 *Wire the unit to the distribution board and have the authority make the final connection*

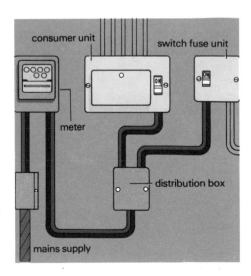

If you are adding a switchfuse unit, the supply will be split at a distribution board

connections to the mains. With the power off they disconnect the meter tails and run them to the distribution board, before connecting the distribution board to the consumer unit.

REWIRE YOUR HOUSE

electricity authority may provide a minimal supply to give you some light and power while you do this. If you are already living in the house, the work will have to be planned carefully so that you can cook, eat, wash and see while you're doing it.

At this stage you must decide how many circuits you are going to have. Since 1947, houses in the UK have been wired with ring mains for sockets and radial circuits for the lights (see pages 244–246). Each floor of the house usually has one power circuit supplying the sockets and one lighting circuit. It may, however, be better to have a separate power circuit for the kitchen since this is an area which uses a lot of electricity.

Planning a lighting circuit

The maximum number of lighting points allowed on a lighting circuit is 12, assuming that each has at least a 100 watt bulb. Where there are more lights than this on your plan or where the total load exceeds 1,200 watts, you will have to have more circuits to cope with the extra load.

Much of the work involved in re-wiring is well within the competence of the average handyman: it involves jobs like lifting floorboards, making holes in joists and walls and screwing things together. But you need to know what you are doing to avoid the two main risks of electricity: electric shock and fire. The first is avoided by *never* working on live circuits or equipment and by having proper insulation and earthing; the second by understanding how to choose the correct cable sizes and components and how to design the system to minimize fire risks, which includes choosing the correct fusing. However, if you're in any doubt about your electrical competence, don't attempt the work: employ a professional. It's not an area where any risks should be taken.

First considerations

The decision to rewire your house is not one to be taken lightly. If the electrical system is faulty it should be replaced as a matter of urgency, but the job involves a considerable amount of upheaval and will take some time to complete satisfactorily. First of all assess the state of your wiring.

There are several ways of recognising old wiring. The first is a number of separate fuse boxes near the meter, some of which may serve only a single socket. Most modern wiring systems have a single fuse box—called a consumer unit (see pages 300–304)—but even if you have one of these, it doesn't mean that the wiring has been replaced. The same applies to sockets and switches—new ones don't guarantee that you have new wiring.

So the next thing is to turn off the electricity at the mains switch or switches and have a look at the wiring itself. The easiest places to look are behind switches and sockets and in the loft space where the up-stairs lighting circuit will be. It's easy to tell the difference between cable with shiny sheathing and PVC insulation and that with old, dull rubber—apart from the appearance, the latter will probably be crumbling and cracking and should be replaced.

The first decision is *when* you should rewire. If you're buying a house (and it's essential to look at the electrical system before buying a house), the best time to rewire is before you get all the carpets down and the furniture in place. It's even better if you can do it with the house empty—the

1 *Old rubber-sheathed single core cables must be replaced with new PVC-sheathed and insulated cable. Do this as soon as possible*

2 *Old-fashioned fuse boxes with double-pole fuses can be dangerous; replace them with a consumer unit when you rewire the house*

3 *If you have to do this to your sockets, you don't have enough of them; you may be dangerously overloading an old radial circuit*

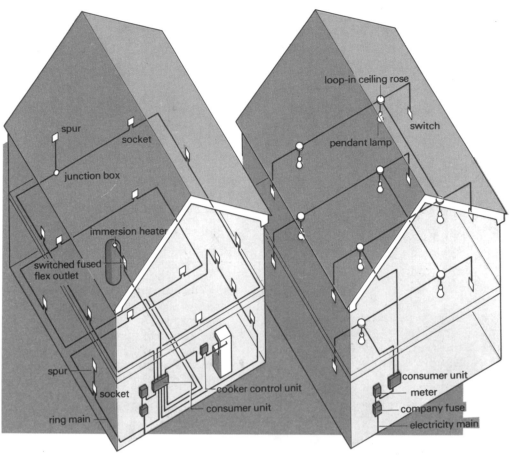

Ring main power circuits (left) and loop-in lighting circuits (right) are the ideal you should aim for when you plan to rewire your house or flat

There are two methods of wiring lighting circuits: junction box and loop-in. Both use 1.0mm² or 1.5mm² cable protected by a 5 amp fuse and are wired as a radial circuit—the power is supplied from the consumer unit via a cable that runs from one light to the next. The difference between the two types is that with junction box wiring, the cable connects a series of junction boxes with separate cables running from each junction box to its respective light switch and ceiling rose, while with loop-in wiring the supply cable connects the ceiling roses with just one cable going from each ceiling rose to its own light switch (in other words, the roses themselves act as junction boxes).

Junction box wiring requires ceiling roses with two terminals and an earth terminal; loop-in wiring needs ceiling roses with three terminals and an earth terminal. Usually the roses you buy can be used for both—you just use the appropriate terminals in each case.

Each method has its advantages and disadvantages: loop-in wiring uses more cable but you save on junction boxes; junction boxes are easier to wire (working on your knees in the loft) than loop-in ceiling roses (above your head in the room) but are more difficult to get at later. For most installations, you will probably use cable most economically if you mix junction box and loop-in wiring methods on the same circuit.

As well as deciding which wiring system to use, you will also have to decide which method or methods you are going to use to run the cable along the ceiling and down the walls. For ceilings, the best thing to do is run the cable between and through the joists in the ceiling space. For walls, you can run cables directly on the surface with mini-trunking, bury it in the plaster or, with hollow stud partition walls, run it behind the plasterboard.

The third decision concerns the number and types of light fittings you have. You shouldn't forget that table, bedside and standard lamps run off the *power* circuit when planning your overall lighting so that you can decide how many fixed lights you want and where you want them. There is a wide choice of lighting fittings, including plain and decorative pendant lights, track lighting, spot lights, wall lights, downlighters, fluorescent lights and so on. Some of these will need special fittings—some decorative pendants, for example, need something more substantial than a ceiling rose to hang from (see pages 267–270).

Replacing the lighting circuit is an ideal time to think about changing the switching arrangements. Apart from altering the position of individual light switches, you might also want to introduce dimmer switches (remember that fluorescent lights need special dimmer switches) or to have two-way switching of, say, hall and landing or bedside lights. Intermediate switching (operating lights from more than two positions) is also possible and there may be opportunities for operating two or more lights from the same switch position.

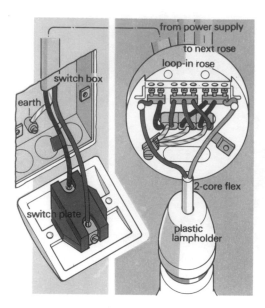

Loop-in connections at a ceiling rose: if the lampholder has metal parts, its flex should have an earth core which is connected to the rose

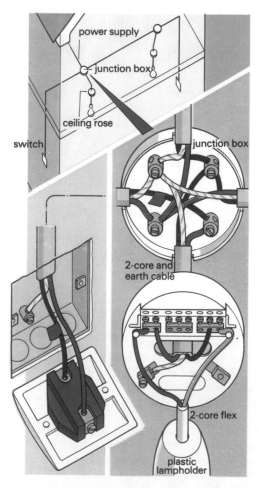

In certain circumstances junction box lighting circuits may be the only answer; you can wire these up by using loop-in ceiling roses

Details of the wiring for all these will be given later.

Finally you should consider what, if any, extras you want to run from your lighting circuit. Typically these might include outside lights, porch lights, electric clocks, extractor fans for the bathroom or kitchen and, possibly, shaver sockets for the bathroom or elsewhere. Check that these won't overload the circuit.

Planning the power circuits

There are two types of power circuit, too: the radial circuit and the ring circuit. Your choice will be dictated by your needs.

With a radial circuit, just one cable goes from the consumer unit to feed the sockets or other appliances on the circuit; with a ring circuit, two cables go from the consumer unit (from the same live terminals)—one to the first socket or fused connection unit in the circuit, the other to the last one. All the intervening socket outlets are connected together in turn in a complete ring. This means that the current is shared by the two cables and a greater load can be carried.

The UK wiring regulations specify one type of ring circuit and two types of radial circuit. Ring circuits must be wired with cable of at least 2.5mm² and can serve an area of up to 100 square metres when protected by a 30 amp fuse or miniature circuit breaker (MCB). One radial circuit, protected by a 20 amp fuse or MCB and wired in 2.5mm² cable, can serve an area of up to 20 square metres; the other, wired in 4.0mm² can serve an area of up to 50 square metres when protected by a 30 amp cartridge fuse or MCB (but *not* a 30 amp rewireable fuse).

The restriction by area rather than by the number of sockets is based on the assumption that you will only use so much power within a given living area at any one time.

As mentioned above, it may be sensible to give the kitchen its own circuit. Not only does this allow for the growing number of kitchen appliances available (many of which, like washing machines, chip friers, kettles and tumble driers have built-in heaters) but also allows you to protect this circuit with an earth leakage circuit breaker (ELCB) which considerably reduces the risk of receiving an electric shock.

For each room in the house, work out the number of socket outlets you think you might want (none are allowed, of course, in bathrooms) and the number of fixed appliances (heated towel rails, extractor fans, washing machines and so on) that you

might want to run off the ring circuits.

Don't skimp on the number of socket outlets: it costs little to have a few extra and it's much better to have too many than not enough. Remember that you're designing for the life of the system and that the number of electrical appliances in use is likely to go on increasing.

As a guide, the following number of outlets (a double socket counts as two outlets) should be adequate to avoid using adaptors and having trailing flexes:
• Living rooms—8 or 10.
• Bedrooms—6 or 8.
• Halls/landings—2 or 4.
• Kitchens—10 or 12.

On the point of boxes, you will need to decide whether to have your sockets (and, for that matter, light switches) surface-mounted or flush-mounted. Flush-mounted

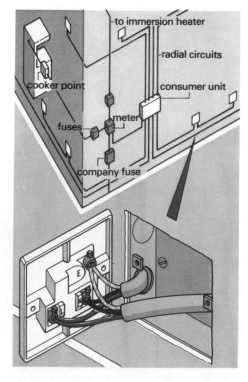

Sockets on a ring main have one cable going in and one coming out; sockets at the end of a spur have only one cable going in

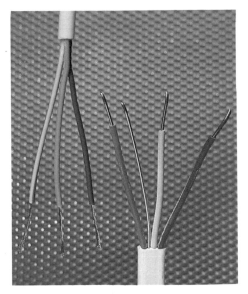

4 *Two types of wire: 0.5mm² two-core and earth flex for pendant lights, and three-core-and-earth cable for two way light switching*

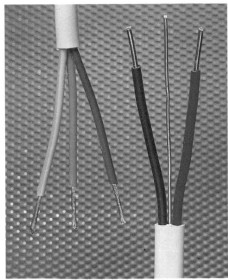

5 *Power circuit wiring: 2.5mm² two-core-and-earth cable for ring mains, and three-core heat-resistant flex for immersion heaters*

Other circuits

The other circuits you're most likely to want are a cooker circuit, an outside circuit and a circuit to supply an immersion heater or an instantaneous electric shower.

A *cooker* has its own supply from the consumer unit which goes to a cooker control unit positioned within reach of the person using the cooker. This has a switch to turn the supply to the cooker off and, sometimes, a 13 amp socket as well though this is not generally a good idea because it invites flexes trailing across the hob. From the cooker control unit, cable is taken to a cable outlet box positioned on the wall behind the cooker where a further piece of cable connects to the cooker itself (the only instance where cable, not flex, can connect an appliance to the mains). The fuse rating at the consumer unit will depend on the maximum capacity of the cooker: for cookers up to 12kW a 30 amp fuse and

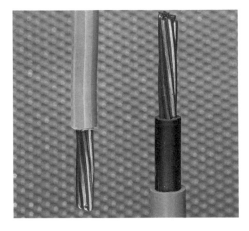

6 *Single-core earth cable, and double-insulated cable for meter tails: this has a colour-coded inner sheath in red or black*

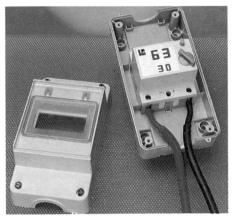

7 *Fit an earth-leakage circuit breaker (ELCB) between the electricity meter and the consumer unit for added protection*

8 *Power circuit hardware: cooker point; one- and two-gang sockets; flex outlets, junction boxes, and socket boxes of varying depths*

sockets, which fit on a metal box sunk into the plaster, look much neater but are harder work as they involve making quite a big hole in the wall and chasing the circuit cable into the plaster. Surface-mounted sockets, which fit on to a plastic box secured to the wall surface, are more obtrusive but you can use cable run on the surface in plastic mini-trunking.

Fixed appliances can be run from fused connection units (FCUs) on the power circuit, either via a flex connected into the FCU or via a flex outlet box. Fused connection units and sockets can also be run as 'spurs' from a ring circuit provided the number of spurs does not exceed the number of sockets or FCUs on the ring and

that each spur supplies only one single or double socket or one FCU.

Bathroom circuits: There are quite specific regulations in the UK covering the use of electricity in any room containing a bath or a shower. The main rules are:

•No socket outlets are allowed.
•No portable appliances are allowed.
•No switches (except cord-operated type) may be within reach of bath or shower.
•Lampholders must be the all-insulated type with a protective skirt, or else fully enclosed fittings must be used.
•Shaver sockets can be fitted, but only the type with an isolating transformer.
•All exposed metalwork must be cross-bonded to earth.

6mm² cable is used; for cookers more powerful than this a 45 amp fuse and 10mm² cable is used. Even if you have a low-powered cooker, it might be sensible to put the higher rated circuit in to cope with any future changes. A split-level cooker can be wired from one control unit provided both parts are within two metres of it.

The UK wiring regulations require that all new sockets installed to supply power *outside* are protected by an earth leakage circuit breaker and are marked '**FOR EQUIPMENT OUTDOORS**'. If the socket is inside the house on a ring circuit, it can have an ELCB incorporated in the socket itself; if you're putting in a circuit for an attached workshop or garage, an ELCB

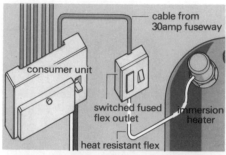

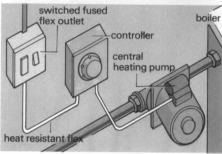

Two common circuits to fixed appliances: in each case use a switched fused connection unit to terminate the fixed wiring and heat-resistant flex running to the appliance

should be fitted to protect the whole circuit. This can be mounted in its own enclosure separate from the consumer unit or can be part of the consumer unit—make sure you choose a unit with enough room for the ELCB to be included and mounted neatly to one side.

Circuits for sheds and workshops not connected to the house or circuits for the garden itself need special precautions to protect them from damage—see pages 320–325.

A circuit for an electric *shower* unit needs to be able to cope with the full rating of the shower. Provided this is 7kW or less a 30 amp fuse can be used, with cable of 6mm² if a rewireable fuse is used, or 4mm² if a cartridge fuse or MCB is used. The cable is run from the consumer unit to a ceiling-mounted pull-cord double-pole switch and then to the shower.

In many electrical installations an *immersion heater* is supplied off one of the ring circuits, but it should have its own circuit wired in 2.5mm² cable and protected by a 15 amp or 20 amp fuse. The cable is taken from the consumer unit to a 20 amp double pole switch (ou can get special ones marked 'water heater'). A timeswitch can usefully be wired into the circuit between the double pole switch and the immersion heater. The flex to the heater should have heat-resistant sheathing and should be open to the air.

Earthing

Traditionally, domestic earthing was supplied via the mains water pipe. But with the increasing use of plastic for water pipes, this can no longer be relied on and most electricity authorities supply a terminal connected to the sheathing of their supply cable from which a 6.0mm² single-core cable is run to the consumer unit to provide earthing. In some rural areas and old installations, however, it is necessary to supply a separate earth via an earthing rod and a voltage operated ELCB.

Your electricity board will tell you if they operate *protective multiple earthing*. This means that they may have special requirements for the connections to the mains and for the size of conductors used in *cross-bonding*, where all metal supply pipes and all exposed metal in the house should be connected to the earthing point for safety.

Wiring

There are, in the UK, complicated rules for working out the sizes of cables you should use in different circuits.

This is because the temperature a cable can reach will depend not only on how much current is flowing through it, but also on how well the heat can escape. The things that affect this are the way the cable is run, the presence of thermal insulation, and the temperature of the air surrounding the cable.

Cable run in conduit or in trunking can carry less current than cable run on the surface or buried directly in the plaster. If the cable is in contact with thermal insulation, a larger size should be used (1.5mm² rather than 1.0mm² for lighting cable in the loft, for example). You should avoid running cable in direct contact with polystyrene insulation and within the airing cupboard and also avoid running it in bunches through holes in the ceiling or wall—keep each cable at least one cable's width from its neighbours.

All connections must be in non-combustible enclosures—mounting boxes and pattresses, for example.

In the UK the electricity authority owns the equipment up to and including the meter. The rest of the installation is your responsibility—and you do not need their permission to alter or extend it. However, they will want to test and inspect it before they connect electricity to a new installation.

You will need to tell them what the likely maximum load of your installation will be.

Fusing

In any circuit there will normally be three fuses. The first line of defence is the fuse in the plug (or fused connection unit) which is rated usually at 3 amps or 13 amps. The second line of defence is the circuit fuse—5, 15, 20, 30 or 45 amps depending on the circuit—and, finally, there is the electricity authority fuse. This is rated at 100 amps and should *never* be tampered with. The fuses are there to prevent excess currents flowing in the wires and thus causing them to overheat. The fuses in the consumer unit are colour coded for the different ratings. Rewireable fuses are the most common and are the cheapest, but they have the disadvantage that they require a current somewhat higher than their actual rating to make them blow. This can sometimes mean that you have to use larger cable in the circuits they are protecting, which isn't a good thing. Cartridge fuses (similar to the fuses used in plugs) blow nearer to their rated current, but the most convenient of all is the miniature circuit breaker (MCB)—a small switch which trips off at a current only slightly greater than its rating and is easy to reset.

Tools and materials

Before starting work, you will need to make sure that you have all the proper tools, equipment and electrical fittings.

You will need two tool kits—an electrical one and a builder's one. The electrical kit should contain:
- Wirestrippers (adjustable ones).
- Wire cutters (diagonal cutters).
- Pliers (two pairs—long-nose and general-purpose).
- Screwdrivers (100mm and electrical).
- Handyman's knife for stripping cable sheathing.
- Red PVC insulation tape.
    The building kit should include:
- Electric drill and masonry bit.
- Wood-boring bits (for making holes in joists).
- Bolster and 6mm cold chisel.
- Hammers (club and claw).
- Screwdriver (150mm).
- Floorboard saw.
- Filling knife and wall filler.
- Small spirit level.
    In addition, you need protective clothing,

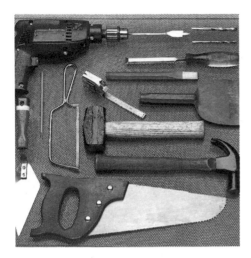

9 *You will need several everyday tools to carry out a rewire — a drill, hammers, saws, chisels, bolsters and measuring tape*

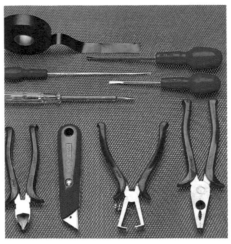

10 *Make a detailed shopping list — cable, wiring accessories and consumer unit — and get several quotes before buying*

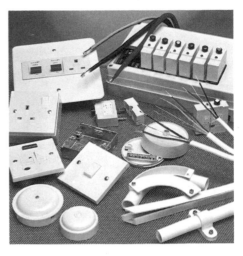

11 *For the actual connection work, you need screwdrivers, wire strippers, side cutters, a sharp knife and some PVC tape*

particular knee pads for working in the loft (and a face mask if it is dirty).

You will also need to find a good source for buying electrical accessories. Compare prices in your local DIY superstores and electrical wholesalers. Use the following as a checklist—you will need to work out the precise quantities yourself:

- **Consumer unit**—at least 8-way, preferably with cartridge fuses or MCBs and perhaps an ELCB as well.
- **Cable**—cheaper in reels for lighting (1.0mm^2 or 1.5mm^2) and ring circuits (2.5mm^2); buy only as much as you need by the metre for other circuits.
- **Sockets**—buy double sockets with switches (sometimes cheaper in packs of 5 or 10).
- **Light switches**—one or two gang.
- **Boxes** for light switches—plaster-depth (16mm) boxes should be adequate for most flush light switches.
- **Lamp-holders**—choose heat-resisting kind, and enclosed type for bathrooms.
- **Ceiling roses.**
- **Junction boxes**—5 amp four-terminal for lighting: 30 amp three-terminal for ring circuits.
- **Fused connection units** for fixed appliances.
- **Cooker control unit and cable outlet box.**
- **Immersion heater switch.**
- **Flex** for pendant lights (0.5mm^2 round two- or three-core, depending on fitting).
- **Cable clips** (different sizes for each cable size being used).
- **Grommets** for metal boxes.
- **Green/yellow PVC sleeving** for covering bare earth wires inside boxes.

- **Special single-core cable** for earth connection (6.0mm^2) and for meter tails (16.0mm^2).
- **Three-core and earth cable** for two-way lighting and running two lights from one (2-gang) switch.
- **Conduit or mini-trunking.**
- **Clock connectors** for clocks/extractor fans.
- **Special boxes** (architrave boxes or BESA boxes for mounting wall lights).

The final thing you will need is some kind of continuity tester for making sure that connections are intact. You could use a multimeter or make up your own tester with a battery and a light or buzzer.

Starting work

Assuming that the whole house needs re-wiring, the work should be divided into four stages: the upstairs lighting (working from the loft), the downstairs lighting and upstairs ring circuit (first floor floorboards up), the downstairs ring circuit (downstairs floorboards up) and finally any special circuits such as cookers, immersion heaters, etc.

You will have to decide at what stage to fit the new consumer unit (if you need one): with whole house rewiring, it's probably best to fit it immediately after the upstairs ring main, connecting the two lighting circuits to the existing fuse boxes as you go.

Depending on the present wiring arrangements, you might also want to fit the cooker and immersion heater circuits just before (or at the same time as) fitting the new consumer unit so that you have hot water and cooking facilities.

Rewiring lighting circuits

Whether you're fitting loop-in or junction box wiring, the procedure is much the same—you simply work from one room to another.

In the planning stages you should have decided where in each room you want the lights and where you want to position the switches, as well as choosing the type of light fitting and switch.

Removing old wiring

After isolating the circuit from the supply (*remove* the fuses—don't just switch off at the fuse boxes) and checking that all the lights are dead, the first thing to do is to disconnect all the light switches and light fittings. Be careful when unscrewing old ceiling roses—you could bring down some of the plaster as well. Remove any wooden mounting boxes that you come across.

Next go up into the loft and unclip the cables from the rafters or disconnect the lengths of metal conduit—you'll have to cut through the cable inside to do this. If there is metal conduit chased into the walls of the room below, it may be much easier to use this for running new cables to light switches: before pulling the old cable out of these, tie a piece of wire or thin cord to the cables at the top of each conduit run.

The cord is attached to a new length of cable which will be drawn down from the loft later on. Make sure that the top and bottom of the conduit are protected by a bush to prevent the cable from chafing.

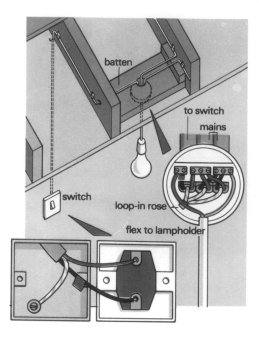

With loop-in wiring, the circuit cable runs from rose to rose. Each rose is linked directly to the switch controlling it

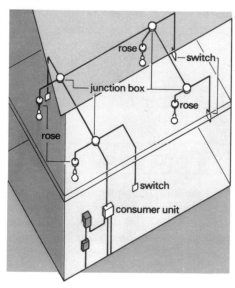

With junction box wiring, the cable runs from box to box. From each junction box separate cables then run to the ceiling rose and switch

There should be a length of conduit to each switch, and one more from the fuse box to the loft. Otherwise, you'll have to chase holes in the plaster for flush-mounted switches or run trunking for surface-mounted ones.

The next thing to do is to mark the position of all the light fittings and switches on the ceilings and walls. For ceiling-mounted lights, drill a small hole from the room below so that you can locate their position in the loft.

You may find that the old ceiling lights were simply screwed to the laths of a lath-and-plaster ceiling—don't copy this, but rather secure the new rose either to a joist or to a piece of wood fixed between the joists. A firm fixing is essential.

Wiring up

With loop-in wiring, the supply cable goes straight to the position of the first ceiling rose or enclosed light fitting; with junction box wiring, it goes to the first junction box—these form an inner 'circle' inside the circle formed by the ceiling roses.

There will be three cables into each loop-in ceiling rose, four into each junction box: supply IN, supply OUT and the cable to the SWITCH, plus supply to the LIGHT with junction boxes. The four terminals are connected as follows:
- **live** wires (red) of IN, OUT and SWITCH
- **neutral** (black) of IN and OUT (+ neutral supply to light)
- **live return** (black) from the SWITCH (+ live supply to the light)
- **earth** wires for all three cables (+ earth to light).

With loop-in wiring, the terminals may be in blocks with the correct number of holes for the number of wires—the light is connected via its flex to the two outer terminal holes. With junction box wiring, a fourth cable is run from the junction box to the ceiling rose where the flex is connected to the cable in the terminals: brown to *live*, blue to *neutral* and yellow/green (where appropriate for metal fittings) to *earth*.

All bare earth wires in junction boxes, ceiling roses and switches should be covered with yellow/green sleeving. The black *live return* from the switch should be marked at both ends by wrapping a small piece of red insulating tape around it to show that it is in fact a live wire.

The switch connections for one-way single-gang switches are the same with either method: the switch will be marked to show which wire goes to which terminal so that the switch turns on the 'correct' way.

Two-way switching

The easiest way to run two-way switching is to use two-core and earth cable from the switch to the loop-in rose or junction box (as with one-way switching) and run a three-core and earth cable from the first two-way switch to the other.

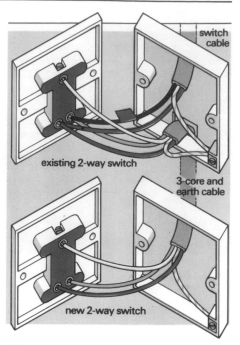

Three-core and earth cable links the two switches in a two-way switching circuit. The cores are colour coded for identification

Wiring a ceiling rose

Wiring a ceiling rose is straightforward providing you know which cable is which—it helps to label them as you go along. Pass all the cables through the backplate of the ceiling rose and then screw it to the ceiling before making the connection to the terminals. Make sure that the ladder you're standing on is secure and is standing level.

The cover of the ceiling rose should be slipped over the pendant flex before this is attached to the two outside terminals: it's easier to wire up the lampholder and strip the rose end of the flex before carrying it up to the ceiling. The two flex conductors are hooked over little lugs in the ceiling rose to carry the weight of the lamp and its lampshade. Make sure you have stripped enough sheathing to allow for this.

Fitting the switch

First you will have to make the hole in the wall to take the flush-mounted switch box—see Fitting boxes. The cable will need to be cut to the correct length to allow you sufficient room to make the connections but no so long that the switch faceplate can't be screwed to its box. This is particularly important if you're using plaster-depth boxes where there is less room behind the switch for the tangle of wires. The earth wire should be connected to the terminal on the box—it earths the fixing screws—and the red and black wires connected to the switch faceplate as described above.

Wall lights

The principle for wiring wall lights is exactly the same as for ceiling lights. The difference is that it will be easier to use a junction box in the loft or ceiling space and that you will need a special box for mounting the wall lights themselves—see pages 256–260 for more details.

Rewiring power circuits

In some ways, power circuits are easier to rewire than lighting circuits. But they need careful planning to get the sockets in the right place and to minimise the amount of cable used for the job.

Work out the number of socket outlets that you need—you can never have too many. You will also need to think carefully about where they're to be positioned. For most rooms, about 300mm above the floor is the usual position though old or disabled people will find it much easier if they're positioned higher up—say 1m above floor height. In the kitchen, the socket outlets should be about 150mm above the work surface (except for floor-standing appliances).

When planning the cable run, allow for any fused connection units for supplying fixed equipment. If you mark the positions of all these and all sockets on your room plans, you can work out how to run the circuit—in particular where the ring is to go and which sockets and connection units are to be fed from spurs connected to the ring.

Removing the old wiring

As with lighting circuits, the first thing to do is to make sure the existing circuit is completely dead by removing all the circuit fuses. Depending on how recently any additions were made to your power circuits, you may be able to use some or all of the existing PVC cable as part of your new circuit. But all rubber- or lead-sheathed cable should be removed, as should all round-pin sockets.

Leave cables which have been buried in walls—unless you're positioning the socket in the same place, in which case you must replace them. You'll have to lift floorboards

12 *Where cables run across the line of the joists, drill holes about 12mm in diameter and thread the cable through*

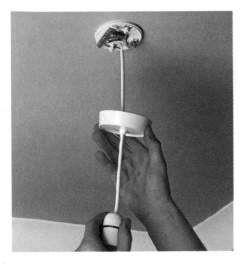

14 *Screw the rose in place and connect up the cables. Then add the flex. Check your electrical connections before you replace the rose cover*

to get at some of the cable which means clearing out at least some of the furniture and lifting up the carpet first.

Go round all the rooms marking the positions of the sockets on the walls with a pencil so that you can make the holes for flush mounting boxes. This can be hard and tedious work and it is probably best to work on one room at a time.

Running the cable

You must run 2.5mm² two-core and earth cable from the consumer unit position to the first and last sockets of the ring on the first floor. Later, when you come to do the downstairs ring the circuit cable will need to be run below the ground floor.

If, as is likely, the consumer unit is in the cupboard under the stairs, it should be

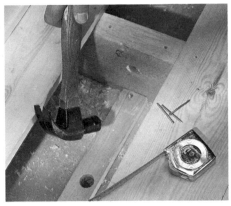

13 *At the position of each ceiling rose, nail a pre-drilled batten between the joists*

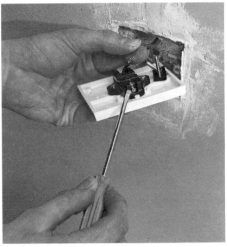

15 *At each switch position connect live and neutral switch cable cores to the terminals. Always make sure the cores are held securely*

possible to run the two cables directly into the space between the ground floor ceiling and the first floor floorboards.

Run the cable into the box for the socket and leave a short length hanging out for making the connections. Run another length of cable into the box, down under the floorboards and along to the position of the next socket. At sockets where you're fitting a spur, a third cable will need to be run from this position to that of the socket or fused connection unit on the spur.

Once all the cable is in place (see Routing cables) the next thing is to make good the plaster round the sockets and where cables have been chased into walls (with surface-mounted sockets, you don't have this problem). You can use metal or plastic conduit to protect the cables but it is acceptable simply to plaster over them—providing they run in straight and

16 *At each socket position, chop out the recess and the cable chase with a cold chisel and lump hammer. Then draw in the cables*

17 *Thread the cables into the box through one of the knockouts, strip the cores and connect them to the appropriate terminals*

18 *After making good, fold the cables neatly back into the mounting box and attach the faceplate. Check that it's level before it is finally tightened*

predictable lines downwards from the sockets (*never* horizontally) and that the cables are secured with clips before you cover them with plaster (you may need to chisel a bit of plaster away to fit the clips). Tuck the wires inside the boxes before replastering.

Wiring up a socket

The ends of each pair of red, black and earth (with yellow/green sleeving) wires should be twisted together using a pair of general-purpose pliers before putting them into the terminals and tightening the screw.

Once all the connections have been made, push the socket back into its box, making sure that the wires are not kinked or squashed, and secure the faceplate.

Routing cable and fitting boxes

Unless you run all the cables along the surface (which is unsightly), you're going to have to go through, across and along joists and through, up and down walls.

Joists: the easiest way to run cable is between the joists and under the floorboards. In the loft and under the first floor the cable should be clipped to the side of the joist at regular intervals. Underneath the ground floor (if it is a suspended timber floor) the cable can rest on the ground or be clipped to the sides of the joists or fixed to support battens nailed at right angles.

Running across joists is more difficult. In the loft, make use of the binders that run over the joists at right angles; below the first floor, you'll have to make holes in the joists. Make a hole with a brace and bit (or electric drill and wood bit) at least 50mm below the top of the joist to avoid damage from floorboard nails.

Walls: cutting channels (chases) in walls to run cables is one of the most time-consuming jobs in electric wiring. It has to be done accurately and carefully. The normal tool is a sharp bolster used with a club hammer. Mark the lines on the wall and cut down both lines before chiselling out between them with a cold chisel.

One problem area is getting the wires behind skirting boards. It's much easier if you take the skirting off, but this creates extra work in making good, particularly if you damage it getting it off. Alternatively, you can use a long masonry drill to make the hole in the wall *and* in the floorboard underneath.

You may have to remove the skirting if you have a solid ground floor so that you can run the cable round the walls behind the skirting.

In a stud partition wall, you may be able to run the cable up the space between the two sheets of plasterboard, but you may hit trouble in the form of noggins running horizontally between the vertical studs.

Mark the position of the box on the wall, making sure that the chase for the cable lines up with one of the entry holes in the box. Use a masonry bit and electric drill to make a honeycomb of holes the correct depth within the marked area to save on the chiselling necessary.

Once you've drilled all the holes, chisel away with your bolster to get a neat, square hole. Carry on chiselling until the box's front edge sits flush with or slightly before the surface.

Now drill and plug two holes in the wall behind the box to line up with the mounting holes in the box. The box should be secured with round-head screws though the plaster used to make good round the box will help hold it in place.

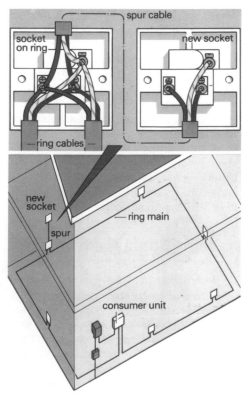

It's easiest to wire spurs from a socket on the ring main. The spur cable simply runs from the terminals of the ring main socket to the new outlet

Heavy duty circuits

Wiring a cooker is straightforward, but positioning the control unit needs careful thought.

You'll probably find that you don't need a very long length of 10mm² (or 6mm²—see page 313) cable, which is just as well because it is quite expensive. The cooker control unit should be positioned so that it can be reached from where you stand in front of the cooker, preferably without having to reach over hot pans. If the control unit has a socket outlet, make sure that any flex runs from it would not be anywhere near the hot cooker rings.

The normal height for a cooker control unit is about 1.5m off the floor. The unit will need quite a large hole in the wall if it is to be flush mounted.

The supply cable is run from a 45 amp (or 30 amp) 'way' in the consumer unit to the control unit position. Another length of the same cable is run down from the cooker control unit to a cable outlet box mounted about 500mm above the floor; the cooker cable is then attached to this box. Unless this is vertically below the cooker control unit, this may involve chasing down to the floorboards and back up again to the outlet box to keep the runs vertical.

The connections inside the two boxes are simple: most control units have three terminals to which the cables coming from the consumer unit must be fitted; the cable running to the cooker or outlet box connects to three more terminals. The same applies to the outlet box, except that the three cores of the cables running from the control unit and the cooker will be connected to common terminals.

You may want to reorganise your cooker supply to power split-level units instead of a free-standing cooker. You can either link both components into a single cooker control unit, or run the circuit cable from the unit first to one component and then on to the other. In the first case, both components must be within 2m of the control unit; in the second case the component furthest from the control unit must be no more than 2m from it.

Immersion heaters and showers

Both of these systems demand their own electricity supplies—15 or 20 amps for the immersion heater, 30 amps for an electric shower—and these must be run direct from the consumer unit. Shower units must have a double-pole switch outside the bathroom or, in the form of a pull cord, inside. The immersion heater should be connected through a double-pole switch with flex outlet. Heat-resistant flex runs from this to the heater itself.

Fitting an ELCB

You may want to fit an earth leakage circuit breaker (ELCB)—also known as a residual current device (RCD)—as part of your re-wiring to protect certain parts of the system.

Some consumer units have ELCBs built in so that you can connect certain power circuits to them—the ones covering the kitchen and garage, say, plus any outside circuits. Alternatively, you can fit an ELCB immediately after the circuit fuseway and run the ring circuit on from there—use either a single 4.0mm² cable or a pair of 2.5mm² cables between the ELCB and the consumer unit and make sure that the circuit beyond is properly earthed—how you do this depends on the type of ELCB you're using. Most are fitted in a separate enclosure which needs to be bought separately.

If you want to protect only one or two sockets, you can use special socket outlets which include an ELCB built in. They're the size of a double socket, but have only one outlet. They're ideal for use in powering appliances being used out of doors.

The type of ELCB needed for these applications is a 30mA one with a loading appropriate for the socket or circuit.

Earthing and cross-bonding

It is absolutely essential that all the mains services—water and gas pipes—be earthed where they enter the house or as near to this point as possible. To do this, you run a 6mm² single-core cable with green/yellow insulation to the pipes, where it is connected with a special bonding clamp; this has a label saying 'SAFETY ELECTRICAL CONNECTION DO NOT REMOVE'

In addition, all exposed metal which could conduct electricity should be earthed. The Electricity Board will advise what is necessary depending on your house and their earthing arrangements (and you must consult them as soon as you can), but as a minimum you should earth the water pipes leading to the hot and cold taps in the bathroom and kitchen, the central heating pipes and the hot water cylinder.

If cross-bonding has already been carried out as part of the previous installation, connect the cables to your main earthing point and have its efficiency checked by an expert. This is particularly important if any plastic plumbing has been used.

Fitting the consumer unit

Installing a consumer unit is a job that can be done in a day—you'll need to have the electricity disconnected.

When you are ready to install the new consumer unit, arrange for the Electricity Board to come in the morning to disconnect the electricity and again the evening to reconnect it. At this point you need to be sure that all your new work is electrically safe, and so you should test each completed circuit. There is a limit to the number of tests you can do yourself, but you should check polarity (all the wires connected to the correct terminals) and continuity (no breaks in the circuit). The first is mainly a matter of inspection; the second requires a simple continuity tester or multi-meter. Don't test for continuity with the power on. An electrician (or the electricity board) will carry out other tests to make sure that the circuit is safe for you.

The actual job of installing a new consumer unit was covered in detail on pages 300–304. Make sure you label each circuit as you connect it up to the unit.

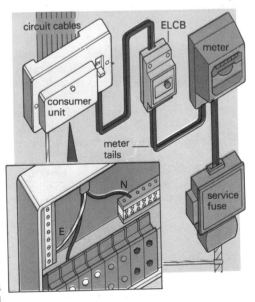

Within the consumer unit, the live cores go to individual fuseways, the others go to terminal blocks

OUTDOOR POWER SUPPLY

To run a power supply underground dig a trench 500mm deep lined with sand. Run the conduit straight up the wall from the trench

earth piled up

supply from consumer unit

mastic sealant

Taking electricity outside your house opens up a huge number of possibilities. It can be used to run power tools in a garden shed; an electric lawnmower anywhere in the grounds; a battery charger in the garage; fairy lights at the bottom of the garden—or even a stereo system to play sweet nothings to the geraniums in your greenhouse.

But don't underestimate the hazards involved: outside the house, electricity is potentially much more lethal. This is partly because the chances of sockets and other fittings getting wet is much higher—and electricity and water just don't mix. It's also partly because there is more chance of the installation suffering physical damage from wheelbarrows or gardening tools.

For these reasons, the rules governing outdoor electric supplies are usually much more stringent than those for indoor wiring—and you should find out what your local electricity code or regulations prescribe. The details given here are based on IEE Wiring Regulations, used in the UK.

First thoughts

Your first consideration should be what sort of a supply you want, and where. It's a good idea to be fairly generous in your estimates, and to allow for any expansions and extensions you think you might need. The most time-consuming part of the job is running the cables to where you want them, and installing ones that have enough capacity for any supplies you might want later could save you quite a lot of effort in future years.

There are four main systems you might consider, and they each are wired in a different way.

Sockets outdoors, mounted externally on a house wall: This is the easiest system to install—you can connect it to an existing circuit inside the house—but it is quite restricting.

Lighting and socket outlets in a garage, greenhouse or shed: You must provide a separate circuit for a supply to any detached outhouse. Between the house and the shed (or whatever) the cable can be run either underground, or slung overhead. Though there are special cables for outdoor supplies, it is probably easiest to use ordinary PVC sheathed twin and earth cable, protected if it runs underground in heavy duty plastic conduit.

Armoured PVC cable and Mineral Insulated Copper Core (MICC) cable are available, but they are expensive and require specialized tools and techniques to connect them to their glands and terminals—definitely a job for a professional electrician. **Other outdoor sockets, mounted throughout the garden:** These are perfectly acceptable providing the sockets are of the waterproof type or in waterproof boxes. Any mounting posts or boxes must be firmly fixed. A separate circuit must be used for these sockets; it must be wired up with PVC cable run through heavy duty plastic conduit and buried in the ground.

Outdoor lighting: It's best if lighting used round the garden, and any pumps used in garden ponds, are run from extra-low voltage supplies: 12V or 24V. These of course need a transformer before they can be connected to the mains supply. Site the transformer in the house or an outhouse, so that all the outdoor cable will be a safe low voltage. Low voltage cables needn't be buried or protected from damage (they aren't lethal) bit it's wise to do so—cutting through a cable is irritating, to say the least.

Types of sockets

• Ordinary plastic sockets, as used in the home, can be used in garages and greenhouses—but they're not the wisest choice as they can be damaged easily. A better choice is an impact resistant, or metal-clad socket—accidental knocks won't damage these robust sockets.

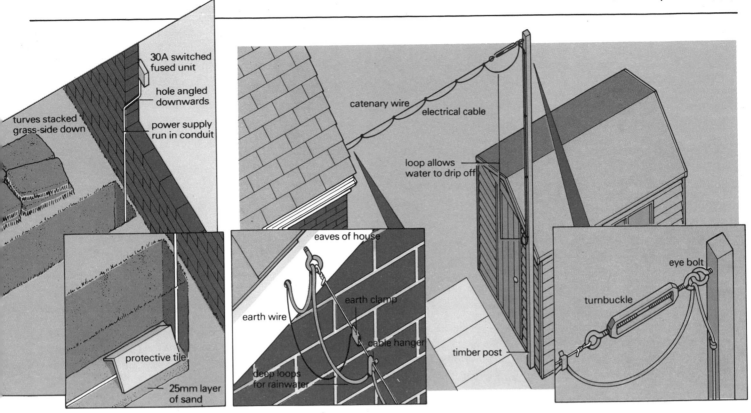

30A switched
fused unit

hole angled
downwards

power supply
run in conduit

turves stacked
grass-side down

catenary wire   electrical cable

loop allows
water to drip off

eaves of house

earth clamp

earth wire

cable hanger

protective tile

deep loops
for rainwater

25mm layer
of sand

timber post

eye bolt

turnbuckle

• For use externally, but in sheltered conditions, a metal socket with a shower-resistant, splash-proof casing may be enough.

• In more exposed conditions, a metal-clad socket fitted into a totally waterproof housing can be used.

• Special waterproof metal sockets are the alternative. These don't need an extra housing, but they can be used only with special plugs, which you would have to fit to each of the appliances you might want to use in the garden.

• For a socket connected as an extension to an existing internal electrical circuit, you should use a socket fitted with an RCD—see Providing protection—unless the whole circuit is fitted with such an RCD.

Providing protection

For electricity supplies outside, a normal fuse (or even a miniature circuit breaker—MCB) is not enough protection against electric shock—there are many potentially lethal faults that a fuse will not react to, and even for those that it does, it may not blow quickly enough to prevent you from being killed. So all circuits for outside use should be protected with a *residual current device*, or *RCD*. This is frequently known as a current-operated earth-leakage circuit breaker (ELCB).

For a separate outdoor circuit, use a *high-sensitivity* RCD, fitted into just that circuit.

High-sensitivity RCDs will 'trip' with a fault current as low as 30mA—well below the level at which you can get a fatal electric shock. And by confining its action to just the outside circuit, you ensure the whole house isn't cut off whenever it trips—a high-sensitivity device may occasionally trip by accident, or during a lightning storm.

Circuit-protection RCDs are available in a number of current-carrying capacities, from 24 amp to 80 amp. For the usual 30 amp outdoor circuit, use one with a 30 amp rating. For a socket fitted to an indoor circuit but intended for use with outdoor appliances, it may be better to use a socket outlet RCD which protects just that socket: again, you should go for a high-sensitivity (30mA) type.

An RCD is not a substitute for a fuse—note that you will need a fuse or MCB in the circuit as well.

When choosing a site for a RCD or ELCB, consider the rest of the wiring as well: it would repay you to place it between the consumer unit and the company fuse so that all the domestic wiring is protected in the event of an electrical fault developing. Remember, however, that if you intend to place the RCD or ELCB in this position, it's the electricity supply authority's job to make connections to the company fuse—if you are in any doubt, consult them or a professional electrician before commencing work. They may also be able to check your wiring before making final connections to the consumer unit.

An overhead supply can be erected using easily available materials. Keep it above minimum height and allow loops in the cable for moisture to drip off outside the buildings

Sockets on a house wall

If you have only a small garden, it's worth considering restricting any outdoor electrics to a socket mounted on the house wall—it's much the simplest job to do.

You can connect a socket mounted on the outside of the house wall to an existing ring mainpower circuit, or a radial circuit, if this won't overload it—see Adding to a power circuit.

First (assuming you have a choice) decide whether you are going to connect the extension to a circuit running at ground level, or one running at first floor level. The decision is basically one of convenience. The socket itself should be mounted about 1.2m above ground level, so that it is less likely to be splashed or damaged—in either case, you'll have to run cable up or down the wall.

Choose a position to mount the socket (or sockets, if you're fitting more than one). Then decide on the type of sockets to use—see Types of socket. (When buying, make sure you get any mounting bases, waterproof covers, and so on that you'll need: explain clearly that you intend to mount the socket out of doors.) It's best to have the cable run indoors as much as possible—running it up or down the inside of the wall until it is directly behind the position of the socket outlet. If you can do this, then start by drilling the hole in the wall for the cable. Make it large enough to take a length of plastic conduit (so that the cable won't chafe on the brickwork) and angle it so that the outside is slightly lower than the inside; then no water can drain into the house. Fit the conduit into the hole, then run a length of cable through it. Connect the cable to the socket, and mount the socket on the wall, following manufacturer's instructions. Make sure the socket is fixed firmly: drill into the bricks or stonework rather than the mortar courses, and use proper wallplugs. If your house is clad with weatherboard, still fix the socket to the brickwork beneath. It is wise to seal the joint between the socket and the wall using mastic, to keep out any moisture.

If you want to run the cable outside rather than on the inside, then you should run it through heavy duty plastic conduit. Use proper fittings to joint the conduit to the piece inserted in the house wall. Then fix it securely to the house wall, and carefully feed the cable through. (See Using plastic conduit.)

Run the cable to the point where you intend to connect it to the existing circuit. For wiring under the floorboards, if the cable run is at right angles to the joists, drill the joists at the mid-point of their depth: do not notch the joists. Cable run over walls can be fixed directly to the wall surface, or run in plastic trunking fixed to the wall. Or you can bury it in the wall. To bury cable on a masonry wall, cut a vertical slot (a *chase*) through the plaster to the wall behind. Do this using a sharp, wide chisel—a bolster chisel and club hammer will do, but especially on old, crumbly plaster, an old wood chisel might make a neater job. If you are leaving the cable exposed on the wall surface, clip it neatly into place. If you are burying it in plaster, a few clips will help to keep it flat and clear of the wall surface. You do not need to run it in conduit, but you can do if you prefer.

On a stud wall, you can usually drop the cable down the cavity behind the plasterboard. Finally, make the connections at the joint box or into the back of an existing socket. Switch on again at the mains, and check that everything works properly.

Replace any floorboards, and make good any plaster chases using a proprietary ready-mix plaster or cellulose filler.

Finally, remember that even the most weatherproof of sockets should not be used while it is raining—unless the manufac-

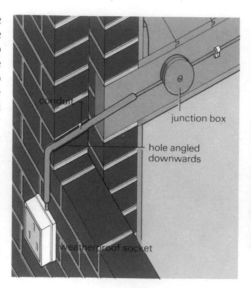

Installing an outside socket can be as simple as one indoors, if you use weatherproof units and prevent water getting into the house

5 *Fit the socket face-plate securely and leave the weatherproof cover in place at all times when you're not using the socket*

turer's instructions *specifically* say that you can. The most that the majority of weatherproof sockets can offer you is the guarantee that they can be installed safely outside to be used in dry weather.

Adding to a circuit

Ring main power circuit: to install one single or double external socket, the easiest thing to do is to run a branch, or *spur* cable from the ring to the new socket. You can connect the spur cable directly to the back

1 *Drill through the outside wall using a masonry bit which matches the conduit—otherwise you'll have to drill from both sides*

6 *You can connect to the ELCB yourself, but you must get the electricity supply authority to connect it to the mains supply*

of an existing socket on the circuit, providing this really is on the ring main and not already on a spur (you cannot connect another branch to an existing spur). Or you can connect the spur to a joint box, fitted into a run of cable—again, providing this is actually on the ring, and is not a spur cable. If you want to connect more than one external socket, it is best to break the ring and extend it.

Whatever method you use, wiring is carried out in 2.5mm² twin and earth cable. The bare earth wire on each cable must be sheathed with green and yellow plastic.

2 *Run the conduit down to the socket location, fit a conduit adaptor to the socket, and cut the conduit to length*

3 *Feed the electric cable through the conduit from inside the house then fix the socket case in position. Trim and strip the cable cores*

4 *Wire up the socket in the normal way, but make doubly sure the connections are tight and the wires cannot work loose*

7 *An ELCB fitted between the company fuse and the consumer unit will protect the entire house from danger if a fault develops*

A single ring main circuit, and its spurs, should not serve an area greater than 100m², which may restrict the positioning of the external socket; in any case, it is sensible to put the socket as close as possible to the circuit.

Radial circuits: Run a branch cable from the *last* socket on the circuit, to each of the external socket outlets in turn. There is a much greater restriction on the area that radial circuits can serve: a circuit wired in 2.5mm² cable and fused at 20 amps can serve only 20m²; one wired in 4mm² cable and fused at 30 amps can serve only 50m².

Using plastic conduit

Plastic conduit is much like plastic plumbing pipe. It can be bent by hand using bending springs—you may have to *carefully* apply some heat for making tight bends or in cold weather—or you can use elbows. The conduit is joined with push-fit fittings—for use outside and underground, joints should be sealed using a special solvent adhesive.

On long lengths, or at tight bends,

Plastic conduit comes in a range of sizes and diameters with adaptors to suit the majority of fittings such as bends, socket outlets and switches

'inspection' fittings should be used. These have a removable cover so that you can check the cable is being fed through the conduit properly, without strain or twisting. After testing the circuit, covers should also be sealed in position.

Straight lengths of conduit over about 8m long should be joined so that the tube does not buckle or split as the temperature changes. Expansion couplings will need sealing when used out of doors or underground, but use a non-hardening mastic, not the normal solvent.

When buying your conduit, tell the supplier what size of PVC-sheathed cable (and how many, if more than one) you plan to thread through it—conduit comes in a range of diameters.

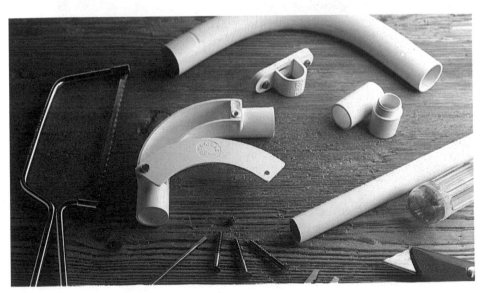

Cables underground

Burying the supply cable gives a neat result, but can be difficult to do under, say, a concrete path. It's also essential to decide at the outset what size of system you want—so you don't need to re-lay the cable later.

Cable run underground should be buried at least 500mm deep—more under flower borders and vegetable plots. It must be protected by running it inside heavy duty plastic conduit. You must cover the conduit with paving slabs or proprietary slabs marked DANGER—ELECTRICITY available from builder's merchants.

Decide where the cable will emerge from the house, and enter the outhouse. Dig a narrow trench between these two points—in as straight a line as possible. The bottom of the trench should be reasonably smooth and soft: if the grounds is full of stones, first lay a 25mm bed of sand.

Assemble your conduit on the surface next to the trench. If the route is long, it may be sensible to thread the cable through each section before you join it to the next. Leave enough cable spare at both ends of the conduit to reach to the first piece of switchgear—if at all possible, do not have any joints in the cable. For a 30 amp supply, you need 6mm² twin and earth cable.

Lower the completed conduit into the trench. The cable must be protected with conduit until it disappears inside the buildings with vertical sections of conduit, properly sealed to the horizontal run in the trench using either elbow fittings or bends. Thread these sections of conduit over the cable, then fix the conduit to the walls.

Pass the cable through the walls, again through properly jointed sections of conduit—see Socket on a house wall.

Don't fill in the trench until you have finished the wiring and tested the supply.

If you are lucky, and your house and outhouse are connected by a brick wall, you can run your cable along this, rather than burying it. It should still be protected inside plastic conduit. You must **not** run cable along a fence—fences can collapse.

Whatever method you use for the cable run, it's best to connect it at the house end to an RCD—which will also act as the isolating switch the circuit needs.

Run the cable from the point at which it enters the house to the consumer unit—see Socket on a house wall. Fix the RCD onto the wall next to the meter or consumer unit following manufacturer's instructions and wire the supply cable to this. Connect the RCD to a new set of metal tails running to the consumer unit. Use a 30 amp fuse (either rewirable, cartridge, or MCB, depending on what your consumer unit is designed to take).

If there's no spare capacity in the consumer unit, connect the RCD to a new switched fuse unit (essentially a single-way consumer unit) and get your electricity board to connect the RCD to the supply.

8 *Decide on the route your trench will follow and mark this out with a string line, avoiding concrete paths and intervening walls*

9 *Dig the trench 500mm deep and fill the base with sand. Assemble and test fit the conduit then run the cable through it*

10 *If you can't get the proper slabs (marked 'DANGER— ELECTRICITY'), use concrete paving slabs to protect the conduit*

11 *Fill in the base of the trench, then fix the conduit to the outhouse wall using saddle clamps before filling and returfing the rest*

Overhead supply

An overhead supply saves you having to dig up gardens and paths, but it can be just as tricky to install as an underground one, and doesn't look so nice.

Overhead cable must be kept at least 3.5m above the ground—5.2m above any driveway. If the house or outhouse isn't high enough, you will have to run the cable between posts either firmly fixed in the ground, or securely bolted to the building.

On short spans of up to 3m, ordinary PVC cable will be able to support itself; on longer spans, you will first have to fix a supporting *catenary* wire, using special eyebolts and straining screws. PVC cable is then slung from this wire.

Start by installing any posts you need to raise the cable. Remember that the cable will sag in the centre of its run—allow an

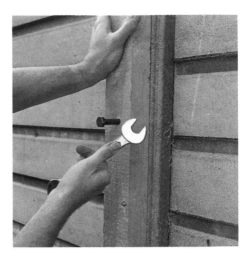

12 *At the outhouse you can either sink a post in the ground or bolt it to the wall so that the incoming supply cable is at the right height*

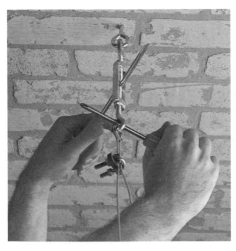

13 *Cut the catenary wire slightly under length, connect it to the turnbuckle, stretch this on the eyebolt and tighten using a screwdriver*

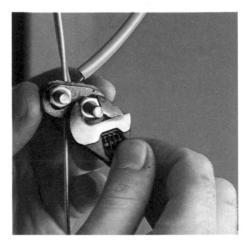

14 *Fix the catenary wire to the turnbuckle using a cable clamp and eye. Use a second cable clamp to secure an earthing wire in to it*

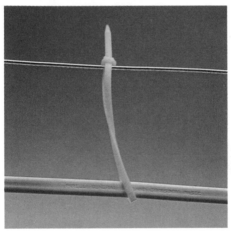

15 *Hang the power cable in loops from the catenary wire using cable ties turned in a figure eight to prevent the cable chafing*

extra 300mm for this.

The catenary itself is a length of galvanized steel wire. At one end, this is firmly bolted to the wall or post. At the other, it is attached to a straining device which allows you to take up any excess slack. The straining device is hooked over an eyebolt fixed to the wall.

To make the loops in the wire requires you to turn the wire round an eye former and secure it with a cleat, both of which are available from hardware stores.

When the catenary is securely fitted, attach the cable to it using cable fasteners at 500mm intervals. At the ends, allow the cable to drop into a loop before passing it through the walls. The loop helps to shake off any rainwater drips that might enter the house or run down the wall. For a 30 amp

supply, use 6mm² twin and earth cable.

The cable can pass into the house or outhouse at this level or you may want to run it down the wall first. As long as it is well above head height, it should not need protection; otherwise, enclose it in plastic conduit to prevent accidental damage.

The catenary itself must be earthed. Connect a separate sheathed earthing wire to the catenary, and run this to the connecting point inside the house.

Connections in the outhouse

It's up to you how you wire up your outhouse. Treat the incoming cable as you

would the 'tails' from the electricity meter inside the house, and follow the normal wiring practice.

In most cases, all you will want in your outhouse is a few socket outlets and a light or two. Providing you have chosen your cable and fuses correctly, then you can connect a radial power circuit direct to an unfused isolating switch rated at 30 amp or more, fitted where the supply cable enters the outhouse. In the radial circuit, put in a fused connection unit (fused at 3 amps) and from this run a normal lighting circuit.

Cable in the outhouse need not be covered but if you think there is any chance of it being knocked or otherwise damaged, then run it in conduit or channelling, or in a trunking system.

If your plans are more ambitous, it would be sensible to connect a small consumer unit to the incoming supply, instead of a simple isolating switch, and run lighting circuits and ring main power circuits off this, following all the usual rules for domestic wiring. If you intend a large-scale installation like this, check how much current it might take—if it's greater than 30 amps, you'll need a larger supply cable, RCDs, and main fuses than those specified in this article.

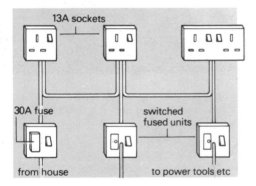

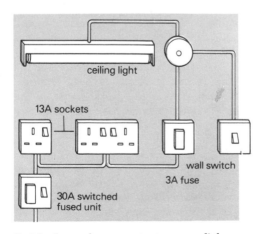

Inside the outhouse protect your radial power and lighting circuit with a 30 amp fuse

GARDEN LIGHTING

There are many different types of outdoor lights, and they can be classified in a number of different ways. Perhaps the most useful way of looking at them is by how and where they can be fixed, since this determines to a large extent how easy or difficult they will be to install.

Wall-mounted lights: The main virtue of lights fixed to a house wall is that they will be easy and cheap to wire up. Several different patterns are available.

The simplest are porch lights—in the shape of old-fashioned carriage lanterns, modern globe lights, 'brick' lights, or the more utilitarian bulkhead lights. All these use normal GLS (general lighting service) bulbs like the ones used in most indoor light fittings. In a clear glass fitting, a 60W bulb will appear very bright in the dark, and may dazzle; though the light will be softer and easier on the eye if the light has a translucent, diffusing, cover. If you use a porch light on an outside wall, make very certain it is designed for outdoor use; lights marked as *jet-proof* will be, but others should be carefully checked.

Spotlights can be mounted on house walls, too, but it is vital that you get a type which is designed for outdoor use—this will use a PAR (parabolic aluminized reflector) bulb which has a specially-strengthened glass front. It is easy to dazzle people with spotlights, so they are best mounted high up, where they can cover a whole area with light. Note that PAR38 bulbs should be available in both spot and flood versions— the spot type covers a smaller area, but gives a more intense light; the flood version will light a larger area but to a lower lighting level overall.

For the brightest light over a large area, a special tungsten halogen floodlight can be used. These are usually mounted high on a building, or on top of a pole, but some types are designed for use at ground level, primarily for floodlighting the front or side of a building.

All the wall-mounted lights have their place in an outdoor lighting scheme—but if you want the best effects, use them carefully. Floodlights and the more powerful spotlights should be kept mainly for utilitarian lighting of drives, paths, yards and so on. But don't forget that patios and barbecue areas need utilitarian lighting too, so that you can see to cook safely. You may well be able to light these areas with judiciously-placed spotlights mounted on house walls. If you can direct the beam through trees or other foliage, to break up the light and provide it with a bit of colour, so much the better.

An alternative trick with spotlights is to mount them low, and shine them up at the house wall—though this may distort the architectural features of the house considerably, it will provide a much softer glow over a particular section of the garden.

Porch lights might provide some of your patio lighting—but be careful to place them where they will not cause glare. The type where the bulb is covered with multi-coloured glass panels might be more restful on the eyes than a clear glass globe—if the style goes well with your house.

Ground-fixed lights: To illuminate parts of your garden away from the house, the safest type of light to use is one that is securely fixed to the ground. One version consists of a steel spike with one or more spotlights mounted on top—you simply drive the spike into the ground wherever you want, and angle the light to illuminate a certain feature (usually a tree, hedge, or shrub). If you change your mind about siting it's easy to pull out the spike and stick it somewhere else (though moving the wiring may be more difficult—see below).

These spotlights are available either as *mains-voltage* or *low-voltage* types. The low-voltage type is based on sealed-beam car headlight lamps; they may be less flexible in beam spread and direction than the mains-voltage types, but they are very much safer and easier to wire (the cable can simply be laid along the ground) and changing their position in the garden is easy. Mains-voltage spotlights can be fitted with a variety of bulbs having different wattages (for varying levels of brightness), beam widths and so on. But wiring them up requires much more care, with the cable being buried well underground—and this makes it more awkward to move the lights once they have been installed.

Another type of light consists of a totally-enclosed and weatherproof bollard with a bulb mounted inside behind a translucent glass or plastic cover. These are part-buried in the ground and can be moved only with some upheaval, so you need to decide carefully first where you want them.

Often, a light mounted at ground level will be all you need in the garden itself—beams aimed upwards at trees and so on will be reflected back to ground level, and bollards, or spotlights aimed downwards, will light the ground sufficiently to make it possible to walk round the garden safely. Remember that you are not trying to create the levels of lighting that you would need inside the house.

If you do need bright illumination, however, you will have to mount a spotlight up high, and aim its beam down to ground level. Unless you have a sturdy brick wall nearby (in which case you can use any of the wall-mounted lights described above) it is best to use only low-voltage spotlights, for safety. These can be mounted on top of a pole or, for better looks, hidden in the upper branches of a nearby tree.

Festoons (or 'fairy lights) are sets of mains or low-wattage bulbs strung on a flex, and wound (carefully) through trees, along walls and so on. These are mainly for decoration, but of course, provide some illumination for lighting the tree and the surrounding ground as well.

Underwater lights: If you want to mount coloured lights in a pond or fountain use special low-voltage complete-sealed lamps.

Providing protection

Whatever type of outdoor lighting you intend to install, protect the circuit with a **residual current device** (RCD), sometimes known as a current-operated earth-leakage circuit breaker (ELCB). This breaks the electric circuit if there is any leakage of current to earth which might cause an electric shock. An ordinary fuse or miniature circuit breaker (MCB) is not sufficient on its own—there are many potentially lethal faults it cannot react to, or won't react to quickly enough.

Use a high-sensitivity RCD fitted into just the outdoor circuit—it is easier to wire in this position, and means that if it trips by accident (as a high-sensitivity RCD some-

times does) it does not disrupt the electricity supply within the house.

Wiring an RCD into a circuit is usually easy—just a matter of connecting the ingoing and outgoing cables to the correctly-labelled terminals. It's best to locate the RCD at a point just before the cable enters the consumer unit.

Rigging up fairy lights

Fairy lights are often only temporary—wired up for a party, say. But it's just as important to make sure that they are safely installed as for a permanent installation.

There are two types of outdoor festoon lighting. One consists of a number of lampholders with miniature bulbs already

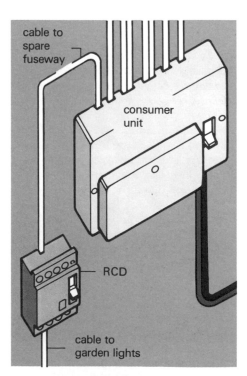

Locate the RCD near the point where the circuit is to enter the consumer unit

1 *Position the festoon lights on the special cable and press the cable over the pins. Seal up the ends of the cable with PVC tape*

3 *Press the festoon cable through a hole drilled in the window frame or wall and seal the hole with mastic to prevent water penetrating*

2 *You can fit normal GLS 40W bulbs in many different colours to the lampholders to achieve a bright, decorative effect*

4 *If the festoon lights are to be switched on from inside the house, the cable must have its own socket fitted with an RCD to protect the circuit*

prewired to a heavy-duty flex. The other consists of a special *festoon lampholder* which you fix to festoon cable. To assemble this sort, use a length of the cable specified by the manufacturers of the lampholders—usually 2.5mm² special festoon cable. Unscrew the top of the lampholder to expose the fixing pins beneath. Press the special cable over these pins so that one pin pierces the live core and the other pierces the neutral core, and screw the cap firmly back into place. Make sure the last lampholder on the circuit conceals the cut end of the cable. Separate the ends of the cable and wrap them with insulated PVC electricians' tape before closing the last lamp holder.

Although 2.5mm² cable can carry a great deal of current, it is wise to restrict the number of lamps to prevent too much voltage drop along its length. An absolute maximum of 40 lamps with a bulb rating of 40W is sensible.

Once you have made up a set of fairy lights, don't remove or reposition any of the lampholders—this will leave holes in the insulation which could let in water and cause a short circuit.

Hang your lights from trees, poles or buildings. Make sure the cable is not under tension and that none of the bulbs could swing against branches or walls—otherwise in a wind they could break, which would be very dangerous. Keep the bulbs high enough so that they are well out of people's reach.

Unless there is a special outdoor socket in your garden, you will have to plug your fairy lights into a socket in your house or outhouse. If the lights are going to be used for any length of time—perhaps over a summer holiday—it is worthwhile leading the free end of the flex into the house through a properly-made hole in the wall or in a window frame. Make the hole with a suitable drill, aiming to have it pointing downwards slightly towards the outside and large enough so that the flex will pass through without chafing. Seal up the hole both on the inside and the outside with a non-setting mastic.

Once inside the house, the flex can be wired to a plug. But don't plug this into an ordinary wall socket—instead, replace the nearest socket with a special socket-outlet fitted with its own high-sensitivity RCD and use only this for your lights.

If you have wired your festoon lights into special festoon cable, you will not be able to wire the end into an ordinary plug. In this instance you must wire the cable into a fused connection unit on a circuit fitted with an RCD for extra protection.

Connecting wall-mounted lights

Try to fix the light at about the level of the first floor—this will make wiring runs short and easy to install.

First drill a hole through the wall of the house—angling it slightly downwards towards the outside—large enough to take a piece of plastic conduit so that the cable will not chafe on the brickwork. If you are careful in positioning, the hole will fall between the floorboards and ceiling at the first floor level. Pass a length of 1mm² two-core and earth cable (*not* flex) through the hole and make the connections to the light. You may be connecting direct to the bulb holder, or to a connector inside the base of the light—if the latter, make sure the con-

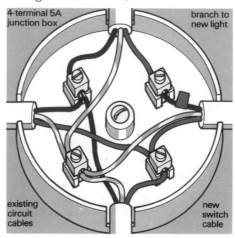

4-terminal 5A junction box

branch to new light

existing circuit cables

new switch cable

A junction box allows you to connect the new light and switch into the existing electricity supply

nections are housed inside a totally enclosed 'termination' box (if the light does not have one, you will have to add one). If the light is double-insulated, it will not need an earth connection, so you must cut back the earth wire to ensure it does not touch any part of the light. If the light is earthed, you must make sure the earth wire is properly connected to the right terminal.

Fasten the light to the wall, carefully sealing all joints and holes with mastic.

You can connect the feed cable to a switch and into the electricity supply in a number of ways. The easiest method is to break into the ground floor lighting circuit and insert a joint box as shown in the diagram, connecting to it both the feed cable from the outside light and the cable going to the switch.

If the wall light is set at a low level, drill through the wall in the same way and take

5 *By removing the back of a low-voltage spotlight it can simply be 'threaded' onto the low-voltage cable supplied*

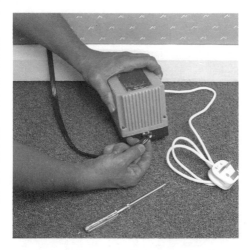

6 *Cable from any low-voltage lights must be connected to a specified transformer before being plugged into the RCD socket*

7 *Push the mounting spike well into the ground. One or more spotlights provide intense decorative lighting among shrubbery*

your supply from the ring main via a 5 amp fused connection unit.

Providing the lights, and any external cables, are kept out of reach there is no real need to fit an RCD to this sort of circuit.

Connecting a bollard away from the house follows exactly the same procedure except that you will have to dig a trench for the supply as you would for any mains-voltage garden fixture.

Installing low-voltage lights

Although low-voltage lights are not electrically dangerous, you still need to exercise some care when installing them.

You can place low-voltage lights anywhere you like in the garden and simply run cables back to the house from each, or you may be able to run several lights off the same cable. Remember that you will need relatively thicker cable to cope with the low voltage—a 40W bulb running at 12 volts takes 3.3 amps, compared to the 0.16 amps a 40W bulb at 240 volts takes, and it is current-carrying capacity that determines the thickness of a cable. The manufacturer's instuctions will explain what is needed. One of the advantages of such lights is that you do not need to bury or protect the cable. But once you have decided exactly where you want your lights it is wise to do so—cutting through the cable is at best irritating, and will probably blow fuses or trip protecting devices in the circuit's transformer. Lay the cables at the bottom of a trench about 500mm deep, on top of a bed of sand—it isn't essential to protect the cable in conduit or with paving slabs as for mains-voltage supplies.

Pass the cables into the house through a hole drilled in the wall, and then seal the opening inside and out. Connect the ends to a transformer. Again, follow manufacturer's instructions on this—they will specify what type of transformer is necessary and how large it needs to be for the number of lights you want.

Connecting mains-voltage garden lights

Mains-voltage lights in the garden may provide you with the best lighting display, but they are the most difficult to wire up.

You must run a separate circuit from the consumer unit to a socket (or sockets) in the garden, and this circuit must be protected by an RCD. Decide where your light is going to be placed and drive a sturdy post,

8 *Drive a sturdy post into the ground where you want the light and wire up a 13 amp weatherproof socket*

9 *Protect the cable along its run in heavy duty plastic conduit. Bury the cable in a trench at least 500mm deep*

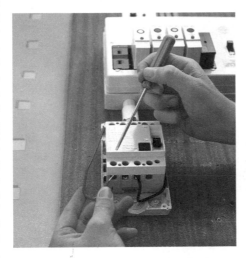

10 *Protect the circuit with a high sensitivity RCD which will break the circuit if there is any current leakage*

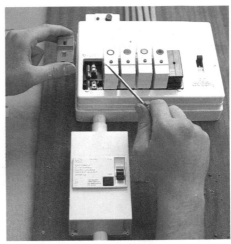

11 *Wire the circuit into a spare fuseway in the consumer unit or a swiched fuse unit linked to the meter*

pressure-impregnated with preservative, firmly into the ground. Fix to this a 13 amp weatherproof socket, mounted on a plastic conduit box. You can, if you wish, include a weathertight switch at this point—but make sure it has a rating of 15A or more. Plan the circuit in the same way as you would an ordinary indoor lighting circuit beginning at the point farthest from the consumer unit and working back to it by the most direct run.

From your post, dig a trench across the garden (at least 500mm deep, and as narrow as you can make it) to the house at a point close to the consumer unit. Connect a length of 2.5mm² two-core and earth cable to the garden socket and, protecting it in heavy duty plastic conduit all the way from the conduit box to within the house, lay it in the trench on a bed of sand for protection.

Before you backfill the trench it is essential that you cover the cable with special tiles marked 'electric live cable' along the entire length of the run as a precaution against someone accidentally cutting through the cable while digging in the garden. With the tiles in place, fill in the trench and compact it. Continue the cable run inside the house in the normal way until it reaches the consumer unit.

Here fit a 15 amp high-sensitivity (30mA) RCD into the wall and wire the supply cable to it, following the manufacturer's instructions. Connect the RCD in turn (still using 2.5mm² cable) to a spare fuseway in the consumer unit, protected by a 15 amp fuse or MCB. If there is no spare fuseway, connect the RCD to a new switched fuse unit (fused at 20 amps) and get the electricity board to connect this.

BURGLAR ALARM

For obvious reasons, many technical details are revealed only in the manufacturer's instructions. Your choice of alarm system depends very much on your requirements, and you are advised to shop around, consulting manufacturers before deciding which system is best. However, except in the most unusual circumstances, there is little to choose between many of the DIY systems.

Preparation and planning

Whatever system you decide on, you must read the instructions carefully and familiarize yourself completely with all the component parts.

Draw a plan of your home to decide where the alarm's sensors—magnetic or pressure pad devices—should be located. Choose where the control unit is to go—in general it should be sited as close to your front door as possible so that you can prime or switch off the system on leaving or entering the house without the alarm going off (though not all systems work in this way). Locate the siren where it can be seen and heard. If you fit it to an outside wall where the sound will be muffled by a tall hedge or outbuilding, you'll lose not only the sound of the siren but also the visual deterrent that sirens provide.

Where valuables are kept in a particular room fit a combination of alarm sensors and stout locks. Remember also that a burglar will generally enter a house by the easiest and least observable route so that is where adequate alarm protection is most needed.

The picture opposite shows a typical layout for an alarm system in a two-storey house. The siren should be mounted high up on an outside wall, and prominently positioned to serve as a deterrent to would-be burglars. The wiring from the control unit passes through the wall in to the back of the siren, leaving nothing exposed and vulnerable. The system's control unit is concealed under the stairs where it is within easy reach of the front door. The sensor on the front door is part of the entry/exit circuit so that it is possible to enter or leave the house without the alarm sounding when it is switched on. The rest of the sensors are divided between two zones: zone 1 is downstairs, zone 2 is upstairs. They can be switched on and off independently to protect

Your first line of defence against intrusion into your home should be strong door locks and lockable window fastenings. But a good burglar alarm is the best deterrent. With modern electronics they have become increasingly sophisticated and harder for burglars to defeat; which has meant a consequent increase in the security of your home.

Burglar alarm systems

Most systems consist of the following:
A control unit: This incorporates the on/off switch and sets off the alarm when one of the sensors detects an intruder. Many incorporate an automatic delay so that you can activate the system, then leave the house through a door on which a sensor is mounted without setting off the alarm.
An alarm unit: This usually consists of a bell or siren mounted in a box and fitted on a

prominent part of an outside wall as a visual deterrent. The alarm (like the control unit) is battery operated so that power cuts don't deactivate it, and is fitted with an anti-tamper device so that any attempt to move or destroy it sets off the alarm.
Sensor units: There are usually two types —magnetic sensors fitted to doors and windows, and pressure pads which are laid under carpets on the likely path of an intruder as he moves through the house. A third, but less common, type of sensor is the infra-red movement sensor. This works a little like radar, detecting movement in a darkened room to set off the alarm. It is less common in DIY installations, but frequently found in professional systems protecting commercial premises.
Wiring: Most wiring consists of two core flex running between the various components of the system, but it is possible to get anti-tamper wiring which sets off the alarm when cut or bridged.

part of the house while the family are in another part. The 'panic button' is mounted beside the bed and activates the siren whether the alarm system is switched on or not.

Tools for the job

You will need a power or hand drill, a 19mm flat drill bit for recessed contacts, a 4mm wood twist drill, No. 10 masonry drill bit, screwdrivers, a sharp chisel, tack hammer, pliers, wire strippers, and, in some circumstances, a long masonry drill bit to bring wires through external cavity walls. In addition to any of the tools you don't have and the kit itself, you will probably also need to buy the appropriate gauge of wiring for interconnection (the instructions will detail this), batteries, cable clips, and pins.

Test the system

Test the major components of the alarm system before attempting installation. This serves a dual purpose—it will enable you to ensure that all the equipment is working correctly and also gives you a chance to familiarize yourself with the components.

Follow the maker's instructions for the connection of batteries and temporary disconnection of the anti-tamper device, if necessary, and then go through each of the specified test procedures as instructed. This way you can be sure that the system will only actuate in 'anger'.

Installing the control unit and siren

The control unit is the heart of the burglar alarm system and controls all its functions.

Site the control unit in a convenient position close to the main exit of your home or wherever the instructions specify. Understair cupboards often provide ideal locations.

Using a masonry bit, drill into the wall at the planned position, plug the holes with wall plugs and screw the back plate to the wall.

Fit the siren on an external wall out of a potential burglar's reach but as close to the control unit as possible. Often this means high up on a front wall close to the eaves.

Ideally, you should run the cable used for connecting the control unit to the siren up through the interior of the house and feed it through the wall directly into the siren.

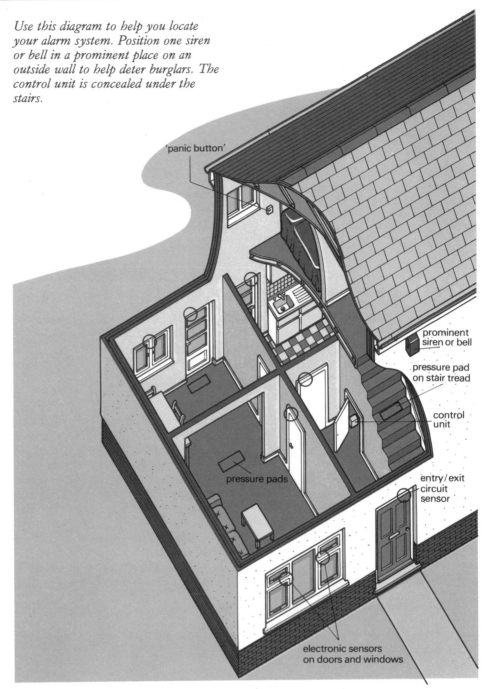

Use this diagram to help you locate your alarm system. Position one siren or bell in a prominent place on an outside wall to help deter burglars. The control unit is concealed under the stairs.

'panic button'

prominent siren or bell

pressure pad on stair tread

control unit

pressure pads

entry/exit circuit sensor

electronic sensors on doors and windows

Follow the maker's instructions closely for this part of the installation as the siren unit will probably include a number of fail-safe and other anti-tamper devices.

With both control unit and siren in position, the two units can be connected.

Wiring

Route all cabling as inconspicuously as possible. Cable can be hidden behind skirting boards, channelled into walls or run under carpets. Ensure that you make good electrical connections—the alarm will fail otherwise.

Measure the length of cable you need— allow a little extra for errors—to make a neat job. Normally 0.5 amp two-core cable is required—this is available at most electrical or hardware stores.

Route the cabling as appropriate between the sensor and the control box. Make sure that enough cable is left to make a connection to the terminals easily.

Use wire strippers to bare the cable. Remove about 5mm of insulation material from each core.

Decide on your major exit/entry route. Normally this will be the front door, but any external door is appropriate. Do not place pressure pads on this route. Normally the

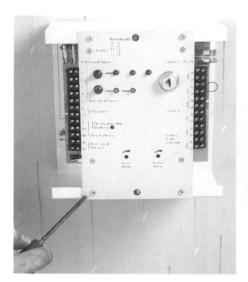

1 *Having bench-tested the system, fit the control unit, preferably out of sight and close to the main entrance of the house*

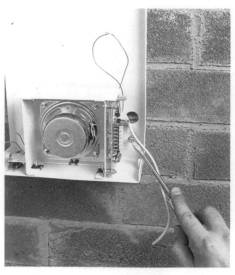

2 *Fit the siren in a prominent spot high up on the outside wall. Try to run the wire straight into it through the wall—leave none exposed*

3 *Make the connections according to the manufacturer's instructions and remember to fit any batteries which are required at this stage*

time allowed for opening and closing the exit door after the control unit is switched on is about thirty seconds, so make sure you can reach the door and leave in that space of time. Not all alarms use this system, however, so check with the manufacturer's instructions beforehand.

Some manufacturers supply 4-core cable for their systems which can be fitted in such a way that cutting it sets off the alarm. Most do not specify which colours of core should be used for which connection—to foil thieves—so choose for yourself, but make a note somewhere for reference in case problems should arise.

Magnetic sensors

Basically these sensors are magnetic switches that will detect if a window or door is opened or closed. The switch assembly consists of two parts—the switch itself, which you fit to the window or door frame, and the magnetic actuator, which goes on the door or opening window. The gap between the two sections should not be greater than 6mm when the door or window is closed.

Hide the sensors from view. An ideal location is at the top of doors and windows.

Using a suitable drill bit or chisel, cut or drill into the centre of the door or window frame edge to a sufficient depth to house the sensor comfortably.

Repeat the process on the fixed frames but add a little more depth to allow for the passage of the cable.

If a flush fit is needed, you will have to chisel away sufficient framework to allow for the sensor flange.

For hidden cables you will need to drill through the outer or upper edge of the fixed frames into the hole previously cut to locate the sensor.

Surface sensors can also be obtained.

4 *Conceal the wiring. Run it under carpets, behind skirting boards and tuck it into the angle of door frames but make sure it cannot get trapped*

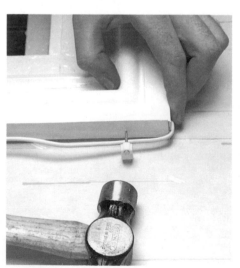

5 *Use cable clips round door and window frames to keep wiring out of sight. The wire itself is thin enough not to be prominent*

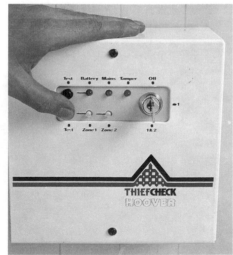

6 *Check the circuits according to the maker's instructions. This may involve nothing more than pressing the control unit 'Test' button*

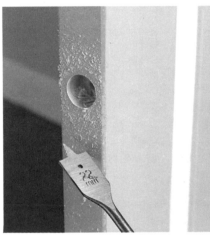

A typical wiring diagram for a 2-zone system, all the wires coming from the control unit. Exact details will vary from system to system so check the manufacturer's instructions before you start work

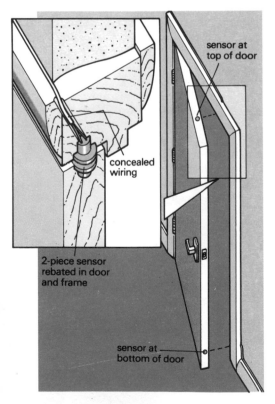

Locations for magnetic sensors in a door or window. They must be inconspicuous, with a gap between the components of less than 6mm

Check each stage of the wiring for continuity—in other words that a circuit has been made. This can generally be carried out at the control panel by operating the zone or selector switch governing the particular circuit. This will simplify any fault-finding that might be needed when the installation is complete.

These are ideal for use where drilling into the door or window frames is not possible—if you have metal frames for example. Consult the manufacturer before you buy.

7 *Using an appropriate wood bit, drill into the edge of the door or window and into the frame immediately adjacent to it*

8 *Drill through the back of the door or window frame into the large hole. Use a drill just thicker than the wire you are installing*

Fitting the pressure pads

A pressure pad is sensitive to weight and will actuate even through the thickness of a carpet when someone is standing on it. Beware though, that the weight of a dog—or even a cat—could cause the pad to operate and sound the alarm.

Ideal locations for a pressure pad are at the threshold of a door, on stair treads and beneath windows. If necessary, a pressure pad can be located directly in front of a particularly valuable item such as a wall safe or free-standing security cabinet.

Place pads directly on the floor and not between underlay and carpet. The surface of the floor must be clean and free from grit or abrasions.

Secure the pads using either adhesive tape or tacks pushed through the fixing tabs on the outside of the pad.

Connect the pads to the control box as instructed in the maker's handbook and test the circuit to ensure that it is operating satisfactorily.

A personal attack button will operate the alarm whether or not the control unit is switched on. Fitted in a bedroom or close to an exit this 'panic button' will help you to summon help if necessary. Be careful not to locate the button where young children might activate it.

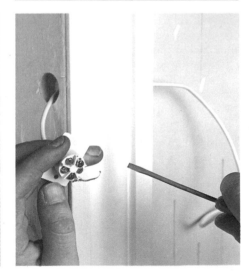

9 *Feed the cable through the back of the frame and bare the ends before connecting the sensors according to the instructions*

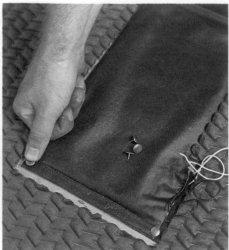

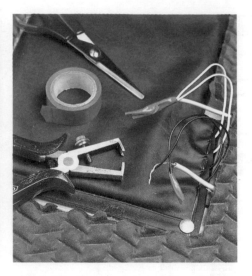

10 *If the carpet has an underlay, cut out a pad-shaped section so that the pressure pad lies flush and doesn't create a visible hump*

11 *Tape or pin the pressure pads in place, taking care not to pin through the sensor elements near the edges of the pad*

12 *Try if you can to run the wiring under the underlay, then tape the connections to the pad following the wiring diagram supplied*

Testing and commissioning

Before fully testing the complete alarm system, follow the maker's instructions for installing any necessary batteries.

You might need assistance to operate pressure pads and magnetic sensors and make sure that all components are properly secured.

Close all doors and windows fitted with sensors and reset personal attack buttons and remove activating keys.

Check, by pressing zone testing buttons, that all the systems are clear.

Now test each pad and sensor by opening doors and windows and applying weight to the pads. If you keep the appropriate zone test button depressed, activation will be indicated by the test light going out.

Repeat the test for all zones by following the maker's setting-up instructions.

A final tip: in case you lose the control keys, leave a spare with a trusted neighbour, or try to get a replacement key cut.

Living with an alarm

Pressure pads can become a nuisance if some form of discipline is not imposed on your family: it is all too easy to forget the alarm is switched on, especially during the day. Your first task must be to educate the family—especially younger members—to check the alarm is not switched on when they are moving around. A common mistake is to lay pressure pads under the carpet near an upstairs WC.

Remember also that the police don't take kindly to false alarms, however much they approve of home owners fitting burglar

alarms. And there is nothing more infuriating to your neighbours than an alarm which comes on while you are away, but cannot be switched off.

If several of your neighbours have alarm systems fitted, it is worth setting up a 'self-help' group: if one of the alarms goes off, arrange between yourselves for someone to call the police to investigate. Quite apart from the security implications, it improves relations between yourselves. Relations will be improved even more if neighbours leave front door keys and alarm keys with trusted friends nearby so that an alarm which goes off accidentally can be switched off.

Prevention, as the police will always tell you, is better than cure. In fitting a burglar alarm system and using it properly, you are doing yourself a favour while at the same time making the police's job of crime prevention much easier.

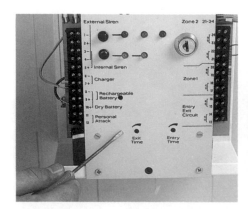

The entry/exit circuit timer may be adjustable using a screw in the control unit

The anti-tamper devices should be tested before commissioning: use the manufacturer's guide

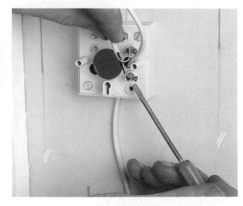

The personal attack button, or 'panic button', can be fitted much like a light switch

CHAPTER 5

HOME CARPENTER

Stylish and easy-to-make projects for every room in the house, from
shelving and storage units to tables, sideboards and an
attractive wall oven and hob unit

PUTTING UP PARTITIONS

A stud partition wall can split one large room into two, or create a small enclosed area in a corner or end of it. The main proviso is that there will be enough space in each part of the room after conversion—although there are more detailed planning considerations.

So before you start, it's important both to measure up the space you have available and to get a clear idea of how the new wall will alter it. If you have difficulty visualizing the effect, it may be worth putting up a temporary screen where you intend to build the wall. If the idea looks practicable, you can plan how to build the wall in detail.

Planning considerations

The instructions given here are for building a light partition wall only, such as might be used to divide a bedroom into two or provide walk-in wardrobes for adjoining rooms. A wall intended to carry heavy items—kitchen units, say, or heavy bookshelves—would need to be built of heavier timber and to be much more strongly supported underneath.

Even so, building a partition wall is one of those jobs where the planning takes longer than the doing. Before you start work, you must know the answers to these questions:
• **What will it stand on?** If you look at your existing floor and it is solid, the partition can stand anywhere on it; fixings can be made with screws and wallplugs. If you are dealing with a wooden floor, the situation is slightly more complicated.

The nail positions will tell you where the floor joists below it are situated. Ideally, a partition should straddle a whole row of joists. If this is not possible, because your partition will be parallel with the joists, it can stand on top of one joist or, at a pinch, *nearly* on top of one.

It is possible to provide extra support by

nailing rows of 100mm × 50mm blocking between two adjacent joists. It is easier, usually, to move the wall a few inches.
• **How will the top be fixed?** Along its top, the partition wall needs to be nailed or screwed to something rigid. Great strength is not needed, because a well built wall will 'want' to stand up, not fall over. But fixing to just lath and plaster or to ceiling tiles will not not be strong enough.

So you can fix to a single ceiling joist, or a row of joists or, at a pinch, to a securely nailed timber ceiling.

If both your floor joists and ceiling joists are parallel to the proposed wall, however, you may find that one set is not immediately above the other. In this case, you will have no option but to install some rows of blocking pieces in the floor or in the ceiling—whichever of the two is the easiest to get at.

So, before you decide on the exact position of the wall, some work with a steel tape and plumbline may be essential.
• **How will I deal with the skirting board?** Theoretically, the easiest way is to remove the skirting board (you drive wooden wedges down behind it) before you build the wall, and cut and replace it later.

But in some houses this is impracticable because the skirting board is 'trapped' behind a built-in cupboard. And in other, old houses it can be a messy job because some of the plaster comes away with the removal of skirting board.

If you decide that removing the skirting is not practicable, you do have an alternative—to build the base of the wall to fit around the skirting board. This does not affect the way you install the skirtings on the wall itself, because they are scribed (not mitred) to fit the existing ones. But it does affect the placing of the studs because, to maintain rigidity at the end of the partition, the end studs should be no more than about 300mm in. So you will need a detailed sketch plan.
• **How will I deal with the coving?** In timber framed houses, the moulding that covers the gap between the existing walls and ceiling is itself often made of hardwood. It can be prised off, trimmed and replaced in much the same way as the skirting board.

In masonry houses, however, the coving may be made of paper-covered plaster (like plasterboard). In this case, you can cut a notch to receive the top plate on one side of

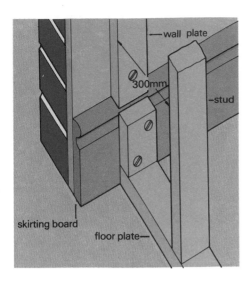

Skirting boards can be dealt with (above) by continuing the wall plate down the face of the board. Use timber of the same size, attached with 63mm No. 8 screws and fixed securely with wallplugs

the room, and remove a length of the coving on the other to fit in your new wall.

Alternatively, the coving may be of solid plaster. In this case it is risky to cut right through it—it tends to shatter. So it is easier to cut only about halfway through it, and shorten your new top plate accordingly. Or, if the plaster is not too thick, you can leave it intact and build round it in the same way you would build round a skirting board.

In Britain, you are not compelled by law to have a window in the room that your new partition creates. You can use 'borrowed light' (see Alternative Ideas) instead. But if you *do* decide to have a window, do not assume that you can knock through an outside wall to provide one; the building regulations on this point are particularly complicated.

In most other countries, you must have a window—often with a glazed area equal to one tenth of the floor area.

So, when you have designed your wall, your next step should be to submit your plans to the building control officer. Take a detailed floor plan, including the siting of the new window if any; a sketch of how the wall is to be supported; and a sketch of how it will be built (adapt the diagram of the frame on this page).

Tools and materials

As this wall is non-loadbearing—you are not removing any existing wall—it can be built from quite light materials.

For the top and bottom plates, use 75mm × 50mm sawn softwood in pieces long enough to span the room you are dividing—a wall with jointed plates is hard to handle. The studs and noggins are also 75mm × 50mm.

For the lintel, use the same 75mm × 50mm timber. You will also want some offcuts of 50mm × 25mm, plus a few scraps of plywood or hardboard, to use as packing pieces.

Most of the frame is fixed with 100mm roundhead nails, but buy 0.5kg (1lb) of 75mm oval nails—they are much easier to use for skew nailing awkward pieces.

Your plasterboard should be 9.5mm thick, in sheets either 915mm or 1220mm wide, depending on which will span the room with minimum waste. Try to buy the taper-edged variety, which produces neater joints than the square-edged type.

You will also need enough plasterboard jointing tape to cover the joints, and some jointing compound (the finer grade) to cover the tape and finish the joint.

Names for the nails used to fix plasterboard vary from one area to another, but if you ask for 'galvanized plasterboard clouts' you shouldn't go wrong.

Unless you want an open archway, you need a new door for the wall. Try to get one that matches the others in the house—size

Build the frame (yellow). Lift it into place and secure it with packing pieces. Level then add the wall plates. Add the noggings, then cut the wood from the threshold

doesn't matter as the wall is built round it. To frame it you need 100mm × 25mm planed softwood and 38mm × 12mm softwood. To hang it you need a pair of 100mm butt hinges and suitable screws—plus a catch and door handles and fittings.

To trim the wall, buy mouldings like those used elsewhere in the room—skirtings, door architraves and coving. Measure the quantities you require, plus a trimming allowance. Buy them from timber or builders' merchants.

Once built, you can finish the wall to match other decorations, so buy paint or paper as required. You also need some filler—although joint finish will do at a pinch—and knotting and primer for the woodwork.

Only 'everyday' tools are needed to build the frame and for finishing the plasterboard. Professionals use a taping knife, a plasterer's trowel, and a plasterer's jointing sponge—a circular plastic foam sponge mounted on a wooden handle which is used

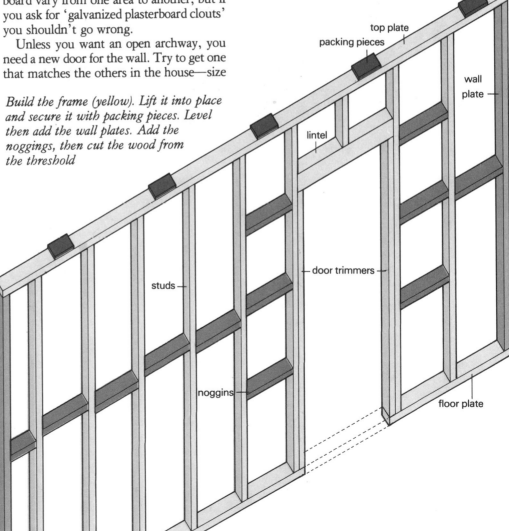

1 *Lay the top and bottom plates on edge. Mark in the position of the double studs for the door—allow a span for frame and door*

2 *Mark the positions of the other studs onto floor and ceiling plates. Use an offcut to keep them the correct distance apart*

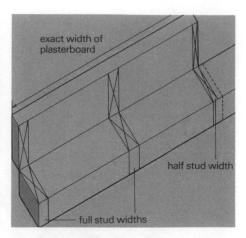

3 *Cut a batten of any size to use as a template. The half stud widths are important—you need to join sheets of plasterboard above a stud*

exact width of plasterboard

half stud width

full stud widths

4 *Nail through the plates into the studs with 100mm round head nails*

5 *Nail on the lintel, then add the trimmers, allowing floor clearance*

6 *Lift the frame into position—you'll need the help of an assistant*

7 *Plumb the frame level, then tap offcuts between the top plate and the ceiling*

to feather off the edges of the joint filler. There's little need for such special tools as long as you're prepared to sand down thoroughly.

Building the frame

The easiest way of building a stud partition wall is to assemble it flat on the floor, then lift it into place. This avoids much awkward skew nailing, and also makes it easier to get the wall plumb.

However, you must take steps to see that the partition does not jam, either on the ceiling or on the walls on either side, as you lift it. To do this, you make the frame a loose fit and omit some components until it has been erected.

For your top and bottom plates, select your straightest lengths of timber. Cut them to length—either a fairly snug fit between the skirting boards (if you are leaving these on) or about 40mm less than the width

between the existing walls (if you are going to remove the skirting boards).

Lay the bottom plate in position on the floor. Using thick pencil marks, mark on the plate the positions of the double studs on either side of the door frame. Make the space between them about 60mm wider than the overall width of the door and frame so that the frame will be a loose fit. (When you install the door frame, you will use bits of hardboard to fill the small spaces on either side, and nail through frame and hardboard into the studs.)

Now mark the other stud positions, working outwards from the doorway. A 75mm × 25mm batten, cut to match the exact width of the plasterboard and with the correct stud spacings marked on it (see diagram) will help you to do this accurately.

Plasterboard must be supported by studs in the middle of the sheet as well as at the edges. For a sheet up to 915mm wide, use one intermediate stud. For wider sheets, use two intermediate studs.

With your bottom plate marked out, lay the top plate on the floor beside it and, using a try square, transfer the stud positions from one to the other—this helps keep the studs straight and plumb.

Next, cut to length all the full length studs. They should be the height from floor to ceiling, less the thickness of the two plates, less 19mm for lifting clearance.

The diagram on page 337 shows how much of the frame should be assembled before you lift it into place. To put this together, you will probably need to get an assistant to help.

Lay both plates on edge. Lay the full length studs (except the end ones) between them, bow sides upwards. Then, using two 100mm nails at each joint, nail each stud simultaneously at both ends, synchronizing your hammer blows so that the plates do not skid about. As you nail, watch that the top surfaces of the plate and studs are flush—to ensure this, you may have to kneel on one or the other.

The trimmers (short studs on either side of the door opening) are cut 5mm longer than your door frame will be deep—again, to help make the door frame a loose fit. The door frame will be the height of the door, plus about 30mm—more if you intend to fit a thick floorcovering. So cut the trimmers about 35mm longer than the door. Nail the trimmers both to the bottom plate and to the adjoining full length studs.

The lintel rests on top of the trimmers. It is nailed through the studs on either side, and also skew nailed to the trimmers (see Skew nailing). This uses more timber than one commonly used method—housing the ends of the lintel into single studs—but is easier and makes a stronger job.

The short length of stud between the lintel and top plate is easily nailed at the top. At the bottom, however, it too will have to be skew nailed into the floor plate.

Now lift the frame into position. Secure it temporarily with two 100mm nails part-driven into the floor, as near as possible to the middle of the bottom plate, and a wedge or two driven between the top plate and the ceiling—preferably under a joist.

Next, check that the bottom plate is straight. Do this by nailing a short piece of 50mm × 25mm wood to each end of the plate and stretching a line taut between them. Check that the distance between line and plate is consistent along the whole length of the plate. If it isn't, force the plate into line with your foot as you nail it, using two 100mm nails hammered into each floor joist (or at about 450mm centres if only one joist is below).

The final stage of erection is to fix the top plate to the ceiling joist(s), at the same time making sure that the wall is plumb. You will need some packing pieces of different thicknesses to wedge between the top plate and ceiling—trim them for a neat fit.

Start by using a plumbline on one of the door trimmer studs. Check that it is plumb in both directions and, when it is, nail through the top plate (and through a packer) into the ceiling above. Do the same on the other side of the door opening. Then work outwards in both directions, plumbing, packing and nailing as you go.

If you find that your nailing is beginning to crack the ceiling, use screws instead.

To finish the frame, first install the components coloured green in the diagram on page 337, then those coloured brown. Finally, cut away the length of bottom plate that is obstructing the door opening.

Skew nailing

Skew nailing is a simple method of joining two pieces of wood which you can use wherever it is not possible to drive a nail straight through two pieces.

Part-drive all nails before you place the workpiece (the component to be nailed) in position. The nails should be at about 50° to the face of the work piece.

As you drive the nails home grip the other side of the work-piece and wedge your foot against it, to stop it moving sideways. If it moves only a few millimetres, it will come back into line as you nail the other side.

Nail heads can be sunk with a nailpunch, particularly if you have a nail on the face, instead of the side, of the workpiece.

Part nailing one end will help

Wedge a foot behind if you can

★ WATCH POINT ★

Don't nail where you intend to install architraves, coving and so on. The trim itself will pull the plasterboard back against the frame—this will prevent any gaps between plaster-board and trim.

Cutting plasterboard

For a straight cut, start by marking out the sheet with a pencil and straightedge—either a steel square or a straight length of batten.

Using the straightedge and a trimming knife, score through the paper and into the plaster on the face ('good') side.

Stand the plasterboard on end, supporting both sides as you do so, so that your cut is vertical. Then bend the sheet back on itself; this will sever the plaster core back to the backing. Finally, trim off the unwanted bit by running your knife down the back of the sheet.

Clamp a block beneath noggins

For a two-way cut—for example, to remove a section that would otherwise cover a doorway—mark out on both sides of the sheet. (If you have trouble transferring the marks from one side to the other, push a

Score the cutting lines on the face side with a trimming knife held against a straightedge

Snap along the line by folding the sheet back on itself—if necessary, over a batten

Sever the offcut by cutting through the cardboard backing. Change blades if the cut tears

bradawl through the sheet to make a hole.)

To cut along the first line, use your knife. Score deeply on both sides until you cut right through the plaster.

To cut along the second line, use the 'cut and bend double' method described above.

Fixing the plasterboard

Now you can hang your plasterboard. Fix it with the ivory coloured side outwards, since it is not going to be skim-plastered.

The most important thing is that the sheets must lie flat against the frame, without any bulges. So start by lifting the sheet about 12mm from the floor, either by resting it on a piece of plywood or by using a foot lift to lever the sheet up.

Start nailing in the middle of the sheet and work radially outward, doing the edges last. Drive each nail so that its head is just below the surface—but not so far that it cuts through the paper.

For a secure fixing, space your nails about 100mm apart around the edges of the sheet, and about 150mm apart down the middle stud or studs.

After the plasterboard is nailed in place, there will be both cracks between the sheets and dents from the nails. All of these must be filled over to get a smooth finish.

On square edged plasterboard, the joints can be merely filled with a little joint finish, using a filling knife. This gives a reasonably level surface, but one which is likely to crack as the timber frame below dries out.

On taper edged plasterboard, however, you can get an almost invisible finish. Start by cutting a length of jointing tape long enough to cover one joint. Take about a cupful of the jointing compound, mix it according to the instructions on the packet or can, and trowel it down the tapered recess where the two sheets join. While it is still wet, use the knife to push the tape into the compound. Make sure there is enough compound behind the tape to ensure good adhesion, and try to avoid trapping air bubbles, which might cause cracking later.

Follow immediately with another coat of compound, this time bringing it level with the plasterboard on either side. Before it sets, moisten the sponge and wipe away any ridges that the knife has left at the sides of the joint. Then clean all your tools and utensils thoroughly.

If the compound subsides or cracks while setting, this indicates either that it is too wet or that you have applied too thick a coat.

Once the compound has set (about an hour), use the plastic trowel to apply a thin

8 *Make an improvised foot lift to lever the sheets into place and off the floor*

9 *Nail from the middle of the sheet, working outwards at 100mm or 150mm intervals*

layer of compound about 200mm wide, then immediately 'feather'—smooth off—the edges with a sponge, slightly moistened.

Let this coat too dry thoroughly. Then apply a second coat, about 250mm wide, and feather the edges with a sponge again.

When dry, sand the surface perfectly flat with medium grade glasspaper on a block.

To fill the nail holes, use either a filling knife or trowel. This can be done with small quantities left over from the joint filler or with filler paste.

Finishing touches

With the framework and panelling complete, the next thing to do is to fit all the trim. This includes skirtings and architraves—and most importantly the door.

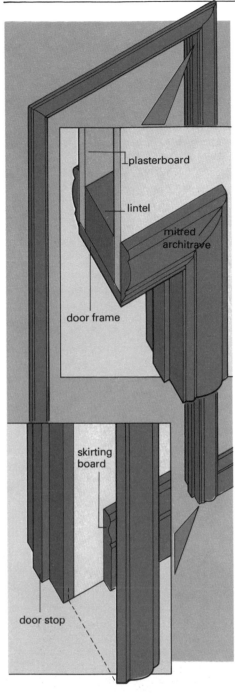

Finishing trim at the door opening (above). The door frame goes in first— it spans the studs and plasterboard. The architrave is mitred, then nailed to the edges of the frame. Fit the doorstop before or after adding the door—it's often easiest to fit the door, then butt the door stop up to it

Before hanging the door, you must make a frame to line the opening in the wall. This is made from 100mm × 25mm planed softwood. Cut one length to span the opening under the lintel, and two lengths the same as the door plus about 5mm clearance—more if the floor is uneven or

you plan to fit a thick floorcovering or deep pile carpet.

Nail the three pieces together and fit the door with a small clearance. Nail an offcut of batten across both sides temporarily to keep them in place, plus another diagonally across the whole frame to keep it square. Fit any frame into the opening and pack out any gaps with slips of hardboard or plywood. Make sure that it is flush with the face of the wall, then nail it firmly in place. Remove the bracing battens.

Decide which way round you want the door to hang. On the side where it opens outwards, measure the thickness of the door in from the edge of the frame. To make the door stop, cut lengths of 38mm × 12mm batten and nail them to the frame, in line with this point.

Cut lengths of architrave to frame the doorway. The corners of these must be mitred. With a narrow moulding you can use a mitre box to guide the saw; alternatively, mark the architrave with a combination square or mitre square. Nail the architrave to the door frame.

It's easiest if you fit the skirting board at this stage. Cut lengths of the board to span the ends of the new wall to the architrave. They don't have to be accurately sawn, but don't make them any shorter.

Use a scribing technique to make the ends of the new skirting to fit over the existing skirting board—if you have removed it, saw it just short of the new wall and re-nail it first.

Hold the new skirting board in place and then use a small wooden block and a pencil to transfer the outline of the existing board onto it. Remove the board and saw along the marked line with a coping saw or similar to deal with the curved outline.

Now refit the board up against the existing skirting. Line up the skirting with the architrave you have fitted round the doorway and mark its width back from the door opening on to the skirting. Remove the skirting, square across from the mark and then saw to length. Finally, nail the skirting to the studs along the base of the new wall.

To complete the trim, cut lengths of coving and nail them to the top of the wall. Where they meet the existing coving, you can use a similar scribing technique to that used for the skirting, although it is difficult to do this accurately.

To complete the construction, hang the door in the frame on a pair of 100mm butt hinges. To do this you will have to cut hinge recesses in both door and frame. Add a catch and door handles at this stage.

Finally decorate the new wall to make it look like a part of its surroundings. Fill any small gaps carefully first. You can paint the plasterboard directly, or paper it as you wish. Before you paint the wood, seal any knots with knotting solution, then prime it thoroughly.

Alternative ideas

If one of the new rooms your partition creates has no window, you can use 'borrowed light'—light from the other room —by glazing the top of your wall.

Studs should be spaced evenly, at least across the glazed area, even if this wastes plasterboard.

To hold the glass in place, and cover the cut edges of the plasterboard, you can choose from several types of moulding—bullnose, bevel edges, architrave or door stop.

To calculate the width of the moulding, allow 4mm for the thickness of the glass and about 4mm for two thin beads of putty (to stop the glass rattling). Deduct the total from the actual, measured thickness of the wall and divide by two.

A small overhang of 1–2mm on either side will help conceal any irregularity in the thickness of the wall. The easiest way is to fix all the mouldings on one side of the wall; then apply putty; then insert the glass; and finally apply the second bead of putty and the 'other side' of the mouldings at the same time. In this way the mouldings can be kept flush with the plasterboard, while the putty helps to take up the irregularities of the fitting.

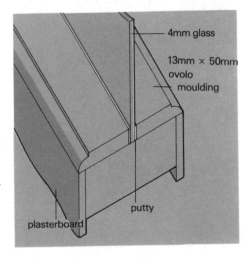

Borrowed light (above) may be necessary if there is no window. You could add a pane of glass between noggins, held and trimmed with a moulding

LIVING ROOM SHELF SYSTEM

These shelves are based on a unitary principle, which means that it isn't difficult to extend them as long, or as high as you want. You can fit them round a corner, or extend them out into the room to form a divider.

There's plenty of space on each broad shelf, and the design helps you to save money on materials. Wide boards are more expensive than narrow ones, so the shelves are all made up from pairs of narrow boards fitted back to back.

To save complicated woodwork and to make an interesting design feature, a small gap is left along the joint between the two. This is narrow enough not to mar the shelves' usefulness, but it serves to lighten them visually. It also allows you to slip in a back panel between the shelves if you want to turn them into a room divider.

The unit shown here is in two sections joined at a corner, but it can easily be adapted to suit your needs.

Each bank of shelves is made in a similar way. There are two halves—front and back—which are mirror images of each other. These are made on the same principle as the dividers sometimes fitted into cardboard boxes. Both the uprights and the shelves have slots cut in them, so they slip one into the other, making a rigid joint.

The uprights and shelves are at regular intervals, so if you want to change the length or the height of a bank of shelves just extend the sizes and cut a further row of slots.

What you need to buy

Most of the materials should be readily available at any woodyard or DIY store. All the shelves and uprights are made from planed softwood (pine) in standard sizes. You need:
- 10.54m of 150mm × 25mm board from which to cut eight uprights 1,015mm long, two uprights 740mm long, and two 470mm long.
- A total of 15.2m of 125mm × 25mm board from which to cut 4 shelves 2,230mm long, 2 shelves 1,495mm long, 8 shelves 1,470 mm long and 2 shelves 760mm long.
- 1.42m of 50mm × 25mm batten from which to cut 2 retaining rails 710mm long.

To put it all together you need 50 50mm × 10mm dowels—you can buy these ready-cut and prepared—four 50mm oval nails and some PVA woodworking adhesive.

Depending on the finish you choose, you need to buy wood stain and varnish, or primer, undercoat and gloss paint.

Cutting the parts

If you haven't bought the timber ready-cut to your requirements, start by sawing all the uprights and shelves to length. Consult the cutting plan on page 343 and make yourself a checklist of the parts you need.

It is important that matching parts are the same length. To ensure this, it's better to cut one of each and to use these as patterns for the rest—rather than marking them all out in one go, which can introduce inaccuracies.

So refer to your list and mark and cut one shelf and upright of each length. Remember to cut shelves from 150mm × 25mm

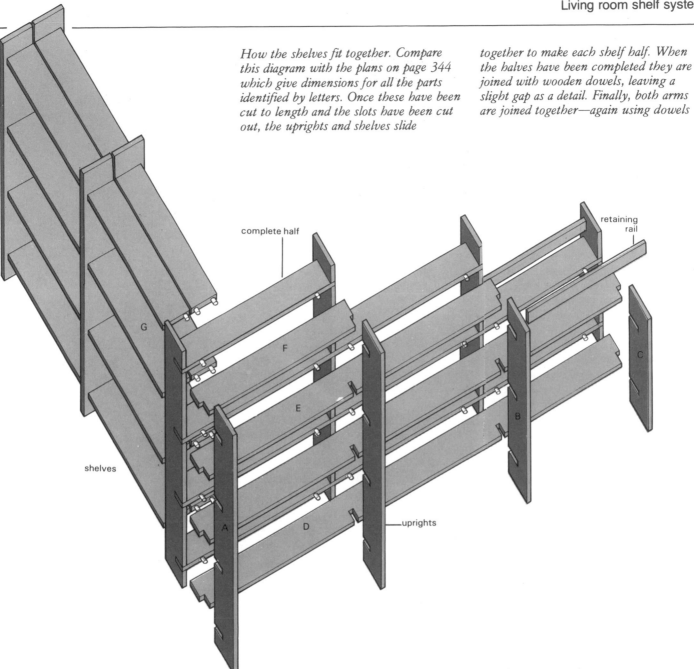

How the shelves fit together. Compare this diagram with the plans on page 344 which give dimensions for all the parts identified by letters. Once these have been cut to length and the slots have been cut out, the uprights and shelves slide together to make each shelf half. When the halves have been completed they are joined with wooden dowels, leaving a slight gap as a detail. Finally, both arms are joined together—again using dowels

complete half

retaining rail

G

F

E

shelves

A

D

B

C

uprights

wood, the uprights from 125mm × 25mm. Mark each lightly with a pencil to identify it. Then use them as templates to mark and cut the rest.

Lay the cut boards down together to check that they are all the same length. If your saw was sharp and you cut them accurately, the ends should be quite smooth and you can finish them off with a few strokes of medium grade glasspaper on a sanding block. If the ends are very untidy, trim them with a plane from the edges towards the centre.

The next step is to make sure that the uprights will fit over your skirting boards. The job involves cutting a notch out of the corner of each upright, the same size as the skirting board. Hold one upright in front of the skirting board, and mark on it how far

up from the floor the skirting board comes. Then hold the upright against the wall above the skirting board, and mark how far out the skirting projects from the wall. The skirting board may vary slightly in height so check the distance against each of the uprights in turn, holding them against their final position on the wall.

1 *Cut all the boards to the lengths required. For greater accuracy, saw oversize and trim with a plane*

2 *Some of the uprights may need to be notched in order to fit them over a skirting board*

Use a try square to extend the marks across the board. Then saw down each line to cut out a notch. Use the cut upright as a pattern to mark and cut each of the others, remembering that only the back ones need to be notched to fit over the skirting boards.

Cut two 710mm lengths of 50mm × 25mm batten to make the retaining rails.

Cutting the joints

When you have cut out all the parts, you can cut the slots which join them together. For each slot you simply make two saw cuts, close together, and then cut out the waste between. The joints at the ends of the shelves are even easier—they are made with two saw cuts like the notches for the skirting.

The important thing is to get the notches in the right place, and to make sure that they are the right width. The cutting plan on the right shows where the slots are in the uprights and in the shelves. But to make sure that you get them in the same place on each board, group matching shelves and uprights together and align their ends. Then mark them all at once.

Mark the positions of the slots on the edges of the boards—make certain this is the opposite edge to the notches on the uprights you have cut. Then, to ensure that the slots are the same width as the wood, take an offcut and use it to mark them.

Square lines across the face and edge of each board, for both sides of the slots, using a try square. None of the slots go right across the boards, so measure off on each how far the slot should go (referring to the diagram on the right) and draw a line at this point. Crosshatch the wood that is to be cut out, to indicate that it is waste.

Cut down each side of the slots as far as the mark. Then take a chisel which is less than the width of the slot and use it to cut out the waste between the saw cuts, down to the mark. Do this for all the slots.

3 *Mark the slots with a try square and offcut to ensure the dimensions are accurate*

4 *Support the wood firmly then saw the slots. Cut out the waste with a sharp chisel*

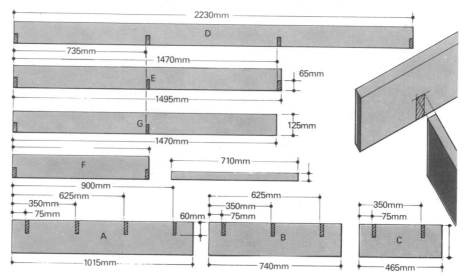

Above: The dimensions of all the uprights and shelves. Slot positions are given to one side only—mark the width with an offcut (inset)

Assembling the shelves

As long as all the slots are cut accurately, the shelves and uprights should join together without any problems. Check all the slots first by sliding an offcut of the wood into them.

If you find any tight spots, ease them with coarse sandpaper wrapped over a batten.

When all seems well, lay out the shelves and uprights together according to the plan. Dry-assemble everything to check that all the parts fit together. If any joints are tight, do not force them, but ease the slot still more. Assemble all four shelf halves in this way. Check that they are square by measuring two diagonals—they should be the same length.

The shelves are now ready for gluing. Take one of the dry-assembled sections and

lay it down. Pull out one of the centre uprights—the others will hold the assembly together. Run a little woodworking glue into each of the slots, then refit the upright.

★ WATCH POINT ★

Refit it as quickly as you can, since the woodworking glue will swell the wood and make it a tight fit if you leave it.

Glue and fit the other centre upright, then the ends, to complete one shelf half.

Before the glue has dried, take the matching shelf half and glue this together too. Put the two completed assemblies against each other back to back. Check that they are

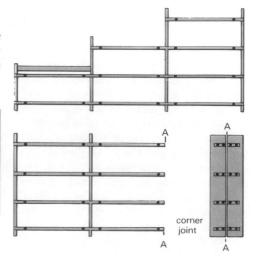

Above: Put the dowels 75mm on each side of the uprights. These joining the two arms are 30mm in from the sides of the shelves

square, and that they match up properly. Pin them together temporarily.

Repeat the process to assemble the other two shelf halves.

Position the two retaining rails on the end shelf, according to the plan on page 344 and check the fit. When you are satisfied, glue the ends and nail in place through the uprights with 50mm oval nails.

Joining the shelf halves

With the shelf halves complete, drill them to take the dowels which join them. These aren't finally glued until you have applied the finish paint or stain.

The plan on page 344 shows the position of the dowels. It's important that the holes on each half match absolutely, otherwise the shelves won't line up. You can ensure this by employing dowel locating pins, which are used in making all sorts of dowelled joints. What you do is to put the pin into one piece of wood, align the second, and press them together. The pin has a projecting point which marks the second piece to show you exactly where to drill the hole.

★ WATCH POINT ★

You can buy proper dowel locating pins, but it's very easy to make your own. All you need are some short— around 20mm—panel pins. Drive a pin into the first piece of wood, leaving a few millimetres projecting. Snip off the head with a pair of wire cutters or pliers to leave a sharp point. After using this to mark the second piece, pull out the pin with pincers or pliers.

Take one shelf half and drive in a pin at every point where you want to fit a dowel. Then take the second shelf half and align the two parts carefully. Press them together to mark the dowel centres. Separate them, and remove all the pins.

Now drill holes for the dowels, centred on each mark. You need a 10mm drill bit. A proper dowel bit is easier, but you can make do with the ordinary twist type. Set the depth stop on the drill, or tape the drill bit, so that you know when the holes are 22mm deep.

Lay each shelf half down flat and drill at all the marked points, taking care to keep the drill square to the wood, until you reach the marked depth.

5 *Smear woodworking glue on the mating surfaces, then quickly slot them together*

6 *The retaining rails are fitted when the assembly is complete; nail them in place*

7 *To ensure the dowels align, drive in pins, snip off the heads and press together*

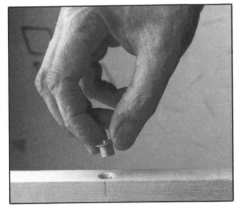

8 *Alternatively, buy dowel centre pins, which are used after drilling one set of holes*

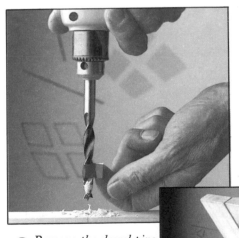

9 *Remove the dowel pins and drill the dowel holes. To ensure that they are the right depth, tape the drill bit*

10 *Insert the dowels but don't glue them at this stage; dry-assemble to check the fit. To maintain an even gap*

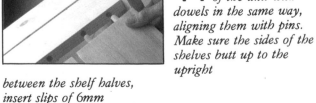

between the shelf halves, insert slips of 6mm plywood. Re-drill any tight holes

11 *Join the two arms of the unit with dowels in the same way, aligning them with pins. Make sure the sides of the shelves butt up to the upright*

Fit dowels to all the holes in one half, without gluing them, and bring the two halves together. Cut some slips of 6mm plywood—or several thicknesses of card, if you haven't any—and insert them into the gap to check that it is even.

When you are satisfied that everything fits, separate the halves and glue down the dowels into one half only. Repeat for the second unit.

After making both units, you can make the corner joint. Once again, this is dowelled, but this time, without leaving any gap. Fit dowel pins and mark the dowel holes in both units as before. This time, drill the holes 25mm deep and dry-assemble to check the fit.

Finishing the unit

You must finish the unit before final assembly, otherwise it won't be possible to reach the surfaces on the inside of the central gap and the paint is likely to run.

The shelves are made in natural pine, so there's plenty of choice when it comes to finishes. But whatever look you choose, ensure a fine finish with thorough surface preparation.

Don't rush this part of the job—the finish will sharply define the edges of the dark shadow line of the gap.

Fill any holes or blemishes with filler—wood-toned if you intend to varnish—and allow to dry. Then sand all surfaces and edges with fine grade glasspaper. Wipe off the dust to avoid spoiling the finish. Seal any knots with a couple of brush strokes of

12 *Prior to applying a finish, fill any gaps or holes and allow to dry. Use wood-coloured filler if you are varnishing. Sand the surface smooth with fine glasspaper. Wipe off dust with a cloth soaked in white spirit*

patent knotting compound. This prevents the resin in the knot from bleeding out and causing blemishes on the paintwork.

The easiest finish is varnish. Thin the first coat a little to help it penetrate the wood, and brush on with even strokes, using a 50mm brush. To avoid runs, don't overload the brush. Make sure too that you don't paint over the projecting dowels joining the two halves of the shelves, or the mating surfaces where the unit is joined at the corner.

Allow to dry thoroughly, then rub down lightly with fine grade wire wool. Repeat using unthinned varnish for at least two further coats.

If you want a brighter finish that allows the grain of the wood to show through, stain the wood with a spirit based stain and allow to dry before varnishing.

Alternatively, you can opt for a painted finish. But it's important to do this properly or it will soon show every knock.

After preparing the surface, give it a coat of wood primer and allow to dry. Rub down lightly, then apply an undercoat to suit your top colour. Let this dry thoroughly, then rub over lightly before applying a first coat of your finishing paint, which should be a good-quality gloss. Let this dry also, then rub down and repeat. The more coats you apply, the better and tougher the result.

Final assembly

When the varnish or paint is dry, you can put the unit together. If you have checked with a dry run first, there should be no problems; but make sure that none of the holes is clogged with varnish or paint—clean them out if necessary with a screwdriver.

13 *If you are painting, prime the bare wood and filler first. If you are varnishing, this can be applied directly; allow to dry, then rub down lightly and recoat*

Smear a little woodworking glue on the ends of all the projecting dowels, then bring the two halves of the unit together. If you are fitting back panels to the units (see Alternative ideas), put them in at this stage. To maintain an even spacing between the shelves, use the same slips of 6mm plywood you used in the dry assembly.

When you have assembled the main shelf sections, you can join them together at the corner—by once again gluing the projecting dowels and the matching surfaces before bringing them together. Allow to dry thoroughly.

Put the completed unit back in place against the wall. It should be stable without any further support, but if you need to fix it, screw it to the wall with a couple of angle brackets screwed to the uprights just below a shelf so they are not visible.

Alternative ideas

Following the basic construction, you can easily make longer or taller shelves as you wish. If you make tall, thin shelves, stabilize them by screwing the back to the wall with brackets on every upright.

Another attractive and practical use for the system is as a room divider. You can make either a straight, or L-shaped section to extend out into the room. And, to prevent things on the shelves from falling off, you can fit solid back panels in the gap down the centre. Make these from plywood—or, even better looking, acrylic sheet—and slot them in before the final assembly. Test the appearance of these panels in a dry run before you assemble the two halves of the unit—try them in different positions. On the top shelves, you can fit extra retaining rails.

MAKE A FILING CABINET

If you're obliged to make use of part of your home as an office or you just want somewhere handy to keep your current bills and documents, you'll appreciate this filing cabinet. It will not only put your affairs in order, but also act as a stylish piece of furniture that you'll be happy to have in any room.

The construction is straightforward: the cabinet is simply a rectangular plywood or blockboard box which stands almost 1.5m high.

The cabinet is kitted out with an array of trays to suit all your likely requirements; alternatively, you can fit shallow wire baskets in their place. There are also handy pigeon holes at the top for storing smaller, but bulky items—anything from ink bottles, erasers, rules and pencils to computer floppy disks, telephone books and other reference material. Located near a desk, the filing cabinet brings everything you're likely to need close to hand.

Materials and tools

To construct the filing cabinet as shown, you'll need two 2,440mm × 1,220mm sheets of 19mm plywood or blockboard from which to cut:
• One 1,422mm × 448mm panel for the cabinet back (A).
• Two 1,422mm × 519mm panels for the cabinet sides (B).
• Three 519mm × 486mm panels for the cabinet top, base and plinth (C).
• Three 500mm × 448mm panels for the intermediate dividers and for the middle plinth panel (D).

Additionally you'll need a 1,220mm × 1,220mm sheet of 12mm thick plywood from which to cut:
• Four 460mm × 448mm panels for the pigeon hole frames (E).

The tray runners, which fit on each side of the cabinet walls, are made from 6mm square ramin (hardwood); you'll need 36 pieces measuring 494mm long.

There are three types of trays you can make yourself:

To make **tray 1**, you'll need: one piece of 35mm × 9mm ramin, 447mm long for the back; two pieces 491mm long for the sides; one panel of 3mm acrylic sheeting measuring 515mm × 447mm for the base; plus an optional divider of 35mm × 6mm ramin.

To make **tray 2**, you'll need one piece of 35mm × 9mm ramin 447mm long for the back; two pieces 491mm long for the sides; one panel of 3mm acrylic sheeting or 3mm plywood measuring 447mm × 340mm for the base; a 35mm × 6mm ramin divider measuring 491mm long; and a piece of 6mm square ramin lipping measuring 447mm long which prevents the tray from sliding back into the cabinet.

To make **tray 3** you'll need: one 447mm × 35mm piece of 4.5mm acrylic sheeting for the back; two 335.5mm × 55mm pieces for the sides; one 335.5mm × 20mm piece for the divider; one 447mm × 6mm piece for the front lipping; and one 447mm × 340mm piece of 3mm acrylic sheeting for the base. See Using acrylic sheet for details of how to work with this material.

The cabinet allows space for 16 trays and you can include as many of each type as you

1 *The panels must be cut out as precisely as possible so double check all measurements and cut the board with a power jigsaw*

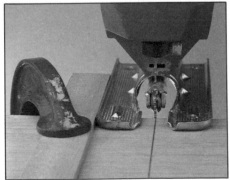

2 *If your saw doesn't have a fence improvise by clamping a strip of wood parallel to the guideline so the sole plate touches it*

3 *Once each section has been cut sand the edges thoroughly using cabinet paper wrapped around a sanding block*

wish, or a combination of types for variety. For the sake of economy, however, you'd be wise to make as many as you can from a single sheet of ply or acrylic.

If you'd prefer to use proprietary wire baskets instead of making your own trays, you'll need the shallow type commonly used in kitchen units: look for baskets 100mm deep, 445mm wide and 500mm from front to back. You should be able to buy these in kitchen specialist shops or large department stores.

Additionally, you'll need PVA woodworking adhesive and 25mm panel pins for assembling the cabinet and acrylic adhesive for making the acrylic trays.

The tools you'll need are: tape measure, try square, straightedge, pin hammer, power jigsaw, tenon saw, electric drill and 4.5mm twist bit, countersinking bit, bradawl, padsaw fitted with a fine toothed hacksaw blade, trimming knife and two sash cramps.

Finish off the cabinet with paint, stain or varnish as you prefer, or a combination of these finishes. It is a nice idea to pick out the front edges of the unit in a contrasting colour, especially if you decide to paint it a bright primary colour, like red.

Cutting out the panels

Consult the materials list to find out how to mark out all the parts of the cabinet from standard-sized sheets of plywood or blockboard. Cutting out the panels must be carried out precisely using a power jigsaw.

Lay the sheet of board on a flat surface and mark out the panels, using a tape measure, try square and long straightedge for accuracy. Cut out the parts with a power jigsaw fitted with a fence to ensure that you don't wander from the guidelines.

When you've cut out all the panels, label them so you know where they belong.

Mark out and cut the thinner 12mm plywood for the pigeon holes in the same way. Sand all the pieces, but don't round off the edges.

Once this is done, you're ready to assemble the cabinet. But before fitting out the unit, cut the halving joints for the pigeon holes (see Making halving joints).

Assembling the trays

There are three types of tray you can make for the filing cabinet: which you choose depends on what you want to store.

The trays are not difficult to make but you'll need to be careful when cutting and drilling the acrylic sheeting (see Using acrylic sheeting).

Study the materials list and diagram so you know exactly how the filing cabinet is constructed. Basically, it consists of a rectangular shell of 19mm thick plywood or blockboard measuring 1,498mm tall × 486mm wide × 519mm deep; the panels are assembled with adhesive and panel pins for simplicity yet the structure is strong enough to fulfil most requirements.

The top 448mm deep section of the cabinet is given over to nine pigeon holes of a convenient size. These are made by inserting an assembly of four strips of plywood connected using cross-halving joints. You can make the pigeon holes whatever size you like, although those shown will cope with most of the items you're likely to want to store.

Below the pigeon holes are two 448mm deep niches fitted with 6mm square ramin runners to hold several paper trays or proprietary wire baskets of varying sizes. The sections are divided by a panel of ply or blockboard, pinned within the outer framework.

The filing trays are made from plywood and can be fitted with coloured or transparent acrylic sheet bases. You can even make a tray entirely from acrylic sheeting if you want to.

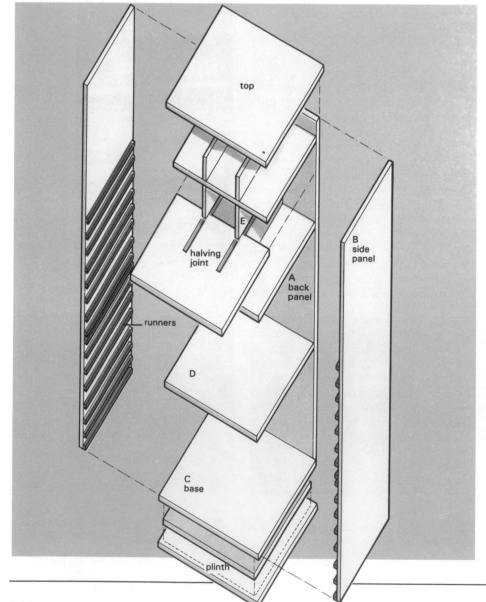

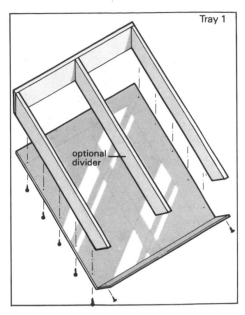

Tray 1 is the deepest tray. It has an acrylic base screwed to the sides

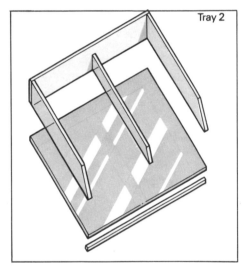

Tray 2 can be made with either an acrylic or plywood base. It has a wooden stop

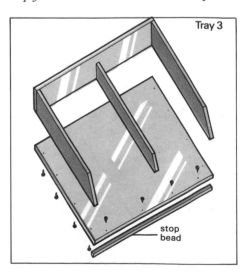

Tray 3 is made completely of acrylic. The pieces are glued together

Tray 1: this is the deepest tray and is ideal for storing large sheets of paper—you can use it with or without the central divider.

First of all cut the acrylic sheet base to size (500mm × 447mm) and drill a row of 3mm countersunk clearance holes around its edge at 100mm intervals to take 19mm No. 4 woodscrews. Bend the tray's leading edge up at an angle of 45° (see Using acrylic sheet).

Saw the back and side pieces of the tray from a length of 35mm × 9mm ramin: the back strip is 447mm long and the two sides measure 491mm. Shape the leading ends of the two side pieces to 45° using a mitre box and tenon saw. If you want a divider, cut a strip of 35mm × 6mm ramin to the same profile as the side pieces.

Stand the three 35mm × 9mm strips, upside down on a flat surface and temporarily tape their corners together. Place the acrylic sheet on top and align all the edges.

Mark the lower edges of the strips through the clearance holes, using a bradawl. Remove the acrylic sheet and drill pilot holes at the marked positions. Reassemble the strips with PVA adhesive and panel pins then invert the frame and screw the acrylic sheet into place. Take care not to overtighten the screws or you may crack the acrylic.

Tray 2: this tray is just the right size to take two reams of A4 size paper—the most common size for typing—side by side. Assembly is virtually the same as for tray 1, except that the leading edge of the tray sides is cut *back* at an angle of 45°, and there's a thin stop bead under the front edge of the base panel to prevent the tray from sliding to the back of the cabinet.

The 447mm × 331mm base can be cut from acrylic sheeting or plywood. If you decide on acrylic, cut out and assemble the components as for tray 1; if you choose wood, simply glue and pin the base to the underside of the side battens. Glue and pin the stop bead of 6mm square ramin under the front edge—an epoxy adhesive will give the surest fixing. You can omit the central divider if you prefer.

Tray 3: this tray is similar to tray 2 except that it is made entirely of acrylic sheeting. The pieces are stuck together with special solvent adhesive. Firstly, mark out and cut the acrylic sheet into the relevant parts.

Peel away the protective paper covering from the part of the acrylic sheet you're going to join, but be careful not to scratch it.

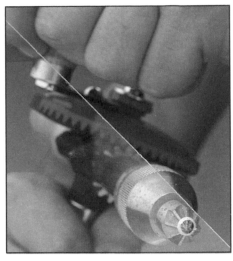

4 *Mark the positions of the screw holes in the acrylic sheet and then drill them*

5 *Cut the leading edges of the wooden tray sides at an angle of 45°. Use a mitre block to help get the angle exact*

6 *Glue and pin the thin stop beading in place under the leading edge of the tray base. This stops it being pushed in*

Using a matchstick, apply a smear of solvent adhesive to the contact areas of the pieces being joined: beware of applying too much, as some adhesives are runny and will remove the sheen from the acrylic sheet. Bring the two pieces of acrylic together and hold under firm pressure for about one minute.

Mark the position of the slots in the plywood panels with a pencil and rule

Cut out the slots using a jigsaw and chisel. Sand any rough edges

★ WATCH POINT ★

Place a set square or try square in the angle between the two butt-jointed pieces, in order to make sure the angle is at 90°.

Allow the adhesive to set fully, according to the manufacturer's instructions (in time the joint will become as strong as the sheeting itself). Place a piece of board over the assembled tray and weight it down with books. Once the adhesive has dried, peel off the protective paper from the acrylic.

Making halving joints

The halving joints which are used to connect the components of the pigeon holes are straightforward to make. Mark out the panels in pairs.

Take the vertical panels (E) and clamp them together with their edges aligned. Remember when marking out these parts, that they're deepest from front to back of the cabinet.

Measure down from the top edges of the panels a distance of 92mm then scribe a line across the face of one sheet and around onto the other panel, using a try square and a

long straightedge to extend the marks squarely.

From this line, measure down 12mm—the thickness of the board—and square a second line around the panels. Now measure down 140mm followed by another 12mm, and square lines around at these marks. Separate the panels and square the lines around each.

Measure along the 12mm deep parallel lines half the front to back dimension of the panels—230mm—and draw a line down the panels at this point. This will give you the depths of the cut-out slots.

Repeat the marking out procedure for the horizontal sections of the pigeon holes, but set the halving joints 141mm in from each side of the panels.

To cut out the lengths of the slots, use a power jigsaw and remove the waste with a coping saw. Sand the slots then test-fit the joints. The pieces should be a tight fit.

Assembling the cabinet

Assembling the cabinet is just a matter of gluing and pinning together the framework. You must be sure to set the tray runners perfectly horizontal if the trays or baskets are to fit properly.

The first job is to mark out the tray

runner positions on the side panels. Lay the panels side by side on a flat surface and measure down from the top edge 448mm. This gives the position of the first shelf. Square a line across the panels at this mark.

Now measure down 19mm—the shelf thickness—followed by 6mm, which gives the location of the top runner. This runner supports the shelf. From the top of this runner, mark off increments of 54mm to the intermediate shelf position, 448mm below.

Measure down 19mm for the second shelf, then continue at increments of 54mm to the bottom of the panel. Square the lines across the two panels using a long straight-edge and pencil with a try square to check that the lines are level.

Glue and pin the 494mm long ramin runners to the side panels at their marked positions. Make sure they're set horizontal on the panels and set back from the front edge by 6mm—this allows for the lipping on some of the trays. If the runners are not perfectly horizontal the trays will not glide freely in and out.

Now glue and pin the side panels to the top and bottom panels, dovetailing the nails at 100mm intervals. If you don't have a workbench, you may need some help to hold the frame steady while you assemble it.

Glue and pin the basic box to the back panel, making sure the edges are flush with

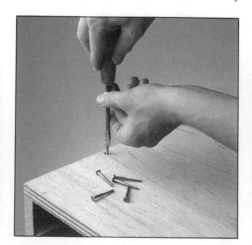

7 *The first step is to mark the positions of the tray runners. Do this carefully as they must be absolutely horizontal*

8 *Once the tray runners have been set in place, pin or screw and glue the top and bottom panels to the sides of the unit*

9 *During the assembly, have a damp cloth to hand to wipe away excess or spilt adhesive before it has time to harden*

the sides. Use sash cramps to hold the cabinet securely while the adhesive dries. The time this will take depends largely on atmospheric conditions.

Draw a 19mm wide margin on one face of the panels C (the cabinet underside and plinth base). Glue and pin panel D (the plinth core) to the plinth base, using the margin as a positioning guide. Apply adhesive to the top of panel D then attach it to the cabinet base by pinning through the fixed panel C—again use the drawn margin as a positioning guide.

Assemble the pigeon hole frames—no adhesive is necessary—and simply slot them into the niche at the top of the cabinet. It's not necessary to pin the assembly in place. Providing you have cut the sections accurately it should fit snugly; otherwise you will have to pin it to the carcase.

Finishing the unit

Sand down the entire unit, using fine cabinet paper and remove all traces of dust with a damp cloth. When the wood is completely dry, you can apply the finish of your choice.

You could stain the unit a deeper colour and then apply two coats of a polyurethane varnish, which gives a shiny, tough and durable finish. Alternatively, you could paint it in a bright gloss paint. Apply wood primer and a coat of undercoat before the final gloss paint finish.

It is possible to wax the filing cabinet, but this is a very fine finish and it is probably only worthwhile if you decide to use a ply with a veneer that has a grain that will respond to this treatment. For example, birch-faced ply would look very good

When working with acrylic sheet, keep the paper on

Mark hole positions on the paper with a sharp bradawl

Drill holes with a wood twist bit. Remove burrs later

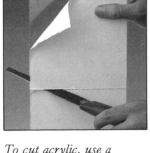

To cut acrylic, use a padsaw fitted with a hacksaw blade

To smooth the cut edges, rub the acrylic on sandpaper

waxed, although it will be a little more expensive than blockboard.

Using acrylic sheet

Acrylic sheeting is easy to use, although you must be careful not to mark the delicate shiny surface during assembly.

Sheet acrylic is covered with a protective paper wrapping. Leave this in place while you mark out and cut the sheet to size.

Mark out the sheet of acrylic using a pencil, tape measure and try square, following the dimensions given.

Clamp the acrylic sheet flat on a workbench, protecting the surface from the cramp jaws with a wood block. Use a

padsaw fitted with a fine hacksaw blade to cut down the guidelines on the waste side, leaving a little excess for filing down later. Work with slow strokes to prevent the blade from sticking.

Once you've cut out the pieces, set them in a vice and file down the edges to the guidelines using an old, flat file. Give a final smoothing with silicon carbide abrasive paper.

You can also drill holes in acrylic. Mark out the hole positions on the paper wrapping: for this project, the screw holes for connecting the acrylic base to the ply tray sides are set 4.5mm in from the edges.

Mount the sheet on a block of wood and clamp them both to a flat surface. Mark the centres of the holes with a sharp bradawl then drill the holes with an ordinary wood twist bit. Remove burrs with a straight-edged piece of metal (the back edge of your trimming knife blade will do).

Once softened by heat, acrylic sheeting can be bent to shape—an electric radiant heater is an ideal heat source.

First remove the protective paper from both sides of the sheet and mark a line where you want the head to be.

On one face of the sheet, tape a 100mm wide strip of aluminium cooking foil on either side of the bending line—the gap between the strips of foil should be 10mm.

With the foil facing the heater warm the acrylic. When the sheet becomes flexible, take it away from the heater and bend it along the line. Check the angle of the bend with a sliding bevel set to 45° and hold it in that position until it cools.

10 *When the base has dried in place you can attach the plinth. This comes in two pieces and is pinned and glued in place*

11 *Tap the sections of the pigeon hole unit together using a wooden mallet. They will be a tight fit so protect the wood*

UNDERBED STORAGE UNIT

Large, bulky items like folded bedlinen, towels and spare pillows take up plenty of room, usually at the expense of cupboards elsewhere around the home. One answer to the problem is to install fitted cupboards; a simpler and considerably less costly solution is to build these underbed storage units and make full use of space that young people, especially, need for toys, records and clothes.

The units are simple plywood box constructions fitted with castors, enabling you to roll them in or out at a moment's notice. Having the castors recessed at the edge keeps the overall height down, while making best possible use of the available space. And, thanks to the hardwood quadrant moulding on the corners, there's no complicated jointing—the whole assembly simply pins and glues together.

Another feature of the design is its versatility. The dimensions given relate to a standard size traditional (not divan) double bed measuring 1.82m × 1.37m (6ft × 4ft. 6in.) and allow for two units on each side. But none of the dimensions are critical so you can easily alter the height, width or depth to suit your own requirements.

How the unit is constructed

The basis of the unit is a box construction of 12.5mm birch plywood. The base is supported by lengths of 9mm hardwood lipping pinned and glued flush with the bottom edges of the side panels. The side panels are butt jointed against short lengths of hardwood quadrant moulding to provide neatly rounded corners. The lift-up lid is

secured to the back panel by a length of piano hinge that's screwed in place.

Cut-outs in the side panels and trimmed-back corners on the base create recessed housings for the castors. The insides of the housings are built up with thin plywood spacer strips and the lower braces, all of which are glued and pinned. The castors are then screwed in place to the undersides of the braces.

The unit is completed by further braces, pinned and glued to the top edges of the front and back panels.

You can vary the design very easily to suit your own bed or personal taste. Use solid timber, for example—pine or a´hardwood—to suit a specific finishing style.

You can also make the unit longer or deeper, or taller or shallower, but try to ensure that altering the size doesn't mean

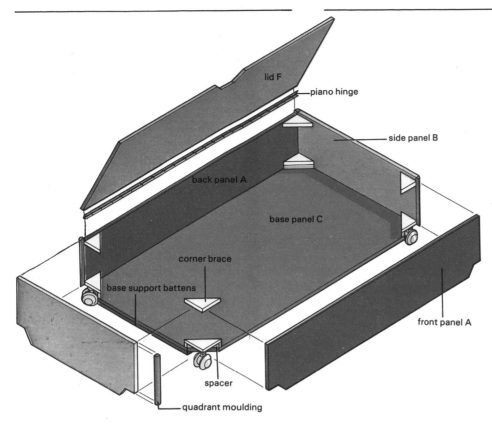

lid F

piano hinge

side panel B

back panel A

base panel C

corner brace

base support battens

front panel A

spacer

quadrant moulding

sawdust to irritate your (or someone else's) skin. Alternatively, line the box with tissue paper. To keep clothes smelling fresh and clean, use a 25mm flat timber bit to drill holes in the base panel or backing panel so that air can circulate freely.

Cutting the parts

It's best to get all the cutting over with in one go. That way, you can ensure that all the parts match up before you get half way through assembly.

Measure and mark out your plywood as described in Measuring and marking ply. If you're building only one unit, follow the diagram on page 354 and cut it in the order specified.

The plywood must be supported a maximum of 50mm either side of the cutting line—a job for which the open jaws of an adjustable workbench are ideal.

If you're using a jig saw without a fence, make your own fence from a straight-edged length of batten. Clamp or pin this parallel with the cutting line, half the width of the saw's sole plate away. Start the cut with the saw tilted up at the back at an angle of 45° and the front of the sole plate resting on the sheet, hard against the fence. As the blade begins to cut, gradually bring the sole plate back to the level; from then on concentrate on keeping the sole plate against the fence and let the saw find its own way through the wood to make the cut.

When you've cut all the main panels, match them against each other and check the fit.

Assuming that all is well, lightly sand off the rough edges, working from the outside in to avoid chipping the surface laminate.

Sand the long edges of the lid a bit more thoroughly so that you take off about 1mm for clearance against the side panels.

Use an offcut to mark out the braces as shown in the picture on page 354. You'll notice that the overall dimensions of the outer 'square' are slightly larger than twice the brace width to allow for the reduction due to the width of the saw cuts.

Cut the braces by hand, for greater accuracy, then clamp them all together. Use a try square to check that they all match and that the corners are true right angles.

Cut the four spacer strips next. Use the long edge of a brace to cut them to length, then turn them on edge and use the brace again to mark the mitred ends. Check that each strip lies perfectly flush with its brace, then pin and glue the four assemblies together and leave them to dry.

having a lot of waste left over. Remember also that a long unit full of heavy items will sag, so fit a stronger bottom and base panel supports. You could even compartmentalize the unit.

What you need

The main construction material for this project is 12.5mm birch-faced plywood, so called because it has a higher than average quality facing veneer which comes up beautifully when stained or varnished. Naturally it is more expensive than the standard WBP grade, but unless you plan just to paint the unit you'll find the extra cost well worth while in terms of looks and finish.

Built to the dimensions given, each unit takes the best part of half a sheet of plywood (1,220mm × 1,220mm). However, it's more than likely that you'll want to build a pair, or even four, units at the same time, in which case you can put the waste to better use: four units take only 1¼ sheets of plywood.

As well as the plywood, you require (per individual storage unit):
• 0.6m of 12.5mm square hardwood (ramin) quadrant moulding from which to cut the four corner pieces.
• 2m of 9mm square hardwood (ramin) lipping to cut the four base supports.
• Four 45mm diameter double-wheeled

castors. If you can't get these at your local hardware store, try an upholstery specialist or furniture restorer. Check that the castors have a screw-on plate fixing and that the screws provided are no longer than 12mm.
• A piano hinge 774mm long, with 12mm No. 6 fixing screws. You'll have to buy the hinge slightly over-size and trim it to fit, using a junior hacksaw.
• A large supply of PVA woodworking adhesive and 25mm panel pins, for securing the joints.
• Plastic wood putty to match the plywood colour for finishing the pin holes.
• Stain, varnish or primer/undercoat and paint for finishing.

Tools: None of the tools for this project are at all specialized, although you do need a sliding bevel and a protractor, rather than a try square, for marking the angles on the cutouts. The correct tool for clamping the panels is a web clamp, but you can improvise this quite easily yourself.

Although you can cut the plywood by hand, it is far easier if you've got power assistance in the shape of a jig saw or circular saw. Both of these tools should be used in conjunction with a fence to stop the blade straying off-line. An adjustable workbench is an invaluable aid to cutting plywood.

If you're going to store clothes, sheets or blankets in the box, you should consider also painting the interior so that there are no splinters to catch in the material, or

353

The cut-outs in the corners of the panels are identical, so measure, mark and cut one, then use it as a template to mark the rest so you can be sure that they will all match exactly: use a try square to mark a rectangle in the corner of the panel, then the sliding bevel set to 45° to mark the angle.

★ WATCH POINT ★

Transfer the cutting lines to the edges of the panel too, so that you have simple visual guides for keeping your saw blade vertical as you cut.

Do the cutting with a tenon saw, then sand the rough edges. Use a marking knife to mark the other panels and when you saw

them take care to keep to the waste side of the line.

Use the completed side panels as templates to mark and cut the four corner pieces of quadrant moulding to length.

Adopt the same procedure to mark and cut the four base supports; mark the ends of these against the angles on the corner cut-outs so that they will lie flush when fixed in place.

Mark the cut-out for the lid in the same way as the corner cut-outs. Drill two holes in the far corners—taking care to keep within the waste—so that you can insert a jig or padsaw blade to make the 'blind' cut. Remove the rest of the waste with two tenon saw cuts and sand down.

When marking up the timber for boxes of different sizes, draw up the sheet of ply or chipboard on graph paper and cut out the

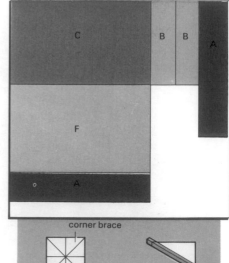

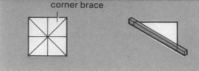

corner brace

silhouettes of the various panels to the same scale. Manoeuvre these on your drawing of the sheet until you get a reasonable layout which enables you to cut out the parts with the minimum of both trouble and waste.

Don't be afraid to use offcuts of softwood or some other material for the spacers and corner braces—if the unit is to be painted or varnished, the difference will be camouflaged, and if the box will be left natural the contrast might be quite pleasing.

Assembling the box

Do this part of the job in stages: the pinned and glued parts need time to dry before they are assembled.

Start by gluing the base supports flush with the lower edges of the front, back and side panels. Hold or clamp the supports in place while you strengthen the fixings by pinning into the panels at 100mm centres.

Pin and glue the four pieces of quadrant moulding to the side panels in the same way. This time, punch the pin heads well below the surface ready for filling.

When all the parts are dry, pin and glue the front and back panels to the side panels. The best way of doing this is to glue the mating surfaces and align the parts, secure them with a web clamp until the glue dries, then pin them for extra reinforcement.

When the box is complete, slip in the base panel. Turn the box on its side so that you can mark the corner cut-offs against the cut-outs in the side panels. Remove the base panel and saw the cut-offs with a tenon saw then glue the base to its supports and leave the entire assembly to dry.

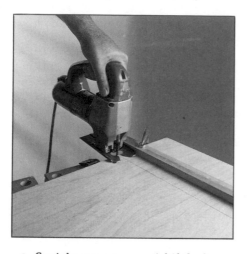

1 *Straight cuts are essential if the box is to fit together properly. Use a timber batten to guide the saw rather than just a fence*

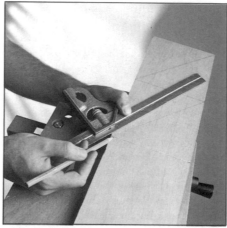

2 *The corner braces must be exactly 90°, so it might pay to invest in an adjustable square or bevel for marking up and measuring*

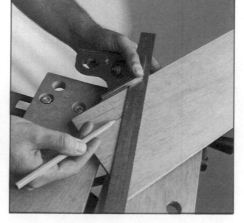

3 *Cut the spacers over-length, pin and glue them to the corner braces, and then saw their ends off flush with the braces*

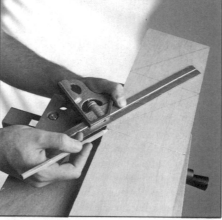

4 *Use the adjustable square again to mark off the corner cut-outs in the front, back and side panels accurately*

Left: You can cut the parts for one box from half a sheet of chipboard or plywood. The excess can be used for the spacers and corner braces—cut these in any pattern you like

If you don't have a web clamp, wrap several lengths of string or twine (which doesn't stretch) around the box and tie off. Twist the lengths tight using a screwdriver, until the panels are brought tightly together; then lock the screwdriver with a piece of wood. Packing will protect the corners.

At this point try the lower brace assemblies for fit. If all is well, glue each one in position and pin through the underside of the base into the spacer strip. Strengthen the fixings by pinning through the side panels as well, this time remembering to punch the heads below the surface (fill the holes later).

Complete the assembly by pinning and gluing on the top braces in the same way. You can align the braces by laying the lid lengthways across the box and then pulling them up against it.

Avoid straining the joints between the corner pieces and side panels by turning the box on end to pin it together.

Before marking and cutting a large panel ensure that all the corners are properly square

Measure lengths and widths to ensure the sides are parallel before drawing long lines

Measuring and marking ply

Marking plywood panels accurately and cutting them to size isn't as easy as it looks, so guard against expensive mistakes by following these tips:
• Always start with a cutting plan. For a single unit, follow the one on page 354; otherwise, draw up your own on a sheet of metric graph paper. The object of the exercise is to minimize the amount of waste and also the amount of cutting, so group panels of the same dimensions together; it helps if you start with the larger ones, then slot the smaller panels in around them. If you are dealing with a full-size sheet, try to arrange the panels so that your first cut divides it roughly in half—it will then become easier to handle.
• When measuring out the panels, leave a 2mm gap between each one to allow for the width of the saw blade. Cut V-shaped marks with a handyman's knife for greater accuracy.
• Double check each and every dimension—and don't assume that the sides of the sheet are square to start with. Check the corners carefully with a try square before you start.

• Do the actual marking out with a knife, held against a long metal rule or straight-edge: it's more accurate than using a pencil and by scoring the surface veneer you minimize the risk of the wood chipping when you cut it. Hold the straight edge carefully to avoid the knife slipping.

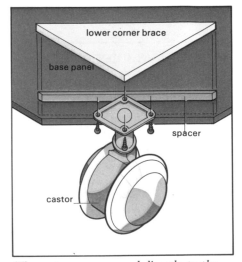

The castors are screwed directly to the lower corner braces. Shop around for castors which won't lift the box too high off the floor

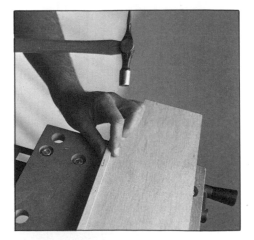

5 *Pin and glue the base panel support battens to the bottom edges of the side panels. Make sure that the two pieces meet exactly at right angles before fixing*

6 *Pin and glue the quadrant moulding to the side panels first, then assemble the box. Punch the pinheads well below the surface, so they can be filled later*

7 *Use a webbing strap to hold the entire assembly together absolutely square until the glue sets hard. Alternatively you can use a sash or corner cramp*

8 *Offer up the base panel and mark off at each corner the cut lines which will match the cut-outs in the side, front and back panels*

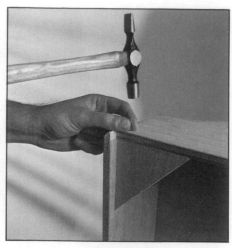

9 *Fit the base panel and lower corner braces before the top ones. Glue them in place and only pin them when the glue has set*

Alternative interior layouts

You may want to store delicate items in the box, such as photographic equipment, jewellery or make-up kits. The problem is to keep the contents tidy and protect them from one another, but this can be done easily by building small partitions into the box structure.

The simplest method of compartmentalization—and the one which offers the best protection for delicate items like cameras and hi-fi equipment—is to fill the box with foam rubber. Simply buy a slab the right size and depth to fit into the box (in two or three layers, if necessary) and glue it in place with a contact adhesive which won't attack the foam. Lay the items you want to store on the foam in a convenient layout, and then cut out their shapes into the foam using a knife.

Alternatively, you can erect timber partitions, but this is more complicated and takes much longer to do. Use the same material as the main side, front and back panels are made of, and cut it into strips the same depth as the front panel. Fix them upright, either along or across the bottom of the box and pin through the sides of the box into their edges.

Where two partitions must cross, cut halving joints so that they offer each other mutual support. For added strength, you can pin through the bottom of the box into the partitions, but this may be hard to do once the main box structure is completed.

You can, in fact, subdivide the box using anything you like: wire stationery trays, shoe boxes, plastic food containers or cutlery racks. You can even make up shoe racks, if the box is deep enough, by screwing a length of timber dowel or brass tube across the box and about 25–35mm off the bottom so that the toes of one pair can fit under the heels of the next pair.

Finishing the unit

If you plan to store items that won't be moved for some time, it's as well to drill extra ventilation holes in the base.

Fit the piano hinge next—to the lid first, then to the edge of the back panel.

Make pilot holes for the screws with a bradawl. When you come to fit the hinged lid to the box, it's a good idea to screw down the leaf at the ends only, then try the lid for fit before you drive in the remaining screws.

Before applying your chosen finish, fill all the pin holes with wood putty and sand the timber thoroughly with fine glasspaper mounted on a block; note that the front edge of the lid can be finished to a slight radius if desired, using a rasp and glasspaper.

Staining offers a number of decorative possibilities, including making a feature of the corner mouldings or matching the lid to the prevailing colour of the castor wheels. But thanks to the birch facing veneer, the unit can look equally as good with a plain varnished finish that will enhance the pattern of the grain.

Apply at least three coats—inside and out—sanding lightly between each one with fine glasspaper or wire wool for a really smooth surface. Be sure that, wherever you do the job, the atmosphere is kept dust-free while the varnish is drying.

Last of all, fit the castors by screwing on their mounting plates. With some designs, the wheels come separately, in which case fit them and check that the castors don't foul their housings before fitting them.

If it's important that the box be reasonably airtight, then dispense with the cut-out in the lid. Instead, buy a proprietary suitcase strap, or make up a strap of your own from rope, leather, plastic, an old belt or whatever's available, and screw this to the lid. As long as the strap doesn't stick out too much, you won't lose any space between the top of the box and the bottom of the bed. And, if you're storing heavy items in the box, fit a strap to the front panel to make moving the unit in and out easier.

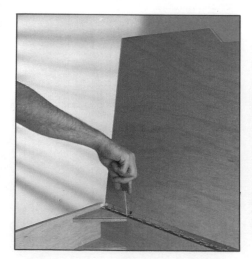

10 *Fit the piano hinge to the lid, then attach it to the back panel with a single screw at each end before driving in the rest of them*

11 *Most castors consist of a plate which must be screwed to the corner brace, and a wheel which simply plugs into the plate*

SPACE SAVING STORAGE

Here's an innovative and exciting way to add an otherwise boring practicality to your home—storage space that doesn't waste space. Planned and co-ordinated, it's both functional and highly decorative. And with just a few basic building considerations—always useful things to know—you could get down to this job before, during or after you've done your other decorating.

At first sight, the project is simply a rather sturdy false ceiling above the smallest room you can find, generally the lavatory. But made with strong, flooring grade tongue-and-groove boards, the ceiling doubles-up as the floor for an overhead cupboard. Cupboard doors provide access from outside the room through one of the walls, and double as features in their own right.

Planning considerations

First of all check that you've got enough height. In the UK, the Building Regulations require that rooms have a minimum headroom of 2.3m—about 300mm above most common door frames. This means that to provide a useable space, your ceilings must be about 3m high. Any windows in the room also affect your choice—make sure that the tops will be lower than the new ceiling level (that is, less than 2.3m high).

The next check is on the floor area. This must be small enough to give a side-to-side span of just 1200mm—floorboards alone will be strong enough to span this width.

There should be few other problems. Pipes and cisterns may get in the way, but with a little adjustment the ceiling would conceal them too. You must of course check that the hole in the wall is in a place which is easy to reach—preferably immediately above the existing door to the room. But don't worry about what the wall is made of—the project can be adapted to fit solid or frame types.

What to buy

The amount of building materials you need will vary with the size of the room, so measure it carefully and make a buying list. All the wood is available in standard sizes from any timber yard or DIY shop, while accessories can be bought from DIY shops or hardware stores.

You need enough 150mm × 25mm

tongue-and-groove floorboards to cover the floor area—bear in mind you'll be cutting them across the short width of the room.

Use 50mm × 25mm battens for the ceiling supports—buy enough to run round all four walls—and buy similar lengths of decorative moulding to trim the joints.

For the door frame, buy a 1m length of

75mm × 50mm timber to make the lintels and some 150mm × 25mm softwood for the frame itself. To trim the frame, you need architrave moulding to match the existing doors and some 25mm × 12mm beading for a door stop. Use a 19mm blockboard for the doors—you can probably find a suitably large offcut. To hang them, you

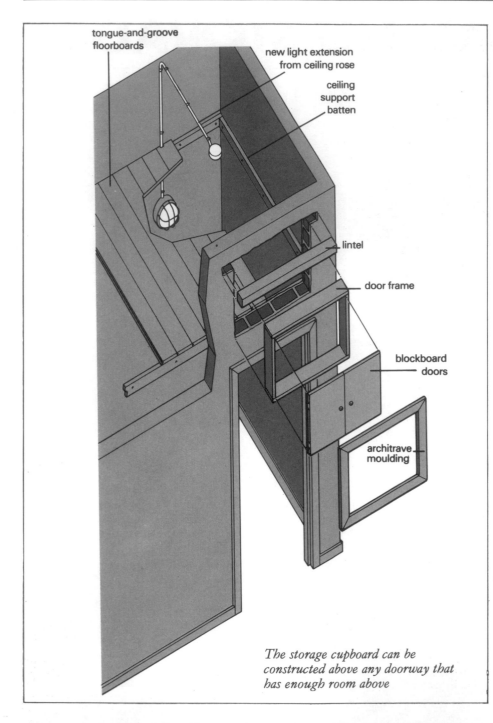

tongue-and-groove floorboards

new light extension from ceiling rose

ceiling support batten

lintel

door frame

blockboard doors

architrave moulding

The storage cupboard can be constructed above any doorway that has enough room above

it, above the door frame. It is mainly concealed by the architrave, and the area around the hole is finished with interior filler or plaster, then painted or papered.

The doors are made from 19mm blockboard fitted with 50mm hinges and magnetic catches. They can be painted, varnished, or even papered to match the decor of the walls.

The ceiling is supported by a 50mm × 25mm batten, screwed to the wall 2.3m above the floor. The panelling is 150mm × 25mm tongue-and-groove floorboards simply nailed in place across the width of the room. The room must not be wider than 1200mm, or the boards will need to have additional support.

To light the room, an extension is taken from the existing ceiling rose with new 0.5mm² lighting flex to a wall mounted light below the new ceiling.

Making the holes

This section covers the hard option—masonry walls. Refer to the diagram on page 360 if dealing with a frame wall.

Tap the wall above the door with your fist—if it sounds dull and solid, it is probably a masonry wall. To check, drill an exploratory hole about 350mm above the door frame with a masonry bit—watch for red brick dust, or grey dust which will indicate concrete blocks.

With a spirit level, extend the width of the lavatory door frame upwards over the hole position. Allow for the thickness of the new door frame, then mark the width of the hole you need to cut. Don't mark the upper or lower lines until you have removed some plaster to reveal one whole brick.

Take up or cover all your carpets and accessories—the job is likely to be messy. Take extra care to cover the fittings.

Working from a step ladder or high table, remove a small area of plaster from the wall

need two pairs of 50mm flush hinges and two magnetic catches, plus the cupboard door knobs of your choice.

You also need a wall mounted light and some 0.5mm² lighting flex—enough to run from the ceiling rose, down the wall to the new wall light.

To put it all together you need a quantity of 50mm oval nails, 63mm No. 8 screws and wallplugs and an assortment of panel pins, as well as a 2kg bag of ready-mixed mortar. The finishing material—whether gloss paint or varnish—depends on your taste and decorations.

How the cupboard fits

A hole, cut through the wall and fitted with two small doors, gives access to the redundant overhead space. The hole is trimmed with a 150mm × 25mm wooden lining that also acts as a door frame; 25mm × 12mm beading is pinned to the frame as a door stop. Decorative architrave—chosen to match the other doors—gives the cupboard an integrated look.

To support the wall above the hole a 75mm × 50mm wooden lintel is built into

★ WATCH POINT ★

Score these vertical cutting lines with a sharp trimming knife—the wallcovering will not tear back beyond the cuts and the plaster is less likely to crumble beyond the scored lines at a later date.

about 400mm above the door with a bolster and hammer. When one whole brick (or block) and mortar course has been exposed,

1 *Remove some plaster to reveal a brick and mortar course: their location determines the upper and lower boundaries of the hole*

2 *Chop the plaster back to the edges of the hole*

3 *Drill the mortar around the first brick. Drive in the bolster to loosen it*

4 *Insert the lintel next placing it on the bricks on either side. Make sure that it is straight, and level it with mortar*

5 *Allow the bedding mortar to cure, then ease out the bricks beneath the lintel, carefully chopping downwards*

6 *Use ready-mixed mortar to pack gaps at the edges. Most will be concealed by the architrave*

measure them so that you can use this dimension to mark in the upper and lower horizontal lines of the hole. Adjust them to correspond to the nearest mortar course, then score them in the same way. Don't make the lower line less than 150mm above the door, and leave at least 150mm between the top line and the ceiling. The size of the hole isn't critical at this stage.

With a bolster and hammer, remove the plaster from both sides of the wall. Drive the bolster at an angle in towards the brickwork in regular, neat chops. At the edges, drive the bolster at a steep angle towards the hole to make a clean line.

Above the topmost line, mark in the position of a 75mm × 50mm wooden lintel set flat to take the weight of the remaining bricks. Make this approximately 75mm longer on either side than the width of the hole. Score the lines and remove the plaster.

When you have removed all the plaster, begin on the brickwork, starting near the top of the proposed hole. Remove only enough bricks to fit the lintel: leave the rest of the opening until later.

★ WATCH POINT ★

Start with a drill and large masonry bit. Repeatedly drill into the mortar all around one of the bricks near the top of the hole. Remove as much mortar as you can by this method then drive your bolster into the joints to loosen more.

Ease out the loose brick. If it refuses to budge, break it up with the bolster but try to keep the surrounding brickwork intact.

Once two or three bricks are out, others should follow with ease. Prise them gently from the mortar, working along the line of the lintel. If you need to cut a brick, chop downwards to splinter it bit by bit.

Now slip the lintel into the gap and level it up with a spirit level. Wedge it in place temporarily with slivers of wood. Mix up some ready-mix mortar with just enough water to make it workable.

Remove the lintel, then trowel a bed of

mortar into either end of the hole. Slide the lintel back into place. Use the spirit level to check and adjust its position, packing mortar underneath or on top. Finally, pack all the gaps with mortar and leave to cure.

When you return to the job, continue removing the bricks from the opening. Leave the sides until last—you will have to trim alternate bricks flush, using the bolster and hammer. After this has been done, pack fresh mortar into any gaps left in the sides with the edge of your trowel. Knock off projecting pieces when the mortar is dry.

Opening up a frame wall

A timber framed wall sounds loud and hollow when you tap it with your fist. At doorways, there is a frame member on each side of the opening, running from floor to ceiling. A shorter one commonly runs from the top of the door frame to the ceiling.

Start your hole by cutting back the panelling to the frame timber on either side. First mark the plasterboard or other wall panel-

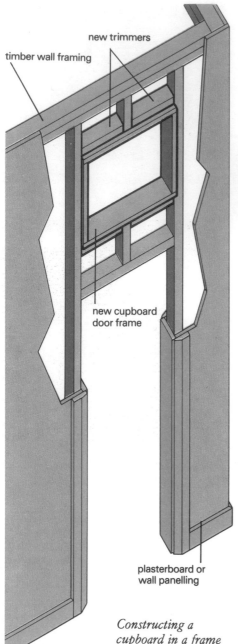

new trimmers

timber wall framing

new cupboard
door frame

plasterboard or
wall panelling

*Constructing a
cupboard in a frame
wall*

ling, then drill small holes to insert a pad-saw—or a thin blade fitted to a trimming knife—and cut along the marked lines. Cut the sides of the hole back to the timber frame. If there is a central one, cut this off level with the horizontal edges of the hole.

To support the top and bottom of the opening, insert 'trimmers' made of wood the same size as the rest of the frame (usually 100mm×50mm). Cut them to span between the sides of the hole and slip them under the wall panelling. They are best held in place with L-brackets screwed to the corners. The cupboard door lining and the doors then fit in the same way as on a masonry wall.

Fitting the door frame

The new door frame also serves to line the hole. Use standard 150mm×25mm planed-all-round (PAR) timber (or a width to fit the thickness of your walls).

Start by holding a board across the bottom of the hole and marking off a length to fit it. Use a try square to level the ends,

7 *Nail and glue the frame together and brace it across the diagonal*

8 *Mark and drill fixing positions, then screw into wallplugs. Plug gaps*

9 *Pin architrave to the frame's edges to conceal the gaps*

then cut two pieces to exactly this length.

Place both pieces together across the bottom of the hole. Hold a further length of the wood up to them and mark the point at which it meets the bottom of the lintel. Cut two pieces.

Join all four pieces with woodworking adhesive and 50mm oval nails. Drive the nails through the ends of the long pieces into the tops of the shorter vertical pieces. Check

---

★ WATCH POINT ★

Brace the frame by nailing a spare length of wood across one diagonal. This will keep the frame square until it is fitted.

---

that the frame is square by measuring the two diagonals—they should be the same.

Drill two 4.0mm countersunk holes near the top of each of the uprights and two at the bottom. Drill two holes in each horizontal.

Place the frame in the hole in the wall and adjust it until it is flush with the wall and level. Wedge it in place with scraps of wood.

Mark through the holes onto the wall by poking a nail through the holes you have made. Remove the frame and drill holes at these points with a No. 8 masonry drill (use a 2.0mm twist bit to drill pilot holes in the wooden lintel). Plug holes with wallplugs.

Screw the new frame into place with 63mm No. 8 screws. Tighten gradually, checking that the frame continues to remain square and upright.

Any roughness on the wall behind the frame does not matter—it will be concealed later on in the construction.

Cut four lengths of architrave moulding all about 100mm longer than the frame they fit over. Cut mitres at the four corners with the aid of a mitre box so that the architrave fits just short of the inner edge of the frame. Nail the architrave to the frame with 50mm oval nails.

Adding the doors

Make the doors from an offcut of 19mm blockboard sheet. Use a tape measure or piece of batten to mark the width and height of the hole and transfer them to the sheet.

Extend the lines with a try square and ruler, then saw it to size. Score the cutting lines with a knife to avoid splintering the surface. Cut the panel down the middle to make two doors, then sand the edges.

Add two 50mm flush hinges to the edges of both doors about 50mm from each

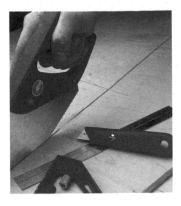

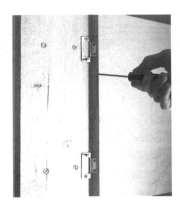

10 *Measure and mark the blockboard. Score lines*

11 *Hinge and fit the doors to the cupboard*

12 *Pin 25mm × 12mm beading to the frame*

13 *Attach catches to doors and frames*

end—see Fitting the hinges (above). Screw the hinges to the frames and test-close the doors. If they have been properly marked and fitted, it's unlikely that the doors will stick. If they do, mark the areas that are sticking and sand until they close smoothly.

Cut a length of 25mm × 12mm beading to fit the width of the door frame. Shut both doors so that they are flush with the front of the frame. Lay the beading flat on the top part of the frame so that it butts up snugly against them. Nail it in place with 25mm panel pins.

Fit the knobs of your choice to each of the doors, then add the magnetic catches. Screw the striking plate to each door, then—one at a time—close the door and align the catch body with the striking plate. Mark through the fixing holes onto the frame and screw the catch body in place.

Fitting the hinges

50mm flush hinges are perfectly adequate for this job. Their main advantage is that you don't need to cut recesses in either the door or the frame—all you need to do is align them properly and securely on the edge of the door, then on the frame.

With a try square, mark points on the hinge edge of each door, 50mm from each end. Place a closed hinge against one mark. Adjust its position until the shoulder sits against the edge of the door, then mark through the screw holes of the inside leaf.

Use a bradawl or 2.0mm drill bit to make pilot holes at these points, then screw the inside leaf home with the screws provided. Do the same for the other hinges.

Place a door in the frame with the hinges closed. Adjust its position to give an equal gap at top and bottom. Then lightly mark the frame to indicate the top and bottom of the hinges themselves.

Open the door, align the hinges with your marks on the edge of the frame, then screw into place. Test-close the door. If it sticks at any point, smooth the area with a sanding block.

Wiring the light

You will need to fit a new light below the position of the lowered ceiling. With most light fittings, all you need to do is replace the existing flex from the ceiling rose with a longer one and connect the other end to a wall light before you install the ceiling.

The boards of the ceiling must be level with the bottom of the door frame, so allow for the thickness of the boards and the support batten below them. Mark this point, then use a spirit level to extend a line round the walls. Mark the position of the light below this.

Before you start any work on the light itself, switch off the fuse board main switch so that there is no chance of getting a shock.

Unscrew the rose cover to reveal the wiring beneath. Whatever the wiring system in use, note the connections of the existing flex to the light, remove the old one and replace it with the new flex in exactly the same position.

Take a length of 0.5mm² (3 amp) lighting flex sufficient to reach from the rose to the light position. Remove about 50mm of the outer sheathing then strip 10mm of the coloured insulation from each wire, and twist the individual strands together. Loosen the terminal screws holding the old flex, then slip the flex from the rose cap. Reverse the process to wire the new flex. Remember: the blue wire goes to Neutral (the old wire may have been black), the brown goes to Live (the old wire may have been red). If cord grips are provided, clamp the wires in them.

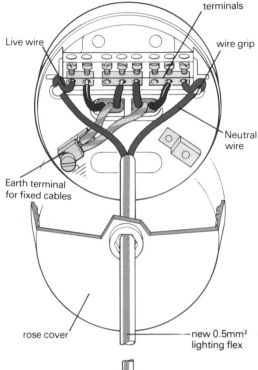

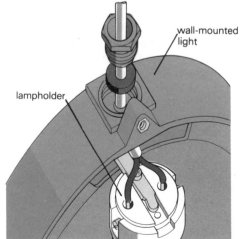

14 *Switch off at the mains. Remove the rose cover and note connections. Remove the old lighting flex and replace it with new flex. Connect to the terminals*

Run the flex across the ceiling and down the wall to the new light position. Cut it to the length required, then bare the wire ends to make the connections to the light itself.

Remove the base from the light, thread the flex through the flex entrance hole and connect the wires to their appropriate terminals.

Mark the light fixing holes and screw the base to the wall, then attach the body.

Switch on the mains supply, then try the light. If it works secure the flex to the ceiling and wall with cable clips.

Installing the ceiling

Start the installation by sawing up 50mm × 25mm battens to fit along the walls, just above the lines you marked, before repositioning the light. Two lengths of wood will be slightly shorter than the wall to allow for an overlap at the corners.

When the batten crosses the flex to the light, cut a notch in the back. Saw part-way through the wood, then cut out the waste with a narrow chisel so that the batten rests against the wall without squeezing the flex.

For masonry walls, drill 4.0mm countersunk clearance holes at 500mm intervals. Hold the battens in place then mark the fixing positions on the walls. Using a No. 8 masonry drill, drill holes at the points you have marked. Insert wallplugs, then screw the battens to the wall.

For frame walls, tap the walls to find the frame members. If necessary, drill an exploratory hole to find one—the rest should be at 400mm or 450mm intervals, which makes them easy to locate. Mark the walls with their positions, hold the battens in place and transfer the marks to the battens. Drill 4.0mm countersunk holes at these points on the battens. Hold them in place and mark the wall in the same way, but drill 2.0mm pilot holes onto the wall. Screw in place as above.

Cover the screw heads with fine surface filler. When dry, sand the filler flat.

Cut the tongue-and-groove boards to fit the width—not the length—of the room.

Measure them as for the support battens. A slightly rough cut at the end will not matter as it will be hidden from view by the battens. Starting at the end away from the door and working from below, drop the boards on to the support battens and nail in place with 38mm oval nails. Slot the tongue of each board into the groove of the next.

As you approach the new opening, it will be easier to work through it. You will probably need to cut the final board along its

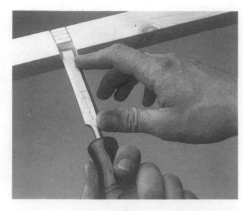

15 *Mark where the batten crosses the flex. Saw two lines partway through, then cut out the waste*

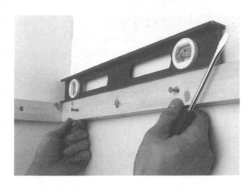

16 *Drill countersunk clearance holes in the batten. Level it, then mark fixing positions. Screw the batten on*

17 *Cut the floorboards. Nail each board to the batten. Slot the tongue of one board into the groove of the next*

★ WATCH POINT ★

To measure the length of a wall without a tape measure, hold two shorter pieces of wood against each other. Slide them apart until the ends touch either side wall, then use both pieces together to mark the wood you want to cut.

length to make a neat fit, so lay the last few boards loosely to check. Measure the gap, or mark it off on a piece of scrap batten, and use this to make the last board. Saw it down its full length.

Lift the remaining unfastened boards slightly so you can fit the tongue of the last board into the groove. Push the boards into place together, then nail them down.

Finishing off

A nice finishing touch is to nail thin decorative moulding to the support batten so that it looks like a cornice. Add it to the corner between the boards and batten, to the

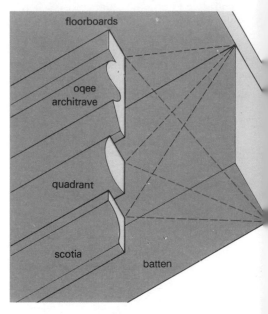

18 *Nail a moulding to the batten. Punch nail heads below the surface with a nail punch and insert filler*

★ WATCH POINT ★

Apply the primer, then rub down with fine glasspaper a second time. The painted surface reveals blemishes far more obviously than an untreated surface does.

bottom of the batten, or to both.

When you have chosen your pattern, nail the mouldings on then punch the heads below the surface. Fill all holes and gaps with interior filler, then rub down with fine glasspaper. Prime all the wooden surfaces.

Alternatively, fill the holes with plastic wood filler then varnish all the surfaces for a natural wood finish.

CUBE STORAGE UNITS

Most cube storage systems look easy to build but aren't, because it's hard to get the panels to fit together squarely. Finishing the edges of the panels can be a problem too; you will normally be restricted to using melamine-faced chipboard with a matching iron-on edging strip.

The cube system (right) solves the fitting problem in an ingenious way: all the panels are cut to the same size and are then butt jointed to edging pieces made from square section hardwood. This also gets round the edging problem—because none of the panel edges are exposed, you can use plywood or blockboard as your main material and then stain, varnish or paint it to match your other furniture.

Another interesting feature of these cubes is that they can be joined to each other to form rigid larger units, which you tailor to fit the available space. This is achieved quite simply by using proprietary plastic male/female connector screws to link the different units together.

A choice of versions

The basic cube is easily modified to make better use of the space inside. Horizontal shelves can be fitted on shelf support studs; or vertical slide-in dividers on sections of hard-wood channel moulding. Taking the work a stage further you can fit a door made to match the other panels and hang it on standard flush hinges. And if you feel really ambitious, add one or more drawers—use proprietary plastic drawer kits faced with the panel material.

If you consult the diagram which shows how the various versions of the cube are put together, you'll see that the parts have been kept to standard sizes as far as possible. This makes it well worth your while setting up a 'production line' rather than trying to build each cube individually. Make full use of the instructions given on templates for cutting and marking out, and this part of the job will automatically become easier. It will also lessen the chances of introducing minor discrepancies between cubes, which could spoil the finished result.

Tools and materials

The basic panel material for the cubes is 12.5mm plywood or blockboard. Both are about the same price, but plywood is slightly stronger and may well have a superior surface finish. If you plan to paint the cubes, make a point of inspecting the surface of every sheet you buy for large knots, dents or chips.

Standard sheet sizes are 2440mm × 1220mm (enough for up to twelve standard panels, plus a door, shelf or divider) and 1220mm × 600mm (enough for up to three panels plus offcuts for drawer fronts). Obviously it makes sense to buy the largest sheet size, but you should also be able to get offcuts that fit the panel dimensions with less waste—ask your timber merchant.

Consult the diagram opposite before making up your cutting list. For each basic cube you will need:
- 5 panels of 12.5mm board (ply or blockboard) measuring 350mm × 350mm;
- about 4.5m of 12.5mm square ramin (hardwood edging);
- a generous supply of 12mm veneer or moulding pins and PVA woodworking adhesive;
- stain and/or polyurethane varnish or primer, undercoat and gloss paint to finish.

For a shelf cube add (per shelf):
- one panel of 12.5mm ply or blockboard measuring 350mm × 219mm;
- four screw-in plastic shelf supports;
- 350mm of 12.5mm × 6mm ramin edging.

For a divider cube add (per divider):
- one panel of 12.5mm board measuring 338mm × 264mm plus 540mm of 12.5mm square ramin channel of 6mm square ramin.

Note: for thinner dividers use 4mm or 5mm ply and narrower section channel moulding.

For a door cube add:
- one panel of 12.5mm board measuring 334mm × 328mm (or 334mm × 334mm if your opt for a handle other than the one shown);
- about 1040mm of 25mm × 12.5mm ramin edging (for the door handle);
- two 25mm flush hinges and a magnetic door catch, plus fixing screws.

For a drawer cube add (per drawer):
- one plastic drawer kit;
- 700mm of plastic drawer runner;
- 3mm white-faced hardboard (drawer base);
- 6mm square ramin to hold drawer base;

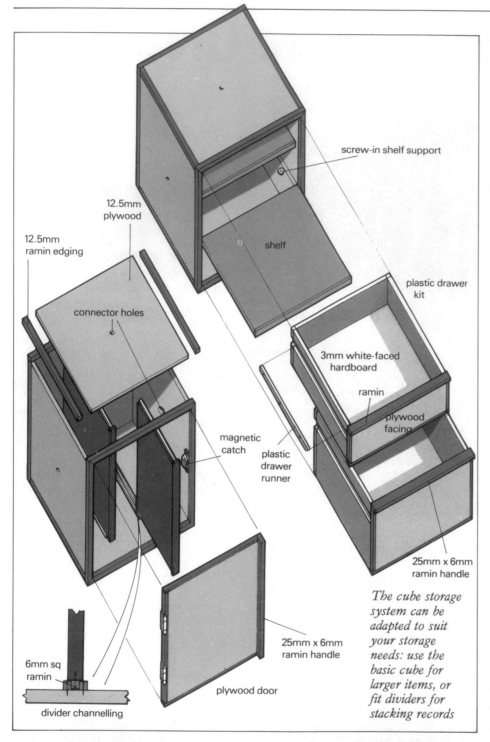

12.5mm plywood

12.5mm ramin edging

connector holes

screw-in shelf support

shelf

plastic drawer kit

3mm white-faced hardboard

ramin

plywood facing

magnetic catch

plastic drawer runner

25mm x 6mm ramin handle

6mm sq ramin

divider channelling

25mm x 6mm ramin handle

plywood door

The cube storage system can be adapted to suit your storage needs: use the basic cube for larger items, or fit dividers for stacking records

and try square to 350mm square, then rule diagonals across it and check that they are exactly the same length.

Cut the template out very carefully and align the edges with the plywood sheet on a flat, firm surface.

Align the edge of the rule with the template and the ply before marking each line. Draw around the template with a pencil to mark the panels and check that they're accurate before scribing over the top with a marking knife. Press down firmly as you run the marking knife along and be sure to keep your fingers behind the blade. Repeat for each panel.

Marking along the template with a marking knife held against a steel rule is not only more accurate than using just a pencil, but also scores the surface of the ply and prevents it chipping when you cut it.

When you come to do the cutting, make sure that the sheet is well supported on each side of the cutting line.

If you're using a jig saw, align the blade with the cut and then clamp a straight-edged piece of wood against the sole plate, parallel with the cut, to act as a guide. Don't try to force the saw through—concentrate on keeping the blade on the line. Be sure to support the sheet with your free hand as you near the end of the cut.

If you are sawing by hand, make sure that the saw is sharp and use long but gentle strokes—too much force will certainly cause the surface to split.

Cut the ramin edging next. On each cube there are four pieces 350mm long with square cut ends and eight pieces 375mm

★ WATCH POINT ★

The template also gives you the chance to mark the central holes for the cabinet connectors—simply punch a hole through the card where the diagonals intersect.

• 12.5mm board for drawer front;
• 346mm of 25mm × 12.5mm ramin edging (for drawer handle).

Construction calls for mainly standard woodworking tools. To mark out the panels accurately you'll need a steel rule, marking knife and try square. You'll find a portable workbench useful for supporting and cutting the panels and you must have a good saw for the cutting work itself—either a sharp panel saw or a power jig saw.

You'll also need an electric drill and 6mm twist bit for making pilot holes for the

cube connectors, and a mitre box for cutting the ramin edging accurately.

Making a basic cube

The hardest part of this job is cutting five panels of plywood to the same size. Take care to get it right and the cube will go together with the minimum of fuss.

The safest way to mark out the plywood for cutting is to make up a template from thin cardboard. Mark this out with a rule

long with the ends mitred. Measure, mark and cut one of each size using a rule, try square, marking knife and tenon saw. Then take the longer of the two and cut the mitres at the ends using a mitre box—be sure to get them the right way round on each strip.

For maximum accuracy, you should now use the two lengths as templates to cut the remaining sections of edging individually. Check the fit of the mitres as you go and sand the cut ends very lightly—just enough to remove any roughness—but beware of rounding off the edges.

1 *Mark out the sheet in 350mm squares then cut out using a panel or jig saw*

2 *Cut the ramin edging to length: you'll need four square ends, four mitred*

3 *Drill a hole for a connector and a counter-sink in the opposite face*

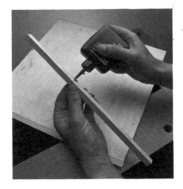

4 *Glue and pin two square-ended ramin strips to opposite edges of panels*

5 *Glue and pin four mitred ramin edging strips around one of the ply panels*

6 *Take the two edged panels and assemble with the remaining unedged panels*

7 *Glue and pin the framed panel to one end of the shell to form a 'box'*

8 *You can test the joining method using plastic screw-threaded cabinet connectors*

Now, using a 6mm twist bit, drill pilot holes for the connectors at the marks you have made in the centre of each panel. Follow by recessing the holes on one side with a suitable countersink to accommodate the connector heads. With the connectors shown, the recess is 16mm in diameter and 3mm deep; with other brands you may have to vary the sizes slightly for a neat finish.

If you want to stain the cubes, do so at this stage, bearing in mind that the edging should be a contrasting colour for best effect. The components will then be ready for assembly, which runs as follows.

Take two of the panels and pin and glue 350mm lengths of ramin exactly flush along two opposing edges on each one. Punch the pin heads below the surface using a centre punch or a nail.

Take another panel and glue and pin four 375mm mitred lengths exactly flush around the edges. Fill any gaps in the mitring (and the pin head recesses) with a mixture of ramin, sawdust and glue.

Take the first two assemblies and the remaining panels. Glue and pin together.

When the shell is dry, take the edged panel and glue and pin it to one open side.

Take the remaining mitred lengths of edging and glue and pin them to the exposed edges.

When everything has been allowed to dry thoroughly, sand down the square edges of the ramin until they are fractionally rounded (1mm radius) and sand the surface of the panels with fine abrasive paper mounted on a wood block. Varnish or paint the cube as you require.

When you've completed a second cube, try out the cabinet connectors. Test-fit a male and female half in adjacent holes in the cubes and screw them together. You may find that they need shortening, in which case note by how much, remove them, and trim with a fine toothed hacksaw. If this damages the thread on the end, restore it by filing off the burrs.

Dividers, doors and drawers

Because the cubes are all a standard size, fitting dividers, shelves, doors and drawers is simply a matter of adding extra parts before and during assembly.

On all the options listed below, start by cutting and edging five panels as for the basic cube. Keep your cutting template handy—it'll help when you come to mark the positions of the fittings. Measure and mark it out with the lines shown in the diagram opposite so that you can use it whatever the version you're building. You can, of course, vary the spacings between the shelves and dividers to suit the shape of the items you're displaying.

Shelf cube: Take one side panel, lay the template exactly over the top and refer to the diagram (left). Measure out and mark the required shelf support positions on the template, then make pilot holes through it into the panel using a bradawl. Press (stud type) or screw (screw type) the shelf supports to the panel, having removed the template, then repeat the entire operation on the other side panel.

Cut each shelf panel to 350mm × 319mm and sand the edges thoroughly. When the basic cube has been assembled, try the shelf for fit and sand or plane as necessary. Then use the width of the shelf as a template to cut a length of 12.5mm × 6mm ramin edging. Glue and pin this to the

365

9 *Mark the shelf support positions on one side; make pilot holes*

10 *Fix the stud shelf supports into the face of the side panels*

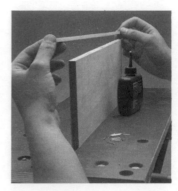

11 *Glue and pin a ramin strip to the leading edge of each shelf panel*

12 *Slide the shelves into the cube so they rest on the shelf studs, edge out*

13 *Mark the positions of the divider channels then nail in place 6mm apart*

14 *Edge the dividers and fix runners. Slide in between channels*

15 *Mark out the positions for the drawer runners and screw them to the sides*

16 *Make up the plastic drawer kits. Slide onto runners*

shelf's front edge then slot the shelf into the cube to rest on its stud supports.

If you should want to alter the shelf positions later to accomodate larger or smaller items, remove the studs where necessary.

Divider cube: Prepare edged panels as for the basic cube. Then cut two lengths of ramin channel to 270mm for each divider, plus 338mm×264mm panels of the materials for the dividers themselves.

Take the cube base panel and lay the template over it. Refer to the diagram on page 364 and align a length of channel exactly with the appropriate line on the template (the shelf positions can be used as divider positions, too). Pin the channel into the base and top panels at 75mm centres, making sure the channel itself stays flush with the back edge of the base panel (not the edging). If you're using 12.5mm dividers it's easiest to make channels from 6mm square ramin strips pinned 6mm apart at each side of the dividers. Fix all the channels in position before assembling the cube.

Try each divider for fit in the cube and sand or plane the edges as necessary. Then cut a length of 12.5mm×6mm ramin edging to trim the front edge. Glue and pin

it in position, and then you can simply slot the divider in place.

Door cube: Make up the basic cube panels and cut the door to size (334mm×328mm with edge handle or 334mm square if you opt for a conventional door). Cut three pieces of 12.5mm×6mm ramin edging to 346mm: mitre both ends of one piece and one end of the other two. Cut the 25mm ×12.5mm ramin handle to 346mm.

Pin and glue the edging around the door so that the handle stands proud (note: if you're fitting a conventional handle simply mitre together four pieces of 6mm ramin). For simplicity you could butt the door edging together instead of cutting mitres.

When the basic cube has been assembled, mark the positions on the centre line of the opposite side. Convert the marks to pilot holes with a bradawl and then screw the hardware in position on the cube.

Try the door for fit and adjust by planing down the hinge edge as necessary. Then mark through the hinge leaves onto the door, convert to pilot holes and screw the door in place. Add the magnetic catch, centred on the centre line of the door. Most have slots so you can adjust the position.

Drawer cube: With this design, you can have three single drawers or a double and a single. Cut the drawer fronts to size (350mm×115mm for a single; 350mm×230mm for a double) plus the ramin edging and handles.

Mitre the side edging strips at one end and the base edging at both, then glue and pin the edging to the fronts. Alternatively, butt join the edging strips.

Cut the plastic drawer sides and back panels to length—this may vary according to the jointing method used—using a hacksaw. Smooth off burrs with glasspaper.

Cut the plastic drawer slides to length (350mm) with a tenon saw and sand the cut edges. Lay your template over a prepared side panel and align the slides with the appropriate lines, keeping them butted against the back edge of the panel (not the edging). Drill pilot holes through the slides and into the panel to take No. 6 roundhead screws, then remove both them and the template. Screw the slides in place. Repeat the procedure for the other side panel. Having assembled the cube in the usual way, make up the drawers and drawer fronts. Then slide the drawers onto their runners.

BUILDING A SERVING HATCH

There is nothing like a serving hatch for convenience, especially if there's no doorway linking the kitchen with the dining area. Making your own is inexpensive, and requires only a few tools and materials.

The real work involves making a hole in the wall in the right place and at the right height, and—in a masonry wall—providing support for the brickwork above the opening. This means adding a lintel. It's not difficult work but it is messy, and it's important to choose a height and size to match your walls and kitchen. In this respect, it's a matter of measurement and alignment.

Once you've made the hole, you just fit a simple timber frame into the opening to line the hatch—make sure that the wood is as wide as the wall is thick. Then add doors and trimmings to match your decor.

You can use one of the wide range of ready-made doors available or make your own, so you can match any decor—from modern to traditional.

Planning considerations

There are several considerations when planning where to put a serving hatch. First you must determine whether your wall is load-

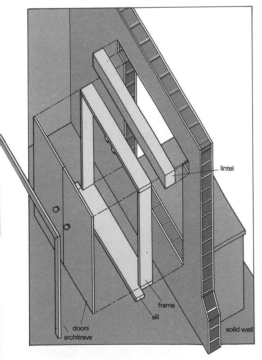

Fit the lintel to support the load above, then insert the 25mm frame and sill. Hang the doors and architrave

bearing and arrange the work accordingly—you'll need suitable supports, both temporary and permanent. But if the wall is a hollow timber framed type, it's more straightforward.

The position of the serving hatch is your second consideration. The centre of the wall is ideal from a structural point of view, but it's not essential. What's important is that the bottom of the finished hatch is level (or nearly level) with your kitchen worktop and that the top is lower than any kitchen fittings—cupboards or shelves, for example.

On the dining room side, try to avoid having to rearrange all the furniture to suit the location of the serving hatch. Accessability is essential so, although the hatch should be close to the dining table, it should not be directly above it.

Buying and hiring

For a serving hatch in a masonry wall, you only need basic tools—a power drill and assorted bits, a long masonry bit, club hammer, brick bolster, spirit level and wood

working tools. But you'll need to hire two expandable steel props—commonly known as Acrows—plus about 2m of 100mm× 100mm timber and some sturdy planks. Get these from a tool hire shop. You need them for temporary support.

You'll need safety goggles and gloves to protect you as you work and plenty of builder's bags to remove the rubble. Dust sheets will also save a lot of clearing up.

You can use a timber lintel, but if the wall carries a heavy load and you're in any doubt, use a pre-stressed concrete lintel instead. There are two types: those for single brick thickness walls, and those for double brick thickness walls. They're both pre-stressed and available from builder's merchants in a variety of lengths. For holes of this size (less than 1.5m) a steel lintel is not necessary.

The amount of timber you need for the lining depends on the thickness of your walls. For the threshold use timber that is about 50mm wider to provide a small sill. Use wood that is 25mm thick.

You also need enough decorative moulding for both sides of the wall. Look carefully before purchasing, and buy some that matches your existing woodwork.

One 20kg bag of ready mixed bricklaying mortar is all you need for the masonry work, but make sure that you've also got enough interior filler to cover any mistakes or small cracks in the walls.

Clearing the plaster

Before you begin the job, prepare yourself and your house for the work that lies ahead. This mainly involves checking and measuring but it also involves making a mess, so begin by folding back carpets and laying dust sheets in the affected areas.

To determine what type of wall you have,

check that the wall is clear of power sockets or light switches. If it's not, turn off the main supply and leave it off. Unscrew the cover plate of the switch or socket and examine the direction of the cables—normally they go up or down, rarely straight across the wall. If you can't tell, carefully chisel away plaster from a small area around the socket until you can see which way they go. If the cables are routed across your proposed opening, they must be re-routed first. Unless you are absolutely certain of the procedure involved, leave this job to a professional electrician.

Score the upper line with a sharp trimming knife to prevent both the plaster from crumbling and the wallpaper tearing beyond this line.

If this line happens to fall directly over the ends of the bricks and mortar joints between them then the position of the vertical line on this side requires no adjustment. If it does not, adjust it to coincide with the end of the nearest brick. Move the right-hand boundary by the same amount, score it and erase the original line.

Work towards the right, removing the plaster to the end of the brick nearest to the

1 *Mark out the proposed outline of the serving hatch. Score along the top line with a sharp knife*

2 *Using a brick bolster and club hammer clear away the plaster from around one whole brick*

3 *Clear away the plaster from the whole area within the new lines. Work in one direction moving across the opening*

tap it with your knuckles. If it sounds hollow it will be a timber frame wall.

If, on the other hand, it sounds solid, then it is most likely to be a masonry wall. It will be brick or blockwork covered by a thick layer of plaster. In this case, drill a hole with a masonry bit about 1.4m from the floor and roughly in the centre of the proposed hatch. If your drill bit is long enough, drill through from one side to the other.

Using this hole as the centre, mark out an area 760mm long by 610m high—use a spirit level and pencil. Before starting work,

Using a brick bolster and club hammer, start chipping away the plaster in the upper third of the marked area, working towards the scored line. Don't worry about clearing the plaster back to the vertical boundaries.

Should the upper scored line fall directly over a mortar course, then the horizontal position of the hatch needs no adjustment. But it is most likely that you will have to raise or lower this top line to take advantage of the nearest mortar course.

After adjusting and re-scoring the top line, adjust the lower line by the same amount. Erase the original line and score the new one to avoid confusion.

Working downwards from the exposed area, remove the plaster to the nearest mortar course of the lower scored line. When you have reached this line the distance between the top and bottom should be between 570mm and 650mm apart.

For the vertical boundaries, first score the left-hand line and start working in the direction of this line.

scored line. The two sides should be between 700mm and 820mm apart.

Clear away any remaining plaster and measure the exact area. Find the centre by drawing the two diagonals and marking where they cross. Precisely in the middle, drill a hole completely through the masonry wall to the other side. Using this hole as a centre point, mark out and score an area with exactly the same dimensions as the other side. Then proceed to remove the plaster from this side. The edges of this side should also fall directly on mortar joints.

Inserting the lintel

It's very important to ensure that the wall—and any load that it carries—is properly supported until the lintel is in place. Once the lintel is installed, the rest of the brickwork can be safely removed.

A brick wall is exceptionally stable—even with a hole in it—but if the wall carries any load at all you must be as cautious as possible. You must insert a 'needle' of timber through the wall above your intended opening and prop it up on either side with adjustable steel props. These will support the load until the lintel can permanently take their place.

Begin by inserting the needle—use 100mm × 100mm timber about 2m long. At a point about 750mm above the top of the proposed opening, remove the plaster from a small area on both sides of the wall. Remove enough to expose at least one whole brick. Using a masonry drill and wearing goggles, drill into the mortar on all sides of the brick. Remove as much mortar as possible by this method, then tap the brick lightly to dislodge it. If it won't budge, drive a bolster into the joint until it will.

Repeat this process on one of the staggered bricks above the first one. If the wall is more than one brick thick—it's unlikely to be a cavity wall though—repeat this process on the other side.

Insert the needle through the hole and support it on either side with adjustable steel props. Lay stout planks underneath the base of the props to spread the load.

Adjust the props and tighten them until the needle is stressed against the top of the hole. Make sure the props are plumb and that the needle is level. If they are, the needle is now ready to carry the load that was taken by the wall.

Mark out and score an area one brick course higher and extending 100mm beyond either side of the proposed hatch.

4 Remove a couple of bricks to create a hole for the needle. Locate it about 750mm above the top line of the hatch

5 Insert the needle and tighten up the props on both sides until the needle is stressed against the top of the hole

6 Lay the lintel on a bed of mortar. Fill the gaps with mortar and allow to cure for at least one day before removing props

---

★ WATCH POINT ★

If you can't remove the brick intact, break it up. Drill into the brick itself, insert a narrow cold chisel and give it a series of heavy blows with a hammer.

Clear the plaster from this area and repeat the procedure on the other side of the wall.

Start to remove the bricks from this course, one by one. Use the method described earlier to remove the first brick and the others should follow with ease. Clean an opening that is large enought to accommodate the lintel but no bigger.

Mix up some ready mixed bricklaying mortar and lay a small bed on either side of the proposed hatch. Insert the lintel and pack under its ends—use more mortar and slivers of wood or slate—until it is perfectly level. Fill any gaps between the surrounding

masonry and the lintel with the rest of the mortar. Leave it to cure for at least one day before you move on to the next stage.

Making the hole

Once the mortar has set around the lintel you can remove the temporary supports and fill the holes you have made. From now on the lintel itself will support the wall and any load that it carries.

Remove the bricks below the lintel and back to your scored lines. Start on a central brick and drill out as before. Now that the masonry is supported, you can use the bolster and hammer more freely. If you encounter a stubborn brick it is wiser to return to the method of drilling out the mortar rather than using force.

On alternate courses at either side of the opening, use a bolster and hammer to cut the bricks in half, leaving them flush with the ends of the uncut bricks.

Use one (or more) of the bricks you remove to fill the hole you made for the needle. Lay a bed of mortar in the hole and squeeze in the brick. Fill any gaps with the

7 Remove the bricks for the hatch opening starting from the centre. Cut the side bricks in half with a bolster

8 Fill the rough edges of the opening with mortar using two battens temporarily nailed to the wall as your guide

remaining mortar. If rough edges extend back more than 50mm from the edge of the opening itself, trowel mortar onto the surface of the bricks to a point about 3mm below the surrounding surface.

Don't worry about the finish around the opening at this stage—most of the rough edges will be either plastered or covered by the wood moulding.

★ WATCH POINT ★

It may be easier to remove the whole brick and chop it in half on a solid surface. Lay a bed of mortar in the hole the brick came from and re-insert the half brick.

Making the frame

You must line the opening with timber of a suitable width. Measure the thickness of the wall—it will determine the width of the timber you use. For the lower surface, add an extra 100mm to the width so that it will overhang into the dining room. Measure the opening from side to side and top to bottom for the lengths you need. Buy twice as much wood moulding for the architrave, as you need it on both sides of the wall.

Cut the wider board 200mm longer than the width of the opening. Cut a notch at each end that is 100mm deep and the same width as the thickness of the wall. This allows it to fit into the hole leaving an overhang on each side. Test fit the threshold into the opening, with the ledge protruding on the dining room side.

For the top of the opening, cut a piece of the narrower board to the same length as the threshold (between the notches). Plane this board to the same width as the wall.

Place the board and threshold together across the bottom of the opening. Hold a further length of the narrower board up to them and mark where it meets the bottom of the lintel. Cut two pieces to this dimension and plane them to the width of the wall. Check to make sure that the ends are perfectly level and square.

Join all four sides using 50mm oval nails and wood glue, driving the nails through the longer horizontals into the ends of the shorter pieces. You should check that all the corners are square.

In each of the vertical sides, drill 4.5mm countersunk clearance holes. Drill two 50mm from the top and two 50mm from the bottom. Drill two similar holes in each

9 *Cut the bottom board 200mm wider then the opening. Cut notches in the ends and test fit the sill into the opening*

11 *Align the frame in the hole using small wooden wedges. Check that the frame is square and level*

end of the two horizontal pieces.

Place the frame in the opening. Level it and make it flush with the wall by tapping small wooden wedges between the frame and the sides of the opening.

Mark through the clearance holes onto the wall beneath—use a long masonry nail—then remove the frame to drill the holes. Use a No. 8 masonry drill and plug the holes with wallplugs. Replace the frame, level it and screw it in place with 63mm No. 8 screws. Check that the frame is level and square as you tighten the screws.

Fitting the doors and finishing

Fit ready made doors—planed to fit exactly—or make your own from blockboard. All you need to do then is to fit two 50mm flush hinges, door knobs and magnetic catches.

Cut the blockboard to fit the opening, then saw it in half to make two doors—the slight gap will allow opening clearance.

Test fit the doors and mark both doors

10 *Mark both the doors and the frame for the position of the hinges.*

12 *Cut and fix the architrave for the sides of the opening first followed by the top. Mitre the corners*

13 *Punch the nail holes and fill them with wood filler before finishing*

and frame for the hinges. Mark points 75mm from top and bottom. Make sure that the doors open into the dining room.

Fit the inner leaves of the hinges to the doors first then to the frame. Fit doorknobs.

Add the magnetic catches to the top of the frame so that each door closes against one catch—hold the door closed and flush with the frame front to mark the catch position. Screw the catches to the frame then fix the striking plates to the doors.

MAKE A COFFEE TABLE

This coffee table has an appealing design that will fit into any house. It is a broad, low table and features spacious racks at each end which are handy for storing newspapers and magazines.

The table is straightforward to build from birch-faced plywood fixed to a softwood frame. The size shown can be made using a standard-sized 1,220mm × 1,220mm sheet of plywood, but there's nothing to stop you making it smaller or larger by scaling the dimensions accordingly.

Birch-faced plywood has an attractive mellow appearance, which you can enhance by sealing it with several coats of polyurethane varnish. However, if you prefer, you can take varnishing one stage further and produce a personalized effect known as decoupage. This involves sticking paper cutouts to the bare wood and overlaying successive coats of varnish.

A variation on decoupage is to paint original motifs on the table using paper stencils as templates. You can cut stencils to create an infinite variety of patterns.

Of course, there's no reason why you can't paint the entire table with gloss paint —or enamel if you want a 'lacquer' finish. Alternatively you can always use melamine-faced and edged chipboard for a ready-made easy-to-clean finish.

Planning considerations

Study the cutting list and diagram over the page to see how you can cut all of the facing panels and the table top from one 1,220mm × 1,220mm sheet. Each component in the diagram has been labelled for easy identification. Label the pieces as you cut them out, so there's no chance of confusing them.

Examine the plywood for defects when you buy and, if you're planning on finishing it with varnish, choose the best-looking side for the table top and leg panels.

The only joints you'll need to make are halving joints to connect the softwood legs to the side rails, and notches in the inner plywood panels to accommodate—and support—the rails.

How it fits together

The softwood sizes given are the 'nominal' dimensions before planing. The actual sizes, therefore, are smaller— probably as much as 5mm on each face. When you're marking out the legs and rails, and cutting the plywood panels to fit, it's imperative that you measure the actual timber for accuracy. Relying on the nominal measurement will result in a poorly-fitting unit.

Materials and tools

To make the frame for the coffee table shown, you'll need:
- Four 342mm lengths of 75mm × 25mm PAR softwood for the legs (**A**).
- Two 1,260mm lengths of 75mm × 25mm PAR softwood for the side rails (**B**).

You will also need a 1,220mm × 1,220mm sheet of 12mm thick birch-faced plywood from which to cut:
- One 1,220mm × 500mm panel for the table top (**C**).
- Two 500mm × 300mm panels for the inner leg cladding (**D**).
- Two 416mm × 70mm strips for the magazine rack bases (**E**).

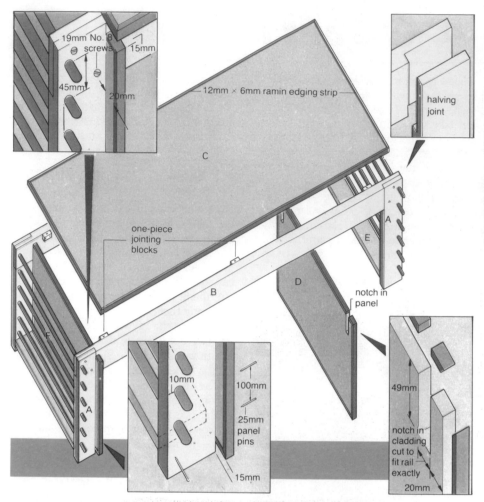

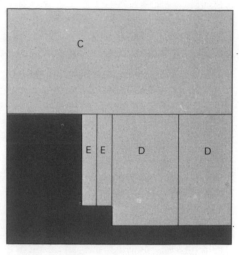

All the plywood components can be cut from a single 1,220mm × 1,220mm sheet. Birch-faced plywood is comparatively expensive but its superior finish is ideal for the table

The rungs (F) which form the outer sides of the two magazine racks are cut from 12.5mm dowelling. The rungs are 500mm long and, as dowelling is usually sold in 3m lengths, you will need to buy six poles.

In addition you'll want sufficient 12mm × 6mm ramin to edge all of the plywood panels—about 6m in total. You'll also require some PVA woodworking adhesive for assembling the halving joints, plus 12 19mm No. 8 countersunk woodscrews for securing them. The panels are fixed using PVA glue and 25mm panel pins. The easiest way of fastening the table top to the base frame is with one-piece plastic jointing blocks—you'll need six.

There are several ways you can modify the design to suit your own requirements. If you would like solid claddings at one or both ends of the table in preference to the rungs, you can cut them from plywood and pin and glue them to the outside edges of the legs. Unlike the inner panels, these would not be notched but they should be trimmed with ramin to match the rest of the table. If you buy a 1,220mm × 1,220mm sheet of plywood, you will have enough surplus timber left over after cutting out the other

components to make a solid cladding for at least one of the magazine racks.

You can make the table using standard woodworking tools. Equip yourself with a try square, marking knife, tape measure, marking gauge, hammer, screwdriver, tenon saw, coping saw, and an electric drill with 12.5mm, 4.5mm and 2mm wood bits. You'll also find a few G-cramps useful when cutting out the plywood panels. You can hire G-cramps quite cheaply if you don't own any.

Although it's quite acceptable to cut the plywood panels to size by hand using a sharp panel saw, you'll find this very tiring and time-consuming. You'd be wise to use a power jig saw (which you can hire) to save both time and energy.

Making the leg components

The table legs are joined to the side rails with halving joints. As these are visible at each end of the unit, it's important that you cut them neatly and squarely.

Mark out four 342mm long legs (A) from nominal 75mm × 25mm softwood

and square round the wood with a try square and marking knife. Don't forget to allow a few millimetres for the width of the saw cut.

Cut the legs to size using a tenon saw, keeping the blade on the waste side of the scribed line. Mark out and cut two horizontal rails (B) from a 3m length of the same timber; these should be 1,260mm long.

To mark out the halving joints, place one piece of timber on top of another, at right angles to it. Align its edge with the end of the lower piece. Use a sharp pencil to scribe the corner piece against the top piece and then continue the line down the sides against a try square. Repeat for one end of each leg and both ends of the two rails.

Set a marking gauge to half the thickness of the wood and scribe a line around the ends of the rails and the top ends of the legs.

You'll need a vice (or workbench with adjustable jaws) to hold the timber upright while you cut the halving joints. Set the first leg in the vice so that it slants away from you. Start to saw down the waste side of the scribed cutting line from the corner, using a tenon saw. Keep the saw horizontal until you reach the depth line, then slant the timber the opposite way and repeat the procedure.

Now set the timber vertically in the vice and saw down the remaining triangle to the depth line. Keep the saw horizontal.

Remove the timber from the vice and set it on a flat surface—preferably on a bench hook—waste side uppermost. Saw down to the depth line, on the waste side, to remove the square of wood. Repeat on the remaining legs and rails.

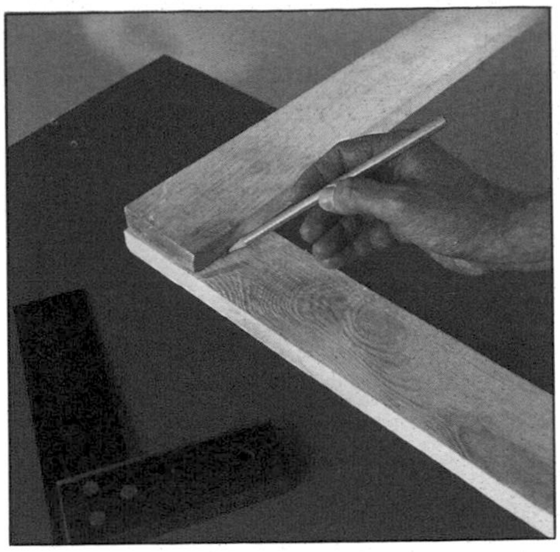

1 *Make the leg-to-side-rail halving joints by first laying one piece on top of the other, aligning them, and marking around*

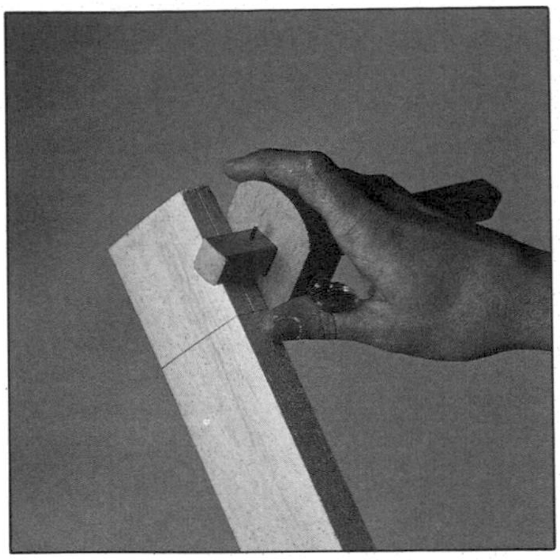

2 *Set your marking gauge to half the thickness of the timber and scribe a line around each of the marked joints*

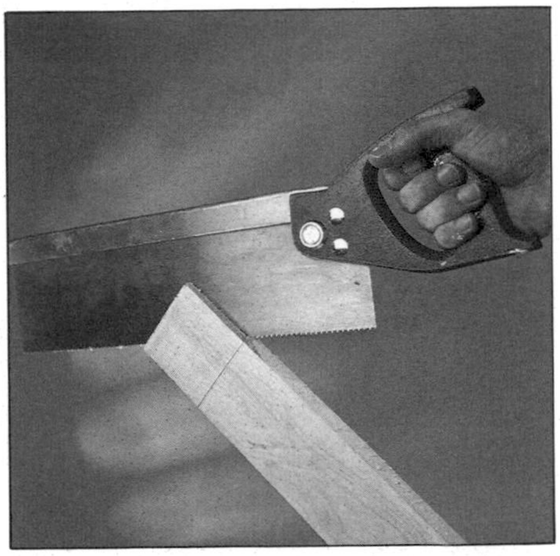

3 *Use a tenon saw to cut the joints. Cut from each corner in turn and then with the saw horizontal to the leg*

Making the table top and panels

The table top and side panels are cut from a standard 1,220mm × 1,220mm sheet of 12mm plywood. Although they'll eventually be trimmed with hardwood edging for neatness, it's vital that you cut the panels perfectly square, as irregularities will be impossible to conceal—even with edging strips.

Mark out the plywood sheet for all components (as shown in the cutting diagram on page 372) using a tape measure and long straight edge.

Support the plywood sheet on a firm, flat surface—ideally a workbench—and start to cut out each panel using a power jig saw.

Don't try to use the jig saw freehand—you're sure to wander from the cutting line. Some models incorporate a 'fence', which guides the blade along the straight and narrow; but if your machine doesn't have one, you can improvise. Measure from the saw blade to the side edge of the tool's metal sole plate. Mark this distance from your cutting line on the plywood and clamp a long, straight-edged batten to the workpiece so the edge is parallel with the line.

When you start to saw, you only have to concentrate on keeping the jig saw's sole plate against your home-made fence to ensure a true cut. Transfer the fence to the other cutting lines when you've made the first cut.

The inner leg panels (D) must be notched on their top edge to take the two horizontal leg rails. Measure 20mm in from each side of the panels, then the thickness of the legs—remember to measure the *actual* thickness; don't rely on the nominal dimension

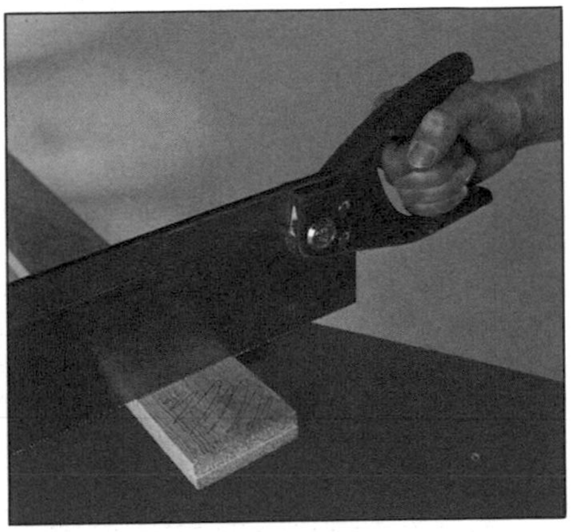

4 *Remove the timber from your vice and make the final cut. The square section of waste should simply fall away*

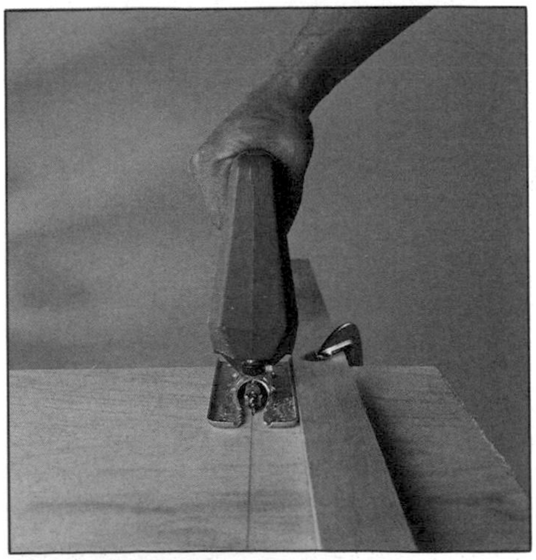

5 *To cut the table top and side panels accurately, use a jigsaw with a fence or improvise with a batten and G-cramps*

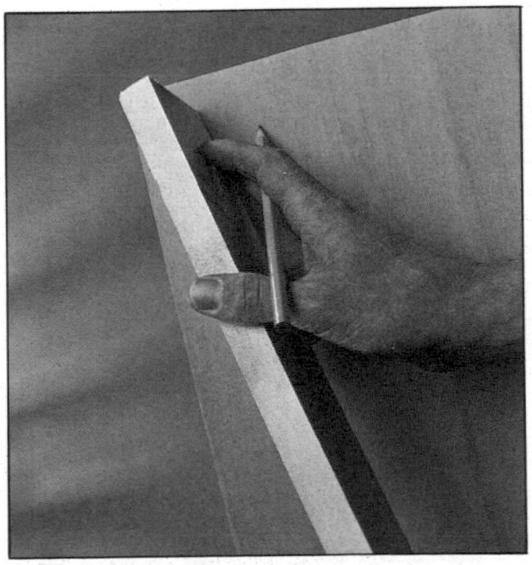

6 *To mark notches for the inner leg panels measure 20mm in from each side and add the thickness of the legs*

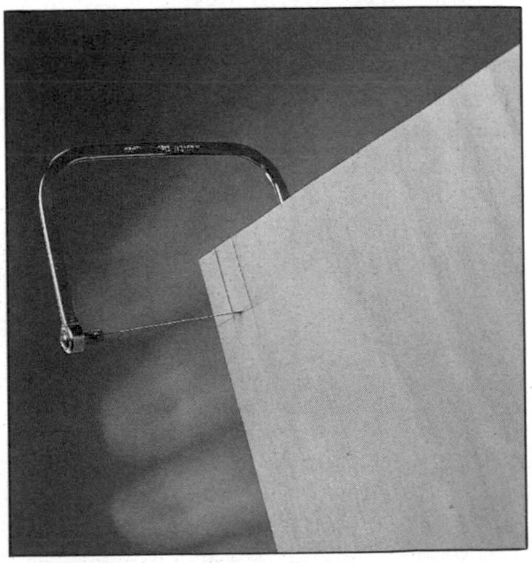

7 *Saw down the width lines of the notch and then cut across the bottom to take out the waste. Sand all the edges smooth*

8 *Cut the ramin edging to length and mitre the ends. Apply glue to it and the top and then pin the edging in place at 100mm intervals*

being accurate. Continue the notch lines over onto the opposite face of the panel.

Measure down 50mm from the top edge of the panels and square this line around to indicate the depth of the notches. Saw down the width lines to the depth line then set the panels one by one upright in the vice or workbench jaws and remove the waste using a coping saw.

Sand the edges of the notches and repeat for the second panel. When you sand down the edges, be careful not to round them off or the ramin trim won't fit. The best way to ensure square edges is to use a wood or cork sanding block with glasspaper wrapped around it; use a medium paper as a coarse one will scratch the wood.

The plywood top is edged all round with 12mm × 6mm ramin, mitred at the corners. Cut the ramin to length in a mitre box and apply PVA adhesive to the inner edge of one long strip and on the meeting edge of the table top. Position the strip then pin it to the ply at 100mm intervals. Make sure the

strip is flush with the face of the table top. Add the adjacent short strip in the same way, checking that the mitres are well-fitting. Continue to fix the beading in this way all round the table top.

★ WATCH POINT ★

To make it easier to fasten the ramin strips to the edge of the panel, tap in the panel pins so they just break through on the other side, then press the strips onto the edges of the ply and hammer the pins home to complete the fixing.

To keep the whole design uniform, the notched leg panels are trimmed with ramin in exactly the same way. This means that you will have to cut and fit small sections of the trim to fit either side of the rails—even though they are partially obscured by the top.

Once you've fitted the ramin strips, wipe off any excess adhesive that's squeezed out with a damp rag.

Assembling the table

The table is assembled using PVA woodworking adhesive and panel pins. First of all you have to complete the leg and rail assemblies, using glue and screws for strength.

Piece together the leg and rail assemblies on a flat surface to check the fit of the halving joints. If there are any slight discrepancies, correct them with glasspaper or by chiselling away small slivers of wood from the meeting faces of the lap joints.

Place a try square in the angle between the legs and rails, to make sure they're meeting precisely at right angles.

Draw a diagonal line from the outer

corner to the inner corner of each rail joint, and drill two 4.5mm clearance holes about 25mm in from the ends of the line.

Mark the leg through the clearance holes using a bradawl and then drill pilot holes.

Apply PVA adhesive to the meeting faces of the halving joint and re-assemble the leg and rail. Drive the fixing screws into the clearance holes to secure the joints.

Repeat the process for the other legs, then clamp or weight the joints and set the assemblies aside for the glue to dry.

★ WATCH POINT ★

To conceal the screw heads, fit plastic screw cups. Slot on the cup before you drive in the screw; then, when the screw has been driven home, fold over the integral cap and snap it shut.

When you have glued and screwed the legs to the rails, mark and drill the holes for the rungs (see Fitting the rungs) and saw the 12.5mm dowelling into 500mm lengths.

Fitting the rungs

The rungs at each end of the table are cut from 12.5mm dowelling and are equally spaced at 45mm centres down the sides of the legs.

The first step in marking the hole centres is to scribe marginal lines down the extreme edges of each leg component. Use your marking gauge set to 17mm for this operation. Starting from the top of each leg, mark off the centres—at 45mm intervals—against the marginal line.

Before you start drilling the series of holes in a leg, place a piece of scrap timber underneath it. Anchor both pieces to your workbench with a G-cramp so that there is no chance of them swivelling around with the drill as you work.

When you drill, keep the pressure on until the bit has gone right through the 75mm × 25mm timber and into the offcut underneath—this will ensure that both sides of the hole are 'clean' and not splintered.

Cut the dowelling into rods 500mm long with a tenon saw and round off the ends with glasspaper. Try slotting the rods through the holes—they should be a tight fit but, if necessary, you can pin them in place when you have constructed the rest of the table.

Scribe marginal lines down the legs and then mark off centres at 45mm intervals

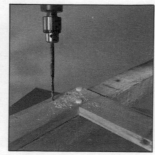

Place a stout offcut under the 75mm × 25mm timber before you start drilling

Cut the dowelling into 500mm rods and round off the ends with glasspaper

9 *Join the leg and side rails with glue and screws. Screw cups with integral caps are a neat way to conceal the heads*

Completing the assembly

Before you start assembling the rest of the table and fitting the various components together, try fitting the rungs into the two pairs of legs and check that they are perfectly horizontal and straight.

Turn the two leg assemblies upside down and slot on the two notched inner panels. Check that they fit squarely on the rails—there should be 15mm of leg protruding beyond the bottom edge of the panels and a 20mm margin at each side.

10 *Turn the leg and rail assembly upside down and fit each of the notched inner panels. Check for correct fit all round*

Apply a bead of adhesive to the meeting faces before fixing the panels with 25mm panel pins at 50mm intervals.

To fit the magazine rack base panels, turn the table on its side and slot in the ply rectangles—they should be a fairly tight fit. Adjust them so they're level with the bottom of the inner leg panel and then secure them by driving panel pins through the legs into their edges.

Lift the table on end and tap panel pins through the leg panel into the edges of the plywood bases. Repeat at the opposite end.

You can now fit the rungs to form the

two magazine racks. If they are not a tight fit, secure them at each end by knocking 25mm panel pins through the legs.

You can now attach the table top. It's fixed with proprietary one-piece jointing blocks screwed to the angle between it and the side rails. Lay the top upside down on a flat surface. Draw a 15mm border against a straight edge down each side, then invert the leg and rail assembly on top. Align the side rails with the border lines and the ends of the rails with the ends of the table top.

Arrange jointing blocks so that they are equally spaced along the inner faces of the side rails; screw them to the table top first, then to the rails. Work from the ends in towards the centre to prevent the leg assembly shifting on the top.

★ WATCH POINT ★

To stop the leg frame from moving as you fix the jointing blocks, it's a good idea to stick it temporarily to the table top using a strong PVC adhesive tape.

Turn the completed table onto its legs and give the entire unit a thorough sanding to remove sharp edges. Apply the finishing treatment of your choice; remember that you will need several coats of varnish or paint to get a really professional result.

11 *Fit the magazine rack base panels by slotting them in place and secure them with panel pins driven through the legs*

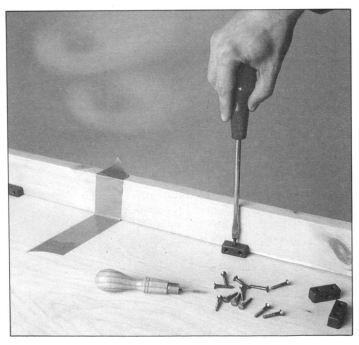

12 *Tape the leg and rail assembly to the table top and then use jointing blocks (work from the end in) to fix on to the other*

EASY-BUILD KITCHEN

When it comes to kitchens, most people would rather add new life to what they've got than go to the trouble of rebuilding the units and worktops from scratch. But with this ingenious system you can do both—at a budget price.

The kitchen on the right may look like an expensive designer's dream. But the system it's based on—using low-cost bricks, chipboard and wood—is actually cheaper to build than ready-made units looking half as good. It's easy to build too: there's no complicated jointing or special techniques to master. And it's versatile: once you've grasped the main constructional principles detailed overleaf you can build new units to fit around your existing appliances, plan a built-in hob or cooker unit, add new features like a breakfast bar, or replan the kitchen from scratch—the choice is yours.

How the system works

In planning the kitchen hard and fast rules are few, but there are some worth careful consideration before you start. One decisive factor is whether the floor is made from solid concrete or from wooden floorboards and joists. If it is solid, you can build the walls straight on to it.

If the floor is wooden—take up the floor covering to see—you may need to strengthen the floor to prevent it bending under the added weight. But if you don't want to go to this trouble, you can build the units to take wooden panels in place of the brick walls—veneered board edged with solid pine, melamine board or plain chipboard clad with imitation brick tiles are all possibilities. If you select one of these, weight should be no problem.

When planning the layout, bear in mind that the heart of the kitchen is the area between the refrigerator, sink and cooker—what is often referred to as the 'work triangle'. This should be small enough to minimize the need for movement, but with enough space to provide work surfaces for cooking and food preparation.

When you have decided on a general layout and what appliances and fittings—like a fridge, cupboard doors and wire baskets—to include, draw a detailed plan of where each item goes. Double-check positions and dimensions, making sure you take account of awkward shapes, like boxed-in service pipes or chimney breasts.

Once you have completed the plans, clear the relevant areas of the kitchen and mark each item's position on the wall and floor. You can then work to these marks.

First, mark the positions of the brick walls on the floor in chalk or pencil, then use a tape measure and spirit level to mark the height of the work surfaces all around the walls. If your floor is uneven, you will level it up automatically by working to the marks of the new work surfaces.

Before you begin building, remove the skirting board by prising it from the wall with a crowbar or claw hammer. Tap your lever between the two, then gently prise the skirting board from the wall at a number of points. Protect the wall surface by levering against a scrap of wood.

The unit walls

If your design includes them, build the brick walls first. Use ready-mixed mortar: a 40kg bag is enough for about 50 bricks.

Each course is made from three bricks. You must cut one of them to make the wall

1 *Build the new walls up to the marks you have made. When dry, paint them with emulsion*

2 *Work to a line drawn level with the top of the new brick walls*

match the width of the worktop. The design uses a worktop 610mm wide which complements the melamine-faced shelves and the dividing walls.

The front edges of the walls must at no point stand proud of the work surfaces, so make sure that the first course of bricks is correctly positioned.

As you build each wall, use a spirit level to ensure it stays upright. Keep a close check too on the finished height. The thickness of the mortar courses must be an even 10mm, so that for bricks with a nominal

thickness of 65mm the actual thickness of each course is 75mm. Twelve courses of brickwork takes the total height to 900mm—the ideal worktop height, and the right height to accept modern standard size under-counter appliances like fridges and dishwashers.

If you are using wooden end panels instead of brick, cut these 900mm long from 610mm wide material. Stand them vertically with the aid of a spirit level and screw them to the walls and floor using 50mm steel angle brackets on the inside face.

Constructing the frames

Both the top and bottom frames of the units are made from the same material—50mm × 25mm PAR (Planed All Round) softwood. Where possible they are simply butt jointed, but you will have to cut notches for dividers and overlaps.

Each frame is made from two long pieces at front and back (rails), joined by shorter crosspieces (struts). Saw the rails to length, having first marked them with a try square.

Referring to your plan, mark out on the rails every point where you will want a divider to fit on the finished unit. You must make a notch at each of these points. The dividers are 15mm thick, so cut notches to accept them in the bottom of both rails.

Use an offcut of the board to mark the sides of the notches and make them approximately 25mm deep. Saw down the sides of each notch, then use a 15mm wide (or less) chisel to cut out the waste. Any roughness in the cutting will be concealed later.

To make the joint, notch the bottom edge of one rail and the top edge of the other at the point where they need to cross. Make the notch as wide as the wood is thick—lay

one on top of the other, and mark either side where you need to cut.

Finally, use a No. 8 twist drill to make screw holes in the back rail so it can be fixed to the wall. For a masonry wall, drill holes at approximately 500mm intervals. On a timber framed wall, work out and mark off where the rail will coincide with the wall studs and drill holes for the screws.

To assemble the frames, cut a series of struts. You will need one for each end of the frame, as well as one to fit above each notch. To make sure the finished frame will be the same size as the worktop, lay the rails together on the worktop. Put them on edge, flush with one side of the worktop, then mark the remaining width on to a piece of your frame timber to get the length of strut.

Assemble the frame again in a 'dry run' to re-check that it is the same size as the worktop. Lay it on top of the worktop and make any adjustments that are necessary to make it fit, then glue it together.

Fit the struts between the rails, using woodworking adhesive and two 50mm oval nails to secure each joint. Fit a strut over every divider position.

Where the frame rests on one of the new brick walls, site the strut level with the bottom edge of the rail—rather than the top

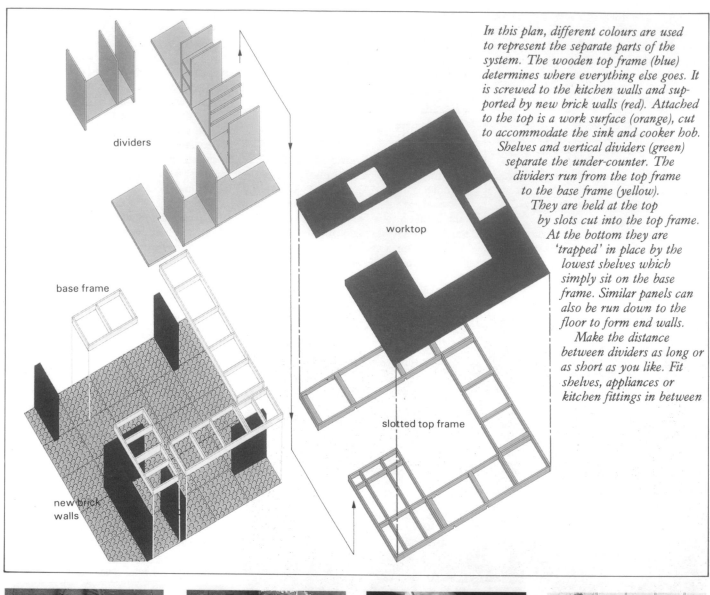

dividers

base frame

new brick walls

worktop

slotted top frame

In this plan, different colours are used to represent the separate parts of the system. The wooden top frame (blue) determines where everything else goes. It is screwed to the kitchen walls and supported by new brick walls (red). Attached to the top is a work surface (orange), cut to accommodate the sink and cooker hob. Shelves and vertical dividers (green) separate the under-counter. The dividers run from the top frame to the base frame (yellow). They are held at the top by slots cut into the top frame. At the bottom they are 'trapped' in place by the lowest shelves which simply sit on the base frame. Similar panels can also be run down to the floor to form end walls. Make the distance between dividers as long or as short as you like. Fit shelves, appliances or kitchen fittings in between

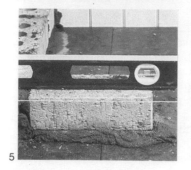

1 Use chalk to mark the floor. Scoop mortar into place, forming a V-shaped recess.   2 Scrape the mortar hard onto the end of the brick. Trim the edges to stop it falling off.   3 To cut a brick, first score marks on all sides. Then strike one side hard to cut.   4 Tap each brick down into the mortar. For long walls, use string to align the front edge.   5 Level across the top of each brick. Make the bubble lie exactly between the lines.   6 To finish the joints, use a rounded stick or 'point' with the edge of your trowel

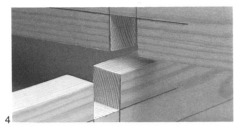

3 *Cut notches in the top frame where you want dividers. Any roughness will be concealed later by the fascia*

4 *Where rails overlap, make similar notches on top of one and on the bottom of the other rail*

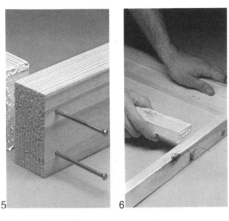

5 *Fix the struts to the rails with woodworking adhesive and nails*

6 *Add support struts to the ends and above each divider slot*

7 *Drill countersunk fixing holes in both the top and base frames. Mark the fixing positions*

8 *Insert wallplugs into the holes you have made and screw the top frame firmly in place*

9 *Screw through the edge of the base frame—use wallplugs for fixing to solid floors*

10 *Alternatively, fit steel angle brackets to the frame and the floor*

edge. You will then be able to drill through the strut, drill holes in the top of the wall, and screw the strut to the top of the wall.

Make the frames for the base, but bear in mind that they will be shorter than the top frames—they sit inside the brick walls rather than on top. Also, they do not require notching because the dividers simply sit on top of the frame.

If you have not built brick walls on both sides of free-standing appliances, like the refrigerator, you will have to let the divider on the other side run down to the floor. To do so, make the base frame shorter by 15mm than the notch above. This will allow you to fit a piece of the board as a 'wall' between the appliance and the unit.

When the frames are complete, prop or locate them in position and mark the places where you need to make fixing holes.

Remove the frames and drill holes to accept screws. For a solid wall or floor, use a No. 8 masonry drill to drill holes 25mm deep and then insert plastic wallplugs. Use 50mm No. 8 screws to secure the rails.

For a timber framed wall use a 2mm twist drill to bore pilot holes in the studs, then secure the rails with 50mm No. 8 screws.

In either case you will need to drill and plug the new brick walls so you can screw the ends of the frames to them. If, on the other hand, you are using wooden end panels you can screw the frames directly to them. Alternatively, it may be easier to use steel angle brackets to make the fixing.

Shelves and dividers

These are all made from melamine-faced chipboard (such as Handiboard or Contiboard) which is 15mm thick and comes in a variety of widths. If you use 610mm wide boards (the same as the worktops), there's less cutting to be done.

For the dividers, measure the height between the base frame and the top of the notches, then cut to these lengths.

If you need to make end walls to fit either side of a free-standing appliance, saw a divider so that it reaches from the notch to the floor. Slot in the divider, then drill and screw it to the base frame.

Cut the bases and shelves in the same way, after measuring the lengths needed between the divider notches.

With the dividers and shelves cut to length, drill holes in the dividers to accept the shelf supports. Use ordinary plastic shelf support plugs which simply tap into holes drilled in the dividers. Drill the holes with the recommended twist bit size and use a piece of tape as a depth gauge.

Slot the dividers into their notches in the top frame and slide them home. Drop the bottom shelves into position—you may need to screw end wall dividers into place.

Fit any fixed items into position as well. If you leave it until later, you may make more work for yourself. At this point, you can

★ WATCH POINT ★

To save time, cut a template from some old card or hardboard to fit your dividers. Measure the position at which you want to install shelves, then drill holes in the template as a marking guide. Note, though, that you cannot use this method if you want your shelves at random heights.

slide the dividers in and out with ease.

For the same reason, take care of any plumbing or wiring connections before the

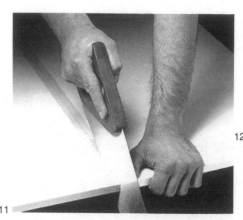

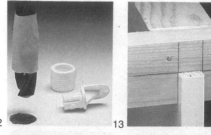

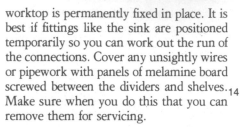

worktop is permanently fixed in place. It is best if fittings like the sink are positioned temporarily so you can work out the run of the connections. Cover any unsightly wires or pipework with panels of melamine board screwed between the dividers and shelves. Make sure when you do this that you can remove them for servicing.

Cutting melamine

For accurate marking, you need a try square, a ruler or other straight edge, a tape measure and a pencil. Use a panel saw or one of the power tools—a circular or a jig saw—for the actual cutting. Make sure your power saw is fitted with a blade suitable for cutting chipboard.

For hand sawing, measure and mark with care. Draw a line across one long side first, then down the two shorter edges, finally joining the marks together across the remaining long side of the board.

Choose a work surface that provides a comfortable and firm working height. A portable bench is ideal but a kitchen stool, raised door threshold, the top stair or one of the walls you have built will do. Any height

11 *Mark, tape over the line, then saw the melamine board for dividers*

12 *Drill holes for shelf plugs. Screw the sleeve into the hole, then tap the plug into the sleeve*

13 *Slot the dividers into the notches in the frame*

14 *Drop the bottom shelves onto the base frame to 'trap' the dividers*

★ WATCH POINT ★

Use a sheet of paper or card if you do not own a try square. Align one edge with the marked edge of the board, then carefully draw along the other without displacing it.

between your hip and your knee is generally comfortable—you can grip the board with knee and hand. You should be able to move your arm in a straight line from the shoulder so that you can use the full length of the handsaw or guide the power saw along the full length of the cut.

When hand sawing, periodically check below the board to see that the blade has not 'wandered'. If it has, twist the handle of the saw in towards the cutting line as you continue sawing. Use a planer file to remove the rough edge, always working inwards to stop further chipping, particularly when working on corners.

The worktops

The work surfaces are pre-finished square-edged kitchen worktops, 610mm wide.

Although these are not as commonly available as round-edged (post-formed) worktops, manufacturers will usually supply to special order. Many stockists will also cut large, standard size boards to the size you need.

Alternatively make your own worktop from a firm base of 19mm chipboard or blockboard. Get the supplier to cut it into 610mm widths, ready for use. Cover it with the decorative laminate of your choice, cut to size and glued with contact adhesive.

Mark out and cut the work surfaces to length to fit on to the top frame. Tape the cutting line and use a fine-toothed saw.

Whichever method you use, you may need to cut holes in the surface to accept a sink and—if you have one—a cooker hob. For both items, the cutting method is slightly different to that used for the shelves and dividers. The cutting line does not run from one side to the other. Instead, it begins and ends in the middle of the worktop. You

Mark off with a square. A combination square (above) is very useful—slide its blade out to use as a ruler or to extend the cutting line

Cover the marks with masking or adhesive tape to prevent the saw splitting the white surface. Tape around all four sides at once

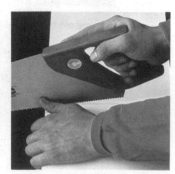

Draw the saw backwards at a low angle to begin the cut. Guide the blade with your thumb until a notch forms over the mark you have made

As you approach the end of the cut, support the offcut end of the board. Finish off with a few short, light strokes of the saw

15 *Use a drill, padsaw and panel saw to cut out holes for a sink or hob*

16 *Brackets and chipboard screws join the worktops to the frames*

will need to drill small holes in order to insert the saw and begin the saw cut.

Mark out the cutting lines in the normal way. Tape over the marks, then drill holes at the corners of your cutting line. At this stage, use a twist drill approximately 10mm in diameter.

Use these holes as a way to begin the saw cut. The ideal saw for this job is a power jig saw, fitted with a blade for cutting chipboard. Insert the blade into one of the holes, then cut along the taped cutting line to the next corner.

If you do not own a jig saw, make a series of holes at each corner. Join them as best you can with a padsaw, until you have a hole big enough to insert a panel saw. When this is possible, complete the cut. Any roughness around the edges of the hole does not matter—the sink, cooker or other appliance will conceal it.

If you need to shave any uneven edges, use a planer file. File in towards the centre of

the chipboard, first from one side then from the other, to avoid damaging the surface. Before you fit either the sink or the cooker, squeeze a flexible sealant around the edges of the hole.

To fasten the worktop, screw L-shaped brackets to its underside (use special chipboard screws here) and to the struts or rails. Begin the screw holes with a nail, small drill or bradawl—chipboard can be difficult to drive a screw into.

The final steps

With the top on, the basic skeleton will be complete and you can add the final touches.

If you are building a sink unit, cut to size and fix in place a narrow melamine board to hide the sink's waste trap and fittings. Drill and screw through the dividers and into the ends of the board to hold it in place, or use one of the many types of connector blocks.

The most prominent finishing touch is the stained wood fascia that covers the edge of the worktop and top frame. This should be at least 75mm wide—enough to cover both items and thus hold the dividers in their notches. You can use plain 75mm × 16mm softwood or one of the range of special mouldings—say, skirting or architrave—providing it is the right size.

Cut the wood longer than you need, allowing for an excess of about 50mm. Where the fascia will form an outside corner, cut mitres on the ends of the two adjoining sections so that you need not see the end grains of the wood. Do this with a mitre box or combination square. Simply butt the ends together at an internal corner.

Use any commercial wood stain to stain the fascia to the colour you wish before you fasten it to the edge of the worktop and frame. A wide range of colours is easily available at most DIY stores or department stores. Apply a number of coats, according to the manufacturer's instructions, then nail or screw the fascia to the edge of the kitchen units.

For the base, stain the wood of the frame rather than add a fascia. But make the colour darker as it is much more likely to get scuffed through wear and tear.

With the units complete, add doors if you want them. Use single-cranked hinges, which screw to the surface. Add magnetic catches and door pulls.

All that then remains is to seal the gap between the worktop and the wall with a clear sealant or a combination of this and decorative wood moulding. Fasten the moulding to the wall with wallplugs and screws. If necessary, use a wood filler to hide the screw heads before you apply a finish to the wood. Then fill any remaining gaps between the moulding and worktop with waterproof flexible sealant.

17 *Where the trim forms an external corner, cut mitres on each of the ends with the aid of a mitre box for accuracy*

18 *Squeeze a flexible sealant along the edge of the worktop before nailing the trim in place. Cover the heads with wood filler*

19 *For doors, use the same 15mm melamine board but with iron-on edging. Fit cranked hinges so you can open the door fully*

20 *Mask the work surface and walls to protect them. Then fill any holes with wood filler and sand down before finishing*

The shelves

Fixed to the wall above your work surfaces, shelves provide handy storage for decorative jars, containers and utensils. Easy to reach and easy to build, they make a bright and practical feature for any kitchen. And they also shed light on your cooking, because concealed lights illuminate the counter top.

The materials are all available in standard sizes—all you have to do is cut them to length. With templates to help with dimensions, there's little room for error here. And there's no complicated woodwork, like planing or difficult joints. The easy-fit components and bright wood stains of this system create a clean, modern look that fits in almost anywhere.

How the system fits together

Though it looks like one continuous unit, the shelving system is made in two distinct parts to make it adaptable and easy to install.

Wall-mounted frames are the rigid support for the whole system. These are made by screwing and gluing the sides (A) on to a top shelf (B) and bottom shelf (C). All the sides are notched to accept the light pelmet (D), then drilled for screw holes and shelf supports. The support batten (E) is glued and nailed to the underside of B.

White-faced hardboard is pinned to the back, then the whole frame is fixed to the wall through E. The continuous pelmet (D) is added later to conceal the light.

Loose-fit shelves (all the same length as B) are the other major part of the system. They are supported by push-fit shelf supports. Two fit inside each frame, the rest run from one fixed frame to another.

Every element of the fixed units—D, E and the hardboard backing—is carried over the loose shelves between them to give the unit its appearance of continuity.

If you want to alter the length of the unit to fit your space, adjust the length of the shelves and the support batten to a maximum of 700mm and a minimum of 400mm each. Divide the available space by the number of units you want, allow for the vertical sides, then estimate the common length of the shelves and the support batten.

Bright red-stained wood and wipe-clean white backing—shelves to suit any home. Hidden lights brighten the worktop too. Build the shelves separately, or as part of a complete kitchen re-design

What to buy

All the materials are inexpensive and readily available from timber dealers and DIY stores. Use standard planed-all-round (PAR) softwood sizes for all the woodwork.

With the exception of C, D and E, use 200mm × 25mm boards throughout. Buy eight 1.5m lengths for this design. You also need five 1.5m lengths of 175mm × 25mm board for C and 50mm × 25mm batten for E. D—the continuous pelmet—is made from 2.7m of 75mm × 25mm board.

For the backing material buy two full sheets (2440mm × 1220mm) of 4mm white-faced hardboard. To attach it to the frame you can use either 10mm panel pins or hardboard pins.

To join the fixed frames together, buy 50mm No. 6 countersunk screws and woodworking adhesive. Chipboard screws

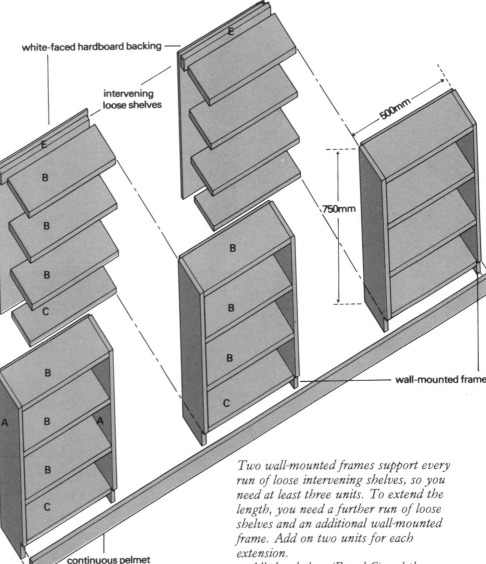

white-faced hardboard backing

intervening
loose shelves

500mm

750mm

wall-mounted frame

continuous pelmet

Two wall-mounted frames support every run of loose intervening shelves, so you need at least three units. To extend the length, you need a further run of loose shelves and an additional wall-mounted frame. Add on two units for each extension.

All the shelves (B and C) and the 50mm × 25mm support batten (E) are the same length, but the white-faced hardboard backing is longer to overlap the edges of the vertical pieces (A).

The sizes shown can be altered to suit your space

will hold better than conventional screws in the end grain of the boards. To nail D in place you need 50mm oval nails.

All you need to complete the units are the shelf supports. Use simple plastic push-fit supports here—the smaller, the better. To finish the surface, use any one of the wide range of wood stains and varnish obtainable from DIY shops. You'll also need a quantity of 63mm No. 8 screws and wallplugs for the wall fixings.

For the concealed lights, use two ordinary strip lights—those with a pull-cord switch are best. To wire them up, you'll need a plug, some lighting flex and a few cable clips to secure the flex.

Cutting the boards

Make a checklist of all the different parts you need. Mark each board after you have cut it to size.
•From a 200mm × 25mm board, cut one 500mm length for a shelf (B), and one 750mm length for a vertical side (A). Use a try square for accuracy, to ensure that the ends are completely square.

★ WATCH POINT ★

If you don't own a try square, use a sheet of card or paper. Align one edge with the side of the board, then mark along the remaining side.

•Use B as a template to cut 14 more shelves. Lay it on top of the uncut board, align the ends and sides, then mark across the top. Lay the shelves on top of each other to check that they are all the same size.
•Cut five 500mm lengths of the 175mm × 25mm board to make the bottom shelves (C) and five 500mm lengths of the 50mm × 25mm batten to make the supports (E).
•Take a small offcut from the 75mm × 25mm timber. Hold this against a corner of A. Mark around it to make

cutting lines for the notch to accept E.
•Cut out the notch with a panel saw. Then use A as a template to cut three more identical vertical sides.

Making the wall-mounted frames

This part of the job is simplified by using templates as described below.
•Make a hardboard template for drilling the holes. Lay A against a small offcut of hardboard, mark round it, then cut the offcut to size with a panel saw.
•Mark shelf positions on the template. For

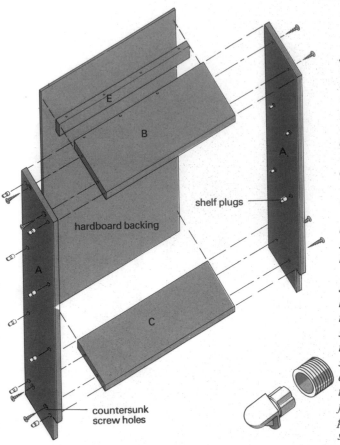

shelf plugs

hardboard backing

A

E

B

A

C

countersunk
screw holes

The wall-mounted frame (left).
Two sides (A) are screwed and
glued to the top (B) and the
narrower bottom shelf (C). E,
the support batten, is glued and
nailed (or screwed) to the
underside of B. The hardboard
backing fits behind—it is glued
and pinned to the frame, then
holes are drilled through those
already in E.

   Shelf support plugs fit inside
and outside the frame.

   The four sides (two of A,
one B and one C), must be
square before you fit the
hardboard backing

Shelf support plugs (bottom
left). There are many suitable
types, but choose the
smallest—they must be less
than half the depth of the wood
so that you can fit one on
either side. With this type the
threaded sleeve fits the hole
first, then the plug itself is
pushed into the sleeve as the
support.

ends, then screw the frame together. Check
that the diagonal dimensions are the same
to ensure that the frame is square.
• Apply woodworking adhesive to one side
and the ends of E. Fit it onto the back of the
frame, on the underside of B. Secure it with
50mm oval nails or No. 8 screws, driven
through the sides of the frame. Make the
other frames in the same way.
• When dry, lay a frame on top of the white-
faced hardboard and mark round it for
cutting. Using a panel saw, cut the sheet
about 25mm narrower than the marked
lines so that it does not overlap the sides of
the frame. Cut four similar sections to fit
behind the loose shelves and the two other
frames.
• If you are putting the shelves up on a solid
masonry wall, drill from the back and

the top and bottom shelves, mark the
positions for two fixing screws 10mm from
the end of the template and 50mm in from
the sides. Site the intermediate shelves
wherever you like. Draw their positions on
the template, then mark the positions of the
shelf supports 50mm in from each side of
the template. They are generally sited immediately below the shelf, but examine the
type you are using. Pierce the hardboard at
all the hole positions.
• Align the template with each side of A in
turn. Mark the wood beneath for reference
with a coloured pen.
• Drill 4.0mm countersunk clearance holes
for the screws. Then drill holes of the

correct size and depth for the supports.
Manufacturers generally specify the size of
the hole to make, but otherwise hold a drill
bit against one to see. It should be fractionally smaller in diameter than the shelf
support plug that you are going to fit.
• To ensure that the hole is the correct
depth, set the depth stop on the drill, or
mark the bit with tape. Screw in the sleeve,
then push in the support.
• Lay two sides (A), a top shelf (B) and a
bottom shelf (C) on edge—and in
position—on a flat surface. Mark through
the clearance holes onto the ends of the
shelves. Drill 2.0mm pilot holes at these
points, apply woodworking adhesive to the

countersink at the front two 4.5mm holes
on the centre line of the support batten.
Make holes 100mm from each end.
• If fixing to a hollow wall, make fixing holes
where the screws will go straight into the
timber framing of the wall. Timber studs
are generally at 400mm or 450mm intervals. Tap the wall, or drill small exploratory
holes where they will later be concealed by
the units, to find them. Mark their positions
and then hold the frames against the wall in
the positions you want the units. Mark
screw holes on each batten to coincide with
the positions of the studs, then drill them
from the back.
• Finish the frames before attaching the

1 *Use an offcut of the
pelmet (D) to mark and
cut notches in the sides*

2 *Make a template to fit A.
Drill and mark holes for
both screws and shelf supports*

3 *Use tape to mark the
depth you need to drill for
the sleeves of the shelf plugs*

4 *Cut the hardboard to fit
the frame. Tape over the
mark to prevent splintering*

backing boards. Rub down the wood lightly with fine glasspaper and a sanding block, to smooth it and remove any marks. Then paint it, or colour it with wood stain and apply at least two coats of varnish to seal it. Do the same to the remaining support batten and the loose shelves.

• Apply glue to the back edges of the frames and put the backing boards in place so that there is approximately a 12mm gap down each side. Fasten the boards securely with 10mm panel pins. Mark through the holes in the support battens with a bradawl, then drill through the backing boards.

• Apply glue to the remaining battens and position one on each of the remaining backing boards, the thickness of a shelf down from the top and with an equal gap at each end. Drill through E into the hardboard.

Fitting to the wall

Attach the frames and the intervening loose shelves to the walls through the holes in E.

Position one frame at a time. Place it against the wall, propped by stools or pieces of wood on the work surface. Using a spirit level, adjust the props until the unit is perfectly horizontal, then mark the fixing positions through the holes you have made in the support batten (E).

For solid walls, use a No. 8 masonry bit to drill the holes, then insert wallplugs. If the wall is particularly hard, a drill with a hammer action may be more effective.

For hollow walls, drill 2.0mm pilot holes into the wall studs and screw into these direct. Use at leat 63mm No. 8 screws and screw into all the studs you can find.

Attach the intervening backing board to the wall by screwing through E in the same manner, but slide the edge of the hardboard underneath the wall-mounted frame. If necessary, loosen the frame's screws to open a gap. Adjust the backing board's position until it is perfectly horizontal and tight against the frame, then tighten all the screws (see fig. 2, below). Attach the final unit in the same manner, then drop the loose shelves into place on top of their shelf support plugs.

Fitting the lights

Connect the wires of a lighting flex to the corresponding terminals inside the light. Attach a fused plug to the other end of the flex and connect it to the nearest socket to test that it functions properly. Remember to unplug before you start fitting the light.

Position the light under any one of the bottom shelves. The loose shelves are best. Just remove one to attach the light, then replace light and shelf together. Alternatively, wire cne light to another and fit one under one loose shelf and one under another to shed light along the full length of the worktop.

Secure the flex to the shelf with cable clips, available from any DIY shop or electrical store. Make sure you get the right size of clip to match your flex.

Trail the flex along the unit, and then in a straight line down the wall to the power outlet. If your light does not have its own built-in switch, you can add an in-line switch to the flex to make it more convenient for switching on and off.

Cut and nail the pelmet in place into the notches on the sides (A). Use a nail punch

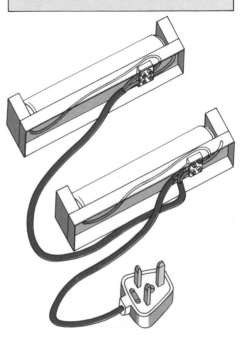

Wire two lights together to spread the light along the length of the worktop. Connect the wires of one length of flex to their terminals inside the light. Twist the wires at the other end to the corresponding ones in a second length of flex, then connect both to the terminals of the other light. Make sure all the connections are secure

to drive the heads below the surface (if you don't own one, use a large nail). Cover the small spots in the wood with wood filler, then stain and finish to match the units.

5 *Level the first frame, mark fixing positions, then attach with screws*

6 *Add the loose backing and batten. Tuck the backing under the last frame*

7 *Drop the loose shelves on to their shelf plugs inside and outside the fixed frames*

8 *Nail the pelmet to the notches in A and then punch the heads home*

DESK AND FOLDER HOLDER

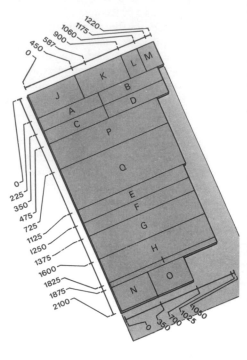

The cutting plan. Mark out a full sheet of plywood as shown, then identify each piece with a letter. Join them up like a kit

Adjustable track systems don't just mean boring office shelves. The supports are immensely strong and infinitely adaptable: add to this a good idea, plus strong lightweight materials in bright colours, and you have attractive yet functional furniture that is really simple to build.

This project uses just one pair of tracks and four brackets to make a compact bureau unit that you can use as a home office, study or hobby centre.

The two units—the desk and the folder holder—are simple box constructions made from plywood panels screwed and glued together. The woodwork is not particularly complicated, and any small mistakes will be concealed by the bright paint finish.

Buying the materials

There are dozens of different track shelving systems and it doesn't really matter which type you use as long as it is strong enough for the purpose. Manufacturers generally give estimates of loadbearing capacity, and you can check this if in doubt. A typical figure for the longest brackets (the longer they are, the less they can safely carry) is at least 100kg—well over the weight of the average adult.

You need two 1,220mm uprights. If you have to buy longer strips, cut them to size with a hacksaw. If the offcuts are a substantial length, keep them for another project. You also need two 550mm brackets for the desk, and two 200mm brackets for the folder holder—or the nearest shorter equivalents.

To fit the uprights to the wall calls for at least a dozen screws. They should be at least 63mm long, and the largest gauge that will fit the holes. If fixing to a masonry wall, buy plastic or fibre wallplugs to suit the screws.

The basic material for the two units is plywood. You will need one full standard sheet—2,440mm × 1,220mm (8ft × 4ft)—of both 15mm and 6mm ply—buy the cheapest as it will be painted over.

To assemble the units you need 38mm No. 8 countersunk screws, 15mm panel pins and some PVA woodworking adhesive, plus a one metre length of piano hinge and suitable screws. To finish them, you need a little filler, primer, undercoat and gloss or enamel paint.

For the pinboard you need a piece of softboard at least 1,100mm × 500mm, 3.5m of 19mm × 6mm ramin and some felt.

1 *Level the first upright using a spirit level and mark the hole positions onto the wall beneath*

2 *Use a marked batten to align the second upright with the top of the first one*

Fitting the brackets

Adjustable shelving systems suitable for this project all work in much the same way. The slotted uprights are screwed to the wall through the countersunk holes in the channels. The brackets then clip conveniently to the holes in the channel at the exact height you want.

The system is simple and effective. But you must ensure that the upright channels are absolutely vertical, at the same height, and parallel to one another. If they are not, the finished unit will not be level, and may not be fixed securely.

First decide exactly where you are going to put the uprights. This depends partly on where you want the unit, and partly on the construction of your wall.

If you are fixing to a masonry wall, you can put the screws wherever you want providing you drill holes and insert suitable wallplugs. On a timber framed wall you are more limited. In most other circumstances, you could fix to a hollow wall wherever you wanted with cavity wall fixings. But with a heavy fitting like this unit, you should screw it directly to the vertical timber supports behind the wall panelling. These are called studs.

Find the studs by tapping the wall, or drill small exploratory holes. They are generally spaced at either 400mm or 450mm centres, so once you have found one you can work out where the others are.

The ideal distance between the shelving uprights is 760mm, but on a stud wall you will have to adjust this to either 800mm or 900mm depending on the location of the studs. This is easy to arrange with a small alteration to the dividers in the desk unit and folder holder.

When you have decided where to fit the uprights, measure 1.75m from the floor

and mark this as the topmost point of the first upright channel.

Put the first upright up to your mark, using a spirit level to ensure that it is vertical. The countersunk fixing holes are generally spaced at 100mm intervals. If this is the case, fix through alternate holes. Mark the positions onto the wall, then drill and fix, using suitably sized wallplugs on a masonry wall.

You must make sure the second upright is exactly level with the first, as well as the correct distance away. To do so, take a long ruler or a straight piece of wood. Mark on it the required distance between the uprights —either 760mm or the distance between the timber wall studs.

Place it on top of the fixed upright, with one of its marks immediately over the centre. Check the horizontal alignment with a spirit level and mark the position of the second upright. Set the upright vertically in line with the mark and check the spacing at the bottom as well. Mark and drill the screw holes and fix the second upright in place.

3 *Mark out the sheet of plywood with a soft pencil then score through the top ply with a sharp utility knife*

Cutting the plywood

Make all the main parts for the desk unit and the folder holder from one standard 2,440mm × 1,220mm sheet of 15mm plywood. Some suppliers will cut the sheet for a small fee if you give them a cutting plan. Otherwise cut it yourself with a hand saw or a power saw, although it may be hard work by hand. The diagram on page 386 shows how to mark out the sheet in the most economical way. Use a soft pencil and a metal rule to transfer the measurements onto the plywood. Identify each part with its key letter.

With the sheet marked out, clear a space for cutting. You need quite a large area, so it may be best to work outside. You will also need form and stable surfaces to support the sheet as you cut it. Long sturdy battens that rest on chairs or workbenches are best— they will support both sides of the cutting line at once.

Try to saw as accurately as possible, cutting directly through the marked lines of your plan. Any minor roughness can be filled and smoothed down prior to painting.

You can fix the pieces together directly afer sawing, but you will get a better fit and a smoother finish if you plane the edges first (see Planing the plywood edges).

Planing the plywood edges

A bench plane as shown is best, but you can use any type. Make sure it is sharp and properly adjusted. Many DIY shops will sharpen and set planes.

Fix the plywood firmly. It's best if you have a workbench with a vice, but if not, clamp it to a sturdy table. Set the boards together side by side, so that you can plane several at once and keep them level.

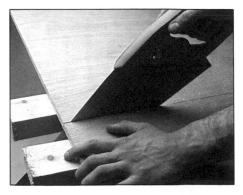

4 *Support long cuts over two sturdy battens placed either side of the cutting line*

Plane with long, firm strokes at an angle. Finish off with finer, parallel cuts

One way to plane a number of boards at once. It ensures they end up the same size

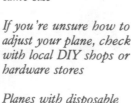

If you're unsure how to adjust your plane, check with local DIY shops or hardware stores

Planes with disposable blades are easier—fully adjustable, and no difficult sharpening

To remove material quickly, set the blade to project about 1mm using the adjusting knob. If you find that the blade judders and digs in, reduce the projection a little or try planing in the opposite direction. As you near the final line withdraw the blade for a finer finishing cut.

Reduce splintering by planing at an angle across the boards. Work in from each side alternately, then finish with a fine cut along the line of the boards.

Making the desk unit

The desk unit is based on a plywood frame made by screwing sections E and F onto the shorter sections A, B, C and D. The inside

dividers (B and C) are positioned immediately above the brackets of the shelving system.

The bottom of the desk is made from 6mm plywood, set back from the edge of the frame and nailed in with 15mm panel pins.

The top is made from two sections, P and Q. P is screwed to the back of the frame. Q becomes the lift-up desk top. The two are joined together with a piano hinge. They overlap the front and sides of the desk by about 30mm.

Assemble all the sections of 15mm plywood that make the desk unit (A to F, and P and Q). Ensure that all the sections of the frame are the same width, and that the

dividers (A, B, C and D) are all exactly the same length—hold them against each other to check.

Drill 4.5mm clearance holes for 38mm No. 8 screws in the ends of sections E and F and at the points where you want the two inside dividers. Use a 4.5mm diameter twist drill to make these holes and a countersink to take the screw heads below the surface.

Transfer the hole positions to the ends of the dividers, then use a 2mm twist bit to make pilot holes to prevent the plywood from splitting when you tighten the screws to make the corner joint.

★ WATCH POINT ★

As you drill the clearance holes, stand a try square on the end next to the drill. The blade will guide you to keep the drill upright.

Apply some woodworking adhesive to the ends of the dividers, then screw the frame together and check that it is square.

Make the base from 6mm plywood. Lay the desk frame on top of the sheet so that two sides are flush with the edges of the plywood. Mark along the two remaining sides. Mark and cut approximately 6mm inside these two marks so that, when you nail the base to the frame, the plywood is set back from the edge.

Apply woodworking adhesive to the edges of the frame, then use 15mm panel pins to nail the base to it. Chamfer, or taper, the edges to further conceal the base.

Screw and glue the fixed back section (P) in place. Use the recommended size of screw to attach a piano hinge first to the desk top itself, then to P.

5 *Fit E and F onto A, B, C and D. Add the thin ply base, then P, then the hinged top*

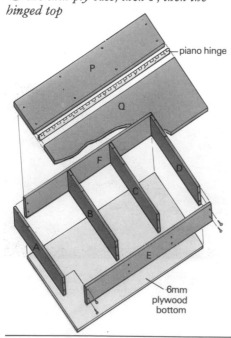

piano hinge

P

Q

F

D

C

B

A

E

6mm plywood bottom

6 *Drill and countersink 4.5mm clearance holes and 2.0mm pilot holes for 38mm No. 8 screws*

7 *Glue the ends and screw together*

8 *Use 15mm panel pins to fix the ply base. Taper the edges*

Making the folder holder

The folder holder is made by screwing J and K onto G and H. I forms the pelmet for the light and is screwed and glued to H.

Dividers and pigeonholes (L, M, N and O) are added to it after the outer frame is complete. The back is made from 6mm plywood, cut to fit the frame.

Assemble all the pieces. Drill countersunk clearance holes for three 38mm No. 8 screws along one edge of H, apply woodworking adhesive to the edge of I, then screw H to I. Drill similar holes through J and K so that you can screw them to the ends of G and H.

★ WATCH POINT ★

To ensure that the holes match at either end, lay J and K on top of each other. Clamp them firmly, mark the top one only, then drill through both at the same time.

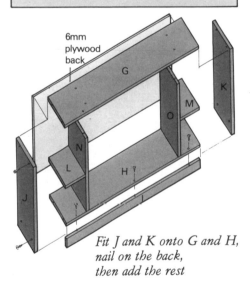

6mm
plywood
back

*Fit J and K onto G and H,
nail on the back,
then add the rest*

Transfer the hole positions to the ends of G and H, then drill 2mm pilot holes to accept the screws. Apply woodworking adhesive and screw the frame together.

With the outer frame complete, attach the two dividers and pigeonholes. Position the dividers above the shelf brackets. Adjust the size of the pigeonholes and fix them using glue and nails or screws.

All that remains is to attach the 6mm plywood back and the pelmet light. For the back, check that the diagonal dimensions of the unit are equal then repeat the procedure used for fixing the plywood base to the desk.

For the concealed strip light, start by

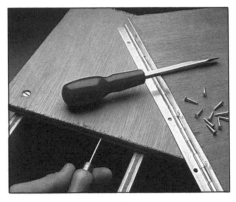

9 *Fit the fixed top (P) with countersunk screws and woodworking adhesive. Cut the piano hinge with a hacksaw, then screw it to the edge of the desk top Q.*

10 *Apply fine-surface filler to rough edges, screw holes and the exposed edges of the plywood. When it is dry, smooth it down with sandpaper*

stripping the insulation on the flex core wires, then attach the wires to the appropriate terminals inside the strip light—these are usually simple plastic connector blocks. Position the body of the light in the centre of the base section just behind the pelmet. Screw the two fixing screws firmly down to hold the light tight against the plywood.

Attach a plug and check that the light works properly. Then unscrew it and paint the unit before replacing the lamp and fixing the unit to the brackets.

Wiring the strip light

Wiring the strip light is just a matter of connecting the wires of a new lighting flex to corresponding terminals inside the light itself. As long as you connect each wire properly—and the plug last—you cannot possibly get a shock.

Ask for a suitable flex when you buy the light. Most require only a two-core lighting flex. This has a Live wire (brown) and a Neutral wire (blue), commonly covered in a flexible protective sheathing. Some flex is

unsheathed—both wires are white but the Live has a ridge or coloured line on one side.

Some lights need a three-core flex which has an Earth wire as well. This is colour-coded green and yellow. Connect the Earth wire to the terminal marked ▨ —there is one in the light and one in the plug.

Start by removing the outer sheathing of the flex. Take great care not to nick the coloured wires beneath. If you do—examine them carefully—start again from scratch.

Underneath the sheathing are the three colour-coded wires. You must strip the coloured insulation from the wires then connect them to a plastic connector block inside the light.

The connector block is divided into three units, each with two screws. One screw holds the wire from the light, the other is intended to hold the corresponding wire from the flex. These are the terminals.

Terminals are marked L for Live (brown), N for Neutral (blue) and ▨ for Earth (green/yellow).

To connect the wires to the terminals you will need a pair of wire strippers and a small screwdriver.

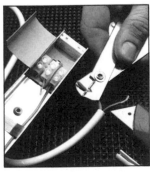

Use the 'V' of the strippers to trim 10mm of insulation

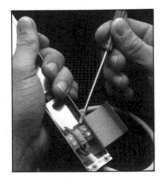

Twist the cores together, then join each to its terminal

For pillar terminals, shape the wire to fit them

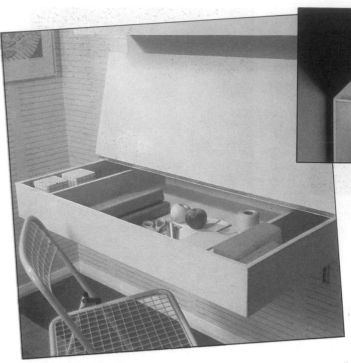

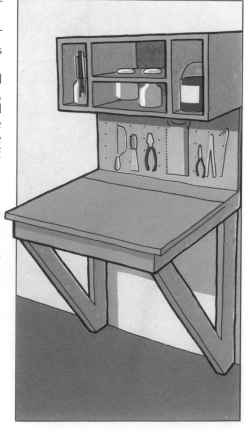

Finish is all-important, so take pains to get it right. Paint the underside of the folder holder white so that it reflects more light onto the desk top. Drill pilot holes for the brackets in the units, fit the brackets, then screw the units in position

The finished desk in use

Finishing off

Fill all holes, rough edges and gaps in the plywood units with fine-surface interior filler. You may need to fill larger gaps with successive layers of filler.

Rub down the wood and filler with fine glasspaper wrapped around a sanding block. Be particularly careful at the edges—make sure that you keep the block at right angles to the surface to maintain the sharp definition.'

Brush off any powdered filler and sawdust. Give the units a coat of primer and allow to dry, then apply an undercoat. Make sure that both the primer and undercoat are compatible with the paint you choose. Rub the undercoat down lightly with fine glasspaper and wipe over with a damp cloth to remove all traces of paint dust.

Apply at least two coats of finishing paint and allow to dry thoroughly before attaching to the shelf brackets. Use 550mm brackets for the desk unit and 200mm brackets for the folder holder. Set them on the uprights so the top of the desk is about 850mm from the floor, with the folder holder about 500mm above it.

Mark and drill holes in the units for the brackets screws. If it is difficult to drive the screws home, put a heavy weight on top of the units to hold them down as you apply pressure.

To fix the pinboard between the two units first screw a batten to the wall below the top unit and between the uprights. Then glue the plywood back to the batten.

Connect the light flex to the nearest power point and check that the light operates properly. Clip the flex up out of the way or run it down inside one of the uprights to conceal it from view.

Alternative ideas

The basic design is so adaptable that it is impossible to give all the variations.

You need not, for example, paint it: wood stains and varnishes will produce different, but just as attractive, effects. Bear in mind though that for either finish you must use high quality birch-faced plywood and mitre the corners to conceal the layers of laminate. The edges will need to be trimmed with a thin edging beading or with suitable iron-on edging trim.

When using varnish or stain, cut all the plywood panels *along* the grain. In this way, the surface will look more like solid wood.

Apart from the finish, you could also change the material you use. Specially faced plywood or blockboard—though much more expensive—can be made to look sleek and professional with a few coats of varnish.

The basic design, strengthened by support legs, can be used in a garage or workroom. Perforated softboard and decorative hardboard are ideal surfaces for hanging tools within easy reach of the work surface

And in a child's room, melamine-faced boards may solve the problem of keeping the unit clean and hygenic. These can be bought in a white or wood grain finish.

Covered desk tops are not difficult, and they can be matched to the felt used for the pinboard—try vinyl-leather, edged with a hardwood trim, or else use an entirely different material for the desk top itself.

The pinboard, too, holds many possibilities. You could consider cork tiles, covered in the material of your choice, as an alternative to softboard. And you could even dispense with the board altogether, fitting a mirror or mirror tiles in its place. Self-adhesive mirror tiles can be glued directly to the wall.

When considering alternative design ideas, bear in mind the extra cost and weight involved. If you are in any doubt about the additional weight, install an extra upright between the two used for this design.

Some alternatives, though simple in idea, need quite extensive changes in construction. For example, to stain the unit instead of painting it means that you must mitre the joints and add dowels to strengthen them too. Unless you have already made mitre joints, don't consider this method. And bear in mind that your cutting will need to be far more accurate and tidy.

WALL OVEN AND HOB UNIT

Installing a hob and wall oven is a job that many people leave to the manufacturer's franchised engineers. Yet even when gas is involved most of the work still comes down to basic carpentry which is well within the capabilities of the average do-it-yourselfer. What this means in practice is that if you plan and build the units and install the hardware ready for connection, you can save a lot of money. In the UK, wiring up all-electric units yourself is legal.

Planning considerations

Before you even look at a manufacturer's brochure, you must work out where your wall oven and hob can go. Don't be too restricted by the position of your present cooker: connections are easily extended or re-routed, though in the case of gas appliances the work must be left to a qualified fitter. These are the points to consider:
• Try to keep the classic kitchen 'work triangle' of sink/cooker and worktop/fridge. A round trip between the three areas should measure no more than 7m.
• The oven and hob should be no more than

2m apart. If they're reasonably close, the connections will be simpler and less disruptive to make. But bear in mind that you need worktop space for both—including heat resistant surfaces on which to lay hot pans and trays.
• Many kitchen unit manufacturers include units for wall ovens and hobs in their ranges. These are a boon if you're doing a large-scale kitchen overhaul, but they don't fit all models and may restrict your choice. If you're fitting the oven and hob into an existing layout, it's almost always easier—and cheaper—to adapt or build on to what you've already got.
• Give priority to the hob's position rather than the oven's—you'll use the hob more. If your existing worktops are neither spacious enough or strong enough to take such an appliance, consider replacing the run with a ready made post-formed worktop at the same time.

What you can do yourself

How much of the installation work you can do yourself depends very much on whether

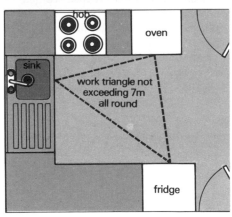

The ideal kitchen layout keeps the distances between the oven/hob, fridge and sink as short as possible. If you have two doors into your kitchen, arrange the layout so that the walkway in between doesn't cut across your 'work triangle'

the appliances are gas, electric, or a combination of both. In all cases you can cut the hole for the hob and construct an eye level cabinet for the oven. Where gas or part-gas appliances are concerned, you then fit the hob and the oven cabinet making sure that there is enough access for the gas fitter to run in and connect supply pipes.

Buying considerations

Choosing a hob and wall oven is largely a matter of studying brochures and picking out the models whose features most appeal to you. Even so, some types require more involved installation procedures than others and it's as well to be aware of these before you make a final choice.

• If you don't have an existing gas supply, running one in could be more trouble than it's worth. You may, for example, have to take out several kitchen units to give the fitter access. If you do have gas, you may need to run in an electricity supply as well. This must come direct from the fuse board or consumer unit, and may again prove to be a disruptive procedure.

• Where electrical appliances are concerned, current rating is the critical factor. Most hobs and single wall ovens are jointly rated at 30 amps, which means that you can use an existing 30 amp cooker circuit for the connections. On the other hand, if you opt for a double oven, you may find that the makers rate this and the hob at 45 amps. If your existing cooker circuit is the 45 amp sort, there's no problem. But if it's only 30 amp—even if the cooker point itself is rated at 45 amps—you have two choices: either you connect the hob to this and run a separate 30 amp circuit for the oven; or you replace the existing 30 amp circuit with a 45 amp one, using larger cable. Unfortunately, both options land you with more work than simply connecting to an existing power point.

Order of work

When the appliances arrive, sit down and work out a strict order of events to minimize the amount of time your cooking facilities are out of action. If you need the services of a fitter, plan for this in the same way so that he's with you for the shortest possible time. In the 'run-up' to installation you can take the following steps:

• Pre-build the oven cabinet in another room. Test-fit both the oven and the cabinet; make any adjustments at this stage so that on installation day you can simply disconnect the old cooker, fit the cabinet to the wall, then connect to the electricity and slide in the new appliance.

• Where appropriate, arrange the new electrical connections. If you are fitting a

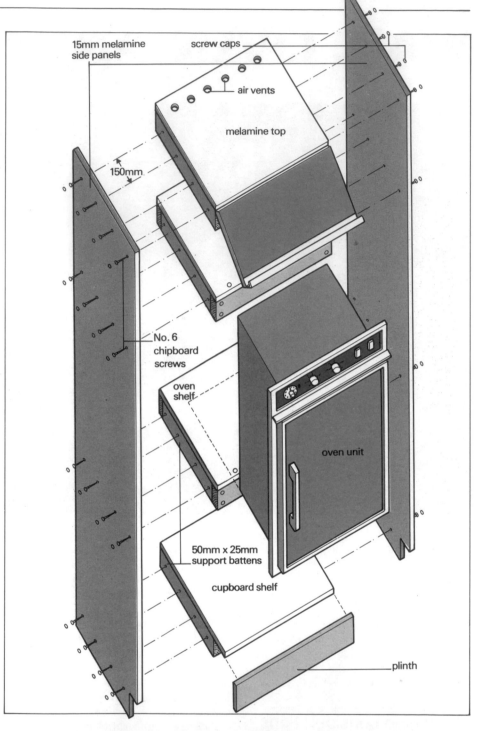

How the cabinet is made: the tops of the side panels are designed to line up with the tops of existing wall cupboards; you could extend them to the ceiling but this would involve scribing a fascia.

The feet of the side panels are cut away at the front to align with your existing unit plinths. When you measure the cut-outs, don't forget to allow for the thickness of the hardboard or thin plywood strip that will run between them.

The oven compartment is formed by two melamine shelves resting on a framework of battens screwed to the side

panels. The shelves don't extend all the way back: there is a slight gap to allow air to circulate freely.

The top panel is drilled along the back edge with at least six 30mm holes which act as vents for the fumes from the oven.

The whole construction is held in place with at least eight metal angle brackets screwed to the side panels and wall. The best and least obtrusive position for the brackets is underneath each of the shelves.

During installation, the cabinet is temporarily braced by off-cuts of batten nailed across the top and bottom corners

new cooker point in place of an existing one, wire your cooker up to this so that you can keep it running until installation day.

• Cut the recess for the hob.

• Choose an 'installation day' on which you can fit both appliances, get gas supplies run in and make any final electrical connections that are necessary.

Oven cabinet

The oven cabinet design featured here is simplicity itself—a box construction in melamine faced chipboard strengthened with 50mm × 25mm softwood battens.

Plan out the size of the cabinet once you know the dimensions of the oven and have fixed on a location. Make a sketch plan, noting the main dimensions, and take this

determined by the oven, the fascia of which must obscure the softwood framing completely and just lip over the edges of the chipboard (see diagram, left).

• **Oven compartment height:** Obviously the oven should be at a comfortable working height, but it's also a good idea to align it visually with something else in the room— the foot of a wall cupboard, say. Most people find that having the foot of the oven at elbow height is ideal.

Once you've determined the height of the oven, you can work out the height of the compartment as you did its width.

• **Cabinet depth:** This is determined by the depth of your existing units rather than by the oven. Most units are 600mm deep and this will give you plenty of room for manoeuvre with the majority of ovens.

Make the depth of the shelves 50mm less than the side panel depth to give you your ventilation gap.

• **Top panel:** This will be as deep as the side panels and as wide as the shelves plus an additional 30mm.

There are plenty of variations on the basic design. The space below the oven can be turned into an extra cupboard by fitting a lay-on door with recessed hinges to match your existing units. In this case any gap between the top of the cupboard and the foot of the oven compartment can be taken up by a fascia of melamine board.

The area above the oven can also be en-

countersunk woodscrews to fix the shelves to the battens. Other requirements include iron-on edging strip for finishing the edges and an offcut of plywood or hardboard for the kickboard on the false plinth.

Construction

Start by marking up and making the cut-outs for the false plinth to be positioned at the feet of the side panels.

Now lay the panels exactly on top of one another and mark off on the front edges where you want shelves to be. Transfer these marks to the inside faces of the side panels using a try square extended with the help of a steel rule.

Use the marks as position guides for the shelf support battens. Cut the battens to length—the width of the side panels minus

1 *Mark plinth cut-outs and tape lines before sawing*

2 *Screw through the melamine to fix the supports*

3 *Drill clearance holes for the kickboard screws*

4 *Scribe the side panels with a pencil taped to a block*

to your timber supplier who will hopefully cut the chipboard panels for you.

Refer to the diagram on page 20 to see how the cabinet is constructed. When you work out your design, bear in mind the following critical dimensions:

• **Side panel height:** This is the same as the tops of your wall cupboards. If you haven't got wall cupboards, aim for a height of around 2.5m.

• **Shelf (compartment) width:** This is

closed—this time by an upward-hinging door held by stays. Alternatively you could leave both areas open and fill in the spaces with extra shelves.

Having finalized the basic box design and decided how many lengths of board you need, make a generous estimate of your softwood requirements. You'll need a supply of 32mm No. 6 chipboard screws to fix the battens to the melamine boards, and a roughly equal number of 38mm No. 6

the thickness of the battening that goes across the front—and drill the panels for No. 6 chipboard screws at 150mm centres.

Lay each side panel on top of the support battens, making sure that they are lined up against their marks. Drill pilot holes into the battens before fixing them in place and then cover the screw heads with plastic caps for protection.

With all the shelf supports in place, lay the side panels on edge and support them a shelf width apart. Drill the side edges of the shelf panels (and the front edges of those either side of the oven compartment) to take No. 6 woodscrews. Fit the shelf panels between the side panels, drill holes through into the shelf supports, and screw them in position. Now fit the front battens, first by screwing into the end of the shelf supports (a little glue on the screws will help them grip), then by screwing into them from the shelves above and below.

To complete the basic cabinet, drill and screw on the top using chipboard screws. Follow by cutting and fixing a piece of hardboard or 4mm plywood to act as the false plinth kickboard. Add any other refinements—doors, extra shelves, upstands at the back of the shelves—at this stage too.

The final job is to brace the cabinet at the back so that it doesn't crack and break when you move it into the kitchen. Do this by nailing thin battens diagonally across the side panels.

Insulation: You can if you wish insulate the inside of the oven compartment by tacking in pieces of insulating board. Research has shown that even the best wall ovens still give off heat, so this is probably a good idea, particularly if you want to use the space above for storage.

Fitting the cabinet

Although you leave fitting the oven until installation day, it's as well to make sure that the cabinet fits at this stage.

Manoeuvre it more or less into position and remove the braces temporarily. Start by checking for obstructions on the wall such as a skirting, pipes and cable. Then mark off against the backs of the side panels where they would strike them and cut suitable clearance notches.

Now try the cabinet hard against the wall. If the resulting gap with the cabinet standing freely on the floor is excessive, the back edges of the side panels must be scribed to the profile of the wall. Do this by running down them with a pencil and a thin block of wood held hard against the wall, then trim back to the scribed lines with a planer file or a plane.

When the cabinet is a perfect fit, screw on the angle brackets.

Arranging the electrics

You have several options when arranging the electrical work, depending on whether or not you have an existing cooker circuit.

Even if you do, you must make sure that it is the correct rating for the new appliances—safety is the overriding factor.

If you have an existing cooker circuit, check its rating by examining the appropriate fuse in the fuse board or consumer unit. If the fuse is colour-coded red, it's a 30 amp circuit; if the fuse is green, it's 45 amps. (Note that if you have a shower, this will also be on a 30 amp or 45 amp circuit. To avoid confusion, switch off the main switch and remove the fuses in turn to find out which serves which.)

If the circuit rating isn't high enough, you must isolate the circuit and install a new one. As the existing cables are almost certainly buried in the wall, the easiest way to do this is by running new cable in plastic conduit (mini-trunking) to a new double switch cooker point located in the best position (see the diagram, right).

If your existing circuit's current rating is satisfactory, turn your attention to the cooker control point. To be of use, it must be no more than 2m from either the hob or the oven; it must also be of the correct current rating. Check the latter point by turning off the main switch and removing the cooker point faceplate—the rating will be given on the back.

Most manufacturers recommend that you connect the hob and oven together and then connect whichever of them is nearer to the cooker point. All the connections must be made in cable of the appropriate rating for the circuit—6mm² twin and earth for 30 amp, 10mm² twin and earth for a 45 amp circuit.

Connections at the appliances must be made strictly in accordance with the manufacturer's instructions, but you can leave these and the connection at the cooker point until final installation (see page 396). Make sure that the point—and its terminal plate—is screwed firmly to the wall before turning the electricity back on.

Adding a new 45 amp circuit

For this you'll need a new 45 amp fuse and fuseholder to match a spare fuseway in your board or consumer unit, plus a surface mounted double switched cooker point. You will also require enough 10mm² twin and earth PVC sheathed cable and plastic conduit to stretch between the two. The conduit is available with angle joints, allowing you to run it unobtrusively along skirting boards.

It may be that you can run the cable

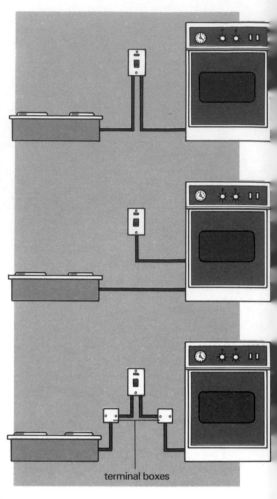

terminal boxes

Consult the manufacturer's instructions on how to wire up your hob and oven to the mains. There are three possible options (above) depending on the type: they can be wired independently (top); the hob can be wired to a junction in the oven which is then connected to the cooker point (middle); or they can be wired up independently via wall mounted terminal boxes (bottom)

under the floor—ground or first floor—so that you only need conduit where it runs up or down walls. This is certainly a neater option, but you'll have to lift quite a few floorboards so bear in mind the disruption entailed. If the cable has to cross joists, feed it through holes drilled one third of the way down—simply notching them could result in the cable being punctured when you relay the floor.

Fasten the backing plate of the cooker point to the wall using screws and wallplugs or cavity fixings as appropriate. Fix the backing part of the conduit along your chosen route using screws, nails or even a strong adhesive adhesive.

Strip back enough outer sheathing on the

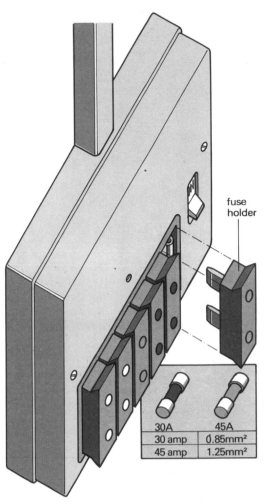

If you are adding a new 45 amp circuit, buy a colour coded fuse holder to match your consumer unit (above) and check the colour of the cartridge or the diameter of the fuse wire

fuse holder

30A	45A
30 amp	0.85mm²
45 amp	1.25mm²

cable to allow you to connect it to the cooker point faceplate. Bare the ends of the live (red) and neutral (black) cores by stripping about 20mm of the insulation; sheath

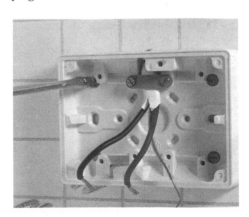

5 *Remove the terminal plate before screwing the back of the cooker point to the wall*

the bare earth core with a length of green and yellow PVC sleeving. Finally, connect the cores to their appropriate terminals on the cooker point faceplate: red to L, black to N and earth to E.

Now feed the cable back along your chosen route to the consumer unit. Where it passes through conduit, simply lay it in the back part and then snap on the cover. 10mm² cable is very thick and stiff but you should nevertheless ensure that it is straight and there are no kinks.

Cutting the hob recess

Cutting a hole for the hob in your worktop is a job that sounds simple in theory, but in practice it's hard work.

If your worktop is the usual thickness—25mm—and you don't own a jig saw, it's worth hiring one. The alternative is a padsaw, but it really is too small for this job.

Take the dimensions for the cut-out from the manufacturer's instructions and follow any specific advice given on positioning. Mark cutting lines on the worktop surface in felt-tipped pen, checking with a rule and try square that the corners are square and that the entire hole is square to the worktop.

If the worktop is laminated, score around the cutting lines with a laminate cutter (you could use a tungsten-tipped tile cutter) held against a steel rule: this will stop the laminate from chipping when you cut it.

Now put pieces of masking tape over the four corners and mark drill holes just inside the lines. The holes you make must be large enough to insert your jig saw blade, so you may have to drill two or even three over each other to achieve the desired result.

Take each cutting line in turn, starting from a corner. Hold the saw firmly but don't try to force it along—concentrate in-

★ WATCH POINT ★

Before you actually start sawing through a worktop, make sure that you've got plenty of spare blades to hand—you'll need them.

stead on keeping it in a straight line and let the blade find its own way through. If you do try to force the blade through the worktop, it is more than likely to bend away from the cutting line and possibly break. Another symptom of pushing too hard is a very hot blade. Remember, too, that the jig saw will create a lot of dust, so clear away any food

6 *Remove the base of the hob and use it as a template to mark your cutting lines on the wall*

7 *Drill holes in the corners large enough to take the blade of the jigsaw, before you begin sawing*

8 *Score along your lines to prevent chipping and then cut out the recess with a jigsaw*

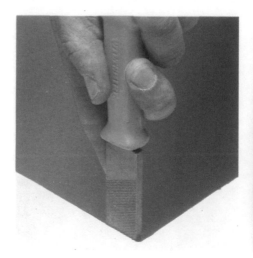

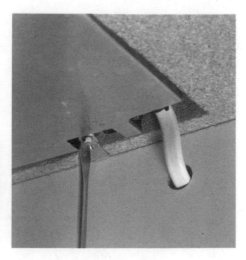

9 *Square up the corners of the recess with a rasp or padsaw. Test fit the hob or hob base and adjust*

10 *Connect the wires to the appropriate terminals in the hob and oven; ensure the cable is locked in place*

11 *Feed the cable out through a hole in the back of the unit and tighten the hob securing clips underneath*

and cover up the kitchen surfaces.

After the hole has been cut, cut back into the corners using a rasp or padsaw. Test-fit the hob or hob base and make any adjustments at this stage. Don't worry if the cut lines are a little ragged: they'll be concealed later by the hob's sealing lip.

Final installation

It's impossible to be specific about what you do on installation day, because so much depends on the nature of the appliances you're installing. But you have one clear priority: to make the changeover from old to new cookers as quickly as possible.

Start with the hob, which may be in two parts or a complete unit, depending on the model. Most simply drop into the recess you have cut and are secured by clips or screws—the instructions will show you how. But check first whether or not you have to prepare the base with an all-round bead of silicone sealant.

Before you actually drop in the hob, connect the linking cable (either direct to the oven, direct to the cooker point, or to both) in accordance with the instructions. Make sure that there's a hole in the back of the kitchen unit for you to feed the cable through to its connection point.

Now fit the oven cabinet. Remove the temporary braces, offer it up to the wall, and mark off the angle bracket fixing holes. Slide the cabinet out of the way and drill the wall to take wallplugs (solid wall) or heavy duty cavity fixings (stud wall). Afterwards, refit the cabinet and secure the brackets with 38mm No. 8 screws.

As with the hob, follow the manu-

12 *When you have secured all the wires in the cooker point, screw the plate back on followed by the cover*

facturer's instructions on how to fit the oven inside the cabinet. Make any cable connections before you slide the oven in and feed the cable out through the back of the cabinet to its connection point.

Connecting the electricity: First of all, turn the electricity off at the main switch on the fuseboard or consumer unit.

Cooker point end: If you are connecting to your old cooker's point, unscrew the faceplate, loosen the terminals and remove the old cable. Replace it with the new cable from the hob or oven, remembering to sleeve the bare earth core with a length of green and yellow sleeving. Follow exactly the same procedure if you are connecting to a brand new cooker point.

Consumer unit end: If you are connecting new cable here, feed it in through the top of

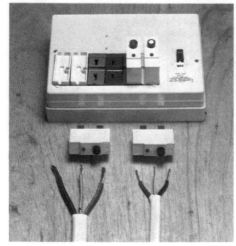

13 *Double check that you have used the proper fuses in your consumer unit: green for 45 amps, red for 30 amps*

the unit and strip off enough outer sheathing for you to be able to connect the cores to their relevant blocks. Sleeve the earth core with more green and yellow sleeving.

The earth core goes to the common earth block; the black core goes to the common neutral block; the red core goes to the circuit's fuseholder. But before you connect the live red core, double check that the fuseholder (and the fuse which goes in it) in the fuseway is the correct rating for the circuit.

Check all the terminal connections, make sure that the cooker point cover is firmly screwed back on, replace the consumer unit cover and switch on to test.

Connecting the gas: Connections to fixed gas supplies will be made by flexible pipe, so the gas fitter will want access to your new appliances.

MAKE AN EXTENDING TABLE

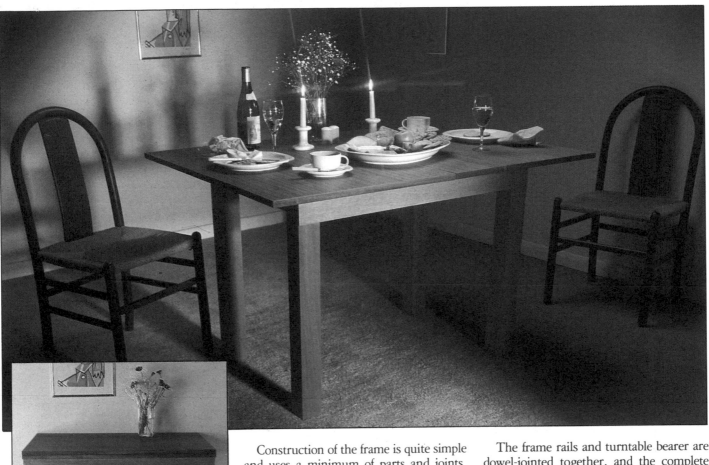

During the day it's a stylish side table that slots neatly into a spare corner or alcove; at night the top opens out to seat four or more in perfect comfort without the need for awkward folding gatelegs.

The transformation is achieved by fitting the double thickness top with hinges and then pivoting it on a cabinet maker's turntable screwed to a subframe within the main frame. You simply open out the flap, release a hidden catch on the underside, and turn the top through 90°. The main frame stays the same, so there are no problems with wobbly legs, and the table is just as easily converted back to its original guise.

Construction of the frame is quite simple and uses a minimum of parts and joints. The example featured here uses high quality birch-faced plywood for the tops and standard sizes of PAR softwood for the base, but you can use other materials—hardwood for the base and home-veneered chipboard for the tops, for instance.

How the table is constructed

Refer to the diagram on page 398 which shows how the table is built. The top consists of identically-sized plywood panels, edged with 3mm ramin lipping or iron-on edging strip and hinged at two points using brass mortise, cylinder, or even counter hinges (the former two are invisible when the top is fully open).

The base frame comprises long and short rails (**B,C**) of 100mm × 25mm softwood, legs (**D**) of 75mm square softwood, and a turntable bearer of 150mm × 25mm softwood. All dimensions are nominal, so be prepared to cope with slight variations in size when you're making the table.

The frame rails and turntable bearer are dowel-jointed together, and the complete assembly is then housed into notches cut in the legs. The leg joints are glued and screwed for extra strength.

The turntable unit is screwed to the bearer and to the lower top flap at a carefully measured pivot point. An ordinary door bolt fitted to one corner of the frame locates in stopped holes drilled in the underside of the bottom table flap to lock the top in either the folded or extended position. The top of the main frame is covered with baize to cushion the table tops during pivoting.

Order of assembly. Although the design is fairly simple, you must follow a strict order of assembly if everything is to line up correctly. The height of the turntable bearer can only be established by locating the main frame against the top, which in turn means building the frame minus bearer in a dry run, marking the bearer joints, then re-assembling the frame with the bearer.

The other tricky stage is securing the turntable to the underside of the top—you have to drill access holes through the bearer so that you can get a screwdriver on the screws fixing it to the table flap.

What you need

The two 19mm plywood top panels each measure 900m × 600mm, so it should be possible to obtain them as offcuts rather than having to buy a full sheet.

Go for a high quality facing veneer, free of large knots and grey/green staining. Birch gives a light, fresh finish that takes well to neutral varnish or coloured stains; the alternatives are mahogany and utile, both of which can be lightly stained and varnished for a more traditional look. Edge the boards with ramin lipping or edging strip. The ramin looks better, particularly when stained in a contrasting colour, but you need to allow for its thickness (generally 3mm) when measuring up to the overall size of the panels.

The main frame parts are standard sizes; you don't need much wood, so it's worth ensuring that the quality is high. If you choose softwood, look for well seasoned parana pine or Douglas fir (British Columbian pine). Hardwood will inevitably be more expensive and may have to be ordered.

It goes without saying that the boards should be straight and relatively knot-free, but take particular care with the leg timber —square section softwood of this size is prone to warps and shakes, which could ruin the look of the table.

The featured turntable is a 57mm one-piece mini unit as found in larger hardware stores and mail order catalogues specializing in cabinet making hardware. Fixings are eight 15mm No. 6 round head screws.

By far the best hinges for the top are 43mm brass mortise hinges, available from the same source as the turntable, but be warned—they are expensive. A less costly alternative is to use 14mm brass cylinder hinges, although the arms on these are more obtrusive. If you don't mind seeing the hinges when the flaps are open, use

The extending table is made up of two components: the folding top panel and the framework beneath. The construction is dowelled except for the legs which are halved and screwed to the side and rails.

You can hinge the two top panels with mortise hinges (shown) or cylinder hinges. Both are invisible when the flaps are unfolded. It is also possible to fit flap hinges.

Extending the table is a simple, two-step operation. First, release the bolt and rotate the folded top anti-clockwise through 90°. Then unfold the top and slide the bolt into the second hole

25mm × 75mm counter hinges.

The locking catch for the top is hidden from view, so any ordinary door bolt with a 6mm pin will do. You also require enough green baize (obtainable from upholstery suppliers) to line the upper edges of the main frame. Red is also available.

Make sure you have a supply of PVA woodworking adhesive, 27mm fluted joint dowels, and 50mm No. 8 screws (for fixing the end rails). The baize should be stuck with a contact adhesive.

Tools for the job. These are straightforward, and most can be found in any general purpose tool kit. You'll find a set of dowel pins useful for marking the rail joints, and if you use cylinder hinges make sure you have a 14mm spurred drill for cutting the housings. This is available from the same source as the cylinder hinges. If you have one, you'll find a carpenter's brace and wood bit best for drilling the hinge housings.

Cutting the frame parts

The pivot measurements in this project rely on the parts being cut accurately, so make

sure your saw is sharp and take extra care when measuring and marking. Remember the rule—measure twice, cut once.

As a general rule, cut one of each component accurately to size and then use this to mark and cut the rest.

Before measuring and marking, choose a face side and edge on each board by running a try square down each of the corners in turn and seeing which forms the most perfect right angle. Mark the 'best' sides and edges with a soft carpenter's pencil, using a continuous curved line so that you can identify them later without any trouble.

Measure to waste wood at either end, so that you can guarantee the ends are cut square. Start with V-shaped pencil marks, then convert them into cutting lines across the face side and edge with a try square— the dimensions are given below.

Support the wood firmly for sawing and be sure to cut to the waste side of the line. You'll find that holding the saw at 30°–40° gives the best results. Start with short, even strokes using your thumb as a position guide; increase the stroke as the saw blade begins to bite, then shorten and quicken it again as you near the end of the

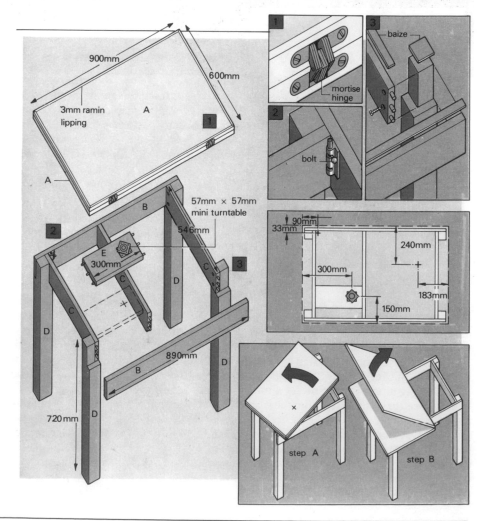

1 *Mark the width and depth of the rail notches on the four 70mm × 70mm legs using a rail offcut as a template*

2 *Measure and mark the position of the dowel holes then drill the holes with a 6mm bit with a depth stop at 15mm*

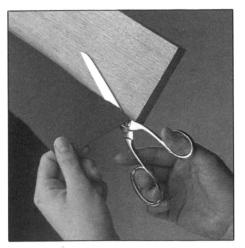

3 *Use a contact adhesive to stick the baize to the top edges of the frame. Trim off the surplus with scissors*

cut supporting the waste piece with your free hand. If one is to hand, you might find that a power or circular jig saw is the best tool for cutting a large panel accurately. A suitable fencing arrangement will be necessary to ensure a straight cut.

Having cut all the parts to size, mark the width and depth of the rail notches around the tops of the legs using an offcut of rail timber as a template.

★ WATCH POINT ★

Mark the notches on all four sides of the legs—it makes it easier to keep the saw cuts straight.

Saw each notch with two tenon saw cuts, keeping to the waste side of the line. Make sure the timber is supported firmly in a vice or adjustable workbench, using offcuts of wood between the jaws to protect the surface. After cutting, try each rail in place; slight adjustments can be made with a planer file or medium abrasive paper.

★ WATCH POINT ★

Check the fit of close-fitting components constantly when adjusting them with an abrasive. This prevents you removing too much material and producing a sloppy fixing.

Drill the dowel holes in the short rail ends next. Prepare each end by scribing a centre line along it using a marking gauge, then

mark off the three hole centres—one in the middle and one 15mm in from each side. Drill the holes using a 6mm bit fitted with a depth stop set at 15mm; make sure the drill is absolutely vertical, if necessary by standing a try square next to it to guide you. A proprietary dowelling jig will take all the guesswork out of getting the hole absolutely vertical.

With all the rails drilled, fit dowel pins in one set of holes and use this rail to mark the corresponding dowel holes in the long rails.

The exact procedure is as follows.

• Lay down a long rail on a flat surface and locate a leg at either end. Adjust until the rail is perfectly aligned in its notches.

• Take your marker rail with the dowel pins and lay it against the inside of a leg so that the end is flush with the long rail. Without disturbing the position of the leg, press the marker rail down hard so that the pins leave a clear impression of the dowel hole positions on the long rail.

• Repeat at the other end.

• Mark the centre rail dowel holes using the turntable bearer as a spacer.

Mark the dowel holes on the other rail in the same way, taking care to mark those for the centre rail from the right end. Then drill all the holes to a depth of 15mm.

To fix the positions of the end rail screw holes, lay each rail in turn in its notches in the legs. Align the parts exactly, then drill paired 2.5mm pilot holes through both components, staggering the holes slightly for extra strength.

Having drilled both rails, remove them and enlarge the pilot holes into 5mm clearance holes. Follow by countersinking the holes to accept the No. 8 screw heads.

Mark and drill the four dowel holes in

each end of the turntable bearer as you did those in the cross rails; note that the holes should be spaced 20mm and 55mm from each side.

Finish by test-assembling the rails and legs upside down in a dry run. If everything fits correctly, glue pieces of baize to the top surfaces of all the parts (trim it when the glue has dried) and fit glued dowels in the holes in the cross rail ends. Lastly set the assembly aside to dry completely.

★ WATCH POINT ★

A length of paper masking tape or coloured plastic tape makes an ideal depth stop for drill bits. Position it 1mm above the desired depth, measuring from the shoulder of the bit and continue drilling until the tape is just perceptible above the surface of the material being drilled.

Cutting and drilling the top

Once again, accurate cutting is important if the boards are to pivot at the correct point. If you use ramin lipping to edge the top, don't forget to allow for its thickness when measuring the top up.

Each panel is 900mm × 600mm. Measure and mark it out with V-shaped pencil marks, leaving waste wood on three sides, then join up the marks into cutting lines using a marking knife and steel rule. Press the knife blade down reasonably hard, so that you break through the surface lamination.

If you cut both panels from the same piece of plywood, remember to allow 2mm between adjacent cutting lines to take into account the width of the saw blade.

Support the plywood firmly on either side of the cutting line before sawing—the jaws of an adjustable workbench make ideal supports—and keep your saw blade centred on the line at all times.

After cutting, trim off the roughness with fine abrasive paper and recheck each panel for squareness by measuring the diagonals. If all is well, apply the iron-on edging or glue and pin on the ramin lipping at 100mm centres and leave to dry.

Mark the pivot position and the two stopped bolt hole centres on the underside of the lower panel following the dimensions given in the diagram opposite. Drill the bolt holes using an 8mm drill bit with a 12mm depth stop.

To prepare for fitting the turntable, set a pair of compasses to the exact distance between the centre of the unit's hub and the centre of one of the fixing holes.

Draw a circle to this radius on the underside of the lower panel, centred about the pivot point.

Finally fit the invisible hinges to link the two flaps as described below.

Fitting invisible hinges

Invisible hinges all work in the same basic way, in that the body of the hinge is screwed into a housing in the board edge while the arm folds into it when the adjoining panel is opened out.

Whether you are fitting mortise or cylinder hinges, begin by laying the two top panels exactly on top of one another, their

Mark the hinge centres on the inside edges of both panels with a marking gauge

Drill the hinge housings with a carpenter's brace and a 9.5mm wood bit

Place the mortise hinge in its housing and fix it in position with brass screws

edges flush, and marking the hinge centres 150mm from each panel end.

Mortise hinge. Offer up each hinge to its centre mark in the fully open position. Carefully mark round the backs of the arm housings onto the board edges, keeping the hinge centred between the two panels.

Cut the housings by drilling a series of closely spaced 9.5mm holes to a depth of 15mm.

Refit the hinges and mark around the outsides of the bodies. Cut the rebates for these by drilling further 9.5mm holes, this time to a maximum depth of 3mm. Afterwards, trim the rough edges of the housings with a chisel or sharp knife.

Test fit the hinge in its housings. When all is well, use a bradawl to make pilot holes for the fixing screws and secure the hinge bodies firmly to the edges of both panels.

Cylinder hinge. Having marked the hinge centre positions on both panels, separate the panels and use a marking gauge to scribe centre thickness lines across the original marks; the cross marks the centres.

Drill the mortises to a depth of 15.5mm

using a 14mm twin spurred bit (you can buy this where you get the hinges). As when drilling dowel holes, ensure that your drill is absolutely vertical and switch it to its slowest speed setting.

After drilling, lay the panels together again and press the hinge cylinders into their respective holes. Using a small screwdriver, tighten the two small locking screws on the edge of each cylinder to hold the hinges firmly in position.

Final assembly

Begin this stage by assembling the legs, long rails and three cross rails in a dry run. The end rails can be held to the legs by temporarily driving in the fixing screws; hold the rest of the frame together with string, using packing pieces to protect the corners.

Lay the top assembly—folded, with the upper face downwards—on a firm, flat surface. Position the frame upside down on top and adjust its position until the top overlaps the legs by exactly 5mm all round. At this

4 *Measure and mark out the top panels with V-shaped pencil marks, score the surface and then cut them out*

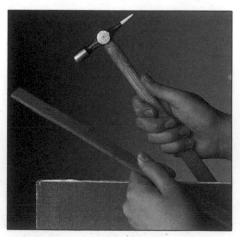

5 *Trim any roughness off the panels then glue and pin the ramin lipping at 100mm centres and leave to dry*

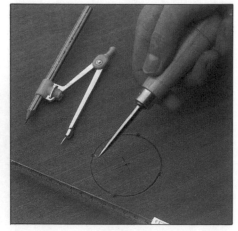

6 *Draw a circle around the pivot point on the table top to match the turntable. Bradawl the screw points*

7 *Assemble the legs, long rails and three cross rails in a dry run. Use string to hold the framework together*

8 *Position the turntable bearer between the end and centre rails. Press it on to a pin in the pivot point of the top*

9 *Having marked the position of the turntable on the bearer, drill the access holes then fix the turntable in place*

point the two separate assemblies are correctly located.

Now tap a pin into the pivot point on the top and snip off the head. Position the turntable bearer between the end and centre cross rails so that it's roughly centred over the pivot point and press down hard so that the pin leaves a clear impression on the surface of the wood. Use a pair of pliers to pull out the pin after use.

Remove the bearer and draw a circle of the same radius as the one on the top, centred on the pivot point mark. Lay the turntable unit on top; adjust the fixing plate until it's square to the sides of the bearer with the screw holes centred over the circle. Use a bradawl to bore pilot holes through the plate and into the bearer.

Keeping the fixing holes centred on the circle, rotate the plate through 45° and re-mark their positions. At these points drill

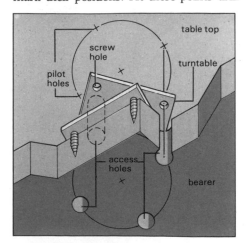

The access holes permit insertion of the second set of turntable screws. Fix them to your screwdriver with putty

8mm holes right through the bearer.

Screw the turntable unit to the bearer using the first set of holes, then relocate the bearer in position in the table frame.

By adjusting the bearer, you should be able to align the screw holes in the unfixed plate of the turntable with the circle previously drawn on the top. Then, by rotating the plate, you can bring the fixing holes directly into line with the access holes in the bearer.

At this stage, poke a bradawl through the access holes in the bearer and the screw holes in the unfixed turntable plate and mark the pilot holes in the underside of the table top. Then, without disturbing the positions of any of the components, mark where the ends of the bearer strike the end and centre rails.

Remove the bearer (don't unscrew the turntable) and fit dowel pins to one end. Dismantle the frame and leg assembly.

Press the bearer against the relevant cross rail (depending on which end you've fitted the pins) and mark the dowel hole centres, using the positional marks you've just made to gauge the bearer's exact location. Afterwards, fit the pins in the other end of the bearer and mark the remaining cross rail.

Drill dowel holes in the cross rails as before, to a 15mm depth. Fit glued dowels in the ends of the bearer and leave to dry.

The base frame can now be assembled for the last time, this time including the bearer. Apply a liberal coating of glue to all the mating surfaces and fit the parts together. Follow by driving strengthening screws into the leg joint and set aside to dry for at least four hours.

Finally, lay the complete frame upside down over the top panel, fit the fixing

10 *With the table assembled, screw the door bolt to the corner of the frame so it aligns with the stopped hole in the top panel*

screws in the unfixed turntable plate and align them with their pilot holes, then drive them home via the access holes in the bearer. Screw the door bolt in the corner of the frame so it aligns with the stopped hole in the top panel.

While the frame is still upside down, use a planer file to round the edges of the feet to a 5mm radius and sand the remaining edges smooth with medium abrasive paper.

Afterwards, give the entire outside frame a thorough sanding with fine abrasive paper mounted on a block.

With the table upright, fill the pin holes in the lipping (where fitted) with wood putty and sand the exposed faces of the top panels as you did the frame.

Having stained the wood as desired, finish with three coats of matt or semi-matt polyurethane varnish.

WALL-MOUNTED DISPLAY CABINET

The trouble with most display cases is that they either look and feel flimsy, or they are so substantial that they effectively hide everything inside. This design is different.

By giving all the boards a bevelled edge, the side panels look lighter than they really are; this has the effect of projecting the interior outwards. And the optional door is even more ingenious: the edges of the frame members are chamfered so that they sit flush within the case, and their mitred joints create a kind of 'picture frame' effect which is sure to show off your collection to its best advantage.

The shelves inside the case rest on push-fit support plugs and are fully adjustable. You also have the choice of building them flat, or angled with lippings, depending on what you want to display.

Materials requirements are straightforward, and call for easily available standard board sizes. The bevels and mitres have to be made accurately if the project is to look good and fit together properly, but don't let this put you off—all you need is some careful marking out and a little skill with a plane.

Planning the job

Study the constructional diagram on page 403 to see how the case is put together. The dimensions given are for a unit measuring 1,100mm × 800mm × 150mm deep, which is a useful size for most purposes and allows you to use 150mm wide boards (preferably parana pine) for the side panels.

You can, of course, adapt the design to make it larger or smaller, but in this case you must take care to ensure that the various components remain in proportion to one another or the whole thing could end up looking top heavy or being impractically large for a normal house.

What you need

For the basic case as shown you require:
• 3.9m of 150mm × 25mm PAR softwood from which to cut the side panels A and B to 800mm and 1,100mm respectively.
• 150mm × 19mm PAR softwood for the

shelves (C and D); each shelf is 755mm long and you're likely to need at least four.
• An offcut of 4mm birch-faced plywood measuring 1,100mm × 800mm for the back panel—with luck, you shouldn't have to buy a full half sheet.
• 32mm × 6mm hardwood lipping for the shelves (angled shelves only).

For the optional door:
• 3.9m of 50mm × 25mm PAR softwood to cut the frame members E and F to 1,105mm and 805mm respectively.
• 3.6m of 9mm square hardwood and 3.6m of 9mm triangular, square or quadrant hardwood moulding for the inner and outer glazing beads respectively.

• A piece of 2mm–3mm perspex or acrylic sheet measuring 1,009mm×709mm for the glazing. Clear acrylic is the more expensive of the two, but gives much better results. Because of the delicacy of the door frame, it is not advisable to use glass.

• A pair of 75mm brass butt hinges and a small magnetic catch or cabinet lock to hold the door in place.

Use PVA woodworking adhesive, reinforced with 12mm, 25mm and 32mm pins to hold the frames together; make sure you have a good supply of these items.

You need a minimum of four shelf support plugs per shelf, but ensure that they're the smaller (and less obtrusive) push-in type so that you can adjust their positions without spoiling the appearance of the unit.

The finish can be stain, varnish, paint or even french polish. Add the final touches to the interior by lining it with baize or a coloured felt, available from haberdashers; use a latex adhesive such as Copydex to glue the fabric to the back panel. You may also prefer to glue it to the upper faces of the shelves as well.

Most of the tools required for this project can be found in any standard DIY toolkit. However, you do require something a little out of the ordinary to cut the bevels and mitres on the panels.

The best tool for this purpose is a circular saw with an adjustable sole plate that can be set at 45°. Smoothing the bevels can be done by hand, using a medium size bench plane, but the job will be much easier if you hire a power planing tool. The best ones have an adjustable fence or sole plate which allows you to plane at a preset angle, plus a V-shaped groove in the sole plate so that the edge of the workpiece acts as a guide.

Whichever method you use for cutting the angles, you'll still need a tool to mark them. Use a sliding bevel and protractor to mark 45° angles accurately, or you could use the 45° set of a combination square.

If you must do the job by hand, ensure that your saw and plane are razor sharp and properly adjusted.

Building the case

The critical part of this job is cutting the four side panels (A,B) accurately, so take care and double-check all measurements.

Start by sawing the panels roughly to size, allowing about 60mm overlength. Then, on each panel, go through these operations, double-checking at every stage.

• Measure off the exact length on the workpiece so that you are left with equal

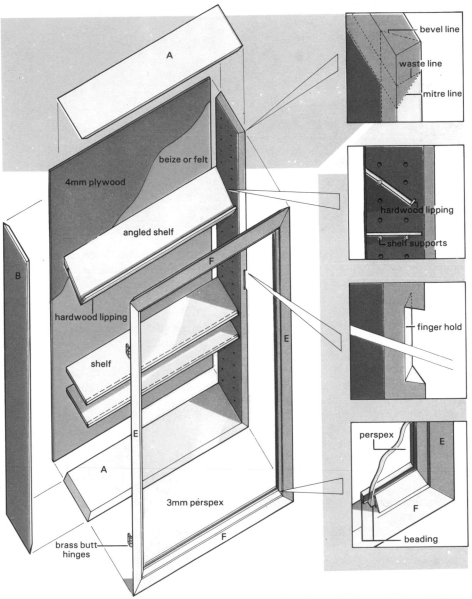

amounts of waste at both ends.

Convert the marks into cutting lines across the board using a try square—wherever possible, take marks from the best sides and edges of the boards. You can decide which are the best by running your square along each, noting the distortions or unevennesses shown against the blade. Mark the best side 'F/S' and the best edge 'F/E'—aim to make these the facing sides of the finished case.

• Clamp the board on edge, set a sliding bevel to 45° and mark the mitring lines back from the cutting lines.

• Lay the board flat on the opposite side to the first cutting lines, and mark a second cutting line which runs across from the mitring lines.

• Clamp the board on end. Set the bevel to 45° and mark off the bevel line on the end grain (make sure that it runs in the right direction).

Mitred and bevelled boards (A and B) are pinned and glued together and strengthened by a plywood backing. The insides of the panels are drilled to accept shelf supports.

There's a choice of shelf styles—sloping or horizontal. Bevel the front edge of the flat shelves to make them look lighter.

The door frame is likewise bevelled and mitred to fit snugly inside the shape of the case, appearing to frame the contents. Butt hinges, a magnetic door catch, a finger hold and felt complete the unit

• Remove the board and set a marking gauge to the width of the bevel by holding it against the marked line on the end grain.

• Hold the board tilted away from you with the gauge at the far end. Roll the gauge until the pin points away from you but is just touching the wood. Now draw the gauge towards you, scribing a line as you go and en-

1 *Mark cutting and mitre lines on the case panels (A/B), then mark the bevel lines on the end grain. Double-check line directions*

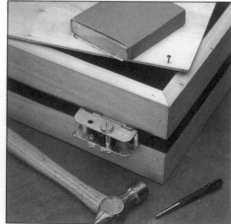

2 *Square off the mitre and length lines, then use a pin marking gauge to scribe a bevel line along the length of each board*

suring that the head stays hard against the edge of the board.

The panel is now fully marked out for shaping and cutting.

Plane the bevelled edge first, as described in Bevelling the edges, then cut the mitred ends.

If you have a jig saw, set the sole plate to 45° and cut the timber clamped flat on the bench with the end protruding. Take care to keep within the waste side of the lines, and finish the cut by sanding with the grain using medium abrasive paper mounted on a sanding block.

If you are sawing by hand, clamp the timber on its side with the non-bevelled edge uppermost and the end projecting from the bench. Hold the saw at 30° and look down over the cut so that you can keep the blade aligned with both cutting lines. As before,

finish the cut by sanding with the grain.

Having cut all the panels, prop them together to test the fit and make any necessary small adjustments. You can check if the box frame is square by measuring the diagonals, which should be equal.

When all is well, measure and mark out the upright panels (B) for their pre-drilled plug holes. The best way of doing this is to mark lines lightly in pencil along and across the timber, then drill the holes where they cross. It's best to drill many more holes than you'll actually need so that you can easily adjust the shelf heights as and when you choose. You need two plugs for each shelf—25mm from the back edge and 60mm from the front. Make two holes at 80mm intervals along the entire length of each side panel (B).

Use a depth stop when you drill, follow-

ing the plug maker's recommendations on size and depth of hole. The least conspicuous type are those shown below—you only need to drill holes for the screws themselves.

Assemble the box by applying glue to the mitred ends of the panels and clamping them together. If you don't have a strap cramp or sash cramps, make your own tourniquet clamp by wrapping string around the frame and then twisting it tight with a screwdriver or a piece of dowel.

Afterwards, strengthen the joints by pinning through each panel at 30mm centres. Take care to drive the pins in straight, and remember to punch their heads well below the surface.

Use the completed frame as a template to mark out the back panel. Convert the pencil lines into cutting lines by scribing them with a marking knife and steel rule so that you score the surface layer of ply and stop it chipping.

Having cut the panel, pin and glue it to the box frame at 50mm centres (it's worth checking at this point that the frame's still square). When dry, sand the rough edges of the back panel until they are smooth against the side panels.

Making the door

The joints on the door frame members are halving joints mitred for greater strength, and making them calls for a very strict marking and cutting procedure.

Although each half of the joint is marked in the same way, one half has a square shoulder while the other has a mitred shoulder. Make those on the rails the square ones and those on the stiles the mitred ones. Mark them with an 'S' and an 'M' respectively.

Start with the stiles; cut them roughly to length with a 60mm excess, then mark the true lengths with an equal amount of waste either end. Follow this procedure on each:
• Square cutting lines across the stile and cross-hatch the waste in pencil.
• Make a mitre line from the cutting line—carry it across the face of the wood.
• Square lines down both edges, against the mitre line.
• Join these lines up on the opposite face of the wood to form a second set of cutting lines.
• Find the half thickness of the wood with your marking gauge: try it from both sides, making small pin marks each time; adjust the head in small increments until the

3 *Cut the bevels and mitres (see Bevelling the edges), then mark the side panels (B) at regular intervals for the shelf support plugs*

4 *Glue and clamp the panels together— make sure they're perfectly square—then pin them. Pin a plywood panel to the back*

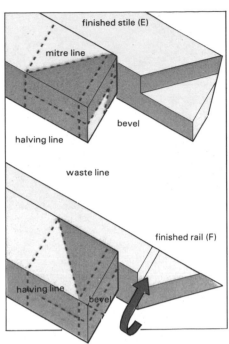

5 *Cut the mitred halving joints on the stiles and rails (E/F) of the door frame. Test fit and adjust with a chisel and glasspaper*

6 *Pin and glue each joint together, testing for square. Trim the end of the stiles to match the bevelled edge of the rails*

7 *Fit hinges in the normal way (use short screws). Pin beading to the front, fit the perspex panel, then add the inner beading*

Marking mitred halving joints is complicated by the bevels—use cut stiles to mark rails

marks line up, then tighten the gauge.
• Scribe half-thickness lines along both edges and the ends, up to the cutting lines.
• Cross-hatch the waste part of the joint as shown in the diagram on the right.
• Mark out and scribe the bevelled edge as you did for the box side panels—make sure you bevel the correct side.

When both stiles have been marked plane off the bevelled edges as described on page 406.

Use a tenon saw to cut each joint half:
• Clamp the timber on end and saw down the half thickness lines as far as the mitred edge lines. Take care to keep the blade absolutely horizontal, and to the waste side.
• Clamp the timber flat, mitred lines uppermost, with the end to be cut protruding. Saw right through the wood, along the mitred line, removing the waste end in the process. (Alternatively you can use a mitre box for this stage.)
• Clamp the timber flat with the shoulder side downwards. Remove the remaining waste with a tenon saw cut across the wood.
• Trim the rough edges of the joint by sanding.

On the rails, mark out the joints in the same way as the stiles, but this time use the stiles themselves (instead of the square) to mark the mitre and half-thickness lines. This ensures that the joint halves match.

Having marked and planed the bevelled edges as before, use the following cutting order on each joint.
• Clamp the timber flat and saw across the mitre down as far as the half-thickness lines.
• Saw off the waste end.
• Clamp the timber on end and saw down the half thickness lines to remove the waste.

When you've completed all the joints,

assemble the frame in a dry run in order to test the fit.

When all is well, glue the frame together using picture framer's corner clamps or a strap cramp.

Try the completed frame for fit in the case; with luck, it should fit perfectly, but you may need to do a little gentle planing or sanding here and there to get the frame edges to lie absolutely flush with the case.

Glazing the door

Start by measuring off the front beading pieces against the inside of the frame, and cut them to length in a mitre box. Check and adjust the fit, then pin and glue the beading in, flush with the front face.

Use a fine-toothed saw to cut the acrylic

sheet to size. Protect both faces against scratches by wrapping the material in paper or cloth and by taping either side of the cutting line. Make sure that the sheet is well supported either side of the cutting lines. After cutting, trim the rough edges with fine sandpaper on a sanding block.

Drop the completed pane on top of the beading in the frame. Cut the rear beading in the same way as the front pieces, then pin and glue it in the frame against the pane.

Fitting out and finishing

Before embarking on this stage, decide whether you want flat or angled shelves and whether or not to finish the inside of the case—this must be done before you fit the shelf studs and baize.

Cut the shelves 60mm overlength, then mark their true lengths with an equal amount of waste at either end. Mark and scribe their bevelled edges as you did the side panels and plane them as described in Bevelling the edges.

Next, mark off the amount by which the width must be cut down on one of the shelves and saw or plane it to size. Use this shelf as a template to mark and cut the others. Finally, saw off the waste at the ends of all the shelves, ensuring that you cut them square.

For angled shelves, you need to cut

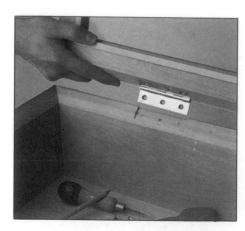

8 *Cut the hinge pockets on the stiles in the normal way; make fine adjustments until the door sits flush. Use short screws again to avoid breaking through the frame*

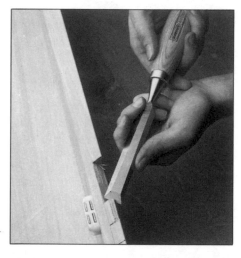

9 *Attach a magnetic or cupboard catch and cut a recess in the case to act as a finger hold so that you can open the door*

10 *Apply fabric adhesive over the backing panel and spread the felt flat on to it. Cut it neatly at the corners as shown*

recesses 20mm in from the back (bevelled) edge to catch the rear support plugs. The best method is to drill 8mm diameter holes in each side, to a depth of 10mm, positioned so that they just touch the lower edge. You can then break and cut out the remaining waste using a small chisel. Complete the shelves by pinning and gluing hardwood lipping along the front.

Cut the door opening recess next—cut it from the front edge of the case. Mark it out using a try square and marking gauge to give accurate cutting lines: you'll notice that the bevel on the recess matches that on the inside edge of the side panel.

Lay the case on its back to cut the recess. Start by making two angled tenon saw cuts down to the depth lines, then gently pare out the waste wood using a sharp chisel.

Despite the unusual frame arrangement, the door is actually hung in the conventional way. Start by marking the hinge leaf positions on the inside (bevelled) edge of the door hinge stile, 150mm from the top and bottom. Use the hinge leaves to trace the outlines of the rebates on the wood.

Mark off the depths of the rebates by holding the leaves against the stile's side edge, then gently pare out the waste wood and screw the hinges in place—use short screws to avoid breaking through.

Offer up the door to the case and mark the hinge positions on the side panel bevelled edge. Double check that the door will still close flush in this position, then cut the rebates as before and screw the hinges home.

If you wish to line the back panel and/or the shelves with baize, cut the material to fit and glue it in place at this stage.

Final fitting adjustments can be made by increasing the depth of one or other of the rebates as required, but take care not to remove too much wood in one go. When the fit is perfect, fit the magnetic catch or cabinet lock to the inside edge of the door

opening recess. Position the shelf plugs as desired, hang the shelves, and the cabinet is complete.

Bevelling the edges

If you have a jig saw with an adjustable sole plate, use this to rough-cut the bevels and then plane them smooth as described below. Alternatively, use a circular saw.

Clamp the workpiece flat on the bench with G clamps so that the edge to be bevelled overhangs. Set the sole plate to 45°, align the blade with the bevel mark on the end grain, and start sawing. Keep well within the scribed line on one side and the edge of the timber on the other.

Power planing: Most power planers have an adjustable guide fence which allows them to plane at a pre-set angle. If yours is so equipped, set it at 45°.

When power planing, it is far better to switch the blade to a shallow cut and make a number of passes than to try to remove too much wood in one go.

Grip the plane firmly with one hand on the handle and the other on the guide knob at the front. Start the motor before you lay it on the workpiece, and then guide it slowly but firmly across the surface in a straight line—don't twist or tilt it or the blade will dig into the wood.

Keep the motor running until you've lifted the plane clear of the workpiece, then wait until the blades have stopped rotating before you put it down.

Hand planing: Hold the plane as shown, gripping the rear handle securely with one hand and using your other fingers to guide the tool along the edge of the workpiece.

Apply a steady, even pressure along the length of the plane and move it down the workpiece in a straight line, keeping your wrists locked. Above all, don't try to press the blade into the wood.

Jig saws—with adjustable sole plates and fences—can be used for bevelling

Circular saws are better as it's easier to keep to the cutting line

Finish up to your marks with a hand plane or power plane

MAKE A SIDEBOARD

One of the problems with building large pieces of furniture is that small mistakes in cutting the parts can soon accumulate to leave you with ill-fitting components and a great deal of expense or time-consuming labour to put things right.

The sideboard featured here is designed to get around these problems by using pre-fabricated components which you can buy off-the-shelf from large DIY centres: drawers and drawer fronts, cupboard doors, side panels and tops. By working out roughly what size of sideboard you want, then finding the correct components, you can 'custom-build' it far more easily than if you were starting from scratch. You simply adjust dimensions to suit the off-the-shelf components.

The remainder of the sideboard is made from standard sizes of PAR softwood, with shelves made from chipboard, plywood or blockboard, finished off with an iron-on edging strip where necessary.

Planning

Before actually buying anything consult the diagram on page 408 so you understand how the unit goes together, then visit local DIY centres and timber yards to find out exactly what is available.

Pine isn't cheap, by any means, but it has the advantage that it needs no edging or other finishing, while the variety of sizes in which it is sold allows you to buy no more than you really need for a particular job (taking the inevitable wastage into account). Doors and drawer fronts, similarly, need little or no finishing and allow an excellent match with the rest of the unit. The drawers themselves can be timber or plastic with whichever system of runners suits you. These, again, can be bought off-the-shelf.

Materials

Taking a sideboard which is 1,500mm long, 600mm deep, and 850mm high (common dimensions for a small to medium-sized unit), you will need the following components: a top panel of 19mm faced ply or pine 1,500mm × 600mm; two drawer fronts of 650mm × 150mm; two 650mm × 450mm doors the same thickness as the drawer fronts; and two 700mm × 450mm side panels. All of these should be in pine.

The main frame of the unit consists of

50mm × 50mm PAR softwood chosen to match the colour of the top and sides (remember that a nominal 50mm × 50mm is an actual size of about 45mm × 45mm, and plan accordingly). The base and shelf can be of any inexpensive sheet material; you will need slightly more than half a standard 2,440mm × 1,220mm sheet so explore the possibility of a supplier cutting the panels to the size you want. This may be cheaper than buying a full sheet.

The components can be glued, screwed and pinned together (but you must reinforce certain joints) while others are made using mortise and tenon joints.

Tools

A standard carpentry tool kit should suffice for this job. You will need a power jig saw with a saw fence or a sharp panel saw; a tenon saw and mitre box; tape measure and try square; pin hammer and 35mm panel pins; screwdriver and 35mm–45mm countersunk woodscrews; a bradawl to mark screw holes; PVA woodworking adhesive; and finally, a finish of your choice.

Marking and cutting components

As always, measuring and marking is one of the most critical parts of the job: get this right and the rest is comparatively easy.

The first thing you must establish is the approximate size that you want the unit to be. Bear in mind that you will be limited, to a certain extent, by the drawer front and door sizes available. Having said that, of course, you can make the unit slightly higher simply by extending the legs.

The overall height of the unit will be the thickness of the top plus the length of the legs. Choose your height (850mm is a common and comfortable working height), subtract the thickness of the top panel, and you've got the length of your legs. Mark off the 50mm × 50mm PAR softwood—on all four faces of the timber—and cut it to length using a tenon saw.

Now cut the mortise slots in the legs. Each leg will have three slots: one at the top for the top rail, one near the bottom for the bottom rail, and third at right-angles to this for the bottom side rail. Remember when marking up the slots that the tenons which fit into them will be half the width of the

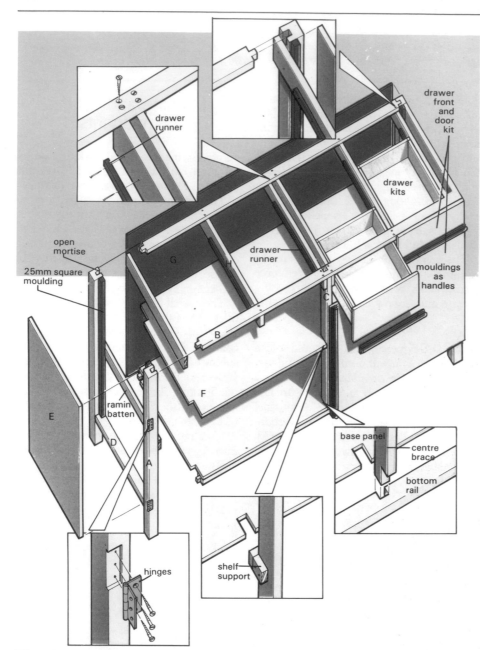

open
mortise

25mm square
moulding

drawer
runner

drawer
front
and
door
kit

drawer
kits

drawer
runner

mouldings
as
handles

G H

B

E

D

A

F

C

ramin
batten

hinges

shelf
support

base panel

centre
brace

bottom
rail

1 *Cut mortises for the bottom rails in the legs—one for B and another at right angles for D. Cut 'open' ones to fit the flush top rails*

2 *Test fit the mortises and tenons— tenons should be half the thickness of the wood used in the legs and half the depth*

The sideboard consists of a frame to which the doors, drawers and top panel are added. The main elements of the frame are the four legs (A), the four top and bottom rails (B), the side bottom rails (D), and the centre brace (C). The legs are handed left and right, and also front and back.

The side panels (E) are identical and are pinned and glued, using ramin battens as reinforcement, to the legs and side bottom rail. The legs and rails are fitted together using mortise and tenon joints, while the centre brace is located by a halving joint at each end.

The base panel and shelf (F) are identical; the base panel sits on the bottom rails round all four sides, the shelf is supported by ramin battens pinned and glued to the inside of the side panels.

Six drawer runner mounting pieces, (H), are screwed and glued to the underside of the top rails, to carry the drawer runners —one is fixed on either side of the centre brace, one at either end. The others are fixed midway between centre brace and the ends.

The top panel is screwed to the front and back top rails from below while the 3mm plywood back panel, (G), is simply cut to size and pinned in place around the outer edges of the unit.

The doors and drawer fronts fit edge to edge across the front of the unit. The outside and bottom edges of the doors are flush with the outside edges of the front legs and the lower edge of the front bottom rail. Short lengths of moulding are attached to the outer edge of the doors and drawers to act as handles.

timber, so make the necessary allowance and consult the diagram on the left for guidance. Then cut the mortises.

Decide how wide the main body of the unit must be (this will be defined by the width of the doors), then subtract twice the thickness of one of the legs to arrive at the length of the top and bottom rails at front and back.

Remember, when marking off the top and bottom rails and the two bottom side rails, that there must be a tenon 25mm long projecting from each end. Allow for this when marking them up.

Mark off one of the rails and cut it to size using the try square and tenon saw. Use this rail to mark off the length of the other three rails. Cut these to size and compare them closely: if there are any slight discrepancies, trim the longer ones down carefully to the length of the shortest.

3 *Measure the distance between the legs and from the top of the legs to the rail—cut a side panel to match for each side*

4 *Cut 12mm plywood to make a base and a shelf. Don't forget to make small cutouts to fit round the legs and the centre braces*

Cut the tenons in the same way as halving joints and check them for size with their matching mortise slots. Mark each rail and its corresponding legs so that you don't get confused later on. Now cut the halving joints in the centre of the front top and bottom rails to accept the centre brace. Clamp them together and cut both pieces at once to get an exact match.

The centre brace at the front of the unit is the last frame member to be cut. Its length is the depth of a drawer front plus the depth of a door (plus the 3mm gaps between drawer front and top panel and drawer front and door). Measure this off carefully and then cut it to size using the tenon saw. Finally, cut the halving joints at each end to match those in the front rails.

The two side frames are composed of the legs, a shelf batten and a bottom rail. As the bottom rail is joined by mortise and tenon,

its length will be the depth of the main body minus the thickness of one of the legs. Measure each leg individually to arrive at an accurate figure, then cut the rails to size, incorporating the length of the tenons.

The two side panels will fit between the bottom rail and the top of the legs and run between the front and back legs. Measure this off and cut the two panels to size using either a sharp panel saw or a power jig saw. If you're using a jig saw, use a timber batten clamped to the timber to cut the line accurately.

Finally, you must cut the bottom panel and the shelf to size. Both the panels run the full depth of the unit, and both must have angled cutouts at their front and rear corners to accommodate the legs. Mark off the corner cutouts and cut them using a tenon saw. Cut the panels to size using the jig saw and timber batten or a panel saw.

Given the overall size of the main body of the sideboard, you can cut the top panel to whatever size you like, within reason. Remember, however, that its overhang at the front shouldn't be so much that it impedes access to the drawers.

Assembling the sideboard

Assembly is a simple, logical process made easy by accurate cutting of the components in the first place.

Start with the side panels; pin and glue lengths of 25mm square moulding along the insides of the bottom, front and back edges, flush with the edges themselves. When the glue has dried, fix the side panels to the lower side rails by pinning and gluing through the moulding into the softwood, flush with the outer edge of the rails.

Now, laying the side panel on a flat surface, offer up the front and rear legs. Check the fit of the mortise and tenon joints between the bottom rail and the legs. When you are satisfied, apply glue to the mating surfaces of the joints and to those where the ramin mouldings meet the legs. While the glue is drying, adjust the joint between side panel and leg so that the two are flush on their outer face. When the glue dries, reinforce all the joints by pinning them using 35mm panel pins.

Choose the height of the shelf and mark off on the inside faces of the two side panels the positions of the shelf support battens. Measure from the tops of the bottom side rails, not from the bottom shelf panel.

Stand both end panels upright with the aid of an assistant and offer up the front and back top and bottom rails. Check the fit of

the mortise and tenon joints, then remove the rails, apply glue, and replace them.

Drop the bottom panel in place to hold the structure square, but don't fix it in place yet. Instead, use rope or webbing clamps at top and bottom to hold the assembly together tightly while the glue dries. Once it has dried, reinforce the joints by pinning.

5 *Glue and pin a moulding to the inside edges of the side panels. Glue the joints, then add the panel, pinning the moulding to the legs*

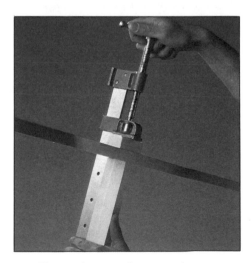

6 *Glue and cramp the centre braces between the top and bottom rails. Cramp the rest of the frame too—make sure it's square*

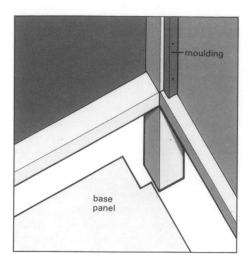

The addition of the base panel will begin to add rigidity and shape to the structure. Pin and glue it to the bottom rails and against the legs and centre brace

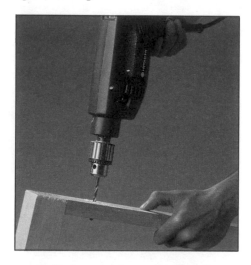

7 *Drill the top rails to accept the drawer runner support battens at the points indicated in the diagram on page 408*

8 *Measure and cut the drawer runner support battens for the top rails— make two more to use as shelf battens on the legs*

Replace the bottom shelf again and, before fitting the upper shelf supports, offer up the central brace. Check the fit of its halving joints with the top and bottom rails, and the cutout in the front edge of the bottom panel. When you are satisfied that the central brace will fit correctly without fouling the bottom panel, apply glue and attach the brace.

Now fix the bottom panel in place by pinning through it into the side and rear bottom rails. The panel will now brace the unit while you turn it on each end in turn to fit the shelf supports. Pin and glue these in place, working to the marks you have already made.

Drill countersunk screw holes at 200mm–300mm intervals into the top rails to take the top panel securing screws.

When you've done this, offer up the shelf. Check that it fits easily; if it doesn't, ease the cutouts using a rasp or coarse glass-paper. Smooth off the edges again with fine glass paper.

Drop the shelf in place, but don't try to pin it to the shelf support battens—you may weaken them. Instead, glue them in place and lay a couple of heavy books at each end to press the mating surfaces together.

One of the tricky parts of this job is fitting the drawer runners. These must be mounted securely to support both sides of the drawer. The simplest types are the tough plastic runners which can be screwed in place to fit the profiles of the grooves in the proprietary drawer sides.

The big problem is to build a secure mounting for them. The best way to do this is to buy a length of 75mm × 25mm (or wider) sawn softwood. Cut this into four identical pieces which will run the depth of the main body of the sideboard, fitting snugly between the front and the back panel. Glue and screw one piece on either side of the centre brace and tight against the top rails—make sure they're fixed at the same points on the back rails.

Fit one of the other pieces to each end of the unit, and one midway between the centre and the end ones, using 35mm countersunk woodscrews. You can now offer up the drawers themselves to find the correct positions for the runners, and screw these in place before fitting the top panel.

Fitting the top panel

Mark on the underside of the top panel the positions of the four legs and the centre line of the panel itself. Mark another centre line

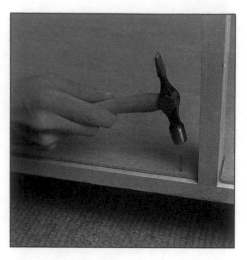

9 *Pin and glue the base panel and the shelf to the rails. You can also add the back panel at the same time, if you choose*

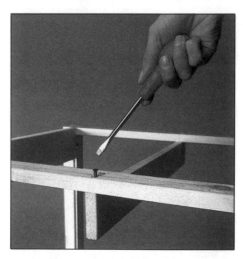

10 *Screw and glue the drawer runner support battens to the top rails— make sure they're square to the top rails*

on both the front and back top rails, then lay the panel bottom side up on a flat, protected surface. Lay the unit on top and match up the centre lines and the legs with the marks on the panel.

Adjust the unit until it is in exactly the right position, then screw the front top rail to the underside of the panel using a 50mm woodscrew, as close to the centre of the rail as possible. With the front rail secured, do the same at the back of the unit, ensuring the pieces don't slip out of alignment.

Once the two rails are fixed, you can drive in the rest of the screws. Stand the unit upright again and use your try square to check that the main body stands absolutely straight. If it doesn't, the back panel will straighten it up and hold it square when it's fitted later on. You are now ready to fit the drawers, doors and back panel.

Finishing the unit

Fitting the drawers, door and back panel is the most satisfying part of the job because you can see the finished sideboard coming to life and taking shape.

Fitting the drawers is easy: you simply slip them into place to check their fit, then remove them and fit the drawer fronts. First assemble the drawers from whichever type of kit you have chosen, then screw the drawer front connecting pieces in place. Make sure that the drawer sides fit between the runner support battens, then cut the base to fit and assemble the parts. Screw the assembly to the drawer front. Measure from the top of the drawer front to the runner groove so that you know where to position the runner—measure the same from the top edge of the rail on to the runner support batten.

Before offering up the doors, screw the hinges to their backs, flush with their edges. You will need at least two hinges for each door, and you may have to chisel out a recess for the hinges in the lower legs themselves. Before doing this, however, screw the doors to the legs, ensuring that both doors are flush with the bottom edge of the bottom rail and that there is a regular 3mm gap between the two from top to bottom. Now examine the hinges carefully: if there is a large gap between the door and the leg to which it is fitted you will have to chisel out the recess.

Mark the hinge position on the outside edge of the leg, then remove the door and hinge complete. Using the pencil marks you have drawn, mark out the edges of the recess using the point of a 25mm wood chisel, then dig out the waste wood using careful chisel strokes, guided by gentle finger pressure. The recess won't be so deep that the hinge's original screw holes are obscured, so you can refix them easily.

The final job is to fit the plywood backing panel to the main body of the sideboard. Start by measuring up the exact dimensions of the main body itself—the panel should fit flush with the bottom of the rear bottom rail and the top of the rear top rail, and about 25mm short of the outside edges of the two rear legs.

Cut the panel to size using either a sharp panel saw or a power jig saw guided by a timber batten cramped along the cutting lines. Lay the sideboard flat on its face on a protected surface and pin the back panel down with two panel pins, one at each top corner. With the aid of an assistant, match the lower corners of the back panel with the

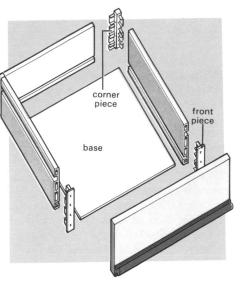

Drawer kits can be easily assembled—just cut the components to fit between the support battens. Then add a drawer front

bottom of the sideboard to ensure that this is properly square, then fix it again with pins at 200mm intervals.

The final stage of the assembly is to pin and glue wood mouldings to the doors and drawers to act as handles. You can fit screw-on knobs instead if you prefer.

Whether you intend to paint, varnish or stain the unit, you should go over all the timber with a fine grade of glasspaper to smooth it off. Sand a very small 2mm radius on the edges of exposed parts like the legs to reduce the chance of splintering.

If you are painting the unit, go over it with a couple of coats of primer and undercoat, then sand down before applying your top coat. It would be wise to remove the doors and hinges and paint these separately.

If varnishing the unit, apply at least three coats, rubbing the first one down with a very fine glasspaper or 0000 grade steel wool before applying the final coats.

11 *If you haven't done so already, pin on the back panel of 3mm plywood. Round off the exposed ends with medium grade glasspaper*

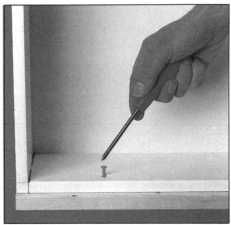

12 *Drawer kits vary in design—you may need to screw through a panel to attach the kit to the drawer front you have chosen*

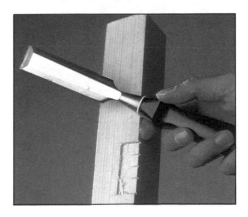

13 *You may need to cut a hinge pocket in the leg so that the door sits neatly, or you may choose to do so for appearance's sake*

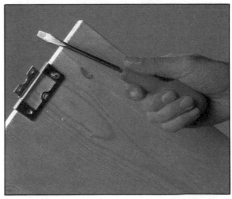

14 *Flush hinges don't usually require hinge recesses. Screw them first to the back of the door and then to the front edge of the legs*

PLAY BOXES

As any parent knows, children have a habit of amassing large quantities of toys, and keeping them packed away tidily when not in use can be difficult. These colourful toy boxes can solve that problem.

They're designed to sit on brackets in an alcove, a corner or a cupboard—just like a shelving system. And although they're all based on single boxes, you just have to add a few details and fittings to turn them into a train engine and trucks that can be taken down and used as toys themselves. Note that small children shouldn't try to lift the boxes down for themselves—and there's a safety lock to stop them doing so. The parts are all made from plywood and battens held together with glue, pins and screws.

The size of the boxes can be adapted to suit any situation, but ideal dimensions are: 750mm long, 225mm wide and 130mm high (excluding the wheels), and the models described here are based on these dimen-

sions. Draw out the panels to scale on squared paper; this will give you an idea of the plywood sheet sizes you need to buy.

To save time when making the boxes, matching pairs of side panels, end panels and frame rails can be cut and drilled together. By marking one piece accurately and clamping it to its partner both pieces can be shaped and/or drilled in one operation that ensures symmetry. The base frame and floor are assembled first, followed by the end and side panels. After this, the bulkheads are added followed by the wheels.

The boxes are ideal for fitting into a handy alcove where simple batten supports can be screwed to each end wall, but they could also be fitted into a tall cupboard (an old wardrobe, for example) or against a corner where a ladder type support would be needed at one end fixed to the floor and ceiling.

Tools and materials

For marking out all the pieces, you'll need a pencil, marking knife, retractable steel tape, try square, a long straightedge, a compass. A tenon saw, a fine-toothed powered jig saw or a coping saw, and a fine-toothed hacksaw will handle all the cutting jobs. An electric drill is essential. A bench stand attachment for the latter will make accurate drilling easier, but if you're careful you can do without it. Wood boring bits in 25mm and 13mm sizes—flat bits are the cheapest type—are needed as are 3mm and 5mm high-speed steel (HSS) bits. A countersink bit will also be useful.

Other useful tools are: a bradawl, centre punch, a round rasp, a half-round fine-cut file, screwdrivers to fit No. 4, No. 8 and No. 10 screwheads, a hammer and nail punch, a smoothing plane, sandpaper and

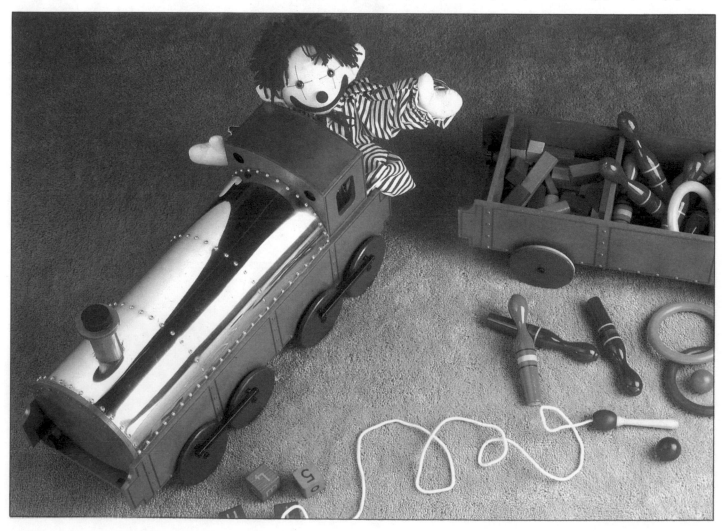

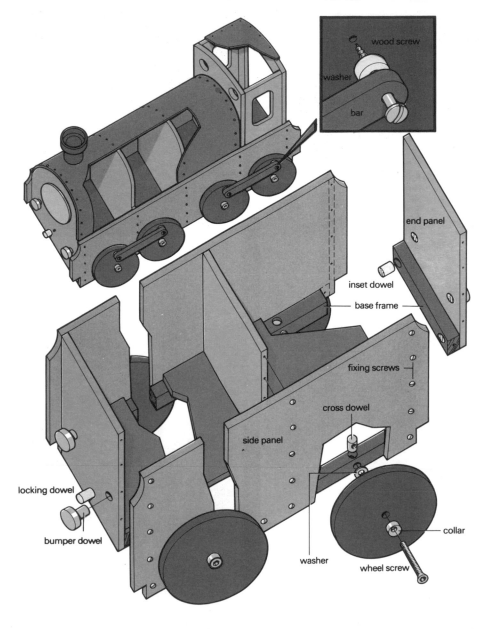

The boxes are made from plywood panels which are glued and screwed together on a simple base frame of softwood battens.

The wheels are made from discs of thick plywood fitted together with screw/dowel connectors

portions of which must be at least 75mm long—are used to link the boxes together to form a train. One hook and one eye are needed per box.

The following screws are required: 10mm No. 4 roundhead, 13mm No. 4 roundhead, 25mm No. 4 roundhead, 25mm No. 8 countersunk, 38mm No. 8 countersunk, and 63mm No. 10 countersunk. The latter are for fixing the wall battens and need wall plugs to go with them. Other fixings needed are: a quantity of 13mm and 19mm panel pins, PVA wood glue and a general purpose impact adhesive.

Making the basic box

The first job is to mark out all the various components of the box, but only one of each matching pair of parts need be marked up accurately. The remainder should only be marked up as rectangles.

The box side panels have cut-outs at their bottom corners that match the dimensions of the wall battens, and their upper corners are curved. Use an upturned saucer or similar round object to draw round the shape. Mark a row of screw holes along the bottom of the panel, a row at each end and two more rows (for dummy rivets) in the middle.

The end panels have dowel hole positions marked 19mm in from each edge, 35mm up from the bottom. In addition you need two screw holes at the bottom, 50mm in from each edge.

The base frame end rails should be marked for dowel hole positions 19mm in from each end, and the side rails with axle centres 150mm from each end and screw holes 10mm in from each end.

The wheels should be marked out with your compasses set at a radius of 62mm.

Cut the base frame rails (note that the end rails sit inside the side rails) and clamp each matching pair together. Mark the positions for the cross dowels at points corresponding to the wheel positions on the side rails.

Cut out the end panels with the jig saw or coping saw, clamp them together and drill 13mm diameter holes at the dowel positions, and 5mm diameter countersunk holes at the fixing screw positions.

Cut out the basic rectangles for the side

The boxes lock onto battens fixed to an alcove, or rest on a supporting ladder secured to the floor and ceiling

sanding block, a few G-clamps, wood filler, steel wool and some blocks of scrap wood.

The materials you need include 9mm plywood for the side and end panels, floors, bulkheads and cab; 3mm (no thicker) plywood for the boiler top, front and cab roof. Alternatively, you could use a thin sheet of brass for the boiler top. You also require 13mm plywood for the wheels. A model shop may be able to supply you with thin plywood.

The locomotive's funnel is made from a 50mm plastic waste pipe connector.

For the base frame and wall battens you'll need 50mm × 25mm prepared softwood. In addition, you need to buy 13mm dowel and 100mm of 25mm dowel. The wheels are attached by M6 'scan' fittings. You'll also need washers to match.

Hook-and-eye fittings—the hook

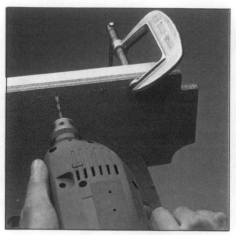

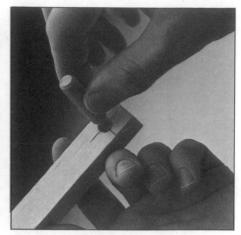

1 *Measure out all the pieces of the box as basic rectangles but only mark two of each shape in detail*

2 *Cut out the details of each panel and clamp them to the appropriate side rail before drilling the screw holes*

3 *Drill the dowel holes in the end rails and glue in the cross dowels. Once the glue has dried, plane off the excess*

panels, clamp them together and then shape the corners as required. Drill 3mm clearance holes at the screw positions around the edge of the panels, but not in the centre—you should leave these blank.

Now take each side panel and clamp it to its respective side rail so that their bottom edges are perfectly aligned and the panel overhang at each end is equal to the thickness of the end panels. Run the 13mm wood bit through the plywood. Mark each panel/rail combination so they can be kept together.

At this stage, you can assemble the base frame. First, glue lengths of 13mm dowel in the holes in the end rails, planing off the excess when the glue has dried. Cut out a 782mm × 207mm floor panel from 13mm plywood. Then glue and screw the base frame and floor panel together, driving the single 38mm No. 8 fixing screw at each end of each side rail into the dowels in the end rails. Mark the fixing screw holes 10mm in from each edge, screw the floor to the base

---

★ WATCH POINT ★

Clamp a piece of scrap wood beneath the plywood when you drill it; this will prevent the plywood splintering as the drill bit breaks through.

---

frame, using 25mm No. 8 countersunk screws.

Next, glue and screw one of the side panels to the base frame and floor panel. Use 25mm No. 4 roundhead screws.

Glue four 25mm lengths of 13mm dowel into the holes in the end panels, fitting them so that their inner ends are flush with the

inner surfaces of the panels. Wipe off any excess glue with a damp cloth. When the glue has dried, glue and pin a 10mm thick piece of 25mm dowel to each to form the buffers.

Glue the end panels to the base frame and first side panel. Drive two 25mm No. 8 countersunk screws through the end panel into the base frame rail and two 32mm No. 4 roundhead screws through the side panel and into the dowels in the end panel. Fit the remaining three screw holes at each end with 25mm No. 4 roundheads.

Glue and screw the remaining side panel to the frame and end panels.

At each end of the box, drill a 13mm diameter dowel hole at the bottom of each end panel so that it is on the panel centreline and passes through the centre of the frame end rail. Glue a length of 13mm dowel into each hole so that it protrudes 19mm from the end panel to act as a lock.

Cut the central bulkheads and six 25mm wide strips from 9mm plywood. Glue and pin the strips to the inside of each side panel so that they are 11mm apart and form slots into which the bulkhead can be dropped so that they can be removed if desired.

Complete the basic box by fitting the dummy 'rivets' to the box sides. Make a pilot hole at each rivet position with the bradawl and fit a 10mm No. 4 roundhead screw. Use the bradawl to make pilot holes for the hook and eye fittings, fitting the hook at one end of the box and the eye at the other.

Drill a 6mm diameter hole at the centre of each wheel and then cut them out with the jig saw or coping saw. Chamfer the edges with sandpaper. Drill a 6mm hole through the side panels and side rails for M6 'scan fitting' screws at the wheel

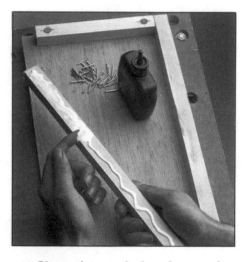

4 *Glue and screw the base frame and floor panel together. Screw through the side rails into the dowels in the end rails*

positions you have marked 150mm in from each end. Then drill 11mm holes up into the side rails of the base frame to accept the cross dowel at a corresponding point.

Test fit the wheels by assembling them in the following order. First insert the cross dowel and align it using a screw driver. Then put the collar onto the screw and slide on the wheel. Next fit a washer and insert the assembly into the hole. Tighten the screw using a hexagonal key and test to make sure that the wheels run freely. You may also have to add a washer to give more clearance from the side of the box or open up the hole slightly with a rasp. Once you are satisfied then take everything out and cut the screw to length so that it won't project beyond the edge of the frame. When everything is as you want it, reassemble all the parts but add a drop of glue into the cross dowel to ensure that the screw doesn't work itself loose during use.

Making the locomotive

The construction of the locomotive is basically the same as the truck with a few obvious differences: the two extra pairs of wheels; the rounded boiler top, the shallower side and rear panels and the cab with its curved roof.

When marking out the front panel, position the dowel hole marks and mark out the curved top by opening your compasses to a radius of 104mm so that the curve begins at a point 250mm above the bottom edge of the panel. There is no need to mark out the tops of the other three boiler bulkheads since these are all clamped to the front panel and cut out in one go. Similarly, the rear panel is clamped to the front for drilling the dowel and screw holes. Don't attempt to mark out the top at this stage.

Mark the curved top of the cab front by opening the compasses to 135mm and placing them on the centre line of the panel, 67mm up from the bottom. Then mark two round window centres 30mm in from each side and 160mm up from the bottom.

The cab sides measure 100mm wide by 250mm high. Mark a horizontal line 35mm down from the top and vertical line 75mm in from the front edge; join the two with a gentle curve, using your compasses or some round object to draw round. Then draw in the 75mm × 50mm side window; the top edge being on the 35mm line, the front edge 19mm in from the front edge of the panel.

When marking out the base frame side rails, mark the axle holes at 260mm and 115mm in from the edge.

Cut and prepare all the components of the locomotive and assemble the base frame, floor, side and end panels in the same way as the truck, gluing and screwing the pieces together.

Then glue and screw the boiler bulkheads in between the two side panels, spacing them at 150mm intervals and securing them in place with 25mm No. 4 roundhead screws. Now mark out the top panel.

Mark out the 3mm thick plywood top,

making sure the grain of the plywood skin runs lengthwise along the boiler. Alternatively, you can use a metal sheet. Draw a line down the centre of the top and another along each side. Draw three more lines on either side of and parallel to the centre line, spacing them equally. Then draw four lines at the positions of the bulkheads. Where the lines cross, drill 3mm screw holes.

Now glue and screw the boiler top to the bulkheads, working from one edge to the other and using 13mm No. 4 roundhead screws. Cut a 100mm diameter disc of 3mm plywood and glue and pin it to the centre of the front panel to make the front of the boiler.

Glue and pin the cab sides to the front panel using 19mm panel pins, and then glue and pin the cab rear panel to the sides. You'll find that the sides stick up slightly above the curved profile of the end panels, so plane them down carefully to match. Measure the cab for the roof, using the same method as the boiler top but adding 6mm to each dimension for a 3mm overhang all round. Then cut the roof from 3mm plywood. Glue and pin the roof to the cab using 19mm panel pins at 50mm intervals.

When the glue has set, the completed cab can be glued and pinned to the boiler rear bulkhead and side panels.

Cut and assemble the wheels and axles in the same way as those for the truck, making sure they turn freely.

The connecting rods are made from 160mm × 13mm strips of 9mm plywood. Lay the locomotive on it's side and tape the wheels to the box to keep them from moving. Mark a hole position at exactly the same place on each wheel 15mm in from the edge. Lay the bar alongside the marks and make corresponding marks on it. Then drill the clearance holes on the bar.

Place a washer over each 38mm No. 8 roundhead screw, insert a screw through each end of each connecting rod and then place another washer over the protruding end of each screw. Finally, screw the rods to the wheels, making sure that they are free to move on the screws. If necessary, remove the rods and open up the holes slightly.

Prepare the funnel by holding it vertically against the top of the front panel and scribing the shape of the top on it with a pencil. Cut out the bulk of the waste material in a V-shape with the hacksaw and then file it to shape with the half-round file. Glue the funnel in place with impact adhesive.

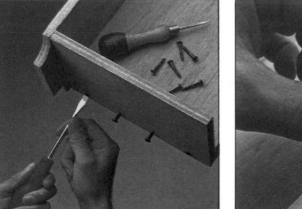

5 *Fix one side panel to the base frame and then add the two end panels. Finally fix the other side panel*

6 *Drill the holes for the wheel fitting across dowels. Insert the dowels and use a screwdriver to line them up*

7 *Test each wheel assembly and make any adjustments necessary to ensure smooth running. Re-assemble the parts*

Finishing the boxes

Punch all the nail heads below the surface of the wood. Fill all nail holes and countersunk screw holes with wood filler and sand it down so that it is flush with the surrounding wood once it has set.

Make sure you sand all the surfaces well

To set the boxes in a corner, build a supporting ladder from 50mm × 25mm batten for the uprights and 25mm × 25mm batten for the cross rails. Cut the uprights so that they extend from floor to ceiling and fix the pairs of rails at the heights you desire. Glue and screw the frame together and secure it to the floor and ceiling using angle brackets

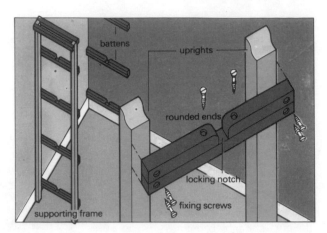

before applying any form of finish, and remove all the dust.

Varnish (whether clear of coloured), or stain and varnish, will allow the pattern of the woodgrain to show through, but the plumbing fitting used for the funnel won't match this. In this case, the funnel can be painted black along with, say, the cab roof. If you are making the boiler cover from a sheet of brass, simply give a polish to bring up the shine.

If you intend painting the boxes, use a tough polyurethane finish which will take plenty of hard knocks, and use the recommended primer, and number of topcoats.

Do not use any paint which has a lead based formulation. If you are in any doubt about a particular brand, contact the paint manufacturers.

Choose bright colours; a final touch would be to stencil the child's name on the sides of the boxes. Stencils can be purchased from art shops, and the letters and numbers applied by stippling through them with a paint brush, or by using an aerosol spray.

Although these boxes are shown in the form of a train, there is no reason why the design shouldn't be adapted to other forms of transport: space ships, boats, lorries with trailers, covered wagons, and so on. Simply changing the profiles of the sides and giving careful thought to the finish could produce all sorts of interesting variations.

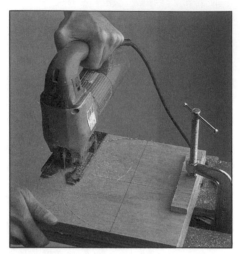

8 *Clamp together all the bulkhead pieces. Mark the top one to use as your guide to ensure that they all match*

9 *Use string to measure the width of the boiler top*

10 *Fix the boiler top in place to the bulkheads*

11 *Cut the pieces for the cab and assemble them*

12 *When the cab is complete, fit it to the box*

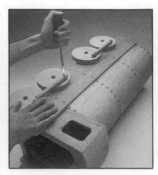

13 *Mark and fix the connecting rods to the wheels*

14 *Mark the rough shape for the funnel cut out*

Fixing the wall brackets

Each end support comprises two short battens which are screwed in place with a 19mm gap between them. This provides a positive location for the 'locking' dowel set into each end panel of each box, which prevents them being pulled from the wall by accident.

Cut each batten to a length of 104mm, leaving the outer ends of the battens square so that they will be flush with the box sides but rounding off the inner ends. Drill two 6mm screw holes in each batten, countersinking them.

Use a spirit level to mark the batten positions on the alcove walls and mark the screw positions on the wall with a bradawl. Then drill and plug the holes, screwing the battens in place. Fix the inner battens in place so that there is 19mm gap between them and the outer battens. Mark, drill and plug the walls, then screw the battens in place.

If you want to set the boxes in a corner, you will need to build a supporting ladder as shown in the illustration at top of page.

MAKE A BATHROOM CABINET

This bathroom cabinet design cleverly shows how you can use inexpensive materials such as melamine-coated chipboard to make your own stylish wall storage unit at a fraction of the cost of buying one ready-made. The cabinet has two particular advantages over many other types. First, it incorporates an open wire tray which offers all the benefits of a solid shelf plus good drainage. Secondly, it provides over-basin lighting which is invaluable if you fit mirrored glass for the sliding doors, as it instantly kills the shadows you would normally throw onto a mirror in this position.

Apart from the basic materials, the construction couldn't be simpler, with the framework held together with butt joints and plastic jointing blocks. The melamine surface means that painting is unnecessary and dirty rings left on the shelves by bottles can easily be wiped away. The boards are readily available from most DIY stores in various standard widths, so you can alter the dimensions to fit in with your own requirements. But a word of warning: don't make the unit too deep, especially if you intend to sit it over a basin, otherwise you'll be continually knocking your head on it.

The design shown is 150mm deep which is adequate for most situations. The other governing factor regarding how big you make the cabinet is the size of the tray you can buy. But if you shop around you should be able to find one suitable.

Tools and materials

The tools you require to build the cabinet are very basic and should include a folding rule, a marking knife and try square. For cutting you will need both panel and circular saws. You'll want a bradawl to mark and start off screw positions and you'll need a drill and 18mm flat bit to drill the wiring access holes. A small electrical screwdriver is necessary for wiring the light fittings and you also require a screwdriver to assemble the cabinet itself. Finally you'll need a spirit level to align everything and a small brush to apply the polyurethane varnish.

The cabinet is made from finished chipboard with a back panel of finished wall-

board. The frame for the back panel is cut from square section beading, and the front edges are finished with half round or double round edging to match the thickness of the chipboard. You need square plastic jointing blocks for the butt joint connections as well as screws and pins.

You'll want six dressing room light fittings—small battenholders in plastic are ideal—and bulbs, and a length of 1.5mm² PVC-sheathed two-core and earth cable. You'll need contact adhesive to fix the edging in place and some polyurethane varnish to finish it off. Also buy some fine glass-paper for smoothing down rough edges.

Building the cabinet

Start by making a sketch of the size of the unit you want to construct and then make up your shopping list of materials. You can use a standard width of chipboard for the sides, bottom shelf and bottom of the wiring cavity.

You can cut down a length of chipboard to form the slightly narrower middle shelf. The top needs to be cut from a wider board as it has to overhang the unit by about 12mm on the sides and front.

To get a neat cut, hold a try square with the stock firmly against the edge of the

board and scribe a line with a sharp knife across the surface of the melamine. Use the try square to continue the line right round the board, and then saw smoothly down the waste side. You may find that the melamine will splinter in places on the underside of the cut, so make sure these edges are concealed within the cabinet during assembly.

★ WATCH POINT ★

Because boards are often stored on end, it's best to cut lengths from the middle section to ensure that the ends are square and free from damage.

Cut two lengths 700mm long from 150mm wide chipboard for the sides. Cut the bottom shelf and bottom of the wiring cavity from 150mm board, each 600mm long. Trim a board down so that it is 175mm wide and cut a 650mm length for the top. Then cut the middle shelf and the lighting panel each to 600mm × 100mm.

Next cut the beading for the wire tray supports and coat it with clear polyurethane matt varnish.

After the front panel has been cut to size mark out the positions of the lights. Six lights equally spaced will provide plenty of light. Use dressing room fittings, which are usually like small battenholders. They take a small round bulb, and the skirt around the socket is so designed that once the bulb is inserted it's impossible to touch any live metal part. Drill 18mm diameter access holes to bring the electricity cables through, and mark the positions of the fixing screws on the front of the panel using a bradawl.

Next, lay the two side panels side by side and use a rule and try square to pencil on the positions of the batten supports for the tray, the bottom and middle shelves and the base of the wiring cavity. Use an offcut to mark the thickness of the shelves and to show where the front panel will go. Then mark the position of all the jointing blocks on the side panels. Hold the blocks in place, use a bradawl to break the melamine to start the fixing holes and drive in 18mm chipboard screws to secure them.

With the jointing blocks attached to the sides you can begin to assemble the unit. Start by screwing on the battens to take the wire tray. Then stand the side panels on their front edges and position the bottom shelf so that it butts against the jointing blocks. Mark through the fixing holes and screw the sections together. Repeat the operation for the bottom of the wiring cavity as well.

The coated chipboard is fixed together with jointing blocks and fitted with mini battenholders wired in series, mirror sliding doors, and a wire shelf

angle cut batten

mini batten holders

fixing batten

faced hardboard

jointing blocks

mirror doors

wire basket

rounded beading

Stand the unit on a level surface and test for squareness by checking the diagonals. Rest the top on the side panels and position the front panel temporarily so you can mark where it goes on the underside of the top and on the base of the wiring cavity. This will enable you to fit jointing blocks to these when the top and front panel are removed. Wire up the light fittings (see Wiring the lights) and then fit these sections permanently in place again by screwing through all the jointing blocks.

Two constructional jobs now remain: fitting a back panel to the cabinet section and then screwing on the middle shelf.

To fit the panel, make up a frame of square-sectioned beading, butt jointing and

pinning through the corners, so that it will fit snugly within the box of the cabinet. Use the partly assembled cabinet as your guide. Check that it's square by measuring the diagonals to see that they are the same. Lay the frame on the face of a sheet of finished wallboard. Alternatively, you can use plywood or hardboard, but this will have to be primed and painted. Score the wallboard surface with a sharp knife and cut it to size with a panel saw. Pin and glue the frame to the back of the unit and secure it by screwing through the beading into the top, bottom and sides of the opening.

Finally, fit the middle shelf to the jointing blocks, driving pins through the back panel into the rear edge for a firm fixing.

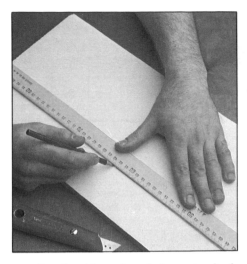

1 Cut the sides to length from standard width board. Cut down an oversize board for the top of the cabinet

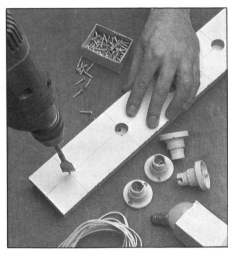

2 Mark the position of the six mini batten holders and then drill wiring access holes. Drill through to an offcut

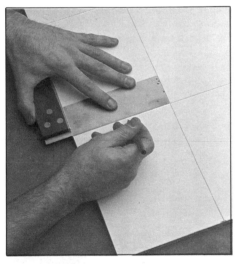

3 Lay the two sides together and use a try square to mark the locations of the shelves and the base of the wiring cavity

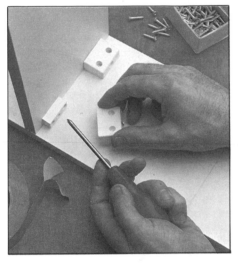

4 Fix the bottom shelf and the bottom of the wiring cavity to the sides of the cabinet using plastic jointing blocks

5 Lay the back panel in from the rear. Fix the beading to the sides and then pin the panel to the beading from inside

6 Finally cut mitres on the ends of the feature strip and fix it to the front edges of the boards with contact adhesive

For an attractive decorative finish, and to stop any exposed chipboard edges becoming subject to damp, fit half or double round beading to all the front and side edges. Normally these will just be straight lengths, but you'll have to mitre external corners when you come to them. Use a mitre block, or a special mitring jig if you can borrow one. Apply several coats of clear matt polyurethane varnish to the face of the beading before fixing it with contact adhesive.

Fitting the glass sliding doors

A unit like this needs two mirrored glass doors, usually 4mm thick. These run in a plastic double channel that you can buy in strips from a glass merchant.

To fit the plastic channelling, you simply cut it to the length you require and screw or glue it in place. Note that there are two depths of channel and that the deeper grooves should go at the top of the door. When fitting the glass this allows you to push the door up into the channel and then to let it drop down into the bottom groove without it falling from the top. Hence the glass panels need to be about 6mm shorter on the depth to allow for this manoeuvring.

To work out the dimensions of the glass, measure the width of the opening, divide it by two and add 15mm; this will take into account that the doors need to overlap in the centre by this amount. To find out how tall they need to be measure the height of the opening and then subtract 6mm. To fit our cabinet each glass door should be 315mm wide and 394mm high.

When buying the glass, get the merchant to burnish the edges so that you can't cut

7 Cut some plastic double channel for the sliding doors. Fix it in place with adhesive at the top and bottom

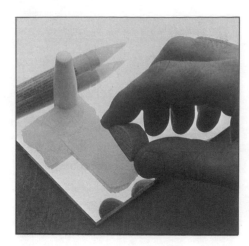

8 *Pre-drill screw holes for the door knobs or fix them in place with adhesive. Mark the hole position with masking tape first*

9 *Once you have completely wired up the light fittings, hang the cabinet and lift the sliding doors into place*

your fingers. Ask the merchant to drill holes through the glass so that you can fit a brass stud or wooden knob. Brass studs come in two parts: you place the shallow dish over the hole on the outside face of the glass, slip a rubber washer over the thread that protrudes through and then screw on a flat backplate to hold everything in place. Alternatively fit a wooden knob with a thin protective soft washer on either side of the glass or simply fix it in place with adhesive.

Wiring the lights

As it's unlikely that you'll want the cabinet lights on while the main bathroom light is off, it's most convenient to wire the cabinet lights so that they are controlled by the main bathroom switch.

The method you use to connect into the

light circuit will depend on how the main light in the room is wired up. But in order to minimize disruption to the rest of the house, do this section of the wiring last.

The individual lampholders are wired up in series. Start with the last one in the line on the front panel. Cut a 225mm length of 1.5mm² two-core and earth PVC-sheathed and insulated cable. Strip back about 25mm of sheathing and take 6mm of insulation off the red and black cores. Sleeve the exposed earth core in green/yellow PVC. Connect this core to the earth terminal on the lamp-holder, and the other two cores to their respective terminals.

Once the connections have been made re-assemble the fitting and screw it to the front panel. Feed the other end of the cable through the next hole and connect this to the second lampholder. You then need to loop in a second length of cable and run this to the third lampholder, and so on.

Now work out how you're going to connect into the lighting circuit. If you've got loop-in wiring you can connect directly to the ceiling fitting (see the diagram on page 421)—exactly what you do will depend on the type of fitting you have. With junction box wiring, you need to connect the cable to the cabinet into the four-terminal junction box feeding the bathroom light and switch, but this may be tricky—there are already four cables in the box. Instead, cut a three-terminal junction box into the cable feeding the bathroom light, and connect the cable to the cabinet into this (see the diagram on page 421). In effect you're splitting the light feed cable into two. However, don't make any con-nections at this stage. Allow about 150mm over at the connection point and then run the cable back to the cabinet site. Ideally chase the cable into the wall above the unit so that it is neatly concealed. And make sure it will miss the mounting battens where it enters the wiring cavity. For ease, and because the run is quite short, you may choose to surface mount the cable as it drops down from the ceiling. In this case run the cable in mini-trunking.

Now mount the cabinet (see Hanging the cabinet) and feed the supply cable through the last hole in the front.

Next turn off the supply to the consumer unit or remove the relevant fuse holder and make the connection to the lighting circuit.

When the connections have been made, screw back the cover over the rose or box, and then turn on the power to check that the cabinet lights work when the main light in the room is turned off. Check the connec-tions if there are any problems.

Hanging the cabinet

Rather than use brackets, the cabinet is mounted on an ingeniously simple inter-locking batten system that is concealed at the back of the wiring cavity.

First hold the cabinet to the wall and mark the position it is to take up. Use a spirit level to make sure it is correctly aligned. Lower the cabinet.

Now cut a length of 75mm × 25mm timber to the internal width between the side panels. Offer this up to the top line of the cabinet marked on the wall, then drop it down the thickness of the chipboard. This is the position of the batten.

Next cut the batten down the middle with a circular saw, angling the cut at 45°. Fix one section of batten to the wall so that the top sloping edge runs down towards the wall. Drill and plug the fixing holes and use at least 62mm No. 12 screws. Then using six 40mm long chipboard screws attach the other section of the batten flush with the back edge of the top of the unit so that the sloping bottom edge will eventually slot into the channel formed by the batten.

To mount the cabinet, simply lift it up and over the batten and allow it to drop down so that the two sections interlock.

Cut a batten at 45° and fix the bottom section to the wall along a horizontal line

Lift the cabinet up onto the batten so that the two sections lock together

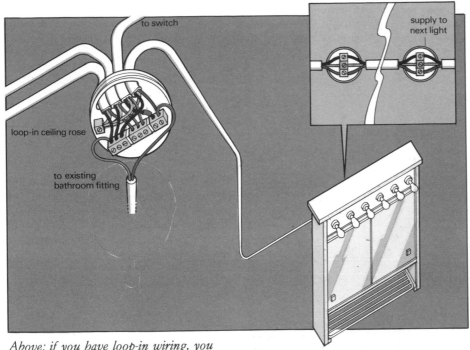

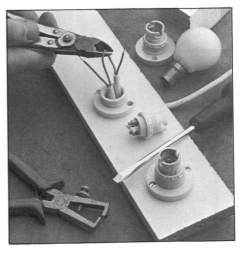

Above: if you have loop-in wiring, you may be able to connect the extra cable from the cabinet lights into the existing loop-in terminals. This means that all the lights in the bathroom are controlled from the same switch

Below: if you have junction box wiring, it may be difficult to connect a fifth cable into the existing box. Use a three terminal box to split the supply between the existing light and the cabinet lights

10 *If you plan to wire the lights via a fused connection unit you could use flex to link them in series; in all other cases, use cable. Start by wiring the last lampholder on the front panel. Use a length of 1.5mm² 2-core and earth cable. Strip back the sheathing and take off 6mm of insulation. Sleeve the earth core in green and yellow PVC sheathing. Then connect each of the wires to their respective terminals*

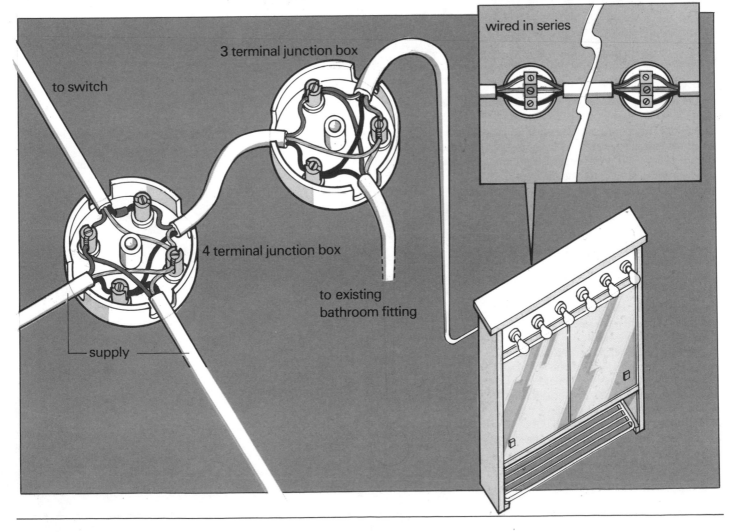

UNDERBASIN UNIT

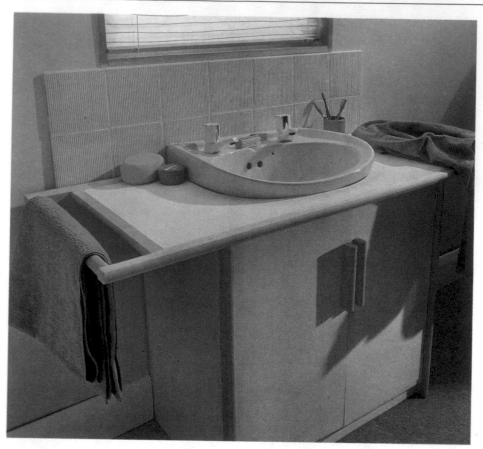

Until a few years ago at least, architects and builders seem never to have spared a thought for the countless odds and ends that accumulate around a washbasin. Cupboard space is always at a premium in bathrooms and bedrooms, and medicine cabinets are usually too full of medicines to cope with such items as shampoo bottles, shaving tackle, talcum power and perfumes.

This project is designed to solve the problem by converting the area underneath a basin—space which normally goes to waste—into a practical cupboard unit, ideal for storing bathroom odds and ends. And at the same time it streamlines the basin area by hiding unsightly brackets and plumbing fittings beneath the basin.

The unit can be fitted around almost any type of pedestal or wall-mounted basin, although with the latter you get more useful shelving space. Height and width don't matter, because the bowl is fully enclosed. In fact, about the only restriction is that you have enough free space below the basin to make the job worthwhile.

You may find one major problem, however: a basin with a complex or compound curve down the front and sides. This makes the job of scribing the cut-outs a little more difficult, but if you follow the directions given you should get a good fit. The same applies to pedestals—you must scribe the shape of the pedestal onto the shelves and cut this out to make them fit; again, by following the instructions you will be able to do it accurately with the minimum of aggravation and waste.

There are plenty of variations on the basin design. The unit shown incorporates a built-in towel rail, made by extending the nosing moulding which is ingeniously used to edge the top and side boards. And it would be a simple job to make a narrower unit with matching mirror—ideal for a vanity basin in a small room.

The main construction material is 19mm man-made board faced with 3mm plywood or plastic laminate. Naturally if you opt for a painted or laminated finish to go with a modern, practical style of decor it makes sense to use one of the cheaper materials—blockboard or chipboard. But for a more homely stained or varnished look, you should always choose a high quality faced plywood.

Planning the job

Assuming that you have the room and that the project is a practical proposition, your first job is to fix the height of the unit: it is this which governs the sizes of most of the parts, and consequently the amount of wood and materials you will need.

Inspect the rim of the bowl closely and decide how much to leave above the worktop surface. The ideal worktop level is

PART	MATERIAL	SIZE	QUANTITY
A (top)	19mm board	990mm × 430mm	1
A1 (facing)	3mm ply or 1.5mm laminate	990mm × 430mm	1 (2 for laminate)
B (sides)	19mm board	740mm × 380mm	2
B1 (facings)	3mm ply or 1.5mm laminate	750mm × 380mm	2 (4 for laminate)
C (front edge trim)	38mm × 25mm softwood nosing moulding	4m total length	—
D (rear edge trim)	38mm × 25mm PAR softwood	4m total length	—
E (towel rail)	25mm dia. softwood		1
F,H,J (fixing battens)	50mm × 25mm PAR softwood	2.6m total length	—
G (lower shelf)	19mm board	716mm × 415mm	1
I (kickboard)	19mm board	716mm × 50mm	1
K (doors)	19mm board	698mm × 357mm	2
L (shelves)	19mm board	716mm × 415mm	2

generally about 25mm down, at the point where the front of the bowl starts to curve away towards the trap. Because the actual contact area of the worktop is only 1.5mm−3mm thick (the thickness of the laminate or plywood facing), you should have little difficulty in achieving a close fit at this height.

Use a spirit level and felt-tip pen to mark a 'height line' around the bowl and then measure to the floor at several points; the measurements should all be the same, but it's worth checking at this stage.

Now study the diagram on page 424 to see what parts go where and work out a cutting list based on your chosen height. The sample cutting list given with the diagram assumes a standard basin height of 800mm, a width of 560mm and a depth of 400mm. In all probability one or both of these dimensions will be the same on your basin, in which case you can simplify things by using the widths and depths which are quoted in the cutting list.

Tools and materials

Make sure that you have a clear idea of what materials you're using and a full cutting list before you go shopping. For a unit of the size shown you'll need a full sheet (2440mm × 1220mm) of 19mm board; work out the total area of 3mm ply or plastic laminate according to which parts you intend to face.

Apart from the boards and timber other items you need are:
• Two pairs of 55mm butt hinges for the doors.
• Two pairs of small magnetic catches.
• 9mm dowels for the towel rail.
• Four pairs of screw-in shelf studs.
• Iron-on edging strip or laminate strip for the doors, shelves and kickboard.
• A large supply of PVA woodworking glue and 50mm panel pins.
• Contact adhesive and 38mm No. 6 screws (laminate facing only).
• Twelve 62mm No. 8 screws and wallplugs for the wall fixing.
• Paint, stain or polyurethane varnish as required for finishing.

Tools for the job are perfectly straightforward and should be found in any well equipped carpentry toolkit. The cut-outs for the bowl (and pedestal, if fitted) can be made with either a power jig saw or a coping saw, although the latter will give you more control. If you choose laminate facings, make sure you have a proper cutter and a metal straightedge to run it against.

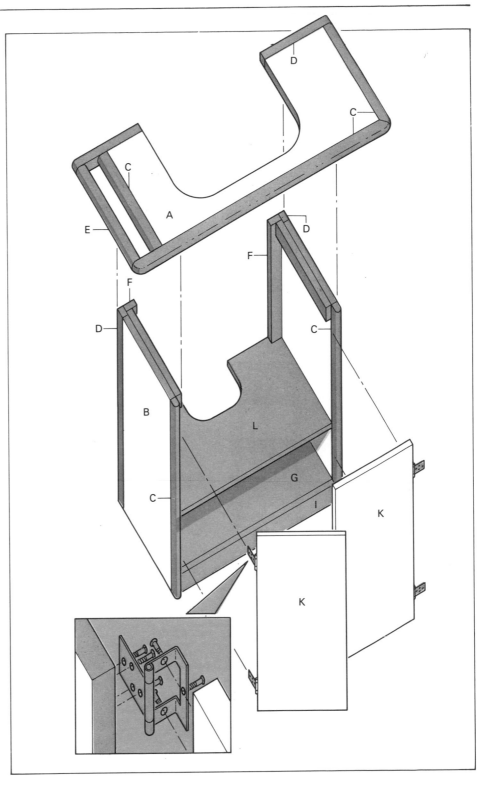

How the unit fits together

The top (A) and sides (B) of the unit are 19mm thick board faced with plywood or laminate (A1, B1) glued in place. Both sides of the board must be faced if laminate is used to prevent warping. Each board is finished with 38mm × 25mm twice rounded softwood moulding (C) on the exposed edges and with ordinary 38mm × 25mm PAR (Planed All Round) softwood (D) on those that are concealed; the wood is glued and pinned in place.

The optional towel rail (which can go on either side of the unit) is made by extending the edge trim outwards and fitting a piece of 25mm diameter softwood round (broomstick) between them.

The sides are screwed to the wall via

The base unit is simple to make, especially if your basin is wall-hung rather than a pedestal type. Remember that you must apply laminate to both sides of the side panels: this prevents them warping, as well as helping to improve the view when the cupboard doors are opened. The bottom shelf is structurally important

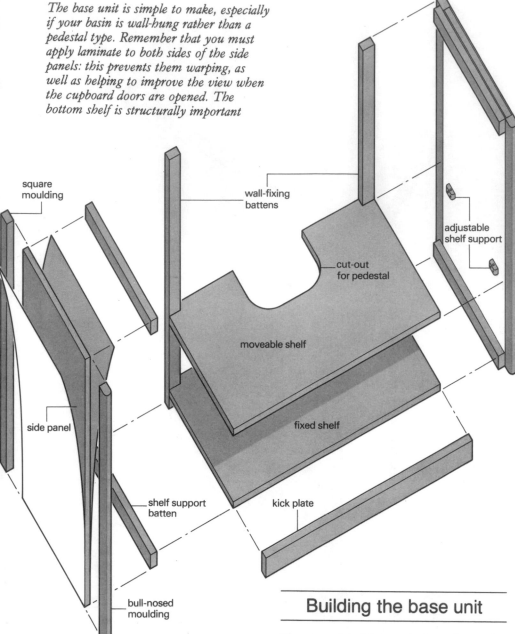

square moulding

wall-fixing battens

adjustable shelf support

cut-out for pedestal

moveable shelf

side panel

fixed shelf

shelf support batten

kick plate

bull-nosed moulding

vertical battens **(F)** pinned and glued to the rear trim. A fixed lower shelf **(G)** stiffens the construction; this is supported on battens **(H)** pinned and glued to the sides and is concealed by a kickboard panel **(I)**.

The top is glued and pinned down into the sides before applying the facing (which then conceals the pin holes).

The double doors **(K)** are hung on butt hinges let in to the sides.

Adjustable shelves **(L)** are supported on screw-in shelf support plugs. They can go at any height, but with a pedestal basin you'll need to saw cut-outs to clear the pedestal itself. The same applies to the fixed lower shelf **(G)**. You will probably have to try the cut-out for the pedestal a number of times until it fits.

Building the base unit

How complex this stage is depends on what sort of finish you want to give the boards. If you plan to use laminate, apply this as and when you cut the boards to size. The same applies to stain, which will be much easier to brush on before assembly.

Start with the side panels of 19mm board. Cut these to your chosen worktop height, minus the thickness of the top itself. Use the panels as templates to mark the facings for cutting—with a marking knife if they're plywood, or in felt-tip pen for laminate.

Cut laminate by running down the cutting line a few times with the cutter held against a steel rule, then snapping off the waste over a metal straightedge. In the case of thin ply, using a marking knife will break the surface and minimize the risk of splintering when you saw it. Even so, make

sure the board is well supported either side of the cutting line.

When cutting thin ply by hand, use a sharp panel saw rather than a rip or cross-cut saw as these, by their very nature, will create splinters and tear the wood.

Assembling the parts

Glue the facings to the side panels using whichever adhesive is most appropriate, spreading it thinly with a notched spreader. Clamp the assemblies using G-clamps and offcuts of wood until all the components are completely dry.

Use the panels again as templates to cut the front (nosing) and rear (softwood) edging to size, and also the two vertical wall fixing battens. Glue the edging strips to the panels (make sure they're the right way round), then reinforce the fixings by pinning them at 100mm centres; punch the pin heads until they are well below the surface of the wood.

Drill clearance holes in the wall fixing battens to take the No. 8 screws. The holes should be at roughly 100mm centres, but it's worth checking beforehand that their positions don't coincide with obstructions below that could make this impossible.

When the panel edgings are dry, pin and glue the battens flush with the rear ones by pinning through from the outside. To do this without weakening the edging fixings, you'll need to support underneath the panels with offcuts of the same batten materials. Take great care to keep the battens flush as you pin them, by holding the assemblies against a wall, or a board clamped to your bench.

Cut the shelf support battens to size. These extend from the rear battens to the front nosing minus 19mm (the thickness of the kickboard). If the insides of the side panels are laminated, drill and screw the battens in place; otherwise pin and glue them. Don't forget to check that support battens are level, by measuring from the bottom at both ends.

Now cut the fixed shelf to size, according to the width and depth of your unit, and glue on laminate facings if required. Use a tenon saw to cut notches in the two rear corners of the shelf, so that it clears the fixing battens and lies flush with the rear edging. If you are dealing with a pedestal basin, make a cardboard template of the pedestal and use this to saw a cut-out in the board. Make the cut-out rather small and test-fit the shelf, enlarging it progressively for a good fit.

1 *Check that the corners of the plywood sheet are square before you start work. Use a try square*

Drill the wall to take plugs or cavity fixings as appropriate, reposition the unit and screw it firmly to the wall.

Making the top

Because the top of the unit has a laminate facing, you don't need to get the cut-out in

2 *Drill the fixing batten screw holes before you fix them to the side panels —not once they're in place*

3 *Cut the mitred joints in the side and rear nosing of the top panel and offer the two pieces up to check their fit*

4 *Make the cut-out in the top panel using a power jigsaw. Don't force the saw through the timber*

5 *Before cutting the other mitred joints at the same end of the top panel, offer up the two nosing pieces; mark them off*

Stand the two side panels upright and lay the shelf between them, on its support battens. Get an assistant to hold the assembly in this position while you pin and glue the shelf in place.

Complete the base unit by cutting the kickboard panel size and pinning and gluing it against the shelf front edge.

Now slide the unit into position underneath the basin and mark the locations of any obstructions that are stopping it sitting flush against the back wall. Make cut-outs for these in the side panels where necessary.

Try the unit again, this time checking that it is level with the battens hard against the wall. Make adjustments by trimming the bottom edges of the side panels with a plane or planer file. When all is well, mark the positions of the fixing screws through the battens onto the back wall.

the 19mm board absolutely perfect. Use a template to cut the facing accurately.

Start by sawing the 19mm board to size then refer to Making the template, for how to transfer the profile of the basin to the board. Cut out the waste and try the top.

Use the template next to mark the cut-out onto your facing material. Make sure that you cut the facing to the waste side of the line so that you still allow yourself enough room for final trimming. Remember, if you are using laminate, to face the underside of the board too.

Try the facings and board together in a final dry run, but don't glue them yet.

Edging the top must be done in strict order if the parts are to join accurately:
• Cut the front nosing roughly to length and mitre the end furthest from the towel rail.
• Cut the longer side moulding approxi-

6 *At the opposite end of the top panel, clamp the nosing in place and use it to mark the cut lines on the towel rail itself*

The top panel is easily made. Only the basin cut-out presents problems. Remember the laminate panels sit flush with the edge nosing

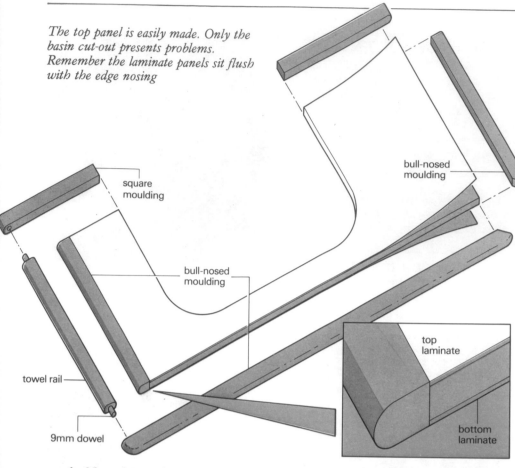

square moulding

bull-nosed moulding

bull-nosed moulding

towel rail

9mm dowel

top laminate

bottom laminate

mately 25mm longer than the width of the top and mitre the front end.

• Try the two pieces for fit where they meet, then pin and glue them to the top leaving enough of a lip to take in the thickness of the facing (ie the nosing should sit flush against the facing when the latter is finally glued in position).

• Cut the front nosing to the correct length and use the top assembly to mark off and cut the remaining edging—the rear pieces and the towel rail side nosing.

• Cut two wall fixing battens to extend from the back of the bowl to the side panel battens. Pin and glue these flush with the backs of the rear edging pieces and drill two clearance holes in each of the battens to take No. 8 screws.

• Pin and glue the rear edging piece on the non-towel rail side and the remaining piece of nosing to the top, leaving a lip for the facing as before. Saw off the long side nosing flush with the rear edging.

• Clamp the other rear edging piece to the top then cut the towel rail dowel to fit between this and the front nosing.

Drill the dowel ends and the edgings to a depth of 10mm and slip glued dowels into the towel rail. Cut a groove along the length of each dowel first to allow excess glue to escape. Apply glue to the rail ends and to the rear edging, then bring all the parts

together and clamp them. Strengthen the rear edging by pinning through into the top in the usual way. When all the parts are completely dry, round off the front corners of the edging and the insides of the towel rail as shown, using a rasp or planer file to leave a perfectly smooth surface that won't catch on delicate fabrics, and is ready for finishing.

★ WATCH POINT ★

Mark the dowel fixing holes by driving a panel pin into the centre of each end of towel rail dowel. Snip the heads off, then slip the dowel into position and press the parts together to mark the wood.

Making the template

The most critical part of the entire job is transferring the shape of the basin to the top board. To do it simply requires a sheet of stiff card which you can cut out to the correct shape, and the exact centre line of the front of the basin.

To find the centre line of the basin lay a timber batten across the basin and clamp it in place. Measure the exact width of the

unit, mark the centre of the batten and, using a carpenter's square, align another batten with this mark so that it overhangs the front of the basin. Mark the centre of the basin front with a chinagraph pencil or felt-tip pen.

Now take a sheet of card, lay it on top of one half of the basin and mark out the rough shape of the cutout from underneath with a pencil. Cut out the shape (try to cut it too small at first), then offer it up to the basin to check the fit. Keep on trimming the card until the shape is exactly right then mark on it the position of the basin's centre line. Check its fit with the other side of the basin.

Now lay the template on a larger sheet, aligning the rear edge of the template with one side of the sheet below. Draw out the basin's half-shape, mark the centre line, then flip the template over, match up the centre line again and draw the other half of the outline.

Cut out the shape of the basin from the larger sheet of card, and offer it up to the basin to check the fit once and for all.

Final assembly

It's best to delay fitting the top for as long as you can so that you have more room in which to mark up the doors and shelves.

Cut the door panels to size by direct measurement from the unit. Allow 1mm clearance for each edging strip (1.5mm if they're laminate) and a further 2mm closing clearance. Try the panels for fit in the unit before using them as templates to cut your chosen facing material.

With the doors faced and edged as required, place them in the unit once more and mark off the hinge positions against the nosing and the door edges.

Screw the hinges to the doors first, then hang the doors against the side panels. When both doors close perfectly—you may have to modify the depths of some of the rebates first—fit the magnetic catches so they close flush with the kickboard edge.

Cut the adjustable shelves to size, notching the rear corners to clear the fixing battens as before.

Having checked that the shelves fit properly, screw in the shelf supports where indicated in the diagram on page 424 and lay them in position.

Now position the top and mark through the fixing battens into the wall. Drill and plug the wall to take the appropriate fixings.

Screw the battens firmly to the wall and pin through the top into the side panels. Finally, glue the top facing in place.

BATH PANEL AND STORAGE

One place that is almost always short on storage is the bathroom—and yet the annoying thing is that usable space is often wasted. A common example is a gap between the end of the bath and the wall. This project shows you how to get the most out of it by installing a removable drawer. It also shows you how to panel in your bath so that you give your bathroom a new, streamlined look together with valuable extra storage space.

The drawer runs on wheels—like a trolley—and is made from melamine, so it's easy to clean and there is no complicated carpentry involved in making it. It is housed in a frame which is fixed to the walls and topped with a melamine board to add a handy shelf to the end of the bath.

The bath panel is made from decorative wall board braced with battens and held in place with magnetic catches—this makes the whole panel easy to remove to gain access to the plumbing.

The project can be adapted to suit many different bathroom layouts. And all is not lost if you don't have enough room to accommodate the storage drawer as well as the panelling—it's easy to adapt the design so you can just box the bath in neatly. But you must think ahead before you start.

Planning considerations

No two bathrooms are alike, so although the idea behind the design will remain constant, its dimensions will vary according to the size of your bathroom. The first thing to do is to take accurate measurements and from these make up your own working drawings—see diagram above. What you will need is a sketch similar to this but showing how the same features will fit into your space. It doesn't need to be very detailed, but it must show the dimensions.

Materials you need

You should be able to get all the materials from any large do-it-yourself store without any trouble.
- The bath panel and facing for the drawer are made from decorative wallboard—Laconite is a popular example. Wallboard is light and has a waterproof surface. It comes in a large range of textures and designs so you should be able to find a pattern you really like. The standard sheet size is 2240mm × 1120mm, which will be ample for the job.
- The drawer and top are made from 16mm white melamine made in different widths from 152mm to 914mm, usually in 2438mm and 1829mm lengths—calculate how much you need from your drawings.
- The edging strip for finishing off the drawer is 19mm wide and is bought by the roll—1800mm should be enough.
- The battening for making the panels and drawer frame is all 50mm × 25mm. Make sure that all the lengths are straight or you will end up with bent panels.
- The runner guides are made from 25mm × 25mm softwood.
- Plastic fixing blocks hold the whole drawer construction together—you will need at least 14. Screws are usually supplied with the fixing blocks when you buy them.
- The drawer wheels should not be more than 40mm in diameter. Fixed wheels are better than revolving castors. These should also be supplied with their own screws; but you may have to buy new ones since the

design requires 16mm chipboard screws.
- Magnetic catches hold the side panel in place. There are several types—get surface mounted ones, preferably with slotted screw holes which will make positioning them that much easier, so count up how many you need from your drawing.
- Corrugated fasteners hold the battens together to make up the panels—buy them in the 30mm size.
- Drawer handles come in lots of different shapes and sizes—the choice is yours. Make sure that your handle or knob can be fixed to melamine—some are attached with a long screw which may come through on the other side and snag your laundry.
- Contact adhesive is used to glue the wallboard to the side panel and front of the drawer. Either buy a large tube or a small tin to make sure you have enough. Spreaders are normally sold with the adhesive but if not, you can make your own by cutting notches in an off-cut of the wallboard.
- Additional materials you need are: 38mm No. 6 chipboard screws for the drawer base

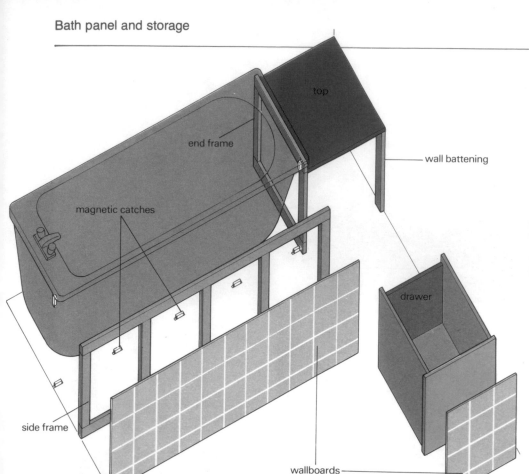

magnetic catches

end frame

top

wall battening

side frame

drawer

wallboards

1 *Measure the frame templates directly from the bath, fitting them underneath the rim of the bath*

2 *Assemble the frames with corrugated fasteners, and then check that the frames are square*

A batten framework fits round the bath. The side frame is held by magnetic catches so it can be removed, and is panelled with wallboard. The end frame supports a top shelf over the drawer

and 50mm No. 8 screws and plugs to fix the battening to the walls (your choice of plug will depend on what type of wall you are screwing into—masonry plugs for a brick wall, cavity plugs for a timber framed wall), 38mm panel pins for attaching the runner guides and PVA wood glue for all the joints.

Tools you need

Most of the job can be carried out with standard carpentry equipment: panel saw, tape-measure, screwdriver, drill and bits, counter-sink, spirit level, trimming knife, hammer, straightedge and bradawl. The only special tool you need is an ordinary household iron to fix the melamine strip.

Panelling the bath

Start by making a frame from 50mm × 25mm softwood, ensuring that it fits accurately around the side and end. This can then be panelled in with wallboard.

Hold the lengths of your frame timber up to the side and end of your bath in turn so that they fit under the rim as shown in the diagram on page 429. Mark the wood off and use a panel saw to cut it to length. Use the two battens you have cut as patterns to make two more similar lengths in order to make the bottom of the frame.

To complete the frames you need a number of vertical struts—all the same length. To find out how long to make them, lay two of your frame lengths one on top of the other and cut a further piece to span the gap between them and the rim of the bath. You need to cut two strips of this length for the end plus a number for the side panel. Here, the vertical struts should be equally spaced not more than 40mm apart—but remember that it is better to insert an extra strut than to leave one out. If you intend to have a join between two panels of wallboard, make sure that you fit an extra strut where the extra join occurs.

To assemble the frames, lay all the pieces flat on the floor and make sure that all the corners are square. Hammer home the corrugated fasteners—two to each joint.

Hold the two completed frames up to the bath to make sure that they fit under it and against each other properly. Use a spirit level to check that they are vertical. Mark the position of the end frame on

the wall and on the floor, then remove both of the completed frames.

Screw two plastic fixing blocks to the back edge of the end frame and two to the bottom edge—all the blocks should be on the side towards the bath. Reposition the frame and mark through the holes in the blocks onto the wall. Drill the wall and insert wallplugs or cavity fixings as appropriate, then screw the frame in place.

The side frame is held up against the bath with magnets placed at each corner behind each strut. To find the positions of the magnets on the floor, wall and end frame, hold the panels up against the bath using a spirit level to check the vertical. Mark off the positions of the magnets, and their corresponding plates, then screw them in place on the frame.

Try the completed frame up against the

bath to check that it fits. Then lay it down on the wallboard to mark the panel for cutting. Lay it on the face of the board—this allows you to align the pattern. Mark up carefully, about 2mm oversize all round, and score the lines with a trimming knife and straightedge. Cut the board with a panel saw, supporting it firmly on both sides of the cut. Smooth the rough edges with glasspaper and a sanding block, then with a plane or planer file after fixing. This allows you to finish the edges to match the frame exactly by using the frame itself as your guide. It's the best way to get a really good fit.

To stick the wallboard to the brace, spread contact adhesive evenly on the bracing battens and onto the rough side of the wallboard. Leave both wallboard and battens until the adhesive is touch dry.

With the end frame in place, carry the

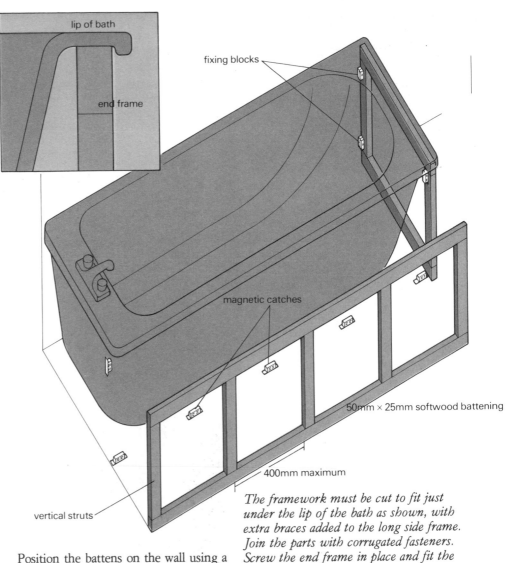

lip of bath

end frame

fixing blocks

magnetic catches

50mm × 25mm softwood battening

400mm maximum

vertical struts

The framework must be cut to fit just under the lip of the bath as shown, with extra braces added to the long side frame. Join the parts with corrugated fasteners. Screw the end frame in place and fit the side on magnetic catches

---

★ WATCH POINT ★

If you have a strong pattern on your wallboard—imitation tiles for example—cut it so that the pattern is complete along the top; it is best to keep cut patterns low down near the floor. Mark the board for 'top' and 'bottom'.

---

framing round onto the wall to support the top panel. Before fitting the top, you must position the runner guides for the drawer.

The drawing (overleaf) shows the general layout, but you will have to cut everything to fit your space accurately.

Start with the wall battens which support the top panel. Cut these from 50mm × 25mm softwood—the one on the end wall is the same length as the end frame; the upright and the one against the back wall should be cut to span the gaps remaining.

Position the battens on the wall using a spirit level to ensure that they are horizontal. When you do this, allow for the thickness of the melamine top above them—it must sit on the battens so that its top edge is just below the lip of the bath.

Mark the line of each batten on the wall, when the first batten is in place, then take

it away for drilling. You need 4.5mm countersunk holes every 300mm or so. Drill and plug corresponding holes in the wall, then screw the battens into place with 50mm No. 8 screws.

3 *Fit the end frame under the bath and screw it to the wall with plastic fixing blocks*

4 *Hold the side frame in place, check it is vertical and mark positions for the magnetic catches*

5 *Remove the frame, mark the dimensions on the wallboard panel and saw it to fit*

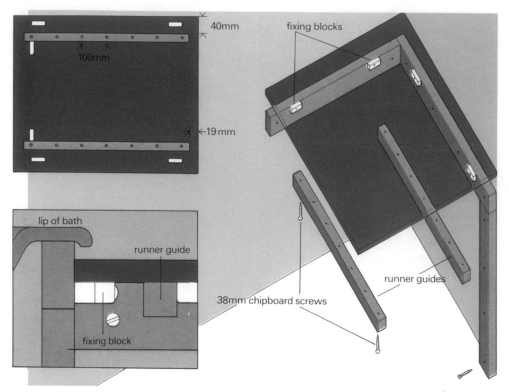

fixing blocks

40mm

100mm

19mm

lip of bath

runner guide

fixing block

runner guides

38mm chipboard screws

Fit the top onto the battens and mark their positions all round. Then remove the top and screw on plastic blocks—two on each side and two at the back to align with the battens. Replace the top and screw it firmly in position. Then screw the runners to it from underneath.

Making the drawer

The drawer is a simple box made from melamine and fitted with wheels. It's easy to make, but measure it accurately for a good fit in the space under the top.

Start with the front panel, which should be cut to fit the opening between the frame and wall batten at each side and between the top and floor—less about 3mm clearance all round. Once again, it's worth making a template to ensure that you get it right.

With this as a guide, you can make the other parts. Cut two sides, the same height as the front and the depth of the top less 50mm. Cut a back, 80mm narrower than the front and 30mm lower. Finally, cut a

The melamine top fits under the lip of the bath, fixed to wall battens with blocks. The drawer runners are screwed to the underside

To make the top, you need a piece of melamine which fits exactly on top of the battens and against the end frame. You can measure this up, but to ensure you get a good fit, it's worth making a template from hardboard or stiff card first. Cut the melamine out with a panel saw. Tape the cutting line to minimize the unsightly splintering of the surface that can happen when cutting laminates.

Before you fix the top in place, add the runners to its underside. They are made from 25mm × 25mm softwood, cut 50mm shorter than the depth of the top. Position them 21mm from the front edge of the panel and 45mm in from the edges. Make sure that they are parallel, then mark along them. Drill every 100mm or so and screw in 38mm No. 6 chipboard screws. Then remove the runners while you fix the top to the battens.

6 *Cut the wall battens to length, level them and screw to the wall at the right height*

7 *A card template cut to fit on the battens will help you to mark the melamine panel*

8 *Position the drawer runners under the top and screw them in place temporarily*

9 *Remove the runners and fix the top with blocks. Finally, refit the runners to the drawer*

★ WATCH POINT ★

Lay an offcut of the melamine on top of the batten when you hold it in place. This will ensure that you allow for the correct thickness.

The drawer consists of five pieces of melamine board and a batten framework. All the parts are cut to fit the space available, leaving the relevant clearances where necessary. The sides are joined to the front with block fixings, leaving a clearance at each side so they align with the runners. The back is fixed between them with a clearance above it for the runners. The batten subframe is screwed inside the main box; the triangles at the corners which support the castors are fixed to give 10mm clearance for the wheels. The base is simply dropped into place on the subframe. To trim the front, it is panelled with wallboard and edged all round with melamine strip

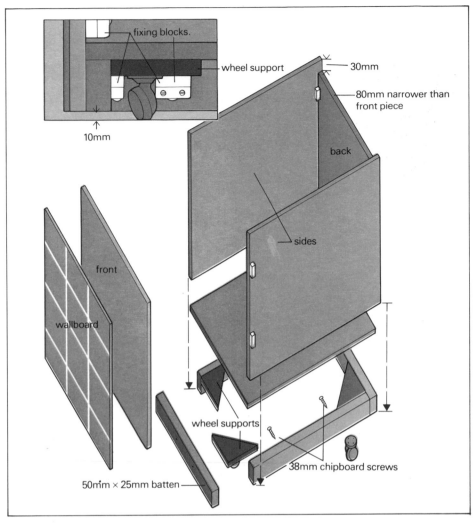

base, the same width as the back and the same length as the sides less 15mm.

To assemble it all, use plastic fixing blocks and battens. The drawing (right) shows how the parts fit together. Screw plastic fixing blocks to the outside of each side, one near the top, one near the bottom, then screw the sides to the front. To make sure they are the right distance apart, lay the back between them and centre it so that both sides are the same distance from the edge of the front panel.

Fit the back in place and secure it with two plastic blocks on each side, one near the top and one at least 75mm up from the bottom. Note that while the bottom edge of the back should be flush with the sides, the top edge is 30mm lower. This allows clearance for the runners above it.

Now cut four lengths of 50mm × 25mm batten to fit inside the drawer assembly as shown in the drawing. They don't need to be a perfect fit as they will be concealed from view. Drill and screw them to the melamine using 38mm No. 6 chipboard screws.

The four wheels on which the drawer runs are mounted on triangular plates which fit inside the corners of the frame. Make the triangular plates from some spare melamine; cut two 100mm squares, then saw them diagonally. Screw the fixing plates of the wheels onto each triangle, making sure that the wheels will have enough room to revolve freely inside the frame.

Line up each triangle inside a corner of the frame so that its wheel projects 10mm below the bottom of the frame. Screw the triangles into position with fixing blocks.

Drop the base inside so that it rests on battens and fix with plastic blocks.

Finally, face the front of the drawer with wallboard so that it matches the bath panel. To do this, cut out a piece of wallboard that slightly overlaps by about 2mm all round.

10 *Assemble the main frame with blocks then screw in the subframe*

Make sure that its pattern will match up with the one on the bath. Score the surface of the melamine with coarse sandpaper to help the glue to bond and then glue the wallboard to the melamine as when making the panel. When it is finally stuck, smooth down the edges of the wallboard with glasspaper or a planer file.

11 *Position the corner supports carefully so the castors project 10mm*

Finish off the edges of the drawer front with iron on edging strips. Lay the strip along the edges of the melamine and wallboard keeping it flush with the front. Protect the surface with brown paper and iron it on. Finish off all exposed edges in the same way. The last part of the project consists of fitting a handle to the drawer.

MAKE A BATH BAR

This bath bar will keep all your bathing paraphernalia just where it's needed and give order to the clutter that's probably already there. The bar is simply fixed to the wall alongside the bath.

Its design incorporates a clever wall fixing method which gives the unit the impression of having no means of support.

The shelves are actually fixed to battens screwed to the wall, but they're located within the thickness of the shelves for neatness. A normal, flat shelf would sag with the arrangement, but the vertical sections act as braces to stiffen the unit.

The bath bar is straightforward to make from plywood (for the shelves and uprights), ramin (for the wall battens) and stout dowelling (for the front trim). Two thicknesses of ply are stuck together to form the lightweight shelves—plus the hidden fixing method—and the surfaces are clad with plastic laminate in your choice of colour. This gives a smooth, waterproof, easy-clean surface—important in the steamy atmosphere of the bathroom. (If you want to use the unit in another room you may prefer to stain, varnish or paint the shelves instead of laminating them).

Materials and tools

Study the cutting diagram on page 433 to see just how the bar fits together. You can cut out all the plywood pieces you need from two 1220mm × 610mm sheets—one 12.5mm thick; the other 9mm thick.

In addition to the plywood you'll need the following:
- Enough sheets of 1.5mm thick laminate to face the top and underside of the shelves and also both sides of the uprights. Two 1220 × 610mm sheets should be sufficient, but if the colour choice isn't good in this size, you may have to buy a larger 2440mm × 1220mm sheet.
- 1 litre of contact adhesive (ideally the emulsion type) to stick down the laminate.
- A 3m length of 12.5mm square ramin (hardwood) for the shelf batten.
- A 3m length of 44mm diameter softwood dowelling for the front edge trim.
- Sufficient 19mm No. 8 countersunk wood-screws to fix the shelves to the battens.
- Sufficient 600 No. 8 countersunk wood-screws to attach the battens to the wall.
- Enough 19mm panel pins to fix the two halves of the shelves together.
- Enough 65mm panel pins to fix the dowel edging trim in place on the shelves.
- PVA adhesive to stick the plywood halves of the shelves together. To mark out, cut and assemble the bar, equip yourself with a try square, tape measure, long straightedge, jigsaw with adjustable sole plate, hammer, screwdriver and tenon saw. You'll also need an electric drill with 4.5mm and 2mm bits, a laminate cutter, trimming knife and fine file, plus a sliding bevel, smoothing plane or coping saw.

How the bar fits together

Each shelf of the bath bar is made from a strip of 12.5mm plywood bonded to a strip of 9mm plywood.

The thinner ply strip overlaps the thicker one at the back by 12.5mm; the ramin wall battens fit in the recess for a flush fitting. The vertical shelf components are made in the same way and the main battens are positioned on the 'shadow' or underside.

The shelves are fixed to the vertical

sections with mitre joints, reinforced with glue and screws.

The unit is intended to be fixed into a return wall at one end, although a mid-wall version can easily be made: it should simply be shorter in length to prevent sagging.

The entire shelf unit is faced with a plastic laminate of your choice, which is applied with contact adhesive.

The front edge of the bar is trimmed with stout 44mm diameter softwood dowelling, which is stained or varnished. The mitred corner joints are rounded off for neatness once the trim has been fixed in place.

Making the shelves

Each shelf is made up from two strips of plywood bonded together. The 12.5mm thick lower half is topped with a thinner 9mm strip, which overlaps at the back to take the wall fixing batten. It's best to cut the ply into strips and stick the two halves together before you cut each piece to the length of the shelf.

Mark out the 12.5mm thick plywood sheet in 137.5mm wide strips, using a tape measure and a long straightedge. Make sure the edges of the ply are sound and straight—any unevenness will make laminating awkward.

Place the sheet on a firm, flat surface—ideally a workbench—and cut out each strip, using a power jigsaw.

Mark out the 9mm thick sheet of plywood for the other shelf components. These strips should be 150mm wide to give the front-to-back dimension of the shelves (including an allowance for the overlap).

You can now stick the two halves of the shelves together, using PVA adhesive.

Lay the 137.5mm wide strips face down on a flat surface and apply a generous amount of PVA adhesive to their backs. Spread it out thinly with an offcut of card, making sure the edges are well-covered.

Position the 150mm wide strips on top and align the edges. Push the panels into a right-angled corner to make sure the edges align: you can make a simple frame from slim battens nailed together in a right-angle, or just use the corner of a room at the level of the skirting board.

Drive in 19mm panel pins to secure the strips together, working from the thin panel side. Space the pins at 50mm intervals, 10mm from each edge. Insert a row of pins down the centre of the strips.

Clamp all bonded strips together with

1 *Measure the ply into strips 137.5mm and 150mm wide and cut them out. Use a batten clamped to the workpiece*

2 *Temporarily pin a length of ramin to each 137.5mm strip. Glue the 150mm strip on top and cramp the two together*

3 *Use a sliding bevel to mark 45° angles on the edges to be mitre-jointed. They can then be cut with a jigsaw*

G-cramps—using battens to protect the ply from damage by the cramp jaws, and to distribute pressure. Set the strips aside for the glue to dry.

When the glue has dried, remove the cramps and mark off the bonded strips in shelf sections. Start at the ramin-edged end, labelling this for later identification.

Measure off the lengths of the shelves—two at 550mm, one at 525mm and one at 400mm—and draw lines across the ply against a try square.

The shelves are mitre-jointed to the uprights, so mark 45° angles on the edges of the strips, using a sliding bevel to set the angle. Continue the lines across the other face of the strips. Notice that the two end shelves are square-ended and the lowest 525mm long shelf is mitred inwards at each of its ends.

Cut out each shelf and label it, then mark out and cut the two short (125mm) and one long (250mm) uprights. Make sure you cut the mitres the correct way round, so that the fixing batten will be on the 'shadow' or underside of the shelf unit.

Sand smooth the cut edges of the shelves and uprights, but don't round them off or you'll find it difficult to fit the laminate accurately in position.

The 400mm long shelf has a cut-out to incorporate a towel rail, and you should cut this now. Measure 75mm in from the front

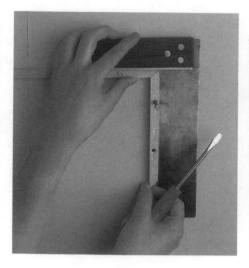

4 *Fix each horizontal and vertical batten to the wall, carefully aligning each mitre with your try square*

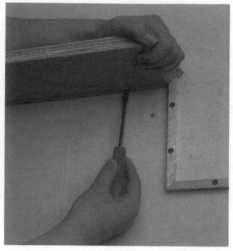

5 *After gluing the overlap and the adjacent edge of the shelf, hold it on its batten and secure the shelf with screws*

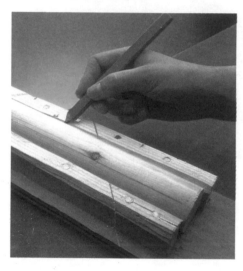

6 *Use your home-made jig to hold the dowel firmly in place while you mark the lines necessary to chamfer the flat*

7 *By fitting an end stop to your home-made jig you can also use it to plane off the chamfer on the dowelling*

edge and draw a line across against a straight edge. Measure 50mm in from each end and draw lines from front to back.

Cut out the recess using the jigsaw freehand—this tool is excellent for cutting around curves. But don't force the blade.

Fixing the shelves

The next part of the job is to assemble the shelves on the wall: all of the finishing—laminating and edging—can be carried out with the unit fixed in position. First you have to attach the wall battens.

To mark the positions of the horizontal shelves, first decide at what level you want the lowest, 525mm long shelf: for con-

venience ·this should be about 350mm above the rim of the bath.

Mark the wall at this point in pencil and continue the line at this height for the length of the bath, using a straightedge.

The overall depth of the unit is 300mm—the height of the deepest vertical. Measure up this distance from your first guideline, subtract 21.5mm to give the baseline of the shelves, then make a second line. Continue the line onto the return wall to indicate the end shelf batten position.

Now measure from the end wall in increments of 525mm, 400mm and two at 550mm—the length of the shelves. Measure 21.5mm back from the lines marking the shorter uprights and 21.5mm in the opposite direction from the long up-

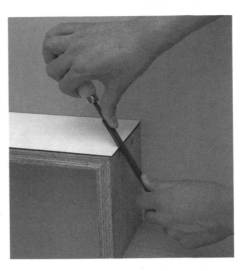

8 *When using your mitre box to cut mitres on the dowelling, use the saw carefully to avoid damaging the slots*

9 *As you position the laminate face panels, press down firmly with a cloth to bond them and eliminate air*

10 *Smooth the trimmed edges of the laminate face panels by quick strokes with a file or laminate trimmer*

right: this gives you the batten positions.

Prise off the ramin battens from the shelves—remember to label them first—and mark and drill 4.5mm clearance holes through their sides to take 35mm No. 8 screws. You'll need four holes per shelf, two per short upright and three per long upright. Space the holes about 70mm apart.

Mark and drill 4.5mm clearance holes to take 19mm No. 8 screws through the overlaps on the shelves—make sure they don't coincide with the holes drilled in the battens—then replace the battens temporarily. Drill 2mm pilot holes into the battens through the holes in the shelves. Countersink all holes by means of a hand countersinking bit.

Offer up the end wall batten to your pencil guidelines and check it for level by placing a spirit level on top. Mark the fixing positions on the wall through the screw holes, then drill the wall and insert wallplugs. Return the batten to the wall and attach with screws.

If your wall is a hollow partition, you'll have to align the vertical battens with a stud: simply screw them to the timber. Attach the shelf battens using screws and special hollow wall fixings.

Fix the other battens along on the long wall in the same way, making sure the mitres are aligned. Check the level of each batten with your spirit level.

As soon as you've fixed the battens to the wall you can attach the shelves, using PVA glue and screws for a firm fitting.

Take each shelf in turn and apply adhesive to the overlap and its adjacent ply edge. Position the shelf on its batten and secure by driving 19mm screws through

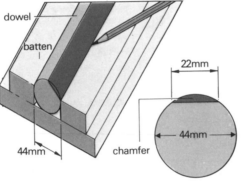

A home-made jig with battens nailed to a softwood base is a useful way of holding the dowel to mark the chamfer

the top into the battens (locating in your pre-drilled pilot holes). Screw the verticals in place in the same way, and check that all mitre joints are fitting accurately.

When all the shelves are fixed, drill pilot holes through the mitres and add screws for extra strength. Check that all screw heads are recessed below the plywood components before fitting the laminate.

Fitting the dowel trim

44mm diameter softwood dowelling is fixed to the front edge of the bath bar with glue and pins. The corners are mitred for neatness and the back edge planed flat to fit against the shelves.

Dowelling isn't easy to mark out and cut unless you have a holder to grip it firmly. You can make a jig from a 600mm long piece of 150mm × 25mm softwood with two 38mm × 25mm battens screwed along

its length, spaced 44mm apart.

Slip the dowel into the channel—it should be a snug push-fit—and use a pencil to mark the chamfer. Draw a line down one side of the dowel against the batten. Continue this line across the end of the dowel, 22mm from the top, and where this line meets the opposite side of the dowel mark a second line down its length against the second batten.

You can either remove the chamfer with a coping saw (holding the dowel carefully in a vice) or with a smoothing plane. If you use a plane to chamfer the dowel, fit your jig with an end stop, clamp the device in a vice and use it as a holder while you plane.

Mark out the length of the trims from the shelf lengths. Aim to cut as many lengths as you can from a single length of dowelling, and remember to label each piece so you know where it fits on the bar.

Use a mitre box or a vice to cut the dowel to length, but be sure to wedge the trim in place while you saw. Make the cuts with a fine-toothed tenon saw.

To make the mitres, simply place the chamfered edge of the dowel against the front edge of the appropriate shelf and mark off the angle on the dowel to correspond with that on the shelf. Then cut the mitres in a mitre box using a tenon saw. Take care to make the cuts at precisely 45°.

Fit each length of dowel trim to the edge of the shelves using PVA adhesive and 65mm pins. Allow the glue to dry, then fractionally round off the corners with medium- followed by fine-grade glasspaper to give a smooth finish. Finally seal the bare wood with stain and polyurethane varnish. or just varnish in gloss or matt finish.

FOLDING DOOR WARDROBE

After the kitchen, your bedroom wardrobe is probably the most important piece of fitted furniture in your home. So any savings you can make are well worth while; even more so if you can improve on what's in the shops.

The clever part about this design is the doors. They look like traditional panelled doors, but where these require a good deal of space to hinge open, the doors on this design need hardly any. The trick is that they are hinged to fold in the middle and then slide aside; so that they only need half the opening space of conventional doors.

If this sounds complicated to make, don't worry. Each panel is just a sheet of melamine board, and they're hinged together along their length with piano hinges—so there's no cutting in of the hinges to do.

There's nothing special about the slider mechanism either; it's just a length of aluminium channelling and a guide pin fitted to the edge of the door. You add the panelled effect later using standard lengths of wooden or plastic moulding—you can add as much or as little as you like.

The space saving ideas don't stop there. Inside the wardrobe there's a special make-up tray, so it will double as a dressing table, too. And so you've room to sit comfortably at it, it pulls out of the cupboard on extending runners then packs neatly away inside when it's not needed.

Inside the wardrobe, the space can be adapted to your needs—whether these are for shelving or hanging space. The shelves are so simple to fit that you can put them anywhere you wish.

Fitting your bedroom space

The wardrobe shown here is fitted into a convenient alcove, thus saving as much space as possible. It's by no means essential to do this; and if you don't have a suitable recess you can fit it against a corner or even in the middle of a wall. When you're working out where to put it, bear in mind that the cupboard depth is just over 650mm and that you need a further 450mm to open the doors.

The width of the wardrobe shown here is 1,855mm, but it is easily altered to suit the width of an existing alcove. The only critical point is that you need to divide the space between four door panels—and it's much simpler and cheaper if these are close to

standard widths of melamine board. It's inadvisable to make the individual door panels much wider than 450mm; if you want a wardrobe wider than that shown it's better to construct a whole new section with a third or even a fourth pair of door panels.

The height of the cupboard is easily adapted to suit your ceiling by the length to which you cut the uprights and the door panels. Its maximum is the length of a standard melamine panel—2,440mm. If your ceiling is higher than this, you need to fit a top panel as well.

Parts you need

Some of these are standard, but most are dependent on the size of the wardrobe you make; so first measure the width of the

space you want to fit. The following check-list assumes that you do not want to make a wardrobe wider than about 1,800mm which can be spanned by two pairs of doors and with one central divider. If you do want to exceed this, you need to count the extra.

For the main assembly you need:
• Two sides and one divider. These are standard 2,440mm × 600mm melamine panels.
• A top rail. This is 150mm × 50mm softwood cut to a little less than the finished width.
• A base plinth. This is 75mm × 50mm softwood also a little less than the full width.
• The upright door jambs. These extend the two side panels and support the doors. Cut from 50mm × 50mm softwood the height of the wardrobe.
• Four door panels. These are cut from

2,440mm melamine panels. To work out the width of each, subtract 110mm from the total width of the wardrobe and divide by four. If you have long saw cuts to make, it's worth asking your timber merchant to prepare these boards to the width you want.

To complete the main assembly you need four piano hinges to match the lengths of the door panels—or shorter lengths to make up to this—plus chipboard screws to suit. You need two pieces of aluminium channel the width of the wardrobe and with a 9mm groove, plus 15mm No. 6 countersunk woodscrews to fix it at 150mm intervals. To fix the parts to each other and to the wall you need 75mm and 50mm No. 8 countersunk screws, plus wallplugs or cavity fixings. You also need about 100mm of 6mm dowelling and various scraps of timber for packing pieces.

The following interior fittings can be added once the main frame is in place.
• For an extra vertical divider you need its height cut from 600mm melamine board.

The structure of the wardrobe is really divided into two main assemblies—the framework and doors (red and blue) and the interior fittings (grey).

The main frame starts with two melamine side panels. These are screwed to the walls on either side, with packing pieces where necessary to keep them vertical. If the wardrobe is not fitted between two walls, then the end panels are screwed to the wall behind, the floor and the ceiling.

The main front frame comprising a top and bottom rail, plus two side uprights is then fixed in front of these panels. The front rails carry the door channels.

A further upright panel is fixed in the centre of the rails to divide the wardrobe.

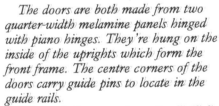

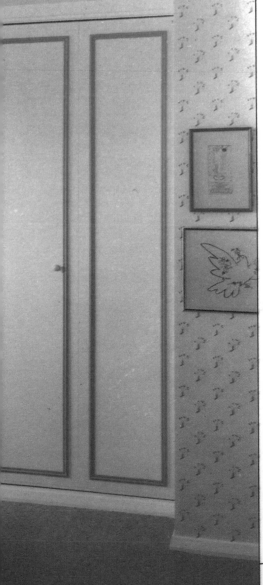

The doors are both made from two quarter-width melamine panels hinged with piano hinges. They're hung on the inside of the uprights which form the front frame. The centre corners of the doors carry guide pins to locate in the guide rails.

The main framework can be divided up as you wish by adding shelves on battens and further uprights between shelves. The sliding make-up tray is made much like a shelf. But instead of permanent fixing, it is screwed to extending drawer runners. Hanging space is made by simply placing a wardrobe rail between uprights or under a shelf.

• Per shelf, you need its width cut from 600mm wide melamine board. To fix it you need two 575mm lengths of 25mm × 25mm softwood; to lip it you need its width in 50mm × 25mm softwood. Don't forget to count the baseboard as extra lengths of shelving—without any lipping.
• The make-up tray needs an extra piece of 600mm melamine—just less than the total span between uprights—plus two 600mm lengths of 50mm × 25mm softwood and two further lengths for lipping.

To assemble these you need 25mm and 15mm No. 6 chipboard screws. For the make-up tray you need a pair of metal or plastic extending drawer runners. For a hanging space you need a suitable length of wardrobe tube plus appropriate end or centre brackets.

Finally to finish off the wardrobe you may wish to use a coping at ceiling level and a skirting moulding along the floor. To trim the door panels buy either ready-made door trims (plastic or wood) or lengths of panel moulding. All these can be fixed with woodworking adhesive and panel pins or alternatively, with contact adhesive.

The melamine needs no finishing at all. You must cover any cut edges, however, with iron-on edging strip. Wooden parts need to be primed, then painted to match.

Assembling the main carcase

Start by fitting the two end panels and the main front frame. These give the wardrobe its shape, so get them square to make the rest of the assembly simple.

If your ceiling height is less than the length of a standard melamine board, cut the side panels to this length first. If you're fitting them over an existing skirting board, you have the option of removing this or cutting back the melamine to fit over it.

Try the panels in place for fit. Push them back firmly against the wall and use a spirit level to check that they are upright. It's not likely that they will fit perfectly first go, so mark them and trim as necessary. You may need to trim the base to fit an uneven floor —alternatively use small packing pieces. If the gaps at the back are only slight, ignore them and just set the boards a bit further forward. If you don't get them square, it will lead to problems in fitting the shelves later.

When you are satisfied with the fit of the panels, remove them to drill fixing holes. If you are fitting them into a deep recess, use a 4.5mm drill to drill clearance holes and countersink them on the inside. If the walls are masonry, put holes at about 600mm intervals—if they're timber framed partition walls, drill to coincide with the positions of the studs. If you're making a free standing wardrobe so that the side panels project, you need to fix the back edge of the panels to the walls—and their ends to the floor and ceiling—using either metal angle brackets or plastic corner blocks. Drill the edges and screw these in place using the appropriate screws. Fit the brackets at a suit-

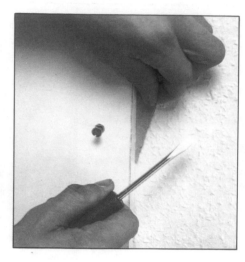

1 *Cut the side panel to size, then drill and screw to walls. Check they are vertical and pack out gaps to avoid distortion*

able height to screw into the timber frame members if the wall is hollow—otherwise you need to use cavity wall fixings.

Replace the side panels in their exact positions and mark the wall for drilling. Remove them again and drill with a 6mm masonry drill or a 2.5mm twist bit for stud walls.

Fit the side panels back and screw them in place with 50mm No. 8 screws—you need to fit wallplugs into the holes in masonry walls. Tighten the screws gradually. If there are gaps behind the panel when it is square and upright, then these may need packing out. Thin slips of hardboard make ideal packing for small gaps. Don't worry about very small gaps, just tighten the screws so that while they hold the panel firmly, they don't distort it.

You can now fit the main front frame. Start with the two uprights which are fitted at each side of the wardrobe. Cut them from 25mm × 25mm softwood. Make them the

full height of the side panels.

Cut the top rail from your 150mm × 50mm timber to the full width of the wardrobe less the thickness of the two uprights together. And cut the base plinth to this width from 75mm × 25mm timber.

★ WATCH POINT ★

To ensure the frame will go in place smoothly, it's best to make it slightly shorter than the full height of the room. It can then be fitted perfectly square by using packing pieces concealed under the rails.

You can fix the top and base rails directly to the floor and ceiling. If you're building into an alcove, the sides can be fixed to the walls; but if they project forward you only have the side of the melamine board as a fixing. So for maximum strength and to keep it square, make up the front frame as a complete assembly, with the corners joined together.

Lay the parts down together on the floor and line them up so that the corners are perfectly square. Drill 4.5mm clearance holes in the uprights and 2mm pilot holes in the rails. Counterbore the clearance holes slightly using a larger diameter bit, then glue and screw them together with PVA woodworker's glue and 75mm No. 8 countersunk screws. Brace the frame square with a batten nailed diagonally across it.

Try the frame in place. Use a spirit level to check its alignment and pack out any gaps to hold it in place. Check that it's square, mark its position, then remove it for drilling.

You can fix it using metal or plastic brackets and screws. But it's just as easy— and neater—to screw through it directly.

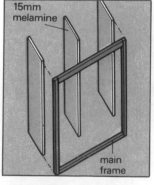

The main frame fits in front of the side panels and any similar matching dividers

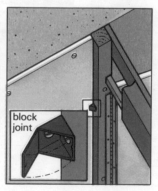

Screw the main frame to walls, ceiling and floor (where possible). If not . . .

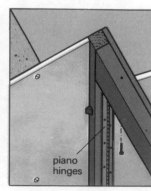

. . . block joints will suffice to hold the frame against the melamine panels

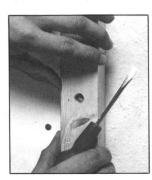

2 *Cut the frame members to length—use a fine-toothed saw and check for square*

3 *Drill and counterbore 4.5mm clearance in the uprights and attach rails*

4 *Wherever possible, screw the main frame to walls, ceiling and floor*

But because the timbers are so thick you would need to use very long screws. To avoid this, make counterbored screwholes using a wider diameter drill bit. Then replace the frame and mark the hole positions with a long nail or similar. Remove the frame to drill fixing holes then plug and secure.

On a projecting end, screw the upright to the edge of the melamine panel as well—either directly or by using plastic blocks on the inside.

Finish off the frame at floor and ceiling level by pinning on a skirting and coving. Use any moulding appropriate to the style of the room and the size of the rails. Prime and paint the bare wood at this stage as it's easier than after the interior fittings are in place.

Fitting out the interior

Whatever interior layout you decide upon, the shelves and dividers are all fitted in the same way, using battens as supports.

The first thing to fit is the central vertical divider. Measure and mark its position on the floor and wall.

The divider is fixed by four shelves, two on either side. Those near the base form a false bottom to the cupboard, while at the top they form a large storage compartment.

Cut the shelves from 600mm melamine. to work out the length required, measure the inside width, deduct the thickness of the divider and cut the remaining piece in half.

Make the support battens from 25mm × 25mm softwood. Screw two 575mm lengths to one side of the divider, flush with its back edge and square across it. Put one with its top edge 60mm up from the bottom edge of the divider, the other at whatever height you want to the top shelf to be. Turn the board over and screw two more pieces exactly on the other side of the melamine.

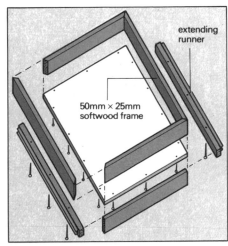

The pull-out tray is made from melamine and fitted with extending runners

extending runner

50mm × 25mm softwood frame

Stand the board in place and mark the height of the top edges of the battens onto the wall and transfer them onto the melamine panels at each end. Screw further 575mm lengths to the end panels and more pieces to the walls to clear the central divider. Screw similar pieces inside the base rail.

With the divider in place, drop the shelves onto the battens to lock it firmly.

Screw the top shelves to the battens, but don't fix the bottom shelves yet if you intend to include any further vertical dividers. If the top of the dividers needs to be fixed, use a bracket or block to screw it to the top rail.

Further shelves can be added wherever you like by supporting them on battens between the divider and end panels. If you want further vertical dividers, lift out the appropriate base panel and cut out a 15mm 'slice' at the point concerned. Then screw support battens to the divider and proceed as before. You may have to cut notches out of this divider to clear battens already in place.

The make-up tray is fitted on two extending drawer runners. Screw these to the panels on each side, making sure they're square and at the same height. Cut a piece of 600mm melamine to fit between them and screw it to the extension rail on each side. Check that it runs freely, then remove it.

Cut four pieces of 50mm × 25mm softwood the same lengths as the edges of the melamine and mitre their corners to form a frame which fits on top. Pin and glue this in place. Cut a further piece the same length as the front edge and fix this underneath to form a fascia and a finger pull. Refix the melamine.

Pin and glue 50mm × 25mm fascia pieces under all the shelves to stiffen and trim them.

Fit a clothes rail by screwing its supports to the inside of the side panels and divider, or under the shelf, whichever is appropriate to the type you buy.

Fitting the doors

Making the doors is simplicity itself. Hanging them should present no problems providing you took care to get the frame square so that they run true. You'll find an

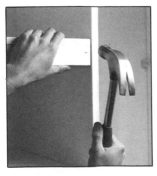

5 *You can fit shelves at any height—draw square lines and attach bearers*

6 *Cut the shelf to fit, and drop on to the bearer—screw down firmly in place*

7 *Pin and glue a softwood fascia on to the ends of each set of bearers*

8 *For the pull-out tray you need a pair of extending metal runners. Fix squarely inside the carcase; fix the inner part to the tray itself*

9 *Screw the wardrobe rail between adjacent panels or to the underside of a shelf*

assistant very useful when you have to fit the doors in place and for holding them steady.

Start by fixing the aluminium channel in place. Cut the two strips to length with a hacksaw so that they fit exactly between the uprights on each side of the frame. Then drill the base of the channels at 150mm intervals using a 4mm twist drill. Countersink the holes on the inside.

Screw the channel to the top and bottom rails about 3mm back from their front edges using 15mm No. 6 screws.

Now measure the exact distance between the top of the lower channel and the bottom of the upper channel. Deduct 6mm from this figure to give you the height of the doors—allowing for an opening clearance. To get their width, measure the distance between the inside faces of the side uprights. Deduct 20mm for clearance and divide by four to get the width of each door panel.

Cut the doors from the nearest available standard size of melamine panel. If you don't have a power saw it may well be worth paying extra to get the timber merchant to cut to the size you need from a large sheet rather than make long cuts by hand.

Edge each panel with iron-on edging strip and trim this off neatly when set. It's not essential to edge the top and bottom of the doors as these won't be seen.

Lay the panels down in pairs one beside the other and align the long edges. Lay a piano hinge along the panels and cut it to the full length of the doors. You can use two shorter lengths and leave a gap if you can't get the exact length. Align the spine of the hinge with the joint between the boards then screw the hinge to the edges of both sheets of melamine using 12mm chipboard screws.

This will give you the two folding doors. Stand them up and check the operation of the hinges. Now take further lengths of piano hinge and screw these to the outer edges of the two doors using 15mm screws.

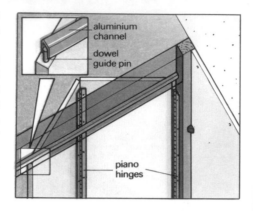

Fit piano hinges in a concertina fashion. Dowel guide pins keep them on line

The spines of the hinges must be aligned exactly down the edge of the board and facing the opposite side to that on which the first hinge was fitted. This will allow the proper 'concertina' action of the folding doors.

On the two corners of the door which don't have hinges fitted, you need to fit guides to engage the track. 15mm in from the ends of the board and in the centre of the thickness of the melamine, drill deep 6mm holes. Cut lengths of 6mm dowel and insert them into the holes. Saw them off to leave about 8mm projecting which will engage in the track and guide the door as it opens and closes.

With an assistant's help, stand the doors upright against the end of the wardrobe. Align the spines of the piano hinges with the front edges of the uprights at each side, then screw the hinges to their inner faces while holding the doors open.

Check the operation and fit of the doors. When all is well add the remaining screws.

Finishing the doors

You don't need to fit any catches, but you do need a doorpull on each side. Use any type you like, but put them near to the fold line between the panels.

For a decorative finish, make use of panel mouldings—either the plastic type sold specifically for bedroom furniture, or ordinary wooden mouldings. Mitre the corners of these neatly and paint them to match other furnishings in the room. Glue in place with adhesive plus panel pins.

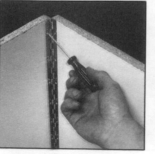

10 *Join doors with piano hinges and fit dowel pins*

11 *Screw aluminium channels to cross rails of the frame*

12 *Hang the doors and engage the dowel guide pins*

FITTED WARDROBE SYSTEM

Built-in furniture is an ideal way to make the best use of space—and a well planned, well made unit can add to the value of your home. But shop-bought systems can work out to be a very expensive buy—and do-it-yourself wardrobes often need a lot of planning, construction and juggling to fit the space that is available.

As far as possible, this wardrobe system combines the best of both worlds. It's based on a simple—but sturdy—framework of melamine boards and softwood battens and—to cut planning down to a minimum—it's mainly built out of modular parts with only one section used to match it to the width of the room. To keep construction as simple as possible it's largely made from standard size materials—so not much cutting. And to keep costs low the number of components for the framework, the doors and fittings is kept to a minimum.

There shouldn't be any problems fitting it to your bedroom. It's width can be whatever you want—and at 2.3m its height is low enough to suit almost any ceiling. All you need is a wall free of major obstructions.

Any wardrobe's appearance depends mainly on its doors, and with this system you have a choice—fit standard sized ready-made cupboard doors or build your own.

Planning considerations

Although planning is kept to a minimum, check the options before you start, and get to know how the system fits together. Then you can tailor a unit to fit your room—and your needs—perfectly. The diagram on page 442 gives details of the wardrobe's main construction.

The system has three basic components which you can mix and match to suit yourself—the unit shown in the photograph uses four of them:
- **The hanging wardrobe** is fitted with a rail and has plenty of space for a variety of clothes plus extra storage below.
- **The two-door storage wardrobe** uses the same basic shell fitted out with shelves for folded clothes and linen.
- **The matching dressing table** has a drawer for storing make up, jewellery and other small items.

Above each unit is a roomy storage cupboard for bed linen, blankets or items you don't use very often, such as suitcases.

And it needn't stop there. There are also designs for an easy-to-make set of shelves to make more use of the hanging wardrobe—plus ideas for fitting out the interior of the storage wardrobe.

You can put all these units together however you want, but it depends on your space. So start by measuring the width of the wall. It will help to draw a simple sketch plan. Each of the wardrobe units is 630mm wide, so you can easily work out how many will fit your wall space.

It's virtually certain that a whole number of units won't span the wall exactly, so to adjust the width you have two options. The first is that the dressing table is of variable width—anything from 500 to 1500mm. This should cover the majority of situations. But if you are left with an awkward small gap to span—usually running along the top of the wardrobe, or at the sides—you can fill this as described on page 445.

The height of the system should be suitable for most ceilings. But in a room with a higher ceiling you can span a small gap with a filling panel or alternatively cover in the top (see page 445).

Based on this information you should be able to refine your sketch to show where each unit fits and the width of the dressing table plus any infill panels. From the sketch you can then work out what materials—and their precise quantities—you need.

Materials you need

What to buy depends on the size of your room and choice of units. But as most of the components are standardized it shouldn't be difficult to work out what you need by looking at your sketch plan and checking off the parts against the list below. Note that this covers the main structure of the wardrobe's framework only—interior fittings are detailed on page 446.

Check which of these parts you need:
- **Plinth frame:** This is all made from 50mm × 25mm softwood. Buy enough to span your room twice plus 475mm for every 600mm width of the unit.
- **Plinth base:** This is made from 600mm wide 15mm melamine faced chipboard. You need a total length to span the whole room.
- **Wall battens:** You need two 2235mm lengths of 50mm × 50mm softwood plus 2235mm of 25mm × 25mm softwood per upright panel.
- **Upright panels:** Each of these is 2235mm long and can be cut from a 2440mm × 525mm panel of 15mm melamine faced chipboard.
- **Shelves:** These are cut from 525mm wide 15mm melamine. Against a wall they are 620mm long; between two uprights they are 600mm long. The shelf above the

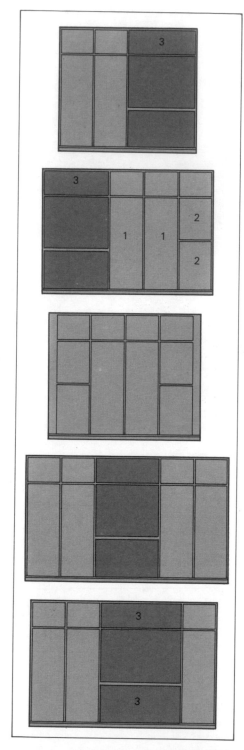

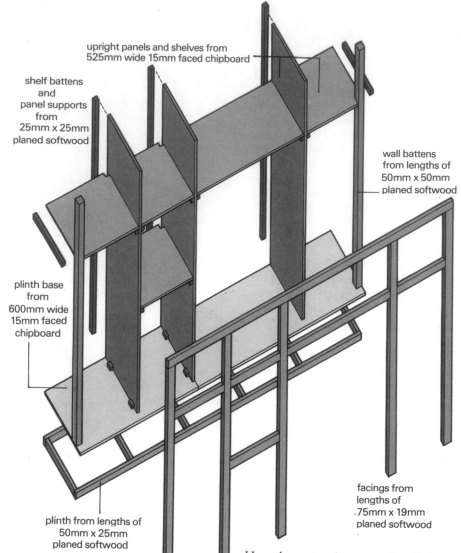

upright panels and shelves from 525mm wide 15mm faced chipboard

shelf battens and panel supports from 25mm x 25mm planed softwood

wall battens from lengths of 50mm x 50mm planed softwood

plinth base from 600mm wide 15mm faced chipboard

plinth from lengths of 50mm x 25mm planed softwood

facings from lengths of 75mm x 19mm planed softwood

Careful choice of hanging wardrobes (1), storage wardrobes (2), and variable sections (3) will fit the system into almost any room

dressing table depends on your room.
• **Shelf battens:** These are 25mm × 25mm softwood. You need a total length of about 1100mm per shelf.
• **Dressing table:** Cut two lengths of 525 mm melamine depending on your room.

• **Top board:** Cut to span your room from 75mm × 19mm softwood.
• **Shelf-facing:** Cut from 75mm × 19mm softwood, 150mm less than the room width.
• **Wall batten facings:** These are 2160mm long from 75mm × 19mm softwood.
• **Upright facings:** These are in two lengths—485mm and 1675mm, both from 75mm × 19mm softwood.

To hold everything together you need glue, nails, screws and plastic block joints. Once again the quantities are variable, but it's worth buying by the box. Get 75mm and 50mm No. 8 screws and 38mm and 25mm No. 6 chipboard screws. Buy ½kg of 50mm oval nails and ½kg of 38mm panel pins. A small bottle of PVA wood-working adhesive is more than sufficient for this job. For wall fixings buy either plastic

How the system is arranged: to fit into irregularly shaped rooms, the wardrobe system isn't fixed directly to the walls. Instead it stands on a plinth on the floor and between battens fitted to the walls. By fitting these carefully to the irregularities of the room and ensuring that their outer faces are perfectly square, you can standardize the wardrobes.

The wardrobe construction could hardly be simpler. The sides are panels of melamine-faced chipboard screwed to the plinths and fixed back to the wall with 25mm battens. Shelves in the same material are added on battens fixed to the sides.

All the front edges are trimmed with pine boards. These serve two functions—they stiffen the structure and make it easier to fit doors.

The dressing table is essentially a sturdier version of the shelves in the units. The cupboard above is of similar construction to the top of the wardrobes—only the door fitting differs

wallplugs or cavity fixings, depending on your walls. Block joints are quite cheap so buy a few extra.

Building the plinth

The first step in construction is to build and level the plinth on which the wardrobe units are going to stand. Before you start, roll the carpet back well out of the way. If it is held by carpet grippers, prise these away along the wall and out for a distance of 600mm on the side walls. When you have finished, the carpet can be rolled back again and cut to fit along the plinth.

The plinth consists of a framework of 50mm × 25mm softwood, glued and nailed together, with a sheet of 675mm wide melamine faced chipboard on top and slightly overlapping the frame at the front.

The sheet of melamine and the front and back battens must span the whole room between the skirting boards at either side. Although this should not be a problem with the softwood, in a large room you will not be able to do this with one piece of melamine—there must be a joint somewhere. If you can, arrange this where it will be least noticeable. If you haven't ordered your wood cut to length, do so at this particular stage.

Construct the frame first. Lay the front and back battens out on the floor. To separate them you need a number of cross bars 475mm long—one for each end, plus one every 600mm. Cut all of these from one pattern, so you know that each batten is identical.

Assemble the ends first. Apply woodworking glue to the ends of the framework's cross bars and nail them with two 50mm nails at each corner.

Check that the frame is reasonably square. If it isn't, it should be simple to push it back into shape at this stage. Now glue and nail it to the cross bars.

When the frame is ready, lay it in position about 50mm from the back wall. Lay the melamine board on top. It helps if you cut it fractionally short. Don't worry at this stage how well the back fits.

The plinth provides the whole basis for the construction, so it's essential that it is flat and level. Hold a spirit level on top of the melamine—on both directions. Adjust with packing pieces slipped beneath or by shaving the bottom of the plinth frame to fit the floor (see Scribing to fit). When you are satisfied that the plinth is flat, screw the frame down using plastic block joints.

Now replace the melamine board. If it

1 *Cut the pieces to length, then nail and glue the corners of the plinth frame together*

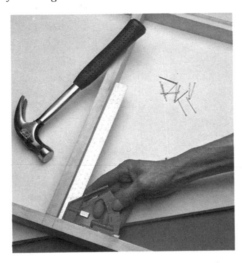

2 *Check everything is square and add further braces at intervals of about 600mm, nailing and gluing in place*

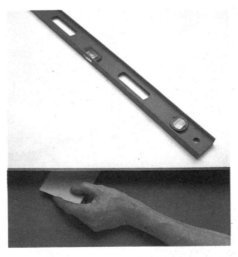

3 *Lay the melamine plinth top and check level. Adjust by packing or shaving the base*

doesn't fit snugly, scribe it to the irregularities of the wall. When the boards fit properly, drill 4mm holes through them

★ WATCH POINT ★

To prevent the wood splitting, stagger the nails so that they aren't both going into the same grain line. It also helps to blunt the points by tapping each a couple of times with a hammer.

and into the frame below at roughly 250mm intervals. Countersink all the holes, then screw the boards down with 25mm No. 6 chipboard screws.

Putting up the wall battens

With the plinths providing a level platform for the structure, it's time to fit the side battens. These must establish true verticals for the wardrobe units to fit against.

Both of these battens are 2235mm long made from 50mm × 50mm softwood. They fit onto the side walls of the structure, so that their front edges are 525mm out from the corners of the room.

Stand each one in turn against the wall with its base on the plinth. The skirting will probably prevent the bottom of the batten from fitting back against the wall—so you will have to notch it out. Mark the width and height of the notch on the wood, then saw it out with two cuts of a tenon saw.

Use a spirit level to check that the batten is vertical, both sideways and front to back.

4 *Make sure the battens are vertical, checking both front to back and side to side*

Look for gaps behind the batten too. If the wall is at all uneven or out of square, the batten has to be scribed to fit against it properly before fixing (see Scribing to fit). Then, line the batten up again and double-check that it is truly vertical.

Drill fixing holes at intervals of about 300mm, starting near the bottom and using a 4.5mm drill bit. Countersink each hole in turn. Hold the batten up and mark through each hole.

In a masonry wall drill 6mm holes at each point and insert plastic wallplugs. In a cavity wall drill 6mm holes and insert cavity fixings—unless you are lucky enough to coincide with a stud position, in which case you can screw directly to it. Screw the battens firmly in place using a quantity of 75mm No. 8 screws.

Putting up the wardrobe sides

Each of these is 2235mm length cut from a 2440mm × 525mm sheet of 15mm melamine faced chipboard. They are fixed to the plinth with simple plastic block joints and to the wall with battens.

Mark the position of each one on the plinth. Those adjacent to the side walls are set with their closest face 620mm away from it. Those in the centre of the unit are set with their faces 600mm apart. .

Stand each panel in turn in position. Use a spirit level to check that it is upright and try it back against the wall for fit. If, as is probable, the wall is uneven, you will have to scribe the back edge to match it (see Scribing to fit). Use a plane or planer file to trim the melamine, then double-check that it fits. Mark each one with a letter so that you can fit it back in the correct position. Draw a line on the wall to show where each panel fits.

Next, screw support battens to the back wall along the lines you have marked. Cut them 2235mm long from 25mm × 25mm softwood, and fix them with 50mm No. 8 screws and wallplugs.

Drill fixing holes along the back edges of the panels to attach them to the battens. Use a 4mm drill bit and set them 15mm from the edge. Countersink all the holes for neatness.

It's easiest if you attach shelf support battens before you screw the sides in place. Refer to the construction plan on page 442 and to your own sketch plan to see where these are required. The main ones are for the division of the top cupboard; these are set 590mm down from the top of the

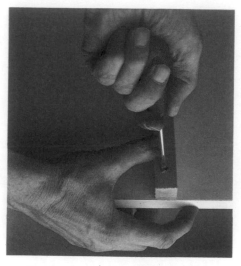

5 *Fix the shelf support battens in place, taking care to get them square*

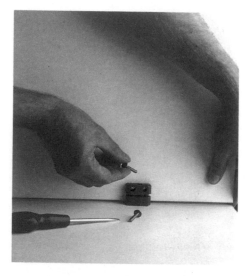

6 *Drill screw holes along the back edge, ready for fixing it to the wall batten*

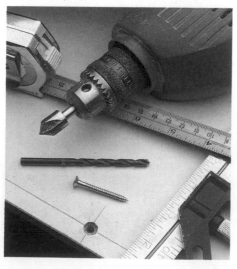

7 *When fixing panels direct, use chipboard screws; countersink the heads*

panels. The divider for the storage wardrobe is set 900mm up from the plinth. Other shelf positions are optional.

All the battens are made from 25mm × 25mm softwood in 500mm lengths. Mark their positions carefully using a try square to make sure they are set squarely across the boards—and mark the boards at each side of a shelf together so that you are absolutely sure both supports are at the same height. The battens must be aligned with the front edge of the panels, not the back.

Screw the battens to the boards with 38mm No. 6 chipboard screws every 150mm or so. Spread a little PVA adhesive on the back of each of the battens for an even firmer fixing.

Now screw the block joints along the base of each of the side panels, flush with the edge. Set two block joints on each, 150mm from the corners.

Stand the panels back up in place—ideally get a helper to hold them upright for you—and mark the positions of the holes in the block joints and along the back edge. If you use a bradawl it should save drilling a pilot hole. Screw the boards firmly in place with 25mm No. 6 screws.

The panels should now stand up by themselves but to steady them further you can temporarily tack battens across the tops of them.

Scribing to fit

Use scribing whenever you have to fit a component snugly against an uneven surface such as an irregular wall or floor.

The first step is to fit the part as closely back to the surface as it will go. It's usually important to keep it in a particular alignment—such as with another component or against a spirit level—so check this point carefully, too.

It's essential that the part does not move while you are scribing, so fix it temporarily or get someone to help you by holding it firmly in place. Mark its position so you can refit it exactly.

To scribe it you need a pencil or marker, plus a block of scrap wood slightly wider than the largest gap behind the part of the structure you are scribing.

Tape the pencil firmly to the block. Then run the block down the wall, keeping it firmly against the surface, so that the pencil marks a line down the edge of the part. This line will be an accurate mimic of the outline of the wall.

Once you have done this all along the

edge you can remove the part and trim it to the line. The best way to do this depends on how close the line is to the edge, and how thick the material is. To remove small amounts you can use glasspaper. For larger amounts use a plane or planer file—you could even use a saw if the material is thin enough to cut easily in this way.

Adding the shelves

The shelves stiffen up the whole structure and complete the main carcase ready for you to fit out the interior and add the doors.

Start by screwing shelf support battens to the walls in line with those on the upright panels. These too are made from lengths of 25mm × 25mm softwood. Cut them to fit the spaces and screw them in place with 50mm No. 8 screws every 150mm or so. In the outer units use a spirit level to make sure that they are positioned accurately along the back and side wall.

The shelves can now be dropped into place. All of them are lengths of 525mm wide 15mm melamine. Those adjacent to the walls are 620mm long. The others are 600mm wide. The shelf over the dressing table, and the dressing table top itself, must be cut to fit the space between the chipboard sides exactly. Cut three panels this size —the dressing table top is made out of a double thickness of melamine.

Try all the shelves in place to check that they fit properly. They may need to be scribed at the back so they slide back flush with the front edge of the uprights. They also need 25mm square notches at both back corners to clear the wall battens.

When you are satisfied with the fit remove each shelf, labelling where it goes so you can identify it later. Then drill a series of 4mm holes along the sides and back of each shelf, 15mm from the edge and at 200mm intervals. Apply woodworking glue to the tops of the battens, put each shelf back in place and spike through all the holes with a bradawl. Drive 25mm No. 6 screws through each hole to hold the shelf down to the batten. But note that while you can do this for the shelf above the dressing table, keep the dressing table boards to one side and don't drill them at this stage.

Once you have fitted all the shelves, apply the pine trims to the wardrobe fronts. These are simply glued and pinned to the edges of the melamine.

Start with the two outer trims on the face of the wall battens. These are 2160mm long and cut from 75mm × 19mm softwood. Use a spirit level to set them

8 *How the front frames and shelves are fitted in the completed frame*

9 *After cutting to fit, nail and glue the softwood trims to the melamine*

10 *Drop the notched shelves onto the support battens*

upright. To do this, you may need to move them out into the room by a fraction if you have scribed the wall batten to fit. Glue the wall batten and nail them in place with 38mm panel pins every 250mm or so. Use a nail punch to sink the heads below the surface of the wood.

To span the top of the unit you need a long board running wall to wall. In the basic design this is cut from 75mm × 19mm softwood, but if doing this would leave a slight gap you could use something wider. The alternative is to fit a coving over the gap afterwards (see below).

Cut the top board to span exactly. Try it in position to check its fit, then glue and pin it to the wall battens and the edges of the upright panels.

There is a similar board spanning the front of the top shelf—this is again cut from 75mm × 19mm softwood but runs between the side trims, rather than above them. Cut this to fit accurately, then glue and pin it to the front of the shelves. It must be positioned so that the shelves run down the centre of the board.

Finally cut short lengths of 75mm × 19mm softwood to trim the uprights between these two boards, and longer ones to run from the plinth up to the lower cross boards. It's more accurate to cut these to fit the space than to measure them. Once again these should be set centrally on the uprights. However, don't just glue and pin them: they have to carry the weight of the doors and need stronger fixings—use plastic block joints at 200mm intervals screwed firmly to both parts.

Concealing awkward gaps

There are two places where you may be faced with an awkward gap around the standard units—at the top or at the side. Fortunately these are usually easy to conceal neatly.

The only time you are likely to have a gap at the side is if you want to fit several wardrobe units and the remaining space is not large enough to construct a dressing table—that is, less than 500mm.

The answer here is not to leave this as a relatively large gap on one side but to set the other units centrally and leave a more manageable gap of 250mm on both sides. The interior of the units so created can then be fitted out with somewhat wider shelving. To get around the problem of needing a wider door, fit a front trim which is oversized by the amount of the gap.

Gaps at the top are even easier to deal

with. It's most likely that you will either have a very small gap—or a very large one in an old house with a high ceiling.

In the first case you can span it with an oversize top board. If this would create difficulties use an ordinary top board and cover the gap afterwards with a wooden or plastic coving moulding.

With a very wide gap, don't even attempt to cover it. Instead, construct the wardrobe completely and panel the top with a sheet of melamine faced hardboard pinned to the top of the uprights to keep the dust out.

Finishing the framework

Once the main framework has been erected you can add the finishing touches, making them as simple or as sophisticated as you like. For example, if you want a simple dressing table you can make a plain shelf using two lengths of faced chipboard placed on top of one another with a timber facing pinned along the front edge. But you can turn it into a proper dressing table with a make-up drawer underneath.

Similarly, you need only fit the inside of the hanging wardrobe with a clothes rail. But you can construct a small set of shelves to take up the wasted space in the bottom.

Inside the storage wardrobe you can fit plain shelves in the two halves or add adjustable baskets.

Decide which interior fittings you want and then incorporate these into your original sketch plan using the construction diagram on page 442 as a guide.

Above: A wide variety of fittings such as sliding baskets adds versatility to the basic framework

Fixtures and fittings

The materials you need fall into two sections—the doors and the interior fittings.
Doors: All of the wardrobe and door fronts fitted to the system are standard size and can be bought ready-made—except for the flap-up cupboard door above the dressing table which is almost certain to be an odd size. You can trim the ends or sides of a standard door; but if the amount to be removed is more than say, 100mm, you will probably find this impossible.

The easy option in this case is to cut a plain panel to the required size from

Below: The main fittings detailed here— dressing table (yellow), shelves (orange), baskets (red), doors (blue)

laminate or plywood and hang this in place of a door. But there's a good chance that you can trim this in style with the rest of the fronts, providing you can buy some smaller doors (see page 450).

Apart from this, for each hanging wardrobe buy a 1680mm × 610mm door, and for each top cupboard a 610mm × 460mm door. The storage wardrobe requires two doors, one 760mm × 610mm door for the top and one 900mm × 610mm door for the bottom.

•**Door fittings:** Buy three 50mm brass or chrome-plated hinges for the large doors and two hinges for each of the others. You also need a matching handle or knob for each door, plus a magnetic catch. For the door above the table buy a lift-up stay.

•**Interior fittings:** The materials you need here vary according to the exact design of your system. So look at your sketch plan and check off the parts against this list:

•**Hanging rails:** For each hanging wardrobe buy an 18mm diameter tube plus two ends and one centre support. If possible buy a little oversize and cut to length.

•**Dressing table:** For the basic dressing table without drawer all you need is a piece of 25mm × 19mm softwood, cut the same length as the front edge of the table.

For the dressing table drawer use a ready-made plastic kit. Buy components to make a drawer up to 525mm deep, 100mm high and roughly half the width of the table (see Self-assembly drawer kits). You also need plastic runners and a hardboard base.

To build a framework for the drawer assembly you need some pieces of 525mm wide melamine faced chipboard and softwood cut into the following lengths:

•For the sides two pieces 525mm long, the same depth as the drawer plus 25mm.

•For the base one piece 525mm wide and the same length as the dresssing table itself.

•Two 525mm lengths of 25mm × 25mm battening to support the base.

•You also need a piece of 150mm × 19mm softwood or melamine the same length as the front edge of the table to make a fascia.

•**Pull-out basket system:** Buy as many standard 545mm baskets as you need. For each basket you need two 525mm lengths of 50mm × 25mm softwood and 25mm × 25mm softwood to act as runners.

•**Freestanding shelves:** This unit is made entirely from lengths of 300mm wide 15mm melamine. If you haven't enough offcuts, all the pieces can be cut from 3.5m of 300mm wide melamine sheet. You need:

•For the sides, two 570mm lengths.

•For the top and bottom panels, two 560mm lengths.

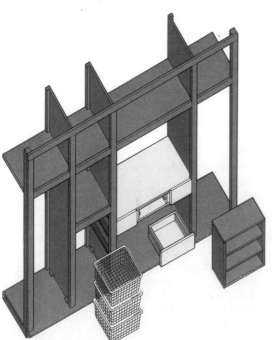

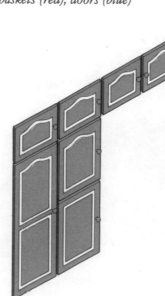

• For the shelves, two 530mm lengths.
Miscellaneous: Buy primer, undercoat and gloss (½ litre of each) for the front facings and support battens, plus paint or varnish for the doors, and general purpose filler

General assembly of the dressing table

Constructing the dressing table

The simple dressing table is built from two layers of faced chipboard lipped with softwood facing. For the dressing table with drawer you need a few additional parts.

To construct the simple dressing table without drawer simply lay the two prepared pieces of chipboard face down on a flat surface one on top of the other. Then drill and countersink screw holes at regular intervals around the outer edge and across the centre. Spread a little glue between the sheets and screw them together.

Turn the assembly over and slot it between the wardrobes so that it is resting firmly on the support battens at either side. Then pin the facing to the front edge of the dressing table.

If you want to fit a drawer to the dressing table, you must erect a solid framework for the drawer to sit in as shown below.

Take the base of the assembly and lay it down flat. Position the two side pieces on it with the gap between them measuring the width of the drawer plus 10mm, and an equal gap on either side. Make sure they are square to the base and level with the front edge. Attach them by fixing two block connectors down the outside edge of each.

Now fit the drawer runners. Position them 55mm up from the base, drill and screw in place.

On the main wardrobe sides, measure down 125mm from the tops of the dressing table support battens. You need two more battens with their top edges in line with these marks, to support the base of the dressing table. Cut these and screw in place.

Drop the base on these supports. Lay a top over it and check that it contacts its supports, plus both side pieces. Remove it, drill and screw the base to support battens.

11 Joint the sides to the base, then screw on the plastic runners

12 Screw support battens to the wardrobes in line with the base and add the assembly. Fit the tops after the base is in place

Now fit the top panel. Drill through and screw it to the supports at each end, and the side pieces where it contacts them—but check that these are upright.

Sand lightly over the upper surface of the top panel and the underside of the remaining top panel. Glue the two together with contact adhesive—the sanding provides a key. Nail on two fascia pieces.

Now fit the drawer together (see Self-assembly drawer kits) and try it for size. If it is satisfactory, remove the drawer and add the front. Drill and insert the screws from inside the drawer so you don't damage the front face. Position the front so that it fits level with the fascia either side. It will then project enough underneath the drawer to provide a hand grip.

Building the wardrobe shelving unit

This freestanding storage unit is designed to be placed in the bottom corner of the wardrobe so it can be used for storing shoes, socks and other items. It is made entirely from melamine faced chipboard, glued and screwed together.

Before you start, examine the construc-

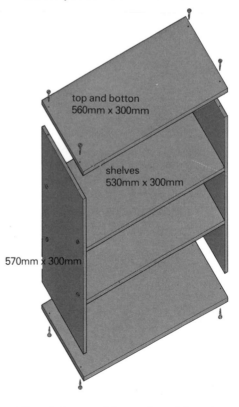

The whole assembly consists of just six pieces of melamine. Measure and drill accurately, and use chipboard screws to put it together

13 *Cut all the pieces to length, joining the outer frame first*

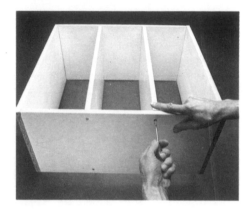

14 *Add the shelves. The cut edges can be lipped with edging*

tion plan. Cut out the pieces and label each of them with a letter or number. Construct the main frame of the unit first by gluing and screwing the two uprights to the top and bottom panels. Mark off the shelf positions at 200mm intervals, then glue and insert the panels and fix them by screwing through from the sides. If you want to add a back panel, glue and pin it in place.

★ WATCH POINT ★

Hold the panels in position temporarily for drilling with a few strips of masking tape. You can then check they are square before finally screwing the pieces together.

Self-assembly drawer kits

Plastic DIY drawer kits—which come in different designs—enable you to construct different size drawers quickly and easily.

All you have to do is to decide the depth and size of drawer you require. The kit

consists of profiled drawer sides with a groove moulded down the outside to accept runners and one on the inside to take the base, plus four snap-fastening corner pieces. There are also moulded plastic drawer runners, if required.

There are two ways to use the kit. The easiest is to make all four sides of the drawer in plastic and add a front trim afterwards. The alternative is to make three sides in plastic—the drawer front itself forms the fourth. This type of construction is more complicated and for this design a four sided construction is used. Apart from the kit itself, you need a piece of hardboard to make the base of the drawer.

The side profile can be cut to length with a fine toothed saw, such as a tenon saw. Use a try square to make the cutting line accurately. When you work out the lengths you need, remember to allow for the thickness of the corner block. The makers give a formula for working this out and it's most important to get it right. Similarly when you come to cut the base of the drawer to size you have to allow for the thickness of the sides—less the slots.

To assemble a four sided drawer first lay out all the component parts of the drawer onto a flat surface. Slot the corner connectors into the back profile. Lift the baseboard into position followed by the two sides. Make sure that the baseboard is located firmly in the slotted recess cut around the inside of the profiles. Finally add the front corner connectors and the front piece of edging profile.

Adding the hanging rails

The hanging wardrobes can be fitted out very quickly—it's just a matter of screwing the hanging rail under the top shelf.

There's a small amount of variation from make to make, but most fit in a similar way. There are two kinds of support brackets. The first is a socket which screws to the side of the wardrobe to take the end of the rail tube. The second is a drop bracket which screws under a shelf and has an arm with a ring on it to accept the tube.

Some rail systems only have one or other of these types of support. It's better to go for one which has both—since this will take the most weight. Fitting is simple, and in most cases the makers will provide full instructions. The important thing is to screw the brackets up firmly and in the correct alignment. If you are using a drop bracket in the centre, its length will determine how far down to fix the end brackets.

15 *Mark the rail tube to the required length. A piece of tape will allow you to use a marker pen and leave a clear line. Allow clearance for the ends*

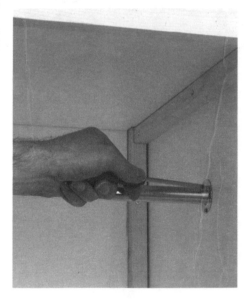

16 *Align the tube carefully down the centre line and at the correct height. Screw on the support brackets at the ends and centre*

Start by finding the centre line across the wardrobe and marking it in pencil. Hold the rail to span the wardrobe and mark the position of the brackets. If you have to cut it to length, use a junior hacksaw. When you mark the cutting line, be sure to make allowances for the amount which is 'lost' in the two end brackets.

Check how the rails fit into the end brackets. Sometimes they drop into them from above after the brackets are screwed in place. Alternatively, some designs have to be slipped over the rail first and screwed in place all together.

17 *Three pull-out baskets make versatile use of space*

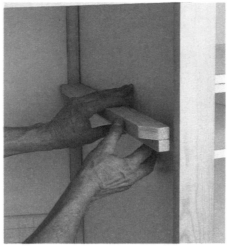

18 *Measure the heights of the baskets and add runners*

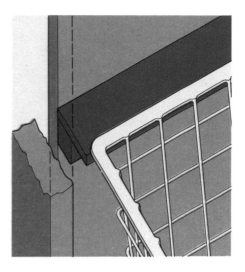

Above: Each runner is made from two pieces of softwood

Fitting pull-out baskets

These provide an alternative to the plain storage cupboard with shelves. They allow you easy access and help keep clothing tidy.

You need to fix packing pieces to either side of the wardrobe to act as runners. They can be made using a 25mm × 25mm batten to support a second piece as shown. The width they need to project depends on the baskets. You must screw them in place to leave a clear spacing of at least 50mm between baskets—so work this out and mark the position of each packing piece before you start. Measure the distance from the bottom of the cupboard every time so you can make certain that each runner is correctly aligned.

Drill and countersink screw holes through each runner at roughly 100mm intervals. Hold each runner in turn in position and spike through the holes with a bradawl to make pilot holes in the chipboard. Then screw the runner into place. When all the runners are positioned, try the baskets for size and check that they slide in and out freely.

If you find that any of the drawers are a little sticky, remove the drawer concerned and rub the top edge of each supporting packing piece with a candle.

Filling and finishing

Before you hang the doors, any gaps in the front facings and support battens must be filled, sanded down and painted. At the same time you can apply a suitable finish to the doors, if they haven't been treated.

Apply the filler with a filling knife, paying particular attention to the gaps between the facings and the walls. Here you may have to build up the filler layer by layer until it is just above surface level. Make sure you fill over the nail heads in the facings, too.

Leave the filler to set hard—this usually takes three to four hours—then smooth down with a piece of sandpaper on a block. Check the surface and refill if it is particularly bumpy. When you are satisfied, remove any excess dust before painting with a soft cloth dampened with white spirit.

★ WATCH POINT ★

You will find it easier to work the filler into very tiny cracks and crevices and remove any excess if you wet the filling knife and run it gently over the surface.

Paint in the order primer, undercoat and topcoat. Leave to dry thoroughly between coats and rub down each with a piece of glasspaper before applying the next.

If the wardrobe and cupboard doors have not been given a surface finish, now is a good time to do it so that all the paint can dry together. Prop the doors up against a nearby wall during painting, with a piece of rag or newspaper wrapped around the top to protect the wallcoverings.

It is worth taking the trouble to get a good finish on the doors. So before you apply the final coat rub the surface down thoroughly with a piece of fine glasspaper or steel wool. Clean off any dust completely with a soft cloth and white spirit and use a

19 *Fill blemishes in the doors and gaps in the frame. Paint mouldings carefully*

20 *When painting large areas of the doors take care to get a smooth finish, working in blocks from left to right*

good quality brush with soft and pliable bristles, to ensure a good result.

Apply the paint evenly and thinly, working in blocks running from the top left hand corner to the bottom right. Finish off by smooth upward movements of the brush to avoid streaking or paint runs.

Hanging wardrobe and cupboard doors

When all the paint is dry you can fit the hinges to the doors and hang them in place.

Sort out the doors so you know what fits where. Then check your construction plan to see which side of each of them is hinged. Mark this in pencil.

The doors are hung on single cranked hinges. These allow the doors to open in their own width without binding. They have the additional advantage of being easy to fit—the metal plates just screw to the back surface of the door and the face of the frame with no cutting in necessary.

Screw the hinges to the doors first. Space them evenly for appearance and to spread the load. Position one hinge 100mm from the top and one 100mm from the bottom of each door. On large, heavy doors it is advisable to fit a third hinge in the centre.

Take care to align the knuckle of each hinge with the edge of the door, and ensure that it is butted up hard against it. Mark the screw holes with a bradawl. With small fixing screws it shouldn't be necessary to drill holes for them.

With all the hinges in place, offer up each door in turn to check its position and mark the screw holes on the frame. With large, heavy doors or when working high up it helps if you have an assistant. Alternatively, prop the doors up for a short period with lengths of wood.

Check that there is a 25mm overlap of the door onto the frame all round, and that the door itself is square. Then mark through the holes in the hinges onto the face of the framework. If you use a bradawl to do this, you can insert the screws directly to hold the door in place.

When all the doors are in place, screw on the handles or knobs you have chosen. Mark them carefully to ensure that they all line up with each other. Don't try to fit them in thin panels; put them in the outer rails where the doors are strongest. Secure each door with a magnetic catch.

The only door which can't be added as simply as this is the flap above the dressing table, which you have to make up first. Cut a panel from plywood or hardboard to stiffen the flap. Depending upon how you fit the doors to it, this can be the same size as the opening—in which case the doors must overlap it by 25mm—or 25mm larger than the opening all round.

21 *Make sure that the doors overlap the front frames by 25mm*

22 *Fit the hinges to the doors then offer each one up in turn. Check that it is square and in correct alignment*

23 *Mark the positions of the hinge holes onto the frame*

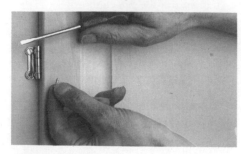

24 *Put in the fixing screws one at a time so that you can adjust the doors*

There are various ways to arrange one or more doors to fit onto the panel; some examples are shown on the right. It doesn't matter if you cut the doors drastically because the panel will support them.

Hang the flap from its top edge. To support it while opened, screw a fall flap stay to the inside of the cupboard.

Finishing off

Once you have cleared up all the dust and mess, roll the carpet into position and recut it to fit in front of the wardrobe units. Trim the carpet back with a sharp marking knife and butt it up against the plinth.

There are a number of additions you can make to the wardrobe system to improve its usefulness and appearance. For example, a mirror could be fixed to the wall behind the dressing table with a light above it.

There are also a number of proprietary wardrobe fittings—shoe racks, sliding rails and drawer systems—which you may want to add to your wardrobes or storage cupboards. These are available from most large DIY retailers and DIY supermarkets —so look around at what is on offer.

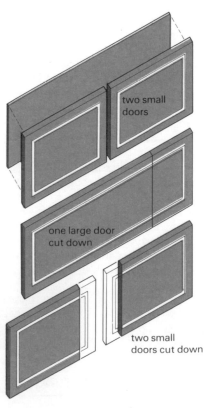

Above: Since you are unlikely to find a door of exactly the size you need for the flap, make a plain panel. To trim it to match the other doors, cover it with door panels cut down as necessary

MAKE A BEDHEAD UNIT

This design has been created with flexibility in mind. The bedhead itself can be as long as or as short as you want it, and adds only 50mm to the overall length of the bed. It features removable upholstered panels which you pad with foam and cover with the material of your choice. And there's plenty of room inside to run the wiring for reading lights, switches and so on.

At 300mm deep, the side units can easily accommodate hi-fi units, speakers, a radio and the like. Leave them with open shelving or fit half doors, and adjust the positions of the shelves to suit what's going inside.

The main construction material is sturdy 19mm plywood, which can be painted, stained or varnished as you wish. The exposed edges are covered with hardwood lipping, and adjacent panels are ingeniously butt-jointed against quadrant moulding to give a truly high quality finish.

Equally ingenious is the way you prepare the panels: simply mark out your sheets of plywood exactly as shown in the diagram on page 453 and then run down the cutting lines with a power saw. This leaves you with a 'kit' of parts that have only to be pinned and glued together.

Planning the construction

The dimensions given here are for a standard size double bed measuring 1600mm wide by 495mm high. Obviously, there's some room for manoeuvre, but if your bed size is significantly different, you need to adjust the lengths of the horizontal bedhead members or the vertical side unit panels accordingly. This in turn will affect the cutting plan given on page 453 and you may therefore need to rearrange the panels so that you're not left with too much waste.

Buying the materials

Start with the plywood. To build the bedhead shown here you'll need one full sheet measuring 2240mm × 1220mm, plus another measuring at least 800mm × 650mm—you may have to buy a half sheet and keep some spare for another project. Because you'll be cutting the sheets with minimal waste allowance it's vital that the plywood you buy has sound edges, free of chips and marks. You need:

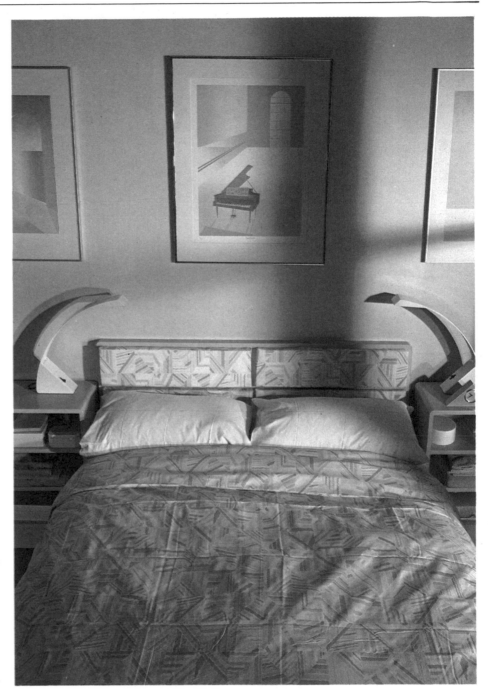

- 2.3m of 19mm ramin (hardwood) quadrant moulding, from which you cut four side unit top edges to 306mm, four bedhead edges to 50mm and four corner reinforcers to 200mm.
- 6.2m of 25mm × 25mm PAR softwood from which you cut eight headboard battens to 768mm.
- 12m (15.6m if you have doors) of 19mm × 6mm ramin lipping to edge the plywood.

- Four pieces of 50mm high density foam measuring 768mm × 156mm plus a latex or contact adhesive to fix it. Buy all this at an upholsterers or specialist foam supplier.
- The fabric of your choice—cut four pieces to 1030mm × 420mm.
- 16 pairs of small magnetic catches.
- A supply of 19mm and 32mm panel pins.
- A good supply of PVA woodworking adhesive.
- Finishing materials—wood stopper or

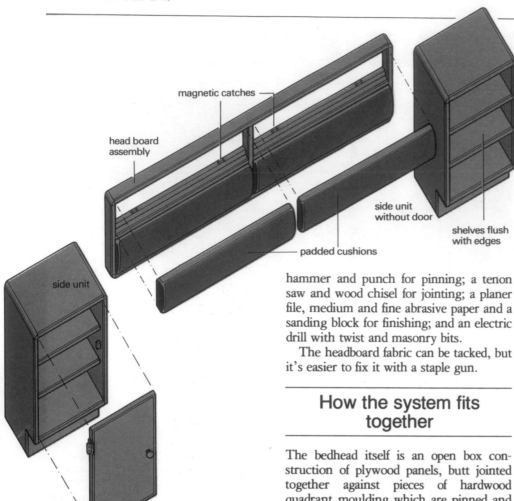

magnetic catches

head board
assembly

side unit

optional door

side unit
without door

padded cushions

shelves flush
with edges

★ WATCH POINT ★

The easy way to do this is by drawing all the panels to scale (1:100) on metric graph paper, cutting them out, and laying them on another piece of graph paper marked out to the size of your plywood sheet. By juggling the various shapes around like a Chinese puzzle, you should soon be able to arrive at the most economical arrangement.

interior filler to cover the pin heads, plus paint, stain or varnish as required.

If you decide to fit doors, don't forget the hardware: buy two pairs of 38mm flush hinges, two round wooden doorknobs and two further pairs of magnetic catches.

Wall fixings can be made with 32mm No. 8 steel woodscrews. If you have a stud wall, aim to screw directly to the studs; otherwise buy standard plastic wallplugs.

Tools for the job

Although the construction of this project is quite straightforward, cutting 19mm plywood by hand is a laborious process and difficult to do with any sort of accuracy. Consequently, it really will pay you to make sure you have a power jigsaw or circular saw equipped with a fence, plus a decent saw table or adjustable workbench so that you can support the sheets on both sides of the cutting line.

Among the other tools you'll need are a tape measure, try square and steel rule or straight edge for marking out; a pin hammer and punch for pinning; a tenon saw and wood chisel for jointing; a planer file, medium and fine abrasive paper and a sanding block for finishing; and an electric drill with twist and masonry bits.

The headboard fabric can be tacked, but it's easier to fix it with a staple gun.

How the system fits together

The bedhead itself is an open box construction of plywood panels, butt jointed together against pieces of hardwood quadrant moulding which are pinned and glued to their edges. Two more panels, halving jointed where they cross, divide the box into four 'compartments'. Square section softwood battens are pinned and glued inside each one, flush with the back, leaving recesses into which you fit the padded headboard panels. The panels are held by magnetic catches; the unit is secured to the wall by screwing through the appropriate battens.

The side units employ the same butt joint/quadrant moulding construction, and feature false plinths cut out of the sides. The tops, lowest shelves and kickboards are all pinned and glued for structural strength, but the centre shelves rest loose on shelf supports.

Cutting the plywood

With a power saw and a proper bench, this job is much easier than you might think. But take extra care with your marking up—mistakes at this stage could prove costly later when the panel edges don't match up.

Refer to the diagram on page 453 showing how the panels can be cut out of standard sized sheets with a minimum of waste.

You'll notice in the pictures that the cutting lines are in fact double, with 2mm between each one. Although this takes longer to measure and mark out, it does enable you to take the kerf—the width of the saw blade—into account while still having clear lines which you can saw by.

If you are building the unit to dimensions other than those given, the usefulness of the marking diagram may be limited and you may have to draw up your own.

Measure out your sheets, section by section, making V-shaped marks in sharp pencil. After each section is completed, measure back against the one before to check for cumulative error.

Do the actual marking out with a trimming knife held against a steel rule. As well as being more accurate, the blade scores through the surface layer of the plywood and cuts down the risk of it chipping when you saw it.

When cutting, simply make sure the saw blade doesn't stray from between the two guidelines. If you haven't got a fence, it may be worth clamping a straightedged batten along the line of the cut; align it by starting the cut then holding the batten hard against your saw's sole plate.

After cutting, smooth—but don't round—the cut edges with medium abrasive paper mounted on a block. Then sort out the four headboard panels and round the edges of these to a radius of about 2mm. Mark all the panels with the appropriate key letter to identify them.

You may find, if you have cut the plywood with a jigsaw, that the cut edges

★ WATCH POINT ★

With a jigsaw, don't try to force the blade through the wood; let it find its own way and concentrate instead on keeping it steady and on line.

1 *Mark cutting lines on the plywood for adjacent parts about 2mm apart using a craft knife to break the surface ply*

2 *The gap between cutting lines allows you to use a power jigsaw without worrying unduly about slightly wavering saw cuts*

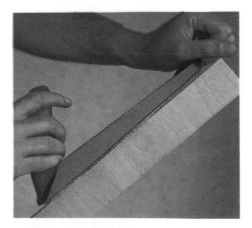

3 *Trim the cut edges down to the marked lines using gentle strokes with a planer file, then sand—but do not radius —the edges*

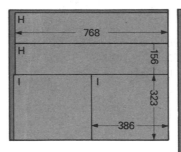

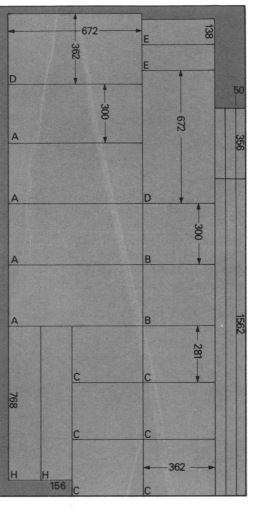

All the major components for the bedhead unit can be cut out of one and a third sheets of 19mm plywood. The square section battens to which the four cushions are fitted are made from 25mm × 25mm PAR softwood

are slightly too wavy to be sanded down easily. Simply smooth them off with a planer file, but don't remove too much material—the edges are apt to splinter so leave a small amount above the cut line for sanding perfectly smooth.

Assembling the side units

Start with the top panels by cutting the hardwood quadrant for the top edges and corner reinforcers to size. Clamp one top panel in a vice with the back edge to your left, using offcuts of ply to protect the workpiece. Glue the side edge and the corresponding edge of a piece of quadrant then lay the quadrant in place, flush with the back edge. Strengthen by pinning in four places, taking care that the moulding doesn't slip out of alignment as you do so. Repeat for all four side edges.

Now cut two pieces of ramin lipping to fit the front edges. It's best to cut them slightly oversized, then try them in place and sand the ends as necessary. Secure the lipping with glue and three equally spaced pins. Afterwards, set the top panels aside to dry.

Tackle the sides next. First mark out and saw the cut-outs for the false plinths, using the same techniques as before. Sand the cut edges smooth, but not rounded. Then pin and glue lengths of ramin lipping to the front edges, flush with the tops.

Mark out the shelf bracket positions on the inside faces of the panels, working from the top edges at all times. Depending on the type of bracket you're using, pin them in place or drill 10mm recesses and glue them.

If you want doors, mark and drill the hinge and catch positions at this stage (see Adding side door units).

Now pin and glue ramin lipping to front edges of the lowest shelves. If the units are being left open, lip the centre shelves too. Finally, mark and drill the wall fixing holes in the back panels where shown in the assembly diagram.

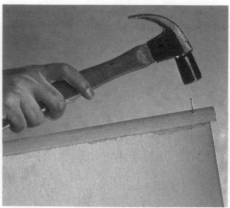

4 *Clamp the shelf side panels together and mark the 'plinth' cutouts simultaneously*

5 *Pin and glue the quadrant moulding to the shelf side panels and punch the heads down*

6 *Use a webbing strap and offcuts to hold the top and side panels while you pin them*

To assemble each unit, start by laying the side panels on edge on the floor with their feet against the wall. Insert the centre shelves between them to give the correct spacing, then tie them in this position—or,

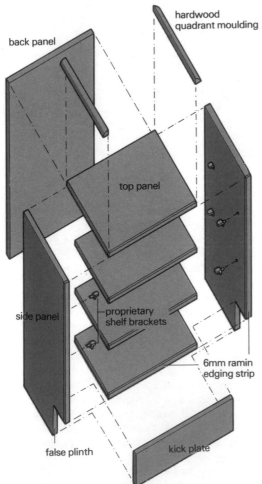

The shelf units are simple in construction. The quadrant moulding overlaps the top and sides to neatly match the lipping along their edges

if you have them, use sash clamps.

Pin and glue the top panel first, using four pins per edge and punching the heads just below the surface of the quadrant. Make sure that the top remains flush with the sides at all times.

Now untie the assembly or remove the clamps and flip it round so that the top is against the wall. Glue the sides of the lowest shelf and ease the side panels apart just enough to slip the shelf into position. Holding it there, turn the unit onto its side and pin through the side panel into the shelf edge at four places.

Complete the side unit by turning it on its front and gluing on the back panel. Use a centre shelf (or if you're fitting doors, an offcut) to support the top of the back while you pin it to the lowest shelf. Then stand the unit upright and pin through the top. Finish by pinning through either side at 100mm centres. Glue the corner reinforcers into the corners between the top and the sides, flush with the back panel.

Adding side door units

Fitting a door to one of the side units is simplicity itself if you use flush hinges—with these, one leaf folds over the other so there's no need to cut recesses.

You can have either full doors, in which case both centre shelves are cut back by 19mm, or fit half doors and leave one of the centre shelves full size.

Mark the hinge positions on the insides of the side panels before you assemble the unit. The leaves should be exactly flush with the edges of the panels, leaving the barrel protruding.

Cut the door to the required size and pin and glue ramin lipping to all four edges.

When this is dry, mark the hinge positions along one edge as you did on the side panels.

If the cut edges are very clean, of course, you could dispense altogether with lipping: simply use iron-on edging strip.

Screw the hinges to the door, then fit the door in place in the unit. Sand the lipping as

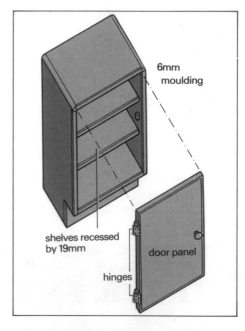

necessary so that the door swings free, then fit a magnetic catch and catch plate. Finish the door by screwing on a wooden knob.

Building the bedhead

As with the side units, assembling the bedhead is perfectly straightforward providing you take care to keep the panels aligned as you pin them.

Start by cutting the edging quadrant to size. Pin and glue it to the side panels as you did on the side units. Make sure the mouldings are flush with the back edges so that you can follow by pinning and gluing ramin lipping to the front edges all the way around the unit.

Make the centre halving joint next. Find the middle of the centre upright and mark a 25mm × 19mm slot across it on what will be the back edge using a pencil and try square. Do the same on the front edge of the centre horizontal member.

Cut the vertical slot lines in the usual way with a tenon saw.

Saw the headboard battens to length by marking and cutting one, then using this as a template to mark and cut the others. Locate two of the battens flush with the back edge of the centre horizontal, separated by the halving slot. Glue them in this position, then pin in four places to strengthen the joints. Fix two more battens to the underside of the horizontal in the same way.

Pin and glue the remaining battens flush with the back edges of the top and bottom panels, using the centre upright as a spacer.

Screw the magnetic catches to all the battens, 150mm from each end, as shown in the diagram. Finish by drilling 4.5mm clearance holes for the wall fixing screws through the battens on the top and bottom panels, level with the catches.

The bedhead is now ready to be assembled. Lay the top, centre and bottom panels front edge uppermost on the floor. Take the centre upright, coat all the mating surfaces with glue, and slot it in position over the centre horizontal panel. At the same time as you are doing this, locate the ends in the top and bottom panels.

Now try the end panels for fit. If this is poor, leave the assembly to dry then sand down any protruding edges with a planer file to get a good finish.

When all is well, glue and pin the end panels in place with the bedhead supported against the wall. Follow by pinning through the top and bottom panels into the centre upright. Make sure all the pin heads are punched below the surface. Then complete the bedhead box by pinning and gluing ramin lipping to the exposed front edges of all the panels—which also gives you the chance to disguise any imperfect joints.

Making the headboards

First measure and mark out the catch plate positions on the backs of the headboard panels and screw the plates in place. Then turn the boards over and glue on the foam padding, following the adhesive manufacturer's instructions. If necessary, trim the foam flush with the edges of the boards using a handyman's knife. If you have access to a staple gun use this to secure the fabric, rather than tacks and a hammer.

Lay each board foam downwards over its fabric covering and adjust until it is roughly central. Fold the first long edge of the fabric over, without pulling it, and take or staple it to the back of the board. Then fold over the other long edge, this time stretching it taut before you fix it. Repeat this procedure with the side edges, pocketing the corners as you fold them.

Finishing off

Thanks to the attractive colour contrast between the ply and its hardwood edging, just about any combination of stain and varnish is possible—as well as an all-over painted finish.

Begin the finishing process by double checking that there are no sharp edges or ill-fitting joints. If you need to sand the plywood, feather the edge evenly or bumps will show up when you apply the surface finish of paint or varnish.

The pin holes must be filled next. If you're painting the bedhead, use fine surface interior filler; otherwise use a wood stopper matched to the colour of the wood (you'll need two—one for the ply, one for the ramin). Press the stopper in with a knife and scrape flush with the surface—it's difficult to sand when dry.

Filler and woodstopper often changes

7 *Pin and glue the quadrant moulding and edge lipping to the longitudinal members*

8 *Clamp the three vertical members together and mark and cut them simultaneously*

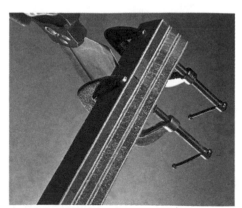

9 *Cut halving joints in plywood using a tenon saw, a drill with wood bit and a keyhole saw*

10 *Wait until the frame is assembled before you cut and fix the softwood battens*

colour once it is stained or varnished, so it is a good idea to experiment with your chosen finish on a piece of scrap board. Leave the filler to dry hard (this will usually take three to four hours) before applying the finish. You may be able to darken the filler or stopper slightly by adding a stain or using some household cocoa. When you apply the filler, sand it down as carefully as possible, so that only a small amount shows. Once it dries, sand thoroughly, working in the direction of the grain to avoid damage.

Before you apply the finish, give all the surfaces a quick sanding with fine abrasive paper mounted on a block. Be sure to clean off all the dust before proceeding. If you're varnishing, remember to do it in a dust-free environment; sand and clean down throughly between coats—three applications should be sufficient. For a fine finish, dilute the first and last coasts with a little white spirit. The first coat will largely sink into the porous wood; the last coat will give a fine, almost dust-free, finish.

The bedhead frame is very simple. The ramin lipping merely hides the plywood's grain—you could replace it with iron-on veneer edging strip, or a carefully applied paint finish

Fitting the unit

Fit the bedhead first. Although there's plenty of room for manoeuvre when it comes to the height you fix it at, it looks best if the centre horizontal aligns with the tops of the side units—giving a height of 394mm if you go by the dimensions in the construction diagram.

Rather than use a spirit level to level the bedhead, it's best to get an asistant to hold it against the wall at the right height, then slide the side units against it and align them before marking the eight screw positions with a bradawl. Having drilled and plugged the wall and screwed the bedhead firmly in place, do likewise for the side units and your installation is complete.

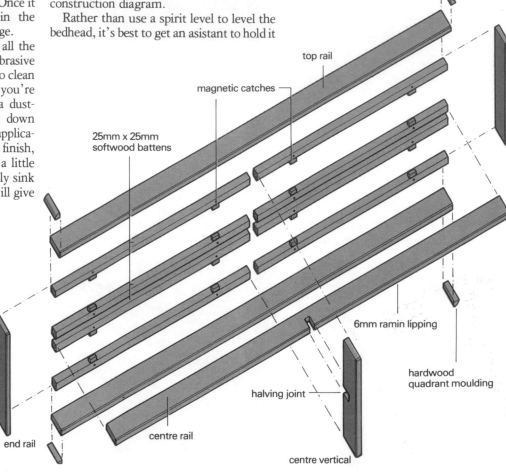

top rail

magnetic catches

25mm x 25mm softwood battens

6mm ramin lipping

hardwood quadrant moulding

halving joint

end rail

centre rail

centre vertical

11 *Use a thixotropic glue to fix the foam. This will not react chemically with the plastic. Press the foam into position as you roll it out*

12 *Fold the material into a neat 'hospital' corner—by tucking the spare material underneath the fold—and staple it down securely*

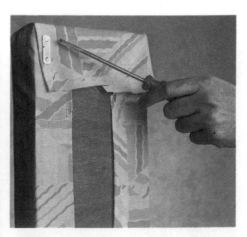

13 *Fit the steel plates for the magnetic catches over the material to ensure a proper match. Try the padded cushions in position and alter as necessary*

CHAPTER 6

OUTDOOR PROJECTS

Brighten up the outside of your home and garden with
some of the clever and stylish ideas here from building
a child's sandpit to making a garden gate

MAKE A GARDEN GATE

Garden gates don't last forever, and if yours is riddled with rot has a badly sagging frame the chances are you'll find it easier to make a new one than to patch up the damage.

The gate design featured here gives you the chance to build something that is completely unique to your home. It uses inexpensive and readily available standard sizes of PAR softwood combined with a straightforward construction method that requires few tools. And you can tailor it to the size of your entrance, avoiding the need to resite the existing posts.

CUTTING LIST			
PART	**BOARD SIZE**	**QUANTITY**	**LENGTH**
A Hinge stile	100mm × 19mm	2	1,067mm
B Latch stile	100mm × 19mm	2	1,017mm
C Inner hinge stile	75mm × 19mm	1	1,067mm
D Inner latch stile	75mm × 19mm	1	1,017mm
E Rail	75mm × 19mm	4	865/1,017/ 1,169mm
F Central brace	100mm × 19mm	1	1,400/1,500/ 1,600mm

G Filler slats are cut from 100mm, 75mm or 50mm × 19m timber as required
Alternative sizes for **E** and **F** give gates of different widths.

Planning the job

The first thing to do is measure the width and height of your gateway, as these dimensions determine the frame size and hence the amount of wood you have to buy. At the same time, check the condition of the posts and the existing hinges and latch—you may be able to re-use the latter. The finished gate will end up fractionally thicker than standard models, so if the latch post is fitted with a stop you should check that

there is enough clearance; if there isn't, the stop must be trimmed down or sawn off and repositioned.

The other decision to make before compiling a cutting list is what slat pattern you will employ. This is what gives the gate its individual character, and as long as you retain the thick central slat (which gives the structure rigidity) you can use any mixture of 100mm, 75mm or 50mm wide boards.

Your best course of action is to sketch out different patterns, roughly to scale, on a

sheet of graph paper and see which looks best. Then you can estimate how much of each size of board you need.

Tools and materials

Make up a cutting list of the wood required, based on your measurements. The cutting list above is for a gate 1,069mm high and gives alternative widths of 900mm, 1,060mm and 1,200mm. If your gateway is not one of these widths, make full use of the accompanying diagram to work out the individual board sizes for yourself.

The basic material is 19mm PAR softwood in 100mm, 75mm and 50mm widths. You can't buy this pre-treated, so each and every length must be soaked thoroughly in preservative between the cutting and assembly stages. Use creosote for a bare, rustic look; otherwise opt for a modern clear preservative or a coloured preservative stain.

All the joints in the gate are pinned and glued (the woodworking adhesive must be waterproof). If you plan to paint the wood you can get away with one of the cheaper urea formaldehyde powder-resin glues such as Cascamite or Aerolite; for a bare finish invest in a more costly resorcinol formaldehyde adhesive like Cascophen.

If you cannot re-use the existing gate hardware, buy a pair of 300mm black japanned steel strap hinges to hang the gate, plus a thumb-latch, sliding bolt or lock to keep it shut. Strap hinges are normally fixed to the gate with a coach bolt and two or three screws per strap, all of which should be supplied. But check that the bolts are at least 62mm long and the screws 42mm.

Make sure you have a large supply of 25mm panel pins to hand for securing the

The construction of the gate is based on two identical frames consisting of hinge stiles (A), latch stiles (B) and rails (E). The frame members are jointed by means of half-lap joints in the rails and stopped lap joints in the stiles, all parts being glued and pinned.

40mm spacers

E

A

B

G

D

E

C

F

E

A

inner stile

B

E

Sandwiched between the frames are the inner stiles (C and D). These create housings into which are pinned the central bracing slat (F) and the filler slats (G). The spacing between slats is a constant 40mm.

After assembly, the central brace is sawn flush with the upper rail, and the hinge stile is bevelled to give a traditional 'gate' finish

joints, plus wood filler for covering the pin holes. For a painted finish, use aluminium primer to stop the preservative bleeding through, followed by two or three coats of gloss paint.

None of the woodworking tools are particularly specialized. But you do have to cut a lot of boards and joints, so make certain that your saw blades and chisel are well sharpened. And you need a vice or adjustable workbench with a clamping facility to cut halving joints accurately.

Making the frames

The two frames are identical in all respects, so you can save time by cutting the component parts in pairs. Before you do so,

however, it's wise to make arrangements for soaking the timber in preservative.

Immerse the timber fully in the preservative as soon as you've cut it to size and made the joints. Leave it for 24 hours if possible, to allow the liquid time to soak in.

Cut the frame parts in pairs—or even fours if you feel confident—having first marked one of each component to the correct length and then clamped the rest to it. Once the timber is clamped up, you might find it useful to mark vertical cutting lines down the edges so that you have a guide for keeping the saw blade straight.

Sand the cut edges lightly to remove any roughness and then cut the lap joints and stopped laps, using a tenon saw and 25mm wood chisel. Note that the bottom housings on the stiles are marked 25mm in from the

1 *Cut paired stiles and rails together so that they match up properly during assembly; use a tenon saw for accuracy*

2 *When cutting the lap joints, make two or three grooves in the waste portion with your tenon saw. This will make it easier to cut out the waste using a 25mm chisel*

ends; the top one on the hinge stile is 50mm from the end, while that on the latch side lies flush. Take care to cut the right sides of the right parts: it helps if you tackle them systematically and label the components of each joint with a number as you go.

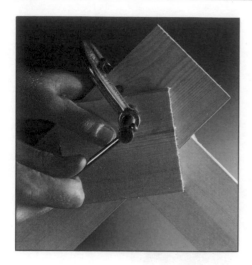

3 *Apply glue to the joints and clamp them. Only pin them when the glue has dried*

When you've tested all the joints individually for fit, assemble the frames in a dry run and measure the diagonals (which should be equal) to check that they are square. Small discrepancies don't matter, providing they're the same in both frames.

Having soaked all the parts thoroughly in preservative and let them dry, pin and glue the frames together using four pins per joint; punch the heads well below the surface and cover the holes with an exterior-quality wood filler. Sand this lightly when it is dry.

The joints must be under pressure if the glue is to set properly, so lay the frames on a flat surface and weight each corner with two bricks or a large stone. Alternatively, clamp them together using G-cramps and timber offcuts. Ensure the joints are properly square.

Cutting the slats

There's no need to make complicated angle measurements when you fit the slats: simply lay them in one of the frames and mark each one out from there.

First of all mark off the lengths of the inner stiles against the frame and cut them to size. Apply glue to the mating surfaces, position them flush with the outside edges of the frame stiles and pin at 100mm centres. As before, punch the heads well below the surface, then clamp securely and leave the entire assembly to dry on a table or flat surface.

The first slat to be fitted is the central brace. Having cut the timber roughly to size, lay it over the frame and align it by referring to the line of the top edge shown in the diagram. Hold it firmly in this position while you mark the lines of the angled cuts against the inner stiles. Convert these edge marks into lines across the board with a try

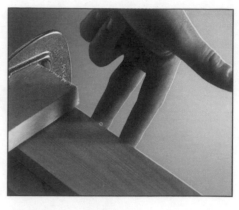

4 *Offer up the cut inner stile, glue it, and clamp it in place. Check that the inner stile is sitting flush with the outer one*

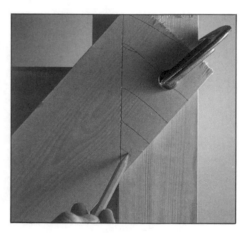

5 *Offer up the central angled stile, clamp it in place accurately, then mark off on the top and edges where to make the angled cuts*

square prior to cutting.

The rest of the slats are marked in exactly the same way, according to your chosen pattern. But first make up two 40mm thick spacers from wood offcuts to simplify positioning.

Relocate the cental brace and then fix it; place the spacers against it, lay down the next slat, and mark off. Continue in this way, taking care not to disturb the previous slat, until all the slats are marked and cut.

Soak the slats thoroughly in preservative as you did the frame parts. After drying them off, lay them back in the frame, readjust the spacings, then glue and pin them in place (use one pin per slat).

Now lay the second frame over the first, having coated the mating surfaces with glue. Pin through the stiles at 100mm centres and then along the rails through the slat ends. Weight the finished assembly with bricks while the glue dries.

When preparing the main frame components, mark them all clearly so that you get the joints in the correct positions

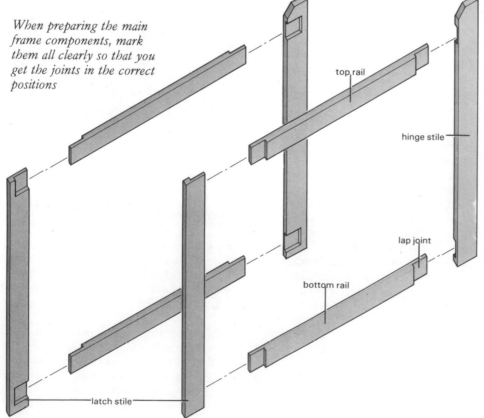

top rail

hinge stile

lap joint

bottom rail

latch stile

6 *Fix the central slat and offer up all the rest using a 40mm spacer to position them. Mark and cut off the excess above the top rail*

7 *Lay the second finished frame above the first and glue the joints. Align the two frames, clamp them together, then pin each joint*

As a last step, saw out the small triangular portion of the central brace which protrudes above the top rail and cut the top of the hinge stile to a bevel; note that the angle of the bevel is the same as that of the brace's top edge. Don't forget to coat the cut timber liberally with preservative.

Gate hardware

There is a wide range of gate hardware available—hinges, latches and so on—but you must choose it carefully. Don't use rising butt hinges: for one thing they're not long enough to support the weight properly, and for another, the gate can be lifted off the hinges easily and stolen!

If you have pets or young children, choose a latch which needs positive action to lock and unlock it—a bolt is fine, if

Latches, bolts and hinges must be galvanized or japanned

troublesome; a traditional gate catch is a better bet as it requires only one-handed operation to open it, but is still secure when the gate is closed.

When you have attached the hardware to the gate, touch up all the screw heads with metal primer (galvanized screws) or black gloss paint (japanned ones) to keep rust at bay.

Fitting and finishing

Before you attempt to fit the gate, make certain that the existing posts are plumb, firmly set in the ground and free from rot.

Check wooden posts for rot at the base by piercing them with a knife or bradawl at around ground level: if the blade penetrates easily, the post should be replaced with a new pressure-impregnated one of similar dimensions (oak is best, but is more expensive than ordinary sawn softwood). Sink the new post in a hole at least 600mm deep and wide enough to accept a 75mm collar of concrete.

8 *With the gate clamped upright, you may need to level off the slats— remember to retreat newly-exposed bare wood if you do so*

Having removed all the old gate hardware, try the new gate in position and note what modifications, if any, must be made to the posts. Once these have been completed prop or wedge the gate as it will finally be hung—nails driven into the posts should help here—so that you can mark the hinge positions.

Hold each hinge up against the gate and hinge post, centre the strap within the rail, and mark all the bolt and screw holes with a bradawl or pencil.

Remove the gate to drill the fixing holes. Those for the bolts will probably be 9mm diameter and must be made with a flat bit. When you come to the screw holes, take care not to drill right through both rails. If a hole doesn't pass through a slat end, glue in a small packing piece of slat timber to strengthen the fixing before you drill.

If the hinges are one-piece, fit them to the gate first, then the posts. With lift-off hinges, simply screw or bolt on the straps and then hang the gate on the pins. When the gate is in position, check that it swings freely; then fit the latches and bolts of your choice.

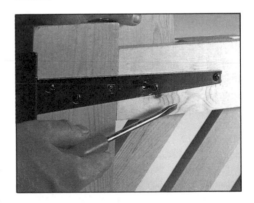

9 *When fitting the hinges, fit a timber packing piece in the gaps between slats to give the screws a better grip*

10 *Support the bottom of the gate at the correct height above the ground while you screw the hinges to the gate post*

CHAIN LINK FENCING

Wherever you need utility fencing around the home, chain link systems offer the perfect compromise between low cost, long life and ease of erection.

As well as being cheaper than most other systems, chain link fencing is versatile, easy to put up, and good at its job of keeping things in—or out. But perhaps more importantly it is tough, durable and virtually maintenance free. Providing it is not maltreated, a chain link fence with steel or concrete posts should last as long as you need it.

Just about the only disadvantage of chain link is its utilitarian appearance. But where looks are important, there's no reason why you can't disguise the harsher aspects of such a fence by choosing coloured PVC-coated wire, painting the posts or training plants up the mesh, for example.

What's available

Chain link fencing comes in several different forms, although most of the systems work in more or less the same way (fig. A). A typical run has two end posts, called straining posts, which are set in the ground with their angled braces pointing in towards the line of the fence (fig. B). Between them, non-braced intermediate posts are set at intervals of 2.5m–3m. The actual chain link mesh is hung from tensioned straining wires running between the straining posts. Fences up to 1m high need only two of these wires—at top and bottom—but an extra middle wire is required for every 1m increase in height.

Mesh: The most commonly used mesh type is plain chain link, which comes in rolls corresponding to heights of between 900mm and 3600mm; lengths of roll vary, but 10m, 20m and 25m are usual. You normally have a·choice of mesh size—40mm, 45mm or 50mm are the most common—and wire gauge (2.0mm–2.5mm is best for domestic use).

When it comes to finish, choose between plastic, galvanized and PVC-coated wire. Typical colours for the latter are green, bronze, white, black and grey. Coated mesh is generally no more expensive, is just as resistant to weathering and looks less utilitarian than the galvanized variety.

One up from plain chain link is decorative chain link, which may take many forms—the most popular style is the 'inter-locking bow'. It is hung just like plain chain link and the choice in heights and finishes is much the same.

Welded chain link is a much stronger mesh which is normally reserved for high security fences, although decorative versions are also available. The thin gauges come in roll form (they are more difficult to work with than their plain counterparts) while the thicker gauges are sold as panels, the sizes of which can be made to order.

Posts: Here you have a choice between concrete, steel (galvanized, painted or PVC-coated), sawn wood and rough hewn hardwood stakes. Each type has its own advantages and a crucial bearing on the look of the fence.

Concrete posts can be found in several guises: as straining posts (the braces either bolt on or they're already attached), intermediate posts, double straining posts (to cope with changes in direction), corner posts (two braces at right-angles) and gate posts. They are pre-drilled to take straining wire fixings, mesh straining bars, hinge brackets and so on. The main advantages of concrete are its strength and weather resistance. Against this, however, concrete posts are heavy to transport and cumbersome, which generally restricts their use in domestic fencing to those below 2m high (although heights of up to 3.6m are widely available).

Steel posts, too, are strong and weather resistant. Their narrow section, which may be square, triangular, or L-shaped, makes them look flimsy on low fences but can be a definite advantage on taller constructions where concrete would look too heavy. The posts are usually pre-drilled to take different fixings; braces for straining posts bolt on and are sold separately. Steel straining posts must always be set in concrete but on firm ground the intermediate posts can simply be driven in with a sledge hammer—another advantage over concrete.

Sawn timber posts—generally in treated softwood, oak or cedar—have a softer, less

A. *There's a choice of mesh available: 1 is chain mesh. 2 and 4 are welded. 3 is light chicken wire. 5 is decorative mesh*

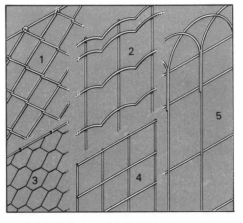

Below: *Chain link fencing, although utilitarian in style, is very cheap to erect*

B. *Fixing methods for the straining wire and the stretcher bars vary from one type of post to another. Concrete and steel posts are pre-drilled to take the various matching fixtures, but wooden posts must be cut and drilled to suit fence height*

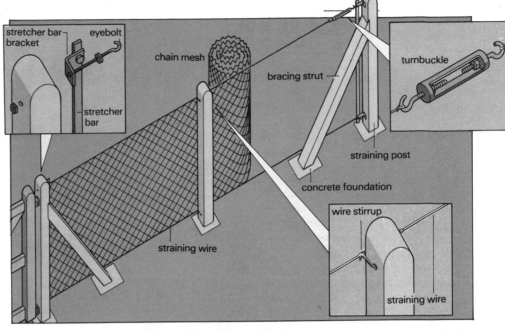

functional appearance but are liable to rot unless well treated with preservative. The straining posts will also have to be drilled to accept the eyebolts, and will have to be braced. Straining posts and braces must be set in concrete; intermediate posts can be driven into firm ground (fig. C).

Gates: Many manufacturers offer chain link gates as part of their ranges, but conventional close-boarded and ranch-style gates are usually just as easy to attach to the posts.

Hardware: This can vary between manufacturers, although it all works on the same principle. You're likely to need:

● Straining wire, which comes in 10m and 25m rolls, often with the fixings included.

● Straining bars—these are threaded vertically through either end of a run of mesh to straighten it. The bars are usually pulled against the straining posts and secured to angle brackets on the wire fixings.

● Wire fixings—at their simplest, for use with concrete or wooden posts and stakes, these are ordinary eyebolts which you fit through the posts and tighten to tension the wire. On some concrete post systems, the eyebolt is fixed and linked to the straining wire via a turnbuckle or bottle screw which can be altered to adjust the wire's tension. With metal posts, the fixing and tensioner are sometimes combined in a single unit called a tensioning bracket; this is bolted to the straining post.

● Intermediate fixings—to secure the straining wire, use wire staples on wooden posts and wire 'stirrups'—custom made from excess wire—on concrete and metal. The mesh is fastened to the straining wires every 150mm using wire 'S' hooks or short lengths of plain 3mm galvanized binding wire.

Planning the job

Assuming that you've chosen a style of fencing, the next thing to decide is the height. As regards the practical considerations, 900mm is perfectly adequate for boundary work, but you should raise this to 1200mm–1800mm for screening part of the garden, or 2750mm–3600mm for something like a tennis court. If you are concerned about

C. *Post holes are best made narrower at the top. Holes for braces are more difficult to estimate. Dig all holes at the same time, set upright posts first, then use braces to adjust the level of the brace post holes. Make sure that the posts are level and vertical*

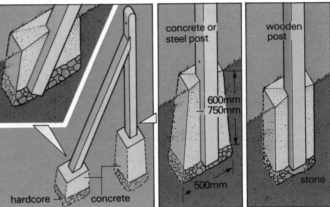

★ WATCH POINT ★

Bear in mind that most suppliers will sell you a 'kit' containing all the hardware relevant to the type of post you intend to use. Where ease of fitting is concerned, there is little to choose between individual systems.

keeping burrowing pets in—or pests out—it's best to erect the fence in a shallow trench, in which case add 300mm to your chosen height.

When it comes to UK regulations, fences sometimes require planning permission. Normally they do not if:

● The fence is under 1m high along a boundary with a road.

● The fence is under 2m high along any other boundary of your property.

Unfortunately, local restrictions sometimes complicate the issue. You may, for example, live on a housing estate where

fence heights were restricted when the original planning permission was granted. Or your fence may constitute an obstruction to the view of drivers on the highway, even if it is on the borders of your property.

About the only way to be sure is by contacting your local authority planning office. It might also be wise, as a matter of common courtesy, to check with any neighbours whose property might be affected by the erection of the fence.

Buying the fencing: Before ordering, make a quick survey of the site. If this is sloping, there may be special considerations (see below). Otherwise, check that the ground is reasonably level along the length of the run and then measure it out.

Another useful tip is to check the soil and subsoil. Drive a stake into the ground at several places along the run to a depth of about 750mm: if you encounter many rocks it may be worth hiring a pick or pneumatic drill, although occasional obstructions can be circumvented by adjusting the post positions.

It helps if you make a sketch plan of the proposed fence. As well as marking on the dimensions, you should also work out the post positions and specify what type is required—straining, intermediate, double straining, corner, gate, and so forth. You'll need to do this reasonably accurately so that you can order the appropriate hardware.

1 Mark fence height on wooden posts; allow for the depth of the hole, the mesh height and an extra 100mm at the top

2 Drill 10mm holes for eyebolts at the mesh top and bottom lines. Make holes 10mm from front edge of posts

The best place to buy chain link fencing is from a specialist supplier but always get more than one quote and don't forget to make the necessary delivery arrangements.

Other materials: As well as the fencing material and hardware, you need concrete and hardcore for bedding the posts. Buy the dry ingredients ready mixed for very small runs, otherwise use Portland cement and 20mm all-in ballast mixed in the ratio 1:5. You need hardcore too, but this can be any broken brick or stone that you happen to have lying around.

Tools for the job: Fitting the wires and mesh should require no more than a pair of adjustable spanners, screwdriver and pliers. Cutting 2.5mm gauge chain link can be done with pliers or pincers, though in most cases you don't need to—you simply unravel one of the interlocking strands (see below).

For sinking the posts, all you really need is a spade and spirit level plus a stringline and pegs; but if you've got a lot of holes to dig (or they're to be small and deep, for steel posts) then it's well worth hiring a post hole borer—a device which looks like a giant wood auger bit with a T-bar handle. Hire a sledge hammer for driving steel or hardwood stake intermediate posts. For wooden posts you'll also want a drill with 10mm bit; a saw, hammer and galvanized nails for securing the braces; and creosote or preservative to protect the timber.

Fixing the posts

This is the critical part of the job, so do it carefully. Above all, don't be tempted to skimp on the post hole depth or you may find that your work quickly comes crashing down.

Start by setting out the line of the fence using a stringline attached to pegs driven into the ground. The line must be level and

6 Cut the brace and the notch, then nail the two together. Pack the base with hardcore, then add the concrete

taut—use enough pegs to stop it sagging—and you should set it about 150mm above ground level. Follow by clearing the site of all vegetation, roots and loose rocks, then mark on the line in chalk—or mark the ground with sand—where post holes will be needed.

Concrete posts

Holes for concrete posts must be a minimum of 600mm deep, increasing to 750mm for fences 1.8m high and 1m for those over 2.25m (your supplier should have taken this into account when you ordered the posts).

If you're digging with a spade, make the holes about 450mm square at the top and taper them out to 500mm square at the base. To use a post hole borer, position the tool at the centre of the proposed hole and put your weight on it while turning the T-bar clockwise—the auger should carve its way downwards with little trouble.

Exceptions to the depth rule are the holes

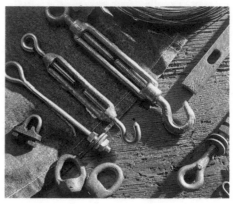

7 Lay out the fixing components—check you've ordered the right type and that you've got the right quantity

you need to dig for the braces of the straining posts—these will work out roughly two-thirds as deep as the main post holes. Dig the main holes first, then hold the braces in place to gauge how much to dig out.

Position each post in its hole and wedge it with a brick or rock while you check the fence height mark against the line (don't forget to allow for the 50mm of hardcore). Remove the post and dig deeper or backfill as necessary, then shovel in 50mm of hardcore.

Replace the post and wedge it again or prop it with timber battening; use your spirit level to check that it is plumb and make sure that the fixing holes are pointing the right way.

Mix up your concrete with just enough water to bind the dry ingredients together—the mix should be slightly crumbly when squeezed in your hand. Shovel the concrete in around the post, compacting it as you go with a stout piece of wood. When you reach the top of the hole, level off and recheck the post for plumb: it should stay in position by

3 *Dig the post holes at your marks on the setting-out line. A post hole borer may prove worth hiring for heavy soil*

4 *Dig adjacent larger holes for the braces, then set all the upright posts in a mixture of concrete*

5 *When the concrete has cured around the upright posts, hold braces in place to mark cutting lines and housing joints*

8 *Fit eyebolts and stretcher bar brackets to each straining post—but don't tighten them up just yet*

9 *Attach straining wire to the eyebolts and then add turnbuckles if you need to make more adjustment*

or notch profile with it held against the post (fig. 5). Don't forget to soak all cut timber thoroughly with preservative before you nail the brace in place (fig. 6). Allow the post to project below the concrete.

When the concrete has cured, check the post for level—on all sides—and also check the lateral alignment of the posts. Shovel a few millimetres of soil over the concrete to disguise it.

Attaching the mesh

Although this is straightforward, the roll of mesh itself will be rather bulky and it may pay you to call in a helper.

Set out all the components to make sure everything's there (fig. 7). The first step is to fit the eyebolts—the straining wire fixings—to the straining posts. On most systems the eyebolts also hold the stretcher bar brackets, so don't forget to fit these, plus washers between every part. Leave the bolts—including the nuts that draw the brackets against the post—loose at this stage (fig. 8).

Take a roll of straining wire, thread it through the eye of the top bolt, and use a pair of pliers to turn it back on itself and twist it about seven times. Alternatively, if a turnbuckle is included, secure the wire to one end of this and fit the other end to the bolt (fig. 9). Leave the turnbuckle on an open 'loose' setting.

Run the wire to the far straining post, pull it taut, and cut it leaving a 150mm excess. Thread it through the eyebolt or turnbuckle and twist as before.

Now tension the wire by tightening the eyebolt nuts or turnbuckles at either end by equal amounts (fig. 10). Be careful when you do this: you don't want the wire to snap. As a rough guide, the tension is

itself, although you may need to prop a straining post until you've concreted the brace hole.

Leave the posts for at least three days, to give the concrete a chance to cure properly.

Steel posts

Holes for steel posts set in concrete can be smaller in diameter than those for concrete posts—say 225mm—but they must be at least as deep in relation to the height of the fence. Sink and station the posts in the same way, having first marked on the fence height, but use smaller pieces of hardcore so they don't sink through it.

Wooden posts

Wooden posts and stakes are best set in concrete, the hole sizes corresponding to those for concrete and steel posts respectively. Before you do so, however, the timber must be treated against rot.

Start by marking the fence height on each post, allowing for an extension of about 100mm at the top (fig. 1): this gives you the positions of the straining wire fixing holes, which you should drill using a 10mm bit (fig. 2).

Next give the posts a thorough coating of preservative, making sure that plenty of the fluid is allowed to drip into the drilled holes. As an added precaution, soak the bottom ends of the posts in a bath of preservative for a further 24 hours.

When you come to sink the posts, set the main strainer posts first (figs 3 and 4), let the concrete cure, then fit the braces and sink or drive in the intermediate posts—use setting-out lines *between* strainer posts for the correct alignment. Braces for stakes can simply be cut at an angle and then skew-nailed to the posts: right-angled offcuts at the bottom will make them more secure. But where sawn posts are concerned you'll make a neater job by sawing an angled housing joint out of the post.

Dig the hole for the brace first, then lay the brace in it and mark off the correct angle

correct when kinks have straightened out and you start to feel appreciable resistance at the eyebolt nut.

Repeat this procedure for all the other straining wires in the run. Then secure them to the intermediate posts by threading further lengths of wire through the fixing holes and twisting the ends around the straining wires, or, with wooden posts, use wire staples to trap it against the posts.

Next take the free end of your roll of mesh and feed a stretcher bar through the end links. Bolt the bar to its brackets on the straining posts. Unwind the mesh along the straining wires—shaking it even as you go—and get your helper to fasten it temporarily to the top one with twists of wire (fig. 11). When you get to the other end of the run, feed another stretcher bar through the line of links that just reaches the straining posts.

Sever the mesh on the far side of the bar by untwisting the top link with a pair of pliers, unpicking the rest of the line, then untwisting the bottom link in the same way (fig. 12). This done, bolt the stretcher bar to its brackets on the straining post (fig. 13).

You should now be able to tension the mesh against the straining wires (and so complete the run of fence) by screwing in the nuts on the eyebolts which force the stretcher bar brackets against the posts. The only job remaining is then to secure the mesh to the straining wires every 150mm, using twists of wire as shown. If the mesh looks dishevelled and unevenly spaced, it's probably too loose. Remove the stretcher, unthread a strand, and move the bar in by one more strand, then repeat the procedure.

Dealing with sloping ground

Chain link fencing is flexible by nature, so minor changes in level rarely present any problems, providing you get the posts level and set the mesh just above the ground.

Where there are pronounced 'humps'—

10 *Tension the wire by tightening the eyebolt at either end or by making adjustments to the turnbuckles*

12 *At the other end of the fence, unravel a strand to cut the wire, then thread through a stretcher bar*

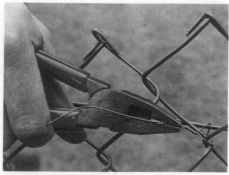

11 *Unroll the mesh from a stretcher bar fitted at one end and then loosely secure with wire twists*

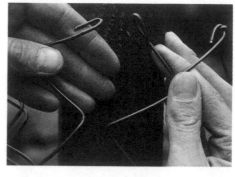

13 *Secure the stretcher bars to their fixing brackets. Staple wire to the intermediate wooden posts*

your setting out line will show them up—it's worth levelling the ground first. The real difficulties occur, however, when there is a marked slope in one direction.

First of all, assess the scale of the problem: on a fairly gentle slope you can erect the fence as normal, with the posts

D. *Deal with sloping sites by setting out a series of 'steps' in line with the gradient. At each change in level erect a two-way straining post. Drill four holes in each post for the straining wires. Erect intermediate supporting posts in the normal way*

straight and the mesh angled between them; on a steeper slope you must 'step' the run into a series of terraces. The latter can involve excavation and levelling.

If you opt for steps, start by deciding how many you need and what length they should be. You can do this by measuring the total length of the run and then sketching it out on paper to see how much soil has to be removed.

When you've arrived at a reasonable compromise between length of terrace and excavation work involved, set out the site by driving in 450mm stakes at each step point and then erect levelled stringlines. This enables you to excavate each terrace more or less level using the line as a guide.

When you come to order the fencing materials, treat each terrace as a separate run with straining posts at either end. You will notice that not only must the intervening straining posts be 'double'; they must also be longer than is usual for the fence height by the height difference between steps, with two sets of straining wire fixing holes (fig. D).

In the case of concrete or steel posts, this can be arranged if you give your supplier a sketch plan of the terrace.

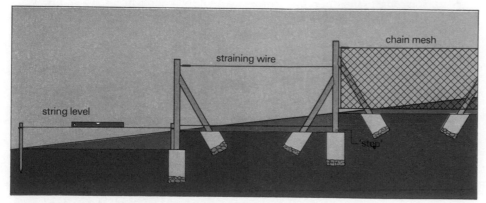

EXTERIOR SUNBLIND

A sunblind or awning is excellent for keeping south-facing rooms cool in summer. It can also be expensive to buy. As awnings must be made to measure anyway, save your money and make a pretty and practical one like this.

Simple awning

Picture windows, patio doors or French windows lighten your home and help open up the view to your garden, patio or courtyard. But if they face the rising or setting sun—or, in the northern hemisphere, they face south—then these windows can let in unwanted glare and heat during the summer months. Apart from the discomfort you might feel, that direct sunlight can also fade soft furnishings, or discolour varnished timber and even some paint surfaces.

One solution—popular throughout most south European countries—is to buy or build an awning. With a wealth of durable materials readily available, and in a variety of patterns and colours, a well-tailored awning can add that summery feeling to your property, neatly finish off the exterior of a window space and provide all the benefits of easily adjusted shade.

Proprietary awnings must be tailor made

Below: *A sunblind can be an inexpensive, attractive addition to patio doors or French windows*

to suit your window or patio door and, while a high standard of finish, materials and design is available, they'll inevitably cost you much more than making one yourself. And the beauty of building an awning is that it is a job every DIY enthusiast can handle without much difficulty.

Planning

Fig. A shows how the awning is constructed and how it is fitted to the wall. Because it is made to measure, you need to work out the dimensions to suit your window.

Choose your awning material carefully. You can safely use such materials as sail-

cloth or canvas (which you will need to treat), woven or proofed nylon. Select a reasonably heavyweight fabric so that it will not 'ripple' in strong breezes and run the risk of tearing when it is tacked to the awning frames. In some cases specific requirements for both design and colour will determine which fabric you end up using.

The easiest material to make the frames with—and the cheapest—is planed softwood batten. You will need to treat the timber with a preservative which can be painted or varnished over.

The mechanism for raising and lowering the awning is very straightforward. You will need a double and a single pulley block on a swivel mounting. These can be bought inexpensively from a chandlery or dinghy shop.

Your next step is to assess how the awning is to be fitted. If the exterior of your house—and in particular the area outside the window or patio door—is roughcast or pebble-dashed, you must provide a smooth surface against which the support frame for the awning can be secured. This means chipping away the finishing until you reach smooth brick or cement; you need to make good with repair mortar. Alternatively, pack out the frame and fill in behind.

Tools and materials

The frames are made entirely from PAR softwood in standard sizes. Actual dimensions will depend on the door or window you are building the frame around. You will need:

● 175mm × 25mm softwood for the wall box.
● 75mm × 25mm softwood for the wall frame.
● 50mm × 25mm softwood for the four moving frames.
● Enough awning material to cover the frames when fully opened, and go down the sides as well. The length of the material is the width of the frame plus twice the length of the frame sides. Its width (around the curve of the awning) is roughly 1.6 times the length of the frame sides. Add a little extra to allow for mistakes. If you can't get one piece large enough, you'll need to get two sewn together.
● Enough 6mm–10mm nylon rope to operate the pulley mechanism.
● 6 steel or backflap strap hinges to hold the frames together.
● 8 angle braces to strengthen frame joints.
● Enough 50mm No. 10 brass counter-

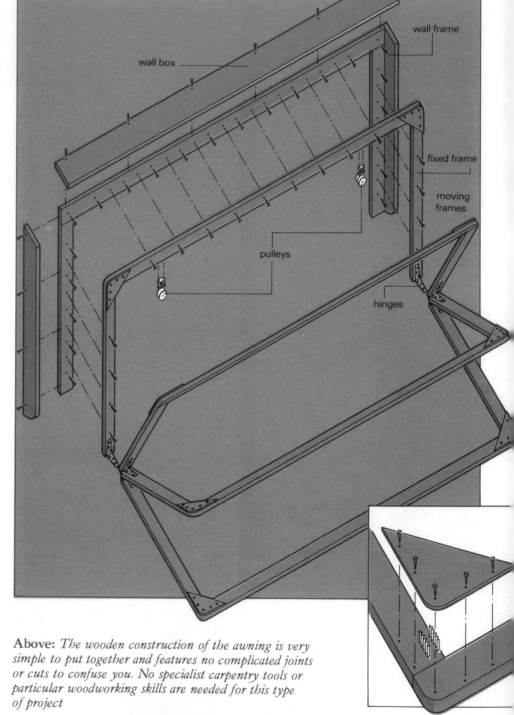

Above: *The wooden construction of the awning is very simple to put together and features no complicated joints or cuts to confuse you. No specialist carpentry tools or particular woodworking skills are needed for this type of project*

sunk woodscrews to hold the wall frame securely in place—you need one every 150mm—with plastic wall plugs to suit.
● Corrugated metal fasteners for frame connections.
● Single or double pulleys to make the pulley mechanism, rope to raise the frames and a cleat to tie off to.
● Woodscrews (38mm No. 8) and PVA woodworking adhesive for frame joints.
● Tacks and decorative upholstery pins to secure the awning material to the frames.

You will also need a tenon saw, a coping saw or power jig saw, screwdriver, drill and bits, a try square, a tack hammer, a 25mm bevel-edged chisel and medium-grade glasspaper for finishing. You must also use a waterproof adhesive such as urea formaldehyde to secure the joints.

Constructing the frames

Begin construction with the wall frame and

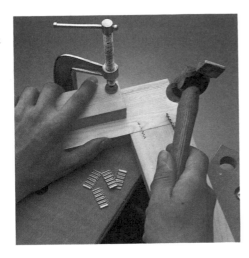

1 *Square up the frame joints and clamp them in place before securing them first with two corrugated metal fasteners*

2 *Pre-drill the corner gussets, and glue and screw them in place. Use a square to ensure the corners are at right angles*

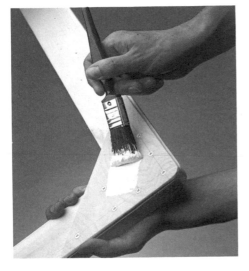

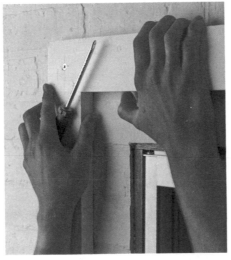

3 *Round off the corners—about 25mm is enough—to prevent the material tearing, then paint all the frames*

4 *Offer up the wall frame, mark its position, drill and plug the holes, then screw in place. Seal behind it with mastic*

Drill all the necessary screwholes and countersink them but do not, at this stage, fit to the wall frame.

Now follow the same procedure to construct four moving frames, checking that, when glued and screwed together, the frame sections remain at right-angles to one another.

Round off the top edges of the moving frames by sanding or with a planer file. In one of the frames, drill and countersink 45mm holes every 150mm. This will be the top-most frame and the holes will be used to fix it to the wall frame.

When all the frame components are completed, they should be treated with a suitable wood preservative then painted or varnished. Use a general purpose wood primer before painting, then apply undercoat and topcoat (fig. 3).

Before offering up and fitting the awning frames, check that all the joints are secure.

★ WATCH POINT ★

The pulley system will be connected up only when the awning material is in place. But when the frame is complete it is a good idea to fit the pulley blocks and securing cleat. The blocks should be screwed to the fixed frame about two thirds of the width of the awning apart. In the lowest moving frame, drill holes the same distance apart to allow the pulley rope to pass through and be knotted.

---

remember that the dimensions of the top rail must allow for the length of the moving frames, plus 20mm clearance at each end. Measure the sections to be cut for the butt joints on both the top rail and side rails. The timber can be cut using a tenon saw, but make sure that the cut ends are exactly square.

Before joining the frame sections together, drill and countersink the screwholes for fitting the frame to the wall. You use 50mm No. 10 screws for this—either stainless steel or brass—so the clearance holes need to be 5mm diameter. Drill one hole every 150mm along the frame.

Arrange the top and side rails so that they are exactly square to each other, then fix them together using corrugated metal fasteners (fig. 1). Ensure, as you do so, that

they remain square. No further support is necessary as this frame will be fixed permanently to the wall.

From 175mm × 25mm planed softwood, cut out the wall box components which will be secured to the sides and top of the wall frame. Where the top and side edges meet, a simple butt joint will be adequate. Here the joints can be glued and screwed together.

★ WATCH POINT ★

If you wish, butt joints can be used and the corners secured with ply gussets (fig. 2) or, to gain additional strength, screw and glue offcut blocks into each corner.

Offer up the wall frame, making sure it is square to the window opening, and mark the positions of the screw holes. Using a masonry bit (No. 10) drill the screw holes in the wall to at least 50mm deep. Offer up the wall frame and check that all the screw holes align.

Once the glue has dried fix the assembly to the wall using heavy-duty plastic wall plugs and for added water protection bed the frame on a sealant mastic (fig. 4). Do not attempt to secure the moving frames until you are sure that the wall frame is firmly fixed to the wall. Each of the moving frames must now be connected together using back-flap or strap hinges.

This is most easily done on a workbench or by laying the frames flat on the floor, fitting two hinges to the fixed frame, then screwing these hinges to the first moving frame (fig. 5). Stagger the hinges slightly so that the screws coming through one side of a frame member do not foul the screws coming through from the opposite side (fig. 6). Ensure the frames remain square and the hinges do not twist them out of shape.

Offer up the completed assembly (you will certainly need an assistant), and fix it temporarily to the wall frame.

Fitting the material

Before attempting to tack material to the awning, it must first be cut—and if wide enough sheets of the material cannot be obtained, lengths must be sewn together.

Open out the moving frames until the lowest frame is roughly horizontal. Now open out all the other frames equal distances apart (you will probably need some help for this) and tack two thin wooden battens across the inside of the ends of the frames, nailing to each one (fig. 7).

The material must first be secured behind the last, fixed frame. Take the frame off the wall frame in order to do this. Allow all the material to hang from the back of the frame, making sure that what will be the outside surface of the fabric is against the back of the frame where it is to be tacked (fig. 8).

B. *Stretch the material over the frame. Thinner fabrics need webbing tape to support the frames. Cut triangular gussets in situ. Fit up the pulley rope as shown*

Lay a strip of webbing over the tape so that it passes over the top edge of the frame and resecure the material by tacking again through the tape or webbing. Tack or staple the awning material to each of the frames in turn making sure the material is pulled taut, but not too tightly (fig. 9). The material must now be cut to match the side triangles.

Tack the material in place one frame at a time, stretching it slightly to prevent creases and cutting off the surplus as you go. Fig. B shows how the material is fitted and how the pulleys are fixed. Do not worry about the edges—they will be covered later. At the bottom of the lowest frame turn the material under the frame and tack it to the back edge. But leave the material slack each side of the holes drilled to take the pulley.

Now the moving frame assembly can be screwed to the wall frame by the holes in the topmost frame, using 38mm No. 8 screws.

With the awning in place you can now glue and screw the wall box top and side covers into position (fig. 11). Make sure that the awning with its material in place does not snag inside the wall box. If the fit is too tight, remove the folding frame assembly and reposition it as necessary until the fit is right.

A word of warning: many canvas-type materials will fray easily when you cut them. This isn't a problem where the frayed edge is tucked away out of sight, but

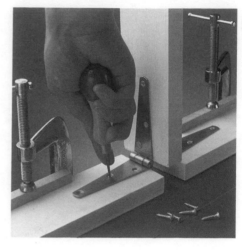

5 *Clamp frame members to a workbench and support intermediate ones while you fix the hinges in place*

8 *Run string lines between the frame corners while you stretch the material over the frames and pin it. Avoid wrinkles*

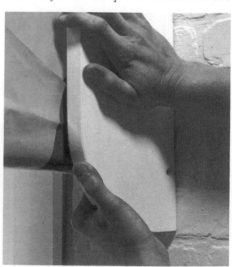

11 *Offer up the wall box components, then glue and screw them to the wall frame using mastic to seal the gap*

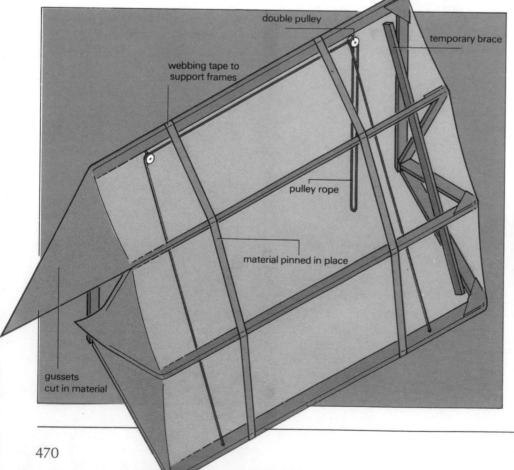

double pulley

temporary brace

webbing tape to support frames

pulley rope

material pinned in place

gussets cut in material

6 *Stagger the hinge positions slightly so that fixing screws on opposite sides of a frame member do not foul each other*

7 *Open out the four awning frames and hold them at the correct spacing with a wooden brace while fitting the material*

9 *Use tacks or staples to secure awning material. Fix first at centre of frame and move outwards to prevent creasing*

10 *Overlap the gussets so that water cannot seep through between them, then tack or staple them in position*

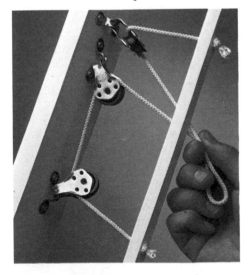

12 *This photograph shows how the single pulley system works. There are many different types of pulley*

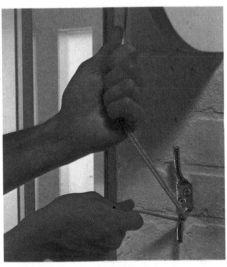

13 *A stout cleat screwed to the wall is enough to secure the pulley rope whether the awning is up or down*

becomes a serious problem at the sides where you must cut the triangular gussets. To counter this problem, buy some plastic or cloth tape—even webbing will do—and lay it over the cut edge of the material before you tack it.

Make sure the tape slightly overlaps the cut edge, and tack it down in the same way as the rest of the material. If you find that the material continues to fray, then untack it, stretch it over the frame and sew a hem on to it. This has the added advantage that it strengthens the material.

The simplest solution, of course, is to choose a rubberized material.

Finishing the awning

Leave yourself enough rope to run, when the awning is open, from the lowest frame to the pulleys, then to the cleat and back to the other pulley, finally ending at the second securing point on the lowest frame.

Now feed one end through one pulley on the double block to the other pulley and then through the hole drilled in the lowest frame. Double knot the rope on the other side, or double it round the frame and tie to the rope as it enters the frame.

Feed the other end of the rope through the spare pulley on the double block and secure, as above, to the lowest frame at the opposite hole. Finish tacking the material on the lowest frame into place around the holes for the rope. Fig. 12 shows how the pulley arrangement should look.

The bottom edge of the awning will look best if it is finished with a matching scalloped or fringed trim. Otherwise, just buy a length of heavy fringing from a soft furnishing supplier. The trim should be put on the lowest frame and tacked in place with a plastic trim over the material.

Now check that the whole system works smoothly and does not snag or catch as the awning is raised and lowered. Apply a small amount of light oil to the hinges, pulleys and pulley swivels. Fix a stout cleat to the wall to wind on the pulley rope when the awning is raised or lowered (fig. 13). Finally, give all screws a fractional turn to ensure they are fully tightened.

Properly made, the awning should not tear or suffer undue damage. But storms and high winds can cause problems such as rips and holes. To repair them, take the awning off the wall and try to stitch the material back together. You may find it easier to iron, sew or glue a matching patch.

If a frame member breaks you may have to remove the material to repair it.

FIT ORNAMENTAL SHUTTERS

Shutters can be used to brighten a plain house front or add charm to a country cottage. You can make and fit them as decorative panels or as working, hinged, flaps to keep the sun's glare from south-facing rooms.

You can buy shutters ready-made, but there is not a great deal of choice. So making them yourself makes sense—especially as DIY shutters are much cheaper than store-bought ones. You can design them to suit the individual style of your house and to fit your window sizes exactly.

When it comes to matching home-made shutters to the style of your house you also get a choice of finishes. You can stain the shutters, leave them natural or paint them to match your window and door frames.

Choosing a style

It is important to choose a style of shutter which matches the style of your house. Modern ranch-style houses call for louvred shutters, ultra-modern houses will need slim-line frames and suburban Tudor homes call for much heavier framing. Mock

Below: *Shutters come in many different styles and can either be purely decorative or they can shield the glare of the sun*

Gothic and those homes built in a rural brick and tile style particularly suit the popular, and easy-to-make, tongued-and-grooved, plain or V-jointed boarding.

The wood required to make your own shutters in this style is readily available in widths of 100mm to 150mm and thicknesses of between 16mm and 20mm. Panelling in these sizes is not too heavy to handle and, if you provide some bracing behind it, sufficiently sturdy for the job.

If you prefer a boarding with a profile, try to use boards of roughly the same dimensions. Do not use man-made boarding for this job—only expensive marine ply is suitable for outside use and even then its

edges need to be sealed. Whichever material you do use, however, make sure that all the surfaces are treated thoroughly with wood preservative.

Choosing the fittings

The right fittings will make all the difference to the finish of your shutters. Although the fittings for fixed shutters serve no practical purpose, to achieve the effect you want the fittings need to look as sturdy as those used for the real things. Working shutters will obviously need sturdy fittings—particularly the hinges. Have a look around your local builders' merchant for old-style fittings—some manufacturers still haven't changed the original designs. Err on the side of heaviness and over-size.

If you feel that the finished shutters will look too plain, consider making some simple decorative cut-outs in them. These can be made by hand but using a powered jig saw makes the job a lot easier. Fig. C shows three typical styles of shutter decoration.

Planning

From the outside of your house, look at the area around the windows to make sure that fitting shutters is feasible. Downpipes, climbing roses and nearby trees may all hinder your plans.

If you have outward opening casement windows, you will only be able to open and close the shutters by going outside—an obvious drawback with windows situated on the first floor.

Imagine how your house will look once the shutters are fitted. Never fit shutters to one window only unless you have a house where that window can be viewed only in isolation.

Plan to make your shutters the same depth as the window opening—even if they're fixed, they should look as though they would cover the depth if needed. But it's not necessary to make fixed shutters exactly half the width of the opening—any discrepancy here is less noticeable and helps you by cutting down on the wood and all the work involved.

A. Shutters can be all things to all houses, but it's important visually to match the shutters to the house. Half-timbered houses don't suit louvred shutters, and modern houses don't suit old oak

Treating the timber

Timber that's going to be used outdoors must be treated thoroughly to protect it for all kinds of weather. Your aim is to get the timber to absorb as much preservative as possible, so make sure the timber is dry. The best time to treat it is after you have cut

★ WATCH POINT ★

One way to ensure that end grain is well soaked is to stand the pieces in a big tin or small bucket of preservative and brush the liquid up them frequently. Leave them for about two days—one each end (fig. 1).

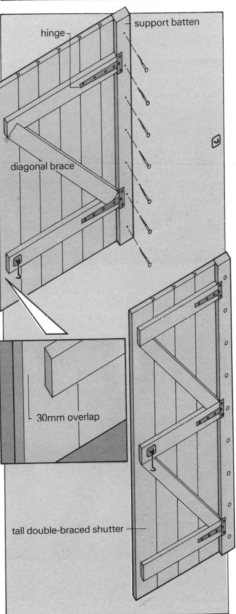

hinge

support batten

diagonal brace

30mm overlap

tall double-braced shutter

the timber to size and made any cut-outs or cut any joints.

Manufacturers' instructions will vary but ordinary preservative should be applied with a big, full brush. But it's not like painting: aim to flood the surface, including any cuts and endgrain.

You can apply preservative yourself or buy timber ready-impregnated—it will cost a little more but reputable builders use it as a matter of course. It's a little more difficult to find for the home builder.

The treatment you choose will depend on how you want your shutters to look. Creosote is the traditional finish and these days you can get it in a range of brownish shades—from light to dark. Remember that you won't be able to paint over it later.

Water-repellent preservatives come in clear, or in a range of colours (fig. 2). They usually have a fungus and insect repellent in them as well. The coloured versions are good if you want the grain to show.

There are also clear, tinted preservatives which can alter the character of timber drastically, making pine look like oak, for example.

Exterior varnishes have been traditional in boat building and there's no reason why you shouldn't use them on your shutters. Opt for matt varnishes, however: glossy shutters will look odd.

Painting is an equally traditional finish for shutters (fig. 3). You'll have to use preservatives under the paint coats, so check when you are buying them that they will allow painting on top.

A word on aesthetic considerations: shutters can look good whatever style you choose, but the wrong choice of colours can be a serious design mistake. Shutters should, if possible, complement doors, window frames and exterior woodwork, so you may find that a totally different colour scheme is required.

Remember that bright primary colours look good in small areas like the door or window frames, while large shutters painted to match may simply look garish. Think about this very carefully and try to make a colour sketch of how the house will look. If you do feel that it is necessary to repaint the door and window frames, don't be put off: the finished overall effect, once the shutters are erected, should be more than the sum of its parts.

B. Working shutters need substantial reinforcement to prevent sagging. An angled brace will do the job (top). Tall shutters need double bracing to stop tongued and grooved boarding from pulling apart

Measuring up

Measure the dimensions of your window openings before you buy any materials. It's the size of the opening in the brickwork or timber that you are concerned with—not the size of the window itself.

Measure the height and width of each opening. Shutters should be made 15mm longer than the height so that if they were shut they would just conceal the top of the reveal. Make working shutters half the width of the opening, less about 5mm for clearance; fixed shutters less than half.

When you are working out the number of boards required, remember that you have to saw off the tongue on one side of each shutter and the groove on the other.

The chances are, with working shutters, that you will end up needing a half or quarter width board in each shutter. You may be able to get around this by using

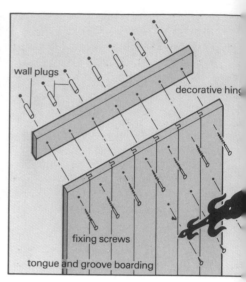

C. *Decorative styles of shutters:*
A. Cut out design in timber. B. Chunky hinges. C. Iron studs

D. *Fake shutters can be screwed to the wall through the backing piece while decorative hinges are screwed to the front*

★ **WATCH POINT** ★

When making fixed shutters, you can save work by letting their width equal a whole number of boards—this saves cutting.

boards of a different width—sizes vary between 100mm and 150mm—or by adjusting the position of the hinges in relation to the opening. But if you can't solve the problem this way you will have to cut a board lengthwise using a ripsaw, then plane off the edge neatly. The cut board should go on the hinge side of the shutter.

Estimate the length of tongued, grooved and V-jointed boarding you will need for each shutter by multiplying its height by the number of boards to make the span. You will also need four 75mm × 25mm softwood boards for the horizontal rails—the width of each shutter less 30mm. Working shutters also need two 75mm × 25mm pieces for the diagonal braces. As a rough guide for their length, simply measure the diagonal of a shutter and multiply by two.

Finally, you will need two 50mm × 50mm pieces the height of the shutter for the side battens to which you fix the hinges.

Assembling the shutters

The shutters are simply panels of tongued-and-grooved and V jointed boarding held

1 *Stand the boards in a bucket of preservative to flood the end grain, and apply to the rest using an old brush*

2 *If creosote is too sombre for you there are other tinted clear preservatives you can use instead*

5 *Mark off and cut the boards using a tenon saw. Cut on the excess side of line and don't splinter protruding pieces*

6 *Saw or plane the tongues and grooves off the edges of the outside boards before screwing the backing piece down*

together at the back with horizontal rails (fig. D). Working shutters also require diagonal braces (fig. B).

Start by cutting the boards all to the same length to suit your opening. Knock the boards together and level them at one end. Square them off at the other end (fig. 4) then saw off the excess (fig. 5). Saw and plane off the tongues of two of the boards and the grooves of two others. These will be the edge boards for the two shutters. Working on a flat surface, one shutter at a time, tap the tongues into the adjacent grooves of the boards to form a single leaf.

Measure and cut the horizontal rails. They should finish flush with the hinge side of the boards about 30mm in from the other side; for working shutters you will need to cut diagonal braces as well, plus two side battens to hinge them to the wall. For medium-sized shutters you can simply butt the slanting ends of the braces against the inner edges of the horizontal rails.

Remember that the diagonals should have their foot near the hinge—then the top effectively props up the outer end of the top rail.

If your shutters are tall and thin you will need to add a third horizontal rail in the middle and use two diagonal braces. And if they are big and heavy, it is sensible to cut a

---

★ WATCH POINT ★

To ensure that the rails and any braces are in the right position, temporarily tack the ends of the rails to the end boards and carefully turn over the whole shutter—the tongues and grooves should keep it all in one piece.

Nail the boards to the rails. As you nail keep a close check to see that the shutter remains square.

25mm deep triangle in the rails to provide a toehold for the diagonal braces. You will also need to trim off their points so they will fit. Alternatively, mitre the end of the diagonal.

With all the timber cut, it is time to treat the wood, as previously described. Make sure you treat each piece individually and don't miss any parts—especially end grain. After treatment let it dry and then start assembling the shutters.

Working on a flat surface assemble the treated boarding, tapping the tongues into the adjacent grooves. With one leaf assembled, mark the position of the horizontal rails and any diagonals and glue and screw or nail them into position from the other side (fig. 6).

Finishing off

Check that the tops and bottoms of the shutters are even and parallel. If there are any irregularities, mark a straight line as close as possible to the edge and use a circular saw or plane to get the top and bottom straight. Don't forget to give another coat of preservative to the end grain.

With the shutters made, it is time to add any decorative details in the form of handles or reproduction hinges or make cutouts or add decorative studs (figs 7 and 8).

You may find certain types of decorative studs and hinges can be fitted after the shutters are erected. If so, this is a bonus: it allows you to arrange the decoration when the shutter is in its proper place, and so choose the pattern which best complements the overall decorative and colour scheme. Remember to match patterns with existing features of the windows such as handles.

Touch up any poorly covered sections with timber preservative, then apply your final coat and any paint. You are now ready to screw fixed shutters directly to the house and to begin hanging working shutters.

Fitting the shutters

Fixed shutters can simply be screwed to the house wall. Remember these shutters are going to be out in all weathers, all year round. So you will need at least three screws per rail—more if the shutter is bigger than average.

Drill and countersink the shutters from the face side through the horizontal rails. Get a helper to hold a shutter in place while you mark through the screw holes directly on to the house wall.

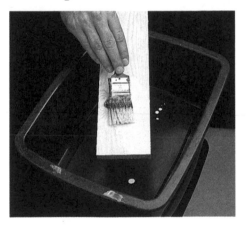

3 *If you wish to paint the shutters first apply a coat of primer, then undercoat and several topcoats*

4 *Knock the boards together with one end squared off. Mark any unevenness at the other end and remove the excess*

7 *Mark positions of decorations so that you can fix mounting screws where they are hidden when the shutter is fitted*

8 *Countersink the screw holes so that the heads will sit flush with the surface. You can conceal them with fittings*

Screw the shutters to the wall, using zinc-plated screws and wall plugs. Stand back and check that the shutters are positioned evenly on each side of the window opening and that they are level. Even if the opening is not quite square it is important that the top and bottom of the shutters are lined up with the most prominent horizontal feature (fig. 9)—the window sill or the eaves if they are just over the window opening—or a row of brickwork over the lintel. Then fit any decorative studs you are using in the screw holes (fig. 10).

With working shutters, it's easier if you do all the preliminaries on the ground. Lay the two shutters in their closed position on a flat surface and separate them with some 10mm to 15mm wide timber scraps to keep the gap parallel. Lay the two side battens on either side and line them with the top (fig. 11). The next task is to lay the hinges in the right position.

Nail a length of 50mm × 25mm timber temporarily across the top and bottom of the shutters and side battens to make the assembly rigid. Fix the hinges with four screws each (fig. 12).

Measure the width of shutters and battens and transfer this dimension to the window opening, making sure that the overlaps on either side are equal. Drill the side battens for the fixing screws and hinges (fig. 13). With a helper, carefully lift up the shutters, side battens and the temporary pieces nailed on top and bottom to hold the assembly over the window. Support it with packing pieces resting on the window ledge, check for level and mark the screw holes through to the wall.

If the wall is brick use a masonry drill and tap in plastic wall plugs. Offer up the assembly and screw the side battens on to the wall before removing the temporary top and bottom ones.

Finishing touches

Because you have added painting and decorative features before you attached the shutters to the wall, the main finishing off work is touching up surfaces, filling and covering screw heads with decorative studs and fixing catches to working shutters.

The main functioning fittings left to add are those which hold the shutters open and hold them closed (fig. 14). The simplest method is to use two sets of cabin hooks and eyes. Close the shutters, hold the catch up to them and mark the position of the two parts and screw the catch into place.

Open the shutters and, using a second identical set, mark the positions on the wall: hook for the shutter cup on one side and cup for the shutter on the other.

If you add a security hasp, make sure it is attached to the inside of the shutters.

9 *Align the shutters with the most prominent feature—the window sill or the eaves—when screwing them to the wall*

10 *It is often helpful and easier to wait until the shutters are erected before fitting the fake hinges and studs*

11 *Lay working shutters side by side with an offcut setting the gap between them. Lay the side battens as well*

12 *Nail battens in place to hold the shutter assembly together temporarily. Then fit the hinges*

13 *Drill and countersink the fixing holes in the side battens before offering up the assembly for fixing*

14 *Working shutters will need catches and hooks so that they can be locked in an open or a closed position*

GARAGE STORAGE UNIT

If you don't have space for a garden shed, you'll probably find that your garage becomes a haven for stepladders, assorted tools, the garden hose, half-used bags of cement plus an array of ironmongery that you can never find when you need it.

This storage system introduces a little order into your chaotic life: there's a compartment for everything in its grid framework, and you can adapt it as you want to suit the items you need to store.

The unit is made entirely from sawn softwood and can be constructed without using any complicated carpentry joints. All the main framing components are simply butted together and nailed for strength.

Designing the unit

Most garages are sufficiently large to accommodate storage space at the back or at one side. Your first requirement, therefore, is to assess what you want to store.

Note down everything you're keeping by its size, as this determines the grid structure you'll need. Assign each large item or collection of materials—ladder, workbench, lawnmower, sheet materials and lengths of timber—to its own compartment. Note down the size of the compartments.

Smaller items such as nails and screws, tubes of glue and assorted hardware can be kept in boxes or screw-top jars and placed on a shelf, along with tins of paint and other containers. Allow for sufficient shelf space when designing the unit.

Lay all your paintbrushes on the floor and measure the area they cover; do the same for tools such as hammers, chisels, saws and power drills.

Translate these measurements as square or rectangular paper cut-outs and piece them together like a jig-saw puzzle to form a large rectangle that's no higher (in real terms) than the garage from floor to ceiling and no wider than the wall you're setting the unit against.

The most important point to note is that there must be sufficient room for the car in the garage once the unit is built. Also, if you're setting the unit on a side wall, check that you'll still be able to open the car doors without hindrance.

The storage system is constructed from a number of shallow frames screwed to the back wall and floor, and attached to the roof joists. The spacing of the frames depends on the width of the compartments you need but you should, where possible, coincide them with a joist. Where this isn't possible you'll have to fit a timber cross piece under the joists, and nail the frames to that.

The frames can be sub-divided to make shallow compartments by nailing cross pieces between frames.

Tools and materials

Because the structure is so simple, you'll need few tools to construct it but equip yourself with the following.
• A tape measure, try square and marking knife for marking out the components.
• A tenon saw and woodsaw for cutting.
• A claw hammer for use in assembly.
• A spirit level for checking that everything is level and plumb.
• An electric drill and assorted wood and masonry bits plus screws, plugs and a screwdriver for fixing to the solid floor (and fitting hinges and clasps).

As for materials, the main framework is of 50mm square sawn softwood and 50mm × 25mm and 75mm × 25mm cross braces. The shelf section consists of 100mm × 25mm sawn softwood on 50mm square battens, and the tool-hanging area is clad with 100mm × 25mm planks.

You'll need an ample supply of 100mm roundhead wire nails and 35mm oval wire nails for constructing the unit, and a supply of timber preservative.

If you're fitting the storage unit into a prefabricated garage for the subframe, 120mm hookbolts, 75mm M10 coachbolts and some 2mm mild steel sheet.

To help you work out how much timber you'll need, draw a scale plan of the unit on squared paper. The plan will also help you when constructing the unit.

Making the frames

The garage storage system is made up from a number of tall, slim, rectangular frames screwed to the back wall and floor, and attached to the roof joists. There are various types of frames to suit the grid system you've designed for your tools.

Where possible, it's best to align each frame with the roof joists, so that you can attach them to the sides of the joists for greatest rigidity. In the case of prefabricated garage kits with pre-cast concrete wall panels and steel joists you'll have to make alternative arrangements (see below).

Measure the height from floor to ceiling and add 100mm to extend up the side of a joist. If your garage has a ceiling—often fireboard is used as cladding—you'll have to cut slots for the frame uprights (see Assembling the framework).

Measure off lengths of 50mm square sawn softwood to make all the frames you'll need and square cutting lines around the wood with a marking knife against a try square. Saw the timber to length.

The unit will probably only need to be about 300mm deep from front to back to accommodate all your materials and equipment. Mark off and cut sufficient lengths of 50mm square sawn softwood to this size; you'll need one per frame.

To assemble the frame, lay two uprights on the floor, pushed up against a wall and spaced about 300mm apart. Place a 300mm long batten across the ends of the uprights, its ends aligned with their sides.

Using the wall as a support, drive 100mm round-head wire nails through the short brace into the ends of the uprights. Drive in two nails per fixing, dovetailed to prevent them being pulled out (see Skew- and dovetail-nailing). Cut a 300mm long offcut of thin wood and tack it temporarily across the opposite ends as a brace.

Repeat the procedure for the other frames. Some frames will need extra intermediate crossmembers to support shelves. Measure between the uprights to give you the correct length for these pieces, mark out and cut them from 50mm square timber, then slot them between the uprights.

A typical garage storage set-up consists of a full-height compartment for tall items such as stepladders, garden machinery and long-handled tools (A). Heavy, unwieldy items such as bags of cement and sand are held within a narrow compartment at ground level (B), while the space above is given over to a collection of plastic washing-up bowls on runners (C) for storing small, light items; the bowls slide in and out like drawers. A broad, deep compartment (D) is ideal for storing sheet materials—chipboard and plywood for example—and long lengths of timber. Part of the framework is hinged to fold down for access. Above is a panelled section fitted out with hooks and clips to hold hand and power-tools plus a portable workbench (E). Next to that is a compartment given over to shelving (F) for holding boxes of nails and screws and tins of paint

1 *Measure and cut one of the uprights to length then use this as a template to mark off the length of the others*

2 *Drive 100mm round-head nails through the short base cross braces into the uprights. Dovetailing will give a stronger fixing*

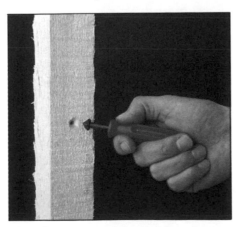

3 *Screw a 50mm butt hinge to the bottom of the fold-down upright. Then attach it to the base batten so that it opens downwards*

Consult your plan to give you the heights at which the shelves must be set and position the battens accordingly—this isn't crucial, as a small amount either way probably won't make any noticeable difference to your grid.

Hold your try square in the angle between uprights and battens to make sure they're square, then dovetail-nail through the uprights into the ends of the battens. These frames don't need additional temporary braces for extra stability.

★ WATCH POINT ★

Key the frames to their relevant positions in the unit to your plan, marking them 1, 2, 3 and so on in pencil. That way there won't be any confusion when it comes to the final assembly.

If you're including a compartment with a fold-down front you can hinge the sections now. Lay two uprights on the floor and brace them temporarily with thin laths at each end. Cut a shelf batten to length and dovetail-nail it between the uprights. Dovetail-nail the base batten to what will become the back wall upright of the frame.

Saw through the front upright directly below the shelf batten. Cut off a further 12mm for clearance. Screw a 50mm butt hinge to the bottom of the timber and attach it to the base batten so that the timber will fold downwards. Secure it at the top in the closed position with an offcut of 50mm × 25mm batten until the frame is secured in its final location. Then fit the hasp and staple.

Before you start to assemble the frames, draw a chalk line across the floor (against a straightedge) to indicate the front of the unit. Use this as a guide to aligning the frames. Mark the frame numbers in the appropriate position on the floor as an added guide.

Prefabricated garages

To fix the frames to the joists and walls of a prefabricated garage you'll need to first make a timber subframe.

Cut 50mm × 50mm uprights to the height of the wall, from floor to joist and deduct 100mm to accommodate the top cross bearer. Cut the 100mm × 50mm cross bearer to the length of the storage unit and fix it to the joists with 120mm hookbolts.

To fix the uprights to the wall you'll need to make U-shaped ties from 2mm mild steel sheet. Cut the sheet with metal shears or a hacksaw into strips 250mm × 25mm.

4 *Drill 6mm clearance holes at 600mm centres through the back uprights for the fixing screws. Countersink the holes*

Position one of the uprights in front of one of the jointing ribs, place the tie over it and mark where it crosses the supplementary holes provided for shelf fixing. Drill 10mm holes through the tie then bolt it to the wall with a 75mm M10 coachbolt.

Take account of the subframe when measuring and marking up the storage framework and skew-nail it to the cross bearer and uprights as described above.

Assembling the framework

The storage system can be assembled by progressively attaching the side frames and filling in between with cross members. It's important to set the frame perfectly level and plumb if the unit is to fit together properly.

Drill 6mm diameter clearance holes for 100mm No. 12 countersunk screws through the back uprights at 600mm

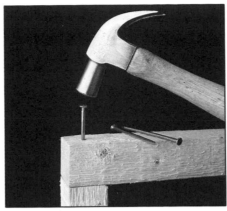

5 *Hold a spirit level against the front and side of each upright to check that the frame is vertical in both planes*

6 *Fit strips of bituminous felt underneath each floor batten to protect the wood from damp. Then screw the base to the floor*

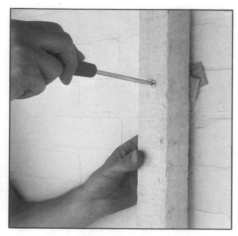

7 *Use thin offcuts of timber to pack out the uprights where the wall is out of true. Position them behind the fixing holes*

intervals. Drill holes through the sides of the outer frame uprights for fixing to the return wall. Drill two holes through each floor batten.

Cut away a panel of ceiling cladding (where necessary) to expose the roof joists at the point where the frame uprights will be fixed; you'll need enough space to hammer.

Starting at the end wall, position your first frame in the corner. (If you're spanning a complete wall, start at the left-hand side—vice versa if you're left-handed.)

Hold a spirit level against the uprights to check that the frame is vertical in both planes. If it's not, this is probably due to the walls or floor being out of true. Don't worry: you can pack out behind the frame.

Temporarily wedge the frame in place with a timber strut and draw around it on the wall, floor and joist in chalk.

Mark the wall through the fixing holes using a large nail or pencil. Mark the floor also. Remove the frame then drill and plug the wall. Repeat for the floor fixing.

Return the frame to the wall and pack it out as necessary with offcuts of timber, so that it's aligned with your chalk marks. It's best to position the packing pieces under a screw hole to hold them firmly in place.

Drive in screws to secure the frame to the

wall and floor. Skew-nail the tops of the uprights to the joists using 100mm nails.

Cut two lengths of 50mm square timber to the width of the first compartment and place them on the floor at right-angles to the frame: the back one running along the wall; the front one aligned with your chalk line.

Take the next frame and position it against the ends of the floor battens. Fix

struts as before while you level the frame with the first one by holding a spirit level across the front—over a long straightedge if the gap is too wide. Secure the frame to the wall, floor and joist as before then skew-nail the floor spacer battens to the uprights.

Continue to fix more spacers and frames, checking that they're aligned with the previously fixed ones. Where two adjoining frames have shelf battens, check that these are horizontal and aligned with each other by spanning the two with a spirit level.

The uprights of some of the narrower compartments—those that contain the plastic bins, for instance—won't match up with a joist position. To support these at the top you'll need to fit horizontal battens spanning the joists at right-angles.

Skew-nail two 50mm square battens to the undersides of the joists, between the nearest full-height frames. Hold the frames in place and mark the uprights to fit snugly under the battens. Cut them to length, slot the frames in place and secure by skew-nailing. Screw the base batten to the floor.

Skew and dovetail nailing

When you're joining two butt-jointed pieces of timber together you can use the dovetail or skew nailing techniques. These methods both give considerable strength to the joint.

Although similar, the two methods are used in different situations.

Dovetail nailing: this is employed when it's possible to drive the nails into the end grain of one component (such as the frame construction in this project).

The end of one piece of timber is butted up to the face of another and nails are driven through the rear face of the second piece into the end of the first piece.

To prevent the two pieces from being pulled apart, two nails are used, driven in at different angles to each other. One is angled to the right, the other to the left, forming the 'dovetail'.

Skew nailing: this is used where you can't gain access to the underside of the joint, and provides the same dovetail effect.

The first piece of timber is butted up to the face of the second and nails are driven through the opposite sides of the first piece at an angle, into the face of the second piece.

It's necessary to support the first piece of timber at one side while you drive in the nail at the opposite side to stop it sliding out of line. You can do this by clamping a block of wood to the second piece, held against the side of the first piece, or simply wedge your foot against it.

You can further increase the strength of the joint by cutting a housing. Use the butting member as your guide for marking and cutting the channel as you would for a halving joint. Allow for the extra length

Skew nailing is used where you can't gain access to the underside of the joint so have to nail through the sides
Dovetail nailing is employed where it's possible to drive nails into the end grain. It's a very secure method

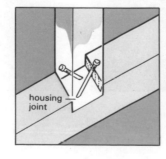

housing joint

when measuring the butting member.

With both methods, it's best to use round-head nails to prevent them being pulled straight through the timber.

Fitting out the frames

You can fit out the frames with shelves, hanging racks for tools and runners to hold containers for storing small items. The components are simply nailed in place.

The hanging rack, which takes your portable folding workbench—plus an array of hammers, chisels, screwdrivers and other tools—is made of 100mm × 25mm sawn softwood planks nailed to the back frame.

Measure the width of the compartment to be clad, and mark out and cut the wood to length using a tenon saw.

Position the first plank at the top of the compartment, its ends resting on two uprights. Hold a spirit level underneath the plank to set it horizontally, then secure it with two 35mm oval nails at each end.

Place the next plank below it, leaving a gap of 19mm, check it's level and secure.

Use the same section timber to make shelves for the unit, again spaced 19mm apart and secured with 35mm nails to the front to back cross support battens.

Attach the necessary hooks or clips to hold tools and equipment to the planked compartment. Draw round each tool in felt-tipped pen, so each has its own home on the hanging board. You'll find it easier to spot its hook or lip when returning the tool to the store.

To retain the fold down section in the closed position, you need to fit a hasp and staple at the top of each folding upright. Position the hasp so that the tongue folds over its own plate and overlaps the top of the upright. Fix each hasp in place and mark the position of the staples. Finally secure the staples and use a bent nail to hold the unit closed.

Plastic washing-up bowls can be used to store a number of smaller items, such as paint roller pads, dust sheets and balls of string. Mount them on runners, one above the other.

Cut to length a number of 25mm square pieces of softwood—they should fit from front to back of the frames.

Nail the runners horizontally to the front and back frame uprights, on the inner faces of a compartment about 400mm wide. Set them about 200mm apart. Secure with 35mm nails, and use a spirit level to position the runners on the opposite side, then slide in the bowls and fill them up.

To hold sacks of sand or cement in their compartment attach an adjustable retaining strap and buckle between two front uprights. In order to protect cement from being affected by moisture coming up from the floor, make a base for the compartment out of 100mm × 25mm softwood nailed to the lower cross battens.

To complete the structure, nail 75mm × 25mm fascia boards along the top of the entire unit, across the two fold down sections of upright (so forming a door), and across the perimeters of each compartment.

Give the entire structure a liberal coat of preservative to discourage rot.

8 *Use an offcut of 19mm thick timber as a spacer for setting the hanging rack planks. This will ensure that they are all evenly spaced. Nail them in place*

9 *Arrange all the items on the hanging racks and draw around each tool with chalk or a felt-tipped pen so that each has its own home to return to after use*

10 *Nail the 25mm square plastic drawer runners horizontally across the drawer frame uprights. Use a spirit level to ensure that they are straight in both directions*

11 *Nail 75mm × 25mm fascia boards along the top of the unit, across the front of the fold-down section, and the perimeter of each compartment*

12 *To ensure a long life for the unit, finish off by giving the entire structure a liberal coat of clear polyurethane preservative to prevent rot*

DECORATIVE PAVING

Pathways are often left until last in the overall design of a garden. They end up as functional elements of the design rather than the decorative accents they could so easily become—with a little thought and planning.

Your garden path need not be a simple strip of concrete. By using unusual materials which blend in naturally with the surroundings, you can create a pathway which is an attractive feature of the garden and is not purely a functional necessity.

Using bricks

Bricks are a natural alternative to concrete, being both easy to lay and very durable, as described in the last section.

Available as special paving bricks or simply as regular building site material—such as hard engineering bricks—bricks come in so many colours and textures that they can blend in with any type of garden.

For instance, patterned red paving bricks provide a subtle contrast to predominantly green and woody shrubs and plants. Just imagine what a simple concrete path would have looked like. The natural texture and warmth of the red bricks adds significantly to the overall atmosphere of the garden. They are by no means a material for just another path!

Similarly a path laid with neutral coloured bricks sets off and enhances the bright flowers which line its length.

In this case bright red bricks would have been distracting. These bricks have been laid in mortar but most paving bricks can be laid simply on a bed of sand that has been well tamped down and compressed.

Paving stones

Unlike brick, paving stones are usually fairly neutral or pastel coloured and to make the most of their special appeal they should be laid out in interesting and different patterns.

They are the ideal paving materials for small gardens and patios and if they are laid as in the picture they can allow quite a bit of greenery to spill over into any confined space. Using grass as a filler between staggered slabs is a particularly effective way of breaking up what might otherwise be a cold expanse of grey across the width of the patio.

The path pictured across the lush green lawn could have been laid simply as a straight line with parallel sides; but how much better to stagger the pattern in semi-geometric steps, giving the effect of a winding pathway without any elaborate curves.

Wooden paths

Usually, the first choice for paving material is some kind of stone, or other hard, rock-like covering. It is not generally realized that deep wooden beams can be just as effective. They are even simpler to lay than bricks—the best kind of wood to use being scrap or driftwood, which is cheap and easily obtainable.

★ WATCH POINT ★

As long as the wooden beams are thoroughly soaked in preservative before they are laid, a properly designed wooden pathway can take many years of wear.

But the ideal bedding material for a wooden walkway is a spread of gravel or small pebbles as illustrated.

Well-seasoned old wooden beams can be embedded in such material either by digging deep grooves in an existing sweep of stones or by laying the wood on the bare ground and then infilling with carefully graded pebbles to pack down the beams tightly against each other. Vary the lengths of each slat to get a ragged edge to the

Left: *Red paving bricks can add a subtle and attractive contrast to a very green-looking garden*

according to size and colour can be bought from specialist garden centres and sometimes from builders' suppliers. If you have the patience, a mosaic path made from finely graded pebbles can look very attractive and almost Mediterranean in style.

A rough stone path is not as easy to lay as it might at first appear. The stones are readily available from quarries and suppliers of rubble and hardcore, but you must choose each stone very carefully, looking for the ones with flat surfaces which can

---

★ WATCH POINT ★

The small pebbles should be embedded in a screed of wet concrete and it is important to choose each stone carefully—setting it against its neighbours so that an even surface is produced overall.

Left: *Rough stone paths are not that easy to lay. The stones must have level surfaces and butt together easily*

Below: *Wooden beams laid crossways can make an unusual-looking path but they need to be kept moss-free*

path and add that characteristically rustic, weathered look.

The pathway which has a bed of stones on one side and a lawn on the other provides a natural link between two different areas of activity in the garden.

The beams have been laid lengthways to create a tidier effect than those laid crosswise and a series of wooden steps links this section of the path to a conventional concrete type around the edge of the lawn.

Wooden paths age very differently from the brick or concrete varieties, developing a thin covering of moss and lichen. Although this can often add to their charm, such growths should be cleared from the actual trodden part of the path as they can be slippery in wet weather. Mossy borders, on the other hand, look delightful.

Pebbles and mosaics

Beds of pebbles are an easy way to cover large areas of ground where plants will not grow, because the ground is shady or otherwise unsuitable. Pebbles graded

then be laid uppermost.

Properly laid rough stone paths look very attractive and are particularly suited for gardens full of bushes and trees. They have an old-fashioned, country feel and lend an air of age and maturity to any garden, however small. Part of their charm is the weeds and plants that sprout up in the cracks, but again such growths are best cut back every so often or they will engulf the whole path and become a safety hazard in damp and wet weather.

Choosing your paving

If you are thinking of relaying one of your garden paths or even laying a completely new one, consider the various areas of the garden through which it will run.

There is no strict rule that says the nature of the path must be the same along its whole length. You can use one or more of the ideas discussed here to blend in the path with the surrounding aspects of the garden.

Above: *An attractive geometric pattern of paving stones can really be the highlight of a rather plain garden*

Above: *Paving stones can be laid with a large space to let grass grow in between them for variety of colour*

Left: *Wooden beams can also be laid lengthwise for a neater, and more uniform, path in the garden*

MAKE A CHILD'S SANDPIT

Sandpits are always a great attraction and when combined with a paddling pool are guaranteed to provide hours of fun. With this design you can make both from the one basic plan.

Sandpits don't have to be very big, which means you should be able to fit one into even the smallest garden. Nor do they have to be expensive and complicated to construct. This design (fig. A) shows just what can be done with basic materials readily available from your local timber yard and hardware store. It also has the advantage that it can be modified to make a toddlers' paddling pool.

You could build both and set them together so your children can have a complete summer play area where you can keep an eye on them and yet there's plenty for them to do.

near to the house and clearly visible from the downstairs windows.

You'll need a flat site as the box rests directly on the ground. A large patio is ideal as it's easy to sweep away any sand that's scattered over the edge of the box. In this instance, saw off the 'drive in' fixing legs shown in the design and use angle brackets to secure the pit. Or you can simply rest it in place if you want to move it around quickly and easily.

A lawn provides another good site but you must bear in mind any adverse effects on the grass.

Try to set the box in a sunny position and keep it away from trees and bushes, which tend to attract insects. And falling leaves are nothing but an aggravating nuisance in damp sand.

What you need

Building the sandpit requires very few tools so a simple kit including a panel saw, screwdriver, drill and bits, and a mallet will suffice. If you are preparing a site in the garden you should also have a spade and rake. Some string and pegs will be useful in marking out the site.

The materials you need for the sandpit are a sheet of oil-tempered hardboard, and some exterior plywood for the top and bottom. The sides are cut from 230mm × 25mm softwood, the legs from 50mm × 50mm softwood, and the seats are cut from 150mm × 25mm softwood. For the framing of the top you'll need 50mm × 25mm softwood.

★ WATCH POINT ★

Make sure the lid is always put on after the children have finished playing in the pit or pool. This is important if for no other reason than keeping animals from fouling the play area. The lid will also prevent the sand being drenched in a downpour of rain. For reasons of hygiene it's probably best to empty the pool after it's been used but the lid will stop debris falling into it. Sandpits and paddling pools not used properly or without some form of supervision can give rise to accidents.

Siting the sandpit

Where you site the sandpit will very much depend on the size and shape of your garden. Remember that the pit isn't a permanent fixture and will only be used in the summer months. You could, if you wanted to, take it up and store it safely away in a shed or garage during the long winter months.

The most important consideration is one of **safety**, particularly in the case of paddling pools. Keep the sandpit or pool

Right: *This versatile sandpit, which can also be made into a paddling pool, will keep children amused for hours*

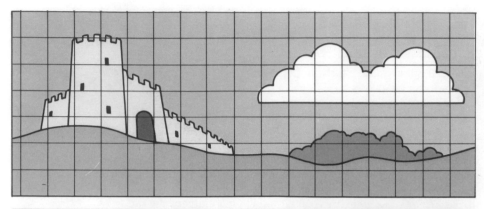

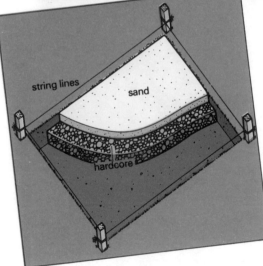

A. *Use the grid as a guide for transferring the design to the sides of the boxes. The castle in the desert is perfect for the sandpit, the tropical island ideal for the pool*

B. *Use string lines to mark out the sandpit and lay hardcore and sand*

important stages. Skimp on this and the pit or pool will not last for more than one summer. Both a sandpit and paddling pool are going to take a fair bashing from children and adverse weather conditions. So before you start any assembly work treat all the timber with a couple of coats of wood preservative. And if you want to change the colour of the wood, try one of the heavily pigmented types. Then later, when the boxes have been made up (and in the case of the pool, before the polyethylene liner has been added) and when all screw and nail heads have been covered up, coat everything with several coats of exterior-grade polyurethane varnish or gloss paint. This will give a tough surface resistant to water. It will also prevent splinters forming on which children could injure themselves while they're playing.

If you are planning to make the paddling pool as well, you will need some heavy-duty polyethylene for the liner and a sheet of vinyl flooring to lay on the base. You need glue and screws to assemble it all and to finish off, some exterior-grade polyurethane varnish or paint. Treat all of the softwood with a preservative after you've cut it but before assembly. Remember, the structure will be outside so even if you haven't made the pool the wood will need protection from the rain.

Finishing treatments

The finishing off work is one of the most

Preparing the site

Lawns and patios will provide you with a ready-made flat site. But if you want to

create a permanent site by itself, from an old vegetable plot or flower bed for example, you'll need to do some thorough preparatory work before you set the sandpit in the chosen place.

First, dig over the site, rake it out and tamp it down firmly. Then check for level in several directions using a spirit level set on a long straightedge. Adjust the ground accordingly. Mark out the position of the sandpit using stringlines or the base of the box itself. Decide on the material you want to use round the box and prepare the area surrounding the box position. Then lay the turf or paving material on the prepared surface.

Next, dig out the site of the box to 100mm−150mm below the surface, fill with hardcore and finish off with a binding layer of sand to allow for adequate drainage beneath the box (fig. B). By providing a dry base you'll help to prolong the life of the sandpit.

Building the sandpit box

Fig. C shows exactly how the sandpit and pool are constructed. Study this first, so you're sure you know how it fits together.

Start by cutting the oil-tempered hardboard base to size. As you'll probably have to buy a 2440mm × 1220mm sheet, the offcut can be used later for the base of the pool.

The rectangle for the base of the sandpit should measure 1500mm × 1200mm. The sides are cut from 230mm × 25mm softwood, the longer ones being 1456mm in length, and the shorter ones being

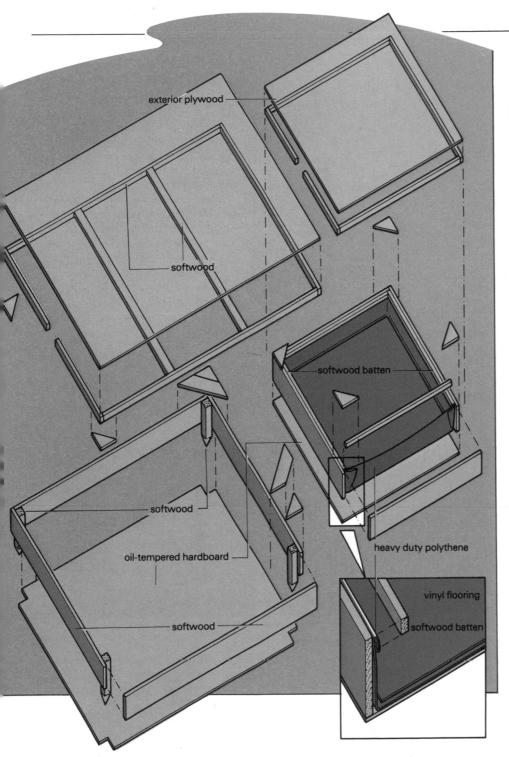

exterior plywood

softwood

softwood batten

softwood

oil-tempered hardboard

heavy duty polythene

softwood

vinyl flooring

softwood batten

1 *Cut pointed ends on the legs—unless you plan to set the box on a paved area, in which case cut them to match the sides*

2 *Mark the screw positions on the legs and longer sides and drill pilot holes. Fix them together after countersinking the screw heads*

3 *Fix the shorter sides to the legs using the base as your guide. If the legs have been cut off they simply act as a corner brace*

1200mm in length. The four fixing legs should be 420mm long cut from 50mm × 50mm softwood. Cut pointed ends on the legs (fig. 1) so they can be driven into the ground. Remember, if you are setting the pit on a patio, cut the legs to the depth of the side of the box so that they simply become corner support battens.

Now glue and screw the legs to the inside faces of the longer side panels so that they are flush with their ends (fig. 2). Use a urea formaldehyde rather than a casein adhesive as the first will withstand all weather conditions. Drive four No. 8 50mm

C. *Both of the boxes are made from lengths of 230mm × 25mm softwood butt jointed at the corners. The legs are cut from 50mm × 50mm softwood cut to match the sides or with pointed ends. There are corner seats which act as bracing cut from 150mm × 25mm softwood, as well as similar spacing blocks for the lid. The base is cut from oil-tempered hardboard with notches cut out as necessary. The lids consist of exterior plywood set on a 50mm × 25mm batten frame. The pool is similar but has no legs. The liner is secured by a batten*

woodscrews through from the panel side to hold the legs in place. Space them evenly and countersink and fill over their heads.

When all the side panels are fixed together you'll have a free-standing unit. Now you have to fit the base. If you are building a box with legs, mark the position of the legs at the corners before taking the side panels off the hardboard (fig. 4). Remove the side panels and cut out the corners of the base along the lines. You will then be able to set the hardboard in position so that the legs pass through the notches cut in the base.

At this stage it's probably best to let the glue dry for a few hours and get on with the job of making the lid (see below). All that remains is to fit the base and the planks across two of the corners. Apart from acting as seats they also give extra rigidity to the top edges of the sandpit (fig. 5).

Hold each plank at an angle across the corners so that the ends of the leading edge rest on the edges of the side panels. Pencil along the underside of the plank where it

Lay the hardboard base on the ground with the shiny side up. Use this as a guide for squareness when you butt up the two shorter side panels and fix them to the other outward-facing edges of the legs (fig. 3). You'll find it easier if you work with the timber upside down so that the top edges of the box are set against the base held on the ground.

meets the side panels to give you the correct angle for cutting off the overlaps. Then glue and screw the seats in place.

Once the glue has dried turn the box upside down to fit the base to the frame (fig. 6). Glue and nail, with broad-headed annular copper-coated nails, to hold the board in place. The shiny side should be the side that eventually comes into contact with the ground. If there are no fixing legs,

simply nail the base straight to the bottom of the side panels.

Now set the box in place in the garden. If it has fixing legs, these will have to be driven in with a mallet. Work so that the box settles down on to the ground evenly so as little strain as possible is put on the joints. Half fill the box with silver sand once it is securely in position.

Making the lid

The lid is made of 6mm thick exterior-grade plywood attached to a 50mm × 50mm softwood batten frame. The lengths of the framing members correspond to the dimensions of the box itself. Cut the top of the lid to match the base.

Make up the frame first on top of the plywood as you did the box, butt jointing and nailing the sections together (fig. 7). This will ensure that the frame and plywood fit flush around the edges. Drive the nails below the surface and fill the holes. Transfer

4 *With care, turn the box upside down and mark the lines for cutting the notches in the hardboard to fit round the supporting legs*

5 *Glue and screw the corner seats in place to help keep the box square. Use two pieces set side by side for each seat*

6 *Turn the box over and fit the hardboard base to the frame with copper-coated nails, keeping the shiny side facing out*

10 *Assemble the basic box by gluing and pinning the butt joints together. Then fit the base as you did for the sandpit*

11 *Cut an oversize square of heavy duty polyethylene and lay it over the box. Then work it well down into the corners*

12 *Lay the square of flooring vinyl so that it sits evenly on the base of the box and holds the polyethylene in place*

the position of the frame to the top surface of the plywood then glue and screw the frame and sheet together (fig. 8).

Because the lid rests on top of the two corner seats, it stands to reason that if left like this it wouldn't sit level on top of the sandpit. Glue and screw small angle braces to the underside of the lid framework to match the two corners of the sandpit which are not fitted with seats (fig. 9).

Leave a 150mm gap in the framework along one side to make it easy to grip the lid to lift it off the box.

Making the paddling pool

The basic principles of the sandpit can be easily adapted to make a small paddling pool. The base of the paddling pool is made of oil-tempered hardboard cut to 900mm square. Cut two sides from 230mm × 25mm softwood 900mm long as well as two shorter sides 856mm long. These are butted together, glued and pinned securely (fig. 10). Because of the size of the pool, internal corner supports are unnecessary. In fact their presence would make it awkward to fit the pool liner. Extra rigidity is given to the framework later by screwing triangular corner seats to the top edge. The pool won't need fixing legs as you'll need to be able to tip it up to run out the water after each use.

Once the frame has been assembled, lay the heavy-duty polyethylene over it, tucking the sheet well down into the bottom corners of the box (fig. 11). Then set the square of heavy-duty vinyl over the base (an offcut will do)—this will help to keep the polyethylene in place (fig. 12). It will also provide a more comfortable surface for your children to stand on. And it can be removed easily for cleaning.

You may find it a little difficult to get the polyethylene to form neat corners. The best method is to pleat it and then use PVC adhesive to hold the various folds in place (fig. 13). Don't be tempted to pin it to the side walls, as this will only cause the paddling pool to leak noticeably when it is full of water.

Finally, you've got to fix the polyethylene to the top of the box above the water line. You could just lap it over the top edge and pin it, but then there's the possibility of the children cutting their feet on the exposed nail heads. Instead, fold the sheeting down until it is just below the top. Screw battens against it to pinch it in position, and countersink the screw heads (fig. 14). It doesn't matter about piercing the sheeting at this level because this will be above the water line when the pool is filled. Now screw on all the corner seats which help give the box its necessary rigidity of structure (fig. 15).

The lid is constructed in exactly the same way as for the sand pit, but, because it is smaller, it will need only perimeter battening: cross battening is unnecessary. Nor will it need extra supporting blocks in the corners as there are already four seats giving the lid a level bedding on which it can firmly rest.

7 Assemble the framework for the lid on top of the plywood using it as your guide to ensure that the frame is square

8 Nail the top of the lid to the framework and drive the heads below the surface. Fill the holes and sand the filler when hard

9 Fix braces to the lid at the corners opposite the seat positions so that the lid sits evenly all round when it is set in place

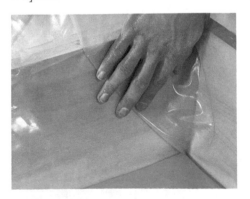

13 Carefully pleat all the corners of the polyethylene liner and use blobs of PVC adhesive to hold it securely in place

14 Trim the edges of the polyethylene with a sharp knife and roll it over. Clamp it to the box by fitting a batten with screws

15 Finally add the four corner angle pieces which act as small seats and also give the necessary bracing support to the framework

PICNIC TABLE AND BENCHES

Eating outdoors in the garden has become increasingly popular over the past few years and a wide range of barbecue equipment and garden furniture has come on to the market. But many of the tables on offer incorporate their benches in one large assembly and consequently they're difficult to clamber over to sit down, and they can't be taken apart quickly or easily for storage during bad weather or the winter. This garden table set, however, has two separate benches and the table has folding legs so that it can be stacked out of the way in a shed or garage when it's not needed. It's simple to set up and easy to make.

Only basic woodworking skills are needed to make the table and benches, all the joints being glued and pinned together. The table shown measures 1,495mm × 750mm and the benches 1,195mm × 400mm, but you can alter the sizes to suit your needs.

Materials

Since the table and benches will spend a lot of time outside, use a hardwood such as beech or elm—this will last longer than a softwood like pine, although it will cost more. All the timber sizes given below are nominal so you may find slight variations.

The table battens are cut from 100mm × 25mm PAR timber. You'll need enough wood for the following pieces:
• Fifteen 750mm lengths for the top battens (A in the diagram shown on the opposite page).
• Two 1,495mm lengths for the side rails (B).
• Two 706mm lengths for the top cross-members (C).
• Four 765mm lengths for the legs (D).
• Two 704mm lengths for the horizontal leg braces (E).
• Four 456mm lengths for the legs' folding braces (F).
• Two 750mm lengths of 25mm dowel (G).
• Two 704mm lengths of 25mm dowel (H).
• Two 658mm lengths of 25mm dowel (I).
• Two 125mm lengths of 75mm × 38mm batten and two 125mm lengths of 75mm × 50mm batten for the leg clamps (J).
• Two 100mm long, 6mm diameter coach bolts with matching wingnuts and washers.
• Eight 50mm chromed No. 8 countersunk woodscrews.

The benches are made from 75mm × 25mm PAR timber throughout and for two you'll need the following:
• Thirty-two 400mm lengths for the top battens (U).
• Four 1,195mm lengths for the top rails (V).
• Four 356mm lengths for the horizontal crossmembers (W).
• Eight 702mm lengths for the legs (X).
• Four 400mm lengths for the horizontal leg braces (Y).
• Eight 410mm lengths for the diagonal leg braces (Z).

In addition to the above materials, you'll need a supply of 18mm and 38mm sherardized oval nails, some waterproof wood glue, some clear wood preservative and good quality exterior varnish.

The legs can be clamped underneath the table making it easy to store in winter

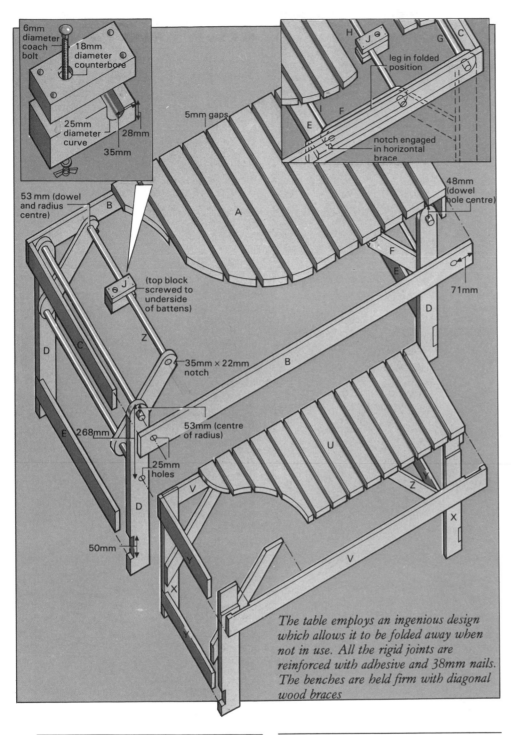

6mm diameter coach bolt

18mm diameter counterbore

25mm diameter curve

28mm

35mm

5mm gaps

H

J

G

C

leg in folded position

notch engaged in horizontal brace

53mm (dowel and radius centre)

B

A

48mm (dowel hole centre)

F

E

J (top block screwed to underside of battens)

Z

35mm × 22mm notch

B

71mm

D

D

C

E **268mm**

53mm (centre of radius)

25mm holes

D

50mm

U

Z

V

X

V

X

Y

The table employs an ingenious design which allows it to be folded away when not in use. All the rigid joints are reinforced with adhesive and 38mm nails. The benches are held firm with diagonal wood braces

Tools

A basic woodworking tool kit is all that is needed to make both the table and benches. It should include a marking gauge, 18mm and 25mm bevel-edge chisels, a selection of wood bits, an electric drill and a half-round file. A pair of sash cramps and four small G-cramps are essential for holding the pieces together during construction—if you don't possess these, you can hire them cheaply from your local tool hire shop.

Cutting out the parts

When cutting out the parts for the table and benches, remember to square all the cutting lines around each piece with your try square and score along each line with a marking knife so that the wood won't splinter when you start sawing.

In most instances it will simplify matters if you cut groups of identical components roughly to length, cramp them all together and saw or shape them in one operation.

Similarly, the holes for the 25mm dowels should be drilled through matching pieces in one operation to ensure perfect alignment. By working in this way, you will only have to mark out one piece of each set as a template.

The table

With the exception of the 25mm dowels and the blocks for the leg clamps (see Making and positioning the clamps), the entire table is made from 10mm × 25mm PAR timber. All the pieces can be cut to their exact dimensions at this stage, apart from the legs and braces which should be cut oversize so that their ends can be rounded off. You may wish to leave cutting the top battens (A) until the supporting framework is made to ensure that they fit properly (each should be 750mm long). If you're building a table to the dimensions shown you'll need 15 of them.

Cut two 706mm top crossmembers (C) and two 1,495mm side rails (B), leaving the latter cramped together after cutting. Using a marking gauge, scribe the centre line on the face of one rail and make a mark on this line 71mm in from each end. Drill a 25mm diameter hole through both pieces at each mark and then widen the holes with a half-round file so that a length of 25mm dowel will turn freely in them. If you don't have a half-round file to enlarge the holes with, you can always taper the ends of the dowels that will slot into the holes instead. In many ways this is easier than filing down the sides of the holes, provided you use a fine glass-paper and follow the grain of the wood. Try not to exaggerate the taper or there will be unsightly gaps when you assemble the table.

Cut two 704mm lengths of batten for the horizonal leg braces (E) and four 765mm lengths for the legs themselves (D). Score the centre line on the face of one leg and mark off along it at 48mm, 53mm and 268mm intervals from one end.

Set your compass point on the 53mm mark and scribe an arc from one edge of the batten to the other. This represents the curved top of the leg. Now measure 715mm along the centre line from the point where it is cut by the arc and square a line across the face of the batten—this is the bottom of the leg. Measure back along the centre line from this point 50mm, align your try square with the mark, and square a line across the leg. Take a piece of scrap 100mm × 25mm batten and stand it on the leg so that its edge is aligned with the line you have just drawn and its face is flush with the edge of the leg. Draw round the off-

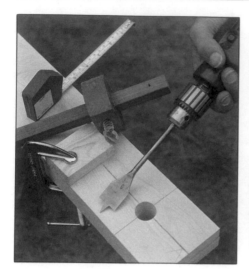

1 *Leave the side rails clamped together after cutting and drill 25mm dowel holes through both*

2 *Enlarge the holes with a half-round file so that a 25mm dowel will rotate freely*

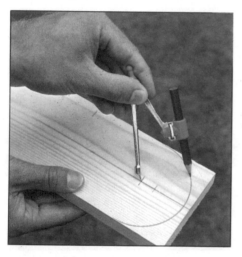

3 *Scribe an arc at the top of each leg and cut out the waste with a jig or coping saw*

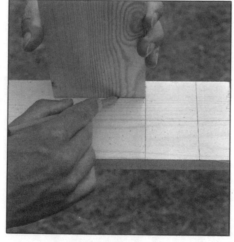

4 *Mark the horizontal brace cutouts on the legs using an offcut of wood as a guide*

5 *Round off the ends of the braces and saw out the 35mm × 22mm notches*

6 *Halving joints are used to connect the legs to the bench side rails*

7 *Set a sliding bevel to 45° and mark the mitres on the diagonal braces*

cut to transfer its profile to the leg. This will be the cutout for the horizontal leg brace.

Cramp the leg battens together and square the bottom line around all four. Similarly, mark the brace cutout lines across the leg edges and on to the face of the outer leg. As before, use the scrap piece to mark the exact profile.

Using a tenon saw, cut right through all four legs at the bottom, taking care to keep to the waste side of your cutting line. When you saw through the edges of the legs to the bottom of the brace cutouts, make several cuts through the waste portion to make removal easier.

Drill 25mm diameter holes through all four legs at the 48mm and 268mm marks and open out the lower one with your half-round file so that a 25mm dowel will turn freely in it. Chisel the waste from the brace cutouts, using a 25mm bevel edged chisel and working in from each side towards the centre. Check that the horizontal braces fit snugly in the cutouts.

Round off the top of each leg separately with a jig saw or coping saw, making sure that you keep the blade vertical all the time.

Now for the folding leg braces (F). First cut four 456mm lengths of batten and mark the centre line on the face of one. Mark off along the centre line 53mm from one end and then 311mm from this first mark. These two points represent the centres for the supporting dowels and also the radii of the shaped ends. Set your marking gauge to the thickness of the wood you are using and scribe a short line, parallel with the edge of the batten, so that it cuts through the arc at one end and finishes in line with a dowel centre. Mark off along the centre line 35mm from where it is cut by the arc, and square a line across the batten. The two lines describe the notch that has to be cut out to make way for the horizontal leg brace when the legs are folded up.

Cramp the battens together and drill 25mm holes through all four at the points marked. Shape the ends of the braces like the tops of the legs. Having rounded the ends, transfer the outline of the notches across the edges of the battens and on to the remaining exposed side. Cut out the waste with a tenon saw.

The remaining pieces for the table are the 25mm dowels; cut two 750mm lengths (G), two 704mm lengths (H) and two 658mm lengths (I).

The benches

The method of marking out and cutting the components for the benches is very similar to that of the table but all the timber is 75mm × 25mm PAR.

The top of each bench is made from 16 battens (U), each 400mm long. These are supported on a frame of two 1,195mm rails (V) with a 356mm crossmember (W) at each end.

The two outer rails must be cut with halving joints to accept the tops of the 420mm long bench legs. Taking each corner in turn, lay a rail down flat and stand a crossmember on top so that it is flush with the end. Mark the rail by running a pencil across the inner face of the crossmember. Then lay a leg on the rail with one edge against the pencil line and mark both rail and leg where each is overlapped by the other.

Set your marking gauge to half the thickness of the wood and score the joint depth on the edges of each piece. Square the face lines down the edges to meet these marks. Cut out the waste with a tenon saw and 25mm bevel edged chisel, working in from each edge towards the centre.

The legs are strengthened by two 400mm horizontal braces (Y) which are let into the legs in the same manner as the table, and four diagonal braces (Z) measuring 410mm long. The ends of the diagonal braces are mitred at 45°—if you don't have a mitre box wide enough to accept the batten, set a sliding bevel to 45° and use this to mark the angled cutting line.

When you have sawn all the pieces to length, clean up the rough edges with some fine glasspaper wrapped round a wooden sanding block.

Before assembling the table and benches, treat all the pieces with two coats of good-quality clear wood preservative.

Assembling the components

Assembling the table and benches is straightforward as all the components are just nailed and glued together. Use sash cramps to hold the frames rigid until the glue sets.

Construct the table and benches on a level uncluttered surface so that as each frame is made, it can be put aside and laid down flat while the glue dries.

The table

The design of the table is such that the various components must be put together in a specific sequence. Begin with the folding leg braces, followed by the leg assemblies, then the table top frame. Finish off by fitting the table top battens and the leg clamps (see Making the clamps).

Assemble each of the folding braces in a dry run before you start gluing the pieces together. Start by connecting two 456mm battens together with a 658mm length of dowel. Slot the dowel through the holes nearest the notches—the ends of the dowel must be flush with the outer faces. Slide a 704mm length of dowel through the other pair of holes, and, with the battens parallel with each other, check that this dowel protrudes by an equal amount at each end. Measure the diagonals to check that the frame is square and then run a pencil around the top dowel on the inside of the side battens and around the lower dowel on each side of the battens.

Dismantle the frame and spread glue on the ends of the dowels between the pencil marks. Then reassemble the frame, wipe off any excess glue with a damp cloth, and set it aside on a flat surface for the glue to dry.

Once you have made the two braces, start on the leg assemblies. Dealing with one pair at a time, slot the protruding dowels of a brace into the appropriate holes in the legs.

Insert the remaining 704mm length of dowel through the top leg holes so that they protrude by an equal amount on each side. Mark the top dowel for gluing as previously described.

★ WATCH POINT ★

If the dowels stick, try rubbing some candle wax on the insides of the holes—this will lubricate the dowels and allow them to rotate smoothly.

8 *Use an offcut to ensure that the dowel protrudes by the correct amount*

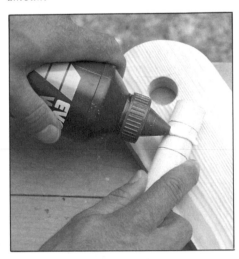

9 *Spread adhesive carefully between the pencil lines before slotting the dowel into its hole*

10 *Complete the brace assembly and then push the legs onto the dowel ends*

11 *When you fix on the horizontal leg braces, reinforce the joints with* nails

12 *The top side rails are the last pieces to go on. Check that the braces swivel*

13 *Finish off the table frame by nailing and gluing the rails to the crossmembers*

Apply glue to the top dowel and the horizontal brace cutouts and assemble the components as shown. Secure the horizontal brace at each end with two 38mm oval nails. Use a nail punch to sink the nail heads below the surface of the wood. Check that the framework is square and pin a scrap batten across the top to hold it while the glue sets.

Having allowed the leg assemblies to dry, move on to the top frame. Glue the two crossmembers to one of the side rails, reinforcing each joint with a pair of 38mm nails. Set this assembly on a flat surface, with the crossmembers uppermost, and fit each leg assembly into its hole in the side rail—make sure the folding brace of each can open inwards towards the centre of the table. Apply glue to the exposed ends of the crossmembers and fit the remaining side rail, taking care to locate the free ends of the leg dowels as you do so. Pin the side rail as before and fit sash cramps across each end until the glue dries.

Glue and pin the top battens to the frame, spacing them at 5mm intervals and using 38mm nails punched below the surface.

The final job, before applying two or

14 *Fix the top battens to the bench frame before adding the legs. Note* the spacer

15 *Sink all exposed nailheads below the surface of the wood using a* nail punch

---

★ WATCH POINT ★

To save yourself the tedious chore of measuring out and marking the position of each slat, cut yourself a 5mm wide spacer from an offcut of 100mm × 25mm batten and use it to gauge the gaps.

---

three coats of varnish, is to fit the leg clamps as described in Making the clamps.

Once you have fixed both the clamps to the underside of the top battens, try opening and closing the legs—you may find that on one pair of legs, the horizontal dowel doesn't engage cleanly in its clamp cutout. If this is the case, don't despair as the simple remedy is to enlarge the bolt hole in the lower half of the clamp into a slot. If you do this, you will be able to slide the block along so that it can cope with any variation in the dowel positions.

If you have to make a slot, leave the block attached to the table while you accurately measure up and mark the exact length you want the slot to be. Then remove the lower

block by unscrewing the wingnut and hold it secure in a vice or in the jaws of an adjustable workbench.

Drill a series of 6mm holes inside the slot outline, making absolutely sure that you keep the drill vertical all the time. Cut out the waste wood between the 6mm holes using a coping saw or fine padsaw. Smooth down the sides of the slot with a strip of glasspaper folded over two or three times.

Reassemble the clamp and test its operation on the table once more.

You may also find a similar discrepancy in one of the folding leg braces when it is in its folded position—the 35mm × 22mm notch may not be long enough to engage the horizontal brace fully. Again, this is easy to put right by increasing the width or depth of the notch with a tenon saw. Be sure to mark and square up cutting lines with a pencil and try square before you start sawing.

The benches

Pin and glue the side rails and cross-members in the same manner as the table. When the glue has set add the top battens, spacing them at 5mm intervals. Don't forget to sink the nailheads well below the surface with a nail punch.

Attach the legs to the side rails with glue, reinforcing each joint with four 18mm nails. Fit the horizontal leg braces across the bottom of each pair of legs, and then glue and nail the diagonal braces between the legs and the top rails. Finally, finish off with a coat of varnish.

Making the clamps

Each table leg assembly is held in the open and folded positions by a wooden clamp screwed to the underside of the table top. Each clamp is made from two 125mm long blocks of wood; one cut from 75mm × 38mm PAR batten and the other from 75mm × 50mm batten. The thinner of the two sections is screwed to the underside of the table top and has a bolt passing through it which secures the lower section with a wing nut and washer. This lower part of the clamp is shaped to fit over the leg brace dowels.

Having cut the wood to size for one clamp, mark the centre line on the face of the upper block and make a mark on this

line 30mm in from one end. With the two pieces cramped together, use an 18mm flat wood bit to bore a hole in the top block at the point marked to a depth of about 6mm (this will act as a counterbore for the bolt head). Then drill a 6mm diameter hole through the centre of this and right through both blocks.

Separate the two blocks and drill a 4.5mm diameter screw clearance hole at each corner of the upper block. Countersink these on the lower face.

To shape the cutout for the leg braces, secure the lower half of the clamp on its side in a vice and drill a 25mm diameter hole down through the wood. The centre of the hole must be 35mm from the end furthest from the bolt hole and 12.5mm down from the upper face. Great care is needed to keep the bit running vertically—if you have one, use a vertical drill stand. If you don't have a drill stand, stand a try square on edge next to the drill and use it as a visual guide to keeping the bit vertical.

Set your marking gauge to 28mm and, with its stop against the lower face of the block, mark a cutting line from the 25mm hole along the edge, across the end grain and along the opposite edge back to the hole. Square another cutting line from the inner edge of the hole on one side, across the upper face and down to the inner edge of the hole on the other side. Cut out the waste with a tenon saw to achieve the shape shown in the picture.

Insert the coach bolt through the hole in the upper block and hammer its head down into the counterbore so that its square shank bites into the wood.

Loosely assemble each clamp, turn the

table upside down and position the clamps centrally on the underside of the top battens.

Open out the table legs so that they are vertical and set the clamps so that they hold the braces in position, clasping the upper dowel. Then, without disturbing the clamps, disengage the braces and fold the legs into the table top—the clamps should engage the lower dowels. Adjust the setting of the clamps as necessary and then mark their positions on the top.

Remove and dismantle the clamps, set the upper blocks back in place and mark the screw holes on the underside of the top battens. Make a pilot hole at each point with a bradawl and screw the blocks to the table with 50mm chromed No. 8 countersunk screws.

If you use brass screws, first cut the thread in each hole with a steel screw of the same size; brass screws are quite soft and will often snap in half if used to cut their own threads.

★ WATCH POINT ★

With a minimum of care your picnic table and benches can be kept looking at their best. At the start of the summer, brush a coating of a colourless preservative onto the exposed wood. The wood will absorb the preservative most efficiently when it is dry. Use furniture wax about once a week during the summer to protect it further. Store indoors or in a dry shed during the winter.

Drill the bolt hole through both pieces and countersink the screw holes

To make the cutout, drill the 25mm hole first and then saw away the waste

With the legs vertical to the table top, mark the position of the clamp

LAY A BRICK PATH

The attractive appearance of brickwork need not just be confined to house building and boundary walls—paths, drives, patios and steps all look great built in brick.

The porous nature of some ordinary bricks makes them unsuitable for paving work. Coming into direct contact with the ground, with no protection against damp, they would quickly become saturated and start to crumble. For this reason you must use either engineering bricks, purpose-made paving bricks or concrete block pavers. They're available in many different forms, all of which are extremely dense and hard—making them impervious to moisture and frost.

Paving bricks and blocks vary in size from about 215×65mm×33mm to 215mm×215mm×35mm and come in a variety of colours. They are not as deep as ordinary bricks, and this saves time and effort when digging the trench for the path.

Best of all are the rough stock bricks which are kiln-burnt longer than other types, giving them a very red appearance and making them more resistant to bad weather conditions.

Alternatively, you might like to consider using old bricks bought from a demolition contractor: if they have withstood 50 years or more without crumbling (in the same sort of situation that they are to be used in now) they are bound to be resistant to frost and moisture—and they may be cheaper than new bricks.

Remove the old mortar on the bricks with a chisel and hammer. You can use the old mortar as hardcore for the foundations.

Brick patterns

Brick paths, drives and patios can be laid in a variety of patterns (fig. A)—basket-weave, herringbone and running bond are popular examples.

Running bond (bricks laid end-to-end and joints staggered from row-to-row) is easy and quick to lay; it's exactly the same as the stretcher bond used for walls, and the bricks can go either across the path or lengthways.

You can make the patterns even more attractive by varying the colours of the

Right: *Laying a brick path is a very straightforward task but the finished result looks attractive and is very hard wearing*

bricks. For instance, in basket-weave bond, you could have one half red and the other in a very pale colour to give a chess board effect or a diagonal pattern. Use a simple run of bricks to form the borders, with either the stretcher (side) or the header (end) faces butting up the edges of the path.

For a more varied appearance you can lay a ragged brick edging, as shown in fig. A, though this uses more bricks than the simpler bonding methods. For wide areas —such as a patio or drive—it is a good idea to start by paving one or two longitudinal

---

★ WATCH POINT ★

Where a path is to curve, fix one peg to the middle of the site and attach a length of twine as long as you want the furthest part of the curve to extend (fig. B). Stretch this taut to another peg, level it, then move the second peg around as a compass as you dig out the foundations. Shorten the twine, and repeat for the inside edge of the path.

---

courses each side to act as a gutter and border.

You can also obtain some interesting effects by laying bricks on edge, although this method uses a lot more bricks and is consequently more expensive.

Preparing the site

Before starting to lay any foundations drive in pegs at each corner of the proposed path. Stretch twine taut between them, check this for level by holding a spirit level on top, then adjust the height of the pegs where necessary so that you have a level guide for the foundations (fig. 1).

A patio or path is not usually expected to take great weight, so most ground can be made to suit the job. If the soil is very firm, try not to disturb it when marking out the area—simply pull out any grass or weeds, fill any hollows and roll the surface flat (fig. 2).

If the ground is soft, you must lay down a layer of rubble or stones, compact it with a roller then cover it with a layer of sand to fill in any voids. You will need to remove

1 *Mark out the path with twine stretched between pegs. Adjust the twine with the help of a spirit level to obtain the right slope*

2 *If you are laying the path on firm ground fill any holes and take away bumps, then roll it smooth with a heavy roller*

3 *To make a sand foundation spread the sand over the site and then smooth it down so that it is about 50mm deep all over*

4 *Now lay the bricks down in the desired pattern, spacing them about 15mm apart and removing or adding sand to make them level*

5 *Protecting the bricks with a piece of wood, tap them with a heavy club hammer to make the surface as level as possible*

6 *Spread sand over the path and brush it well into the cracks, leaving a trough of about 30mm deep between the bricks*

some extra soil to allow this.

Where soft patches occur in otherwise firm ground, fill them with rubble, compact it well and roll it level. In extremely wet conditions, or where the site is below surrounding ground level, it is a good idea also to install a 25mm wide sub-soil drain in a bed of clinker beneath the hardcore. If possible, the drain should have a slight gradient and discharge into a soakaway (a rubble-filled pit, which filters the water away). However, it is a good idea to consult your local building inspector at the planning stage if this is necessary.

Ideally, all paths should have a gradient of 25mm in one metre to ensure rapid drainage of rainwater. To obtain this, check that the marking-out pegs are level then adjust their heights so that the twine between them slopes right away from the house. As you use the twine as a guide for digging the foundations, the gradient will eventually be transferred automatically to the bricks themselves.

7 *Finally spread a dry mortar mix over the path, brush it into the joints then sprinkle with water using a watering can with a fine rose*

A gradient of 25mm every three metres is sufficient for a level patio, but a site which slopes dramatically away from the house also needs a soakaway at the far end—a shallow, gravel-filled trench will do the job.

When the patio site slopes heavily towards the house, bring the adjoining edge

★ WATCH POINT ★

A paved patio which butts up to the house must be at least 150mm below the level of the damp proof course (DPC) so that rainwater cannot splash up to the wall above it and so cause a damp problem indoors. For the same reason water should not be allowed to collect where the patio joins the house.

up to ground level with hardcore and insert a vertical DPC against the wall of the house. This can be a strip of bituminous felt.

Bedding material

The site for paths and patios needs to be excavated to about 100 to 150mm, depending on which bricks you use. Though bricks

Large, flat areas often look as if they are concave—turning up at the edges. To avoid this, introduce a slight camber of, say, 25mm every three and a half metres by gradually lowering the marking-out lines from the middle of the site outwards.

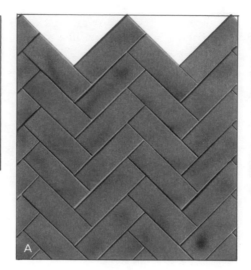

can be laid directly on to a well-tamped bed of clay or gravel, the path is best protected against subsidence by laying a sub-foundation of concrete. Make the concrete bed from one part cement to six parts all-in ballast and with just enough water to make the mix workable.

Lay the concrete to a depth of between 50mm and 75mm and set up formwork of timber planks on edge, nailed to wooden pegs driven into the ground outside the area of the path, to mould and retain the wet mix until it's hard. The surface need only be roughly levelled at this stage, as the mortar in which the bricks are laid will help to take up any irregularity.

Hardcore is not really necessary for paths and patios, but is for sites where the subsoil is soft. At least 100mm thickness of broken bricks or concrete should be laid—plus a layer of small chippings or stone dust and sand as the final layer. Alternatively, over the hardcore, 100 to 150mm of weak concrete can be laid, made up as described above.

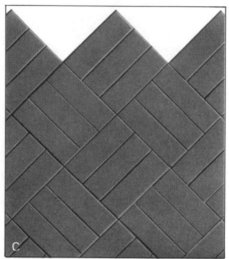

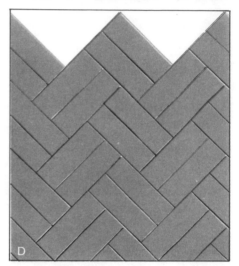

Laying bricks on sand

Where the ground is naturally hard, a brick path can be laid loose on a bed of sand (fig. 3)—although you may have to excavate to a depth of 180mm before you reach sufficiently firm and level subsoil. In this case level off as much as possible, roll out the area, then spread a layer of sand over the site.

Lay down the bricks in the desired pattern, spacing them about 15mm apart and removing or adding sand as is necessary to get them to the required level (fig. 4).

You can compact the bricks into the sand bed by laying a stout length of wood over the rows in a manageable area, and tapping with a club hammer (fig. 5). This is fine for small areas but for a larger surface you'd be wise to hire a plate compactor: this machine, fitted with a rubber sole plate, will vibrate the bricks quickly and evenly into a

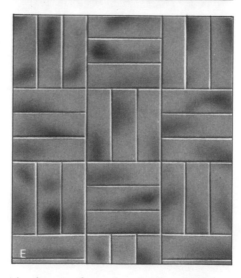

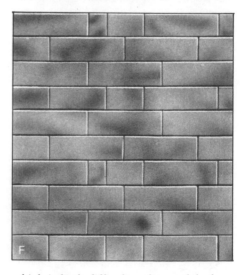

A. *Among the various brick patterns you can lay are (A) single herringbone bond (B) raking bond (C) diagonal basketweave (D) double herringbone bond (E) basketweave bond and (F) a mix of half bond and Flemish bond. You should bear in mind that the more complicated patterns will require some brick cutting* *which is both difficult and wasteful of material not to mention expensive. It should not be attempted if you do not feel confident enough to complete the job in a professional manner. If this is the case it is better to attempt only the easy patterns or you will only be disappointed with the result*

firm, level surface.

When you have laid all the bricks, spread sand over the surface and brush it well into the cracks (fig. 6). Pass over the surface once more—using club hammer and wood block, or plate compactor—to firm up the joints properly.

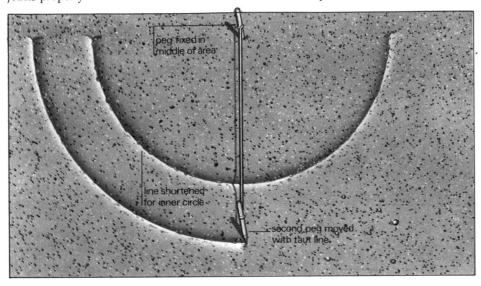

B. *To mark out a curved path, scratch the lines with this makeshift compass. Simply shorten the line to mark the inner edge*

Laying bricks on mortar

Before you start to lay the bricks, prepare two lengths of board, about 2m long × 125mm wide, and prop these at the side of the path as the bricks are being laid. Move the boards along as you work and lay a straightedge, with a spirit level on top, across them to act as a gauge to keep the surface level.

Use a guideline stretched taut along the length of the site to indicate their correct height; place this to the right if you are right-handed and to the left if you are left-handed.

Start at the lowest point of the proposed path and lay the bricks by pressing them into the mortar bed and tapping them gently into position with the handle of your club hammer until they're level: check this by holding a straight-edged length of wood

over them. It will help you to have a scale plan of your chosen design handy so that there can be no confusion over the pattern.

Brick borders

Adding a border to a brick path or patio serves three purposes—it makes the work look more attractive, helps to hold the bricks together and prevents grass and weeds from encroaching on the path.

Always use new, purpose-made bricks—soil piled up against them will make them more vulnerable to decay.

Another sensible precaution is to build the mortar up around the outside of the border bricks, as far as you can without ruining the appearance of the path. A raised border of, say, two courses would give even more protection. Lay these in the normal way, adhering to a recognized bond.

Brick steps

All the bricks suitable for paths are equally suitable for steps, although you must be careful to choose a type that does not become slippery when wet and therefore dangerous.

Before deciding how many steps to make, determine the height and horizontal width of the slope or incline by banging in a post—at least as high as the ground you are measuring—at the foot of the slope. Use another piece of wood to run from this to the level ground right at the top of the slope (fig. C).

When you have checked that the horizontal piece is level, measure exactly the height at which the posts meet. Measure the horizontal distance between them as well, then divide the proposed number of steps into this measurement to give you the width of the treads.

Before finally deciding on the number of steps, consider your proposed number in relation to the gradient of the slope: if it is steep, the riser should not be too high and the tread should be as wide as possible—at least 300mm.

Normally, it is possible to divide the height equally into steps with risers of about 100mm. But if this leaves too narrow a tread, reduce the height of the risers slightly.

The next stage is to roughly cut out the shape and number of steps and dig a trench to form the footing of the first riser. Continue this trench around the sides of the steps in preparation for the building of the side walls.

Next, excavate the steps to allow for a riser equivalent to the depth of two courses of the bricks you are using plus a 50mm mortar bed and two 15mm mortar joints. Excavate gradually, checking for level all the time.

When you are satisfied that the steps have been correctly cut and are level, fill in the trench with a 1:5 mix of cement and all-in ballast. When this is set—and it will probably take at least a day—the first riser and tread can be laid. For this, you need a mortar mix of 1:3 cement and builders' sand. Lay the first course of bricks for the riser in a stretcher bond on a 50mm bed of mortar and lay the next course on a 15mm bed.

For laying the front course of the tread, single bull-nose bricks are satisfactory, although for comfort and safety the nosing should be of a small radius. If you use conventionally shaped bricks, adjust the level of the mortar to allow for a slight drainage gradient and also to stop water gathering.

Lay the front course flush with the second course of the riser and complete the tread in the normal stretcher bond. Carry on this way until all the steps are complete, remembering to check each course for level before moving on to the next. Fig. C shows how the entire flight of steps can be made.

To prevent subsidence of the soil from the steps and to give them a more attractive appearance, you should now build a side wall. Check that the ground is level before you begin, then build the wall in a stretcher bond using the same bricks for uniformity.

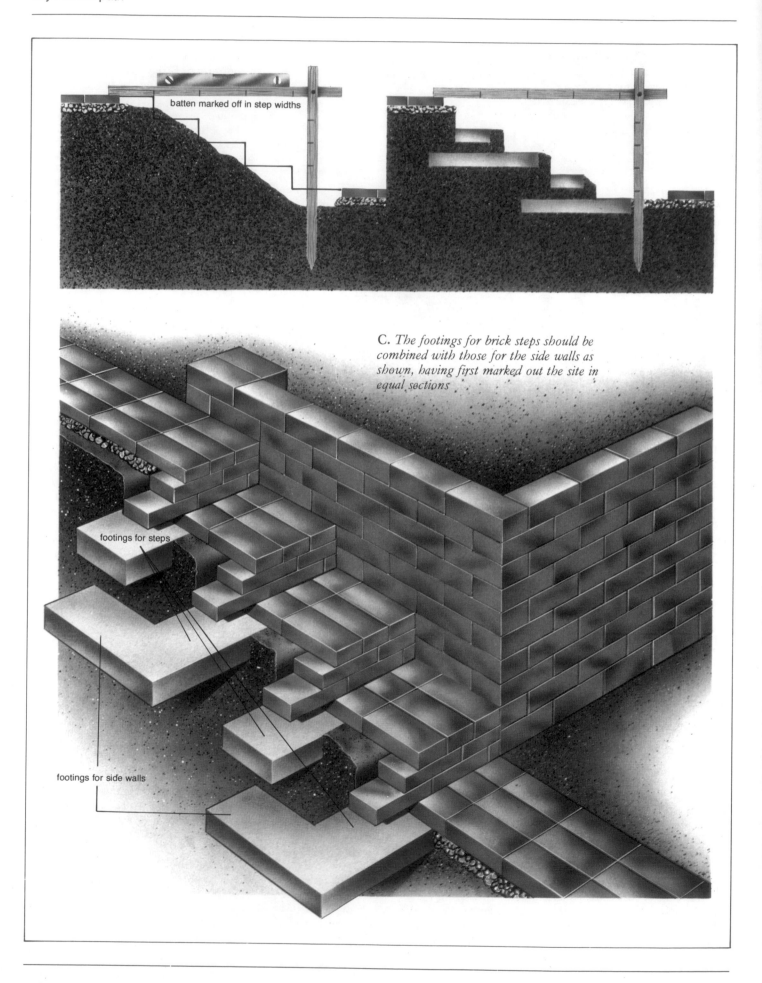

batten marked off in step widths

C. *The footings for brick steps should be combined with those for the side walls as shown, having first marked out the site in equal sections*

footings for steps

footings for side walls

BUILD A GARDEN SHED

If you lack storage space for your garden tools, a timber shed could solve all your problems. They're available in a range of sizes to suit all gardens and are no problem to build providing you follow one or two basic rules.

A garden shed is always useful as a place to lock away your garden tools and equipment, bikes and deckchairs, as well as a place to pot plants and store them over winter. A larger shed with good window light and good headroom can even be used as a small workshop.

Most garden buildings are wooden, but you can also get metal sheds and sheds with concrete-panel walls. Metal sheds will last a lifetime, but they are utilitarian and, unlike the more natural-looking timber shed, are out of place in most gardens. Concrete-panel sheds are really an alternative to building in brick and are considerably more expensive than a wooden building.

Choosing a size

The most popular size for a shed is just over two metres deep by about one and a half metres wide. This gives plenty of storage space and room for a narrow waist-height shelf or a fold-away workbench. If you want a shed just for storage, or if space is very tight, you might consider a much smaller shed of about one metre square with double doors. Although not large enough to step into, the advantage of such a shallow shed is that storage is easy to organize and there are no dark depths for things to get lost in.

A shed of about three metres by two and a half metres with plenty of window light (and perhaps an electricity supply) will give you enough room for a permanent workbench.

The size of shed you choose may be influenced by where you intend to site it—think carefully about this. Sheds are often put at the far end of a garden where they are out of sight; but it may be more convenient to have a shed much nearer the house where there is a dry mud-free path and it is fairly easy and not too expensive to fix up an electricity supply.

Choose a site which is level and avoid parts of the garden that tend to be wet or boggy. Position the shed out of the main lines of view from the house; if it has to be built in sight, arrange rambling plants such as evergreen clematis or honeysuckle, to

Above: *Garden sheds are now readily available in kit form. They are easy to build and different sizes can be obtained to suit your garden*

soften the harsh lines of the design.

If you want to use your shed as a growing house, make sure the windows get good sunlight, otherwise put your shed in shade so that the more sunny parts of the garden can be used for flowerbeds. Think about the way the door will open and aim to have the opening away from the prevailing wind.

Buying a shed

Before committing yourself to buying a particular shed, have a look at a sample that has been erected (even mail-order firms have showrooms where their sheds are available for inspection). Look for a shed

that has all the features you want and then check that the structure is sound. Fig. A shows three popular types.

Take particular note of the following points:
● **Roof:** There are two types of roof: apex—with sloping sides either side of a ridge; and pent—with a slope in only one direction. Pent roofs are used on shallow sheds and on low-priced ones of average size—they look best when a shed is installed with a wall or fence behind; a shed with an apex roof looks good whether free-standing or alongside a wall.
● **Cladding:** The wooden cladding of the shed walls can be simple overlap, rebated or tongued-and-grooved. Overlapping cladding is most economical and used on cheaper sheds; rebating gives better waterproofing and, provided good quality timber is used, tongued-and-grooved is more weatherproof still. You may come across

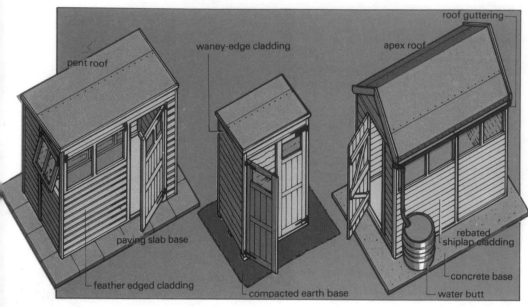

Labels on illustration A:
pent roof · waney-edge cladding · roof guttering · apex roof · paving slab base · feather edged cladding · compacted earth base · rebated shiplap cladding · concrete base · water butt

A. *Three types of garden shed and how they are constructed. The more elaborate the construction, the more expensive the shed, and therefore the more durable it will be*

shiplap cladding, this can be rebated or tongued-and-grooved—the name describes the shape of the board.

● **Floor:** A boarded floor on framing bearers is available as an optional extra with most sheds. These are useful if you are installing the shed on sleeper walls or if you want a floor which is 'warm' underfoot. A shed on a concrete slab base can be constructed without a boarded floor.

● **Timber:** Sheds are available in redwood, whitewood and Western Red Cedar. The first two are softwoods, which need treating with preservative for durability. Some sheds are sold untreated for you to do yourself, but a shed will last longer if it's professionally treated and it is worth paying the extra for a shed that has been pressure-impregnated with a preservative.

Western Red Cedar is naturally durable. Left untreated it weathers to an attractive grey; if you prefer the timber to be light brown you will need to revive the surface with an occasional brushed-on cedar treatment.

● **Doors and windows:** Apex roof sheds usually have the door at the centre on one end. Pent roof sheds may have the door on an end or on the front. A front-opening door is ideal for a shed to be used only for storage, but if you want a workbench or a shelf for plants, an end door is better as it leaves the long side uninterrupted. Doors are normally single ledged-and-braced, but sometimes part glazed durable doors are offered. The windows are normally along one side.

If you want to use your shed partly as a growing house look for a shed with windows at 45° above a cantilevered shelf to give even light to plants. If you want

opening windows for ventilation, look for top-hinged ones which can be left open in the rain.

To check the structure of the shed, shake the walls, slam the door, and jump on the floor—if it bends or feels fragile look for

another shed. Check fixings as well: are nails straight, holes properly drilled and so on?

In your shed kit you should get:
● **prefabricated panels:** sides, ends, roof slopes, floor (if required) and door;
● **window frames** (these may be glazed);
● **ironmongery:** nuts, bolts and hinges;
● **door lock:** with the better kits;
● **instructions** for assembly.

You may also need:
● **preservative** if the shed is not pretreated —buy either a proprietary timber preservative or traditional creosote;
● **rag bolts or expanding anchor bolts** to secure the shed to the base;
● **concrete** for a solid floor—mix cement: damp sand:coarse aggregate in the ratio 1:1⅔:2⅔;
● **lock** for door if not supplied;
● **cup hooks** and shelf brackets;

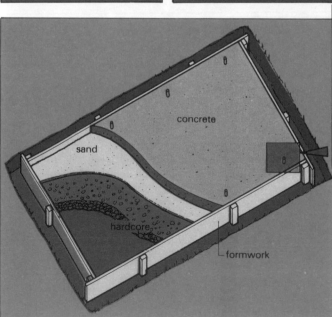

Labels: matching water levels · plastic tube · spirit level · straight batten · concrete · sand · hardcore · formwork

B. *(far left) When preparing a shed site, if the stakes are far apart, use a clear, water-filled tube to check the level. When water levels match, the ground is even*

C. *(left) When stakes are close together use a spirit level*

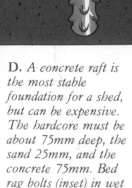

Label: rag bolt

D. *A concrete raft is the most stable foundation for a shed, but can be expensive. The hardcore must be about 75mm deep, the sand 25mm, and the concrete 75mm. Bed rag bolts (inset) in wet concrete to secure walls*

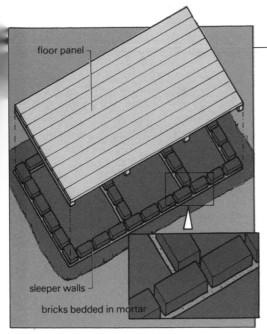

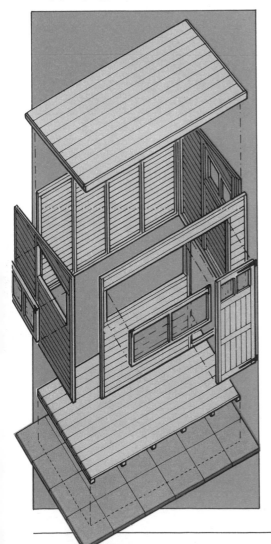

E. Sleeper walls, a single layer of bricks high and embedded on mortar, will support most sheds easily. Leave gaps between bricks to allow air to circulate freely and prevent dampness which would almost certainly lead to rot in the floor—this should be laid on bitumen damp proofing felt

F. The major components of a typical garden shed kit with a pent roof. Apex roof models are only slightly more complicated. The base is of level paving slabs butted tight together; these should overlap the shed base. Construction is simple, all the components being nailed or screwed together

● **bitumen damp-proof course:** available in roll form.

Tools

Make sure that you have all your tools to hand before you start work. You will need:
● **a spanner** of appropriate size;
● **hammer** and pins for glazing;
● **trowel,** spade, wheelbarrow (for concrete);
● **side forms** and stepladder;
● **brace and bit** or electric drill and bit (if holes aren't predrilled) and a putty knife.

Preparing the site

It's important to choose the correct site for your shed. One of the main requirements is that it should be level.

One of the best ways of checking levels is to use a water level (fig. B)—a length of polyethylene tube like that supplied for home brewing, full of water with a cork in each end. You can use this to set stakes to exactly the same level—the stake tops are level when the water level at each end of the tube coincides with each mark.

For a small job like a shed base it may be just as easy to set pairs of stakes level by laying a batten and spirit level across the pair (fig. C)—but beware of cumulative errors with this method.

Stakes can easily be prepared by sawing at a steep angle through a length of rough sawn batten. Wooden tent pegs are an alternative. Use nylon string rather than hemp, as this may well rot or stretch if it is left in the open.

Laying the floor

Laying the floor is the first job to be done, and the one which makes most difference to the finish of your shed. Mark out roughly the site for your shed and set string guidelines around the area to be cleared. Clear any vegetation and remove the fertile topsoil for use elsewhere in the garden. If the area is grassed, lift the turfs in pieces

300mm × 100mm, roll them up and keep to use elsewhere.

For a solid base establish the exact size that the base needs to be and move your stringlines to suit these critical dimensions. At this stage it is important to work precisely—if the base ends up too large it will collect water and the puddles will rot the lower timbers of the shed. The slab is usually made 38mm smaller than the shed itself. Take care to get the corners at 90°.

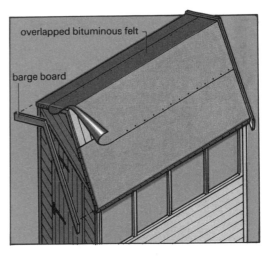

G. On an apex roof lay roofing felt starting from the 'bottom' of the roof, with a single piece covering the ridge, then add fascias

On some soils it is possible to lay a concrete slab directly on the subsoil, but an unstable soil, such as shrinkable clay or peat, needs a 75mm layer of hardcore beneath the concrete (fig. D).

Find a source of clean hardcore such as builders' rubble from which the perishable bits such as paper and wood have been sorted. Before laying the hardcore, dose the soil liberally with weedkiller to prevent plant growth breaking up the foundations.

★ WATCH POINT ★

To check that your rectangle is exactly true measure the diagonals—these should be equal.

Break up the hardcore with a sledgehammer into pieces small enough to mingle without voids, then compact it well.

Level the hardcore surface with a layer of sand (a 50kg bag will cover 3 sq metres) or, if you are not laying hardcore, lay the sand on the subsoil about 25mm deep. Place a sheet of 250 gauge polyethylene over the sand to extend beyond the stringlines and weight it temporarily with bricks. Fix a formwork box over the polyethylene to hold a depth of 75mm concrete in the area bounded by the strings.

Arrange planks on to and across the formwork as access for a wheelbarrow so that you can pour the concrete evenly in the area to be filled. Use a stout timber to ram the mix well into the corners and for firm edges work along the formwork. Use a plank on edge to 'saw' the concrete level with the formwork, top up any hollows and saw again.

While the concrete is still wet, work out where the base will sit and position rag bolts to secure the edges of the shed—two or three on each side is usually enough.

You can leave the concrete with its sawn finish or, for a floor that can be swept more easily, smooth the surface lightly with a trowel about an hour after the concrete has been placed.

Board flooring

A board floor can be laid directly on a firm subsoil, but it is much better to provide a solid base—a concrete slab as above or sleeper walls around the perimeter and under the main bearers (fig. E). The walls need only be one brick (or block) high. Often you can lay them straight on compacted earth, but the base is more secure if you bed the bricks on mortar—the mortar is also useful to take up any unevenness in levels. It is essential that the sleeper walls are level to provide equal and even support

1 *Whichever type of base you finally select, lay a damp proof course over it before laying the floor panels and their timber bearers*

2 *Skew-nail through one floor panel into the timber bearer supporting the adjacent one, then nail the adjacent battens together*

5 *Use coach bolts to secure the walls firmly to each other, tightening the nuts from inside where they won't be affected by rust*

6 *Fit the windows then the roof supports, screwing them in place from inside the shed where water cannot drip into the holes*

9 *Offer up the roof panels, nailing them to the roof supports once you are satisfied they butt together and cover the entire shed*

10 *Overlap the bituminous felt generously, with the overlap running 'downhill' to allow rain to run off without soaking the timber*

3 *While an assistant holds the wall panels up from the 'outside', nail them temporarily together inside, ensuring they are square*

4 *When the walls are square, nail them to the floor while your assistant supports them from outside in the vertical plane*

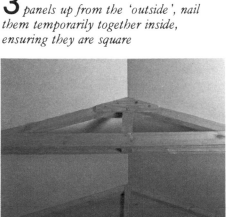

7 *Apex roofs must be tough, especially on a large shed. Extra bracing is necessary to prevent sagging and leaks*

8 *Don't rely on nails and screws to carry much weight. Ensure that roofs and rafters are supported by the vertical frame members*

11 *Lay the bituminous felt roof covering on the roof panels and nail the fascia board in place on the higher edge of the roof*

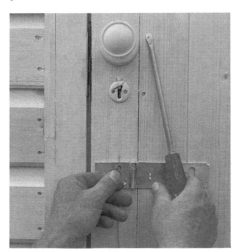

12 *To protect tools and garden furniture (and to satisfy your insurance company) fit proper door and window locks before you store things*

to the floor. Lay the bricks with larger joints than for normal bricklaying and leave the spaces between them clear of mortar so air can circulate underneath.

A popular alternative to concrete slabs and sleeper floors is a layer of concrete paving slabs. These come in a variety of sizes and colours so choose the type you prefer and buy enough to overlap the shed base all round.

Clear the site, remove the turf if you wish, and level and compact the earth. Apply a liberal dose of weedkiller to prevent vegetation growing up between the slabs. Mark the exact size of the base with stakes and string, and lay the slabs one by one, using the stringlines and a spirit level to ensure they are all horizontal and on the same plane. Fill hollows with fine hardcore or gravel.

Use a couple of extra slabs as a 'doorstep' to prevent the grass being worn away outside the shed door and to prevent puddles forming after rain.

Before installing the floor on a concrete slab, paving slabs or sleeper walls, lay strips of bitumen damp-proof course under the bearers to halt rising damp.

Assembling the kit

By making sure that you have all the parts of your kit ready (fig. F) before you start and sorting out the fixing you will need at each stage, you'll find assembling the shed is quite a simple process.

First of all, lay the floor on the base (fig. 1). With a boarded floor screw down to the framing bearers (joists) underneath the boards; with a concrete floor you will need to use masonry anchor bolts if you haven't already set rag bolts in the concrete. Nail the floor panels on to the timber bearers (fig. 2).

Unless you're prepared to mess around with temporary braces, you will need a helper to hold the wall panels while you fix them together. In some sheds the panels are simply bolted together through predrilled holes, but it is only a little more time consuming to use screws in pilot holes you make yourself with a hand drill or a brace and bit. There are normally three fixing points at each corner of the shed. The panels are arranged so that the bottom batten slightly overlaps the edge of the floor (or concrete base). When all four side panels are in place fix the panels to the floor.

With the frame secure, you can fit the windows (fig. 6), the roof bearers (figs 7 and 8) followed by the roof panels (fig. 9). They may be notched to fit over the wall panels. Fixing is either by metal angle brackets or by screwing through the purlins and top battens of the panels. Access to brackets is normally a little easier.

With some sheds the roof panels are supplied prefelted so all that remains at this stage is to tighten the panel fixings and then finish off. If the roof is not prefelted, fix the felt supplied. It will normally be a one metre wide lightweight bitumen felt surfaced with tiny mineral granules.

Lay the felt horizontally, starting from the lower edge. Allow an overlap of at least 25mm on all nail edges (fig. 10) and nail the felt to the roof panel framing timbers at 100mm intervals. Use 19mm galvanized large-headed clout nails if nails are not supplied. Do this on both sides of an apex roof and then lay the crown felt to go over the ridge board and down each side to overlap the lower felts by at least 75mm (fig. G). Some kits include bitumen adhesive to seal this joint, but it isn't strictly necessary; nailing through both layers of felt into a roof purlin is usually adequate.

In areas where torrential rain and heavy winds are common it is a good idea to seal the overlap between layers of roofing felt. Lay a course of mastic between the two layers along the line where you will nail the upper one to the roof panel.

Finish the roof by nailing on the fascia boards (fig. 11) and any capping supplied. Fit the felt over battens if any are supplied. All these timbers are very exposed, so give them an extra preservative treatment (by soaking if possible) to ensure durability.

Finishing the shed

The quality of finishing greatly enhances the durability and character of the shed so don't cut any corners. Hang the shed door using the hinges supplied—usually black japanned tee hinges (they should be about a third of the door long). The holes for the hinge screws may be predrilled; if not you will need to do this job yourself. Get someone to hold the door while you mark the positions. Remember to allow a clearance of

13 *Secure the glass (or clear acrylic sheet) with putty on one side and sprigs or headless pins on the other, forcing the sheet against the putty*

15 *Although the timber should be pre-treated it is wise to add a further coat of preservative—it's available in a variety of colours*

6mm at the bottom.

If you bolt the hinges on (with the nuts on the inside) it makes it difficult for anyone to remove the door from outside. The same applies to a hasp and staple fixing for a padlock. This is the minimum security you will need for a shed, although a sturdy door lock is better (fig. 12). Note that household insurance policies often exclude garden equipment stolen from unlocked outbuildings.

Windows will usually need glazing, although most shed suppliers provide the glass. If you break a piece, replace it with horticultural glass—optically this is not as good as the float glass used for house windows but it is cheaper.

Putty may be supplied for bedding the glass at the back only, with special sprigs to hold it in place (fig. 13). If putty is sticky rub it on a clear sheet of paper to remove excess oil.

Nail vertical battens to both sides of the corners to protect the vulnerable end grain

14 *Fit vertical battens at the corners to protect the end grain of the cladding panels from the weather, and as an extra brace*

of the cladding panels (fig. 14).

If your shed was not pre-treated with preservative use an old brush and apply creosote or preservative liberally (fig. 15); work from the bottom of the shed up to the roof so that splashes won't stain untreated parts. Take care not to splash plants or get the chemicals on your skin. Creosote is poisonous to plants, but preservatives are usually not.

Shelves and hooks are the finishing touches inside. Make sure any shelf bracket is properly supported by a strong framing member of the shed. Use spring clips to provide tidy storage for long-handled equipment such as rakes and brooms and store them head up with any teeth facing the wall.

Timber sheds—especially old, dry, weathered ones—burn easily. If you install an electricity supply, ensure that this is properly earthed and that the components are regularly maintained and not overloaded: sparks and overheating can char the timber and cause fires. Electricity should only be installed by a competent person. If you're not exactly sure what to do, seek expert advice.

When storing plants over the winter, take care over the use of paraffin heaters. These are normally quite safe, but make sure they cannot tip over accidentally and start a fire.

If using the shed as a work room, you will inevitably need some sort of heating during the winter months. Portable gas heaters are perfectly safe if used properly: ensure there is adequate ventilation and that the burners operate correctly—carbon monoxide kills. Also make sure that the gas bottle is disconnected when not in use. Gas leaks can cause an explosion.

Finally, if storing lawnmower fuel or weedkiller, *label the containers clearly.*

BUILDING A GREENHOUSE

In temperate climates, the growing season for many plants in the open is short, and this is bound to restrict your choice of plants and flowers. But a greenhouse can alter the situation completely, enabling plants of many kinds to be grown all the year round. In colder climates, an even greater variety of plants can be propagated and grown if the greenhouse is continually heated, as this will allow you to grow many different exotic examples from warmer regions all around the world.

Building your own greenhouse is not a very complicated job, and it permits you to design and tailor the building to suit your individual needs, the requirements of the site, and the type of plants that you wish to grow.

This section gives you information on the different types of greenhouse you can construct and the step-by-step pictures show you how to build the easy lean-to style of greenhouse which is pictured on this page.

Basic considerations

One of the first things to decide is the type of crop to be grown, noting any special requirements; for example, indoor carnations grow best in tall greenhouses, and need more ventilation than most crops. If you are uncertain about the most suitable greenhouse for your needs consult a nursery or an experienced gardener. However, for average purposes, it is usually a matter of selecting a convenient and sunny spot, either making use of an existing wall to build a lean-to greenhouse, or alternatively siting it apart from other buildings as a free-standing unit.

The size and type of greenhouse best

A. Below: *A lean-to greenhouse is a pot planter's paradise and an asset to any home. In it you can be 'outside' and relax even when the weather is bad—and it is far cheaper than an extension*

suited to your needs are partly governed by the space available, the site itself, the crops and the final cost.

The lean-to type, best sited on an east–west axis in the sun, is usually cheaper to make, to heat (because of its better insulation), and to maintain than a free-standing model of similar size and construction. The mini greenhouse variation can be either a lean-to or free-standing type (see below).

Available space may be further restricted by planning regulations. Structures in front of the building line between the house and the road are normally prohibited in the UK. On the other hand, small greenhouses which are less than 3m high and which do not occupy more than half the garden area are not usually subject to planning consent. Unless you are absolutely certain of the planning regulations in your area, you should consult the local council before starting work.

Design and construction

All buildings have a number of important design and construction requirements, and in the case of a greenhouse there are six main considerations.

● **Appearance:** This is influenced by the design and also by the construction materials—usually wood and glass.

● **Strength and durability:** A greenhouse should be capable of withstanding the worst possible conditions of wind, sun, storms, frost and snow. Timber glazing bars, for example, should ideally not be less than 20mm deep for a 1m span, and the depth should be increased by 12mm for each additional 500mm of span.

● **Light:** Maximum light is of course necessary all the year round so avoid narrowly spaced glazing bars, aiming for intervals of between 450mm and 750mm.

● **Ventilation:** This is critical; the total ventilator area should ideally not be less than 15 per cent or one-sixth of the floor space.

● **Ease of construction:** It is very important that a greenhouse project does not demand great expense on tools and materials, and in this respect a timber frame is a good choice.

● **Low maintenance:** Costs need to be kept in mind, and simplicity of design, combined with sound construction techniques, are of great importance.

Comparison with kits

When deciding whether to erect a proprietary kit greenhouse, or to build a home-made unit, the acid test for most people boils down to cost; but to make a valid comparison you have to take into account many factors, including quality, design, construction and durability. Often the kit price excludes such items as the base, the glass and delivery, so the comparison must be made on the cost of the different greenhouses erected on site complete. This way you can make a fair assessment of relative costs.

Different models

Although the following describes how to build two lean-to types of greenhouse, a free-standing span or apex type with a high central ridge or a mini greenhouse can also be made with certain modifications.

Timber is excellent for the main structure because it is versatile and easy to work with, and presents few problems with either glazing or cladding. Also, less condensation forms on wooden frames than on metal ones because they retain a more even temperature. Given the occasional treatment with paint or preservative, timber structures can last 20 to 30 years and more.

Softwood should be treated with a horticultural grade of preservative containing copper naphthanate. Special attention should be paid to joints and those parts of the building which are in contact with the ground. These should be soaked for a few days in a container of the solution. Long timbers such as bottom plates can be laid on a long sheet of polyethylene gathered along the corners and edges to form a receptacle or bag into which preservative is poured.

Although it costs about 50 per cent more, cedar wood is a timber which requires little treatment or maintenance because it has a natural oil which resists

1 First prepare the site, providing an even bed of hardcore which should be well tamped down, and paint the back wall with a weatherproof agent

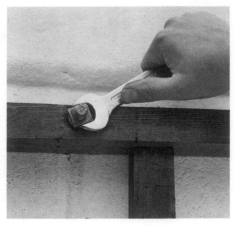

2 Having cut the back horizontal and vertical timbers and applied a timber preservative, fix the horizontal wall plate with long coach bolts

6 The bottom plate of the front frame is a structural component and so it should be firmly fixed to the building blocks with wall anchors

7 At this stage apply a liberal amount of timber preservative to the bottom plate, making quite certain that you treat all cuts and end grain

decay and is ideal for outdoor use.

Both the lean-to greenhouse designs are made up of four sections—two ends, the front and the roof. The designs as shown are adequate for a greenhouse with an eaves height of 1.52m, a ridge height of 2.13m and a width of 2.33m. This should allow considerable freedom of movement, but the measurements can easily be adapted to your own requirements, especially the length. However, if and when altering sizes, keep in mind the standard sizes of cladding materials: this avoids needless cutting and subsequent waste. Also, when building larger structures, heavier timbers and bracing are necessary for extra strength.

The four frames of the greenhouse can be assembled in one or two ways. The frames can be made up separately, then bolted together and screwed to the wall. Alternatively, the wall timbers or studs can be

screwed to the wall first, and the framework then constructed in situ. The frame can later be glazed or clad with PVC corrugated roofing sheet. Standard 4mm thick glass is adequate for glazing and this should be installed in 'modules' as nearly square as possible. This means in effect that the glass is panelled. For instance, on the roof, each run of glass between timbers consists of three panes of overlapping glass. This avoids the use of large panes of glass which are both vulnerable and difficult to install.

3 *Once the loadbearing wall plate has been fixed the vertical back frame can be secured to the wall using masonry nails*

4 *Lay a single course of lightweight building blocks then mortar treated posts into the hollow corner blocks. Make sure that the posts are vertical*

5 *In order to save much wasteful trimming of the cladding material, it makes sense to use it as a guide when actually building the structure*

8 *Once the preservative is dry, set the bottom plate on the building blocks. Make sure that it is flat, then render the building block course*

9 *The PVC roofing sheets can be secured to the structure either with battens or in grooves—the latter being easy to make with a circular saw*

10 *The essence of the greenhouse structure is that the frame is self-bracing. The front top plate is thus nailed to the front corner posts*

Making the four frames is very simple. The essence of the separate parts is that they are self-bracing, in other words they have an intrinsic strength in their unassembled state. The following is only a guide, however, and you should feel free to modify the construction if you want to change the dimensions.

End frame: Using planed softwood timber, cut the base, top, back and front to size then make half-lap angle joints at the ends using a tenon saw and chisel. Make T-halving joints to take the upright and horizontal timbers; these in turn are then cut to size with half-lap joints at the ends. The joints in the top rail must, of course, be cut to the appropriate angle.

In all cases, paint the prepared cuts with preservative before putting them together. Drill and countersink two screw holes at each joint to take the appropriate screws.

Do, however, avoid drilling too deep or the screws will have an insufficient grip. Finally, assemble the timber sections and screw them together, making sure that the bottom corners are perfectly square.

End frame with door: Preparation and assembly of the parts is the same as for the first end frame, but with three differences. The lower horizontal timber cross rail from the front stops at the centre upright instead of running through to the back. This allows for the door. Also necessary is a projecting vertical door stop fixed behind the centre upright and aligned with the door.

The door itself is made from two uprights, fixed to three cross pieces with half-lap joints at the ends and T-halving joints in the centre. Drill and countersink the appropriate screws as before. Then fix three 150mm 'T' hinges to the cross members of the door. The door should not actually be

hung until the end frames are fastened to the wall, but check that the door fits the frame before erecting the structure and adjust as necessary.

Front frame: Cut the four upright timbers to the correct length, making T-halving joints in the centres. Then cut the top, centre and base members, with half-lap end joints, plus two evenly spaced T-halving joints on each. Paint all joints with preservative and allow this to dry before drilling and countersinking to take two screws at each joint. Finally, assemble and screw the timbers together, making sure that the corners are square and that the bottom plate is laid flat side down like those of the end frames. If you decide to put a door in the front frame, follow the instructions given above. As before, do not hang the door until the structure is complete, but do make sure that it fits the frame before moving on to assemble the greenhouse.

Roof: Repeat as for the front frame, with the addition of a ventilator seating. Cut the ventilator seating timber with half-lap joints at each end and screw this securely into the extended half-lap joints of the two centre timbers. Because of the sloping roof it is necessary to chamfer the back timber by about 7°, just sufficiently to allow it to butt squarely against the wall when fixed to the wall plate. Make the ventilator frame in the same way as the door, with the necessary size adjustments. Fix two 150mm strap hinges to the roof frame for the ventilating system and make sure that it is a good weatherproof fit.

Foundations

The base of the greenhouse must be raised above the ground level, to keep it clear of surface water.

If you are building on soil then you will have to dig a foundation to provide a base, the top of which should be at least 25mm above ground level (fig. 1).

It may be that there will be an existing foundation of sorts, in the form of a driveway, path or patio. Provided this consists of paving slabs or concrete laid over a hardcore base it will be adequate, although the level will still have to be raised to the proper height.

One way of doing this is to fit a formwork of 25mm × 25mm battening around the base and fill it with concrete. If you use this method, you must ensure that the new concrete bonds well to the existing surface by coating the latter with a solution of PVA bonding agent.

An alternative is to 'build' the base by laying paving slabs or a layer of bricks—with mortared joints in between them—on the top of the existing surface.

Whichever method you choose, the finished surface must be painted with a proprietary waterproof sealing compound.

A far simpler method of isolating the timber frame from the ground is to build a single course of lightweight building blocks

★ WATCH POINT ★

The base must be absolutely level when finished otherwise the wooden frames of the greenhouse will be at staggered heights when you come to assemble them and therefore they will not fit.

11 *Where thin section timbers are butt or halving jointed it is best to secure them with a screw. Always drill holes to avoid splitting the wood*

12 *Housing joints are normally skew-nailed, but a galvanized steel angle bracket screwed under the joint provides added strength*

14 *The PVC sheet can be cut using an abrasive disc fitted to a circular saw or saw attachment. Use a stout length of timber as a fence*

15 *When fixing the PVC cladding, support the sheets from below and from behind then drill through them and into the supporting timber*

17 *The window sill is fixed above the bottom cladding to provide a weather seal. All metal fittings must be of a type suitable for outdoor use*

18 *One great advantage of cladding the greenhouse with PVC roof sheeting is that it can be stretched or squashed up to take up minor adjustments*

13 *Alternatively, screw through joints after drilling and plugging the end grain of the longitudinal timber to avoid splitting it with the screw*

16 *Use pre-formed polystyrene eaves filler strips when fitting the roof to provide rigidity and also to draughtproof the greenhouse*

19 *With the end of the roof butted against the backing wall, the joint can be made weathertight with a timber batten, mastic and self-adhesive flashing*

on top of a shallow 150mm concrete foundation, then lay the bottom plates on the frames. Using this method, the two front corner posts, suitably preserved, may be anchored into hollow blocks, and the rest of the structure constructed about these (fig. 4). If the course is continued around the floor area, there will be a step at the base of the door. If you feel that this is a disadvantage, the blocks and bottom plate can be constructed with a cutout for the door. However, without the step it will be very difficult to both keep the door away from the rot-inducing soil, and to make the greenhouse draughtproof.

The receiving wall

The wall to which the greenhouse is attached should, ideally, be absolutely vertical. Unfortunately few walls are. If the wall is less than 12mm out of plumb, the gap can be filled with a bricklaying mortar. But, if it is over 12mm or you do not want a wedge-shaped mortar gap, then you will have to shape three lengths of 50mm × 50mm timber (two vertical battens support the two end frames, and the horizontal batten—the wall plate—supports the roof) so that they form a vertical surface to which the greenhouse frame will be attached. Use a scribing technique to transfer the wall profile on to the timber: hold the wood vertically against the wall and scribe down its length using a pencil attached to a block of wood, which you run down the wall. Saw or plane down the scribed line. Lay a thick layer of sealing mastic or compound along the wall and the timber where the surfaces will meet, screw the timber firmly to the wall with wall plugs or large bolts.

Construction

All the joints should be both glued and screwed, using a PVA waterproof adhesive and either brass, galvanized or japanned screws. The glass or PVC sheeting can be housed either between narrow wooden battens or in glazing grooves cut with a plough plane, router or power saw (fig. 9).

Assembly

Drill the back plate of one end frame and fix it to the vertical timber attached to the wall, then do the same at the other end frame. Move the front frame into place, drilling

and fixing the base to the bolts (which are set in concrete). Drill and screw the ends of the front frame to the respective front timbers of the end frames. The shell of the greenhouse is then ready to receive the roof frame. This should be drilled and fixed to the end and front frames as well as to the wall plate and, when fitting it, you should make quite sure that the frame is flush with the wall to avoid distortion.

Cladding with PVC

To clad the frame first lay one sheet of PVC roofing on the ventilator (if fitted), bedding it down on foam eaves filler and fixing it with screws and washers. Then fix the casement stay and hinges. Carefully position and secure the remainder of the PVC sheets to the roof, using eaves filler, and securing them with screws and washers.

Fix PVC sheeting to the door frame in the same way as to the ventilator, then fix the door in place, making sure that it opens and closes freely. When covering the ends, it is necessary to measure carefully then cut the PVC sheet to the required shape using a fine-toothed saw.

Glazing

The method of overlapping glass panes is quite simple. First press a bed of putty along the glazing beading shelf, then press the bottom pane of glass into the putty. Press from the edges of the pane, not the centre, or it may shatter. Now hold the next higher pane where it will be fixed, and mark the sides of the structure where the bottom of the pane will be located.

Put the pane aside for the time being and drive a 25mm nail into each side of the woodwork immediately next to the lower pane, level with the marks, until just about 6mm of the head is still protruding. You now have two metal stops on which the next pane can rest while it is puttied in position. The process is repeated for successive panes. There are several types of proprietary clips that are made for joining overlapping glass sheets, but they all suffer from the same disadvantage—the final pane often has to be cut to fit. The nail method, on the other hand, allows you as little or as much overlap as you need.

Where a structure abuts against a wall you must provide a run-off for rainwater at the junction point. This flashing could be zinc, lead or copper fitted in a groove cut in a mortar joint, but a simpler alternative is to use self-adhesive flashing, which you simply press into the angle over a coat of flashing primer.

Door catches, handles and the ventilator stay add the finishing touches, along with weatherboarding, which should be nailed over the roof ends and then treated with preservative.

Variations on the theme

Mini greenhouse: A smaller version of the lean-to greenhouse, this is tended from the outside and has one or more opening doors at the front. Usually, this type of greenhouse is essentially a modified lean-to in which similar methods of construction to the basic design are used, with twin doors placed centrally and no end door.

The internal height should be at least 1500mm so that shelving can be fitted to double the effective area, allowing 700mm headroom for the plants situated on each level.

Apex or span: This is a free-standing model which rises to a central ridge and it can be constructed along the lines of two lean-to's placed back to back.

The necessary modifications include a central ridge with capping, a central door in one end, and side and end bracing to provide rigidity.

An alternative design

The glazed and boarded greenhouse illustrated (right) has been designed very simply so that it can be constructed with a minimum of time and effort. The generous eaves height of 1520mm and a ridge height of 2130mm ensures adequate headroom, especially around the edges at bench or staging level where plants are sited. And the width of 2330mm allows considerable freedom of movement.

The timber section for the standard-sized greenhouse should be at least 50mm × 50mm for all structural components and 75mm × 50mm for the door posts. The door battens should be 25mm × 25mm and the glazing beading should be 16mm × 16mm.

The measurements can be adapted according to your requirements, especially the length. If the design is extended in this way some extra reinforcing will be necessary mid-way along the roof and side. A glazing bar can be replaced by a 75mm × 50mm timber and a cross bar at the side would add rigidity and strength. A similar stout piece of timber should be inserted mid-way along the side section.

Throughout the design two main glass widths—460mm and 610mm—are used. The window and roof glass, it must be noted, is installed in 'modules' as nearly square as possible. This means in effect that the glass is panelled. For instance, on the roof each run of glass between timbers consists of four panes of overlapping glass.

In the case of a PVC-sheet-clad greenhouse (below) the timber section should be at least 50mm × 50mm. The hardwood corner posts should be 75mm × 75mm, but you can get away with 50mm × 25mm for the wall plate and vertical wall timbers.

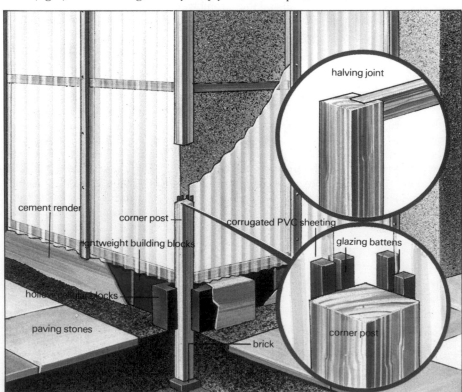

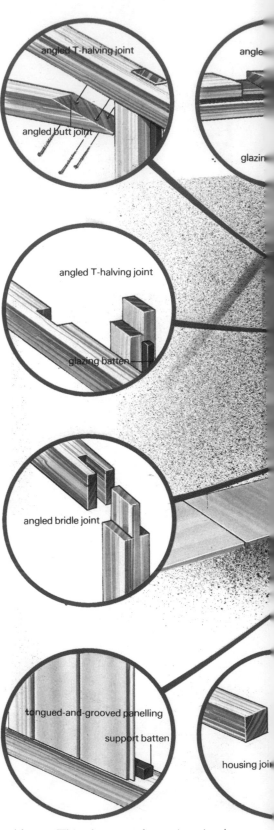

Above: *This glass greenhouse is a simple construction and can be built quickly. A PVC sheet clad greenhouse (left) features slightly different timber sections*

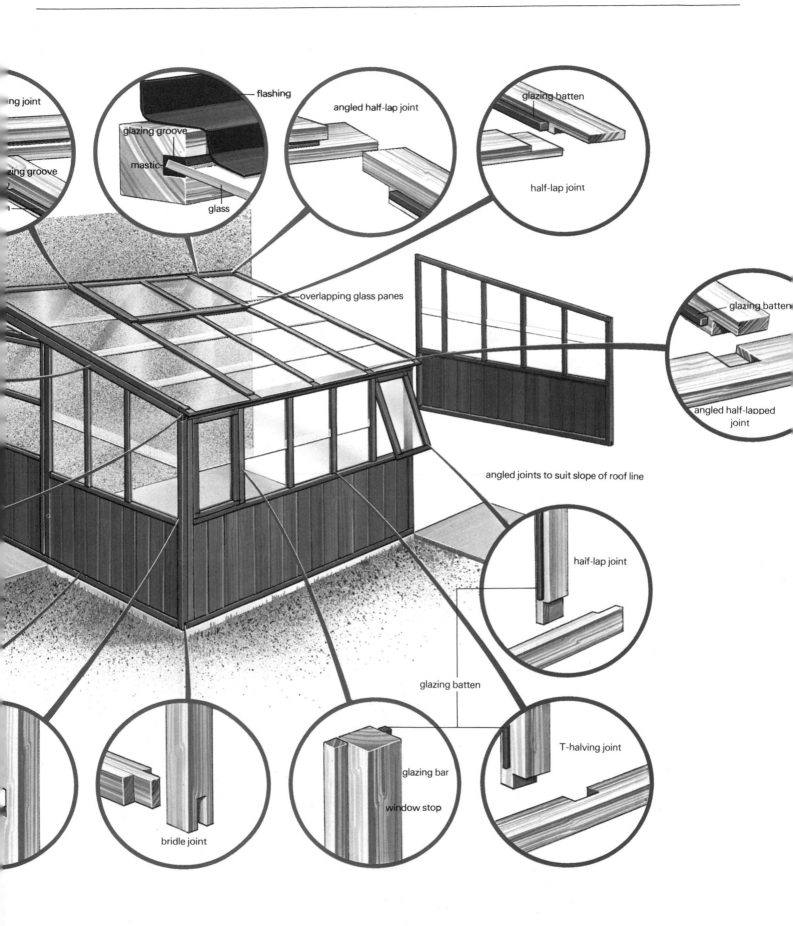

ing joint

zing groove

flashing

glazing groove

mastic

glass

angled half-lap joint

glazing batten

half-lap joint

overlapping glass panes

glazing batten

angled half-lapped joint

angled joints to suit slope of roof line

half-lap joint

glazing batten

glazing bar

window stop

T-halving joint

bridle joint

KIDS' CLIMBING FRAME

There are two things which you can safely guarantee where children are concerned. One is their natural tendency to climb anything within reach and the other is the tedious regularity with which they fall over. The solution to this problem is to build a climbing frame which offers vital security and stability.

Half the fun of this climbing frame lies in its ability to change shape and cope with an array of bolt-on 'goodies' such as ladders, ropeways, swings and so on, which exercise the child's imagination as well as its body.

There are a number of essential factors to be considered with any climbing frame. It should never be too high for the child—two metres is a staggering altitude for a four-year-old but within reach of a child twice as old. Only you can determine, however, the parameters which best suit your own off-spring—bearing in mind that children grow frighteningly fast. A climbing frame should also be sturdy, secure and should not offer any sharp edges or extensive protrusions which could cause an injury in a fall. And, of course, *supervision* is the final keystone to safety. Certainly no toddler should be allowed on a climbing frame unsupervised.

A demountable frame is an excellent choice. It can be stowed away during the winter months and simply erected for use when the sun comes out. For this reason a timber construction based on a modular principle is probably the most convenient and, comparatively, the least expensive. But before examining a typical construction, what are the alternatives?

Materials

It is tempting to use materials like scaffolding poles and clamps which you can cut to length. But this approach offers a number of hazards to the young climber. Sawn-through steel tubing, even if filed down, presents dangerous corners which, if not cutting young skin open in a fall, could cause serious grazes. The dangers are doubled if scaffolding clamps are used. In a swift descent back to earth, these could inflict serious injuries.

But not all forms of scaffolding are excluded and, in a number of cases,

Right: *This climbing frame can be great fun for young children and it is not difficult to construct*

products available on the market can serve purposes extra to the needs of children. Some scaffolding frames intended for DIY use represent a much safer alternative. Some types consist of open-frame steel panels about one metre wide by 600mm high. Each panel is self-supporting—in other words it is cross braced, rigid and secure. The panels simply slot together forming obstruction-free assemblies which, commonly, are used to construct tower platforms for exterior maintenance work.

While the height that these structures can reach is not recommended for junior members of the family, various low-level box structures can be easily erected to make an exciting and extensive climbing frame.

In some cases the frame components can be extended with short poles, curved inter-connections and so on, to make portable garages or workshops over which tailor-made awnings fit for weather protection.

Such assemblies have a multitude of uses but—needless to say—they are not necessarily cheap.

Modular frames

The featured climbing frame is simple to make, inherently flexible in layout and, because only one type of standard component is used, can be extended to suit the funds available, the demands of the

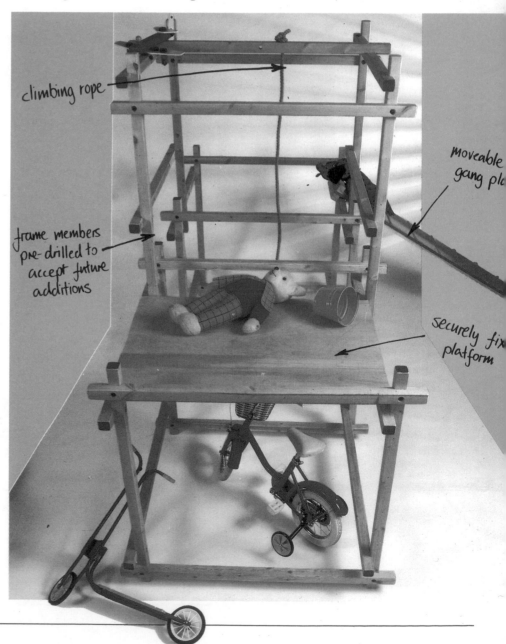

climbing rope

frame members pre-drilled to accept future additions

moveable gang pla

securely fix platform

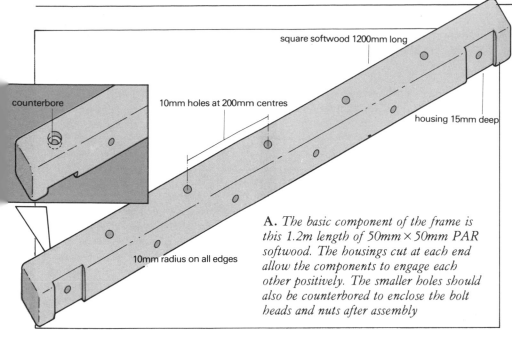

square softwood 1200mm long

counterbore

10mm holes at 200mm centres

housing 15mm deep

10mm radius on all edges

A. *The basic component of the frame is this 1.2m length of 50mm × 50mm PAR softwood. The housings cut at each end allow the components to engage each other positively. The smaller holes should also be counterbored to enclose the bolt heads and nuts after assembly*

children, and the time available for manufacture.

The basic component is a 1200mm length of 50mm × 50mm PAR (planed all round) softwood to reduce splinters, which has a wide housing cut in one of the surfaces at each end. Bolt holes drilled through adjacent sides along the length of the component allow you to bolt the pieces together in an infinite variety of combinations, and to dismantle the assembly quickly and easily—either for storage during the winter or for some sort of change.

The dimensions given are a compromise between strength and cheapness; you could make the components from 75mm × 50mm timber, or even from 50mm × 25mm timber if you have a very young child, while you could equally easily reduce the length of the components to give a smaller overall size of frame. The choice is yours. However, if you intend to use the frame for access work around the house as mentioned earlier, you should choose timber of 75mm × 75mm cross section.

With the components assembled, you arrive at an open cube construction which is 1200mm along each edge. Two or three of these (or as many as you wish) form a large sturdy frame to which you can fix slides, swings and ladders.

Tools and materials

The featured design consists of three frames. To build this number you must buy 44m of 50mm × 50mm PAR softwood. Try to buy the timber in lengths which are multiples of 1.2m.

The two featured accessories are a 'gang plank'/slide, a simple swing and a platform. To build the platform you need a sheet of 19mm marine ply (for weather resistance) of 1.2m × 745mm. To build the slide you need a 2m × 300mm length of the same material. To make the end braces for the slide you need two 300mm lengths of 50mm × 50mm PAR softwood and, for the 'rungs' on the gang plank, eight 300mm lengths of half-round ramin moulding.

To assemble the unit you use 70mm black iron coachbolts and nuts, each with a 10mm diameter shank. Use 110mm bolts with 75mm × 75mm timber.

To make the components you will need:
● a power drill with 10mm wood bit and a 25mm flat bit
● a cross-cut saw or jig saw and a tenon saw
● a tape measure, try square and steel rule
● medium- and fine-grade glasspaper
● screwdriver and 20mm No. 8 brass woodscrews
● a suitable socket wrench or box spanner
● paint or varnish, as you prefer
● a mitre box with right-angle slots.

Making the frames

The frame members are easily made, and when they are all complete you have broken the back of the job.

Start by cutting the timber into 1200mm lengths. Sand the cut ends and radius them slightly using a planer file followed by medium-grade glasspaper to remove any sharp edges (fig. 1). At the same time give all the edges a 10mm radius as well.

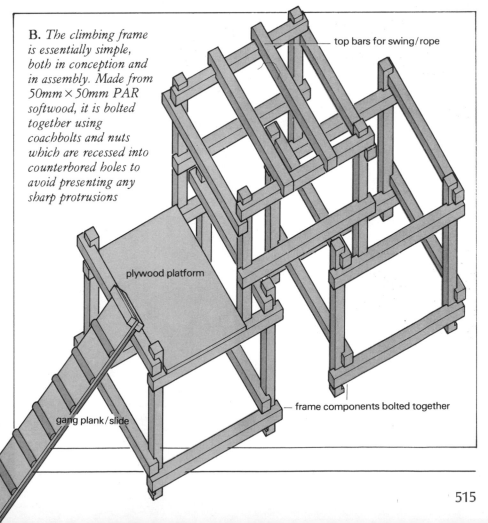

B. *The climbing frame is essentially simple, both in conception and in assembly. Made from 50mm × 50mm PAR softwood, it is bolted together using coachbolts and nuts which are recessed into counterbored holes to avoid presenting any sharp protrusions*

top bars for swing/rope

plywood platform

gang plank/slide

frame components bolted together

At each end of the same side you will need to cut out a housing 75mm wide by 15mm deep. Measure 40mm in from the end of the timber and, using a try square, mark a line across the width. Next measure 50mm along from that line and repeat the process (fig. 2).

Continue your pencil lines down both sides of the timber and mark a point 15mm down from the edge. Pencil this depth line in too. Secure the timber in a vice and, using a tenon saw and mitre box, cut down to the 15mm depth at each end of the housing, remembering to cut on the waste side of the pencil lines. Check as you do so that the saw is cutting evenly on both sides. Stop sawing just short of the bottom marks. Repeat the process across the width of the

housing at 10mm to 15mm spacings. This will make chiselling easier and prevent you from splitting the timber.

Gently mark the pencil lines at the bottom of the housing with your chisel, then start removing the timber from the top of the housing, working down and approaching from both sides. Ensure that your chisel stays horizontal to your work and finish off with light chisel strokes to smooth off the timber (fig. 3). Sand or rasp the bottom completely smooth, and repeat the process at the other end of the 1.2m length.

Using the 10mm twist bit, drill the bolt holes along the main frame. These should be spaced at 200mm intervals and alternate from top to bottom and side-to-side as shown in fig. A. Make sure that the holes are drilled at the exact centre of the timber face, and that your drill bit remains at right-angles to the surface.

Treat each frame section with a wood preservative before painting or varnishing it: make sure the compound can be overpainted when you buy.

Each of these frame components can now be bolted to one another, the housing helping to steady the structure. Add a washer under each nut, which should be

1 *Cut the frame members to the same length and radius the edges, first with a planer file, then with glasspaper to remove splinters*

2 *Mark the positions of the housings at each end of the components, and check that each one matches every other component*

3 *Cut the housings using a tenon saw and mitre box, then a wood chisel to shave the bottom of the housing to the correct depth*

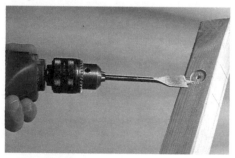

4 *When drilling the bolt holes, start off by drilling a narrow pilot hole, then use the flat drill bit to drill the counterbores*

★ WATCH POINT ★

Before drilling the bolt holes through the housings, first drill a central pilot hole right through the wood using a 3mm twist bit. Reverse the timber and, using your pilot hole as a guide, drill down to a depth of 8mm using the 25mm flat bit (fig. 4). Then drill right through with the 10mm twist drill (fig. 5).

tightened with a socket or box spanner (fig. 6). Remember that if you use a frame section as a cross member as shown in fig. B the spacing between the housings must be matched by the gap between other frame members. This means, for example, that in a simple tower structure one of the horizontals secured between two uprights will be 'inside' the frame while its opposite number on the far side will be 'outside'. This won't affect the overall stability of the structure in the least.

5 *When the counterbore has been drilled you can then enlarge the rest of the hole to the full 10mm diameter using an ordinary twist bit*

6 *Fit the components together, knock in the coach bolts using a ball-pein hammer and tighten the nuts using a socket or box spanner*

Making the gang plank

A gang plank (fig. C) is easier to build than a ladder, as well as being cheaper and safer for the child. It can also double up as a slide, simply by turning it over.

Mark off a strip 2m long and 300mm wide on a sheet of 19mm marine ply, and mark the cutting lines with a sharp knife to break the surface ply and prevent splintering when you saw it. Cut the panel using either a panel saw or a power jig saw with either a saw fence or straightedge to guide the sole plate.

Sand down the cut edges but do not radius them at all. Using your try square mark pencil lines across the piece at 200mm intervals. To these lines fix 'rungs' from half-round sections of a hardwood such as ramin. Cut these to 300mm in length and drill three countersunk screw holes through their curved surfaces. Lay the rungs on the pencil lines and mark the positions of the screw holes in the top surface with a bradawl.

Fix the rungs down using pins and waterproof wood glue, and ensure that the heads are knocked well down (fig. 8).

At one end of the plank you must fix two 300mm timber battens, one on each side to form a grossly elongated 'T' shape. These battens will hook over the frame members to hold the plank securely in place whichever way up it is. Cut the battens from 50mm × 50mm PAR softwood and drill three counterbored screw holes 12mm deep along the length of each. As they will be on opposite sides of the same thin piece of timber, offset the holes slightly from one piece to the other so that the screws won't meet each other (fig. 9).

Fix the battens in place using waterproof

★ WATCH POINT ★

On the slide surface of the plank you can either apply several coats of paint or varnish to create a very smooth surface, or you can glue in place a length of plastic laminate which is easier to look after. Fit slim side rails to prevent splinters (fig. 10) and round off the edges (fig. 11).

wood glue and 50mm No. 8 brass woodscrews, then sand them smooth. Don't radius their edges—this will only make them slip off the frame.

Adding accessories

There's no limit to a child's imagination, and it may take a little ingenuity to satisfy

an active, boisterous ten-year-old. Adding some simple accessories such as a swing, a climbing rope or a platform at the top of the gang plank can make the frame even more fun to play with.

Because of the bolt holes drilled through the main frame members you can fix accessories like swings or climbing ropes almost anywhere within the bounds of

7 *When marking cutting lines for either the slide or the platform, use a sharp knife to prevent the cut edges from splintering*

8 *Pin and glue the gang plank rungs in place and be careful to punch the pin heads well down before filling their holes*

10 *Screw down the slide's side rails flush with the edges to cover any splinters and fill the counterbored screw holes*

safety and common sense. The simplest swing consists of an old car tyre (thoroughly cleaned of rubber deposits and road grime first) suspended by a single rope from one of the higher cross members. More elaborate swings can be created from two lengths of rope and a single softwood plank. Alternatively, you can install a climbing rope—a single length of thick hemp rope with knots tied in it at regular intervals.

When making a swing use weather- and rot-proof nylon rope—you can buy it very cheaply at a yacht chandler's or (in the form of a car tow-rope) from a motor accessory shop.

To make a swing seat use PAR softwood rather than ply as solid timber is stronger round the edges. Buy an offcut at least 25mm thick and 150mm × 400mm in size and drill a 10mm hole on the exact centre line of the plank and not less than 30mm from the end.

Feed one rope through each hole, tie in it as big and tight a knot as you can to prevent it slipping back out again (fig. 12), and seal the cut end of the (nylon) rope by melting it with a flame. Then hang the swing from one of the frame members by passing the other ends of the ropes through a couple of

9 *Fit the two end battens on opposite sides of the top end of the gang plank, again using screws in counterbored holes for safety*

11 *Round off the corners of the side rails so that they can't splinter or otherwise hurt the children when they are using it*

bolt holes 400mm apart. Tie good, tight knots at the top, too (fig. 13).

A platform can be fun as well as useful—it makes it easier for the child to get to the slide, for one thing. Use 19mm marine ply cut to 1200mm × 745mm; any other board will warp. Apply several coats of marine varnish or exterior-quality paint and take care to flood the grain round all four edges. Screw the platform across two of the horizontal frame members using 50mm No. 8 brass woodscrews, ensuring that the screw heads are countersunk and then filled (fig. 14).

Finishing touches

Many owners will prefer to leave the frame out in the garden all year, some for only the summer months. Whichever is the case, the unit will get very wet—especially if it stands on grass. The best way to ensure a long life is to treat it with at least two coats of a water-repellent preservative stain. These stains come in several shades, are non-toxic and are easy to maintain—you simply brush on extra coats as needed. If you don't mind touching up scuffs and chips, you could use yacht varnish or exterior-quality paint. In this case, preparation is vital. All components should be sanded smooth and knot holes or indentations filled with a plastic filler. Apply several coats of wood preservative, then cover this either with the varnish

12 *Fix the rope to the swing seat by passing it through a hole near the edge of the timber and tying a tight figure-of-eight knot*

13 *You can use a figure-of-eight knot or a bow-line to secure swings or climbing ropes to the cross bars of the climbing frame*

14 *Cut the platform to whichever size you or your child wants and fix it using countersunk woodscrews. Remember to fill the screw holes*

15 *If you are erecting the climbing frame outdoors, coat all the components with preservative. Don't use creosote*

★ **WATCH POINT** ★

Whatever treatment you choose, remember to flood the endgrain of the frame components with preservative. Where the unit sits on grass or wet soil you may also wish to lay strips of bituminous felt under the feet of the lower frames to prevent too much water being drawn into the timber.

---

or with a complete treatment of primer, undercoat and finish paint.

If your garden isn't big enough for the climbing frame, or if you don't want such a big structure on the lawn, you could erect the frame indoors in a suitable 'playroom', or even keep it in the corner of the children's bedroom.

If you're going to do this, however, think of the carpets: lay some offcuts of 19mm plywood or blockboard under the feet of the frame to prevent deep and permanent marks

from appearing. There is also the question of balance to be considered —any slight inaccuracies in the length of the various legs will be offset in the garden as the frame 'sinks' slightly into the grass; in the bedroom they may cause the frame to rock slightly, so pack the feet out a little to stabilize it.

Part of the beauty of this frame is that it can also be erected on the side of a hill, even one with a marked slope. The technique is to bed the feet of the various frame members into the soil so that they stand four-square, with each adjoining frame slightly higher or lower than its neighbour to match the slope. For safety's sake you should brace the frame using a couple of lengths of rope and stout timber tent pegs driven into the ground 'uphill' from the frame to prevent it toppling over.

C. *The gang plank is simpler and safer than a ladder. The laminate slide surface on the other side is strictly optional*

half-round moulding
at 200mm centres

plywood

laminate

battens 50mm × 50mm

edge strips 25mm × 12mm

BUYING MATERIALS

Much of the art of tackling DIY successfully lies in having the right quantity of materials. Buy too little and you may ruin the job—if you're forced to go out and buy more wallpaper to finish a room, you may find it's from a different batch and the colour varies; buy too much, and you'll simply have wasted money on materials that you may never be able to use again.

Calculating how much you need isn't always easy, however. It's often difficult to gauge quantities of unfamiliar materials, and if you've measured in metric but have to buy in imperial sizes, you'll have another problem to contend with. The way round these difficulties is to plan in advance, do some basic research before you measure and buy, make allowance for wastage and take advantage of the guidance below.

Type	Length mm	Height mm	Thickness mm	Number per sq. m
brick	225	75	112.5	60
screen wall block	300	300	100	11
light aggregate block	450	225	60–225	10
aerated concrete block	450 525	150 225	50–225	15
dense aggregate block	450	150 225	60–225	15 10

Bricks and mortar

It is easier to work out the number of bricks, or whatever, if you include an allowance for the mortar joint—about 10mm—around each brick. Use the chart to calculate the numbers required for your wall—it includes most of the common building materials.

Remember always to allow for cutting and wastage that will occur. If you want to know the actual size (all sizes quoted are nominal) subtract 10mm.

Mortar is made up of cement, soft or builders' sand and water. It is possible to change the characteristics and properties of the mortar by including various additives.
- **Plasticizer:** this makes the mortar more workable.
- **PVA adhesive:** makes the mortar adhere to any other surface better.

- **Waterproofing agent:** improves water resistance.

If you need only small quantities of mortar it is simpler to buy a bag of ready mixed dry ingredients rather than buying the ingredients separately and mixing them up yourself. If you need no more than 1 cu m of mortar, buy the ingredients separately from your local builders' merchant. Use the table to help you calculate the quantity of mortar you will need, remembering that 10kg of mortar is enough to lay 15 bricks.

Intended use	Masonry cement	Soft sand
brick/dense block laying	1	4–5
lightweight block laying	1	4–5
brick/dense block (severe exposure)	1	3
lightweight block (internal walls)	1	6

Concrete mixes

Mixing large quantities of concrete is a formidable task, the time and effort involved is huge, so it is best to get the concrete delivered to your home ready mixed for use. Look in the Yellow Pages or your local directory under Concrete—Ready Mixed, for specialist concrete firms.

Concrete consists of cement, sharp sand, gravel aggregate and water. But the ingredients are bulky and extremely heavy. To give you some ideas of the sort of quantities you will be dealing with:
- 2,170kg of dry ingredients (with a low water content and using a 20mm aggregate) in a standard 1:2:4 mix makes 1 cu m of wet concrete.
- 1 cu m of wet concrete is enough to pour a slab measuring 3.3m × 3m × 100mm.
- A standard bag of cement weighs 50kg, add to this 100kg of sand and 200kg of aggregate to make 0.17 cu m of wet concrete.

Timber and boards

Wood is sold in a wide variety of sizes and shapes and what you buy really depends on the use to which the wood will be put. There are three kinds of finish to wood.

- **PAR (planed all round):** the sawn wood is planed smooth on all its faces. This makes it slightly smaller all round than the sawn timber.
- **Sawn:** this timber is sawn to a series of standard sizes—it then dries, making it slightly smaller than the nominal size quoted. Because it is not planed all the surfaces are rough.
- **Planed both sides:** this timber has two sides planed (opposite sides) the other two are left rough (the narrow edges).

Because of these size differences you should always use the actual size of the timber when measuring up.

Standard sizes of man-made boards

There are four types of man-made board that are readily available:

- **Hardboard.** This is sold in three thicknesses, 3mm, 4.5mm and 6mm, in widths from 610mm to 1,220mm and lengths from 1,830mm to 3,050mm.

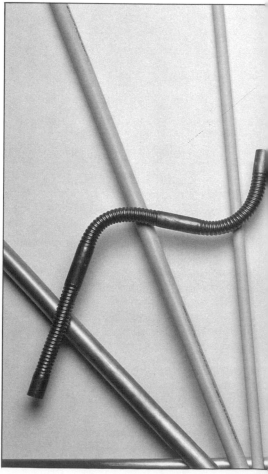

The proportions of the dry ingredients varies depending on what you want the concrete for. Use the table to help you decide what you will need for your job.

Intended use	Cement	Sharp sand	Shingle 20–5mm	Shingle 10–5mm
foundations drives, floors	1	2.5	3.5	—
foundations wet ground	1	1.5	2.5	—
reinforced lintels/fence posts	1	2	3	—
paths	1	2	—	3
blocks, paving slabs	1	2	—	3
setting in fence posts	1	2.5	3.5	—
screed	1	3	—	—

When you are estimating the quantities you will need for a job remember that any foundations you might dig are unlikely to be accurate so always err on the generous side when ordering either the dry ingredients or the ready mixed cement. The same applies when you come to estimate the quantities that you'll need for paths and edgings when using concrete as an anchoring for fence or gate posts, posts for washing lines, rotary clothes driers and other such items.

Whether you are mixing your own concrete or using ready mixed, you'll need to make provision for taking delivery. In the case of ready mixed particularly, make sure you can use the material straight away.

It is possible to make concrete using cement and all-in-one ballast. The table gives you the proportions you will need.

Intended use	Cement	Ballast 20mm	Ballast 10mm
foundations drives, floors	1	5	—
foundations wet ground	1	3.5	—
reinforced lintels and fence posts	1	—	3.5
paths, edgings	1	—	4
blocks, paving slabs	1	—	4
setting in fence posts	1	5	—

- **Plywood** is sold in 3mm, 6mm, 9mm, 12.5mm and 19mm thicknesses, and in 2,440mm × 1,220mm or 1,220mm × 610mm sheets.
- **Blockboard** is sold in 12.5mm to 25mm thicknesses, 915mm, 1,220mm and 1,525mm widths and 1,830mm, 2,440mm and 3,050mm lengths.
- **Chipboard** is sold in thicknesses of 12.5mm and 19mm, widths of 610mm and 1,220mm and lengths of 2,440mm.

Natural timber

Natural timber is sold in standard metric lengths which start at 1.8m, increasing at intervals of 300mm to a maximum of 8m. Some of the most common types and sizes are listed below, but of course your timber merchant or large DIY store will cut to order.

- **Planed square section softwood:** 12.5mm, 19mm, 25mm, 32mm, 38mm, 50mm, 75mm, 100mm.
- **Planed softwood boards:** 12.5–32mm thick and 12.5–225mm wide.
- **Sawn softwood:** smallest 12.5mm × 38mm, largest 300mm × 300mm.
- **Softwood quadrant:** 12.5–50mm.
- **Hardwood dowel:** 6mm, 9mm, 13mm,

16mm, 19mm.

You can of course buy various sizes, shapes and quality of skirting board and architrave. It's a good idea to shop around for these and all the other wood as quality and price can vary enormously.

Pipe sizes

It is possible to buy adapters that have imperial size fittings at one end and a metric size fitting at the other which solves the problem of fitting new sections of piping to existing pipework.

All new piping, whether copper or plastic comes in metric sizes. The measurement refers to the external diameter of the pipe. The old imperial measurement referred to the internal diameter of the pipe which is why equivalents don't seem to be very good. Copper piping equivalents are:

Metric	Imperial
15mm	½ inch
22mm	¾ inch *
28mm	1 inch

*denotes incompatibility

Plastic piping is measured in the same way as copper piping. Equivalent sizes are:

Metric	Imperial
22mm	¾ inch
32mm	1¼ inch
40mm	1½ inch
50mm	2 inch

If you are in any doubt that your piping is imperial or metric—it is impossible to tell by looking—use compression fittings to join the old and new piping. These are safer than capillary fittings where the gap between fitting and pipe is critical.

Paint quantities

The volume of paint you will need for a given job is dependent on a number of variables, not least the way you paint. It also depends on the condition of the surface to be painted, the quality of the paint, the porosity of the surface and whether you are trying to cover a dark base with a lighter colour.

However, it is possible to give some idea of coverage, but bear in mind these are only averages, and unless your surface is in good general condition it is wisest to buy more than the stated volume. This is especially true if you are getting a colour made up especially for you. It may prove impossible to mix exactly the same colour if you need more.

Paint	Amount	Area
primer	1 litre	15 sq m
undercoat	1 litre	15 sq m
emulsion	1 litre	18 sq m
oil-based	1 litre	17 sq m
non-drip	1 litre	17 sq m
exterior	1 litre	6 sq m
varnish	1 litre	10 sq m

Standard sizes of paint tin are: 250ml, 500ml, 1 litre, 2.5 litres, 5 litres.

Measuring wallpaper

There is a method of working out how many rolls of paper you will need for a room. Start by counting how many widths you will need, add up all the lengths and from this work out how many rolls you will need. A standard roll measures 1,005 × 530mm. If the paper you have chosen has a large pattern repeat you should allow an extra roll.

Very often ceilings need to be papered. A simple way to calculate how much paper you will need is the following: measuring in metres, measure the length of each strip, count up the number of strips, then multiply these two figures together and divide the answer by ten. If the answer isn't a whole number round it up to the nearest whole number.

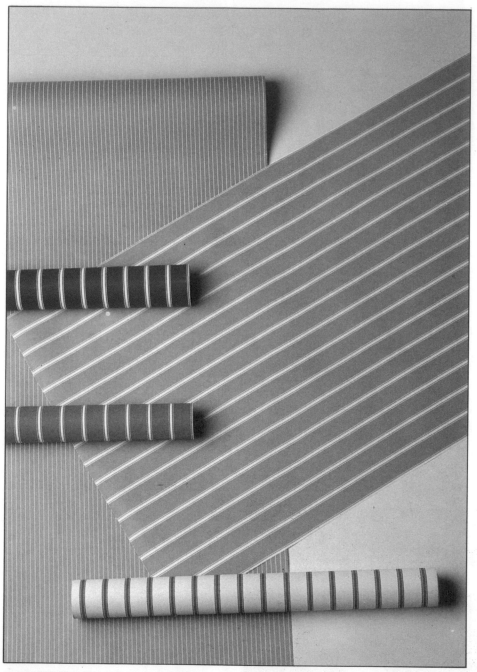

Tile count

Working out how many tiles you'll need for a wall can also be a problem, but not if you use the chart below. All you have to do is measure the area to be tiled and multiply this by the number given for the size of tile you are to use. The tiles listed are all the commonly used ceramic, mosaic and quarry tiles.

Always allow a few extra tiles for breakages when cutting. And don't forget that ceramic tiles have special edge and corner tiles. It is much more difficult to calculate tile numbers for irregularly shaped tiles. However, manufacturers usually indicate a coverage figure.

Size (mm)	Number needed per sq. m
50 × 50	400
100 × 100	100
108 × 108	86
200 × 100	50
152 × 152	44.5
216 × 108	43
300 × 300	11.2
600 × 600	2.8

Buying glass

Glass is sold in a variety of thicknesses. This is a modern trend replacing the practice of selling it by weight. You can buy glass from 2mm thick to 12mm thick. 4mm is the most common thickness and this is used for windows.

When measuring frames for glass always check diagonal measurement to see if the frame is square. Measure the opening across the width and height of the frame, not forgetting the rebates in which the glass fits. If the frame is very uneven take a paper pattern. Remember to give height before width when ordering the glass.

To fix the glass you will need putty. This is sold by weight and as a rough guide allow 125g per 300mm of pane perimeter.

Height from skirting	Distance around room in metres (including doors and windows)												
	10	11	12	13	14	15	16	17	18	19	20	21	22
2–2.2 metres	5	5	5	6	6	7	7	7	8	8	9	9	10
2.2–2.4 metres	5	5	6	6	7	7	8	8	9	9	10	10	10
2.4–2.6 metres	5	6	6	7	7	8	8	9	9	10	10	11	11
2.6–2.8 metres	6	6	7	7	8	8	9	9	10	11	11	12	12
2.8–3 metres	6	7	7	8	8	9	9	10	11	11	12	12	13
3–3.2 metres	6	7	8	8	9	10	10	11	11	12	13	13	14
3.2–3.4 metres	7	7	8	9	9	10	11	11	12	13	13	14	15

Glass thickness	Use
2–3mm	picture frames
4mm	windows up to 2 sq. m
5–6mm	windows up to 3 sq. m; framed external doors
10mm	windows over 3.3 sq. m; all glass doors if toughened
12mm	windows over 3.3 sq. m; all glass doors if toughened

Nuts, bolts and screws

If you don't want to split the wood or damage your screw it is very important to have the right sized hole in the wood. The same applies for a secure fixing.

Screws are measured by length (in mm) and diameter (by gauge number). The most common gauges are 4, 6, 8 and 10. The chart gives clearance hole and pilot hole sizes for these gauges.

Screws are commonly sold by weight, although it is becoming more usual to find them in packs of 25, 50 or 100 screws, especially at DIY stores.

The main problem with nuts and bolts is that there are several different standards, so when you want to know what bolt will fit a hole you need to know the specification of the bolt.

There are two main systems. **ISO Metric** and **Unified**. There are two others probably still in existence but no longer in use. These are **British Standard (BS)** and **British Association (BA)**. Each system uses a different way to measure the bolt diameter.

Screw gauge	Pilot hole	Clearance hole
4	bradawl	3mm
6	1.5mm	4mm
8	2mm	4.5mm
10	2.5mm	6mm

Use the table to help you decide what bolt you'll need to fit a given hole diameter.

Hole size mm	Nearest bolt size Metric	Unified	BS	BA
10	M10	—	—	—
9.5	—	3/8 in	3/8in	—
8	M8	5/16 in	5/16 in	—
6.5	—	1/4 in	1/4 in	—
6	M6	—	—	0BA
5.5	—	No. 12	—	—
5	M5	No. 10	—	2BA
4.5	—	No. 8	—	—
4	M4	—	—	4BA
3.5	—	No. 6/5	—	—
3	M3	No. 4	—	6BA

INDEX